𝔐𝔲𝔰𝔦𝔠
IN THE
RENAISSANCE

by
GUSTAVE REESE

REVISED EDITION

New York
W · W · NORTON & COMPANY · Inc ·

ML
172
.R42
1959

TO M. D. HERTER NORTON

who prompted the writing
of this book
and its predecessor

1602

Contents

Preface   xiii

*I THE DEVELOPMENT OF THE CENTRAL MUSICAL
LANGUAGE OF THE RENAISSANCE IN FRANCE, THE
LOW COUNTRIES, AND ITALY*

1. Social Background in Burgundy (1363–1477) and in the
   French Crown Lands (Reign of Charles VI); French Mu-
   sic between Machaut and Dufay; Italian Music of the Early
   Quattrocento   3

2. Composers, mainly of Northern France, in the Period of
   Dufay   34

3. Music of France and the Low Countries in the Period of
   Busnois and Ockeghem; an Outpost at Naples   97

4. The Frottolists and their Contemporaries in Northern and
   Central Italy   153

5. Josquin des Prez and his Contemporaries from France and
   the Low Countries, in particular Obrecht, Agricola, Isaac,
   Compère, Brumel, Pierre de la Rue, and Mouton   184

6. Secular Vocal Music of the Post-Josquin Period: Claudin,
   Janequin, Gombert, and their Contemporaries as Writers
   of Polyphonic Chansons; Verdelot, Festa, Arcadelt, Willaert, Rore, and their Contemporaries as Writers of Italian
   Madrigals   288

7. Sacred Vocal Music of the Post-Josquin Period: Gombert,
   Clemens non Papa, Willaert, and their Contemporaries   335

8. Secular Vocal Music of the Late Renaissance: Arcadelt, Le
   Jeune, Lassus, Sweelinck, and their Contemporaries as
   Writers of Polyphonic Chansons; Palestrina, Monte, Marenzio, Monteverdi, and their Contemporaries as Writers
   of Italian Madrigals   380

9. Sacred Vocal Music of the Late Renaissance: Italian Composers, including Palestrina at Rome and the Gabrielis at

Venice; French and Netherlandish Composers, including
Goudimel in his Relation to the Genevan Psalter and
Lassus at Antwerp   448

10. Instrumental Music of the 16th Century: The Italian Pro-
     duction, including the Lute-Books Printed by Petrucci and
     those Written by Francesco da Milano, Galilei, and Moli-
     naro, the Keyboard Works of the Cavazzonis, Merulo, and
     Andrea Gabrieli, and the Ensemble Compositions of Gio-
     vanni Gabrieli; the French and Netherlandish Production,
     including the Lute-Books of Le Roy and Besard and the
     Keyboard and Ensemble Collections Printed by Attain-
     gnant; Music in the 16th-Century Theater   519

II THE DIFFUSION AND DEVELOPMENT OF THE
MUSICAL LANGUAGE OF THE RENAISSANCE IN THE
HISPANIC PENINSULA, GERMANY, EASTERN EUROPE,
                  AND ENGLAND

11. Spain and Portugal: The Musicians of the 15th Century, in-
     cluding those of Ferdinand and Isabella; the 16th-Century
     Polyphonists, including Morales, Guerrero, and Victoria;
     the Writers of 16th-Century Instrumental Music, including
     the Six Great *Vihuelistas* and Cabezón   575

12. Germany: Pre-Reformation Vocal Polyphony, including the
     Lochamer, Glogauer, and other Miscellaneous *Lieder-
     bücher,* the Franco-Netherlandish Element as Represented
     by Isaac, and the Music of Heinrich Finck; Monophony—
     The Meistersinger; Instrumental Music through the 16th
     Century, including the Keyboard Works of Paumann,
     Schlick, and Hofhaimer and the Lute Pieces of the New-
     sidlers   632

13. Germany: Music of the Reformation, including the Collec-
     tions of Walter, Rhaw (1544), and Eccard; 16th-Century
     Catholic Polyphony from about 1520, including the Music
     of Senfl and the Franco-Netherlandish Influence as Repre-
     sented by Lassus and Monte; Secular Polyphony, includ-
     ing the Ott and Forster *Liederbücher* and the Collections
     of Hassler   673

14. Music in Hungary, Bohemia, Poland, and the Adriatic
    Coastal Areas of the Southern Slavs   714

15. England: Music from c. 1450 to c. 1535, including the Carols
    and the Works of Fayrfax and Taverner; the Composers
    of Sacred Music with Latin Text from c. 1535 to c. 1635,
    including Tallis, Byrd, and Philips; Sacred Music with
    English Text from c. 1535 to c. 1635, including the *Booke
    of Common Praier noted,* the Early Psalters, and the An-
    thems of Tomkins and Gibbons   763

16. England (c. 1535 to 1635): The Madrigals, including those of
    Morley, Weelkes, and Wilbye; the Ayre; Instrumental Mu-
    sic, including the Lute Works of Dowland, the Keyboard
    Works of Byrd, Bull, and Farnaby, and the Ensemble
    Compositions of Tye, Morley, and Gibbons; Music in the
    Theater   815

APPENDICES

1. Bibliography   884

2. Index   947

List of Plates

PLATE I   *facing page* 62

Signatures of Renaissance composers: Guillaume Dufay, Johannes Regis, Juan del Enzina, Jacques Arcadelt, Philippe de Monte, Roland de Lassus, Giovanni Pierluigi da Palestrina, Tomás de Victoria, Marc'Antonio Ingegneri, Claudio Merulo, Gregor Aichinger, Jan Pieterszoon Sweelinck, Christopher Tye, Thomas Tomkins

PLATE II   158

Verbum caro factum est, a 2. Marquetry (with *trompe l'oeil* effects) by Fra Giovanni da Verona in the Church of Monte Oliveto Maggiore, Siena

Four-part canon. Marquetry by Fra Vincenzo da Verona now at the Louvre, Paris

PLATE III   222

Miniature from the Paris copy of *Le Champion des dames,* showing Dufay and Binchois

Johannes Martini. Miniature in Florence, Bibl. Naz. Cent. MS, *Banco rari 229*

Lassus' Coat of Arms

Luca Marenzio as Saturn and Gio. del Minugiaio as Mars. From Buontalenti's drawings of the *intermedi* of 1589

PLATE IV   366

Title-page of Monteverdi's copy of Zarlino's *Istitutioni harmoniche,* bearing the composer's signature

Autograph note written by Glareanus in the tenor part-book of Munich, Univ. Lib. MS 322–325, in which he praises the usefulness of singing sacred songs—as illustrated by many examples drawn from the Scriptures—but warns of perverted spirits who turn the best and most honorable pursuits into their very opposites

PLATE V   382

Tenor part of *Kyrie II* of Gheerkin's *Missa Panis quem ego dabo*
from the fancifully ornamented MS Cambrai 124

Superius of Arcadelt's *Nous voyons que les hommes font tous
vertu d'aimer,* reworked in the 19th century into the *Ave Maria*
foisted upon the composer (from LeRoy & Ballard's *Chansons à
quatre parties,* 1554)

PLATE VI   542

Organ design from the treatise of Henricus Arnaut of Zwolle (d.
1466)

Interior of the Church of the Incoronata at Lodi, the birthplace of
Gafori, with organ altered by Giovanni Battista Antegnati in
1544

PLATE VII   670

Players on the oliphant, fife and drum, and trumpet. Detail from
The Feast of Herodias by Israel van Meckenem (d. 1509)

Singers, with open choir-book (the man appears to be beating the
tactus), and harpist. Detail from *Danaë and the Shower of Gold,*
16th-century tapestry (School of Philip van Orley and Jan van
Roome)

A trumpeter, two shawm players, and two cromorne players. From
the woodcut series, *Triumph des Kaisers Maximilian I.,* by Hans
Burgkmair and other artists of Augsburg and Nuremberg

PLATE VIII   846

Page from Fuenllana's *Orphenica Lyra,* showing transcriptions for
vihuela of vocal music by two of his fellow Spaniards

John Dowland's Autograph of His Lute Piece, *My Lady Hunsdon's Allmande,* from MS 1610.1 at the Folger Shakespeare Library, Washington

Preface

I F THERE were such a thing as polyphony in prose, it would obviously be a godsend to the writer of history, whatever it might be to the reader. The historian would be spared his persisting struggle to reconcile the chronological thrust with the regional spread—the development, over the years, of one kind of growth with the diffusion, over vast areas, of many kinds of growth simultaneously. However, language being less adaptable to contrapuntal treatment than music, the solution that is most suitable to the historian's problems has to be discovered from case to case. For this study, the most fitting method has seemed to be one that might, with Browning in mind, be called the *Ring and the Book* technique. Part I deals at some length with the central musical language of the 15th and 16th centuries, which was developed in France, Italy, and the Low Countries, while Part II deals primarily with the music of other lands. This distinction has nothing to do with the comparative intrinsic merit of the various bodies of music, but only with the separation of local dialects from the central language. Indeed, such local productions as the 16th-century music of Spain and England provide artistic expressions quite in a class with the best music of France, Italy, and the Low Countries. The method of first taking into account only the central language has the advantage of permitting the main technical developments of the centuries under consideration to be described, as it were, in a straight line. Thereafter, the entire period is traversed again for each country dealt with in Part II. As a result, the same musical forms and processes of composition are treated several times, but each discussion is entered from a different approach and with the admixture of something individual—that is, national. The method offers advantages not only to the one whose task it is to sort out a huge amount of varied material, but also to the one who studies it: the student has the main historical outline presented to him more than once, but each time with important changes in the details by which it is filled in.

Much of the music dealt with in this book is still the subject of intensive investigation. It has seemed to be a matter of prime importance, therefore, to analyze many compositions in whole or in part, so that style trends might be made clear from a presentation of basic facts. In other words, at least as much emphasis has been laid upon the marshalling of evidence as upon the drawing of conclusions. The latter, we trust, are nevertheless introduced with sufficient frequency to provide the reader with ample sign-posts. This, in a general way, is the policy followed in André Pirro's *Histoire de la musique de la fin du XIVe siècle à la fin du XVIe*.

A conscious effort has been made to interweave the beginning of this book with the author's *Music in the Middle Ages* and its latter part with Manfred Bukofzer's *Music in the Baroque Era.* This accounts for what might otherwise seem too frequent references to *Music in the Middle Ages* early in the new work—references intended, of course, to underline relationships between developments traced in the two volumes. On the other hand, there has been an attempt to make this book reasonably well-rounded within itself, and such a goal has been sought also in individual sections. Here numerous cross-references are provided in the interest of readers who may consult the book as a reference tool rather than as something to be read straight through. We hope that especially such readers will find assistance also in the rather detailed index.

In dealing with the various composers, preference has been given to what seemed suitable procedure in the context, and with respect to the information at hand, rather than to uniformity of method. Attempts to indicate the chronology of a man's output have not often been intensively pursued. To do otherwise would have considerably delayed the completion of a book that was supposed to be published several years ago. Also, a limit obviously had to be put to waiting for the appearance of relevant works whose issuance is expected. (For instance, we have been able to consult only the first two volumes of *Die Musik in Geschichte und Gegenwart.*)

Multiple footnote references (where possible) to transcriptions of compositions into modern notation have evidently been found serviceable by users of *Music in the Middle Ages,* and the same procedure is therefore followed here. Not only has it sometimes led an investigator, working in a library with modest resources, to a transcription he might not otherwise have found, but it has proved helpful, where facilities were good, to lecturers wishing to assemble several copies of a composition in a classroom. The present volume includes no record list similar to the one contained in its predecessor, but we hope to make a *catalogue raisonné* of Renaissance recordings available elsewhere in due course.

For permission to use transcriptions into modern notation and other copyrighted material from books and articles, grateful acknowledgement is made to the following publishers:

American Institute of Musicology (Armen Carapetyan): quotation from an article by Dr. Carapetyan, *The Musica Nova of Adriano Willaert,* published in the *Journal of Renaissance and Baroque Music;* here reprinted on p. 323f.

American Musicological Society: material from Dr. Dragan Plamenac's paper, *Music of the 16th and 17th centuries in Dalmatia,* published in the Society's *Papers* for 1939; here incorporated in the section on Dalmatian music beginning on p. 757.

The Mediaeval Academy of America: Exx. 28 and 39, taken from Dr. Helen Hewitt's edition of *Harmonice Musices Odhecaton A.*

Michigan State College Press: Ex. 157, taken from Dr. Milton Steinhardt's *Jacobus Vaet and his Motets.*

Möseler Verlag: Exx. 22, 30, 45, 48, 68, 69, 74, and 165, taken from six *Hefte* of *Das Chorwerk.*

Editions de l'Oiseau-Lyre (Louise B. M. Dyer), Paris: Exx. 5*a, b* and 6 *a–c,* taken from *Les Musiciens de la cour de Bourgogne* by Jeanne Marix.

Oxford University Press: Exx. 179, 181, 182, and 189, taken from Vols. I, IV, V, and VI of *Tudor Church Music;* Ex. 188, taken from No. 49 in *Tudor Church Music,* octavo edition; and the quotation from Canon Fellowes' *English Cathedral Music from Edward VI to Edward VII* that appears on p. 814.

Princeton University Press: Exx. 70*a* and 108, taken from Dr. Alfred Einstein's *The Italian Madrigal;* also the quotation appearing on p. 159.

Stainer and Bell: Ex. 183, taken from Vol. III of the *Collected Works of William Byrd.*

Where a musical example is said to be printed "after" a modern edition, a change of some sort has been made—for example, in the barring (as in Ex. 98) or in the application of *musica ficta* (as in Ex. 43*a*) or in the division of time-values (as in many examples).

During the thirteen years that this book has been in the writing, it has been my singular good fortune to have the help of a large number of friendly and generous people. Among my colleagues, nobody has been of greater assistance than Dr. Dragan Plamenac. He placed at my disposal for a long period many unpublished transcriptions into modern notation and has frequently offered suggestions that have added greatly to the value of the book. Professor Charles Warren Fox and Professor Oliver Strunk likewise placed at my disposal transcriptions they had made, and they too gave helpful suggestions on various occasions as did Professor Manfred Bukofzer, Dr. J. M. Coopersmith, the late Dr. Alfred Einstein, Rev. Dr. Laurence Feininger, Dr. Federico Ghisi, Professor Otto Gombosi, Dr. Ruth Hannas, Professor Erich Hertzmann, Professor Edward Lowinsky, Professor Arthur Mendel, and Professor Curt Sachs.

Professor Mark Brunswick placed me very specially in his debt by allowing me to borrow, for no less than eight years, a valuable portion of his library.

When the first versions of Chapters 12 and 13 were written, Mr. Nathan Broder collaborated with me in preparing them and, indeed, bore the heavier share of the burden. In the nine years that have since elapsed, a number of changes have been made in these chapters, but considerable portions of them remain virtually unchanged. Dr. Willis Wager similarly collaborated with me in writing a substantial part of Chapter 11 in its original form. Here, too, much remains practically as it appeared in the early version. Dr. Everett B. Helm helped me plan several sections on the madrigal, which consequently were well under way before the publication of Dr. Einstein's monumental work on the subject. Dr. Joseph Kerman was most kind, both in making the material in his excellent dissertation on the English madrigal available to me and in helping me to adapt some of it for the purposes of this volume.

Miss Luise Haessler and Mr. Eric Ganley expedited my perusal of several works in Dutch. Various kinds of assistance from Miss Elizabeth Lansing and Dr. Hans Tischler also merit grateful acknowledgement.

A very special debt is due to those friends who were, or still are, students of mine in the Graduate School of New York University. Dr. John M. Ward, who has long since emerged from the latter group, was a pillar of strength when the sections on Spanish instrumental music, English lute music, and English music in the theater were prepared. Of all those who have aided me, few have given more actual time than Mrs. Marion L. Versè, who has made transcriptions into modern notation and assisted me in gathering material at libraries, in drafting sections of the book (especially in Chapter 9), and in many other ways. Mr. I. Leroy Domingos, at various times over a period of seven years, has helped me in a multitude of ways with a spontaneity and whole-heartedness that are unforgettable. Portions of Chapter 7 are, in fact, our joint work. Mr. Roland Partridge cleared a number of difficult paths with me, notably the one that led to the section on Tinctoris. Miss Eleanor Lawry assisted me with high competence and gave ungrudgingly of her time when Chapter 10 was under way. Miss Mary Schieffelin worked with me most effectively in the forming of certain passages on the French chanson. Mrs. Peguy Lyder and Mrs. Donald Quimby were of substantial assistance in connection with the sections on English 16th-century sacred music with Latin texts, and on the English ayre, respectively. Mr. Theodore Karp has given generously of his time for numerous purposes, including that of co-operating with me in the writing of the section on Compère. Hurdles were surmounted also in the company of Dr. Josephine Shine, Dr. Milton Steinhardt, Mr. Theodore Seder, and Mr. Oscar Dike.

Other students, past and present, to whom I extend my thanks include Miss Gloria Bader, Mr. George Below, Miss Maude Brogan, Mr. Montague Cantor, Miss Anne Carlin, Mr. Norman Cherry, Mr. Ronald Cross, Mr. Albert Cohen, Mr. Irwin Grace, Mrs. Philip James, Mr. George Michael, Miss Genevieve Oswald, Miss Eileen Southern, Mr. Jennings L. Thompson, Mr. James Thomson, Miss Ethel Thurston, and Miss Mary Van Vleck.

Of all those who have been students of mine, none has given more time and energy than Dr. Catherine V. Brooks. As a former librarian on the staff of the Music Division of the New York Public Library, she placed her professional skill at my disposal on countless occasions. The section on English virginal music is more hers than mine. She has helped in the preparation of "copy," the reading of proof, the preparation of the index—in short, in practically every phase of work on the book. Her enthusiasm and drive have materially expedited its completion.

During a stay in Los Angeles, I was very kindly helped with the proof-reading by Dr. Alice Ray, Mr. Gerhard Singer, and Mr. Robert Trotter.

Mr. Wolfgang Weissleder has directed his skill to the making of the copies that were photographed to provide the musical illustrations.

The staff of W. W. Norton & Company—in particular Mr. Robert Farlow and Mr. Willis Parker—have indulged my idiosyncrasies with kindness and forbearance.

Nobody has had more of those idiosyncrasies to contend with than my wife, and I owe her a debt such as I am afraid I can never properly discharge for her patience and good humor in confronting them and for her resourcefulness in coming to the rescue time and again.

The library facilities upon which I have made the greatest demands are unquestionably those of the Music Division of the New York Public Library, and I owe an expression of gratitude not only to its Chief, Dr. Carleton Sprague Smith, but also to the members of his splendid and accommodating staff. The members of the Music Division of the Library of Congress have also responded to many requests, and I acknowledge with pleasure my debts to Dr. Harold Spivacke, Chief of the Division, to Mr. Edward N. Waters, and especially to Mr. Richard S. Hill. I likewise owe thanks to the British Museum, in particular to Mr. A. Hyatt King; to the Bibliothèque Nationale at Paris, in particular to Mme. Nanie Bridgman; and to the Biblioteca G. B. Martini at Bologna, in particular to Professor Napoleone Fanti. All have replied graciously and promptly to the numerous communications I have addressed to them.

JANUARY 1954   *Gustave Reese*

Preface to the Revised Edition

IN THE five years since this book first appeared, the healthy state of musicological research has yielded new data on various matters—for example, on the lives of Ciconia, Obrecht, and Josquin, and on the production of Pierre de la Rue and Antoine de Févin. While the need for a thoroughgoing revision of the book seems not yet to be indicated, it nevertheless appears desirable to take advantage of the exhaustion of the third printing to turn the fourth one into a revised edition and to incorporate into it, within the limits imposed by the continued use of existing plates, certain new facts that have come to the author's attention. Obviously no attempt has been made to take into account all the pertinent new periodical articles, books, and editions, although it has been possible to refer to a fair number of these.

I am indebted for valuable suggestions to the reviewers and to my colleagues and students.

G. R.

JUNE 1959

Part One: THE DEVELOPMENT OF THE
CENTRAL MUSICAL LANGUAGE
OF THE RENAISSANCE IN
FRANCE, THE LOW COUNTRIES,
AND ITALY

Chapter 1: SOCIAL BACKGROUND IN BUR-
GUNDY (1363–1477) AND IN THE
FRENCH CROWN LANDS (REIGN OF
CHARLES VI); FRENCH MUSIC BE-
TWEEN MACHAUT AND DUFAY;
ITALIAN MUSIC OF THE EARLY
QUATTROCENTO

The Two Renaissance Periods in Music

ANY line dividing the music of the Late Middle Ages from that of the
Early Renaissance must inevitably be an arbitrary one, like any drawn
between these two great periods themselves. Some musical traits, to
be sure, are clearly medieval, while others are typical of the Renaissance. But
the former still recurred long after the latter first appeared, and the musicians
of some nations felt the Renaissance spirit later than did those of others. Most
of this book will regard the Early Renaissance as beginning with the opening
years of the 15th century and the Late Renaissance [1] as extending through
the 16th century into the early years of the 17th, these approximate delimita-
tions being made with some variation from country to country. Moreover, it
will look upon the Early and Late Renaissance as distinct style-periods, related and differentiated by about as many similarities and dissimilarities as
were afterward to exist between the Classical and Romantic Eras.

Two great musical developments, rich in promise, had unfolded during
the Middle Ages, one reaching, the other approaching fruition. The former
grew from a strong trend toward organized, measured rhythm. Having
achieved its goal, it enabled Renaissance art to attain a rhythmic fluidity and
complexity that part-music has never surpassed; the counterpoint of rhythms
was often more important than that of melodies. The second development
gave scope to the tendency—which could take root only after the older trend
had for some years made music in two or more parts possible—to base polyphony on the third rather than on the perfect consonances. In this chordal
field, it was left for both Renaissance periods to realize more fully the potentialities of the triad (favored in its first inversion in some English music
of the late Middle Ages) and to regulate dissonance, which in medieval and

---

[1] The author prefers the term "Late" to "High," since the latter may suggest an unwarranted
implication that the music of the 15th century is inferior to that of the 16th.

Renaissance writing alike appears mainly as the product of ornamental notes.

Early Renaissance music still revealed some of the sharp contrast between voices that had dominated much medieval polyphony, but certain of the older techniques that had contributed toward producing this contrast, as well as other surviving style-features, were now used with new meaning.[1a] The small total range that characterized medieval polyphony, and which helped to bring about frequent crossing of the voices, had made desirable a sharp differentiation of the individual parts—whether in rhythm, in melody, or in the timbres of the performing media. But as a wider total range came into use in the Early Renaissance, crossing became less frequent and differentiation between the voices less sharp. The growing homogeneity of the voices eventually resulted in the establishment of imitation as a standard technique of the Late Renaissance. As to form, there was a reaching out in the Early Renaissance after larger structures, and in the hands of a master like Josquin—who helped to close the Early Renaissance and usher in the Late, much as Beethoven was to be a connecting figure between the Classical and the Romantic Eras—these structures attain a high degree of integration and span a wide and imposing arc. Western music as a whole, owing largely to the singular brilliance of the composers originating from Northern France and the Low Countries and to the international prestige that led to their being engaged and emulated throughout western and central Europe, achieved a cultural unification it has never since matched. Composers, especially in the 16th century, spoke one musical language—which, however, had local dialects—, a language used to express a spirit that was regarded by the people of the era themselves as new.[1b]

Early Social Background in the Various French Areas

Before the Anglo-French struggles that raged, with interruptions, between 1337 and 1453, France had led western Europe in music; during this so-called Hundred Years' War, other countries threatened her leadership—Italy in the 14th century and England in the first half of the 15th. But Italy did not outstrip her; and, if for a while England did, there was a center of French culture and civilization, the duchy of Burgundy, that was in turn to surpass England. Though torn by civil strife and invasion, the main center

---

[1a] E.g., the old *cantus-firmus* technique. Reapplication, but with new artistic purpose, of this and other devices of the Middle Ages will naturally be examined in the course of the present book.

[1b] Discussion of the views regarding the nature of the new era in history that were held by its own people, and also an account of the terms that they applied to it, are included in SchraR. Regarding the position of music in Renaissance culture, *see* Low M.

of French culture—the territory held by the crown—did not actually go into temporary eclipse until after the disaster of Agincourt in October, 1415. During the reign of Charles V (1364–1380) and even during most of the unhappy reign of the intermittently insane Charles VI (1380–1422), the crown lands continued to cultivate music with vigor.

Burgundy, at different times (and with varying territorial possessions) a kingdom, a county, and a duchy, returned to the French crown in 1361, upon the death, without heirs, of Duke Philip of Rouvre. In 1363, however, King John II conferred the duchy upon his fourth son, Philip the Bold, a younger brother of the future Charles V.[1c] Philip married Margaret, the heiress of Flanders, Artois, Brabant, and the counties of Rethel and Nevers, thus consolidating a power eventually to become formidable to the kingship itself. Philip's son and grandson, John the Fearless and Philip the Good, succeeding to the duchy in 1404 and 1419, added, by marriage, purchase, or conquest, the Franche-Comté, the rest of what is now Belgium, the provinces of Zeeland, Friesland, and North and South Holland, also the counties of Bar-sur-Seine, Mâcon, and Auxerre, and the towns of Abbéville, Amiens, and Saint-Quentin. Thus an extensive domain existed, broken, however, into two parts —one north, one east of the French crown lands—by the intervening counties of Alsace, Lorraine, and Champagne. Charles the Bold, the last duke of the line, who ruled from 1467 to 1477, lost his life in wars resulting from his attempt to remedy this defect.

The large Burgundian holdings within France itself were held in fief from the crown. But the dukes, after the competent King Charles V died, were dissatisfied with a state within a state, and finally aimed to free themselves entirely from royal authority. Philip the Good so far faltered in his allegiance as to side with the English against the France of Joan of Arc. Charles the Bold definitely hoped to form a kingdom of his own.

The Burgundian possessions were frequently embroiled in war; but they suffered less than the crown lands, and were therefore better able to foster the arts. The wealth derived, especially from Flanders and Brabant, enabled the dukes to maintain at Dijon, their capital, one of the most magnificent courts in Europe. The Flemish sculptor, Claus Sluter, became *Ymagier* to Philip the Bold in 1390, and it is to him that Dijon owes the tomb of Philip and the Well of Moses, with its statues of the prophets. In 1425, Jan van Eyck was at the court at Bruges, as painter and *valet de chambre* to Philip the Good. It was under this Philip, who belonged to the school of plume and panoply, that the duchy attained its greatest splendor. If the ostentatious display of wealth smacked somewhat of vulgarity, the court at Dijon nevertheless resembled a sort of fairyland. Women wore hennins—the cone-shaped headdresses, from the tops of which hung long butterfly veils. Their gowns

[1c] The musical inclinations of the father and both sons are touched on in ReMMA, 383f.

were often adorned with wide borders of fur and their throats with golden neck-bands.[2]

Opulence was not confined to the court, however. The *bourgeoisie,* especially in Flanders, was rich and powerful, and was destined to influence the development of music.

In the 14th century, the kings and princes of Europe instituted "chapels" which, in imitation of the Papal Chapel, were well staffed musically. These became even more the fashion in the 15th century. Every potentate, big or little, had his musicians, who usually went with him if he journeyed abroad. All four rulers of the Burgundian line were notable patrons of music. The accounts preserve the names of many musicians employed by Philip the Bold and details regarding instruments that he purchased. They show us also that in 1384 he acquired a book of motets [2a] from a certain Jehan Macon, a singer at the Sainte Chapelle in Paris, and we may therefore deduce that the works of Parisian composers formed at least a part of the repertory performed before him; for that matter, he spent more time in Paris than in his own domains. When he died in 1404, one of his musicians was Perrinet de Fontaines who, as Pierre Fontaine, was to figure as the creator of attractive chansons.[3] A certain *valet de chambre* of John the Fearless, called upon to take part in the divine service in 1408, was apparently the composer Tapissier.[4] John, in 1412, took over from his uncle, the Duke of Berry (brother of Charles V and Philip the Bold), four choirboys and, at their head, the highly esteemed Nicolas Grenon.[5] Besides Grenon and Fontaine, figures of further interest named in a list of singers paid by John in 1415 include Guillaume Ruby and Richard de Bellengues (also called Cardot).[6] But it was under Philip the Good that music was in its heyday at Dijon. Of the three chief composers of the period—Dunstable, Dufay,[7] and Binchois—the two last-named were in his employ, Binchois for about thirty years. Grenon, Fontaine, and Ruby are among the older men who remained in his service; Hayne van Ghizeghem and the Englishman Robert Morton are among the younger ones who entered it. Consideration of the activity of these various ducal musicians will extend into our third chapter. Philip had his son, the Count of Charolais, the future

---

[2] For further historical and social background, *see* A. A. Tilley, *Medieval France* (1922); C. A. H. Guignebert, *A Short History of the French People,* Vol. I (English transl., 1930); and esp. J. Huizinga, *The Waning of the Middle Ages* (English transl., 1924) and O. Cartellieri, *The Court of Burgundy* (English transl., 1929).

[2a] Could this have been the MS described in DrozU; BesS II, 235ff? The MS appears, from the small surviving fragment, to have dated from 1376 and to have once been owned by the later Philip.

[3] For a study of Philip the Bold's musicians, *see* BrenV, 3ff; *see also* MarM, xi. For broader surveys of music at the Burgundian court, *see* MarH; DahnkM, 199ff.

[4] PirM, 29. Cf. ReMMA, 333, 358.

[5] PirM, 28.   [6] PirM, 33.

[7] Pronounced Dü-fah-ee (accent on third syllable), not as in modern French. Cf. StaD, 7; DTO VII, xix; RB III, 44f.

Charles the Bold, instructed in music; the boy played the harp at the age of seven. Charles emulated his father as a music patron, including among his musicians the important Antoine Busnois. He tested his own mettle occasionally as both singer and composer.[8]

While the supremacy of the Burgundian court during much of the 15th century is clear, other centers of French civilization cultivated music also. Thus, in 1410, the composer Richard Loqueville is mentioned as in the service of Duke Robert of Bar; he played the harp and taught the instrument to the duke's son and the chant to the choirboys of the chapel.[9] The Duke of Berry was especially partial to organ music.[10] Duke John V of the independent duchy of Brittany (with which Loqueville seems to have had some ties[11]) maintained singers and instrumentalists at his capital of Nantes.[12] In 1401, King Charles VI founded a Court of Love,[13] a sort of literary society whose members occupied themselves, in the late trouvère tradition, with both music and poetry. At least one of its members—Jehan de Villeroye, also called Briquet—is known as a composer.[14]

In 1407, Charles turned his attention to a group that was active on a less lofty social plane—its members being professionals rather than titled amateurs—when he sanctioned the new constitution of the Confraternity of St. Julien des Ménétriers. This body, whose members were instrumentalists headed by a *roi des ménétriers,* had been organized in 1321, and by 1335 had prospered sufficiently to complete a hospital for poor musicians. Its membership originally included *jongleurs* and *jongleresses,* but under the constitution of 1407 the guild was placed on a higher professional level: before teaching or otherwise pursuing his calling, a musician had to pass an examination and be pronounced *"suffisant"* by the *roi* or his deputies.[14a]

Transfers of musicians from one French center to another were frequent, as were the instances in which French musicians went abroad and foreign ones came to France. During the reigns of Charles V and Charles VI, the various French courts, including that of Burgundy, showed a special predilection for German performers.[15] But it was the contacts with Italy and England that were to prove particularly vitalizing to French composition.

The courts were naturally not alone in fostering music. We have some idea of how many singers the chief cathedrals employed in certain years. Cambrai in 1386 had ten *vicaires* and six boys; Chartres in 1390, thirteen *heuriers;*

---

[8] About Charles as amateur musician, *see* DoorM, 24f; PirH, 115.
[9] PirG, 322.   [10] PirM, 21.   [11] Cf. DannS, 58.
[12] For a study of music at the court of the Breton dukes in the 14th and 15th centuries, *see* LauM.
[13] About which, *see* MarH, 98f; A. Piaget in *Romania* XX (1891), 417ff; XXXI (1902), 597ff.
[14] PirM, 24f; a chanson by Villeroye pr. StaD, 82. Jehan Carité, another member, may be the Charité named in the Oxford MS described on p. 10 *infra;* but *see* DannS, 11f.
[14a] Cf. BernhM. About modern literature on the guild, *see* A, Loft in JAMS IV (1951), 264ff.
[15] PirA.

Notre Dame in Paris in 1398, seventeen or eighteen *clercs de matines*.[16] (The three terms are varying local designations, all meaning "singers of the psalmody of the Office."[17]) Cambrai, already celebrated as an ecclesiastical center, was to become famous also for its music. Pierre d'Ailly, formerly chancellor of the University of Paris, became Bishop of Cambrai in 1396. He appears to have been a man of musical sensibility and to have stimulated cultivation of the art there.[18] In a letter addressed in 1428 to the chapter at Cambrai by Philip of Luxemburg, the writer paid tribute to its cathedral by saying, "It surpasses all others and may well serve them as a model, with the beauty of its chant, the magnificence of its lighting, and the delightful clangor of its bells."[19] The Sainte Chapelle in Paris continued to maintain its *maîtrise,* or choir school, as it had done since at least 1299, the date of the earliest surviving mention of music there.[20]

Relative Musical Roles of France and the Low Countries

After what has been said in describing the stage upon which Binchois and Dufay (for part of his career) were active, it would be redundant to insist at length that the once frequently encountered name, "First Netherlands School," is misleading. The term, like "Second Netherlands School" and "Third Netherlands School"—all introduced more than a century ago by Raphael Kiesewetter[21]—served, for a time, to classify certain composers, bound together by chronological position and some common traits, and thus to facilitate the study of their work. But the area now known as the Netherlands, though it contributed such masters as Obrecht and later Sweelinck, was not the dominant factor in producing the composers of Kiesewetter's three schools. Many musicians of the first one clustered about the court of Burgundy, and some historians have therefore regarded them as constituting a "Burgundian School."[21a] However, since the main composers, all French by heredity and culture, came not from the land between Lorraine and Provence that constituted the basic duchy of Burgundy, but from the area now surrounding the Franco-Belgian border, it would be better, if one wishes to classify them by nationality, to designate them as northern French.[21b] (A few late 14th- and early 15th-century songs with Dutch or Flemish texts[22] seem to lie outside the main current.) As at other courts, moreover, musicians

[16] PirR, 56.   [17] PirGM, 164.   [18] Cf. PirE, 30; BorQS, 19.

[19] HabD, 42; about 15th-century music at Cambrai Cathedral, *see also* HouH, 82ff, 421f; VanP, 80. Interest was not restricted to sacred music; cf. PirH, 55.

[20] *See* BrenM, 12; about the Sainte Chapelle in the 15th century, *see ibid.,* 25ff.

[21] In KiesT.

[21a] Designating the music of the first school as "Burgundian" seems to have begun with GurB, and the term *"Burgundische Epoche"* was introduced in BesM, 184. "Burgundian School" was first used in literature in English in LangN and LangM, 176ff.

[21b] Cf. HandMG, 249f.

[22] For examples, with discussion, *see* WolfAL; LenN; BäumkN; CouG.

kept passing to and from that of Burgundy, and nothing is known to indicate that a special Burgundian style was developed, as distinguished from French style in general.[23] In Kiesewetter's "Second" and "Third" schools, the fundamental culture was still French and the influence of what is present-day Belgium was also deeply felt, being exerted with especial force on the "Second" school. This has led to the occasional adoption of "Flemish" and "Franco-Flemish" as descriptive terms, respectively, for the last two schools.[23a] But in the "Second" school, quite as well as in the "Third," the Walloon contribution was very important, composers native to what is now Belgium including many from areas other than Flanders.[23b] The term "Franco-Flemish," however, has its virtues if applied to a group consisting partly of people who are French (in the broad cultural sense) and partly of Flemings; but it should be noted that the term excludes the Dutch. Certain modern writers, instead of either of the above-mentioned terms, simply use "Netherlandish." [23c] "Netherlands" (= "Low Countries") had no official meaning in the 15th century; in the 16th it represented territory embracing, approximately, the Netherlands and Belgium of today, plus part of Northern France, to a little beyond Cambrai—just the area that produced most of the musicians for whom a group name would be useful.[23d] But, granted that this area produced the chief musicians of the last two schools, it is still wrong to exclude the lands belonging to the French crown, where the activities of such a giant as Ockeghem mainly took place. "Netherlands School," even in its 16th-century sense, unfairly minimizes the role of France. "Franco-Netherlandish" is better, and is probably an acceptable designation for the later schools if, here again, one wishes to use a term with national connotations and is willing to overlook an anachronism with regard to the 15th century.[24] But perhaps it is just as well to avoid all the hairsplitting to which historians' use of national names for the successive generations has given rise, and simply to name them after their leading composers.

While in the early 15th century, as in the 13th and 14th, the French were a great nation in the field of music, their international position was no longer so exclusively that of disseminators; they were also recipients. They combined Italian and English elements with French elements, producing a music that may be called international and bringing about a shift from the more pronounced nationalism of 14th-century music. The English elements in use as late as the middle of the 15th century are discussed in ReMMA (Chap. 14), which goes farther chronologically in describing the music of England than it does in dealing with that of France and Italy. Before discussing the

---

[23] Cf. FédorovB.   [23a] Cf. LangN; LangM, 176ff.   [23b] Cf. ClercxB, 114ff.
[23c] E.g., Besseler and Van den Borren.
[23d] Cf. BorQS, 21; also the 2 studies there cited.
[24] As we do not hesitate to do in this book (at least for the area covered by the modern Low Countries, i.e., the Netherlands and Belgium), where that avoids circumlocution.

music of the Dufay–Binchois generation, therefore, it is desirable to go back to the music of those two countries at about the turn of the 15th century (interpreting "turn" broadly), that is, to a period which, musically, still belonged essentially to the Middle Ages.

French Music between Machaut and Dufay

In French music, the period between Machaut's death (c. 1377) and the beginning of Dufay's activity (c. 1420) was a transition between two peaks. For the earlier years, we have but few composers' names, recorded in such sources as Chantilly MS 1047 and the Apt MS (which seems to preserve at least some of the repertory of the papal court at Avignon).[25] Very few names are given in the Reina MS at Paris.[26] Fuller information is afforded by Modena, Bibl. Estense *a. M.* 5. 24 (*olim* lat. 568; dating from shortly after 1400) and such later MSS (in which works by Dufay and his generation appear beside those of older men) as Bologna, Liceo mus. Q 15 (*olim* 37; dating from approximately 1430), the Aosta MS, and Oxford, Bodleian, MS Canonici misc. 213 (both from 1450 or somewhat earlier).[27] The last, of north Italian origin, preserves about 325 pieces; it consists of 10 fascicles, Nos. 5 to 8 being important for the first two decades of the 15th century.[28] The seven Trent Codices, Nos. 87 to 93 (87 and 92 being the oldest, 91 the most recent) were compiled at Trent, then under Germanic control, between 1440 and 1480. Their huge repertory, however (dating mostly from c. 1420 to c. 1480), includes a few works bearing the names of men active during the period under discussion.[29]

The fact that the various MSS fall into two groups, chronologically, means that the contemporary music in them represents two generations of com-

---

[25] Both receive brief attention in ReMMA (pp. 337, 357f, 411, 415). Contents of the Chantilly MS are listed in WolfG I, 329ff (emendations in LudGM, 611); those of the Apt MS are pr. in GasMA (but *see* de Van's review in Acta, XII [1940], 64ff). Concerning both MSS, *see also* MGG II, 1085ff (also I, Pl. XXVIII), and I, 569f, respectively. About sources in which part of the Avignon repertory may be preserved, *see* BorQS, 18.

[26] Contents of this MS (part of which dates from the early 15th century), listed in WolfG I, 261ff; but *see also* LudGM, 616.

[27] For lists of the contents of these 4 MSS, *see* respectively, PirrE, 116ff; VanB; VanAM; ReaneyO. Such men as Machaut and Landini continue to appear in the Modena MS. For an article on the pieces with French text in the Bologna MS (touched upon in ReMMA for the sake of its English music), *see* TorF. About other relevant MSS, *see* DannS, 13f.

[28] Cf. BesS I, 240. It is with these fascicles that DannS (a study of the years immediately before Dufay) is mainly concerned. StaD gives 50 pieces, mostly secular, from this MS; MarM gives 30; BorP prints all its contents having Latin text except those by Dufay or those pr. in StaD or (after the Trent MSS) in DTO VII; further items in DannS; CW XIX, XXII; etc. StaD has 8 pp. of facsimile; ApelN, 3 more (and 2 duplicates of facsimiles in StaD); MarM, 1 more. For a paper on the MS, *see* BorCC.

[29] About these MSS, cf. ReMMA, 410. A thematic index of MSS 87–92 is pr. in DTO VII, 31ff; a 2-page unpaginated errata list for this index was supplied with DTO XI¹. The index to MS 93 is pr. in DTO XXXI, viiff.

posers.[29a] The ensuing discussion, in the course of associating certain composers with certain MSS, will show who were the most significant figures of each
generation.

The Chantilly and Modena MSS, containing many examples of highly
complicated notation—a type sometimes called "Mannered" [30]—, were possibly compiled for pedagogical use.[30a] While much older MSS (e.g., Harley
978) contain verbal instructions, i.e., *canones* (canons, rules),[31] for the performance of a polyphonic piece, it is now that we first meet, in any profusion,
directions explaining—or veiling—the significance of notes by means of
some play on words.[32] In short, puzzles, such as were to amuse various 15th-
century composers, including Dunstable,[33] were well on the way. "Musicians
. . . began to indulge in complicated rhythmic tricks and in the invention
of highly involved methods of notating them. . . . Here we find compositions
written in the form of a circle or a heart . . . an indication of the strong hold
upon the imagination of the composer that the purely manual business of
writing exercised in those days." [34] The overrefinement evident in the
Mannered Notation reflected a high degree of sophistication in the music
itself, producing a type of composition (to which the term "Manneristic
Style" has been applied [35]) that constitutes the final stage in the development called, rather loosely,[36] the *ars nova*. By c. 1450, white notes—not then
new—were generally adopted in France and Italy for the minim and all
larger values, and the worst of the old intricacies of notation were discarded. White mensural notation [37] became standard for the music of the
entire period covered by this book, except for such instrumental music as
used tablature.

Several composers of the years between Machaut and Dufay are known
to us only by name and by examples of their work; even where factual data

---

[29a] Cf. ApelFM, 1.

[30] Described in ApelN, 403ff; cf. ReMMA, 346 (fn. 41), 358 (fn. 78). *See also* ApelFM, 7ff;
ApelF.

[30a] Cf. VanP, 84f, 87, 90.

[31] It should be borne in mind that *canon* did not have its present meaning until later; what we
call "canon" was called *fuga*. This caused no confusion, since the thing we term "fugue" did not
yet exist. The *canones* (rules) applied to a melody that was written out only once. They directed
that, e.g., (*1*) after being read as written, the melody was to be performed in augmentation or
diminution, or perhaps in contrary or in retrograde motion (i.e., in mirror or in crab fashion);
or (*2*) the melody was to be performed as a *fuga*, at a designated interval (unison, fifth, etc.),
each new entrance to occur after a specified lapse of time. As the *fuga* gained in favor and the
augmenting, etc., of tenors died out, the term "canon" shifted from the rule itself to the one
sort of thing the rule still required (incidentally leaving the term "fuga" available for a new
use).

[32] For a rare, earlier example, *see* Ludwig's ed. of Machaut, III, 71; WolfMS, 23.

[33] For some examples of his puzzles, *see* OH II, 33f.

[34] ApelN, 403. A facsimile of a piece written in heart shape (from the Chantilly MS) is pr. in
ApelN, 427, and WolfMS, 100; transcr. in HAM, 51; ReaneyE, 9. Further about early *canones*,
see WolfH I, 426f; DannS, 31.

[35] E.g., in ApelFM, 10ff.   [36] Cf. ReMMA, 331.

[37] Mentioned incidentally in ReMMA, 345; discussed at length in ApelN and WolfH I.

do reach us, they are scant. Among the men represented in the Reina MS, although most of them are not actually named,[38] are Pierre des Molins, Jacques (or Jacopin) de Selesses (or Senleches), Grimace (Grimache), and Grenon. The *En atendant* of Selesses [39] may be singled out as illustrating the extreme rhythmic complexity in which late 14th-century music sometimes indulged. Grimace's three-part *Alarme, alarme* [40] is interesting as an example of a love song written in the style of a battle piece and employing a theme resembling a military signal. Chansons of this type, comparing the beloved to a fortress to be taken by force and drawing amusing parallels, continued to be produced by later composers.[41]

Gacian Rayneau (= Reyneau), represented in the Chantilly MS, was active at Barcelona as late as 1429 (*see* Chap. 11). Among the ten pieces [42] by Solage in this MS is *Corps femenin,* in which the *ballade* is shown achieving the considerable length of 151 measures (one of Machaut's longest *ballades* had extended to only 44).[43] Jean Vaillant, whose *Dame doucement* is dated 1369 in the same MS, is still traceable in the early 15th century, when he taught music in Paris; [44] his *virelai, Par maintes foy,* with its charming birdcalls, is the source of Oswald von Wolkenstein's *Der may mit lieber zal.*[45] Information regarding Jean Tapissier shows that he too was known at the time to the Parisians, a glimpse of whose musical life is afforded by a retrospective passage in *Le Champion des dames,* Martin le Franc's poem of some 24,000 verses, dedicated to Philip the Good and dating from 1441–1442. The poem contains a whole canto on the state of the arts in France. Two of the six stanzas dealing with music read: [46]

Tapissier, Carmen, Césaris	*Tapissier, Carmen, Césaris,*
N'a pas longtemps si bien chanterrent	*Not long ago so well did sing*
Qu'ilz esbahirent tout Paris	*That they astonished all Paris*
Et tous ceulx qui les frequenterrent;	*And all who came foregathering.*
Mais oncques jour ne deschanterrent	*But still their discant held no strain*

[38] They have been identified through copies of the same works in other MSS that do give the names.

[39] Facsimile from Modena, Bibl. Estense a. M. 5. 24 (*olim* 568). in ApelN, 423; transcr. in HAM, 49; ApelFM, 81* (cf. *ibid.*, 31). 4 other pieces by Selesses, *ibid.*, 77*, 79* (facsimile on Pl. VI), 83*, 84*.

[40] Pr. ApelFM, 122*; GasA, 787.

[41] The type exists in independent poetry also; cf. Molinet's "Dialogue du gendarme et de l'amoureux" (in *Les Faictz et Dictz de Jean Molinet,* Noël Dupire, ed., 3 vols., 1936–1939).

[42] All pr. in ApelFM, 45*ff (Pls. IV and V give 2 in facsimile).

[43] Cf. *ibid.*, 6.   [44] PirM, 2f, 9.

[45] Cf. ReMMA, 379. For Vaillant's piece, *see Zeitschrift für deutsche Bildung* II, 550; ApelFM, 114*; another Vaillant piece, *ibid.*, 128*.

[46] After Van den Borren's transcript (BorD, 53f) from a MS at Brussels. Note comments he quotes from Pirro and those he makes himself, explaining the discrepancies between his version and those printed elsewhere (StaD, 13; OH II, 23, 41; etc.). Note especially substitution of *aveugles* for *Anglois* in line 1 of the last stanza that he prints; the poet's reference is to the blind viol-players at the Burgundian court (cf. p. 51 *infra*), not to the English. For an article on a MS of the *Champion* at Grenoble (with 10 plates reproducing miniatures), *see* JaC.

En melodie de tel chois	*Filled with such goodly melody—*
Ce m'ont dit qui les hanterrent	*So folk who heard them now maintain—*
Que G. Du Fay et Binchois.	*As Binchois sings, or Dufaÿ.*
Car ilz ont nouvelle pratique	*For these a newer way have found,*
De faire frisque concordance	*In music high and music low,*[47]
En haulte et en basse musique,	*Of making pleasant concord sound—*
En fainte, en pause, et en muance,	*In "feigning",*[48] *rests, mutatio.*[49]
Et ont prins de la contenance	*The English guise they wear with grace,*
Angloise et ensuy Dunstable	*They follow Dunstable aright,*
Pour quoy merveilleuse plaisance	*And thereby have they learned apace*
Rend leur chant joyeux et notable.	*To make their music gay and bright.*

Tapissier is among the contributors to the supposed Avignon repertory, others of significance being Chipre, Perrinet (Pierre Fontaine), Jean Granet, and Tailhandier. Tapissier and his two companions in the *Champion*—Carmen [49a] and Césaris—are all represented in Bologna, Liceo mus. Q 15, and Oxford, Canonici misc. 213. An organist Césaris is known to have obtained a small organ in 1417 from Yolanda of Aragon, Queen of Sicily, for the cathedral at Angers.[50] Further information regarding Loqueville and Grenon (both also represented in the Oxford MS) shows that they taught music at the Cambrai Cathedral, the former from 1413 apparently until his death in 1418.[51] The latter became canon at Saint Sépulcre in Paris in 1399 (and subdeacon and deacon in 1401),[52] instructed the choirboys at Laon (1403–1408), then taught grammar to those at Cambrai for a short time,[53] served the Duke of Burgundy (1412; cf. p. 6), returned to Paris (1418),[54] taught music at Cambrai (1421–1424),[55] was at Rome as a singer in the Papal Choir (1425–1427), and eventually returned north, being traceable at Cambrai as late as 1449.[56] Other names appearing in the Oxford MS, and also in the lists of the pope's singers through 1428, include those of Guillaume Legrant (1419–1421) and Pierre Fontaine (1420–1428).[57] (*See also* pp. 38ff.) The Hasprois of the MS is undoubtedly the Jo. Asproys who was among the singers of the antipope at Avignon in 1394.[58]

Baude Cordier, though not known to have been a papal singer, is another musician who spread French influence to Italy. In a charming poem (in *rondeau* form),[59] added after the piece in the Chantilly MS that is written

[47] "High" and "low" here mean "loud" and "soft" (cf. ReMMA, 385).
[48] I.e., in applying *musica ficta*. [49] "Modulating" from one hexachord to another.
[49a] For data on him, *see* MGG II, 850ff.
[50] PirM, 29f. Fuller data on Césaris in MGG II, 983ff. [51] PirH, 55, 57. [52] PirM, 20.
[53] PirH, 55. [54] PirM, 33. [55] HouH, 82. [56] Cf. MarH, 67, 155.
[57] Cf. HabD, 59f; HabR, 32.
[58] Cf. HabR, 25. He may also be the Jehan Simon who became a minstrel to Charles V in 1380 (cf. PirM, 2f). *See also* PirH, 55.
[59] Pr. WolfG I, 334f; MGG II, 1665.

down in the shape of a circle (cf. p. 11), he states that he comes from Rheims and that his music is known in Rome. The piece itself consists of a canon *a 2* (actually a round) supported by a free third part, and thus resembles the Italian *caccia* more than the French *chace*.[60] Perhaps we have here an example of Franco-Italian interaction, of which there will be ample evidence later. There are several chansons by Cordier in the Oxford MS.[61]

Of special interest, as illustrating how widespread French influence was, is Turin, MS J II 9, originating from Cyprus and dating from between 1413 and 1434. All the contents[62] are anonymous, but they show that the MS was the product of a circle whose musical training was French. Cyprus was still an outpost of western culture, as it had been under King Peter I, who figures in Machaut's poem *La Prise d'Alexandrie*.

The period under consideration retained traits familiar from French 14th-century music at its height, and added to these not only several features borrowed from abroad but some that were new. The *formes fixes*—the *rondeau, virelai,* and *ballade*—continued in use, but with modifications and with a shift in popularity from one form to another. Thus, the *ballade,* prime favorite with Machaut and in the Chantilly MS, yielded pride of place to the *rondeau* in the Oxford MS, as Table I shows.[63]

Table I

	Machaut (polyphonic examples only)	Chantilly MS	Oxford MS, fascicles 5–8
Rondeaux	21	18	78
Ballades	41	68	19
Virelais	8	10	8

The *rondeau* tended to lengthen. In the Oxford MS, its refrain ordinarily has four or five lines as compared with two or three in Machaut. Where the refrain has four, the form of the resulting *rondeau quatrain,* as it is called, is —by lines—*ABCDabABabcdABCD*.[64] This is merely an expansion of the

[60] Cf. ReMMA, 365. For a facsimile, *see* AuP, Pl. XXII; for transcrs., AuP, 21; RieH I², 352 (cf. Handschin in MD III, 84).

[61] He is represented in the Apt MS too, though he is not named there; cf. BesM, 150. The heart-shaped piece from the Chantilly MS (fn. 34) is also his. For his *Amans amés, see* HAM, 51; ReaneyE, 14; facsimile in MGG II, 1665.

[62] For list, etc., *see* BesS I, 209ff. For some transcrs., *see* BesM, 146; WolfH I, 369, 376. Facsimile in ApelN, 419. *See also* BukMR, 76 (= BukOH, 55).

[63] After MGG I, 1125.

[64] As in ReMMA, repetition of a letter represents musical repetition; a new letter, new music. Capital letters indicate text repetition (i.e., presence of refrain lines); lower-case letters, use of fresh text (i.e., presence of strophe lines). Unless otherwise stated, changes or repetitions of letters bear no relation to the rhyme scheme, as they do in the discussions of some other writers. (Cf. ReMMA, 169, fn. 14.)

rondeau pattern applied by the *trouvères*.[65] The *rondeau* with five-line refrain (*rondeau cinquain*) corresponds in this manner: *ABCDEabcABCabcde-ABCDE*. The rare *rondeau sixain*—some purely literary examples exist by as early a poet as Christine de Pizan (d. 1430)—is found in musical setting also. In MS copies, the music is, of course, written out only once; but in *rondeaux quatrains*, a repetition sign ⸭ (or something similar) appears after line 2; in *rondeaux cinquains*, after line 3. There normally are sustained time-values at this point. These two types remain standard for the rest of the history of the form.[66]

The old *virelai* stanza pattern—section 1 with refrain text, section 2, section 2 with fresh text, section 1 with fresh text, section 1 with refrain text [67]—continues essentially unaltered; but with Grenon's *La plus belle et doulce figure* [68] we encounter a *virelai* that consists of only one stanza, rather than of the several that were customary in the past. This one-stanza type, which came sometimes to be called *bergerette*,[69] was to enjoy considerable vogue later. (Modern writers are likely to refer to examples of the type by either name.) Occasionally two-section compositions appear in a musical source with only one set of words for section 1 and two sets for section 2. Such pieces are likely to be *virelais* with incomplete texts—a fact demonstrated by the appearance of some of the same works with complete *virelai* texts in other sources.

With the dwindling in popularity of the traditional grand *ballade*, examples with only one or two stanzas sometimes replace the formerly favored three-stanza type. However, we continue to find (if we analyze by line) the musical-poetic stanza structure preferred by Machaut: *ababcdE* (with the rhyme scheme *ababbcc*). That is, we encounter what the Germans would call two *Stollen* and an *Abgesang* (producing the *Bar* form), the *Abgesang* concluding with a refrain [70]—only theoretically, of course, where limitation to a single stanza makes a functionally repetitive refrain impossible [70a]. But there is much variation in rhyme order and in length and number of lines.

---

[65] Cf. ReMMA, 222. The smaller 8-line form is poetically identical with the "triolet" of modern English prosody, which applies the term "rondeau" to quite another form.

[66] As earlier, so in the 15th century, some *rondeaux* reach us as mere refrains, e.g., StaD 82, 134; MarM, 19.

[67] I.e., with the form—by section and not by line—*AbbaA*. Certain modern writers call the *b* section the "residuum." In some sources, to be sure, the term appears at the head of this section if, the first section being long, *b* begins on a new left-hand page. Since section 1 comes to a full stop, some such word is useful to show that the new page presents a continuation. The term is also found, however, in connection with other forms, and should therefore not be regarded as a specific designation for the *b* of the *virelai*.

[68] Pr. MarM, 4.

[69] E.g., in Pierre Fabri's *Le Grand et Vrai Art de pleine rhétorique* (1521), where Busnois is wrongly credited with inventing the type and where a roundabout description is given by means of a comparison with the *rondeau* (*see* A. Héron's edition, II, 71).

[70] So that the form—by section and not by line—may be represented by *aabC*.

[70a] If, however, a source gives only one stanza, it may indicate the beginning of what is intended as the refrain by means of a fermata (as is done by the source with respect to Ex. 1) or in some other way.

In all these *formes fixes,* each line of text, as in the past, is set as an individual unit.

The growing reciprocal influence of France and Italy is evident in *ballades* by Hasprois [71] and Cuvelier (*Ne Geneive, Tristan, Yssout* [72]) containing melodic sequences such as frequently occur in Italian *trecento* music [73] but less characteristically [74] in French music. The sequences occasionally appear in melismas, thus bringing these coloratura passages—often requiring virtuoso performers—closer to Italian than to French models. A *ballade* by Grenon,[75] rich in melismas of the less organized kind favored by the French, nevertheless shows the Italian touch, in the state in which the piece reaches us, through the presence of a contratenor by Matteo da Perugia. Besides the Italianate melodic sequences there are isorhythmic sequences (i.e., repetitions of short rhythmic patterns to fresh melodic content) [76] such as earmark much 14th-century French music. There are even isorhythmic *rondeaux,* in which the second section is isorhythmically related, in all voices, to the first.[77] A steady rhythmic flow, replacing Machaut's frequent contrast between flowing and sustained passages, is an important feature of the newer style. The latter portion or all of the *clos* ending of the recurring section of the *ballade* is often related to the ending of the refrain by means of musical rhyme (i.e., musical identity), as in Machaut's *ballades.*[78] Dissonances are numerous and conspicuous. Also present sometimes is a profusion of sharps and flats, as in the *Bonté, bialté* of Césaris,[79] in which work, however, the accidentals do not give rise to semitonal progressions on a single degree (i.e., from C to C-sharp or B to B-flat).[80] Music histories, etc. (including ReMMA), commonly embrace both such progressions and the profuse employment of accidentals, without such progressions, under the single term "chromaticism," although the two are quite different musical phenomena. To avoid confusion, we shall retain "chromaticism" as a generic term, covering both; but we shall also employ specific terms to distinguish between them: "degree inflection" for the former and "accidentalism" for the latter.

The *texture* in which a vocal top line (or, as this part is interchangeably called, treble, superius, cantus, or discantus) is supported by a subordinate, instrumental tenor and contratenor was much in vogue. This treble-

---

[71] Pr. DannS, 125, 128.

[72] The beginning pr. BesM, 145. For the identity of Cuvelier (the Cunelier of some historians), *see* PirM, 2.

[73] Cf. ReMMA, 369.   [74] Cf. BesM, 145.   [75] Pr. MarM, 1; WolfME, 33.

[76] The passage from Cuvelier cited in fn. 72 contains isorhythmic sequences as well as melodic ones, as does his *ballade,* pr. WolfG III, 155. The original notation of all transcrs. in WolfG III, cited in this and other footnotes, is approximated in WolfG II.

[77] About 5 such pieces, *see* ApelFM, 7; for 2 of them in print, *see ibid.,* 130*, 131*.

[78] Cf. ReMMA, 353. (About rhyme, *see also ibid.,* 107f.)

[79] Pr. ReaneyE, 30; WolfME, 27; WolfH I, 348 (*see* comments in DannS, 52, about the transcr.); discussed in FiB, 7. Flats appear before B, E, A, and D, while F is sharpened.

[80] About a fairly early ex. of such a progression, *see* ReMMA, 421.

dominated style, unsuitably termed by some historians the *"ballade* style," suffered no such decline as did the *structure* known as the *ballade* form. (*"Ballade* style" is likely to produce the misleading impression that the kind of writing it represents is limited to the *ballade* form, whereas it is present among *rondeaux* and *virelais* also.[81]) Indeed, this style almost ousted others from the chanson repertory: writing *a 2,* to which Machaut devoted much attention, now appeared comparatively seldom. Even the "Mannerists" had, in principle, adhered to the style: their love of intricacy, to be sure, produced complex lower parts, the contratenor often rivaling the superius in maintaining variety and rhythmic animation; but the superius nevertheless was normally predominant. After these composers, the style came more and more to be applied to much shorter pieces than the great *ballades* of their time and of the earlier 14th century. The shift to this briefer type is one of the important developments in French music of c. 1400 to c. 1420. Preludes, interludes, and postludes become shorter, and syllabic passages take precedence over melismatic ones. The contrast that once existed between the vocal and instrumental parts becomes less sharp.

Besides the treble-dominated style, the French composers of the time used the following survivals from the past in their chansons: (1) the conductus style, with all parts moving more or less simultaneously, point against point; [82] (2) the Italian *ballata* style,[83] with vocal cantus, vocal tenor (i.e., a tenor with text), and usually an instrumental contratenor; (3) a style generally resembling that of the motet *a 3* or *a 4* musically, with upper voices that are free or in imitation—occasionally in canon, probably owing to the influence of the Italian *caccia*—and with a rhythmically less animated tenor; (4) the polytextual style, also, of course, deriving from the motet.[84]

We have also, from this period, a few examples of a new style that was to prove short-lived in its application to complete pieces—writing *a 2,* in which both parts are not only independent but of equal importance; they may have either the same text or different texts. An example by Césaris, a double-*rondeau* (i.e., one with two texts),[85] illustrates also the survival of some old musical traits: the avoidance of a steady rhythmic flow, through the juxtaposition of slow-moving and fast-moving phrases, and interference with clear-cut

[81] Handschin, in RB I, 95, suggested the substitution of *"cantilena* style" (which has its virtues), but retracted in RB VI, 10f. This term, like "free-treble style," is restricted to pieces with original main melodies, but, since the same texture is sometimes found where the main melody paraphrases a *cantus prius factus,* we prefer "treble-dominated style." One can always make clear through the verbal context whether the melody is new or not. It should be added that, while by far the greater number of pieces with treble domination are *a 3* in the period under discussion, the four terms mentioned are all intended to apply to writing *a 2* likewise.

[82] For an example by Grenon, *see* DannS, 133.

[83] This style seems to have entered French music about the turn of the century, but to have made headway slowly. For a French example, *see* MarM, 7.

[84] For examples by Césaris of style 3 and of styles 3 and 4 combined, *see* DannS, 131, and StaD, 96, respectively.

[85] Pr. DannS, 136.

sectional divisions through not allowing the two parts to have their cadences simultaneously. It is well defined phrase formation that was to prove characteristic of early 15th-century music.

The following little piece by Loqueville,[86] touching upon the fortunes of itinerant musicians, illustrates several points that have been mentioned: the treble-dominated style, the new, brief *ballade* form, and clear-cut phrase formation. In illustrating the last point, it reveals the distinct rhythmic grouping—regular enough not to be at variance with the modern conception of the bar-line in transcriptions into present-day notation—that had characterized French music ever since the days of the rhythmic modes and had been present likewise in Italian *trecento* music, a kind of distinct grouping that was to continue for a while in French music, but was to yield in the middle of the 15th century (*see* Chap. 3) to a new rhythmic style introduced from the north. The delightful play of "hemiola" such as we find in this piece (and likewise in Exx. *5a, 6a–c*, and *7b* and *c*) occurs frequently throughout Renaissance music; this is the device in which rhythmic groups of $\frac{3}{4}$ and $\frac{6}{8}$, or their equivalents, are combined either successively in the same voice or simultaneously in different voices.[87] While each of the two lower parts here has a flat in the signature, the highest part has none.[87a] The question of conflicting signatures will be discussed in Chapter 2. The piece is obviously intended for voice and two instruments.

EXAMPLE 1. *Quant compaignons s'en vont juer*—Loqueville (Oxford, Bodleian, Canonici misc. 213, f. 90ʳ).[88]

---

[86] For a *rondeau* of his, *see* DannS, 130; for a Credo, BorP, 134. For a brief discussion of other pieces, *see* PirH, 56f.   [87] Cf. SachsRT, 190.

[87a] The absence of a signature in the upper staff of Ex. 1 is therefore deliberate.

[88] An accidental added above or below a note (or within parentheses) indicates that, while it

> When comrades sally forth to play
>   In divers countries here and there,
> They do not banquet every day
>   On roasted capon or fat hare
> Save if with gold they are supplied.
> For just as sure it does betide
>   That if a comrade lose his gains
> *He ends with sorely wounded pride,*
>   *His feet held fast by two stout chains.*
>   (Translated by G.R.)

It has been pointed out (pp. 11f) that music of the time occasionally attained extreme rhythmic complexity. Intricacy was sometimes present in other respects also, to an extent that the modest character of Example 1 would never lead one to expect. An anonymous *rondeau* in the Reina MS, *Passerose de biaulté*,[89] contains an early example of mensuration canon.[90] Philippe de Vitri's four prolations,[91] still fairly new when the Reina MS was compiled, show most interestingly how a system of notation, called into being by the requirements of musical creation, may sometimes suggest to such creation, in turn, steps it would otherwise probably not take. In a modern (i.e., post-Renaissance) mensuration canon, the various parts, beginning simultaneously, give forth the same melody, but in different time-values, the values in one part bearing a fixed relationship to those in another (e.g., being in one part consistently double those in another);[92] such a procedure fits naturally into our system of notation. In the *ars nova* notation, however, evolved by de Vitri out of the older Franconian system, more interesting relationships—possible in our notation, but not likely to occur to a composer using it—suggested themselves quite readily. Here a breve could be divided either into two semibreves (*tempus imperfectum*) or into three (*tempus perfectum*); a semibreve into either two minims (*prolatio minor* or *imperfecta*) or into

---

is absent in the source, its application was (or may have been) required by the practice of *musica ficta* (cf. ReMMA, 380ff). Except in some "scientific" editions of old music, it has become customary to replace the various time-value symbols of the old notation with modern ones of shorter apparent value. But instead of dividing the original time-values (by 4 or some other figure) this procedure actually gives their equivalents in modern notation, since, over the centuries, the significance of note-symbols has changed with respect to duration. Cf. ReMMA, 275f; CW XIX, 3; BesV, 9, 16f; SachsRN; SachsMH, 139f (includes a comparative chart). It is sometimes necessary also (though not in Ex. 1) to replace the original time-signature, since it may not correspond, in its modern significance, to the true rhythm of the music; cf. SachsRT, 241ff.

[89] Not by Trebor, as stated in WolfG I, 266; cf. LudGM, 616. The Trebor piece with the same title (from the Chantilly MS) is pr. ApelFM, 65*.

[90] I am indebted to Dr. Oliver Strunk for bringing this piece to my attention. For a mensuration canon in Trent MS 87, *see* BukMC, 167; for a quite elaborate one in Old Hall, *see* the anon. Credo (which may be by Pycard; cf. BukMR, 54) pr. RamsO II, 101 (*see also* ApelN, 432ff and App., No. 64).

[91] Cf. ReMMA, 343.

[92] *See*, e.g., Schoenberg's canons in *A Birthday Offering to Carl Engel* (1943), 201ff.

three (*prolatio maior* or *perfecta*). By pairing these methods of time-division in all four possible ways, de Vitri obtained his *quatre prolacions,* and it is one of their incidental virtues that they provide a means for obtaining the interesting relationships mentioned. Thus, if in a canon one part is in *tempus perfectum, prolatio minor* ($\frac{3}{1}$; modern equivalent: $\frac{3}{4}$; cf.fn.88), and another part is in *tempus imperfectum, prolatio minor* ($\frac{4}{2}$; modern equivalent: $\frac{2}{4}$),[93] the former part will be in irregular augmentation of the latter: the breves (or modern half-notes) of the part in *tempus imperfectum* will be increased by half in the part having *tempus perfectum,* with certain exceptions,[94] but all smaller time-values will remain the same in both parts. That is what happens in the two lower voices of *Passerose de biaulté.*

EXAMPLE 2. Opening of *Passerose de biaulté*—Anon. (Reina MS, f. 65ᵛ; transcr. by Oliver Strunk).

⁹MS has e

Another piece in the Reina MS, preserved also in the Chantilly MS, employs canon with change of time-interval. In the refrain of this composition—*Plasanche ortost acux,* a four-part *virelai* by Jean de Picquigny—the device is used quite simply,[94a] but it was to become a subtle means of adding elasticity to passages in canon as time progressed.

As in the 14th century,[95] secular music occupied the chief attention of composers early in the 15th. But they did not entirely neglect the sacred motet. Like the musicians of many other periods, however, their use of the designation "motet" was extremely vague. Originally[95a] the term had stood for a type that was an outgrowth of organum, itself an accretion to the liturgical chant. In modern times, the word, from the strictly liturgical standpoint, has become increasingly applicable only to compositions which, like the earliest motets, may lead an existence within the liturgical framework (i.e., they may

[93] The other two prolations are *tempus perfectum, prolatio maior* $\left(\frac{9}{2}=\frac{9}{8}\right)$ and *tempus imperfectum, prolatio maior* $\left(\frac{6}{2}=\frac{6}{8}\right)$.

[94] E.g., where a breve is followed by one semibreve; observe the two half-notes on g and the one on b-natural in the middle voice in Ex. 2. *See* ApelN, 108, Rule 3.

[94a] After rests and 3 preliminary notes, the superius becomes the *comes* in a canon introduced 2 measures earlier by the second voice. The canon continues at the 2-measure time-interval for 5 measures. But then, partly by eliminating rests, the superius contracts into 1 meas. what the second voice had spread over 2, and the canon continues at a distance of 1 meas.

[95] Cf. ReMMA, 357.   [95a] Cf. *ibid.,* 312.

be sung at a church service) without, however, becoming a part of it. But just as in the 13th century, when the motet was new, a piece could belong to the species if it was written in the style of the church motet but had a purely secular text not even loosely connected with the church service (e.g., No. 33b in HAM), so in the 15th century, which occasionally went to the opposite extreme, some works were regarded as motets even though their texts were definitely liturgical. Thus, the index of Modena, Bibl. Estense, *a.* X. I, 11, includes, after the line *"hic incipiunt motetti,"* not only nonliturgical works but also settings of the *Ave Regina coelorum* and the *Alma Redemptoris Mater.* If we survey the centuries, we find that a motet may have one text, or two or more simultaneously sung texts; the words may be in Latin or in a vernacular tongue, or two different languages may be sung at the same time. Turning from matters of function and language, we find that the music, though most often polyphonic, is on occasion monophonic.[96] Moreover, pieces labeled *"motectus"* (or something similar) survive in a form apparently intended for instrumental use (at least, there is no text), whatever the original form may have been. It is clear that the meaning of "motet" has altered so frequently and so drastically over the years that no single definition will apply to all the kinds of composition it has designated. While in this book "motet" will most often refer to a vocal piece that is polyphonic and has a text that is both sacred and in Latin (without, however, being a part of the Ordinary of the Mass), no attempt will be made to apply the term with a consistency not found in the sources themselves.

French music of the period under consideration produced no stylistic rebirth of the motet. Instead, in the main, old French traits reappear with an admixture of Italian elements. The tenor motet still prevails—i.e., the kind (standard since the 13th century) that is polytextual and has a tenor (1) evolved from a pre-existent melody and (2) generally moving more slowly than the upper parts. The isorhythmic type of tenor motet, a characteristically French art expression since the days of Philippe de Vitri,[97] continues to flourish. Thus, the *A virtutis—Ergo beata—Benedicta*[98] of Césaris gives each of its four voices an extended rhythmic pattern (or *talea*) of its own, each pattern being sounded four times and each repetition having fresh melodic content, so that the antiphon melody[99] that serves as tenor is given forth only once. The *Eya dulcis—Vale placens*[100] of Tapissier is similar in plan, except that it has three *taleae*. It must date from before 1417, since it mentions, as existing, the Church schism (1370–1417), which at first resulted in the setting up of two rival popes and later of three.[101] Certain passages display the so-called *tuba* style, which is characterized by fanfare effects. It is often found in music of

---

96 *See*, e.g., the Gregorian *Manuel des maîtrises* (1926).   97 Cf. ReMMA, 337ff, 354.
98 Pr. BorP, 174; ReaneyE, 32.   99 Liber, 1606, 1686.   100 Pr. StaD, 187; ReaneyE, 72.
101 The isorhythmic motet by Carmen, pr. BorP, 167, also refers to the schism.

the time.[102] The isorhythmic principle is applied in various ways. Thus, the three upper parts of Grenon's four-part *Ave virtus—Prophetarum—Infelix* [103] begin by each singing a long *talea* and repeating it once. They then go through this procedure three more times, each time with new material. Meanwhile, the lowest part, or tenor, which is entrusted with the final fragment of the popular medieval sequence *Laetabundus*,[104] performs its melody once during the two appearances of *talea*-group A; then it repeats the melody once, in halved time-values, during the two appearances of *talea*-group B; then it repeats the melody twice, with the values further halved, once during each appearance of *talea*-group C; finally, with the values still further halved, it does the same thing during each appearance of *talea*-group D. The tenor, therefore, has six *colores* (melodic repetitions [105]); as is normal, there is no *color* in the upper parts. The piece ends with a brief coda. The way in which the complete tenor is to be evolved from the fragment, which is written out but once in the MS, is indicated by means of a verbal canon (cf. p. 11).[105a] While other kinds of motet come to us from this period, the preference for the isorhythmic type is marked; the song-motet, which was to be favored a little later, seems still to be unknown. DannS selects out of the Oxford and Chantilly MSS 29 motets by Frenchmen (Hubertus de Salinis,[106] Tapissier, Carmen, Césaris, Grenon, Loqueville, Gilet Velut, Alain,[107] and one clearly French Anonymous) and treats them, for purposes of analysis, as providing a cross section of the French motet of the time: no less than twenty-four are isorhythmic. Five have an *introitus* (introduction) that stands outside the isorhythmic scheme;[108] some of these *introitus* are instrumental rather than vocal (cf. p. 42).[109]

The two top parts of Carmen's four-part *Pontifici decori speculi* [110] execute a canon throughout while the other two are free and provide support, so that one may fairly regard the influence of the Italian *caccia* as present (cf. p. 17). It is to be detected in other motets also. Crab canon, no stranger to 14th-century French music,[111] is to be found in a motet by Loqueville.[112] Passages

[102] Further about some passages in *tuba* (= trumpet) style, *see* BorD, 143. There is undoubtedly a relation between these passages and the current use of the slide-trumpet (cf. pp. 35f).

[103] Pr. BorP, 194.

[104] About sequence form, *see* ReMMA, 187–192; about *Laetabundus*, see esp. p. 189.

[105] This is the standard meaning; but the meanings of both *color* and *talea* vary. See AfMW, VIII (1927), 210ff.

[105a] *Nova vobis gaudia*, a simpler isorhythmic motet by Grenon, with 4 *taleae* and 2 *colores*, is pr. MarM, 233. For another simple ex. by him, *see* BorP, 203.

[106] Latin Salinae is Castellane (Basses Alpes) or Seillars (Var). Examples of Hubertus pr. ScherG, 26; BorP, 276.

[107] The inclusion of this composer in a group of Frenchmen is questionable; cf. ReMMA, 411. On the other hand, Mayshuet and Pycard, represented in Old Hall, may be French rather than English; cf. BorQS, 99; ReMMA, 411; BukMR, 71 (= BukOH, 51).

[108] Machaut had already used such an *introitus* (cf. ReMMA, 354).

[109] DannS, 62f, tabulates various characteristics of these 29 pieces; the data on the relation of *color* to *talea* are not wholly dependable.

[110] Pr. StaD, 88 (facsimile, *ibid.*, Pl. 2); ReaneyE, 54.   [111] Cf. ReMMA, 351.

[112] Cf. DannS, 65.

in hocket appear now and then, but the device is less favored than it was formerly.[113] Instead of whole pieces being devoted to it, as in Machaut's *Hoquetus David,* it becomes absorbed in the general polyphonic structure,[114] as in Velut's *Benedicta viscera—Ave Mater.*[115] In the motet, as in other types of composition, anomalous dissonances still occur. That the motet is sometimes affected by secular forms is nothing new; the *rondeau* had entered the realm of the motet as early as the 13th century.[116] Almost the only really forward-looking trait appearing in the motet of the period is a more uniform treatment of the two highest parts (the triplum and motetus), which makes itself felt in the 14th century. There is, to be sure, no close melodic relationship between the parts (cf. p. 4), but the rhythmic differentiation between them, characteristic of the motet of de Vitri's day, becomes less sharp.

From the standpoint of quantity, music for the Ordinary of the Mass suffered, like the motet, from the preference for secular music. No complete Mass reaches us from after Machaut's until shortly before those of Dufay. But we do have examples of settings of individual sections by Tapissier, Loqueville, Grenon, Guillaume Legrant, Velut, Cordier, and others. As is proper in strictly liturgical polyphonic Mass settings, no part-music is provided in the Gloria and Credo for the words *"Gloria in excelsis Deo"* and *"Credo in unum Deum,"* since the celebrant renders them, using the established formulas.[117] The individual sections continue to be written in motet, conductus, or treble-dominated style, as formerly,[118] i.e., in no special style of their own. But the MSS give directions which indicate that a change that was to have a fundamental effect on the art of composition was applied, toward the end of this period of transition, to the method of performing certain settings of Mass sections. The innovation originated in Italy or England, more probably the former, and will therefore be discussed again presently. But the French adopted it also. To grasp its significance fully, one must recall that when passages of organum were interpolated in medieval performances of plainsong the purely monophonic plainsong passages were sung chorally, but the polyphonic organum insertions were sung by a group of soloists.[119] This is the opposite of what we would expect today: with a combination of monophony and polyphony present, we would think first of the former as being assigned to a soloist and of the latter as being assigned to a chorus. But the old practice makes sense. Part-music was new in the days of organum.

---

[113] About 13th- and 14th-century hocket, *see* ReMMA, esp. 320ff, 355f.

[114] Cf. SchneiderH, 394f.

[115] Pr. BorP, 217. (Other works by Velut in DTO VII, 221; StaD, 194). *See also* Césaris' *A virtutis* (cf. fn. 98).

[116] Cf. ReMMA, 317f.

[117] The Gloria and Credo of the Machaut Mass had been treated the same way (cf. ReMMA, 356). It is because of the omission of the above-mentioned words that a liturgical polyphonic setting of the Gloria is sometimes referred to as an *Et in terra* (or just as an *Et*) and a setting of the Credo as a *Patrem omnipotentem,* i.e., by the next words.

[118] Cf. ReMMA, 356ff.   [119] *Ibid.,* 264f.

Dealing with the unaccustomed and comparatively difficult was an undertaking for superior soloists; choristers could continue with the familiar and easier task of singing in unison. There is nothing to show that choruses took part in the performance of polyphonic music prior to c. 1420. The old MSS of such music are only big enough for three or four people to sing from. Large MSS, such as were set on a lectern for all the choristers to sing the plainchant from, begin to be repositories of part-music only in the early 15th century. The directions referred to above as being given by the MSS consist of the words *"Unus," "Duo,"* and *"Chorus."* Since *Unus* appears in polyphonic passages, it can only mean that those passages were to be sung by soloists. Ordinarily, of course, it could be taken for granted that polyphonic music was for soloists, but, if a chorus was called for anywhere in a piece, it became necessary to distinguish the music for soloists from that for chorus. *Duo* sometimes replaces *Unus* in passages *a 2;* that it likewise refers to soloists is obvious from its employment in contradistinction to *Chorus.* In a number of pieces, presumably the earlier ones, words are provided only in the top part of the sections marked *Chorus;* the lower parts are textless, and may therefore well have been meant for instruments. This, too, would make sense. Choristers trained to sing in unison could more easily join in performing a polyphonic piece if allowed to continue singing in unison, with instruments on the other parts, than if they had to divide and sing all the parts themselves. There are examples, however, of a more venturesome nature. A Gloria and Credo by Guillaume Legrant [120] contain not only sections *a 2* marked *Unus* but also passages, marked for chorus, that have text in all the parts. In the Credo, the writing for soloists is more complicated rhythmically than that for the choristers, which is predominantly chordal. In compositions such as these, full-fledged choral music has arrived.[121]

Italian Music of the Early Quattrocento

In Italy, the force of *trecento* music did not spend itself until after the first quarter of the *quattrocento* had elapsed.[122] In the course of these years, Dufay's Italian forerunners and older contemporaries produced much of the music he must have heard during his sojourns in the peninsula, from c. 1420 on. The names of about three dozen native or Italianized composers have

[120] Pr. BorP, 123, 127; *see ibid.,* xxviii, xxx. In both pieces, Legrant makes much use of accidentals, and in meas. 189–200 of the Credo calls for no less than 3 tritones. There was also a Jean Legrant; for printed examples, *see* DTO XI¹ 88, 89 (= DisK, 22); StaD, 164, 167, 169; WolfQM, 158.

[121] Further on the earliest choral polyphony, *see* DannS, 82ff, and BukMR, 176. The section *a 2* in Dunstable's *Alma . . .* (pr. ReMMA, 418ff) is marked *Duo,* and both parts have text; in the passages *a 3,* only the top part has text. Dunstable alternates chorus and soloists in other works also. In view of his death in 1453, however, these works may well belong to later years than those discussed above.

[122] Cf. ReMMA, 362.

reached us from this period; several, however, can be linked to only one composition, some to none at all.

The leadership in Italian music, which during the *trecento* had belonged to Florence, was held during the first quarter of the *quattrocento* by

> *. . . Venice where the merchants were the kings,*
> *Where St. Mark's is, where the Doges used to wed the sea with rings.*[123]

After the turn of the century, the Serene Republic was the dominant political and cultural power in northern Italy. Zucchetto, the first known organist of St. Mark's, had been appointed in 1316; [124] but the glory of Venice as a musical center had its beginnings with the founding of the singing school at the cathedral in 1403.

The leading composer in northern Italy was undoubtedly the foreigner, Johannes Ciconia. He was born c. 1340 at Liége, where his activity in various positions can be traced from 1372 to 1385. After a sojourn in Padua, apparently beginning about the turn of the century, he died there in December, 1411.[125] At least thirty-seven of his works reach us: Mass sections, motets, a canon, and secular pieces (two with texts in French, eight in Italian).[126] Some of his motet texts, referring to specific events and people, show him to have had relations with both Padua and Venice, which conquered Padua in 1406. He appears to have written at least some of the texts himself: one is in praise of the University of Padua, and several pay homage to dignitaries of church and state, including the Doge Michele Steno, who reigned from 1400 to 1413. Motets of this kind are typical of the period; religious motets are rare. Ciconia has left us, in addition, a treatise, *Nova musica,* a part of which, "De proportionibus," exists also in separate MSS.[127] From one of these we learn that he was a canon of Padua in 1411. Ciconia, appearing early in the *quattrocento,* foreshadows the process whereby, later in the century and throughout the 16th, the Franco-Netherlandish spirit was to merge with that of Italy.

The texts used by other composers show that they, too, provided music for Venice or other north Italian cities: Antonio da Cividale del Friuli (An-

---

[123] About the ceremony of wedding the sea with rings on Ascension Day, as a symbol of the naval supremacy of Venice, *see* Pompeo Molmenti, *Venice: Its Individual Growth from the Earliest Beginnings to the Fall of the Republic* (English transl., 1906), I, 214.

[124] Cf. IMAMI I, xix.

[125] The biographical facts have been assembled by S. Clercx-Lejeune, in her paper, *Johannes Ciconia de Leodio,* read before the International Musicological Society at Utrecht on July 5, 1952, and in subsequent research. Such facts are given also in GhiF, 86ff; GhiB, 25ff; AudaL, 84ff; WolfN, 205ff; DrozM, 286f; BorQS, 28f; MGG II, 1423ff.

[126] For a list, *see* KorteS, 8f (more accurate than the one in WolfN, which, however, offers a thematic index); to Korte's list should be added the 8 items named in both PirrL (1949), 135, 137, and BonacN, 615; the 2 named in GhiI, 183, but probably not the 4 queried items in BonacN, 615. Note that the motet pr. in WolfG III, 79, is not by Ciconia. "Ciconia" is Latin for "stork"; what the composer's real name was is uncertain; it was probably one of the forms used in Liége dialect for the French word *cigogne* (= stork). Many variants of the name appear in the archives. Cf. Clercx-Lejeune, *op. cit.*

[127] Descriptions in LafE I, 375ff, 387f; WolfN, 200ff.

tonius de Civitate Austrie [128]), who was evidently active at Florence also, since he wrote a work apostrophizing it, has left us a motet (perhaps an epithalamium) [129] dated 1423, addressed to Giorgio Ordellafi of Faenza and his wife; Antonio Romano is the composer of a motet [130] on the election of Doge Tommaso Mocenigo in 1414, while Cristoforo da Feltre (Christoforus de Monte [131]) wrote another [132] on the election, in 1423, of Francesco Foscari (the elder of the two Foscari of Byron's play and Verdi's opera). Likewise assignable to this group, among others, are Beltrame Feraguti, Grazioso da Padova, Bartolomeo Brolo (Bartolomaeus de Brolis [133]), Bartolomeo da Bologna, Corrado da Pistoia, Matteo da Perugia, and Ludovico da Rimini. These men wrote Latin motets, Mass sections, and some chansons in French style (though at times with Italian text), while the indigenous *trecento* forms—the madrigal, *ballata,* and *caccia*—exerted their influence also.

The motets, though structurally indebted to French models, reveal native traits too. About twenty-five north Italian motets survive with attributions to composers (ten to Ciconia). None of the tenors of these motets has been definitely identified as a *cantus prius factus,* so that, instead of borrowing tenors like the French, it appears that the Italians invented them. With this practice, there came into favor the principle (no doubt suggested by older methods of tenor construction) of frequent repetition, with modifications, of a melodic nucleus. The modifications included making insertions between salient notes of the nucleus, the insertions being subject to change in the various repetitions. Also, the tenor notes, instead of being long drawn out as in the standard French motet, are roughly in the time-values next larger than those of the upper voices. A good example of both features is provided by Bartolomeo da Bologna's *Quae pena maior.*[134]

The old liking for strict imitation, expressed in the *caccia* canons of the *trecento* is now evident not only in a piece like Ciconia's canon *a 3* at the fifth, *Quod jactatur,*[135] but also in motets making use of imitation in the usual sense. At the beginning of a composition, to be sure, as in the old *caccia,* the entry of the second imitating voice may be delayed until after a very long time-interval—so long, indeed, that *stretto* may actually be absent, as in

---

[128] On the significance of "Civitas Austrie," cf. *Enciclopedia Italiana* X², 513, or P. C. E. Deschamps, *Dictionnaire de géographie ancienne et moderne,* col. 288, under *Castrum Forojuliense.* In naming the composer, the sources usually give "Civitate" as "Civitato."

[129] Pr. BorP, 188. Another dated motet (1422) that survives as a fragment is pr. BorP, 186. For information regarding Antonio, *see* MGG I, 550f.

[130] Pr. ScherG, 23.   [131] Cf. AmbG III, 510.

[132] Pr. DTO XL, 6 (for an additional example by Cristoforo, *see* WolfG III, 172). There is information about other ceremonial motets in KorteS, 10ff; AmbG III, 510.

[133] DTO XXXI, 138, conjectures that the reference is to Broglio, in the Swiss canton of Ticino.

[134] Pr. WolfG III, 164. Further on Italian tenor technique, *see* KorteS, 23f; FiF, 7.

[135] The single voice given in the source is pr. in WolfN, 208, with directions for realization of the canon. *See* comments in BorD, 340f. For another canon, undoubtedly emanating from the same circle (despite its French text), *see* BukMC, 169 (incorrect in GhiIM, 9).

Ciconia's three-part *O felix templum*.[136] In this work, however, the composer departs from the procedures of the old *trecento* type—though still under their influence—by assigning imitation so frequently to the two highest parts at phrase-beginnings that, in the absence of a *cantus firmus* or an isorhythmic plan, the device acts as a form-producing element (cf. p. 88). It is noteworthy that such a result seems not to have been yielded by imitation until some two centuries after it had been produced by canon. Ciconia may well be the man who introduced the kind of motet that features imitation in this way [136a]— a kind, however, that had to be reintroduced later before gaining wide acceptance, although Ciconia did have some immediate effect on other composers. The influence of the *caccia* makes itself felt in the lowest part likewise: it is a supporting voice, assuming no important share in the imitation. But it differs from its precursor significantly by combining, with notable success, the qualities of a supporting voice—even from the harmonic standpoint— with those of a good melodic line. Such a tenor may be regarded as a substitute for the *cantus firmus* of a typical French motet. When writing *a 4*, e.g., in *O virum omnimoda—O lux—O beate Nicholaë*,[137] Ciconia produces a similar result through close interaction of the tenor and contratenor. It is likely that supporting parts of this type were played on slide trumpets.[138] The use of small motifs not only in imitation, but also in repetition or sequence, particularly at cadences, is conspicuous in both *O felix templum* and *O virum*. Of special interest in the former is the frequent recurrence, with slight modifications, of the initial note-group.[138a] This foreshadows the more developed head-motif technique (see Chap. 2).

The isorhythmic motet is found in Italy, but seems to have been unpopular among native composers. We have four examples by Ciconia—not surprising in view of his northern origin. He departs from the French model, however, in calling attention to the appearance of a new *talea* by introducing it with a long-sustained time-value. Also he builds his new *talea* on closely related thematic material, so that a kind of melodic-variation technique joins the isorhythmic technique.[139]

Furthermore, there exist motets that show the influence of the *trecento* madrigal by being pieces *a 2* with both a repeated first section and a concluding section in contrasting rhythm.[140] *Ballade* form is represented, e.g., in Corrado da Pistoia's three-part *Veri almi pastoris*,[141] as is treble-dominated style.[142] Ludovico da Rimini's motet, *Salve cara Deo tellus*,[143] contains two

---

[136] Pr. BorP, 243. *See also* BorP, 188. [136a] Cf. BesEP, 19f.
[137] Fragment in KorteS, 29; BesM, 204. [138] Cf. BesEP, 20ff; MGG II, 1430.
[138a] Cf. BorQS, 91f.
[139] *See* the motet pr. in BorP, 180; cf. also KorteS, 33ff.
[140] *See* KorteS, 40f. [141] Pr. WolfG III, 161.
[142] E.g., in Feraguti's motet in honor of Francesco Malipier of Vicenza (BorP, 249). Other motets by Feraguti in BorP, 253, 257.
[143] Pr. DTO XL, 14; more correctly in DiseP, 75.

passages in *fermata*-marked block-chords, a kind of writing to which we shall return in Chapter 2. This composition is a setting of a Latin poem by Petrarch in praise of Italy.

Among the Italians, as among the French, there are, from this period, settings of individual sections of the Ordinary of the Mass, but no complete setting. In Italy, too, the Mass sections lack forms specifically their own and are cast in forms borrowed from the secular and the motet repertory. Some pieces reveal conductus texture. Clear phrase formation, with simultaneous cadences in all voices, is typical in northern Italy.[144] The most interesting aspect of the Italian works, as of their French counterparts, is the contrasting of sections for soloists and for chorus. A Gloria of Ciconia's [145] represents an intermediate step between choral singing in unison over two instrumental parts and choral singing in all parts. Here passages for two soloists alternate with passages *a 3* in which the two upper parts are for chorus while the lowest one is instrumental.

As already stated, choral polyphony may have originated in Italy. The Italian codices, Modena, *a*. M. 1, 11–13 (= lat. 454–456), are outstanding early examples of the use, for part-music, of large MSS, such as many people could sing from. Moreover, *a*. M. 1, 11 and 12 (dating from the second half of the 15th century) "call for two choirs which sing, polyphonically, alternate stanzas of the hymns or alternate lines of the psalms. Each choir has its own manuscript; two books are needed, each containing only one-half of the composition. We have here the beginnings of polychoral composition, almost a hundred years before Willaert, generally regarded as its inventor, wrote his famous psalms for double chorus." [146]

Mass sections, as in the *trecento*, exist in both madrigal and *caccia* style.[147] Others, in treble-dominated style, are plentiful.[148] The music of one of these, a Gloria by Bartolomeo da Bologna, is in large part the same as that of the same composer's *ballata, Vince con lena*.[149] If, as is likely, the *ballata* antedates the Gloria, the latter is one of a few Italian works of the time that forecast the eventual application of the parody technique to complete Masses (cf. p. 202), for it draws on the entire polyphonic complex of its prototype. No mere *contrafactum* is here present,[149a] since more takes place than the substitution of one text for another; the Gloria contains additional music. Ciconia again displays his predilection for neat construction by adopting *abbc* form in another setting (in treble-dominated style) of the Gloria,[150] a text normally

---

[144] For a good example, *see* a Sanctus by Grazioso da Padova in VanM I, 26; WolfG III, 147.
[145] Pr. BorP, 82. Cf. BukMR, 180.   [146] *Ibid.* 181f.
[147] *See* ReMMA, 368; KorteS, 50ff, 61.
[148] *See*, for example, the Gloria settings by Antonio da Cividale (WolfG III, 174) and Grazioso (VanM I, 21); also Bartolomeo da Bologna's Credo (BorP, 44).
[149] Pr. StaD, 60 (facsimile, *ibid.*, last plate); cf. ReMMA, 345. The Gloria pr. BorP, 37.
[149a] Cf. ReMMA, 218.   [150] Pr. HAM, 59; BorP, 88.

given a through-composed treatment. This liking is shown also in still another Gloria,[151] in which he obtains unity through subtle application of the melodic-nucleus technique to the tenor.

EXAMPLE 3. Extracts from tenor of Gloria—Ciconia (after DTO XXXI, 1).

Do-mi-ne De - - - - us   Qui tol-lis pec-ca-ta mun-di, mi-se-re-re no-

bis. Qui tollis pec-ca-ta mun-di, su-sci-pe de-pre-ca-ti-o - -nem no - - - stram.

This Gloria is paired with a Credo (anonymous, but undoubtedly Ciconia's),[152] the two being musically linked through the varied use of several fragments common to both. Matteo da Perugia, in a Gloria that has a highly florid superius,[153] seeks unity through a device borrowed from the French motet: the tenor, from *Et* to *deprecationem meam,* is repeated, with the time-values halved, from *Qui sedes* to the end. An anonymous Gloria is unusual in being based on a Gregorian Agnus;[154] a polyphonic Mass section, if built on a plainsong setting for the Ordinary, normally draws on one having the same text (cf. p. 66). In this instance, the Agnus is the one now found as part of Mass XVII, i.e., as part of a group of settings constituting an Ordinary.[155] Until rather recently, however, such groups appeared in chant-books quite rarely. (Even the term *"Ordinarium Missae"* is comparatively modern.) It was usual for all Kyries to be placed together, all Glorias together, etc. But a few 15th-century chant-books present special sets of considerable interest (cf. p. 242[156]).

An important source of early 15th-century secular pieces with Italian text is an incomplete MS at Lucca,[157] of which fragments exist also at Perugia.[158] Oxford, Canonici misc. 213, figures among several other sources. Of the three *trecento* forms with Italian texts, the *ballata*—Italy's equivalent of the *virelai* —remained more alive than did the madrigal and *caccia.* Among the *ballate,* one may no doubt include not only such examples as Ciconia's *Dolce for-*

---

[151] See analysis in KorteH, 51ff. For a facsimile of an additional Gloria by Ciconia, *see* WolfMS, 5.   [152] Pr. DTO XXXI, 3; analysis in FiF, 7f.

[153] Pr. IMAMI, Ser. II, I, 235.   [154] Pr. IMAMI, Ser. II, I, 263. The work may be Matteo's; cf. *ibid.,* 47ff. See also VanP, 88.

[155] The Kyrie, Sanctus, Agnus, and Benedicamus of Mass XVII pr. Liber, 6off. This Mass, being for the Sundays of Advent and Lent, lacks a Gloria. The Credos in the Liber appear by themselves, on pp. 64–73, 90–94. (Credos II, V, and VI are really versions of Credo I.)

[156] Also WagE III, 435ff; BukMR, 227.   [157] For studies, *see* PirrL, BonacN.

[158] Large portions of GhiB, GhiF, and GhiI deal with the Perugia fragments; GhiA treats of a Pistoia fragment at one time mistakenly thought to have come from the Lucca MS; music from both the Perugia and Pistoia materials pr. GhiIM. Other fragments from the same period exist at Parma, Padua, Siena, and elsewhere.

tuna [159] and Bartolomeo da Bologna's *Vince con lena,* which are extant with complete texts, but also certain two-section pieces that survive with apparently incomplete texts, such as the anonymous *Gentile alma benigna,*[160] which reaches us with one set of words for section 1 and two sets for section 2 (cf. p. 15). It is in this state that Paris, Bibl. Nat., nouv. acq. fr. 4379, preserves Ciconia's setting [161] of Leonardo Giustiniani's "O rosa bella," a poem shown by literary sources [162] to be a *ballata.* Very likely a *ballata* is present even in an example like Randulfo Romano's *Perche la vista,*[163] which comes to us having a single set of words not only for section 1, but also for section 2—with both *aperto* and *chiuso* endings, however, indicated in the music for section 2. The *ballate* include two anonymous examples—*Mercè, mercè, o morte* and *Amor amaro*—which in one writer's opinion are "without doubt . . . the most beautiful and expressive pages of the Ars-Nova of the early 15th century." [164] Ciconia's *Cacciando un giorno,*[165] one of the pieces in *trecento* madrigal form, keeps alive the *caccia* tradition also, not only through the text, which draws upon symbols of the hunt, but, to a lesser extent, through its music, which contains two passages of imitation and a brief snatch of canon.

French influence is shown in Italian secular music both through the setting of Italian poems in French *rondeau* form and through the setting, by Italians, of French poems. Structurally, *O celestial lume* [166] by Bartolomeo Brolo (fl. probably as late as c. 1430–1440) is simply an Italian *rondeau.* Its mellifluous melody, however, is more Italianate than French. This piece appears in the Oxford MS, as does *O dolce compagno* [167] by Domenico da Ferrara, another Italian composition showing French influence, but differently: only the superius and contratenor are written out; a verbal canon, however, explains that the tenor is to be derived by singing the superius backward. These parts, in their behavior, recall the superius and tenor of Machaut's *Ma fin.*[167a] More-

159 Pr. WolfG III, 77.   160 Pr. DTO XI[1], 115.

161 Pr. DTO VII, 227, after Rome, Bibl. Vaticana, Cod. Urbin. lat. 1411, where the second set for section 2 is missing. 2 anon. settings of the same poem, pr. *ibid.,* 224, 225.

162 E.g., the volumes of Giustiniani printed at Venice c. 1472 and in 1485. To conform with the old prints, the order of lines as given in DTO VII, 234, should be changed to 1–4, 7, 8, 5, 6 (lines 1, 2, should then be repeated to round out the *ballata* form); as might be expected, there are also variants in individual words. (The setting that is ascribed to Dunstable in Cod. Urbin. lat. 1411 and to Bedingham in Porto, Bibl. Munícip. 714, and which is anon. in several other MSS, therefore either ends on a half-close or is based on a misunderstanding of the structure of the poem. Cf. ReMMA, 423, fn. 166.)

163 Pr. StaD, 181.

164 GhiI, 189; music pr. GhiIM, 17, 19.

165 Pr. GhiB, 35; GhiIM, 3. Mod. editions of Ciconia not yet cited pr. GhiIM, 2 (*I cani;* tenor only), 6 (but *see* BukMC, esp. p. 170; facsimile in GhiB, 19), 10, 11 (only tenor complete), 21 (superius only), 23; ApelFM, 108*. It is doubtful that Ciconia wrote the pieces pr. in GhiIM, 2 (*Chi vole;* superius only), 5; BukMC, 169 (incorrect in GhiIM, 9); these are among the 4 whose authenticity is queried in BonacN (cf. fn. 126).

166 Pr. StaD, 83 (facsimile, *ibid.,* Pl. 5). Other examples of Brolo pr. DTO XXXI, 28; BorP, 292, 293; EDMR IV, 80.

167 Incorrectly transcr. in StaD, 160; facsimile, *ibid.,* last plate.

167a Cf. ReMMA, 336.

over, as in Machaut's piece, the first half of the contratenor is repeated back-ward to supply the second half.[168]

Matteo da Perugia, active at Milan, was, as already hinted, much affected by French influence. Of his extant secular works, which all survive in Modena, Bibl. Estense, *a*. M. 5. 24, twenty-two—by far the larger portion of them—have French texts.[169] Similar examples reach us by Brolo and Antonio da Cividale. While late 14th-century intricacy is still at times present in Matteo, he exercises moderation. The contratenor tends to become a sup-porting voice, like the tenor, rather than a rival of the superius in maintaining rhythmic animation and variety. As a result, Matteo is an important figure in the transition toward the style of the Dufay period.[170]

Turning from northern Italy, we find a much less varied repertory in cen-tral Italy, where Rome had suffered from the schism, and in the south. Be-tween 1389 and 1409, the Papal Choir had been manned almost entirely by musicians from Liége. The lists of singers for 1410 to 1418, however, give the names of musicians from northern France. The Council of Constance, which opened in November, 1414, and did not close until April, 1418, had elected Martin V as pope in November, 1417, thereby ending the schism. The Papal Chapel benefited from the consequent stabilization of Italian condi-tions, and in the early 1420's it developed into an important music center, attracting musicians from all European countries.

The accounts show that the Italian composer, Nicola Zacharia (Zacharie, Zacarie, and other variants), became a papal singer in 1420.[171] This musician should not be confused with Antonio Zachara da Teramo, represented in the Lucca MS, Bologna Liceo mus. Q 15, and elsewhere.[172] Other composers belonging to this general area include, at least according to the evidence af-forded by their names, Antonello (Amarotus) da Caserta, whose works appear to the largest extent in Modena, Bibl. Estense, *a*. M. 5. 24, and Filippo da Caserta, who is represented in the Chantilly and Reina MSS as well as in Modena and who wrote the Neapolitan treatise on mensural notation printed in CouS III, 118.[173] That treatise includes [174] an interesting passage on *trayn*

---

[168] The explanation in DiseJ, 16, produces the same result as that described above, but is unnecessarily complicated. The piece is not "a simple fauxbourdon chanson," as claimed in KorteS, 71 (on fauxbourdon, cf. pp. 64f, *infra*).

[169] These 22 pr. ApelFM, 1*–30* (1 of them likewise in VanP, 91; 13 likewise in IMAMI, Ser. II, I); *see also* KorteS, 13f. The *Plus onques dame* pr. in WolfG III, 167, as Matteo's is actually anon. (cf. LudGM, 631f, but also ApelFM, 25); this rhythmically subtle *virelai* is much in the French post-Machaut manner.

[170] Cf. ApelFM, 13f.

[171] Cf. HabR, 32. HabD, 57f, indicates that he remained in the choir until 1424; he was also in it for 8 months in 1434 (cf. *ibid.* 67).

[172] One man has the first name Antonio and is described as coming from Teramo; the other has the first name Nicola and is described (HabR, 32) as coming from Brindisi. Concerning their separate identities, *see* further GhiI, 185; GhiB, 27f; GhiF, 91ff; PirrL (1951), 135ff.

[173] CouS III, 23, doubts that the theorist and the composer are one. But cf. VanP, 77, 85.

[174] CouS III, 123.

or *traynour,* the combination, in different voices, of conflicting rhythmic groups, e.g., four notes against three, etc.[175]

The motet *Laetetur plebs–Pastor* [176] by Nicola Zacharia opens with a long passage in imitation, such as we find in Venetian music, but practically abandons imitation thereafter. A Gloria *a 2* of his [177] favors clear-cut phrase formation; but the southern Italians, unlike their northern countrymen, seem more generally to have preferred avoiding simultaneous cadences in all parts.[178] A Credo *a 4* by Zachara da Teramo,[179] which paraphrases Gregorian Credo I, appears as a *Patrem du vilage* in Bologna MS Q 15 and as a *Patrem Dominicale* in Trent MS 87. Both *"du* [or *de*] *vilage"* and *"dominicale"* recur, applied to settings of this Credo, throughout the Renaissance. Zachara's setting divides the chant, embellished, between the two upper voices: "migration" on the part of borrowed melodies was by no means rare at this time.[180] The paraphrasing of plainsong material by elaborating it in the highest voice—a technique applied with great eloquence by early 15th-century English composers [181]—was destined to assume great importance in Renaissance music. When chants were subjected to mensuration, a loss of some of their original fluidity resulted; figuration, employing short-note embellishments, etc., provided a certain amount of compensation for this. Paraphrasing, or otherwise reworking pre-existent material, often rises to the status of original composition, as becomes evident if one compares the six anonymous Kyries in Trent MS 90 that set an identical plainsong Kyrie (the one belonging to Mass IV) but elaborate it differently.[182]

Nicola Zacharia has left us a *caccia* of much brilliance, *Cacciando per gustar,*[183] depicting a market scene and vividly incorporating the cries of the vendors of oil, eggs, mustard, and other wares. In addition, his secular works include not only such an Italian *ballata* as *Sol mi trafigge 'l cor* and a composition of the same type combining French and Italian, but a piece in French *ballade* form with Latin text.[184] Zachara da Teramo had a liking for fantastic, picturesque verse. The *ballata, Deus deorum Pluto,*[185] has a macaronic Latin-Italian text bristling with "terrible and barbarous names . . , taken from

---

[175] Illustrated in the *virelai* cited in fn. 169.   [176] Pr. BorP, 284.   [177] Pr. WolfQM, 154.
[178] Cf. KorteS, 80.

[179] Pr. DTO XXXI, 16; *see* comments in FiF, 12. The work, which is among the Credos ascribed to "Zacar" in Bologna MS Q 15, is attributed to "Zach. de Teramo" in Trent MS 87, a circumstance that enables us to determine which composer should be credited with the several works given to "Zacar" in the former source. One of the Glorias likewise given to "Zacar" in Q 15 was included in Old Hall; see BukMR, 38, 40 (= BukOH, 516f).

[180] *See* BukMR, 46ff (= BukOH, 522ff), on the frequent division of such melodies in English music (the Zachara example, however, shows that the technique is not peculiar to it).

[181] Cf. ReMMA, 418ff.

[182] The 6 settings pr. DTO XXXI, 62ff; the plainsong pr. Liber, 25.

[183] Pr. MarrF, 6; WolfF, 618.

[184] Pr. WolfG III, 151; PirrL, 151; WolfG III, 168, respectively. Concerning the rhythmic complexity of the last of these, *see* SachsRT, 196f.

[185] Pr. GhiIM, 14; other *ballate* by Zachara, *ibid.,* 13 (fragment; transcription faulty; *see* paper by Dr. Plamenac referred to in Chap. 4, fn. 122a), 15.

the infernal mythology, and [is] intended as an enthusiastic prayer to Pluto, king of the demons." [186] Just as Bartolomeo da Bologna turned *Vince con lena* into a Gloria, Zachara turned *Deus deorum* into a Credo and produced still other Mass sections that reworked part-compositions of his own, belonging to the secular repertory.[187]

The preference for French texts in the works of Filippo and Antonello da Caserta and the strong Francophile tendency in their music are very probably the results of a direct connection between both of these men and France. Their compositions provide further evidence of that Franco-Italian interpenetration which was to contribute substantially to the international character of the music of the Dufay generation.[188] From our survey of developments in France and Italy immediately preceding this generation, we turn to the compositions it produced, works that simultaneously bade farewell to the Gothic spirit and hailed that of the Renaissance.

---

[186] GhiI, 185.

[187] Cf. PirrL (1949), 129. BolC IV, 245, which gives a defective list of contents of Q 15 (under its old no., 37), misleadingly adds to the composer's name portions of the titles of the compositions.

[188] For *ballades* by Filippo, *see* WolfG III, 158; ApelFM, 98*, 100*. For *rondeaux* by Antonello, *see* ApelFM, 42* (facsimile in ApelN, 415), 43*; 5 *ballades,* 31* ff; a *virelai,* 40.* Further on early *quattrocento* secular music, *see* LiuQ; KorteS, 65ff; BorQS, 120f; GhiB, F, I, IM, SF; BorAI; PirrD.

Chapter 2: COMPOSERS, MAINLY OF NORTHERN FRANCE, IN THE PERIOD OF DUFAY

D UFAY—one of the great exponents of French music, regardless of period, a master in the line of lofty figures that had already included Perotin and Machaut—dominated the art of composition unchallenged from c. 1425 to c. 1450, when, though still at the height of his powers, he was approached in eminence by Ockeghem, the leader of a new generation. In the preceding years, however, Dufay was far from a lone figure. His contemporaries included, besides such an exquisite composer as Binchois, a host of lesser luminaries. If Loqueville had been active during Dufay's youth, Fontaine and Ruby (mentioned in passing in Chap. 1) helped, like Grenon, to form the background not only of his early manhood but of his middle years.

Composers in the Papal Chapel at about the Time of Dufay's Entry; the Basse Dance

Fontaine, whom we have found serving the first three dukes of Burgundy from at least c. 1404 and who was in the Papal Choir, 1420–1427, came from Rouen. Beginning with 1436, the Burgundian account books list him as a chaplain, i.e., as a member of the chapel choir. His name is omitted after 1447. Fontaine's *rondeau, Pour vous tenir,*[1] survives *a 3* in a MS at Parma, while in Oxford, MS Canonici misc. 213, it is provided with an additional superius. In the latter source, the piece has two texts, the second one being *Mon doulx amy tenés.* What we find in this version, however, is not a double *rondeau* in the usual sense, but rather two different three-part *rondeaux* that have two parts in common: while one superius has only the *Pour vous tenir* text and the other only the *Mon doulx amy tenés* text, the tenor and contratenor (which are not provided with complete texts) present incipits reading respectively *"Pour vous et mon doulx"* and *"Pour vous et mon."*[2] The Oxford MS, in its copy of this piece, has a dotted line connecting one of the words with a note, to show that they belong together. This MS uses such lines similarly in some other works. In melismatic cadences, the MS in-

[1] Pr. MarM, 13.
[2] In MarM, the music incipits in original notation are given in the order in which the voices appear in the Oxford MS, but in the transcription into modern notation the editor has reversed voices 2 and 3 so as to place the alternative superius voices on the higher staves. Therefore, to obtain *Pour vous tenir,* combine voices 1, 3, and 4 of the transcription; for *Mon doulx amy,* combine voices 2, 3, and 4.

dicates that, contrary to later custom, the final syllable is generally introduced not on the final note but on one of the preceding notes.[3] Apparently the relation of text and music was not always as haphazard in early 15th-century music as the many more obscure MSS would indicate (cf. p. 75). There is an interesting feature in the contratenor of *Pour vous tenir—Mon doulx amy:* the range extends down to F, i.e., to a whole tone below the lower limit of the Guidonian gamut.[4] Similarly, the highest limit theoretically available in the past, the tone e″, is exceeded by Fontaine when he ascends to f″ in *De bien amer.*[5] Adam von Fulda, the German theorist and composer of the second half of the 15th century,[6] credits Dufay with adding three notes above and three below the accepted gamut.[7] However, the sporadic use of the new lower notes fails to produce a real bass region, such as we shall find in the music of the Ockeghem period; the range is still predominantly high and the timbre light, as in the past. The structural tenor continues to lie high. (To be sure, the notation of Renaissance music does not represent absolute pitches, and a piece of the Dufay period may well have been performed lower than the written symbols would indicate to us. However, the subsequent exploration of the lower register by the next generation, in writing, shows that the music of the Dufay period was at least relatively higher.) A quite exceptional low note—D—occurs twice in one version of Fontaine's three-part *rondeau, J'ayme bien celui qui s'en va.* Among the MSS preserving the piece is Escorial V.III.24 (which originated at the Burgundian court in the second quarter of the century); in this source the part containing the D's is marked *"Contra Tenor Trompette."* But in Bologna, Liceo mus. MS Q 15, the piece survives in what seems to be its original form. Here the contratenor descends no lower than G. It is possible that the contratenor of the Escorial MS, which is not so much a new part as a remodelling of the old one, is by Dufay. The instrument specified is the slide-trumpet of the time, from the modern standpoint actually a type of trombone,[8] which, beginning in 1468, is traceable under the name sackbut, though the instrument itself dates back perhaps to the 14th century. It is noteworthy that in

---

[3] *See* BorP, iii; on the underlaying of text in the Trent MSS, *see* AdlerT.

[4] The ranges spanned by the music discussed in this book are so much greater than those dealt with in ReMMA that pitches will here be designated by one of the modern letter-systems (i.e., the first one illustrated in ApelH,586) rather than by the Odonian symbols used in the earlier book. When the reader checks a statement about range made in the present volume against modern practical editions, he should remember that they (unlike purely scholarly editions) sometimes transpose a work.

[5] Pr. WolfG III, 83.

[6] Not to be confused with the Adam represented in the Oxford MS, Canonici misc. 213 (*rondeaux*, pr. StaD, 52, 54, 57; the last 2 also in DisK, 6, 8); about his possible identity, *see* PirH, 90.

[7] GerS III, 342, 350. *See* BorD, 81f, 342f.

[8] Concerning the early history of the instrument, *see* SachsCT and esp. BesEP, which discusses Fontaine's piece in detail and gives both the Bologna and Escorial versions on p. 35; the latter version is also pr., but with errors, in AuI, 527.

the Escorial MS there is no question of a part that may possibly call for the instrument (cf. pp. 21f, 27); the source actually demands one. It was not usual to "orchestrate" to the extent of requiring particular instruments for specific parts. As in the past, in most music, sacred or secular, a player apparently executed any part within the scope of his instrument, and did not hesitate to double a singing voice or substitute for it. The doubling instruments—the viol, harp, lute, sackbut, cromorne, and portative organ were likely choices—undoubtedly often continued during interludes, etc., while the singers paused. It is probable, also, that chansons, as well as other types of music, sometimes received purely instrumental performances.[9] We have some precise information concerning instruments of the time. Henricus Arnaut of Zwolle (d. 1466), at one time physician and astrologer to Philip the Good and later to Charles VII and Louis XI, left a treatise [10] setting forth in detail the structure of several keyboard instruments (including an organ), the harp, lute, etc. It is interesting to note that the keyboard of the organ shown in the Van Eyck altarpiece at Ghent (1432) is almost completely chromatic.

Of special significance is Fontaine's *Sans faire de vous departie*,[11] for its tenor is practically identical with a *basse-dance* melody of the same name, preserved in Brussels MS 9085.[12] This magnificent MS—its heavy black pages bear notes of gold and silver—supposedly belonged to Margaret of Austria (1480–1530), the granddaughter of Charles the Bold, but apparently originated before her time. The contents, consisting mostly of *basses dances,* include several identifiable melodies adapted from works of an earlier day. Other chansons of the period that are drawn upon include Binchois's *Triste plaisir*.[13]

The earliest known mention of the *basse dance* occurs in a Spanish poem.[14] The first French source to refer to it is Nicole de la Chesnaye's *La Nef de Santé,* written some time before 1477 and printed in 1507.[15] The Italian equivalent, the *bassadanza,* enjoyed a vigorous life. The meaning of the name has been variously interpreted; [16] since the dance was performed with gliding steps, the word *"basse"* (low) may well allude to this fact.

The Brussels MS contains fifty-nine items. It opens with a theoretical discussion of the *basse dance,* presents its music in the form of one-line melodies, and supplements these by letters representing the appropriate dance steps. Nearly all the tunes appear in a series of undifferentiated blackened breves;

---

[9] Pictures yield some information about the roles of instruments in the performance practice of the period; cf. SachsBD. Some, provided by ivory carvings, may be deduced from RoksI, 82ff.

[10] Pr. CerfI.

[11] Pr. MarM, 14. Other *exx.* by Fontaine *ibid.,* 9, 10, 12. For fuller biographical data, *see* MarH, 165ff and *passim.*

[12] Published in facsimile in ClosBD. We shall use the old spelling, *dance,* in this book.

[13] *See* GurB, 159ff; HertzS, 406ff (which lists several more).

[14] Cf. SachsW, 311.   [15] *See* HertzS, 403.

[16] For a summary of 3 different views, *see* FerandM, 401f.

the few items given in more varied mensural notation are not examples of the *basse dance* proper.[17] Some time between 1488 and 1496, at Paris, Michel de Toulouze printed, without an author's name, *L'Art et instruction de bien dancer*,[18] the text and musical contents of which are largely the same as those of the Brussels MS. The inclusion of two pages of normal mensural notation lends this book considerable interest in the history of music printing, a subject to which we shall return in Chapter 4.[19] The bulk of the music, however, is in the same kind of breves that appear in the MS. Scholars have attempted to discover a clue to the true rhythm implied by these undifferentiated notes,[20] and for that purpose some have gone beyond an examination of the tunes alone and have studied the dance itself. The inclusion of relevant material in some of the more than a dozen dance instruction-books of the Renaissance [21] that reach us from several countries has helped to make that possible.

The true *basse dance* belonged to a family of related dances, differing rhythmically from one another. The French sources name two: the *basse dance* proper and the *pas de Brabant* (the Italian *saltarello*); the Italian sources name more (cf. p. 177). The same *basse-dance* melodies, usually underlying a polyphonic texture, could accompany dances of one related type as readily as those of another. The undifferentiated breves were actually played without a change of time-values in an individual piece, each note carrying a step-unit of the choreography. But the *basse dance* proper, the "imperial measure," was slower moving than the related dances (whether French or Italian), and the breves doubled their value when they were applied to it; hence the peculiar notation.[22] The rhythm of the *basse dance* itself was duple (on the higher level) but each beat was divisible into a group of three.[23] It became the custom to follow the dignified *basse dance* by the quicker *pas de Brabant,* thus producing a contrasting pair of slow and fast dances such as was to be quite common throughout the Renaissance.

Pictorial representations on tapestries and in miniatures supplement the literary accounts in providing evidence concerning dance music. Several show instrumental ensembles playing for the dancers. It is clear that two shawms and a slide-trumpet formed a common group, while the harp, lute, and flute made up another (but there were other combinations also). The former group consists wholly of *hauts instruments,* the latter of *bas instruments* (cf. Chap. 1, fn. 47). These two types were associated with different kinds of dance events. The *hauts instruments* were employed for big festive occasions and were usually played from a balcony or loggia; the *bas instruments* were for

[17] SachsW, 319ff. [18] Facsimile reprint in TouA. [19] Further about this point, *see* MeM.
[20] A convenient summary of the pioneer suggestions of Closson (ClosBD, ClosD), Riemann (RieR), Blume (BlumeS, 36ff), and Wolf (in his review of ClosBD in *Die Musik,* XLV [1912], 296)—which, though superseded, are of interest—may be found in KinJ, 350ff.
[21] Descriptive list in MichelD.
[22] For further details, *see* Gombosi in Acta VII (1935), 26; BukMR, 198ff, esp. 201f.
[23] SachsRD; SachsW, 318ff; GomD, 299f.

more intimate dance entertainments and were placed near the dancers.[24] The *basse-dance* melody itself was played as the tenor, and above it the higher parts were improvised or, more rarely, composed. At least in some instances, improvisation apparently resulted in an approximation of parallel organum.[25] If the dance melody was derived from a chanson, it was the tenor (the original rhythm, of course, being disregarded) that was drawn upon,[26] as in the instance of Fontaine's *Sans faire de vous departie.*

The January, 1428, list of papal singers, the first that omits Fontaine, is also the first to eliminate Grenon and five of the six French choirboys who had been in his charge. (He had brought four of these with him from Cambrai in 1425.) Barthélemy Poignare, who remained with a singer's full rank, is known as the composer of a Gloria preserved in Trent MS 87.[27] Gualterius Liberth, represented in the Oxford MS (the pieces there ascribed to Gualtier and Gautier are probably his, too) appears as Gualterus Liberti (cf. p. 93) on the register for December 20, 1428.[28]

Foliot (Philippe de la Folie), who was in the choir from 1424 to 1428, figures also at the Burgundian court of Philip the Good.[29] Guillaume Malbecque [30] and Jean Brassart joined the Papal Choir in 1431. Malbecque matters little: he was probably one of the many musicians who were primarily singers and merely tried their hand at composing once in a while, even if they had no special gift or training. This was not true of Brassart, who was a superior musician (*see also* Chap. 12). His *O flos fragrans* [31] survives in several MSS, the earliest one assigning text to the superius only, later ones giving it to all voices. The piece thus illustrates, through its history, what was to become a growing tendency to treat all parts so that they could be sung if desired, even though a *cappella* performance was not required. Brassart's four-part *Fortis cum quaevis actio,*[32] in honor of St. John the Baptist, is a long work that comes to a complete halt about halfway through and then starts afresh; i.e., it is in two movements. (These were called *partes* in the Renaissance; it is customary to retain the Latin word *"pars,"* instead of using the English "part," to avoid confusion with "part" meaning "voice." The designations *"prima pars"* and *"secunda pars,"* while common in the sources, are sometimes omitted there.) Another point exemplified by this motet, a point

[24] Further concerning these ensembles, *see* GomD, 290ff; HertzS, 403f; SachsW, 317.

[25] Cf. PirD, 14; ApelR.

[26] For further details, *see* GomD, 294f, 301; SachsW, 317.

[27] Incipits pr. DTO VII, 31, No. 30.

[28] Cf. HabD, 60; StaD, xv. RieH II¹, 104, and RieL, 1034, are wrong in stating that there are 2 works by "Gualterius Liberth" in Bologna, Lic. mus., 37 (= Q 15).

[29] For biographical data, *see* MarM, xiv; MarH, *passim*. The piece, printed *a 2* and credited to him in MarM, 237, must be by a later Foliot; it is really a double canon and can hardly date from before Josquin (communication from Dr. Bukofzer). For details concerning singers not known as composers, *see* PirH, 66.

[30] A *rondeau,* pr. StaD, 179.

[31] Pr. DTO VII, 102 (where word 3 is wrongly given as *"flagrans"*).

[32] Pr. *ibid.,* 97. Other works of his, pr. BorP, 243; DTO VII, 95; XL, 83; DèzE, 77 (= OsN, 525). For biographical details, *see* DrozM, 286f; AudaL, 70ff; MGG I, 223ff.

very common in early 15th-century sacred music, is the opening upper-voice duo. Thirty-two measures are sung by the two highest parts, before the others enter.

The name of Arnold de Lantins, who served in the Papal Chapel for a few months in 1431–1432, indicates that his family probably came from the town of Lantin, in the province of Liége. We have some thirty works by him, among them a complete Mass *a 3*.[33] In view of the artistic excellence of Machaut's Mass, it is strange that no subsequent composer is known to have written a complete setting of the Ordinary until early in the 15th century, when such works begin to appear in profusion. It is fair to assume, on stylistic grounds, that Arnold's Mass is one of the earlier of these new compositions. Machaut had based his Kyrie, Sanctus, Agnus, and *Ite missa est,* each on a different plainsong, which was assigned to the tenor in long notes, in old *cantus-firmus* fashion. (There is no plainsong in the Gloria or Credo.[34]) As one means of achieving unity, Machaut had used a recurrent motif, introducing it in various voices.[35] The application of a recurrent motif to paired Mass sections (i.e., two sections not belonging to a complete setting of the Ordinary) may be present in the Old Hall MS. (Whether pairing is intended in this MS or in others of the time that are similarly organized [36] is hard to determine because all Kyries are placed together, all Glorias together, etc., as in plainsong MSS; cf. p. 29.) Here the Gloria and Credo of two apparent Gloria–Credo pairs, attributable to Leonel Power,[37] begin with similar initial motifs (and have other features in common also, reminding one of the Gloria–Credo pair by Ciconia mentioned on p. 29).[38] A Sanctus and Agnus by Leonel [39] give the impression of being paired also, but since they are based on the Sanctus and Agnus of Gregorian Mass XVII, which are themselves akin, it would be rash to assume a deliberate relationship. Arnold, who prefaces his Sanctus, Benedictus, and three Agnus settings by intonations [40] assigned to the middle voice, may be drawing on Mass XVII also.[41] He does not, however, lay out the plainsong in motet-like *cantus-firmus* manner like Machaut. Indeed, while some fleeting correspondences with the plainsong may be found

[33] Preserved in Bologna, Liceo mus. Q 15, and in Oxford, Canonici misc. 213. Pr. BorP, 1–36.
[34] The claim, made in HandZP, 542f, that the Credo is based on Credo I seems to be far-fetched.
[35] Cf. ReMMA, 356. For a detailed study of this Mass, *see* Gombosi in MQ XXXVI (1950), 204.
[36] E.g., to a large extent, Trent MS 90; cf. DTO VII, 58ff.
[37] In each "pair" one piece is ascribed to Leonel and the other is anon.
[38] Cf. BukMR, 44f, 59f, 64 (= BukOH, Pt. I, 520f; Pt. II, 39f, 43).
[39] Pr. RamsO III, 76, 136.
[40] *I.e.*, by bits of actual plainsong, unmeasured and unaccompanied by countermelodies.
[41] The identical intonation introducing the Sanctus, Agnus I, and Agnus II, while more like the setting of the first word of the Sanctus in Mass IX, is nevertheless much like the opening of both the Sanctus and the Agnus of Mass XVII. The identical intonation introducing both the Benedictus and Agnus II (but at different pitch levels) is the same as the setting of the word "Benedictus" in Mass XVII.

in the middle voice of the polyphony from the Sanctus on, the resemblances to the Chant material are so slight that their presence may be merely fortuitous. At most, one could only say that the Chant is very freely paraphrased. No plainsong seems to be incorporated in the first three movements. But, in a way that recalls Machaut's recurrent motif, Arnold introduces, in varied forms, the same passage—a motto or "head-motif,"[42] as historians have called it—in the highest voice at the most important places. Moreover, this passage bears a striking similarity, no doubt deliberate, to the opening of the intonation prefixed to the Sanctus, Agnus I, and Agnus III. The fabric of Arnold's setting is mostly that of treble-dominated style; all three voices usually enter simultaneously. In the Kyrie and Sanctus, the liturgical texts are subjected to troping.[43] The Gloria is noteworthy for its assignment of a *"tuba"* to the lowest part.

The words of two of Arnold's motets, *Tota pulchra es* and *O pulcherrima mulierum,* are from the Song of Solomon.[44] It is only in the 15th century that it gradually became common for the motet—in the basic sense, let us remember, not a liturgical form (cf. pp. 20f)—to draw on Bible texts; in fact, in the first half of the century, examples are still rather rare. The second of these motets of Arnold's contains the following purely chordal passage:

EXAMPLE 4. Passage from Arnold de Lantins' *O pulcherrima mulierum* (Oxford, Bodleian, Canonici misc. 213, f. 80ᵛ; complete piece in BorP, 269).

Introducing such writing—whether at the end of a work or in its course, whether the chords are in root position or in first inversion—is not unusual at this period. Dunstable used block-chords in his Song of Solomon motet, *Quam pulchra es;*[45] Dufay had a strong liking for them.[46] Fermatas, such as those provided for Arnold's composition by both the Oxford MS and Bologna, Lic. mus. Q 15, first appear in passages of this sort early in the century. In the Oxford MS, Arnold's authorship of the piece is indicated by "Arnoldus de ntins"; the note represents *la* in the *hexachordum molle.* Of the twelve chansons by Arnold in the same MS, five bear ascriptions that

---

[42] *Kopfmotiv, motif de tête, motif initial.*   [43] Concerning tropes, *see* ReMMA, 185ff.

[44] Pr. BorP, 262, 269. Another sacred piece, *ibid.,* 267. To be sure, the former text is used for a liturgical antiphon, but in an adapted form that is not the one set by Arnold.

[45] Pr. DTO VII, 190; ScherG, 29; Grove II, 112.

[46] For some exx., *see* BcsM, 208; PirH, 60; CW XIX, 7, 12. For some exx. by Binchois, *see* DTO XXXI, 44f, 57, 59, 61.

begin the name Lantins with *la* in the *hexachordum durum*.[47] Rebuses of this type recur; the *fa* in Dufay's name is also sometimes playfully represented by a note.

Other Early Contemporaries of Dufay; Cadences

While one may suppose that the contemporary Hugho de Lantins was related to Arnold, we have no data on this point. By him, too, thirty works survive. He undoubtedly spent some time in Italy, for he has left us four pieces with Italian text.[48] One of these, *Tra quante regione,* was written in honor of Cleofe Malatesta, who married Theodore Palaiologos (Despot of the Morea and son of the Byzantine Emperor Manuel II) at Mistra near Sparta, on January 19, 1421.[49] Hugho's rondeau, *A madamme playsant et belle,*[50] is a happy example of the use of free canon; this appears between the outer parts, first at the octave below, then at the fifth below. A ceremonial motet, *Christus vincit,*[51] celebrates the success of Francesco Foscari in enlarging the domains of the Serene Republic. Hugho's motet *Celsa sublimatur—Sabine presul* [52] is an unpretentious example of the isorhythmic type, with an introduction and two *taleae.* Of three Glorias bearing his name in the Oxford MS, one,[53] in *caccia* style, has the tenor singing in canon at the fifth below the superius. In addition to the two flats of the signature, flats are applied as accidentals to both A and D—an unusual procedure at the time. (Accidentalism, such as that mentioned on p. 16, had not taken firm root.) In one of the other Glorias,[54] the text is divided successively among the three voices in such a way that one sometimes enters with fresh text shortly before its predecessor has finished the only enunciation of the previous text passage. Such antiliturgical distribution of text, designed to achieve brevity, occurs likewise in other works of the period.[55] The third Gloria [56] is of interest for those passages in $\frac{6}{3}$ writing which, placed at cadences in the course of the piece, create a certain impression of unity. A fourth Gloria,[56a] ascribed to Dufay in the Oxford MS, is attributed to Hugho in both Bologna, Lic. mus. Q 15 and the Aosta MS (it is anonymous in two Trent MSS). It is probably his.

[47] 14 chansons by Arnold are pr. in BorPL, 11ff (1 also in WolfG III, 82; another—the charming *rondeau, Puisque je voy*—also in HAM, 75). Two of the pieces are dated Venice, 1428.
[48] Cf. p. 52 *infra.* The pieces are pr. BorPL, 61ff.
[49] Cf. A. Zakythinos, *Le Despotat grec de Morée* (1932), 189. Pompeo Litta, *Famiglie Celebri Italiane,* Vol. X, gives the wrong date and incorrectly names the groom "Tommaso." Further concerning both Hugho and Arnold, *see* BorL; BorPL, Intr.; PirH, 67ff; AudaL, 69f.
[50] Pr. BorPL, 36; StaD, 174; ScherG, 36; DisK, 14; cf. ApelN, 133. BorPL contains 13 additional chansons by Hugho (1 in HAM, 76). For facsimiles of 2 of these, *see* ApelN, 141, 177.
[51] In Bologna, Bibl. Univ. 2216. This motet is the earliest known polyphonic setting of the *Laudes Regiae;* about this point and the music of such *Laudes* generally, see BukML. For a description of this Bologna MS, *see* BesBU.
[52] Pr. BorP, 215.   [53] Pr. BorP, 118.   [54] Pr. BorP, 115.   [55] Cf. ReMMA, 421.
[56] Pr. BorP, 110.   [56a] Pr. DTO XXXI, 15.

There are many cases of conflicting ascription in the music of the period, and unfortunately such a preponderance of evidence does not always exist.[57]

Johannes de Limburgia, who, to judge by his name, came from the ancient duchy of Limburg, a region not far from Lantin, has left us about fifty compositions.[57a] A Mass of his reworks a long head-motif with interesting melodic and rhythmic variations.[58] Gembloux, also nearby, was evidently the place of origin of Johannes Franchois. A Gloria and Credo of his [59] are notable for the amount of imitation in them.[59a] The Credo provides fairly early examples of the innumerable instances in which, in polyphonic settings, *ascendit in coelum* and *descendit de coelis* are respectively illustrated by ascending and descending passages. An *Ave Virgo* by Franchois opens with a 42-measure *introitus,* which amounts to an independent instrumental piece *a 3,* quite different in structure from the vocal section that follows. The designation *"Trumpetta Introitus"* in the lowest part shows that at least this part is to be played by a slide-trumpet in the introduction.[59b] The vocal section, which is isorhythmic, consists of two *talea* patterns, each presented twice. This section is given in alternative versions, one *a 5,* one *a 4.* As the motetus and the triplum are the same in both versions, they appear in the MS only once, along with the supplementary parts.[60]

While very little precise information about the performance practice of sacred polyphony has come down from the early 15th century, that provided in *Ave Virgo* is not an isolated instance. A *Gaude Virgo* by H. Battre appears in Trent MS 87, with directions specifically indicating that certain passages are to be sung by *mutate [mutatae] voces* (changed voices) and others by *pueri* (boys).[61] There is evidence that, in actual performance then as later, gifted vocalists sometimes invented cadenzas to display their skill. A Gloria by Estienne Grossin (Grossim), in the form in which it is preserved in Trent MS 87, contains an elaborate close showing, apparently, the sort of coloratura passage a singer may have interpolated rather than what the composer had

---

[57] In judging preponderance, one should consider not only numbers but "authority." Since both the Bologna and Oxford MSS are "authoritative," the preponderance in the above instance is purely numerical.

[57a] 2 motets, pr. DTO VII, 213; WolfG III, 85; another in facsimile in MGG II, Pl. 6. The motet pr. in DufayO I¹, 29, may also be his.

[58] *See* the table in BesM, 200.

[59] Pr. BorP, 93, 99 (alternative Amen on p. 108). Cf. BorQS, 48f, 107f, 163.

[59a] Another Gloria-Credo pair (pr. DPLSER, *Ser. I,* No. 11), anon. in the source, is attributed by R. D. Laurence Feininger to Franchois on the grounds of the similar handling of this technical feature.

[59b] *See* further BesEP, 15ff.

[60] The group embracing 3 such parts consists of the tenor, alius tenor, and contratenor; the group of 2, of the solus tenor and contratenor cum solo tenore. This arrangement led the DTO editor of the composition to the false assumption that it is *a 7,* and it is so printed in DTO XL, 19. 3 chansons by Franchois, pr. BorPL, 72ff (1 also in WolfG III, 84).

[61] This is 1 of 6 motets by Battre pr. in DTO, XL, 89ff; other works by him, pr. DTO XXVII¹, 88; XXXI, 38, 41. All his known compositions are preserved toward the end of Trent MS 87, in the so-called "Battre fascicle."

originally written.[62] (One need not conclude, as have some writers, that highly florid writing necessarily required the participation of instruments; melismas would have seemed eminently vocal to singers accustomed to Gregorian Chant.) A Mass by Grossin, lacking only an Agnus, has a contratenor designated as for slide-trumpet.[63] Grossin, represented in Canonici misc. 213, in part by the airy *rondeau, Va t'ent souspier,* became chaplain at St. Merry in Paris in 1418 and *clerc de matines* at Notre Dame in 1421.[64]

Musical activity at Notre Dame continued on its old high level. Foliot had been a choirboy there in 1405. Even at smaller places like Toul and Noyon, the choir schools appear to have given excellent instruction. Jacques de Templeuve, first chaplain of the Burgundian court under John the Fearless, had been trained at the choir school of Chartres Cathedral. The school of Rouen Cathedral seems to have formed particularly good musicians. Fontaine had probably been a choirboy there; Guillaume Ruby definitely was.

Ruby is mentioned in the Rouen archives as having played the organ in 1399. In 1400 he was in the Royal Chapel of Charles VI. As a musician of the Burgundian court, he first appears in the service of John the Fearless in 1415, but seems to have remained only briefly. He was again at court, in the employ of Philip the Good, from 1430 to 1451 (*see also* pp. 92f).[65]

Contemporary with Fontaine and Ruby at the Burgundian court was Jacques Vide, who is first mentioned (as a *valet de chambre*) in 1423. He was Philip the Good's secretary in 1428 and disappears from the accounts in 1433. Of his surviving chansons, *Il m'est si grief* and *Amans doublés* [66] may be singled out as making particularly liberal use of dissonance. Canonici misc. 213, the only source preserving the charming *Las, j'ay perdu mon espincel,*[67] gives music—complete in itself—for the superius and tenor only; the staves for the contratenor are left blank. Since this is a carefully prepared MS, perhaps no music is actually missing. The empty staves may, in their own way, describe the words "*Las, j'ay perdu . . .*" and thus present an example of symbolism, bordering on *Augenmusik,*[67a] that dates from many years before this technique came into general use. In *Vit encore ce faux Dangier,*[68] a *rondeau cinquain,* the effect of a *rondeau sixain* is obtained through the repetition of line 1 of the refrain text at the end of that text; [69] the melody used in the superius at this concluding point is the same, so far as intervals

---

[62] Cf. FiF, 9; the Gloria is pr. in DTO XXXI, 7.

[63] Cf. VanAM, 14, 26–31, 39f, 43, 45; BesEP, 13, 16ff.

[64] PirM, 33. For the *rondeau, see* StaD, 172. Other works of his are pr. in DTO VII, 208; XXXI, 9. About the chanson pr. in DTO VII, 255, and CW XXII, 9, *see* fn. 294.

[65] Cf. MarH, 137ff, 174f.

[66] Pr. DisK, 10 (with a fourth part in MarM, 21), 12 (= MarM, 17), respectively.

[67] MarM, 23.

[67a] As suggested to me by Dr. Dragan Plamenac.

[68] MarM, 26. MarM contains 4 additional pieces by Vide; DTO XI¹, 94, another. For biographical data, *see* StraM VII, 59; MarM, xiv; MarH, 161f.

[69] This necessarily calls for a repetition of line 12 after line 16.

are concerned, as that sung at the beginning, but the rhythm is subtly modified to agree substantially with a pattern introduced three times previously. In other ways, too, the piece is remarkable for its tightly knit writing.

All the standard cadences of the period are illustrated in Vide's few chansons. There are several examples of the "under-third" cadence (sometimes wrongly called the "Landini sixth" by modern writers). Familiar from 14th-century music,[70] it is still common in the 15th century. Also common is a cadence in which consecutive fifths are avoided by crossing the parts, one of which leaps up an octave. The two types may be combined.

> EXAMPLE 5. (*a*) Cadence of line 2, Vide's *Espoir m'est venu* (after MarM, 20). (*b*) Medial cadence, Vide's *Vit encore* (after MarM, 26). (*c*) Final cadence, Dufay's *Las! que feray?* (after StaD, 147).

Another close used in the Dufay period, now sometimes called the "Burgundian cadence," may be described, in modern terminology, as employing two different and simultaneously sounding leading-tones, obtained by raising not only the seventh scale-degree (if not already a semitone below the final) but also the fourth.[71] These degrees are occasionally preceded or followed by ornamental notes.

> EXAMPLE 6. (*a*) Penultimate cadence, Vide's *Il m'est si grief* (after MarM, 23). (*b*) Final cadence, Fontaine's *Sans faire de vous departie* (after MarM, 15). (*c*) First cadence, Binchois's *Qui veult mesdire* (after MarM, 71).

(*See also* Ex. 1, meas. 2f in system 2 and end.) The Phrygian cadence,[72] whether at the normal pitch-level or transposed, is comparatively rare; but it occurs both unadorned and embellished.

---

[70] Cf. ReMMA, 350, 367.
[71] The name "Burgundian cadence" is not too appropriate, for the close was already common in Machaut. Doubling of the leading-tone in the usual sense occurs at this time also (cf. p. 61).
[72] Cf. ReMMA, 381.

EXAMPLE 7. (*a*) Final cadence, Dufay's *Adieu quitte le demourant* (after DTO XI¹, 77). (*b*) Final cadence, Vide's *Espoir m'est venu* (after MarM, 20). (*c*) Medial cadence, Dufay's *Bien doy servir* (after DTO XI¹, 78).

(*See also* Ex. 1, meas. 5f.) The diminished triad in root position in Example 7*c* is noteworthy; it should undoubtedly remain unaltered.[73] The last chords of our cadences are typical in omitting the third, as do such chords in earlier music; but its appearance is not too rare at the termination of cadences other than full closes.[74]

The various modes produced cadences of different types. These cadences and also cadence-like passages in the course of a phrase (for brevity, we shall use the term "cadences" for both) are the main reasons for the use of conflicting signatures, such as were mentioned on p. 18. Signatures of this sort are present in five of Vide's chansons. They appeared in the 13th century and persisted until the 16th. Of the various explanations offered by modern scholars,[75] Edward Lowinsky's [76]—which may be paraphrased (with some quotations) as follows—is the most convincing. In pieces *a 3,* the lowest voice often has a signature of one flat, while the upper voices have no signatures; or both lower voices may have signatures of one flat, while the discant has none. Occasionally the two lower voices show two flats while the discant has only one. Other combinations are rare. The following cadences—whose $\frac{6}{3}$-chord successions terminated by an $\frac{8}{5}$ chord remind one of old English discant and of such a subsequent practice as fauxbourdon (cf. pp. 64f)—may be found in 14th- and 15th-century pieces *a 3.*

EXAMPLE 8. (LowS, 235).

I	II	III	IV	V	VI	VII
Dorian	Phrygian	Lydian	Dorian transposed	Phrygian transposed	Lydian transposed	Common form of Lydian

[73] Cf. ApelN, 10.

[74] For exx., *see* Ex. 1 (meas. before 2nd double-bar); CW XIX, 9 (last meas.), 15 (system 3), 14 (system 4).

[75] E.g., in FiK, 15; JepK, lxiii; ApelP.

[76] In LowS. By courtesy of Dr. Lowinsky, the quotations printed in our text are borrowed from that article, with his exx. renumbered.

These are merely the skeletons of cadences, which actually appear in varied forms. "Nevertheless, it is obvious that none of them requires a B-flat in the discant or in the middle part; only in the tenor is it ever definitely needed. This is the main reason for the frequent occurrence of the signature ♮♮♭ in early polyphonic music." [77]

A new cadence of four chords appears in the 15th century (Ex. 9a) and becomes one of the chief cadential formulas of the Renaissance. In the late 15th century and in the 16th it occurs with increasing frequency transposed once more to the flat side (Ex. 9b), or a 4, or both (Ex. 9c). "The original form of this harmonic progression is the Mixolydian cadence." (Ex. 9d)

EXAMPLE 9. (LowS, 243).

Once transposed   Twice transposed   Twice transposed (a 4)   Untransposed

"The four-chord Mixolydian cadence has a counterpart in a four-chord Dorian cadence in normal position or transposed."

EXAMPLE 10. (LowS, 244).

Early in the course of the 15th century, the signature ♮♭♭ took precedence over the previously prevailing ♮♮♭. The reasons leading to this shift lie in the gradual alteration of harmonic structure, as evidenced by the change of cadential formulas. The most important change is from the cadences with $\frac{6}{3}$ chords before the close to the I-V-I cadence. A second table of cadences (Ex. 11) now replaces our first one (Ex. 8).

EXAMPLE 11. (LowS, 245).

Mixolydian transposed Dorian   Lydian   Dorian transposed

[77] In this discussion, ♮ indicates the absence of any signature in an individual voice.

At the same time the cadential formulas undergo the change described, the following new cadences appear:

EXAMPLE 12. (LowS, 245).

"The two upper voices are identical with the outer parts of the Phrygian cadences in Example 8. The bass is so constructed that no diminished fifth results.[78] In other words, these are the Phrygian cadences in the new style. It is plain that the new cadences IV and VI demand a B-flat signature for the middle voice." The old cadences with $\frac{6}{3}$ writing, "which require a B-flat in the lowest voice, are still in use together with the new formations. Thus we arrive at the signature ♮♭♭." The same is true of the new table of cadences as of the old: the formulas are mere skeletons and in practice take on varied forms; e.g., cadence II often appears in the form shown in Example 13a, which demands a B-flat in the lowest voice.

Another reason "contributing to the frequency of the new signature ♮♭♭ . . . is the gradual ousting of the cadence with two different but simultaneously sounding leading-tones by the cadence with only one leading-tone," as shown in Example 13b.

EXAMPLE 13. (LowS, 246).

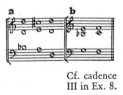

Cf. cadence
III in Ex. 8.

While the cadence types furnish the main reason for conflicting signatures, there are other reasons also. If a part had no B at all, "a signature of B-flat was superfluous. If it had only one or a few B-flats, they could more easily be indicated by individual accidentals than by a key signature that had to be repeated at the beginning of each line." If a part having a flat in the signature was imitated in canon a fifth higher, obviously the imitating voice needed no flat in its own signature. "With the emergence of the technique of imitation, the correspondence between conflicting signatures and differing tonal levels in the different voices becomes more frequent." That technique, how-

[78] Such fifths and augmented fourths also have an effect on conflicting signatures; cf. LowS, 235ff.

ever, as already pointed out, did not assume structural importance, on a large scale, until after the Dufay period.

Vide was that rarity for his time—a composer who was not also a singer. While, as we have seen, the accounts list him as Philip's *valet de chambre* and secretary, they do not show him to have been a singer in the choir. Philip the Good took great pride in his chapel singers and fastidiously supervised their selection. In 1447, after trying out Jehan Pullois, master of the choirboys at Antwerp, a man who from that year to 1468 was to be a member of the Papal Choir, the Duke declined the services of this quite respectable composer (d. 1478).[79] The Burgundian test periods sometimes lasted long. It was only after appraising Robinet de la Magdalaine (Robert le Pelé) for the whole of Easter week in 1448 that the Duke engaged this singer, who had been admired in Rome and Rouen; Robinet has been identified[80] as the author of one of the *Cent nouvelles Nouvelles,* the set of tales formerly attributed to Louis XI.

Dufay: Biography

The records do not tell under what circumstances Dufay became, at least officially, a singer of the Burgundian court. Indeed, although we are fairly well supplied with biographical facts concerning him, there are some important gaps. For example, we do not know exactly when or where he was born; this may have happened shortly before 1400 in some town near what is now the Franco-Belgian border.

In 1409, Nicolas Malin, the master of the choirboys at Cambrai Cathedral, visited Douai, Lille, and Béthune in search of talent; and a register—the first document that seems to mention Dufay—records that soon thereafter a certain priest received 77 sous "for minding the said Willelmus before he was admitted to the service of the altar." Grenon, whom we have found arriving at Cambrai in 1408 to teach grammar (cf. p. 13), was still there on Dufay's arrival, but left before the boy was inscribed among the choristers. Another musician known by surviving works, who was there at about this time, is François Lebertoul.[81] Loqueville succeeded Malin in 1413 (cf. p. 13) and may well have had a hand in preparing the young Dufay to become a composer not only of sacred but also of secular music.

[79] Cf. PirRM, 17; MarM, xiif. For further data on Pullois (Pulloys, Pyllois), *see* SaarB, 180ff; BurbM, 189 (not wholly dependable); for compositions, *see* DTO VII, 259; XI[1], 92–94, 117 (= CW XLV, 12).

[80] *See* MarG, 285. For an article on Robinet, *see* PirRM. Whether the Rubinus, whom the *Glogauer Liederbuch* credits with *Der pawir schwanz* (pr. in EDMR IV, 86; EitT, 49), or the Rubinet to whom 6 chansons are ascribed in Florence, Bibl. naz. centr., Banco rari 229, is Ruby or Robinet or some still other composer, is unclear. (The title, *Der pawir schwanz,* means "The Peasants' Dance"; cf. p. 116.)

[81] A motet of his from Canonici misc. 213 (which also contains some of his chansons), pr. BorP, 273. *See also* BesM, 190.

It is recorded that in the summer of 1420 a "Guillaume de Fays" was in the service of St. Germain l'Auxerrois at Paris.[82] This may refer to our composer. Beginning with the same summer, Dufay is traceable in Italy. Of his about 200 surviving works, the earliest to which an approximate date can be assigned is *Vasilissa, ergo gaude*. This piece, addressed to Cleofe Malatesta on the occasion of her departure for Byzantium to marry Theodore Palaiologos (cf. p. 41), praises both the bride and the groom.[83] Since she left for Greece on August 20, 1420, the music must have been written before that date.[84] Another composition from about this time is the epithalamium, *Resveillés vous, et faites chiere lye,* of 1423, which celebrates the marriage of Carlo Malatesta (brother of Cleofe) and Vittoria Colonna, niece of Pope Martin V.[85] The Malatesta family ruled over Rimini and Pesaro, and it is clear that Dufay was in their employ until at least 1426. This sojourn must have given him an opportunity to become acquainted with Italian polyphony of the *trecento* and early *quattrocento*.

It would seem that, after leaving the Malatestas, Dufay returned north again. The text of *Adieu ces bons vins de Lannoys,* dated 1426 in Canonici misc. 213, suggests that he may have held some post at Laon; [86] he bids goodbye to the good wines of the place, to the ladies, and to *tous compaignons galois.*

Dufay's presence in Italy is once more attested, in 1427, by a leave-of-absence sent from Bologna in his behalf by Cardinal Louis Aleman to the chapter of St. Géry at Cambrai, where Dufay was serving as deacon. In December, 1428, his name appears in the lists of the singers in the Papal Choir and remains until August 1433.[87] Some of his colleagues there have already been mentioned.

Probably assignable to 1433 is Dufay's *ballade, C'est bien raison,* in praise of Nicholas III of Ferrara, Marquis of Este,[88] who had relations with both the French and Burgundian courts. He is best known to us today as the husband of the luckless Parisina (the heroine of Byron's poem), beheaded in 1425 by order of Nicholas, together with her lover Hugo, the Marquis's son. Dufay was in the employ of the Court of Savoy [89] from at least as early as February,

[82] *See* PirH, 61.

[83] DTO XXVII¹, 102 (which refers to Theodore as Tommaso, accepting, as do some other modern sources, the errors in Litta; cf. fn. 49), misinterprets line 12 of the text as indicating that Theodore is already dead (but the adverb *coelitus* means "from heaven," not "to heaven") and it therefore dates the piece some time after the marriage; actually Theodore survived Cleofe by 15 years (cf. Zakythinos, *op. cit.,* 190, 225). Cleofe's being addressed by the Greek term *vasilissa* (βασίλισσα, queen) is, of course, explained by the bridegroom's parentage.

[84] Cf. BesND, 160ff.   [85] The date, 1416, usually given, is incorrect. See BesND, 162f.

[86] He was to become the recipient of 2 benefices from the diocese of Laon in 1430. The piece, incomplete in the MS, pr. PirH, 62.

[87] HabD, 60ff; HabR, 33.

[88] The Estes did not become Dukes of Ferrara until 1452. The beginning of the piece, pr. BesM, 193. Regarding Dufay's association with the court of Ferrara, *see* BesND, 166f.

[89] The duchy included—besides Piedmont and modern Savoy—Geneva and the land north of the Rhône between Geneva and Lyons.

1434, until March, 1435, but during this period made a trip home to visit his mother. Duke Amadeus VIII of Savoy, a direct ancestor of the modern Italian ex-royal line, resigned in favor of his son Louis in the course of 1434, retiring to his "hermitage," the château of Ripaille on Lake Geneva, but assuming the active role of antipope as Felix V in 1439. Dufay functioned first as chaplain, then as director of the chapel, serving chiefly Louis and his wife, Anne of Cyprus, who were ardent music lovers.[90]

Dufay's name reappears in the lists of the pope's singers between June, 1435, and June, 1437. But his duties now were not centered at Rome. With the death of Martin V in 1431, there had begun the troubled pontificate of Eugene IV, who had been compelled in 1434 to flee to Florence, which he left in 1436 for Bologna, returning to Rome only in 1443. While in the Pope's service, Dufay acquired several canonical prebends in the north, the most important being the one that went with his appointment as canon of Cambrai Cathedral in 1436, but he was allowed to remain in Italy. Prebends were on occasion granted to church musicians to supplement their incomes and were an important factor in establishing their financial stability. In theory, the receipt of such a benefice should require residence at its seat, but in practice this was regularly waived in cases of the kind in question.[91]

In 1438, Dufay provided the three-part motet, *Magnanimae gentis laudes,*[91a] upon the occasion of the signing of a treaty of alliance between the Swiss cities of Berne and Fribourg. Thereafter he becomes somewhat difficult to trace until 1454, or slightly later, when his relations with Cambrai begin to grow progressively closer, although he does not, as was once thought, remain practically fixed there.[92] The archives show him to have been in the town occasionally before 1437, but just as his appointment as canon there in 1436 left him free to remain in Italy, so his retention of the post did not prevent frequent absences later. His will [93] shows that, all told, he lived seven years in Savoy. It has been held, therefore, that part of the interval between 1438 and c. 1454 must have been spent there, and the archives of the Savoyard court and a letter of Dufay's (cf. p. 58) bear this out. These archives refer to him as *cantor illustrissimi domini Ducis Burgundie,*[94] and it is possible

---

[90] Cf. CordD; BorD, 41ff; BorQS, 35ff. Dufay was *maître de chapelle* at the marriage of Louis and Anne on February 8, 1434. Turin MS J II 9 (cf. p. 14) must have been brought from Cyprus to Savoy by Anne (*see* BesS I, 210).

[91] Cf. BorQS, 37. For a whole study of Dufay's *"carrière bénéficiale,"* see BaixC.

[91a] Pr. DufayO I², 77. Regarding errors in the surviving form of the text, the circumstances under which Dufay wrote the piece, etc., see BesND, 167ff.

[92] Cf. GrunN, 76; KühD, 115; BorGD, 175; BorQS, 42f.

[93] The original Latin is printed in HouH, 409ff; HabD, 119ff. There is a French transl. (with some errors) in ProdE, 13ff.

[94] Cf. CordD, Pt. II, 35; BorD, 361; BorF, 284. A note in the Papal Archives, dated October 17, 1446, pertaining to Dufay's acquiring the canonry of St. Waudru's (St. Waldetrudis'), Mons, provides additional evidence by referring to him as chaplain of the Duke of Burgundy. The Burgundian archives themselves, however, have yielded no record of his formal employment. *See* BorF, 285.

that he passed a substantial part of the interval at the Burgundian court also. (It is known that he was at the court on a diplomatic mission in 1446.[95]) There is some indication of his presence there in Martin le Franc's *Le Champion des dames*. Isabella of Portugal had become Philip the Good's third wife in 1430, and in 1435 he had brought from the Hispanic peninsula two blind viol-players—Jehan Fernandes and Jehan de Cordouval; the poet praises the blind players at the Court [96] and says:

J'ai veu Binchois avoir vergongne	*The shame-faced Binchois I have seen*
Et soy taire emprez leur rebelle,	*Silent before their rebec-tones*
Et Dufay despite et frongne	*And frowning Dufaÿ in spleen*
Qu'il n'a melodie si belle.	*Since no such melody he owns.*

It has been suggested that a composition of Dufay's, entitled *Portugaler,* may have been written in honor of Isabella.[97]

At Cambrai, Dufay continued his contacts with the outer world, supervised the music of the cathedral, and contributed new works to its repertory. Students gathered about him, and the influence of Cambrai as a musical center increased.

Dufay lived the life of a great personage, esteemed at home and abroad. In 1458 he visited Besançon, having been asked to function as arbiter there in a musical debate. Of much interest is a letter sent to him by Antonio Squarcialupi, organist of Santa Maria del Fiore at Florence and owner of the famous Squarcialupi Codex, one of our main sources of *trecento* music.[98] The letter,[99] dated May 1, 1467, shows that Dufay had sent singers from Cambrai to Piero de' Medici and that they had been found excellent by both Piero and the organist; Piero, according to Squarcialupi, regarded Dufay as the chief ornament of the age; his son Lorenzo felt likewise and loved Dufay's compositions passionately. Lorenzo wished to have one for himself and had written a *canzone,* which poem he requested Dufay to set to music and which Squarcialupi enclosed.[100]

The composer's will is dated July 8, 1474, and he died on the following November 27.[101] One of the provisions of the will asked that, if possible, *"motetum meum de Ave Regina Celorum"* be sung during his dying moments—a wish that could not be carried out; to approximate fulfilment, however, the motet was performed in the chapel after the blessing of the body.

[95] Cf. PirH, 87; DufayO II, xxiii.

[96] These are the players referred to in Chap. 1, fn. 46. It is more probable that they were Spanish than Portuguese; *see* esp. A. Van den Linden in RB IV (1950), 74ff; also PirD, 8; BorD, 55f.

[97] But *see* DèzB, 304; pr. *ibid.*, 305. *See also* p. 659, fn. 134, *infra.*

[98] Cf. ReMMA, 362ff.

[99] Printed several times. For original Latin and German transl., *see* KadB, 13ff; French transl. in ProdE, 27ff.

[100] If Dufay made the setting, it seems not to have survived.

[101] For fuller biographical data, *see* BorD (this fine monograph should be read in the light of BorQS, 31ff); BorF; PirH, 54ff.

Dufay: Chansons and Related Works

Unless prompted by unusual circumstances, such as Lorenzo's request, a work with Italian text, at this period, is likely to have been written only in Italy; for, although a piece with French text, e.g., the epithalamium of 1423, might possibly be intended for use primarily outside French-speaking countries, other languages, except Latin, did not enjoy a similar international prestige. Dufay's pieces with Italian texts, therefore, may safely be assigned to his Italian period. Of his six Italian songs in the Oxford MS, one, *Quel fronte signorille,*[102] is actually headed by a statement that it was written at Rome. (With an additional phrase of music, this evidently much liked piece appears in the same MS and elsewhere, adapted to a French *rondeau* text, *Craindre vous vueil,*[103] and in Munich MS 3232a, with a Latin text.) *Donna, i ardenti ray,* preserved on the same page as *Quel fronte,*[104] is noteworthy for its use of binary rhythm, far less common during most of Dufay's period than ternary rhythm; the date of this MS shows the piece to be an early one, but Dufay's compositions in binary rhythm are more likely to belong to his later years. *Vergine bella,*[105] another of the six, is a setting of stanza I of Petrarch's Canzone 49. Although Jacopo da Bologna had written music to Petrarch's *Non al suo amante* in the 14th century, this is the earliest known setting of a portion of the celebrated poem that was to inspire Rore and Palestrina also. Dufay writes a setting of large proportions, such as we have found in the old grand *ballade,* but here the music is through-composed. There is more equality of the voices than is usual in contemporary settings of vernacular texts. The melodic lines are evidently affected by the spirit of *trecento* music. It is not hard to imagine what a revelation the flowing melodies of Landini's countrymen, and probably of Landini himself, must have been to the young Dufay, "reared in the rather severe tradition of Richard de Loqueville and Nicolas Grenon, a tradition still quite impregnated with the rationalism of the French *ars nova.*" [106] Such Italian traits as enter *Vergine bella* and other Dufay compositions, however, do not make them real examples of Italian music. The presence of these traits there, and in works by some other northerners who had come to the peninsula, simply served to bring Italian elements into the developing Franco-Netherlandish style, and the main composers

---

[102] Pr. StaD, 148 (cf. ApelN, 134); facsimile in StaD, Pl. 6, and ApelN, 103.

[103] Pr. CW XIX, 18; less well in DTO VII, 250. Cf. BorD, 259f; DèzB, 303 (note 2); and PirH, 70, where a claim is made that the text forms an acrostic on the name, Caterine Dufay; in Canonici misc. 213, however, the acrostic yields the first name "Cateline." It is impossible to say whether the French or Italian piece came first.

[104] And therefore presented in the facsimiles mentioned in fn. 102. The facsimile of another Italian song, *La dolce vista,* is pr. (after Vatican, Urbin. lat. 1411) in BannM, Tavola 130c in the vol. of plates.

[105] Pr. CW XIX, 7; BorD, 305. Old notation (after Bol., Bibl. Univ. 2216, with variants after Bol., Lic. mus. Q 15) in LisioU. *See also* HabS (with facsimile); LisioM; BorQS, 34.

[106] BorQS, 22.

remain firmly within the current of Franco-Netherlandish music history, even though some modern writers who favor the term "Burgundian" (cf. p. 8) refer to them as belonging to an Italo-Burgundian (rather than to a merely Burgundian) School. Notwithstanding a piece like *Vergine bella*, Dufay and his countrymen on the whole treated Italian texts largely in the chanson style.[107] Dufay's *Donna gentil'e bella*, in the Mellon Chansonnier (at the Yale University Library),[108] is a regular *rondeau*, like Brolo's *O celestial lume*.

The more complex character of *Vergine bella* may be due to the semi-sacred nature of its text, for it was in their sacred music that Dufay and his contemporaries were most aspiring. Whereas, for example, they used the most advanced structural technique of the day in their *cantus-firmus* Masses (cf. pp. 66ff), in their chansons they tended to be conservative; though Dufay, even in his early motets, commonly wrote *a 4*, his chansons normally are *a 3*. In the 15th century, secular music, though important, lost the leadership it held in the 14th.[108a] (Popular histories are so apt to regard it as axiomatic that secular music is always more venturesome than sacred, that these points take on a certain corrective value.) The rising moneyed *bourgeoisie* must have exerted a conservative, if not retarding, influence on secular composition. All this, however, did not prevent the chansons—both Dufay's and those of other composers—from including gems of exquisite charm.

The *rondeau*, as might be expected, is the form most frequently used in Dufay's chansons. The *ballade*, if less often employed, is represented by some choice specimens. *Malheureux cueur* [109] and *Helas, mon dueil* [110] are examples of the still rarer *virelai*. There are also a few chansons that are free to the extent that they draw on none of the *formes fixes*.

The texts are of the same general nature as those of other chansons of the period. If conventional and still utilizing the trouvère idioms and situations of two centuries earlier, and if not of the artistic value of Machaut's poems, they nevertheless possess a certain charm, though of a somewhat bourgeois quality. Love, of course, is the favorite subject, especially love that gives the singer cause to complain. The mood is often one of melancholy, of a gentle dissatisfaction with life, of resignation. But there are also songs of happy love, May songs, New Year songs, drinking songs. A number of Dufay's chansons, like some by other composers of the time, are preserved in MSS that give only the first words of the text, but scholars have occasionally been able, with such a clue, to track down the full text in old collections of poems. Important

---

[107] Cf. BesM, 194.   [108] For a special study of this MS, *see* BukU.

[108a] In view of the pioneer character of Ciconia's *O felix templum*, this would be true even with respect to the use of imitation. In early 15th-century music this, as we shall see, does appear to be employed more in secular than in sacred compositions. But the available evidence would seem to point to sacred music as the field in which the path was first broken.

[109] Pr. CW XIX, 20.   [110] The beginning, pr. BesM, 211.

in this connection are the *Jardin de Plaisance,* published c. 1501 by Antoine Vérard, and the song MS of the Cardinal de Rohan.[111]

The number of voices supplied with text varies. *Malheureux cueur* and *Las! que feray* [112] are examples in which only the superius has it; *Ce jour de l'an* [113] is an example in which it is given to all three. Often the superius and tenor have text, while the wordless contratenor is obviously instrumental, as in *Adieu m'amour* and *Vostre bruit.*[114] *Estrinez moy* [115] might be called a *rondeau* in dialogue: the superius sings all the text of the refrain except the last line, which is given to the tenor. Introductions, interludes, and postludes, in which all parts are without text, as in *Hé compaignons* and *Je me complains,*[116] seem to be wholly instrumental. (The last of these is dated July 12, 1425, in the Oxford MS.)

Understandably enough, where only the superius has text, one is apt to find the treble-dominated style in Dufay's chansons, as in those of other men. But more characteristic of Dufay are pieces in which superius and tenor alike have important melodies (whether they both have text or not) and the contratenor is a filling-in part, that is, where the so-called discant-tenor technique is applied. It is the tenors of such chansons—among those of Dufay one might single out *Le serviteur* [117] and *Se la face ay pale* [118]—that yield *cantus firmi* for future Masses. Where all three parts have text, the predominance of the superius is naturally still further decreased: the contratenor shares some of the importance of the other voices, and we see the beginnings of a process that was to culminate in the kind of polyphonic chanson that became typical in the 16th century.

In secular music it appears that usually the tenor was newly composed, like the other parts. But there are exceptions. For example, it seems clear that the tenor of Dufay's *La belle se siet au pié de la tour* [119] is derived from a pre-existent melody. The poem, recounting trenchantly the tale of a young girl whose father wishes to hang her lover, has a musical history of its own, spanning two centuries. In modified form, it was destined to enjoy popularity as the text of a folk song, under the title *La Pernette.* Of the four melodies with which the poem (in varying forms) became linked, the one used by Dufay is the earliest; indeed, it survives in a MS of Namur believed to be older than

---

[111] Modern facsimile ed. of the former in JP I; the latter pr. LoepL.

[112] Pr. StaD, 146.   [113] Pr. *ibid.* 102.

[114] Pr. CW XIX, 22 (= HAM, 73), 25 (= DTO XI¹, 83; EDMR IV, 66), respectively.

[115] Pr. GurB, 162.

[116] Pr. StaD, 127, 108, respectively. *See also* CW XIX, 14 (= DTO XI¹, 80); HAM, 73; etc.

[117] Dufay's chanson consists of voices 1, 3, and 4 of the five voices pr. in DTO VII, 238. The clef of the superius is printed a line too low from meas. 17 on. The ascription there made to Isaac is also wrong; cf. HewO, 146. About the attribution to Dufay, *see loc. cit.* For a facsimile after Pavia, Bibl. Univ. MS 362, *see* JepK, xviii (anon.).

[118] Pr. in StaD, 140; DTO VII, 251, 252 (version *a 4;* obviously by a later musician; it is a transposition as well, and presents a very early ex. of a sharp in the signature); BushL, 68 (with facsimile).

[119] Pr. StaD, 122.

his composition.[120] Dufay disposes the melody in long time-values, after the manner of a motet tenor, while the other two parts sing above it. Some of their passages have a recitative-like quality that helps to give the work an atmosphere not so much of drama as of a legend declaimed by an ancient minstrel. The piece is through-composed.

An effect related to oratory is obtained likewise in *Resveillés vous:* [121] Dufay lays emphasis upon the words "Charle gentil" (which refer to Carlo Malatesta) by setting them to *fermata*-marked block-chords (cf. p. 40). Important words, including names, are similarly underscored in many other works of the time.

The treatment of the tenor in *La belle se siet* resembles that used in a species of 15th-century chanson called the motet-chanson (not to be confused with the song-motet; cf. p. 94 [122]). This is a mixed type, employing a secular French text for the two upper voices and a Latin text for the lowest part. The result is simply an example of what is normally called, in discussions of music of an earlier period, a bilingual motet. Dufay's *Je ne puis plus—Unde veniet* [123] is a specimen of this type.[124]

The *ballade, Ce jour le doibt,*[125] adds an *envoi* of 4 lines to the 3 stanzas that had formed the usual type of earlier days. This appendage apparently calls for a repetition of the last four phrases (plus the postlude) of the music. In other respects, the musical form—with each stanza having a repeated opening section followed by a longer unrepeated section—is normal; likewise normal is the presence, at the end of each stanza, of the one-line refrain (which closes the *envoi* also). The relation of the superius and tenor of this lovely May-song is interesting: the former reproduces in shorter time-values, and with slight modifications, several passages that the latter gives forth in longer values. *Se la face ay pale* is an example of the *ballade equivoquée,* i.e., of a *ballade* whose text lines end with the same final syllables, repeated in a different sense, rather than with rhymes. Although the piece is provided with three stanzas and a normal refrain, it departs from the standard form musically by having no repeated section, the setting, though repeated for each stanza, being itself through-composed. The popularity of this piece is attested to by its presence in sources from the Germanic areas of the time. Two keyboard arrangements are included in the *Buxheimer Orgelbuch* (cf. pp. 658ff); the chanson likewise appeared in Strasbourg MS 222 C. 22, which was burnt

---

[120] Further about its history, *see* GéroC, 3, 85; GéroB, xvi, xxiii, 107.

[121] PirH, 59.

[122] If the term "motet-chanson" is adopted, uniformity would seem to call for "chanson-motet" instead of "song-motet"; the latter, nevertheless, appears preferable, since it helps to produce terms which, showing greater contrast in their formation, can more readily be differentiated.

[123] Pr. StaD, 143.

[124] Further about the motet-chanson (and also the song-motet), *see* SteB, 51ff; HewO, 69ff.

[125] Wrongly pr. as *Le jour s'endort* in DTO XI¹, 85; ScherG, 35. Cf. RdM VII (1927), 49; BorFA, 9.

during the War of 1870. (The MS contained 207 items, 52 of which survive in copies made by Coussemaker; some of the pieces reach us, also, in other old MSS.[126]) In both sources, Dufay is represented by additional compositions as well.

Par droit je puis [127] presents the curious aspect of a *rondeau* in *caccia* style: the two upper parts are in canon and are supported by a *contratenor concordans cum omnibus*. In the chansons as a whole, snatches of imitation are not uncommon. Thus, in the *rondeau, Donnez l'assault,* a love song written in the style of a mock battle-piece (cf. p. 12) and therefore rich in fanfare effects, imitation *a 2* occurs at the opening of section 2.[128] The same thing is found at the beginnings of lines 1 to 3 of *Mon cuer me fait,*[129] and there is imitation *a 3* at the beginning of line 5. The beginnings of lines 2 to 4 of *Pour l'amour de ma doulce amye* [130] are also set to imitative writing. The setting of line 4 involves imitation at the fourth; all three voices take part, and it is noteworthy that the second and third entries are modified in a way showing a nascent, though no doubt unconscious, feeling for tonal answers. At the opening of *Franc cueur gentil* [131] all three voices again participate, but here the reason for the slight change is chordal; imitation occurs also at other points in this *rondeau*. The three-part *rondeau cinquain, Vostre bruit,* has imitation *a 2* at the opening of every line. The widely disseminated *Le serviteur,* a three-part *rondeau quatrain,* introduces lines 2 to 4 with imitation *a 3*. Among other Dufay chansons employing imitation are *Pouray-je avoir vostre mercy* and the charming New Year's songs, *Bon jour, bon mois* [132] and *Ce jour de l'an*. Such snatches of imitation, however frequent, merely decorate the counterpoint, cast in the *rondeau* mould, and do not give the pieces their basic form (cf. p. 88). At least some of these Dufay chansons with imitation are probably later works: two are *a 4,* and one exhibits the tonal-answer feature. One ascends to f″ (cf. p. 35).[133]

Some clue as to date—applicable, of course, to sacred music as well—is provided also by the extent to which chains of $\frac{6}{3}$ progressions are present— if there is much writing of this type, the work is probably an early one (cf. pp. 46f). The rhythm of the music offers still another clue. Generally speaking, composite ternary rhythm (*tempus imperfectum, prolatio maior*) was in favor early in the century, simple ternary rhythm (*tempus perfectum, prolatio minor*) during the second quarter, and binary rhythm (*tempus im-*

---

[126] For a full account of the MS, *see* BorS; for a special article on its Dufay and Binchois items, BorC; for a study of its *musique pittoresque,* BorM.

[127] Pr. StaD, 115.

[128] Pr. DTO XI[1], 82 (*a 3*); BukU, 35 (*a 4*). (A repeated-note pattern is imitated *a 3* at the opening of section 1.)

[129] Pr. StaD, 118.   [130] Pr. *ibid.,* 157.   [131] Pr. CW XIX, 19; DTO XI[1], 83.

[132] Pr. StaD, 152, 134 (= CW XIX, 16), respectively.

[133] For other chansons reaching f″, *see* StaD, 150; BorD, 291; KiesG, Supp., xi.

perfectum, prolatio minor) beginning with the second third.[134] The *virelai* form enjoyed a revival of interest in the latter part of the century, and it is indicative that both specimens mentioned on p. 53 display binary rhythm—*Malheureux cueur* in its section 2, section 1 being in simple ternary rhythm. Other chansons in binary rhythm are *Belle vueilles moy vengier, Ne je ne dors, Dieu gard la bone sans reprise,* and *Du tout m'estoie.*[135] The last of these reveals another late trait—the non-quartal technique, described on pp. 103f. *Belle, que vous ai je mesfait* is an example in which each of the three parts is in a different rhythm, apparently to illustrate, at a time when such descriptive touches were rare, the confused state of mind of the singing lover who bemoans the indifference of his fair one.[136]

Reports reach us of the manner in which chansons were sometimes performed at court entertainments. The *Mémoires* of Olivier de la Marche and the *Chronique* of Mathieu d'Escouchy describe the Banquet of the Oath of the Pheasant, at which Philip the Good and the Knights of the Golden Fleece vowed to undertake a crusade against the Turks to recover Constantinople, which had fallen to them in May, 1453; the crusade, however, was destined never to be carried out. The banquet, held in February, 1454, at Lille, took place in a great hall whose walls vanished under splendid tapestries depicting scenes in the life of Hercules. The chroniclers, besides describing the silken costumes, the elaborate table decorations, and the perfumes that scented the air, tell of the masques that were performed and of the part that music played in animating them, as well as in endowing the table decorations with the power of sound. "In that hall there were three tables; on one there was a church, in which there were a sounding bell and four singers who sang and played on organs when their turn came." On another table there was a huge pastry so formed that it could house "twenty-eight living persons playing on divers instruments." Later, on the main table, "three little children and a tenor sang a very sweet chanson, and when they had finished a shepherd played on a bagpipe in most novel fashion." We learn also of two trumpeters who sounded a fanfare while mounted on a horse that was led back and forth the length of the hall. Appropriately enough, considering the Order of the Knights, there were masques about the adventures of Jason. Before the first, "those in the church sang, and in the pastry there was played a *douchaine* [cromorne [136a]] with another instrument and soon thereafter four *clairons* sounded very high [loud] and made a very joyous fanfare. These *clairons* were

---

[134] About the Latin terminology, *see* pp. 19f *supra.* The principles applied there and in ReMMA, 343f, to black notation were applied to the later white notation also.
[135] The first 3 pr. ThibaultQ (the second also in EDMR IV, 37); the last, in GomO, Supp., 1. *Cent mille escus,* pr. in AmbG II, 554, and OH II, 52, with ascriptions to Dufay, is also in binary measure, but the piece is not his (cf. Chap. 3, fn. 59).
[136] The piece pr. DTO XI¹, 77; cf. BorD, 251ff.
[136a] Cf. SachsDD.

behind a green curtain, hung over a great scaffolding built at the end of the hall. When their fanfare was ended, the curtain was suddenly drawn, and there, on the scaffolding, was seen the personage of Jason." After this masque "organs were played in the church for the length and extent of a motet, and shortly afterwards there was sung in the pastry, by three sweet voices, a chanson, named *Sauvegarde de ma vie.* Then, through the door, after those in the church and those in the pastry had each performed four times, there entered into the hall a wondrously great and beautiful stag: upon the stag was mounted a young lad, about twelve years old. The child held the two horns of the stag with his two hands. When he entered into the hall, he began the upper part of the chanson, very high and clear: and the stag sang the tenor, without there being any other person except the child and the artifice of the said stag; and the song that they sang was named *Je ne vis oncques la pareille.* While singing, as I have narrated to you, they made the rounds before the table, and then returned; and this interlude seemed to me good. After this interlude of the white stag and the child the singers sang a motet in the church, and in the pastry a lute was played with two good voices, and the church and the pastry always did something between the interludes." [137]

A *rondeau, Je ne vis oncques la pareille,* reaches us—anonymous in nine sources, ascribed to Dufay in one, and to Binchois in another—and is probably the chanson sung at the banquet. To be sure, the piece [138] is *a 3* and the account mentions only two performers. Perhaps the contratenor was omitted.

At the height of the banquet, an elephant was led in by a giant; the animal bore a little castle on its back, and in the castle was a woman robed in white satin and wearing over it a black mantle in token of mourning. She represented the Church and gave utterance to a lament bemoaning the fall of Constantinople and appealing to Philip and the nobles for help. A four-voice *Lamentatio sanctae matris Ecclesiae constantinopolitanae* by Dufay is preserved.[139] It is undoubtedly one of the four *"lamentacions de Constantinoble"* which, in a letter dated *"le xxii^e de fevrier"* (the year was probably 1454), sent from Geneva to Piero and Giovanni de' Medici, Dufay says he wrote during the past year.[140] The superius of the surviving piece—which is a motet-chanson in two *partes*—has a French text, while the words of Jeremiah, "All her friends have dealt treacherously with her, among all her lovers she hath none to comfort her" (Lamentations I, 2), sound in the tenor in Latin. They are sung once in each *pars,* each time to a modified form of the Tone used in the chanting of the Lamentations in Holy Week,[141] the plainsong here serving as *cantus*

---

[137] The *Chronique* is pr. in Vols. 118, 120, 126, and the *Mémoires* in Vols. 213, 219, 220, 240, of the *Publications de la Société de l'Histoire de France.* The above quotations are a condensation from Vols. 120 and 219. *See also* MarH, 37ff; Georges Doutrepont, "A la cour de Philippe le Bon. Le Banquet du faisan . . . ," in *Revue générale* (Brussels), LXX (1899), 787.

[138] Pr. CW XIX, 24; DTO XI¹, 102.

[139] *Pars I,* pr. PirH, 84; complete piece in BecherD, 126f.

[140] Cf. GrunN; KühD, 114f.   [141] *See* Liber, 626.

firmus. Pars I ends with three voices sustaining notes in the final chord, while an inner voice moves for two more notes; continuing activity of an inner part at the close, common later, was rare at this time. The French text does not agree exactly with any portion of the lengthy *Complainte de la dame* as recorded by either chronicle; very likely the *Complainte* is one of the other three "lamentacions," mentioned by Dufay in his letter.[142]

Dufay: Mass Compositions

We observed in Chapter 1 that secular music was preferred early in the 15th century, that Mass sections not incorporating plainsong and written in treble-dominated style were fairly common, and that *quattrocento* Italy was emulating *trecento* Italy in producing such sections in early madrigal and *caccia* style. We noted also the rarity of an example like the Credo of Zachara da Teramo, which paraphrased a Gregorian melody. Although, with the Dufay generation, secularized Mass sections continued to appear, paraphrasing of the Chant became much more widespread. This arose out of a new church-liness, which also led not only to a large production of complete Masses but to such other ambitious undertakings as series of Magnificat settings for the eight Tones and cycles of hymns for the whole Church year. Nevertheless, the real artistic significance of the Chant was not grasped; as in the preceding period, it was regarded as in need of improvement. Such extensive elaboration was therefore sometimes applied to it that the borrowed melody can hardly be recognized.[143]

In a setting of the lovely *Kyrie Orbis factor* chant,[144] Dufay alternates the monophonic plainsong with polyphony *a 3,* the chant being here paraphrased in the superius. In another independent Kyrie [145] based on the same melody, the chant, slightly elaborated, lies in the middle voice, and the setting makes frequent use of the $\frac{6}{3}$ technique—a combination of characteristics that had been known in 14th-century English music.[146] Another Kyrie *a 3,*[147] preserved in two Cambrai MSS (also in two Trent MSS), is written in treble-dominated style, without plainsong. In each of the last two Kyries mentioned, there is one setting of the words *"Kyrie eleison,"* to be sung three times for the first three invocations; one setting of *"Christe eleison,"* to be similarly repeated for the next three invocations; and another setting of *"Kyrie eleison,"* likewise

[142] For modern editions of Dufay works with French texts, not yet cited, *see* BecherD, 133; DTO VII, 251; XI¹ 84 (= DisK, 26), 87 (2 pieces); BesBF, 261, 262; StaD, 105 (= KiesG [1846 ed.], App., xii, with wrong ascription to Binchois), 113, 132, 138, 155. DufayO IV will contain all Dufay's *rondeaux, virelais,* and *ballades.*

[143] *See* FiF, 21.

[144] Pr. Liber, 80 (and named after the insertion that had been added to the Kyrie text before troping was banned from the liturgy); Dufay's setting pr. DPLSER, Ser. 1, No. 7, 1.

[145] Pr. DèzM, 10; DPLSER, Ser. 1, No. 7, 4.

[146] Cf. ReMMA, 404.   [147] Pr. CW XIX, 13. About 2 other separate Kyries, *see* fn. 166.

to be repeated for the last three invocations. Automatically, therefore—and this is true also of the first of the Kyrie compositions mentioned—each invocation is given a closed musical section, a procedure by no means uncommon in the early part of the century. (It had been applied long before, of course, by Machaut.) In the first of our three compositions, the plainsong has the odd-numbered invocations, so that Dufay provides only one polyphonic setting each for Kyrie I and Kyrie III, but, by the same token, two for the *Christe*—each even-numbered invocation here having a closed setting of its own. Occasionally, as in his *Missa Sancti Jacobi* (to be discussed presently), Dufay writes a different closed setting for each of the nine sections. (Arnold de Lantins followed the same procedure in treating the troped Kyrie of his Mass.) But in addition to these methods, Dufay sometimes writes continuous music for each group of three invocations, as in the *Missa sine nomine* (also to be discussed), this being the procedure that was soon to be adopted as the normal one.

Dufay's independent Gloria settings include one,[148] based on the Gloria of what is now Gregorian Mass XI, that alternates plainsong and polyphony. The monophonic chant of another Gloria, with a similar alternation, is notated mensurally in Trent MS 92 but as plainsong in certain other sources. This composition, in which the Gloria of Gregorian Mass IX (*De Beata Virgine*) [149] is paraphrased in the superius, has inserted in it the words of the six medieval Marian tropes (the *Spiritus et alme,* etc.). The practice of intercalating these tropes in settings of Gloria IX was standard and was to continue until the Council of Trent (cf. pp. 448f). *Fermata*-marked block-chords appear impressively. In four passages, they are used to underscore the closing trope lines in praise of the Virgin; in two of these passages a fourth voice is momentarily present.[149a] In the Gloria with the designation *"de Quaremiaux"* ("for Lent")—a true *Gloria breve*—the structural device is a seven-fold repetition (with appropriate rhythmical modifications) of an *ostinato* formula in the tenor [149b] Another Gloria preserved in Trent MS 92 is remarkable for the way in which, throughout its length, it varies the three motifs of its first eleven measures.[150] Still another Gloria, the delightful *Et in terra ad modum tubae,*[151] is in *caccia* style. The two upper parts sing in canon throughout. The two lower ones are suitable for slide-trumpets, but the words *"ad modum"* may indicate that only tone-painting is intended—that this pair of

---

[148] Pr. DPLSER, *Ser. I,* No. 7, 5.

[149] Pr. Liber, 40. Dufay's setting pr. DTO XXXI, 81 (*see also* FiF, 34).

[149a] Some other Glorias based on Mass IX and having the same tropes, ibid., 67, 108. About these tropes, *see* WagG, 34f; KabisM.

[149b] Pr. DPLSER, *Ser. I,* No. 10.

[150] Cf. FiF, 31f; for the piece, *see* DTO XXXI, 75.

[151] Pr. DPLSER, *Ser. I,* No. 3; DTO VII, 145. Trent 90, one of the sources preserving this work, contains 2 more Mass compositions calling for *tuba* (cf. the thematic index to the first 6 Trent Codices, printed in DTO VII, 31ff; *see* Nos. 891 and 1123–26).

voices is to be performed by other media, but the sound of trumpets suggested.[151a] These parts have a motif of their own, appearing first in this form:

Each lower part, alternating with its fellow, plays the motif twice in succession. It appears altogether twenty-five times before it is subjected to modifications, thus producing a striking *ostinato* effect. The two parts continue to alternate without overlapping until they approach the end. (In other words, so far as sound is concerned, the music is *a 3* until near the close.) The motif is then subjected not only to melodic alteration but to rhythmical changes that bring about a gradual shortening in its length, until the diminution and the continuing alternation produce a passage in hocket. After the hocket, the two lower parts sound simultaneously, in company with the two other voices. What had, so far as actual sound was concerned, been music *a 3*, now becomes music *a 4*. The enriching of the texture and the increased impetus produced by the rhythmical changes in the lower parts result in an effective climax, achieved, though it be, in almost naive fashion.[152] Early 15th-century composers in general apparently preferred the Gloria to other Mass texts for canonic treatment. (Pycard's Gloria in the Old Hall MS is even in double canon, an early example of this species.[153])

A Credo *a 4* of Dufay's, preserved in several sources, has in Bologna, Lic. mus. Q 15, the words of an Italian song added under the Latin of a trope inserted in the Amen passage:

EXAMPLE 14. Extract from trope passage in a Credo of Dufay's in Bologna, Lic. mus. Q 15 (after BesBF, 213).

O Ma-ri- a, no-li fle - re, jam surrexit Christus ve - re.
La vi - la - nel- la non è bel- la se non la do-mi-ni - ca.

One is tempted to conjecture that this is a snatch of Italian popular song.[154] In the penultimate chord of this Credo, a chord which we would now designate as a dominant, the leading-tone is doubled at the octave, a not altogether rare procedure at the time.[155] Another Credo introduces both imitation of rhythmic motifs (cf. the isorhythmic sequences mentioned on p. 16) and snatches of melodic imitation.[156]

[151a] Cf. BesEP, 14.

[152] The Apt MS contains a Gloria (pr. in GasMA, 79) by a musician whose name, provided by the scribe, has been read as "Dufay"; he suggests (GasMA, xiii) that this may be an early work by the composer (cf. also PirH, 59). However, Ludwig (LudD, 427) has deciphered the name as "Susay" and proposed Pierre de Susay (traceable before 1350) as the possible composer; DannS, 9, points to the later Jehan de Susay as a more likely choice. *See also* G. de Van, in Acta, XII (1940), 65f, who reads the name as "Gusay."

[153] Cf. StrunkOH, 247ff (= BukMR, 83ff).

[154] *See* Handschin in RB, I (1947), 97f; VatV I, 12. [155] Cf. PirH, 73f.

[156] The piece is pr. in DTO XXXI, 73. *See also* FiF, 30f.

Among the Mass sections assignable to Dufay's Italian period is a *Sanctus papale,* the name of which indicates that it was written for the Papal Choir. At the end of the copy in Trent MS 92, a verbal notation links this Sanctus and an Agnus Dei [157] that follows shortly after it. But the compositions are not closely related musically. Their texts, however, are both troped, which shows that intercalating other words into those of the Mass had penetrated into the papal liturgy itself. The insertions stretch the two sections far beyond their normal length, apparently for the practical reason that the elaborate pontifical ceremonies required certain musical settings to be of considerable duration. The word *"Sanctus"* is first sung in plainsong; then part of the trope, marked *Duo,* is sung by two soloists; the second *Sanctus* is evidently for three soloists; then comes another portion of the trope, set *a 3* and marked *Chorus;* the third *Sanctus* is *a 4;* the rest of the setting is predominantly *a 3,* but at *Osanna I* there is a momentary subdivision of the voices, resulting in five parts. Similarly, in the opening *Duo* a third voice enters briefly to help sing a portion of the word *"Virgine."* Subdivision appears here and there in Dufay, sometimes with exquisite results. While it is reasonable to suppose that the music is most often choral where such departures from strict part-writing occur, the entrance of a third voice in the opening *Duo* of this Sanctus shows that any general assumption on this score would be unwarranted. In this piece, as in other early Dufay works, the unregulated dissonance of the previous generation occasionally reappears. Near the end there is a syncopation in which the positions of the consonance and dissonance with relation to the first beat of the measure are the reverse of what later became the rule: the sustained note enters as dissonant on the last beat of a measure and becomes consonant on beat 1 of the next. The borrowed chant melody of the initial *Sanctus* is paraphrased several times in the course of the setting. The tenor of the Agnus, which is *a 3,* is borrowed from Gregorian Mass IX. The first two words are sung in plainsong; then the same melodic fragment is sung against the other parts, first with the notes in normal order and then in reverse order; thereafter the melody unfolds without further retrograde motion.[158]

If the Sanctus and Agnus just described are not musically related, there are two Gloria–Credo pairs in Cambrai MS 6 (one set reappears in Trent MS 87) that do reveal an attempt at unification. The initial phrases in each pair are the same. Dufay makes a similar effort to link a Gloria, Credo, and Sanctus in Bologna, Lic. mus. Q 15, and a Sanctus and Agnus Dei in Trent MS 92.[159] A Kyrie, Gloria, and Credo in the Bologna MS [160] are loosely related by the identity of their last two chords.

---

[157] The pieces, pr. DTO VII, 148, 153.

[158] For additional comments on these settings, *see* WagG, 86f, 96f; BorD, 152ff.

[159] Cf. PirH, 75f. The tying together of the Trent pairs may be noted in the thematic index printed in DTO VII, 31ff; *see* Nos. 8 and 9, 1368 and 1567.

[160] Fol. 164 ᵛ–166 ʳ. All pr. in DPLSER, *Ser. I,* No. 1.

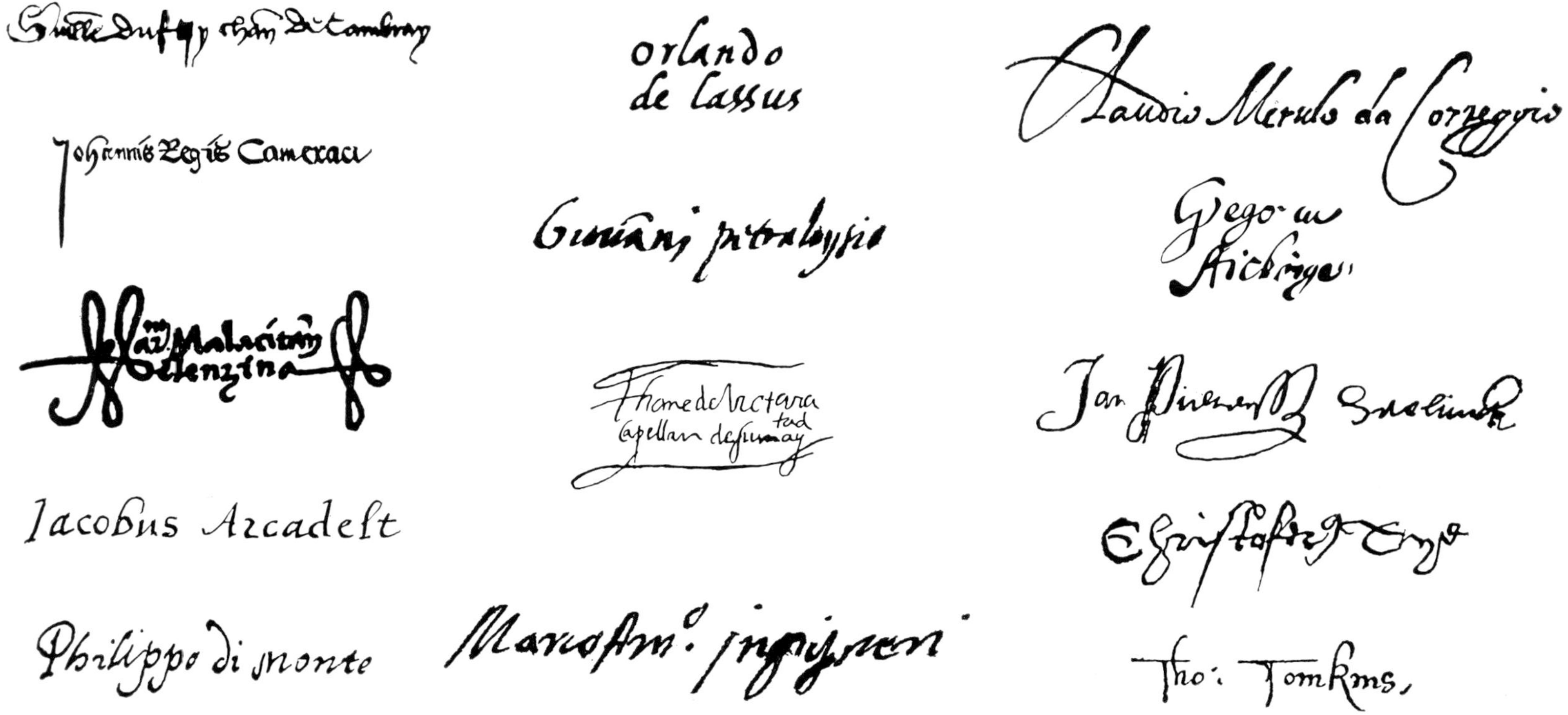

SIGNATURES OF RENAISSANCE COMPOSERS

Claudio Merulo
Gregor Aichinger
Jan Pieterszoon Sweelinck
Christopher Tye
Thomas Tomkins

Roland de Lassus
Giovanni Pierluigi da Palestrina
Tomás de Victoria
Marc'Antonio Ingegneri

Guillaume Dufay
Johannes Regis
Juan del Enzina
Jacques Arcadelt
Philippe de Monte

PLATE I

Eight complete Masses reach us that are unquestionably by Dufay, and there are others that may be his also.[161] Of the eight, three give every indication of being the earlier works. These are preponderantly in the treble-dominated style. One, a three-part *Missa sine nomine*,[162] achieves a certain unity by presenting the same sequence of changing time-signatures in the Kyrie, Sanctus, and Agnus, and by having the superius and contratenor open the Sanctus with the same melodic material with which they had begun the Kyrie; moreover, the superius melody in question closely resembles the intonation of the Agnus. The Kyrie text, in one source, is embellished by a trope that is noteworthy for word repetitions, unusual (unless liturgically required) in Franco-Netherlandish works of the first half of the century. A diminished fourth occurs in the Gloria as a melodic interval (no rarity at this period); in short, the restrictions of the Palestrina style still lay far in the future, in this respect as well as in several others. This section is divided into four subsections, separated by interludes that are perhaps instrumental and in which use is made of snatches of imitation, many of them purely rhythmic.

The second early Mass survives without title in Trent MS 90. Passages in this work are identical with extracts quoted in the *Proportionale* of Tinctoris, who indicates that they come from Dufay's Gloria and Credo *de Sancto Anthonio*. The composer's will mentions as works of his own both a *Missa Sancti Anthonii de Padua* and a *Missa Sancti Anthonii Viennensis*. Quotations, stated as coming from the Gloria of the former work, are made in a letter of c. 1532 from the Italian theorist Giovanni Spataro to his colleague Pietro Aron (cf. Chap. 4, fn. 164). These excerpts do not appear in the Gloria in Trent MS 90, and it is consequently fair to assume that the work preserved in this source is the *Missa Sancti Anthonii Viennensis*. The composition is *a 3*.[162a]

The third early Mass, the *Missa Sancti Jacobi*,[163] is probably named for St. Jacques de la Boucherie in Paris; a connection between Dufay and the rector of that church, Robert Auclou, is shown by an acrostic on the rector's name and title contained in the words of an isorhythmic motet [164] probably written by the composer c. 1426. The Mass, very likely dating two or three years later, includes four settings for the Proper as well as a complete Ordinary. Some sections are *a 4*, some *a 3;* duos are interspersed. The sections of the Ordinary are unified by an identical sequence of three different time-signatures and by

---

161 The anon. *Missa La mort de Saint Gothard* is almost certainly his; cf. BesND, 174. This Mass, as well as the anon. Masses *Veterem hominem, Christus surrexit* (incomplete), and *Puisque je vis* are pr. by Dr. Laurence Feininger as works of Dufay's (on stylistic grounds) in MPLSER, Ser. I, II; but concerning the *Missa Veterem hominem*, see M&L XXXV (1954), 183.
162 Pr. DufayO II, No. 1. Kyrie also in DèzM, 3; Gloria also in DTO XXXI, 71; Agnus also in DèzM, 5.
162a Cf. BesND, 173f; DufayO III, i; the work is to be pr. *ibid.*, II, No. 3.
163 Pr. DufayO II²; Kyrie also in ScherG, 33; Credo also in DTO XXXI, 76; Communion also in BesF, 109.
164 Pr. DufayO I², 28; cf. *ibid.*, xxi.

a concurrent alternation of *"Chorus," "Duo,"* and *"Chorus."* Identifiable plainsong melodies underlie all sections except the Gloria, Alleluia, and Credo.[165] The handling of the chant varies from motet-like *cantus-firmus* treatment in the tenor of the Offertory to elaborate paraphrase in the superius at the end of the Introit. Besides the plainsong intonations taken for granted in the Gloria and Credo, many are written in at other points, sometimes in the superius, sometimes in the tenor, in either event being (as is normal) in the voice that continues with the chant. The Communion of this Mass, for which only two voices are written out, is of especial historical importance, since it contains what is believed to be the oldest example of fauxbourdon. In one source preserving the piece,[166] there is not only the direction *"faux bour- don,"* but a Latin rhyme stating: "If you seek a third part, take the notes from the highest one and begin at the same time proceeding a fourth below." This verbal canon actually sums up the whole method applied in performing faux- bourdon. Whatever the written-out lowest part (the tenor) may do, the un- written middle part (the contratenor) always moves in parallel fourths with the superius.[167] The choice of the fourth was undoubtedly prompted by the fact that it made possible the inclusion of the superius in both $\frac{8}{5}$ and $\frac{6}{3}$ forma- tions. By the same token, the composer had to contrive the tenor in such a way that every chord (not counting ornamental notes) would be either an $\frac{8}{5}$ or a $\frac{6}{3}$.[167a] The technique provided more opportunity to change from one chordal structure to another than did English discant, in which the two upper voices entered with a fifth and octave above the first note of the lowest part in each phrase and proceeded so as to form $\frac{6}{3}$ chords with the lowest voice until the last note of the phrase was reached, when there was a return to a root-fifth-octave chord. Another, and an important, difference is that, whereas in English discant the *cantus prius factus* was in the lowest part, in fauxbourdon the main melody was in the highest one. Still another difference is that, whereas English discant began as an improvisation technique, the results of which were later applied to written composition, fauxbourdon—so far as we know about it from the actual sources—was always a form of written composition. (It would not be quite right to except even the middle part and look upon it

[165] Cf. Liber, 1304, 25 (Dufay uses the plainsong only in the last invocation of each subsec- tion), 1327, 21, 48, 1392.

[166] Bol., Lic. mus. Q 15. It contains 18 fauxbourdon pieces, of which 2 (including the Com- munion) can be shown to be older than the rest; cf. BesBF, 11f (= BesD, 29). Of the remaining 16, 9 are by Dufay, 1 being a Kyrie; portion pr. in BesBF, 19; BesD, 37. For another Kyrie in fauxbourdon by Dufay, a fine example, *see* DTO XXXI, 80.

[167] The liberties taken in some modern "realizations" of fauxbourdon pieces seem to be un- warranted. Cf. BesBF, 22f (= BesD, 40). Also the use of "fauxbourdon" to designate written- out successions of $\frac{6}{3}$ chords is incorrect; to be an example of genuine fauxbourdon a piece must be notated in two parts to which a middle part is to be added; the most that would be justified in using this term in references to such $\frac{6}{3}$ successions is to call them "fauxbourdon-like."

[167a] After the initial stage of fauxbourdon, an effort might be made also to give the tenor melodic interest. See BesBF, 184f, and the Dufay ex. pr. *ibid.,* 264.

as the result of improvisation, since it really came into existence through the application of a rigid principle.)

Fauxbourdon was a Continental creation—possibly produced by Dufay himself; [167b] it was undoubtedly an attempt to apply to written composition the sonorities heard in the performance of English discant. It is probably for this reason that Martin le Franc refers (cf. pp. 12f) to Dufay and Binchois as having *"prins de la contenance angloise."* These composers had ample opportunity to come under English influence, for the English conquerors maintained chapels on French soil; Dunstable himself was probably in the service of the Duke of Bedford there.[168] Here is the ending of Dufay's Communion: [169]

EXAMPLE 15. Close of the Communion of Dufay's *Missa Sancti Jacobi* (complete piece in BesF, 109; DufayO II², 31).

In our example, the notes taken from the Chant are starred. (A similar procedure is followed at other points in this book.) The considerable amount of figuration that appears in the final cadence is typical of the treatment of cadences generally in paraphrase writing; but, as here, correspondence with the plainsong is as a rule restored with the last note of the phrase.

The great extent to which fauxbourdon gradually permeated early 15th-century music was to have an important effect: composers, influenced by its mellifluousness, were led to avoid the harsher asperities of earlier days and to smooth out the harmonic texture even when they were not writing in actual fauxbourdon.

A Mass *a 3* by Reginaldus Liebert,[170] a contemporary of Dufay's, resembles his *Missa Sancti Jacobi:* it provides music not only for the Ordinary but for seven portions of the Proper, it makes much use of plainsong intonations, and it employs fauxbourdon (in part of the Sanctus and in the Agnus). Plainsong material is unquestionably paraphrased in nine sections and may be present

[167b] Since the above was written, FiZ has appeared, advancing arguments against both these points, but they are not very well thought out nor, to the present writer, do they seem headed in the right direction.

[168] Cf. ReMMA, 412; BesBF, 15 (= BesD, 32).

[169] Inconsistencies between the above account of fauxbourdon and that in ReMMA, 398ff (first 7 printings), are due to the more recent appearance of BesD, BesF, and BesBF, q.v. for further details, including the derivation of the term "fauxbourdon."

[170] Perhaps the Reginaldus who succeeded Grenon at Cambrai in 1424; cf. HouH, 82. The Mass is pr. in DTO XXVII¹, 1. A *rondeau* by Reginaldus is pr. in StaD, 176; DTO XI¹, 90; DisK, 15.

in the remaining three,[171] the paraphrase being characteristically in the superius, though not exclusively; in the Kyrie, for example, the plainsong "migrates" from one voice to another.

The five other Masses that can be definitely ascribed to Dufay belong to the *cantus-firmus* type, extremely important throughout the 15th century. This is true also of the *Missa La mort de Saint Gothard* which, of four anonymous Masses held to be Dufay's, is the one regarded, at least by one authority,[171a] as most likely to be his. All six of these works are *a 4*. In the type in question, a *cantus firmus* is repeated, though not necessarily continuously, from the beginning of a Mass to its end. (Suspension of the *cantus firmus* at certain points, such as the *Christe, Pleni,* Benedictus, and Agnus II, was more or less standard—this being less common, however, in the *Christe* than in the other sections.) Throughout the history of this type of Mass, composers evidently felt that a plainsong melody that provided a setting for a particular portion of the Ordinary should not be pressed into service in connection with another portion (cf. p. 29). They therefore normally refrained from drawing upon chants that set the Kyrie, etc., for persisting *cantus firmi* and preferred melodies—secular as well as sacred—that by comparison were neutral. Normally, the chosen melody was assigned to the tenor, which presented it mainly in time-values longer than those prevailing in the other voices, while these voices wove constantly fresh polyphony. Plainly, *cantus-firmus* treatment was an outgrowth, after about two centuries of development, of the same basic idea that underlay the 13th-century motet tenor. But in the 15th century this idea took on a new meaning, producing unified compositions comparable in magnitude to symphonies. While French and Netherlandish composers were to produce many *cantus-firmus* Masses, the type seems to have originated among the English. The Gloria and Credo of Dunstable that have the same melody twice in the tenor of each [172] represent an intermediate step toward the form that restates a single *cantus firmus* through all five sections. In each movement of Leonel Power's three-part *Missa super Alma Redemptoris Mater,*[173] one of the earliest works approaching such a form,[174] the tenor—here the lowest voice—renders the first half of the *Alma* melody, the rhythmic configuration that is imposed upon this chant fragment (a configuration that quite disregards the phrase divisions of the original) being the same in all

---

[171] The plainsong melodies that underlie the sections of the former group and may underlie 2 sections of the other group are pr. with their paraphrases, one above the other for comparison, in DTO XXVII¹, 95ff. (*See also* FiK, 8ff.)

[171a] Heinrich Besseler; cf. fn. 161.   [172] Cf. ReMMA, 421.

[173] Pr. DPLSER, *Ser. I,* No. 2.

[174] For the incipits of another, the *Missa Rex saeculorum* (without Kyrie), ascribed to Power in Trent MS 92, *see* DTO VII, 60 (No. 901), 76 (No. 1404), 62 (No. 984), 77 (No. 1446). The work, however, may be by Dunstable, since the Gloria is twice attributed to him in the Aosta MS; cf. VanAM, 24ff, Nos. 40 and 65.

movements. This work, in being *a 3,* in employing a sacred melody as *cantus firmus,*[175] and in having the *cantus-firmus*-bearing tenor as the lowest part, resembles all the earliest known English Masses. Power omits the Kyrie, a feature common in English Masses (cf. p. 765). In view of the progressive tendency we shall find in works by Dufay, it is fair to assume that he was probably the first Frenchman to essay the *cantus-firmus* Mass. Furthermore, a new feature may be his "personal creation." [176] The *cantus firmus* had, in rare cases, lain in the next-to-the-bottom voice in old music *a 3* [177] (we have, moreover, noted on p. 59, a Kyrie *a 3* of Dufay's that places the borrowed chant there); but the Dufay Masses in question differ, not only from music of this type, but also from the English Masses just mentioned, by placing the *cantus firmus* in the next-to-the-bottom voice in music *a 4.* This disposition now becomes standard. In the 1440's the *cantus firmus* in Dufay's motets had begun to rise from its traditional position in the lowest voice (cf. p. 80), and the *Missa Caput,* which gives stylistic evidence of being the oldest of his *cantus-firmus* Masses, probably dates from the early part of the decade. Establishing the tenor as next-to-the-bottom part did not yet mean that the range necessarily corresponded to that of the tenor voice: the part was often written in the alto clef, and this practice still sometimes recurred late in the Renaissance. (The voice newly placed at the bottom was at first called by a great variety of names.) Partly because the *cantus firmus* was disposed in long time-values, partly because it was now an inner voice, it was unlikely to be heard very clearly unless it was performed on some such instrument as the slide-trumpet (either alone or doubling the singers), a quite possible procedure, at least in the early days of the type. In any event the repeated melody exerted enough unifying power to make the *cantus-firmus* Mass one of the great examples in the history of the organization of musical materials. That power, obviously, made itself felt all the more if the listener was able to identify the *cantus firmus* readily, and there was, therefore, a marked tendency to select *cantus firmi* from among melodies that were well known.[178] It became fairly normal, not only in *cantus-firmus* Masses, but in *cantus-firmus* motets, for the tenor to be the last voice to enter. This made it possible for the first notes of the *cantus firmus* to appear in another voice in anticipatory imitation (cf. p. 76). The added part, the *contratenor secundus,* not only increases the sonority in this kind of music, but provides a foundation with some of the functions of a bass. Obviously, it is easier to write an original part that will serve such a function than to make a pre-existent melody do so.

[175] Cf. BesBF, 152. [176] Cf. DufayO III, v. [177] Cf. ReMMA, 404; WolfG III, 191ff.
[178] For further suggestions concerning the motives governing the choice of *cantus firmi, see* Dent in the *Festschrift für Johannes Wolf* (1929), 24.

The application of *cantus-firmus* treatment to individual Mass movements as if they were a group of unrelated motets (i.e., without obtaining unity by carrying over the same *cantus firmus* from one movement to another) had occurred, as we have noted on p. 39, in the work of as early a composer as Machaut.[179] In a sense, the term *"cantus-firmus* Mass" might have some suitability for a composition using a *cantus firmus* in this way. It is normally reserved, however, for Masses employing *cantus-firmus* treatment as a unifying device. In still another sense, the term might fit any Mass which, like Reginaldus Liebert's, is based on borrowed melodies. Liebert's work, however, with its pre-existent material appearing in elaborated form mostly in the superius and not being presented in long notes, is better called a paraphrase Mass.[180] There is much less paraphrase in the superius of the *Missa Sancti Jacobi,* which might be regarded as a combination of paraphrase Mass and Mass using the *cantus-firmus* technique in purely motet-like manner.

Undoubtedly Dufay's *cantus-firmus* Masses are later than the three thus far discussed. Of the newer group, the Masses on *Caput, Saint Gothard,* and *Se la face ay pale* seem to belong to his middle period of Mass writing. These works reveal traits characteristic of the mid-15th-century four-part Mass generally—quite possibly as a result of Dufay's own initiative—in their frequent use of upper-voice duos, a "solid, instrumental treatment of the *Tenor,"* and a "disparity in the figuration of the upper and lower voices, which form two distinct architectural groups." [181] This disparity is very much in the spirit of the Early Renaissance.

The *cantus firmus* of the *Missa Caput* [181a] derives from the antiphon *Venit ad Petrum,* as it appears in the Sarum use.[181b] Each of the five sections of the Mass is divided into two segments, the first being in ternary rhythm, the second in binary. Since the *cantus firmus* appears complete in each of these segments, every section presents it in two rhythmic forms. The binary one repeats, near the end, a phrase of music that the ternary one has used but once; otherwise the forms correspond. With a few minor changes, this twofold presentation of the *cantus firmus* remains constant from section to section. The upper voices open each of the five sections with a brief head-motif *a 2,* the other voices being silent. There is considerable contrasting of writing

---

[179] *See also* ReMMA, 356, regarding the 14th-century Tournai Mass.

[180] Compositions of its type are sometimes called plainsong Masses but, since the *cantus firmi* of *cantus-firmus* Masses are often likewise taken from plainsong, the term is not very fortunate.

[181] DufayO II[1], i.

[181a] Facsimile after Trent MSS 88 and 89 in DTO XIX[1], 3ff; transcription into modern notation, 17ff. About defects in the underlaying of the text, *see* UrVG, 366. The preface is poor, especially the section claiming that the superius is derived from the *cantus firmus.* There are also errors in the treatment of the music. The Mass is pr. likewise in MPLSER, *Ser. I,* II, No. 1, and will be pr. in DufayO II, No. 4.

[181b] Cf. BukMR, 226ff.

a 2 and *a* 4. The Kyrie is troped, but lacks the final subsection. Its style indicates that it may well have been composed after the rest of the Mass. If the work originally consisted of the other four movements only, this fact would strengthen the possibility—suggested by the use of a melody from the Sarum repertory—of its connection with England. Indeed, it may be modeled on a lost English Mass, since the *cantus-firmus* treatment departs in certain respects from the kind that is normal for Dufay.[181c] Imitation plays a secondary role. The presence of $\frac{6}{4}$ and seventh chords in the Sanctus, measure 21, is of some interest.[182] A passage in the Gloria (meas. 130–142) recurs modified in the Agnus (meas. 115–127).[183] Two excisions occur in the text of the Credo. The practice of omitting passages from the Credo—certainly a strange one from the point of view of later periods—is to be found applied in many Early Renaissance Masses. Perhaps the explanation lies in the efforts that were being made by the Papacy to bring about a reconciliation with the Eastern Church.[183a] The possibility that phrases of chant were inserted is ruled out by the existence of examples in which there is no break in the polyphonic interlocking at the points of omission. Nor is there any wholly consistent plan in the cuts.

The *Missa La mort de Saint Gothard* [183b] is distinctive in presenting its *cantus-firmus* in straightforward form only in Agnus III; in the other portions of the work it appears in somewhat altered, freer forms. The melody, like *La vilanella non è bella* (cf. Ex. 14), gives the marked impression of being a popular one.[183c] Basing a Mass on a secular melody, as in this instance and in the next Mass to be discussed, which is unquestionably Dufay's, may be his own innovation.

In his *Missa Se la face ay pale* [184] Dufay uses the tenor of his own *ballade* (cf. pp. 54f) as *cantus firmus*. An analysis of this Mass will illustrate, in greater detail than has been attempted heretofore in this study, the possibilities inherent in *cantus-firmus* treatment, as well as other aspects of early 15th-century Mass writing.[185] Here is the melody:

181c For the details, *see* BukCR.

182 *See* BukMR, 275, about the $\frac{6}{4}$ chord in DTO XIX¹, 38, meas. 75. Such chords appear with some frequency at this time; cf. HayE, 15ff.

183 Cf. BukMR, 278.   183a *See* HanMC.

183b Pr. MPLSER, *Ser. I*, II, No. 8; to be pr. also in DufayO II, No. 5. Our not describing the other 3 anon. Masses mentioned in fn. 161 is due to the necessity, imposed by space limitations, of selecting material for analysis, rather than to any stand taken against their authenticity.

183c *See* DufayO III, iv; *see also* BesBF, 212ff, which discusses still another popular melody that Dufay incorporated into a Gloria.

184 Pr. DufayO III, 1; DTO VII, 120; MPLSER, *Ser I*, II, No. 4 (the work being here followed by 2 anon. compositions, because of their stylistic similarity to it); *see, ibid.,* iiiff, for a table of errors in the DTO edition.

185 The work illustrates so many points that it is discussed here once more, even though it has already been analyzed in BorD, 104; WagG, 89; and (from the harmonic standpoint) KorteH.

EXAMPLE 16. Tenor of *Se la face ay pale* as it appears in the *Missa Se la face ay pale*—Dufay.

* This three-note group, which does not appear in the chanson, is omitted in the Gloria and Credo.

At the beginning, the tenor is treated in such fashion that each of its measures corresponds to two measures of the other parts.

EXAMPLE 17. Opening of the *Missa Se la face ay pale* (superius and tenor only).

This anomaly arises from the fact that Dufay applied the proportional system to his tenor, thereby modifying its rhythm according to a series of possibilities of a semimathematical order. With this system a given tenor may, in the course of an extended work, appear in normal basic time-values,[186] in diminished or augmented values, in duple or triple measure, etc. If the tenor is to reappear from one end of the Mass to another without changing anything but its "proportions," it need be written only once—in *integer valor* (i.e., with normal time-values)—the requirements for its various modifications being indicated by verbal canons. It will readily be recognized that the principle of proportions, like the idea of repeating the *cantus,* had already operated on a more modest scale in the field of the motet (cf., e.g., p. 22).[187] The instructions affecting the Mass under examination require the following:[188]

1. Segments *a* and *b* of the melody to be augmented in the first section of the Kyrie, and *c* in the third (the tenor is absent from the *Christe,* which consists of free writing *a 3*), so that each tenor note has twice its *integer valor* (hence the correspondence between each single measure of tenor to two measures in the other voices);

---

[186] Which are not necessarily the first ones that appear.
[187] Actually, the germ of the idea goes back to the 14th century; cf. ReMMA, 354.
[188] Cf. DTÖ VII, 278.

2. The entire tenor to appear three times in succession in the lengthy Gloria, each time in a different proportion: in tripled time-values through *Filius Patris,* so that each measure of tenor corresponds to three measures in the other parts, all voices—as in sections 1 and 3 of the Kyrie—being in triple meter; in doubled time-values from the second *Qui tollis* through *Jesu Christe,* but with the tenor still in triple meter ($\frac{3}{4}$ in the reduced time-values of our examples) while the other parts are in duple meter ($\frac{2}{8}$), so that each measure of tenor still corresponds to three measures in the other parts; and in normal time-values (i.e., with each measure within the limits of the prevailing *integer valor*) from *Cum Sancto Spiritu* to the end, so that one measure of tenor equals one measure of the other parts;

3. The entire tenor to appear three times in succession again in the Credo, in the same proportions as in the Gloria;

4. Segment *a* of the melody to appear in doubled time-values against triple meter in the other parts (as in the Kyrie) from shortly after the beginning of the Sanctus through *Dominus Dei Sabaoth,* after which the tenor rests from *Pleni* through *gloria tua; b* of the melody to appear, again in doubled time-values against triple meter, in *Osanna I,* after which the tenor rests through the Benedictus; and *c* to appear, still in doubled time-values, in *Osanna II,* but with the other voices now in duple meter (as in the second sections of the Gloria and Credo, the rhythmic interrelations that prevailed there now naturally recurring);

5. The tenor to behave in the Agnus exactly as it did in the Kyrie, so that the first and last sections of the Mass form counterparts to each other.

The above analysis shows that the tenor rests throughout the *Christe, Pleni,* Benedictus, and Agnus II. This procedure, as has already been pointed out, was common in *cantus-firmus* Masses; and it was to remain standard practice for the Renaissance Mass to employ less than the full complement of voices in these passages, even where no *cantus firmus* was involved. (Perhaps "standard" is too strong a word to use with regard to the *Christe.*) Later, such treatment was often accorded to the *Crucifixus* also.

The fact that the *cantus firmus* is treated rigidly in the *Missa Se la face ay pale,* but freely in the *Saint Gothard* Mass, does not, in itself, throw light on chronology. The two types of treatment had both already existed in the oldest English *cantus-firmus* Masses.[188a]

Another unifying device applied on a large scale in the *Missa Se la face ay pale* is the head-motif. The one used by Dufay is indicated in Example 17 by a bracket. It occurs in the superius in the first three measures of the work and reappears thereafter in that voice at many of the more important places, subject to melodic and rhythmic modifications which, however, leave it quite recognizable. While this means of unification was not new, Dufay endows it with greater richness in his *cantus-firmus* Masses. As in similar works, the head-motif, sounding above the other parts, makes itself felt as a unifying device more strikingly than does the *cantus firmus,* the latter more subtly than

188a *See* O. Strunk in JAMS II (1949), 108.

does the former. The *cantus firmus* may be regarded as an internal device, the head-motif as external.

Dufay displays great imagination and craftsmanship in clothing the skeleton furnished by the *cantus firmus* and head-motif, particularly in the fresh countermelodies that he writes against the repetitions in the tenor.[189] Chordal writing is absent; the style is polyphonic throughout. Variety is obtained by the introduction, into the four-part texture, of passages sometimes *a 2,* sometimes *a 3.* The writing shares the general character of music of the time in being in layers: the head-motif is confined to the superius; the *cantus firmus* lies in the tenor, practically never appearing in the other voices. Interrelation between the parts is limited to the passages in canon, which appear here and there but are mostly brief. Of special interest is the snatch of canon in the Credo at measure 249, for it is between the tenor and contratenor: for a moment a bit of *cantus firmus* sounds in a part other than the tenor. (The same thing, involving three voices, happens in measures 6–9 of a *Benedicamus Domino* by Dufay.[190]) The short fanfare at the middle of section *C* of the *cantus firmus* also makes fleeting appearances in other parts. But the kind of Mass in which the *cantus firmus* permeated the whole texture is still a thing of the future.

With its clarity and simplicity of design, the *Missa Se la face ay pale* may be regarded as representing a classical phase in Dufay's writing.

The remaining *cantus-firmus* Masses bearing Dufay's name—those on *L'Homme armé, Ecce ancilla Domini,* and *Ave Regina coelorum*—differ from their companions in presenting all four voices in a "harmonious equilibrium" that "characterises the Mass technique of the later XVth century; both *Tenor* and *Bassus* form part of the polyphonic structure, no longer content to provide a simple harmonic base for the melismatic evolution of the upper voices. The use of duets is more discreet, and there is a fulness of sound which well bespeaks the mature manner of the Master." [191] The *cantus firmi* of these works are much elaborated, but to those of the last two named— drawn from Marian antiphons—no verbal canon is applied.

The *Missa L'Homme armé* [191a] may be the first in the long list of Masses based on the tune that serves as *cantus firmus,* although there is some possibility that the work was antedated by Ockeghem's Mass of the same name.[191b]

---

[189] DTO VII gives the impression that there are consecutive unisons in meas. 36f of the Kyrie and in meas. 144 of the Credo; but this is due to faulty transcription (cf. the editions in DufayO and MPLSER). Dufay may very well have intended the consecutive fifths in meas. 34f of the Kyrie to be rendered unequal through *musica ficta,* as is suggested by the b-flat in the tenor shortly before.

[190] Pr. DTO XXVII^1, 24.

[191] DufayO II^1, ii, where, to be sure, the quoted passage is meant to refer only to the *Ecce ancilla* and *Ave Regina* Masses. But it is applicable likewise to the *L'Homme armé* Mass which, in other ways also, shows signs of being a late work.

[191a] Pr. DufayO III, 33; MPLSER, *Ser. I,* I, No. 1. Kyrie also in AmbG II, 556 (with errors); Kyrie I and Agnus III also in HAM, 71f.

[191b] Cf. DufayO III, vi.

Masses were to be built on the melody for generations to come by numerous composers, including such masters as Obrecht, Josquin, and Palestrina. A 15th-century MS has been found at Naples, containing no less than six anonymous Masses erected on it (cf. pp. 149f) and preserving one stanza of the secular text.[192]

EXAMPLE 18. The *L'Homme armé* melody (after facsimile—printed in GomB, 612—from Naples Bibl. Naz. VI E 40).

Oh, the man, the man at arms
Fills the folk with dread alarms.
Everywhere I hear them wail,
"Find, if you would breast the gale,

A good stout coat of mail."
Oh, the man, the man at arms
Fills the folk with dread alarms.

The source of the melody is uncertain; according to Aron's treatise, *Il Toscanello in musica* (1523), Busnois was believed to be its composer.[193] Since this musician was active during Dufay's last years, it would have been possible for the aging master to borrow from him. However, the Mellon Chansonnier contains a chanson in which the melody appears (divided between tenor and contratenor), and this setting is in a style that places its anonymous composer in the generation of Dufay and Binchois. Perhaps Aron's contemporaries credited the creation of *L'Homme armé* to Busnois only because he wrote a Mass on it that was particularly famous.[194] That the Mellon version is the original *L'Homme armé* is highly unlikely. Since the text of the rather square-cut melody is not a *rondeau, virelai,* or *ballade,* and the music fits the words one note to a syllable without any melisma whatever, we may well have a folk tune here.[195] A word of caution may be in order, however, against leaping to conclusions generally about alleged folk origins of 15th century melodies. The original mode of the tune may well be Mixolydian, as in Example 18 and in the Mellon chanson. However, the melody appears so often in transposed Dorian in polyphonic settings—e.g., in Dufay's Mass—that the possibility that this was the original mode should at least be considered.

[192] See PlamH; GomB; PlamM. (Although, in the second of these, its author argued that the words must have been grafted upon the melody and must originally have belonged to the superius of a lost 3-part chanson in which this melody served as tenor, he now agrees with the view expressed by Dr. Plamenac in PlamH and PlamM that text and tune belonged together from the beginning.)
[193] See AronT, lib. I, cap. 38. (The passage is quoted in PlamM, 378; AmbG III, 614.)
[194] About the "authority" of this Mass, see StrunkH; also pp. 107f, 197, *infra.*
[195] Cf. PlamM, 181, 183.

In the Kyrie of Dufay's work, the *cantus firmus* (differing slightly from Ex. 18) appears once complete, modestly elaborated, the first portion and the *da capo* in ternary rhythm, the middle section in binary rhythm; at the end there is an extra repetition of the first portion with the time-values halved. The *cantus firmus* is presented, with interruptions, twice in the Gloria, thrice in the Credo; in both it is elaborated somewhat more than previously. In the Sanctus, it is introduced without the *da capo* up to *Sabaoth* and it is absent from the *Pleni,* the *da capo* returning for *Osanna I;* it is again absent in the Benedictus (*a 2*), but is given complete in *Osanna II*. It receives its most varied treatment in the Agnus. In Agnus I it appears complete; in Agnus II (*a 3*), it is first absent, but is then divided, in modified form, between the two lower voices; in Agnus III, it is first presented backward and then, with shorter values, in normal form. The last five measures are the same as the last five of the Kyrie.

EXAMPLE 19. Agnus I from Dufay's *Missa L'Homme armé* (after MPLSER, *Ser. I,* I, No. 1).

The original application of the text, which is reproduced in the above example, gives the impression of haphazardness. This feature is common in 15th-century MSS. It has been suggested [196] that poor word-note correlation such as this may bespeak rendition by trained soloists: during performance the correlation could be left to the judgment of the individual soloists, a state of affairs that had to be changed, when choral performance became more usual, to avoid chaos. In measure 7, note 3 in the alto illustrates a form of dissonance common in the Renaissance. Moreover, it appears here in a pattern approximating one of the configurations that were to become classic with Palestrina, though this type of dissonance was used with considerably more freedom by other composers, including Dufay (observe the last note of the superius in measure 10). This is the dissonance which Fux, in the 18th century, was to call the *nota cambiata*.[197] It is approached conjunctly from a consonant note above and is normally quitted by a descending leap of a third to another consonant note, the note on either side being relatively accented. In the classic treatment represented in Example 19 the consonant note after the *nota cambiata* is followed by an unaccented passing-note above it and this leads to an accented harmony note.

The superius of the Mellon *L'Homme armé* has a separate text in which a certain man is mentioned as both Maistre Symon and Symonet le Breton. This is the friend of Dufay's who predeceased him by one year and whose portrait the composer's will directed be placed on the altar during his own obsequies. Symon was himself a composer, but a second-person reference to him in the superius occurs in a way that makes him an unlikely source of this setting.[198]

The *Missa Ecce ancilla* [199] is known to date from not later than 1463: an entry shows it to have been copied out in that year for the Cambrai choir. Its *cantus firmus* draws not only on the *Ecce ancilla* antiphon, but on the *Beata es, Maria*.[200] The elaboration is not the same in all presentations. In the Credo, the *Ecce* melody is followed by the *Beata* and returns at the close; in every other major section, the two chants each appear once. The tenor has the peculiarity, shared by the tenors of a few later Masses, of retaining its original text. Also unusual is the extent to which *Osanna II* is developed—a feature all the more noteworthy since, in Renaissance Masses, the music for *Osanna I* usually serves for *Osanna II* also; the direction in the sources is ordinarily

[196] WagG, 77.

[197] Jeppesen and most modern writers follow Fux's precedent; however, Padre Martini, and, in the present day, such a writer as A. T. Merritt, use the term to designate a passing-note inserted on the first half of an even-numbered beat between a consonance above it on the preceding beat and another below it on the second half of the same even one (the beat being represented in their examples—which follow 16th-century practice—by the half-note).

[198] For a *rondeau* by Symon, *see* JepK, 58.

[199] Pr. DufayO III, 66; MPLSER, *Ser. I,* II, No. 9.

[200] Cf. Liber 1417, 1538v.

"*Osanna ut supra.*" Still another departure from the norm is the use, in this Mass, of two distinct head-motifs.[201]

The *Missa Ave Regina coelorum* [201a] is based on the same melody as Dufay drew upon in the motet *a 4* mentioned in his will (cf. pp. 51, 82). The entire chant, elaborated, is presented in the Kyrie, which (strangely, in a late work) provides a closed setting for each invocation. Of the eight incises of the original melody, the opening one, given twice (as incises 1 and 2) in the plainsong, receives three presentations in Kyrie I, the elaboration being different in the second presentation. In the *Christe,* the next two incises (as a pair) likewise appear three times, and again there is a different elaboration in the middle. The rest of the plainsong, unrepeated, is divided between the first and last invocations of Kyrie II, there being no chant in the second invocation. The second *Christe* invocation is given in alternative versions. The first in *a 3,* with the two upper parts in canon, the lowest one bearing the words "*Concordans cum fuga.*" The other version, *a 2,* has the same superius, the lower part, marked "*Concordans sine fuga,*" resembling the bottom voice of the version *a 3* only at the beginning and end. Invocation 1 of Kyrie II is written *a 2,* with an optional bass, "*Concordans si placet.*" In all the movements the tenor is used with great freedom, being subjected to various elaborations. There are some passages of imitation. Each of the five major sections opens with a three-part head-motif, which is of unusual length (nearly eight measures) and in which the lowest part heralds the delayed *cantus firmus* by means of anticipatory imitation. Permeation of the head-motif by the *cantus firmus* is to recur in the works of later men. Dufay's *cantus firmus* also infiltrates the other voices, especially the superius, appearing at times in duos and trios. Permeation by the tenor, new c. 1470, was to take on great importance in the work of Josquin, as was a quasi-polychoral feature introduced at the close of Dufay's Gloria and Credo: here the two lower voices echo what the two upper voices have just sung. His voices are not always simultaneously in the same meter. Of much interest is a passage in Agnus II that looks as though it may have been based on all three voices of a trio passage in the motet *a 4.* If the motet was written first and the taking over of the polyphonic complex was deliberate, we have here another anticipation—perhaps we should say another early example—of the parody-Mass technique (cf. pp. 28, 112f, 202f, 240f).[202]

Dufay's will mentions a *Requiem pro defunctis* which he had written and which he ordered sung the day after his funeral. It is doubly unfortunate that this work has vanished, since it was probably the first polyphonic setting of the Requiem Mass; before the 15th century, this service had always been

---

[201] Further concerning this Mass, *see* BorQS, 146ff.
[201a] Pr. DufayO III, 91; also twice, after different sources, in MPLSER, *Ser. I,* II, No. 7.
[202] Further about this Mass, *see* BorQS, 157ff; BorF, 290.

sung in plainsong. The *Missa Sancti Anthonii de Padua,* likewise named in the will (cf. p. 63), seems to be lost also. Since the term *"Missa"* was used in the 15th century to designate not only an Ordinary but a cycle for the Proper, we cannot be sure that this missing work was of the former type.

Trent MS 88 contains sixteen anonymous cycles for the Proper.[203] They include three Introits and one Alleluia that recur in Trent MS 90, the Alleluia there bearing the name of Dufay. On circumstantial evidence, eleven of these cycles have been ascribed to him.[204] Thirteen Introits from this group present a striking point of interrelationship: all of those that are in any one Tone have both the same *Gloria Patri* and a verse setting that is at least partly the same, the Introits in question being indicated in Table II (some cycles have more than one Introit; where this is so, a letter after the cycle number in the table shows which Introit is involved).

Table II

Tones	1	3	6	7	8
Cycles	V, IXb, XII	Ib, VI	XI, XIIc	VIIb, IXa	Ia, II, VIIa, XIV

In addition the Graduals of three cycles are interrelated, as are the same sections of two others and the Alleluias of two more.[205] Cycle XV, for Easter, includes a *Victimae paschali,* in which the first member of each double verse [206] is set polyphonically, the unpaired opening verse and the second member of each double verse being left for performance in plainsong.

Dufay: Motets

Dufay's motets and related works include some of his finest compositions. The isorhythmic technique is employed in several of them, in varying degrees of complexity. In the *introitus* of the *Vasilissa, ergo gaude,*[207] written for the departure of Cleofe Malatesta to Greece in 1420 to marry the son of the Byzantine Emperor (cf. p. 49), the two upper parts sing in canon unaccompanied; when the canon is abandoned, the piece proceeds isorhythmically in all four voices, with two *taleae.* There is no *color* in the tenor, which appropriately enough in view of the occasion for which the work was composed, derives its melody from the Gradual *Concupivit rex.*[208] The motet *Apostolo glorioso—Cum tua doctrina—Andreas,*[209] dating from 1426, likewise opens with an *introitus* and is thereafter isorhythmic in all parts. Here, however,

---

[203] Pr. MPLSER, *Ser. II,* I (cycle 2 also in DPLSER, *Ser. I,* No. 4). *See also* LippP, 27ff.
[204] MPLSER, *Ser. II,* I, preface.   [205] Cf. *ibid.* vi.
[206] About the last of these cf. WagE I, 235.
[207] Pr. DufayO I², 1; DTO XXVII¹, 30, with some errors in text.   [208] Pr. Liber 1230.
[209] Pr. DufayO I², 11; DTO XL, 22.

there are two *talea*-patterns, each presented twice. As in Franchois's *Ave virgo* (cf. p. 42), more voices are provided than are to be used at once. The motet appears to be *a 6*, but is to be performed, optionally, *a 3* or *a 5*: one voice (the solus tenor) is a "reduction" of three of the others (the tenor and two contratenors) and may be substituted for them. In the process of "reducing," Dufay is much more careful than Franchois to preserve the recognizability of the *cantus firmus*. This melody is an antiphon for the feast of St. Andrew; [210] the upper parts sing in Italian verse about the apostle's activity in Greece and his martyrdom at Patras. Only the tenor is isorhythmic in *Supremum est mortalibus*.[211] This work lauds the virtues of peace and belongs to the spring of 1433, when Eugene IV and Sigismund signed a treaty that reconciled their differences and led to the crowning of the latter as Holy Roman Emperor. The words *"Eugenius et rex Sigismundus"* are set to *fermata*-marked block-chords, which cause the two names to stand out impressively and are deliberately used for that reason. (The word *"rex"* shows that the composition antedates the imperial coronation in May.) In the tenorless introduction and at certain other points when the tenor is silent, the three upper voices proceed in fauxbourdon.[212] (No more than three voices ever sing at one time.) The composition has been singled out [213] as the earliest datable motet employing fauxbourdon. The highly attractive *Salve flos tusce gentis—Vos nunc etrusce —Viri mendaces*,[214] dating from c. 1435, hails the city of Florence and its young women. The work is for four voices, two of which are tenors. It presents four *talea*-patterns, each twice. Only the tenors are isorhythmic in the two statements of the last *talea*-pattern; all the voices are isorhythmic elsewhere. The paired tenor melodies appear four times in all, once in each twofold presentation of a *talea*-pattern. The time-values of the first tenor statement are halved in statement 2 and are reduced by a third in statement 3; the values of statement 3 are halved in statement 4.

About two years older than *Supremum est mortalibus*, the motet *Ecclesie militantis—Sanctorum arbitrio—Bella canunt—Ecce nomen Domini—Gabriel* [215] was written upon the election of Eugene IV as pope. After an introduction *a 2*, the composition is *a 5*. There are two chant-derived tenors—one,

---

[210] Pr. Antiphonale, 487.

[211] Pr. DufayO I², 23; DTO XL, 24.

[212] Incidental use is made of fauxbourdon also in the strange fragment, *Juvenis qui puellam*, the words of which propound both sides of an argument concerning a curious case of annulment of marriage. Dufay's tombstone (which is in the Museum at Lille) refers to him as *baccalarius in decretis* (Bachelor of Canon Laws). Possibly he wrote this piece in a mock-serious mood while pursuing his studies, in Savoy, and the argument should be regarded as a travesty. (The piece is pr. in WolfG III, 86; regarding its date—between 1441 and 1446—, see BesND, 170ff. The text is transl. into French and discussed in BorD, 179ff. Photograph of the tombstone opp. p. 20 in BorD and opp. p. 280 in BorF; also in MGG II, Pl. 23).

[213] In BukE, 129.

[214] Pr. DufayO I², 61. For the source of the *cantus firmus*, see Officium, 53. The text is apparently by Dufay. About the passage ending *"Guillermus cecini, natus est ipse Fay,"* see BorQS, 31.

[215] Pr. DufayO I², 82; DTO XL, 26.

on the name "Gabriel," alluding directly to the pope, who had been Cardinal Gabriel Condolmieri—, each sounded six times. The first statement is reduced by a quarter in the third statement, but returns undiminished in the fifth one; each even-numbered statement reduces its predecessor by half. Above the paired tenors, the contratenor sings its own melody three times, once to each twofold presentation of the tenors; and, above this three-part *ostinato*,[216] the two top parts weave a counterpoint of constantly fresh melody. There is a brief coda.

On March 25, 1436, the Florentine *duomo*, Santa Maria del Fiore, was consecrated by the pope. In celebration of the notable event, Dufay wrote his four-part motet, *Nuper rosarum flores*,[217] which was performed during the ceremony. Dufay very likely participated; perhaps Brunelleschi, whose great cupola was still in the process of construction, was among the auditors. At the point in the text where Eugene IV is referred to as the successor of St. Peter, the word *"successor"* is illustrated by imitation between the superius and contratenor; word-painting, however, is not common in Dufay.[218] We know, from the account of an eyewitness, that many string and wind players were in the procession at the consecration and that they filled the edifice with their music during the elevation of the host.[219] Some undoubtedly joined in performing the motet. Here again there are two tenors; both are derived from the opening of the Introit *Terribilis est locus iste*,[220] but the identical melody is given a different rhythmic configuration in each (so that a free canon results), and the lower tenor shifts it down a fifth. Passages *a 2* for the upper voices (which open the work) are alternated four times with passages for all the voices. Each resulting two-part plus four-part pair forms a section, corresponding to a stanza of text. In the first section, the tenors are in *integer valor*, but their time-values are variously diminished upon repetition, producing the relation 6:4:2:3 for the whole piece. The upper voices, on first impression, seem to be free, except for a snatch of canon in the third passage *a 2*. Actually, however, they elaborate the same melodic material differently in the four-part portion of each section. Here we have a variation technique, recalling one employed by Ciconia (cf. p. 27). Example 20 (presenting upper voices only) gives first a brief extract from section 1 and, below it, the corresponding extract from each of the other three sections, showing how the variation technique was here applied.[221]

---

[216] Which, obviously, has its isorhythmic aspect. However, the term "isorhythmic motet" is perhaps most usefully confined to works which, isorhythmic in one or more parts (normally including the tenor), have faithfully repeated melodic material only in the tenor. If there is coincident repetition of both melody and rhythmic pattern (proportionately varied or not) in one or more parts, it is simpler merely to call this repetition an *ostinato*.

[217] Pr. DufayO I², 70; DTO XXVII¹, 25; HalbG, 26.

[218] The other exx. include the division of the voices on the word *"dividas,"* momentarily producing 4 parts in the 3-part *Iuvenis qui puellam*. Cf. BorMM, 81.

[219] DufayO I², xxvii; HabR, 34.   [220] Pr. Liber, 1250.

[221] Further about this motet, *see* ReeN; BesE, 144ff; SteB, 12; etc. The variation technique

EXAMPLE 20. From Dufay's *Nuper rosarum flores* (after BesE).

In all the motets so far discussed, the lowest part (a tenor) has a *cantus prius
factus*. Owing to the presence of two plainsong tenors in *Ecclesie militantis*,
the next-to-the-lowest part also has a pre-existent melody. Both the lowest parts
have such a melody in *Nuper rosarum flores* also, since these voices are based
on the identical chant. But the *cantus-firmus*-bearing tenor is the next-to-the-
lowest voice by virtue of a low-lying tenor II in *Supremum est* and in *Fulgens
iubar—Puerpera pura—Virgo post partum* (also an isorhythmic motet),[222]
dating from the 1440's. In these compositions, however, the tenor asserts its
old prerogative of being the lowest voice in the final chord. But in *Moribus—
Virgo*,[222a] dating from c. 1446, the shift to the new order is complete.[222b]

Dufay's other motets and related works include various compositions in
honor of the Virgin. Such compositions became quite numerous in the 15th
century. By the early 13th century, many guilds and confraternities had come
into being. In Italy, there prevailed among them the custom of singing canticles in the evening before the statue of the Virgin. These canticles were
called *laude* by the Italians, and the members of the confraternities formed
expressly to sing them were called *laudesi*.[223] "The idea of an evening service
of a popular character sung before the statue of Our Lady, spread throughout
Europe. In particular the 'Salve Regina' . . . was consecrated by usage to this
rite, and we find traces everywhere of its being sung, often by choirs of boys,
for whom a special endowment was provided, as a separate evening service.
In France, this service was commonly known as *Salut*, . . . in England and

---

discussed above is now sometimes called isomelic; as we shall see, the term is also applied (perhaps more happily) to the technique described on pp. 92f, *infra*.
[222] Pr. DufayO I², 52.   [222a] *Ibid.*, 41.   [222b] Cf. BesBF, 173.
[223] Concerning a diversion of the *laude* from their original purpose, *see* ReMMA, 237f.

Germany, simply as the *Salve*." [224] The music rendered at these services was
not restricted to the four great Marian antiphons; but, when new works were
wanted for 15th-century singers functioning under *Salve* endowments, polyphonic settings of these antiphons were especially favored.

Among Dufay's Marian motets, *Inclita stella maris* [225] is remarkable for the
mensuration canon in its two upper parts. Four voices are provided; the
piece may be performed solely by the two canon voices, or by the voice that
has the unaugmented canon melody together with contratenor I, or by the
two canon voices with contratenor I, or *a 4*.

Dufay's setting *a 3* of *Alma Redemptoris Mater* is a particularly exquisite
example of paraphrase. The much loved antiphon of Hermannus Contractus
(d. 1054), upon which many a piece of medieval polyphony had been
erected,[226] continued to inspire 15th- and 16th-century composers to similar
endeavors. Dufay's work begins with the opening melisma of the old melody
very slightly elaborated in the superius, which sings unaccompanied.

EXAMPLE 21. Opening of Dufay's *Alma Redemptoris Mater* (complete
    piece in HAM, 70; CW XIX, 10; DTO XXVII[1], 19) and of the
    plainsong antiphon (transposed; after Liber, 273).

Thereafter the two lower voices enter. The composer, in the process of paraphrasing, limits the superius throughout to a rounding out of the chant, inserting at the proper places cadences that apply traditional formulas of the
period. There is almost no imitation, but rather a strong prevalence of free
counterpoint—the lower voices being subordinate—which, from the words
"sumens illud" to the end, gives way to *fermata*-marked block-chords. If in
Resveillés vous and *Supremum est mortalibus* Dufay used such chords to underscore the names of prominent persons (i.e., for extramusical purposes),
here their presence is plainly due to their eminently right musical effect. In
the last three chords, a reinforcing voice suddenly sounds immediately below
the superius with an altogether charming effect. To judge by the quality of
this antiphon and of the motet *Flos florum*,[227] Dufay must have taken particular pleasure in applying to sacred composition the treble-dominated manner with its main top part and two subordinate parts. Whereas in the *Alma*
Dufay's main melody is an elaboration of a *cantus prius factus,* in the *Flos*

[224] CE II, 466. *See also* UrK, 161; SteB, 72.   [225] Pr. DufayO I[1], 5.
[226] Cf. ReMMA, 127f, 318f, 339, 415, 418.
[227] Pr. DufayO I[1], 11; CW XIX, 5; StevensM, 14.

florum it is apparently an original invention. The latter piece ends like the former with a passage in *fermata*-marked block-chords. The melody of the superius includes an effective diminished fourth on the word *"recens."* The three-part *Ave Virgo* [228] has a rich and flowing superius over two less active voices, and has the external aspect of a treble-dominated composition. But the tenor, though unidentified, has much the appearance of being a chant melody treated as a *cantus firmus.*

However elegantly Dufay wrote sacred music in the treble-dominated manner, the *cantus-firmus* style remains standard in his motets and closely related works, as in those of contemporaries. It will be noted that all such Dufay compositions discussed before the *Alma* belong to the *cantus-firmus* type. If paraphrase is applied only to the superius of that work, it is used in both the higher voices of the three-part *Anima mea liquefacta est,*[229] while the chant melody [230] that is being paraphrased in both these parts is simultaneously laid out in *cantus-firmus* fashion in the tenor. In other words, each of the three voices treats the same melody in a somewhat different way, there being enough similar passages in the two higher voices to produce much more imitation than is usual in Dufay.

Of particular grandeur is the *cantus-firmus* setting *a 4* of the *Ave Regina.*[231] The text is troped with such interpolations as *"Miserere tui labentis Dufay"* ("Have mercy on thy dying Dufay"), and it is therefore clear that this is the *Ave Regina* referred to in the composer's will (cf. pp. 51, 76).[232] The will designates performance by singers and the writing is, in fact, of a vocal character in all parts (cf. p. 38). The complete *Ave Regina* plainsong, embellished, is assigned to the tenor, a second contratenor lying below it. The *Ave Regina* plainsong is rather sequence-like (*aa'bcb'cde*) but this fact is not reflected in Dufay's countermelodies, which remain unrepeated. The tenor has occasional long rests, during which the other voices present trio or duo passages, these at times being based on the chant. Indeed, the *cantus firmus* permeates the other parts to a degree that foreshadows later practice. The composition is in two *partes,* the first being in ternary meter, the second mostly binary. The ternary passages are markedly more florid than the binary ones, and this difference in the treatment of the two meters is general for

---

[228] Pr. DufayO I¹, 19.   [229] Pr. DTO XXVII¹, 20 (*see* criticism in DèzB, 302).

[230] Pr. ProcessionaleM, 275. The text of this antiphon to the Virgin is based on the Song of Solomon V, 6–8.

[231] Pr. BesC, 10; Music Press No. 116 (ed. by M. Bukofzer), p. 6. The piece is given also in old notation (obviously defective), after San Pietro MS B 80, in HabD, App. 1 (with 2 transcriptions of *pars I* only). Music Press No. 116 contains also a 3-part *Ave Regina* by Dufay (facsimile after Canonici misc. 213 in ApelN, 119), not based on the plainsong. For the incipit of another 3-part *Ave Regina,* ascribed to Dufay in Modena, Bibl. Est. *α*. X. I, 11 (*olim* Cod. VI. H.15; also Lat. 471), *see* DTO VII, 45, No. 443.

[232] Also mentioned in his will is the motet pr. in DufayO I¹, 14. (The suggestion made in DTO XL, 105, that the anon. piece pr. *ibid.,* 75, is the work referred to in the will is incorrect.)

the period. Dufay maintains the rhythmic flow at a steady pace in each *pars;* even in *pars I* he uses fewer arabesques than in his early writing. Harmonic progressions and the treatment of dissonance conform, as in other later works, with newer standards and are far removed from the practices of the pre-Dufay generation.[233]

Dufay's compositions in sequence and hymn form illustrate the systematic alternation of plainsong and polyphony. In his lovely setting [234] of *Laetabundus,* the double versicles of the sequence form [235] are so treated that the first verse of each pair is sung as chant, while the second verse consists of polyphony *a 3* in which the superius paraphrases the melody that has just been heard by itself. Dufay follows the reverse procedure in his handling of the *Veni Sancte Spiritus,*[236] where the chant is in the middle voice. The sequence, which had been one of the first forms to be treated polyphonically, continued in the favor of composers throughout the Renaissance.

In Dufay's hymn settings, the strophic form of the originals is preserved. Most often Dufay writes genuine three-part polyphony, but, for three hymns, only the outer parts are notated and the singers are expected to provide a *contra au fauxbourdon;* two other hymns likewise survive in fauxbourdon versions, but come to us, in addition, having the outer parts supplied with a free contratenor; [237] for two more, alternative versions reach us, not only for the contratenor but for the lowest part as well: here one setting harmonizes the superius in fauxbourdon, while the other combines the same superius with two entirely different lower parts of a more polyphonic nature. *Ad coenam Agni providi* [238] appears in two sources with a real polyphonic setting *a 3* for the odd-numbered stanzas and a fauxbourdon setting for the even-numbered ones. But usually the odd-numbered stanzas are all sung to the same

---

[233] A setting of one of the other great Marian antiphons, the *Salve Regina* (pr. DTO VII, 178), is ascribed to Dufay in Munich MS 3154, but its authenticity has been convincingly attacked in DèzS. Also of doubtful authenticity are the motets pr. in DufayO I¹, 27, 29 (cf. fn. 57a); I², 91. (This vol. of DufayO contains 6 genuine Dufay motets not yet cited.)

[234] Opening pr. DèzM, 9.   [235] Cf. ReMMA, 187ff.

[236] Cf. the *Victimae* described on p. 77. The *Veni* is pr. in DTO XXVII¹, 29.

[237] The free contratenor for *Christe Redemptor . . . Ex Patre* may not be Dufay's, but it does seem that the one for *Ave maris stella* is genuine and that Dufay wished to offer a choice of 2 versions.

[238] Now sung to the text *Nunc Sancte nobis Spiritus;* cf. *Liber,* 808 (*see also* Chap. 9, fn. 79). Many old hymn melodies have, since the pontificate of Urban VIII (1623–44), been sung to texts somewhat or entirely different from those with which they were associated in Dufay's time, the melodies occasionally being slightly altered. (The adapting of a single melody to various hymn texts is, of course, facilitated by the fact that so many such texts have the same metrical structure.) Thus his *Aurea luce = Decora lux* (Liber, 1522); *Conditor alme siderum = Creator alme siderum* (Liber, 324); *Hostis Herodes = Crudelis Herodes* (Liber 464); *Iste confessor = Christe sanctorum* (Antiphonale, 725, [218]); *Jesu nostra redemptio = Salutis humanae sator* (Liber, 852; also given with the *Jesu nostra redemptio* text in Graduale, 140*); *O lux beata trinitas = Iam sol recedit* (Liber 312, 915); *Sanctorum meritis = Sacris solemnis* (Liber, 920) or *Panis angelicus* (VP, 6); *Ut queant laxis = O nimis felix* (AntiphonaleM, 926; slightly varied). *See also* fn. 242. Some of the melodies may be found with their old texts in the *Hymni antiqui* section at the end of the Antiphonale; also in AntiphonaleM.

complete unisonal plainsong and the even-numbered ones to the same complete polyphonic version (this plan being reversed in only a few examples). The paraphrasing of the chant appears in the superius of all but two pieces, in which this occurs in the middle voice. The degree to which the original melody is subjected to figuration varies greatly; in the *Conditor alme siderum* the melody is taken over literally except at two cadences; in the *Ave maris stella* it is considerably embellished. A number of Dufay's hymn settings obviously enjoyed widespread favor, for they appear in German as well as Italian and French sources; several survive in as many as five MSS and some in still more. In all, settings of twenty-two hymns reach us.[239] They constitute a cycle for the whole year,[240] written for the Papal Choir c. 1430. All but three are retained in Cappella Sistina Cod. 15, which dates from as late as c. 1500, showing that the compositions continued to be used by the Choir (some, to be sure, in "up-to-date" versions) seventy years after they were written. "The spirit wafted to us from these little treasures is that of the Early Renaissance. . . . The master, who was . . . still able to erect the Gothic motet with its powerful sound, created, in these song-like productions that proclaim the Renaissance in music, highly intimate works of art, in which Franco-Burgundian eloquence and Italian feeling for sound achieved marvellous artistic unity."[241]

EXAMPLE 22. Dufay's Christmas Hymn, *Christe Redemptor omnium,
Ex Patre,*[242] with alternative contratenors (after CW XLIX, 5).

---

[239] All but 1, which is undecipherable, are pr. in CW XLIX which, in addition to the authentic hymns, prints, in an appendix, 8 more that have been attributed to Dufay, but without full justification. (Some, for example, borrow Dufay's superius but add two new lower parts.) DTO VII, 159ff, prints 12 of the authentic pieces; the 2 pr. in DTO XXVII[1], 22, 29, are of the type consigned to the appendix of CW XLIX. Isolated hymns are published also in ScherG, 33; BesM, 201; DèzM, 7, 8 (= WolfME, 37); HabD, App. 13.

[240] The nearest earlier approach to this seems to be a set of 10 hymns *a 3* in the Apt MS; 9 have the paraphrased chant in the superius, 1 in the tenor. In each, the same setting serves all odd-numbered stanzas. Cf. GasMA, 56ff, 174.   [241] CW XLIX, 2.

[242] Text not to be confused with the hymn for All Saints' Day, *Christe, Redemptor om-*

Two Dufay settings of the Magnificat—in Tones 6 and 8—survive in a fairly large number of copies.[244] They are *a 3,* but open (as is normal) with the first word in plainsong. Thereafter the writing is polyphonic throughout, thus contrasting with the practice, sometimes followed in the 15th century (cf. p. 91) and normal in the 16th, of alternating plainsong and polyphony. The formulas, used when the Magnificat is rendered in Tones 6 and 8 in plainsong, provide Dufay's superius with its basic melodic material. (In the *Magnificat sexti toni,* the plainsong appears briefly in the tenor also.) However, the composer varies the rather uninteresting formulas with skill and imagination, and, to avoid monotony, gives contrasting treatment to the twelve verses of the text. He does this by dividing the verses into four groups of three; in each group he sets verse 1 in fauxbourdon, verse 2 in free polyphony *a 2* and verse 3 in free polyphony *a 3.* The sections that have similar texture have also similar content (section 1, however, opening with the intonation, corresponds in its polyphonic portion only with the latter part of sections 4, 7, and 10). Since the text is in prose, some adjustments have to be made in the music, upon repetition, to accommodate the varying number of syllables, and these are carried out with much elegance. In the *Magnificat sexti toni* there are three main divisions after verse 1.[245] The music for this verse, which serves as an introduction, is not repeated. The settings for verses 2 to 5, however, constituting division 1, are repeated for verses 6 to 9 (division 2), and the music for verses 2 to 4 returns once more for verse 10 and the *Gloria Patri.* Here again, of course, the repetitions are made with adjustments.

Dufay was the greatest composer of his generation. He wrote in all the

---

um, Conserva, which employs the same melody (now sung to *Jesu, Redemptor omnium;* cf. Liber, 365). Dufay provides music for both texts, setting the melody quite differently each time.

[243] For an Engl. transl., *see* Hymns Ancient and Modern (1909 ed.), 72.

[244] These settings are pr. in DTO VII, 169, 174. The earliest known polyphonic Magnificat was English; cf. p. 772.

[245] For the chant formulas for the Magnificat, *see* Liber 211f. Further about Dufay's Magnificats, *see* DèzB, 300; PirH, 80; BorD, 161ff.

forms and used all the techniques of his day, and examining his works is—notwithstanding their superiority and personal character—tantamount to viewing a cross section of contemporary European production. Only one composer of continental origin could, at the time, seriously rival his supremacy, and that only in the field of the chanson. This composer was Binchois.

Binchois

Gilles de Binche, called Binchois, was the particularly bright and enduring star in the Burgundian constellation. He was born c. 1400 at Mons in Hainaut, the son of Jean de Binche, counsellor to two successive rulers of Hainaut—a man, therefore, of some consequence. Gilles is found at Paris in 1424 in the service of William de la Pole, Earl (later Duke) of Suffolk, husband of Geoffrey Chaucer's granddaughter Alice and himself a musician and poet. A bilingual motet on Binchois's death, by Ockeghem (cf. Chapter 3), offers some further information concerning his youth.

En sa jonesse fut soudart	*In youth he plied the soldier's art,*
De honnorable mondanité,	*Thus worldly paths he nobly trod;*
Puis a esleu la milleur part,	*Later he chose the better part,*
Servant Dieu en humilité.	*In humble manner serving God.*

If the evidence of Dufay's relations with the Burgundian court is meager, we know that Binchois served it for about thirty years, beginning c. 1430. He gradually advanced from fifth to second chaplain and obtained some rich ecclesiastical prebends. It has been claimed,[246] but without documentation, that after completing his service at the Burgundian court he visited the court at Naples. His death took place at Soignies near Mons, in 1460.[247] Tinctoris ranked Binchois with Dufay and Dunstable,[248] and his fame was to last far into the next century. A miniature in one of the MSS of the *Champion des dames* (reproduced as an illustration in this book) represents Dufay and Binchois together,[249] and they undoubtedly knew each other.

While Binchois did not have the versatility of his greater contemporary, he was a chanson composer of the finest quality. Some of his chansons, e.g., the endearing *De plus en plus,*[250] have a dewy freshness that reminds one of the polyphonic *rondeaux, virelais,* and *ballades* of the 13th century and indicates why, in Ockeghem's lament, he is called *"le père de joyeuseté";* others are

---

[246] In MME I, Intro., 16. Ettore Li Gotti, *L'Ars Nova e il Madrigale* (in *Atti della Reale Accademia di Scienze, Lettere, e Arti di Palermo*, Ser. IV, Vol. IV, Part II [1944], 339) mentions an Italian piece (*Deducto se'*) as the work of Binchois, but it is anonymous; *see* BinchC, 5*. (All Binchois chansons for which citations are given in the ensuing pages are pr. BinchC also.)

[247] For further biographical data, *see* ClosB; PirH, 87ff; MarM, xivff; MGG I, 1853ff.

[248] CouS IV, 154.   [249] There is some possibility that a portrait by Jan van Eyck also preserves the likeness of Binchois. *See* PanofE.

[250] Pr. HAM, 74; ScherG, 36; CW XXII, 7; StaD, 80; DisK, 17; OckW I, 78.

tinged by a gentle melancholy that recalls Machaut, but are free of his occasional overripeness. Although written for aristocratic court circles, Binchois's music often has a comfortable, bourgeois character that lends it an agreeable air of informality. In fact, bourgeois influence was penetrating into art generally. The wealthy merchants of Flanders had to be pleased—their features appear with increasing frequency in the works of the painters—and even the art of the court was bound to feel the effect. Flanders was coming markedly to the fore. "Just as once Dijon had eclipsed Paris, so Dijon was now to recede in favour of Bruges, Ghent and Brussels. . . . The Netherlands exercised a wonderful power of attraction over Philip the Good. . . ."[251] The cultural foundation of the music, however, remained quite unshakenly French.

For his texts Binchois drew on the most famous practitioners of the *seconde rhétorique*—i.e., (of poetry)[252]—whose writings were favored at the Burgundian court: Charles d'Orléans, whose *rondeaux* "rank second to nothing of their kind," is the poet of *Mon cuer chante;* the text of *Triste plaisir* is by Alain Chartier, and that of *Dueil angoisseux* by Christine de Pizan.[253] The lyricists of the time (who apparently were often the composers) continued to write about characters in the *Roman de la Rose:* Malebouche is mentioned in Binchois's *Nous vous verens bien;*[254] Dangier and Malebouche in *Quoyque Dangier.*[255] The text of *Rendre me vieng* seems to spell the name "Robin Verel" as an acrostic.[256]

Binchois's chansons achieved wide recognition. Some of them are preserved in many MSS. The stanzas of Jean Molinet's extensive poems *Dialogue du gendarme et de l'amoureux* and *Oraison à la Vierge Marie* have the characteristic of beginning and ending with the incipits of popular chansons, and Binchois's are well represented among them.[257] As already noted (cf. p. 36), *Triste plaisir* was to yield a *basse-danse* melody—as was also *Mon doulx espoir.*[258] The tenor of *Dueil angoisseux* was to become modified into the *cantus firmus* of a Mass preserved at Trent;[259] that of *De plus en plus* was to underlie a Mass by Ockeghem, and that of *Comme femme desconfortée*[260] was to be borrowed by several composers. The *ballade, Je loe amours,*[261] became especially liked in Germany; we shall encounter it again in Chapter 12.

[251] O. Cartellieri, *The Court of Burgundy,* 215. The term "Netherlands," of course, is here used in the broad sense that it had before the separation between Belgium and what is now called the Netherlands. Cf. p. 9.

[252] Prose was the *première rhétorique* in the terminology of 15th-century littérateurs. Cf. BukU, 33f. Modern writers have frequently misinterpreted the two old expressions.

[253] The first pr. in MarM, 65; AmbG II, 565. The second pr. in OH II, 46; DrozP, 29; StaD, 72; CW XXII, 14. The third pr. in DrozP, 25; CW XXII, 8; DTO VII, 242.

[254] Pr. StaD, 67.   [255] Pr. MarM, 73.   [256] *Ibid.,* 74.   [257] *Ibid.,* xv.   [258] *Ibid.,* 66.

[259] Pr. DTO XXXI, 127; discussed in FiF, 56f.

[260] Pr. DrozT, 70 (anon., but ascribed to Binchois in the Mellon Chansonnier).

[261] Pr. MarM, 52.

Technically, most of Binchois's chansons are quite simple. The heights attained in the best give way sometimes to a certain mediocrity in others. The superius of *Adieu, m'amour et ma maistresse*,[262] for example, is a mere perfunctory stringing together of cadence formulas. The music of *Je me recommande humblement*[263] consists of slightly embellished $\frac{6}{3}$ successions. As might be expected, the *rondeau* form is preferred, but there are some fine *ballades*, such as *Adieu, mon amoureuse joye*.[264] Almost all the chansons are *a 3*, but *Files a marier*, with its admonition to young girls, is *a 4*.[265] Ternary rhythm predominates, but binary rhythm appears also, as in *Seule esgarée*.[266] Text usually is limited to the superius, which has the main melody while the other parts act as supports, but *Amoureux suy*[267] is an example with words in two parts, while the May song, *Vostre alée*,[268] has them in three. *Vostre alée* is altogether extraordinary for its time: each of the five phrases begins with imitation in all three parts,[268a] so that the piece is an example of pervading imitation (*Durchimitation,* through-imitation, continuous imitation), a type of writing not to become common until much later (cf. pp. 249f). However, since the piece is a *rondeau,* the form of the composition does not derive from the imitation, as does that of the later works referred to;[268b] rather, the imitation decorates the form (*see also* pp. 105, 123). More typical of Binchois's generation is the *rondeau, Margarite, fleur de valeur,* in which all the voices begin together and imitation is used sparingly (at the opening of section 2).

EXAMPLE 23. *Margarite, fleur de valeur*—Binchois (MS Escorial V.III.24, f.52ᵛ) [268c]

[262] Pr. CW XXII, 5; MarM, 30; ParrishM, 49.　[263] Pr. DTO XI¹, 71.
[264] Pr. DTO VII, 241; CW XXII, 6.
[265] Pr. HAM, 74; MarM, 46. Binchois's piece survives with incomplete text. For an unrelated anon. setting of the complete text, *see* PlamS, 532; cf. *ibid.*, 518f.
[266] Pr. MarM, 77.　[267] Pr. *ibid.*, 33.　[268] Pr. *ibid.*, 81; AmbG II, 563; CW XXII, 15.
[268a] This is a more systematic and thoroughgoing use of the device than any described thus far.
[268b] Or that of some music of the Ciconia period; cf. p. 27.
[268c] The piece is also pr. complete in CW XXII, 9; WolfG III, 91.

Daisy, most prized flow'r of the year,
Thou queen of all the flowers blowing,
May God this day, His gifts bestowing,
Grant every wish thou holdest dear

And from dishonor keep thee clear
And safe when Spite her darts is
   throwing,
Daisy, most prized flow'r . . .

Sad be the heart, the days be drear,
Of any wretch in fervor owing
To sing thy charm serene and glowing,
For of thy praise no praise is peer.

Daisy, most prized flow'r . . .

(Transl. by G.R.)

In *Jamais tant que je vous revoye*,[269] there is an example of the strange practice, followed without consistency by 15th- and early 16th-century musicians,
of inserting a flat before f″ even though the musical context makes it clear
that no lowering is called for. The explanation lies in their concept of *musica
ficta.* The gamut, extending from G to e″ in the form that had become
standardized by the 13th century, embraced no chromatic alterations except
the flat on b and b′. "All tones included in the system had a legitimate place
on the so-called hand of Guido; [270] all other tones were thought of as belonging to *musica ficta.* This means that f″ was one of the tones having no place
on Guido's hand and therefore assigned to *musica ficta.* To illustrate this, a
flat was put before f″, not with the intention of lowering it, but only to indicate that here we had *fa fictum,* a tone by means of which the limits of
legitimate *musica vera* had been transgressed and the land of *musica ficta*
reached." [271]

Binchois and the other Court musicians are at their best in their secular
works, notwithstanding their daily duties as singers at divine service. In fact,
they did not hesitate "to introduce the chansons into the church; a sacred text
was substituted for a frivolous one, and the forbidden work became a *saincte
chansonnette.*" [272] Thus, a *rondeau* by Binchois exists not only with the text
C'est assez [273] but with the text *Virgo rosa venustatis.* There is ample reference to sacred music in the archives, however. Some of this, e.g., Binchois's *Passions en nouvelle maniere,* has been lost. What is left consists mainly of motets, hymns, Magnificats, and Mass sections, often in treble-dominated style.
While Binchois's motets and related works are mostly unpretentious, his
Nove cantum melodie,[274] in two *partes,* is a full-fledged isorhythmic work.
Pars I presents one *talea* three times; *pars II* has two *taleae,* each appearing
three times. The tenor is given once against each threefold presentation of the
taleae; in its second and third appearances, the original time-values are reduced

269 Pr. StaD, 64.   270 Cf. ReMMA, 151.   271 LowS, 254f, q.v. for the evidence.
272 MarM, xvii.   273 Pr. *ibid.,* 40.   274 Pr. *ibid.,* 212.

by a half and a third respectively. This motet (written on the birth, in 1430, of Philip the Good's son, Antoine) is of additional interest because, in its text, Binchois enumerates his colleagues at the Ducal Chapel—among them Fontaine, Ruby, Foliot, Symon le Breton, Nicaise Dupuis, who as a choirboy had been trained by Grenon, and Richard de Bellengues (cf. p. 6), who was to live to the age of ninety.[275] *Domitor Hectoris* [276] is a motet in honor of the Holy Cross and, at the point where the wood of the Cross is apostrophized, Binchois employs *fermata*-marked block-chords. At the beginning of his *Ave Regina coelorum, Mater Regis*,[277] the superius and tenor paraphrase the plainsong of the antiphon (not to be confused with the familiar antiphon, *Ave Regina coelorum*, which continues with *Ave Domina*).[278] Chant melodies according to the Sarum use underlie Binchois's *Gloria, laus, et honor* [278a] and one of his two settings of *Inter natos mulierum*.[278b] In treating the hymn *A solis ortus cardine*, Binchois places the plainsong [279] in the tenor and adds two voices that help to produce fauxbourdon-like cadences at three points. The setting of the hymn *Ut queant laxis* [280]—drawing not on the melody used by Guido d'Arezzo, but on one employed also by Dufay (cf. fn. 238)—provides only two voices and calls for the addition of another in fauxbourdon; the given voices, however, are close together (often in thirds) so that the third voice must evidently be added, abnormally, a fourth *above* the higher notated part.[281] The *Da pacem* and *Te Deum* settings [282] are likewise given only two written voices, with the indication that a third is to join them in fauxbourdon; but here adequate space is allowed between the voices for the insertion of the added part a fourth below the higher given one, in the usual way. Of great significance historically, if not for its strictly musical value, is Binchois's *In exitu Israel*. This is a highly fauxbourdon-like setting of Psalm CXIII (114) [282a] with the *Tonus peregrinus* [283] in the superius (free writing appearing only at the end). The noteworthy point is that here we have a psalm setting that is at the same time fauxbourdon-like and in chordal recitative, mostly with one chord to a syllable (mild floridity being present only at cadence

---

[275] A chanson of his, pr. StaD, 85.   [276] Pr. VanAM, 66.   [277] Pr. MarM, 189.
[278] Cf. Liber, 1864.   [278a] Pr. MarM, 194; plainsong in FrereG, 83.
[278b] Pr. MarM, 209; plainsong in FrereA, 573.
[279] Liber, 400; for Binchois's piece, *see* MarM, 188.   [280] Pr. WolfME, 38; MarM, 226.
[281] Cf. BukE, 73.   [282] Pr. MarM, 192, 219 (cf. Liber 1867, 1834), respectively.
[282a] References to Catholic psalm settings will give the Catholic number first in Roman figures and then the Protestant number, if different, in parenthesis in Arabic figures. (*See also* Chap. 7, fn. 102a *infra*.) The Protestant numbering is the same as the Hebrew. The Catholic numbering differs as follows: IX = 9 and 10 combined; X–CXII = 11–113; CXIII = 114 and 115 combined; CXIV and CXV jointly = 116; CXVI–CXLV = 117–146; CXLVI and CXLVII jointly = 147. Psalms I–VIII and CXLVIII–CL are the same in both systems. It will be noted that, where there is a difference, the number in the Catholic system is the lower one. The verse numbers also differ occasionally.
[283] In the form in which it is applied to the same psalm in Liber, 1885; for Binchois's piece, *see* MarM, 196. The plainsong intonation is wrongly based on Tone I rather than on part 1 of the *Tonus peregrinus;* the error, however, is present in the source—a point kindly verified for me at Modena by Dr. Dragan Plamenac.

points) and with much immediate repetition (this being brought about by the presence of the psalm-tone). Thus the piece represents a transitional stage between early fauxbourdon, using mainly $\frac{6}{3}$ chords, and Italian *falsobordone,* which, commonly applied in 16th-century psalmody—though first appearing earlier—, employed mainly chords in root position but was similarly chordal (with florid cadences), recitative-like, and given to repetition.[284] (Cf. pp. 166, 491f.)

Binchois's Magnificats on the first four Tones [285] make much use of fauxbourdon-like writing, each harmonizing its respective Tone without much elaboration. All the Magnificats except the one in Tone 3 set the complete text; this work omits the odd-numbered verses (except the first), which are therefore intended to be performed in plainsong. The Magnificat in Tone 2 sets the verses alternately *a 2* and *a 3.*

Binchois appears not to have employed the *cantus-firmus* Mass technique. His Mass sections either paraphrase Gregorian melodies or reveal treble-dominated style without traceable borrowings from plainsong.[286] Even where the sections borrow from the Chant, the result recalls that Binchois's real domain is the chanson. The absence of the deep earnestness that marks Dufay's sacred music, however, does not prevent Binchois's Mass sections from often having a considerable charm of their own. In no instance do the sources show that any of these compositions are to be combined to form a complete Ordinary. A certain Kyrie, Gloria, and Credo, however, are rather clearly indicated as belonging together.[287] The middle voice of the Kyrie,[288] entirely *a 3,* paraphrases the Kyrie [289] of Mass VIII (the *Missa de Angelis*). The Gloria and Credo (which incorporate no Gregorian melodies) specify in Bologna, Lic. mus. Q 15, that the passages *a 2* are for soloists and those *a 3* for chorus.[290] A Gloria and Credo at Trent are tied together by technical characteristics.[291] The superius of a Sanctus and Agnus,[292] also at Trent, draws on plainsong Mass XV; the superius of another such pair [293] paraphrases the chant of Mass XVII. The latter Agnus is remarkable for its time in being written for three low voices, the lowest descending to E. It is in setting the shorter Mass sections —the Kyrie, Sanctus, and Agnus—that Binchois is most successful; to this

[284] Further about the early stages of *falsobordone, see* BukMR, 185; FerandM, 180f.
[285] All pr. in MarM; 1 also in ScherG, 37.
[286] For some of the former type, *see* the Kyrie in MarM, 154 (in which the superius paraphrases the Kyrie of Gregorian Mass IV), the Kyrie in DTO XXXI, 49 (in which the tenor paraphrases the Kyrie of Mass IX), or the Agnus in EinSH, 271; DTO XXXI, 50 (in which the superius paraphrases the Agnus of Mass XVIII); for some illustrations of the latter type, *see* the Glorias in DTO XXXI, 42, 46.
[287] Pr. *ibid.,* 48; BorP, 53, 63; also in DPLSER, *Ser. I,* No. 5, 1–21. The indications are described *ibid.,* preface.
[288] Pr. on top in DPLSER.
[289] Traceable to the 14th century; cf. BesM, 173. Pr. Liber, 37.
[290] Cf. BorP, xiii, xvi; also BukMR, 180.
[291] Pr. DTO XXXI, 55, 58; about the technical characteristics, *see* FiF, 26.
[292] Pr. DTO XXXI, 53, 55. [293] Pr. DTO XXXI, 51, 53; DPLSER, *Ser. I,* No. 5, 22, 25.

composer of graceful chansons they give greater opportunity to speak the musical language that rises most readily to his lips.[294]

Rouge; Frye

The Ruby named in Binchois's *Nove cantum melodie*, undoubtedly identical with the Guillaume Ruby mentioned in the Rouen archives (cf. p. 43), may be the G. le Rouge whose *bergerette, Se je fays dueil,* is preserved in the Mellon Chansonnier. "Ruby" would be explainable as derived from the Latin form of "Rouge".[295] He could very well also be the W. de Rouge represented in Trent MS 90 by a *Missa Soyez aprantiz*.[296] The Germanic source of the MS may account for the initial, the W standing for "Wilhelm" (Guillaume); but W could equally well stand for "Willelmus," a name we have found applied to Dufay without reference to the German language (cf. p. 48). The Mass is *a 3* and has its *cantus-firmus*-bearing tenor as the lowest voice. To that extent, therefore, the work is in early style (which would support the theory that Ruby and Rouge are one). In the Kyrie, the *cantus firmus* is the original form of the tenor of *Soyez aprantiz,* a *ballade* by Walter Frye. In the succeeding movements, the intervallic relationships of this tenor are kept practically unaltered, but the rhythmic configuration [296a] is changed for each presentation. The isorhythmic technique is here provided with a counterpart; whereas in the former the rhythmic pattern remains the same but the melodic content may vary, in the latter the melodic material remains the same but the rhythmic pattern varies. This technique has been called isomelic.[297] It was perhaps suggested by the kind of application of the isorhythmic technique in which *taleae* and *colores* do not coincide, so that a tenor, upon repetition, has a new rhythmic shape.[298] The isomelic technique continued to be used for many years. Other examples from the period under discussion are

---

[294] Besides the pieces seeming definitely to be by Binchois, thus far cited in complete transcriptions into modern notation, further works of his appear in such notation in MarM (41 items, of which 2 are also in CW XXII and 1 in BesM, 196; the additional motet which MarM, 227, credits to Binchois, on the authority of Trent MS 92, is attributed to the Englishman Sandley in the more trustworthy MS, Modena *a.* X. I, 11); CW XXII, 4 (= StaD, 74; DisK, 18), 9 (= DTO VII, 255, where it is indicated as possibly by Grossin on the authority of Trent MS 87; but the piece is attributed to Binchois in the Oxford MS; the indication in DTO VII, 35, No. 152, that this chanson is given to Grossin also in Bol., Bibl. Univ. 2216, is not borne out by BesBU, 59; WolfG I, 201, or MarH, 228), 11 (= StaD, 77; DisK, 20), 12 (= DTO VII, 245), 13 (= DTO VII, 246), 13 (a second piece), 16; DTO VII, 91, 244; XXVII¹, 89; XXXI, 44, 50 (first piece); StaD, 69. The chansons in Hugo Riemann, *Sechs bisher nicht gedruckte dreistimmige Chansons . . . von Gilles Binchois . . .* 1892 (7 in number, despite the title) are all available in better editions elsewhere. The motets pr. in DTO VII, 94; XL, 51, 61, assigned to Binchois in certain sources, are all more probably by Dunstable (cf. MarH, 233).

[295] Cf. BukU, 27. In view of the initial, however, Ruby is presumably not the "P. Rubeus" to whom 2 pieces are ascribed in Bol., Lic. mus. Q 15. (*See also* fn. 80.)

[296] The Mass appears without title in this MS; the title is given (garbled and in the Gloria only) in San Pietro B 80, but there the composer is unnamed.

[296a] I.e., not just the rhythmic proportions. See the tenor incipits in DTO VII, 63, Nos. 1031–35.

[297] Cf. fn. 221.   [298] Cf. ReMMA, 339.

two anonymous Masses based on the *O rosa bella* that is attributable to Dunstable.[299] Rouge shows a liking for upper-voice duos at the beginnings of sections and subsections. When, in the Gloria and Credo, there is anticipatory imitation of the *cantus firmus* by the superius, that voice presents the melody in rhythmic configurations still different from the various ones applied to it by the tenor.[300]

Nothing definite is known about the life of the composer of *Soyez aprantiz* —at least not under the name of Walter Frye. If Rouge and Ruby are one, his being traceable up to 1451 and his having written a Mass on this chanson jointly furnish some clue regarding the period of Frye and show that it may be wrong to consider him (as have certain historians) a member of the Busnois–Ockeghem generation; in fact, he may well have been one of Dufay's older contemporaries. In view of the provenance of the MSS in which he is principally represented, he very likely spent a part of his career at the Burgundian court. *Soyez aprantiz* is anonymous in two sources,[301] but its music appears in the Mellon Chansonnier with an ascription to "Walterus Fry" and with an English text (*So ys emprentid in my remembrance*).[302] The presence of such a text indicates that the composer was very likely an Englishman, as does the inclusion of Frye's motet *Sospitati dedit* in a MS "of English origin that contains an exclusively English repertory." [303] The English word "free" has included "fry" and "frye" [304] among its different spellings, and the name "Fry" (variously spelled) is commonly accepted by genealogists as meaning "free" and as referring to the original bearers' having been bondsmen and having been released—that is, to their being *liberti* (the Latin term was used in legal writings[305]). These facts suggest that Walter Frye may have been the Gualterus Liberti who was in the Papal Choir in 1428 (cf. p. 38). The *rondeau, Tout a par moy,*[306] was to serve as the basis of works by Tinctoris, Agricola, and Josquin. *Ave Regina . . . Mater Regis* was a great favorite. Its superius and tenor appear bodily in a Flemish painting of the Madonna

299 They are pr. DTO XI¹, 1, 28 (in 2 versions). Another anon. *Missa O rosa bella* appears *ibid.*, 13. For analyses, *see* LedH, 239ff.

300 For a fuller description of Rouge's Mass, *see* ReeI. Another Mass by "Lerouge" is mentioned by Tinctoris; cf. CouS IV, 171. (But Tinctoris seems not to refer, as has been claimed, to a "de Rubeis," allegedly identical with Ruby.)

301 The Laborde Chansonnier and Montecassino MS 871N. Concerning an attribution to "Bellingan" (= Bedingham) in another MS, *see* BukU, 25.

302 A *Sois emprantis* is referred to by Ramos de Pareja (cf. pp. 586f) in his *Musica practica* (RamosM, 65). He says that Tristano da Silva (a Spanish musician; cf. RamosM, 14; MME I, 39, 41f) permits consecutive fifths if one of them is diminished and one perfect, and he states that such a progression occurs in the chanson. The observation recurs in Pietro Aron's *Lucidario*, Lib. II, fol. 7ᵛ, where a work by Verdelot is also cited. Aron gives an example, which is not from Frye's composition; that piece, however, does contain two passages (meas. 3, 6) that illustrate the point if one applies *musica ficta*.

303 BukU, 25. (The MS is Pepys 1236; cf. p. 773 *infra*.) About the possibility that 2 anon. *ballades*, with English texts, in the Mellon MS, are by Frye, *see ibid.*, 24f.

304 Both pronounced frē (not frī) in Middle English.

305 *See*, e.g., Du Cange, *Glossarium mediae et infimae latinitatis*, IV, 99.

306 Pr. PlamS, 530. (Ascribed to Binchois in 1 source, but to Frye in 2.)

and Child, in which they are painted into a MS held by a singing angel.[307] The many MSS that preserve it include several predominantly secular collections. This helps to make it an ideal example of what modern musicology terms a "song-motet"—i.e., a relatively small motet *a 3*, distinguished by simplicity and an intimate, songlike character, and often appearing in mainly secular sources. The term is based on criteria of scope and function rather than upon stylistic traits; it provides a classification different from the one designated by the style-defining expression "motet in treble-dominated style," so that a work may well fit into both categories. Song-motets might be used in private chapels or for devotional services at home. The text of the *Ave Regina* is not that of the familiar antiphon, nor quite that of the one set by Binchois, but of a responsory formerly sung at Compline from Candlemas to Maundy Thursday.[308] No identified chant is incorporated. The liturgical function of the text affects the form of the music. While the original basic form of the plainsong responsory of the Office had been *AbA* (but with various repetitions), later on only the final portion of *A* was generally repeated, so that the basic form became modified into *aBcB* (*aB* = old *A;* *c* = old *b;* *B* = last part of old *A*).[308a] Frye's piece has this structure, which appeared rarely in polyphonic music before c. 1520, but was to become common thereafter.

EXAMPLE 24. *Ave Regina*—Walter Frye (after Florence, Riccardiana, MS 2794, the Laborde MS, and the *Buxheimer Orgelbuch*).[309]

[307] For a list of MS sources, *see* PlamS, 102f, 245f. One of the sources, the *Schedelsches Liederbuch* (described in MaiM, 125ff; *see also*, p. 634 *infra*), contains 3 additional motets ascribed to Frye and, since it is of German provenance, has been the apparent basis for a claim that he was a German (OrM, 304; MosG I, 336); however, the evidence as to his English origin, given above (after BukU), is of greater weight. The painting showing the *Ave regina* is reproduced in PirH, opp. p. 80; BesM, opp. p. 200.

[308] *See* Franz J. Mone, *Lateinische Hymnen des Mittelalters*, II, 202. The text differs from that of the less familiar antiphon simply by repeating lines 3 and 4 at the end.

[308a] For the details, see WagE I, Chap. VIII; *see also* p. 491 *infra*.

[309] Vincent, in making the transcription of the piece pr. in VincM, 679, based on the Laborde MS, in which the superius of *pars I* is missing, "restored" the latter portion of the missing voice on the basis of the *aBcB* form. In the application of accidentals in Ex. 24, the 3 intabulations in the *Buxheimer Orgelbuch* have been taken into account (except at the beginning of meas. 1), but these 3 are themselves not in complete agreement.

"Hail, Queen of the Heavens, Mother of the King of the Angels: O Mary, flower of virgins, like the rose or the lily: utter prayers to the Lord for the salvation of the faithful. O Mary, etc."

Since Frye is generously represented in MSS of Burgundian origin, he may well have been active at the Burgundian court. One of these MSS, Brussels 5557, contains, in the section that seems to be the "original nucleus" of the MS,[309a] his Masses *Flos regalis* (*a 4*), *Summe Trinitati* (*a 3*), and *Nobilis et pulcra* (*a 3*). The first two lack the Kyrie, a fact providing an additional indication that the composer was English (cf. p. 765), and in all three the Credo is truncated, a feature common in English Masses, though not peculiar to them. The trope, *Deus creator,* is inserted in the Kyrie of the *Missa Nobilis et pulcra.* Frye uses the *cantus-firmus* technique,[310] and in the first two Masses the *cantus-firmus*-bearing part differs from its equivalents in Power's *Missa super Alma* and in Rouge's Mass and resembles those in the Dufay *cantus-firmus* Masses (cf. p. 67) by being the next-to-the-bottom voice. (In the other Mass, the two lower voices cross frequently.) The rhythmical character of Frye's tenors at times approximates that of the other voices. This happens less typically in the Dufay generation than in that of Ockeghem. However, examination of the works shows that in certain other respects they are in a style characteristic of the older group.[311]

[309a] Cf. KennO, 89.

[310] For the originals of the *cantus firmi* (from the Sarum chant repertory) of the *Missa Summe Trinitati* and *Missa Nobilis, see* FrereA, 572, and Pl. X of the last fascicle.

[311] For example, the frequent use of the kind of octave-leap cadence illustrated in Ex. 5, a

We opened this book by saying that any line drawn between the music of the Middle Ages and that of the Renaissance must be arbitrary. It is clear that Dufay and his contemporaries still used medieval forms—even though the spirit of the Renaissance had, in the eyes of some modern scholars, already made itself felt in the music of 14th-century Italy.[312] The great innovation of the time, the *cantus-firmus* Mass, was itself, from the technical standpoint, only a vastly extended application—first, it would seem, by Englishmen, then by such an essentially French genius as Dufay—of the principle of the 13th-century motet-tenor. But this Gothic device, of French invention, was shifted from the motet to the Mass for a new purpose: to give rise to the first highly organized cyclic form, a form in which the device reached its apogee and last significant use. The fauxbourdon technique, making use of chordal formations already typical of English discant, was also only partly new; more important than any element of novelty, however, was its influence in developing a taste for smoother harmony, according to what we may today call premodern standards. Canon had already been favored in *trecento* Italy. Roughly, we may say that in the early 15th century the special accomplishment of northern French polyphony was not so much to introduce novel elements as it was to bring about a fusion of Italian canon, English sonority, and French form.

cadence employed sparingly in the Ockeghem period. For fuller (but slightly inaccurate) data about these Masses, *see* BorQS, 210ff.—Since this book was first printed, Hugh Baillie has found that Walter Frye joined a London guild of musicians in 1456 (see PRMA LXXXIII [1956], 20), thus providing strong evidence that Frye was indeed English. Another recent contribution on Frye is an article by Sylvia Kenney in JAMS VIII (1955), 182.

[312] Cf. ReMMA, 360.

Chapter 3: MUSIC OF FRANCE AND THE LOW COUNTRIES IN THE PERIOD OF BUSNOIS AND OCKEGHEM; AN OUTPOST AT NAPLES

IF, IN the main, Dufay and some of his contemporaries were more strikingly modern in sacred than in secular music, the composers of the next generation, with the notable exception of Ockeghem, were the reverse. Thanks to the later master, the Mass continued to flourish, but the motet, though represented by some fine examples, assumed a subordinate position. Most of the composers in question are found at their best and most prolific in their chansons, preserved in large numbers in the *chansonniers* of the period.

The Chansonniers; Hayne van Ghizeghem and His Lesser Contemporaries at the Burgundian Court

Often richly illuminated with decorative initials, borders, and miniatures, the *chansonniers* are beautiful visually as well as important musically. Among those that preserve French secular poems of the time, a large proportion (some of which we have already encountered) present the verse in musical setting.[1] More noteworthy collections, dating from c. 1470 to c. 1500, include the following (listed by size; Nos. 2 and 11 are the earliest, No. 1 the latest): (1) the Pixérécourt MS (Paris, Bibl. nat. fonds fr. 15123) now containing 169 pieces; (2) the Dijon Chansonnier, with 161; (3) the one at the Colombina Library, Seville, with 123, to which should be added 38 pieces formerly part of the MS, but now included in Paris, Bibl. nat., nouv. acq. fr. 4379, and 6 pieces split between the two MSS; (4) MS IV. a. 24 at the Escorial, with 118; (5) the Laborde Chansonnier at the Library of Congress, Washington, with 106; (6) the Nivelle de la Chaussée MS, with 64; (7) MS 287 extrav. at Wolfenbüttel, with 57; (8) the Mellon Chansonnier, with 57; (9) the Chansonnier Cordiforme with 43; (10) MS 362 in the University Library at Pavia, with 43; (11) the Copenhagen Chansonnier, with 33 compositions.[2] Our refer-

[1] Thus, of the 90 *chansonniers* listed in JP II, 105ff, 66 contain music; and the list neither is nor claims to be complete.

[2] Complete reproductions of Nos. 5 and 8 are available in microfilm in O. Albrecht's *Music Microfilm Archive*, Reel 4. Transcriptions of 50 compositions from No. 2 are printed in DrozT and of 6 more items in MoD; for a special study of the MS, *see* MoD (which has a more complete index of the contents than appears in DrozT [the latter omits Nos. 4, 78, 123, and 158 of the MoD list and changes the text-incipit of No. 149], but omits 1 item given there: *Prenez . . . ,*

ences to the earlier MS Canonici misc. 213 and to the Trent Codices have shown that MSS with a miscellaneous repertory often yield many polyphonic chansons also. Some chansons were so popular that they appear in many different sources. Thus *De tous biens plaine* by Hayne van Ghizeghem, is found in twenty MSS (including 8 of the 11 listed above) and in two early prints.

The writing in the *chansonniers* is mainly *a 3;* settings *a 4* increase in the later sources. Text may occur in one or more voices, or only incipits or titles may be given. The preferred language is, of course, French, but there are also some secular examples in Italian, Spanish, English, and Flemish. Though the contents are mainly secular, a few sacred pieces with Latin text are included, because of their small dimensions and because they were intended for use in private chapels rather than in church performances; that is, they are song-motets (cf. p. 94). A celebrated example, the *Ave Regina* of Frye, has been mentioned a few pages back. Another popular song-motet was the *O gloriosa Regina* [2a] by Johannes Touront.

If the new *chansonniers* continued to include works by Dufay and Binchois, this was due more to the lasting esteem in which these masters were held than to any lack of contemporary composers. The younger musicians included a group, with Busnois at its head, that held forth at the Burgundian court and further added to its glory.

When Philip the Good died in 1467, the musicians in his employ [3] included Constans de Languebroek, Gilles Joye, and Robert Morton. Constans, who had served since 1442 and was highly reputed, became the teacher of Hayne van Ghizeghem; he died in 1481.[4] Joye, who entered the chapel in 1462 and died in 1484, was a theologian and poet as well as a musician.[5] Morton, an Englishman, became a singer in the chapel in 1457; in 1465 Philip granted him a short leave-of-absence to serve the future Charles the Bold, then still Count of Charolais. In 1470, i.e., not until after the accession of Charles,[6] of whom

---

since it is no longer in the MS, though listed in its table of contents). Transcriptions of all pieces in No. 11 are pr. with commentary in JepK. For data on Nos. 1 and 3–10, *see,* respectively, WolfH I, 458 (also JepK, lxxi); PlamS (also AngCF); AuI, 528ff; BushL (also VincR); the Catalogue of Sotheby & Co. for March, 1939; DrozT, viii, xiiiff (also JepK, xxivff; the total given on p. xxx is correct; the table in DrozT is defective); BukU (also the *Yale University Library Gazette*, XV [1940], 24ff); PicotC IV, 314ff (also PorchC); and MarchiP, 202ff (slightly defective; *see also* JepK, xxixf). About related MSS, *see* esp. JepK, lxxiff. The dating of No. 4, given in AuI, 517, is incorrect; cf. JepK, lxxiii. The AuI, 517, dating for Escorial V. III, 24, is likewise wrong; cf. p. 35 *supra* and esp. BesS I, 241f (which provides other corrections also). A complete ed. of No. 9 (also called the Jean de Montchenu Chansonnier), by G. Thibault, is announced for early publication.

[2a] Preserved in 10 sources; cf. PlamS, 258f, No. 106. Pr. DTO VII, 219; BesC, 7; VincM, 675. Another piece by Touront, pr. DTO VII, 217. Further on him, *see* esp. SteB, 52ff, 106, 110ff, 115.

[3] See list in DoorM, 23; MarH, 260.

[4] For fuller data, *see* MarH, 199ff; for music, MarM, 90, 92.

[5] For fuller data, *see* MarH, 213; for some music, MarM, 87, 89; PlamS, 541; another chanson may be seen in Music Microfilm Archive, Vol. 1 (cf. fn. 2), as No. 23 in the Mellon MS and as No. 46 in Laborde.

[6] Cf. MarH, 210.

Morton was evidently a favorite, he was raised to the status of a chaplain. He died in 1475. Morton's chanson, *L'Homme armé,*[7] is much like the anonymous setting *a 3* in the Mellon MS (cf. p. 73), except that it adds a bass, which causes some V-I cadences to appear where there were fauxbourdon-like cadences in the earlier version.[8] His *rondeaux, N'aray-je jamais mieulx* and *Le souvenir de vous*[9] were much admired, as their survival in many sources shows. A piece *a 3* that reaches us textless in Perugia, Bibl. com., MS 431 (G 20), is found as a Spanish *villancico* in the *Cancionero de Palacio* (cf. pp. 576, 582ff).[9a] A motet of his, also textless in the Perugia source, recurs, adapted to a German text, in a German MS of the 1460's (cf. p. 634).[10] This *"chappellain anglois"* was evidently one of the better composers at the Burgundian court in his day.

The charming text of an anonymous *rondeau* in the Dijon MS, *La plus grant chiere,*[11] describes the welcome accorded to Morton and Hayne van Ghizeghem during a visit they paid to Cambrai. The people honored them by observing the old custom of offering the *mais,* i.e., by planting leafy branches in front of their dwelling. The poet reports that, at the planting, both musicians sang and performed on *"bas instrumens."*

Hayne's name first occurs in the archives of 1457, when Constans was repaid for undertaking the charge of *"un jeusne filz appelé Hayne van Ghizeghem."*[12] In 1467 he was a singer and *valet de chambre* to Philip the Good, and, upon the duke's death that year, remained in the employ of Charles the Bold. The next year he entered Charles' military service, which may explain his small output—all secular—and his brief career; he last appears at the siege of Beauvais (1472), disastrous to the Burgundians. Guillaume Crétin, in his *Déploration*[13] written after Ockeghem's death c. 1495, lists Hayne among composers no longer living and calls upon him to play on his lute, in the afterworld, the master's motet, *Ut heremita solus.*[14]

Hayne's chansons form a small corpus uneven in quality but unified in style —all in binary rhythm, in *rondeau* form,[14a] and originally *a 3*. Of those unclouded by conflicting ascriptions, six are *rondeaux quatrains;* six, *rondeaux cinquains;* and one—*La regretée*[15]—a *rondeau septain* (three other pieces are textless). Hayne may have been the poet of most of his chansons, but the

---

[7] Pr. MarM, 96; LedH, 425 (the comments about this piece in LedH, 233ff are not trustworthy).

[8] Cf. BukU, 19.

[9] Pr. JepK, 4 (= JosqMS III, 124), 37, respectively.

[9a] Pr. MarM, 93; MME V, 34; cf. MME X, 23f (text).

[10] For the motet, *see* MarM, 240; cf. BukU, 26. MarM contains 4 Morton works not yet cited. *See* further, PirH, 115f, 118.

[11] Pr. MarM, 86.

[12] MarG, 277f. The name exists in several forms. Gijseghem is a village in Flanders. Several scholars have confused the composer with an older homonym (his father?); cf. MarG, 277.

[13] Pr. in *Oeuvres poétiques de Guillaume Crétin,* ed. by Kathleen Chesney (1933), 60ff.

[14] Further biographical data in MarG; MarH, 205ff.

[14a] Except for 1 *bergerette;* cf. p. 275, fn. 508.   [15] Pr. MarM, 115.

text of one—*Allez regretz* [16]—is by Duke Jean II de Bourbon, cousin and brother-in-law of Charles the Bold and patron of Villon. This chanson enjoyed considerable fame, and in the late 15th century Nicole de la Chesnaye had the characters in his *La Condamnation des banquets* dance to it; similarly, a few decades later, Rabelais had minstrels play Hayne's *Les grans regretz* [17] for dancing.[18] Many of Hayne's chansons—e.g., *Plus n'en aray* and *Pour ce que j'ay jouy* [19]—begin with imitation *a 3*, but no piece consists entirely of points of imitation, like Binchois's *Vostre alée*, nor is any in canon throughout. *La regretée* starts with imitation *a 2*, the lowest part being free. But the older type of opening, with all parts entering at once, is present in Hayne also. Every part, whether with or without text, tends to have long, supple, rounded curves and is singable even though instruments must have often engaged in performing these pieces. Although the bass of the lovely *A la audienche* [20] touches D, Hayne does not explore the lower range. Chains of parallel thirds, etc., occur, but are not overworked. The gentle *De tous biens plaine*, by all odds his most popular chanson, is probably an early composition [21] and—like *Amours, amours*,[22] and *A la audienche* [23]—was later "modernized" by the addition of a *si placet* (i.e., an optional) [24] part. The tenor of this chanson (*see* Ex. 35) became a favorite *cantus firmus*, being used in motet, Mass, and additional chanson compositions by Busnois, Compère, Agricola, Obrecht, Josquin, and others.[25]

In periods when pre-existent music was frequently drawn upon as a basis for new compositions, any piece often singled out in this way might help to shape the character of a musical culture. Thus, the 13th century had produced a whole body of compositions based on the *In seculum* tenor. It was not until the late 15th century that secular polyphony began to make comparably wide use of pre-existent melodies, and then it favored not only *De tous biens plaine*, but also a singularly attractive anonymous *rondeau*, *J'ay pris amours a ma devise*, that survives in the Dijon MS and seven other sources.[26] The same superius and tenor appear in the Laborde MS and in Paris, Bibl. nat. nouv.

[16] Pr. HewO, 341; DrozP, 49; GomO, Suppl., 3; MaldP XIII, 34 (with substitute text and wrong attribution to Compère); VillaT, App. I, 2 (facsimile after Turin MS qm III, 59, on p. 1).

[17] Pr. MarM, 118; HewO, 370; MaldP XI, 46 (with substitute text and attribution, after 1 source, to Agricola; however, the piece is ascribed to Hayne in 3 sources; it is anon. in 6 others).

[18] Cf. MarG, 281; *Oeuvres de Rabelais* (Burgaud des Marets and Rathery eds.), II, 464f. Rabelais includes the composition in a large list of pieces popular in his time. Concerning Rabelais and the chanson generally, *see* CarpenR.

[19] Pr. MarM, 124, 125, respectively.

[20] *Ibid.*, 100; HewO, 411.   [21] Cf. MarG, 285, fn. 24.

[22] Pr. EDMR IV, 55; DTO VII, 257; HewO, 237; the latter 2 with *si placet* part.

[23] Cf. HewO, 411, fn. 4.

[24] For *De tous biens*, see DrozT, 20; MoD, App., No. 5; AmbG, II, 576; JepK, 7; HewO, 263; GomO, Supp. 24; SmijO, 144; the last 3 with *si placet* part.

[25] All Hayne's known chansons but 1 are pr. in MarM and HewO jointly; duplications, not yet cited, in AmbG V, 14 (with attribution to Ockeghem after 1 source; 2 give the piece to Hayne; in 3 it is anon.); GomO, Supp., 5; EDMR IV, 57. (About *Suis venu*, in MarM, 129, cf. fn. 59 *infra*. *J'ay bien choisi*, ascribed to Hayne, *ibid.*, 111, is given to Busnois in the Pixérécourt MS). *See also* GomC. A complete edition of Hayne, by Otto Gombosi, is in preparation.

[26] Cf. HewO, 139f; pr. DrozT, 3; ObrWW, 94.

acq. fr. 4379; but there is a new contratenor, lying above the tenor,[27] rather than below it as did the contratenor in the evidently earlier Dijon version. In Trent MS 1947–4, still another contratenor—quite florid and probably instrumental—is substituted.[28] An unknown wag's travesty of the chanson, *J'ay pris ung poul* [= *pou*] [28a] *en ma chemise,* in Florence, Bibl. naz. cent., Magl. XIX, 176, has a superius based on, but not identical with, the old one. The many reworkings were to include an anonymous piece *a 4,*[29] combining— with two new parts—the superius of *J'ay pris amours* and the tenor of *De tous biens plaine.* Other compositions that the period liked to use as raw material will be mentioned from time to time; the prototypes preferred by the 16th century were to be, in a large degree, different, a fact that contributed toward making the musical culture of that century distinctive. But the *L'Homme armé* melody was to prove irrepressible.

Busnois

This melody and the tenor of *J'ay pris amours* are among the *cantus prius facti* reworked by Antoine de Busnes, called Busnois.[29a] When Charles the Bold succeeded his father, he already had Busnois in his employ. Molinet paid tribute to the composer by means of a poem in which the only rhyme syllables were *bus* and *nois;* Busnois, himself a poet as well as a musician, addressed a poem in *rondeau* form to Molinet.[30] Tinctoris dedicated his *Liber de natura et proprietate tonorum* to Ockeghem and Busnois jointly, and elsewhere singled out these *"moderni"*, with Regis and Caron, as "among all those whom I have heard, foremost in composition." [31] Priest as well as court musician, Busnois held several church posts, being at the time of his death, in 1492, *rector cantoriae* of St. Sauveur at Bruges.[32]

Busnois set some of his own verse to music. He preferred, in the texts he wrote or chose, love themes of the more melancholy kind. His loved one was Jacqueline d'Hacqueville, whose name he incorporated, with varying spellings, into some of his own texts. The incipit of *Ja que lui ne s'i attende* [33] gives her first name; that of *Ha que ville et abhominable,*[34] her last. Her whole

---

[27] This version pr. DTO XIV¹, 185; ObrWW, 92.
[28] This version pr. DiseJ, 20; *see* comments *ibid.,* 19ff.
[28a] Bowdlerized into *"plus"* in the Pixérécourt MS.
[29] Pr. HewO, 230.
[29a] The setting of *De tous biens plaine* pr. under his name in KiesT, App., 58, is anon. in the source—the collection, *Canti C,* printed by Petrucci, in which the piece is No. 85—and is probably ascribed to him in KiesT because No. 81 is credited to Busnois in *Canti C* and Nos. 82–84 bear no attributions; evidently the last musician named was regarded in KiesT as the composer of all subsequent works up to the next piece provided with an ascription.
[30] For the 2 poems, as well as Molinet's answer to the second, *see Les Faictz et Dictz de Jean Molinet* (Noël Dupire, ed.) II (1937), 795ff.
[31] CouS IV, 16, 154.
[32] For further biographical data, *see* esp. DoorM, 30; PirH, 114ff; MGG II, 515ff.
[33] Pr. JepK, 60.
[34] Pr. as anon in DrozT, 28, but ascribed to Busnois in 2 MSS. *See also* p. 106 *infra.*

name appears as an acrostic in *Je ne puis vivre ainsi*,[35] as do the words "*A Jacqueline*" in *A vous sans autre*.[36]

Busnois's mastery of small form and his refined treatment of detail appear to advantage in his secular music. His name appears on seventy-one chansons, of which eight are found with conflicting ascriptions. The remainder include thirty-four *rondeaux,* thirteen *virelais* (of the one-stanza *bergerette* type, whose invention was wrongly attributed to him; cf. p. 15, including fn. 69), one *ballade,* six pieces in free form, and nine whose form cannot be determined because complete text is lacking.[36a] All of the texts are in French, except for two in Italian and one in Flemish (the *ballade*).[36b] One of the Italian songs is the famous *Fortuna desperata,* on which Josquin and Obrecht were to base Masses.[36c]

Busnois wrote *rondeaux* besides those of the *quatrain* and *cinquain* types. *Ha que ville* is a three-line *rondeau* in the Dijon MS,[37] while *C'est bien maleur*[38] and *Quant ce vendra*[39] are *rondeaux sixains*. The scheme of the former is *ABCDEFabcABCabcdefABCDEF* (as in Binchois's *Comme femme,* cf. p. 87), whereas that of the latter is *ABCDEFabcdABCDabcdef-ABCDEF*—that is, in the former, groups 2 and 3 consist of three members, but in the latter they consist of four; the form of the *rondeau sixain* was not entirely standardized.

In some *bergerettes,* e.g., Example 25,[40] the refrain is in triple, section 2 in duple, rhythm. (It is worth noting that Busnois's avoidance of compound rhythm—*tempus imperfectum, prolatio major* [$= \frac{6}{8}$]—coincides with Dufay's reduction of its use in his later period in favor of *tempus perfectum, prolatio minor* [$= \frac{3}{4}$].) This contrast, though not always present, becomes a noteworthy feature of the *bergerette*.[41] If it appears in two-section pieces that are textless, or have incipits only, these pieces may be identified as *bergerettes* rather than *rondeaux,* which do not present a structural change of meter. Absence of metrical contrast, however, does not indicate that such a two-section piece is necessarily a *rondeau.*

Contrast often occurs also between the texture of the *bergerette* refrain and that of section 2, the former being more complex and melismatic than the latter, the change in character being connected with the above-mentioned shift from triple to duple rhythm (cf. pp. 56f). A fifth or even a complete triad may be found at the close of section 2, but the refrain normally ends on a unison or octave.

[35] Pr. DrozT, 64.   [36] *Ibid.,* 34.
[36a] For a list of the chansons, *see* BrooA.
[36b] Pr. LenN, Supp., 24; cf. BrooA.
[36c] Pr. JosqMS I, 105. Long regarded as anon., the piece is ascribed to Busnois in the great MS at the Segovia Cathedral; cf. BrooA. It also underlies numerous chanson adaptations.
[37] But LoepL, 355, gives a *rondeau-quatrain* text that fits the music better. Cf. BrooA.
[38] Pr. DrozT, 40.   [39] *Ibid.,* 5.   [40] *See also* DrozT, 54 ($=$ JepK, 24), 78.
[41] Cf. the anon. chansons in BushL, 70; JepK, 54; etc.

EXAMPLE 25. Extracts from the *bergerette, Je ne puis vivre ainsi*—Busnois (after DrozT, 64).

Busnois, instead of following the custom of having all the parts strike their concluding notes simultaneously, sometimes, as in *Mon mignault—Gracieuse* and *Acordés moy,*[41a] likes to have an inner voice continue moving at a final cadence against the sustained notes of the other parts (cf. p. 59).

The under-third cadence is still common, the Burgundian and octave-leap cadences less so. But even the first type was growing archaic, and the leading-tone-to-tonic progression, with the root of V leaping to the root of I in the bass, gained in favor. Evidence of the shift is provided by Busnois's *Quand ce vendra.* In the latter part of the century, as we have noted, writing *a 4* began to supplant writing *a 3* in secular music, as it had already done in sacred music. *Si placet* parts modernized quite a number of chansons originally *a 3.* Later, *si placet* parts were normally the work of a second hand. However, it is possible that in Hayne's and Busnois's day such a part was provided by the original composer.[42] (In this event, some works may have been composed *a 4* in the first place, to satisfy the newer taste, but one part may have been deliberately written so that it could be easily dispensed with if desired.) Now, *Quand ce vendra* exists in a version *a 3*[43] in the Dijon Chansonnier and in one *a 4* in the Mellon Chansonnier; in the former version there are two under-third cadences, but both are discarded in favor of simple leading-tone-to-tonic progressions when the piece is modernized by the addition of a *si placet* voice. The opportunity for color contrast offered by writing *a 4* is recognized by Busnois who, in his *Je ne demande autre degré,*[44] for example, groups the voices in various ways.

In its earlier version, *Quand ce vendra* is an example of what has been called the non-quartal style, evident in a small but clearly discernible body of works

41a Pr. HewO, 258 (= GiesS, 76), 290, respectively.   42 Cf. BukU, 19.   43 Pr. DrozT, 5.
44 Pr. HewO, 311; ObrMS I, i (after p. 48). Busnois has left us also a three-part *Je ne demande lialté.*

a 3 of c. 1460 to c. 1520. No major composers appear to have written solely in this style, but some, including Busnois, reveal a special fondness for it. In its strictest form, no essential fourths appear between any two voices, so that each pair constitutes good counterpoint by itself, according to the standards of the time; where fourths do appear, they result from the presence of passing-notes, suspensions, anticipations, etc. In a less rigid form, the style admits fourths at cadence points and in passages of strict imitation.[45]

Conventional melodic figures that recur in the music of the period may be illustrated by examples from Busnois: an ascending initial pattern with a dotted-note figure and repeated notes, and a descending broken-triad figure followed by an ascent and descent of a second.[46]

> EXAMPLE 26 (*a*). Opening of superius of *A qui vens tu tes coquilles*—
> Busnois, (*b*) Opening of tenor of *Corps digne—Dieu quel
> mariage*—Busnois.

In *Corps digne—Dieu quel mariage*,[47] there is considerable writing in parallel tenths (cf. p. 179). The use of this facile device, as well as of parallel thirds and sixths, tends to become a mannerism with Busnois. (Its presence in pieces *a 3* may sometimes be attributed to the application of the non-quartal technique.[47a]) But sequence, which, depending on its treatment, may likewise be regarded as a facile device, is sometimes handled by Busnois most felicitously. In the superius of *C'est bien maleur,* a sequence pattern of binary character creates a delicate rhythmic conflict within the prevailing ternary meter.[47b] In the setting of line 3 of *Je ne puis vivre ainsi,* a composition of altogether extraordinary beauty, the two upper voices, engaging in canon over a contratenor, present a six-beat phrase, which is twice repeated in sequence, but with its first beat omitted; as a result, the two later appearances in each canon voice are five-beat phrases, with interesting effect upon the rhythmic structure.[47c] The contratenor adds clarity and intensification to the interplay of rhythms by parallelling the dux (with some minor variants) a tenth below. In the same piece, the entry of the middle voice and the continuation of the superius produce a conflict of non-synchronizing accents (cf. Ex. 25). The rhythmic intricacies of this elegant composer go well beyond the use of hemiola favored by the previous generation, but have nothing in common with the eccentric complexity of the late 14th century.

---

[45] Further about this style, *see* FoxNQ.

[46] Further about the first figure, *see* BukU, 21f; about the second figure, JepK, xxf. The second figure is often found in triple meter and with a sustained note at the beginning instead of 2 repeated notes.   [47] Pr. KiesT, App., 60; SmijO, 27.

[47a] Cf. FoxNQ, 42ff. As there noted, long series of consecutive tenths were specifically approved by certain theorists.   [47b] *See* DrozT, 40, meas. 8f.

[47c] See DrozT, 65, systems 1 and 2. In the last appearance, the length of the final note of the phrase is modified (differently in each voice), but the five-beat character is not destroyed.

On the contrary, the balance of his phrase structure and the grace of his melodic line are enhanced by them.

In the latter part of the century, there was increasing exploration of the lower ranges. We have already found a striking sporadic example in Binchois (cf. p. 91), but in Busnois and Ockeghem the expansion downward becomes general. As a result of this increase in total range, the voices tend to pull apart and to cross one another less often, thus preparing the way for the growth of imitation as the most characteristic feature of Late Renaissance music (cf. p. 250). Busnois not uncommonly descends to F; in *Joye me fuit* [48] he goes down no less than four times to D. Low registers are not limited to the bass. In the four-part *Acordés moy,* not only does the bass reach F, but the altus does so too. All the voices of the three-part *Bel Acueil* [49] lie low.

EXAMPLE 27. Opening of *Bel Acueil*—Busnois (from Mellon Chansonnier f. 1ᵛ; transcr. by Oliver Strunk).

Bel Acueil, the constable of Love,
Who well knows how to serve his writs . . .

Imitation—sometimes in two, sometimes in all three voices—is a favorite device of Busnois's. It is usually at the octave or unison, but occasionally at the fourth below or fifth above. He employs it so much that he may be regarded as preparing the way for the general use of pervading imitation that was soon to come.[50] *Bel Acueil* and *A vous sans autre,* both *rondeaux quatrains,* exhibit this device as consistently as does Binchois's *Vostre alée* (cf. p. 88). "From a condition in which all voices set out homophonically, through stages in which imitation was brief and merely incidental, then with two voices consciously imitating each other above a harmonic bass,[51] the technique has now arrived at its third stage, in which each voice enters alone and in which the Contra joins in the imitation. The former harmonic function of the Contra, that of serving as 'bass' for the whole, has receded somewhat into the background—and the melodic principle has proved stronger than the har-

---

[48] Pr. DTO VII, 247; DrozT, 50.
[49] Pr. after the Dijon MS in DrozT, 36 (cf. differences in Ex. 27).   [50] *See* BorQS, 280.
[51] For a good anon. example of this type in the Dijon MS, *see* DrozT, 56.

monic." [52] However, in many Busnois chansons the contratenor, after entering in imitation with the other parts, retires to its usual subordinate position. Busnois prefers literal imitation, but, in the contemporary anonymous four-part *Garison sçay*,[53] there is an example of a leap of a fifth, from the final to the dominant, being answered (as in later tonal imitation) by a leap of a fourth, from the dominant to the final. (The remaining two voices of this remarkable piece also answer by leaps of fourths, these, however, involving other pairs of scale-degrees.) Among the passages illustrating Busnois's imaginative use of imitation is one in *A une dame*,[53a] in which an imitating voice paraphrases its antecedent. In one setting of *Quelque povre homme*,[53b] the end of a contratenor phrase is imitated by the opening of the succeeding tenor and superius phrases. In *Acordes moy,* Busnois three times employs imitation in pairs—an outstanding trait of the style of Josquin des Prez; in two instances the device is so handled as to produce brief passages of double counterpoint. Strangely enough, although Busnois uses a mainly advanced technique in this piece, he resorts in it likewise to so old-fashioned a device as hocket; such mixtures of the old and the new are not uncommon in his music.

It is noteworthy that the increasing use of imitation in the late 15th century and the widening of the total compass go hand in hand. In the 13th-century motet the voices moved, roughly speaking, within the same range, but tended to be strikingly contrasted with one another melodically. In the 14th century, a desire was sometimes evident to relate the parts more closely.[53c] But in the 15th century, when sufficient range was available within which the voices could be placed one distinctly above the other, they renounced much oftener the sharply contrasting melodic character that had helped them to stand out as individual entities when they occupied the same musical space. In the late 15th century the stratiform quality of polyphonic writing gradually shifted from the realm of melodic contrast to that of range. Melodic independence of the parts, frequently singled out as a prominent trait of 16th-century polyphony, is actually evident to a considerably greater degree in the polyphony of much earlier years.

In *Ha que ville* Busnois provides his superius with alternative sets of companion voices: in one set they consist of free countermelodies, while in the other, in conformity with the prescription *Trinus in unitate,* they repeat the melody of the superius in canon at the unison.[54] In view of the repetitious nature of the *rondeau* form, perhaps some statements of the superius melody were intended to be supported in one way, some in the other.

Text illustration is rare in Busnois. However, in *Terrible dame,*[55] for which

[52] HewO, 66.   [53] Pr. JepK, 26.   [53a] Pr. BukU, 39.   [53b] Modern ed. in BrooB, Supp., 103.
[53c] Cf. ReMMA, 364.
[54] DrozT, 28, gives only the freer version; LafE II, 26, only the canon—which cannot be combined with the 2 free parts.
[55] Portion pr. PirH, 120.

four parts are written out, there is a dialogue between a lover and his mistress, and Busnois illustrates his text by giving the lover's lines to the lower voices, while the upper ones are silent, and by giving the lady's lines to the upper voices, while the lower ones are silent. The direction *"faulx bordon"* in the source indicates that a voice should be added a fourth below the upper voice of each pair, in those passages that are written *a 2.* In *J'ay pris amours tout au rebours,* Busnois applies the words *"tout au rebours"* by inverting almost exactly, in his own tenor, the tenor of *J'ay pris amours.*[56]

The popularity of Busnois's chansons in their day is attested by their wide dissemination in MSS, many existing in at least five sources.[57] The German *Glogauer Liederbuch* (cf. p. 635) contains *Pour entretenir mes amours* [58] and *Au povre par necessité,* the latter in the form of a *saincte chansonnette, Regina regnantium.*[59] *Quant ce vendra* appears as a *saincte chansonnette* also: the Trent MSS present it twice—both in its version *a 3* and in its Mellon version *a 4*—in the guise of a *Gaude Mater;* they contain also an anonymous Mass (lacking the Agnus) based upon it.[60]

Fewer examples of Busnois's sacred music survive than of his chansons. The *Missa L'Homme armé,*[61] written c. 1475, was destined to be cited by Tinctoris and Ramos.[62] The note-values of the *cantus firmus* (cf. Ex. 18) are never augmented or diminished, but variety is provided by change of meter. The melody is presented once each in the complete Kyrie, in the Sanctus (through *Osanna I*) and, inverted, in the complete Agnus, and twice each in the Gloria and Credo—being suspended during the *Christe,* again at *Et incarnatus est,* and during the *Pleni,* Benedictus (to *"Domini"*), and Agnus II. (The second appearance in the Credo is abbreviated; the fragment heard in *Osanna I* recurs, since this subsection returns as *Osanna II.*) In Kyrie, Credo, and Agnus alike, the interruption in the *cantus firmus* comes at the end of the first statement of the high-lying motif that is sung twice about half-way through the tune; but the interruption comes after statement 2 in the Sanctus (cf. p. 197

[56] The Busnois piece pr. HewO, 305; ObrWW, 96. (HewO, 100, is not quite correct in accounting for Busnois's use of the words, *"tout au rebours."*)

[57] Cf. BrooA.   [58] Pr. EDMR IV, 64.

[59] Pr. *ibid.,* VIII, 64. The *Liederbuch* contains also 2 pieces for which there are conflicting attributions—*Cent mille escus,* pr. *ibid.* IV, 67 (= AmbG II, 554; OH II, 52; given in both places with wrong ascription to Dufay; some sources ascribe the piece to Caron; cf. PlamS, 110f), and *Je suis venut,* pr. AmbG II, 573 (= OH II, 56; MarM, 129, here given with ascription to Hayne, but *see* BukU, 41, fn. 96). For other chansons by Busnois, *see* SmijO, 185; DTO VII, 236 (there anon.) 246; XI¹, 74; KiesT, App., 56; DrozT, 22, 94; JepK 16, 42 (there anon.), 44 (= BesM, 212; given with facsimile after Dijon); HewO, 235, 270, 286 (all 3 survive with conflicting attributions; cf. *ibid.,* 131, 142, 144, respectively); PlamDP, 14; BrooA (5 pieces). Further on Busnois as a chanson composer, *see* BrooA, BrooB, PerleB, McalS.

[60] Cf. BoerB, 8; DTO VII, thematic index, Nos. 502, 711–714, 1189.

[61] Pr. MPLSER, *Ser. I,* I, No. 2; the Kyrie, pr. SmijO, 18. I am indebted to Dr. Strunk for access to his MS score of this Mass before the MPLSER ed. was published. About a *Missa O crux lignum* by Busnois, *see* HabV, 120; about an anon. Mass that may be his, *see* BorQS, 206. The *Missa Ecce ancilla* credited to Busnois in Grove I, 504, is Dufay's.

[62] Cf. StrunkH, 25.

regarding Obrecht's similar treatment of the melody). At several points where the tenor is silent, Busnois introduces two-part canon. The *cantus firmus* does not, to any considerable degree, spread from the tenor to the other voices, but, in the *Tu solus altissimus* portion of the Gloria, the descending-fifth figure is imitated in all voices on each of its three appearances. At the beginnings of the five major sections, the second highest voice opens in anticipatory imitation of the *cantus-firmus*-bearing tenor, the entrance of which is delayed. The former voice is combined, at these points, with the superius, which always has the same material. The resulting head-motif, taking the form of a duo of the upper voices, shows Busnois sharing Dufay's predilection for opening with such a passage. Busnois's second highest voice bears the designation "Contra," and this term is applied to the lowest voice also. Here we see a step in a process—brought about by writing *a 4*—that was to produce our terms "alto" and "bass," for the contratenor split, so to speak, into two parts: the contratenor altus and the contratenor bassus, eventually called merely altus and bassus.

Of two Magnificats in Brussels MS 5557, one bears Busnois's name; the other, which is anonymous, may be his also. In both, after the normal intoning of the word *"Magnificat"* in plainsong, all the rest is polyphonic. The anonymous work is *a 3;* the other sets the various verses *a 2, 3,* and *4.* In each, there is paraphrasing of the plainsong, and repetitions of musical sections help to produce unity. Only the outer parts are notated in the *Deposuit potentes* of the Magnificat that is definitely Busnois's, and performance in fauxbourdon is called for. The general style characteristics, therefore, are much the same as in the Magnificat of the Dufay period.[63]

Brussels MS 5557 contains also five motets and three smaller sacred works by Busnois (one incomplete). Another motet, *In hydraulis,*[64] survives in Trent MS 91 and Munich MS 3154. This motet, in two *partes,* was written c. 1465 in honor of Ockeghem, who, in *pars II,* is praised as first among all the singers of the court of France. At the end, Busnois mentions himself as an "unworthy musician of the illustrious Count of Charolais." The textless tenor, which is sometimes silent for fairly long stretches, consists of a three-note *ostinato,* repeated at different levels: d-c-d, a-g-a, d'-c'-d', d'-c'-d', a-g-a, d-c-d. This combination appears four times in all, in two different rhythmic configurations. While *ostinato* tenors had, of course, been used in motets as early as the 13th century, they then constituted the lowest voices; Busnois's *ostinato* differs in that the tenor is here an inner voice.[65]

Busnois builds his three-part *Anima mea liquefacta est*[66] over a chant tenor, *Stirps Jesse.* Its entrance is delayed, and here again Busnois has his *cantus firmus* anticipated by an upper voice—this time, the superius. The extract

---

[63] Further about these 2 Magnificats, *see* BorI, Instalment I, 67, and esp. BorQS, 212ff.
[64] Pr. DTO VII, 105.
[65] Further about this motet, *see* SteB, 21ff; BorQS, 225ff.
[66] Pr. SmijO, 22. *See* further BorQS, 244f; SteB, 17.

from the Song of Solomon that provides the text ends with the words *"quia amore langueo,"* and on *langueo* Busnois writes a long, sinuous melisma.

In a four-part *Regina coeli,*[67] Busnois paraphrases the plainsong melody in the tenor and "alter tenor," the former imitating the latter in canon at the fourth above, while the upper parts are free. In a setting of the *Victimae paschali,* there is an extension of register—this time upward—to g''.[68] Of special interest is the motet, in two *partes, Anthoni usque limina,*[69] dedicated to Busnois's patron saint, St. Anthony Abbot. The text is probably by the composer, whose name it suggests: its first three syllables give *"Anthonius,"* and it ends with *"ut . . . fiat in omnibus noys"* ("so that . . . understanding may come upon all"; *noys* is Greek νοῦς ["understanding"] in Latin letters). The tenor, not written out in the MS, consists of the single note d' which, according to a verbal canon, is to be emitted at various points by a bell—or perhaps by some sound imitating a bell. Tinctoris objected to *ostinati,* but allowed them *campanarum aut tubarum imitando* (cf. pp. 6of regarding Dufay's *Gloria ad modum tubae*).[70] The motet is mainly *a 3,* not counting the bell, but an additional voice enters momentarily in each *pars.* The piece contains passages of canon both *a 2* and *a 3.*[71]

By the time of Busnois's departure from the Burgundian chapel in 1482, it had passed into new hands. Developed by Philip the Good and inherited by Charles the Bold, it descended, upon the latter's demise in 1477, to his daughter, Mary of Burgundy. Later in that year Mary married Maximilian of Austria, afterward Emperor Maximilian I. When she died, five years later, he acted as guardian of their children, Philip the Handsome and Margaret of Austria, and as regent of the Low Countries (Burgundy itself reverted to the French crown). It was he, therefore, who maintained the chapel until Philip took it over in 1494.

Caron, Faugues, Regis, Barbireau, and Lesser Figures

One of the four MSS preserving Busnois's *Missa L'Homme armé*—MS Cappella Sistina 14[71a]—is of great importance to the whole subject of *L'Homme armé* Masses. It contains also the first two movements of Dufay's Mass on this old melody and the entire Masses on it by Caron, Faugues, and Regis. (It is the sole source for the work by the last of these.)

Caron was associated with Cambrai, at least for a time, for he served at its

---

[67] Pr. SmijO, 16. About another *Regina coeli* by Busnois, *see* SteB, 20; BorQS, 247ff (exx. 1 and 3 on p. 250 should be interchanged).

[68] Cf. SteB, 79; BorQS, 245.   [69] Facsimile and transcr. in BoerB.

[70] CouS IV, 151. Busnois was evidently not greatly concerned about such limitations; cf. not only *In hydraulis,* but DrozT, 66, system 3, meas. 4ff, and, for a varied *ostinato, ibid.,* 29, systems 2–4.

[71] Further about this motet, *see* BoerB; BorQS, 238ff; SteB, 22f, 54ff. Regarding other motets by Busnois, *see* BorI, Instalment I, 67; BorQS, 235, 247f, 251; SteB, 75ff, 89. A complete edition of Busnois is in course of preparation by Catherine V. Brooks.

[71a] Described in HabD, 72ff.

cathedral as an altar boy.[72] While music continued to flourish with vigor at the Burgundian court, at Cambrai it was cultivated with constancy but more modestly. The records show that an unnamed Mass by Caron was copied there for the use of the choir in 1472.[73] His first name, according to Tinctoris, was Firmin; according to other sources, Philippe.[74] He was esteemed not only by Tinctoris [75] and Hothby (cf. p. 178),[76] but by such later theorists as Hermann Finck and Sebald Heyden.[77] The extent of his representation in Italian MSS and his settings of Italian words, e.g., *Fuggir non posso,*[78] suggest a stay in Italy. His rather Busnois-like *Mort ou merci vous requiers,*[79] with its examples of three-part imitation, shows Caron to have been abreast of the newer trends of the day. His quite enchanting *Helas que pourra devenir* survives in no less than eighteen old sources.[80] Originally a three-part composition, it was later provided with a *si placet* altus. With regard to its text, too, it was subjected to change: a *rondeau cinquain* text, strangely enough, was made to fit the music, set in the first instance to a *rondeau quatrain;* the piece survives in addition as a *saincte chansonnette,* with the words *Ave sidus clarissimum.*[81] There is much canon between the superius and tenor, first at the octave above, later at the fifth below. Variation occurs in the time-intervals at which the voices imitate (cf. p. 20), occasionally in a single phrase of canon, with intricate rhythmical relations at times resulting. Thus, in the setting of line 2, different kinds of conflicting accents result—at the opening, from Caron's having the canon take place after one time-unit and, in the course of the phrase, from his reducing the time-interval by half.

EXAMPLE 28. Extract from *Helas que pourra devenir*—Caron (after HewO, 246; *si placet* altus omitted).

[72] HouH, 83; HabD, 43.   [73] HouH, 84; HabD, 44. *See also* SteB, 7, fn. 10.

[74] Cf. EitQ II, 341. The composer has been confused with Jehan Caron, who was *sommelier* (cellarer) of the oratory of the Burgundian Court, 1436–1474. (About him, *see* MarH, esp. 129, 196f.) Jehan's never having risen above this lowly post would indicate that he possessed no marked ability; this circumstance, combined with the difference in first name and the fact that the composer is widely represented in MSS and must therefore have been highly regarded, hardly supports the theory that Jehan and the composer were one.

[75] Cf. CouS IV, 77, 146, 152, 154, 172, 200.   [76] *Ibid.,* III, xxxi.   [77] Cf. AmbG II, 423, 508.

[78] Pixérécourt MS, fol. 36ᵛ. The *Tanto l'affanno,* pr. EDMR IV, 52, probably originated as a piece with French text. Cf. PlamS, 246f, 250f.

[79] Pr. DTO VII, 235 (anon.; after Trent 89; but the piece is credited to Caron in the Mellon and Pixérécourt MSS). The first two words are incorrectly read as *Mort-on* in MarH, 196, and are there suggested to be a play on the name of Morton. The further hypothesis, there advanced, that Jehan may have composed the piece, since he and Morton were at the same court, fails, at least on the evidence of the incipit. The work is elegantly written and is no doubt by Firmin (Philippe).

[80] Cf. PlamS, 108f.

[81] Pr., *a 3,* with this text, in EDMR IV, 92, and with the altus and both *rondeau* texts in HewO, 246 (also, with the altus and the *rondeau-cinquain* text, in DTO VII, 248; without text in TorreS, 554); *see* further, HewO, 84.

The frequent variation in the time-interval throughout the piece invests the canon with an altogether charming element of fancy.[81a]

Also popular enough to survive as both a chanson and a *saincte chansonnette* —and both *a 3* and *a 4*—is the *rondeau cinquain, Accueillie m'a la belle* (the first word is *Saoulé* in the Dijon MS and Trent MS 1947-4), which has the text *Da pacem, Domine* in Trent MS 91.[82] A *Rosa playsant*,[83] attributed to Caron in a MS at Florence, appears in *Canti C* (printed by Petrucci in 1504) as by "Philipon" (cf. p. 117) and in MS 2856 at the Bibl. Casanatense, Rome, as by Dusart. Among Caron's several Masses, there is one based on *Accueillie m'a*, as well as a four-part *Missa L'Homme armé*.[84] In the latter, the rhythmic treatment of the *cantus firmus* approximates that of the other voices much of the time, though the traditional long values occur also. The old melody, presented in Dorian transposed, is considerably elaborated. Duos of the upper voices, at the openings of all movements (except the Kyrie) and in their course, recall earlier practice. Imitation is confined almost wholly to passages *a 2*. The instances, apparently deliberate, in which isolated measures are too long or too short (according to the mensuration indicated by the time-signatures), are more numerous than was usual at the time in a single work.[85]

Faugues is among the composers admired by Tinctoris, who indicates[86] that the composer's first name was Guillaume, as does a treatise at the Escorial.[87] Among Faugues's surviving Masses—all his known works are in this form—is a *Missa super Basse danse*.[88] His *Missa L'Homme armé*[89] presents the old tune in canon at the fifth below in all passages that are *a 4*. It may well be the oldest example of a canon Mass.[90] The melody appears in the Dorian mode untransposed in the altus and in the Dorian once transposed in the tenor. It is melodically embellished at times and is stated in various

[81a] Consistency with our other exx. requires the time-values in Ex. 28 to be one-half of those in HewO; in addition, each of our measures embraces 2 in HewO. In terms of the HewO transcription, the canon proceeds as follows. First it is at the octave at a time-interval of 3 meas. In meas. 15 (with which our ex. commences) it is at the fifth below; the distance begins as half a meas., but the fifth note in the superius, which is a half-note, is answered by a quarter-note in the tenor, so that the distance is reduced to a quarter of a meas. This continues into meas. 29, where a 2-meas. cadence begins. At meas. 31, the canon resumes at a distance of 1 meas. The dotted half-note in the superius in meas. 35, however, is answered in the tenor by a plain half-note. The same thing happens to the dotted half in the superius in meas. 36 and to the one in meas. 37, so that the time-interval is again reduced to a quarter of a meas. and the conflicts of accent return. This continues into meas. 44, where a cadence begins. The canon resumes in meas. 47 at the time-interval of half a meas. The third note in the superius, a quarter-note, is answered by a half-note, so that the time-interval becomes three-quarters of a meas. This keeps up into meas. 50, but the half-note in the superius in meas. 51 goes unanswered, so that the time-interval again becomes a quarter of a meas. This interval continues into meas. 58, and the rest of the piece is free.

[82] Pr., *a 3*, with both texts, in DTO XI¹, 75; *a 3*, after Dijon, in DrozT, 12; *a 4*, after Trent 1947-4, in DiseJ, 4. For other chansons, see GomO, Supp., 2; EDMR IV, 65. See also fn. 59 *supra* and BukU, 22.   [83] Pr. SmijO, 62.

[84] Pr. MPLSER, *Ser. I*, I, No. 3; Kyrie I also in AmbG II, 580; Agnus also in SmijO, 33.

[85] Further regarding Caron, see MGG II, 859ff.   [86] CouS IV, 77.

[87] Cf. RiaC, 65.

[88] Cf. DTO VII, 67 (Nos. 1151-55).

[89] Pr. MPLSER, *Ser. I*, I, No. 4. The Kyrie is given *a 3* (i.e., without the canon worked out) in AmbG II, 567 (Kyrie II, *a 3*, also in KiesG, App., xvi).

[90] Cf. FeinK, 53.

meters. This Mass survives not only in MS Cappella Sistina, No. 14, but in an earlier version at Modena. Comparison of the two versions gives some insight into the working processes of Faugues, who was evidently concerned about unifying this composition through means additional to the use of a *cantus firmus*. In the older form, the music for Kyrie II serves also at the end of the Gloria; there is a return to Kyrie I within the Credo and to the *Christe* (but with cuts) in the *Osanna;* the Sanctus reintroduces Kyrie I, with a different opening duo. In the later version, the form is simplified: the music of Kyrie II recurs in the *Cum Sancto Spiritu,* the *Confiteor,* and the *Osanna;* the Sanctus is newly written. The repetition at the *Confiteor* is introduced by music closely resembling that previously used before the *Cum Sancto Spiritu.*[90a] Further divergences between the two versions add to the evidence of Faugues's careful craftsmanship.[91] A passage from a Mass *a 4,* based on Dufay's *Le serviteur* and ascribed to Ockeghem in Trent MS 88, is quoted by Tinctoris—who, however, names Faugues as the composer.[91a] Since several attributions in the Trent MSS have proved undependable, but the authority of Tinctoris is highly regarded, the work is now generally credited to Faugues. In the several long introductory duos between the upper voices, the second voice occasionally anticipates the *cantus firmus* in imitation. The Credo is an example of a continental setting that makes a substantial excision in the text (cf. p. 69). In this Mass, as in the *Missa L'Homme armé,* unity is sought through repetition —a device, incidentally, not used to this end in the other Masses ascribed to Ockeghem—for the polyphony that closes the Gloria closes the Credo also.[91b] Dufay's tenor is stated eight times (being twice interrupted) with a literalness sometimes found in Ockeghem, but not in what are presumably his maturer works; and this Mass is clearly the product of its composer's ripe experience. In one important respect, however, the work resembles the *Missa Fors seulement* of Ockeghem (cf. pp. 126ff) : it foreshadows the coming parody Mass (cf. pp. 202f, 240f) by drawing on all three voices of its prototype; indeed, it goes even further than the *Missa Fors seulement,* for at times it draws on those three voices simultaneously. The old superius is often considerably— and imaginatively—paraphrased. The manner in which the pre-existent material is reworked in Kyries I and II (the *Christe* is free) illustrates the procedure followed in the work as a whole (Table III).[91c]

[90a] Cf. p. 16, meas. 119–143, and p. 9, meas. 79–103; *see* Plamenac in *Notes,* VI (1949), 485.

[91] *See* the preface of MPLSER, *Ser. I,* I.

[91a] Cf. CouS IV, 146; CouT, 382; BesV, 6. The Mass is given (with the attribution to Ockeghem), in facsimile and modern notation, in DTO XIX[1], 81ff. DTO XIX[1] presents also an anon. Mass *a 3* based on *Le serviteur.*

[91b] The openings of the *Osanna* and Agnus III are also alike.

[91c] As pointed out in Chap. 2, voices 1, 3, and 4 in DTO VII, 238, give Dufay's chanson. In comparing the Mass with the chanson as there printed, one should bear in mind that the clef of the superius is placed a line too low on p. 239. (We follow the meas. numbering in DTO XIX[1] for the Mass, though here too there is an error: an extra meas. is included between meas. 20 and meas. "25.")

Table III

Material from the chanson	Places where applied in Kyrie
Measure 1–9 superius	Measure 1–12 superius
1–33 tenor	1–47 tenor
2–5 contratenor	3–7 contratenor II
17–19 superius	23–24[b] contratenor I
18–19 superius	21–22 superius
20–25 superius	25–30 superius
20–22 contratenor	25–27 contratenor II
27–30 superius	35–41 superius
31–end superius	43–47 superius
1–end superius	134–end superius *
1–2 tenor	134–135 contratenor I (transposed down a 4th)
1–end tenor	134–end tenor
3–8 contratenor	138–144 contratenor II
10–11 contratenor	147–148 contratenor II
15–18 contratenor	154–157 contratenor II
21–26 contratenor	160–165 contratenor II

* Highly elaborated, with brief omissions and interpolations.

An additional Ockeghem-like feature is the drive to the cadence at the end of the Kyrie (cf. p. 122). The *L'Homme armé* Mass shows Faugues to have been venturesome; if the *Serviteur* Mass is actually his also, it adds substantially to his stature as a modern in his day.

Johannes Regis (c. 1430–85) is traceable at Soignies in 1458; appears to have become *magister puerorum* at the Church of Our Lady in Antwerp [91d] in 1463; later became secretary to Dufay, who names him in his will; in 1474 became a priest and went to Mons; and in 1481 was again at Soignies, where at some time he became a canon and where he died.[92] His works were an integral part of the repertoire at Cambrai during Dufay's old age.[93]

Although few of his works survive—two Masses, one Mass section, eight motets, and two chansons [94]—his style can be deduced from them. The form in which his special characteristics are most clearly seen is the motet. He prefers to write this in two *partes,* the rhythm being ternary in *pars I,* binary in *pars II*—a type already found in Dufay's great *Ave Regina* and destined to enjoy favor into the time of Josquin.[95] All the Regis motets, save one, are *a 5,*

[91d] "Our Lady" was not elevated to the rank of a cathedral until 1559.
[92] For fuller biographical data, *see* LindenR, Chap. I.
[93] Cf. HouH, 84, 422; HabD, 44, 52.   [94] Cf. LindenR, 14ff; BukU, 23.
[95] Cf. BesM, 215f; LindenR, 29.

and the *cantus firmus,* when present, is entrusted to the tenor, which may be any one of the three inner voices. This part begins in long-sustained notes, but is later subjected to figuration and then shares the rhythmic character of the other voices, which Regis presents in ever changing combinations. The music has a fine sonority, suitable for festive occasions. The *O admirabile commercium,*[96] except for the fact that it has three *partes,* may be regarded as typical of Regis' style. A three-part *Ave Maria*[97] is a little song-motet. The chansons[98] are of less interest than the motets.

The *Missa L'Homme armé* of Regis[99] differs from its predecessors in plainly using the old melody for a symbolical purpose. Of the four voices, the two outer ones are always given the normal words of the Ordinary, but the two inner ones (the contratenor I and tenor) often have, instead, the opening of the text of the *Dum sacrum mysterium*—the antiphon at the Magnificat in the Feast of the Dedication of St. Michael the Archangel—, this text at times receiving relevant additions. Regis follows the plan, inconsistently, to be sure, but quite frequently, of assigning the text of the Ordinary to the inner voices when they do not have *L'Homme armé* material, but the text of the *Dum sacrum mysterium* when they do have such material. The protecting Archangel, the head of the heavenly host, is clearly the "armed man." Regis draws upon plainsong as well as upon the *L'Homme armé* tune. He does not use the melody of the *Dum sacrum mysterium* itself, but he does introduce other Chant material associated with this Feast: the Tone for Mode I, as it is applied to the verse (*Milia milium*) of *Factum est silentium,* and the antiphon, *Dum committeret bellum.* The former appears in the alto in both the Gloria and the Credo;[100] the latter in the tenor in both the Sanctus and Agnus I.[100a] In *Osanna II* the tenor appears to have part of the melody of the *Pueri Hebraeorum* for Palm Sunday,[101] while the *L'Homme armé* melody returns in contratenor I. That voice, which often executes, with the tenor, the earlier part of the *L'Homme armé* tune in canon at the fifth below, assumes throughout a heavy share of the tenor's traditional role as bearer of the *cantus firmus.* This tune appears in "normal" values, in diminution, in augmentation. The openings of all five movements vary the same three-part head-motif, which ends with a *fermata*-marked block-chord. Regis' Mass, obviously intended for the Feast of St. Michael, provides an understandable explanation for the

[96] Pr. LindenR, App. (The *Verbum caro* used in the tenor is not the Chant melody now current; cf. SteB, 109.) *See also* the opening of *Clangat plebs* in BesM, 214.

[97] Pr. CPC, No. 24. Further on Regis' motets, *see* SteB, 24ff.

[98] One is Pr. KiesS, App., 11; KiesT, App., 62.   [99] Pr. MPLSER, *Ser. I,* I, No. 5.

[100] In meas. 41–52 (p. 5) plus meas. 49–77 (p. 8) and in meas. 53–64 (p. 10f) plus meas. 51–76 (p. 14). For the plainsong (from the Sarum repertory), *see* FrereA, 553, col. 1.

[100a] In meas. 17–28 (p. 15f) plus meas. 16–27 (p. 16f) and in meas. 13–24 (p. 20f); the presentation in Agnus I is incomplete. For the plainsong (also from the Sarum repertory), *see* FrereA, 557, col. 2.

[101] Liber, 583. Selection of this melody for use at this point may have been prompted by the fact that the last words of the *Pueri Hebraeorum* are *Hosanna in excelsis.*

employment of a secular melody; but similar instances, it must be stressed, are not readily found. Regis' *Missa Ecce ancilla Domini* is based mainly on two *cantus firmi—Ecce ancilla Domini* and *Ne timeas—*but five other plainsong melodies are also drawn upon. The various *cantus firmi* are most often presented in pairs. These *cantus* are all antiphons of Advent and retain their own texts. The borrowed melodies are not only elaborated, but subjected to modification to facilitate their combination.[102] Regis, in retouching his material for such an end, was illustrating an attitude general among the Flemish masters, an attitude that goes far toward belying the charges of pedantry too often leveled against them without sufficient cause.

Regis is one of several composers mentioned in Crétin's *Déploration* as welcoming Ockeghem upon his arrival in the afterworld.

Là Dufay, le bon homme survint,	*There worthy Dufaÿ stepped to the fore,*
Bunoys aussi, et aultres plus de vingt,	*Also Busnois and over twenty more,*
Fedé, Binchois, Barbingant et Donsta-ble,	*Dunstable, Barbingant, Fedé, Bin-chois,*
Pasquin, Lannoy, Barizon tres nota-ble,	*Pasquin, the famous Barizon, Lannoy,*
Copin, Regis, Gille Joye et Constant,	*Copin, Regis, Gilles Joye and Constans too;*
Maint homme fut aupres d'eulx es-coutant,	*Full many folk about them listening drew,*
Car bon faisoit ouyr telle armonye. . . .	*For good it was to hear such har-mony. . . .*

Of these musicians who died before Ockeghem, two—Pasquin and Copin—are obscure figures; Lannoy, Fedé, Barbingant, and Barizon call for further comment.

Lannoy may be the Colinet de Lannoy who composed *Cela sans plus,*[102a] a celebrated piece on which many later compositions were based, and *Adieu, naturlic leven myn.*[102b]

Jehan Fedé was vicar of St. Amé at Douai, his birthplace, in 1439 and 1440. He appears to have been a papal singer from 1443 to 1445 (an entry refers to "Joh. Sohier, alias Fede"[103]); a singer at the Sainte Chapelle in 1449; in the employ of Charles VII in 1452 and 1453; a *contratenorista* at St. Peter's in 1466; and a member of the chapel of Louis XI in 1473 and 1474, having, in 1472, become a canon of the Sainte Chapelle under the name of "Sohier le clerc."[104] Both sacred and secular works by Fedé come down to us.

Under the name of Barbingant there survive a three-part *Missa Teribilment* and four secular compositions. The Mass is based on the anonymous *bergerette,*

---

[102] Further about this Mass, *see* LindenR, 20ff; BorQS, 203ff.
[102a] Pr., with facsimile after 1 source, in WolfH I, 395; further about the piece, *see* GomO, 75ff.
[102b] Pr. LenN, Supp., 21.   [103] HabD, 11.
[104] Cf. PirH, 101; BrenM, 32. (There is some doubt that all these facts apply to the same man; *see,* e.g., HabR, 49; EitQ III, 402.)

Terriblement suis fortunée,[105] and, like the Faugues *Missa Le serviteur,* it foreshadows the parody Mass. In this instance, however, the superius and tenor of the chanson form the basis of all five Mass sections, only the contratenor being unrelated to the model. Of the secular pieces, the four-part *Der pfoben swancz* (meaning "The Dance of the Peacocks"),[106] composed before 1461, was destined to be drawn upon by several later composers. On the words *"ma maistresse,"* appearing in the refrain, the superius of the three-part *rondeau, Au travail suis,*[107] quotes amusingly, and almost literally, the opening of Ockeghem's *Ma maistresse.*[107a] Barbingant has been regarded by some as identical with Jacobus Barbireau,[108] but certain circumstances—the alleged inferiority of the works ascribed to Barbingant, the fact that the pieces so credited in one source do not recur elsewhere with attributions to Barbireau, and the failure of "Jacobus" to appear in conjunction with "Barbingant"— have been pointed out [109] as indicating that two different men are involved. Whatever its significance may be in this connection, it should be pointed out also that not only Crétin, but also d'Amerval and Tinctoris, refer to "Barbingant" but not to "Barbireau."

Barbireau, from 1448 to his death in 1491, was choirmaster at Our Lady in Antwerp, where his tenure saw the number of singers grow from 38 to 69.[110] Perhaps he was more important as choir director than as composer, and the Antwerp of his day more influential in the field of performance than in that of composition. Late in Barbireau's life Emperor Maximilian sent him on a diplomatic mission to Buda (cf. p. 723). Under the name of "Barbireau" there survive three Masses, one motet, and three chansons. The range of the four-part *Missa Faulx perverse* lies low, the bass sometimes reaching D. A Mass,[111] mainly *a 5,* is named after the antiphon, *Virgo parens Christi,* the melody of which is given to the middle voice; the antiphon words, rather than those of the Ordinary, appear in that voice, except briefly in the *Osanna.* The writing *a 5* is varied by passages for both smaller and larger groups. The four-part *Missa Pascale*—actually only a combination of Kyrie I, *Christe I, Christe II,* and Kyrie II—divides the plainsong of the *Kyrie Lux et origo* between the superius and tenor.[112]

---

[105] Pr. DTO XI¹, 112; further on this Mass, *see* DanisP. The account in LenPM, 412f, is not quite correct. All Barbingant-Barbireau works for which citations are given on this page and the next are contained in BarbirO also.

[106] Pr. ScherG, 43; EitT, 60 (defective; *see* SaarB, 90); cf. EDMR IV, 88.

[107] Pr. OckW I, 42. Cf. PlamJO, 33, about conflicting ascription to Ockeghem.

[107a] Pr. OckW I, 124.

[108] If this is correct, there are more than 40 variants of the name of this one man; cf. SaarB, 1.

[109] By Van den Borren in RB, I (1947), 136.

[110] Cf. BurbM, 254; also p. 118 *infra* concerning the size of the choir in 1443–44.

[111] Kyrie pr. SaarB, 211.

[112] Original notation of Barbireau's *Kyrie I* given in RoediN, 42; modern notation of *Christe II,* in GomO, Supp., 9. Further on Barbireau's Masses, *see* SaarB, 38ff.

The text of Barbireau's long motet *a 4, Osculetur me*,[113] in two *partes*, is taken from the Song of Solomon. It is the only known setting of the *Osculetur* passage from this period, the *Anima mea liquefacta est* and *Tota pulchra es* passages having been the favorites of composers of the time. Barbireau's chanson, *Gracuuly* [= *Gracieulx*] *et biaulx*, illustrates harmonic—not merely melodic—sequence.[114] *Scon lief* [115] was to be used by Obrecht as the basis of one Mass and fleetingly in a *quodlibet* Mass. But the most famous of Barbireau's works is the three-part *Een vroylic wesen*.[116] This mostly chordal piece, with imitation between the superius and bass at the beginning, was extremely popular in the 15th and 16th centuries. It survives in many sources: in its original form, in various vocal arrangements, with text in German or French instead of Flemish, in organ and lute versions, in a Mass setting by Isaac. Its vogue was especially great in Germany—so much so that, before Barbireau's authorship was established, some modern scholars believed it to be a German rather than a Flemish song.[117]

"Barizon" must be Philippe Basiron, also known as Philippon; [118] otherwise Crétin would be applying *"tres notable"* to a figure modest enough to have sunk into complete obscurity. Basiron is represented in the Copenhagen Chansonnier by a fine *bergerette, Nul ne l'a tele*.[119] This is one of those examples of the form in which the binary rhythm and quiet motion of *pars II* contrast with the ternary rhythm and greater activity of *pars I* (the refrain). *Pars II* is provided with two closes—that which leads back to a repetition of this section terminating on the dominant while, interestingly, that which leads back to the opening of the chanson ends on the *finalis*. A four-part chanson [120] of Basiron's combines the superius of Ockeghem's *D'ung aultre amer*, which it presents in its own superius, and the *L'Homme armé* melody, which it assigns to the tenor. Basiron drew on this old melody also as the basis of a Mass, described as new in a document of 1484.[121] In both compositions he presents the tune in Dorian transposed. It appears in canon *a 2* in the Mass, but less frequently than in the *L'Homme armé* Mass of Faugues. Among several other Basiron Masses is a *Missa de Franza*,[122] printed by Petrucci in 1508.[123]

---

[113] Pr. SmijO, 40.   [114] Cf. SaarB, 161f.   [115] Pr. ObrMS IV, 128.

[116] Pr. LenN, Supp., 28; LandL, 26; DTO XIV¹, 5.

[117] Further on this piece, *see* SaarB, 101ff; FoxF.

[118] Petrucci's ascribing to "Philipon" the *Rosa playsant* credited elsewhere to Caron (cf. p. 111) may therefore well involve an attribution to Basiron. But, since Caron's first name is occasionally given as Philippe, it should not be overlooked that "Philippon" may sometimes apply to him.

[119] Pr. JepK, 14.   [120] Pr. SmijO, 30.

[121] *See* Luigi N. Cittadella, *Notizie amministrative, storiche, artistiche relative a Ferrara*, I (1868), 716. The Mass is pr. in MPLSER, *Ser. I, I*, No. 8.

[122] Agnus II pr. CommB VIII, 14; fragment of *Osanna* in OH II, 60.

[123] *See* further SaarB, 171f; GomO, 9. For another chanson, *see* VincR, Ex. 1.

Ockeghem: Biography; Chansons and Related Works; Motets

The great master of the period (however excellent Busnois may have been), Johannes Ockeghem,[124] is mentioned as a compatriot by Jean Lemaire de Belges, who refers to himself as a native of Hainaut.[124a] Ockeghem was born c. 1420 and died at Tours, c. 1495. From June 24, 1443, to June 24, 1444, he was among the twenty-five singers who served on the *cantoris* side at Our Lady in Antwerp; the twenty-six singers on the *decani* side provided the psalmody.[125] Pullois was among the singers. Ockeghem was a chorister, from 1446 to 1448, in the chapel of Duke Charles of Bourbon; in 1453 we find him similarly occupied in the Royal Chapel, where his service very likely began somewhat earlier. From 1454 on, he had the distinction of acting as first chaplain and composer to three successive kings of France—Charles VII, Louis XI, and Charles VIII, adding the post of *maître de la chapelle du Roy* in 1465. He became also treasurer of the Abbey of St. Martin at Tours, an appointment conferring very high favor upon him, for St. Martin was the wealthiest and most important monastery under the kings of France, who, from the time of Hugh Capet, were its abbots. Ockeghem travelled, in 1469 and 1470, in Spain and, in 1484, in Flanders. His popularity among his fellow-musicians is attested not only by the texts of Busnois's *In hydraulis* and Compère's *Omnium bonorum plena* (cf. p. 227), but likewise by an impressive *Déploration* on his death, composed by Josquin to a French poem by Molinet, a work to which we shall return. Molinet wrote an epitaph in Latin verse on him also.[126] A lament by Erasmus, "Ergo ne conticuit," was set to music by one of the several musicians named Johannes Lupi.[126a] The *Déploration* by Crétin has already been mentioned.

None of Ockeghem's works are actually dated. However, his lament on the death of Binchois (cf. pp. 86, 121) can, of course, be dated 1460; and his Requiem may be presumed to be later than Dufay's, of which a scribe is known to have made a copy in 1470. But beyond this we have no guidance other than features of style.

A few works attributed to Ockeghem in certain sources are ascribed to other men elsewhere. Making allowance for this fact, we may reckon the surviving output at about twenty chansons; eleven complete Masses; two Masses containing only the Kyrie, Gloria, and Credo; one Mass containing only the first two sections; an isolated Credo; a Requiem; and ten or fewer

---

[124] About the various forms of the name, and the correct one, *see* CauN.

[124a] Cf. ClercxB, 122ff. The claim—widely printed, e.g., in BurbM, RoosO—that Ockeghem was born at Termonde, in East Flanders, is apparently wrong.

[125] The *cantoris* side of the choir is on the north, by the cantor or precentor; the *decani* side, on the south, by the dean's stall.

[126] Pr. BrenPM, 27.

[126a] The poem is pr. in StraM I, 101f. For further biographical data, *see* BrenV, 22ff; PirH, 100ff; ClercxB, 126ff.

motets. This is not a large amount. Other works are known to have existed, but do not reach us. Even so, Ockeghem's production seems to have been small in relation to the great reputation he enjoyed among his contemporaries. He is sometimes regarded as the head of a Flemish School that flourished in the latter part of the 15th century. However, his association with France lasted so long that he may just as legitimately be credited to that country as is the North German Brahms to Vienna. If he brought Netherlandish influence to France, he was just as certainly affected by the old traditions of the milieu in which he worked. The clarification that followed the period of the Chantilly MS continues to show effect in his music, but not in the same way as in Dufay: in Ockeghem it has more influence on texture than on form. There is a strong tendency toward asymmetry. While Ockeghem's style, to be sure, is based somewhat on that of Dufay, as is Busnois's, the clear phrase formation, generally found in Dufay, is often conspicuously and, beyond doubt, deliberately avoided. Ockeghem prefers, as Dunstable frequently did also, to keep the flow of polyphony constant. He reveals an affinity with Dunstable likewise in the great freedom with which he applies the technique of paraphrase. The use of chromatic tones declines, even more than in Dufay, in favor of modal diatonicism.[127] The spirit is more that of the north, less that of Italy; more that of developed flamboyant architecture, less that of Santa Maria del Fiore.

Ockeghem's secular pieces, though fine works, are less characteristic than his motets and Masses. The influence of the Dufay-Binchois chanson is here basic. The *rondeau,* both *quatrain* and *cinquain,* is well represented, and there are several *bergerettes.* Most of the compositions are rather melancholy. Practically all are *a 3;* the exceptions are a gymel on *O rosa bella,* in which Ockeghem adds one voice to the old superius,[128] and the four-part *Petite camusette,*[129] *Je n'ay dueil,*[130] and *Qu'es mi vida,* this last being a reworking *a 4* of a piece *a 3* by the Spaniard, Cornago.[131] As in Busnois, the compass frequently extends downward into the bass region and the parts cross less often than in the earlier chansons. The middle part of *Fors seulement l'attente* [132]

[127] Cf. ApelN, 106.

[128] The gymel appears as the 2 top parts of what is wrongly pr. as a piece *a 4* in DTO VII, 233; the opening rests should be omitted. (The piece *a 4* is made up of Ockeghem's gymel combined with Hert's setting *a 3* of *O rosa bella,* Dunstable's superius being common to both. Communication from Dr. Manfred Bukofzer.)

[129] Pr. GomO, Supp., 8; *see also* SmijA, 119. The piece may really consist of a superius "added to a pre-existing organism" *a 3;* cf. PlamJO, 36f.

[130] Pr. AmbG V, 10; MaldP XXI, 19 (with wrong ascription to Pierre de la Rue).

[131] Communication from Dr. Dragan Plamenac.

[132] By "middle part" is here meant the one which—however it is otherwise named and notwithstanding its brief crossing of the highest part—really lies at the middle. Actually the sources are inconsistent in their disposition of the 2 upper voices from the standpoint of notation: e.g., Capp. Giulia XIII 27 treats the middle part as tenor (information from Dr. Plamenac), while the Wolfenbüttel Chansonnier is among the sources that assign the tenor's position on the page to the highest part—the one that enters last. For the sake of simplicity, we shall, in all references to this piece, regard the highest part as the superius and the middle part as the tenor. The chanson

—a celebrated piece in its day—never crosses the lowest part (though it does cross the superius), while the middle part of *L'autre d'antan* [133] never crosses the superius (though it does cross the bass); on the other hand, the middle part occasionally crosses both outer parts in *D'ung aultre amer*.[134] Fauxbourdon-like passages occur here and there. Fourths, as essential harmonic intervals, however, are otherwise used sparingly between any two voices. Binary rhythm is far more common than ternary. *Fors seulement contre ce que ay promis* [135] (which, with a few changes, adopts the superius of *Fors seulement l'attente* as its lowest voice, adding two new parts), *Petite camusette,* and *Je n'ay dueil* have text in all parts, and completely vocal performance is implied; the other pieces seem primarily intended for one singer with instrumental support. Imitation appears occasionally, as in *Les desleaulx, Quand de vous seul, Ma bouche rit,*[136] and *Petite camusette.* It can hardly, however, be regarded as characteristic of Ockeghem.[137] Canon, on the other hand, he handled with such skill, on the rare occasions when he employed it, that his examples assume a prominence out of proportion to their number. *Prennez sur moi votre exemple amoureux* [138]—the well known *Fuga trium vocum in epidiatessaron* (canon in the fourth above, for three voices)—is celebrated because it is not only a good canon, but also an outstanding example of what Glareanus was to term *catholica.* These works were written in such a manner that they might be performed in any one of several modes. Although examples are rather rare, the concept of the *catholicon* was by no means new in Ockeghem's day, there being monophonic examples in as early a work as the 10th-century *Musica enchiriadis.*[139] A second *catholicon* of Ockeghem's will be more fully discussed presently. *Prennez sur moi* was a great favorite; it is even found reproduced in wooden inlay in the *grotta* of Isabella d'Este (cf. p. 157).[140] Theorists continued to reproduce the piece in their treatises, as late as 1590. Its fame, however, should not blind one to the fact that some less spectacular Ockeghem chansons are still finer works. Two of them, *Ma maistresse* [141] and *L'autre d'antan,* are referred to by Tinctoris; [141a] others include *Ma bouche rit* and, if it is his, the lovely *Malheur me bat.*[141b]

is pr. in DrozT, 48; GomO, Suppl., 12; GiesS, 2 (DrozT following the Dijon MS, GomO and GiesS following St. Gall, Stiftsbibl. 461, both of which MS sources have the highest part as tenor; GomO and GiesS, however, print the voices in the order of their pitch level).

[133] Pr. DrozT, 32; AmbG V, 12. (*See* comments in PlamM, 381f.)

[134] Pr. DrozT, 72; SmijO, 12; JosqMS II, 140; JepK, 52 (facsimile after Wolfenbüttel Chansonnier on p. xvii).

[135] Pr. GiesS, 4; GomO, Supp., 14. Held not to be genuine Ockeghem, *ibid.,* 18f (*see also* Gombosi in JAMS I, [1948] 49f), but accepted as genuine by Plamenac.

[136] Pr. DrozT, 16, 62, 9 (= HewO, 335; GomO, Supp., 6;.EDMR IV, 61; WolfME, 39; MfMG VI, Supp. No. 8).

[137] The claim made in RieH II¹, 125, that true pervading imitation begins with Ockeghem, is without convincing proof (but cf. p. 123).

[138] Pr. (with differences) in LeviO, 440; JepK, 62; DrozT, 1; etc.

[139] Cf. esp. LeviO, 464; ReMMA, 137, Ex. 28.

[140] *See* Pl. II in DrozT.   [141] Pr. OckW I, 124; HAM, 78.   [141a] CouS IV, 152, 156.

[141b] Pr. HewO, 353; GiesS, 60; JosqMS II, 66; ObrMS I, 189, 191. About the conflicting ascriptions, *see* HewO, 158. It should be added that Aron gives the piece to Ockeghem; cf. StrunkR, 214.

Although Ockeghem's predilection for imitation is less conspicuous than Busnois's, it is one of the factors making his chansons markedly more polyphonic than those of the Dufay–Binchois type. Every voice has a carefully worked out melodic interest of its own; a textless lower voice is never a mere filling-in part. Melodic considerations outweigh all others. The clear-cut phrase formation of the typical Dufay–Binchois chanson gives way to continuous flow: there is a preference for not having all the parts begin and end their phrases simultaneously; and the resulting overlapping subordinates not only the cadences but also such harmonic quality as their presence inevitably produces.[142]

While Ockeghem's powerful individuality found the framework of the chanson too small to permit his genius full scope and revealed itself most clearly in his Masses and motets, and while it must be admitted that in the secular field he is not the equal of Busnois, his chansons do include some of the important examples of the time and long remained in favor.

The lament a 4 on Binchois's death [143] carries on the tradition of the old bilingual motet: the superius has a French *ballade* text (*Mort tu as navré*) while the tenor employs Latin. At the close, it sings "*Pie Jhesu, Domine, dona ei requiem,*" thus slightly paraphrasing the ending of the *Dies irae* text. The Chant melody that sets these words is paraphrased also. The 13th-century *Dies irae* had not yet become a fixed portion of the Mass for the Dead (cf. p. 130), but missals of Arras (1491) and Tournai (1498) testify to its use in France (it was more widely sung, however, in its native land, Italy [143a]), and Ockeghem obviously applied this material with symbolical intent. The musical structure of this beautiful composition is governed by the *ballade* form of the French text. The style is rather old-fashioned, perhaps deliberately so in honor of the deceased.

The several Marian motets are of great musical interest. These include an *Alma Redemptoris Mater,* an *Ave Maria,* and two *Salve Regina* settings, all a 4, and an *Intemerata* and *Gaude Maria, a 5.* The *Alma* is in two *partes.* The second voice paraphrases the plainsong throughout, and touches of the plainsong are found also in the highest and lowest voices, especially the latter. These touches, however, do not always involve imitation; they are sometimes concerned with different paraphrases of the same melodic material. There is a long melisma in all voices on the penultimate syllable, and Ockeghem here obtains a delicate effect by assigning to the superius a new paraphrase of

---

142 For further discussion of Ockeghem's chansons, *see* GomO, 5ff, 17ff, 85f. For printed Ockeghem chansons not yet cited, *see* DrozT, 98; AmbG V, 16; also, for works differently ascribed in different MSS, GiesS, 54 (by Compère?); AmbG V, 14 (= MarM, 103) (probably by Hayne; cf. fn. 25).

143 Pr. MarM, 83; MoD, App., No. 3; ApelH, 392, wrongly ascribes to Ockeghem "the earliest example" of a polyphonic setting of the Lamentations of Jeremiah, perhaps through a misunderstanding of a statement in BrenV, 75, about lost laments by Ockeghem, Busnois, and Hémart, mentioned in 1475 in the accounts of Cambrai Cathedral, these works having probably been occasioned by Dufay's death the previous year.

143a Further concerning its origin, *see* p. 504 *infra*.

the opening plainsong notes. The voice bearing the complete plainsong has
the same rhythmic character as the other parts, as in normal paraphrase
motets, even though, since this voice is an inner one, it would have been more
in keeping with convention to employ longer values. Ockeghem's paraphrasing of the plainsong in this voice contrasts with Dufay's paraphrasing
of it in his superius (Ex. 21).

EXAMPLE 29: Opening of second voice of *Alma Redemptoris Mater*—
Ockeghem (complete piece in BesN, 5; *pars I* in BesV, 21).

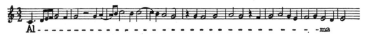

Whereas Dufay's paraphrase of the chant unfolds calmly and gently, Ockeghem's varies from a somewhat impetuous beginning to a broad, more even
treatment. Ockeghem does not add many more notes in the course of his
paraphrasing than does Dufay in his, but there is a greater change in the
character of the melody. Ockeghem obtains a climax at the close of each *pars;*
whereas long rests occur in the various voices in the earlier portions of each,
only short rests occur at the end of *pars I* and, at the end of *pars II,* all the
voices are piled on, entirely without rests. In addition, Ockeghem brings
the shorter values to the fore at these closes. His careful treatment of climax,
in the form of a drive to the cadence,[143b] is evident in other works also and is
a characteristic of his style.

The *Ave Maria* is not based on any known plainsong. It is typical of Ockeghem in that the voices overlap at most of the cadences. The voice having the
cantus prius factus, if one is present, is again rhythmically of the same general nature as the other parts. All four voices are kept busy throughout.[144]

The pre-existent melody [145] is treated in different ways in the two *Salve
Regina* motets: in one [146] the old melody is allotted to the bass and at times to
the superius and tenor; in the other, to the superius and at times to the two
other upper voices. In the first of these settings, which is in three *partes,* the
voice that has the plainsong is of the same free rhythmic character as the other
voices, but in the second setting the tenor—which, however, is not the principal, chant-bearing voice—is disposed in long notes, in old-fashioned style.
Ockeghem, never a perfunctory composer, is here seen attempting the unusual. In fact, he often gives the impression of deliberately seeking the unhackneyed, of wishing constantly to come to grips with new procedures and
problems.

[143b] The treatment of this feature in music of the period is discussed in ClementC.
[144] Further about this motet, *see* SteB, 61.
[145] Which, as pointed out in PlamJ, closely resembles a 15th-century version of the antiphon,
published by P. Wagner in the *Gregorianische Rundschau,* II (1907).
[146] Opening pr. BesM, 238.

The five-voice *Intemerata Dei Mater*,[147] in three *partes*, is not based on any known pre-existent material, but the tenor melody is treated like a *cantus firmus*, at least to the extent that its entrance is delayed while anticipatory imitation of it appears in the superius. Contrast of timbre is conspicuous, especially at the opening of *pars II*, where the three upper and three lower voices answer one another antiphonally (the middle voice serves in both groups). In all *partes* Ockeghem treats a little stepwise descending motif that has the rhythm ♩. ♫|♩, which is presented—sometimes in augmentation, sometimes in *stretto* (usually in two voices, but near the end in four)—against rhythmically varied, but simple, countermelodies. At the end of each *pars*, Ockeghem builds up a climax in much the same way as he does in the *Alma*. The bass lies quite low, at one point touching C.

The name of the composer of *Gaude Maria* is given as "Johannes Okegus" in the only source, which dates from 1538. Erasmus employs that name with reference to Ockeghem.[147a] The source, in which a *Coeleste beneficium* is similarly ascribed, consists of a set of part-books at Regensburg. Part-book notation, in which each voice has its own book, seems to have come into existence c. 1460, the earliest known example being apparently the *Glogauer Liederbuch*. But the old choir-book arrangement—which at first (beginning c. 1225 with the early motet) had all voices on one page, but not in score (i.e., with the upper parts written in columns, one beside the other, and with the tenor extending across the bottom of the page), and which later spread the voices, each as a separate unit, over facing pages—persisted until the mid-16th century, although the part-book arrangement had become increasingly popular.

The *Gaude Maria*, in three *partes*, is a responsory and has the same words and music at the ends of *partes I* and *III* (cf. Walter Frye's *Ave Regina*). It differs strikingly in style from the better known works that bear some form of Ockeghem's name, in that it consists almost entirely of a series of points of imitation. As a consequence the texture greatly resembles that of certain works by composers of the Josquin generation. However, it is the simple repetition pattern of the responsory rather than the chain of imitation-points that provides the basic structure of the piece. In the recurrent ending, the plainsong *cantus firmus*,[148] which is in the middle voice, permeates, through the use of imitation, the bass, alto, and superius. While, in this passage, the bass has the plainsong fragment, it is paired with the *vagans,* which has a rhythmically more active theme; when the tenor has the fragment, it is paired with the alto, which now has the rhythmically active theme. In other words, we here have imitation in pairs, another feature characteristic of the Josquin generation (cf. pp. 257f). In view of the lateness of the only source, there may be some doubt that the work is really Ockeghem's. But, since Ockeghem lived until c. 1495, at which time Josquin was a middle-aged man,

[147] Pr. SmijO, 3.　[147a] Cf. PirH, 102.　[148] For its current form, *see AntiphonaleM,* 1195.

it is quite possible that he was here adopting the style of the younger genera-tion. Moreover, it is difficult to imagine who else the highly gifted "Okegus" could have been. If the piece is actually by Ockeghem—a likelihood enhanced by the nature of the melodic lines, which alternately soar and surge in the typical Ockeghem manner—he underwent a development comparable to Verdi's.[149]

The *Motetti C,* printed by Petrucci in 1504, includes an anonymous four-part *Ut heremita solus,*[150] which is probably Ockeghem's, since Crétin mentions a motet of that name in connection with the composer (cf. p. 99). The tenor is notated as a complicated puzzle.[151] It moves in sustained values, while the other voices play about it in intricate arabesques.

Crétin mentions also a 36-part canon by Ockeghem. Virdung, in a letter dated 1504, describes a 36-part work by the master, and there are still other old references to the composition. It is possible that this is the same as the anonymous *Deo gratias*[151a] printed by Petreius in 1542 and by Neuber in 1568. But Virdung states that the piece consisted of six canons *a 6,* while the *Deo gratias* is made up of four canons *a 9.* Whoever wrote the *Deo gratias,* it is not free of monotony, continually repeating, as it does, the tonic and dominant of F major. Of the 36 voices, no more than 18 ever sound at one time.[152]

Ockeghem: Masses

Ockeghem's genius is shown even more clearly in his Masses than in his motets. He is one of the leading masters of the form, of which he is chrono-

---

[149] I am indebted to Dr. Plamenac for lending me his unpublished transcriptions of this motet, the *Ave Maria,* and the first *Salve Regina.* At what was undoubtedly the first modern rendition of the *Gaude Maria,* which took place in New York on April 30, 1949, Dr. Plamenac, who directed, provided most valuable prefatory comments of a historical and explanatory nature. Further about *Gaude Maria* and *Coeleste beneficium, see* PlamJ; SteB, 39ff, 107f.

[150] Pr. ScherG, 44.

[151] It is given twice, with an alto clef and with the time-signature O at the beginning. The signatures C and O each occur once in the later course of each presentation. The time-signatures divide the tenor (excluding the final note) into 3 equal segments (each containing 108 semi-breves, in the original notation, in presentation 1; 54 semibreves, in presentation 2); but this di-vision has no effect on the free flow of the other parts. (In ScherG, in which various time-signatures are freely applied by the editor, the divisions are: meas. 1–40, 41–75, 76–115; 116–135, 136–162, 163–186.) The remaining symbols on the staff are all two- or three-letter syllables and notes. These notes all lie within the *hexachordum durum.* In the first presentation they are longs; in the second, breves. Three obscure verbal canons provide the keys to the riddle. Every letter in each syllable is to be replaced, according to the demands of the time-signature, by a perfect or imperfect *longa*-rest in the first presentation, by a perfect or imperfect breve-rest in the second presentation. Each note is to be given two companions, where possible. These are normally to consist of the degree above the note and the fourth above that. If the rise of a fourth takes the melody out of the *hexachordum durum,* a descent of a fifth is to be substituted. Where an augmented fourth, or diminished fifth would result (either through a direct leap or with an intervening note), the second note is omitted. This gives the whole melody. The syllables com-bined with those derived from the notes (*ut, re,* etc.) provide a line of Latin text which, however, is apparently not intended to be sung to the music. Cf. ScherR.

[151a] Pr. RieH II[1], 239.

[152] Further on this work, *see* PlamA; FeinK, 45ff; BorQS, 220ff.

logically the greatest exponent after Dufay. It has sometimes been held [153] that a composer's motets reveal his individual style more effectively than do his Masses, since he is free to choose his motet texts, while the text of the Ordinary is fixed. This conclusion is undoubtedly correct with regard to some composers—for example, Lassus. But it is just as true that certain other composers are both at their best and at their most characteristic in their Masses; and, like Obrecht and Palestrina, Ockeghem is of their number.

Among the sources preserving Ockeghem's Masses, Chigi MS C. VIII. 234 at the Vatican is of special interest. Its thirty-nine compositions include no less than thirteen of his works in this form, besides two of his motets. The MS is a magnificent one, decorated by fine miniatures and fantastic pictures in the borders.[153a]

As might be expected of so inquiring a mind, Ockeghem sets the Mass in a number of ways, some of them new. That he could handle the standard *cantus-firmus* technique with distinction is shown by such works as his four-part *Missa L'Homme armé* and *Missa Caput*. He treats the famous *cantus firmus* of the former [154] in straightforward manner, without embellishment other than the appendages, two being rather elaborate, that are affixed to most presentations. The manner in which this melody is notated [154a] by the master provides some evidence that his *L'Homme armé* Mass may be older than Dufay's (cf. p. 72). The *cantus firmus* (given once in the Kyrie, twice in the Gloria, twice complete and once without its *da capo* section in the Credo, once in the Sanctus, but with interruptions during the *Pleni* and Benedictus, and once in the Agnus, but with an interruption during Agnus II) is entrusted to the tenor throughout; in the Credo and Agnus, however, this part lies below the bass. In these movements as elsewhere, the tenor is notated in the Mixolydian mode, but in the Credo a verbal canon indicates that the melody is to be sung a fifth lower, it thus being placed in the Ionian mode (since B remains natural), while in the Agnus a verbal canon calls for a transposition to the octave below; here a flat is added in the signature, so that the mode becomes Dorian transposed. Except for the descending leap of a fifth, which is imitated twice in the Credo—all the voices taking part in one instance—the *cantus firmus* does not permeate the other voices. Imitation not

[153] E.g., in SmijA, 111.

[153a] A description of the miniatures, with 2 facsimiles, is contained in J. Ladmirant, "Trois manuscrits à miniatures de l'Ecole flamande conservés à la Bibliothèque Vaticane" in *Bulletin de l'Institut historique belge de Rome*, XVII (1936), 69. *See also* MGG II, 1190ff.

[154] Pr. OckW I, 99 (facsimiles of Kyrie and *Et resurrexit*, after Vat. Chigi MS C. VIII, 234, *ibid.*, Pls. III, IV) and MPLSER, *Ser. I*, I, No. 6. The latter follows a MS—Capp. Sist. 35—that was intended for use by the Papal Choir and therefore manipulates the Credo so as to introduce, before the *Et incarnatus est,* a break that provides for the kneeling down of the curia, a break not present in the former, which follows the Chigi MS, presumably giving the original version intended for use elsewhere (cf. the pref. to MPLSER, *Ser. I*, I). So far as general practice is concerned, the "genuflexions now indicated at such words as 'Et incarnatus est,' 'Et Verbum caro factum est,' and the like, are . . . of comparatively recent introduction" (CE, VI, 426f).

[154a] Involving the *error Anglorum; see* DufayO III, vi.

involving the tenor appears only slightly oftener and then merely *a 2*. An f″-flat (cf. p. 89) is twice written out in the superius. Interest in contrast of timbre is notable in Agnus III, where various two-part combinations appear before all four voices join for the close. Climaxes are achieved by increased motion at the ends of sections and subsections.

The *Missa Caput* [155] has the same *cantus firmus* as Dufay's similarly named Mass. Except in its Kyrie, Ockeghem's work, like Dufay's, divides each of its main sections into one segment in ternary rhythm and one in binary. The metric scheme in the Kyrie is: Kyrie I, ternary; *Christe,* binary; Kyrie II, ternary. The Kyrie is given special treatment in other ways also: whereas each of the remaining movements begins with a fairly long upper-voice duo in Dufay style—the duo incorporating a head-motif—this opening movement has the four voices enter almost simultaneously, and the head-motif is absent; moreover, whereas each of the other movements presents the *cantus firmus* twice (as in Dufay's Mass), the Kyrie presents it but once. The Credo is notable for some instances of simultaneous singing of different portions of the text ("telescoping"), apparently to achieve brevity.[156] Ockeghem's *cantus firmus* does not permeate the other voices to any greater extent than does Dufay's, but the upper voices of his work are somewhat more richly decorated than are those of the older master's, though they have less amplitude than characterizes the lines in most of Ockeghem's other Masses. The superius, in particular, seems to have a somewhat English quality. Whereas Dufay places the *cantus firmus* within the polyphonic texture, Ockeghem assigns it to the lowest part. The *cantus firmus,* after a fairly extended rest, ends each major section and some subsections with a single utterance or a once-repeated utterance of the *finalis;* while conclusions of this sort are not rare at this period, their systematic use as a unifying device, as in this Mass, is unusual. Ockeghem's predilection for approaching the cadence with increased motion and with dotted figures is particularly evident at the end of this work.[156a]

The five-part *Missa Fors seulement* [157]—a powerful work consisting of only a Kyrie, Gloria, and Credo—employs a different, though related, technique. Ockeghem presents as *cantus firmus* mainly the superius of his *rondeau, Fors seulement l'attente,* but also, on occasion, its tenor. (Perhaps the fact that Ockeghem used the highest part of his chanson as the tenor of his Mass is responsible for the designation of the former voice as the tenor in some chansonniers. However this may be, it *is* the pre-existent highest part that serves as the tenor of the *Fors seulement* Mass. Basing a Mass on such a part soon becomes less extraordinary; cf. p. 199.) In the Kyrie only the old superius is borrowed for *cantus-firmus* purposes, its part I (up

[155] Pr. OckW II, 37; DTO XIX¹, 59 (complete facsimile after Trent 88, *ibid.,* 49).
[156] Cf. ReMMA, 421; also p. 41 *supra.*
[156a] *See* further BorQS, 196ff.
[157] Pr. OckW II, 65 (facsimile of Kyrie, *ibid.,* Pl. XI).

to meas. 41 of the chanson) appearing in the tenor of the Kyrie I and *Christe* —with a brief interpolation in the *Christe*—and part II in the contratenor of Kyrie II. However, the first phrase of the chanson tenor appears at the very opening of the Kyrie, though not as *cantus-firmus* material, being sung in imitation by the contratenor and superius; the contratenor then paraphrases the beginning of phrase 2 of the superius, before proceeding freely. The chanson contratenor is also quoted, though briefly, its measures 1–7 being presented by measures 1–7 of the Kyrie bass I, its measures 28–30 appearing in measures 30–32 of the Kyrie tenor and constituting the interpolation referred to above. In the Gloria, *Fors seulement* material, this time derived only from the superius and tenor, is again worked into the free polyphony as well as being transformed into a *cantus firmus* for the tenor. The material is distributed among all five voices of the Mass, as illustrated in Table IV.

Table IV

Material from the chanson	Places where applied in Gloria
Measure 1–10 tenor	Measure 1–7 (with insertion) contratenor
10–17 superius	1–6 *vagans*
1–4 superius (= 1–4 tenor)	7–9 superius
1–10 tenor	9–15 superius
18–22 superius	15–18 bass
21–41 superius	25–39 (with insertion) tenor
30 (note 2)–41 tenor	45–53 tenor
42–54 tenor	63–76 tenor
49–54 tenor	68–73 contratenor
53–65 superius	77–101 (with 12 inserted meas. of rest) tenor
59–60 tenor	83–84 contratenor
55–59 tenor	97–99 superius
61–end superius	106–124 (repetition in meas. 119–123) tenor
67–end superius	113–122 (repetition in meas. 117–121) contratenor
60–end tenor	125–136 *vagans*

In the Credo, the chanson tenor and superius are once more both drawn upon to produce the *cantus firmus,* but this time the result is all entrusted to one voice—the higher of the two tenors (Table V). The other Mass movements each have but one tenor; although all three movements are *a 5,* the voice designation is not entirely the same for any two.

Table V

Material from the chanson	Places where applied in Credo
Measure 10–70 superius	Measure 1–68 tenor I
49–61 tenor	101–117 tenor I
49–61 tenor	134–155 tenor I
61–end superius	189–end tenor I

In this movement, the voices other than the tenor I yield only fleeting reminders of the chanson. Throughout the composition, the *cantus firmus* is seldom subjected to variation, and, to this extent, the work is a traditional *cantus-firmus* Mass. The transference of the *cantus firmus* from one voice to another in the Kyrie is likewise nothing new. But the composition is venturesome in its employment, in the *cantus firmus,* of material from more than one voice of the chanson; and also (however slight this may be) in its simultaneous use, in two voices of the Mass, of material from two voices of the chanson. Here again, as in the *Missa Le serviteur* and *Missa Teribilment* the reworking of more than one part anticipates the later parody Mass.[158] Ockeghem employs a rather large amount of imitation (particularly in the Credo), so that the work is probably a late one; the imitation, however, has no effect on the basic structure of the composition. This Mass is a striking study in the lower ranges: at least three voices always lie in the tenor compass or lower, and even the superius frequently goes below c′ and descends to g. Differently constituted voice groups provide contrast. In the Gloria, a group made up of the three lowest voices underlines the text at "*miserere nobis, qui tollis peccata mundi . . . ,*" the setting of these words being soon followed, appropriately enough, by the return of the higher voices at "*Tu solus altissimus.*"

A still different application of the *cantus-firmus* technique is illustrated by the four-part *Missa De plus en plus* and *Missa Au travail suis,* which treat the pre-existent material with the greatest liberty. The tenor of the former Mass [159] derives from that of Binchois's lovely *rondeau cinquain.* The borrowed material is paraphrased throughout and is never presented twice in quite the same form. The whole tenor appears once each in the Kyrie, Gloria, and Credo, with a return at each close of as much music as accompanies line 1 in the chanson. The melody is more highly elaborated in the Kyrie than at any other point in the Mass. In the Sanctus the tenor presents the tenor of section 1 of the *rondeau, tacet* during the *Pleni,* sings the tenor of section 2 of the *rondeau* during the *Osanna,* engages in a free duo with the superius on the word "*Benedictus,*" and then *tacet* until the repetition of the *Osanna.*

[158] But it does not quite make the *Missa Fors seulement* a parody Mass, as sometimes claimed.
[159] Pr. OckW I, 57.

Agnus I (= III) twice presents the tenor of *rondeau* section 1 before pro-
ceding with the rest; Agnus II is built on the tenor of *rondeau* section 2
(minus the first note); both Agnus settings end with a return of the music
for line 1. The tenor permeates the other parts very seldom. Imitation is absent, but snatches of canon appear in the Gloria—at *Tu solus altissimus,* where
the canon, slightly free, is at the lower seventh—, in the Sanctus, and in Agnus
I. The Gloria, Credo, Sanctus, and Agnus II open with upper-voice duos
in Dufay fashion. Each of these, except the duo in Agnus II, reaches a full
fermata-marked cadence before the lower voices enter. All four voices open
the Kyrie and Agnus I simultaneously. Different voice-groupings provide
contrast of timbre. A fifth voice appears momentarily at the end of the Kyrie,
but not even here is the third from the root present in a movement-ending
chord, though it does appear at the end of Kyrie I. Ockeghem takes advantage
of the full range of all voices by writing long, sweeping scale passages, occasionally allowing them to cross, although he generally keeps them clear of
one another. There is the typical impetus at section endings.

The tenor of the Kyrie of the *Missa Au travail suis* [160] presents, with slight
changes, the tenor of the similarly named Barbingant [160a] *rondeau,* the superius of which, as we have seen, had itself quoted the opening of Ockeghem's
Ma maistresse. In the four other major sections of the Mass, the first ten notes
of the tenor are derived from Barbingant, but the rest of this voice is freely
invented. At the opening of most of the sections, as at that of the chanson,
the tenor permeates the other voices. Imitation—some of it, however, quite
fragmentary—appears in all five sections, but only at the beginning of the
Kyrie do all voices take part; moreover, Ockeghem, when using imitation,
takes liberties with his motifs for harmonic reasons. Brief passages in canon
occur at several points. Whereas the chanson is in ternary rhythm, the Mass
is entirely in binary rhythm, except in the last 14 measures, where—and this
is typical of Ockeghem's tendency to do the unexpected—no borrowed material appears. The third is included in the final chord not only of several subsections but also of several major sections; at four cadences, the final chord has
an extra voice. Contrast of textures is notable in this Mass: there is an almost
regular alternation of passages *a 2* and passages for all four voices (writing *a 3*
is uncommon). Ockeghem, who sometimes seems to delight in going counter
not only to established practice, but also to what are plainly his own underlying style characteristics, breaks up the cantus into several segments (each
ending with a full close), in a manner frequently found in Josquin. While
this Mass contains some passages in thirds or tenths, the painstaking craftsman Ockeghem does not use them to excess. The four voices lie in fairly well-
differentiated strata, so far as range is concerned, but there is some crossing
even at cadences. The cadence of Agnus II lies exceptionally low, the superius

[160] *Ibid.,* I, 30.   [160a] But cf. fn. 107 about conflicting ascription.

itself ending on as low a note as *a*. Except for the Credo, the sections are quite short.

They are not so short, however, as those of Ockeghem's five-part *Missa sine nomine* (consisting of only a Kyrie, Gloria, and Credo).[161] Here again, then, Ockeghem does something unusual for his time (but cf. p. 765). The work is, for all practical purposes, a *Missa brevis* of the type that became much favored in a later day. The Gloria, based on the melody of plainsong Gloria XV, employs the paraphrase rather than the *cantus-firmus* technique. The tenor may have a variant of Kyrie XVI in the first section; in the last section, it has a quotation from Credo I in the form of an intonation on *"Patrem omnipotentem,"* but for the most part it "perseveres" in this movement "in a monotonous but metered psalmody." [162]

Ockeghem's *Requiem*,[163] which applies the paraphrase technique almost throughout, is the oldest polyphonic *Missa pro defunctis* extant, Dufay's being lost (cf. p. 76). Before the Council of Trent (cf. pp. 448f), the liturgical form of the Mass for the Dead differed from present practice, being, in fact, subject to variation from one locality to another. In France, the *Dies irae* did not become an established portion of the Requiem Mass until the mid-16th century; among the Franco-Netherlanders, the *Si ambulem* (with the response *Virga tua*) and the *Sicut cervus* [164] were used in place of the present-day Gradual and Tract. Polyphonic Requiems were almost never complete in the Renaissance. Ockeghem's setting ends with the Offertory, and (the MS preserving the work being a good one) it appears that this may be all that was written and that the last four movements were to be sung in plainsong. All known Renaissance Requiems apply paraphrase or *cantus-firmus* treatment to the chant.[165] But there is no uniformity in them with regard to either the number of Gregorian intonations used or the voices to which they are assigned. Where Ockeghem introduces intonations, however, he places them in the superius. His setting reveals many ingenious traits. In the plainsong Kyrie, the first eight invocations all employ the same melody; the first half of the last invocation has new music, but the rest is sung to the same material as served for the second half of each earlier invocation. Ockeghem varies his setting to produce *a a′ a a″ a‴ a″ a″″ a″″″ b* form (the second half of *b* treating its chant fragment differently from the several ways in which that fragment is handled when appearing in the concluding portions of the various *a*'s). Invocation 1 is set *a 3*, and settings *a 2* and *a 3* alternate for the remaining invocations, except that a fourth voice is added for the second half of the last one, showing yet

161 *Ibid.,* II, 77.   162 Cf. *ibid.,* xxxi.

163 Pr. OckW II, 83 (facsimiles of 3 passages, *ibid.,* Pls. XII–XIV).

164 I.e., portions of Psalms XXII (XXIII) and XLI (XLII). About the various forms of the pre-Tridentine Requiem, etc., *see* WagG, 16ff, 56. *See also* FoxR.

165 Cf. Liber, 1807ff. For the melodies of the *Si ambulem* and *Sicut cervus,* see Graduale, 126, 212 (= Liber, 753).

another means whereby Ockeghem seeks to obtain an impressive final cadence. Throughout this work, he sets successive movements and subsections contrastingly. The Offertory is divided into four subsections, differing not only in style and number of voices but also in time-signature; this is the only portion of the composition in which the chant occurs in a voice other than the superius. The paraphrasing of the Chant melodies varies from simple to quite ornate, but always changes their character. There is little canon in this work and practically no imitation. The melodic writing is more restrained than is usual in Ockeghem Masses, except in the duos, where there are long arabesques, and the Offertory, where it is sometimes very elaborate. The bassus, though it does not descend below G, lies in the bass range; the tenor is often nearly as low, and the other two voices are by no means high. There are a long passage *a 3* lying below c' and a duo with both voices in bass range, the texts of both passages dealing with the infernal regions; word-painting occurs elsewhere also.[166]

The four-part Masses *Mi-Mi, Cuiusvis toni,* and *Prolationum* appear to be freely composed—"appear to be," since, 15th-century technique being complex and full of surprises, there is always the possibility that pre-existent material may lurk behind a paraphrase that obscures it beyond recognition.[166a] Each work is remarkable in a different way. The first [167] (called *Missa Quarti toni* in one source [168]) is a full-length Mass, written not only without an identified, basic *cantus prius factus* but also, unlike the other two works, without a specific technical purpose. In its use of evidently free writing, the composition is not unique among Ockeghem's Masses, but it is a particularly felicitous example.[169] On the words *"Patrem omnipotentem,"* the superius momentarily quotes Credo V (or I?), and the bass opens the Benedictus with a possibly fortuitous quotation of Kyrie XI,[170] but neither passage has structural significance. The name, *Missa Mi-Mi,* derives from the descent from e to A in the bass at the beginning of each major section (also at the openings of Agnus II and III and, decorated, at that of the Benedictus), these notes being *mi* in the natural and soft hexachords respectively; Kyrie II opens with the same leap in the tenor. At various phrase endings, including the last, the leap occurs in reverse for cadential purposes. It is slightly possible that this *Mi-Mi* motif derives from *Petite camusette,*[171] but if it does it still has no significant effect on the free character of the writing, owing to its brevity and its few appearances. The work lays no great stress on imitation, symmetry,

[166] Cf. OckW II, xxxiii.   [166a] Cf. BorQS, 183.

[167] Pr. OckW II, I (facsimile of Kyrie, after Vat. Chigi MS C. VIII. 234, *ibid.,* Pl. I); CW IV.

[168] Hence the listing of this title as that of a separate work in BrenV, 68; cf. OckW II, xvi.

[169] Other examples are provided by the three-part *Missa Quinti toni* and *Missa sine nomine,* pr. in OckW I, 1 and 15, respectively (facsimile of Kyrie of latter, *ibid.,* Pl. I); for discussion, *see* PirH, 106f; BorQS, 183ff.

[170] Cf. PirH, 110.

[171] Cf. RoediN, 44f, 8of. On its resemblance to the later *Aus tiefer Not, see* BesE, 151f.

or contrast, though it is not without them; external means of giving shape to the composition are secondary. "The centre of gravity lies throughout in music-making itself."[172] The individual melodic lines are ample, intense, quasi-improvisational. A noteworthy relation between text and music may be found at *"mortuorum"* in the Credo. Here there is an early example of what historians have called *Augenmusik* (eye-music)—a kind of writing, destined to become popular with the Italian madrigalists, whereby a composer, addressing himself to the performer rather than to the listener, describes the text he is setting by means of the notation he employs: Ockeghem applies black notation to the word in question.[173] There is little crossing of parts in this work, and none at cadences, save for the end of the first subsection of the Credo. The last cadence note is frequently delayed or repeated, a practice often followed also by Josquin. The lower ranges are much explored. Chordal writing is employed sparingly, but to good effect. The use of chains of thirds and tenths is strikingly rare. Impetus is created toward the close of sections and subsections, where Ockeghem delights in dotted rhythms. The sweeping melismas at these points are highly impressive.

EXAMPLE 30. *Missa Mi-Mi*—Subsection close before the *Et incarnatus*—Ockeghem (after OckW II, 9; CW IV, 14).

---

[172] CW IV, 3.   [173] Cf. OckW II, xvii.

This Mass shows Ockeghem, the supreme technician of his generation, producing one of his finest works without recourse to the devices of musical ratiocination.[174]

The name of the *Missa Cuiusvis toni* [175] implies that the work was designed for performance in any mode—i.e., that it is an extended *catholicon*. Since in each authentic mode and its corresponding plagal the collocation of tones and semitones is similar with relation to the *finalis,* and since the *tessitura* of each of Ockeghem's four voices remains fixed, "any mode" can mean no more than "any of the four *maneriae*." [175a] The music is written out but once, the change of mode being effected by changes of clef and key-signature on the part of the singers. Ockeghem himself supplies, in lieu of these elements of notation, only a circle with a question-mark to indicate the line or space where the *finalis* appears.[176] The composition, which may have been written to test choir-singers' knowledge of the modes,[177] is not only a technical tour de force, but also a work of genuine artistry, though slightly rigid in comparison with that other tour de force, the *Missa Prolationum. Cuiusvis toni* is unified by the opening motif of the superius, which is not restricted to head-motif use but recurs frequently in varied form throughout the Mass, always in the same voice except for brief appearances in the contratenor and tenor in Kyrie I. The opening theme of the contratenor is treated somewhat similarly, though less extensively.

The *Missa Prolationum* [178] is not only without a *cantus firmus* but also without a head-motif, though the function of such a motif is partly filled by the presence, at the opening of most sections, of a slowly moving, variously broken F-major or A-minor triad; unity of style is obtained by the use of canon throughout. The Kyrie I, *Christe,* Kyrie II, Gloria, Credo, Sanctus, *Pleni,* and *Osanna,* i.e., the sections leading up to the liturgical climax achieved by the elevation of the host, progress, section by section, from mostly double canon at the unison, at the second, at the third, etc., to double canon at the octave. The resulting canon cycle foreshadows such later cycles as appear in certain Palestrina Masses (cf. pp. 479f) and in Bach's "Goldberg" Variations, and is the first example of its kind. (Simply as a canon Mass, however, it may have to yield precedence to Faugues's *Missa L'Homme armé.*) After the *Osanna,* Ockeghem continues to apply double canon: in his Agnus I, at the fourth; in his Agnus II and III, at the fifth. The Mass takes its name from the four prolations of Philippe de Vitri (cf. pp. 19f). Each voice is in a different prolation, and some section-openings, like the one incorporated in Example

[174] Further about this Mass, *see* BreidS, 88ff; BorQS, 195f; PirH, 109f.
[175] Pr. OckW I, 44. There are various reprints of isolated sections.
[175a] Cf. ReMMA, 153.
[176] Further on the notation of this Mass, *see* esp. LeviO, 454ff. *See also* BorQS, 190ff.
[177] Cf. AmbG III, 178.
[178] Pr. OckW II, 21; complete facsimile, *ibid.,* Pl. II–IX.

31, and for similar reasons, produce canon in irregular augmentation. The double canons consist of one canon between the two upper voices, both employing minor prolation, and another between the two lower voices, both employing major prolation. In each pair, the time is perfect in one voice, imperfect in the other. Thus, where normally written longs, breves, and isolated semibreve pairs occur in a context of ordinary longs and breves, the voice in perfect time moves in irregular augmentation in relation to its companion in imperfect time. But in a passage with only short notes—minims and blackened longs, breves, and semibreves [179]—the voice in perfect time moves at the same speed as the one in imperfect time. With this in mind, Ockeghem uses two main devices: (1) In Kyries I and II, Gloria, Credo, and *Osanna,* all voices begin simultaneously in long notes. The voices in imperfect time gain on those in perfect, and the resulting double mensuration canons are in irregular augmentation. When the two *dux* voices are far enough ahead of the two *comes* voices to produce the distance that Ockeghem wants, only short and blackened notes are used, and the rest of the section is in ordinary double canon. (2) In the *Qui tollis, Et resurrexit,* Sanctus, and Agnus I and II, the *comites* begin with a series of rests in long values. Sometimes the rests are of equal denomination but, the prolations being different, the *comes* in imperfect time gains on the one in perfect time, and enters sooner. Sometimes the denominations are just dissimilar enough to counteract the effect of the different prolations and to permit the part that moves faster (in rests) to enter with the one that moves more slowly. But the notes of all these voices are short or blackened, so that the canons are entirely ordinary ones. The only portions of these sections that are in irregular augmentation are, strangely enough, the ones in which the singers count rests before entering. (Perhaps Ockeghem wrote this Mass for his own choristers, as a test piece in measuring notes and rests in the four prolations.) The passages in rests are in augmentation on paper, in theory, and for the performers, but not, of course, in actual sound. It remains to be said that the *Pleni* is a normal single canon *a 2,* the Agnus II a normal augmentation canon *a 2,* and the *Christe* and Benedictus normal canons in which one pair of voices alternates with the other. These sections are the only ones employing fewer than all four prolations, one prolation being used in the *Christe* and two in the others. Only the *dux* voices of this Mass are notated, the others are to be derived from them. The intervals of the various canons are indicated in the MS in three ways: (1) Since every melody is to be sung in two prolations, except in the *Christe,* two time-signatures appear in each given part at the opening of each other section or subsection, these signatures being so placed on the staff as to show the

---

[179] Basically the blackening of a note reduces its value by one-third; for details, *see* ApelN, 126ff. The blackening of the notes that set *"mortuorum"* in the *Missa Mi-Mi* is abnormal; its purpose is purely symbolic, and the rhythm is unaffected. (This does not mean, however, that the symbolism of *Augenmusik* is always unaccompanied by rhythmic change.)

interval desired. (2) Two clefs are vertically aligned to indicate the interval, where it is possible to place both on lines (i.e., in the canons at the third, fifth, and seventh), this method being supplementary to the first. (3) Verbal directions are given, these, however, being useful only in connection with the *Christe,* in view of the employment of the other methods also. This Mass is a tour de force of ingenuity, but it would be a great mistake to regard it as nothing more. The complexities of notation and composition are "not detrimental to the work's purely musical qualities" and this fact "is in itself proof of the author's high mastery." [180]

EXAMPLE 31. *Missa Prolationum—Kyrie I—*Ockeghem (after OckW II, 21).

Probably no major composer has been more misrepresented by popular histories than Ockeghem. Far from being the pedant sometimes depicted, he reveals a romantic vitality, a love for the experimental, the unexpected, the irregular, that stamp him as a composer of marked originality. At the same time, he possesses "a quality of mildness and gentleness in his feeling and in his mode of expression" and "melodic grace." [181] When he uses involved techniques—not, be it noted, on frequent occasions—he contrives, as in the *Missa Prolationum,* to produce music of artistic excellence, aside from the ingenuity displayed. His occasional discarding of pre-existent material evinces the forcefulness of his creative urge, as his approach to the parody technique in the *Missa Fors seulement* indicates his sensitiveness to tendencies foreshadowing the future. If he was not the first composer to employ pervading imitation for structural purposes, as Riemann once thought, *Gaude Maria*

[180] D. Plamenac in OckW II, xxi. Further on this Mass, *see* BreidS, 95ff.
[181] Otto Kinkeldey in *Speculum,* XXIII (1948), 725. (KrenekO appeared from the press too late to be taken into account in the above discussions.)

at least shows him applying that device expertly and keeping abreast of newer trends in still another way. While polyphonic overlapping was certainly nothing novel, his liking for it established a "seamless" texture as one of the traits most favored during the rest of the Renaissance wherever Franco-Netherlandish influence was strong.

Some Minor Composers

Brussels MS 5557 credits Ockeghem with a Mass based on the anonymous *rondeau, Pour quelque paine,* but the attribution is in a hand much later than that which penned the music. Moreover, the work reappears in Cappella Sistina MS 51 (which dates from 1471 to 1484) credited to Cornelius Heyns.[182] Otherwise unknown, Heyns seems on the basis of this Mass to have been a skilful composer. In some respects the *cantus-firmus* treatment differs from that found in Ockeghem's known Masses: the melody is presented not only in augmentation, in a few sections, but in augmentation combined with inversion in the Sanctus and in cancrizans motion in the Agnus I.

The composers of the seventeen Masses, separate Gloria, and six separate Credos in Cappella Sistina MS 51 include (besides Heyns), Busnois, Caron, Faugues, Basiron, Vaqueras, Vincenet, and others.[183] Bertrandus (or Bernardus) Vaqueras was among the singers in the Papal Chapel from 1483 to 1507 and is probably identical with the Bertrandus who had sung at St. Peter's in 1481–1482.[184] Glareanus included, in the *Dodecachordon, partes I* and *II* of Vaqueras' three-*pars* motet, *Domine non secundum,* which paraphrases the plainsong for the Tract for Ash Wednesday.[185] Vaqueras is one of the many composers of *L'Homme armé* Masses. His setting [186] is *a 5,* the *cantus firmus* being presented in canon *a 2.* The governing mode continues to be Dorian transposed, even though the nature of the canon changes from one movement to the next. The canon is at the fifth (from g) in the Kyrie, at the fourth (from d) in the Gloria, at the fifth (from c) in the Credo, and at the second (from g and f respectively) in the Sanctus and Agnus. In the Kyrie, the note-values of the *comes* are double those of the *dux,* some of the melody, however, being omitted in the *comes* as a result. The mensural relationship is equal in the other movements. The canon is tri-sectional in the Gloria and Credo, the lower voice being the first to serve as *dux,* then the upper voice, then the lower again. The *cantus firmus* appears no oftener than once in each movement, this being made possible by the long passages during which it rests. Vincenet's works include four pieces in the Mellon MS, one being the *rondeau cinquain, Ou doys je secours,* in which strain 5 reintroduces, in slightly varied

---

[182] Cf. OckW II, xxxiv; PlamJO, 34ff. For the Mass and chanson, *see* OckW II, 98, 116. Extracts are printed under Ockeghem's name in RieH II¹, 231–34; RieM, 23.
[183] Cf. HabV, 21.   [184] Cf. HabR, 54ff; EitQ X, 18f.
[185] For the plainsong, *see* Liber, 527; for the motet, PubAPTM XVI, 189.
[186] Pr. MPLSER, *Ser. I,* I, No. 10.

form, the melodic material of strain 1. Of the remaining three numbers, one has a Spanish text, one is a *rondeau* with an Italian text (cf. p. 30), and the other is *Fortune par ta cruaulté*,[187] which survives in as many as twelve sources. This is one of the innumerable Renaissance pieces dealing with the goddess Fortuna and her inconstancy.[188]

The goddess is presented with her characteristic attribute, the wheel, in the *rondeau, Au hault de la roue de fortune*,[189] by Jean Cornuel, also known as Verjust (d. 1499). His active career led him to St. Peter's, Milan, Cologne, and Hungary, but unfolded mainly at Cambrai. Somewhat of a poet, Cornuel, like Busnois, exchanged verses with Molinet.[190] The latter (b. 1435, d. 1507) had ample opportunity, as Burgundian court poet, to become acquainted with the chief musicians of the day. As has been shown by the various references that have been made to his verse, he knew a number of them, and many of their works, intimately. He may even have dabbled in composition himself: the *rondeau, Tart ara mon cueur*, is ascribed to "Molinet" in two sources.[191] Crétin's *Déploration* contains an exhortation to Molinet, which was apparently heeded, to mourn for Ockeghem in poetry. Besides representing certain composers as already in the afterworld and as welcoming their famous confrere, Crétin calls also upon several surviving musicians, telling them to write a *Ne recorderis,*

Pour lamenter nostre maistre et bon pere. . . .	*And thus lament our master and good father. . . .*
La perte est grande et digne a recorder.	*The loss is great and should be chronicled.*

"Verjust," who survived Ockeghem but briefly, is among the minor figures addressed, as is Jehan Fresneau; [192] the prominent composers of the younger generation include Agricola, Verbonnet (= Ghiselin; cf. p. 266), Prioris, Josquin, Gaspar (= Weerbecke), Brumel, and Compère. Since the *Déploration* refers to Ockeghem as *"nostre maistre,"* historians sometimes regard these younger men as his pupils, but it is obviously dangerous to base conclusions on such feeble evidence.[192a]

Tinctoris

The generation of Busnois and Ockeghem boasted a third figure of prominence, the theorist, Johannes Tinctoris (c. 1435–1511), whose authority has

---

[187] Pr. EDMR IV, 68; HewO, 347.

[188] On this subject, *see* LowG. Several technical features of *Ou doy* show that Vincenet can hardly be identical (as is claimed in EitQ X, 91) with the Johannes Vincenot who entered the Papal Chapel in 1426 and was still there on Dufay's arrival (cf. HabD, 59f). *See* further, BukU, 21f.

[189] Pr. DrozN, 187.   [190] Further about Cornuel, *see* DrozN, PirJC.

[191] It may, however, be by a slightly later homonym; cf. JepK, xxxivf. For the piece, *see ibid.*, 12; DrozP, 60; DTO XIV¹, 197. Regarding Molinet's relations with music, *see* esp. BrenPM. About music in his *Chroniques*, see LdnM.

[192] About him, *see* BrenV, 39, 42; EitQ IV, 75.   [192a] Cf. SteB, 7, fn. 11.

already been cited several times.[193] His reputation for learning prompted Trithemius to admit him—the only full-fledged musician—into the *Cathalogus illustrium virorum Germaniae . . .* (fol. 73ᵛ), 1495. (It is worth noting that Trithemius includes the Low Countries under the term *"Germania";* cf. pp. 207, 212.) Abbot at Sponheim, in the Rhine region, Trithemius was a leading German humanist. Broad knowledge together with an interest in occultism earned him, as it did his contemporary, Dr. Faustus, a reputation as a sorcerer. The biography reads:

Johannes Tinctoris of Brabant, born in the city of Nivelles [near Brussels] and canon of the church of that city, doctor of both laws [canon and civil], formerly archicapellanus *and* cantor *of King Ferrante of Naples, a man very learned in all respects, an outstanding mathematician, a musician of the highest rank, of a keen mind, skilled in eloquence, has written and is writing many remarkable works, through which he makes himself both useful to his contemporaries and worthy of memory to posterity. Among them I have only found, regarding music, three books on the art of counterpoint; likewise one book on the Tones; and one book on the origin of music. He has written many remarkable letters to various personages. He has drawn up a table in which he has included all the most ancient musicians and has called Jesus Christ the greatest singer. He is still living in Italy, writing various works, being about sixty years old. Written under King Maximilian, in the year of our Lord 1495.*[194]

Although Tinctoris, according to this notice, was a canon at Nivelles, this, of course, did not prevent his residing in Italy.

The registers of Cambrai Cathedral for 1460 show a Johannes Tinctoris to have been connected with its musical organization.[195] If, as is likely, this is the theorist, he and Dufay (then in charge of the choirboys there) undoubtedly met. According to his own report, Tinctoris at one time—evidently before his Neapolitan period—taught the choirboys at Chartres. There he must have come into contact with Gilles Mureau (d. 1512), who became an *heurier* at the Cathedral c. 1462 and canon c. 1472, and by whom some chansons, but no sacred music, survive with ascriptions.[196] In various treatises, Tinctoris refers to himself as master of arts, teacher of mathematics, and professor of law, and it is fair to assume that he pursued at least some of his university studies while still in the north. The precise date of his entering the service of the

---

[193] "Tinctoris" is Latin for "of the dyer." It is the only form of the name used by the musician himself. StraM IV, 10ff, deduced a Flemish transl., [van den]Vaerwere, from it, but without adequate foundation. There were a few men named Johannes Tinctoris in the late 15th century (*see*, e.g., the various students of this name, listed in Edmond de Reusens, *Matricule de l'Université de Louvain*, I [1903], for the years 1429–1453), with resulting confusion on the part of several biographers. The most serious confusion (in StraM IV, 2–25) identifies the musician with a homonym of Poperinghe in Flanders. AudaL, 88ff, and BorJT, 289ff, refute StraM.

[194] Latin text reprinted in CouS IV, iii; CouT, ix; and, more accurately, BellerT, 57.

[195] *See* Pirro in RM VII, No. 8 (1926), 323.

[196] About Mureau, *see* PirGM. For a chanson of his, *see* DrozP, 43. The piece pr. in HewO, 235, may also be by him; cf. *ibid.*, 131 (also fn. 59 *supra*).

Spanish ruling house at Naples is unknown, but it must have been before
Beatrice of Aragon, daughter of King Ferrante, became Queen of Hungary
in 1476 by virtue of her marriage to King Matthias Corvinus; five treatises
by Tinctoris and a motet of his bear dedications to Beatrice or make other
mention of her, and some of the references show that the works they belong
to were written before this event—two dedications qualify her as a "virgin." [197]
The *terminus a quo* is probably not earlier than 1473, since Eleonora, sister
of Beatrice, in that year married Hercules I, Duke of Ferrara, one of the greatest music patrons of the Renaissance; no work of Tinctoris' mentions Eleonora,
and it is unlikely that her name would have been consistently omitted if she
had been at Naples.

Under Ferrante (= Ferdinand I), Naples—despite wars with the An-
gevins and the Turks—was a brilliant cultural center, as it had been under
his father, Alfonso the Magnanimous (= Alfonso V of Aragon). Jacopo
Sannazaro, destined to become a favorite poet of the later Italian madrigalists, was the chief organizer of the court entertainments.[198] Giovanni Pontano,
the greatest Latin stylist between Petrarch and Erasmus, served as chancellor.
The best scribes obtainable built up, at high fees, one of the finest libraries in
Europe. The place was a hive where artists and musicians, native and foreign,
were busily at work. The foreigners, understandably enough, included Spaniards, among them probably the composer Cornago (cf. pp. 576f), who had
served under Alfonso and is represented in MS Monte Cassino 871 N,
a MS evidently of Neapolitan origin. The fact that they included also
Tinctoris helped to turn the musical circle at Naples into an outpost of France
and Burgundy.

While proof of the tradition that Tinctoris founded a public music school
in Naples is lacking, it seems that, despite the activity in Alfonso's day, he
was the true initiator of a Neapolitan musical culture.[199] In 1487, Pontano
authorized him in the king's name to go to France and Burgundy to procure
singers.[200] We do not know that he went at this time, but he did visit the
north during his years in Naples. In 1492 he was living at Rome; [201] he may
have left Naples permanently by that year, since Trithemius refers to him, in
1495, as "formerly" in Ferrante's service. He died in 1511.[202]

Whether he was a strikingly original thinker or not, Tinctoris was a true
musical encyclopedist. His twelve treatises form a *"summa"* that affords insight not only into the musical theory of his own day (and earlier), but into

---

[197] Actually Beatrice used the regal title after her formal betrothal in 1475 (A. Berzeviczy,
Béatrice d'Aragon . . . [French ed., 1911], 95f), so that these works may antedate that event
and not merely the marriage.
[198] Concerning these, *see* Benedetto Croce, *I Teatri di Napoli. Secolo XV–XVIII* (1891), Chap. I.
[199] Cf. PannOM.
[200] For Pontano's letter in the original Italian, *see* StraM IV, 56f; FlorM, I, 28. French transl.
by A. de La Fage in *Revue et Gazette musicale de Paris*, XVII (1850), 257.
[201] Cf. ScherB, 174.   [202] For further biographical data, *see* esp. BorJT.

that of the entire Renaissance. They appear to have been conceived as a whole in a logical sequence and to have been written mainly in that order. The works [203] are (1) *Diffinitorium musicae;* (2) *Expositio manus;* (3) *Liber de natura et proprietate tonorum;* (4) *Tractatus de notis et pausis;* (5) *Tractatus de regulari valore notarum;* (6) *Liber imperfectionum notarum musicalium;* (7) *Tractatus alterationum;* (8) *Scriptum super punctis musicalibus;* (9) *Liber de arte contrapuncti;* (10) *Proportionale Musices;* (11) *Complexus effectuum musices;* and (12) *De inventione et usu musicae.* No. 1 is on musical terms, Nos. 2 and 3 on the tonal system, Nos. 4 to 8 on mensural notation, Nos. 9 and 10 on polyphonic technique, No. 11 on esthetics, and No. 12 on history and performance. All seem to have been completed at Naples within about ten years, c. 1474 to c. 1484. A few can be more closely dated: No. 1 was written before 1476 (possibly in 1474 or still earlier; it was printed c. 1494); No. 2 is a product of c. 1475; No. 3 was finished on November 6, 1476, and No. 9 on October 11, 1477; No. 10 is mentioned in the prologue of No. 2 and is therefore earlier; No. 12 took form c. 1484 (1480–87). No. 1 reaches us both in MS and early print, Nos. 2 to 11 only in MS, No. 12 only in print.

No. 1,[204] dedicated *ad . . . virginem . . . Beatricem,* is the most discussed of Tinctoris' works though not the most important. The print of c. 1494 was produced at Treviso (near Venice) by Gerardus of Lisa,[205] also a Fleming and a musician, who c. 1470 had set up one of the first printing presses in Italy. His activities as teacher and as *maestro di cappella* at the cathedral curtailed his production as a printer; he specialized in artistic editions for a small circle of discriminating patrons. The *Diffinitorium,* the first dictionary of musical terms printed though not the first written,[206] is a small work defining 300 terms. Although not all the definitions are clear (especially those dealing with older music), it is evident that Tinctoris aimed at lucidity and method. In treating of music within his experience, he wrote informatively. A *motetum,* he says, is a composition of moderate size, using words on any subject, but more frequently on a sacred subject (an excellent definition; cf. pp. 20f). A *cantilena* is a short form with words on any subject, though more often about love. (Since, according to this definition, a cantilena text may at times be sacred, Tinctoris would no doubt approve of the modern term "song-motet." His definition casts additional light on the inclusion of song-motets in *chanson-*

---

[203] All but No. 12 pr. CouS IV; also in CouT; No. 12 pr. WeinT, 27 (references to translations, etc., will follow). On the treatises in general, *see* KornT; BorJT, 299ff; PannT. The most important source is Bibl. royale de Belgique, MS 4147.

[204] Pr. CouS IV, 177; CouT, 467; ForkL, 204; BellerT, 55 (with German transl.; *see* criticism in BalmT); BaloT (with English transl.); TinctorisT (with French transl.); LichtD III, 297; HamilD, 143.

[205] Facts determined from a study of the printer's type used; cf. *Catalogue of Books Printed in the XVth Century in the British Museum,* Part VI (1930), 886, under Pallavicinus, Jacobus, and Tinctoris. The British Museum copy is identical with those at Gotha (BellerT, 59) and Treviso (AlesL, esp. 9ff, 33). Further on Gerardus, *see* AlesO, esp. 32, 53.   [206] Cf. ReMMA, 147.

niers.) *Res facta* is a composed work, i.e., not one improvised *super librum;* etc.

No. 2. expounds the Guidonian solmisation system [207] (Tinctoris calls it *"solfisatio"*), but replaces the term "hexachordum" by *"deductio."* Mutation is explained partly by means of an ingenious diagram.

No. 3,[208] the treatise dedicated to Ockeghem and Busnois (cf. p. 101), deals with the modes not only in plainsong but in polyphony. Of special interest is Tinctoris' discussion of the combination of quite different modes (*commixtio tonorum*) or of modes belonging to the same pair, i.e., an authentic mode and its own plagal (*mixtio tonorum*). Each kind of combination may be either successive, involving one voice, or simultaneous, involving more than one. Tinctoris, here and elsewhere, is evidently trying to account theoretically for the new and multifarious nature of the music of his time. He is perspicacious about the relation of mode and polyphony, stating clearly that mode is attributable to a single melodic line only. The tenor provides the modal foundation for the whole, but each part is, by itself, authentic or plagal, *mixtus or commixtus.* (If a part-composition is to be assigned to a mode at all, it is the mode of the tenor, but only because that is the most important voice.) It is almost as though Tinctoris divined that the system of the church modes was to remain valid solely for monophony and that, as soon as polyphony began to develop, harmonic relations began to develop also, and were to lead gradually to a new tonal system—that of major and minor.

Nos. 4 to 8 [209] together form a logical, extended treatise on mensural notation, dealing respectively with (a) notes and rests; (b) *modus, tempus,* and *prolatio;* (c) the way in which a note loses part of its normal value (becomes "imperfect") by reason of its context: (d) the way in which, again because of the context, a note adds to its value (becomes altered); and (e) the points of division, perfection, and augmentation.[210]

No. 9,[211] the most important treatise in the group, is dedicated to Ferrante. It is divided into a prologue and three books. The prologue [212] indicates Tinctoris' acquaintance with ancient writers, from Plato and Aristoxenos to Boethius and Isidore of Seville, but also considerably less than the old medieval respect for *auctoritas;* whatever may have been said in times past about the music of the spheres, Tinctoris will not believe that music can be produced by anything except terrestrial instruments.[213] He is very much a man of his own time; only the compositions of the last forty years, he says, are worth

---

[207] Pr. CouS IV, 1; CouT, 1; extended discussion in BalmT, 5ff (with German transl. of extracts).

[208] Pr. CouS IV, 16; CouT, 39; extended discussion in BalmT, 118ff (with German transl. of extracts).

[209] Pr. CouS IV, 41–76; CouT, 104–198.   [210] On these various subjects, *see* ApelN.

[211] Pr. CouS IV, 76; CouT, 198.   [212] English transl. in StrunkR, 197ff.

[213] Which would include the voice; cf. ReMMA, 118.

listening to. The composers flourishing in his own day he regards as almost innumerable, and he singles out Ockeghem, Regis, Busnois, Caron, and Faugues, all of whom can boast of having had as teachers the recently deceased Dunstable, Binchois, and Dufay. He so rejoices in their music and is so instructed by it that he emulates their style in his own compositions. It is clear that Tinctoris was aware of a break between the music of the early 15th century and the music preceding it. If he had been in a position to establish a dividing line between medieval and Renaissance music, he would undoubtedly have placed it c. 1425. Book I opens with a definition of "counterpoint," to which a further explanation is added in Book II, Chapter XX. The second passage makes it plain that "counterpoint" is not only a generic term, embracing both improvisation (*super librum cantare*) and written music (*res facta*), but also a specific term, used as a synonym for "improvisation." The earlier passage states counterpoint (in the generic sense) to be a regulated combination, produced by setting up one voice against another; it is from the placing of note against note, or point against point, that the term *"contrapunctus"* is derived. If the combination sounds sweet to the ear, it is consonant; if harsh, dissonant. Tinctoris lists twenty-two consonances (in his system, which spans three octaves, the addition of one or two octaves to a simple interval produces a separate item). The unison, fourth, fifth, octave, and their compounds are perfect consonances; the major and minor thirds and sixths and their compounds, imperfect. But Tinctoris has little liking for the fourth and its compounds—in music *a 2*, indeed, he removes them from the category of consonances—and would almost exclude them from improvised counterpoint. If such counterpoint is in more than two parts, however, he states that a fourth may appear—especially in the penultimate chord—between the tenor and an upper voice, provided the interval is supported by a fifth between the tenor and the lowest voice; an accompanying example *a 4* indicates that the fourth may in fact be presented by any two upper voices, as long as the lowest voice sounds a fifth under the bottom note of the interval. Tinctoris, of course, mentions the constant application of the fourth by the two upper voices in fauxbourdon. In *res facta,* he says, it is used if supported below by a conjunct fifth, third, tenth, or twelfth, and he concedes that it sounds better when thus complemented. He treats of the compounds in much the same manner.[214] It will be noted that the constituent voices in the permissible uses of the fourth never include the bass. Although Tinctoris' discussion of the fourth does not correspond to the non-quartal style mentioned earlier, it evidently does reflect the same contemporary attitude toward the interval that brought this style into being. Another consonance concerning which Tinctoris

[214] The above interpretation differs from that in BorJT, 307; but cf. FerandM, 155ff (which corrects some exx. printed with errors in CouS and CouT). The discussion in JepCP, 10, is incomplete.

has misgivings is the sixth, whether major or minor;[215] in his judgment, a sixth removed from its context has more roughness than charm; it should be excluded from music *a 2*, both improvised and written. Book II deals with the dissonances. At first, fifteen of them are referred to:[216] the second, tritone, seventh, and their compounds. Then a second group of twelve "false consonances" is introduced: the diminished and augmented fifth and octave and their compounds.[217] (The tritone appears in the first group rather than the second, perhaps owing to the equivocal status of the perfect fourth.) The *semitonium chromaticum* is mentioned in various connections, including, as might be expected, the diminished and augmented octave. If counterpoint is *simplex* (note against note), dissonance should not be employed, but, if it is *diminutus* (i.e., if it admits of two or more notes against one), dissonance of the first class may be used under circumstances that are described, rhythmic conditions being taken into account. False consonances, however, should not be used; but Tinctoris admits that they are found *"apud infinitos compositores etiam celeberrimos,"* and he presents examples from Faugues (the passage from the *Missa Le serviteur* cited earlier as evidence of that composer's authorship), Busnois, and Caron.[218] The examples all illustrate the use of the diminished fifth (between the bass and an upper voice),[219] but not the false octave. Tinctoris disapproves, however distinguished the composers, and quotes the famous line in which Horace states that "even Homer nods." One important difference is pointed out between dissonance treatment in *res facta* and in improvisation: in the former, the voices, whatever their number, must observe their mutual obligations to one another according to the rules (a five-part *Deo gratias* is offered as an illustration);[220] in the latter, it suffices if the improvised lines are made to fit the tenor. Nevertheless, if the singers have some understanding among themselves in advance, that is worthy of praise rather than blame. (Improvised) counterpoint may be set against either a plainsong tenor or a mensural one: if the former, certain methods are specified for applying note-values to it; in some churches, however, the plainsong and counterpoint are sung unmeasured, a procedure producing a beautiful result, but requiring great skill, especially on the part of the tenor. The frequent attention paid to improvisation by Tinctoris, and by other theorists, attests to the prominent role it played in the musical life of the time. Many effects eventually adopted in written music were undoubtedly first achieved experimentally in

---

[215] Not just minor, as stated in JepCP, 10; *see* CouS IV, 88f; CouT, 229ff.

[216] The table in CouS IV, 122, and CouT, 314, omits the major 21st, called for by the text (also the penultimate word before the table should be *discordantiae*).

[217] The table in CouS IV, 124, applies the brackets incorrectly.

[218] As given in CouS IV, 146; CouT, 383, some notes are wrong.

[219] In view of Tinctoris' testimony, the editorial ♮ (making the fifth perfect) in DTO XIX[1], 105, meas. 170, should be ignored.

[220] Pr. in modern notation (and with corrections of errors in CouS IV, 129f; CouT, 337ff) in FerandM, 149.

improvisation. It is reasonable to suppose, for instance, that the $^6_5$ chords, encountered rather often in *res factae* a little later, were an outgrowth of such a development. Book III presents eight general rules.

(1) A perfect consonance should be used at the beginning and end, but an imperfect consonance may be employed at the opening, if the music starts on an upbeat, and at the end (except that the consonance must not be a sixth or a compound thereof) if several singers are improvising. (In other words, if a piece was improvised, it might end with a third or a compound of a third.)

(2) A part may accompany the tenor with several imperfect consonances of the same size (i.e., with parallel thirds or sixths) but not with successions of like perfect consonances (e.g., parallel octaves or fifths), unless—and this is interesting—these are required by strict imitation or a particularly beautiful effect results.

(3) If a tenor reiterates a note, concords of the same kind, perfect or imperfect, may be repeated against it. "However, where other concords can be interpolated, the singing of this kind of counterpoint over the *cantus planus* [i.e., in improvisation] is diligently to be avoided." But in *res facta* one may have repetition, especially of thirds and sixths, if it makes for smooth setting of the words.

(4) The added part should have a small range and move conjunctly, even if the tenor leaps. But there may be exceptions in the interest of beauty.

(5) A cadence should not be introduced on any note—high, medium, or low—if it breaks up the development of the melody.

(6) The same melodic note-group should not be repeated in improvisation (i.e., there should be no *"redicta"*), especially if the *cantus firmus* has such repetition. However, in written music *redictae* are permissible in imitations of bells, trumpets, etc.[221]

(7) One should avoid two or more consecutive cadences on the same degree, even when the *cantus firmus* seems to lend itself to this. *Cantus firmi* calling for such resemblances to *redictae* should be selected only when necessary.[222]

(8) One should seek variety by using different note-values and cadences, by writing sometimes conjunctly, sometimes not, both with and without syncopations, canon, rests, etc. This rule is applicable most to a Mass, less to a motet, least to a *cantilena* (this being the simplest type). Tinctoris mentions examples from Dufay, Faugues, Regis, Busnois, Ockeghem, and Caron.

While this treatise in part restates earlier rules, the spirit of a new period breathes from many of its pages. The apparent preoccupation with vertical

---

[221] Cf. pp. 60f. Part of Tinctoris' example is given in modern notation in RieG, 319.
[222] The example illustrating Rule 7 is given in facsimile, after MS at Brussels, in ApelN, 153 (A), where it is accredited to the *Proportionale* (but cf. CouS IV, 152; CouT, 397).

relationships is in keeping with the increased care, taken since early in the century, in the handling of consonance and dissonance. It does not, however, represent a conscious shift of interest from the polyphonic to the harmonic aspects of music: a knowledge of the linear aspects could to some degree be taken for granted in Tinctoris' day.[223]

No. 10,[224] like No. 9, bears a dedication to Ferrante. The introduction [225] opens with a brief traditional survey of music history, from Jubal on, in the course of which occurs the reference to Christ mentioned by Trithemius.[226] Treating of his own time, Tinctoris observes that the chapels instituted by the great princes have considerably advanced the art of music. It is here, too, that he mentions the English, led by Dunstable, as having originated a new art, and that he names Dufay, Binchois, Ockeghem, Busnois, Regis, and Caron as the illustrious continuators of that art. The body of the treatise offers a detailed exposition of the Proportional System. Proportion, he says, is the mutual relation between two quantities—in music, the mutual relation between two notes. It exists whenever notes are made to have a bearing on one another, whether the notes are successive ones in a single voice or simultaneously sounding ones in different voices. The equal proportions are the simplest and require no special sign. The various other proportions include the *genus multiplex*—in which (in modern terms), if the ratio is expressed as a fraction, that fraction can be reduced to a whole number—and the *genus superparticulare*—in which, if the ratio is expressed as a fraction, the numerator of the fraction is one more than the denominator. Thus, with respect to the former type, a measure in one voice may correspond to two measures in another (cf. p. 70 regarding Dufay's *Missa Se la face ay pale*); this would be an example of *proportio dupla* and would be indicated by a number placed over another number having half its value (e.g., $\frac{2}{1}$ or $\frac{4}{2}$ or $\frac{6}{3}$). The second type may be illustrated by *sesquialtera* or *emyolia* (hemiola), in which the greater number contains the lesser number one and a half times (e.g., $\frac{3}{2}$)—that is, in which binary and ternary groups may be combined either successively or simultaneously. (In our example on p. 18, the binary and ternary groups do

---

[223] Further about this treatise, *see* KornT, 17ff; FerandM, 148ff; BorJT, 307ff.

[224] Pr. CouS IV, 153; CouT, 401. Dedication in English transl. in StrunkR, 193ff. The 4 examples given in facsimile, after MS at Brussels, in ApelN, 153 (B–E) equal examples pr. in CouS IV, 155 (col. 2), 158 (col. 2, no. 1), 161 (col. 2), 155 (col. 1), which equal, respectively, CouT, 406 (no. 2), 414 (no. 2), 423, 405. All these examples—also the 1 mentioned in fn. 222—are defective in CouS and CouT.

[225] Which names among his titles that of King of Hungary. Music historians have considered this an error on Tinctoris' part or the result of confusion caused by Beatrice's marriage to Matthias. Actually, Tinctoris adopted the exact official list of titles used on the great seal and in all formal documents of Ferrante's reign. Cf. Nicola Barone, "Intorno allo studio dei diplomi dei Rè Aragonesi di Napoli," in *Atti dell'Accademia Pontaniana*, XLIII, Ser. II, Vol. 18, Mem. No. 9 (1913), 7, 9; Camillo Minieri-Riccio, *Saggio di Codici Diplomatico*, 2 vols. (1879), *passim*.

[226] Although he does not name No. 10 as one of the Tinctoris works known to him. Regarding a late medieval reference to Jesus as a *Doctor in arte citharizandi*, *see* PirE, 28; on the antecedents of such a concept, *see* L. Schrade, *Die Darstellungen der Töne an den Kapitellen der Abteikirche zu Cluni*, in *Vierteljahrsschrift für Literaturwissenschaft und Geistesgeschichte* VII (1929), 229 (cf. BorJT, 310).

not have the same length; three two-beat groups equal two three-beat groups. On the other hand, it is obviously possible for two-beat and three-beat groups to be equal, e.g., where the latter are triplets. Tinctoris, unfortunately for us, is one of the various theorists who use the terms *"sesquialtera"* and "hemiola" interchangeably, although two different things are represented. It would be helpful if each term were to apply to just one of them in some such manner as this:

HEMIOLA   SESQUIALTERA

In one of these, notes of the same denomination retain their value; in the other they do not.[226a] If a greater number of notes in a countermelody is to be brought into correspondence with a smaller number in a tenor, the larger figure should appear above the lesser one (as in the fractions given above); but, if the situation is reversed, the lesser should appear above the larger. The proportional theory is developed by Tinctoris in the most complicated detail; we find him here a musical mathematician, at times explaining proportions that can have had little to do with actual practice, though they may have been studied for purposes of exercise. Of the principles expounded, those of augmentation and diminution (simple and double) and of *sesquialtera* are the most valuable.[227] Of interest from the historical standpoint is Tinctoris' passing mention that, while the tenor is usually the fundamental voice, the superius may at times serve as such and even the contratenor may on rare occasions do so. Among the numerous examples in the *Proportionale* is a quodlibet (i.e., a potpourri made up, for amusement, out of snatches of well-known pieces) that combines fragments of *O rosa bella, L'Homme armé,* and other material.[227a] Examples of the quodlibet entertained the Renaissance society of various countries.

No. 11,[228] less concerned with actual musical practice and less interesting than the other treatises, deals with the effects of music, of which Tinctoris names twenty. Examples: music delights God (no. 1); it excites the soul to piety (no. 6); it elevates the earthbound mind (no. 11); it makes work easier (no. 15). In discussing no. 18, "Music increases convivial pleasures," Tinctoris observes that singers and all types of instrumentalists—pipers (on *tibiae,* i.e., shawms, cromornes, etc.), drummers, organists, lutenists, recorder-players, trumpeters—add to the magnificence of great banquets. In no. 19, he

---

226a *See* SachsRT, 190.
227 Further about the Proportional System, *see* esp. ApelN, 145ff; WolfH I, 415ff; TiraG.
227a For a study of this quodlibet, *see* BrenH.
228 Pr. CouS IV, 191 (incomplete, after Brussels MS), 195 (complete—except for prologue, preserved in Brussels MS—after a MS at Ghent); CouT, 504 (after Brussels), 513 (after Ghent).

names some composers expert in musical effects and includes Obrecht. This is the only place where he mentions this master, who, although he predeceased Tinctoris, belongs stylistically more to the Josquin generation than to that of Ockeghem.

Of No. 12, a work divided into five books, we have left only a printed copy of some extracts.[229] The work opens with a letter to Johannes Stokhem, then at Beatrice's court in Hungary. Stokhem, perhaps born near Liége, had met Tinctoris in that city. After serving Beatrice, he is found as a singer in the Papal Choir in 1487,[230] when the apparently younger Gaspar van Weerbecke and Josquin were members also. Though little music comes down with ascriptions to Stokhem, he seems to have been a figure of some consequence: Petrucci included no less than four chansons of his [231] in the *Odhecaton* (cf. p. 155), one being *a 5*. Tinctoris, in his letter, states that he has finished the treatise but is not hastening publication and that he is sending Stokhem two chapters each of Books II, III, and IV. This is what survives. The battle of Otranto is mentioned at the end of the text, so that the treatise must date from between that event (1480) and Stokhem's entry into the Papal Choir. The printing was done by the press of del Tuppo at Naples, which was idle from 1482 to 1485,[232] but may have produced the work in 1481–82 or 1485–86. Chapters 19 and 20 of Book II concern singing: the former deals with the singers of the Old Testament and of classical antiquity, the latter with those of the New Testament and Tinctoris' own period. He comments on a special kind of plainsong—*cantus regalis*—in which added notes ornament the *cantus planus*. A good singer, he says, must have *ars, mensura, modus, pronunciatio, et vox bona*. In naming the best singers he has known, he singles out Ockeghem as the finest bass; most of the others are from the same area. Chapter 8 of Book III deals first with the history of the *tibiae*, the material out of which they are made, and their structure. In his day, the shawm (*celimela*) is well-nigh perfect, the cromorne (*dulcina*) less so. Since the ranges of the *tibiae* resemble those of human voices, these instruments have been divided similarly into soprano, tenor, and contratenor. The tenor type is commonly called *bombarda;* the contratenor part, especially if low, may be played on the brass *tuba*—named *trompone* by the Italians and *sacque-boute* by the French. Chapter 9 is partly devoted to the past history of the use of the *tibiae;* in his own time they are widely employed at church festivals, weddings, banquets, processions, and

[229] Reprinted in WeinT, 27. See also HabT; WeinU; BorJT, 311ff; BainesT.
[230] Cf. HabR, 56.
[231] Pr. HewO, 228 (= TorreS, 547), 255 (*see* comments *ibid.,* 97; also CouS IV, 149, ex. 1), 261 (= TorreS, 550), 399 (= ReO, 76). Regarding other works, *see* esp. AmbG III, 262. For further biographical data, *see* BergVM; the Belgian *Biographie nationale,* XXIV, 87f; PirH, 222; AudaL, 73.
[232] Cf. *Catalogue of Books Printed in the XVth Century in the British Museum,* Part VI (1930), 868. Del Tuppo's name does not appear, but a comparison between the facsimile in WeinT and a facsimile of work known to be del Tuppo's, given in the said *Catalogue,* Part VI, Pl. LXVIII* (ex. 85 G), bears out the claim made in WeinT, 8, that del Tuppo was the printer.

similar public and private occasions. In soldiers' camps and in the towns, they are heard day and night. He praises, as the best *tibia*-player of the day, a Godefridus, who served Emperor Frederick III (d. 1493). In Book IV, Chapters 4 and 5, Tinctoris turns to the *lyra* or *leutum* (lute) and its variants: the viol, rebec, guitar, citole, and *tambura* (an oriental lute-like instrument, played by the Turkish invaders). Strange as it may now seem to class all stringed instruments—whether bowed or plucked—under the ancient term *lyra,* the procedure conformed with the Renaissance deference for classical antiquity. Tinctoris credits the Catalans with having invented the guitar. In Chapter 5 he writes, after the usual bow to the ancients, about the best contemporary lutenists. The greatest of these, in his opinion, is Pietro Bono, at the court of Duke Hercules of Ferrara.[233] Others could play pieces not only *a 2* but also *a 3* or *a 4*—a difficult feat. Tinctoris mentions a German, Heinrich, recently in the service of Charles the Bold, as one of them. With regard to players on the *viola cum arculo* ("bowed viol"), he recounts having heard, at Bruges, two Flemish brothers "no less erudite in letters than expert in music," Carolus and Johannes. They performed two-part music "so skilfully and beautifully" that no melody ever pleased him more. These brothers have been identified [234] as Jean and Charles Fernand of Bruges. The latter taught literature at the University of Paris; as instrumentalists, both served Charles VIII of France. Concerning bowed instruments, the viol and the rebec, Tinctoris had a strong personal opinion: they were *his* instruments—his, he writes, because more than the others they incite his soul to piety and fill his heart with a burning fire, opening it to the contemplation of things above. He prefers to have them kept for sacred music rather than for worldly things and public festivities. Subjective as this opinion may be, it is valuable as supplementary evidence that instruments were used in the performance of sacred music.[234a] Tinctoris does not end the chapter on this spiritual plane; he proceeds to say that the guitar was little used because of its thin tone, that women played it more than men, and that in Catalonia the former employed it in singing love songs.

Tinctoris is the central early figure in the line of great, representative Renaissance theorists, a line that includes his foreign contemporaries Ramos de Pareja, Gafori, and Aron, and such later writers as Glareanus, Zarlino, Cerone, and Morley. As such a figure, and because of the wide scope of his writings, Tinctoris provides a key to the history of the musical theory of the whole

[233] Substantiation of Tinctoris' opinion exists in letters from c. 1480 to 1488. Beatrice requested Bono "on loan" from Hercules I. Bono was in Vienna after August, 1486. He was known in Milan. In 1496, a poem by Battista Guarino called him *"cithariztam rarissimum."* See HaraPB; MottaM, 53; MosPH, 72; StraM VI, 110ff; GomV, 112f; CanM, 661f; FökM, 10f; MGG I, 117ff.

[234] PirE, 46. *See also* César Du Boulay, *Historia Universitatis Parisiensis,* V (1670), 869f.

[234a] RoksE provides data on late 15th-century employment of instruments of the *tibia* class for such purpose.

period. The very fact that he stands on the border line of the Middle Ages and the Renaissance gives those writings an added interest.

Though significant mainly for his treatises, Tinctoris survives likewise as a composer. His four known Masses include one *a 4* based on the *L'Homme armé* tenor,[235] a work sometimes referred to as the *Missa Cunctorum plasmator,* after the first words of the trope inserted in the Kyrie. There are two extraneous texts in the Sanctus: a troped extract from the *Te Deum* and a free mosaic of the two *Pueri Hebraeorum* antiphons of Palm Sunday; both texts are introduced with a certain appropriateness, since in the original chants they are associated respectively with the words *"Sanctus"* and *"Hosanna in excelsis"* (cf. fn. 101) and are so associated in the Mass. Tinctoris treats the *cantus firmus* with considerable liberty and applies successfully, throughout the Mass and in all voices, his own rule regarding the desirability of variety. The other three Masses consist of a work *a 4* (without Kyrie and Agnus) and two *a 3,* one of the latter being dedicated to Ferrante.[236] Additional sacred compositions include two motets [237] and one of the settings of the Lamentations printed by Petrucci in 1506. Among Tinctoris' secular numbers are versions of *De tous biens plaine* and *D'ung aultre amer,* both, together with a few other works of his, preserved in the important MS at the Segovia Cathedral; [238] a *Vostre regart* and *Helas* [239] that were once popular enough to come down in several sources; and an Italian piece, *O invida fortuna.* Presumably a number of the examples in the treatises are by Tinctoris also.[240]

The print that contains Tinctoris' setting of the Lamentations preserves also a setting by one of his colleagues at Naples, the Catalan, Bernardo Ycart (Hykaert, etc.), whose name appears (with those of Tinctoris and others) in a list of singers in the Royal Chapel in 1480.[241] Theorist and composer, he is mentioned by Gafori. He is represented by several compositions in the Faenza MS, Bibl. Com. Cod. 117, discussed on pp. 174, 178, and by a chanson in the Pixérécourt MS.[242]

The Biblioteca Nazionale at Naples possesses a MS, VI. E. 40, in which there are six anonymous *L'Homme armé* Masses, dedicated *"ad serenissimam Ungarie Reginam,"* Beatrice. The composer was evidently Franco-Nether-

235 Pr. MPLSER, *Ser. I,* I, No. 9; Agnus also in SmijO, 97.

236 About these Masses, *see* JepG, 21; BorJT, 315.

237 One pr. WolfME, 42 (cf. also GomO, 11f); about the other, *see* BukU, 22f.

238 Cf. AngI, 10, 14f; MME I, 108, 110f.

239 Pr. DrozT, 46, and HewO, 331 (= GomO, Suppl., 11; EDMR IV, 63), respectively.

240 Further about compositions, *see* BorJT, 314f.

241 StraM IV, 29. About the nationality of Ycart (sometimes regarded as Flemish), cf. MME I, 24, 136. Monsignor Anglés has had the kindness to write us: ". . . the name Ycart or Icart is typically Catalan and can be found today all over the country; the name occurs very frequently in Barcelona."

242 But not, as often stated, in Paris, Bib. nat. MS fr. 15103; cf. Dr. Plamenac in MQ XXXIV (1948), 292f. *See* further, RoncB, 35f; AmbG III, 145 (note that the Ferrara MS there referred to is the present Faenza MS); MME I, 24f, 136.

landish or under Franco-Netherlandish influence, to judge from the style of the music,[243] and may well have been associated with the circle just discussed. The six works constitute an extraordinary cycle: the tenor of each of the first five—all *a 4*—consists of a different portion of the *L'Homme armé* melody, the portion being indicated in each Mass by a verbal canon; the final Mass of the cycle—which is *a 5*, the added voice singing the *cantus firmus* in canon at the fifth above the tenor—employs the entire song. The MS gives the secular words as well as those of the Ordinary (cf. p. 73), and it is from this source that the text of the grand old tune has been recovered.[244]

Music in Plays

The dramatic and quasi-dramatic interludes presented at the Banquet of the Oath of the Pheasant in 1454 (cf. pp. 57f) had their counterparts in the plays that continued the tradition of the liturgical drama of the Middle Ages. During the 15th century these plays—mysteries and related types [245]—grew to tremendous proportions and often required several days for a full performance. Interpolations of plainsong and polyphony—secular as well as sacred, instrumentally performed as well as vocally—played an important part.

In Arnoul Greban's *Mystère de la Passion*,[246] dating from c. 1450—a huge work which it took four days to perform [247]—the chanting of part of a Kyrie by a choir of angels follows immediately after a lamentation over the crucifixion by God the Father. The *Mystère de Saint Louis* (1472) [248]—a presentation of which required three days—incorporates examples of plainchant also. Three characters, the Bishop of Soissons, the Abbot of Saint Rémy at Rheims, and the Dean of Rheims, sing a litany *"tant qu'ilz veulent,"* to quote the rubric. After a victory over the Saracens, a cardinal calls for the singing of a *Te Deum* and the *Vexilla Regis*. Various chants succeed one another at short intervals towards the close, the last being again the *Te Deum*. In *La Vie et passion de Mgr. Sainct Didier* (1482), the *Veni Creator Spiritus* is introduced. Such hymns were undoubtedly rendered in fauxbourdon.[249]

The interpolation of sacred polyphony into the plays may be exemplified by the performance of a motet, *Sanctorum meritis,* on the second day of the *Mystère de Saint Louis*. Gabriel directs the angels to sing the motet as they bear the souls of slain knights to heaven, and the rubric states that they do

[243] Dr. Strunk has kindly loaned me the scores he has made of 4 of these Masses.
[244] By Dr. Plamenac. For further details, *see* PlamH; PlamM.
[245] For the sake of simplicity, no distinction will be made here between mysteries, miracle plays, and moralities.
[246] For the text, *see* the Gaston Paris and Gaston Raynaud edition, 1878. *See also* Gustave Cohen, *Le Théâtre en France au moyen âge,* I (1928), 46, 48ff.
[247] It was expanded in 1486 to such an extent that it required 10 days; cf. Jean Frappier and A.-M. Gossart, *Le Théâtre religieux au moyen âge,* 10.
[248] For the text, *see* the Francisque Michel edition, 1871.
[249] Cf. PirH, 124 (where further exx. are cited of the use of plainsong in the mysteries).

so *"jusquez a tant qu'ilz soyent en paradis."* Greban's Passion contains a motet sung by demons. Astaroth assigns the parts thus:

Sathan, tu feras la teneur	*The tenor, Satan, you will do*
Et j'asserray la contre sus;	*And I the contra shall essay;*
Belzebuth dira le dessus	*The top part's for Beelzebub*
Avec Berich a haulte double	*While Berick sings on high a duplum,*
Et Cerberus fera un trouble	*And Cerberus shall sound a triplum*
Continué, Dieu scet comment.	*Continuous, the Lord knows how.*

(A pun is perhaps intended by the word *"trouble."*)

Lucifer urges Astaroth and his other "little devils" to babble and mutter their notes and to chatter like monkeys or hungry old crows. Diabolic ensembles are found also in the *Mystère des Actes des apostres* by Arnoul Greban and his brother, Simon, as well as in an *Incarnacion* played at Rouen in 1474.[250]

Both motets and chansons are called for in Greban's Passion in the following speech of God the Father, in which He rejoices as Jesus arrives in paradise:

Angles, par ung chant solennel,	*Angels with a solemn chant*
Esmouvez nous dame Musique	*Summon Dame Music here before us,*
Applicans dame Rethorique	*Bringing Dame Poetry to bear*
A doulx et armonieux sons;	*On sounds harmonious and sweet;*
Chantez nous motés et chansons	*Motets and chansons sing to us,*
Fulcis de doulce melodie,	*Full of the sweetest melody;*
Et briefment chacun lays nous die	*And let forthwith each render lays*
Les plus somptueux qu'il pourra,	*As sumptuous as may be found,*
Et nostre cour s'esjouira	*And in your voices' harmony*
En l'armonie de vos voix.	*Our heav'nly court shall then rejoice.*

It is understandable that the Passion should make frequent mention of music, since Arnoul Greban was himself a musician, serving about the midcentury as organist at Notre Dame in Paris and as director of its *maîtrise*.[251]

The singing of chansons is indicated at various points in the *Mystère de Saint Louis:* a rubric calls by name for a certain *Gente de corps, belle aux beaus iex;* the full text is given for *Adieu les damez de vaillance.* At the end of the fourth day of Greban's Passion, God the Father asks the angels to sing *"doulces chansons."* The word *"silete"* follows. This word and the term *"pose"* appear frequently in the Passion and in other mysteries. The exact meaning is obscure, but some sort of interlude seems indicated. In the *Mystère de Roy Advenir,* the *silete* is assigned to the organist, who, before God speaks, admonishes the audience to maintain silence. The *silete* is sometimes sung, sometimes entrusted to instruments. There are examples for organ, trumpets, minstrels, "other instruments," etc.[252] In the Passion, the *silete* just referred

---

250 Cf. *ibid.*, 126.   251 Cf. SteinG.   252 PirH, 129. Further about the *silete, see* SchulerO, 46ff.

to undoubtedly provided the angels with the opportunity to comply with the injunction of God the Father.

Instruments are mentioned often. In the *Mystère de Saint Louis,* the Count of Provence directs the minstrels to perform*"ung beau motet"* on wind instruments as the characters go to church for the wedding of St. Louis and Margaret. After the ceremony the characters withdraw to an inn for the marriage celebration, and the minstrels play again. Food is served, and the rubric states: *"Les menestrez jouent pendant qu'on disne."* The minstrels presumably provide music also when, shortly thereafter, the *"Orliennaise"* (a particular *basse dance?* [253]) and a *sauterelle* are danced. Trumpets were often used in scenes of great pomp or of a military nature, and they are played while Queen Margaret and the King of Cyprus dine. At the coronation of the Sultan's son, the Caliph orders the minstrels and trumpets to sound, and the rubric says: *"Les trompectes, menestrez, tabours et tous instrumenz c'on peut avoir doivent sonner. . . ."*

At Seurre, in 1496, before the play began, a group of musicians marched through the streets performing on instruments both *hauts* and *bas.*[254]

Abundant quotations of chanson-text fragments are found not only in edifying plays and mysteries, but also in the numerous farces of the period. Some of these farces are so full of snatches taken from well-known chansons—such as *Dueil angoisseux* (cf. p. 87)—as to foreshadow the vaudevilles and burlesque plays of the 18th century.[255]

---

[253] No. 15 in ClosBD?   [254] Pir H, 129.

[255] *See* G. Cohen, *Recueil de Farces françaises inédites du XVᵉ siècle,* 1949, xxxf, 447. Among the texts quoted we find also pieces (e.g., *A la duché de Normandye, Av'ous point veu la Perronnelle*) appearing in the monophonic chansonniers of Bayeux and Paris fr. 12744 (cf. pp. 205ff).

Chapter 4: THE FROTTOLISTS AND THEIR CONTEMPORARIES IN NORTHERN AND CENTRAL ITALY

ITALIAN creative ability in the field of music seems to have declined after the first quarter of the *quattrocento*, not to recover its vitality for some fifty years. As far as we can now tell, Bartolomeo Brolo (cf. pp. 26, 30) was the only Italian composer of consequence active during this interval. However, the *chansonniers* mentioned in Chapter 3 include a number of compositions with Italian text. The Seville Chansonnier contains no less than twenty-four such pieces; the Pavia, Wolfenbüttel, Cordiforme, and Mellon MSS are among other *chansonniers* that preserve additional examples. To be sure, some of these are by northerners—for instance, old Italian pieces by Dufay reappear —but it is fair to assume that at least a good portion of the anonymous Italian works are by Italians.

There was no lack of musical activity other than composition. Italians such as Squarcialupi (d. 1475) filled important posts as performers. Also, the practice of reciting poetry to an improvised instrumental accompaniment was widespread. Often poet and improvisator were the same person. Leonardo Giustiniani (d. 1446), poet of the *ballata, O rosa bella,* was skilled in this art. Rafaelle Brandolini, writing at the time of Leo X, reports that Lorenzo de' Medici had welcomed improvisators. Baccio Ugolini (who had performed the title role of Politian's *Orfeo* in 1471) delighted Lorenzo by extemporizing *"ad lyram."* Other improvisators include Rafaelle himself and his brother, Aurelio (d. 1491). The services of Atalante, who had been taught how to play the lute by Leonardo da Vinci, were sought for the leading part when *Orfeo* was to be performed before the Duke of Mantua in 1490. The Spaniard Chariteo (Benedetto Gareth) was admired for the simple and soft manner in which he intoned Vergil.[1]

Early Music Printing

In the 1470's a new blossoming of native composition occurred. At about the same time the recently invented art of printing was applied to monophonic music. Early in the 16th century it was also applied, on a large scale, to polyphony. Since much of the polyphonic music that was printed then dated

[1] Further about these improvisators, etc., *see* RubL, 2; LafE I, 61ff; PirL, 2f; PirH, 166.

153

from the later decades of the 15th century, our sources for the art forms of that period include early prints as well as MSS.

Among the most important of these sources are the prints of secular music published by Ottaviano de' Petrucci,[2] especially, for present purposes, those devoted to Italian music. Whatever the contribution of Michel de Toulouze may have been (cf. p. 37), Petrucci is the man whose position as a printer of music is analogous to that of Gutenberg as a printer of books. Even though Petrucci was not the first to print music or even the first to do so from movable type, he was the earliest to accomplish printing in an important way with respect to music other than plainsong. Printed music naturally gained wider circulation than MSS. The appeal to a larger audience is reflected in Petrucci's departing from custom by providing solutions to verbal canons.

Three tasks faced the early music printers. They had to represent (1) monophonic Gregorian Chant, (2) polyphonic music, and (3) short musical examples in theoretical or other works.[3] This they did by means of wood blocks, metal blocks, or movable type. Printing music by the last-named method apparently originated in Italy, though experiments in the other processes occurred earlier in other countries.

The first known printed book meant to include music is the *Psalterium*, printed by Johann Fust and Peter Schöffer, Gutenberg's associates, at Mainz, in 1457. Only the text and three black lines of the staff were printed; the fourth line was drawn by hand in red, and the notes were also written in manually. Hand-written insertions continued to be made in many liturgical works, even after the general adoption of music printing, since individual copies from large editions could thus be made to conform with local traditions.[4]

The earliest attempt to depict actual music in print appeared in the *Collectorium super Magnificat* of Charlier de Gerson, produced at Esslingen in 1473 by Conrad Fyner. Here, *sol, fa, mi, re, ut,* mentioned in the text, are represented, without staff lines, by five black squares placed in a diagonally descending row and preceded by the letter *f* as an F clef.[5]

To return to Italy: a Roman *Missale* completed at Milan by Michael Zarotus of Parma on April 26, 1476, is the earliest known instance of the printing of music from movable type.[6] Gothic-style (lozenge-shaped) notes are used; however, the printing of the music is not continued throughout. Six months later another *Missale,* also employing movable type but using Roman-style (square) notes, was produced by Ulrich Han (or Hahn) at Rome.[7] In both

---

[2] For biographical data, *see* SchP and VernO.

[3] *See* MeP, 172. This is one of the best historical studies of music printing.

[4] For facsimile of a page with music inserted by hand, from a 1459 print of Fust and Schöffer, see *Catalogue of Manuscripts and Early Printed Books . . . Library of J. Pierpont Morgan,* I, opp. p. 10.

[5] Facsimiles of this page in KinsP, 61, Pl. 1; MeP, 172; LittC, 6; SquireP, 105; etc. LittC, 5f, also has a transl. of Gerson's text.

[6] MeN, 86.   [7] For a page in facsimile, *see* MolD, 8.

books, double-impression printing was employed: the staves were printed in red in one impression, the plainsong notes in black in another.

Mensural note-shapes seem to have been printed for the first time in Franciscus Niger's *Grammatica brevis*, produced at Venice in 1480, by Theodor von Würzburg. It is not clear whether these were printed from type or from a metal block. Three note-shapes are drawn upon to illustrate five poetic meters. There are no staves, but the ascending and descending spacing of the note-heads probably indicates that melodies were intended.[8] In 1487 there appeared, in Nicolo Burzio's *Musices Opusculum*, produced at Bologna by Ugo de Rugeriis, the first known, complete, printed part-composition.[9] This was made from a wood block. It is noteworthy that printing from movable type, a more advanced technique, preceded printing from blocks.

Among the liturgical incunabula printed in Italy are several examples by Ottaviano Scotto.[10] The presses yielded also various books on theory, to which we shall return later.

A petition, addressed by Petrucci to the Signory of Venice and dated May 25, 1498, requested the exclusive privilege for twenty years of printing music for voices, lute, and organ.[11] Not until May 14, 1501, however, did Petrucci's first publication appear. This was the famous *Harmonice Musices Odhecaton A*, which is the earliest printed collection of part-music.[12] It includes compositions by Ockeghem and Busnois, as well as by several composers to be discussed in Chapter 5. It was followed by *Canti B* and *Canti C*, published in 1502 and 1504,[13] respectively. Together with the *Odhecaton*, these form a series particularly rich in Franco-Flemish chansons. All three are in choirbook form, like most of Petrucci's later prints of secular part-music. His aim was evidently to offer "raw material," from which copies for specific performance requirements could be derived. He printed sacred music in partbook form, however, for direct practical use.

Ten out of a series of eleven Petrucci books (1504–1514) preserve a treasury of *frottole* (Book X is lost). The earliest piece of the type to find its way into print, however, is the *Viva el gran Re Don Fernando*, a *barzelletta* (= *frottola*) celebrating the Spanish conquest of Granada and rejoicing that the power-

---

[8] Facsimile in MeP, 174; LittC, 15. The same notes, placed on a four-line staff, are incorporated in a larger musical example in Niger's *Vergiliana Opuscula*, 1500 (facsimile in MeP, 177).

[9] Facsimile in LittC, 17; Grove, IV, 254.

[10] Facsimile of a page from his *Missale Praedicatorum*, Venice, 1482 (double impression), in RieNN, Pl. 14a. A bibliography of incunabula containing music meant for performance (as distinguished from the theoretical works listed in CazaT and WolfH II, 478) has been begun by Kathi Meyer. *See* MeL. Further on music in incunabula, *see* FlowM; KinP; MantN; PatP; ReP.

[11] For English transl. of petition, *see* ReO, 40.

[12] This is available in facsimile (PetrO) and in modern transcription (HewO). For information regarding the work, *see* HewO, pref.; ReO; etc. Facsimiles from other Petrucci prints are given in many sources, e.g., KinsP, 72; MeP, 184; SquireP, 121. His surviving publications are listed and described in SartP (review, with corrections, in *Acta* XX, 78ff).

[13] They were actually dated February 5, 1501, and February 10, 1503, but with reference to the Venetian calendar, in which the year began on March 1 (cf. CastP, 17, 23, 40, 64).

ful city *"de la falsa fè pagana è disciolta e liberata."* [13a] Probably first sung at Naples, it was included in a Roman publication of 1493 that was devoted primarily to a play commemorating the event.[14] A few of Petrucci's pieces are by Andrea Antico, who not only composed, but also worked as a type cutter, printer and publisher.[15] In association with Giovanni Battista Columba, an engraver, and Marcello Silber (alias Franck), a printer, he produced in 1510, at Rome, his first published collection of *frottole,* the *Canzoni nove con alcune scelte de varii libri di canto.*[15a] Venice had temporarily become an unfavorable scene for artistic enterprise, owing to the serious defeat inflicted upon the republic by the League of Cambrai in 1509. However, shortly before 1520 Antico apparently returned to Venice, where he later brought out some prints in partnership with Ottaviano Scotto. In connection with works produced by partners, it is often hard to determine the exact role of each. Some printers not only did their own work, but also commissioned the printing of certain editions from other shops and printed for others as well. In 1513, Antico secured papal privileges for the printing of music and soon thereafter emerged as a serious competitor of Petrucci.[16]

The Frottola and Related Types

The term *frottola* (derived from *frocta*—"a 'mixture' of unrelated thoughts and facts" [16a]) has been used in both a generic and a specific sense, with resulting confusion. For example, Petrucci, in his *Frottole . . . Libro Quarto,*[17] included *strambotti, ode,* and sonnets, as well as *frottole* proper. He did, however, separate the categories in the table of contents. Almost all the Italian secular poetic forms of the period from c. 1470 to 1530—i.e., the forms just mentioned plus the *capitolo* and *canzone*—were covered by the designation, used generically. These pieces replaced the *rondeau* and *bergerette* in the favor of courtly circles, especially in northern and central Italy. As we shall see, they are every bit as much *formes fixes* as the *rondeau,* etc. It is strange to find them coming into fashion in Italy just when the *formes fixes* were dying out in the north.

The birthplace of the new art was Mantua,[18] with the courts of Ferrara

13a About the possibility that *"barzelletta"* is a corruption of *"bergerette,"* see MGG I, 1163.
14 Cf. EinIM I, 35ff. The piece is pr. *ibid.,* 36; BarbiC, 611; PubAPTM V, 131.
15 For data on Antico, see EinIM I, 41, 59; ZenA; ZenN; GravA; TomasA; SCMA IV, pref., which includes a facsimile page of his work.
15a Described in EinAAC.
16 The license was printed in certain editions of Antico's *Canzoni sonetti strambotti et frottole, libro tertio* (pr. SCMA IV, following the print of 1517)—for example, in the undated ed. described in EIF, 18. No copy of an actual ed. of 1513 (mentioned in PirH, 159ff) seems to be extant; *see* MQ XLI (1955), 381.
16a EinIM I, 60.
17 Pr. complete (except for 2 *frottole,* pr. FerandF, 322, 324), together with *Lib. I,* in PetrF. (Cf. the review in M&L, XVIII [1937], 315).—Since this book was first publ., *Lib. I–III* have been pr. in IM, Ser. I, I.
18 About music in Mantua in the 15th century and down to 1517 *see* BertolM, 7–31.

and Urbino playing auxiliary roles. Of the several factors favorable to its growth, the most formative was undoubtedly the patronage of the highly intelligent marchioness of Mantua, Isabella d'Este, daughter of Hercules I of Ferrara, niece of Beatrice of Aragon, and music student of Johannes Martini. Like most women of her circle, she had received instruction in dancing as well as in music, but unlike them, she made the arts an integral part of life rather than a superficial one. In what was once her study in the ducal palace at Mantua, Ockeghem's *Prennez sur moi* (as has been mentioned on p. 120) may be found worked out in marquetry. Many of the great artists of Italy stood on terms of mutual respect and friendship with her. Leonardo da Vinci, Titian, and Castiglione paid her homage.[19] Ariosto (in *Orlando furioso,* canto XIII, stanza 59) called her "that friend of illustrious works . . . liberal and magnanimous Isabella."

The recitation of poetry was completely enjoyable to Isabella and her circle only when given a musical setting. Serafino dall'Aquila (d. 1500), the leading poet of *strambotti,* served at Mantua at the height of his fame, in 1494. Like many poets of the time, he was skilled in singing verses to his own accompaniment on the lute. Some of the anonymous settings of his *strambotti* that have come down to us may well be based on his own performances, a number, no doubt, being his own compositions. After Serafino, the most prolific poet of amorous lyrics was Galeotto del Carretto (c. 1470–1531). He was one of the numerous authors who regularly sent verses to Isabella to have them set to music by one of the two great frottolists at her court.[20]

These composers, Bartolomeo Tromboncino (died c. 1535) and Marco Cara (died c. 1530),[21] were the direct cause of Mantua's renown as the center of the new art. Their fame was already high when, c. 1495, they began their activity at Isabella's court. Tromboncino,[22] who was a man of stormily emotional temperament, often found himself in trouble, eventually murdering his unfaithful wife and her lover. In time, however, his talent earned him forgiveness even for this.

There is much evidence of the high esteem in which Tromboncino's abilities were held. His music was performed at the brilliant festivities attending the wedding of Lucrezia Borgia with Isabella's brother, Alfonso d'Este, at

[19] *See* RubL, 9; EinIM I, 38.

[20] About Serafino, cf. M. Menghini, *Le rime di Serafino de' Ciminelli dall'Aquila,* 1894. About Galeotto, *see* RubL, 10f, 33. For a survey of 15th-century Italian lyric poetry, *see* Vittorio Rossi, *Il Quattrocento (Storia letteraria d'Italia,* VI, 1933), 541ff.

[21] For details of their lives, *see* EinIM I, 42ff.

[22] For *frottole* (in the generic sense) by him, *see* PetrF (25 pieces with ascriptions; about a piece there anon., but apparently his in part, *see* EinB, entry under 1505¹, fn. 7 [cf. in addition our fns. 82 and 83 and their text]; of the 25, 1 is also pr. WolfME, 55; SchwartzN, Supp., 7; BesM, 220; 3 others are also pr. HAM, 97; SchwartzN, Supp., 5; ScherG, 68); SCMA IV (8 pieces—perhaps 10 [cf. our fn. 24 and its text about 1 of the doubtful pieces]); EinIM III, 7 (a different version in GaspI, 627), 10, 12 (= RubL, 60), 14, 317 (= EinAA, 165), 318 (= EinF, 620); EinAAC, 337; RubL, 43, 49, 53, 57; KörL, 158, 159, 160, 161 (all lute-song versions); SchwartzN, Supp., 3; IMAMI II, xvii. *See also* fns. 27, 51, 52b, 62.

Ferrara in 1502. One of the interludes (*intermedi*) sung there during a performance of Plautus' *Asinaria* was *"una musicha mantuana"* by Tromboncino, and on the day following the wedding was heard ". . . another composition of Tromboncino's in which a *barzelletta* was sung in praise of the married couple. . . ." [23] In the same year, in celebration of the marriage agreement reached by another high-born couple, Carretto wrote his *Nozze di Psiche e Cupidine,* in which a *barzelletta* by Tromboncino (or Cara?) served as an interlude. [24]

Baldassare Castiglione in his classic description of Renaissance court life, *Il Libro del Cortegiano* (printed in 1528, but written between 1508 and 1516), praised Marco Cara. [25] That his admiration was reciprocated is attested by the fact that Cara set to music one of Castiglione's sonnets, *Cantai, mentre nel cor lieto fioria.* [26] Another example of the fascinating interplay of personalities which enriches the art history of this period is Tromboncino's setting, published in 1518, of a poem by Michelangelo, *Come haro dunque ardire.* [27]

On the whole, very little is known concerning the Italian frottolists. We are not even certain of the place of origin of Filippo da Luprano, [28] one of the most prolific. Michele Pesenti [29] (not to be confused with Michele Vicentino, [30] also a frottolist) and Giovanni Brocco [31] were from Verona. Antonio Caprioli [32] came from Brescia. Francesco d'Ana [33] (died c. 1503) was, at first, organist at San Leonardo in Venice, and then from August 20, 1490, second organist at St. Mark's. Lodovico Fogliano, [34] whose *Musica theorica* (1529) comes much closer to propounding the system of just intonation than did the earlier treatise of Ramos (cf. p. 586), [34a] composed, as did his brother, Gia-

[23] Quoted from Marin Sanuto's diaries (IV, 229) in EinIM I, 46.
[24] Cf. RubL, 33; the piece is pr. in SCMA IV, 56.
[25] See *The Book of the Courtier,* a transl. by L. E. Opdycke (1929 ed.), 50. For a study of this book from the musical standpoint, *see* BukB. StrunkR, 281ff, gives extracts from Hoby's English transl. of 1561.
[26] Pr. SCMA IV, 61. Other exx. by him pr. PetrF (21 pieces with ascriptions; about 1 piece anon there but apparently his in part, *see* EinB, entry under 1505¹, fn. 7 [cf. also our fns. 82 and 83 and their text; likewise fn. 22]; of the 21, 1 is also pr. p. 163 *infra*; 1 is pr. in ScherG, 70 [in lute-song version]; another in BruL I, 18 [in lute-song version; same version in orig. notation in WolfN II, 60]; still another in KiesS, 14); SCMA (7 pieces); EinIM I, 101; RubL, 39; GaspI, 629; CesM, 249; TorreS, 450, 481 (both given as anon.; but cf. EinB, entry under 1526², fns. 4, 5), and perhaps 520 (= GanF, Supp., No. 9; there ascribed to P. Michele (= Pesenti; the "P." = Prete [priest]); cf. EinB, entry under 1516¹, fn. 1). *See also* our fn. 53.
[27] Pr. EinIM III, 18; TromM, 1; A. Gotti, *Vita di Michelangelo Buonarotti* (1875), II, 99.
[28] Exx. by him pr. PetrF (12 pieces); FerandF, 322, 324; SchwartzN, Supp., 1; SCMA IV, 67; KrV, 8 (No. 13). About his possible identity, *see* EinIM I, 40.
[29] Exx. pr. PetrF (24 pieces); 1 also in EinSH, 272; SchwartzN, Supp., 6; another in GanF, Supp., No. 7; TorreS, 573; still another in RieH II¹, 360; TorreS, 434; CW XLIII, 7); cf. also near end of our fn. 26. ChilS, 25, may likewise be Pesenti's; cf. EinB, entry under 1510¹, fn. 1.
[30] Exx. pr. SCMA IV, 14 (= GanF, Supp., 10); 52.
[31] Exx. pr. PetrF, 1, 12; WolfME, 57. *See also* fn. 54.
[32] Exx. pr. PetrF (12 pieces); 1 also in FiB, 11); another in FerandM, 354); RubL, 63; SchwartzN, Supp., 7.
[33] Exx. pr. PetrF (10 pieces); EinIM III, 536 (= RubL, 51); WolfME, 53; AmbG V, 536.
[34] Exx. pr. EinIM III, 54 (2 pieces); likewise fn. 39. *See also* RoncF.
[34a] About Fogliano's ratios, *see* RieG, 334ff.

erbum caro factum est, a 2. *Marietry* (*with* trompe l'oeil *effects*) *Fra Giovanni da Verona in the hurch of Monte Oliveto Maggiore, Siena*

he Superius has been identified by Dr. Pla-nac as that of the setting a 3 found in MS nc. 27, f.º 109ᵛ–110ʳ, of the Bibl. Naz. Cent., Florence)

Brogi

RENAISSANCE MUSIC IN RENAISSANCE MARQUETRY

zzavona

Four-part canon. Marquetry by Fra Vincenzo da Verona now at the Louvre, Paris

For *Ockeghem's* Prennez sur moi *in marque-try, see* DrozT, *Plate II; for* J'ay pris amours, *see* NA II, *Plate VII*

PLATE II

como.[35] Many other names could be added, for compositions of the *frottola* family were written by laymen and priests, nobles and commoners alike.

The style of such compositions was half popular, half aristocratic. Popular tunes were often used, but in a manner designed to please the cultivated listener. Such material attracted the frottolists as "an object of mirth and mockery, though also of a secret yearning to descend into the lower sphere of supposed vulgarity." [36] They incorporated into their pieces the beginnings of many popular songs and the complete versions of others.[37] Thus the well known *De voltate in qua e do bella Rosina* forms the refrain of the *frottola, Poi ch'el ciel e la fortuna,*[38] and a quodlibet by L. Fogliano [39] contains, among other popular tunes, *Fortuna d'un gran tempo, Scaramella,* and *Che fa la ramacina,* melodies we shall re-encounter.

Sometimes a frottolist was, in the old tradition, both poet and composer. Thus, in Petrucci's *Frottole Libro Primo,* we find several *frottole* with the superscription *"Michaelis cantus & verba."* [40] In treating texts generally, the composers paid attention to rhythmic nicety and correct accentuation, producing settings that are predominantly declamatory and syllabic. Word-painting was not common, but a good example appears in *Rusticus ut asinum* [40a] (in which the use of Latin heightens the effect of travesty). A passage in black notation, denoting a change of meter on the words *"oyme, oyme, cur moreris, asine?"* effectively depicts the cries of the peasant who has lost his donkey. In addition, the black notation provides an early Italian example of "eye-music" (cf. p. 132).

The melodic line of the typical *frottola* has small range and many repeated notes. The contrast to the Franco-Netherlandish style is striking at the cadences (other than the last), where the feminine rhymes so prevalent in Italian are set to repeated notes (rarely to a step or leap). The contrast is heightened by the Italian fondness for clear-cut phrases, in which all voices begin and end together. *Cantus firmi,* in the very few instances in which they occur, may lie in any voice. Thus, in Petrucci's Book I of *frottole,* the superius of Tromboncino's *Non val aqua al mio gran foco* appears also as the alto of Cara's *Glie pur gionto el giorno* and as the bass of *L'aqua vale al mio gran foco* by "Michael." In Book IX, a composition by Rasmo (= Erasmus Lapicida [41]; cf. pp. 165, 641) uses the superius of Cara's *Pietà, cara signora* as its superius and the superius of Tromboncino's *La pietà chiuso ha le porte* as its tenor.[42]

The role of imitation and of contrapuntal decoration in the *frottola* type is generally a modest one. The writing is normally chordal and *a 4,* with the

---

[35] An ex. pr. CW XLIII, 11. *See also* RoncS.   [36] EinIM I, 87.   [37] See JepVF.
[38] Pr. EinW, 360.   [39] Pr. TorreS, 461.
[40] Cf. PetrF, 26 (No. 37), 27, 28, 29, 30 (Nos. 41, 42), 31.
[40a] Bibl. nat., Rés, Vm⁷ 676, fol. 73ᵛ–74. Concerning this MS, *see* BridgmM.
[41] For the 3 pieces, *see* PetrF, 14, 8, 23.   [42] C. SchwartzF, 458.

superius carrying the main melody and the bass having many leaps of fourths and fifths and acting as a harmonic foundation. Apparently these two voices were written first and the inner ones were added to serve as harmonic fillers.[43] This procedure indicates an attention to chordal considerations much greater than that given them by the Franco-Netherlandish composers of the time. The Italian cultivation of harmonic color results in the deliberate use of certain chord progressions. In addition to those resulting from leaps of the fourth or fifth in the bass, there is frequent use of progressions related by the interval of a third. Dissonance treatment in the Italian forms shows a greater use of fourths than in the northern practice. As in music of the early Dufay period, one often finds, at cadences, the bass leaping upward an octave from the penultimate note to the *finalis,* while the tenor crosses, descending stepwise to the root of the chord (cf. Ex. 5). This is one of the few traits of the *frottola* type more archaic than those of contemporary Franco-Netherlandish practice. The V-I progression that results is often present at cadences in other configurations also. Common likewise are extended pedals, usually inverted, sometimes double, at the end.[44]

The *frottola* melodies show a number of favorite rhythmic patterns. Many begin with the figure ♩ ♩ ♩ | ♩,[45] which was destined to take on considerable importance. Four of the most popular opening patterns, which also occur in a number of variants are these:

♩♩|♩ ♩♩ ♩|♩ ♩ [46]   ♩♩♩|♩♩♩ [46a]

♩ ♩|♩ ♩ |♩♩ |♩ ♩ [47]   ♩ |♩. ♪♩ ♩ |♩ ♩ [47a]

In general, a complete text was laid only under the superius, the other parts having only incipits. The various methods of performing music mentioned by Castiglione [48] presumably were applied to the *frottole.* He liked especially performance by solo voice with plucked string accompaniment [49]— one of the predecessors of *seicento* monody. Examples for such rendition are provided by the *frottola* transcriptions of Franciscus Bossinensis, published by

[43] *See* LowSS, 21, quoting Einstein. Also cf. p. 181 *infra* regarding the slightly different, obsolescent succession reported by Aron.
[44] For exx., *see* esp. PetrF, 16, 48, 84. Further on Italian harmonic practice of the time, *see* JepI, xxxvff.
[45] Exx. pr. SCMA IV, 10, 16, 36. In this pattern, and those that follow, the barring may vary in modern transcriptions.
[46] Exx. pr. PetrF, 6 (Nos. 8, 9), 40 (No. 59).   [46a] Exx. pr. SCMA IV, 24, 25, 27, 29, etc.
[47] Exx. pr. PetrF, 14 (No. 20), 18 (No. 26).
[47a] Exx. *ibid.,* 1 (No. 1), 9 (No. 12), 88 (No. 71). Further on rhythmic patterns, *see* JepI, xxxiff.
[48] *See The Book of the Courtier* (cf. fn. 25), 86f; or StrunkR, 284f.
[49] To be sure, he used the expressions *"cantare alla viola"* and *"cantare alla viola per recitar."* However, since there was not only the *viola da arco* (i.e., the bowed viol), but also the *viola da mano* (i.e., the vihuela [cf. pp. 619f] or the lute), there is no reason to assume that Castiglione meant the former. On the contrary, the Renaissance translators of the *Cortegiano* into English, French, and German refer, at this point, to the lute, while the Spanish translator refers to the *vihuela.* It has been suggested (in BukB), at least with regard to the English (1561) and German (1565) translations that the lute is mentioned in place of the viol to accord with local preferences for the plucked instrument. But the weight of evidence appears not to support this view. Cf. WardV, App. to Chap. 1.

Petrucci (cf. pp. 163, 522).[50] Solo instrumental performance of *frottole* was also cultivated. In 1508, Joan Ambrosio Dalza included several *frottole* in his *Intabulatura di Lauto,*[51] and in 1517 Antico published his *Frottole intabulate da sonare organi,*[51a] the first organ tablature printed in Italy (cf. pp. 528, 534). There is also evidence for *a cappella* rendition: e.g., an illustration in Antico's *Canzoni nove* (1510) shows four men singing from a choir-book.[52]

Although many *frottole* are inconsequential, it would be a mistake to dismiss them lightly as a whole. To be sure, most *frottole* consisted of settings of trivial texts. Many of these were not intended to have value as independent verse, but were mere *poesia per musica*. Frivolity was often the keynote, love poems were likely to be parodies; but that did not prevent the unpretentious little pieces from having, as a class, musical importance of their own. Through them Italy influenced the art of the northerners, and through them lay the way to the more flexible and expressive madrigal. The texts improved as new *frottola* collections appeared. While no famous Italian poet was drawn upon in Petrucci's Book I (though it did contain a setting of "Integer vitae"), several such poets are represented in the later Books: for example, Politian in Book II, Galeotto del Carretto in Book III, Bembo in Book VII, and Petrarch, abundantly, in Book XI.[52a] A setting by Tromboncino of Dido's letter to Aeneas in Ovid's *Heroides,* VII, may be the first love letter in music.[52b]

A defect of the *frottola* is the heaviness of its texture, which is ill suited to the lightness and gaiety of its tunes. Cara sought to remedy this defect when he set a sonnet "S'io sedo a l'ombra" [53] in a monophonic style with the support of only a few chords.

In general, the musical sonnet is the most regular and schematic of the forms. Such a composition was designed as a vehicle for the setting of any poetic sonnet, regardless of content: it is not unusual to find above the music some such superscription as *"Modo de cantar sonetti."* [54] Cara's *Sonno che gli animali* illustrates the general practice of using only three musical units to set the quatrain and tercets, disposing them *abbc abbc abc abc.*[55]

The *strambotto* has eight lines of text, frequently of a serious nature. The

[50] For a facsimile page from the *Tenori e contrabassi intabulati . . . Lib. I, see* PirH, 177; for 2 facsimiles from *Lib. II, see* SartFB, opp. pp. 240, 241.

[51] PirF contains comparative versions of Tromboncino's *Poi che volse la mia stella* according to Petrucci's Book III (*a 4;* also pr. EinIM III, 75), F. Bossinensis' *Tenori . . . Lib. I* (voice and lute), and J. Dalza's *Intabulatura . . .* (lute solo).

[51a] From 6 transcriptions from this work with the original versions *a 4,* see JepO, App., 3ff.

[52] Facsimile in PetrF. Further about performance, *see* PetrF, xii; RubL, 5, 32; JepI, xlixff.

[52a] Cf. EinI, 84.   [52b] Pr. EinL, 49.

[53] Pr. EinIM I, 101, with commentary. There is some possibility that the piece is by Tromboncino, since Petrucci's Book V adds the initials B.T. in the index.

[54] For a textless sonnet with such a superscription, *see* PetrF, 58.

[55] The piece is pr. SCMA IV, 3; the sonnets pr. *ibid.,* 55, 57, illustrate the same point. (SCMA IV underlays only lines 1, 2, and 14 of sonnets following the general practice, complete texts being given in the pref. matter and adaptation to the music being left to the user.) SCMA IV, 61, is irregular in that it provides new music for the tercets, the form being *abbc abbc dde dde;* RubL, 51, has the form *abbc abbc def def.* Brocco's setting of Petrarch's "Ite, caldi sospiri," as pr. with incorrect directions in ScherG, 69, seems to be irregular in still another way, but is actually regular; cf. MQ XLI (1955), 382.

rhyme pattern is the one invented in the 14th century by Boccaccio and later called *ottava rima: abababcc*. The musical pattern often is simply *abababab*,[56] but there are variants using more than two musical units.[57] Many pieces are too slight to be of interest, but some compress a notable amount of musical expressiveness within their few measures.

EXAMPLE 32. *Io son l'ocello che non pò volare*—Tromboncino (Petrucci, *Frottole Lib. VIII;* transcr. by A. Einstein).

Io   son lo - cel - lo   che non   pò   vo - - la - re,
Io   son quel se - gno   do - ve   a   sae - - ta - re
Io   son stan - cho   no - chier in   al - - to   ma - - re
Io   son co - lui   che   più de nul - la   cu - - ra

Non me es - sen - do   ri - ma - - sto   pen - - na a ku - - na;
Se   sfor - za - no   le stel - le a - - du - - na a du - - na;
Tem - pe - sta - to   dal ciel   e   da   fortu - - na;
Poi che dal ciel o - gni u - no ha   sua   ventu - - ra.

"I am a bird who can no longer fly, having no feather left to me; I am the target at which the stars thrust themselves one by one; I am the tired mariner on the high seas, tossed about by heaven and by fortune; I am he who no longer cares at all, since each one's destiny is given him by heaven."

The *oda* had an indeterminate number of stanzas of four lines each, the last line being of a different length from the others. The several possible rhyme schemes made this kind of ode a form of chain verse. A common rhyme scheme was *abbc cdde . . . xyyz*. There were four musical phrases repeated as a unit for each stanza.[58]

The *capitolo* consists of an indeterminate number of tercets, sometimes with a concluding quatrain. Each tercet-line has its own music, repeated in each stanza. A final quatrain, when present, has its own music for line 4.[59]

The *frottola* proper varies, but differs from these other forms in possessing a refrain. A typical *frottola* has a poem with a four-line *ripresa* and six-line strophes; its music consists of two units, each of two phrases. The four phrases set the four lines of the *ripresa;* the first two phrases, performed twice,[60] plus the last two phrases set the six lines of each strophe. After each

---

[56] For some exx. in this form, *see* RubL, 45; WolfME, 53, 54, 57; PetrF, 50 (No. 9), 52 (No. 11), 53 (No. 13), etc.

[57] The *strambotti* in SCMA IV have the form *ababbcd*, except the one on p. 25, which has the rhyme scheme *ababcbdd* and the musical pattern *abbcdefg*.

[58] Exx. pr. RubL, 47; SCMA IV, 38; HelmH, 308.

[59] For a Tromboncino *capitolo, see* RubL, 49.

[60] Indicated in Petrucci's prints, etc., by repetition signs. These have dots on both sides of the

strophe, the *ripresa* recurs as a refrain, complete or in part. In the latter event, the part retained is likely to consist of the first half, extended, and is given in the source after the complete *ripresa*. A slight departure from the norm is represented by Cara's *Oimè il cor*. This has eight-line strophes, and phrases 3 and 4 must therefore be repeated, in each strophe, for lines 7 and 8.[61] The piece is one in which the strophes are followed by a shortened *ripresa*. Example 33a shows Cara's *frottola* in its original form; Example 33b gives it in Franciscus Bossinensis' transcription for voice and lute, preceded by its *ricercare* (cf. p. 522), also by Bossinensis.[62]

EXAMPLE 33. (*a*) *Oimè il cor*—Marco Cara (after PetrF, 1) and (*b*)
    arrangement of it by Franciscus Bossinensis, preceded by his
    ricercare for the piece (from *Tenori e contrabassi intabulati
    . . . Lib. I*, Petrucci, 1509; transcr. by D. Plamenac).

vertical lines. Dots to the right of such lines do not indicate repetition of the following section.
    [61] The same is true of the Tromboncino *frottola* pr. in ScherG, 68, but the form is incorrectly indicated on p. 9 of the ScherG *Quellennachweis* (cf. PetrF, xxxi).
    [62] For a Tromboncino *frottola* with a similar transcription and *ricercare, see* FerandM, 382ff. (The original *frottola* = PetrF, 17.)

"Alas the heart, alas the head! Who does not love does not understand. For him who errs and makes no amends, after the error repentance remains.

Oimè, dio, che error fece io
ad amar un cor fallace,
oimè, dio, che'l partir mio
non mi da per questo pace.
Oimè, el foco aspro e vivace
mi consuma el tristo core;
oimè, dio, che'l fatto errore
l'alma afflicta mi molesta:
   Oimè el cor, etc.

"Alas, O God, how have I erred
to love a faithless heart; alas, O
God, that, for this, my parting
hence grants me no peace. Alas,
the bitter and living fire consumes
my mournful heart; alas, O God,
how the error I have made troubles my afflicted soul. *Alas the
heart, etc."*

The *canzone,* of all the generic *frottola* forms, has almost the least structural regularity. The number of strophes varies from piece to piece, as does the strophe structure, although the latter is constant in a single *canzone.* At the end there is sometimes a *commiato*—a short envoy, containing the author's parting words to his poem, or something similar. The only standardizing feature is the use of a combination of seven- and eleven-syllable lines. The irregularity of the rhymes, the rhythmic variety, and a high standard of literary content distinguish the *canzone* [63] from the more popular forms— the *strambotto* and *frottola* proper.

The *villota* possesses no structural regularity at all. According to one hypothesis,[64] this type dates back to the first half of the 15th century and enjoyed its heyday c. 1480. Neither claim is supported by proof. However, the early *villota* does belong to the *frottola* period. A common feature, throughout its history, is that in some way it incorporates a popular or street song into its texture.[65] Pieces of the type tend to have nonsense syllables in the text, to be dance-like, and to have sections in contrasting duple and triple meter. A separate section that sometimes concludes a more developed *villota* and contrasts with the main body by means of a more rapid pace is known as a *nio.*[66]

The *justiniana* (= *giustiniana*) is a setting *a 3,* for solo voice with instru-

[63] Exx. pr. RubL, 53, 57, 60, 63.
[64] Advanced in TorreS (cf. also TorreP); but *see* reviews in M&L, XXL (1940), 392; RMI, XLIII (1939), 645; also KinT.   [65] Cf. EinIM I, 340; II, 744, 748ff.
[66] Exx. of the *villota* pr. SCMA IV, 18; PetrF, 92 (by Compère; cf. p. 224, *infra*); AmbG V,

mental support, of verse by Leonardo Giustiniani (d. 1446), a setting characterized not so much by special structure as by a highly melismatic top part and effects resembling the stammering of a transported lover. Archaic at Petrucci's time, it is represented by some examples in his Book VI.[66a]

The general trend after 1510, as evidenced by the contents of successive *frottola* books, was in favor of the more serious forms, the *canzone,* sonnet, and *oda.* The last known printed collection of *frottole* appeared in 1533, but their essence nevertheless continued alive in other forms. The lighter types of *frottola* developed into the *villanesca,* while the more serious forms were infused with Franco-Netherlandish style trends to bring forth the madrigal.[67]

Sacred Music; the Laude

Although Tromboncino, Cara, and their fellow frottolists were essentially composers of secular music, they wrote some church music also. Petrucci printed two collections of Lamentations of Jeremiah, both in 1506, and Tromboncino, Weerbecke (cf. pp. 217ff), and Erasmus Lapicida are represented by settings [68] in Book II. Book I (alluded to on p. 149), which contains some material other than Lamentations, ends with a *Passio sacra,* not a real Passion despite its opening word,[68a] by Francesco d'Ana.[69] Two actual settings of the Passion, both anonymous—one according to St. Matthew, the other according to St. John—, probably Italian and dating from the last quarter of the 15th century, are preserved in *a.* M. 1, 12, at Modena (cf. p. 28).[70] The St. John Passion is the simpler. The words of Jesus and the Evangelist are not provided with music, the other solo roles are written out to the plainsong formula material assigned to the *Synagoga* in the Gregorian Passion,[70a] and the choral sections—those for the *Turba* (the term designates not only the "crowd" in the literal sense, but any group)—are set in fauxbourdon with the same formula material in the discant. The St. Matthew Passion likewise provides no music for Jesus or the Evangelist. It presents, however, in addition to sections *a 3,* one ostensibly *a 8* (though only two voices are active at a time) and two really *a 6,* the plainsong in all three sections being in the tenor.

---

134 (by Josquin; cf. p. 230); TorreS, 471, 507. For further references on the *villota, see* the bibliography in ApelH, 794.

66a The poet had provided music for some of his own verse. Further on the type, *see* RubJ.

67 Further on the *frottola, see* EinF, EinIM, RubF, JepF, SchwartzF, SchwartzN, and SchwartzP. EinB (which brings up to date the portion of VogelV listing the collections containing works by more than one composer) includes bibliographical data on *frottola* prints.

68 A fragment of Tromboncino's setting (in a chordal, almost syllabic style, with melismas reserved for cadences) is pr. in TorA I, 19–30. For the underlying chant, *see* Liber, 626.

68a Cf. KadP 4f.   69 Pr. complete as 2 motets TorA I, 13, 17.

70 Cf. MosV, 11f (with exx.; 1 also in BukT, 2; BukMR, 186).

70a Cf. Officium, 111–42, 255–81, 321–47, 497–518. The part of the *Chronista* (= Evangelist, Narrator) is there indicated by the letter C (except at the beginning where no indication is given), that of Christ by a cross *pattée,* and that of the *Synagoga* (a figure representing all the remaining dramatis personae) by the letter S. The parts of Christ, the *Chronista,* and the *Synagoga* were sung on three different levels as early as the 13th century; it was not until the 15th century that they were assigned to separate performers. Cf. SchofN, 518. Although the practice has varied over the centuries, it is most usual for each of the 3 parts to have an opening and a closing formula, for Christ and the *Synagoga* each to have also a formula for questions, and for the Evangelist to have one with which to introduce the words of Christ.

This Passion, too, contains fauxbourdon passages. Historians have divided Passion compositions into two classes: the motet type and the dramatic type. In the former, the consecutive narrative is set forth and polyphony is applied, without distinction, to texts drawn from the *Christus, Chronista,* and *Synagoga* parts, the appropriate formulas being introduced into the polyphony. In the latter type there is a sharper distribution of the various roles. The parts of the *Christus* and the *Chronista* are sung in plainsong, polyphony being provided for the *Synagoga* part alone (but not necessarily just for the portions of it that represent groups), so that the formula material of only this part is dramatically suitable for polyphonic reworking. The two Passions of the Modena MS obviously belong to the dramatic type. Besides the fauxbourdon passages mentioned above, the St. Matthew Passion in this MS includes also passages written in the different style that later came to be designated by the Italian cognate of "fauxbourdon"—*falsobordone* (cf. pp. 90f)—i.e., a declamatory style employing many repeated chords and having chord-roots in the bass. The style, because of the repeated chords, was especially suitable for use in settings of psalm-tones and similar formulas. Indeed, it undoubtedly resulted from the creation of such settings, and these evidently came into being in the course of improvising before written examples first appeared.[70b]

The *frottola* had an equivalent in the religious, non-liturgical form of the *lauda.* The practice of singing songs of praise in the evening before the statue of the Virgin had been cultivated by religious fraternities in the Middle Ages (cf. pp. 80f). During the 13th and 14th centuries, companies of *laudesi* were to be found in all the larger towns of Italy. Florence, the chief center, had at least nine of them. According to an account of c. 1546, such a fraternity, consisting mostly of artisans, met in a church every Saturday, after nones, to sing *a 4* half a dozen *laude.* The singers changed with each piece; and afterward, to song and organ music, the service ended with the unveiling of a picture of the Madonna.[71]

The writers of *lauda* poetry seem to have been legion and of various stations and occupations; new texts appeared constantly. The poetry was generally less sophisticated than that of the *frottole,* but its forms were often derived from secular counterparts. Thus we have *laude* which conform to the rhyme-scheme and structure of the *frottola* proper, *strambotto, capitolo, oda,* etc.[72]

The music of the *laude,* in general, changed with the fluctuating fashions, so that examples from MSS of different periods vary considerably.

Only a few monophonic *laude* survive from the 15th century. However, one should not be misled, by their rarity, into underestimating the extent to which monophonic *laude* were cultivated at this time.[73] But the main artistic interest lay in the polyphonic settings. The 15th-century MS, Ital. Cl. IX, 145, at the Marciana in Venice, contains five anonymous two-part *laude,*[74] each

[70b] Cf. BukT, 31; FerandM, 177f, 180.   [71] Cf. JepI, xv.
[72] Further on this point, *see ibid.,* xxviii.   [73] Further on this point, *see ibid.,* xxf.
[74] Described in JepV; JepI, xxi. Two pr. *ibid.,* xxii.

presumably by "a humble Franciscan" who also wrote the words. They are written in a linear style and are plainly by competent composers. In contrast, the same MS contains some cruder two-part *laude,* such as might have been devised and sung in circles where, without adequate training, the writer still wished to follow the polyphonic fashion. They are less free in style, adhering rather to the old *cantus-firmus* principle.[75] Another MS, from the last quarter of the century,[76] contains a three-voice *lauda, Ubi karitas et amor,*[77] set in a chordal style indicative of the Italians' early and well-developed sense for harmony. Some *laude* are preserved also in paintings of the period. One was painted into a large altarpiece (c. 1504) by Lo Spagna, now in the gallery at Perugia.[78] Two pieces, which though textless appear to be *laude* of c. 1500, are shown in Carpaccio's *St. Jerome in his Oratory.*[79]

The largest known collection of polyphonic *laude* of the time is formed by Petrucci's *Laude Libro primo . . .* of 1508 and *Laude Libro secondo* of 1507 (concerning the inconsistency between the volume numbers and the dates, *see* JepI, lix).[80] Many of the composers represented we already know as frottolists: Tromboncino, Cara, Giac. Fogliano, Luprano. Others, such as Innocentius Dammonis, wrote in the religious genre exclusively. Dammonis was evidently the chief *lauda* composer: Petrucci's print of 1508 is devoted entirely to sixty-six pieces of his.[81]

The music of these *laude* shares with the *frottola* settings the stylistic traits that have been discussed and which may be said to constitute the Italian style of this period. It is interesting to note that the *lauda, Sancta Maria ora pro nobis,*[82] is set to the same music as the *strambotto, Me stesso incolpo;*[83] the latter is anonymous in Petrucci's *Frottole Libro Quarto* (1505) but the former is credited to Cara and Tromboncino jointly in the *lauda* print of 1507. Also, we find that one musical setting was sometimes used for various *lauda* texts. Petrucci's second *lauda* book includes *Vengo a te, madre Maria* [84] and *Senza te alta regina;* although the first is ascribed to Giac. Fogliano and the second to D. Nicolo, both *laude* are set to identical music.

The same music would not have been applicable to various texts if it had expressed the words. It was, actually, neutral, and this is strikingly illustrated by the use of the same music for the *lauda, Jesu, Jesu* and for a *canto carnascialesco, Visin, visin.*[85] A greater textual contrast could hardly be found anywhere.

The Canti Carnascialeschi

These *canti carnascialeschi,* or carnival songs, were sung in Florence during the carnival season. The Florentines celebrated not only the pre-Lenten revelry,

---

[75] Two pr. *ibid.,* xxiv.   [76] Described in GuerrC.   [77] Pr. JepI, xxiv.
[78] Cf. DentL, 66f, where it is reprinted.
[79] Reproduced as frontispiece to IMAMI II; detail of music opp. p. xxxiv.
[80] All the music of the second book and a selection from the first are pr. in JepI.
[81] Further about Dammonis, *see ibid.,* lvi; LowS, 256f.
[82] Pr. JepI, 31.   [83] Pr. PetrF, 64. On *strambotto* parodies among the *laude,* see GhiSL.
[84] Pr. JepI, 6.   [85] Pr. GhiCC, 110, with both texts. Facsimile of *Visin, ibid.,* opp. p. 56.

but also the *Calendimaggio,* which began on May 1 and ended with the Feast of St. John on June 24. An essential part of the festivities was the singing and dancing of the *canzona a ballo* in the streets by masked merrymakers. (*"Canzona a ballo"* denotes in its widest sense any secular song that is danced as well as sung.)

Under Lorenzo de' Medici, whose rule began in 1469, the carnivals had become infused with a more intense life. He strongly encouraged the celebrations, and, following his lead, the court took a much greater part in them than previously. Lorenzo has been accused of acting as he did in order to induce the people to forget their lack of political liberty. It is more likely, however, that he was simply indulging his love of display and magnificence and delighting both the populace and himself by the grandeur of his contribution to the festivities.

Torchlight processions with decorated cars of masqueraders were the main feature of the carnivals. Some of the *carri* represented the city's trade and craft guilds, others depicted legendary scenes or the triumph of classical conquerors. Lorenzo increased the number of these chariots and the lavishness of their decoration. The triumphs emphasized the power and glory of the Medici, while the mythical representations—in contrast to the more popular displays arranged by the guilds and crafts—gave scope for Lorenzo's court of nobles, poets, and artists to exercise their talents.

Lorenzo himself wrote poems to be sung not only by his courtier-actors, but also by the guilds. His *Trionfo d'Arianna e Bacco* and his *Canto di uomini che vendevano bericuocoli e confortini* ("Song of the Sweetmeat Sellers")[86] are among the most famous of the *canti carnascialeschi* and epitomize the two main types—the mythical; the local and topical—into which they mostly fall.

The second type, of course, had the more popular appeal, consisting as it did of songs describing the various guilds or depicting daily life. Double meanings, involving an obscene twist, were common. The names of some of the songs are almost enough, by themselves, to evoke the vigorous, turbulent life of 15th-century Florence. In the *Canti de' sartori,*[87] *de' profumieri, de' facitori d'olio, de' molinari,*[88] *dei poveri che accattano per carità,*[89] the elegant tailors and perfumers of Florence, the oil-makers, millers, and beggars who filled the crowded streets, live and ply their trades again. The *Canto d'uomini che vanno col viso volto di dietro* ("Song of the men with their faces turned backward") embodied some political gibe, while the *Canti della malmaritata, delle donne giovani e di mariti vecchi, delle vedove,*[90] *dei giudei battezzati*[91] (Songs of the unhappy wife, of the young wives with old husbands, of the widows, of the baptized Jews) were intended to be comic.

---

[86] Heinrich Isaac (cf. pp. 169f) is supposedly the musician who set this text. Only a fragment survives; cf. EinIM I, 33.

[87] For a facsimile, *see* GhiCC, Fig. C, before p. 57.   [88] An ex. of this type pr. GhiCC, 112.

[89] An ex. pr. MassonC, 1. Text by Lorenzo de' Medici.

[90] An ex. *ibid.,* 46.   [91] An ex. *ibid.,* 22.

Textually, the *canti carnascialeschi* [92] descend from the old *cacce,* which also were topical, descriptive, and full of double meanings. Musically, however, they are chordal and strophic like the Mantuan *frottole.* The *canti carnasciales-chi,* however, or, as they are sometimes called, the Florentine *frottole*—includ-ing, as they did, chariot songs, serenades, processionals, etc.—were all sung in the open, as were, on occasion, the *laude* and the *frottole.* Open-air per-formance may well have determined the chordal character of this *popolaresca lirica.* The public nature of the performance, the necessity for rising above the clamor of the crowd, and the acoustics of the *piazze,* all encouraged the use of resounding chords rather than polyphony.

One of the earliest and most famous collections of *canti carnascialeschi* (and, until the discovery of Florence, Bibl. naz. centr., Banco rari 230 [*olim* Magliab. XIX, 141] [93] in the 19th century, almost the only known source) is that made in 1559 by Anton Francesco Grazzini, known as Il Lasca. It is entitled *Tutti i Trionfi, Carri, Mascherate e Canti Carnascialeschi.*[94] The term *"mascherata"* obviously comes from the custom of singing pieces so named during carnival masquerading.

The *canto carnascialesco* varies greatly, both in structure and in degree of complexity. A common scheme is this: [95]

Text rhymes	|abba|	|cd|	|cd|	|a|
Music	$\frac{4}{4}$ a	b	b	$\frac{3}{4}$ c

During its golden period under Lorenzo de' Medici, the *canto carnascialesco* on the one hand was the property of the whole community, many of the *canti* being anonymous, and on the other hand was enriched not only by the poems of Lorenzo himself and of his herald Battista dell'Ottonaio, but by the com-positions of his musicians Alexander Coppinus [96] and the Netherlanders, Heinrich Isaac (c. 1450–1517) and Alexander Agricola (cf. pp. 207ff).

Of these, Isaac is the most interesting, partly by reason of his privileged position at Lorenzo's court. He arrived in Florence c. 1484, having possibly been called there for the specific purpose of assuming Squarcialupi's old post as organist of the Cappella di San Giovanni (the Baptistery).[96a] Later, he became organist at the churches of Santa Maria del Fiore and the Annunziata. As music teacher to Lorenzo's sons, he had among his pupils the future Pope Leo X.

Isaac's career, as we shall see, took him to several countries. He was an

---

[92] The texts are collected in *Canti carnascialeschi del Rinascimento, a cura di Charles Singleton* (*Scrittori d'Italia,* 1936).
[93] For description of contents of this, as well as other sources, *see* GhiCC, App. II.
[94] Described in GhiCC, 22ff.
[95] Cf. Lorenzo's *canto* in MassonC, 1.
[96] For *canti* by him, *see* MassonC, 16, 74, 98, 101; GhiFM, 14.
[96a] Cf. GhiCC, 40f (in the light of Grove II, 740).

international master, equally at home in the composition of Masses, motets, French chansons, German Lieder and *canti carnascialeschi*. His *Ne più bella di queste* [97] is a song in praise of Florence, and another piece, *Palle, palle,*[98] a textless composition, takes its name from the six balls or pills found in the Medici family crest. A *cantus firmus* is presented three times, each new appearance lying a step higher than its predecessor, except for the last three notes of the melody, which are always given at the same pitch-level. Perhaps the tune derives from the party cry of the Medici.[98a] Unfortunately none of the actual *canti carnascialeschi* that Isaac wrote survive complete, but we do have a *Calendimaggio* song of his, *Or'è di Maggio.*[99] His *Fammi una gratia* [99a] reaches us in a MS (Florence, Conserv. B. 2440) [99b] that would appear to preserve a repertory especially connected with the court of Lorenzo.[99c] Included is an anonymous setting of Lorenzo's *Un dì lieto giamai* [99d] and compositions by Alessandro and Bartolomeo (Florentine organists),[99e] Francesco Ajolla (= Layolle; cf. p. 300),[99f] Agricola,[99g] and others.

In 1492, Isaac set to music Politian's lament on the death of Lorenzo, *Quis dabit capiti meo aquam.*[100] Two years later the temporary fall of the Medici and the rule of the monk Savonarola radically affected the *canti carnascialeschi*. Some of the well-known melodies were newly fitted with sacred and penitential words. This was the period when Savonarola's reformatory zeal led to the Burning of the Vanities in the Piazza della Signoria. Among the many art treasures that were irretrievably lost were musical instruments and probably also secular songs.[101]

After Savonarola's fall in 1498, the carnival returned, but in more sober form. The country had been invaded by the armies of France and of Emperor Maximilian. In the prevailing atmosphere of uncertainty, the carnival songs remained solemn and penitential, while to the processions was added the *Trionfo della Morte*. The nearest approach to the old spirit was made by the *canti dei lanzi,*[102] which made fun of the armies of the Emperor. Some, classifying the soldiery according to their special functions, as halberdiers, pikemen, fusiliers, and the like, are closely akin to the old guild *canti*. The

---

[97] Pr. DTO XIV¹, 40.

[98] Pr. DTO XIV¹, 98; facsimile, *ibid.*, vii. (*See also* SIM X, 322.)

[98a] However, it does not reappear in the *Canto delle palle,* pr. GhiFM, 19.

[99] Pr. DTO XVI¹, 206.   [99a] *Ibid.*, 37.

[99b] Described in GanF; but *see* EinIM I, 129.   [99c] Cf. *ibid.*, 31, 130.

[99d] Pr. GanF, Supp., No. 4, as the work of Bernardo Pisano; but *see* EinIM I, 130. About Pisano, *see* pp. 313f, *infra*.

[99e] The former is apparently not identical with Coppinus or Agricola; cf. GhiCC, 59f. An ex. of his pr. GanF, Supp., No. 5; a portion pr. AmbG V, 531 (text omitted). Exx. by Bartolomeo, pr. *ibid.*, 530; GanF, Supp., Nos. 1, 6; WolfGM I, 85.

[99f] Ex. pr. *ibid.*, No. 2; portion pr. AmbG V, 533 (text omitted).

[99g] The *Amor che sospirar,* mentioned on p. 208.

[100] Pr. DTO XIV¹, 45; for another lament, *see ibid.*, 49.

[101] Savonarola, however, was not unfavorable to music, so long as it was religious. Cf. ChilSM.

[102] Five pr. MassonC, 89ff.

soldiers are impersonated in the songs and, as a result, most of the texts are written in a mixture of Italian and German; all are bibulous and obscene.

Even after the Medici were restored in 1511, the carnival did not regain its old gaiety, but became a grave court ceremonial; the *canti carnascialeschi* lost their popular spontaneity and grew more literary in character. But by this time (although they continued on into the 17th century) the *canti*, especially by virtue of their structural freedom, had made their distinctive contribution to Italian music.[103]

The Sacre Rappresentazioni, etc.

If the *canti carnascialeschi*, performed before Lent and some time after Easter, in the *Calendimaggio*, were of a frivolous nature, more serious matter was provided for performance during Lent by the *sacre rappresentazioni*. These religious plays derived from two sources. One was the type of *devozione* (or dramatized *lauda*) that was an enactment, as a play in verse, of the events of Holy Thursday and Good Friday. (There were also *devozioni* associated with Christmas.) The custom of offering these presentations had spread throughout *trecento* Italy. The other source was the elaborate celebration in Florence of the feast of her patron saint, John the Baptist.[103a] This was celebrated yearly with processions—which included cars decorated to represent religious subjects—and with tableaux and mimes on specially erected stages in all the public squares. Such spectacles might include a Resurrection, with a tomb bursting open with a loud explosion, or an Assumption of the Virgin by singing angels. The spoken drama of the *devozione* and the mimetic and musical spectacles of the feast of St. John fused into the *sacra rappresentazione*.

The *rappresentazioni* were usually enacted in church—and even here with the aid of spectacular scenic effects. Brunelleschi designed a Heaven in the vaults of a certain church, with doors that rolled back with a sound like thunder to reveal the Eternal Father enthroned in glory among the heavenly host.[104] The action, taken from any sacred story, was ushered in by an *annunziazione*. Such a prologue formed the subject of a remark by Vincenzo Borghini (d. 1580) that throws some light on the use of music in the *rappresentazioni* and hence on their position in the history of music as well as of drama. "The plays were sung, and for a while this was regarded as a good thing. . . . The first person to suppress song in the *rappresentazione* was l'Araldo, at the beginning of the 16th century. That does not mean his play was not sung, but that the introduction to it was spoken, which at first seemed rather strange,

---

[103] Further concerning the *canti carnascialeschi*, see GhiC; GhiCC; MassonC; MGG II, 764ff. For reprints of *canti*, see esp. MassonC, CW XLIII, GhiFM, and GhiCC.

[103a] See J. A. Symonds, *The Renaissance in Italy*, II (of Modern Library ed.), 251.

[104] Cf. AncoO I, 421f. This is the chief work dealing with the *sacre rappresentazioni*.

though it afterwards grew in favor. . . And it was an extraordinary thing how the old usage of singing was abandoned quite suddenly. . . ." [105] This implies that music had once played an even greater role than is indicated by the surviving texts [106] of 15th- and 16th-century *rappresentazioni*. Here we find many references, chiefly in the form of stage directions, to musical interpolations. In the prologue to the *Rappresentazione di San Giovanni e Paolo*, written by Lorenzo de' Medici, c. 1471, the angel says:

Senza tumulto sien le voci chete	*Now, without tumult, keep your voices quiet,*
Massimamente poi quando si canta.[107]	*Most in particular when there is singing.*

The stage directions of the *Rappresentazione di Santa Margherita* require St. Margaret to sing a *lauda* beginning *O vaghe di Jesù* to the music of the secular piece, *O vaghe montanine*.[108] There are many other references to the singing of *laude* in these plays. In the *Rappresentazione di Santa Eufrasia* we read: "While the madonna sleeps, the sisters sing this *lauda*":

O Maria del ciel regina	*Mary, O thou queen of heaven,*
Viva fonte e vera pace . .[109]	*Thou true peace and living fountain . . .*

Such singing may well have been in parts. A more secular episode occurs in the aforementioned *Rappresentazione di Santa Margherita* when "Young huntsmen sing this song":

Iamo alla caccia, su alla caccia!	*Let us go hunting, hey for the hunting!*
Su su su su, ognun si spaccia!	*Soho, soho, everyone hurry!*

Then, "when the song is over, the horns sound." [110] The religious nature of the stories of the *rappresentazioni* did not preclude colorful and vigorous treatment. In Lorenzo's *San Giovanni e Paulo* there is a battle scene that was quite possibly accompanied by Isaac's *A la bataglia*.[111] Little orchestras of lutes and viols were often used. The action was sometimes interrupted by

105 Cf. AncoO I, 322f. The above transl. is, save for the first sentence, that contained in Romain Rolland, *Some Musicians of Other Times* (1915; a transl. of RollM), 31. L'Araldo may have been Lorenzo's herald, Ottonaio.

106 43 of them pr. AncoS.   107 AncoS II, 237.

108 Cf. the setting in TorreS, 515; GanF, Supp., No. 11.   109 AncoS II, 316.   110 *Ibid.*, 129f.

111 Pr. DTO XVI¹, 221; GhiMI, 269. Cf. PirL, 2; text of GhiMI. (It should be pointed out, however, that Lorenzo's play dates from 1471 [cf. SolA I, 1], whereas Isaac entered his service only c. 1484. But the composition may have been interpolated in later performances. The statement, made in several reference books, that the music for the entire play survives at Oxford, is incorrect; cf. GhiMI, 264.) Further on the *battaglia* and other program music, *see* GläB; BrenE (containing, on p. 750f, a short 15th-century *battaglia* [facsimile in IMAMI I, opp. xciv]; BrenE is incorporated in BrenV, but without this ex.).

interludes in which dances were performed. Thus, in the *Santa Margherita,* a character dressed in a costume with bells on it is asked to *"saltar . . . alla moresca."* [112]

The *Maggi,* the country cousins of the more sophisticated, court-patronized *sacre rappresentazioni,* probably preserve for us evidence of what the latter originally were like, for, while the *rappresentazioni* evolved, the *Maggi* remained highly traditional—so much so that they often bore as sole musical instruction *"da cantarsi sull'aria del Maggio."* The stanzas were always written in *abba*-rhymed verse.

The subjects treated were much like those of the *rappresentazioni,* but included a greater number of legendary and historical stories. The type of spectacle was more violent, battles, jousts, and storms at sea forming staple sources of delight. The comic element was represented by the *buffone.* [113]

The interpolation of music by Tromboncino in a performance of Plautus' *Asinaria* (cf. p. 158) is an example of the role music played in dramatic activities at court. In an *intermezzo* to Plautus' *Casina*—presented at the same wedding celebration as was the production of *Asinaria* referred to—music was executed by six viols. [113a] We know likewise that when Politian's *Orfeo* was performed at Mantua c. 1471, music (now lost) was provided by a certain Germi for a *canzone,* choruses of Dryads and of Bacchantes, and a prayer of Orfeo's. Owing to the influence of Lorenzo de' Medici, pagan themes had already made their way into the *trionfi* and *sacre rappresentazioni.* It is from the latter, transformed by classic elements, that this *Orfeo* grew—a link between the religious and pseudo-classic drama of Italy. At first, *Orfeo* consisted of several scenes, but was later divided by Politian into five acts, following the precedent of the classical drama. Plays of the new type, sometimes called *ecloghe* or *farse,* proved highly successful, and were imitated at various Italian courts during the late *quattrocento.* In 1482, musical and choreographic *intermedi* were provided for Niccolò da Correggio's *Cefalo.* [114] The music for *Dafne,* presented in 1486, was by Giampietro della Viola. Giampietro's surname, taken from the instrument, signifies that he was an improvisator on it. Similarly, every famous piper or flutist of this period had, as his surname, *Piffero* or *Piffaro.* [114a]

Instrumental Music

The scarcity of instrumental music surviving from 15th-century Italy might cause us to underestimate its importance in its day. But literary sources show

[112] AncoS II, 132.
[113] For further reading matter on the *rappresentazioni* and *Maggi, see* the bibliographies appended to the articles on these subjects in the *Enciclopedia Italiana.*
[113a] Cf. IMAMI I, xlviii.
[114] Further about *Orfeo* and *Cefalo, see* CanM, 658; RubL, 32; PruB, 29f.
[114a] Cf. EinIM I, 35, 43.

that it was used often—in church services, festivities, receptions, social gatherings. For example, at the celebration of the wedding of Costanzo Sforza and Camilla of Aragon at Pesaro in 1475, the guests heard not only two antiphonal choruses of sixteen singers each, but *"organi, pifferi, trombetti ed infiniti tamburini."* [115] When Galeazzo Maria Sforza, Duke of Milan, went to Florence in 1471, he took along forty players of "high" instruments. [116] The nobility retained numerous instrumentalists to accompany their singers and to render solos and ensemble music. Instrument collections in the various palaces included lutes, viols, harps, flutes, etc. [117]

The *sacre rappresentazioni* were preceded by instrumental preludes, which followed the prologue. [118] Pictures show children playing instruments in the performance of such dramas; there is evidence also of a children's instrumental ensemble functioning at Ferrara in 1472. [119]

Beginning with the 14th century, and perhaps earlier, bands of wind instruments had been employed by such cities as Florence and Lucca. [120] Civic records include references to trumpeters, *pifferi,* and bagpipe players. The usual wind band seems to have had about eight or nine players. [121]

The oldest print of Italian organ music extant dates from 1517 (cf. p. 161), but many collections of such music must have existed in the 14th century; an inventory of the Cathedral Library at Treviso mentions a *"liber pro organis"* as far back as 1364. [122] Faenza, Bibl. Com., Cod. 117, a MS of the early 15th century, contains an extensive collection of keyboard transcriptions of vocal numbers by some of the most outstanding French and Italian composers of the 14th century and the beginning of the 15th—including Machaut and Landini—as well as organ-Mass sections which, if perhaps not earlier than the oldest German equivalents (cf. pp. 659f), are written with riper art and therefore indicate an older tradition in Italy. Various techniques appear in the Faenza repertory. For example, the superius of a vocal original may be embellished while the old tenor is retained practically intact, or a tenor may be taken over and a new ornate superius be composed above it. [122a]

Organ-Mass music presented a strange phenomenon in that large portions of the sacred text were never heard by the congregation. They were, instead, represented by purely instrumental organ music, in which the plainsong melody was incorporated, often in such free manner that the choir could not pos-

---

[115] KinO, 165f.   [116] MottaM, 32. About some other large groups, *see* PirH, 144.
[117] For details, *see* PirH, 136ff.
[118] About the use of instruments in these *rappresentazioni, see* AncoO I, 327.
[119] ElsU, 18. About other instrumentalists in 15th-century Ferrara, *see* VenA, 747f.
[120] Cf. CelleF, XXXIV, 587, 591; XXXV, 562ff, 579; ElsU, 9. About such a band that began activity in the 13th century at Siena, *see* CelleS; about pipers there in the 15th century, *see* BoneJ.
[121] Cf. the Bolognese bands mentioned in FratV, 189.   [122] AlesO, 9.
[122a] PlamF (which includes 4 exx.), supplemented by *New Light on Faenza Codex 117,* a paper read by Dr. Plamenac on July 5, 1952, at the Congress of the International Musicological Society, held at Utrecht (to be published). An edition, by Dr. Plamenac, of all the instrumental pieces contained in Faenza is in preparation.

sibly have sung along with the organ.[123] The musical procedure in this type of Mass calls for alternation of plainsong, rendered by the choir, and the instrumental passages just described.[123a]

Another keyboard piece of about the same period is a transcription of Landini's *Questa fanciulla* in Paris, Bibl. nat. MS fr. nouv. acq. 6771.[124] In addition, some interesting fragments survive in a letter that is dated 1537 and contains several passages from a book written in Padua in 1409. These passages seem to be extracts from organ settings (*a 2, 3,* or *4*) of Chant melodies.[125]

The oldest Florentine organ of which we know was built c. 1299.[126] Beginning with the *trecento,* the fame of Tuscan organ builders spread through the peninsula. Venice produced a great builder in Fra Urbano, who constructed a famous organ for St. Mark's in 1490 and remained active at least forty years. This instrument was added to the earlier organ there, so that the *quattrocento* saw Venice able to boast of antiphonal organ-playing, a position shared by Naples.[127] At Brescia, the Antegnati family achieved a fame they were to maintain through four generations. In addition, numerous Germans and Frenchmen competed in Italy with native organ builders.[128]

Italian organs of the period—and until as late as the mid-18th century—revealed in general the same traits. They usually had but one manual (the first Italian organ with two manuals was built at Rome in 1499). There were only three to five pedal-keys, which furnished a downward extension of the manual.[129] The normal range of the manual was F-f'''. From c. 1480 on, *tasti scavezzi* (split keys) provided slightly different pitches for D-sharp and E-flat, G-sharp and A-flat. The registration, consisting chiefly of mixtures, did not permit marked tonal contrasts. Thus Italian organs were mechanically less advanced than those of France or Germany and were long to remain so—a strange fact, in view of the relative importance Italian organ music was destined to achieve in the 16th century.[130]

Fifteenth-century Florence, as we have seen, was the home of the celebrated organist Squarcialupi [131] and a place where Isaac played organ likewise. We have the names of several *quattrocento* organists active at St. Mark's. Francesco d'Ana's service as organist at St. Mark's has already been noted.[132]

---

[123] About the method of working out organ settings of plainsong, cf. SchraC, 521.
[123a] Further on the organ-Mass, *see* ScherA, 37ff; ScherZ; SchraO; also *infra.*
[124] Cf. ReMMA, 367.
[125] *See* JepO, 19ff (facsimile on p. 20). For further possible organ music of the *quattrocento, see* JepO, 22.
[126] Cf. JepO, 32.   [127] MosPH, 99f; LafE, 62.
[128] Further about such builders, *see* RoksMO, 112ff; JepO, 24ff.
[129] About the early history of the pedal in Italy, *see* IMAMI I, xxiv; FrotO I, 40.
[130] Further on Italian organs of the period, *see* JepO, 35ff.
[131] Cf. ReMMA, 372; *see also* p. 51 *supra* and WolfG I, 228ff.
[132] For a list of the Renaissance organists at St. Mark's, *see* WintG I, 198f; CafS I, 53–55; corrections in IMAMI I, xxxix, lxxiv. Further on Italian organists of the 15th century, *see* FrotO I, 67ff.

Stringed keyboard-instruments were favored in the home, especially, it would seem, in the accompaniment of *frottole*. Some late 15th-century makers of *cembali,* etc., are known by name.[133] The Antegnati, famous in the 16th century not only for their organs but also for their lutes and viols, may deserve credit for the high standing of Brescia as a lute- and viol-making center from c. 1495 on.[134] Tinctoris states that the viol was used generally "for the accompaniment and ornamentation of vocal music and in connection with the recitation of epics."[135] But 15th-century Italy no doubt saw it used also independently and in viol and mixed ensembles.[136]

Dance Music

The keyboard music mentioned above consists of transcriptions of vocal music. Transcriptions as well as imitations of such music constitute one of the three main categories of Renaissance instrumental music, the other two being dance and improvised music [137] (the last category overlapping the other two and the second overlapping the first). Examples of 15th-century dance music survive in the Italian dance treatises of the time. These examples are monophonic. Domenico of Piacenza, dance master at Ferrara, whose pupils spread his art all over Italy shortly after 1450, was clearly a central figure. Among his disciples was Guglielmo Ebreo of Pesaro (perhaps identical with Giovanni Ambrogio da Pesaro [137a]) who taught at Florence and whose book [138] is one of several known Italian dance manuals of the period. It includes a number of tunes as well as choreographic directions for many dances, two of which are credited to Lorenzo de' Medici and many to Domenico. Another dance theorist of the time whose treatise likewise includes tunes is Antonio Cornazano.[139]

Although in Spain, c. 1460 to 1480, and later in France, the sequences of steps in the *basse dance* tended to become fixed, in Italy every dance composition (in the choreographic sense) tended to be an individual creation. The Italian dances discussed in the manuals are all court dances and fall into two main classes. One, the *bassadanza,* is allied to the French *basse dance.* But whereas in France the various fixed steps had to be grouped into fixed sequences which in turn were combined freely to make up the whole, in Italy the dance was much freer: the sequences themselves were formed from a free combination of the fixed steps. The *bassadanza* tunes, like their French cousins, were written in undifferentiated blackened breves, and for the same reason: each tune was meant to serve as a *cantus firmus* underlying improvised

---

[133] Cf. GoehlG, 54f; RoksMO, 119.   [134] LütgG I, 29.   [135] WeinT, 45; HabT, 74.
[136] GomVD, 58.   [137] Cf. FischerI, 383.   [137a] Cf. MichelD, 122f.
[138] Described in KinJ; text, after 1 of the sources, in GuglielT.
[139] Text in CornazL.

or composed upper parts to provide music for various related dance types differing from one another rhythmically. There were four such types in Italy, the rhythm distinctive of each being maintained throughout. Of the four, the *bassadanza* proper and *saltarello* were the equivalents of the French *basse dance* proper and *pas de Brabant* and were likewise combined in pairs. To the two former the Italians added the very rapid *piva* and the slower *quaternaria* or *saltarello tedesco*. These were not considered fashionable, but were used for occasional sections of the *balli*, to be described presently. As in the French counterparts, the addition of upper melodies to the *cantus firmi* resulted in instrumental ensemble music played by variously constituted groups, a slide-trumpet and two or three shawms being a frequent combination. It is interesting that Cornazano refers to the top part as the *sovrano;* we here have an early instance of the term "soprano" in its modern sense.[140] Among the *cantus firmi* provided by Cornazano is one that he calls *Il Re di Spagna*. This melody, which appears in sources of various nationalities and which is probably Spanish in origin, is the only one known to appear in both a French and an Italian dance manual, thus bridging "the gap between the Italian *bassa danza* and the French *basse dance*." [140a] The tune survives also incorporated in various polyphonic settings. One of these, *a 2*,[140b] reaches us with a Spanish title in a MS of Italian origin [140c] and with an Italian title in another source.[140d]

The second main class was the *ballo,* which expressed dramatic content through pantomime.[141] (The French repertoire contains some *balli* too, but they are mostly of Italian origin.) The changes in action demanded by the content, brought about a sectional arrangement of the music (not present in the *bassadanza*) and might call for every type of step and rhythm. The changes are the probable reason, also, why mensural notation was used for the *ballo* melodies (except in sections written in *bassadanza* measure). Sometimes these melodies were sung instead of played. This, however, does not mean [142] that the melodies for *balli* were, as a matter of principle, drawn from pre-existent vocal parts and that the *bassadanza* tunes, which were not intended for singing, were necessarily drawn from a repertoire more closely connected with instrumental performance.[143]

---

[140] Cf. KinJ, 363f.
[140a] BukMR, 198. The tune as given by Cornazano is pr. *ibid.,* 205; CornazL, 29; as given in the Toulouze print it is pr. in TouA.
[140b] Pr. BukMR, 199.
[140c] Perugia, Bibl. Comunale 431; about its origin, *see* JepK, lxxii.
[140d] Bol., Lic. mus. Q 16 (*olim* 109).
[141] For a fine example, *see* GomD, 303ff.
[142] As modern investigators once thought; the mistaken notion has been corrected in KinDT (which contains the repertoire of Italian dance tunes).
[143] Further about the *bassadanza* and *ballo, see* GomD, *passim;* SachsW, 298f, 306ff, 328ff; KinJ, 345ff (the bibliography on pp. 371ff is augmented in BukMR, 212ff).

The Theorists

The last quarter of the 15th century was a fruitful period for music theory. This was due in part to the ease with which ideas could be exchanged as a result of the invention of printing. In fact, a number of treatises come to us in incunabula. Much of the literature grew from controversies among the theorists and these often developed into long and bitter feuds. ". . . a, so to speak, music-theoretical madness . . . had seized all Italy at the time. One discussed music theory as today one discusses sport or the theatre." Treatises on the subject reach us in quantity, as do letters regarding it, exchanged by leading specialists of the day.[143a]

The theorists active in Italy c. 1480 included—besides Tinctoris—the Englishman John Hothby (d. 1487), the Spaniard, Bartolomé Ramos de Pareja (cf. pp. 586f), his pupil Giovanni Spataro (c. 1458-1541), Franchino Gafori (1451-1522), Francesco Caza,[144] and Nicolo Burzio (cf. p. 155). Of these, Ramos, Tinctoris, and Gafori (Gafurius) are the leading figures. The important Pietro Aron (c. 1470 [145]-c. 1545) belongs to the following generation. Hothby spent so much of his life in Italy that he figures more in the musical history of that country than of England. He seems to have settled in Florence c. 1440. His *Calliopea legale* [146] is probably his chief work.

Gafori was born in Lodi and received his early musical education in church circles. One of his teachers was the monk, Johannes Bonadies,[146a] who copied into the Faenza MS mentioned on p. 174 theoretical writings and music of various kinds, including compositions by Hothby and a Kyrie by Bonadies himself.[146b] In 1473, Gafori went to Mantua for a time, later to Verona. In 1477, he settled in Naples, where he became involved in public disputes with several famous musicians, among them Tinctoris. He remained in Naples until an outbreak of plague and war with the Turks forced him to leave. For a time he occupied posts in Monticello and Bergamo. In 1484 he went to Milan to become choirmaster in the cathedral and to teach in a public music school which Lodovico Sforza (il Moro) had founded. He remained at Milan for the rest of his life.

[143a] JepKC, from which the above quotation is taken, reports 112 such letters, mostly written by or to people mentioned in this chapter.

[144] For a facsimile ed. of his *Tractato vulgare de canto figurato* with German transl. and comments, *see* CazaT.

[145] Not 1490, as usually stated; cf. BlumeJ, 60.

[146] The original Italian with French transl. pr. CouH, 295. For 3 other treatises by Hothby, *see* CouS, 328ff. Further about him, *see* KornH; SmtC.

[146a] Known also as Godendach. BorCB, 253f, considers the man a Fleming, "Godendach" the original name, and "Bonadies" a Latinization.

[146b] RoncB, Pl. opp. p. 40, gives a facsimile of the complete Kyrie. Kyrie I is pr. in MarpB II, 242; MartiniS I, 188 (with old notation); ForkA II, 670; also in FerandM, 180, where (as in AmbG III, 147) a third part is regarded as missing, owing to a misreading of the direction: *cantetur* [not *contratenor*] *cum organo*.

Gafori's theoretical writings comprise five main works.[147] Of these the *Practica musicae* (1496), in four books, is probably the most important from the standpoint of comment on contemporary practice. In it are Gafori's famous eight rules of counterpoint,[148] here summarized: (1) A polyphonic piece should, in general, begin with a perfect consonance. (2) Two perfect consonances of equal size may never follow one another in parallel motion.[148a] (3) Between two perfect consonances of like size at least one imperfect consonance should be inserted. (4) Perfect consonances of differing size may follow one another (Gafori illustrates with examples in contrary motion only). (5) Consecutive octaves and fifths produced in the course of voice-crossing are permissible. (6) The tenor and cantus should proceed in contrary motion and the contratenor should move in parallel motion to one of these two, but this rule is not hard and fast. (7) At cadences the perfect consonance should be preceded by the most closely related imperfect consonance, i.e., a major sixth should move to an octave, a minor sixth to a fifth (by oblique motion) or octave, a third to a unison or fifth. (8) Each composition should end in a unison [between tenor and cantus] or in an octave or double octave.

The *Practica* contains likewise Gafori's theory of proportions[149] and his description of the strange practice of singing in consecutive seconds and fourths, at the Milan cathedral, on occasions of mourning.[150] It also mentions the "famous procedure in counterpoint, in which the notes in the bass move in tenths with those of the superius, the tenor moving in concord with both other parts." [150a] A picture on fol. a 1 provides a feature of special interest. A boy choir is depicted with its master; in the foreground one boy beats time while the others sing from a large volume placed on a lectern. Gafori, unfortunately, has no section on time beating, but he does equate the time-value of a semibreve to the "pulse beat of a quietly breathing man"—i.e., to M.M. 60 to 80.[151] This information, important on other grounds, is relevant here also, because from the time of Adam von Fulda's *Musica* on—for example, in Lanfranco's *Scintille di musica* (1533) and in Angelo da Picitono's *Fior angelico di musica* (1547)—there is evidence that time was customarily marked by a lowering and raising of the hand,[151a] the complete down-and-up motion being

[147] For lists of the works in their various editions, *see* HirB, 65ff; MGG IV, 1240 (which is more complete). GafT is a facsimile ed. of one of them: the *Theorica musica,* 1492.

[148] In Book III, Ch. III. For a German transl. of the rules, with discussion, *see* RieG, 337ff.

[148a] The context indicates that this does not apply to fourths.

[149] Further about Gafori's treatment of mensural theory, *see* PraetM.

[150] Cf. RieG, 348. Riemann's error in linking this practice with a 13th-century account of "howling in seconds of the Lombards" is discussed in FerandH.   [150a] Transl. in FoxNQ, 40f.

[151] Cf. *Practica,* III, 4. The semibreve in question, of course, is that of the Renaissance; the present comment has nothing to do with modern transcriptions dividing original time-values. ApelH, 731, and ApelN, 191ff, fix the metronome rate of the semibreve at above 48 to 60. The pulse rate of a normal person, however, is about 70; 60 to 80 allows for some latitude and agrees, for example, with SachsRN. Allowance must be made also for deliberate deviations from the norm; cf. p. 622.   [151a] Sometimes, however, by a raising and lowering; cf. SachsRT, 217f.

called a *tactus;* and, in its normal form, a *tactus* took up the time-value of a semibreve.[152] While the hand was the usual means of beating time for singers, theorists point out that, since instrumentalists needed their hands for playing, they could just as well mark the *tactus* with their feet.

In Gafori's treatise on instruments, *De harmonia musicorum instrumentorum* (1518), fol. 67ᵛf, he advocates the adoption of a range of four octaves, from C to c‴, in the construction of keyboard instruments. Somewhat later, in 1533, the recommended range was increased further, to encompass G₁ and e‴, in the *Recanetum de musica aurea* of Stephanus Vanneus.[153] Gafori informs us, in the *De harmonia . . . instrumentorum,* that he had Latin translations made for his use of various treatises in Greek, including those of Aristides Quintilianus and Ptolemy.[154] He thus differs from his predecessors, who apparently had obtained their knowledge of ancient music theory mainly by way of Boethius. There was also in his library a copy, with his marginal notes,[155] of at least a part of the Latin translation of Plato by the famous Platonist, Marsilio Ficino. (Ficino himself [156] was a performing musician as well as a theorist, and the author of commentaries on Plato that include discussions of Plato's concepts of music.[157]) Portions of Gafori's *De harmonia . . . instrumentorum* intensified an already existing controversy with Spataro [158] and resulted, two years later, in the printing of the *Apologia Franchini Gafurii Musici adversus Joannem Spatarium et complices Musicos Bononiensis.*

Gafori was, like Tinctoris, a composer; but, though he was prolific, none of his compositions appear in early music prints. They survive chiefly in three

---

[152] The above description of the *tactus* agrees with Sachs RN, 368 (but not with SachsRT, 219, where the minim, rather than the semibreve, is equated with M.M. 60 to 80 in normal *tactus*). Within the allowances mentioned in fn. 151, the speed of the *tactus*—i.e., of the hand motion itself—was unvarying. Normal binary meter (*tempus imperfectum, prolatio minor*—cf. pp. 19f) included 2 such *tactus;* normal ternary meter (*tempus perfectum, prolatio minor*) included 3. To mark essential deviations from the standard tempo of the actual music performed in the course of the hand motions, the semibreve could be replaced by a breve (*tactus alla breve*) or by a minim (*tactus alla minima*). (Though theoretically the mensuration signature ₵ indicated *tactus alla breve,* in practice after c. 1500 it came to indicate normal *tactus; see* ApelN, 192, and SachsRT, 224.) In *sesquialtera,* the 2 beats of the *tactus* corresponded to 3 minims in sound—thus replacing the 2 "normal" minims by a minim triplet; in *proportio tripla,* each of the 2 beats of the *tactus* corresponded to 3 seminimins—thus replacing each of the 2 "normal" minims by a semiminim triplet. (Contemporary terminology, however, is inconsistent.) These, as well as the many other and more complicated variations of the basic tempo, were indicated by suitable time-signatures. Further on the subject, *see* esp. SachsRT, 217ff and 228ff. Ornithoparchus' *Micrologus* (1517), II, 6 (= p. 46ff of Dowland's Engl. transl. of 1609) is particularly helpful, among early sources dealing with *tactus; see also* TiraG, TiraM, AudaT, AudaP, PraetM (not all of these are in agreement with each other or with the foregoing). Concerning misunderstandings in the once widely accepted SchünF, *see* SachsRT, 220f.

[153] Cf. LowMS, 64.   [154] Cf. AmbG III, 153f.

[155] Now at Harvard; *see* KinG. About his annotated copy of Anselmi's treatise on music, see HandAT.   [156] For his treatise, *see* FiciF I, 56ff.

[157] Further on Ficino and music, *see* KinG, 380f; KristM, 269ff.

[158] His *Dilucide et probatissime demonstratione de maestro Zoanne Spatario . . . , contra certe frivole et vane excusatione da Franchino Gafurio (maestro de li errori) in luce aducte* (1521) is available in facsimile with German transl. and comments on the controversy, etc., in SpataroD. Regarding letters written by or to Spataro on music theory, *see* JepKC. Compositions of his pr. TorA I, 31, 35; JepI, 4.

Milanese MSS of c. 1500—compiled and copied upon his initiative and therefore often called the Gafori codices [159]—that contain a large repertory of
sacred works by various composers active at Milan. In all, we have thirteen
Masses, twenty-eight motets, eleven Magnificats, six antiphons, two litanies,
and one *Stabat Mater* by Gafori. In general, he indulges less in display of
craftsmanship than do the Franco-Netherlanders. In the Sanctus [160] of his
Missa Trombetta, Gafori appears to have used as a model Dufay's *Gloria
ad modum tubae* (cf. pp. 6of), since he builds the two lower voices in identical
fashion on the same alternating *ostinato* figure. (It is not impossible that the
Dufay influence was still felt at this date: one of the Gafori codices includes
the *Te Deum* of Binchois.) The significant difference is in the two upper
voices, which had been set in canon by Dufay, but are treated in free counterpoint by Gafori. Another Mass, in Tone 8, is actually called a *Missa brevis* in
the table of contents of one of the codices, this being an early instance of the
use of such a designation.[161]

In his motets, Gafori shows a liking for the pairing of voices used by his
contemporary, Josquin. Influences of the *frottola* style are apparent in the
harmonic vertical approach to composition. His harmonic boldness sometimes leads him to violate convention. Thus, in a certain point of imitation
in his motet, *Beata progenies,* the third voice to enter begins on a major
seventh over the bass.[162] Another motet, *Salve decus genitoris,*[163] is a composition in honor of the unscrupulous but brilliant Lodovico il Moro. Duke
Galeazzo Maria Sforza had been assassinated in 1476, and Bona of Savoy
then became regent during the minority of their son, Gian Galeazzo. In 1481,
Lodovico (the uncle of Gian Galeazzo) usurped her power, becoming actual
duke of Milan in 1494 after the sudden death of his nephew and remaining
in power until he was driven out by Louis XII of France in 1499. In the meanwhile he had been a generous patron of the arts, including music.

Pietro Aron (Aaron), writing a generation later than Gafori, was more
consciously a man of the Renaissance. Of his five treatises, four were written
in Italian.[164] The Latin contribution, *De institutione harmonica* (1516), was
attacked by Gafori. It is in this work that the first mention is made of composers having, in general, abandoned the successive manner of composition
(he gives the order as: cantus, tenor, bass, alto) in favor of the simultaneous

---

[159] For details about them, *see* JepG; concerning a fourth codex, damaged by fire, that survives
in part, *see* SartQ.
[160] Facsimile in CesM, 222; transcr. of the *Pleni* and *Osanna* I, *ibid.,* 223; of the *Pleni* only, in
IMAMI II, xxxix. 2 Masses pr. GafW I.
[161] Cf. JepG, 22, last item.   [162] Cf. CesM, 220.
[163] Facsimile of first part in CesM, 228; transcr. of whole piece, *ibid.,* 229. CesM contains further information on Gafori's compositions.
[164] Gafori's *Angelicum ac divinum opus musicae* (despite its Latin title) was written in
Italian also, but with an apology for its use. The above figures are correct: in LichtD IV, 121, and
elsewhere, the Latin treatise is regarded as a transl. of the Italian *Compendiolo,* but *see* SchmidlD
I, 72. Music-theoretical writing of Aron's is preserved also in a considerable correspondence, involving him, Spataro, Giovanni del Lago, and others; cf. JepKC; WolfBA.

or vertical method.[165] In advocating, in the same treatise, the division of tonal material into octaves rather than into hexachords, he followed the lead of Ramos, whose chief predecessor in this regard appears to have been Joannes Gallicus [166] (active at the court of Mantua after 1442; not to be confused with the 16-century Leipzig theorist, Joannes Galliculus). Aron was conspicuously progressive in favoring, in his best-known treatise, *Il Toscanello in musica* (1523),[167] the written indication of accidentals at all times and uniform rather than conflicting signatures.[168] The *Toscanello* is a general manual, including extended discussion of mensural notation, intervals, *genera,* counterpoint, chordal formation,[168a] etc.[169]

Aron's *Trattato della natura et cognitione di tutti gli tuoni di canto figurato* (1525) [170] is an early source providing criteria for identifying mode in polyphonic music. In Chapter II, he says that a singer should judge the mode of a piece from the tenor (unless plainsong is present in some other voice) since this is the "firm and stable part." This statement, however, should be regarded in the light of the musical examples he offers in Chapters IV through VII, one chapter being devoted to each authentic and plagal pair, i.e., to each *maneria.*[170a] In these examples he illustrates types of codas (to use modern terminology) that composers may add, in the various modes, after the cadence proper has been reached. While, at the close of every such cadence, the tenor has the final of the mode, the bass has it likewise. Moreover, while in no instance is the final given at the end of the coda to the tenor (which always has either the third or the fifth),[171] it consistently appears there in the bass. Thus, if Aron's text makes little of the role of the bass in determining the mode, his examples do otherwise. (The same might be said of his treatment of the superius.) But the text indicates that it is definitely the tenor that determines whether the mode is authentic or plagal. For example, Aron points out the difficulties that result if the tenor is compelled to descend to the lower range of mode 2 and implies that the mode is not present if the tenor does not make the descent. Actually, the assignment of a polyphonic piece to the mode of its tenor is a rather artificial procedure. Since the ranges of human voices in neighboring classifications lie about a fourth or a fifth apart, it is obvious that parts written for such ranges will tend to lie in different modes (cf. p. 186).

---

[165] Further on this point, *see* LowMS, 67; FerandH, 320f.

[166] Cf. LowMS, 75f. For the passage in Gallicus, *see* CouS IV, 373.

[167] There were several editions; the spelling was *Thoscanello* in the first edition.

[168] Further on these points, *see* LowS, 230, 259ff.

[168a] BushCF, 243, gives a chart based on the consonance tables compiled by Aron, Ornithoparchus, Zarlino, Tigrini, and Morley, in which their practices regarding chordal formation are compared.

[169] Further about this treatise, *see* RieG, 349ff.

[170] Extract in English transl. in StrunkR, 205ff.   [170a] Cf. ReMMA, 153.

[171] We are referring here to the order of degrees above the final, not to dominants, etc. (The two modes of each *maneria,* of course, have the same fifth degree, etc., even though their dominants are different.)

While these modes will not always be alternately the authentic and plagal forms of the same pair, they will be so quite often. Yet the mode of the complex will be considered that of the tenor regardless of the number of voices. For instance, in a piece for SATB that has such alternation, if the tenor is in an authentic mode the superius will be in it also, but if a second altus is added, the superius will be in the plagal mode; nevertheless, according to the criterion set up, the polyphonic complex will be regarded as in the authentic mode in either event, merely because that is the mode of the tenor. To be sure, so far as modal color is concerned, the division between authentic and plagal modes tends to disappear in polyphony anyway. But what distinction does exist is certainly to the modern ear largely dependent upon the character of the superius. Aron's procedure, however, whether artificial or not, provides a convenient tool; whereas Tinctoris, with good reason, had for all practical purposes regarded mode as assignable to individual lines only (cf. p. 141), Aron's ascription of mode to a polyphonic complex does provide a terminology that makes it possible to comment upon the modal character of a polyphonic piece without circumlocution.

One can easily see that Aron, in such varied ways as his use of the vernacular, his desire for a consistent indication of accidentals, his disapproval of conflicting signatures, and his emphasis on a practical terminology, proves himself a Renaissance man in touch with the progressive musical thinking of his day.

Chapter 5: JOSQUIN DES PREZ AND HIS CONTEMPORARIES FROM FRANCE AND THE LOW COUNTRIES, IN PARTICULAR OBRECHT, AGRICOLA, ISAAC, COMPÈRE, BRUMEL, PIERRE DE LA RUE, AND MOUTON

IT WOULD be difficult to overestimate the intrinsic and historical importance of much of the music to be discussed in this chapter. In the Josquin period practically every basic feature of Renaissance music that did not already exist made its appearance. The art impulses of Italian and Franco-Netherlandish music, which had interpenetrated one another throughout the Early Renaissance, now did so to a greater extent. A fusion was in process that produced the underlying musical style of the Late Renaissance. Whatever came afterward—even the music of such giants as Palestrina and Lassus—was only a continued treatment of what was already present in every essential feature.

No one man could alone have been responsible for all the characteristic qualities of the new music. Historical forces combined to mould them. But these forces were able to find particularly brilliant expression because a large group of singularly gifted composers were all vigorously active at about the same time. Obrecht, Agricola, Isaac, Compère, Josquin, Brumel, Pierre de la Rue, and Mouton were the brightest lights in an especially luminous constellation. And Josquin was a star of the first magnitude.

As might be expected, in view of the merging of styles that took place, the new men included many who left the north to sojourn, for longer or shorter periods, in Italy. Chapter 4 has shown that this country, if she could not at the time boast many composers of really powerful stature, did have a large cultivated class, including munificent patrons, and Italian taste affected the music of the Franco-Netherlanders active there. These musicians were eagerly sought by both courts and churches, and were often engaged by emissaries sent northward for that express purpose. Partly owing to the favorable reputation of northern musicians, dating from the time of Dufay and still earlier, these new descendants upon Italy were warmly welcomed. As we have seen (pp. 169f), Agricola and Isaac were employed in Florence, during the last third of the 15th century, by Lorenzo the Magnificent. There Aron met not only these composers, but also Obrecht and Josquin.[1]

Petrucci's output as a whole, notwithstanding its inclusion of no less than eleven books of *frottole,* gives much more space to Franco-Netherlanders than to Italians. The contents of the *Odhecaton* and of its companion collections, *Canti B* and *Canti C,* though international in scope, were, as pointed out in the preceding chapter, mainly Franco-Netherlandish. The same is true of most of Petrucci's other anthologies—e.g., his *Motetti A* of 1502. (Here, incidentally, in the first printed motet collection, there is the same confusion as prevailed both before and after regarding the exact meaning of motet: liturgical texts appear in the company of texts that are non-liturgical.) As for the collections representing individual composers, they too show the Franco-Netherlanders greatly in the ascendancy.

The Changing Status of the Modes

Among the various traits that mark this period is the increased prominence accorded to what we would call the major and natural minor modes. These had, of course, been used long before—with the B consistently flattened—as variants of the Lydian (or Hypolydian) and Dorian (or Hypodorian) modes, the major mode appearing in such instances as the *Alma Redemptoris Mater* and the secular pieces given in ReMMA, Examples 55, 58; the natural minor in such instances as the Kyrie of Mass XI and the secular piece given in ReMMA, Example 56. But the theorists did not recognize these variants as independent modes until the Swiss, Glareanus—as late as 1547 (twenty-six years after Josquin's death)—published his *Dodecachordon* (from δώδεκα, meaning "twelve," and χορδή, meaning "a string"). In illustrating that treatise he drew heavily, in his passages on the "new" modes, as well as elsewhere, on composers of the Josquin generation. Wishing to graft his additions on to the old ecclesiastical system, with its grouping of eight modes into four authentic–plagal pairs, Glareanus divides major and natural minor each into such a pair. Natural minor becomes Aeolian and Hypoaeolian (Modes IX and X); major becomes Ionian and Hypoionian (Modes XI and XII). The former pair has its final on A, the latter on C. The basic ambitus of each authentic mode, of course, extends an octave upward from its final; that of each plagal mode, an octave from the fourth below its final.[2] Glareanus mentions hypothetical modes (XIII and XIV) on B, but dismisses them as impractical, since their scales cannot, like those of the other modes, be divided

---

[1] Aron, *De Institutione Harmonica* (1516), III, 10.

[2] For Glareanus' discussion and his exx. of the 4 "new" modes, *see* GlarD, 104ff, 256ff; 124ff, 319ff; 115ff, 288ff; 137, 354ff (= PubAPTM XVI, 82ff, 203ff; 96ff, 278ff; 90f, 240ff; 104f, 314ff). (PubAPTM XVI is a German transl. of GlarD; an English transl. of Bk. III, Chap. 24, is given in StrunkR, 219ff; a complete English transl. in MilleGD. For an article on Glareanus' musical exx. generally, *see* ScherN.)

into a perfect fifth plus a perfect fourth, or the reverse.[3] The twelve modes that consequently remain account for the title of his book. Although his system of a dozen modes was widely accepted, some theorists continued to feel that the eight-mode system sufficed. Like them, Glareanus realized that the old system, by permitting the flattening of B in the Dorian and Lydian pairs, provided for the intervallic configuration of the Aeolian and Ionian pairs.[4] But the presence or absence of the flat actually changed the mode, and Glareanus' tabulation set up an independent modal pair for each intervallic configuration. In any event, it is plain that in polyphony only five modes mattered for practical purposes. Glareanus himself emphasizes that the Lydian pair, as modified into Ionian and Hypoionian, has almost completely supplanted the unmodified pair.[5] Moreover, the distinction between an authentic mode and its plagal is, in polyphony, an academic one (cf. p. 183). This leaves, as the really fundamental modes of Late Renaissance polyphony, the Dorian, Phrygian, Mixolydian, Aeolian, and Ionian. But actually, Glareanus does not deal so much with the mode of a polyphonic complex as with the modes of its individual voices (cf. p. 141). He realized that in such a complex the different ranges of adjacent voices will frequently tend to place them in different modes, these rather often being the authentic and plagal forms of the same pair (cf. pp. 182f).[6]

Obrecht: Biography; Secular Works

Of the three examples of Obrecht presented in the *Dodecachordon*, two are used to illustrate the Aeolian mode. Jacob Obrecht (= Hobrecht [6a])—the only real Dutchman among the leading masters of the period and perhaps the finest of them all after Josquin himself—belonged to a family that had its origin at Bergen op Zoom in Holland. *Mille quingentis,*[7] a motet in which he laments the death of his father Willem in 1488, states that he himself was born on St. Cecilia's day (November 22). Other evidence indicates that the year was 1450 or 1451 and the place either Bergen op Zoom or Sicily.[8] It

---

[3] Cf. GlarD, 112f & 276ff, 152f & 342ff (= PubAPTM XVI, 88ff & 227ff, 101f & 303ff). He does not, as stated in Grove II, 73, call them the Locrian and Hypolocrian modes, but the Hyperaeolian and Hyperphrygian. The reader should bear in mind that some modern publications, e.g., ProsM, also count 14 modes, but make the B modes Nos. XI and XII; the C modes, Nos. XIII and XIV.

[4] The flattening of B in the Mixolydian pair merely produced normal Dorian and Hypodorian transposed. The B, of course, was not flattened in the Phrygian pair.

[5] Cf. GlarD, 328, 280 (= PubAPTM XVI, 288, 231).

[6] Cf. GlarD, 250f (= PubAPTM XVI, 197f). For a special study of modal usage in 15th-century Masses, *see* WienM.

[6a] This spelling represents West Brabant dialect; *see* PiscaerO, 329f.

[7] Music pr. ObrMT, 179; text, SmijTM, 133.

[8] Cf. RB XI (1957), 126, and PiscaerO, 329f. The claim that our Obrecht was admitted to the University of Louvain in 1470 (cf. PirH, 192, and the source there cited) is not correct, since the baptismal name of the father of the student in question is given in the records as Jacob, not Willem (cf. SmijMQ, 215). This undermines the conclusion, advanced in Baker's *Biographical Dictionary of Musicians* (5th ed.), v, 1175, that Obrecht was born in 1452.

has been claimed that Obrecht was a singer in the service of Hercules I at Ferrara in 1474, but the evidence [9] is far from conclusive. About 1476, he had Erasmus as one of his choirboys at Utrecht, and in 1479 became choir director at Bergen op Zoom. From there, he went to Cambrai, where he was active at the Cathedral from September 1484 to November 1485. He had already been appointed a *succentor* at St. Donatian in Bruges. A short leave of absence having been granted him at Bruges, he accepted the invitation of Hercules I to go to Ferrara, but was again at his post in 1488 [10] and remained there until 1491, the year that Barbireau died. Obrecht may have succeeded him at the Church of Our Lady in Antwerp, but the records do not mention him until 1494, and then not as *Magister choralium* (the post Barbireau had held). Instead he seems to have been, at least nominally, a chaplain until he died of the plague in Ferrara in 1505. During his last years he can be traced briefly in Bergen op Zoom and in Bruges.[11] Tinctoris praises him in the *Complexus*.[12] The eldest figure in the painting, "The Three Ages of Man," variously ascribed to Sebastiano del Piombo, Giorgione, Lorenzo Lotto, and others, was once thought to preserve the composer's likeness,[13] but has since been shown to represent Hubert Naich.[13a]

Obrecht's secular works include sixteen or seventeen with titles, texts, or incipits in Dutch, eight in French, one or two in Italian, and four without title or text (two being canons).[14] Regardless of a composer's nationality, such a preponderance of Dutch is most unusual for this time: the old prestige of French was challenged solely by the rapidly growing prestige of Italian. Most of the pieces provide only incipits, so that sometimes one cannot be sure of the literary form—or, consequently, of the form of the music.

La tortorella may be a *strambotto* for which we have only an incomplete text: pair 2 of its four known lines is set to an only slightly modified form of the music that served for pair 1.[15] *Weet ghij wat mynder jonghen herten deert?* ("Do you know what grieves my young heart?"),[16] which reaches us with only an incipit for text, is in *abb* form and may therefore be a *bergerette;* the way in which the *a* ends, however, makes this doubtful.

Among Obrecht's works based on pre-existent *rondeaux* is a setting [17] *a 4*

[9] Given in StraM VII, 496.   [10] Cf. SchrevB, 160f.
[11] Further data in PirH, 192; GomO, 128; StraM III, 181ff; MQ XLIII (1957), 500; RB XI (1957), 125, 157.
[12] CouS IV, 200.   [13] Cf. PruP; EinIM I, 155f, Pl. opp. p. 158.
[13a] Cf. SindH. *See also* RB XI (1957), 134.
[14] 18 pieces pr. in ObrWW, those on pp. 2 (= HewO, 274) and 45 (= *La Stangetta* in HewO, 325) being of uncertain authenticity; 10 more, from the Segovia MS mentioned in Chap. 3 (discovered after the publication of ObrWW, ObrMT, and ObrMS), in SmijO; 4 more from the Segovia MS listed in AngI, 9f, 12, and MME I, 107–9, of which 1 (No. 36) is of rather doubtful authenticity (cf. HewO, 143, 218), *Myn hert* (pr. ObrWW, 64) is by la Rue; cf. p. 273 *infra;* GomO 123ff. The canon pr. ObrWW, 53, as a secular work is really from the Credo of the *Missa Salve diva parens;* cf. BesV, 18. (Some of the other untitled, textless pieces may, of course, also eventually prove to be sacred.)
[15] The piece is pr. in ObrWW, 43; AmbG V, 36 (after a MS giving only 2 lines).
[16] Pr. SmijO, 80.   [17] Pr. ObrWW, 14; AmbG V, 29; GiesS 12.

of the superius of Ockeghem's *Fors seulement l'attente* (cf. pp. 119f), the melody being transposed down a fourth and given to the contratenor; Obrecht's own superius begins with the opening of Ockeghem's tenor, but this melody is soon abandoned.[18] The setting retains the ground plan of the original and, though textless in the sources, can be performed as a *rondeau*.[19] This is true, in addition, of Obrecht's *J'ay pris amours*,[20] in two *partes*, an extraordinary work. In *pars I,* the superius of the anonymous *rondeau, J'ay pris amours* (cf. pp. 100f), serves as the first half of the superius, the old tenor as the second half of the bass, this voice of Obrecht's having a repetition of measures 1–5 of the original tenor appended at the close as a coda; in *pars II* the old tenor functions as the first half of Obrecht's altus and as the second half of his tenor. Obrecht's settings, compared with the models which they rework, tend to reveal a more modern feeling for tonality and harmonic structure; and in his *J'ay pris amours,* transposition is employed to produce a I-IV-V-I key-relationship: in the first half of *pars I,* the borrowed melody is at its original level, A (Aeolian); in the second half, the other borrowed melody, whose original level was also A, is transposed down to D; in the first half of *pars II,* it is shifted up to E; and in the second half, it returns to A.[20a] It is especially interesting that the feeling for tonality should become evident here in conjunction with the use of the Aeolian mode.

Obrecht's recasting *rondeau* material into a shape other than that of a *rondeau* is indicative of the attitude of his whole generation. Although the *formes fixes* were not dead, they were moribund, and composers sought to replace them by freer structures which, however, were still influenced by the old forms to the extent that they were often built on repetition patterns. But these patterns were not stereotyped, and Josquin, in particular, showed considerable imagination in employing a great variety of them. Art music with vernacular texts, to be sure, had known departures from the *formes fixes* in the past, e.g., in Dufay's *La belle se siet* and *Vergine bella,* but now the "regular" pieces had become the exception and departures were the rule. The content of these freer forms became increasingly motet-like in texture: with most composers the fabric was heavier than it had been or was to be from c. 1525 on; the chanson *a 4* definitely superseded the chanson *a 3* and, although the superius and tenor were still the main voices, the contratenor and altus more nearly approximated them in interest, and few reminders were left of the old treble-dominated style or of the rather sharp contrast between melodic lines that had once been common. The minim, which had already begun to replace the semibreve as the normal time-unit, now did so definitely.

---

[18] *See* further GomO, 30ff.

[19] *Helas mon bien* (ObrWW, 17; GiesS, 62) also has the appearance of a *rondeau.*

[20] Pr. ObrWW, 19.

[20a] It should be noted that we are here concerning ourselves only with the levels of individual parts.

Among Obrecht's pieces in the freer forms are *Lacen adieu* and *Ic en hebbe gheen ghelt*,[21] in which unity is obtained by repeating at or near the end a passage first heard in the central portion. *Se bien fait*[22]—one of the more motet-like pieces from the standpoint of texture—is tied together by the four-measure phrase that opens the bass part and recurs within it five times, exactly or varied, against different countermelodies. The first section of *T'saat een meskin*[23] presents in long notes, mostly in the tenor, briefly in the altus, what appears to be a Dutch folk tune. This tune has the form *aba* and underlies the *aba'* form of this section of the setting. It is clear that several of the Dutch pieces owe their patterns, at least in part, to the fact that they are based on folk or popular airs. *T'saat een meskin* and two other pieces[24] have material from the first section manipulated afresh in the second, in this respect being akin to *J'ay pris amours*.[25] In *T'Andernaken*,[26] the tenor—which apparently derives from a pre-existent melody[27]—repeats its opening section; but Obrecht's piece is not a *ballade*, for he provides each presentation of this section with different countermelodies. Moreover, the pre-existent text (omitted by Obrecht, whose setting—like many of his other secular pieces—is undoubtedly instrumental[28]) does not have the same line at the end of each stanza.[29] The "gay, quick notes of the accompanying voices . . . cavort about" the tenor, but the charm of the piece is slightly diminished by a general tendency of Obrecht's toward overuse of such facile devices as melodic sequences and (recalling Busnois) parallel tenths or thirds. Such tenths are present in profusion also in *Meskin es hu*,[30] which survives both *a 3* and *a 4*—the tenor of the version *a 3* (evidently a Dutch folk song) being divided, in the version *a 4*, between the tenor and altus, which render portions of it alternately; the procedure is related to the old practice illustrated in Franchois's *Ave Virgo* (cf. p. 42) and Dufay's *Apostolo glorioso* (cf. pp. 77f).

In his four-part *Cela sans plus*,[31] Obrecht presents, in canon between the inner voices, the tenor of Colinet de Lannoy's popular chanson. That composer had already treated his tenor melody in canon, with the time-interval varying from two measures to six and back to two again. Obrecht, with his technical mastery, saw that it was possible, without altering the melody radically, to rearrange the changing time-intervals in an increasing order, from two measures to four to six. Varying the time-interval in canon was a device much liked by Obrecht, and one that he used with great skill. In the

---

[21] Pr. SmijO, 76, 92, respectively.   [22] Pr. AmbG V, 40; ObrWW, 34.

[23] *Ibid.*, 7; HewO, 407; HAM, 82; GiesS, 102.   [24] Pr. SmijO, 70, 86.

[25] *See* analysis of *T'saat* . . . in HewO, 102.   [26] Pr. ObrWW, 3; HewO, 366.

[27] Text, with attempted reconstruction of the pre-existent tune (made from Obrecht's tenor) in DuyL II, 1050ff; text also in ObrWW, xvif.

[28] Cf. HewO, 80f.

[29] The Dutch chanson pr. in SmijO, 95, is also no *ballade*, the repeated opening section being too brief.

[30] Pr. HewO, 421; AmbG V, 34; ObrWW, 1.   [31] *Ibid.*, 12.

four-part *Tant que nostre argent dura*,[32] modified canon appears in the two lower voices. One of the untitled textless canons is accompanied by verbal instructions showing that the given melody is to be worked out *a 3* at the unison and that its semibreves are to be extracted, are to have their values multiplied by six, and are thus, in their original order, to form a fourth part beginning an octave below the others.[33] (The composer seems to have enjoyed extracting a melody in some such way as this; cf. p. 198.) The other pieces without title or text [34] are characterized by considerable use of sequence. This device is at times harmonic as well as melodic in *La Stangetta* (which is of uncertain authenticity; it may be by either Obrecht or Weerbecke).[35] The composition may be named after a member of the Cremonese family of Stanga; instrumental works—and this is evidently one—occasionally derived their titles from the names of the persons to whom they were dedicated.[36]

While imitation is not absent from Obrecht's secular works—it appears, for example, in *Se bien fait*—its presence is rather rare, and to that extent these works are somewhat old-fashioned. A number of historians, because of a certain conservatism in Obrecht, place him midway between Ockeghem and Josquin or even group him with Ockeghem and Busnois. However, the strong feeling he occasionally reveals for tonality shows him to be sensitive to newer trends, as do his infrequent use of the *formes fixes,* his shift to a motet-like type of chanson, and his adoption of the minim as the normal time-unit. "Progressive" features, as will presently be shown, appear in his sacred works also. If he nevertheless looms as less of a modern than does Josquin, this must be at least in part due to the fact that he died earlier.

Obrecht: Motets

In Obrecht's motets,[37] the conservative tendency is seen in frequent recourse to *cantus firmi* in long notes, in a predilection for polytextuality, and in a rather rare use of imitation. But here again we shall find Obrecht concerned, in an inquiring spirit, with "modern" methods of unifying his compositions.

No less than three settings of the *Salve Regina* survive, one each *a 3, a 4,* and *a 6*.[38] In all, the plainsong, at least part of the time, serves as *cantus firmus* in

---

[32] *Ibid.,* 36.
[33] The piece is pr. *ibid.,* 57 (cf. xxii); for the other untitled, textless canon, *see ibid.,* 54, or GiesS, 106.   [34] Pr. ObrWW, 48, 50.
[35] Cf. fn. 14. Beginning at meas. 37, the tenor presents the same 5-note motif 4 times, with the time-values successively halved.
[36] Cf. DiseM, 309; HewO, 76.
[37] 18 (including a Magnificat) pr. ObrMT (the *Pater noster* there ascribed to Obrecht is by Willaert; the *O vos omnes* is by Compère; the *Si oblitus fuero* is by Ninot le Petit [*see* SmijV, 180]; *see also* fn. 40); 1 in SmijO, 65; 9 more listed in AngI, 8ff, and MME I, 107. We shall deal later in this chapter with the Passion which, though ascribed to Obrecht in certain sources, is not actually his.
[38] Pr., respectively, ObrMT, 145 (= AmbG V, 46); SmijO, 65; ObrMT, 1.

sustained notes, is elaborated, and permeates the other voices. The chant is entrusted to the tenor in the settings *a 3* and *a 6,* but to the altus in the work *a 4* (except briefly at the end, where it is given to the tenor). The piece *a 3* sets all the text, divided into seven sections, while the other two compositions set only the text of sections 2, 4, 6, and the first half of 7, plainsong obviously being intended to alternate with the polyphony. Obrecht's tendency toward overuse of parallel tenths is sometimes in evidence, but also much ingenuity in reworking the same material.[39] In writing a motet on the *Alma Redemptoris Mater,*[40] Obrecht assigns the plainsong, paraphrased, to the bass; bits of imitation sometimes involve this chant, sometimes are independent of it. In *Haec Deum coeli,*[41] the *Ut queant laxis* melody mentioned on p. 83, fn. 238, is sung in slightly free canon *a 3* (without the *Ut queant* text) against two other parts. The tenor of Obrecht's *Mille quingentis* (cf. p. 186) renders, three times, the opening of the Introit to the Mass for the Dead, which Obrecht transposes from the original Lydian mode to the Phrygian.[42] Old as the technique of tenor-repetition may be, Obrecht's use of it accords with the other ways in which he and his contemporaries show a liking for tying a composition together. In *O beate Basili,* a *cantus firmus* is presented twice, first in canon between the tenor and altus, then in the superius. This *cantus firmus* bears some resemblance to one of the *Iste Confessor* chants[43] for the Common of Doctors and for the Common of a Confessor Bishop; since St. Basil ranked as both a Doctor and a Confessor Bishop, the choice of this chant as a basis for Obrecht's motet would be quite appropriate.

The four-part *Ave Regina coelorum, Mater Regis* achieves unity through the *aBcB* pattern. The appearance of this pattern here is not surprising, for the tenor is identical with that of Frye's *aBcB* setting *a 3* of the same text (cf. pp. 94f).[44] Obrecht's composition, since it lays out the tenor in long notes, has, of course, a different aspect from Frye's, in which all three voices are equally active. Obrecht's harmony is fuller, bits of imitation are present as are the ubiquitous parallel tenths, the bottom part descends lower than Frye's. The design of the five-part *Factor orbis* is somewhat similar, but the repeated section, on each appearance, has a different text and a different rhythm,[45]

---

[39] Cf. BreidS (on the setting *a 3*).

[40] Pr. ObrMT, 157; *Ego sum (ibid.,* 165) is a *contrafactum* of this piece.

[41] *Ibid.,* 46; VNM XLIV, 1. The text is stanza 2 of *Quod chorus vatum;* chant pr. VP, 103.

[42] The reprint in ObrMT, 179, follows Petrucci's *Motetti C* (1504), which gives the piece without text but with the title *Requiem.* This should not mislead one, as it evidently does WagG, 56, into believing that a Mass for the Dead by Obrecht survives. A further error in WagG, p. 161f, treats this piece as though it were the Introit of a Requiem Mass by Josquin.

[43] The one pr. in *Liber,* 1177. For the motet, *see* ObrMT, 85.

[44] Obrecht's motet is pr. *ibid.,* 64, after Petrucci's *Canti C,* which gives only the first few words of text for each *pars.* Wolf, in editing ObrMT, has underlaid the correct text, but it would seem improperly, since he does not repeat the last 2 lines of *pars I* at the end of *pars II,* which he evidently should have done in view of the disposition of the text in Frye's motet. Obrecht's work is given with the wrong text in AmbG V, 20.

[45] Cf. meas. 73–87 of *pars I* and 86–126 of *pars II* in ObrMT, 15ff.

and there is a coda. This piece may be designated as a sacred quodlibet: the words for each voice consist of a mosaic, pieced together from various texts, these belonging mostly to antiphons, and the five voices only occasionally have the same words; various Chant melodies are drawn upon. Thus, in *pars I,* tenor I sings, in long notes, the text and melody of *Canite tuba;* [46] in *pars II,* it first treats the *Erunt prava* and then (freely) the *Crastina die;* [47] finally it has the text of *Veni Domine,*[48] but (as a result of the application of the *abcb* pattern) it sings them to the latter part of the *Canite tuba* melody; his *Veni* text, however, has already appeared with its own melody in *pars I* (tenor II, meas. 13).

Polytextuality is not uncommon in Obrecht motets. *Beata es, Maria* (in two sections) has a single text in its first section but is polytextual in its second, where the altus has both a text and a melody derived from the sequence, *Ave Maria . . . Virgo serena.*[49] In each section, the tenor presents as *cantus firmus* a *Beata es, Maria* melody also employed as a motet tenor by Brumel. Obrecht's five-part *Salve crux arbor,*[50] in three *partes,* is likewise polytextual but, instead of progressing from monotextuality to polytextuality (like *Beata es*), reverses the process. Here, too, the tenor repeats its melody, but in no two of the four presentations is the rhythm the same; there is much use of canon and imitation.

A *Parce, Domine* printed by Petrucci *a 4* is given *a 3* by Glareanus, who says that this is the original form.[51] The piece, like Obrecht's *Si sumpsero,*[52] survives in several sources, including some that present instrumental transcriptions; these motets obviously enjoyed a certain popularity.

Obrecht: Masses

Obrecht's Masses—a collection of five of them was printed by Petrucci in 1504—constitute, in bulk, more than two-thirds of his output.[53] Four-part writing is the general rule. (In the following discussion, all the Masses are *a 4,* unless otherwise stated.) It is in these compositions that the master's genius is seen at its best. The *cantus-firmus* principle, which predominates, is worked out in various ways and receives some of its happiest applications at his hands. But if it is an old principle that underlies most of this music, Obrecht, in his Masses as in his secular pieces and motets, on occasion shows himself alive to the more forward-looking tendencies of his time.

---

[46] Antiphonale, 219.   [47] *Ibid.,* 219, 226, respectively.   [48] *Ibid.,* 213.

[49] Pr. VP, 46; for the motet, *see* ObrMT, 69.   [50] Pr. *ibid.,* 29.

[51] The motet appears *a 4* in ObrMT, 95; *a 3* in PubAPTM XVI, 207; RoksT, 24; ForkA II, 524; ReissmA I, 5; KiesT, 28; ParrishM, 56.

[52] Pr. ObrMT, 175; MaldR, XIX, 17 (cf. ReT, 102 [No. 304]).

[53] While ObrWW and ObrMT each consists of 1 vol., ObrMS comprises 5. To the Masses there printed (*recte* 22, but Wolf breaks 1 into 2 incomplete Masses; cf. fn. 59), 3 more should be added; *see* MME I, 107; AngI, 8. The Kyries of these 3 Masses pr. SmijO, 51ff. *See also* RoediN, 76, 83f.

The *Missa super Maria zart*[54] is an example of Obrecht's Masses built on a single *cantus firmus* of monophonic origin. The melody is a German Marian song, which Obrecht treats with much ingenuity. He divides it into twelve segments (*see* Ex. 34*a*)[55] and presents them in long notes in the tenor in accordance with this plan: Kyrie I—segments 1, 1, 2; *Christe*—tenor *tacet;* Kyrie II—1, 2, 1, 2; Gloria—3, 3, 3, 4; *Domine Deus* and *Qui tollis . . . miserere*—tenor *tacet; Qui tollis . . . suscipe*—4, 4, 4, 5, 6, 5, 6, 5, 6; Credo—6, 6, 7, 8, 7, 8, 7, 8 (varied), 7, 8, 9; *Qui propter nos* and *Et incarnatus*—tenor *tacet; Et resurrexit*—8 (5 times), 9 (9 times, the last and antepenultimate 9's being varied); Sanctus—9, 10, 9, 10, 9, 10; *Pleni*—tenor *tacet; Osanna*—11, 12, 11, 12, 11, 12, 12; *Benedictus*—tenor *tacet*. Time-values are frequently diminished upon repetition of a segment. Of the sections that apply the *cantus-firmus* principle, only the Agnus presents the entire melody, so that it is not until this point is reached that—in a climactic way—the principle produces its usual unifying effect. This it brings about, not in the customary manner, but by a summarizing, as it were, of all the segments heard before—a method that had a special attraction for Obrecht, who used it to good purpose in other works also. In Agnus I of the present Mass, the complete melody is sung straight through by the bass. In Agnus II, although the tenor *tacet,* the whole melody is divided in "migrating" *cantus-firmus* fashion among the other voices (with suitable transpositions), the segments being distributed thus: altus—1, 2; bass—1, 2; cantus—3; bass—4; altus—all the rest (5 being repeated, the second time a fourth lower).[55a]

EXAMPLE 34 (*a*) Melody of *Maria zart* (after BöhA, 705; WackerK II, 814) and (*b*) Opening of Agnus II of the *Missa super Maria zart*—Obrecht (after ObrMS II, 103f).

[54] Pr. ObrMS II, 41.
[55] In numbering the segments, we disregard the orig. repetition of segments 1 + 2 (i.e., segment 3 is the first one after the repetition), but we do regard it in comments about uses of the complete melody straight through.   [55a] Obrecht changes the last note of segment 1.

"Mary, thou gentle one, of noble stem, a rose without thorns, thou hast restored with might what had been lost in days gone by through Adam's fall: St. Gabriel promised thee power. Help, so that my sin and guilt be not avenged; bestow clemency on me, since the consolation existeth not of gaining mercy through my own merit. And in the end, pray, turn not from me in my dying hour."

In Agnus III, the melody is given complete to the superius, but segment 4 is modified in a way that extends its compass upward, and a still stronger climactic effect is obtained by transposing segments 1, 2, 5, and 10 an octave higher than the pitch-level of the rest. The *cantus firmus* does not enter in the Gloria until meas. 22 or in the Credo until meas. 19; late entries of the *cantus-firmus*-bearing voice, such as we have noted on p. 67, are common in Obrecht and in other composers of the time, and it becomes increasingly the custom for this voice to be the last one to enter. In the *Missa super Maria zart,* the *cantus firmus* frequently permeates the other voices in passages in imitation. All the tenorless subsections resemble Agnus II in drawing on the pre-existent melody, the amount of it introduced and the kind of treatment, however, varying considerably. Thus, in the *Qui propter nos* only one segment (9) appears briefly, in *cantus-firmus* fashion, whereas the *Domine Deus* and first *Qui tollis* each anticipate the effect of the Agnus somewhat by presenting the entire melody—but freely paraphrased. The paraphrasing of segments 1 through 5 in the bass of the *Et incarnatus* is fairly elaborate and becomes evident only if one ignores all notes smaller than a semibreve. Obrecht's predilection for melodic sequences is much in evidence in this work, e.g., at the words *"Adoramus te,"* The *Christe* presents an example of modulation, leading the composer far enough into the realm of accidentalism to call for the insertion, in the source, of a flat before D.[56]

Unlike the foregoing, the *Missa super Sub tuum praesidium* and the *Missa diversorum tenorum* are both based on several *cantus firmi*. In each of the five major sections of the former,[57] the text and the melody (with melismas added at the cadences) of *Sub tuum praesidium*,[58] an antiphon in honor of the Virgin, are sung once by the superius. The Kyrie is *a 3*, and the number of voices increases by one in each major section (so that the Agnus is *a 7*). In the Credo, a third text, *Audi nos,* consisting of two lines, is presented four times in the discantus II, the same melody serving for each line, but the time-values changing in each of the eight statements. In the Sanctus the added text is, instead, the *Mediatrix nostra,* this appearing in both the discantus II and the tenor, two complete presentations being given in each (as well as two fragmentary ones in the discantus II and one in the tenor), the two voices usually singing portions of the melody alternately. In the last major section, the first added material is provided by the *Celsus nuntiat* (in the discantus II and the vagans) and the *Supplicamus nos* (in the altus I), each being presented once in Agnus I and once more in Agnus II (with a partial further repetition of the *Celsus nuntiat* in the vagans); the opening of the *Regina coeli* (in the discantus II and the vagans) and the close of the *Salve Regina* (in the altus I) provide the added material in Agnus III. The simultaneous use of different pre-existent melodies in this work naturally limits the opportunity for the introduction of imitation. The rhythmic motion is often very active, the frequent employment of short time-values being quite marked. The progressive piling on of additional voices helps to build up a most impressive climax.

Of the *Missa diversorum tenorum,* which reaches us without an Agnus, portions exist in two sources, only part of the Sanctus being common to both.[59] Among the melodies drawn upon are several found in polyphonic chansons we have already encountered. Thus the *cantus firmi* of Obrecht's Kyrie I,

[56] Cf. CreV, 119ff; BorD, 290.   [57] Pr. ObrMS II, 1.   [58] Pr. Liber, 1861.

[59] The Kyrie and Sanctus are pr. in ObrMS IV, 85, after Capp. Sistina MS 35, as the *Missa Carminum* (the designation, in the absence of any in the source, being that of the ed., J. Wolf; neither of the Tracts given by him belongs to the Mass; one is an anon. piece, the other by de Orto; cf. SmijMC, 193f); the Gloria, Credo, and Sanctus (through *Osanna I*) are pr., after Milan. Archivio del Duomo 2268 (one of the Gafori codices), as the *Missa Adieu mes amours I* in ObrMS IV, 1 (the designation, chosen because of the presence of the *Adieu mes amours* melody in part of the Credo, is again the editor's; the source, however, does give a title in this instance, i.e., *Missa diversorum tenorum;* cf. JepG, 23). The additional Sanctus pr. as an appendix in ObrMS IV, 35, is unrelated to the Obrecht Mass; cf. JepG, 23. Perhaps, as in Obrecht's *Missa Libenter gloriabor,* to be mentioned again presently, the music of the Kyrie was to serve again for that of the Agnus (cf. SmijMC, 194). Concerning the fact that what Wolf prints as two different incomplete Masses are really part of one Mass, *see* further JepG, 23; GomO, 116ff.

Qui tollis, Credo opening, *Qui cum Patre,* Sanctus opening, and Sanctus continuation (before the *Pleni*) correspond, respectively, to the tenors of Dufay's (or Binchois's) *Je ne vis oncques,* Busnois's *Joye me fuit,* Ockeghem's *Petite camusette,* and Busnois's *Acordés moy,* the superius of Barbireau's *Scon lief,* and the tenor of Busnois's *Mon mignault—Gracieuse.* At *Et resurrexit,* Obrecht draws on the popular *Adieu mes amours* melody [60] (on which he also based a separate Mass [61]). This work clearly has some of the aspects of a quodlibet. In the Credo, a substantial part of the text is omitted (cf. pp. 69, 112). Although this Mass has in common with the *Missa super Sub tuum praesidium* the feature that it is based on several pre-existent melodies, it does not share with that work the procedure of having one of the melodies bind the whole structure together.

Obrecht's *Missa Caput* and, if we concede that the borrowed melody is a folk tune, his *Missa L'Homme armé* are each, like the *Missa super Maria zart,* written on a *cantus firmus* of monophonic origin; but they differ from that Mass—and resemble Ockeghem's *Missa Caput*—by showing clearly that they are modeled upon other composers' polyphonic treatments of the *cantus-firmus* material. The *Missa Caput* [62] is based on the same melody as are the similarly named Masses of Dufay and Ockeghem; but, whereas Dufay places it in his tenor and Ockeghem in his bass, Obrecht gives each voice an opportunity to sing it: the tenor has the melody in the Kyrie and Credo, the superius in the Gloria, the altus in the Sanctus, the bass in the Agnus.[63] Each of the major sections, other than the Kyrie, is divided into a segment in ternary rhythm and another in binary rhythm, exactly as in the *Caput* Masses of Dufay and Ockeghem. (After a Kyrie I in ternary rhythm and a *Christe* in binary rhythm, Kyrie II, missing in Dufay and given in ternary rhythm by Ockeghem, is written by Obrecht in binary rhythm.) Obrecht obviously knew the two earlier Masses. The altus of his Gloria opens with as much as the first seven and a half measures of the superius of Dufay's Gloria, thereby quoting more than just the head-motif.[64] On the other hand, like Ockeghem, he departs from Dufay's twofold presentation of the *cantus firmus* in all movements by giving it only once in the Kyrie. There is at times great

[60] For a fuller list of the pre-existent melodies used in this Mass, *see* GomO, 117ff.

[61] When Wolf gave the title *"Missa Adieu mes amours I"* to the part of the *Missa diversorum tenorum* preserved at Milan, he appended the figure *"I"* because he knew of the survival of the altus and bassus of the other Mass—he adds a *"II"* after its title—in a private collection; cf. ObrMS V, unpaginated introduction before p. 157. All the voices of this work survive in Jena Choir-Book 32; cf. RoediN, 83f. All the voices of some movements survive in the Segovia MS; cf. No. 4 in MME I, 107; AngI, 8. That this is the same as Wolf's *Missa Adieu . . . II* may be seen by comparing the incipits he gives of the altus and bassus (in the introduction cited) with the Kyrie I given in old notation (after Jena) in RoediN, 83, and with the Kyrie pr. (after Segovia) in SmijO, 54.

[62] Pr. ObrMS IV, 189.

[63] For conflicting views concerning the authenticity of the alternative Agnus, pr. *ibid.,* 250 (with the *cantus firmus* in the tenor), *see op. cit.,* introduction before p. 189; GomO, 85.

[64] Cf. BukMR, 301.

rhythmic activity in Obrecht's Mass, and individual voices occasionally have arabesques that recall the music of the two earlier masters; but the harmonic aspect has quite another character, being definitely that of a later period. In fact, this Mass differs so considerably from its predecessors, and they so much from each other, that nothing could illustrate more strikingly the extent to which various compositions may be essentially original, though all are erected on the same *cantus firmus*.

In his *Missa L'Homme armé*,[65] Obrecht follows the lead of still another forerunner—Busnois. The general plan of the Mass is, indeed, so close to that of Busnois's that the work has been described [66] as a "parody" of the earlier composition ("parody" here not having the limited technical meaning generally assigned to it in this book; cf. p. 202) and also as "a tribute, on Obrecht's part, to the 'authority' of his model." Obrecht disposes of the tenor material in much the same manner as Busnois had done: thus, he has the *cantus firmus* interrupted by tenorless sections at exactly the same points in the Kyrie, Credo, Sanctus, and Agnus (cf. p. 107). These tenorless sections are of the same length as Busnois's, and the two Masses are likewise of equal length in their entireties. Despite all this, however, Obrecht's Mass has its own striking individuality. The mode of Busnois's Mass is Dorian, except in the Credo, where it is Hypodorian, both modes being transposed; the *cantus firmus,* as one might therefore expect, is erected on G everywhere except in the Credo; here it is erected on D. Obrecht similarly makes a change in the Credo, but his prevailing mode is Hypoaeolian, while his mode for the Credo is Aeolian. The *cantus firmus,* again as one might expect, is erected on E everywhere except in the Credo; here it is erected on A. Where it is built on E, the melody, taken out of its polyphonic context and considered by itself, is squarely in the Phrygian mode. It is easy to understand why Glareanus, in the *Dodeca-chordon,* never examines the mode of a polyphonic work as such, but solely that of each separate part.[67] (It is also easy to see that, modally, Phrygian melodies may well be closely allied to Hypoaeolian melodies, the former bearing a dominant relationship to the latter.) Obrecht introduces a delicate touch in the Credo, from *Et resurrexit* on, by recalling the Phrygian character of the *cantus firmus* in the other movements through an occasional flattening of the note b. After the *cantus firmus* is interrupted during the *Et incarnatus est,* it resumes—repeating, as it should, the fragment sung before the halt, but now an octave lower, apparently to add somberness to the setting of the word *"Crucifixus";* the low register is retained through *"Filioque procedit."* For his Agnus I, Obrecht takes the melody through the end of statement I of the medial repeated motif and not only inverts it, like Busnois, but presents it backward; he treats the rest of the melody the same way in Agnus III. A head-motif relates Obrecht's Kyrie I, *Qui tollis, Pleni, Osanna,* Agnus II,

---

[65] Pr. ObrMS V, 53.   [66] In StrunkH.   [67] Cf. ApelAT, 63, fn.

and Agnus III. His countermelodies and canons are new, and his use of imitation more extensive than Busnois's.

When Obrecht chooses as a persisting *cantus firmus* a melody that came into being as part of a polyphonic piece, or at any rate achieved standard form as part of such a piece, he likes—in the manner of Ockeghem in the *Missa Fors seulement* and Faugues in the *Missa Le Serviteur*—to introduce some of the pre-existent countermelody material also. The drawing upon two out of a total of three pre-existent voices is illustrated in the three-part *Missa sine nomine* and the four-part *Missae Malheur me bat* and *Ave Regina coelorum*.

The first of these [68] is based on the tenor of Hayne's most famous chanson and is therefore actually a *Missa De tous biens plaine*. Obrecht modifies the tenor somewhat, reducing the number of time-values to three, and obtains this *cantus firmus:*

EXAMPLE 35. *Cantus firmus* of the *Missa De tous biens plaine*—
Obrecht; derived from Hayne van Ghizeghem (from ObrMS V; time-values not divided).

The Kyrie divides this into three segments, assigned successively to the lowest voice (in Kyrie I), the middle voice (in the *Christe*), and the lowest voice again (in Kyrie II). The Gloria treats the *cantus firmus* simply, merely presenting it twice in the lowest voice with long rests between phrases. But the movement is noteworthy for the content of its superius. Through *"Filius Patris,"* this consists of Hayne's old superius, with free interludes added between phrases, Hayne's melody being sung mostly while the *cantus firmus* is silent; from *"Qui tollis"* to the end, Obrecht's superius engages in modified canon at the fifth with the second presentation of the *cantus firmus* by the lowest voice, the liberties consisting mostly of changes in time-value and, as a result, of changes in time-interval. The Credo is quite extraordinary in a semi-Schoenbergian way that recalls the textless, untitled canon described on p. 190. The *cantus firmus* is set forth according to the length of the note-values: first all the longs are executed, then all the breves, then all the semibreves. The presentation is completed at the end of *"descendit de coelis."* Then the same procedure is repeated, but this time the marshalling of the notes begins at the end of the *cantus firmus* and continues backward. This presentation is completed, with slight changes, at *"per prophetas,"* after which the *cantus-*

[68] Pr. ObrMS V, 157; StevensM, 71.

firmus notes are given in normal order, but in ternary rhythm (binary rhythm having prevailed from the beginning of the Mass to this point). In the Sanctus the *cantus firmus* is divided into eight sections and, up to *"Sabaoth,"* these are given forth by the lowest voice in the following order: 1, 8, 7, 6, 5, 4, 3, 2. The *Pleni* and Benedictus are *a 2*, without *cantus firmus*, but this appears in the lowest voice in *Osanna I* in normal form, and in the middle voice in *Osanna II* in ternary rhythm. In Agnus I, the *cantus firmus* is in the middle voice in normal form; in Agnus II (*a 2*) it is in the lower voice with the values halved; in Agnus III it is in the outer voices in a canon at the unison, ingeniously modified, by changes in the time-interval. The treatment of the *cantus firmus* in the Credo and Sanctus of this Mass, as in other works by Obrecht, may seem unduly intricate, even pedantic, to those insufficiently familiar with Netherlandish music. Actually, his procedures are no more complicated than those frequently employed by Bach; they are simply different. It is clear that Obrecht, having always in mind the musical result, carefully considered the inherent possibilities of his *cantus firmus* and —in this work—saw that its notes would yield a good melody, not only in their original order, but also in the permutations described. His treatment of the *cantus firmus* in this work, as in others (e.g., the *Missa super Maria zart*) is not an arbitrary, pedantic procedure, but rather an analytical, artistic one.

Obrecht employed various means of unification in addition to the *cantus firmus* in the composition under consideration. Thus a figure sung by the highest voice in measures 5–6 of the Kyrie is frequently repeated, throughout the work, in normal position, in inversion, at the original pitch-level and at others. Toward the end of the Kyrie, the highest voice is given a striking motif, consisting of an ascending leap of a fourth presented three times in sequence, and this motif is most effectively reintroduced, in the lowest voice, at about the middle of Agnus I, while the highest voice is silent and the middle one has sustained notes of the *cantus firmus,* so that the motif is clearly audible.[69]

The *Missa Malheur me bat*[70] is based on the chanson attributed to Ockeghem. At the chanson opening, the superius and tenor are briefly in strict imitation, but what follows shows it is the former voice that Obrecht chiefly draws upon. This melody he divides into nine segments,[70a] each used as *cantus firmus* of a different four-part subsection of the Mass through Agnus I. He quotes the melody complete only in Agnus III. The general plan, therefore, recalls the Mass on *Maria zart,* but the assignment of the *cantus firmus*

---

[69] *See* further GomO, 45ff.

[70] Pr. ObrMS I, 141; facsimile of the Sanctus, after Petrucci's print, in ScherNO, 92ff.

[70a] (1) meas. 3–7 of the chanson; (2) meas. 8–11; (3) meas. 12–19 (note 1); (4) meas. 19 (note 1) to 26 (note 1); (5) meas. 26 (note 1) to 33 (note 1); (6) meas. 33 (note 2) to 38 (note 1); (7) meas. 38 (note 1) to 43; (8) meas. 44–48 (note 1); (9) meas. 48 (note 1) to end.

to the superius throughout provides a marked difference. Each segment appears three times in succession—except segment 6, which is given four times—in order to supply enough *cantus-firmus* material for the subsection it serves. Kyrie I is in ternary meter and therefore, since the chanson is in binary meter, does not retain the original configuration; no two presentations in this subsection are rhythmically alike. In the treatment of segments 2, 4, 7, and 8, the original values of the chanson appear in the last presentation of the series and are preceded by augmentations (regular or irregular), the first double and the second normal. Segment 6 is also first presented in double augmentation and finally in its original values, but has two statements in normal augmentation in between, instead of one. The manipulation of segments 3, 5, and 9 represents other variants of the norm. The chanson tenor is used as *cantus firmus,* in original values, in the three-part *Crucifixus* (the music of which serves for the Benedictus also) and Agnus II, this melody being given to the tenor in the former and to the bass in the latter. At one point or another, motifs from the chanson permeate all voices of the Mass. This work is distinguished by great clarity in both its harmony and its period structure. Modally it is most interesting: though the mode of the underlying chanson is Phrygian, Obrecht manipulates his material so as to make the mode of the Mass Aeolian. This he accomplishes mainly at the points where the chanson has cadences on the final of the mode: here he treats the concluding E chords as dominants and adds extensions ending on A chords. At some points he substitutes an Ionian cadence. Real Phrygian cadences do occur during this Mass, but, strangely enough, not at places corresponding to their appearance in the chanson. A slightly embellished *ostinato* on E and A provides Agnus III with a most effective bass. (*Ostinati* are prominent likewise in Obrecht's Mass on *Der pfoben swancz* [cf. p. 116], which is related to the *Missa Malheur me bat* in certain other respects also.[71]) Wholly aside from any technical considerations, this is one of the loveliest of Obrecht's Masses.[72]

The *Missa Ave Regina coelorum,*[73] like Obrecht's similarly named motet, is built on the old song-motet by Frye. In the Mass, as in his own motet, Obrecht borrows Frye's tenor (often discreetly elaborated), but the earlier superius melody—retaining its original position in the highest voice—is drawn upon too, its first nine and one-third measures appearing in measures 58–77 of the *Patrem* and its measures 1–21 in the whole of the Benedictus. Normally, Obrecht places Frye's tenor in his own tenor, but in the Agnus he assigns it to the bass, Frye's *pars I* being drawn upon in Agnus I and his *pars II* in Agnus III. In Agnus II, measures 1–19 of the *cantus firmus,* paraphrased, appear in slightly free canon between the tenor and bass. The *Qui tollis* of the Gloria has already treated the entire *cantus firmus* in much the same way, but the

---

[71] Cf. GomO, 116, which identifies the tenor. The work is printed as a *Missa sine nomine* in ObrMS V, 1.

[72] Further about this Mass, *see* GomO, 91ff.   [73] Pr. ObrMS III, 141.

canon is freer. The opening of the Credo handles a fragment of Frye's tenor similarly, but the upper pair of voices precedes the lower pair in anticipatory imitation, so that the *cantus firmus* permeates all the voices at this point. Imitation and canon play especially large roles in this Mass; *ostinato* technique is prominent in the *Et resurrexit*. At various places, Obrecht uses, as a head-motif, measures 11–15 of the superius of his own *Ave Regina* motet, this being material that does not appear in Frye's composition.

In another group of Masses Obrecht draws on all the voices of his polyphonic models. To this group belongs one of his best works—undoubtedly from his most mature period—a Mass [74] based on Busnois's three-part *Fortuna desperata* (cf. p. 102). The old tenor [75] serves as Obrecht's tenor in (1) the Kyrie I (which gives only measures 1–15 of the melody; (2) Kyrie II, which presents the whole 58 measures of the melody; (3) Gloria, which opens with measures 1–30 sung backward, continues with measures 31–58 sung in normal order, and, from the *Qui tollis* on, repeats this procedure; (4) Credo, which forms a pendant to the Gloria by opening with measures 31–58 sung backward, continuing with measures 1–30 in normal order, and, from *Et incarnatus* on, repeating that procedure; and (5) Agnus I, which presents the melody once in normal values and once with the values halved. Obrecht's bass sings the old tenor in the *Osanna;* his superius opens the Sanctus with it, but then continues with measures 1–15 of the old superius; this pre-existent melody is sung complete by Obrecht's superius in Agnus III, first in normal values, then with the values halved. A fragment of the *Fortuna* tenor is used in anticipatory imitation in the altus and superius at the beginning of the Mass. The three old voices are almost never drawn upon at the same time, but they do appear together at the openings of Kyrie II and Agnus III (each time with a free fourth voice), thus momentarily approximating the parody technique.[76] The *Missa Forseulement* likewise introduces all three voices of its model—Ockeghem's *Fors seulement l'attente*—but here again the polyphonic complex is not extensively reworked as such: this is an inferior composition, perhaps intended only as a sketch.[77] A generally similar borrowing procedure appears in the *Missa Si dedero,*[78] based on Agricola's song-motet *a 3* (cf. p. 211). The drawing upon Agricola's three parts, however, assumes considerable proportions, not only in Obrecht's passages *a 4,* but also in his tenorless ones. The latter provide complete presentations of the chanson tenor, superius, and bass in the altus of the *Pleni,* the superius of the Benedictus, and the bass of the Agnus II, respectively. Even so, the pre-existent voices are practically never all borrowed at once; but a simultaneous quotation of the three does occur briefly in Agnus I.[79] Obrecht applies to Agricola's tenor the same partitioning process, but without the complete melody at

---

[74] *Ibid.,* I, 85; VNM IX.   [75] Called *"Altus"* by the editor in JosqMS I, 105.
[76] *See* further GomO, 112ff.   [77] Cf. GomO, 32ff; for the Mass, *see* ObrMS V, 133.
[78] Pr. *ibid.,* III, 1.   [79] In meas. 51–53; cf. Agricola in ObrMS II, 57, meas. 68–70.

the end, that he applies to the *cantus firmi* of the *Missa super Maria zart* and *Missa Malheur me bat*. The *Missa Si dedero* is of special interest as a very early example of a type of Mass that was to assume great importance—a type based on pre-existent sacred polyphony, polyphonic models before having been customarily secular.[80]

The parody principle makes a real appearance throughout a whole subsection in still another Mass based on a composition *a 3*, the Mass modeled on the *Rosa playsant* of "Philippon" or Caron or Dusart (cf. p. 111). The principle—which we have already found applied at an early date to individual Mass movements (cf. pp. 28, 33) and which we have traced through Faugues and Ockeghem in a separate development that gradually yielded a technique capable of being employed on a larger scale—may well have received its first considerable use within the framework of a complete Ordinary in this Obrecht Mass. (The term *"Missa parodia"* is the only one, now employed for the various Renaissance Mass types, that was actually used in the 16th century. It was included by the German, Jakob Paix, in the title of his Mass based on Crecquillon's *Domine, da nobis,* 1587.[81]) The distinctive feature of this type of Mass is that it is based, not on a single melody, like the normal *cantus-firmus* and paraphrase types, but on the several voices of a polyphonic model, the simultaneous appearance of all the voices, at least on occasion, being characteristic though not indispensable. This type was to be greatly favored by 16th-century composers. To be sure, the method lent itself easily to perfunctory treatment, and there are parody Masses in which composers make no important contributions of their own. However, there are others in which they handle the borrowed polyphonic material with great skill and imagination.

In every one of the five major sections of the *Missa Rosa playsant*,[82] the three voices of the chanson are simultaneously reworked at least briefly. In the tenorless *Pleni,* all three recur together in their entirety in elaborated form, the chanson tenor being paraphrased in the Mass contratenor instead of appearing in *cantus-firmus* form.

EXAMPLE 36. Opening of the chanson, *Rosa playsant* (Caron?) (after SmijO, 62) and of the *Pleni* of Obrecht's Mass based on it (Segovia MS, fol. 32ᵛ–33; transcr. by A. Singer).[82a]

[80] Cf. RubMM, 7.   [81] Cf. AmbG III, 45.
[82] Kyrie pr. in SmijO, 58. The contratenor that appears in the chanson as pr. *ibid.,* 62, is an added part given in *Canti C;* the piece survives *a 3* in Florence, Bibl. naz. centr., Banco rari 229 and in the Casanatense MS at Rome.
[82a] Since Ex. 36a belongs to the period covered by Chap. 3, consistency with the method of transcription used there would require a further division of the time-values by 2. However, consistency within the ex. itself is of more moment for present purposes.

The *cantus firmus,* as such, being absent, this *Pleni* provides a genuine application of the parody technique. But, since the Mass *as a whole* derives its form from the reappearance of its *cantus firmus,* the work is really a *cantus-firmus* Mass, incorporating a tenorless section in parody style, not a true parody Mass, which would have to be indebted to the parody technique for its fundamental structure. (The distinction is similar to that between a composition that employs pervading imitation, but derives its form from being cast in the mould of a *rondeau,* and a composition that owes its structure primarily to the pervading-imitation principle. Cf. p. 88.) As far as *cantus-firmus* treatment is concerned, Obrecht here again applies the partitioning method. The old tenor is divided into nine segments, the first two being presented twice and the others each three times; a segment is never repeated with the same rhythmic configuration. The Mass tenor *tacet* in the *Christe, Pleni,* Benedictus, and Agnus II; but the chanson tenor is paraphrased complete in the Benedictus just as it is in the *Pleni;* these are the only two points in the Mass at which the chanson tenor appears in its entirety. The historical importance of this Mass is paralleled by its high intrinsic musical quality.

In the Missa *Je ne demande,*[83] Obrecht builds on a four-part model—Busnois's *Je ne demande autre degré*—and takes advantage of this fact to draw on all four voices, though he refrains from really reworking the whole polyphonic complex at one time. He applies the partitioning method to Busnois's tenor in his own tenor, presenting the borrowed material there in complete form only twice, once each in Agnus II and Agnus III. By means of sequence patterns of five time-units, he produces in the *Qui tollis* (without change of signature) a remarkable passage in quintuple meter, contrasting with the prevailing binary meter.[84]

EXAMPLE 37. Extract from the *Qui tollis* of the *Missa Je ne demande—* Obrecht (after ObrMS I, 8ff).

[83] Pr. ObrMS I, 1.   [84] Cf. ScherT, 475.

*Note the unresolved suspensions

The last six measures of this example present an excellent illustration of the organization of eight-beat units into three plus three plus two—a combination that was very popular about 1500.[84a]

Obrecht's Masses abound in further interesting details. Thus, in the *Missa Sicut spina rosam*,[85] the bass of the Agnus is derived from that of the Kyrie of Ockeghem's *Missa Mi-Mi*.[86] If, in using the same music for both the *Crucifixus* and the Benedictus of the *Missa Malheur me bat,* Obrecht, like Faugues, tries to supplement the unifying force of the *cantus firmus* by that of polyphonic repetition, he accomplishes this in the *Missa Libenter gloriabor* through reapplication of the music of the three divisions of the Kyrie to the three divisions of the Agnus [87] (cf. pp. 341, 348). But the most conspicuous technical feature of Obrecht's Masses is undoubtedly his imaginative treatment of the *cantus firmus,* especially his breaking of the melody into segments and his employing each one repeatedly, reserving a complete consecutive presentation for the tenor at the end or for some other voice in a tenorless section. The *L'Homme armé* Masses of the Naples MS, of course, follow a related procedure with regard to a whole cycle of compositions (cf. p. 149f), but Obrecht applies the method within the frame of individual works. Indeed, this breaking up and reassembling of the *cantus firmus* may be regarded as one of the prominent traits of his style, together with his approximation and final attainment of the parody technique, his tendency to abandon the *formes fixes* in his chansons, his liking for changing the time-interval in canon, his feeling for tonality, and his clear harmony. In addition to the technical proficiency

[84a] Cf. SachsRT, 247ff; also the pattern on p. 333 *infra*.   [85] Pr. ObrMS III, 101.
[86] Cf. BesE, 151, fn. 2. (It is less likely that Ockeghem borrowed the bass from Obrecht.)
[87] Cf. MME I, 107; the Kyrie pr. SmijO, 51.

shown in his music, its sheer loveliness makes him one of the greatest figures in a great generation.

The Monophonic Chansonniers

The *Adieu mes amours* melody, on which Obrecht based one Mass and part of another, was a great favorite in his time. Josquin, Weerbecke, and Mouton are among those who incorporated it into chanson settings. Like the discants and tenors of *J'ay pris amours* and *De tous biens plaine,* it belongs to a body of melodic material that was reworked often enough to help mould, in a modest way, the musical culture of a generation or more.

Two monophonic *chansonniers* of the time reach us—Paris Bibl. nat. fr. 9346 (*Le Manuscrit de Bayeux*)[88] and Bibl. nat. fr. 12744.[89] Many melodies frequently incorporated in polyphonic works of the Josquin period appear also in one or the other of these *chansonniers; Adieu mes amours* is found in the Bayeux MS. The two MSS, between them, contain 206 monophonic pieces.[90] The latest date that can be assigned any of these chansons is that of the battle of Fornovo (July 5, 1495), mentioned in *Et que feront povres gendarmes.*[91] Though many chansons date from the last quarter of the century, some texts can be traced in such early MSS as Canonici misc. 213. Whereas the chansons of MS 9346 originate largely from the Ile-de-France and Normandy, those of MS 12744 represent a wider geographic distribution.

The contents of these MSS mirror the contemporaneous shift from the *formes fixes* toward the free chanson. There are but two *rondeaux*[92] in the Bayeux MS and none in MS 12744. However, the opening strophes of two poems in the latter MS are made up of the refrains of *rondeaux quatrains,* but the later portions bear no resemblance to the models.[93] The *virelai* is well represented; forty examples occur in MS 12744 and thirty-five in the Bayeux MS.[94] There are fourteen *ballades* in MS 12744, but only three in the Bayeux MS.

One of the *virelais,* famous in its time and contained in both MSS, is *Hellas, Olivier Bachelin.*[94a] It deals with the imprisonment by the English of Olivier Basselin, the almost legendary originator of *vaux-de-vire* (*voix-de-ville*),[94b] a

[88] Modern ed. in GéroB.
[89] Modern ed. in ParisC. Facsimiles included in first issue and in AuP, Pl. XXIII.
[90] MS 12744 contains 143 chansons, including 2 pairs of parodies, and MS 9346, 100; 35 are common to both sources.
[91] Pr. ParisC, text, 126; music, 69.
[92] One of these, *Triste plaisir,* provides new *additamenta* to the refrain by Chartier, whose poem had been set by Binchois.
[93] Cf. ParisC, Nos. XXIII, LIX, with LoepL, Nos. 377, 585, respectively.
[94] These figures include several *virelais* of irregular structure. Cf. analysis of *Ma seulle dame* in HewO, 54f.
[94a] ParisC, text, 57; music, 32; GéroB, 45.
[94b] Cf. TierC, 226ff.

special kind of monophonic chanson, a collection of which was published by J. Chardavoine in 1576 (cf. pp. 389f).

A few melodies attained such popularity that they were set to more than one text. In MS 12744, the lovely melody of *L'amour de moy* serves also for *Jamès je n'auré envie*.[95] A single melody underlies both *En venant de Lyon* and *Lourdault, lourdault*,[96] though the former has a coda not appearing in the latter. The melody of *Adieu mes amours*[97] reappears with the text, *Ilz sont bien pelez*.[98] The melody of one *Vray dieu d'amours* poem recurs in the company of another *Vray dieu d'amours* poem that has substantially the same first strophe and shows certain other resemblances also.[99] Other interrelationships are often less clear. Though the opening melodies of *En l'ombre d'un buyssonet* and *Il fait bon fermer son huys*[100] are similar in a number of respects, later melodic materials reveal no relationships. It is possible that some resemblances are caused by the chance juxtaposition of similar stock-motifs, on which these melodies are constructed.[101]

Partly owing to the ornamented nature of many of these melodies, it has been suggested that they are voice-parts extracted from polyphonic compositions.[102] But a study [102a] of 114 polyphonic treatments of 68 texts contained in the two Paris MSS, 93 settings clearly employing 54 tunes found in these sources, has revealed only two instances in which a monophonic version will actually fit into a polyphonic setting. There seems to be greater reason to regard the monophonic chansons that appear also in polyphonic compositions as pre-existent bases for the latter rather than as transcriptions arranged from them. (A MS does exist, however, that contains 22 melodies, most of which, unlike the melodies of the two Paris MSS, are easily traceable to polyphonic compositions of the period. This source is the Tournai Chansonnier,[103] noteworthy also for its beautiful miniatures. In addition to the tenors forming the major portion of the collection the MS includes a bass and superius voice-part; it may well constitute an assemblage of favorite parts from polyphonic works.[103a])

Of special interest, in MS 12744, is the quodlibet, *Mon seul plaisir*.[104] The

[95] ParisC, text, 30, 52; music, 15, 29, respectively. *L'amour de moy* is also pr. GéroB, 30, after the Bayeux MS. The chanson has been made familiar to modern concert audiences in arrangements by Vaughan Williams, Tiersot, and others.

[96] ParisC, text, 85, 69; music, 49, 39, respectively.

[97] Pr. GéroB, 100.   [98] Pr. ParisC, text, 130; music, 71.

[99] Cf. *ibid.*, text, 9, 123; music, 4, 68, respectively.

[100] *Ibid.*, text, 20, 27; music, 10, 13, respectively.

[101] Further about such motifs, *see* GéroL, 2802ff.

[102] Cf. GéroB, xxxviif; HewO, 14; BukMR, 173. Gérold claims further that the polyphonists, drawn upon by these two MSS, had themselves drawn upon pre-existent folk material (his complex, and debatable, theory thus postulating three stages).

[102a] ReC.   [103] Two facsimiles pr. TourC, opp. p. 35; 3 more in LenN, after p. 173.

[103a] Mention should be made also of a collection of 17 tenors, bound into Bibl. nat. n. a. fr. 4379. Every one of these can be traced to a polyphonic original; cf. AfMW VII (1925), 233; ReC, 4.

[104] Pr. ParisC, text, 71; music, 41.

four strophes of its poem incorporate 19 quotations from text incipits [105] of famous chansons, including *Comme femme, J'ay pris amours, Ma bouche rit, Par le regart,* etc. However, neither the melody in MS 12744 nor the polyphonic setting of the same text by Ninot le Petit (cf. p. 278) is based on musical quotations from these chansons. Other melodies in the two Paris MSS, such as *Bergerette savoysienne, L'amour de moy,* and *Si congié prens,* have achieved greater fame than the quodlibet, thanks in part to the fact that they survive in fine polyphonic settings by leading masters of the period.

Agricola

Among the composers who used melodic material also appearing in the monophonic *chansonniers* is Alexander Agricola (likewise called Alexander Ackerman [*sic*] or simply Alexander, etc.). He may have been a Fleming by birth, though some doubt exists on this score; his art, however, is clearly Netherlandish. In January, 1472, a certain Alexandro was in the service of Galeazzo Maria Sforza at Milan.[106] The month before, this duke had written to King Matthias Corvinus of Hungary, recommending Pietro da Vienna *ex Alamania,* the cousin of his singer Alexander.[107] If, as is likely, this Alexander is our Agricola, the words *"da Vienna"* may apply to him as well as to his cousin and support the theory of a German origin, though they may just as well apply only to Pietro; the expression *"ex Alamania"* by itself would not necessarily indicate such an origin, since Flemings established in Italy or Spain were fairly often referred to as coming from *"Alamania,"* [108] a designation that might quite aptly include their country in the days of its subjection to the German emperor. The name "Ackerman" also offers inconclusive evidence, since it is not only the German but also a Flemish equivalent (the standard spelling being "Akkerman") of the Latin "Agricola." [109] In 1531, Jacques de Meyere, referring to Flanders as a prolific producer of singers, heads a list of them with the name "Alexander." Also, Agricola's epitaph includes these words: *"Quis Belgam hunc traxit?"* The evidence seems, on the whole, to weigh more heavily in favor of Flanders than of Germany as the scene of birth.

On June 10, 1474, a laudatory letter from Galeazzo Maria,[110] mentioning several years of service rendered by Alexander de Alamania, gave the musician leave to try his fortune elsewhere. (His name, however, still appears in a Milanese register of July 15; cf. p. 217.) Undoubtedly this is the same Alexander who had been in Florence in 1470 and appears there again in 1474 with

[105] A partial list is given in JP II, 112ff. *See also* LoepL, xviiif.
[106] Cf. PirH, 201.   [107] Cf. MottaM, 531f.
[108] Cf. DelpA, 103.
[109] The standard German, of course, is "Ackermann."
[110] Pr. StraM VI, 13.

a certificate addressed by the duke to Lorenzo the Magnificent. But Alexander eventually proceeded to the Low Countries, serving briefly at Mantua on the way; his name appears in the accounts of Cambrai Cathedral for 1475–76. He later made a second visit to Italy, returning north in 1500, when he entered the service of Philip the Handsome. Philip had married Joanna, the daughter of Ferdinand and Isabella of Spain, in 1496, and, upon the death of Isabella in 1504, the young pair became King and Queen of Castile, León, and Granada. As a result, relations between the Low Countries and Spain, in music as in other fields, became increasingly closer. Agricola accompanied Philip on voyages to Spain and also to Paris. During a second trip to Spain, in 1506, Philip died of a fever, and it is the general belief that Agricola died then likewise. At all events, the musician's name disappears from the court rolls after June 8, 1506.[111] But the epitaph mentioned above (printed by Rhaw in Wittenberg in 1538),[112] while it states that Agricola died near Valladolid in Spain at the age of 60, unfortunately does not give any date.[113] His works include nine Masses, two isolated Credos, some twenty-five motets, and about ninety-three secular pieces.[114]

Agricola composed *canti carnascialeschi,* as is attested by his *Canto de' facitori d'olio.*[115] His *Amor che sospirar,*[116] written in a simple Italian chordal style, is interesting as one among a number of pieces that show northerners in the process of assimilating Italian traits and combining them with those of their own Franco-Netherlandish tradition, as they developed the style that Ockeghem had bequeathed to them.

Petrucci included chansons of Agricola's not only in the *Odhecaton* but in *Canti B* and *Canti C*—nineteen of them and, in addition, a song-motet. These chansons include more *rondeaux* and *bergerettes* than one would expect at this time, but no *ballades.* The tenor of the three-part *Royne des fleurs,*[117] a lovely piece, varies a *bergerette* found also in the Bayeux MS.[118] Agricola modifies the *bergerette* form to present in *pars II,* not the same musical unit twice, but two units which, though different, are nevertheless related. *L'heure est venue—Circumdederunt* [119] is both a *bergerette* and a motet-chanson at the same time. Other motet-chansons include *Belles sur toutes—Tota pulchra es* and *Revenez tous regretz—Quis det ut veniat.*[120] Several chansons

---

[111] The attempt to prove that Agricola must have died in 1506 is made in MfMG XV (1883), 111ff. It is not so conclusive as some historians seem to think.   [112] Facsimile in DelpA, 104.

[113] For further biographical data, *see* esp. DelpA (which, however, has several incorrect dates); PirH, 201f; MGG I, 158f. Grove I, 48, states: "A letter of Charles VIII of France   . . proves that he [Agricola] was in that king's service, and left it . . . for that of Lorenzo de' Medici; he was at Milan till June 1474. . . ." But Charles VIII was born only in 1470 and ruled 1483–98.

[114] Cf. MGG I, 159f, which gives titles.   [115] Cf. GhiCC, 48.

[116] About one-third pr. in AmbG V, 532. Dr. Otto Gombosi, who is preparing a collected edition of Agricola, has kindly provided me with a complete copy.

[117] Pr. HewO, 337.   [118] Pr. GéroB, 5.

[119] Pr. HewO, 389; BoerC, 79; MaldP XXIII, 25, 27 (cf. HewO, 164; ReT, 88, Nos. 19–20).

[120] Pr., respectively, in ScherG, 49, and MaldP XI, 43 (cf. BorI, 122, No. 18, also 126, No. 7; ReT, 91, No. 101).

draw upon earlier composers. *Comme femme* [121] borrows Binchois's tenor; this Agricola piece, with its striking use of octave leaps, runs, and arabesques, illustrates a certain quality of restlessness, evident in the composer elsewhere also. The tenors of Agricola's settings of *Tout a par moy* (one *a 4* and one *a 3*) are faithful to Frye's tenor (cf. p. 93). The setting *a 4* [122] is an interesting example of *ostinato* treatment. In the first section, the contratenor presents a five-measure fragment (based on the tenor and used with slight variation) four times; then it uses the first four notes of this fragment nine times as a short *ostinato*—five times at the original pitch-level, three times a fifth above, and once a fourth above (for the medial cadence). In the second section, a four-note *ostinato* (taken from the opening of the second section of Frye's tenor) occurs ten times on the same pitch-level. The setting *a 3*, which survives without text, illustrates pleasantly Agricola's liking for decorative figuration and runs, as the following example shows:

EXAMPLE 38. Extract from the three-part *Tout a par moy*—Agricola (after Florence, Conserv., B. 2439 f. 65ᵛ; transcr. by D. Plamenac).

Agricola's four-part *Je nay dueil* [123] opens with all the voices imitating the first six notes of the bass of Ockeghem's chanson of the same name. The melodic lines are affected at many points by this six-note pattern, but are all, including the tenor, essentially new. Three different compositions [124]—two *a 4* and one *a 3*—are built on Ockeghem's *D'ung aultre amer*. The two four-part chansons adopt Ockeghem's tenor, one with a little more liberty than the other. The tenor of the composition *a 3*, in meas. 1–9, makes very free use of the beginning of Ockeghem's superius; then, in meas. 9–14, it makes free use of the opening of his tenor; and finally proceeds with almost entirely new music. *De tous biens plaine* was set by Agricola several times. One setting, *a 3*,[125] provides Hayne's tenor with countermelodies in equal time-

---

[121] Pr. AmbG V, 180. Agricola wrote still another *Comme femme;* cf. PirH, 209.
[122] Pr. SmijO, 107; JosqMS III, 56.
[123] Pr. HewO, 302; MaldP XXI, 23, 29. Cf. BorI, 123, No. 19; ReT, 103, No. 333.
[124] Pr. SmijO, 101, 103, 105.   [125] Pr., in part, PirH, 208.

values; another,[126] *a 4* (with a contratenor added by an anonymous hand), makes more use of imitation and changing rhythms. Agricola's *Ales regrets* [127] likewise has a tenor derived from Hayne. The newly composed upper parts are typical of the composer in their restlessness and undulating figuration. The tenor of Agricola's *Se congé prens* presents the *Si congié prens* melody of Bibl. nat. fr. 12744.[128] Agricola's *L'Homme banni* [129] bears no relation to the similarly named piece ascribed to Barbingant.

Petrucci, in 1504, printed a collection containing five four-part Masses by Agricola: *Le serviteur, Je ne demande, Malheur me bat, Primi toni,* and *Secundi toni.* The *Missa Malheur me bat* is based on the tenor of the chanson. Agricola treats it with the greatest liberty. The tenor begins the Kyrie [130] in sustained notes, soon assuming the rhythmic character of the other voices, quite as in the chanson; but, whereas Agricola is faithful to his source up to the rhythmic change and for a few notes thereafter, he completes Kyrie I with melodic material of his own. The tenor of the *Christe,* fairly close to the model, nevertheless contains free interpolations; in Kyrie II, it now retains the model, now rejects it. The *cantus firmus* appears mostly in the tenor in the other sections of the Mass, but is sometimes assigned to the bass or alto instead. Much as in the Kyrie, Agricola not only changes the *cantus firmus* rhythmically but decorates it with new notes, omits others, or abandons it entirely. Hocket technique—now an old-fashioned device—is present in the Sanctus.[131]

The *cantus firmus* is treated with even greater liberty in the *Missa Je ne demande,* based on the tenor of Busnois's *Je ne demande autre degré* (cf. p. 103).[132] Here again the borrowed material is sometimes embellished, sometimes simplified. On occasion the other voices imitate the tenor; in still other passages, the tenor emancipates itself entirely from the *cantus firmus* and imitates the other voices. The termination of the *Christe* is one of the places where the tenor departs from the *cantus firmus,* but it remains faithful to Busnois's tenor through the rest of the Kyrie. The Gloria [133] is of special interest. Here the discant and altus of the Mass simultaneously paraphrase

[126] Pr. GomO, Supp., 32.

[127] Pr. HewO, 323; GiesS, 94; discussed in GomC, 103, 106.

[128] Cf. HewO, 142.

[129] Pr. HewO, 321; GiesS, 96; BerH, 114. For other chansons, *see* WolfME, 46 (*Oublier veuil tristesse,* given without words after a textless source); PlamJO, 37; HewO, 244 (= BoerC, 63), 357, 377, 392; GomO, Supp., 53. (Concerning MaldP XXI, 15, *see* BorI, 122, No. 9; ReT, 91, No. 103.) For a facsimile of 2 voices of Agricola's *Se mieulx, see* StaE I, Pl. 103; cf. also HewO, 152. A textless double canon in St. Gall MS 461 is ascribed to Agricola in the index of GiesS, but is printed as anon. on p. 1 (also in BerH, 111); it is listed as anon. in the description of the MS in GeerV, 235f; however, it is accepted as Agricola's in MGG, 160.

[130] Pr. GomO, Supp., 57; Kyrie I only in PraetM, 73; WagG, 271.

[131] Portions of the Sanctus and Agnus are pr. in PirH, 204; AmbG III, 133. Further discussion esp. in GomO, 86ff; PirH, 203ff.

[132] Kyrie and Agnus II pr. in GomO, Supp., 68, 72. Agricola's *Missa In myne zyn* is likewise based on a melody employed by Busnois; cf. PirH, 206.

[133] A portion pr. BesM, 240.

both the discant and the tenor of the model. It is, in a way, odd that a composer like Agricola, conspicuously given to original creation, should in this Gloria be among the first to clear the path toward a type that relies as heavily on borrowing as does the parody Mass; but even here he is engaged in doing something unhackneyed.[134]

As has already been seen, Agricola's bent toward originality is strangely combined with an occasionally retrospective attitude. Old-fashioned hocket, the presence of which has been noted in the *Missa Malheur me bat,* recurs in the Kyrie II of the *Missa primi toni.*[135] Similarly, old-style $\frac{6}{3}$ progressions are used in the *Quoniam tu solus* of the *Missa secundi toni.*[136]

The *Missa Paschalis super Je ne vis oncques* derives its name partly from the fact that the Kyrie and Gloria are based on the plainsong *Missa Lux et origo* (*Tempore Paschali*) and partly from the circumstance that the Credo is based on *Je ne vis oncques la pareille,* the two upper voices, at the opening, borrowing from the superius of the original.[137]

Of particular beauty is the three-part motet *O quam glorifica luce,* based on the Gregorian hymn [138]—one of the compositions included in Petrucci's *Motetti A* (1502). Several fragments of the plainsong, which Agricola embellishes gracefully, are made the basis for points of imitation *a 3,* but this device does not obtain throughout. The four-part *Nobis Sancti Spiritus* [139] also makes use of imitation. This motet is contained in an important MS, Bologna, Lic. mus. Q 19 (also known as the Rusconi MS), which dates from 1518.[140] The four-part *Sancte Philippe* [141] is of a different nature: the tenor at first moves in long notes; then its function is taken over by the superius; finally all parts have the same general rhythmic character. *Si dedero,*[142] a song-motet, must have been very popular; aside from instrumental transcriptions, it survives in nineteen sources, including the *Odhecaton.*

The variety in Agricola's writing is remarkable and reminds one of Ockeghem, as do his urge to write freely and the energy of his melodic lines. At a time when the Italian influence was simplifying the texture of music in the direction of chordal writing, Agricola's liking for arabesques and runs stands out conspicuously (in spite of an occasional piece in the Italian manner) and produces a somewhat "Gothic" effect in the midst of the rapidly unfolding Late Renaissance.

[134] Further on this Mass, *see* esp. GomO, 93f; PirH, 205f. The *cantus firmus* is treated freely in the *Missa Le serviteur* also. Cf. AmbG III, 249. *See also* AmbG III, 249.
[135] Cf. AmbG III, 249; PirH, 203.   [136] *Ibid.*
[137] Cf. PirH, 207. For the Benedictus, *see* CPC, No. 37.
[138] The motet is pr. in CPC, No. 38; for the plainsong, *see* VP, 43.
[139] Pr. MaldR III, 19.   [140] For a list of contents (defective), *see* BolC III, 3f.
[141] Pr. MaldR III, 21.
[142] Pr. HewO, 339; ObrMS III, 55; MaldR XIX, 16 (cf. HewO, 154). For another motet, *see* MaldR XXIX, 1 (the piece printed as Agricola's *ibid.,* III, 25, is anon. in the source; cf. ReT, 91, No. 99). Concerning the motet printed as Agricola's in RieH II[1], 192, *see* fn. 342.

Isaac

Heinrich Isaac (Ysaac, Yzak, etc)—whom like Agricola we have met in Florence (Chapter 4)—was born probably c. 1450. Though historians once thought him to be German by birth, the evidence of his final will indicates that he was a native of Brabant or East Flanders. His having often been called Arrigo Tedesco is not in itself evidence of German birth, since "Tedesco" was applied to people from the Netherlands as well as from Germany, just as "Alemania" was applied indiscriminately to the countries themselves. The first mention of Isaac occurs outside his native land, in an Innsbruck document of 1484. It is possible that he only stopped at Innsbruck briefly on his way to the court of the Medici, for he is thought to have arrived in Florence at about that time. His duties in the service of Lorenzo the Magnificent have already been described. The overthrow of the Medici and the rise to power of Savonarola, in 1494, caused Isaac to leave Florence. In 1497 he became court composer to Emperor Maximilian I at Vienna, whose tastes and generosity as a patron matched those of Lorenzo. Isaac remained in this service until his death. During the latter part of his life he was permitted to travel extensively. Though he spent much time at Innsbruck, where Maximilian had one of his several seats, Isaac sojourned also in Constance, Ferrara, Florence, and elsewhere. He was allowed to settle in Florence in 1515, though still receiving pay from Maximilian, and it is there that he died, in 1517.[143] Isaac's Netherlandish origin and his periods of residence in Italy and Germany, as well as his use of pre-existent Italian, German, and French or Netherlandish melodies, have caused some modern writers to read into his works a chameleon-like response to change to environment. However, susceptibility to different national characteristics is not so great that it prevents a unifying personality from making itself felt.

Some works of Isaac's Italian period have already been considered. In addition to them, many other secular and sacred compositions of his were written or published in Italy. He is represented in the *Odhecaton* by five pieces, *Et qui la dira, Hé logerons nous, La Morra, Helas que devera mon cuer,* and *Benedictus,*[144] of which the last three appear to be instrumental *tricinia.*[145] The first, *a 4,* contains several passages in which the greater length or height of certain notes in relation to those about them produces a particularly fine counterpoint of rhythmic accents.[146] In Example 39, to consider only two of the voices, the superius has its accents on beats 1, 5, 8, and 11, while the

[143] For further biographical data, *see* esp. C. S. Terry in Grove II, 739ff, and the works there cited.
[144] Pr. respectively, in HewO, 242, 307, 315, 327, 379; also, respectively, in DTO XIV¹, 72 (= DTO XVI¹, 205; GiesS, 82), 76, 90 (= RieM, 31), 75, 112 (= , with added altus and other changes, PlamA, 44).
[145] Cf. HewO, 74f.
[146] Cf. JepP, 57f; MorrC, 19.

altus has them on beats 3, 7, 10, and 13. Thus Part *a* of the Example might be
barred (from the modern standpoint) as in Part *b*.

EXAMPLE 39. Extract from *Et qui la dira*—Isaac (complete piece pr. in
HewO, 243; SmijO, 197).

Many examples of such rhythmic flexibility, as well as of the type in which
all the voices are accented simultaneously but not at regularly recurring intervals, may be found in the works of Isaac and his contemporaries. Rhythmic
elasticity was to continue as one of the main characteristics of 16th-century
style.

Et qui la dira is in free *AbA* form and, like much of Isaac's secular music,
is based on a popular tune, this one [147] appearing in the Bayeux MS. There
is a good deal of strict imitation in the two lower voices. *Hé logerons nous*
likewise repeats the opening section at the close. These pieces illustrate the
tendency of the time to break away from the old *formes fixes,* but without
abandoning repetition schemes. *Helas*—which seems to take Caron's *Helas*
as its point of departure [147a]—uses canon at varying time-intervals. The
piece consists of five points of canonic imitation, the canon being maintained
until almost the end of each point and being alternately *a 3* and *a 2* (the third
voice supporting the two-part canons freely). The time-intervals are, in order,
three measures, a minim (in the original time-values), a semibreve, a minim,
and a semibreve. Three pieces are credited to Isaac in *Canti C. Par ung jour
de matinée,*[148] *a 4,* has the altus and tenor in strict canon at the fifth below.
The textless *Tart ara* [149] is based on the three-part chanson of the same name
ascribed to Molinet (cf. p. 137). Isaac adopts the tenor of the model and
builds round it two new voices, on motifs derived from Molinet's superius.

[147] Pr. GéroB, 102.   [147a] As pointed out to me by Mr. J. C. Thomson.
[148] Pr. DTO XIV¹, 101; SmijO, 195.   [149] DTO XIV¹, 107.

He uses different mensural signatures for the inner voice and for the outer voices; the practice of employing different signatures simultaneously was already old-fashioned and was soon to die out. Of Isaac's three settings of *J'ay pris amours,* the one in *Canti C,*[150] which is *a 4,* retains the old tenor; another, also *a 4,*[151] is based on motifs drawn from both the superius and the tenor of the model. The remaining version, *a 3,*[152] is a resetting of the superius of the original, with a tenor in free counterpoint and a contratenor cleverly fashioned out of repetitions of the five-note motif with which the superius begins. The superius of the four-part *En l'ombre—Una musque—Sustinuimus pacem* [153] presents twice the *A l'ombre d'ung buissonet* [154] melody found in the Bayeux MS (the first time without the final phrase); the tenor simultaneously paraphrases the *Une mousse de Biscaye* melody [155] that is included in Bibl. nat. fr. 12744 and then repeats six times (at two alternating pitch-levels) an adaptation of the music of one of the later lines. *Mon pere m'a donné mari* is one of several contemporary polyphonic treatments of a popular song having a text that presents the plaint of the *mal mariée.*[155a]

In contrast to the imitative and contrapuntal texture of Isaac's chansons, his Italian pieces are mostly written, as one might expect, in the chordal style characteristic of the *frottola* and *canto carnascialesco.* His *Questo mostrarsi adirata* [156] is a setting of a text by Politian. *La più vagha et più bella* [157] corresponds in musical form, but for a more extended final section, to the type of *canto carnascialesco* for which a pattern is given on p. 169. The quodlibet, *Donna, di dentro dalla tua casa,* incorporates several popular tunes—including *Fortuna d'un gran tempo* and *Dammene un pocho di quella maza crocha.*[158] Busnois's *Fortuna desperata* is drawn upon by Isaac at least twice. His setting *a 3* [159] places the old tenor melody in the highest voice, adding graceful and lively countermelodies. The other setting, *a 4,*[160] places the old superius in the highest part and contains fragments of the old bass in the lowest one; the piece recalls the major scene of Isaac's activity as an older musician, for the middle voices derive from the German song, *Bruder Conrat.*

In 1506, Petrucci issued the *Misse henrici Izac,* containing five Masses *a 4: Chargé de deul, Misericordias domini, Quant j'ay au cor, La Spagna,* and *Comme femme.* The first of these is based on an anonymous *bergerette* in the Pixérécourt MS and other sources, the third on a chanson by Busnois, and

[150] *Ibid.,* 77.   [151] *Ibid.,* 78.   [152] *Ibid.,* 29.   [153] Pr. GiesS, 50.   [154] Pr. GéroB, 119.
[155] Cf. ParisC, text, 14; music, 7.
[155a] Isaac's piece is pr. in DTO XIV¹, 96. (For an anon. piece with parallel text, in which the husband complains of his wife, *see* VNM XXX, 1.) Further on the *mal mariée, see* HewMM.
[156] Pr. DTO XIV¹, 42; EinIM III, 2.   [157] DTO XIV¹, 38.
[158] Cf. JepVF, 67. The quodlibet pr. SmijO, 191; AmbG V, 351; DTO XIV¹, 35. Concerning the term "*maza crocha,*" *see* PlamS, 527.
[159] Pr. DTO XIV¹, 74.
[160] *Ibid.,* 73. A *Fortuna* setting (pr. *ibid.,* 134) that transposes the old tenor to the Phrygian mode may also be Isaac's. DTO XIV¹ and the Supp. to it in XVI¹ contain additional exx. of Isaac's French and Italian secular music.

the last on the Binchois *rondeau*. In the *Missa Chargé de deul*, Agnus I,[161] which has the tenor of the *bergerette* refrain in its own tenor, is noteworthy for the variants to which phrase 1 of the borrowed melody is subjected in the other voices as this subsection progresses. These variants appear too long after that phrase has been sung by the tenor to be imitations of it; their function is to produce a unifying effect. All the variants are provided with little prefixes that slightly veil their entry.[162] The *Missa Quant j'ay au cor*[163] begins with not only its tenor but also (for a brief space) its superius quoting the corresponding voices of the chanson. The *Missa Misericordias domini* contains several passages in which Isaac's skill in the use of conflicting accents is shown most brilliantly, e.g., in the *Christe*. The Benedictus includes a passage in which two voices have non-synchronizing five-beat sequences against the prevailing binary meter of the other parts.

EXAMPLE 40. Extract from the Benedictus of the *Missa Misericordias Domini*—Isaac (from *Misse henrici Izac*, Petrucci, 1506; transcr. by J. C. Thomson; text underlaid as in the original).

At certain points in this Mass there are short recitations on one chord in root position, in *falsobordone* style. The *Missa La Spagna* has as its *cantus firmus* the very famous *basse dance* melody that we have found in Cornazano's dance manual (cf. p. 177).

Petrucci, in his *Motetti a cinque* (1508), credited three motets to Isaac. In *Motetti C,* however, he had already printed at least two Isaac motets without ascription, one of these being *Rogamus te*. This work is based on the four-note solmisation figure, *la mi la sol*. A textless version of this piece, bearing the syllables as its title, is also extant.[164] This motet is closely related to a Mass by Isaac that evidently belongs to his German period (cf. p. 648). There is a reminder of Isaac's early relations with the Medici in another motet, the six-part *Optime pastor*, written to celebrate the accession to the papal throne, in 1513, of Leo X who, as a son of Lorenzo the Magnificent, had been a pupil

---

[161] Pr. OH II, 98, with the tenor placed above the altus.
[162] Cf. WagG, 280, where, the discussion being based on OH I, the altus is referred to as the tenor.
[163] Kyrie pr. SmijO, 182; for Kyrie I in the orig. notation after Jena MS 31, *see* RoediN, 74.
[164] Pr. DTO XIV¹, 87; GiesS, 46. Cf. DaT, 69; StraM, 87f; SmijE.

of Isaac's in earlier days. This work employs the *Da pacem* and the *Sacerdos et pontifex* simultaneously as *cantus firmi*. Duos contrast with full-voiced chords; the closing section is brilliant and lively.[165]

It is desirable to consider here a work that belongs to Isaac's German period and which for this reason would otherwise be reserved for Chapter 12—his monumental *Choralis Constantinus*.[166] Commissioned in 1508 by the Cathedral Chapter at Constance,[167] this is the first polyphonic setting of complete Propers of the Mass spanning the whole church year. It includes the Propers for all Sundays and for certain feast and saints' days as well, and there are also five settings of the Ordinary at the end of Book III. Since the work is a milestone in the history of music for the Proper,[167a] treatment of it at this point will make more meaningful the subsequent discussion, in Part I of the present book, of developments bearing upon music for that portion of the Mass. In this great series, Isaac is completely the Netherlander. The music is written in from two to six parts, but most of it is *a 4*, with the ecclesiastical melody (according to the Constance use) sometimes in one voice, sometimes divided between two or more voices, sometimes developed in imitation, sometimes combined with another borrowed melody. The character of the highest voice is not the same in Book III as in Books I and II, where the Chant melodies are mostly in the discant: in Book III they are mostly in the bass, so that the highest part becomes freer. The style in general is increasingly florid in Books II and III, where greater use is made of involved devices of mensural notation, cryptic proportions, and abstruse passages of hemiola, especially at the beginning of Book III. The *cantus firmus* is occasionally in notes of equal value, but is much more often embellished to give it the same rhythmical character as that of the other voices. Despite the freedom with which Isaac handles the *cantus firmus,* he seldom alters it so much that it becomes unrecognizable, and he remains especially close to the original at beginnings and other points of structural importance. There are few examples of canon. An often rather unvocal line, with a wide range, abrupt changes in register, and few rests, may point to the use of instruments. The music of each composition is usually continuous—at least, it is not broken into small clearly marked sections—except in the Tracts, sequences, and proses, where well-defined sections correspond to the lines and strophes of the text. In most of the examples of sequence, Isaac, like Dufay (cf. p. 83), writes polyphony for only one unit of each double versicle,[167b] leaving the

---

[165] Cf. AmbG III, 396.

[166] Book I pr. in DTO V¹; Book II in DTO XVI¹; Book III in IsaacC. Isolated pieces pr. EisZ, 39, 114, 127; SmijO, 186; etc. The correct title should probably be *Choralis Constantiensis;* cf. LippP, 35.

[167] Cf. NedK, 455.   [167a] About its significance in that history, *see* esp. EisZ, 31ff; LippP, 34ff.

[167b] Here, as elsewhere in discussions of sequences, "double versicle," of course, refers not necessarily to 2 verses in the sense of 2 lines, but to 2 literary units (2 lines, 2 whole stanzas, 2 half-stanzas) of parallel structure, each of the 2 units being sung, in a pure plainsong performance, to the same Chant melody.

other to be sung in chant. Sequences with single lines of text as versicle-units predominate, and in these it is usually the even-numbered lines that Isaac sets polyphonically. Next most frequent as units are halves of six-line stanzas; in these he leaves the first three lines in plainsong and sets the second three in polyphony. There is little consistency in the number of lines that make up other types of stanzas, or in the sections of them that are chosen for polyphonic treatment; Book III shows more variety in this respect than Book II. The fact that there is only one sequence in Book I, while Book II contains 24 and Book III 22, is probably due to the inclusion in the latter books of the services for festive occasions and saints' days, to which sequences are most appropriate. For his sequence texts Isaac draws upon writers (among them Notker, Abelard, and Adam de St. Victor) whose dates range from the 11th century to the 15th.[168] In the Introit settings, the antiphon is sung polyphonically, the first half of the psalm verse is sung *choraliter,* and the second half of the verse is again polyphonic; the doxology is never set, but was probably sung in plainsong; no repetition of the antiphon is indicated. In all the *Choralis Constantinus* settings, the voices have a large measure of independence, and they are woven by means of a variety of contrapuntal devices into the flexible, continuous texture characteristic of the Netherlanders. There are occasional passages of homophony for expressive purposes. Expressive significance, however, does not seem to play an important role in Isaac's use of dissonance, which on occasion appears melodically in the leap of a minor seventh or, in a chord, unprepared. In Book III the treatment of dissonance is much closer to that of the Palestrina period than it is in the first two books. One interesting detail is his use of the third in final chords: in Books I and II it appears seldom at the end of the last section, but often at the close of previous sections; in Book III, its appearance at the final cadence is less rare. Except for the general absence of contrapuntal intricacies such as puzzle canons, the work is a tour de force of Netherlandish technique and reveals Isaac's great skill, power of invention, and thorough command of his native style. Isaac died before he had quite finished the *Choralis Constantinus,* and it was completed by his pupil, Ludwig Senfl (cf. p. 689).[169]

Weerbecke and some Lesser Figures

Even before Isaac assumed Squarcialupi's old post at Florence, musical activity at Milan, under the rule of Galeazzo Maria Sforza, had been largely in the hands of Franco-Flemings. Nearly all the 18 *"cantori de camera"* and 22 *"cantori de capella"* named in a Milanese register [170] dated July 15, 1474, were from Flanders or Picardy.

---

[168] Further on the sequences, *see* CuylerS.
[169] Further on the *Choralis Constantinus, see* esp. CuylerCC; BlaI; MosG I, 424ff.
[170] Pr. MottaM, 322f.

Heading the list is "Gasparre vice abbate." This is Gaspar van Weerbecke (= Weerbeke), who was born c. 1445 at Oudenarde (near Ghent), and who is first found in the ducal service in 1472.[171] The duke, from one of whose letters we learn that Weerbecke was a cleric of Tournai, sent him to the Franco-Netherlandish area on two occasions—in April, 1472, and January, 1473—to recruit singers for service at Milan. In 1481 the composer left that city for Rome to join the Papal Choir, where he remained until 1489. He revisited Oudenaerde in 1490 and was accorded a great reception and a gift of wine. During the following years his name figures in documents of both the court of Milan and the chapel of Philip the Handsome. In 1499, he returned to the Papal Chapel, and his name remains on the rolls of its singers until 1509. After that there is a gap in the archives, but he is still designated *"Cantor Capelle pape"* in a record of his entry into the confraternity of the German Campo Santo at Rome in 1514.[172]

Petrucci held Weerbecke in sufficiently high regard to devote a book of five Masses to him, entitled *Misse Gaspar* (1507). The first of its contents, the *Missa Ave Regina coelorum,* illustrates the continued writing of bitextual Masses: the tenor has the words of the antiphon, while the other three voices have those of the Ordinary. In 1508, Petrucci included Weerbecke's *Missa N'as tu pas* [173] (based on an anonymous chanson in *Canti C*) in his *Missarum diversorum auctorum liber primus.* Economy in the use of voices seems to be a trait of Weerbecke's style, and in this Mass he seldom employs them all simultaneously for any great length of time, but often treats them in pairs. Although he likes simplicity and clarity, he shows his skill in canon in Agnus II of this composition, and his mastery of mensural complexities in the *Missa O Venus banth* (included in the 1507 print). Among his other Masses are a *Missa brevis* [174] (characteristically enough) and a *Missa Princesse d'amorettes,* noteworthy for the broad melodies that open its Kyrie and Agnus.[175]

Of the thirty-three pieces in Petrucci's *Motetti A,* no fewer than nine are by Weerbecke. One of them, the four-part *Virgo Maria,*[176] opens and closes in a chordal style reminiscent of the *lauda* and *frottola;* the final double-pedal recalls them also. The middle section is in moderately florid counterpoint, mostly *a 2* and *a 3*. It is not surprising that part of one of the Weerbecke motets

---

[171] The Gasparo who in 1469 was rector of the ducal church of San Gottardo at Milan (cf. StraM VI, 30) was not—as claimed in EitQ X, 200, and Grove V, 678—identical with Weerbecke; MottaM (cited, strangely enough, by both EitQ and Grove) shows, on p. 325, fn. 1, that this Gasparo, whose duties at San Gottardo included those of keeper of the watchtower, died in 1470. (The Grove article is defective in still other ways.)

[172] Cf. HabR, 115. Further biographical data in MottaM, 304ff; CesM, 191f, 195f; StraM II, 65ff; VI, 1ff; VII, 140ff; DoorM, 158; list of works in CrollW, 69.

[173] Agnus I pr. OH II, 93; other excerpts in WagG, 142ff.

[174] Kyrie I in orig. notation in RoediN, 46.

[175] Kyrie I in orig. notation *ibid.,* 78; complete Kyrie pr. SmijO, 171; opening of Agnus pr. in PirH, 212.

[176] Pr. AmbG V, 183; CPC No. 36. Another piece from *Motetti A (Mater digna Dei)* pr. CPC No. 43.

Petrucci had already issued—the *Verbum caro factum est,* contained in the *Motetti B* (*De passione* . . .) of 1503—should have been reprinted in his second book of *Laude* with a substitute text.[177] The *Ave mater omnium,* which appears in Petrucci's *Motetti Libro Quarto* (1505), was reproduced by Sebald Heyden in his *De arte canendi* (1540) as an example of Mode II. The Gafori codices contain (besides one of the Masses printed in 1507) nineteen Weerbecke motets, sixteen of which form two cycles belonging to a special type of Mass (cf. p. 227). The last of these sixteen is a *Tota pulcra es,* in which Weerbecke reworks a number of motivic germs with considerable ingenuity.[178] The sumptuous Chigi MS C. VIII. 234 (cf. p. 125) preserves a five-part *Stabat mater* by him that is simple but eloquent.[179] The sequence form, which one might expect to find in association with this text, is not followed. Weerbecke is represented in Petrucci's second book of Lamentations by a setting that has the liturgical melody discreetly paraphrased in the superius.[180]

As mentioned on p. 190, *La Stangetta* may be by Weerbecke.[181] But few secular compositions reach us under his name.[182] It has been suggested[183] that, since "Gaspar" on occasion appears in archive entries as "Jaspar" or "Jaspart," Weerbecke may be identical with Japart, of whom nothing is known, except that he was a friend of Josquin's, and to whom the musical sources attribute secular pieces only. This seems hardly probable, however, since some of these sources, e.g., *Canti C,* supply Japart with a first name of his own, Johannes. One of the Japart pieces in the *Odhecaton* is a four-part *J'ay pris amours,*[184] in which the superius of the old chanson is provided with new lower parts. In a four-part *De tous biens plaine*[185] in *Canti C,* Hayne's tenor is printed in normal form in the contratenor part, but is accompanied by the enigmatic inscription *"Hic dantur antipodes,"* calling for its inversion. In a chanson in *Canti B,* Japart combines Hayne's tenor, uninverted, with the superius of the *Je cuide* that is anonymous in the *Odhecaton* but may be his own work.[186] Additional pieces likewise resorting to enigmatic inscriptions

[177] For the motet, *see* SmijO, 174; for the *lauda* version, JepI, 90. *Pars II* of the motet—the portion excluded from the *lauda*—is an *Ave verum,* musically different from the *Ave verum,* also by Weerbecke, that begins on fol. 42^v of the same motet collection. *See also* CrollW, 79, where there is information about an additional motet turned into a *lauda.* For another Weerbecke motet from *Motetti B, see* SmijO, 178.

[178] *Pars II* pr. CesM, 202; facsimile after Gafori cod. *ibid.,* 201.

[179] About a quarter is pr. in StraM VI, opp. p. 42, with altered time-signature (which, however, the rhythm of the piece justifies).

[180] Cf. the setting pr. in ScherG, 54, with the chant in Liber, 626.

[181] There is an attribution to "Uuerbeck" in the 1501 printing of the *Odhecaton,* but Petrucci may have doubted its correctness, since he left the piece anon. in the 2 later printings. The ascription to Obrecht appears in a source of less central origin.

[182] About some that do, *see* CrollW, 75f. The chanson, *O Venus bant,* though ascribed to Gaspar in the Seville Chansonnier, is credited to Josquin in St. Gall, MS 463, and in all 3 printings of the *Odhecaton.* Perhaps the Seville attribution resulted from confusion with Weerbecke's *Missa O Venus banth.* Further about Weerbecke's music, *see* PirH, 210ff; AmbG III, 250ff; CrollW.

[183] Cf. StraM VI, 104; PirH, 124.   [184] Pr. HewO, 265; GomO, Suppl., 51.

[185] Pr. *ibid.,* 34.   [186] Cf. HewO, 130.

or combining pre-existent melodies seem to indicate that this amiable but minor composer had a special penchant for such procedures.[187]

The Milanese register headed by "Gasparre vice abbate" includes "Raynaldino" among the singers *de capella* and "Jacotino" among the singers *de camera*. Raynaldino may well be the Renaldo or Renaldino who is represented by several well written compositions in Bologna, Lic. mus. Q 19.[188] He may also well be the Magister Rainaldus, found at Rieti (between Rome and Perugia), 1471–1472;[189] the Raynaldus Odenoch de Flandria, who was a singer at the Treviso Cathedral, 1477–1488; the Raynaldus francigena, who was *magister cantus* at Padua, 1489–1490; the Raynaldus de Odena or de Honderic, who sang in the Papal Choir, 1491–93;[190] and the Raynaldo francigene, who died at Parma in 1529, being then a singer in the Church of the Steccata,[191] where he was succeeded by his son Ernoul Caussin, an active composer.[192] Perhaps he is the "Franci" to whom the index of Petrucci's *Motetti de Passione* ascribes a *Parce Domine,* anonymous in the body of the print.

Jacotino, born in Picardy and traceable at the Milanese court from 1473 to 1494, is one of the three or four musical Jacotins traceable within a period of some eighty years. Perhaps he is the composer of two motets printed by Petrucci. Or these may be the work of a Jacotin whose real name was apparently Jacob Godebrye[193] and who, in 1479, became chaplain at Antwerp, where he died in 1529.[194]

Martini

The *cantori de capella* include also Zohanne Cornuel (Jean Cornuel; cf. p. 137), Alexandro (Agricola) and, listed one right after the other, Aluyseto, Zohanne Martino, and Juschino—Loyset Compère, Johannes Martini,[195] and Josquin des Prez. Weerbecke very likely engaged this brilliant trio for Milanese service on one of his earlier recruiting trips to the north. The stipend for each was five ducats monthly—next to the lowest rate (Weerbecke and Raynaldino received 12; Jacotino, Cornuel, and Alexandro, 10). However, the highest *yearly* salary paid to a papal singer in 1474 was 36 ducats,[196] so that

[187] Other Japart exx. pr. *ibid.,* 233 (= GiessS, 70; ScherG, 66), 267 (= BoerC, 65), 272, 284 (= BoerC, 67; TorreS, 554), 292; ScherNO, 75 (facsimile after *Canti C* on p. 90). Japart has some claim on HewO, 277, as do also Obrecht and Isaac (cf. *ibid.,* 143); 2 sources ascribe HewO, 286, to Japart while 1 assigns it to Busnois and 1 to Pirson (= la Rue) (cf. *ibid.,* 144); 1 source attributes HewO, 270, to Japart and 1 to Busnois.

[188] 7 of them are pr. after this MS in MaldR I, 25; XI, 40, 43, 44, 49; XII, 3, 4, with attributions to Rinaldo del Mel, even though the MS is dated 1518 and Mel was not born until c. 1554. Cf. ReT 81, 109. (BolC III, 4, citing fol. 177 of Q 19, is quite wrong in assigning to Renaldo the additional name of Benedictus. What appears on this fol. is a superscription referring to the Benedictus of a Mass by A. de Févin.)

[189] Cf. SaccR, 123.   [190] Cf. CasCP, 12f.   [191] Cf. PeliP, 197.   [192] *Ibid.,* 141f.

[193] Cf. LesAC, *Notices,* No. 3.   [194] Concerning him, *see esp.* SaarB, 178f.

[195] There are various spellings: the first name is often Giovanni or Zohanne; "Martini" is not necessarily an Italianization—it occurs also as a Flemish surname, as do some variants.

[196] HabR, 49; *see also* CesM, 193.

the rate was very generous for any singer who—like Josquin and, no doubt, Compère and Martini—was still quite young. Since the documents yield no facts about Martini after 1492, he probably was the first of the three to die. He was called a Fleming by the Italians and may be the Johannes Martini from Armentières (near Lille), mentioned among Flemish singers by Jacques de Meyere.[197] He clearly became an important figure in his day, and the facts concerning him will cast light on a number of other musicians and on activity in several countries.

In 1475, Martini, already in the service of that truly princely patron of music, Duke Hercules I of Ferrara, received a monthly increase of 2 ducats over whatever he had been previously getting there.[198] Queen Beatrice of Hungary—still, apparently, the ardent music lover whose taste had been formed by Tinctoris—in 1488 wrote to the duke,[199] her brother-in-law, that she wished to obtain as organist the famous Messer Paolo; she understood that he was serving Sigismund, Archduke of Austria, and she asked Hercules' assistance. This he promised, adding that his *"musico Martini"* was a friend of Messer Paolo's. The latter was the great Paul Hofhaimer, who was organist at Innsbruck (cf. p. 641). Relations were strained between the houses of Austria and Hungary, and an intermediary like Hercules was needed. In September, 1489, Beatrice becomes insistent; her organist has died, and she asks the duke to send *"Zohane Martino per indurre* [persuade] *messer Paolo."* [200] Martini, according to Hercules' reply [201] dated October 15, 1489, has praised Paolo *"grandamente"* and has stated that he and Paolo are close friends; Martini will be sent. Yet, on December 24 Martini has still not left Ferrara, because, writes the Duke, Martini has heard that Paolo is with Maximilian. But he adds that Martini *will* be sent when Maximilian "returns to the court of the aforesaid Duke of Austria." [202] The journey may well have been made —though the published letters do not tell us so—since Maximilian, presumably accompanied by Hofhaimer, visited Sigismund at Innsbruck in March, 1490. Moreover, several of Martini's works survive only in Munich MS 3154, originating from Innsbruck.[203] In any event, the project failed, for Hofhaimer never entered the service of Beatrice, who, when the death of King Matthias

[197] *Rerum Flandriacum tomi X,* 1531. Modern ed. in *Recueil de chroniques. . . Société d'Emulation de Bruges, 2me Série,* 1842; citation of Martini on p. 83. Meyere mentions a Thomas Martinus and his two brothers, Joannes and Petrus. About a motet by a Thomas Martini, see AmbG III, 263; there is an *Anima mea liquefacta est* credited to Thomas Martin in the *Motetti e canzone, Libro I* of c. 1521 at the Morgan Libr., New York.

[198] ValC, 451. The Duke wished a Don Martino d'Alemagna to come from Constance to organize his chapel in 1471, but ValC, 420, does not regard him as the same man. Gustave Gruyer, *L'Art ferrarais à l'époque des princes d'Este,* I (1897), 114ff, has been cited as merging the two, but does not do so.

[199] Letter pr. FökM, 15.   [200] Letter pr. GomV, 113.

[201] Pr. Albert Berzeviczy, "Aragoniae Beatrix," in *Monumenta Ungariae Historica,* XXXIX (1914), 142.

[202] Pr. FökM, 16; *see also* GomV, 114.

[203] Cf. CW XLVI, 2.

Corvinus left her a widow, became so embroiled in political intrigues that her cultural activities were necessarily curtailed.

Martini's own letters are all to Isabella d'Este and date from her first three years at Mantua. Isabella, aged 16, had married Francesco Gonzaga in February, 1490, and Martini's earliest letter [204] is dated September 2. He writes that her father, the Duke, wishes him to come and instruct her in singing. He is eager to do so, but begs her to wait a fortnight so that he may provide himself with necessities, etc. The kindly and somewhat intimate tone indicates a teacher–pupil relationship. With a later communication [205] he sends Isabella a secular composition; like a good *maestro*, he tells her to sing it often *"per pigliarne* [to take advantage of] *la practica."* Further letters mention sending singers to her. Only one is named, Carlo di Lounay, who has *"villamente"* left the Marchesa's service without permission. Martini had sent Carlo to Isabella and takes his part, adding that he is a good contralto and has left to accompany Alexander (Agricola?). Carlo reappears in the service of Pietro de' Medici in 1493, when his singing is much admired. Later he apparently re-enters Isabella's employ, for in 1499, again in trouble, he writes to her from Bologna, asking forgiveness for having taken away a book.[206]

Petrucci printed several works by Martini—hymns and secular pieces.[206a] One of the latter is the widely disseminated three-part *La Martinella*,[207] in which there is much imitation between the two upper voices over a free bass. In *Canti B*, Petrucci brought out Colinet de Lannoy's *Cela sans plus* with a *si placet* bass by Martini [208] that greatly strengthens the original chanson. This version is also preserved in Rome, Bibl. Casanatense 2856, which likewise contains twenty-two of Martini's own works,[209] among them *La Martinella*. One of the chansons in this MS is his *Toujours bien*,[210] a charming piece much like *La Martinella* in style. Also among them is a textless four-part canon, the canon being at the octave below in one pair of voices and at the fifth below in the other, though all employ the same melody.[211] The various other MSS preserving secular works by Martini include the beautiful Cappella Giulia MS XIII. 27 (cf. p. 286). Florence, Bibl. Naz. centr., Banco rari 229, contains as many as seventeen secular pieces by Martini.

Among Martini's works in Munich MS 3154 (cf. p. 221) are a *Salve Regina*,[212] *Magnificat Secundi Toni*,[213] and *Ave maris stella*,[214] all *a 4*. The first of these uses the double *cantus-firmus* technique: melodic material from the *Salve Regina* is at various places combined with other *cantus firmi—Da pacem,*

---

[204] Pr. in facsimile in BertolM, 14.   [205] *See* CanM, 663.
[206] *See loc. cit.;* facsimile of date line and signature in BertolM, 16.
[206a] The surviving examples are included in anthologies, but Petrucci is known to have devoted at least one publication entirely to Martini: the *Hymnorum Lib. primus Jo. Martini;* the words *"Lib. primus"* may indicate that there was also a *Lib. secundus,* which is likewise lost; cf. E. Lowinsky in JAMS, II (1949), 122; VernO, 112; SartP, 128.
[207] Pr. EDMR IV, 62; DTO VII, 223.   [208] Thus pr. ObrWW, 83.
[209] Listed in AmbG III, 263.   [210] Pr. ChilT, 66, with facsimile.
[211] This is the canon pr. in LafE II, 32, without mention of a source.
[212] Pr. CW XLVI, 1.   [213] Pr. *ibid.,* 14.   [214] Pr. *ibid.,* 19.

Miniature from the Paris copy of Le Champion des Dames, *showing Dufay and Binchois.*

Johannes Martini. Miniature in Florence, Bibl. Naz. Cent. MS, Banco rari 229 (*this page written in gold on red parchment*)

Orlandi Lassi, quicunq; insignia cernis,
Siste parum; vigili singula mente nota.
Vt sol illustrat totum pulcherrimus orbem,
Orlandum mundi sic plaga quæq; canit.
Herculeo credunt animantia cuncta leoni,
Cedit at Orlando Musica turbe libens.
Crux monstrat veteris tibi relligionis amicum,
Cætera tu tacito pectore volue, licet.

Lassus's Coat of Arms

With scythe: Luca Marenzio as Saturn; in helmet, Gio. del Minugiaio as Mars. From Buonstenti's drawings of the intermedi of 1589 (cf. pp. 569f; also Aby Warburg, Gesammelte Schriften I, 261ff, 394ff, esp. 275, 426f)

PLATE III

Vexilla Regis, Veni Sancte Spiritu, etc. The Magnificat sets polyphonically the odd-numbered verses, except, of course, for the opening word which, like the even-numbered verses, is left to be sung in plainsong; the *cantus firmus,* broken up, shifts from one voice to another. In the *Ave maris stella,* after a brief introduction in which the altus and bass sing mostly in contrary motion, the discantus and tenor paraphrase the plainsong, sometimes in imitation. Imitation is present also in the *Salve* and Magnificat, appearing both *a 2* and *a 3*. Martini's use of it is quite skilful and will bear comparison favorably with Josquin's. In each of these two works *a 4,* Martini obtains variety by setting one verse *a 3*.

In the earliest Gafori Codex there is a four-part Magnificat in Tone 8 by Martini. In the next, there are three Masses by him (each including a Gloria, Credo, and Sanctus only)—a *Missa Coda de pavon,* based on Barbingant's *Der pfoben swancz,*[215] a *Missa Ma bouche rit,*[216] based on Ockeghem's chanson, and a *Missa Io ne tengo.*[217] The three Masses of Martini's in Cappella Sistina MS 35 include a *Missa Cela sans plus* and a *Missa La Martinella.* Trent MS 91 opens with his *Missa Cucu.*[218] This work incorporates in the tenor (the second highest voice) the descending minor-third call of the cuckoo. The following example shows it at three different pitch-levels.

EXAMPLE 41. Extract from *Missa Cucu—Cum Sancto Spiritu—*Martini (Trent MS 91 f. 4ᵛ; transcr. by K. Geiringer).

Compère

Loyset Compère, whose name precedes Martini's in the Milanese register of 1474, had served as a choirboy at Saint Quentin. In 1486, he became *chantre ordinaire* to Charles VIII and, later, canon and chancellor at Saint Quentin, where he died in 1518.[219]

---

[215] *See* SaarB, 95.

[216] Cf. the extracts from the Mass pr. in CesM, 21f, with the chanson pr. in HewO, 335; DrozT, 9; etc.

[217] These 3 Masses recur in Modena MS L 456. About other works by Martini at Modena, *see* EitQ VI, 361; SteB, 95.

[218] About a motet in this MS that may be by Martini, *see* SteB, 65.

[219] For further biographical data, *see* esp. DelpC.

The works assignable to Compère's Italian period presumably include those with Italian text. Of these *Scaramella fa la galla*[220] is a *villota*, though an exceptionally refined one: at the opening, the other three voices imitate, in diminution, the melody assigned to the tenor; beginning with beat 2 of the concluding section, the notation sets forth, with a ternary time-signature, the same tenor melody as it had given with a binary signature but with mostly the same time-values[221] in section 1. The second presentation of this melody omits all the rests found in the first presentation. The tune, like that of *Che fa la ramacina*, of which Compère also made a setting,[221a] is among the popular melodies incorporated in the quodlibet by L. Fogliano mentioned on p. 159.

In his chansons, Compère, unlike several of his more up-to-date contemporaries, favors the *formes fixes*, at least in pieces of a serious nature, written *a 3*. Some lighter chansons, *a 4*, although they depart from the old established types, still preserve well-defined forms: *Lourdault, lourdault*—which draws upon a text (but not upon the accompanying melody) found in Bibl. nat. fr. 12744[222]—is in three-part form, the opening section being modified upon its return, while *Alons ferons nos barbes*[223] presents the slightly more complex *abcc′a′b′d* pattern. The four-part *Ung franc archier*[224] uses a pre-existent popular air,[225] which Compère sets in canon *a 2*. Whereas binary rhythm predominates in the chansons, there are a few in ternary rhythm, among them the ingenious three-part quodlibet, *Au travail suis*,[226] which combines the textual and melodic incipits of *Au travail suis* (Barbingant), *Presque transi* (Ockeghem), *Par le regart* (Dufay), *De tous biens plaine* (Hayne), *D'ung aultre amer* (Ockeghem), and *Malheureux cueur* (Dufay).

Though pervading imitation is more usual in the lighter chansons *a 4*, such as *Nous sommes de l'ordre de Saint Babouin* and *Vostre bargeronette*,[227] it appears also in works *a 3*. Thus, all voices participate in imitation in *Mes pensées*,[228] while two voices are in imitation over a supporting contratenor in *Disant adieu*[229]—an interesting example of non-quartal harmony (cf. p. 104). More typical of Compère than imitation at the beginnings of all text lines is imitation at the beginnings of most of them, as in *Venez regrets*.[230] This chanson is based on Hayne's *Allez regrets;* however, Compère does not borrow Hayne's tenor literally, but departs from it at cadences and toward the end. In *Le grand désir d'aymer*,[231] all voices enter together at the be-

[220] Pr. PetrF, 92; RieH II¹, 351; TorreS, 522.
[221] The deviations occur at the end.
[221a] Pr. CW XLIII, 9; PetrF, 92.
[222] Cf. p. 206. *See* SmijO, 119, for Compère's piece. The musician Jean Braconnier, who was called Lourdault, may have acquired the name from having had this piece addressed to him; but there were other musicians of the period similarly named; cf. PirNB.
[223] Pr. HewO, 275.   [224] *Ibid.*, 279.
[225] Cf. WeckCP, 63ff.   [226] Pr. OckW I, 43.
[227] Pr., respectively, in HewO, 299 (= AmbG V, 186), 309.
[228] *Ibid.*, 345.   [229] *Ibid.*, 403. Another ex. of pervading imitation is pr. in DrozP, 55.
[230] Pr. HewO, 333; GomC, 104 (further information *ibid.*); pr. as *Venez ami* (cf. BorI, 126; ReT, 96, No. 195) in MaldP XIII, 30; RieH II¹, 347.
[231] Pr. BordTC, No. 2.

ginning of the chanson, but imitation plays some role at the openings of later lines.

Only three line-openings are marked by imitation in *Le renvoy*,[232] but the chanson is of interest for other structural devices. The music for line 3 is compounded of sections of the music for lines 1 and 2, with a cadence added. In *Sourdés regrets*,[233] lines 1 and 2 present five musical motifs, four of which, repeated in different combinations, form the rest of the piece. *Se mieulx*[234] consists entirely of a series of variations on the material that accompanies line 1.

The *formes fixes* are again prominent in Compère's motet-chansons, of which *Royne du ciel—Regina caeli*[235] is an exquisite example. Each line of the *rondeau quatrain* (whose content is closely related to that of the Latin text) is introduced by imitation in the two upper voices, while the contratenor presents the first few notes of the Marian antiphon in a fourfold sequence, each new presentation lying a step higher than its predecessor. Though the chant-bearing voice is here in long values, it assumes the character of the upper voices in much of *Malebouche—Circumdederunt me viri mendaces*[236] (the symbolism of having a tenor concerning *viri mendaces* accompany a *rondeau* about *Malebouche* is both obvious and charming). The opening of *Le corps—Corpusque meum*[237] is much like that of Hayne's *De tous biens plaine*. The three-part *O vos omnes,* a motet-chanson in Brussels MS 228, with the text *O devotz cueurs* in the upper voices, appears elsewhere as a song-motet, with Latin text only;[238] this little work, for all its seriousness, is a fine example of the airy lyricism that characterizes Compère.

Compère's short motets include a five-part *Virgo caelesti*,[239] unified by the threefold presentation, in diminishing values, of an ascending hexachord in tenor I; tenor II sings a Gregorian melody. The latter half of the four-part motet, *O bone Jesu*,[240] consists entirely of block-chords in root position, the bass being occasionally embellished by non-essential tones. The chordal aspect is displayed with greater grandeur in the impressive *Crux triumphans*,[241] one of Compère's larger motets. The *Crucifige,* a setting of verses in a series of rhymed texts based on the main episodes of the Passion, is powerfully dramatic. At various points in the piece, the motivic material is reminiscent

---

[232] HewO, 381.   [233] Pr. MaldP XXIII, 17.

[234] Pr. HewO, 329; SmijO, 121; GiesS, 98. Other exx. of similar construction pr. HewO, 364, 403. For other chansons by Compère, *see* HewO, 317 (= GiesS, 54), 343; MaldP XIII, 32 (= MaldP XXIII, 15; CW III, 21); *see also* fn. 562. The chanson pr. HewO, 400, after the *Odhecaton*, where it is ascribed to Compère, bears an attribution to "Petrequin" or some variant thereof in 3 MSS, and it is therefore more probably by Pierre de la Rue, one of whose sobriquets was Petrequin (cf. p. 266).

[235] Pr. HewO, 395; HAM, 83.   [236] Pr. HewO, 319.   [237] *Ibid.*, 361.

[238] Pr. (as anon.) with French and Latin texts in MaldP XXIII, 23; with Latin only, in BesN, 10; RoksT, 19; ObrMT, 173; ScherG, 49; HAM (1949 ed.), 80 (with incorrect attribution to Obrecht in last 3). For another Compère motet-chanson, *see Plaine d'ennuy—Anima mea,* pr. with partly substitute text and wrong ascription to Pipelare in MaldP XIII, 37; CW III, 23 (cf. BorI, 125; ReT, 114, No. 554).

[239] Pr. SmijA, 113.   [240] Pr. SmijO, 116.   [241] Pr. KillK, 195.

of the Gregorian Tone assigned to the *Synagoga* in the chanting of the Passion in Holy Week, but this may be coincidental. If deliberate quotations of the Gregorian Tone are present, Compère's treatment of its cadence is extremely free. (In the last system, meas. 3, alto, the second note is actually b″ in the source; perhaps it should be a″.)

EXAMPLE 42. *Crucifige*—Compère (*Motetti de Passione* . . . , Petrucci, 1503; transcr. by T. Karp).

"Crucify, crucify, crucify, they cry aloud, in the third hour. Mocked, he is clothed in a garment of purple, on his head is placed a crown of thorns, and he carries the cross on his shoulder to the place of punishment."

The text of *pars II* of Compère's *Omnium bonorum plena*,[242] which may be translated as follows, is of unusual interest:

O thou who art replete with all good things, thou, comfort of sinners, whose province it is to pray and utter supplications for those unhappy sinners who have turned away from God, pray to thy Son for the salvation of singers. First for Guillaume Dufay, moon of all music, light of singers, hear me, O Mother, for Dusart, Busnois, Caron, masters of song, for Georget de Brelles and Tinctoris, cymbals of thy glory, and for Ockeghem, des Prés, Corbet, Hémart, Faugues, and Molinet, and for Regis and for all singers, as well as for me, Loyset Compère, beseeching thee with a pure heart to intercede for these masters, whom I recall, O Virgin, . . .[243]

The words *"Omnium bonorum plena"* translate Hayne's *De tous biens plaine*, and Compère has based his motet on the tenor of the chanson, given forth by the motet tenor once in each *pars*. Hayne's superius is drawn upon also in the opening portion of *pars I*. The use of material from Hayne's love song in this motet to the Virgin is undoubtedly meant to have a symbolical significance.[244]

The Gafori codices at Milan contain, in addition to two Magnificats, etc., by Compère, two "substitution" Masses of his. Such works consist entirely or mainly of a series of motets, each intended to replace a liturgical Mass movement (both the Ordinary and the Proper being involved). In the *Missa Hodie nobis*—obviously for Christmas—Compère replaces the Introit by the motet *Hodie nobis de Virgine;* supplying no Kyrie or substitute, he proceeds to replace the Gloria by *Beata Dei Genitrix,* the Credo by *Christus natus est,* and the Offertory by *Genuit puerpera.* The Sanctus is retained. *Memento salutis* is used after the elevation, *Quem vidistis pastores* replaces the Agnus, and *O admirabile commercium* the *Deo gratias.* All movements are *a 4.* The *Missa Ave Domine Jesu Christe* comprises eight motets, *a 4* and *a 5.* Very likely the *Missa Galeazescha* (probably named for Gian Galeazzo Sforza), anonymous in one Gafori codex, is also the work of Compère, as three of its motets reappear, credited to him, in another of the codices. "Substitution" Masses seem to have been, characteristically, in one mode throughout, and thematic relationships are often found between different movements. The frequent absence of a Kyrie or Agnus or a substitute for them suggests a connection between these Masses and the Ambrosian rite.[245] But it is also possible that these motet cycles were intended for use in Low Mass according to the Roman rite.[245a]

---

[242] Pr. DTO VII, 111.

[243] De Brelles, Dusart, and Hémart were *maîtres* at Cambrai; cf. HouH, 82; concerning Corbet (Courbet), *see ibid.,* 83.

[244] For further details, *see* BorQS, 2ff.

[245] For details, *see* JepG, 16f. About some substitute motets in a MS at Munich, *see* MaiM, 20.

[245a] Miss Josephine Shine who, in her paper *The Motets of Mouton* (read before the American Musicological Society at New Haven, Conn., on December 29, 1952) made incidental mention of the probable connection between the growing production of motets and the increasing spread of Low Mass, intends to undertake a fuller study of this probably important subject.

The normal Masses of Compère include a *Missa Allez regrets*,[246] based on the same Hayne chanson that he had drawn upon in *Venez regrets*. Though the superius and tenor of Kyrie I are almost identical with their chanson counterparts, greater freedom is displayed in later movements. The ascending hexachord, characteristic of Hayne's superius incipit, at times receives extensions, at times is broken by intervening rests. In Compère's *Missa L'Homme armé*,[247] the *cantus firmus,* when present, is always placed in the Phrygian mode in at least one voice. But at the opening of the Sanctus (up to *Sabaoth*) and in each *Osanna,* as well as in Agnus I and III, the *cantus firmus* appears in canon (between the two lowest voices in *Osanna I;* between the two middle voices in the other sections), the canon never, however, being at the unison or octave, so that the mode is always other than Phrygian in the paired voice. In the Gloria, the rhythmic treatment of the *cantus firmus* occasionally produces at least rhythmic imitation of what happens in other voices. The superius takes over the *cantus firmus* briefly in the *Crucifixus*. The *cantus firmus* of the *Pleni* is derived by presenting the first phrase of the *L'Homme armé* melody in sequence, successively on E, F, G, and A. In the Benedictus, this same phrase appears in sequence, successively on E, D, G, E, A, and B. In the same section the bass sings in canon, sometimes with one voice, sometimes with another. The plainsong of Credo I is paraphrased in the Credo simultaneously with the singing of the *L'Homme armé* melody in the tenor; at times the paraphrase is worked out in imitation, usually involving only the two higher parts. The Mass as a whole has a clear and light texture.

Compère's frequent use of the *formes fixes* and his strong predilection for the melodies of such a composer as Hayne make him, in a way, the last of the Busnois-Ockeghem group stylistically, at the same time as he is a member of the generation of Josquin. Indeed, the airiness often present in his writing recalls the period of Dufay and Binchois.

Josquin: Biography

Josquin, the greatest of the singer-composers of the Milanese register of 1474, was probably born c. 1445—a countryman of Hainaut, if we may credit Ronsard (1560).[248] Culturally and in every other sense that really matters, he was a Frenchman. The proper spelling of his name—Josquin des Prez—may be found in an acrostic in the text, very likely by the composer, of his motet *Illibata Dei Virgo*.[249] According to Hémeré, Richelieu's librarian, Josquin was a choirboy in the collegiate church at St. Quentin, but Hémeré gives no dates. The stay at St. Quentin is confirmed by a contemporary MS at St. Gall,

[246] Pr. CompèreO I, 26. Kyrie I pr. in original notation in RoediN, 6. Incipit of Benedictus pr. PirH, 228. For further information, cf. *ibid.*

[247] Pr. CompèreO I, 1. Kyrie pr. SmijO, 113. I am indebted to Dr. Strunk for having loaned me his MS score of this Mass before it appeared in CompèreO.

[248] Cf. p. 293. About Josquin's birth date, see SartJ, 58, but in the light of RB XI (1957), 157.

[249] Pr. JosqMT I, 140.

which calls Josquin *"Veromandus"*: St. Quentin was the capital of the county of Vermandois, south of Hainaut.[250]

Josquin seems to have gone to Italy as a youth and to have reached artistic maturity there. In the years 1459–72 he was a singer at the Milanese *duomo*,[250a] from which he may have gone directly to the chapel of Galeazzo Maria Sforza; his presence there, however, is first documented in the register of 1474 (cf. pp. 217, 220). He was still at Milan in 1479, serving Cardinal Ascanio Sforza (brother of Lodovico il Moro) who, although an ardent music lover, paid his musicians poorly, a fact alluded to by the composer in some of his works. Serafino dall'Aquila also expressed himself on the subject in a sonnet [251] addressed to Josquin while both (together with the painter Pinturicchio) were in the cardinal's service. The composer was a singer in the Papal Choir, with short interruptions, from 1486 to at least 1494 and was perhaps the Josquin paid by the court of Lorraine in the spring and summer of 1493.[252] He may have sojourned for brief periods (possibly in 1487–88) in Florence and Modena.[253] The archives show that, in 1499, he was at Ferrara in the employ of Hercules I.[254] An undated letter to the duke from his secretary proposes the engagement of Isaac instead of Josquin, because Isaac "is able to get on with his colleagues better and composes new pieces more quickly." [255] The letter continues: "It is true that Josquin composes better, but he does it when it suits him and not when one wishes him to." In 1501, Josquin was in France: the duke's agent reported then to his master from Blois, stating that he had seen the composer. Ghiselin (cf. p. 266f) brought Josquin back from France to Ferrara in 1503.[256] At some later date Josquin was active at the court of Louis XII, remaining there until the king's death (1515). An amusing piece [257] from this period contains a part designated *vox regis*: Louis was a poor singer, and the part Josquin wrote for him consists of but a single note repeated all the way through. In his last years Josquin was canon of St. Gudule in Brussels and provost of the chapter at Condé. Here he remained until his death in 1521. Epitaphs formerly existed at Condé and Brussels, and the latter city once also possessed the composer's portrait. This painting is reproduced as a woodcut in Opmeer's *Opus Chronographicum* (1611). Opmeer describes Josquin as "with a frank countenance and attractive eyes." [258]

Adriaen Petit Coclico, in his *Compendium musices* (1552), gives what purports to be an account of Josquin's manner of teaching. Coclico states that he was a pupil of the master, but he was given to making excessive claims (cf. p. 512). The description that he gives rings true, however, and, if he did not

[250] Cf. PirH, 171; SmijJP, 98; SmijE, 316ff; BlumeJ, 57.   [250a] Cf. SartJ, 59ff.
[251] Pr. EinIM I, 55.
[252] Cf. PirH, 172. But "Josse, priest, of tall stature and a handsome man," the excellent low bass engaged from the choir of Antwerp Cathedral for service at Ferrara—allegedly, though erroneously, c. 1480—cannot be Josquin, as has been claimed; cf. ClercxB, 119.
[253] BlumeJ, 60; SmijA, 122.   [254] ValC, 422; PirH, 173.
[255] StraM VI, 87; SmijJP, 100f; SmijE, 313.
[256] PirH, 173; BertolM, 25.
[257] Pr. PubAPTM VI, 426; ForkA II, 599.   [258] BlumeJ, 64f.

actually study with Josquin himself, it may well be that he derived reliable information from someone else's first-hand experience. He says:

My teacher Josquin . . . never gave a lecture on music or wrote a theoretical work, and yet he was able in a short time to form complete musicians, because he did not keep back his pupils with long and useless instructions, but taught them the rules in a few words, through practical application in the course of singing. And as soon as he saw that his pupils were well grounded in singing, that they had a good enunciation, that they knew how to embellish melodies and how to fit the text to the music, then he taught them the perfect and imperfect intervals and the different methods of inventing counterpoints against plainsong. If he discovered, however, pupils with an ingenious mind and promising disposition, then he would teach these in a few words the rules of three-part and later of four-, five-, six-part, etc., writing, always providing them with examples to imitate. Josquin did not, however, consider all suited to learn composition; he judged that only those should be taught who were drawn to this delightful art by a special natural impulse.[259]

Josquin: Works with French or Italian Texts or Titles

Josquin's secular works include a small group of *frottole*—using the term in its generic sense. It is fair to assume that all of them belong to the early part of his career, and the evidence is strong with respect to some, since they are ascribed to Jusquin d'Ascanio, i.e., to the Josquin of Ascanio Sforza. One of these is the macaronic *In te Domine speravi*,[260] found not only in Italian sources but in one from Spain. This is a true *frottola,* corresponding to the norm described on pp. 162f. The charming *El grillo è buon cantore,*[261] imitating the chirp of the cricket, applies the *frottola* form more freely. It is possible that the text of this piece alludes to Carlo Grillo, a singer of Galeazzo Sforza's before 1474.[261a] Another Italian piece, *Scaramella va alla guerra,*[262] has in its tenor a slightly altered version of the *Scaramella* melody found in the tenor of Compère's piece (cf. p. 224). A setting *a 3,* probably by Josquin, of *Fortuna d'un gran tempo* is included in the *Odhecaton;* each part has its own key-signature, and the composition presents difficult problems in the application of *musica ficta.*[263] This piece, like *La Bernardina,*[264] reaches us textless; both may be instrumental *tricinia.*

Josquin was the greatest chanson composer of his time. To what extent he was an innovator in that role is not clear: it is quite possible that his importance, like Dufay's with respect to the *cantus-firmus* Mass, rests less on being a pathfinder than on being the best early exponent of a new type. Standing at the crossroads, he, together with Obrecht and others, is faithful at times to the old *formes fixes,* but more characteristically breaks away from them. As we shall see, his free chansons—like those of other composers of the

---

[259] Engl. transl. adapted from SmijJP, 105f. About Josquin as teacher, *see* further RoksJ; also CreAC, 267f.   [260] Pr. PetrF, 37; BarbiC, 311; HAM, 98; MME V, 110.

[261] Pr. ScherG, 69.   [261a] See RB XI (1957), 158.   [262] Pr. AmbG V, 134.

[263] For a study of these problems, *see* LowG, where the piece is printed both with and without added accidentals; pr. also in HewO, 375; TorreS, 458.

[264] Pr. ScherG, 61; KiesS, App., 13; KiesT, App., 64.

time—take an occasional cue from the old forms, at least in their recourse to repetition schemes. In applying a great variety of such schemes, Josquin discloses considerable ingenuity. As might be expected, the influence of the motet is frequently evident. Another prominent trait of style, in his chansons as in his other works, is his strong tendency to employ canon.

Out of the fifty-two compositions with texts or titles in French that have been seen by the author and that are either known to be by Josquin or may be his (five attributions are debatable), eight of the twelve *a 6* include sustained canon, as do also seven of the seventeen *a 5*, six of the sixteen *a 4* (including one presumably for instruments), and one of the seven *a 3* (also presumably such a piece).[265] Of the four voices of *Plus nulz regretz*,[266] the lower pair presents most interesting deviations from strict canon. Not only does Josquin change the time-interval here and there, as do Obrecht and others, but, in addition to allowing himself a few minor liberties, he varies the phrase endings of the *comes,* as compared with those of the *dux,* by means of extension or abbreviation. Josquin's imagination is in evidence in his use of imitation, especially where he does not apply it literally. Sometimes, as in *Du mien amant* (see Ex. 43*a*), he manipulates paired imitation on two motifs in such a way that the motif that enters first in the initial statement enters second in the later statement, the two melodies being so constructed that they fit one another contrapuntally in either arrangement. In *Faulte d'argent* (see Ex. 43*b*), two motifs first enter simultaneously but, in the later entry, successively; moreover, the individual voices of the original pair are imitated at different intervals, one at the octave and one at the fifth.

EXAMPLE 43. Extracts from (*a*) *Du mien amant*—Josquin (complete piece in JosqWW I, 59), (*b*) *Faulte d'argent*—Josquin (complete piece in JosqWW I, 38; HAM, 93).

265 Pieces *a 6* with canons: JosqWW I, 3 (with practically no *stretto,* however), 9, 28, 36, 41, 43, 51 (= CommB XII, 53), 54 (= PubAPTM VI, 89); pieces *a 5: ibid.,* 1, 13 (= PubAPTM VI, 94), 15 (= PubAPTM VI, 98; MaldP XXII, 19), 17, 26, 45, 59, 68, 70; pieces *a 4: ibid.* 53; HewO, 418; ScherG, 60, 61; PubAPTM VI, 113; *CantiC,* cxxxiii; piece *a 3:* HewO, 349 (= BoerC, 82; canon not maintained throughout). Pieces of debatable origin: HewO, 359; 383; GomO, Supp., 18; JosqWW I, 81 (= PubAPTM VI, 108; cf. fn. 301 *infra*); piece cited in fn. 263. Presumably instrumental pieces: canonic—HewO, 349 (= GiesS, 100; BoerC, 82); ScherG, 61, top; non-canonic—WolfME, 51; HewO, 60; GiesS, 6 (= GomO, Supp., 18), 34; the pieces cited in fns. 263, 264.
266 Pr. JosqWW I, 74.

b

Among pieces in the *formes fixes,* it is rather surprising to find, especially since Josquin rarely wrote in them, an occasional example of the antiquated *ballade,* e.g., *Bergerette savoyenne*[267] and *Une musque de Biscaye.*[268] The explanation, in these instances at least, lies in the fact that he is writing not entirely new chansons, but settings of *cantus prius facti* that appear to have been quite popular.[269] *Entré je suis*[270] is also *ballade*-like in structure, but it has only one stanza of text, and it is impossible to say whether a refrain is present and whether the piece is a true *ballade. La plus des plus*[271] shows Josquin writing a *rondeau.* In *Adieu mes amours*[272] the two lower voices present, in somewhat free canon, the text and melody of the pre-existent monophonic tune, the *bergerette*-like form of which is retained by Josquin, except that he omits the refrain at the close. (The music of *Je sey bien dire*[273] also follows the *abba* plan, but without the canonic element.) Josquin writes out the music of *Adieu mes amours* in full, and, in the course of doing so, introduces minor changes in repeated passages. The altus has the *bergerette*-like text also, but in one source the superius has an independent *rondeau* text, which, however, has no effect on the structure of the music. *Du mien amant* is a *bergerette* of the normal kind.

Of the forms employing repetition, though not in *forme-fixe* manner, *aba* appears in *Faulte d'argent.* Generally similar are *Regretz sans fin*[274] and *Tenez moy en vos bras*[275] with the pattern *AbA,* and *Plus n'estes ma maistresse*[276] with the pattern *AbA'; Petite camusette,*[277] the tenor of which borrows a brief fragment from the tenor of Ockeghem's *Petite camusette,* also has the *AbA* design, but with an introduction and coda. *Basiés moy,* which exists both in a double-canon version *a 4* and a triple-canon version *a 6,* has the form:

[267] Pr. HewO, 240.
[268] Pr. LafE II, 28; BordTC, No. 1; JosqMS II, 119. *See also* fn. 155.
[269] For the monophonic form of *Bergerette . . .* ; *see* ParisC, text, 7; music, 4.
[270] Pr. PubAPTM VI, 113.
[271] Pr. HewO, 355.
[272] Pr. HewO, 249; AmbG V, 131; LafE II, 29; ObrMS IV, 38; TorreS, 540; SmijO, 156; BerH, 131.
[273] Pr. AmbG V, 129.   [274] Pr. JosqWW I, 9.
[275] Pr. *ibid.,* 33.   [276] Pr. *ibid.,* 76.
[277] Pr. *ibid.,* 43; ELAM XI, 13; CommB XII, 50; SmijO, 158.

introduction, *aa'*, coda, this form being determined by the presence, in one canon pair, of a tune found also in the Bayeux MS.[278] In other chansons, the structure *aabbc* appears, as in *Incessament livré*,[279] sometimes with the second *a* or the second *b* modified, as in *Parfons regretz*[280] and *Plusieurs regrets*,[281] respectively. (The first and third of these pieces are among the canon chansons.) In the five-part *Je me complains*,[282] the superius and *quinta pars* (in canon at the fourth below) have the design *aab*, the other parts varying their earlier material during the second *a*. The music of line 2 of the five-part *Cueur langoureux*[283] modifies that of line 1; the text of line 2 is repeated to new music, the superius, which sang before, now being silent; thereafter every line except the last (which ends with several pedal-points) is given in two settings, the first with, the second without, the superius. (The superius and middle part are in canon.) Measures 6–24 of the rich-textured 100-measure *Se congié prens* are repeated, with changes to new words, in measures 29–51 and 73–94,[284] this design, however, being the result of the presence of the *Si congié prens* melody found in Bibl. nat. fr. 12744. The charming *Allegez moy*,[285] which incorporates a canon *a 2*, has a refrain after line 2 and before the coda. *Plaine de dueil*[286] is a strophic song with no exact repetition in the course of the one musical setting that serves for all the stanzas; the likewise strophic *Plus nulz regrets*,[287] with three stanzas (stanza 2 being half the length of the others and presumably intended to be sung to the second half of the music) has, in the course of its setting, only two brief repetitions. The liking for symmetry, manifested in many ways in Josquin's production, is pleasantly evident in the structural schemes of his chansons.

Josquin's secular works include also through-composed, motet-like chansons. Some of these are built on *cantus firmi*, certain of the pieces belonging to the group of those already mentioned that incorporate canon. In his *De tous biens playne*,[288] Josquin adds a canon *a 2* to Hayne's superius and tenor; the meter is ₵ and the canon is at the time-interval of a minim (in the original values) so that there is a constant and interesting clash in accentuation. Among other *cantus-firmus* compositions we find *L'amye a tous*,[289] the middle part of which is the tenor of *Je ne vis oncques la pareille;* round this Josquin weaves particularly lovely polyphony in which only momentary use is made of repetition.[290] The old *L'Homme armé* tune,

---

[278] The settings are pr., respectively, in JosqWW I, 53, 51 (= CommB XII, 53). For the popular melody, see GéroB, 120.

[279] Pr. JosqWW I, 13; PubAPTM VI, 94.   [280] JosqWW I, 5.

[281] *Ibid.*, 15; PubAPTM VI, 98. *See also* JosqWW I, 17 (= PubAPTM VI, 102).

[282] *Ibid.*, 26.   [283] *Ibid.*, 1.

[284] The piece is pr. *ibid.*, 28. *See also ibid.*, 23, where the music of meas. 10–20 is repeated, with modifications, in meas. 36–43 (to fresh text).

[285] *Ibid.*, 36.   [286] *Ibid.*, 7.   [287] *Ibid.*, 74; MaldP XXII, 5.   [288] HewO, 418.

[289] JosqWW I, 65.

[290] Another ex. with only brief repetitions *ibid.*, 63; MaldP XV, 27; PubAPTM VI, 105.

basis of so many lengthy Masses, is once more turned into the tenor of a gay little secular piece; [291] but Josquin never proceeds perfunctorily: the melody undergoes a "sea change" from ternary rhythm to binary. The free treatment of the tune includes omission of the final A section of the original *AbA* form. The superius of Josquin's *Ma bouche rit* [292] takes over Ockeghem's superius bodily, adding a little decoration, while Josquin's bass, in its entirety, is built on just the opening of Ockeghem's tenor repeated as an *ostinato;* Josquin's text consists of only the first line of Ockeghem's, repeated over and over. The superius of Josquin's (or Ghiselin's?) evidently instrumental *Fors seule-ment* [293] derives from the contratenor of Ockeghem's *Fors seulement l'attente.* (There is another *Fors seulement* setting that may be by Josquin too.[294]) There are traces of the *cantus-firmus* technique in *Cela sans plus,*[295] the opening of Colinet's piece being presented, inverted, in long notes in part of Josquin's tenor. One of the two *En l'ombre d'ung buissonet* pieces by Josquin that are printed in Antico's *La Couronne et fleur des chansons a troys* (1536) has in its superius the melody found in the Bayeux MS. (The other one [296] and a third Josquin *En l'ombre*—a double canon in *Cantı C*—are constructed on different melodies.[297]) A piece that has its *cantus firmus* "drawn out of the vowels of the words" ("*cavato dalle vocali . . .*"), to borrow Zarlino's expression, is *Vive le roy.*[298] The term "words" applies here to the title, for the composition, undoubtedly instrumental, is textless. Since *v* was interchangeable with *u* and *y* with *i,* the vowels are represented in the *cantus firmus* by the solmisation syllables *ut-mi-ut-re-re-sol-mi.* This series is presented three times in the second voice: in the natural hexachord, in the hard one, and again in the natural. The other voices form a canon *a 3,* inde-pendent of the *cantus firmus* and based on thematic material from an anony-mous chanson *a 3* of the same title that survives in the Seville Chansonnier.[299] It is believed that this lively and attractive piece was intended as an act of homage to Louis XII. Among the through-composed chansons that seem to be written without the use of pre-existent material are *Vivray-je toujours, Madame helas, En non saichant, J'ay bien cause de lamenter,* and *Mi larés vous tousjours languir*—the first three syllables being amusingly set by the scale de-grees *mi, la* and *re* in four of the five voices.[300]

Examples of the motet-chanson in Josquin's production include the setting *a 5* of *Cueurs désolez;* [301] the *quinta vox* of this highly dramatic piece sings

---

[291] MaldP XX, 16; WeckC, 394; ChilS, 21; SmijO, 155.   [292] JosqWW I, 47.

[293] GomO, Supp., 18; GiesS, 6.   [294] Cf. GomO, 17, fn. 2.

[295] HewO, 349; BoerC, 82; GiesS, 100.   [296] Pr. as anon. (after St. Gall 461) in GiesS, 68.

[297] The melody in ParisC, music, 10, is not involved. *See also* TierE, 237ff.

[298] ScherG, 61; cf. DaT, 72f. For Zarlino's discussion of this type of theme, *see* ZarI, 329.

[299] Pr. PlamS, 538; cf. *ibid.,* 524f.

[300] Pr. MaldP XIV, 27; HewO, 359; JosqWW I, 21, 83 (= AmbG, 125), 85, respectively.

[301] JosqWW I, 72; the setting *a 4* (*ibid.,* 81; PubAPTM VI, 108) is perhaps by Appenzeller; cf. p. 305 *infra.*

the plainsong *Plorans ploravit in nocte* against powerful through-composed music in the other parts. These examples include also two laments, *Nimphes, nappés* and *Nymphes des bois*.[302] In the former, *a 6*, two voices sing, against the eloquent polyphony of the remaining voices, a canon that is built on one of the plainsong *Circumdederunt* melodies which, in this canon form, was a favorite *cantus firmus* of Josquin's (cf. p. 255). The other lament, *a 5*, is a moving *déploration* on the death of Ockeghem (and is therefore datable c. 1495). It is in two *partes*. In *pars I*, the tenor sings the Introit, *Requiem aeternam* (up to the verse). It is silent in most of *pars II*, but joins the other voices in a final *Requiescat in pace*. The French text, assigned to the other parts, calls upon Josquin, Brumel, La Rue, and Compère to don mourning and weep great tears for the *bon père* whom they have lost. The whole composition is symbolically written in black notes, so that we have here another early example of eye-music (cf. pp. 132, 159). *Pars I* is evidently intended as an imitation of the style of Ockeghem, while *pars II* is chordal and has more clearly defined phrases.

The variety represented in Josquin's chansons, especially with regard to formal structure, is, like the richness of their polyphonic texture, remarkable. Appreciation of their value was by no means limited to his contemporaries and immediate successors, for these compositions were destined to experience a strong revival at about the middle of the 16th century (cf. p. 300).[303]

Josquin: Masses

Josquin's Masses as a group represent him in conservative vein; nevertheless, they collectively illustrate all the Mass techniques of the Renaissance—not only those of his own days, but of days to come, for which he opened up new possibilities. Here, as elsewhere, his technical virtuosity is such that contrapuntal complexity in no way interferes, in his best work, with apparent spontaneity. Though at his very best as a motet composer, he is still a key figure in the field of the Mass.

Contemporary esteem for Josquin's Masses is attested by Petrucci's having devoted to them as many as three books, including his earliest Mass print (1502; the other books appeared in 1505 and 1514). Petrucci published no more than one such book for any other composer, none achieving a second printing at his hands, whereas he reprinted each of the first two Josquin books once.[304] Prints devoted to one man's music—Masses or otherwise—were to be rather rare throughout the first half of the 16th century.

---

302 Pr., respectively, in JosqWW I, 54 (= PubAPTM VI, 89), 56 (= MaldP XII, 11; BuH II, 481; EB XVI, 8; JosqMT I, 152 [*Requiem;* text in tenor only]).
303 Further about Josquin's chansons, *see* esp. UrJP, 36ff.
304 Cf. SartP, 32f, 48ff, correcting earlier writers.

The often cited *Missa Hercules Dux Ferrariae,* evidently an early work though printed in 1505, illustrates the rigid *cantus-firmus* technique. A *pièce d'occasion* honoring the duke,[305] it shows Josquin at rather less than his finest, but, nevertheless displays several characteristic traits. The *cantus firmus,* based on the solmisation syllables, *re ut re ut re fa mi re,* is *cavato dalle vocali . . . ,* being derived from the vowels of the words, *Hercules Dux Ferrariae* (Josquin disregards the *a* of the diphthong at the end). It is used mostly in long notes. Voices other than the tenor rarely have the *cantus firmus,* which, after the initial anticipation in the superius, is hardly ever presented in imitation. At first, the tenor enunciates this subject in three-statement units, statement 1 beginning on d, 2 on a, 3 on d′. This continues through *"non erit finis,"* in the Credo. Then the three-statement unit appears once in *cancrizans* motion, as it does later in Agnus I. The Benedictus is set in three short sections: the word *"Benedictus"* for AT; *"qui venit"* for TB; *"in nomine domini"* for ST. In each the tenor states the *cantus firmus* once, the ascending pitch-pattern being maintained. The division of this Mass into short subsections is typical of Josquin. There are frequent instances of imitation *a 2* in relatively short, melismatic passages; and many of the larger sections begin imitatively. In a single voice, short figures are often repeated exactly or sequentially. Sequence occurs strikingly in Kyrie II, where a three-note figure, consisting of a leap of a third down followed by a repeated note, receives, in the superius, four presentations beginning on successive descending scale-degrees, and then appears in the bass, where the beginning notes describe a descending octave-scale and where the figure is finally repeated on various degrees. The five major sections of the Mass end on complete triads. The under-third cadence is used occasionally at other points.

The rigidity of the *Missa Hercules* is exceptional in Josquin. The *Missa L'Homme armé super voces musicales* (printed in 1502),[306] another *cantus-firmus* Mass, is probably also early, since Josquin's music seems to have become less involved as his career unfolded and this Mass displays intricate contrapuntal devices. These, however, serve as genuine means of musical communication and do not degenerate into mere rhetorical flourishes. The introduction of fragments of the melody in voices other than the tenor foreshadows the permeation, in later works, of all the parts by a basic melody.

Josquin presents his imaginatively elaborated version of the famous song fully at least once each in the course of the Kyrie, Gloria, Credo, Sanctus, and Agnus III, and its first two periods in Agnus I. In each of these six sections

[305] The Mass is pr. JosqMS II, 19; Kyrie I in old notation in RoediN, 4. The composition would seem to date from before 1499—the first year in which Josquin, already about 50 years of age, is definitely known to have been employed by Hercules (cf. p. 229). Perhaps it will some day be shown that he actually entered the Duke's service prior to 1499 or else that, as a result of special circumstances, he wrote the Mass before doing so.

[306] Pr. JosqMS I, 1; PubAPTM VI, 1; Kyrie I in old notation in RoediN, 80.

the melody opens on a different degree of the *hexachordum naturale* (and ends on the note on which it begins except in Agnus I), commencing with c and proceeding in order to a. It is from the fact that the melody appears on these degrees (*voces musicales*) that the Mass derives its name. As the melody ascends from section to section, the tenor crosses the altus with increasing frequency; at points in the Sanctus and Agnus I it rises even above the superius. In Agnus III the melody is finally assigned to the uppermost voice, in greatly augmented note-values. Since key transposition is not involved, the *L'Homme armé* tune changes mode, in *catholicon* fashion, with each new presentation, the modal series consisting of Ionian, Dorian, Phrygian, Lydian, Mixolydian, and Aeolian. Josquin, however, did not permit the progress of the *cantus firmus* through all these modes to destroy the modal unity of his Mass, which throughout retains its anchorage in the Dorian mode. All the sections close with essentially the same form of the Dorian cadence, the first four sections on a D-octave without third or fifth. In order to make this possible, Josquin planned his music so that the statement of the *L'Homme armé* tune would end long enough before the close to permit additional free writing leading up to the Dorian cadence in those sections in which the tune did not lie in the Dorian mode. In the Gloria, where it does lie there, Josquin preserved balance by concluding the last statement of the *cantus firmus* four measures before the close. Only in the final Agnus did Josquin permit the *cantus firmus* to continue up to the very end—the *finalis*, a, constituting the fifth of the only root-fifth Dorian chord that concludes a section of the Mass.

In Kyrie I the superius anticipates the *cantus firmus* in notes half the value of those in the tenor. At the beginning of the *Confiteor* the *cantus firmus* appears very briefly in imitation in all voices. The *Qui tollis* and *Et incarnatus* have the tune in *cancrizans* motion. (The section after the *Et incarnatus*, from *Et in Spiritum* to *in ecclesiam*, is included in only one of the several sources; it is probably not by Josquin. This Credo, therefore, seems to belong to the group of settings that omit part of the text.) The three-part *Pleni*, which lacks the *cantus firmus*, is a regular canon except in meas. 42–50, where the canon is broken by a little free material. The Benedictus, also lacking the *cantus firmus*, is, like that of *Hercules Dux,* in three sections, each *a 2*. These sections are mensuration canons, one voice simply doubling the note values of the other in regular augmentation. Agnus II is a riddle canon *a 3* (the tenor rests once more): the three voices are to be derived from the single notated part, by reading each part in a different mensuration. A head-motif appears at the openings of Kyrie I (in the altus, which, however, is the functional top part at the moment), Gloria, and Agnus I. In each instance, it serves as a counterpoint to the initial *L'Homme armé* notes, which are sung by a voice that does not have them in their *cantus-firmus* function. In the Credo, the two upper voices contain some reminders of plainsong Credo I.

Here, as in most of his works, Josquin employs a basic scoring *a 4*. He varies the texture, however, not only by changing the number of voices kept active in sections *a 4*, but by introducing short sections with different scoring, as in the *Pleni*, Benedictus, and Agnus. The use of short sections with reduced scoring is a Josquin trait. This breaking up of the form into small units, however, does not produce a halting effect, but rather the impression of a chain of carefully matched segments designed to balance one another. Structure, in his Masses as in his other works, is a primary concern of Josquin's.

Petrucci's print of 1502 contains another Mass on the same *cantus firmus*, the *Missa L'Homme armé sexti toni*.[307] Though not so brilliant as the other, this Mass is technically less retrospective: the given melody is entrusted with relative frequency to voices other than the tenor; original material is found in the tenor; the melody is notably elaborated. It is presented in imitation in all voices at the beginning of Kyrie I and in three of the four voices at several other points in the Mass. Imitation in pairs opens the *Hosanna*, and the imitation at the fifth, by the bass, of the tenor's *cantus firmus*, continues with almost canonic exactness throughout this section. In the *Pleni* the first syllable of *"terra"* in the altus is set with a luxuriant 25-note melisma. In Agnus III the number of parts is increased to six; this section is a double canon of altus I and II and superius I and II against long notes in tenor and bass, which sing portions of the melody and related figures. The range of this Mass is low: D is found in the bass, and no note higher than c″ in the superius.

The *Missa La Sol Fa Re Mi*,[308] also from the 1502 book, has, as its *cantus firmus*, a, g, f, d, e, and transpositions. This *cantus*, according to Glareanus, originated in mimicry of the facile promises of an unnamed potentate (could it have been Cardinal Ascanio?) who used to put off requests with the words, *"Lascia fare mi."* [309] Whether the story is reliable or not, a *villotta* by Ruffino d'Assisi contains a popular Italian tune [310] employing the same solmisation pun (the notes are to be read in the hard hexachord):

EXAMPLE 44. Opening of the popular tune, *Lassa fare a mi* (after JepVF, 73).

The simple but not ungraceful theme is used frequently in long notes in the tenor in traditional *cantus-firmus* style, but appears also in short notes, taking on the same rhythmic character as the other voices, in some instances as an

[307] Pr. JosqMS I, 109; Kyrie I in old notation in RoediN, 79.
[308] Pr. JosqMS I, 35; Kyrie I in old notation in RoediN, 80.
[309] Cf. GlarD, 441 (*recte* 440); PubAPTM XVI, 398.
[310] Ruffino's *villotta* is pr. in TorreS, 471. Further on the use of this tune, *see* JepVF, 73. The idea of a pun on these syllables was certainly not original with Josquin. Cf. PirH, 172, for an anon. poem containing the same pun.

ostinato. The theme is at times assigned to voices other than the tenor: it is presented in imitation by all voices in the *Christe* and *Hosanna I.* The rhythm of the figure is varied in many ways, recalling the isomelic compositions of Dufay and others. The *Pleni,* scored *a 4* but using all voices together only at the end, is imitative almost throughout. The imitation begins with the *la-sol-fa-re-mi* figure in superius and tenor. At the end of phrase 1, Josquin, apparently in a playful mood, gives the altus the figure a, g, c, a, b (still *la, sol, fa, re, mi,* but with a change of hexachord after note 2); the other voices take up this figure and all voices toy with it until the cadence of the section is reached. Besides the five-note theme, plainsong melodies appear in the Gloria and Credo. Mass XV is drawn on in the superius of the Gloria as far as *"Adoramus te,"* and fragments are quoted thereafter, once in imitation. The Credo draws less exactly on Credo V. This Mass is more chordal than the *Missa Hercules* or the two *L'Homme armé* Masses, but this does not preclude a number of extended melismas and sweeping vocal lines.

The intermediate stages leading up to the full-fledged parody type are illustrated in Josquin's Masses, as in those of his predecessors. His *Missa Malheur me bat* (printed in 1505) [311] borrows from the three-part chanson attributed to Ockeghem; but only at the opening of the Sanctus, for eleven measures, does it take over all parts simultaneously. Josquin draws upon the chanson superius, at the opening of the Mass, for his own superius. His altus, at this point, detaches and presents three times the five-note figure with which the chanson contratenor begins. The tenor and bass then follow the superius and altus in paired imitation. The tenor of the chanson is presented in its entirety in the Kyrie tenor. It is given no oftener in the tenor of the Gloria, but is here lengthened by repetition of phrases and figures from the original. The chanson superius [312] furnishes the superius of the entire Credo, being sung twice, the first time extended by repetition of phrases. The Sanctus, after the eleven-measure quotation at its opening, proceeds freely up to the *Pleni.* The chanson contratenor provides the altus of the two-part *Pleni* and four-part *Hosanna.* The Benedictus is divided into three short sections, in each of which the upper part is derived from the opening measures of the chanson contratenor. In Agnus I and part of the six-voice Agnus III, the chanson tenor is disposed in long notes in old-fashioned *cantus-firmus* style. In Agnus III, at the same time, the superius of the model provides the superius of the Mass, while altus I and II on the one hand and tenor II and the bass on the other execute a double canon, recalling Agnus III of the *Missa L'Homme armé sexti toni.* Agnus II, using no material from the model, is a canon at the second. This Mass, unlike Obrecht's, retains the Phrygian mode of the chanson.

311 Pr. JosqMS II, 39; Kyrie I in old notation in RoediN, 5.
312 Not the tenor, as stated in PirH, 184.

The *Missa Fortuna desperata* (printed in 1502) [313] displays a more schematic combination of the *cantus-firmus* and parody techniques. Ingenious use is made of the three voices of the model as *cantus firmi* in different parts of the Mass, while at the same time these *cantus* often have, as counterpoints, material also derived from the model. The tenor of the model [314] is repeated four times by the Mass tenor in the course of the Kyrie and Gloria, the last time with the values of the original diminished. Throughout the Credo, Josquin employs the superius of the model as his own superius, presenting it four times, with note-values again diminished in the last appearance. In the Sanctus, the bass of the model, transposed a fifth upward, becomes the altus. This voice is silent during the three-part *Pleni,* but in the *Hosanna* it reintroduces the chanson bass-line for its last appearance as a *cantus firmus,* completing the neat scheme by diminishing the note-values once more. The bass of Agnus I (= II) gives out in greatly augmented values an inversion of period I of the superius of the model. The bass of Agnus III is once more the tenor of the model, this time in long notes. Against these *cantus firmi,* the beginning of the polyphonic complex, sometimes with voices interchanged, appears at the opening of all the major sections of the Mass except the Agnus. At the end of each of the first four major sections, the most characteristic effects of the final cadence of the chanson are likewise retained. While the texture of the Mass is mainly polyphonic, chordal writing is strikingly introduced in the *Christe,* which contrasts markedly with the Kyrie settings. The opening of Agnus II is the same as that of the *Hosanna* of Obrecht's *Missa Fortuna desperata,* but this passage is not known to exist in any of the chanson settings, so that presumably Josquin borrowed from Obrecht or vice versa.[315]

It is in the *Missa Mater Patris* (printed in 1514) [316] that the parody technique is used by Josquin on a comparatively extensive scale. Whereas the preexistent polyphonic complex is drawn on sparingly in the Masses *Malheur me bat* and *Fortuna desperata,* the *Missa Mater Patris,* which is based on a motet *a 3* by Brumel (cf. p. 262), draws on its model (though not always on all voices) in the three subsections of the Kyrie, at the opening and close of the Gloria and Credo, at the opening of the Sanctus and Agnus I, and nearly throughout Agnus III. For the rest, however, the mainly four-part work is preponderantly free. When a relation with the model exists, it is almost literal—wholly so in practically all of Agnus III (*a 5*), except for the introduction of two additional voices. The low range of the model is retained. There is no *cantus firmus* in this Mass: relying upon the parody technique for its fundamental structure, it appears to be the earliest example of a true parody

---

[313] Pr. JosqMS I, 81.

[314] The reader is reminded that the tenor is called the *"Altus"* by the editor in JosqMS I, 105.

[315] Cf. GomO, 115, where Obrecht is held to be the more likely borrower.

[316] Pr. JosqMS III, 1; Kyrie, pr. SmijO, 135. I am indebted to Dr. Oliver Strunk for having drawn my attention to the stylistic significance of this Mass before its publication in JosqMS.

Mass, as distinguished from a mere parody movement, whether independent or part of a larger work (cf. pp. 28, 33, 76, 203).

Just as there are *cantus-firmus* Masses that point in the direction of the parody Mass, there are others in which the *cantus-firmus* technique leads into highly developed paraphrase writing. In these works the permeation of the polyphonic complex by the *cantus firmus* is so considerable that, if one did not examine the tenor, one might believe the technique employed to be that of the paraphrase Mass pure and simple. Analysis reveals, however, that, in such works as the Masses *Ave maris stella, Gaudeamus,* and *Da pacem,* and in parts of the *Missa de Beata Virgine,* it is only in the tenor (or its canonic *comes*) that the pre-existent melody is present in complete form. These four works, by virtue of their style, seem to point the way to the genuine paraphrase Mass that is one of Josquin's greatest masterpieces, the *Missa Pange lingua.*

The Dorian plainchant setting of the hymn, *Ave maris stella,* furnishes the basis of Josquin's Mass of that name (printed in 1505).[317] At the beginning of the Kyrie, Gloria, and Agnus and of a number of subsections, the chant is imitated in all voices, the tenor having the same rhythmical movement as the other parts. After the opening measures of these points of imitation, the tenor proceeds more or less literally with the chant, whatever may happen in the other voices. This melody occurs once in the Kyrie, twice in the Gloria—incomplete, though used several times—and with considerable ornamentation in the Credo, once complete in the Sanctus, once in the *Hosanna,* where the chant receives its most literal statement, and once each in Agnus I (complete) and III (incomplete). Besides these presentations by the tenor, which occasionally occur in sustained notes, the melody is at times used quite extensively by the superius, thus helping to create the impression of a paraphrase Mass. In Agnus III the superius proceeds in canon with the tenor. This Mass makes extensive use of imitation. Almost every phrase of the Gloria opens with it. In the Credo, the chordal-syllabic character that is normal on the words *"Et incarnatus est de Spiritu Sancto"* is preserved without sacrificing imitation—here in pairs, with the chant motif in superius and tenor. In the three-part *Pleni* (the tenor *tacet*) Josquin disposes the words in four text phrases: *"Pleni sunt coeli," "et terra," "gloria tua," "gloria tua,"* set by musical phrases that can be easily distinguished in spite of overlapping and cadential elaboration. Each musical phrase begins with a characteristic motif that is used in imitation in all voices.

The *Missa Gaudeamus* (printed in 1502),[318] which resembles the *Missa Ave maris stella* in matters of external construction, is based on the Introit, *Gaudeamus . . . Mariae,* transposed from its original Dorian to the Mixolyd-

---

[317] Pr. JosqMS II, 1. Kyrie I in old notation in RoediN, 5.
[318] Pr. JosqMS, I, 57. Kyrie I in old notation in RoediN, 85.

ian. A motif, which is an ornamented, mensural version of the plainchant on the first word of the Introit, is used imitatively in all voices at the Kyrie and Gloria openings. The tenor of the Kyrie continues to follow the plainchant beyond the initial motif, as in various sections of *Ave maris stella*. In the Gloria, however, through *"Filius Patris,"* this voice repeats the motif eleven times as an *ostinato*. The beginning of the chant is recalled once more on *"Patrem omnipotentem"* in tenor and superius, set in imitation in pairs against bass and altus. In the Credo as a whole, the tenor, carrying the chant, fulfils a genuine *cantus-firmus* function, though it is silent from *"Et incarnatus"* to *"non erit finis."* The opening motif of the Mass appears somewhat altered in the Sanctus and augmented in the *Hosanna,* where the repetition of it by the altus is as insistent as that by the tenor in the Gloria. Still another version of the opening motif appears in the imitation that begins Agnus I.

The *Missa Da pacem* (first published, in 1539, by J. Ott at Nuremberg) [319] employs the plainsong *Da pacem in diebus nostris* as its *cantus firmus,* partly in long time-values, partly in time-values approximating those of the other voices; in the four-part Agnus II, the *cantus firmus* is used in canon *a 2* and in the six-part Agnus III in canon *a 3*. There is considerable permeation of the *cantus firmus* in the other voices, and all the major sections open with the same four measures of polyphony, in which the three voices that have thus far entered sing the opening phrase of the plainsong in imitation. Full chordal effects are often achieved without the loss of independence of the parts, as in the remarkably eloquent *Et incarnatus*.

The *Missa de Beata Virgine* (printed in 1514),[320] being based on chant settings of portions of the Ordinary, naturally lacks the kind of unity (shown in the other Josquin Masses described), that results from having all movements constructed on a single pre-existent piece. The Kyrie and Gloria are based on those of the present plainsong Mass IX. The Credo is derived from Credo I, and the Sanctus and Agnus from those of Mass IV. The Gloria contains the Marian tropes, which we have found usual in separate chant settings of Gloria IX (cf. p. 60) and which were normally retained, until after the Council of Trent, whenever settings of this chant were incorporated in Masses *de Beata Virgine*.[320a] As pointed out on p. 29, until rather recently chant books seldom grouped their Kyries, Glorias, etc., into Ordinary sets, usually placing together, instead, all settings of a single text. But the exceptions, though rare, are sometimes striking. The J. P. Morgan Library, in New York, has a Kyriale prepared for Carlo Pallavicino, Bishop of Lodi (1456–97), that contains a whole series of Ordinary sets. Its Mass *In honorem Beate Marie Virginis* is made up of the Kyrie and Gloria of the present Mass IX—the Gloria

[319] Pr. CW XX, 5; JosqMS IV, 29.

[320] Pr. CW XLII, 5; JosqMS III, 125. Kyrie I in old notation in RoediN, 17.

[320a] As was usually the case; but there is an occasional exception, such as the Mass by Finck described in Chap. 12.

being provided with the Marian tropes—and (through cross-references to other parts of the MS) of the Sanctus of Mass XVII and Agnus of Mass IX. (As in current chant books, the Credos are grouped separately.) With the exception of the Agnus, this choice was eventually to become almost standard in polyphonic settings. The selection of chants in Josquin's Mass, though it differs even more widely, is still related. The varying selections undoubtedly represent different local practices.

All the voices in Josquin's Kyrie and Gloria take part in elaborating the chants, the tenor being no more important than the superius and being sometimes less faithful to the plainsong. There is much imitation. The technique is definitely that of the paraphrase Mass. This technique returns very freely in Agnus II (*a 2*). But in the Credo, Sanctus, Agnus I, and Agnus III, a fifth voice is added to the four-part texture—this voice always being in canon with the tenor and the melodic material consisting of elaborations of the various chants. Although the rhythmic character approximates that of the other voices and although those voices sometimes imitate the plainsong, it is only the tenor and its canonic *comes* that have complete statements of the borrowed material. These movements, therefore, employ the *cantus-firmus* technique, and the Mass as a whole embraces two styles.

Much variety is produced by the number of voices kept active. The effect is that of vocal "orchestration," especially striking in the longer sections. The conclusion of the Gloria furnishes an impressive example of climax writing, with a figure derived from the *cambiata* of measure 2 below recurring with increasing frequency as the voices gather momentum.

EXAMPLE 45. Extract from *Missa de Beata Virgine—Gloria—*Josquin (after CW XLII, 17).

In the Credo, at the words, *"Qui cum Patre et Filio,"* there is an interesting passage employing *sesquitertia* (i.e., four against three). Here, for several measures, Josquin has what amounts to one measure of triple meter in the superius against two of duple meter in the other voices.

According to Glareanus, it was when Josquin and Brumel were "approaching their last years" that each wrote his *Missa de Beata Virgine*. "But Josquin excelled by far, in my opinion, . . . and so acquitted himself in this contest that it seems to me . . . that finer music cannot be created." [321]

Like the *Missa Ave maris stella* and *Missa Gaudeamus,* the *Missa Pange lingua* [322] (first published by Ott in 1539) is a fantasy on a plainsong. In the Kyrie, the paraphrase of the complete chant is treated imitatively in all voices, though in Kyrie I the version used in the bass and altus differs from that of the tenor and superius. Nearly every phrase in the Kyrie begins imitatively, especially in the *Christe.* In the Gloria the superius paraphrases the first period of the chant and the beginning of the second, and in one way or another is imitated by the remaining parts. The opening of the chant is imitated in all parts at the beginning of the Credo. The first notes reappear in the superius at *"Et incarnatus"* and in the superius and altus at *"Crucifixus."* Throughout the rest of the Mass, elements of the chant constantly appear and disappear, the paraphrasing taking on extraordinary variety and being conducted with such freedom that at times only reminders of the plainsong are present, though quotations are quite literal at the beginnings of movements. Extensions and transformations of the melody at times lack the melismatic ornaments characteristic of Josquin's earlier Masses. Concomitantly, chords become more varied. The chordal style of this Mass naturally throws the superius into relief. This is not to say, however, that the inner voices function as "fillers." At *"Et in unum Dominum,"* the plainchant of Credo II appears in the tenor, with anticipatory imitation at the fifth in the altus; a partial statement by the superius follows. As in the *Missa de Beata Virgine,* the voices are often paired, with relatively long passages in which only two voices sing.

Among Josquin's other Masses, it is worthy of note that the *Missa L'Ami Baudichon* [323] is based on a popular tune, which is incorporated likewise in the anonymous chanson, *Souviegne vous de la douleur,* in the Dijon Chansonnier; [324] that the *Missa Una musque de Buscaya* [325] derives its name from the popular melody which Josquin treated also in a chanson setting (cf. p. 232); that the *Missa Faysant regrets* is constructed on section II of Frye's *Tout a par moy;* [326] that the *Missa Alles regrets* [327] is based on the chanson by Hayne; that the *Missa Di dadi* is written on the tenor of Morton's *N'aray-je* (the Mass derives its name from the faces of dice, pictured to indicate the mensural proportions governing the relationship of the tenor to the other

---

[321] GlarD, 366; PubAPTM, XVI, 326.

[322] Pr. CW I, 5; AmbG V, 80; JosqMS IV, 1 (including Agnus II, not in CW and AmbG). Chant in Liber, 957.

[323] Pr. JosqMS II, 67.   [324] Pr. MoD, App. No. 6.   [325] Pr. JosqMS II, 93.

[326] The Mass is pr. JosqMS III, 33. Kyrie I in old notation in RoediN, 4; *Hosanna* and Benedictus pr. BuH II, 499f. In JosqMS III, xiii, it is claimed that Josquin's Mass is based on Agricola's 4-part *Tout a par moy* (*see also* PirH, 186). As stated on p. 209 *supra,* Agricola's piece is constructed on Frye's earlier one of the same name. That Josquin based his Mass directly on Frye is shown by the fact that he uses no material peculiar to Agricola, but does begin the superius of his Agnus III with an extensive quotation of material peculiar to the opening of Frye's superius. The tenor borrowed by Josquin is, of course, common to both chansons.

[327] Pr. JosqMS IV, 61; Kyrie I in old notation in RoediN, 46.

parts); [328] and that the *Missa D'ung aultre amer* [328a] is built on the tenor of Ockeghem's chanson. The Sanctus and Agnus of this last Mass employ also the plainsong of Gregorian Mass XVIII; [328b] in the Josquin Mass, the replacing of the Benedictus with *pars I* of the motet *Tu solus qui facis mirabilia* (cf. p. 258) is somewhat remindful of the "substitution" Mass. But the substitution bears a relationship to traditional procedure. The custom of singing a motet in honor of the Sacrament, in connection with the transubstantiation, took hold c. 1500,[329] and the insertion of a portion of *Tu solus* is related to that custom.[329a] The *Missa ad fugam* and the *Missa sine nomine* [330] consist of canon cycles.

The mention made by some historians [331] of a Requiem Mass *a 4* by Josquin results from a mistaken attribution to him of the motet, *Requiem (= Mille quingentis)*, by Obrecht and from slips of the pen, referring to this motet as a *Missa pro defunctis*.[331a] Moreover, a six-part Requiem in 14 sections that appears under Josquin's name in Leyden, Gemeentearchief, MS 863, is not his, but is the Richafort composition mentioned on p. 335.

In setting the text of the Mass, Josquin is primarily concerned with large-scale ideas rather than with individual words. When one examines his treatment of Latin texts, one quite often finds this French composer influenced by his native language rather than by the humanistic concept of the proper handling of Latin accent. As might be expected, some clichés of word-painting appear—an ascending line on *"ascendit,"* uniform treatment of the voices on *"simul,"* etc. Occasionally, there is an attempt at less ordinary text delineation, as at the end of the passage on *"non erit finis"* in the *Missa Ave maris stella,* where the altus ascends scalewise through a tenth.[332]

Josquin's Masses, by drawing on Gregorian Masses and on antiphons, responsories, hymns, and the like, on polyphonic works both secular and sacred, and on *soggetti* made from solmisation syllables associated with words, epitomize the polyphonic settings of his time.

---

[328] For facsimile material including such dice faces, *see* ApelN, 184, 186 (where, however, the bibliographical information is incorrect). The Mass is pr. JosqMS III, 93.

[328a] Pr. JosqMS II, 121.

[328b] This is true as well of the independent Sanctus and Benedictus (pr. *ibid.,* 136) in which Josquin (as in his *Victimae pascali;* cf. p. 251) draws on the superius of *D'ung aultre amer.*

[329] For details, *see* WagG, 17f.

[329a] A motet (pr. JosqMS II, 139), included in Petrucci's *Fragmenta missarum* directly after the Benedictus mentioned in fn. 328b, is probably related to the custom likewise, although it does not involve substitution.

[330] The former is pr. JosqMS III, 61, and its Kyrie I is given in old notation in RoediN, 75; the latter pr. JosqMS III, 167; Kyrie I in old notation in RoediN, 7; extracts in BuH II, 490; *Pleni* also pr. PubAPTM XVI, 404f.

[331] *See,* e.g., WagG. 161; PirH, 188.

[331a] One should guard against the possible further confusion that may arise from the existence of Josquin's lament on Ockeghem, in one source, with the Requiem text only (cf. fn. 302).

[331b] *See* MGG VII, 201.

[332] Further about Josquin's Masses, *see* WagG, 145ff; PirH, 179ff; AmbG III, 215ff; GomO, 51ff; 88ff, 108ff; OsJ, 178ff.

Josquin: Motets

Splendid as are Josquin's chansons and Masses, it is in his motets that his art is seen at its greatest. If the restriction to one text, imposed upon Mass composers, acted as no hindrance to Ockeghem or Obrecht—or, later, to Palestrina—Josquin needed the large variety of text, available to the motet composer, to express the many-sidedness of his genius and to inspire in him fully the venturesomeness that makes him an outstanding exponent of new techniques as well as a summarizer. He is by no means the conservative in his motets that he seems to be in certain of his Masses. Some of the "modernities" about to be discussed in connection with the motets are occasionally present in the Masses and also in the secular works, but it is in the motets that they receive from Josquin their most distinguished treatment. However brilliant his contributions in all three fields, it is particularly owing to the motets that he is one of the two or three greatest composers of the periods that have customarily been grouped together under the term "Renaissance." Palestrina's higher prestige is mainly due to the widely held and no doubt correct opinion that his music is more suitable for devotional purposes; but, master that he is, Palestrina must yield first place to Josquin as a historical figure and must admit him to a place at least of companionship on purely musical grounds.

It has been pointed out (p. 40) that motets did not often draw on scriptural texts until quite late. The earliest dated source containing a motet setting of a psalm, rather that settings in fauxbourdon-like or falsobordone style, is a MS of 1507 in which there is such a work by Brumel (cf. p. 262). The earliest dated source containing a Josquin psalm is Book I of Petrucci's Motetti de la Corona, printed in 1514, which includes Memor esto verbi tui (Psalm CXVIII [119]). This psalm is in two partes, which Josquin ties together by presenting, at the end, a most interesting variant of the opening. Pars I begins with the tenor and bass singing, in canon, a melody consisting of a two-measure motif, immediately repeated; the four measures then recur in sequence a third higher and are followed by a freely varied version of the motif, sung once, a third higher than that. Thereupon, the two upper voices imitate the lower pair. At the end, Josquin reintroduces the opening words and uses the same motif, slightly changed and with the values halved. Here it is the two upper voices that enter first. Instead of either pair waiting for the other to sing the entire melody as before, they now alternate in each presentation of the motif. A climactic effect is achieved: the sequence a third above the initial statement is sung only once in each pair; statement 3, at the additional third, is sung once in each pair, as at the opening, but this time without elaboration; the varied version, having been deferred, is now presented twice, a third higher still, the second statement being immediately prefixed by a repetition of sequence 2.

EXAMPLE 46. Beginning and end of *Memor esto verbi tui*—Josquin (after JosqMT II, 3, 11).

This work contains passages that recall psalm-tone 1, but their appearance may be due merely to the fact that the composition is written in the Dorian mode. However, in *Laudate pueri* (Psalm CXII [113]) [333] the presence of psalm-tone 5 in the tenor, at the opening, is unmistakable, even though B-flat replaces B. At the close of the *Gloria Patri,* Tone 5 returns in the same voice, and then, at the very end, the first three words of the psalm are repeated and the Tone recurs, now transferred to the superius. The Tone occasionally permeates the other voices. At the opening of *Deus in nomine tuo* (Psalm LIII [54]) [334] the tenor paraphrases psalm-tone 4. We shall find that several psalm settings of this period incorporate the psalm-tone corresponding to the mode of the composition, but, since a Tone is not introduced in every setting, it is less likely that this happened because composers were trying to establish a special genre than because they—as worshippers accustomed to hearing the

[333] Pr. PubAPTM VI, 65.   [334] Pr. CommB VI, 59; JosqMT II, 127.

Chant—naturally associated the psalms with the Tones. In the main, motet settings of psalms employ the same techniques as are found in other motets.

Josquin's celebrated *Miserere* (Psalm L [51]), written for Duke Hercules I, was printed by Petrucci in 1519. But since the Duke died in 1505, the piece must antedate that year.[334a] This powerful work *a 5*, in three *partes*, is built on an exceedingly simple *cantus firmus*, undoubtedly suggested by the general nature of the psalm-tones. The melody is given out, at the opening, by the superius, altus, tenor I (with slight elaboration), and bass.

EXAMPLE 47. Opening of *Miserere*—Josquin (complete piece in JosqMT II, 58; CommB VI, 68; BordA, *Motets,* I, 122).

At the end of each verse (and of one half-verse) [335] this melody is repeated by tenor II. It appears eight times in *pars I*, first on e′-f′-e′ and then one degree lower at each successive repetition until an octave has been spanned. By means of an ascent from the low point thus reached, exactly the reverse procedure is followed in *pars II*. In *pars III*, tenor II, beginning at its original point, descends stepwise until it reaches a-b-a. The method reminds one of Busnois's *In hydraulis*. Against the *cantus firmus* Josquin, varying the number of parts employed and occasionally interrupting the polyphony with stark *falsobordone*-like passages (in which Tones 3 and 4 are sometimes recalled by tenor I), writes countermelodies of great eloquence. *Domine, Dominus noster* (Psalm VIII),[336] like the *Miserere*, also employs an *ostinato*, which, however, remains stationary; also as in the *Miserere*, tenor II has a long organ-point at the close. Terminal organ-points, probably suggested by Italian influence, are a trait of Josquin's style.

[334a] This is not in itself proof, of course, that the piece is older than the two psalms mentioned on p. 246, which may also have been fairly old by the time they were included in a dated source. In estimating chronology, the dates to be compared should obviously be like in kind.
[335] As numbered in Liber, 734.   [336] CommB VII, 34.

We have two settings by Josquin of the *De profundis* (Psalm CXXIX [130]), both masterly. One, printed in 1520 and also in the *Dodecachordon*,[337] is noteworthy, aside from its purely musical value, for the clefs in which it is written. Among the Renaissance practices that became wholly or partly standardized in Josquin's day, possibly owing to his own efforts, is that of using the soprano, alto, tenor, and bass (SATB)[338] clefs in writing *a 4*, which type of writing also now definitely became "classic." Departures were of course made with respect to both the clef combination and the number of voices employed, but these departures were recognizable as such. In the *De profundis* in question, Josquin uses the clef combination MTBarSub. Whatever this combination may have signified in other connections (cf. p. 531), it seems clear that Glareanus regarded Josquin as not wishing the piece to be transposed up from the low register in which the clefs, if literally interpreted, place it, for he states: "Here, indeed, I should like everyone to note how the beginning of this composition presents the expression *'De profundis'* to us—with what effect and what gravity—in such manner that it has not moved the modes higher, from their normal position, as is customarily done in such cases elsewhere."[339] The piece is predominantly in the Phrygian mode and is written without any signature. The quoted passage calls attention to the fact that Josquin has not employed a signature of one flat and transposed the music up a fourth; by implication it also indicates that, in Glareanus' opinion, the music should not be removed from its low register by anyone else.

In Josquin's motets, the replacing of the old *cantus-firmus* technique by the device of pervading imitation, i.e., by a series of fugue-like expositions, gets well under way. With his love of variety, he uses both methods in the motets, as elsewhere, but in these works the examples of pervading imitation are particularly felicitous. The setting *a 4* of *Dominus regnavit* (Psalm XCII [93]), in two *partes*, provides a fine illustration. The words are arranged in short text-phrases, and practically every text-phrase has its own melody, at least the beginning of which is sung by each voice in turn. The chain of points of imitation, rarely broken, is varied in its components: some points present imitation in pairs, others are in ordinary imitation, still others are canonic. Time-values are occasionally varied in successive entries. Particularly noteworthy are points of imitation in which tonal answers are present—a leap of a fourth here answering a leap of a fifth, or the reverse—Josquin thus employing a method that was not to become common until the next generation. One point of imitation, on text beginning with the word *"Elevaverunt,"* takes this striking form:

[337] Pr. JosqMT III, 20; PubAPTM VI, 75; XVI, 332; RieH II¹, 260 (transposed). The other is pr. in CW XXXIII, 10.

[338] From this point on, the following abbreviations will at times represent the various clefs: V (violin or treble), S, M (mezzo-soprano), A, T, Bar (baritone; either C-clef on line 5 or F-clef on line 3), B, Sub (sub-bass; F-clef on line 5), Γ (G on line 3). Shortly after Josquin, V commonly took the place of S.

[339] GlarD, 364; PubAPTM XVI, 325.

EXAMPLE 48. Extract from *Dominus regnavit*—Josquin (after CW XXXIII, 6).

Obviously, an expansion of the total range (cf. p. 105) had to precede such writing. It provided the space within which imitation could really flourish and reduced the reason for the sharp contrast that was often favored in the Early Renaissance (cf. p. 4). The parts could stand out clearly despite their homogeneity, since the need for crossing had lessened, and the way was open for the development of imitation into the chief characteristic of Late Renaissance music.

The two *De profundis* settings are among the other Josquin motets that employ pervading imitation, but they do so less consistently. A piece (not a psalm) in which such imitation does appear with complete consistency is *Rubum quem viderat Moyses*.[340] In *Qui habitat in adjutorio* (Psalm XC [91]), Josquin provides a tour de force that may be regarded as a companion piece to the *Deo gratias* attributed to Ockeghem. To be sure, Josquin's work is only *a 24* while the *Deo gratias* is *a 36;* but, whereas the latter work never has more than 18 voices active simultaneously, Josquin at times actually has all 24 voices singing together. His work is a quadruple canon, each canon being *a 6*.[341] This complex structure, like that of *Deo gratias,* is achieved only by renouncing harmonic variety, but, while there is a dominant chord on the last beat of each measure in *Deo gratias,* Josquin conceals the limitation in his harmonic resources by having no such persisting coincidence on any beat.[342]

Josquin's motets include several settings of sequences. He handles the

---

[340] JosqMT I, 29. See also *Tribulatio et angustia* (JosqMT III, 95; PubAPTM VI, 62).
[341] The canon for the sopranos, pr. ForkA II, 593.
[342] Further about this canon, *see* RieH II[1], 250. For other psalms by Josquin, *see* CommB VI, 43 (= JosqMT II, 81; CW XXXIII, 17), 48 (*pars I* also in ForkA II, 580); VII, 41, 68; JosqMT II, 118 (*pars I* in BuH II, 503); MaldR XIX, 15 (cf. ReT, 102, No. 304; pr. also, in accordance with 1 source, as Agricola's—and with a part added in Petrucci's *Canti C*—in RieH II[1], 192).

liturgical form in various ways, normally paraphrasing a borrowed plainsong melody. In his treatment of the *Veni Sancte Spiritus*,[343] with its five double versicles, he adheres to sequence form strictly for pairs 3 and 4, i.e., the second versicle of each pair is set to the same music as the first; he varies the endings somewhat in pair 1, more extensively in pair 6; in the last pair he comes closest to writing a new setting for the second versicle: the plainsong is still paraphrased, but some of the countermelodies are changed. His handling of the old melody, therefore, differs from Dufay's (cf. p. 83). The setting is for six voices, two of which have free melody while the others move in double canon, one pair having the plainsong paraphrase.

Josquin liked particularly to vary his treatment of each section of a sequence melody upon its repetition, as he did in the last double versicle of the *Veni Sancte Spiritus,* thus producing what have been called [344] variation-chain sequences. The type may be his invention. His five-part *Inviolata integra* and four-part *Victimae paschali laudes* are particularly fine examples.[345] He divides the first of these into three *partes,* throughout which the sequence melody [346] is presented in canon between the quintus and altus. Josquin divides the second composition into two *partes: pars I* paraphrases the unpaired versicle that opens the plainsong and also the first double versicle; *pars II* paraphrases the rest. The elaborated plainsong is sung sometimes in the tenor, sometimes in the altus, briefly in the bass, several of the repetitions involving variation. In *pars I,* the plainsong has pitted against it, in the superius, the superius of Ockeghem's *D'ung aultre amer,* which thus comments symbolically (the secular text is not used) on the words, *Victimae paschali;* in *pars II,* the superius of Hayne's *De tous biens plaine* is sung by the motet superius to the text of Mary's answer to the injunction, *"Dic nobis, Maria,"* the application of material from Hayne's chanson having here much the same symbolical meaning as it has in *Omnium bonorum plena* (cf. p. 227). The other countermelodies add to the variation character.

Another variation-chain sequence by Josquin—one highly regarded during the Late Renaissance—is his setting of the *Benedicta es coelorum Regina*.[347] This melody,[348] among those eliminated from use at Mass by the Council of Trent, has three double versicles. Josquin sets the first two pairs *a 6,* the first versicle of the last pair *a 2,* and the last versicle again *a 6.* Some of the countermelodies that he writes against the embellished plainsong are of a striking nature and figure prominently in works based by later composers on this famous motet.

[343] Pr. JosqMT III, 37; CW XVIII, 16.
[344] In StrunkM, 156.
[345] Pr. JosqMT II, 111 (= PubAPTM VI, 46) and I, 136 (= SmijO, 140), respectively.
[346] Liber, 1861; Josquin's version is slightly different.
[347] Pr. JosqMT III, 11; SmijO, 146; BesN, 14; VNM XXXVIII, Supp. II, 1.
[348] Pr. VNM XXXVIII, Supp. I; *Cantus varii* (1902), 365; etc. The *Benedicta es* melody was derived from one (pr. in A. Schubiger, *Die Sängerschule St. Gallens* [1858], No. 24) associated with the text *Benedicta semper sancta sit Trinitas* and dating from the 10th century or earlier.

EXAMPLE 49. Openings of Verses 1 and 2 of *Benedicta es coelorum Regina* in the plainsong version and in Josquin's setting (after BesN, 14).

"Blessed art thou, Queen of Heaven, Thou art called the brightest star of the sea . . ."

Other variation-chain sequences, or related works, include *Mittit ad Virginem* —a very lovely example—, *Christum ducem,* and *Praeter rerum seriem.*[348a] In the text of the second of these, the last line of each double versicle is the first line of a well-known hymn—e.g., *Conditor alme siderum*—a fact that is reflected in the melodic content of the music. *Praeter rerum seriem* takes on special interest from the fact that it applies the variation-chain technique to a melody of which a two-part setting had long before been included in one of the so-called "Notre Dame" MSS—Wolfenbüttel 677,[348b] in which it appears in fascicle 11, the "English" fascicle.[349]

[348a] Pr., respectively, in JosqMT I, 14, 21 (cf. fn. 379, *infra*); II, 21 (= CW XVIII, 23).

[348b] *See* fol. 194[v] in the J. H. Baxter facsimile ed. (*An Old St. Andrews Music Book,* 1931). The relationship, discovered by Mr. Alvin Johnson, was pointed out in the course of his paper on Rore's Masses, read at New Haven in December, 1952 (cf. p. 375, *infra,* fn. 166). In Wolfenbüttel 677, the identical music is used for the two halves of each double versicle. Salinas (*De musica libri septem,* p. 287) mentions the melody as being sung unisonally in his day "in France, in the Mass of the Blessed Virgin, by young boys and by virgins consecrated to God." For another Josquin motet showing sequence-like features, see JosqMT I, 114.

[349] Cf. ReMMA, 393f, and esp. the material by Handschin there cited.

In the well-known four-part *Ave Maria . . . virgo serena*,[349a] Josquin paraphrases, in imitation *a 4*, the first double versicle of the plainsong sequence *Ave Maria*,[349b] but thereafter proceeds freely, paying no attention to the sequence structure. At the beginning he reveals the keenness of his musical insight through the change of a single note in the borrowed material. The plainsong begins with three reiterated notes. Josquin obtains a much more effective opening—especially in view of the imitation—by replacing the initial note with one a fourth lower; when he reaches the second half of the double versicle, he is content to imitate the melody in a more faithful paraphrase of its original form. (Obrecht, when he introduces the same sequence melody in his *Beata es, Maria* [cf. p. 192], does so late in the composition, making no change in the opening note.)

Josquin's *Stabat Mater*,[350] like the *Ave Maria . . . virgo serena* and like Weerbecke's *Stabat Mater,* also does not follow the sequence form. To all outer appearances, this is a free composition; but there are points of resemblance between it and a *Stabat Mater* in Dammonis' *lauda* collection that may indicate that both works draw on an identical lost *Stabat Mater* melody.[351] Josquin introduces a touch of symbolism in his work by adopting, as his *cantus firmus,* the tenor of Binchois's *Comme femme desconfortée* (cf. p. 87). The writing is preponderantly chordal, giving the effect of choral recitative, and treats the text in a strongly dramatic manner.

Josquin shows a liking for Latin texts that are metrical. The *Stabat Mater* provides a rhymed example from the Middle Ages. An unrhymed one from classical antiquity, whose choice reflects the influence of the humanistic Renaissance, is *Dulces exuviae,* the eloquent passage in the *Aeneid* that leads up to the death of Dido. Humanistic influence, however, does not induce the composer to observe syllabic quantities strictly, though he and his contemporaries offend less in the handling of Latin quantity than had their predecessors. Josquin's selection of these lines from Vergil established a precedent followed by many later composers.[352]

The paraphrase technique present in the sequence settings is variously applied in other Josquin motets. The paraphrasing of a complete melody, as in Dufay's *Alma Redemptoris Mater,* was no longer as popular as it had been. But it takes place in the superius of Josquin's splendid *Salve Regina.*[353] The

349a Pr. JosqMT I, 1; PubAPTM XVI, 318; MaldR II, 12; CasR II, 10. (Textual discrepancies in the sources are reflected in the various reprints.) An anon. version *a 6* is pr. JosqMT I, 5. (Actually, the headings in JosqMT ascribe the version *a 6* to Josquin and give the one *a 4* as anon.; however, the introductory notes show that the reverse is correct.) Except for the 2 added parts, the version *a 6* is identical with the one *a 4*. Further on this piece, *see* WernJ.

349b VP, 46.

350 Pr. JosqMT II, 51; AmbG V, 61; MaldR III, 27; BordA, *Motets,* III, 91.

351 Cf. JepI, xxxiv; for Dammonis' piece, *see ibid.,* 118.

352 Cf. StrunkV, 485ff.

353 Pr. separately, as ed. by H. T. David, by Music Press, N. Y. (MP 93); also JosqMT III, 26.

second highest voice enters, after a rest of three measures, with the first four notes of the plainsong imitated at the fifth below; then, after a similar rest, it repeats these notes an additional fourth lower. Alternation at these two levels continues throughout the piece, *ostinato* technique thus being combined with paraphrase technique. Still another *ostinato* appears, at the opening, in the bass. The remaining voices (and the bass most of the time) engage in imitation or free counterpoint. In his *Alma Redemptoris Mater*,[354] Josquin paraphrases the plainsong, in canon, in the altus and tenor. Imitation is ingeniously used in this fine motet, the outer parts several times singing in imitation against the canon. In another work—a double motet[355]—Josquin combines the *Alma Redemptoris Mater,* paraphrased (in two partly different ways) in the superius and bass, with the *Ave Regina,* paraphrased (in two partly different ways) in the altus and tenor. At the opening, the two melodies are presented in double counterpoint: they are first sung simultaneously by the upper voices; when the two lower voices repeat them in paired imitation, the positions of the upper and lower melodies are reversed. The melody of the *Ave Maria* appears in the four-part *Missus est Gabriel angelus*[356]—quite appropriately, since the text consists of the story of the Annunciation according to St. Luke. The melody, delicately paraphrased, is introduced at the point at which part of the *Ave Maria* text is spoken by the Angel Gabriel. Other excellent paraphrase motets are Josquin's *Ave Maria . . . benedicta tu,* his *Domine non secundum peccata,* the *Liber generationis,* and *Planxit autem David.*[357] The second of these is a work in four *partes,* which paraphrases the melody of the Tract for Ash Wednesday, the first two *partes* being *a 2* and the last two, *a 4.* The third, printed in 1504, which sets St. Matthew's account of the genealogy of Jesus, is an early example of the Gospel motet, a type that was late in gaining a foothold.[358] The last, David's lament for Saul and Jonathan, is prefaced by twenty-four measures of free writing, which recall the opening of the *Stabat Mater.* Thereafter, the superius paraphrases the Tone for the Lamentations of Holy Week; then the tenor does likewise; after this, the superius has the formula in long notes, transposed up a fourth. The Tone, paraphrased, permeates all four *partes* of this moving work.[359]

Josquin's motets with a *cantus firmus* in the tenor include numerous examples not yet mentioned. In them, the rhythmical character of the tenor tends to approximate that of the other parts, though, as we have seen, *cantus*

---

[354] Pr. JosqMT II, 77.   [355] *Ibid.,* I, 105.

[356] *Ibid.,* I, 82; MaldR XVI, 47.

[357] Pr. JosqMT I, 12 (= ParrishM, 60), 51, 59 (= PubAPTM XVI, 338), 95 (= PubAPTM XVI, 377), respectively.

[358] Cf. CW XXIII, 2. For the plainsong on which Josquin's setting is based, *see* JosqMT I, 173. Another Gospel motet of Josquin's, *In principio erat verbum* (JosqMT III, 106; CW XXIII, 4), includes a free paraphrase of the Gospel Tone in Liber, 107.

[359] Further about it, *see* UrJP, 26f.

firmi in long notes are still found. *Huc me sydereo—Plangent eum*[360] presents another such *cantus.* Here the plainsong[361] is given forth three times, each repetition being in time-values shorter than those that prevailed before. Josquin is fond of tenors whose texts, like that of the tenor in this motet, differ from the text shared by the other voices but comment on it. *Lectio Actuum Apostolorum*[361a] provides a variant: while the other voices tell of the descent of the Holy Ghost and the gift of tongues, as recounted in Acts II, the tenor sings as *cantus firmus* the antiphon, *Dum complerentur,*[362] whose brief text is, with slight change, a part of this biblical passage. The tenor of the five-part *Missus est Gabriel*[363] has the same words as the other voices, but nevertheless alludes to them, symbolically, through its melody, which is the tenor of Busnois's *A une dame j'ai fait veu.* Both of these motets, like *Huc me sydereo,* have their *cantus* in long notes. In the celebrated *Ave verum,*[364] in three *partes,* the rhythmic treatment of the tenor, which has the plainsong,[365] is mainly like that of the other voices. This piece has the special feature that the first two *partes* are each subdivided into a duo followed by a trio, the latter repeating the music (but not the text) of the duo and notably changing the effect by means of the added voice. In *Virgo prudentissima,*[366] the *cantus firmus* is, somewhat amusingly, modified at the words *"ut sol,"* the original notes being replaced by new ones whose solmisation names correspond with the text syllables; the new notes are imitated in the other voices. The triple motet, *O bone et dulcis Domine Jesu—Pater noster—Ave Maria,*[367] has two simultaneously sounding *cantus firmi.* The tenor presents the plainsong for the *Pater noster,* while the bass sings the melody of the *Ave Maria,* at first strictly, then freely. Josquin particularly liked to treat a single *cantus firmus* in canon. The canon on *Circumdederunt me,* which served in *Nimphes, nappés,* was a particular favorite of his (cf. p. 235). It reappears in the six-part motets *Sic Deus dilexit* and *Christus mortuus,*[368] and it is striking that the melody was later used by Gombert (though not in canon) in his lament on the death of Josquin (cf. p. 305). The melody does not derive from one appearing in the present Roman chant-books, but from one peculiar to the Sarum use.[369] This tenor, with its grim text, is among those employed by Josquin to comment on the words of the other parts.

---

360 Pr. JosqMT II, 11.   361 Cf. Liber, 735.   361a Pr. JosqMT II, 99.   362 Cf. Liber, 884.
363 Pr. JosqMT II, 89.
364 Pr. JosqMT I, 48; *pars I* also in PubAPTM XVI, 240; EC, *Partie I,* III, 1266.
365 Liber, 1856.   366 Pr. JosqMT I, 133.   367 *Ibid.,* I, 85.
368 Pr. in CommB VIII, 8, 11, respectively. The canon serves also in another Josquin motet *a 6* that reaches us with two different texts; *see* CreAC, 106f, 124ff.
369 Printed in *Manuale ad usum celebris Ecclesie Sarisburiensis . . . per Desiderium Maheu* (1526), fol. 117. It may be found in a modern ed., but with English text only, in G. H. Palmer, *The musick for the mass for the dead adapted to the English text from the Sarum Manuale* (1902; 2nd ed., 1930), 12. It is interesting to note that the tenor of Josquin's *Ave nobilissima* (JosqMT II, 29) likewise draws on a Sarum melody (*see* FrereA II, 418).

EXAMPLE 50. Opening of the *Circumdederunt me* canon used several
times by Josquin as a *cantus firmus* (transcr. from *Sic Deus
dilexit* in *Thesaurus musicus, Tomus tertius,* Montanus and
Neuber, 1564).

The canon used as a *cantus firmus* in *Ut Phoebi radiis* [370] is an elaborate
solmisation pun. The lines of the poem open successively, with *ut, ut re,
ut re mi,* etc., until the whole *ut . . la* series is achieved; stanza 2, beginning
its lines with *la, la sol, la sol fa,* etc., reverses the procedure. The syllables are
so combined with the rest of the text as to produce meaningful Latin, and
Josquin, of course, sets them with their musical equivalents. The bass, which is
the *dux* of the canon in *pars I,* is kept in the natural hexachord; the tenor,
which is the *dux* in *pars II,* in the soft hexachord.

Josquin's liking for canon, so often evident in his chansons and Masses,
naturally led him to compose still other canon-motets than those already
mentioned incidentally in discussions of other motet types. The six-part *In
nomine Jesu* [371] presents double canon throughout its length against two free
voices. On the other hand, a canon at the close of *Ave Maria . . . Virgo serena*
is so simple in its effect as to be almost folklike. Apparently he wrote canon
as readily as Bach wrote fugue and was no more motivated by pedantry in
using his favorite device than was Bach. Each man merely employed a technical medium particularly suited to his genius.

Glareanus gives as a motet of Josquin's an *O Jesu fili David,*[372] in which
the superius and tenor sing in canon a melody identical with the German
folk song, *Wohlauf, gut g'sell, von hinnen.* The theorist refers to the melody
as being taken from a German and French folk song. Actually, the "motet" is
a *contrafactum* (by Glareanus?), since the piece had been published (with an
attribution to Josquin) in *Canti B* as a polyphonic chanson, *Coment peult
haver joye.* Whether the text of the tune was originally French or German
is unknown. *O Virgo Genitrix* [373] is another chanson turned into a motet,

[370] Pr. JosqMT I, 110; cf. DaT, 69f. *Illibata Dei Virgo* (cf. p. 228) also has a tenor made of
solmisation syllables; the figure *la-mi-la* is given in the soft hexachord, alternately untransposed
and once transposed. For some other Josquin motets with monophonic *cantus firmi, see* JosqMT I,
24, 27, 29, 31, 33, 70; PubAPTM VI, 36. For others with *cantus firmi* in canon, *see* JosqMT I,
147; II, 42; CW XXIII, 12; also the *Alma Redemptoris Mater* discussed near the top of p. 254.
[371] Pr. PubAPTM VI, 32.
[372] Pr. CW XXX, 5; HawkH II, 467; PubAPTM XVI, 316.
[373] Pr. *ibid.,* VI, 83.

the music being that of *Plusieurs regrets* (cf. p. 233). *Tulerunt Dominum meum* presents another instance of text substitution, this piece being musically the same as *pars I* of *Lugebat David Absalon,* printed in 1564 by Montanus and Neuber.[374] *Lugebat . . .* is in genuine writing *a 8.*

Another Josquin motet on David and Absalom, *Absalon fili mi,*[375] is notable for its remarkable, twice-stated setting of the words, *"sed descendam in infernum plorans."* This may be analyzed (in modern terminology) as presenting a series of five major chords whose roots progress by (theoretically) descending fifths, but with certain interpolations. These interpolations take place after the first three chords in the series and in each instance present the relative minor of the preceding chord.[376] Near the beginning of this powerful and dramatic motet, a suspension on a major seventh, which would obviously sound quite harsh inserted in the typical sound-context of the period, helps to establish a mood of lamentation; this mood is enhanced by the presence of numerous melodic minor seconds. It has been held that Josquin at times used the strongly dissonant suspensions on both the major seventh and the minor second with expressive purpose.[377] The latter species appears in *Ave Christe, immolate.*[378]

Josquin appears not to have written motets in *aBcB* form, but he does make some use of identical musical endings to fresh text. In the four-voiced *Qui velatus facie fuisti,* in six *partes,* the endings of *partes I* and *II* are musically alike, as are those of *partes IV* and *VI.*[379] There are other long Josquin motets in many *partes,* e.g., *Vultum tuum deprecabuntur.*[380] The number of *partes* here is seven, *pars V* being *Mente tota,* which achieved fame individually; it exists in seven sources without its companions, and Masses were based on it by such later composers as Févin and Willaert. *Vultum . . .* is especially rich in examples of paired imitation, which is used in it in several different ways: (1) with the second voice of each pair imitating the first, so that all have basically the same material (meas. 124ff, 569ff; in certain other works, e.g., *Dominus regnavit,* this procedure is modified so as to involve two identical canons); (2) with each pair having two different melodies, the paired voices in some instances entering simultaneously (meas. 68ff, 221ff), in some succes-

---

[374] *Tulerunt . . .* is pr. in CW XXIII, 22. The comments *ibid.,* 3, and in AmbG III, 224 (fn.), are incorrect.

[375] Pr. (in different keys, these in turn differing from the key of Ex. 23 mentioned in the next fn.) in PubAPTM VI, 57; OH II, 77.

[376] Cf. LowC, 24f (which includes a discussion of the key signature and clefs), 55, Ex. 23; CreV, 114f. When LowC, 25, applies the term "modulation" to the series of chords, it is done with a special connotation; cf. *ibid.,* 15f.

[377] Cf. AmbG III, 214, 301.

[378] Pr. CW XVIII, 8; CommB VIII, 1; BordA, *Motets,* I, 41.

[379] The motet is printed in JosqMT I, 41. *Pars VI* (*Christum ducem*), which constitutes a sequence motet by itself (cf. p. 252), exists independently also. Its formal relation to *pars IV* would argue in favor of its being an integral portion of *Qui velatus* (but *see* UrJP, 28f, *contra*).

[380] Pr. JosqMT I, 117.

sively (meas. 468ff); (3) with a second statement in which the upper melody remains the same as it was before but the lower melody is inverted (the original time-interval of one measure between the voices, moreover, being replaced by simultaneous entries; meas. 358ff). In addition, we have found elsewhere (4) imitation with the melody that entered first in pair 1 entering second in pair 2 (cf. p. 231), and (5) imitation employed in such a manner as to produce double counterpoint (cf. p. 254). Some of these methods are abundantly represented in Josquin's work as a whole. Imitation in pairs is clearly an earmark of his style, but he applies it with the variety of a great artist; he does not allow a characteristic to degenerate into a mannerism.

In striking contrast to his writing in imitation is Josquin's almost purely chordal writing in such motets as *O Domine Jesu Christe* and *Tu solus, qui facis mirabilia.*[381] In both, *fermata*-marked block-chords recur—frequently in *Tu solus.* Although only *pars I* of this motet is incorporated in Josquin's *Missa D'ung aultre amer* (cf. p. 245), *pars II* likewise introduces material from Ockeghem's chanson. *Pars I*, like Weerbecke's *Verbum caro*, was reworked into one of the pieces in Petrucci's second book of *Laude.*[382] *O Domine* and *Tu solus* show that Josquin possessed a fine feeling for chordal color and harmonic effect, even if he did not indulge it to the same extent as, for example, Palestrina was to do.

Conflicts of accentuation in simultaneously sounding voices, moderately but tellingly used by Josquin, appear with striking effect in his *Benedicite omnia opera Domini,*[383] largely, though not solely, as the result of passages in canon at a distance of one time-unit. Such conflicts are delicately employed also in *Ecce tu pulchra es, amica mea.*[384]

Josquin's prevailingly binary rhythm is provided with contrast, in many pieces, by a section in ternary rhythm, this often occurring toward the end and being followed, in many instances, by a return to the original meter. A different kind of play between the two meters is illustrated by *Magnus es tu, Domine,*[385] the first *pars* of which occurs notated in three sources in binary rhythm, in three others in ternary. The difference, however, is more visual than aural: the first group of sources doubles the values and makes a binary measure of each of the three time-units constituting a measure in the second group; the rhythm is still actually *di tre battute. Magnus es tu* has an ascending leap of a minor seventh on the last utterance of *"supernorum"* ("lying on high"), a leap which even a word like this would be unable to justify in the restrained style of Palestrina.[386] Other intervals excluded from his style, but

---

[381] Pr. *ibid.,* 35 (1st 3 *partes* also in ScherG, 58), 56 (*pars I* also in JosqMS II, 131), respectively.
[382] Cf. JepI, lxvii, 40.   [383] Pr. JosqMT III, 86; CommB VI, 66.
[384] Pr. JosqMT II, 1; CW XVIII, 4.
[385] Pr. JosqMT I, 88–94; PubAPTM XVI, 221; *pars II* (*Tu pauperum refugium*) also in BesN, 12; HAM, 92. The piece is ascribed to Josquin in most sources; but *see* JosqMT, *Bundel III,* xiv.
[386] For another minor seventh, *see* JosqMT I, 87, meas. 63.

present on rare occasions in Josquin's, include the minor tenth [387] and major sixth.[388] Sometimes,[389] after a leap of an octave, Josquin continues in the same direction, even though no break is present between the end of one word or phrase and the beginning of another.

Josquin's treatment of mode occasionally produces unusual effects. Glareanus writes that the composer often does not hesitate to close a work, which is in other respects Aeolian, with an Ionian cadence, and he prints a canon *a 2* by Josquin as a case in point.[390] Most of *Memor esto* is squarely in the Dorian mode, but each of the 2 *partes* ends with a Phrygian cadence, the first with a plagal extension. (Such extensions were to become quite common; evidently composers felt that the Phrygian cadence by itself was somewhat lacking in finality.) Glareanus observes [391] that while, in the *Missa Gaudeamus,* Josquin transposes into the Mixolydian mode an Introit melody originally in the Dorian mode, he concludes it in the Aeolian.

While Josquin treats mode freely, he shows a growing feeling for tonality in the modern sense. In a number of compositions, e.g., *Germinavit radix Jesse,*[392] the initial notes assigned to the various voices in the first point of imitation constitute, if combined, the final chord; or its dominant, as in *Tribulatio et angustia;* or its subdominant, as in *Qui velatus facie fuisti—* the third from the root being omitted in all these instances. However, such tonal relationship is by no means always present. Thus, in *O admirabile commercium,*[393] the final chord—unusual, at the time, for its inclusion of the third—consists of B-flat, b-flat, d', and f'', but the initial notes of the first point of imitation are, in order of entry, a', d', a, and d. Moreover, the initial notes do not always add up to a triad: thus, in *Rubum quem viderat Moyses,* in which the final chord comprises A, a, e', and c'' (sharp?), the initial notes are d, g, g'', and c'.

The esteem in which Josquin was still held long after his death, at least in some quarters, is indicated by the following passage from Cosimo Bartoli's *Ragionamenti accademici,* printed at Venice in 1567:

I know well that Ockeghem was, so to speak, the first who in these times redis- *covered music, which had almost entirely died out—not in other wise than Dona-* *tello, who in his times rediscovered sculpture—and that Josquin, Ockeghem's* *pupil, may be said to have been, in music, a prodigy of nature, as our Michelangelo* *Buonarotti has been in architecture, painting, and sculpture; for, as there has not* *thus far been anybody who in his compositions approaches Josquin, so Michel-*

---

[387] *See ibid.,* I, 67, meas. 301; II, 26 (= CW XVIII, 28f) on *"scrutator."*

[388] *See ibid.,* I, 2, meas. 46; 141, meas. 25f. A descent of a major seventh is followed by an ascent of a major sixth on *"lucifer,"* ibid., 7, meas. 66f, but in a voice that may not be by Josquin; cf. fn. 349a.

[389] E.g., in PubAPTM XVI, 196, meas. 11 of *pars II.*

[390] GlarD, 257; PubAPTM XVI, 204.   [391] GlarD, 164; PubAPTM XVI, 121.

[392] Pr. JosqMT I, 31.   [393] *Ibid.,* 24.

angelo, among all those who have been active in these his arts, is still alone and without a peer; both one and the other have opened the eyes of all those who delight in these arts or are to delight in them in the future.[394]

Brumel

Antoine Brumel—whose *Missa de Beata Virgine,* as we have seen, is reported by Glareanus to have been written in competition with Josquin's—became *heurier* of the Cathedral at Chartres in 1483 and was a member of the choir at Laon in 1497. He was *maître des enfants* and canon at Notre Dame in Paris, 1498–1500. Perhaps he moved direct from Paris to Lyons, where he served the Italian Duke of Sora. In 1505, Alfonso I of Ferrara, who was this Duke's brother-in-law, sought to engage Brumel as his *maestro di cappella* for life. We know from a letter of Brumel's that he eventually became *maestro* at Ferrara, but there is no reliable evidence to show when this happened.[394a] A Jachet Brumel, who is conjectured to have been his son, was organist at the court in 1543.[394b] Glareanus, by stating that Antoine wrote the *Missa de Beata Virgine "in extrema . . . senecta,"* indicates that the composer lived to a ripe old age. The same theorist is of the opinion that Brumel excelled more through industry than natural gifts, but actually his music is often of superlative quality.[395]

Sixteen complete Masses by Brumel survive. His *Missa de Beata Virgine* [396] and Josquin's employ different chants in their Sanctus and Agnus settings, Brumel's being based on Gregorian Masses IX and XVII, respectively, both of Josquin's on Mass IV (cf. p. 242). In other sections, the borrowed plainsong is alike in both Masses. The selection used by Brumel is the one that was to appear in the Medicean edition of the Chant (cf. p. 458, fn. 39) [396a] and must therefore have had a certain currency; it differs only slightly from a selection—whose frequent appearance in later polyphonic *de Beata Virgine* Masses seems to indicate that it was even more widely favored—in which Sanctus XVII replaces Sanctus IX. Brumel embellishes or simplifies the Chant melodies and handles them rather freely. At times he employs old-fashioned *cantus-firmus* technique, with the borrowed melody in the tenor in long notes, at other times the plainsong is paraphrased in the superius only. At still others, it is paraphrased in both the superius and the tenor in imitation; in certain passages, it is imitated in all the voices. Whether the tenor or the superius is the leading voice with regard to the plainsong is, on occasion, dubious. In short, the Mass employs both the *cantus-firmus* and the paraphrase techniques. The imitation is sometimes in pairs, but rhythmically it tends

---

[394] For the Italian text, *see* StraM VI, 84; EinIM I, 21.
[394a] *See* MQ XLI (1955), 383f.   [394b] Cf. StraM VI, 102.
[395] Further biographical data in PirB, 349f; PirH, 232f; PirGM, 165; HewO, 73; StraM VI, 95ff; MGG II, 398 ff. *See also* GlarD, 152, 456; PubAPTM XVI, 114, 412.
[396] Pr. MMRF VIII, 1.   [396a] As pointed out to me by Mr. Lloyd Biggle.

to be less strict than Josquin's. Troping, present of course in the Gloria, is applied also in the Benedictus. Despite Glareanus' preference for the Josquin Mass, this one is likewise a fine work, its last three movements being particularly beautiful. A nameless Mass,[397] in Bologna Lic. mus. Q 19, likewise has no one theme all the way through, but not primarily because different Chant melodies are drawn upon: the work is a composite. The Kyrie comes from another nameless Mass in Rome, Bibl. Ap. Vat., MS Pal. Lat. 1982, and the Gloria and Credo from a *Missa Descendi*.[397a] The tenor of the Sanctus and Agnus is the melody that serves in both the Sanctus of plainsong Mass VIII and in the antiphon *O quam suavis*,[397b] and these sections perhaps come from a lost *O quam suavis* Mass of Brumel's. Since the melody appears in his Agnus as well as in his Sanctus and since, as pointed out on pp. 29, 66, it was not normal for a chant for one part of the Ordinary to serve in a polyphonic setting of another part, it is likely that Brumel thought of his tenor as deriving from the *O quam suavis* rather than from the plainsong Sanctus, even though the association of words and notes in his own Sanctus setting is close to that of the chant. The tenor of Brumel's *L'Homme armé* Mass [398] carries the popular melody in sustained notes. The *cantus firmus* is treated freely, and new material is interpolated. At times the old tune appears, embellished, in anticipatory imitation in the other voices, but in the main these are independent of the tenor. Brumel's Mass *Je n'ay dueil,* surviving also with the designation *Missa festivale*,[399] is based on Agricola's chanson of the former title. The four-part texture of this Mass is varied by sections *a 2* and *a 3*. Among Brumel's remaining Masses are the *Missa Et ecce terraemotus* for as many as twelve voices,[400] the *Missa super Dringhs*,[401] whose name (given by Glareanus, at one point, in Greek letters) has not yet been fully explained; and others based on *Victimae paschali;* [402] *Bergerette savoyenne;* [403] *Bon temps,* an anonymous chanson in *Canti B;* [404] and *A l'ombre d'un buyssonnet*,[405] the melody being the one used by Josquin for his chanson in *Canti C.* The last of these, *a 4,* is notated in two parts only, the other two voices duplicating these in canon. Brumel's *Missa pro defunctis* is

---

[397] Pr. MaldR X, 35; XI, 3. For the Kyrie I of another nameless Mass, in old notation, *see* RoediN, 82.

[397a] The plainsong source of the *Descendi* tenor is pr. in LiberR, 252. Cf. RubIL, 75f.

[397b] Pr. Liber, 38, 917, respectively.

[398] Pr. BrumO I; Kyrie pr. GomO, Supp., 45.

[399] 2 extracts from the Credo, also the Sanctus and Agnus, pr. in AmbG V, 146ff.

[400] For a brief description, *see* SchmidtgG, 236.

[401] The opening of the Credo is pr. in WagG, 176; the *Crucifixus* in BuH III, 529; *Pleni* and Benedictus in PubAPTM XVI, 412ff (the latter also in ScherG, 631); one of the Agnus settings in PubAPTM XVI, 414. PubAPTM XVI, 308, gives still another Benedictus—a canon *a 2*—as coming from this Mass, but no such attribution is made in GlarD, 346; the same piece is presented as an ex. in Gregor Faber, *Musices practicae erotematum . . .* , 82 (also pr. WeckC, 112).

[402] Kyrie I, in old notation, in RoediN, 77.

[403] It is just possible that Brumel had Josquin's setting in mind when he wrote this Mass and not merely the tune in Bibl. nat. fr. 12744; cf. BorPM, 155ff.

[404] Kyrie I, in RoediN, 77; the chanson in ObrMS IV, 126.

[405] Cf. FeinK, 53; TierE, 240.

unusual for its period in that it includes a polyphonic setting of the *Dies irae*.[406]

Brumel's *Laudate Dominum* is one of the earliest motet-settings of a psalm that can be given an approximate date (cf. p. 246). While Petrucci included Josquin's psalm, *Memor esto,* in the same publication of 1514 in which he printed *Laudate Dominum,* the latter piece can be traced back further to 1507, the date of MS Cappella Sistina 42, in which the work is likewise preserved.[407] This impressive composition contains several points of imitation (some in pairs), changes of meter, and instances of conflicting accentuation, produced by canon at a time-distance of one beat. Brumel's *Regina coeli* [408] is a lovely paraphrase of the Marian antiphon, the melody being given to the tenor but being made to permeate the other voices also. Paraphrase and permeation of the texture by the plainsong are again present in the *Lauda Sion,*[408a] in which Brumel provides settings for the odd-numbered verses only. The *Mater Patris,*[409] upon which Josquin's Mass of the same name is based (cf. p. 240), is a song-motet; among the sources in which it survives is not only the *Odhecaton* but a MS at Munich that contains an autograph of Glareanus.[410] The short and simple *Sicut lilium,*[411] with its clear-cut phrases, is interesting partly for the unmistakable resemblance between its opening and that of Josquin's *Planxit autem David.*[412] *O Domine Jesu Christe,*[413] which likewise contains several instances of simultaneous cadences in all parts, is nevertheless richer polyphonically. In a textless piece *a 8,*[414] presented by Faber as an example in his *Musices practicae erotematum Libri II* (1553), each voice is in a different Tone.

The superius of Ockeghem's *Fors seulement l'attente* serves as the tenor of a chanson that survives with conflicting ascriptions to Brumel and Agricola, but is undoubtedly by Brumel.[415] The piece contains interesting suspensions of the seventh and ninth from the bass, with delayed resolutions.

EXAMPLE 51. Close of *Du tout plongiet—Fors seulement*—Brumel (complete piece in ObrWW, 85; GiesS, 16; MaldP XXI, 28).

[406] Further on Brumel's Masses, *see* PirH, 233f; AmbG III, 243f.

[407] Cf. HabV, 19, 119. *Pars* I of the motet is pr. in MaldR XI, 4; ForkA II, 629; KiesT, 48. I am indebted to Dr. Strunk for having brought Brumel's priority to my attention.

[408] Pr. AmbG V, 172.   [408a] Pr. SmijO, 161.

[409] Pr. HewO, 351; SmijO, 138; JosqMS III, 29.

[410] Cf. HewO, 157, 111, in the light of WolffH I, 455. Further about this motet, *see* DiscC.

[411] Pr. RoksT, 44.   [412] Cf. *ibid.,* xxii.   [413] Pr. MaldR II, 43.   [414] Pr. LafE II, 121.

[415] Cf. GomO, 19ff. The piece is pr. after Regensburg, Cod. Pernner, in ObrWW, 85; after St. Gall 461 in GiesS, 16; and after Brussels, Bibl. roy. No. 228 (where it is bitextual), in MaldP XXI, 27, with an unjustifiable ascription to la Rue; cf. BorI, 121 (No. 17); ReT, 103f (No. 334).

Brumel's *Vray dieu d'amours* [415a] works out, partly in agreeable points of imitation *a 3*, the *Vray dieu d'amours* melody that occurs twice in Bibl. nat. fr. 12744, with somewhat different texts (cf. p. 206). The tenor of Brumel's *Jamès que là ne peut estre* first renders the opening phrase of *Je ne vis oncques* in normal form and then presents it backward.[416] Brumel's occasional liking for clear-cut phrase structure is expressed in the chordal *Tous les regrets*.[417] A setting of *T'Andernaken* shows him overusing sequences and a repeated rhythmic figure.[418] But, despite such occasional weaknesses, Brumel, though evidently not the equal of Josquin, Obrecht, or la Rue, is one of the better composers of his generation.

Eloy; Prioris

The literary works in which Brumel is mentioned in the company of Alexander Agricola and Josquin (among others) include not only Crétin's *Déploration* on the death of Ockeghem, but also the *Livre de la Deablerie* [419] by Eloy d'Amerval, printed at Paris in 1508. In this poem, Satan and Lucifer exult over the prospect of future evil deeds and are opposed in a long passage that includes the names of great musicians of the time. After a verbal bow to Dunstable and Dufay,[420] Eloy lists

> *Robinet de la Magdalaine,*
> *Binchoiz, Fedé, Jorges* [421] *et Hayne,*
> *Le Rouge, Alixandre, Okeghem,*
> *Bunoiz, Basiron, Barbingham,*
> *Louyset, Mureau, Prioris,*
> *Jossequin, Brumel, Tintoris.*

Eloy was himself a composer as well as a poet. While *magister puerorum* at Sainte-Croix in Orleans, he wrote a series of French and Latin motets on the liberation of Orleans by Joan of Arc. These were performed on May 8, 1483, the 54th anniversary of the original thanksgiving procession. The music, unfortunately, is lost, but the texts survive.[422] Eloy later served at St. Bartholomew's in Béthune. His five-part *Missa Dixerunt discipuli* is polytextual, the *cantus firmus,* which presents both the text and the music of the antiphon, *Dixerunt discipuli,* being sung by the tenor while the other voices sing the words of the Ordinary.[423]

Likewise mentioned by both Crétin and Amerval is the Netherlander Johannes Prioris. Active for some years in Italy, he was organist at St. Peter's

[415a] Pr. GiesS, 64.   [416] Cf. PirH, 234.

[417] Pr. with substitute Flemish text in MaldP X, 45; cf. BorI, 126; ReT, 94 (No. 155).

[418] Cf. GomO, 73.

[419] Ed. by C. F. Ward and pr. in *University of Iowa Studies, Humanistic Studies* II (1923).

[420] Ward, *op. cit.,* 226, says "du Say"; but *see* BorD, 76, fn. 3.

[421] Jorges = Georget de Brelles (cf. p. 227).   [422] *See* further BrenPM.

[423] For the antiphon, *see* Liber, 1748; for the Kyrie and Agnus of the Mass, *see* KiesG, App. xx, xxii. Further about Eloy, *see* BrenEA.

in 1490 and, in 1507, was *maître de chapelle* to Louis XII. He was still alive in 1512.[424] The only Mass of his surviving in an old print (1532) is a Requiem *a 4*,[425] but other Masses reach us in MS. Throughout the polyphonic period, the Requiem, as far as its basic plan is concerned, continued to be what it had been in Ockeghem's day: a part-setting of the corresponding Gregorian melodies. Of the five Requiem sections set by Ockeghem, Prioris omits the Tract, but he adds music for the Sanctus, Agnus, and Communion. His Gradual, like Ockeghem's, is the *Si ambulem,* and it paraphrases the same Chant melody; otherwise Prioris adapts Gregorian material now normal in the Mass for the Dead—employing the Sanctus melody, however, in an early version.[426] Except for the intonations, which are assigned to the tenor, the plainsong lies in the superius throughout, but is imitated in the lower voices, mainly in the verse of the Gradual, the Offertory, and the Communion. A portion of the Gradual is *a 2,* but elsewhere all four voices are kept active. Prioris varies repetitions in the chant felicitously and provides them with different countermelodies. Two Magnificat settings of his in Tone 4 and one in Tone 6 [427] reveal quite free elaboration of the Gregorian formulas; settings are provided for the even-numbered verses, it obviously being intended that the singers are to render the odd-numbered ones in plainsong. *Dulcis amica Dei,*[428] a little song-motet that survives anonymous in several sources and was evidently a favorite in its day, is shown by the ascription in Cambridge, Magdalene College, MS Pepys 1760, to be by Prioris. *Mon cueur et moi,*[429] an attractive *rondeau cinquain,* survives in Florence, Conserv. B. 2439, and in three of the great *chansonniers:* the Wolfenbüttel, Laborde, and Copenhagen MSS; *Mon cueur a demy,*[430] a *rondeau quatrain,* is found in the Dijon and Laborde MSS. Prioris, like Compère, must be one of the latest figures represented in these collections. A piece [431] provided, in the Laborde MS, with the Italian incipit, *Consomo la vita mya,* but with no further words, occurs also in MS Pepys 1760 with two lines of verse that reappear in a *strambotto* text, included in a quite different setting [432] in Antico's *Canzoni . . . et frottole Libro tertio.*[433]

De Orto; de Opitiis; Ghiselin

Marbriano de Orto (Ortho, etc.; d. 1529), was a singer in the Papal Chapel at the time of Prioris' service there, his name being listed in the rolls from 1484

[424] Further biographical data in EitQ VIII, 71; PirNB, 252; Grove IV, 256.
[425] I thank Dr. C. W. Fox for having loaned me his MS score of this work.
[426] About which *see* WagE III, 456 (incl. fn. 3).
[427] Verse 2 of each of these 3 is given in old notation in RoediN, 33 (2 exx.), 35.
[428] Pr. VincM, 681; WagG, 246; RoksT, 15; MaldR XVI, 44 (somewhat lengthened and with an added 4th part, as in Cambrai MS 124).
[429] Pr. JepK, 34; BushL, 73 (with facsimile).   [430] Pr. DrozT, 74.
[431] Pr. BukMR, 211; RoksT, 52; VincM, 682.   [432] Pr. SCMA IV, 33. Cf. BukMR, 210.
[433] Further about Prioris, *see* AmbG III, 256 (but in the light of EitQ VIII, 71); RoediN, 16; BorI, 123 (No. 20).

to 1494. He became a canon at Comines in 1487 and dean of St. Gertrude at Nivelles in 1489. He was engaged as a singer to Philip the Handsome in 1505 and accompanied him to Spain in 1506. Archduke Charles, the future Charles V, in 1515 made de Orto his first chaplain.[434] Petrucci printed a book of five Masses by de Orto (1505), a setting of the Lamentations (1506), a *Kyrie de Beata Virgine* (in the *Fragmenta Missarum,* 1505), motets, and chansons. Works of his survive in MS also.

The Masses of 1505 are based on the plainsong *Missa Dominicalis* and on chansons: the *Missa J'ay pris amours*[435] has two settings of the Credo; the *cantus firmus* of the *Missa La bella se sied* is that of Dufay's chanson;[436] the *Missa Petita camuseta*[437] is built on the same five-note motif that is imitated by all the voices at the beginning of Okeghem's chanson. In this last-named Mass, for example, the Agnus III assigns the motif to the tenor four times in stepwise descending sequence, the time-values of each appearance being half those of its predecessor, the theme beginning in long notes, in old-fashioned *cantus-firmus* style. In his *L'Homme armé* Mass,[438] also included in the 1505 print, de Orto usually assigns the popular melody to the tenor, but in the Credo it is entrusted to the bass (here labelled *bassus tenorizans*), and the superius and altus are at times given it also, anticipatory imitation being brought into play.

De Orto is one of the composers who set Dido's *Dulces exuviae.*[439] His four-part *Ave Maria,*[440] a song-motet, opens the *Odhecaton.* It bears only a fleeting resemblance to the Gregorian antiphon (at the words "*Dominus tecum*"). (The chant is more easily discernible in his setting of the Tract, *Domine non secundum peccata nostra.*[440a]) The *Odhecaton* contains also de Orto's chanson, *Venus tu m'a pris,*[441] and the composer is represented like-wise in *Canti B* and *Canti C.*[441a]

The young Archduke Charles made a festive entry into Antwerp in 1515 in the company of Maximilian, and on this occasion Benedictus de Opitiis wrote two works, *Sub tuum praesidium* and *Summae laudis, o Maria* in honor of the grandfather and grandson. The works were printed from wood blocks in a sumptuously illustrated album.[442] The composer functioned as

---

[434] Further biographical data in DoorM, 152; PirH, 214f; HewO, 94f. Perhaps de Orto's surname came from the small town of Ortho in Belgium; cf. PirH, 215, fn. 1.

[435] Agnus II pr. PubAPTM XVI, 279.

[436] Cf. StaD, 10. (This is a different melody from the *La belle se siet* in the Bayeux MS; cf. GéroB, 106f.)

[437] Kyrie I in PirH, 219; in old notation in RoediN, 80; Agnus III in AmbG V, 198.

[438] Pr. MPLSER, *Ser. I,* I. Further about de Orto's Masses, *see* esp. PirH, 215ff.

[439] Cf. BurbE, 24.

[440] Pr. HewO, 219; AmbG V, 193 (cf. BoerC, 44f).

[440a] Pr. ObrMS IV, 101 (cf. SmijMC, 193f). For the chant, *see* Liber, 527.

[441] Pr. HewO, 401.

[441a] For other secular pieces, *see* GiesS, 30, 42.

[442] Facsimile in OpitiisL; modern ed. in OpitiisS. *See also* BorDO; BurgL; VerhM; MGG I, 1631ff.

organist at Our Lady in Antwerp from c. 1514 to 1516, when he left for England. There is no trace of him after 1522, although efforts have been made, apparently without justification, to identify him with the Benedictus Ducis whose career in Germany is traceable from 1532 on and whom we shall find again in Chapter 13.

The Verbonnet mentioned in Crétin's *Déploration* is the same person as Johannes Ghiselin. Two of the five works printed by Petrucci in a collection of Masses by "Joannes Ghiselin" (1503) appear elsewhere under the name Verbonnet; [443] moreover, a setting of *Een vrowelic wesenn* in Florence, Conserv., B. 2439, bears the ascription "Jo Gysling, alias Verbonnet." [444] The composer was at the court of Ferrara in 1491, 1503, and 1535. His Masses are based on chansons; e.g., the *Missa La belle se sied* [445] draws on the same melody as does de Orto's, the *Missa Je n'ay dueil* uses motifs from Ockeghem's and Agricola's chansons.[446] Ghiselin's motets include a *Vita dulcedo* (the text taken from the *Salve Regina*), in which the superius recalls *Je ne vis oncques;* [447] his *Tota scriptura* [448] is distinguished for the way in which it is evolved out of a small amount of motivic material. Among Ghiselin's chansons there is a four-part *Fors seulement l'attente,*[449] in which the tenor derives first from Ockeghem's tenor, then from Ockeghem's superius. Ghiselin's setting of *Een vrowelic wesenn* has Barbireau's bass in the lowest voice. A piece by Ghiselin in Florence, Bibl. naz., MS Panc. 27, is of special interest in that it incorporates the *Spagna* tune.[450] The textless, perhaps instrumental, three-part *La Alfonsina* [450a] may be named after Duke Alfonso I of Ferrara (cf. p. 190). Midway in the composition there is a striking passage in which the superius descends a tenth stepwise, mostly in long notes, while the lively lower voices proceed in sequence, etc.[451]

Pierre de la Rue

Pierre de la Rue (Pierchon, de Vico, Petrus Platensis [451a]), who like Prioris figures in the early history of the polyphonic Requiem, was born in Picardy, perhaps at Tournai. An entry in the Burgundian court accounts for 1477 may apply to him.[452] The first definite date that we have for him is November 17,

[443] Cf. PirP, 52.

[444] SaarB, 133, questions the statement made to this effect by earlier writers; an examination of a microfilm of the MS, however, shows it to be correct.

[445] Kyrie I, in old notation, in RoediN, 82.

[446] Cf. PirH, 224.   [447] *Ibid.*   [448] Pr. RieH II¹, 255.

[449] Pr. GomO, Supp., 16 (with ascription to Ghiselin); GiesS, 10 (with ascription to Verbonnet); cf. GomO, 24. Regarding another *Fors seulement* that may be either Ghiselin's or Josquin's, cf. p. 234.   [450] *See* GomH, 57.   [450a] Pr. HewO, 387; AmbG V, 190; GiesS, 92.

[451] Another ex. by Ghiselin in PubAPTM XVI, 162; BellerM, 67.

[451a] Among still other variants of the name is Petrequin (cf. p. 225), a form that has given rise to the theory that it represents Guillaume Piétrequin of Bordeaux, who would thus be established as another composer of the time; see LesJ, 159. However, it has been shown in RobynsJ, 41 and 149, that this theory is probably incorrect and that the name represents la Rue.

[452] Cf. CW XI, 2.

1492, when he was engaged as a singer by Maximilian. He was in the service of Philip the Handsome from 1496 until the latter's death in 1506, and subsequently in that of Philip's sister, Margaret of Austria, whom Maximilian appointed Regent of the Netherlands in 1507 in behalf of her brother's infant son, the future Charles V; but for a brief gap, Charles continued Margaret as Regent until her death in 1530, although he had been declared of age in 1515. La Rue's employment by Philip and Margaret centred his career at Brussels. However, he twice visited Spain, in 1501-02 and 1505, in Philip's retinue. He is found, in 1510, at Malines,[452a] in the chapel of the ten-year-old Charles. The last two years of the composer's life were spent at Courtrai, where he died in 1518.[453] After his death, Margaret had two richly illuminated MS volumes prepared, one devoted to Masses *a 4* by la Rue, one to Masses *a 5*.[454] His surviving works include over thirty Masses, besides motets, Lamentations, and chansons.

La Rue's Requiem[455] is an outstanding work. The text set by him, like that of the other polyphonic Requiems thus far discussed, varies from the one that later became standard. He provides polyphony for the Introit, Kyrie, Tract, Offertory, Sanctus, Agnus,[455a] and Communion, thus proceeding like both Ockeghem and Prioris with respect to the first, second, and fourth of these; like Ockeghem with respect to the third; and like Prioris with respect to the last three. His Tract, like Ockeghem's, uses the *Sicut cervus* text, not the *Absolve, Domine* text that has since become customary.[456] Gregorian intonations figure in five sections; in all seven, plainsong is polyphonically set in one way or another. In the *Osanna* and Agnus it is treated in *cantus-firmus* fashion; but it is encountered much oftener in very free paraphrase, the derived motifs being at times worked out in imitation. Some sections are *a 4*, some *a 5*. A predilection, shown by la Rue in many works, for introducing occasional short passages *a 2*, is evident here also. The composition is conceived in dark, glowing colors, set forth by the extraordinary use, not only of the lower registers of each voice, but of low voices as well. Several different clef combinations appear. The lowest part is written in the Γ clef and not infrequently descends to B_2-flat; the lowest clef combination is TBar$B\Gamma$. The Tract lies higher. The clef combination SATB, the highest in the whole Mass, is here employed, as also—appropriately, as far as word-painting goes —in the Communion (*Lux aeterna*).

452a The city had had a vigorous musical life in the 15th century; cf. DoorCM.

453 Concerning la Rue's last years at Courtrai and his will, see CaulM, 39ff. Further biographical data in DoorM, 155f; PirH, 228; RobynsJ, 13ff.

454 For a facsimile, in color, of the Kyrie of the *Missa O gloriosa Margaretha*, from one of these MSS, *see* SmijA, opp. p. 152, or BesM, opp. p. 248.   455 Pr. CW XI, 5.

455a La Rue uses the same music for Agnus I and III. CW XI prints Agnus III and II in that order, and fails to give any explanation with regard to the performance of Agnus I.

456 The editor of CW XI seems not to have recognized the Tract function of the *Sicut cervus* or the presence of its appropriate chant (cf. Liber, 753). Concerning other relations between la Rue's Requiem and Ockeghem's, *see* OckW II, xxxiif.

The five-part *Missa Ista est speciosa, Missa de Sancta Cruce* and *Missa Pascale* [457] represent the type of Mass in which there is little motivic relationship between the *cantus firmus* and the surrounding polyphony. The *Ista est* melody appears to have been much favored in the 15th century; [458] the *cantus firmus* of the *Missa de Sancta Cruce* is the Introit of the Mass for the Finding of the Holy Cross. [459] In each of these la Rue Masses the *cantus firmus* is decorated in a different way when it is repeated, and such imitation as exists between it and one or another of the surrounding voices is limited to material that appears in the decorative passages. It is difficult to know, at these points, whether the *cantus firmus* is permeating the polyphony or is itself being affected by it. The *Missa Ista est* is rather rich in dissonance: there is an example, interesting for the time, of a retardation in the superius, combined with a simultaneous suspension in the bass, near the beginning of the *Qui tollis*. The *Missa Pascale* uses seven *cantus firmi* taken from music for the Easter season, and while the tenor renders one of these in the first portion of the Credo, the contratenor paraphrases Gregorian Credo I. [460] A *cantus-firmus* melody seems to permeate the polyphony only in the *Christe*. In some passages, notably the *Et resurrexit* there is considerable imitation between the tenor and the other voices, but no *cantus firmus* is present.

In the Masses *Ave Maria, Conceptio tua,* and *De doloribus* [461] the *cantus firmi* permeate the polyphony to such an extent, owing to the frequent use of imitation, that the works at times have the aspect of paraphrase Masses. In the *Missa Ave Maria,* la Rue derives his *cantus firmus* from the opening phrases of the plainsong, which he sometimes presents in long notes, but usually allows to partake of the rhythmic variety of the surrounding polyphony. A touch of symbolism appears in the Credo, at the words *"Et ex Patre natum,"* where the tenor has not only the melody of the *Ave Maria* fragment but also its text. [462] La Rue replaces the conventional treatment of the words *"descendit de coelis"* by a cadence that achieves great beauty through the manner in which the final chord is gradually built up by the several voices.

[457] Pr. in RueM, 37, 164, 103, respectively. Kyrie I of each, in old notation, after MSS at Jena, in RoediN, 1, 26, 8, respectively.

[458] It appears in the superius of an anon. motet preserved in Trent MS 91 (cf. DTO VII, 69, No. 1204) and in the *Glogauer Liederbuch* (cf. EDMR IV, 109, No. 120); also in the tenor of an anon. motet in MS Munich 3154 (cf. SteB, 109).

[459] Liber, 1454.

[460] For 5 of the *cantus firmi, see* Liber 778, 782, 771, 777, and 761; concerning the other 2, *see* RoediN, 9.

[461] Pr. in MMRF VIII, 77; RueM, 7, 71, respectively. The opening Kyries are given in old notation in MMRF VIII, after p. 76; RoediN, 9 (2 items), respectively. The text of the plainsong on which the *Missa Conceptio tua* is based is now altered; cf. Liber, 1627. About the *cantus firmus* of the *Missa de doloribus, see* RoediN, 10.

[462] Further about symbolism in this Mass, *see* BrenP, 21ff. For the prayer version of the plainsong, *see* Liber, 1861; for the antiphon version, *ibid.,* 1679.

EXAMPLE 52. Extract from the *Credo* of the *Missa Ave Maria*—Pierre de la Rue (after MMRF VIII, 100).

La Rue's liking for occasional passages *a 2* is much in evidence in the *Missa Conceptio tua* and *Missa de doloribus*. He has left us two *L'Homme armé* Masses: one containing canons all the way through, except in the duo passages,[463] and one that likewise uses canon, but less consistently.[464] The latter begins and ends with mensuration canons in irregular augmentation. Kyrie I, *Christe,* and Kyrie II each expand one part into two, against free lines, whereas Agnus III expands one part, with notable virtuosity (in view of the mensuration aspect), into four. At various points throughout the Mass the secular song, rhythmically varied and melodically paraphrased, permeates all the four parts. In Agnus I all three lower voices sing the melody, each in its own rhythmic variation. Like Agnus III of this *L'Homme armé* Mass, the *Missa O salutaris hostia* consists of one line expanded canonically into four, only here the whole Mass is so written.[465] Throughout the five-part *Missa de Feria*,[466] tenors I and II, whenever present, sing a canon at the fifth above, except in the Sanctus, where the canon is at the fourth above, while the three other voices present an accompaniment making much use of imitation, sometimes imitating the canon itself.

La Rue's fine *Missa Ave sanctissima Maria* [467] is written for three voices, each being expanded canonically into two. The work, the oldest six-part Mass Ordinary known (but cf. p. 245), is also the first Mass known to use canon *a 6*. It is a parody on a motet similarly written for three voices expanded into six, published in 1534 by Attaingnant, with an attribution to Verdelot.[468]

---

[463] Cf. FeinK, 59. This Mass survives in MS Capp. Sist. 34 and Jena MS 2, being anon. in both according to Dr. Walter Rubsamen. HabV, 13f and 87, in cataloguing the former MS, ascribes the Mass to la Rue on circumstantial but fair evidence; RoediN, 1 (which gives Kyrie I in old notation), in cataloguing the latter MS, again gives an attribution to la Rue, relying on HabV.

[464] Cf. FeinK, 61; Kyrie and *Et incarnatus* pr. GomO, Supp., 36, 39; Kyries I and II also in HAM, 95 (defective in early printings). I am indebted to Dr. Oliver Strunk for lending me his MS score of the whole work.

[465] Cf. FeinK, 59; Kyrie I and *Pleni* in PubAPTM XVI, 402, 188.

[466] Pr. RueM, 195. The tenor of the Credo is based on Gregorian Credo I.

[467] Pr. RueM, 135; better in DPLSER, *Ser. I B,* No. 1; *see also* RoediN, 8, 12.

[468] Motet pr. ScherG, 93; SmijT III, 166; MaldR XVIII, 13. Facsimiles of T and B (after Brus-

The motet survives also in the earlier MS 228 at Brussels. Only on the words *"Patrem omnipotentem factorem coeli"* does la Rue retain exactly the music of the beginning of the motet; here he uses it as an introduction to the rest of the Credo and emphasizes its introductory character by setting it off from what follows by a *fermata* in each part. Elsewhere throughout the Mass the borrowed material is molded to suit the immediate purpose, even (e.g., in Kyrie I) when this involves reversing the order of phrases in the upper voices to achieve chord progressions that are more natural to the mode of the Mass, which is not that of the motet (the Mixolydian replaces the transposed Dorian).[469]

La Rue's *Missa De Sancta Anna* resembles Josquin's *Missa D'ung aultre amer* both by providing a motet in honor of the Sacrament and by having it substitute for a portion of the Sanctus. La Rue's motet is an *O salutaris hostia*,[470] and it replaces *Osanna I*.

An isolated four-part Credo by la Rue, entitled *Patrem L'Amour de moy*,[471] is based on a tune in Bibl. nat. fr. 12744 and in the Bayeux MS,[472] but without treating it in old-fashioned *cantus-firmus* style. There survives, in *Canti C* and other sources, a delightful anonymous four-part chanson, which assigns this melody to the tenor and has the other parts imitate it much of the time. La Rue introduces enough material that is peculiar to this chanson to show that he knew it, but his setting is essentially an imaginative fantasy on the basic monophonic version, as a comparison of the following extract with that version makes clear.[473]

EXAMPLE 53. Extract from the *Patrem L'Amour de moy*—Pierre de la Rue (after MS Cappella Sistina 36, fol. 4ᵛ; transcr. by C. V. Brooks).

---

sels 228) in Marcel Françon, *Albums poétiques de Marguerite d'Autriche* (1934), frontispiece. MaldR ascribes the motet to la Rue, but it is anon. in the source there followed. RubMM, 8, regards the attribution to Verdelot as wrong, on the grounds that he would have been too young for la Rue to base a Mass on a work of his.

469 According to Dr. Walter Rubsamen, the reference in BorI, 70, to a setting *a 10* of this Mass is incorrect; the version catalogued there is actually the one *a 6* mentioned above.

470 Pr. AmbG V, 144; BordA, *Motets*, III, 68. For Kyrie I, in old notation, *see* RoediN, 15, the title of the Mass there being given as *Felix Anna*.

471 Opening section pr. in old notation in RoediN, 18.   472 Cf. p. 206.

473 Further on la Rue's Mass settings, *see* WagG, 166ff; PirH, 230ff. For other Mass movements, *see* AmbG V, 137; SmijO, 123; ScherG, 64 (*Christe* also in PubAPTM XVI, 230); RoediN, *passim* (*see* RoediT, 134f).

Among la Rue's motets is the moving four-part *Vexilla Regis—Passio
Domini.*[474] The second voice sings a text taken from the Passion according to
St. Matthew and consisting of Christ's "My soul is sorrowful unto death:
tarry ye here, and watch with me," preceded and followed by words of the
Evangelist. The music of this voice consists of an adaptation of the appropriate
Gregorian formulas for the Chronista and the Christus.[475] The superius
paraphrases the *Vexilla Regis* sparingly but effectively, and this hymn melody
affects the tenor also; the bass is free. A most eloquent composition results,
for all its brevity. In *Lauda anima mea* (Psalm CXLV [146]),[476] the *Tonus
peregrinus* appears in the tenor at the opening and elsewhere later. Among his
settings of the *Salve Regina,*[477] one [478] is a canon *a 4,* the melody of which contains fragments of the plainsong. A second,[479] also containing such fragments,
is a free fantasy on them. Still another contains, in the superius, passages borrowed from Dufay's *Par le regart* and from *Je ne vis oncques.*[480] There is a
fine balance of different kinds of texture—imitative, freely contrapuntal,

474 Pr. SmijO, 127; MosV, 52; MaldR XVIII, 17.
475 The Christus formula is not the one used in the current *Officium majoris hebdomadae;*
it may be found, however, in the *Cantus ecclesiasticus sacrae historiae Passionis . . . Jesu Christi,*
publ. by Pustet in 1868.
476 *Pars I* pr. ForkA II, 616.   477 Cf. MaiM, 58f.   478 Pr. MaldR XVIII, 3.
479 Pr. *ibid.,* XIX, 23; XXIX, 17; CPC, No. 34.   480 Cf. PirH, 230.

chordal; paired, polyphonic *a 3*, polyphonic *a 4*—in the noble *Gaude Virgo*.[481] There is much writing for paired voices in *Delicta juventutis;*[482] the restraint with which la Rue adorns the melodic lines helps to give the piece an air of solemn grandeur.[483]

Some of la Rue's chansons are of the motet-chanson type, e.g., his *Plorer, gémir—Requiem*.[484] While such a piece as *Tous les regrets*[485] is a *rondeau*, la Rue's chansons seem to show a strong aversion to the *formes fixes*. In his setting *a 4*[486] of the superius of Ockeghem's *Fors seulement*—round which he weaves four points of imitation independent of the old melody—la Rue destroys even the division into two sections that is typical of the *rondeau:* he causes two entries in the third point of imitation to precede Ockeghem's medial cadence and one to follow it, thus completely bridging the gap. Sometimes he avoids a repetitive form altogether, as in *De l'oeil de la fille du roy, chacun est en doute et effroi*,[487] which, in view of the opening words, may well have been addressed to Margaret of Austria. However, he does resort to repetition schemes and, in the process, seeks to vary the patterns. In *Pourquoy non,*[488] which is unusual for its period in that it has two flats in the signature, the music of line 1 is repeated, intensified, for line 2. The musical openings of certain other chansons recur at the end, as in *Ce n'est pas jeu*,[489] where the repetition is somewhat altered. Another type of repetition, in which a musical phrase from the middle of the chanson returns at the close, but with different text, is exemplified by *Autant en emporte le vent*.[490] *A vous non autre* and *D'ung desplaisir,* on the other hand, each end with a repetition that is both textual and musical (though less than a full line is involved).[491] The ending of the last phrase of the lovely *Au feu d'amour*[492] is related, through partial

---

[481] Pr. MaldR XVIII, 7.   [482] Pr. CW XI, 21.

[483] Further about la Rue's motets, see PirH, 230; AmbG III, 240f. Regarding the motets ascribed to la Rue in MaldR XVIII, 18, 20; XIX, 3, 5, 7, 10, 12, 15, 20, see ReT, 102f; *see also* BorI, 121, 123f, 127. For extracts (all settings of verse 2) from Magnificats, see RoediN, 29, 30, 34, 35 (= MaldR XXIX, 23), 36.

[484] Extract pr. PirH, 229. Another example, *Cueurs désolez—Dies illa, dies irae,* pr. MaldP XXII, 15, and CW III, 34, as by la Rue, has the *Dies illa, dies irae* verse of the *Libera me* of the Burial Service (Liber, 1767) in the fourth voice. (The melody is not from the *Dies irae,* as the "correction" in CW III would indicate; cf. pp. 504f *infra*.) Whether the piece is really by la Rue, however, is doubtful (cf. Bor I, 124, No. 36; ReT, 104, No. 342).

[485] Pr. MaldP XX, 16 (with garbled text; cf. BorI 121, No. 2; also 126, No. 6; ReT, 103, No. 320).

[486] Pr. GiesS, 14. La Rue wrote also a setting *a 5.*

[487] Pr. MaldP XX, 18. Repetitive form is avoided also in the chanson pr. MaldP XXIII, 11 (there given as anon., but *see* BorI, 124, No. 45; ReT 87, No. 13).

[488] Pr. HewO, 252 (facsimile, after Brussels MS 228, following p. 42); CW III, 29; MaldP XXI, 13.

[489] Pr. MaldP XX, 21; *see also Trop plus secret,* pr. *ibid.,* XXI, 5 (with changed text; cf. BorI, 121, No. 7; ReT, 103, No. 325).

[490] Pr. CW III, 27; MaldP XXI, 11. The text in Brussels, Bibl. roy., MS 228, is not quite the same as in these reprints, but the above statement holds good.

[491] The pieces are pr., respectively, in MaldP XXIII, 13 (as anon.; but *see* BorI, 124, No. 46; ReT, 87, No. 14); CauQ, 6. The repetition is slightly varied in *A vous.*

[492] PubAPTM XXIII, 68; RieM, 48.

repetition, to the ending of phrase 1. Effective use is made of imitation in this piece as also in the moving *Incessament mon pauvre cueur lamente* and *Cent mille regretz,*[492a] in both of which two out of the five voices are in canon.

The four-part *Mijn hert heeft,*[493] with its Middle Dutch text, is based on an anonymous setting *a 3.*[494] La Rue does not so much add a new voice as he ingeniously makes four parts out of the old three: the anonymous version keeps its three voices busy most of the time, whereas la Rue allows them to rest occasionally and redistributes some material among the several voices. He removes a number of the old embellishments—his tendency to decorate sparingly is again evident—and turns the lowest voice into somewhat more of a functional bass, though it is still primarily melodic.[495]

While la Rue seems not to have enjoyed an international fame comparable to that of Josquin, he was nevertheless one of the important composers of the time, and the fine quality of his serious art—serious even in his comparatively lighter secular works—amply justified the favor in which he was held by Margaret.

Longaval; Pipelare; Divitis; Some Lesser Figures

All four parts of la Rue's *Mijn hert heft* are drawn upon in a Mass [496] by Johannes Gascoing. Some historians have regarded him as identical with Matthieu Gascongne (cf. pp. 300, 348), but he is probably an earlier composer.[497]

There is a Passion in three *partes* that is attributed in some sources to Obrecht. However, these sources, which are German, all date from thirty or more years after Obrecht's death; of two Italian sources, earlier and therefore presumably more authoritative, one now at Florence ascribes the work to Longaval, one now at Rome to Jo. à la Venture. An Antoine de Longueval served Louis XII and Francis I from 1509 to 1522, being mentioned as *maître*

492a Pr. JosqWW I, 70, 68, resp. (but neither is by Josquin; cf. introductory notes, xii; RubIL, 77).

493 Pr. SmijO, 129; MaldP XI, 41 (as anon., but *see* BorI, 122, No. 15; ReT, 88, No. 27); XXI, 21; ObrWW, 64 (as a dubious Obrecht work).

494 Pr. GomO, Supp., 84. For another anon. setting *a 3, see ibid.,* 86; for a setting thereof *a 4, see* MaldP XIV, 38 (cf., BarthaN, 565).

495 Other chansons are attributed to la Rue in MaldP XX, 23; XXI, 3, 7, 9 (= CW III, 32), 17; XXII, 3, 10, 12, 13, 23, 25, 27; XXIV, 1 (this one hypothetically), but their authenticity has not been established (cf. BorI, 121ff; ReT, 91, No. 95, and 103f). The piece credited to la Rue in MaldP XXI, 19, is by Ockeghem; the one credited to him *ibid.,* 27, is by Brumel (cf. fn. 415 *supra*); the 2 credited to him *ibid.,* 23, 29, are really 2 sections of 1 piece by Agricola (cf. BorI, 122f; ReT, 103f, Nos. 333, 335). MaldP and MaldR are valuable collections, since they make available in modern print a large repertory of music, much of which is not elsewhere accessible in that form. However, many of the attributions are wrong, and Maldeghem had an exasperating bent for substituting texts, especially in secular pieces, so that it is often difficult to know just what composition one is examining. (Cf. ReT.) There will be several occasions, later in this book, to refer to the shortcomings of Maldeghem's editions.

496 Kyrie I in old notation in RoediN, 3.

497 *See* RoediT, 133. For verse 2 of a Magnificat by Johannes, in old notation, *see* RoediN, 38.

de chapelle in 1517; [498] a few additional works credited to him survive. Johannes à la Venture is unknown in any other connection and is very likely identical with Longaval (French *à la venture* = Flemish *longeval;* [499] "Longueval," of course, would be a Gallicization instead of a translation of the Flemish). Although several sources refer to the Passion as *"secundum Matthaeum,"* it actually derives its text from all four Gospels, and this fact is made clear by the two Italian MSS [500] at the outset.

EXAMPLE 54. Opening of the Passion probably by Longaval (from MosV, 12f; after Florence, Bibl. naz. centr. II. I, 232).

The combination of the names of all four Evangelists is made in order to prepare for the introduction, at the proper time, of the Seven Last Words of Christ on the Cross: of the seven Words, three are found in Luke and John and one in both Mark and Matthew, from which Gospel the basic text of Longaval's Passion as a whole is drawn. The practice here applied was followed in many later Passions also.[501] Longaval's work,[502] a motet-type Passion, is based on the Chant formulas assigned to the *Chronista, Christus,* and *Synagoga* in the rendition of the Passion in Holy Week.[503] Each of the four voices draws on the Chant; only the tenor, however, has formula material belonging to all three roles. *Falsobordone* texture is occasionally present. Nevertheless, the writing becomes fairly polyphonic at times, even though imitation is seldom employed. Passages for different voice combinations provide contrast and a certain

[498] Cf. BrenM, 65, 68f.   [499] Cf. BorFA, 11; SmijMP, 184.
[500] Facsimile of the opening after the Rome MS in SmijMP.
[501] Cf. KadP, 13.
[502] Pr. both *a 4* and in a version *a 6* of c. 1560 (cf. MosV, 12) in ObrP; the version *a 4* also in KadP, 246.
[503] ObrP, following original source material, prints the version *a 4* with the letters E, C, and T at formula entrances. These stand, respectively, for Evangelista (= Chronista), Christus, and Turba, the last term being employed as synonymous with Synagoga, since it is applied to passages that set the words of individuals as well as passages that set the words of groups. (MosV, 12, is wrong in saying that C stands for Cantor. It is wrong also in stating that the superius never has the plainsong. In addition, it gives our Ex. 54 as by Longheval immediately after discussing the Passion allegedly by Obrecht, without recognizing that the two are the same.)

amount of dramatic effect: although consistency is not adhered to, most passages for individual characters are written *a 2* and most of those for groups, *a 4*.[504]

Matthaeus Pipelare of Louvain was choir director of the Illustrious Confraternity of Our Lady at 's-Hertogenbosch, c. 1497 to c. 1500.[505] That the last two syllables of his name should occasionally be represented by notes in the old MSS is, of course, inevitable. Among his chansons is a four-part *Fors seulement*[506] which, although it borrows no voice literally from Ockeghem's *Fors seulement l'attente*, nevertheless makes unmistakable references to the famous old piece. Pipelare's *Ick weedt een molenarinne*[507] employs repetition toward the end, but is not in any of the *formes fixes*. There is a four-part *Een vrolic wessenn* based on Barbireau's superius, that is probably also Pipelare's.[508] A five-part *Missa Fors seulement* by Pipelare uses as *cantus firmus* the tenor of his own chanson.[509] In his four-part *L'Homme armé* Mass,[510] he employs the old melody, sometimes complete, sometimes in segments, transferring it from voice to voice, but assigning it mostly to the tenor; in the final Agnus an added part sings in canon with the bass. However, in the *Missa Mi mi*,[511] all the voices share the *cantus prius factus, Petite camusette;* the Agnus draws on Gregorian Mass X. Chant melodies are incorporated also in a *Missa de Feria* and in a polytextual *Credo de Sancto Johanne evangelista*.[512] The motet, *Memorare Mater Christi*,[513] is a *Hymnus de septem doloribus dulcissimae Mariae Virginis* and is written *a 7*, each voice representing a different *dolor;* the third voice sings the tenor of the Spanish *villancico, Nunca fué pena mayor* ("Never was there greater pain") (cf. p. 581), thus alluding symbolically to the sorrows of the Virgin, the subject of the text sung by the other voices.[514]

A singer, Crispiaenen, is mentioned in the records of the Confraternity at

---

[504] A chanson by Longueval is pr., with substitute text, in MaldP I, 33. The original incipit is *Alleregres;* however, the tenor is not that of *Allez regrets* but of *Les grans regretz* (cf. HewO, 160; ReT, 111, No. 487).

[505] See SmijI XIII, 214f, 217f, 220ff. Concerning the musical life of the Confraternity, *see* esp. SmijM.

[506] Pr. ObrWW, 88 (after Florence, Bibl. naz., MS XIX, 164–167); MaldP I, 12 (after Brussels, Bibl. roy. 228, but with substitute text) and XXI, 25 (transposed); cf. BorI, 122. An elaborated, evidently instrumental version is pr. in GiesS, 8 (after St. Gall, 461) and MosL, 126 (after the *Liederbuch* of Arnt von Aich; cf. p. 638).

[507] Pr. MaldP XIV, 7 (the Dutch text there given is that of the original with more modern spelling; cf. LenN, 87).

[508] Cf. SaarB, 111ff. The motet-chanson attributed to Pipelare in MaldP XIII, 37, and CW III, 23, is by Compère (cf. 225, fn. 238, *supra*); the chanson ascribed to him in MaldP XIII, 35, and CW III, 25, is the *b* section of a *bergerette* credited to Hayne in Riccardiana MS 2794.

[509] Compare the chanson tenor with that of the Mass as given in RoediN, 3 (Kyrie I is given *ibid.*, 2f, in old notation).

[510] Kyrie I in old notation *ibid.*, 42. I am indebted to Prof. Oliver Strunk for having loaned me his MS score of this Mass.

[511] Kyrie I in old notation in RoediN, 44.

[512] Cf. *ibid.*, 46, 12 (portions of the works are given in old notation).

[513] Pr. MaldR XI, 31.

[514] Further about Pipelare, *see* AmbG III, 187, 259; SaarB, 60; EitQ VII, 455. For verse 2 of a Magnificat, in old notation, *see* RoediN, 31.

's-Hertogenbosch in 1497. This may be Crispin van Stappen, who, in 1492, had become a singer at the Sainte Chapelle in Paris. In October of that year, he became *maestro di cappella* at the Cathedral in Padua. Some months later he obtained a post in the Papal Chapel, where he remained until 1507, except for a brief return to Padua (appointment to a canonry at Cambrai in 1504 did not require renunciation of his Roman post). He was listed as a member of the Confraternity in 1506—which is not necessarily proof that he was in its service. In 1524–25, he was *maestro di cappella* at the Casa Santa di Loreto. He died at Cambrai in 1532.[515] A song of departure from Padua, written by Van Stappen in the form of a *strambotto*, begins *"Vale, vale de Padoa, o sancto choro."* [516] Petrucci's *Canti C* includes his *Gentil galans de gerra*, in which the contratenor spans a twelfth; a piece that combines the *De tous biens plaine* melody with the antiphon *Beati pacifici;* and the motet *Virtutem expulsus,* which is unusual in that it is set for three sopranos and bass.[517] Petrucci's *Motetti B* (*De Passione . . .*) includes an *Ave Maria,*[517a] in which the plainsong serves as *cantus firmus.*

Born at 's-Hertogenbosch was Nicolas Craen, who became a singer at St. Donatian in Bruges in 1504. Glareanus thought well enough of him to include his three-part motet *Ecce video coelos* [518] in the *Dodecachordon.* There is a *Si ascendero* of his in *Canti C.*

Antonius Divitis (Van Rijcke, Le Riche, etc.) was born at Louvain, c. 1475. Early in 1501 he became a singer at St. Donatian and, in June, its choirmaster. He studied for the priesthood and celebrated his first Mass in 1502. He remained at St. Donatian until 1504 and then served as choirmaster at St. Rombaut, Malines, until 1505, when he entered the chapel of Philip the Handsome as a singer. Like Agricola and la Rue, he accompanied Philip on the latter's final trip to Spain. Divitis' name is next found in the list of members of the chapel of Louis XII of France at the time of the king's death in 1515. An Antonius Richardus was a member of the choir at St. Peter's in 1526, and this may be Divitis. If so, it is the last date we have for him. His few extant works include two Masses, two Magnificats, a small group of motets and Mass fragments, and a chanson.[519] The *Missa Si dedero* is based on Agricola's song-motet; the *Missa Quem dicunt homines,* on a famous motet in two *partes* by Jean Richafort (cf. pp. 336f).[520] In the latter Mass, Divitis draws on selected passages of both *partes* of the motet, sometimes applying a process of simplification, as in the *Qui tollis,* built on material in our Example 75,

[515] For biographical data, *see* PirB, 353; PirH, 222; SmijI XIII, 214f; XIV, 62; XVI, 4, 10 (fn.); XVI, 97; BrenM, 41f; RB I (1946–47), 134; NA XVIII (1941), 16ff.
[516] Pr. WolfME, 54.   [517] *See* further, AmbG III, 261; PirH, 222f.
[517a] Pr. SmijO, 199.
[518] Modern ed. in PubAPTM XVI, 285. For another motet, *see* SmijO, 111. Further about Craen, *see* AmbG III, 261f; EitQ III, 92.
[519] For further biographical data and list of works, *see* DoorD.
[520] Dr. Charles Warren Fox has kindly loaned me his score of the Kyrie, Gloria, and Credo of the Mass. For the Kyrie I of the *Missa Si dedero* in old notation, *see* RoediN, 18.

sometimes elaborating, sometimes quoting fairly literally; original material is occasionally interspersed, as in the *Christe*.[521]

Pierre Moulu (probably born in the late 15th century), referred to by Ronsard[522] as having been a pupil of Josquin's, must have had an element of the fantastic in his character. He wrote a *Missa duarum facierum* (printed in Petreius' *Liber XV missarum,* Nuremberg, 1539), the "two faces" of which are revealed by rendering the work either with observance of all the rests or by disregarding those greater than crotchets (cf. the description of Compère's *Scaramella* on p. 224). The presence, in a given passage, of dispensable rests in certain voices but not in others requires, of course, parts that can be adjusted to one another at different time-intervals, as in Example 55. Moulu obtains smooth polyphony either with or without the rests, though the composition must be regarded more as a tour de force than as a work of art.[523]

EXAMPLE 55. *Missa duarum facierum*—Kyrie I, in its alternative forms with and without long rests—Moulu (from *Liber quindecim Missarum,* Petreius, 1539; transcr. by C. W. Fox).

---

[521] Further about Divitis, *see* AmbG III, 267f. For part of an independent Credo and the *Et exultavit* sections of the 2 Magnificats, all in old notation, *see* RoediN, 7, 31, 38.

[522] In the preface mentioned on p. 293 *infra*.

[523] *See* further AmbG III, 278; RieH II[1], 271f.

[524] "Remove the other rests, but the minims continue in gentle song."

Another Mass is so composed that the singers may vary the number of written parts they actually perform.[525] A motet of Moulu's, *Sicut malus,* attained considerable popularity, becoming the subject of several keyboard transcriptions.[526] Another motet of his, after mentioning such composers as Dufay, Busnois, Obrecht, la Rue, and *"Josquin incomparabilis,"* goes on to include less well-known men—among them "Nynot," Bruhier, and Forestier.[527] The first of these, usually called Ninot le Petit, is represented in several Petrucci prints, as well as in Florence, Conserv., B. 2439, and other sources. His *Si oblitus fuero* is a particularly eloquent work.[528] Bruhier's known compositions include a Mass, a few chansons, and a duo for two basses on *L'Amour de moy* (printed in Rhaw's *Secundus Tomus Biciniorum* of 1545).[529] Among Mathurin Forestier's works are a *L'Homme armé* Mass and a *Missa super Baise moy,*[530] the latter being written on the *Baisés moy* melody that appears in the Bayeux MS and upon which Josquin drew also.[531]

Antoine de Févin

Antoine de Févin (Févim, etc.)—called by Glareanus *"felix Jodoci aemulator"* ("happy emulator of Josquin") [532]—was probably born c. 1480 at Arras, where his father was alderman in 1474. Louis XII, in a letter written in 1507, praises Févin's chansons highly. When Févin died at Blois in or c. 1512—probably at an early age, since Glareanus refers to him as *"egregius iuvenis"* ("excellent youth")—he was a singer in the king's service.[533] Jean Daniel (= Maître Mitou), organist at St. Maurice at Angers c. 1530, includes Févin—together with Alexander (Agricola), Prioris, Josquin, La Rue, Loyselet (Compère), and such younger men as "Richard fort" (= Richafort), Gascongne, Mouton, Moulu, Lafage, Claudin, and others—in a list of musicians he knew, named by him in a *noël*.[534] Févin is mentioned also by Rabelais.

We have nine Masses by Févin, fourteen motets, several Lamentations, three Magnificats, and seventeen chansons. He has more pieces in Cambridge, Magdalene College, MS Pepys 1760, than anyone else, but no clear proof links it with him directly.[535] Two Lamentations are given to Robert de Févin (a relative?) in its body but to Antoine in its index and in other source material. The *Misse Antonii de Fevin,* printed by Petrucci in 1515, contains five Masses;

---

[525] Cf. AmbG III, 279.
[526] Cf. RihM; for *pars I* of the motet and 1 keyboard transcription of it, *see* RoksT, 47.
[527] Cf. HewO, 103.　　[528] Pr. ObrMT, 97; cf. p. 190 *supra,* fn. 37. Further about Ninot, *see* HewO, 75, 103; 1 piece pr. *ibid.,* 288.
[529] Cf. AmbG III, 192, 128.　　[530] Kyrie I in old notation in RoediN, 11.
[531] Further about Forestier, *see* AmbG III, 263.　　[532] GlarD, 354; PubAPTM XVI, 314.
[533] Further biographical data in DelpF; KahF; PirNB, 252; PirH, 235.
[534] Pr. H. Chardon, *Les Noëls de Jean Daniel* (1874), 7.
[535] A defective list of contents is given in *Bibliotheca Pepysiana III: Mediaeval Manuscripts* (1923), 36ff. The inventory of Févin's works given in KahF, 2nd instalment, 144ff, omits many items in this Pepys MS. Mr. Edward Clinkscale, whose Ph.D. dissertation on Févin is in progress at New York University, has kindly provided certain data incorporated in the above passage.

despite its title, however, the volume attributes two of them to other composers, one of these being Robert. Among the three Masses ostensibly by Antoine
is the *Missa Sancta Trinitas,* based on a motet by that composer, but actually
written by Mouton (cf. p. 284). The *Missa Ave Maria* [536] is based on Josquin's
Ave Maria . . . Virgo serena. However, Févin is not a mere imitator. Thus,
whereas Josquin opens with the same time-interval—two measures—between
the various entries and with all the voices presenting the motif on the identical
scale-degrees, Févin departs from both procedures. His superius imitates the
altus on the same scale-degrees, but after two and a half measures; in the lower
voice-pair, the appearance of which is delayed for six measures, the tenor
imitates on the scale-degrees previously sung by the upper pair, but the bass
enters a fifth below—and after the time-interval of only half a measure. The
Missa Mente tota [537] is constructed on the fifth of the seven *partes* of Josquin's
Vultum tuum deprecabuntur. Each of the five major sections of the Mass
and several subsections open with Josquin's initial material, but with changes
in the order of the entry of the parts, etc. Free fantasy is engagingly exercised
both here and in the reworking of other pre-existent elements. These contrast
strikingly in the original—especially a theme consisting of a rising leap of
a minor third, followed by conjunctly ascending notes, and a theme in ternary
rhythm, opening with repeated notes, both these themes differing strongly
from the opening one (a *do-do-ti-do* motif)—and Févin takes good advantage
of the opportunity thus offered to obtain variety.[538] Févin's motet, *Sancta
Trinitas,*[539] referred to above, since it was transcribed for both lute and
keyboard (cf. pp. 522, 559f), must have been much liked. The two *partes* of
the Song of Solomon motet, *O pulcherrima mulierum,* seem to have been used
separately as well as together, since they exist both ways in the sources.[540]
The first word of *pars II, Descende in hortum meum,* leads to the writing
of a seemingly inevitable descending figure, but this does not mean that the
treatment is perfunctory; indeed, the opening has a quite poetic character.
The Févin Lamentations include an eloquent setting of the *Gimel: Migravit
Judas* for Maundy Thursday. The chant-notes for *"Gimel"* (indicated by
asterisks in the following extract) are given forth by the tenor, while against
them the superius sings elaborate, mournful melismas of the kind that were
characteristically applied to the Hebrew letters in polyphonic Lamentations.
After *"migravit Judas,"* the chant "migrates" to the superius.

[536] Pr. CPC, No. 47; Benedictus also in RoksT, 8.   [537] Pr. MMRF IX, 62.
[538] For the Kyrie I of Févin's 6-part *Missa de Feria,* in old notation, *see* RoediN, 1; for the
Introit of his Requiem, up to the verse, *see ibid.,* 14. RoediN contains also, again in old notation,
the settings of verse 2 from 2 Févin Magnificats.   [539] Pr. RoksT, 28.
[540] The entire motet survives with conflicting attributions to Févin and Bauldewyn (1 source
each) and is anon. in 2 sources; *Pars I* appears alone with conflicting attributions to Festa
and Mouton (1 source each); *Pars II* (pr. AmbG V, 208) appears alone, ascribed to Févin in 1
source. It is obvious that the piece must be regarded as an *opus dubium.* The author is indebted to Mr. Alexander Main and to Mr. Edward Clinkscale (whose dissertation, cf. fn. 535,
will provide full details) for the information given in this fn.

EXAMPLE 56. *Gimel: Migravit Judas* from the Lamentation for Maundy Thursday—Antoine de Févin (from Cambridge, Magdalene College, MS Pepys 1760; transcr. by C. V. Brooks).

Mouton

The most gifted of Josquin's emulators, perhaps, was Jean Mouton, the teacher of Willaert and as such an important link between Josquin and the Venetian School. His birth took place in the township of Haut-Wignes (Holluigue) [541] in the vicinity of Samer, near Boulogne. From 1477 to 1483, he was a choirboy at Notre Dame at Nesle (near St. Quentin). In 1500, he was director of the choirboys at Amiens Cathedral, and in 1501 he held a similar position at Grenoble. In 1513, he was a member of the chapel of Louis XII, and after Louis's death he remained in the service of Francis I, during whose reign the chapel was to prosper brilliantly. Glareanus, who met Mouton at court sometime between 1517 and 1522, was most enthusiastic about his music and wrote that it was "in the hands of everyone." In the *Dodecachordon,* Glareanus praises Mouton's style and uses several of his works as examples. The composer was greatly admired by Leo X. He died as canon of St. Quentin in 1522.[541a]

Glareanus' expression, *"facili fluentem filo cantum"* ("melody flowing in a supple thread"), aptly characterizes an outstanding trait, the remarkable smoothness of Mouton's melodic line. A follower of Josquin, he applies the master's devices to a different type of melody, one that frequently moves stepwise and, when it leaps, often does so by small intervals, even in the bass.

Mouton seems to have written few secular pieces. Of special interest among them is the double canon, *Qui ne regrettroit le gentil Févin,*[542] which is a *déploration* on Févin's death. Other chansons by him include a four-part *Jamès, jamès, jamès* [543] in the *Odhecaton;* a three-part *Dieu gard de mal* in

---

[541] Not Hollingue, as sometimes stated; cf. RoyM, 241.
[541a] For further biographical data, *see* esp. DelpM; RoyM; Lesure in RB V (1951), 177f.
[542] Pr. PlamDP, 19.　[543] Pr. HewO, 296.

MS Pepys 1760 at Cambridge; a four-part *Adieu mes amours,* which survives in Basle, MS F. X. 1–4; [544] and a four-part *La, la, la, l'oysillon du boy* in a print of 1536. [545]

Among the links connecting Mouton's music with Josquin's are the settings the two men made of *Dulces exuviae.* Mouton appropriates the superius that Josquin wrote for Dido's parting words, but the lower voices are, for the most part, new. [546]

The *In illo tempore* by Mouton in Antico's *Motetti Libro quarto* of 1521 incorporates portions of the plainsong melodies of *O filii* and *Victimae paschali.* [547] Mouton's *Reges terrae* contains examples of such old devices as the under-third cadence and *fermata*-marked block-chords. This responsory for Epiphany [548] is in two *partes,* each ending with a group of Alleluias, the two groups being identically set, so that the form is *aB* (*pars I*) *cB* (*pars II*), a pattern already encountered in sporadic examples by Frye and Obrecht and in a variant by Ockeghem. In the early 16th century this kind of setting of the responsory became established as the typical large polyphonic form for the Office. [549] The first print containing the *Reges terrae* dates from 1534, twelve years after Mouton's death. But the 1521 Antico print had already presented a *Iocundare Ierusalem* by Mouton, likewise a responsory, displaying the same repetition features. [550] In this print there appeared a Richafort motet also in the *aBcB* form, on the liturgical text *Emendemus in melius* (cf. p. 337), of which the *B* section consists of normal words instead of *Alleluia* exclamations.

Mouton shows particular interest in reworking motivic material. In the four-part *Sancte Sebastiane,* [551] the opening motif is imitated in all voices in long notes. This motif returns, in two voices, as one of the pair of motifs on which the second point of imitation is built; the first notes have the same values as before, the later notes being augmented. In a subsequent point of imitation, the original motif is used in *stretto*-like entries, with the note-values halved. At the very end, the motif recurs in the bass (only) in the values

[544] Pr. BerH, 66.   [545] Pr. MMRFO, No. 3074.

[546] Cf. StrunkV, 485ff, where the endings of both works may be compared.

[547] Among other motets incorporating chant are 2 in the *Motetti e canzone, Lib. I,* of c. 1521, at the Morgan Libr., New York: *O salutaris hostia* (based on Liber, 941) and the 6-part *Salva nos, Domine,* containing a canon *a 2* on the Benedictus antiphon of Sunday Compline (Liber, 271). *Gloriosi principes* (in the book of Mouton motets printed by Le Roy and Ballard, 1555) is built on an adaptation of the Gregorian *Petrus Apostolus* (found in the *Antiphonarium Romanum juxta breviarum Pii Quinti,* Paris, 1696) as *cantus firmus.* Cf. ShineM.

[548] The liturgical text is now *Reges Tharsis.* The motet is pr. CPC, No. 45.

[549] Further concerning the polyphonic responsory, *see* StrunkM, 158.

[550] Moreover, it seems similarly to have only "*alleluia*" exclamations as text in the recurrent musical passage. The repetition of the last words of the *a* section, "*adorare eum*," at the beginning of the reappearance of the musical passage, may be a printer's error; cf. first fn. on p. 9 of ed. by H. T. David, pr. separately by Music Press, New York (MP No. 91). The liturgical text is now *Surge, illuminare* [not *Iocundare*] *Ierusalem.*

[551] Modern ed. in ShineM, No. 14.

it had in its second presentation. In the four-part *Factum est silentium,* Mouton derives no less than seven motifs from material contained in the first three points of imitation. Here is the subject of the first point with its three derivatives.

EXAMPLE 57. Motifs from *Factum est silentium*—Mouton (complete piece in ShineM, No. 5).

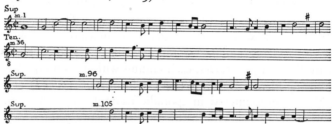

Similar relationships occur in other works sufficiently to indicate that Mouton was deliberately applying a technique designed to achieve unity.

Two serene and joyous Christmas motets of Mouton's, *Noe, noe psallite noe* [552] and *Quaeramus cum pastoribus,*[553] were to attract composers later in the century, when Arcadelt wrote a Mass on the former and Willaert and Morales each produced one on the latter, upon which Cabezon also composed a long keyboard fantasia.

Mouton was fond of canon and used it expertly. The *Nesciens Mater virum* and *Ave Maria, gemma virginum,*[554] both *a 8,* consist of quadruple canons, written with the utmost smoothness. Two of the five voices of the *Tua est potentia* are in canon at the fourth below.[555] The altus and bass of a four-part *Ave Maria* [556] are in mirror canon. The same kind of canon appears not only between the outer voices of the four-part *Salve Mater Salvatoris,*[557] but also briefly, at the beginning, between the inner voices. Here again, all is accomplished with polish and elegance. Glareanus includes this piece and the *Nesciens Mater* as examples in the *Dodecachordon,* as well as Mouton's *Miseremini mei* and *Domine, salvum fac regem.*[558] He also gives, and erroneously ascribes to Mouton, the *Per illud ave* from Josquin's *Benedicta es*

[552] Pr. SmijT II, 86.

[553] Pr. separately as No. 7 in *Anthologie de Musique Sacrée des Maîtres Anciens, Chants Latins* (ed., H. Expert) Paris, Procure Générale.

[554] Pr. SmijT III, 43 (= PubAPTM XVI, 419), 173, respectively.

[555] Mod. ed. in ShineM, No. 16; MinorM, No. 16.

[556] Pr. separately by Music Press (D.C.S. No. 40). For a 3-part *Ave Maria* by Mouton, *see* CPC, No. 41.

[557] Pr. ScherG, 65; PubAPTM XVI, 417; HawkH II, 482.

[558] Pr. PubAPTM XVI, 281 (= SmijT I, 176), 253, respectively. The former piece, even though ascribed to Richafort by Petrucci, is undoubtedly by Mouton; cf. RubIL, 73.

coelorum Regina; he mentions, however, that some attribute it to Josquin.[558a] Mouton did write a *Benedicta es,* but its *Per illud* section reads as follows:

EXAMPLE 58. *Per illud* section of the *Benedicta es, coelorum Regina*— Mouton (from *Motetti de la corona, Libro primo,* Petrucci, 1514; transcr. by J. Shine).

"Through that *Ave* addressed to thee and by thy gracious response the word was made incarnate, through whom the whole world was saved."

The *Domine, salvum fac regem,* a "God save the King" for Francis I, is one of several "political" motets by Mouton. Other such pieces include *Non nobis, Domine,*[558b] composed in 1509 on the birth of Renée, second daughter of Louis XII, *Quis dabit oculis,*[559] a lament on the death of Renée's mother, Queen Anne, in 1514, and *Christe Redemptor, O Rex omnipotens,* containing the lines *"Fit regi felicitas, reginae fecunditas"* (printed in 1521).[560]

Petrucci printed a book of five Masses by Mouton in 1515. Several of these, as of his other Masses, use the *cantus-firmus* technique, but with admixtures of other techniques. The rhythmical character of the *cantus firmus* normally approximates that of the other voices. The first Petrucci Mass, *Sine nomine,* proves to be a *Missa Benedictus Dominus Deus,*[561] based on the tenor of a Févin motet. This voice is silent in the midst of *pars I* of the model, and when Mouton reaches the corresponding point, in the first three movements of his Mass, he fills in the gap by presenting the motet altus in either his own altus or his bass. In both this Mass and the following, *Missa Alleluya,*[561a]

558a Also ascribed to both men, and likewise to Moulu, is a *Quam pulchra es (pars I* pr. BuH II, 535); cf. RubIL, 88.
558b Ascribed to Mouton in one source and to Gascongne in a later one. Cf. RubIL, 73.
559 Pr. MPI II, 113.
560 For other Mouton motets, *see* CommB VIII, 16; SmijT I, 150, 196; III, 98; CPC No. 42; ShineMM; perhaps MaldR XVII, 47 (cf. RubIL, 83).
561 Modern ed. in MinorM, No. 2.   561a *Ibid.,* No. 1.

Mouton marks off certain section endings by immediate musical repetitions to fresh text. The composer's liking for reworking motivic material is strikingly evident in the Kyrie of the second Mass. The third Mass paraphrases the *Alma Redemptoris Mater*.[561b] Mouton uses a recurrent opening *a 2* in four of the five major movements. In the Credo (the remaining movement), a fifth voice adds plainsong Credo I to the polyphonic web while the paraphrasing of the *Alma* continues. At the opening of the *Qui tollis,* two fragments are paraphrased in counterpoint. The next Mass, also *Sine nomine* in Petrucci's collection, is actually the *Missa Dictes moy toutes vos pensées*.[561c] Mouton bases the work on the tenor of a Compère chanson,[562] doubly transposed. The borrowed material permeates the superius and the other voices to such an extent that the composition gives the impression of being a cross between a *cantus-firmus* Mass and a paraphrase Mass. The last work in the collection, *Missa Regina mearum*,[562a] appears elsewhere as *Missa de Alamania*.

Mouton uses the *cantus-firmus* technique more strictly in the *Missa Tu es Petrus*,[562b] the Gregorian melody [562c] being restricted to the quintus, where it appears nineteen times. (This is his only known Mass *a 5*.) A *Missa Tua est potentia* [563] is constructed on the melody which, in Mouton's own motet, is treated in canon. The *Missa L'oserai-je dire* [563a] is written on a melody that is found in the Bayeux MS and in anonymous polyphonic settings in the *Odhecaton, Canti C,* etc. Only portions of the basic melody of the *Missa Faulte d'argent* [563b] are related to the tenors of Josquin's chanson and of a *Faulte d'argent* by N. Beauvoys in Florence, Conserv., B. 2442, these two also being different, but related; the Mass melody bears a closer resemblance to the tenor of a *Faulte d'argent* by Antoine de Févin in Pepys MS 1760.

Two Masses display *cantus-firmus* technique while incorporating short passages approximating parody style at the openings of the major movements: the *Missa Sancta Trinitas*,[563c] based on Févin's motet, and *Missa Verbum bonum*,[564] which is based indirectly on a plainsong sequence by way of a motet setting of it by Therache (cf. p. 285). The sequence is one that had been treated polyphonically as early as the 12th century.[564a] There is also one real parody Mass, that on Richafort's *Quem dicunt homines*.[564b]

Two Masses should be cited for special technical interest. A Jena MS con-

---

561b Pr. MMRF IX, 1.

561c Modern ed. in MinorM, No. 3. This Mass and the preceding one were printed not only by Petrucci but also in Antico's *Liber quindecim missarum,* 1516.

562 Modern ed. in MinorM, No. 14.   562a *Ibid.,* No. 7.   562b *Ibid.,* No. 10.

562c Pr. *Liber,* 1515.   563 Modern ed. in MinorM, No. 11.

563a Kyrie I in old notation in RoediN, 3, where the bibliographical data are not quite correct.

563b Modern ed. in MinorM, No. 5.

563c *Ibid.,* No. 8; Kyrie II and close of Credo pr. in BuH II, 531f. Ascribed by Petrucci to Févin (cf. p. 279), but to Mouton in MSS at Coimbra, Vienna, 's-Hertogenbosch, and the Vatican; anon. in MSS at Tournai, Vienna, and the Vatican.

564 *Ibid.,* No. 12.   564a Cf. ReMMA, 270.   564b Modern ed. in MinorM, No. 6.

tains a *Missa L'Homme armé,*[565] in which the old tune serves as *cantus firmus* in canon *a 2;* there are, in addition, three canons *a 3,* one *a 4* and one *a 7.*[565a] In the *Missa sine cadentia* [565b] of Cambrai MS 20, Mouton apparently attempts to avoid the traditional cadence formulas of the period.[566]

Carpentras and Some Lesser Figures; Leo X

Another Mass based on *Verbum bonum* is ascribed to "Ruphinus," very likely Fra Ruffino Bartolucci d'Assisi (cf. p. 238), *maestro* at the cathedral of Padua (1510–1520) and later at the "Santo" there. This Mass, for two choirs, each *a 4,* is of special interest, since it helps to bridge the gap between the earliest known polyphonic writing for antiphonal choirs in the late 15th century (cf. p. 28) and that of Willaert. Nine psalms by Ruffino, likewise for antiphonal choirs, survive also, as do ten such psalms by Francesco Santacroce, who was a member of the Padua Cathedral during Ruffino's term there.[566a]

In 1514, Petrucci printed Book I of his *Motetti de la corona,* and in 1519 he brought out three more books in the same series. Mouton is generously represented in the first two collections and is included in the third as well. Other familiar names that appear are those of Josquin, Loyset, Jacotin, Brumel, Divitis, Longueval, and Févin; and among the works of theirs that Petrucci selected are several we have already discussed. But a group of younger men comes to the fore likewise, most of whom—Richafort, de Silva, l'Héritier, Lafage, Bauldeweyn, Festa, Willaert—we shall discuss in Chapters 6 and 7. Additional names include those of Hylaire (= Hilaire Penet), Pierkin Therache, and Carpentras. Penet, a cleric at Poitiers and a singer to Leo X, from 1514 to 1522, has left us a few works, one being a motet, *Descendit angelus,* on which Palestrina was to base a Mass. By Therache, who served in the chapel of Louis XII, we have at least one Mass and a small group of motets.[567]

Carpentras is of greater moment. Evidently born before Févin (perhaps c. 1470), he had attained such a ripe old age by the time of his death in 1548 that he survived men like Verdelot and Festa, who artistically belong to a later period. His original name was Elzéar Genet, the name by which he is better known being derived from Carpentras, Vaucluse, whence he came. He spent most of his career in the papal service, but was at the court of Louis XII some time between 1508 and 1513. In 1508, he was a papal singer under Julius II and in 1513 became *maestro di cappella* under Leo X, by whom he was highly regarded. He is among the musicians mentioned by Rabelais in

---

[565] Kyrie I in old notation in RoediN, 6.   [565a] Cf. FeinK, 64.
[565b] Modern ed. in MinorM, No. 9.
[566] Further about Mouton, *see* ShineM; MinorM; BrenJM; AmbG III, 284ff; PirH, 235ff.
[566a] About Ruffino's and Santacroce's polychoral pieces, *see* esp. AlesP; further about Ruffino, *see* NA XVIII (1941), 31; TebAP, 2; EinDM, 507, 509.
[567] About him, *see* further AmbG III, 246f; EitQ IX, 392f.

Book IV of *Pantagruel*.[568] Antico's *Canzoni . . . et frottole, Libro tertio*, contains three pieces by Carpentras,[569] all recalling somewhat the standard texture of the general *frottola* type; but the old Italian equivalents of the *formes fixes* are absent. One piece is a *canzone* and all three compositions are of the structurally freer kind that was to lead the way to the madrigal. Carpentras composed other secular music also. In his later years, however, he concentrated his efforts on the writing of sacred music, four books—one each of Masses, Lamentations, hymns, and Magnificats—appearing between 1532 and 1537. These are of moment not only for their musical content, but for their connection with the history of music printing (cf. pp. 289f). Of the five works included in the Mass book, all named after French secular pieces, the *Missa A l'ombre d'ung buissonet*[570] is based on the similarly named melody found in the Bayeux MS and drawn upon by Josquin for one of his chansons in Antico's *Couronne et fleur* of 1536 (cf. p. 234). The melody appears in all movements of the Mass, though not continuously and not disposed in old-fashioned *cantus-firmus* manner. It is chiefly the Lamentations that maintained Carpentras's reputation far into the *cinquecento*. These works, intermingling *falsobordone*, passages of imitation, and the customary melismas upon the pronouncement of the Hebrew letters, were for many years cherished by the singers of the Papal Chapel.[571]

Pope Leo X, one of the most generous of the great Renaissance patrons of music—as befitted a son of Lorenzo the Magnificent—was himself a composer. The training he had received from Isaac in his boyhood in Florence not only helped to form his discriminating taste, but enabled him to write with the skill of a cultivated amateur. He incorporated the tenor of Colinet de Lannoy's *Cela sans plus* into a smoothly written setting *a 5*.[572] A canon by him is preserved in Perugia, Bibl. comunale, MS 431.[573] The sumptuous MS, Cappella Giulia XIII. 27, opening with Isaac's *Palle, palle* (cf. p. 170) and containing works by Ockeghem, Josquin, Agricola, Hayne, Compère, and others—including Colinet, represented by his *Cela sans plus*—may well have been made for the Pope.[574]

After the death of Josquin, the function of 16th-century music was to develop further the style which, in all its essentials, was present in his work

---

[568] For further biographical data, *see* ReqG; PerG; QuitG; HabR, 61; Grove II, 364f; MGG II, 867ff.

[569] Pr. SCMA IV, 10, 16, 22.   [570] Pr. BordA, *Messes*, III, 124; discussed in TierE.

[571] Cf. BaiP II, 187ff, but in the light of fn. 81 in Chap. 9 *infra*. For extracts from the Lamentations, *see* AmbG V, 212ff; AlfiR VII, 389; for a motet, BordA, *Motets*, III, 144. *See* further AmbG III, 281ff.

[572] For the music and a discussion, *see* HabM; *see also* WeinKK.

[573] Cf. JepK, lxxii (the citation of a facsimile in WolfH I, made immediately after the statement about the canon, does not apply to that piece, but merely refers the reader to an ex. illustrating the appearance of the MS). A canon *a 4* that follows directly after the canon *a 3*, but without an ascription, may also be the Pope's (communication from Dr. Knud Jeppesen).

[574] For a general article on Leo X and music, *see* PirL.

and in that of his contemporaries and to disseminate it throughout Europe. Netherlanders, such as Lassus and Philippe de Monte, were to spend the greater part of their careers spreading it in Italy and Germany. And, through their missionary work and that of several of their countrymen, the Franco-Netherlandish style became so firmly grafted upon shoots abroad that vigorous developments flourished on foreign soil, producing masters such as Palestrina, Victoria, Senfl, and Byrd—all of whom, however, expressed themselves in a language which, whatever the individual traits it displayed, had its main immediate source in the body of music produced by Josquin des Prez and his generation. The substituting, by these older men, of the homogeneity that results from imitation for the sharp contrast between melodic lines that predominated earlier; their employing freer, ever varying repetition schemes instead of the stereotyped patterns of the *formes fixes;* their beginning a shift from the writing of Masses on monophonic models to basing them on polyphonic complexes; their developing a heightened feeling for chordal sonority and especially for tonal centers—these various steps, among several others, led them through the gateway of the Late Renaissance to a vantage ground from which the path pointed clearly to the territory still to be traversed.

Chapter 6: SECULAR VOCAL MUSIC OF THE POST-JOSQUIN PERIOD: Claudin, Janequin, Gombert, and Their Contemporaries as Writers of Polyphonic Chansons; Verdelot, Festa, Arcadelt, Willaert, Rore, and Their Contemporaries as Writers of Italian Madrigals

SOCIAL and political conditions in France in the early 16th century were particularly favorable to the growth of secular music. As we have seen, the 15th century had witnessed the rise of a new and wealthy *bourgeoisie*. This group, partly from the natural curiosity and vigor inherent in its character, partly, too, from a very human desire to ape courtly tastes, had taken advantage of the cultural opportunities offered it. Other and more specialized influences also contributed to the development of the chanson—foremost, that of the Italian Renaissance, whose propagation in France was furthered by royal inclinations; these brought not only French military expeditions into Italy but Italian art into France. Of great importance, as well, was the growing influence of popular art on cultivated art, c. 1500, an influence that aided in the creation of increasingly free verse forms.

While some of the texts employed by the Josquin generation had still adhered to strict formalism, the poetry of the first decades of the 16th century sought greater liberty. The change was due largely to Clément Marot (1496–1544), son of Jean Marot. The father was one of the *rhétoriciens—* poets who, under the influence of the Italian humanists, had attempted to revive classical ideas in poetry; while giving up the cut-and-dried rules of the *formes fixes,* they had nevertheless retained a certain rigidity, inimical to the kind of musical composition that was coming into favor. Adopting traits that sometimes approximated those of folk texts, Clément used a more direct and colloquial language and favored short stanzas, without, however, adopting any stereotyped scheme. The alternation of masculine and feminine rhymes became firmly established at this time as an enduring characteristic of French poetry. Ronsard later was to emphasize this feature as of first importance in the composition of song texts.[1]

---

[1] Cf. HertzC, 8; also Pierre de Ronsard, "A Brief on the Art of French Poetry" (abridged transl.) in *The Great Critics,* James H. Smith and E. W. Parks, eds. (1939), 179.

The new chansons enjoyed wide dissemination, greatly aided by the activities of several famous French printers. From the period between Petrucci's *Canti C* and the production of these Frenchmen, only a few prints are known that constitute chanson collections, e.g., two issued by Andrea Antico in 1520. The style of one of these, the *Chansons a troys,* "is very similar to that of the late *rondeau.*" [2] The chansons in the other, the *Motetti novi et chanzoni franciose a quatro sopra doi,* are double canons for four voices, with one exception, a canon *a 4.* In short, these collections adhere to established tradition.

Attaingnant and Other Printers

In 1525, an important advance in printing was made by Pierre Haultin of Paris (d. 1580). Whereas Petrucci had printed the staff and the notes separately, Haultin achieved one-impression type-printing: he made type-pieces in which small fragments of the staff were combined with the notes, and with these pieces the whole composite of staves and notes was built up. His method fathered, in principle, the kind of music type-printing still occasionally employed. However, it was not at once universally adopted: double-printing re-emerged sporadically for more than 250 years.

Haultin's type was used by the Parisian publisher Attaingnant, among whose important publications (1528–1549)—sacred and secular, vocal and instrumental—there are about seventy collections that contain nearly 2000 chansons (including, however, some duplications).[3] It is significant, particularly in relation to chansons and madrigals, that Attaingnant was probably the first printer to insist on the careful placing of words under their appropriate notes.[4] Haultin's system was applied also in the type made by Guillaume Le Bé for the famous house of Ballard. Robert Ballard together with his half-brother Adrian Le Roy established in Paris, in 1551, a firm that was to print Lully in the 17th century and Couperin in the 18th and was to retain its privileges until the revolution of 1789.[5] Another innovation is attributable to the type-founder Etienne Briard (working at Avignon, c. 1530).[6] Instead of the square and lozenge-shaped noteheads generally used for mensural music at that time, he employed oval ones. The first printer known to have adopted this reform was Jean de Channey of Avignon, who employed Briard's type when printing Carpentras's four publications of Lam-

---

[2] HertzC, 7.   [3] Cf. MGG I, 786f; EitQ I, 230f; CauP; HertzW, 16f.

[4] For facsimile reproductions from Attaingnant prints, see *inter alia,* AttainC I–IV (instrumental); frontispieces of MMRFBT III, VIII (vocal). For further biographical data, etc., see RihA; LauC, xiiff; AttainC V; LesA; MGG I, 766ff.

[5] For further details, *see* LauC, xxiff.

[6] E. G. Peignot, *Dictionnaire raisonné de bibliologie, Supplément* (1804), 140, does not, as stated in Grove I, 467, contest Briard's priority in favor of Robert Granjon.

entations and other sacred music between 1532 and 1537 (cf. p. 286).[6a]

Important, in addition, was Jacques Moderne—known, because of his obesity, as "Grand Jacques"—who founded a music house at Lyons and among whose famous publications is the *Parangon des chansons* (eleven books,[7] 1538–1543). He was probably the first to print choir-books in which two voice-parts face in opposite directions on each page, to enable people sitting on either side of a table to sing from the same volume.[8] Noteworthy, too, is Nicolas Du Chemin (c. 1510–1576), whose issues appeared in Paris from 1540 to 1576 and included a seventeen-volume chanson collection.

Music publishing flourished also in the Low Countries, notably in Antwerp and Louvain. Tielman Susato (died c. 1561), one of the best-known Belgian printers, established himself in Antwerp, c. 1529, as music copyist, flutist, and trumpeter, and later as publisher. In 1543, he produced the *Premier Livre des chansons à quatre parties . . .* , including eight chansons by himself.[9] Hubert Waelrant (c. 1517–1595), an important composer, and the printer Jean Laet in 1554 established a publishing house, which continued to operate until Laet's death in 1597.

The collections issued by Pierre Phalèse of Louvain (c. 1510 to c. 1573) include both French and Flemish chansons, as well as lute music. At first a publisher employing independent printers, he undertook his own printing in 1552. After his death, his son moved the firm to Antwerp.[10]

The reign (1515–1547) of that typically Renaissance monarch, Francis I, corresponds closely to the first period of the 16th-century chanson. Then and later the chanson drew on Italian and Netherlandish elements, spicing them with native French grace and wit. Its textual charm—of varying shades of respectability—was calculated to delight the courtiers of Fontainebleau and Paris. Despite the extremely broad humour evinced,[11] many of the chanson composers wrote serious motets and Masses and even held positions in the Church.

The two earliest collections published by Attaingnant, apparently the first prints of polyphonic chansons of the sort to be discussed—indeed, the first prints of polyphonic music in France—appeared in 1528. The older one is actually dated April 4, 1527, but under a calendar in which the year began on Easter eve. Of this collection, only two parts remain. Nevertheless, its con-

---

[6a] The contract between Carpentras and Channey was signed Jan. 2, 1531; Carpentras was to pay; the quantity called for is 500 copies. Cf. ReqG, 8. The claim, often made, that ligatures were discarded in these prints, is shown by microfilm copies to be false; information kindly provided by Dr. Glen Haydon and Dr. Hans David.

[7] Reference books give the number variously; but *see* EitQ VII, 12f.

[8] For 2 pp. of facsimile, *see* MfMG V; *see also* comments, *ibid.*, 116.

[9] Further on Susato, *see* BergS or [Belgian] *Biographie nationale*, XXIII (1921–24), 279ff.

[10] For further data and many facsimiles of music printing by 16th-century Belgians, *see* BergT, GoovH. On Phalèse, *see also* LauC, xviiff.

[11] Because of which, certain modern editions, e.g., MaldP and ELAM, sometimes bowdlerize texts, occasionally replacing the originals entirely.

tents can be largely reconstructed from later sources in which some of the same pieces recur. The second collection survives complete but bears no date; this, however, can be approximated through circumstantial evidence.[12]

One of the first Attaingnant collections that are not only dated but also extant in complete form is the *Trente et une chansons musicales* (1529).[13] The two main composers included in it are Claudin de Sermisy, whom the music books usually name just Claudin, and Clément Janequin, to whom the entire second collection had been devoted. Despite the latter's greater fame today, and probably in his own time, we may well consider Claudin at least his equal among chanson composers of the type which, with certain differences, they both represent. These composers have been said [14] to comprise a Paris school.

Claudin de Sermisy and Some Minor Figures

Sermisy (c. 1490?–1562), a composer of Masses and motets as well as of chansons, was in 1508 appointed a singer in the Royal Chapel of Louis XII, becoming *sous-maître* under Francis I. He and Louis Hérault shared the post in 1547 and retained it under Henry II. In 1533, Claudin was made a canon of the Sainte Chapelle (where he had served briefly in 1508), thus being assured a substantial salary. With Francis I he traveled to Italy (1515), and he was among the musicians who delighted their hearers when Francis and Henry VIII met at the Field of the Cloth of Gold (1520).[15] Of the thirty-one songs in Attaingnant's first collection of 1528, Claudin is represented by no less than seventeen. About 160 chansons of his were printed in the collections of the period. A number, as will be seen later, became so popular that they were arranged for lute and keyboard and were adapted to sacred texts. In an entertaining quodlibet [15a]—or *fricassée,* as the French came to call this type of composition—, printed in 1536, there are about fifty quotations from popular chansons of the time, and Claudin is represented by more pieces than can be attributed to any other single composer.

Claudin's chansons support the claim [16] that many features of the French chanson, which was markedly to influence the Italian instrumental *canzona* (called *alla francese*), were themselves partly derived from the Italian *popolaresca lirica* (cf. p. 169). Italians contributed in person to the vogue of this kind of lyricism in France, for many were employed among the musicians of the *chambre* and those of the *écurie* at the French court,[17] which, in pa-

---

[12] About these 2 prints, *see* CauP.   [13] Pr. MMRF V.   [14] Cf. HelmS, 239.

[15] For further biographical data, *see* BrenD, 8ff; BrenM, 106f and *passim;* PirH, 317ff; LesAC, *Notices,* No. 1.

[15a] Pr. LesAC, 19; cf., *ibid., Notices,* No. 7.

[16] Cf. IMAMI II, ixff; also LassoW XII, xxvii; HelmS, 241.

[17] Cf. IMAMI II, xii; PruM, 241f, 245.

tronizing Italian culture, did not confine its favors to Leonardo da Vinci and the visual arts. This vogue is attested to by the *Heptaméron,* attributed to Francis I's brilliant sister, Marguerite d'Angoulême, which incorporates in "Nouvelle 19" a translation of the text of Michele Vicentino's *Che fara la, che dira la.*[18] On the other hand, the Italians continued receptive to the music of the north. (In fact, while influences operated in each direction, those exercised by the north on Italy were, as we shall see presently, much the more powerful.) Thus, two duos by Claudin appear in the *Canzoni francese . . . ,* published in 1539 in Venice by Antonio Gardane—himself a Frenchman—who inserted also some duos of his own, written to French texts. The subtitle of the volume includes the important words: *"buone da cantare et sonare"*—an early instance of an indication in a title that the contents are apt for either voices or instruments.[19]

Claudin's own interest in Italian art is shown by his having set such an Italian text as *Altro non è il mio amor* and a French translation (*Allez, souspirs enflammez au froit cueur*) of Petrarch's *Ite caldi sospiri, al freddo core,* which we have already found attracting the frottolists; the Italian influence is seen in Claudin's sacred music also—e.g., in his *Missa O passi sparsi.*[20]

In contrast to typical Franco-Netherlandish music, the characteristic secular work of Claudin and of some of his generation, like that of the frottolists, is predominantly chordal in style, song-like, with syllabic treatment of the text. While melodic grace is by no means lacking, there is a strong tendency to use rapidly repeated notes, producing a light declamatory effect, and the whole is characterized by terseness, precision, simplicity, airiness, and a generally dance-like quality. An initial rhythmic figure, which some historians have come to associate with the chanson of this period, may be found in Claudin, for example, in his *Jouissance vous donneray,*[21] which was very popular in the 16th century.

EXAMPLE 59. *Jouissance vous donneray*—Claudin de Sermisy (from
   Trente et sept chansons . . . , Attaingnant, c. 1529, and other
   sources; transcr. E. Hertzmann).

[18] PirP, 52; PirH, 165. Pr. SCMA IV, 52 (with ascription to Vicentino; Pirro's attribution to Pesenti seems incorrect).

[19] *See* ExFR VIII, prefatory note entitled *Source;* Gardane duos pr. 1, 4, 19, 22. Four more pr. ExA, 12, 14, 16, 18; a chanson *a 4* pr. LesAC, 54.   [20] Cf. PirH, 320.

[21] Pr. as anon., and with substitute text, in MaldP XVII, 4. For a reproduction of a painting of 3 women performing this piece (the superius part is painted into the picture), *see* BergT 15; SachsMH, Pl. XIII.

Joy, dearest lover, thine shall be,
And I shall lead thee tenderly
Where hope would have thee seek thy
    pleasure;

Alive I shall not part from thee,
And still when death has come to me
My soul its memories shall treasure.
       (Transl. by G. R.)

As we have observed, this initial rhythmic figure occurred often in the *strambotti, ode,* etc., of the period immediately preceding Claudin. It reappears frequently in the chansons of his time: in Attaingnant's *Trente et sept chansons . . .* (undated, but c. 1528–30) twenty-three pieces begin with the figure and six more with variants of it.[22] With occasional exceptions, e.g., *Jouissance,* it introduces a narrative chanson, recounting some gay anecdote. Indeed, in secular vocal polyphony it is a special mark of 16th-century narrative compositions generally, a fact that will assume added significance in connection with the Italian madrigal.[23] Another idiom, illustrated in the superius of measures 6–7 and 11–13 above, "is a particularly happy invention because it fits words with both masculine and feminine endings." [23a]

Ronsard, in a preface written for a *Livre de meslanges,*[24] mentions Claudin, among others, as a *"disciple"* of Josquin; if the term is warranted, Claudin's chansons reveal him more as a follower of Josquin the frottolist than of Josquin the Franco-Netherlander. It may well be that Ronsard's attribution of pupils to Josquin is of the same nature as Crétin's attribution of pupils to Ockeghem. Claudin achieves mention also in Rabelais's *Pantagruel* (Book 4),[25] as do several other composers treated in this chapter—for example, Willaert, Gombert, Janequin, Arcadelt.

A large group of Claudin's contemporaries wrote chansons in much the same style as his. This showed a preference not only for chordal writing, but for having it *a 4*. However, Pierre Cléreau included in his output many

[22] *See* MMRFBT VHI.
[23] Cf. EinN, esp. 482ff.
[23a] LaudP, 49.
[24] English transl. of the preface (after 1560 ed.) in StrunkR, 286f; French text (after 1572 ed.) in RMR, 77; ExF, vii; etc.
[25] *Oeuvres de Rabelais,* Burgaud des Marets and Rathery, eds., II (1858), 35.

chansons that are *a 3* but share the general features of this style, notably chordal writing.[25a] The simplicity of the style produced music especially suitable for performance by amateurs. (In the realm of theory, the needs of the amateur were cared for by such material as the *Nouvelle Instruction familière* of Michel de Menehou,[25b] which, printed in 1558, concerned itself with rudiments; a chanson of the Paris type, written by Menehou, concludes the little work.) Variety of color is often gained by contrasting brief two-part passages with passages for two other voices or for larger groups. The two upper voices often move in progressions of thirds. Imitation, even of short duration, is most sparingly used. In Claudin's *C'est une dure departie*,[26] however, two voices sing an extended canon.

All the post-Josquin composers, both those of the Paris type and those more given to polyphonic writing (men to whom we shall return presently), in the main avoided involved rhythmic and contrapuntal devices, including canon—whether crab, mirror, mensuration, or ordinary. In fact, there was a reaction against complexity, and this, technically, is the chief significance of the second quarter of the century in the field of music. The complications once present in some quantity, such as difficult notation, puzzles, etc., begin to vanish. Ligatures are much less frequently used. Mensuration becomes very simple: *alla breve* meter (*tempus imperfectum diminutum*) is by far the commonest. Change of time-signature occurs rarely and, when it does, appears simultaneously in all voices: having different signatures in different parts, as, for example, in Ockeghem's *Missa Prolationum,* is considered old-fashioned. The counterpoint of rhythmic accents and general rhythmic flexibility do continue, but they are allowed to make themselves evident from the old pages by virtue of the implications of the music itself without special intricate notation.[27]

Structurally, the Claudin type of chanson often follows a repetition scheme that is in fact its outstanding technical feature. In this scheme, which is applied to a seven-line poem, the music for lines 3 and 4 of the text is a repetition of that for lines 1 and 2, and both the text and the music of the last line are repeated. The music for this last line is frequently the same as that for lines 2 and 4. A normal chanson pattern of the time, then, would be *ababcdEE*,[28] as in Claudin's *Secourés-moy*.[28a] The basic pattern may be varied. Thus, in Claudin's popular *D'où vient cela*,[28b] the music for line 6

25a Cf. CauC; a chanson *a 4* pr. LesAC, 65. For biographical data, *see ibid., Notices*, No. 24.
25b Pr. MeneN.
26 Pr. MMRF V, 63; BlumeS, App. B, 28.
27 Cf. KemJC, 44ff.
28 *E* sometimes refers back to *a*, still oftener to *b*. *See also* BarthaP, 509, 516.
28a For a transcr. for solo voice and lute, pr. by Attaingnant in 1529, *see* LauC, 29.
28b Pr. CommB XII, 16; BlumeS, App. B, 22; voice and lute transcr. pr. LauC, 32.

is a repetition of that for lines 1 and 3. Related also are such patterns as *ababcDD* and *ababcdab*, illustrated, respectively, by Claudin's *Vivray-je tousjours* [28c] and *Il me suffit*.[28d] Unrelated patterns, however, occur in quite popular numbers such as Claudin's *Languir me fais*,[28e] which has the form *abca*. (This chanson, *Secourés-moy*, and *D'où vient cela* are among Claudin's settings of poems by Marot.) Despite the avoidance of the old *formes fixes*, the liberal use of repetition no doubt reflects their continuing influence, as in the chansons of the Josquin–la Rue generation. The Claudin type of chanson is characterized also by clearly defined phrase-formation. Since this type of chanson normally adhered to the old custom of setting each line of text as a separate unit, it yielded clear-cut forms which, as we shall see, lent themselves more readily to instrumental transcription than did the Italian madrigals, whose forms, resulting from an attempt to reflect not so much the structure of a poem as its meaning, were highly variable.

Chanson composers in Claudin's day seem to have drawn upon pre-existent melodies less frequently than in the time of Josquin. However, continuation of the practice is illustrated, for example, by a setting made by Claudin of the *Sur le pont d'Avignon* melody that is encountered in a polyphonic setting in *Canti C* [28f] and by a setting,[28g] by the obscure D'Oude Scheure, of *De tous biens plaine.*

Janequin

The Renaissance liking for realistic tone-painting, evident in varying degrees of naïveté and effectiveness in both vocal and instrumental music, appears in a distinctive manner in the program chansons of Clément Janequin. Born apparently at Châtellerault (near Poitiers), Janequin early entered sacred orders. Antico included three of his pieces in the *Chansons a troys* of 1520 (cf. p. 289).[28h] As already noted, Attaingnant had printed a whole collection of Janequin in 1528. (He was to devote two other prints to the composer subsequently and one to Janequin and Passereau together.) Janequin was active at Bordeaux c. 1529. In one of his pieces, *Chantons, sonnons, trompetes,*[29]

[28c] Pr. MaldP XVII, 10 (with substitute text; cf. ReT, 90, No. 73); voice and lute transcr. pr. LauC, 14.

[28d] Pr. CommB XII, 12; MaldP XIV, 14; WintK I, App., 137; transcr. for voice and lute pr. in LauC, 35.

[28e] Pr. CommB XII, 15; MaldP XVI, 18 (with substitute text; cf. ReT, 89, No. 41). MMRF V contains 10 Claudin items not yet cited (2 also in BordC, 1 being likewise in MMRFR I, 47; 1 also in ELAM X, 2; 1 in MaldP XVII, 15). For other Claudin reprints, see MMRFO Nos. 3078, 3080; ExA, 28; PubAPTM XXIII, 109, 110, 112 (= MaldP XV, 24); CauQ, 8; KemM, 223; DaF, 6; LesAC, 2, 4, 13, 35, 40; MaldP XVII, 12, 20; the MaldP reprints are given as anon. and have substitute texts; cf. ReT, 88, No. 30; 90, Nos. 64, 70. See also fn. 69 *infra*.

[28f] Not the folk tune now popular.

[28g] Pr. CouN, Supp. 9; MaldP XIX, 9 (with substitute text).

[28h] See LesJ, 158. [29] Pr. ExFR I, 1; JanequinT, 10.

he provided a welcome-song for the occasion when, in 1530, Francis I's sons returned to France from Spain, where they had been held as pledges of their father's fidelity to the treaty of Madrid. Beginning shortly thereafter, Janequin held successive posts in Anjou, including that of *maître* of the choir school of the Cathedral of Angers. Subsequently he enjoyed the protection of the first Cardinal of Lorraine, Jean de Guise (d. 1550)—the too worldly but generous patron of Erasmus, Marot, and Rabelais. By 1548, apparently owing to the good offices of Charles de Ronsard, brother of the poet, Janequin had become curate of Unverre (near Chartres), but he lived in Paris. From c. 1555 he was also under the protection of François, Duke of Guise, nephew of the Cardinal mentioned above. In certain works,[30] Janequin celebrates victories of the duke. In 1555, the composer is described as "singer in ordinary of the King's Chapel," and thereafter he became "composer in ordinary" to the king, apparently being the first musician to hold this title in France. In 1559 he mourns, in a dedication, his "age and Poverty"; he died c. 1560.[31] Whether he was poor or not, his fame and popularity were extraordinarily widespread. This is attested to by the numerous imitations and instrumental transcriptions of his chansons that appear in contemporary French, German, and Italian publications, notably of *La Guerre* (= *La Bataille de Marignan*).[32] Susato, in his *Dixiesme Livre* (1545), published a version with a fifth part added by Verdelot.[33] Janequin's program music is by no means limited to martial activities, as is shown by such titles as *Le Chant des oiseaux*, *Le Caquet des femmes*, *La Chasse*, *Les Cris de Paris*,[34] etc. The first two of these and *La Guerre* are alluded to in a laudatory sonnet on Janequin, by Jean-Antoine de Baïf, printed by Le Roy and Ballard in one of their collections (the Adrian of line 1 is, of course, Le Roy):

> *Why, Adrian, have you required of me*
> *Some lines as foreword to this book, to do*
> *It honor? Well then take them, though, beshrew,*
> *The author's name alone were guarantee!*
> *For where does one not hear the sound, the plea,*
> *Of this voice-weaver, this musician, who,*
> *Drugging his hearers with a nectar brew,*
> *Compels their souls the body's cage to flee?*

[30] *Le Siège de Metz* and *La Guerre de Renty* (modern reprints by Rouart, Lerolle & Cie., the former appearing singly, the latter coupled with Le Jeune's *La Sortie des gendarmes*).

[31] For further biographical data, etc., *see* LesJ; LevrJ; JanequinT, i; CauJ; CauG.

[32] *See* BrenV, 143ff, which gives much interesting data about the piece.

[33] Pr. CommB XII, 85. Janequin's own version pr. MMRF VII, 31; MMRFR I, 65; BordT, No. 2. MMRF VII is a modern reprint of Attaingnant's collection of 1528 devoted to Janequin (cf. pp. 290f).

[34] The pieces are pr. in MMRF VII, 1 (= BordT, No. 1); JanequinD, No. 1; MMRF VII, 62; ExFR, III (= CommB XII, 1; BordT, No. 3), respectively.

> If he with heavy chords motets compose,
>   Or dare to reproduce alarms of battle,
>   Or if in song he mimic women's prattle,
>   Or imitate birds' voices in design,
> Good Janequin in all his music shows
>   No mortal spirit—he is all divine.

Transl. by Lorraine Noel Finley.
(For the original French, see CauJ, 24.)

A point in *Le Chant des oiseaux,* at which simultaneous false-relation would result if *musica ficta* were applied, has been cited [34a] as evidence that, in vocal music, the Franco-Netherlanders before 1550 used the modes in pure form. It is quite likely that no accidental is needed in this instance: while it is true that false-relation is at times clearly indicated in music by the composers in question,[35] examples are less frequent in it than in contemporary English writing.[35a] But to argue that a large group of men avoided *musica ficta* just because it would cause false-relation in a few isolated cases, is weak indeed. It may as easily, perhaps more correctly, be held that one way a composer had of indicating that he did not wish *musica ficta* applied to a note occurring in a context normally requiring it, was to double that note. The *Chant des oiseaux* is especially charming, as is *L'Alouette* [36] with its representation of the call of the lark, but *La Guerre,* because of its fame, may be singled out as an example of Janequin's descriptive methods. The music imitates vividly the confused noises of the battle (fought against Swiss mercenaries employed by the Milanese): drum-beats, fanfares, rallying cries. *Parlando* or patter effects, common to chansons of the time, are present. Janequin also uses short, rapid declamatory phrases, tossed from one voice to another in suggestion of a violent *mêlée,* with frequent repeated notes and hocket-like figures. There are occasional extended reiterations of a single harmony, with its tones merely redistributed among the several voices. The piece has no great melodic or harmonic originality; emphasis is placed, rather, on lively and varied rhythms (*see* Ex. 60a). *La Guerre* (like some other Janequin works) is quite long, differing in this way, as in its emphasis on descriptive effects, from chansons of the Claudin type. It is in two *partes,* with the text of *pars II* almost entirely onomatopoeic (*see* Ex. 60b).

[34a] In CauM.
[35] As in Vaet's *Ecce apparebit;* see p. 700f *infra. See also* RoksT, 13, meas. 2. The latter ex. is drawn from the field of instrumental music, in which, it should be noted, CauM admits *musica ficta* is used, at least sparingly. Urging caution in the application of *musica ficta* (in itself a laudable principle), CauM, 60, cites also, from a piece by Cléreau (cf. p. 294), an ex. allegedly showing the occasional persistence of modal purity beyond the mid-century. It is held that the passage is in Dorian once transposed, that f' occurs between two appearances of g', but that the f' cannot be raised because it is tripled. The passage *is* mainly in Dorian transposed. However, the f' is not a 7th degree where it occurs, but a 1st degree, there being, at this point, a V-I cadence in Ionian transposed, so that there is no point in raising the note in any voice.
[35a] Cf. pp. 783; 824, fn. 34 *infra.* [36] Pr. HAM, 109; MMRF VII, 105.

EXAMPLE 60. Extracts from *La Guerre*—Janequin (after MMRF VII, 39f, 42).

"The fleur-de-lis, flower of great price, is there incarnate. Sound, trumpets and clarions. . . . Follow Francis, King Francis: Alarm, alarm, alarm, alarm! Follow the crown! *Fan, fan,*" etc.

While recognizing the boldness of Janequin's *"magnifique fresque sonore,"* [37] we should remember that programmatic effects were not really new to music (cf. p. 32); nor did they fail to be present, though perhaps to a less striking degree, in other works of the period.[38]

Janequin's large chanson production—286 examples survive—was not limited to program pieces or even to the chordal type. In fact, he treated many phases of the chanson and has left us numerous graceful works in more conventional style, such as *Si j'ai esté vostre amy* (which contains a canon, almost throughout, between superius and tenor), *Qu'est-ce d'amour* (one of several settings of poems by Francis I himself), *Tu as tout seul* (with text by Marot), *Pour quoy tournés vous vos yeux* (with text by Ronsard; in this work binary rhythm is delightfully varied by short passages in ternary rhythm), *Ce moys de mai,* and *Au joly jeu.*[39] Of all Attaingnant's composers,

[37] JanequinT, i.   [38] *See* BrenV, 83ff.

[39] Pr., respectively, in ExR, 1268; JanequinT, 19, 65, 118; MMRF V, 72 (= BordC, No. X), 82 (= MMRFR I, 54; BordC, No. IX). Chansons by Janequin not yet cited pr. MMRF V, 9, 76 (= MMRFR I, 60), 93; VII, 120; ExA, 32, 36; ExFR I, 8, 12, 17, 20; JanequinD, No. 2; JanequinT (26 items); PubAPTM XXIII, 64, 66; SquireM II, 35 (= MMRFR I, 51; ExF, 29; TierR, 126; BordC, No. XI); MaldP XIX, 14 (cf. BarthaN, 565); LesAC, 23, 29, 38, 46; ExF, 21 (= TierR, 119), 25 (= TierR, 122); facsimiles of the last 2, after the 1552 print of Ronsard's *Les Amours,* in Pierre de Ronsard, *Oeuvres complètes,* P. Laumonier, ed., IV (1932), 230, 236, respectively.

Janequin is the only one who not only set an Italian text but did so in madrigal style.[39a]

Certon and Some Other Composers of the Paris School; the Group at Lyons

The three leading representatives of the Paris school include also Pierre Certon. The man of this name who became a *clerc de matines* at Notre Dame in 1529 and barely escaped imprisonment for his questionable conduct, is probably our composer. *Clerc* at the Sainte Chapelle in 1532 and *maître* from before 1542 until his death in 1572, Certon has left us almost 200 chansons. These include works that are especially witty, often based on brief narrative texts. The entirely chordal *Fuions tous d'amour le jeu* and *La, la, la, je ne l'ose dire* [40] are happy examples of his art.

Most of the other composers of the Paris type, when compared with Claudin and Janequin, appear as minor figures. However, their works include many of great charm. Pierre Sandrin's *Douce mémoire* [40a] enjoyed a deserved popularity, as did *D'amours me plains* [40b] by Rogier Pathie, organist of Mary of Hungary's court chapel in the Netherlands. Hesdin's *Ramonez moy ma cheminée* [41] illustrates the disfavor into which the *formes fixes* had fallen for purposes of musical structure: its text is a simple *rondeau*, but (except that the music of the last two lines repeats that of the first two) the setting ignores this fact entirely.[42] Passereau's use, in his witty *Il est bel et bon*,[43] of descriptive matter—which here takes the form of barnyard cackle —reminds one of Janequin's music. The piece, though basically chordal, con-

---

[39a] Pr. LesAC, 26. Cf. LesJ, 159.

[40] Pr. CauQ, 32, and EinSH, 282 (= PubAPTM XXIII, 28; ELAM X, 6), respectively. Other Certon pieces, pr. MMRFO, No. 2979; DaF, 2, 8; PubAPTM XXIII, 24, 26, 30; ExA, 30 (= CommB XII, 76); LesAC, 31, 49, 58; ExF, 1 (= TierR, 98; BordC, No. I), 6 (= TierR, 102); facsimiles of the last 2, after the 1552 print of Ronsard's *Les Amours*, in Pierre de Ronsard, *Oeuvres complètes*, P. Laumonier, ed., IV (1932), 190, 196, respectively. For further biographical data, etc., *see* BrenM, 333f; PirH, 320ff; DouM II, 2f; LesAC, *Notices*, No. 11; MGG II, 976ff.

[40a] Pr. OrtizT, 86; PubAPTM XXIII, 103; other exx. *ibid.*, 105, 106, 107 (= ELAM X, 16); CauQ, 15, 22; EinIM III, 241; LesAC, 60. For biographical data, *see ibid.*, *Notices*, No. 22.

[40b] Pr. PubAPTM XXIII, 101; MaldP, XIX, 12 (with substitute text). For 7 different lute transcrs. (vertically aligned for comparison), *see* KosackL, 122. About Pathie, *see* StraM, VII, 439ff; MME II, 11f, 181 (text); etc.

[41] Pr. PubAPTM XXIII, 55; ELAM X, 20; another chanson pr. LesAC, 42. This composer may be the Nicolle des Celliers (called "Hesdin") who was master of the choirboys at the Cathedral of Beauvais and who died in 1538; *see, ibid., Notices*, No. 15.

[42] The text of Janequin's *L'Alouette* is related to another *forme fixe*: it derives in part from the anon. 14th-century *virelai, Or sus, vous dormés trop* pr. ApelFM, 117*, but this circumstance produces no effect on the structure of the music as, indeed, it has little chance to do, since the portion of the *virelai* text that is borrowed belongs entirely to the first section.

[43] Pr. MMRFO, No. 3075. Other Passereau chansons pr. LesAC, 8, 16; PubAPTM XXIII, 95; one that may be his or Janequin's pr. CauQ, 11. The composer was a curate at St. Jacques de la Boucherie, Paris; cf. CauJ, 19.

tains several passages of imitation. The number of these little masters is legion. It will perhaps suffice here merely to add mention of Courtois, Jean Maillard, Godard, Garnier, Conseil and Gascogne.[44]

Lyons was to a considerable extent a musical outpost of Paris, and Moderne was the counterpart of Attaingnant. Among the composers published mainly by Attaingnant, but represented in Grand Jacques's *Parangon,* are the old dependables, Claudin, Janequin, and Certon. But Moderne, too, had a group that clustered primarily about him. Most important, probably, was Francesco or François de Layolle, who made his career partly at Florence, partly at Lyons. The Layolle represented in Florence, Conserv., B. 2440 (cf. p. 170), was perhaps his grandfather.[44a] The younger Layolle's varied output included chansons, and Attaignant did not disdain to reprint, in 1539, *Ce me semblent choses perdues,*[44b] which had appeared in Book IV of the *Parangon* in 1538.[44c] Among Layolle's companions in Books I and II was the minor but colorful figure, Eustorg de Beaulieu, who as a poet has left us a repertory of early Protestant song-texts (but without the music).[44d]

Richafort; Crecquillon; Clemens non Papa

Although the chanson composers of the Paris-school type dominated the French musical scene during the earlier part of the 16th century, we may regard their production as a brief (but important) "intermezzo"[45] in the development of the chanson from Josquin to Lassus. During the initial decades of this "intermezzo" the older style was so little regarded that, after Petrucci's *Canti C,* there is no printed collection containing chansons by Josquin until the *Selectissimae . . . cantiones* of 1540 (printed by Kriesstein at Augsburg), in which the chansons of his mature style were published for the first time. Thereupon the neglect of the master ended, and Susato's seventh book of chansons, devoted entirely to him, appeared in 1545. But, whereas Claudin's style no longer holds sway in printed collections after 1540 (only in the one significantly called *Chansons anciennes* by Du Chemin in 1550 is real interest still shown in his secular works), Josquin's chansons appear often in Le

---

[44] Exx. by these composers pr. in CauQ; PubAPTM XXIII; ELAM X; MMRF V; MaldP XVI, 34 (cf. BarthaN, 565, or ReT, 89, No. 48); etc. Further about the chordal-type chanson, *see* KemW. *See also* MGG II, 1055ff.

[44a] About the identity problem, *see* esp. EinIM I, 279f.

[44b] Reproduced in the facsimile mentioned in fn. 8.

[44c] *See* further, on Layolle, TricouL, 6ff.

[44d] *See* esp. BridgmB, 1 chanson pr. *ibid.,* 69 (preceded by facsimile after Moderne's print, showing same features as those described on p. 290 *supra*); only other surviving chansons pr. BeB, 23, 26.

[45] Cf. BarthaP, 508.

Roy and Ballard's *Meslanges* of 1560 to 1572. The tradition of the motet-like Franco-Netherlandish chanson had been carried on during the period of the Claudin–Janequin supremacy by several composers, among them Jean Richafort and a group whose works appear infrequently in the Attaingnant prints of 1539 to 1549, but in far greater number (as befitted the Netherlandish origin of many of these men) in the collections of Susato. Among the musicians of this group may be named Jehan Le Cocq (= Gallus),[46] Cornelius Canis,[47] Pierre de Manchicourt,[48] the long-lived Jean Guyot (Castileti),[49] Thomas Crecquillon, and Jacobus Clemens non Papa (= Jacob Clement). In contrast to Claudin and Janequin, all these composers, including Richafort, not only wrote chansons in a polyphonic style with some frequency but, after c. 1540, produced chansons in five or more parts.

An amusing example of the works *a 5* is the Richafort setting of the 11th-century goliardic lines parodying the famous sequence, *Verbum bonum et suave,* which begin as follows:

Vinum bonum et suave	*Wine that's of the best and sweetest*
Bibit abbas cum priore	*Drink the prior and the abbot,*
Sed conventus de peiore	*While the monks of humbler habit*
Bibit cum tristitia.	*Drink the poorer sullenly.*

That such a parody is not unique is shown by Guiard's *Or ouez les introites de taverne,* included in Attaingnant's *Vingt et huyt chansons musicales,* 1533.[49a]

In the more polyphonic pieces of the various composers belonging to this group, the motifs are flowing rather than declamatory; through-composition and imitation are much favored. Richafort's four-part *Sur tous regretz* and his five-part *D'amours je suis desheritée* [50] illustrate this style, as do Clemens' *La belle Margarite* for five voices, two of which are in canon, and his six-part *Languir me fais.* The last named treats much more polyphonically the melody appearing in the superius of Claudin's chanson of the same name.[51] Crecquillon shows a marked fondness for the more contrapuntal chanson, as in the following example.

[46] Not to be confused with Handl, whose name is also Latinized into Gallus; cf. pp. 736ff. *See also* p. 327 *infra.* Exx. of Le Cocq pr. in CommB XII, 28, 30, 43.

[47] For his 5-part *Ta bonne grace, see* BuH III, 309. Voices 3 and 4 sing a canon at the second, while the other voices make some use of imitation. Canis is the Latin form of the composer's real name, de Hond (cf. StraM I, 42; VII, 354); but he should not be confused with the de Hondt whose first name was Gheerkin; cf. p. 306. *See further* MGG II, 748ff.

[48] Ex. pr. in CommB XII, 56.

[49] Ex. *ibid.,* 58; for studies of him, *see* WauG, LyG; or *see* MGG II, 900f.

[49a] *See further* SchmidtgI.

[50] The former pr. in PubAPTM II, 213 (= MaldP XV, 37); the latter is preserved in Cambridge, Magdalene College, MS Pepys 1760.

[51] These Clemens chansons pr. in CommB XII, 68, 72, respectively. Another polyphonic ex. pr. MaldP I, 14 (= SmM, 104; orig. text lacking in both places; cf. ReT, 94).

EXAMPLE 61. Opening of *Si mon travail*—Crecquillon (from Crecquillon, *Le Tiers Livre des chansons a quatre parties* . . . , Susato,
1544).

"If my pain can give you pleasure while another gives you greater joy, fear not
to displease me . . ."

However, these composers did on occasion write in the style of the other
camp. Clemens' *Entre vous filles de quinze ans* has the Claudin–Janequin
texture; *Je prends en gré* not only has this texture but repeats the music of
lines 1 and 2 for lines 3 and 4 and restates the final line to the same music (at
least in the outer parts; the inner voices are musically changed).[52] Crecquillon's *Qui la dira* is predominantly chordal.[52a] The techniques of the two
groups were not of necessity mutually exclusive: Richafort's *De mon triste
deplaisir,* and Crecquillon's *Ung gay bergier, Contrainct je suis,* and *C'est a
grand tort* [52b] all have the Paris type of musical repetition to new text at the
beginning and to the same text at the end but are markedly polyphonic in
texture. Similar in texture and with repetition of the last line are Richafort's
Il n'est sy doulce vie and Clemens' *Frisque et galliard.*[52c] These two men
and Crecquillon are figures of considerable importance, especially in the field

52 Pr. CommB XII, 63 (= WagG, 359); MaldP XIV, 30, respectively. Repetition at the end
occurs also in the mainly chordal *Une fillette* (pr. PubAPTM XXIII, 31); modified repetition in
the gay *La, la, maistre Pierre* (CommB XII. 65; ELAM XI, 19).
52a Pr. MaldP XIV, 17. MaldP XXIV, 26 (cf. ReT, 97), which is very mildly polyphonic, has
repetition at the end; MaldP XIV, 16, without such repetition, is also mildly polyphonic.
52b Pr. CommB XII, 13 (= MaldP XV, 32; cf. ReT, 114; substitute text removes repetition of
final line); CommB XII, 25 (= RieH II¹, 464); MaldP VIII, 42; I, 17, respectively.
52c Pr. MaldP XV, 35 (substitute text removes repetition of final line); PubAPTM XXIII, 33,
respectively.

of sacred music. The popularity of Clemens' chansons, however, was so great that some of them were reprinted by the house of Phalèse as late as 1643. His works in this genre, as well as those of Crecquillon, were heavily drawn upon as sources of transcriptions for voice and lute for Part II of the *Hortus Musarum* (1553; cf. p. 555). Both men were prolific composers of chansons —more so, it would seem, than Richafort.

The last of these musicians (born c. 1480; died 1548, the same year as Carpentras [52d]) is the oldest of the three. Mentioned by Ronsard as a Josquin pupil, he is traceable as director of the Chapel at St. Rombaut, in Malines, as early as 1507. Richafort was, in 1531, in the service of Mary of Hungary, regent of the Netherlands, and, from 1542 to 1547, director at St. Gilles, Bruges.[53]

Crecquillon became director of Charles V's chapel c. 1540 and later held prebends at Louvain, Namur, Termonde, and Béthune, where he died c. 1557.[53a]

The words "non Papa" were added to "Jacobus Clemens" apparently to distinguish the Latin form of the composer's name from that of a poet, Jacobus Papa. It is likely that Clemens was born on the island of Walcheren in 1510, but that his early creative years were spent in Paris, since his works were first printed in collections issued in 1539 by Attaingnant. His return to the Low Countries may be dated c. 1545, for nine of his chansons were included by Susato in the latter's *Huitiesme Livre* . . . of that year. The close of his life was probably spent in Ypres and Dixmude. He died in 1557 or 1558.[54]

Gombert

Motet-like in the Franco-Netherlandish sense and in this respect similar to the more characteristic chansons of the composers just mentioned, are the secular works of Nicolas Gombert, who was born some time between 1480 and 1500, apparently in southern Flanders (not, as has been suggested, in Bruges). It is possible that he studied with Josquin during the latter's retirement in Condé. In 1526 his name appears on the rolls of the imperial chapel singers; from c. 1529 on, he was *magister puerorum* and, as such, accompanied the emperor on journeys from Spain to northern Italy, Austria, and Germany.[55]

52d A dialogue contained in a *"conversatie-boekje"* of c. 1540–1550, designed to teach the French language to Flemings, mentions "Richafort" as having died in 1540 (*see* LenN, 157), but this cannot refer to Jean Richafort, still traceable in 1548; it may well apply, however, to his brother, Guillaume, also a musician, who is not traceable after 1539 (cf. DoorR, 110).

53 For further biographical data (including the question of name) and a list of works, *see* DoorR; about the list, *see also* Chap. 7, fn. 3, *infra.*

53a For further biographical data, *see* MGG II, 1781ff.

54 Further biographical data in KemJC, 11ff (corrections in CreC); MGG II, 1476ff.

55 EppN, 8ff, queries Gombert's alleged trip to Spain. However, evidence of a sojourn there is provided by Spanish compositions by Gombert (cf. p. 585); *see also* SchmidtgG, 37ff; 100, fn. 211.

(References to the appearance of the chapel singers at different localities under imperial control—e.g., Madrid, Vienna, Brussels—should not be interpreted as indicating the existence of separate organizations.) He probably spent the last years of his life in Tournai, dying not prior to 1556.[56]

Gombert's early chansons display, as special features, general avoidance of phrase repetition, also imitation, not always strict, in which the voices often enter after time-intervals which, for the period, are extraordinarily brief.[57] The specifically French influence, however, appears occasionally in clear-cut cadence formations. All these traits are illustrated in *Amours, amours;*[58] it is noteworthy that, although Gombert's basic thematic material is here repeated (*aabbca*), it invariably appears in a new setting and even the tenor undergoes small alterations.

The *Selectissimae . . . Cantiones* (1540), of significance as the earliest large chanson collection offering a majority of pieces *a 5* and *a 6*, included Gombert's six-part *En l'ombre d'ung buissonet,* a triple canon, and *Qui ne l'aymeroit,* a quadruple canon.[59] In the first of these tours de force, Gombert's predilection for imitation at close time-intervals is most strikingly illustrated—in this case, in strict canon.

EXAMPLE 62. Opening of *En l'ombre d'ung buissonet*—Gombert (from *Selectissimae . . . Cantiones,* Kriesstein, 1540; complete piece in MaldP XI, 20).

This composition is based on the Josquin setting of *En l'ombre d'ung buissonet* that appears in *Canti C.* In his later chansons, Gombert seems to have avoided canon.[60] In them he still favors close imitation and usually avoids exact phrase repetitions, but the structure becomes less neat and concise, more broad and motet-like. A fine example of the type is his *Le bergier et la bergiere,*[61] in which, however, repeated notes underscore, in declamatory fashion, the words of alarm, *"le loup emporte noz moutons."* In contrast to most of the cadences in the early *Amours, amours,* all those in this chanson overlap.

Gombert's *Chant des oiseaux* and *Chasse de lievre* may be profitably com-

[56] Further biographical data *ibid.,* 18ff.
[57] *See,* e.g., the opening of *Tu pers ton temps* (SchmidtgG, 227).
[58] Pr. SchmidtgG, App., 48.   [59] Pr. MaldP XI, 16; cf. ReT, 99, No. 250.
[60] Cf. SchmidtgG, 226; BarthaP, 518.   [61] Pr. CommB XII, 39.

pared with Janequin's pieces on like subjects and are interesting as further examples of program music. The Gombert "Bird Song" [62] published in 1545 (Janequin's appeared c. 1528), uses the same text and thematic material as Janequin's; but Gombert's chanson (which is *a 3*) shows a more advanced technical skill, both harmonically and in the variation of thematic material.

As Josquin composed a lament on the death of Ockeghem, so several were written on his death; but whereas the words of the early threnody were mainly in French, those of the new ones were entirely in Latin. Gombert, in his setting *a 6* of one of the elegies, *Musae Jovis*,[63] draws on the older master's favorite *Circumdederunt* tenor, but presents it as a single melody rather than as a canon. While retaining a clearly recognizable relationship to Josquin's *cantus firmus,* Gombert's modifies it, chiefly through melodic expansion, though even the contour is slightly altered. The new cantus appears four times in the course of the piece, each time in a different mode; each of the last three presentations applies diminution differently to the time-values of the first. The cantus is written down in the form of a puzzle; no doubt this archaic device was used as an additional gesture of deference to Josquin.[64]

Identity Problems; the "Wolf Pack"

Gombert has at times been confused with a composer Nicolas, apparently a Frenchman, of whom we know nothing,[65] and also with Nicolas de la Grotte,[66] a later composer (cf. pp. 389f). Even greater confusion has reigned regarding Benedictus Appenzeller, many of whose works were once assigned to the German, Benedictus Ducis (cf. pp. 266, 679f).[67] A chanson collection,[68] devoted entirely to Appenzeller, was printed in 1542, but two of the pieces had been published as early as 1529 in Attaingnant collections, one piece [69] appearing there as anonymous and the other [70] as the work of Josquin, who may have been Appenzeller's teacher: the younger man, like Gombert, has left us a lament [71] on Josquin's death, drawing on half of the *Musae Jovis* text. Appenzeller produced both Claudin- and motet-like chansons.

[62] Pr. *ibid.,* 78. Further about these Gombert chansons, *see* SchmidtgG, 229; BrenV, 175ff.

[63] Pr. JosqK, 8.

[64] Further about Gombert's secular works, *see* BarthaP, 516ff; SchmidtgG, 219ff; AmbG III, 301f. For exx. not yet cited, *see* PubAPTM II, 216, 219; SchmidtgG, App. 50, 52, 56, 63; MaldP XI, 23; XIV, 19, 21, 23, 25; XVI, 35 (cf. BarthaN, 565); XVII, 3. (Several text changes in MaldP reprints; even a substitution of Dutch for French text in first item listed. Cf. ReT, 98f. The piece ascribed to Gombert in MaldP, XIV, 27, is probably not his; cf. SchmidtgG, 371.)

[65] Cf. BarthaP, 521ff.   [66] Cf. DrozC, 133.

[67] A summary of the evidence on the problem of identity is given in BarthaB, 6ff. *See also* SquireW, SpittaD, BorDO.

[68] Described in SquireW, 269.

[69] Pr. MaldP XIX, 7 (there anon.; ascribed to Claudin in Cambrai MS 124, but *see* BarthaP, 526).

[70] Pr. JosqWW I, 81.

[71] Pr. JosqK, 4; MaldP XIV, 34; BuH II, 513. Other Appenzeller chansons pr. MaldP XIV, 40,

Many similar problems of identity, some as yet unsolved, occur among musicians of the 16th century. Bibliographical evidence and stylistic analysis supplement biographical clues in establishing distinctions. We can assign separate identities to some *"Doppelmeister,"* although it is not always possible definitely to ascribe individual works.[71a] For example, while it has been established that works signed merely "Benedictus" are attributable to Appenzeller rather than to Ducis,[72] it is as yet difficult to say which of the local Cambrai worthies, Gheerkin de Hondt or Gheerkin de Wale, wrote the works signed "Gheerkin." [73] As for the works signed merely "Lupus," or with a variant thereof, the situation is more complicated, since more than two composers are involved. There was a Lupus Hellinck of Utrecht and, later, Bruges (d. 1541) and also a Johannes Lupi or Lupus of Cambrai (d. 1539). The real name of the latter was Jennet or Jehan le Leu. ("Lupi" is, of course, merely the genitive form of "Lupus.") From the capitulary acts of Bruges we learn that Hellinck was a choirboy at St. Donatian from 1506 to 1511 when, because his voice had changed, he was transferred to another position. If we assume that his change of voice took place when he was about sixteen, we may deduce that his birth occurred c. 1495. On similar grounds we may establish J. Lupi's date of birth as c. 1510, since he served as choirboy at Cambrai until about 1526. The Johannes Lupi who is known to have served as an organist at Nivelles in 1502 must therefore be a different person; he would qualify chronologically as the "Lupus" who, according to Vincenzo Galilei, went as an established musician from the Franco-Netherlandish area to Italy in 1513, attracted by the court of Leo X.[73a] There is evidence also of a Johannes Lupi who was active at Our Lady at Antwerp and died c. 1547. There is no specific indication that either of these men was a composer. (Such proof does exist with regard to J. Lupi of Cambrai.[74]) However, it is quite possible that the Lupi of Nivelles is the composer of certain compositions assignable to dates too early to permit their having been written by the Lupi of Cambrai. One of these compositions is the Lament on the death of Ockeghem by "Johannes Lupi"—if, as it is fair to believe, the Lament was written shortly after Ockeghem's death.[75] (*See also* p. 118.) When dates are unavailable, it is difficult to determine the exact authorship of pieces as-

---

42, 44; XV, 3, 8 (2nd piece), 12, 14, 18, 22; XVI, 30; XVIII, 5; *see also* fn. 81 *infra*. Many of the MaldP reprints have substitute texts; cf. ReT, 89 (No. 46), 100. MaldP looks upon Appenzeller and Ducis as identical and translates "Ducis" into "Hertoghs" (cf. ReT, 76). In captions or indexes or both, it ascribes 12 pieces to "Hertoghs" that are anon. in the source; cf. ReT, 100. Further on Appenzeller, *see* BarthaB; BarthaP, 507, 525ff; SquireW; MGG I, 567ff.

[71a] For a special study of 16th-century *Doppelmeister, see* HuD.

[72] *See* BarthaB, 66.

[73] Cf. CouN, 75f. Exx. by "Gheerkin" pr. MaldP XV, 42–52 (6 items); XXV, 5 (= XV, 51; CouN, App., 15).

[73a] Cf. LowBV, 178f.

[74] Cf. LenN 155ff (esp. 158f); StnT, 129ff (esp. 135). The evidence occurs in the dialogue mentioned in fn. 52d.

[75] Cf. AlbH, 64.

signed to "Johannes Lupi" or "Johannes Lupus" and, even more so, that of works bearing only a surname. In addition to the names already mentioned, one finds references to Lupus Lupius, Wolf, Wulframus, Le Leup, etc. The problem of identifying the various members of this "wolf pack" becomes even more complex with the appearance of another partial namesake, Didier Lupi Second (cf. p. 393), about whom we have practically no data other than those afforded by the publications printed under his name. A chanson collection published at Lyons in 1559, in ascribing the contents, distinguishes between "Lupus" and "Lupi Second." [76]

It seems that Lupus Hellinck knew Clemens non Papa and that there was musical interchange between them.[77] While Hellinck wrote some excellent sacred music, he seems, on the basis of the works known to be his, to be less important as a composer of secular music than the Johannes Lupi who emerges as a fine representative of the typical early 16th-century chanson.[78] The most famous chanson that may be by the latter is *Je suis desheritée*, credited to "Lupus" in an Attaingnant collection of 1533, but to the Frenchman, Pierre Cadéac, in a collection of 1539, also printed by Attaingnant. When a printer gives different attributions for the same piece, it is hard to know whether to accept the earlier one as authentic, on the grounds of chronological priority, or the later one, on the supposition that the printer was making a deliberate correction. On *Je suis desheritée* parody Masses were to be based not only by various composers of the time (cf. p. 341) but, later on, by Palestrina and Lassus.[79]

Settings *a 2* and *a 3* of the *Je suis desheritée* melody [79a] were printed in 1545 and 1559, respectively, both credited in the sources to "Jacotin." Other chansons of the period bear the same attribution.[79b] This may refer to the Jacques or Jacotin Le Bel who was a singer in the Royal Chapel from 1532 to 1555.[79c] A Jacotin Level had been in the Papal Chapel from 1516 to 1519.[79d] If this is the same man, he must have enjoyed an unusually long singing career.

Secular Pieces with Middle Dutch Texts

As earlier, the cultural boundaries between France and the Netherlands remained, at the mid-century, relatively fluid, in music as in the other arts.

---

[76] *See* EitQ IV, 338. [77] *See* ZfMW, XIII (1930), 157f.
[78] Cf. AlbH and the pref. of CW XV.
[79] The Cadéac or Lupus setting pr. CW XV, 6; ScherG, 115; PubAPTM XXIII, 20. About the several different settings, *see* BarthaP, 513. (For Cadéac's *L'oeil trop hardy, see* PubAPTM XXIII, 22). CW XV contains 9 additional chansons attributable to J. Lupi; other such chansons in MaldP XVI, 3 (= CommB XII, 18; PubAPTM XXIII, 72), 6 (= PubAPTM XXIII, 75), 8 (= CW XV, 22), 9, 11; XXIV, 24; PubAPTM XXIII, 74. The piece ascribed to "Lupus" in MaldP XVI, 5, is anon. in the source; cf. ReT, 108, No. 441.
[79a] The former pr. DaF, 4; the latter pr. ScherG, 116.
[79b] 3 of them pr. PubAPTM XXIII, 63; MMRF V, 105; LesAC, 6.
[79c] *See* LesAC, *Notices*, No. 3 (note the correction of EinIM I, 266).
[79d] Cf. SaarB, 179f.

Composers such as Clemens set chansons with texts in the speech of the Lowlands as well as of France. Susato's *Premier Livre* . . . of 1543 (cf. p. 290) was apparently the first collection of polyphonic chansons printed in the Netherlands. A MS of Flemish provenance, copied c. 1550, contains many French works previously published by Attaingnant.[80] In 1551 appeared the first of Susato's seven *Musyckboexkens* under the title *Het ierste musyck boexken mit vier partyen daer inne begrepen syn XXVIII nieuwe amoreuse liedekens*. . . .[81] (It is noteworthy that he terms these chansons *"zeer lustich om singen en spelen op alle musicale Instrumenten"*; he had similarly described some of the chansons previously published by him in French.) This volume contains works by Susato himself, Hellinck, Jerome Vinders (who wrote still another lament on the death of Josquin [82]), Willaert, Antoine Barbé,[82a] Josquin Baston,[83] Gheerhart, and anonymi. A later collection, *Een duytsch musyck boeck* (1572),[84] reprints three of these works and contains chansons by Jan Belle, Clemens, Gerardus Turnhout,[84a] Joan de Lattre, Ludovicus Episcopius (*sic*), Noel Faignient [84b] and others. Five of these pieces are *a 5* and one *a 6*. As we have seen (p. 301), such writing for more than four voices began to gain favor c. 1540.

In contrast to the older Netherlandish style, one finds here a tendency, destined to grow, toward chordal texture, and there is a general resemblance to the French chansons. Identifiable *cantus prius facti* are sometimes present, complete or in part. The older fondness for melismas begins to disappear; this is especially noticeable in Jan Belle.[85] Although most of the 16th-century Middle Dutch chansons prefer binary rhythm, ternary snatches, in strict chordal style, are frequently introduced (often at the close of narrative chansons), either for contrast or for textual emphasis. Contrast is also attained by setting off the upper voices against the lower (or, rarely, ST against AB), and a passage presented by one group is likely to be repeated by the other or by the whole ensemble. A feature particularly favored by Episcopius [86] is the use of pedals, even of double-pedals, at the octave.[87]

---

[80] *See* ThibaultF.

[81] Pr. VNM XXIX. For 20 pieces from the second *Musyckboexken*, see LenN, App., 53ff; among the composers are Hellinck, Nicolas Liégeois (= Champion; cf. p. 338 *infra*), Baston, and Appenzeller. Further on the first 2 books, *see* BorMN, 379ff; the third book is discussed on p. 564 *infra*; books 4–7 are devoted to the *Souterliedekens*, cf. p. 355.

[82] Pr. JosqK, 1.

[82a] A chanson of his pr. CommB XII, 35. *See* further MGG I, 1231.

[83] For a 6-part Lament of his (with Latin text) on the death of "Lupus," *see* MaldP XII, 3. The 2 middle voices sing the Gregorian melody to *Requiem . . . Domine* in canon 6 times to fresh countermelodies.

[84] Pr. VNM XXVI.   [84a] For a study of him, *see* DoorT.

[84b] Other Dutch chansons of his pr. LenN, App., 110, 113; French chansons pr. MaldP XXVIII, 17, 19.

[85] Dutch chansons of his pr. VNM XXVI, 3, 37, 40, 43, 46.

[86] Dutch chansons of his pr. *ibid.*, 20, 62, 67, 78, 91, 111, 116 (ascribed to Turnhout on this page, but correctly to Episcopius in index; cf. DoorE, 345). Further about him, *see* DoorE; DoorL; AudaL, 130; LenN, 120.

[87] For other exx. of 16th-century Middle Dutch chansons not included in VNM XXVI, XXIX,

Willaert and Rore as Chanson Composers

Among Franco-Netherlandish composers who spent a major part of their lives in Italy and whose secular works are mainly Italian madrigals, but who also contributed to the literature of the chanson, are Arcadelt, Willaert, his pupil Rore, Verdelot, and Berchem.[88] The bulk of Arcadelt's chansons date from 1553 and later—i.e., from a period after the one that yielded his madrigals—and will be discussed in Chapter 8.

Adrian Willaert (born c. 1480–1490) was a native of Flanders, more likely of Bruges than of Roulers, which has also laid claim to him.[89] As a youth he was sent to the University of Paris to study law, but soon shifted to music, becoming a pupil of Mouton. The main scene of his activity was to be Venice. His chansons show an interesting counterbalance of Franco-Netherlandish and Italian influences. Changes in the development of the two styles are reflected in the course of Willaert's chanson production.[90] The Franco-Netherlandish influence is evident from his earliest chansons, appearing in the *Motetti novi et chanzoni franciose . . . sopra doi* of 1520 (cf. p. 289), which reveal a close kinship to Mouton; these chansons consist mostly of strict double-canons that pair off the two upper and two lower voices. Extraordinary skill is shown by *Mon petit cueur,* in which the same double canon at the fourth below is resolved in two different ways: in both, canon 2 enters one measure after canon 1; but, in one resolution, the upper voice in each pair enters a half-measure after the lower voice, while, in the other resolution, the lower voice in each pair enters two measures after the upper voice.[90a] The purely musical result is agreeable notwithstanding this tour de force. Somewhat less complex, in the same collection, is Willaert's first *Petite camusette* setting (the second appeared in 1540), in which a canon *a 2* is allotted to the lower voices, the two upper ones working out the same melodic material more freely.[91] Willaert set still other texts that Josquin had used and carried on his tradition as a chanson composer.[92] In Willaert's Netherlandish-type chansons from c. 1530 to 1536, the tenor receives *cantus-firmus* treatment, the other voices being in a similarly broad, but strongly melismatic, style; the melismas, however, have no text-illustrating significance. In this final period, from c. 1540 on, this polyphonic type is further de-

---

see PubAPTM XXIII, 9, 11; LenN, App., 21–129. Further regarding Middle Dutch chansons, see LenP; LenN; introductions to VNM XXVI, XXIX.

[88] Chansons by Berchem pr. MaldP XXIV, 20; PubAPTM XXIII, 9, 11. See further MGG I, 1675ff.

[89] Cf. LenW, 109; LenAW, 208f.   [90] See HertzW, 3ff.

[90a] The piece is pr. (with some text change), after Cambrai 124, in MaldP XIV, resolution 1 on p. 4, resolution 2 on p. 3 (transpositions on pp. 6, 5). The print of 1520 contains still another double canon (anon.) on *Mon petit cueur*, also with 2 resolutions.

[91] For a table comparing Willaert's 2 tenors with Ockeghem's, Josquin's, and that of an anon. composer, see HertzW, 82.

[92] Cf. BarthaP, 510.

veloped. Typical of this period is *Jouissance vous donneray,* composed to the same text as Claudin's chanson, but in a strongly contrasting polyphonic style in which Claudin's clear-cut cadences and syllabic text setting yield to broadly flowing and melismatic declamation. Willaert, at the opening of his richly sonorous piece, assigns a fragment of Claudin's tenor melody to the highest voice; the tenor part then continues with the rest of the melody, expanding it through interpolations; all the voices share in its development as the composition unfolds.[93]

EXAMPLE 63. Opening of *Jouissance vous donneray*—Willaert (after *Livre de meslanges* . . . , Le Roy and Ballard, 1560, and *Mellange de chansons* . . . , Le Roy and Ballard, 1572; transcr. by E. Hertzmann).

The Italian influence on Willaert's chansons may likewise be traced through three periods of development. At its full flowering, one finds—instead of the broad melismatic polyphony of the Netherlandish type—concise and predominantly syllabic settings, which even in canonic examples tend to a more chordal style, a more lively rhythmic precision, and a closer relationship of text and music.[94]

Cipriano de Rore (1516–1565), a native of the Low Countries (probably Antwerp) despite his Italianized name, was one of the finest composers among Willaert's pupils in Venice. He received his first musical instruction as a singer in the choir at Antwerp under the direction of Antoine Barbé, and sang there until, his voice having changed, he went to Italy c. 1534.

[93] For a comparative study of different settings, by various composers, of 14 individual chanson texts, etc. (including *Jouissance* and *Petite camusette*), see BarthaP, 511ff.
[94] Cf. HertzW, esp. p. 28, last column. Other Willaert chansons, pr. WolfME, 67; SmM, 86. For a list of Willaert's works (not up to date), see EitAW, 113ff.

Quantitatively, he is a minor figure in chanson history, only eight pieces by him with French texts being known to us.[95] Renée of France, daughter of Louis XII and wife of Hercules II of Ferrara, at whose court Rore served, was an ardent Protestant, and her court became a refuge for Marot, Calvin, and other French religious exiles. *En vos adieux*,[96] probably composed in her honor, is not merely a madrigal with French words. It is a true chanson in that the musical setting parallels the form of the verses instead of being moulded by their ideas (cf. p. 295). Moreover, with slight changes the music for lines 1 and 2 recurs for lines 3 and 4, and the last line is repeated to the same music. *Helas, comment voulés vous*,[97] with which this chanson is coupled and which has the same repetition scheme, contains an interesting example of expressive degree-inflection—favored in Italy from about the middle of the century—at the words *"les yeulx en pleurs."* [98]

Literary Background of the Cinquecento Madrigal

The development of the Italian madrigal in the early 16th century was an intricate process, affected by earlier Italian secular forms, the French chanson, and sacred music, and at the same time by literary currents and changing social conditions. No study of the music apart from the texts can do justice to the madrigal, since, although at first composers were satisfied with conveying the general mood of the most significant lines, they later, in addition to intensifying the representation of varying moods, gave considerable attention to detailed word-painting, which was often highly artistic in practice even though naïve in principle. Actually, the madrigal came to be a genuine, small *Gesamtkunstwerk*, going so far as to include visual elements, yielded by the "eye-music" procedures already mentioned. The evolution of madrigal music went hand in hand with increasing discrimination on the part of composers in their choice of texts.

During the *frottola* period, Italian lyric poetry had declined, indulging in preciosity, bombast, and sentimentality. Even Serafino dall'Aquila (cf. p. 157) and Antonio Tebaldeo, whose names are outstanding, produced mostly distorted echoes of Petrarch, the great model of lyric writers. When the revival of letters came, its chief figures were the master of narrative poetry, Ariosto, and the prose authors Castiglione and Machiavelli, rather than lyric poets. In Petrucci's first *frottola* book names of well-known poets are rare. However, the frottolists themselves showed increasing regard for literary quality, often drawing upon such poets as Politian and Petrarch (cf. p. 161 [99]).

---

[95] *See* EitC, 41, 57, 73; MusiolR, 50. [96] Pr. ELAM XI, 27; SCMA VI, 82.
[97] ELAM XI, 32; SCMA VI, 84.
[98] Another chanson pr. LesAC, 62 (pr. with altus missing in MaldP XI, 7).
[99] *See also* RubL, esp. Ch. I and VII; EinI, 84.

While, of course, some newer lyric poems of literary merit appeared, it is concentration not upon them but upon Petrarch that most clearly reveals the rise in literary taste among musicians.[100]

Cardinal Bembo was the person chiefly responsible for raising literary standards among writers as well as among readers and listeners. Pietro Bembo (1470–1547) was a Venetian nobleman and scholar. He filled the post of papal secretary in Rome from 1512 to 1520, and was nominated Cardinal by Paul III in 1539. Intensely interested in literature, Bembo aimed to restore to the Italian tongue the prestige it had lost after the passing of Dante and Petrarch, and to place it once more on a level with Latin. He was the first to compile rules of Italian grammar—in his *Le Prose della volgar lingua*,[101] which also deals with problems of form and style. He wrote most of his works in Italian, and strove to achieve the utmost purity of language. While he imitated Boccaccio in his prose, Petrarch was his model of poetic perfection. His most important work, *Gli Asolani,* dedicated to Lucrezia Borgia and published in 1505, consisted of prose dialogues on love, interspersed with Petrarchesque *canzoni.* Although Bembo's own verse fails to achieve real greatness, the influence of his lofty ideals was felt throughout the century.

Among established forms of higher lyric verse cultivated at the time were the old *canzone,* sonnet, *sestina* (cf. p. 332), and *ballata.* To these was added the new madrigal, not to be confused with the *trecento* form of the same name.[102] The 16th-century literary madrigal is very similar to the *canzone;* in fact, it may be defined as a *canzone* of one stanza. Bembo states in his *Prose* that there are no definite rules governing either the number of verses to be used in a madrigal or the manner of rhyming them. This leaves as the only formal criterion the number of syllables that may appear in a line. Most frequently, as in a *canzone,* a madrigal has lines of eleven or seven syllables, or a combination of both. In some instances, verses of eleven and seven syllables alternate. Verses of five syllables are rare. In practice, the madrigal has from six to sixteen lines, but it averages about ten. The last two verses often form a couplet.

Poems in the various forms mentioned—as employed by both old and contemporary poets—provided, along with a few of the old, *trecento* madrigals, the basis for the musical-madrigal literature of the 16th century. Throughout the century, Petrarch, whose *Canzoniere* appeared in as many as 167 editions between the end of the 15th century and the beginning of the 17th,[103]

---

[100] Further about Italian lyric poetry in the 16th century, *see* Adolf Gaspary, *Geschichte der italienischen Literatur*, II (1888), 480ff; Giuseppe Toffanin, *Il Cinquecento (Storia Letteraria d'Italia)*, VII (1929), 340ff; Jefferson B. Fletcher, *Literature of the Italian Renaissance* (1934), *passim.*

[101] Published in 1525. Gian Francesco Fortunio published his rules in 1516, but they were written after Bembo's.

[102] Cf. ReMMA, 362ff.   [103] EinMD, 405.

was by far the most popular poet with composers. Some *ballate* from Boccaccio's *Decameron* were provided with music, among them *Io mi son giovinetta,* first set by Domenico Maria Ferabosco (1513–1574).[104] Other authors of poems selected for musical settings were Michelangelo, three of whose madrigals were set by Costanzo Festa and Arcadelt; Bembo, whose poems in *Gli Asolani* lent themselves well to madrigal composition; Jacopo Sannazaro of Naples, the author of the pastoral romance *Arcadia* (the model of Sir Philip Sidney's poem of the same name); Ariosto, stanzas of whose *Orlando furioso* (original 40-canto version published in 1516) were drawn upon by composers and taught the musical madrigal "to express passion and ardour"; [105] Giovanni Guidiccioni, the poet of Arcadelt's most famous madrigal, *Il bianco e dolce cigno;* and Luigi Cassola, whose "poesy of serenades" was often set—there are eight examples by Arcadelt alone. Mere *poesia per musica* such as had often been set by the early frottolists disappears for at least fifty years; the poetry assumes primacy and the music is composed for it. Nevertheless, it must be admitted that not all the texts chosen were of high caliber: the *cinquecento* literary madrigal displays in particular a profusion of exaggerated, high-flown metaphors. Superficially imitating Petrarch, it everlastingly complains of unrequited love.

General Musical Character of the Early Cinquecento Madrigal;
Social Background

Turning to the purely musical aspect (in discussing which we shall, unless otherwise stated, use such terms as madrigal, *canzone,* etc., in the musico-literary rather than the specifically literary sense), we find that the transition from the *frottola* family to the madrigal is clear in its main outline if not in all details. As has already been said, the most serious type of composition within the *frottola* group merged directly into the madrigal, while the lighter, more folklike type of *frottola* was the predecessor of the *villanesca,* (cf. p. 165). By "more serious type" is meant primarily the *canzone.* In fact, from 1520 to 1530 many pieces were printed under the designation *canzone* which in effect were almost madrigals. The *Musica di messer Bernardo Pisano sopra le canzone del Petrarcha* (Petrucci, 1520) sets "the lofty poetry of Petrarch" in a "rich garb of motet-like polyphony." [106] *Che debb'io far,* from this book, might well be described as a motet with Italian text. Pisano provides a setting for strophe 1 of this *canzone* and a separate setting for the

104 Pr. EinIM, III, 56, BonaB, 431; IMAMI IV, 89, with Galilei's lute transcr. Further about lute transcrs. of this work, *see* ChilC. Biographical data, etc., on D. M. Ferabosco in ArkF, 221f; LiviF, 125f; EinIM I, 307ff.
105 EinI, 89.
106 EinDM, 153. (Of the 17 pieces in the collection, 7 set poems by Petrarch.)

commiato. All seven strophes of the main body of the *canzone,* therefore, were sung to the music of strophe 1.[107] No special effort is made to express the content of the text. Several phrases begin with imitation, usually in three of the four voices. On the words *"e l'aspettar,"* the bass and tenor enter imitatively on the formula of a leap of a fourth upward to a dotted note followed by a descending line, a formula which became common enough in the madrigal period to be called an idiom (cf. Ex. 64). Lightly polyphonic writing is found also in Tromboncino and Cara—e.g., in the former's setting of Michelangelo's *Come haro dunque ardire.*[108]

As far as we know, the specific term "madrigal" first appears in 16th-century music in the collection *Madrigali de diversi musici libro primo* (1530),[109] an earlier edition of the famous *Madrigali novi de diversi excellentissimi musici* (1533). It is noteworthy that, in this collection, the publisher Valerio Dorico printed the parts separately, each with complete text, thus departing from the practice, more usually applied to collections of this general sort in the past, of printing the voices in choir-book arrangement with the complete text only under the cantus. Dorico's example was followed in later madrigal publications.[110] While Dorico, at Rome, is among the chief music printers of the new generation in Italy, as are the Germans Giovanni de Buglhat and Hucher at Ferrara, Venice remained the chief scene of Italian music printing. Besides the family of Antonio Gardane (cf. p. 292; from c. 1557 on, he called himself Gardano), that of Ottaviano Scotto (cf. p. 156) continued to operate there extensively.

In considering the French secular current evident in the madrigal, it should be borne in mind that Attaingnant's copious output of chanson publications had begun in 1528. The flow of this current into Italy is tangibly symbolized by the appearance of French chansons in Italian collections of the early 1530's. Janequin's *Bataille* was reprinted by Dorico in 1531, and a lute version of it was issued by another publisher in 1536 (cf. p. 526). Presumably the first Italian print devoted entirely to chansons of the typical 16th-century kind was Antico's *Primo Libro de le canzoni francese* of 1534; many collections containing instrumental transcriptions of chansons appeared in succeeding decades.[111] Through prints like these, as well as through men like Arcadelt, who composed both chansons and madrigals, the *frottola* current

---

[107] Setting of strophe 1 pr. JepL, 86. Concerning other *canzoni* by Pisano with separate setting for the *commiato, see* EinDM, 153. For other pieces by Pisano, *see* EinIM III, 3; GanF, App., No. 3; about No. 4, cf. Chap. 4, fn. 99d.

[108] Pr. EinIM III, 18; TromM, 1; also in A. Gotti, *Vita di Michelangelo Buonarroti* (1875), II, 99. Other exx. showing a tendency toward polyphonic decoration, though less marked than in the Pisano ex., in RubL, 53, 57, 60, 63; SCMA IV, 22.

[109] The alto part of this ed. was found in 1929, in the Biblioteca Colombina at Seville; *see* JepL, 77.

[110] *See* CesE, 14f. (The Pisano print of 1520 had the arrangement followed by Dorico.)

[111] Cf. IMAMI II, xlif.

returned via the roundabout route of France (cf. pp. 288, 291f) to the peninsula, where the spring had by now almost run dry.

How does a madrigal differ from its prototypes? At first it greatly resembled them, being mildly polyphonic like the *canzone* or chordal like the Claudin-Janequin type of chanson. The beginnings and endings of phrases in the early madrigal are most often clearly marked, as in both prototypes. Nevertheless, its abandonment of strophic form and the use of imitation in many examples did bring it, externally, close to the motet. The madrigalists gradually replaced the apparent polyphony that prevailed in the *canzone* by real polyphony, such as is found among the Netherlanders, i.e., by a polyphony revealing intricate and purposeful part-writing and an equal musical importance of the voices. But alongside the northern polyphonic technique the old chordal technique of the *frottola* survived, albeit in a subordinate position, and affected the madrigal through its emphasis on warmth, color, and melodiousness, thus helping the madrigalists in their efforts to express the content of the texts. As a result, the madrigal never reached the academic eruditeness sometimes evident in the motet. The text was assigned to all voices and was set with equal care in each.

In short, the 16th-century madrigal may be said to have the following traits: (1) music composed to set a text of literary quality rather than a text written merely to be set to music (*poesia per musica*); (2) music intended to express the content of the text; (3) as a result of this, a non-strophic (through-composed) form, on the principle that the same music will not suffice to set the varying content of successive stanzas, the actual form differing from piece to piece and being suggested even more by the content than by the structure of the poem; (4) individual voices that are equal and all engaged in precise and beautiful declamation of the text (as distinguished from the voices in a *frottola,* with its assignment of the most prominent role to the superius); (5) a texture that may be polyphonic or chordal (and syllabic) and that, when it uses imitation, does so because this enhances the rhythmic independence of the voices or illustrates the text rather than because it is intrinsic to the madrigal.

The development of a type combining voices of equal importance and Italian poetry was brilliantly furthered by the presence in Italy of numerous Franco-Netherlandish musicians. The glorious culture and wealth of 16th-century Italy attracted many foreigners, who found especially favorable reception there from nobles able to afford the finest music as an ornament to their courts. Venice in particular became a great cultural center, and its sumptuousness and splendor virtually compelled secular music to flourish.[112] Many musicians wrote works dedicated to nobles from whom, presumably, they had obtained or hoped to obtain appointments; while those attached to courts

[112] For a description of musical activity in Venice at the time, *see* PirH, 254ff.

more or less permanently [113] often composed, to order, occasional pieces for celebrations and madrigals that set poems to a *"madonna"* for whose favors a nobleman might sue. *"Madonna"* was frequently a courtesan, accomplished like the *hetaira* of ancient Greece. Especially in Rome, Venice, and Florence, these "honorable courtesans" were wooed by nobles and wealthy persons.[114] Madrigals addressed to a *madonna* were often serenades and as such were meant to be performed out of doors, primarily by voices, and—like most other madrigals—with one voice on each part. During the first half of the century, since *madonna* did not take part in the singing, madrigals scored for men's voices were common; even the parts written in the soprano clef could have been sung falsetto.

Although some *madonna* madrigal texts are blunt, as are also some *villanella* and *strambotto* texts, others might do homage to a lady of quality just as well. The increasing frequency in setting Petrarch's poems idealizing Laura reflects the growing refinement of taste. The cult of "neo-Platonism," interpreted as the pursuit of ideal beauty, had long been present in Italian letters. In the 16th century it was, so to speak, secularized, through combination with the perennial motif of romantic love between the sexes, into a veritable cult of woman. As the century advances, this influence is evident in the choice of texts by poets who idealized feminine beauty; the coarser type of text tends to die out.

Not all madrigals of low vocal range were serenades, of course. Some were written for the private entertainment of small groups of men singers. With the exception of serenades, pieces for court events, and the like, the madrigal in general was performer's rather than listener's music. In Part 1 of the *Dialogo della musica* (1544) Antonfrancesco Doni [115] gives the music of several madrigals, sung by the interlocutors, who are four men. In Part 2, seven men and one woman sing compositions in varying numbers of parts. *"Madonna"* little by little relinquishes her role as a silent listener; moreover, she gradually ceases to be the main subject of madrigals, and scoring for mixed voices becomes normal.

Verdelot

The right to be called "father of the madrigal" belongs to either Philippe Verdelot or Costanzo Festa—it is not certain which. (The latter is not to be confused with Sebastiano Festa, who belonged to the *frottola-canzone* generation.[116]) The other outstanding early masters of the form are Arcadelt and Willaert.

Little is known of Verdelot's life. It is likely that he is identical with Philippe

---

[113] Cf. AnthA, esp. p. 225ff.   [114] Cf. CaraM, 215ff.

[115] Whose *Libreria* makes him "the first musical bibliographer" (EinIM I, 195). Further on Doni, *see* EinAD; MalD.

[116] A *canzone* by S. Festa pr. RubL, 66.

Deslouges.[116a] Vasari, in his life of the painter Sebastiano del Piombo, calls Verdelot a Frenchman. The composer spent many years during the first half of the century in Italy, where he was active in both Venice and Florence. He appears to have died c. 1540.[116b] Verdelot is represented in the *Madrigali de diversi musici . . .* of 1530. His first book *a 4* must have appeared in or prior to 1536, since that year saw the publication of Willaert's arrangements for solo voice and lute of twenty-two Verdelot madrigals contained in it. Book II of madrigals *a 4* was published in 1536 and Book III in 1537; both contained also works by Festa and others. Four books of madrigals *a 5* were published c. 1535 to 1540, one of which was devoted entirely to Verdelot; and in 1541 appeared a book *a 6* containing eighteen madrigals of his. While he wrote madrigals in varying numbers of parts, he was especially happy in writing *a 5* and *a 6*. Many reprints of Verdelot's madrigals were issued shortly after their first appearance. Verdelot is one of the composers of this period whose works won sufficient esteem from the later composer-publisher Claudio Merulo (cf. pp. 417, 540f) for him to re-edit them for his own generation.[117]

Verdelot's style reflects the manifold trends that converged in the madrigal: comparison of some of his works with others reveals nearly opposite poles represented by these trends. *Donna leggiadr'e bella* [118] is chordal and syllabic almost throughout, while *Dormend'un giorn'a Bai* and *Ultimi miei sospiri* [119] make conspicuous use of imitation; but, even in works where polyphony is highly developed, completely chordal passages occur. *Divini occhi sereni* [120] presents a mean in the balance of chords and polyphony. What Dr. Einstein calls "polyphonically animated homophony" is more characteristic of his writing than is any other style, as it is also of the writing of Festa and Arcadelt.

Three voices open the five-part *Quant'ahi lasso,*[121] in which one can hear two groups, a high one for the lady's voice and a lower one for the man, a genuine dialogue. Two voices sing in imitation a phrase that includes the upward-fourth idiom found in Pisano, while the phrase in the lowest voice includes an inversion of this formula.

EXAMPLE 64. Extract from *Quant'ahi lasso*—Verdelot (after WagMP, 464).

116a For the evidence, *see* SchmidtgG, 170. 116b Cf. EinIM I, 156; but also LowBV, 187f.
117 Cf. CatM, 8off. For details of Merulo's ed. of Verdelot, *see* EinC.
118 Pr. PubAPTM III, 235.
119 Pr. WagMP, 461, and MonteO V, App., respectively. The latter also with Dutch text in MaldP XI, 37; cf. ReT, 116, No. 600. 120 Pr. PubAPTM III, 237. 121 Pr. WagMP, 464.

The idiom appears to have been a favorite of Verdelot's, and he uses it elsewhere, both with and without imitation. Verdelot's normal intervals of imitation are the octave, fifth, and fourth, but in *Si liet'e grata morte* [122] the second voice enters a fifth below the first and the bass a fifth below the second, thus giving rise to imitation at the lower ninth.

Between phrases there may be simultaneous rests in all voices; a cadence concluded by all voices together, but not separated from the following phrase by rests; a cadence with one or two voices carried into the succeeding phrase against simple sustained notes; or interlocking in northern motet style. In *Dormend'un giorn'* and *Ultimi miei sospiri,* phrases 1 and 2 equal phrases 3 and 4, in chanson fashion, notwithstanding their polyphonic character. *Dormend'* also has repetition of the last phrase of music with the last line of text.

I vostr'acuti dardi and *Madonna qual certezza* [123] are examples of madrigals in sharply divided sections (too short, however, to be regarded as *partes*). In the former piece, in two sections, the penultimate phrase, though not the same as the first, is obviously related to it; in the latter, in four sections, section 4 concludes with the same two final phrases as section 1. Structural repetition appears also in the lovely *Con lagrime e sospir,* [124] where phrase 2 recurs toward the end.

Repetition may serve a different purpose in *Madonna non so dir.* [125] For once the poet does not implore the lady's favors, but makes it clear that *"un bel si"* and *"un bel no"* are equally acceptable. Evidently as a bit of text delineation, these expressions are identically set (except for *Stimmtausch* in the two upper voices), as are the lines:

Se'l ser un si, un si scriverò'n rima,   If it is yes, a "yes" I in rhyme shall spin you;
Se'l ser un no, amici come prima. [126]   If it is no, as friends we shall continue.

Word-painting is rare at this early period; many opportunities composers would later have seized upon are passed over. In *I vostr'acuti dardi,* however, the sigh is unmistakable on *"ahi, ahimè";* and the rising semitone in the superius on *"mi fa(n)"* foreshadows the wider adoption by madrigalists of the old practice of pairing syllables of texts with notes bearing the corresponding solmisation syllables. In *Quant'ahi lasso,* the word *"morte"* is coupled with a mild suspension, thus:

---

[122] Pr. EinC, 249; *see* p. 253.
[123] Pr. PubAPTM III, 243 (= ELAM XI, 38) and EinIM III, 21, respectively; the second, after Willaert's arrangement for voice and lute, pr. TagA I, 1.
[124] Pr., in Willaert's arrangement, EinIM III, 319; TapS, 18; BruL I, 20.
[125] Pr. CW V, 13.
[126] The second of these lines is then repeated to different music.

EXAMPLE 65. Extract from *Quant'ahi lasso*—Verdelot (after WagMP, 465).

Donna leggiadr'e bella, scored for TTBB, extols the charms of the beauty to whom it was addressed. Two Verdelot madrigals, evidently commissioned, incorporate the name of Tullia of Aragon, one of the most celebrated courtesans of Rome, who for a time lived in Venice.[127]

Costanzo Festa

Costanzo Festa entered the service of Leo X in 1517 as a singer in the Papal Chapel. His first known work dates from 1514. In 1543, he was reported too sick to follow the Pope to Bologna; he died in 1545.[128] Festa was a prolific composer of secular music. Madrigals of his were printed in many important collections of the time, e.g., in the *Madrigali de diversi musici . . .* of 1530 and in some of Verdelot's and Arcadelt's books. In 1543, Gardane published Festa's own madrigal book, *Il vero Libro di Madrigali a tre voci di Constantio Festa.*[129] The composer was the leading writer of madrigals *a 3.*

[127] Texts in EinIM I, 175f. Further about Verdelot, *see ibid.,* 154ff; 247ff; Van den Borren in the [Belgian] *Biographie nationale,* XXVI (1936–37), 595ff; additional madrigals, pr. EinIM III, 24, 26, 29; ScherG, 95.

[128] Further biographical notes in MPI II, ixf; also, with list of works, in CamF. The list fails to note the dubiousness of certain attributions; cf. fn. 129.

[129] Another madrigal book reprinted by Gardane in 1541 (no copy of the original print is known) bears the title: *Di Constantio Festa Il Primo Libro de Madrigali a tre voci. Con la gionta de Quaranta Madrigali di Ihan Gero, Novamente ristampato. . . . Aggiuntovi similmente Trente Canzoni Francese di Janequin. . . .* Strangely enough this book contains (outside of the chansons) only 42 madrigals, so that—since one is ascribed to Parabosco and the title states that 40 are by Gero—just one madrigal appears to be attributable to Festa, in spite of the prominence given his name in the title. Which one this is, is not indicated. In 1553 another reprint appeared, under Gero's name; the lists of madrigal titles in the two prints are identical except for two titles which are omitted from the later reprint (cf. VogelV I, 235, 284). These are the Parabosco and *Afflitti spirti,* which therefore is presumably by Festa. This situation has led to considerable confusion in the ascription of the contents of these prints to Festa and Gero. Other prints add further complications: e.g., *Madonna io v'amo* (pr. BuH III, 246), which is included in both the 1541 and 1553 prints and in Festa's 1543 book, appears with an ascription to Festa in several reprints of the last as well as in Merulo's 1568 ed. of it; but in a 1541 Petreius print it is given under Gero's name (cf. VogelV I, 234ff; EinB, entry under 1541[1]). Conflicting ascriptions to Festa and Gero are not confined to the prints already named. Thus the two-part *Amor, che mi consigli* (pr. TorA I, 53) is attributed to Festa in a collection of *canzoni,* etc., of 1531, but is included as Gero's in this composer's first madrigal book *a 2* (also 1541; cf. VogelV II, 378; I, 285, respectively). (Inclusion in Gero's book *a 2* throws some doubt on the suggestion that has been made that the piece was intended as a double canon.) The madrigals pr. in FestaM, 1, 3, 6, 8,

In the 1540's there appeared in madrigal writing a new trend, which has been attributed to the influence of the *villanesca*.[130] This trend manifests itself in increased rhythmic animation and the use of shorter note-values, resulting in the adoption of the common-time signature. Varied rhythmic patterns abound, especially syncopations; and semiminims, which were previously used in the main for melismatic purposes (cf. p. 378), are supplied with separate syllables. Since small note-values occur as a matter of principle, these compositions are called *madrigali a note nere, madrigali a misura di breve,* or *madrigali cromatici,* the last term referring not to chromaticism but to the fact that the prevailing notes were not white but black, and to that extent "colored." In other words, the semiminim, in pieces of this kind, replaced the minim as the normal time-unit. Works by Festa are found in at least four collections of such madrigals (1543-1549). Once established, this type of writing appears also in collections not designated *"a note nere,"* etc. In *Veggi'or con gli occhi,* syncopation and "black notes" characterize the following passage:

EXAMPLE 66. Extract from *Veggi'or con gli occhi*—Festa (from FestaM, 30f [original values halved]).

The style in such a madrigal as *Quando ritrovo la mia pastorella*[131] is predominantly chordal, with phrases clearly marked; the voices are not equal in importance. This piece, which begins with the "narrative" formula (cf. pp. 292f) and has the last line of text repeated to the same music, is virtually a chanson with an Italian text. It is, incidentally, Festa's best-known work in the English-speaking world, being widely reprinted with the English text *Down in a flow'ry vale,* a free translation by Thomas Oliphant (1799-1873).[132]

Festa's *Così suav'è'l foco,*[132a] a particularly fine composition, opens with paired imitation and is polyphonic throughout, as is *Quanto più m'arde.*[133] In the latter work, the minor seconds in the superius on *"dolor duol"* and *"morte m'ancide"* and the comparatively low register of the passage setting these words are clearly expressive of the text. *Donna ne fu ne fia,*[134] scored for ATTSb with the alto part not rising above f', begins, like *Quando ritrovo,*

---

belong to the works attributable to either Festa or Gero. (Those in FestaM, 15, 21, 25, are attributable to either Festa or Arcadelt.)

[130] *See* HertzW, 44ff.   [131] Pr. HAM, 140.

[132] Cf. his *La Musa Madrigalesca* (1837), 328f. Stanza 2, often given in modern prints, does not appear here, and presumably was added by a later hand.

[132a] Pr. EinIM I, 36.   [133] Pr. FestaM, 17.   [134] Pr. WagMP, 487.

with the "narrative" formula. The first two lines of the text are repeated at the end, the first to the same music as at the beginning and the second to an imitative phrase based on the altus of the chordal second phrase. The closing phrases of *Se grato o ingrato* exhibit an unusual repetition scheme: phrases 4 and 3 from the end are identical; a new phrase is then introduced, followed by a single modified presentation of the repeated phrase. This madrigal contains an example of the common practice of lowering what we would call the root of a leading-tone triad in root position, in order to avoid a harmonic diminished fifth: [134a]

EXAMPLE 67. Extract from *Se grato o ingrato*—Festa (after PistF, 14).

Arcadelt as Madrigalist

In Florence, a center of madrigal writing no less important than Venice and Rome, the leading madrigalist of the middle thirties was the Netherlander, Jacques Arcadelt (born c. 1504; [135] died probably after 1567). His first madrigals appeared in 1537, one in a collection *a 3,* printed by Scotto, and one in Verdelot's Book III *a 4.* In January, 1539, Arcadelt, then at Rome, was admitted to the Julian Chapel, and after some months there he became a member of the Sistine Chapel. The same year saw the publication of no less than four books of his madrigals *a 4.* About 1542, a Roman banker commissioned him to set music to two of Michelangelo's madrigal poems—which, however, failed to please the great Florentine.[136] In 1542 a madrigal book *a 3* was published and in 1544 a fifth book *a 4.*[137]

Arcadelt's madrigals show notable affinity with the French chanson. To be sure, polyphonic passages alternate with chordal ones, but the polyphony is simple, as in *Voi ve n'andate.*[138] Usually phrases within his madrigals are clearly marked, as in the most famous of them, the exquisite *Il bianco e dolce cigno.*[139] The influence of the chanson is seen here also in note repetition and in the repetition of the last line of text to virtually the same music, this being based on the familiar upward-fourth idiom.

[134a] Further on Festa, *see* esp. EinIM I, 157ff; 257ff; additional madrigals pr. *ibid.*, III, 33; MaldP XXVI, 19 (cf. ReT, 92f).

[135] Cf. EinIM I, 159.

[136] Cf. *ibid.*, 161f, 272. The pieces pr. TromM, 8 (= A. Gotti, *Vita di Michelangelo Buonarroti* [1875], II, 110; MaldP XXVI, 13); 12 (= Gotti, *op. cit.*, 116; MaldP XXVI, 1).

[137] Further biographical notes in KlefA, Chap. I; list of works (not up to date) in EitA, 123ff, 129ff, 137ff, 153ff.

[138] Pr. CW V, 16; MaldP XXV, 12.   [139] Pr. SquireM, 2; BuH, 303; MaldP XXV, 9; *etc.*

Among madrigals prompted by events of the day—whether of rejoicing or of mourning—are Arcadelt's *Ecco, d'oro l'età,* composed for the wedding of Margaret of Austria (niece of the famous Regent of the same name) and the Duke of Parma in 1542, and the impressively beautiful *Deh, come trista* for the death of a Florentine nobleman, perhaps Alessandro de' Medici.[140] The writing, particularly in the latter, is in polyphonic motet style.

Most of Arcadelt's madrigals are *a 4.* Harmonically unrevolutionary, his writing is still completely diatonic. His pure vocal style, free of the kind of leaps we have come to associate with instrumental writing and painstaking in its adjustment of music to text, laid the ground for the madrigals of Palestrina. His treatment of dissonance, however, is not always as orthodox (from the standpoint of what became normal 16th-century style) as Palestrina's. Thus, we find in the altus this example of a c′ that is approached as a passing note and quitted as a suspension.

EXAMPLE 68. Extract from *Voi ve n'andate*—Arcadelt (after CW V, 18).

Of the identified texts of Arcadelt's madrigals, twenty-four are from poems by Petrarch in various forms.[141] Two of these are *trecento* madrigals: *Hor ved'amor* and *Per ch'al viso.* Their musical treatment, however, is wholly in the style of the *cinquecento:* the pieces are through-composed and therefore have nothing at all in common with the musical madrigal of the *trecento.*

The lyrical melodiousness of Arcadelt's madrigals and his predilection for four-part writing show that the Italian musical temperament exerted a strong influence on him. His immense popularity in Italy—his first book of madrigals *a 4* was reprinted thirty-three times by 1654, and many spurious pieces appeared bearing his name—was probably due to the fact that he, more than any other Netherlander working in Italy at the time, reproduced in his madrigals some of the lucidity of the Italian *frottola.* The music makes an immediate appeal and is easy to sing and personal in quality.[142]

[140] Ed. by Everett Helm, 1946, pr. by Music Press, Nos. 82, 81, respectively. The latter also in HelmH, 316.

[141] The 21 remaining texts whose poets have been identified are taken from Boccaccio, Bembo, Lorenzo de' Medici, Ariosto, Michelangelo, Guidiccioni, and Luigi Cassola. Further about Arcadelt's texts, *see* KlefA, 19ff.

[142] Further on Arcadelt, *see* esp. HelmM; EinIM I, 159ff, 264ff; MGG I, 603ff. Madrigals by him not yet cited, pr. *ibid.,* III, 38, 41 (= MaldP XXVIII, 2), 44, 125 (a *canzone* setting in 5 *partes*); EinGA, 7; CW V, 19 (= OrtizT, 69; the well-known *O felici occhi*); ScherG, 96; OH

Willaert as Madrigalist

Willaert, who was in the forefront in so many fields of musical endeavor, was a leader also in the development of the madrigal. Once he had, in 1527, established himself as *maestro di cappella* at St. Mark's (cf. p. 370), his fame spread rapidly and musicians were eager to study with him: in addition to Cipriano de Rore, his pupils included Zarlino and Vicentino.

The gradual synthesis of Italian and Franco-Netherlandish traits is well illustrated in Willaert's madrigals, which show a clear evolution of style. The earliest examples were printed in Verdelot's Book II of 1536. Here, as in the chanson and related *frottola*-type, the setting is predominantly chordal; imitative passages appear only occasionally. The various phrases are still plainly marked. The upper voice is melodically the most important, although the other voices, in contrast to those of the *frottola,* are also independently conceived. However, we often find fauxbourdon-like progressions of parallel sixths and thirds. Willaert's emphasis is on color, and he is therefore much interested in harmonic experiments, as is evidenced in his treatment of the bass, which abounds in leaps. Much has been made of his occasional use of rudimentary chromaticism.[143]

Willaert's later madrigals reveal a greater predominance of Netherlandish traits. Phrases are not sharply defined; the end of one phrase and the beginning of the next overlap in motet fashion, thus departing from the style of his early period. All voices are of equal importance; although in the bass leaps with harmonic implications are still conspicuous, the emphasis now is more on line than on color. Chordal passages are used mostly for the sake of expression. An example of such a madrigal is *Quanto più m'arde,*[144] published c. 1540. The writing is imitative, especially in *pars II. Qual dolcezza giammai,*[145] printed in the same collection, is a dedicatory madrigal, in which Willaert makes the five voices produce the effect of two choruses of different ranges. The text mentions *"la bella Pecorina."* This is Polissena Pecorina, who herself played and sang, besides sponsoring musical entertainments in her home. Doni writes in a letter to Marchese Malvicino of Piacenza:

The music of liuti, Stromenti, Pifferi, Flauti, and of voices which one hears in your excellency's and Colombo's houses is splendid; and the music made by viols at S. Guido dalla Porta's is marvelous. But you would have been amazed if you heard the divineness which I witnessed here in Venice. There is here a gentle-

---

II, 124; SCMA V, 4 (actually the chanson, *Quand je me trouve,* the music of which first appeared with the text *I vaghi fiori;* cf. EinB, entry under 1549[1]); MaldP XXV, 16, 19; XXVI, 4 (= EinW, 363), 7, 10, 16, 21, 24, 27; XXVII, 1, 4, 10, 13, 16, 19, 22; XXVIII, 6, 9, 12. (The pieces ascribed to Arcadelt *ibid.,* XXVI, 19; XXVII, 7, 25, 28; XXVIII, 4, are not his; cf. ReT, 92f.) *See* the list given in KlefA, 122ff, about certain madrigals ascribed to Arcadelt in some sources but not in others, including a few madrigals just enumerated.

[143] Cf. KrI, 35ff; CaraM, 204ff.　　[144] Pr. WagMP, 455.　　[145] Pr. *ibid.,* 449.

woman, Polisena [sic] *Pecorina (consort of a gentleman from my own city). . . .
At her house I heard one evening a concert of viols and voices at which she played
and sang with others. The "perfect maestro" of the music was Adriano Willaert
whose diligent inventions are no longer usual with composers. His music is so
well unified, so expressive* (dolce), *so appropriate* (giusta), *and it so wonderfully
adorns the words, that I confessed not to have known what music was in all my
days save for that evening. . . .*[146]

Willaert's madrigals printed in 1542 in Scotto's *Madrigali a quattro voci*
follow the *note nere* trend already found in Festa.

In 1559 appeared the *Musica nova*, edited by Willaert's pupil Francesco
Viola,[147] the only known collection of the time containing madrigals by
Willaert to the exclusion of other composers. It also includes motets by him.
The *Musica nova* is apparently a later printing of a collection (of which no
copy has survived) published about fifteen years earlier and dedicated to La
Pecorina.[148] The secular texts stem almost without exception from Petrarch.
The declamatory character of the *Musica nova* pieces approaches the recitative style, partly as a result of many note-repetitions.[149] The voice-leading
displays an intricacy of polyphonic writing surpassing Verdelot's and that
of other madrigal composers of the time. Chord progressions in which the
roots descend by thirds, not uncommon in Arcadelt and Verdelot, are here
very frequent. The five-part *Mentre che'l cor*,[150] from this collection, is a
sonnet, set in two *partes,* one for the octave and one for the sestet. This
procedure, characteristic of Willaert,[151] was to remain so for the madrigal
generally. *Mentre che'l cor* also provides an early example of word-painting.
Melismas appear with obviously descriptive intent on several words, e.g.,
"*cantando,*" on which various short melismas occur, leading us up to this
climactic one in the middle voice:[151a]

EXAMPLE 69. Extract from *Mentre che'l cor*—Willaert (after CW V, 7).

Corteccia and Some Lesser Madrigalists

Along with Festa, other native Italians contributing to early 16th-century
madrigal composition were Alfonso della Viola (not to be confused with

[146] Quoted from CaraM, 202f.   [147] He is the composer of a book of madrigals *a 4* (1550).
[148] *See* HertzW, 51; CaraM, 201ff; RieH II¹, 385f.   [149] Cf. HertzW, 51.   [150] Pr. CW V, 5.
[151] *See* HertzW, 53. However, Willaert divides a sonnet *a 7* (pr. EinIM III, 63), also from this
collection, by setting quatrain I *a 4,* quatrain II for the remaining 3 voices, and the sestet for a
varying vocal "orchestration," ending *a 7.*
[151a] Further on Willaert as a madrigalist, *see* esp. HertzW; EinIM I, 319ff. For additional
madrigals by Willaert, *see ibid.,* III, 59; RieH II¹, 387 (= MaldP XIII, 42).

Francesco Viola), Giandomenico Martoretta, Girolamo Parabosco (probably died c. 1557), Domenico Maria Ferabosco (cf. p. 313), and Francesco Corteccia (b. early 16th cent. in Arezzo; d. 1571). Books of madrigals *a 4* by Alfonso della Viola were printed in 1539 and 1540, and he is represented in a collection published by G. Scotto in 1562. As a writer of music for stage works, he will be met again in Chapter 10. Martoretta's works, which appeared from 1544 to 1566, include a Book II of madrigals (1552), noteworthy for containing *Laura soave vita,* which is provided with two alternative sets of clefs and labelled *"Duo toni"*: the piece may be performed in either the Phrygian mode or the Mixolydian. There is a similar example in Martoretta's Book III (1554).[152] A madrigal book *a 5* by Parabosco appeared in 1546. Four pieces by him are included in Doni's *Dialogo.*[152a]

Early in his career, Corteccia went to Florence. He published two books of madrigals *a 4,* in 1544 and 1547, and one of madrigals *a 5* and *a 6,* also in 1547, all of which were dedicated to Cosimo de' Medici. He composed a series of madrigals that were sung in costume at the wedding of Cosimo and Eleonora of Toledo in 1539 (cf. p. 567). In some of his works *note nere* are conspicuous.[152b]

Of special interest is the *strambotto*-like *Io dico e dissi e dirò* (*Orlando furioso,* Canto 16, stanza 2). Improvisation to instrumental accompaniment such as Brandolini described (cf. p. 153) was still being practiced. Epics and elegies in *ottava rima* were recited to partially improvised music—"partially" since such music was based on pre-existent patterns (cf. the old French *chanson de geste* [152c]). These patterns were applied with such changes as the improvisator considered appropriate to the content of individual stanzas. When *Orlando furioso* appeared, it imparted new impetus to this practice, being intoned in many sections of Italy. Some of the melodic formulas that were used were named after the localities with which they were associated; thus, we find the terms *Aria di Firenze, Aria di Genova,* etc. In Corteccia's *Io dico e dissi,* a formula from Florence is presented four times in the superius while the lower voices sing fresh counterpoint against it (Ex. 70a).[153] Since the various formulas were designed for the rendition of *ottave rime,* they could be and were applied to other poems having the *ottava-rima* pattern. The melody that was to prove the most popular of the group—compositions continued to be written on it well into the 17th century—seems

[152] Cf. KrZC, 112; KrV, xiv; LeviO, 462f; *Laura soave* pr. KrV, 24. The suggestion, made in KrZC and KrV, that these pieces may have a bearing on the *chiavette* problem (cf. pp. 531ff *infra*) is unfounded.

[152a] A madrigal of his, pr. EinIM III, 151. *See also ibid.,* I, 444ff.

[152b] *See* the exx. in TorA I, 113, 117.   [152c] *See* ReMMA, 203f.

[153] Other Corteccia madrigals, pr. EinIM III, 47, 52, 321 (incomplete; cf. *ibid.,* II, 841); MaldP XXVII, 25 and 28 (cf. ReT, 92f).

originally to have been applied to Canto 44, stanza 61, of *Orlando furioso,* beginning *Ruggier, qual sempre fui,* and was fittingly called the *Aria di Ruggiero* (Ex. 70*b*). It was most often assigned to the bass but sometimes to the superius. While the *Ruggiero* melody occurs in vocal music (cf. p. 428), it comes down to us incorporated chiefly in instrumental compositions, as we shall see in Chapter 10.[154]

EXAMPLE 70. (*a*) Extract from the superius of *Io dico e dissi e dirò*— Corteccia (complete piece in EinAA, opp. 168; EinIM III, 49), (*b*) The *Ruggiero* melody.

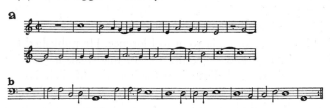

In 1548 appeared *Madrigali di Giovanni Nasco a 5 voci.* Nasco (= Maistre Jhan of Verona), a Netherlander, had recently been appointed *maestro* of the important Veronese *Accademia Filarmonica.* Later he became *maestro di cappella* of the Treviso Cathedral. Other madrigal books by him, containing pieces in as many as eight parts, appeared during the 1550's. His secular works comprise also *canzoni* and *villanesche.*[155]

Countless other early composers of madrigals include Hubert Naich,[156] the younger Fr. de Layolle, Andreas de Silva, and Antonio Barré. Layolle must have entered fully into the art life of Florence: Andrea del Sarto painted him into a fresco of the Adoration of the Magi at the Santissima Annunziata, and Pontormo made a fine portrait of him; he, in turn, taught music to Benvenuto Cellini.[157] De Silva was a singer in the Papal Choir in 1519, and in the record for that year is called "our composer." [158] In 1522, he received a payment for services from the Duke of Mantua.[158a] Vincenzo Galilei includes him in a list of Flemings and Frenchmen.[159] Barré, a Frenchman, is listed as an altus in the Julian Chapel records of 1552. Three years thereafter he pub-

---

[154] Further concerning the *Ruggiero,* etc., *see* esp. EinAR; EinAA; EinIM I, 206.

[155] A piece by Nasco, pr. ChilS, 26. Further about him, *see* EinIM I, 192f, 307, 455ff; TurrN; TurrV; AlesC, 159ff.

[156] A madrigal of his, pr. PubAPTM III, 239.

[157] Cf. EinIM I, 280; TricouL, 6f.

[158] *See* HabR, 69. This has led to his being called composer to the Papal Choir before Palestrina filled that post.

[158a] Cf. BertolM, 34. Further biographical data in LowBV, 175ff.

[159] Cf. LowBV. A madrigal by de Silva, pr. PubAPTM III, 246.

lished a madrigal book *a 4,* containing works by himself and others, and later he set up his own printing house, first at Rome, then at Milan.[160]

A northerner whose madrigals have often been confused with Festa's (cf. fn. 129) was Jhan Gero. His personal identity has been a subject of confusion also, for he has wrongly been considered the same as Jehan Le Cocq (cf. p. 301) and consequently the same as Maistre Jhan of Ferrara (since Le Cocq and Jhan have been regarded as one, though without adequate evidence). Gero's first madrigal book appeared in 1541. His name is prominent in *note nere* writing. In his *Io mi credea scemare,*[161] at the phrase *"s'io mi son morto o vivo,"* the word *"morto"* is illustrated by a marked slowing down of the time-values and *"vivo"* by an ascending leap of an octave. The use Gero makes of syncopation in *Amor io sento* [162] is noteworthy. Maistre Jhan, a shadowy figure, was *maestro di cappella* to both Alfonso I and Hercules II.[162a] A few madrigals of his have come down to us.

Several other *Doppelmeister* are found among northerners of this period: Ivo and Ivo de Vento, Jachet Berchem (cf. p. 309) and Jachet of Mantua, Matthaeus Le Maistre and Hermann Matthias Werrecore.[163] All but Le Maistre contributed to the development of music in Italy. Ivo lived several decades earlier than Ivo de Vento. Madrigals by him are found in various early collections, beginning with Verdelot's of 1538.[164] While Jachet of Mantua wrote much sacred music, Berchem appears to have written primarily secular music.[165] In 1546 and 1555 Berchem published books of madrigals *a 5* and *a 4,* respectively, and in 1561 three books of settings of stanzas from the *Orlando furioso,*[166] which he dedicated to Duke Alfonso II of Ferrara. Le Maistre served as *Kapellmeister* at the court in Dresden (cf. p. 682), while Werrecore was active in Milan. Sacred and secular works by the latter appeared in print during the 1540's and 1550's—including the *Bataglia Taliana,* composed in honor of Francesco Sforza after this duke had won a great victory in the 1520's.[167] This was an Italian counterpart of Janequin's *Bataille.*

---

[160] Madrigals by Barré pr. WagMP, 468, 476. The first is a through-composed setting of 4 stanzas of *Orlando furioso* (Canto 32, 18ff). *See also* MGG I, 1340f.

[161] Pr. TorA I, 109.

[162] Pr. WagMP, 481. Other madrigals by Gero pr. *ibid.,* 478, 483; TorA I, 87, 105; SmM, 134; cf. also fn. 129. For 4 French duos, *see* ExA, 20, 22, 24, 26.

[162a] Cf. WeyF, 84ff. Concerning the identity problem, see further *ibid.;* EinIM I, 307.

[163] For an examination of the *Doppelmeister* problem in connection with some of these composers, *see* HuD, 178ff.

[164] *See* HuI, 15ff.

[165] *See* esp. EitJ. Berchem has been confused also with Jachet Buus and Giaches de Wert.

[166] Further about them, *see* EinIM II, 564ff. Madrigals by Berchem pr. EinIM III, 123; MaldP XI, 25, 29 (both with substitute Dutch texts; cf. ReT, 80, 93); XXVII, 7, and XXVIII, 4 (cf. ReT, 92f.).

[167] Published separately, 1931, by A. Tirabassi; *pars I* also in KadM, App., No. 1. About the disputed identification of the battle, *see* EinIM I, 743f. Further about Werrecorre, *see* HabW; IMAMI I, xciif; BorTM, 39f; BrenV, 146ff.

The native Italian, Pietro Taglia, was also active at Milan, where madrigal books of his were printed in 1555 and 1557.[167a]

Vicentino and His Experiments

One of the most striking contributions of the Italian madrigal—the development of chromaticism to a high degree—was heralded and championed by Nicolò Vicentino (1511–1572). A pupil of Willaert's, this apostle of "advanced" music spent most of his life in the service of Cardinal Ippolito d'Este of Ferrara, accompanying his patron during his long residences in Rome. He is famous chiefly for his book, *L'antica musica ridotta alla moderna prattica* (1555), in which he tries to apply what he believes to be the ancient Greek diatonic, chromatic, and enharmonic genera [167b] to the polyphonic music of his time. His enharmonic system divides the whole tone into five parts. This book contains a number of his compositions. He wrote also five books of madrigals *a 5*.

Some revolutionary intent is shown by the title page of his Book I of madrigals (1546), which declares the contents to be written "in the new manner rediscovered by his most celebrated teacher." It would thus seem that Vicentino may have received his initial stimulus to the frequent use of accidentals from Willaert.[168] Actually, however, although these appear often in the 1546 book, most of them serve quite "normal" purposes, such as raising degree 7 in cadences. But Book V (1572; the intervening books are lost) reveals Vicentino as an extreme chromaticist. Rarely employed accidentals such as D-sharp, D-flat, and A-sharp are common. Even a melodic augmented third, E-flat to G-sharp, occurs. Further striking departures from the old tonal system are represented by cadences on triads built on D-sharp, F-sharp, B, D-flat, and A-flat.

Dolce mio ben, in *L'antica musica . . . ,* illustrates Vicentino's method of notation: a dot over a note raises it by a small *diesis* (as in the first progression of the outer voices in Ex. 71); a large *diesis,* which corresponds to the small semitone, results either when notes appear to be written a semitone apart, but the lower one is raised by a dot (as on *"consu-"* in the superius in the example), or when the notes are written on the same scale-degree, but one is sharpened or flattened and the other is natural (as on *"fanno,"* in the bass); if one note is sharpened or flattened and the other one is natural, and the notes are on adjacent scale-degrees, they call for a large semitone (as on

---

[167a] *See* further EinIM I, 424ff.   [167b] Cf. ReMMA, 23ff.

[168] For more details, *see* KrI, 100f. Grove V, 495, quotes the title page of Vicentino's Book I as containing the phrase *"unico discepolo"* to Willaert, and then remarks that, as he certainly was not *"unico,"* he may not even have been a *"discepolo."* Actually, the title page reads: *"del unico Adrian Willaerth discipulo."*

"tanto" in the tenor [168a]). A small whole tone is indicated either by notes appearing to be a semitone apart, but with a dot raising the higher one, or by two notes on the same scale-degree, one being sharpened and the other flattened; an ordinary whole tone is indicated in the usual way.[168b]

EXAMPLE 71. Extract from *Dolce mio ben*—Vicentino (after KrI, 155).

Vicentino says that a piece noted in this fashion may also be performed in other ways, for example, by surpressing both the chromatic and enharmonic accidentals or only the latter.

Vicentino's theories met considerable opposition, both in his own time and subsequently, from theorists such as Zarlino, Giovanni Battista Doni, and Artusi. On one occasion he entered into an open debate with the Portuguese theorist Lusitano and was declared vanquished by the judges.[169] He has been charged with ignorance even with regard to the true nature of the Greek genera. Whatever may be said against him, however, his chromaticism pointed the way to the liberation of music from the diatonic restrictions of the modal system.[170]

Rore as Madrigalist

Vicentino's precepts regarding chromaticism found considerable support in the works of his contemporary, Cipriano de Rore. Like many another Netherlander, Rore spent most of his life in Italy, occupying various court and church positions. He studied with Willaert and, like Vicentino, may have been inclined toward chromaticism by this master. Rore's first three books of madrigals *a 5* appeared in Venice in 1542 to 1544. He left Venice, in or c. 1547, for the court of Hercules II, Duke of Ferrara, and c. 1550 succeeded Vicentino as *maestro di cappella* there. In 1558 he went back to Antwerp to visit his parents, and stopped off at Munich on the way. During his absence, Hercules II died and Alfonso II engaged Francesco Viola as *maestro di*

[168a] Appearing as the second voice in our example.
[168b] This is "natural" if neither note bears an accidental; it is "accidental" if either or both bear one. A large whole tone is written either like a normal whole tone, but with a dot over the higher note, or in the form of a diminished third.
[169] For a full account of this dispute, *see* HawkH III, 90ff.
[170] Further about Vicentino, *see* ZenckN.

cappella. However, Margaret of Austria, Regent of the Netherlands, who held her court at Brussels, made him an offer of employment, which he accepted, and this was followed by a similar offer from her husband (cf. p. 322), Duke Ottavio Farnese of Parma. The duke, returning to Parma in 1561 after a visit to Margaret, was accompanied by Rore, who became his *maestro di cappella*. However, Rore remained only a short time in Parma, having received an invitation to succeed Willaert at St. Mark's. He assumed his important duties there in 1563, but soon grew dissatisfied and wrote to Duke Ottavio complaining of the heaviness of his duties, of the disorder resulting from the division of the *cappella* into a *cappella grande* and a *cappella piccola* (cf. p. 370), and of the *poca provisione;* and he asked permission to return to Parma, where he wished "to live and die." He went back in 1564. His death occurred the next year.[171]

Rore was from the beginning much concerned with delineating the changing mood of the text (though not especially with depicting specific objects or actions). He wrote no *villanesche* or any madrigals of a frivolous nature, but concerned himself with serious and noble texts, such as those from Petrarch and from tragedies presented at the court of Ferrara.[172] With him the madrigal takes on a more dramatic aspect—as opposed to the lyricism of his predecessors—and his passionate utterance not only draws to a close the "age of innocence" of the madrigal [172a] but points the way to the future. "Since no musician could help being influenced by Rore, and since it became important in the madrigal to illustrate every idea and every image and all the emotional value of the text as sharply and directly as possible, the construction of the madrigal underwent a change." [173] Musical form became even more dependent upon the expressive needs of the poetry—less upon its form—than it had been in the early madrigal, with its fairly constant mood and technique from the beginning of a piece to the end. Rore often disregarded the structure of the line as well as the rhyme and line division, and did not feel it necessary that the musical line should correspond to the poetic line.

He used chromaticism interestingly, though only occasionally. A certain amount appears in the collection which, in its second edition (1544; first ed., 1542), bore the title, *Primo libro di madrigali cromatici a 5*. This, however, is not the reason for the title; *"cromatici"* refers only to *note nere* (cf. p. 320). The collection, indeed, is significant as one of the early books *a note nere*. Only later on did Rore approach the audacious methods of Vicentino, and even then he made no attempt to compose in intervals smaller than a semitone.

[171] For further biographical data, *see* MusiolR, 4ff; SCMA VI, pref.; PirH, 253; RossiR (containing letters).
[172] E.g., SCMA VI, 41.   [172a] Cf. EinIM I, 424.   [173] EinN, 477.

The Latin ode, *Calami sonum ferentes,* written for four basses, opens imitatively with an ascending chromatic subject:

EXAMPLE 72. Opening of *Calami sonum ferentes*—Rore (complete piece in BuH III, 319; CommB XII, 119; MusiolR, App., 19).

"Reeds bearing sound, light with the Sicilian meter."

Although most of the ode is based on imitation, the middle portion is chordal; it contains some chromatic changes of harmony that may well have furnished a starting point for the chromatic experiments of Gesualdo. The piece enjoyed great fame in the 16th century and exerted a wide influence.[174]

Although his music is delicately attuned to the sense of the text, most of his madrigals maintain a closely knit contrapuntal texture recalling motet technique.

EXAMPLE 73. Opening of *O morte, eterno fin*—Rore (after EinGA, 13).

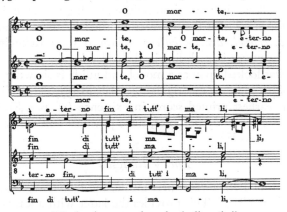

"O death, eternal end of all evils."

He contrives basses which, although they serve a harmonic role, nevertheless approximate the melodic character of the other parts. The harmonies tend toward complexity, and frequent crossing of voices makes the texture even more intricate. Some of his madrigals, however, show a tendency toward simplification in the further interest of dramatic expression:

[174] Another secular piece with Latin text, pr. MaldP XII, 29.

EXAMPLE 74. Extract from *Dalle belle contrade*—Rore (complete piece in CW V, 26; HAM, 143).

Ben son dubbio s'e cortele tue dolcez-ze poi chian-chor ti go. — di,

["Ah, cruel love,] your delights are uncertain and brief, so that it pleases you [also for joy to end in weeping."]

Comparative simplicity marks also Rore's highly attractive *Anchor che col partire*,[174a] by far his most famous madrigal.

Madrigal cycles result from Rore's treatment of Petrarch's *canzone, Vergine bella, che di sol vestita,* and his *sestina, A la dolc'ombra*.[175] Dufay had set the first stanza of the *canzone* (cf. p. 52). Rore turned each of its ten stanzas and its *commiato* into a separate madrigal. For nobility of conception as well as for musical beauty, these pieces are among Rore's best. The *cinquecento* produced a number of other fine cyclic *canzone*.[175a] *Sestina* settings were not new in Rore's day. The poetic form, dating back to the troubadour Arnaut Daniel [175b] (d. 1199), attracted Late Renaissance composers, especially the Italians, who, however, sometimes drew only on isolated stanzas. Rore sets each of the six-line stanzas as a separate *pars,* but omits the *commiato*. Petrarch's text follows the normal procedure of using the same six line-ending words in all the stanzas in the order established by the Provençals: *abcdef, faebdc, cfdabe, ecbfad, deacfb, bdfeca,* followed by a three-line *commiato* using two of the words in each line in the order *be, dc, fa*.

That Rore was looked upon as a model and guide is shown by the publication in score of his collected madrigals *a 4* as late as 1577. This edition, presenting one of the earliest printed scores in existence (cf. p. 538), was unquestionably designed for study purposes, since practical editions were published in separate part-books.[176]

The Villanesca

Another form of Italian vocal part-music, the *villanesca,* developed at the side of the early madrigal. This provides the latter with a less polished, more folklike counterpart. *Villanesche* appeared also under other names in 16th-

---

[174a] Pr. SCMA VI, 45; EinIM III, 112; MonteO VIII, App.; TagA I, 65.
[175] Pr., respectively, in WagCR (1 piece from the cycle also in ScherG, 103; 2 in MaldP XI, 8, 12) and SCMA VI, 12ff (3 also in WagMP, 490ff).   [175a] *See* further EinIM I, 432ff.
[175b] Cf. ReMMA, 237. For an ex. by Daniel, with music, *see* F. Gennrich, *Troubadours, Trouvères, Minne- und Meistergesang* (1951; in *Das Musikwerk*), 16.
[176] Further about Rore, *see* EinIM I, 384ff; EitC; MusiolR; pref. of SCMA VI; HolR; WagMP. 29 madrigals by Rore not yet cited pr. in SCMA VI (1 also in WagMP, 496 [= CW V, 21]; *pars II* of *Mia benigna fortuna* also in EinIM III, 114). Other Rore madrigals pr. KrV, 35, 38; CW V, 28; MonteO XXIII, App.; MusiolR, App. 1, 7, 11, 14, 16, 18, 22; EinIM III, 92, 103, 117. About early uses of score in MS, *see* L. Ellinwood in MQ XXVII (1941), 188. *See also* LowSS.

century prints. Late in the century related light forms emerged, and the name of one form was rather often applied to a piece in another such form, with resulting confusion, a subject that will prove of more moment in Chapter 8. The *villanesca* type originated at Naples and spread rapidly to other areas. The form is that of a *strambotto* enlarged by a refrain after each two lines, this refrain being variable in structure and length from one piece to another: poetic form—*ab* + refrain, *ab* + refrain, *ab* + refrain, *cc* + refrain; musical form—the same, except that *cc* repeats the music of *ab*. Departures from this pattern are frequent, however.[177] For example, immediate repetitions of *a* and of the refrain are common. Many *villanesca* texts are love poems, some of which outdo the madrigal in bewailing lovers' woes. Double meanings occur, as well as instances of unequivocal obscenity. Musically, the *villanesca* is simple and chordal, with syllabic underlaying. Both popular elements and parodies thereof are evident. This ♩ ♩♩|♩ ♩ ♩ |♩ is a typical rhythmic pattern. *Villanesche* were often sung to the accompaniment of instruments, mainly the lute.[178]

The first known book devoted entirely to *villanesche,* an anonymous collection *a 3,* dates from 1537. The next work of this type to appear was Giovane Domenico da Nola's *Canzoni Villanesche* (1541), which quickly became famous and gave impetus to the development of the form. Nola, the chief early *villanesca* composer, was born during the first quarter of the century, in the Kingdom of Naples, in the capital of which he was for many years *maestro di cappella* at the Church of La Nontiata. Nola's earlier *villanesche* are *a 3,* with the melody in the superius. *Madonna, voi me fare* illustrates the parodying of the madrigal, found in some *villanesche.* Lines might be borrowed from older poems, or exaggerated texts or inappropriate musical settings might be used for the sake of caricature. In this composition, which recalls the *"madonna"* madrigals, the opening words are repeated several times, set in dignified style, and then reach the not very exalted development, *"una camisa, madonna, voi me fare,"* with parallel fifths on the first three syllables.[179] The *villanesca a 3,* in fact, made quite frequent use of parallel fifths, as in Nola's *Tre ciechi siamo,*[179a] belonging to the *mascherata* subtype, from which the following is taken.[180]

ve - ga-vi pie - ta - de!

---

[177] For more details, *see* ScheerV, 15ff.   [178] For more details, *see* MontiV, 32.
[179] For more details, and fragments of this piece, *see* EinV, 221f.
[179a] Pr. EinSH, 285. Other *villanesche* by Nola pr. CW VIII, 11, 12, 13 (cf. fn. 185); EinIM III, 80, 86. Madrigals by Nola pr. TorA I, 127, 133, 141. *See also* p. 430, *infra.*
[180] Further on Nola, *see* esp. EinIM I, 366ff. For more detailed discussion of the use of consecutive fifths, *see* ScheerV, 35ff. On parallel fifths as a parody technique, *see* EinV, 215; EinW, 371f. A *villanesca a 4* containing parallel fifths, by Werrecore, not Le Maistre as stated, pr. KadM, App. No. 2.

Pieces in this style, deliberately crude and primitive in effect, apparently reflected, in written composition, the practice—known as *sortisatio*—of improvising vocal polyphony to pre-existent melodies. The earliest known mention of it occurs in the *Opus aureum* (Cologne, 1501) of the French theorist, Nicolas Wollick. Two examples given by the German writer, Heinrich Faber, show a note-against-note style, with occasional passages in unison and in parallel fifths. *Sortisatio* seems to have fallen out of favor toward the middle of the century; [180a] though originally applied to plainsong, as well as to secular melodies, it was later restricted more to the performance of pieces of a popular nature.[180b]

Villanesca collections *a 3* were brought out in 1545 by Tomaso Cimello (who includes a parody of Janequin's *Bataille*) [181] and by Vincenzo Fontana; [182] and one by Giovan Tommaso di Maio was printed in 1546.[183] The earlier year saw collections *a 4* published by Willaert and Perissone Cambio,[184] isolated examples having appeared earlier. In pieces *a 4* the tenor has the melody, which is sometimes a tune taken from the superius of an older, three-part *villanesca*. Willaert's *Cingari simo*,[185] with a tenor derived from a Nola superius, is an early example illustrating the artistic elaboration—without the use of parallel fifths—that this form was to undergo. The writing is much like that of the more chordal madrigals *a note nere*. In order to facilitate memorizing, *mascherate*—sung in costume, presumably without written music available—were composed with the utmost simplicity.

[180a] *Sortisatio* continued to be of importance, however, in the training of singers.
[180b] Further about *sortisatio, see* FerandS.
[181] Exx. pr. CW VIII, 14, 15 (= BesM, 300; ScherG, 97); EinIM III, 90.
[182] Ex. pr. *ibid.*, 81.
[183] 2 *villanesche* pr. *ibid.* III, 78, 79; a *strambotto, ibid.*, I, 355.
[184] *Villanesche* by Perissone pr. CW VIII, 20 (cf. fn. 185); BuH III, 215 (= KiesS, *Beilage,* 16); EinIM III, 146, 149. Further on Cambio, *see* esp. *ibid.*, I, 438ff.
[185] Pr. EinW, 370f. CW VIII contains 3 pairs of *villanesche a 3* and *a 4* employing the same melody in the superius and in the tenor respectively; *see* 11, 20; 12, 16 (= EinIM III, 88); 13, 18. Those given on pp. 16 and 18 are by Willaert. For other *villanesche* by him, *see* CW V, 12; VIII, 5, 8; octavo ed. by E. Thomas, Universal Edition No. 2686. For a discussion of his *villanesche, see* HertzW, 68ff.

Chapter 7: SACRED VOCAL MUSIC OF THE POST-JOSQUIN PERIOD: Gombert, Clemens non Papa, Willaert, and their Contemporaries

Such printers as Attaingnant and Susato, mentioned in Chapter 6 as publishers of chansons, have left us a rich store of sacred polyphony also. They were preceded, however, by a group of pioneers who contributed to our supply of liturgical incunabula containing chant. Many examples are found in four Paris libraries—the Bibliothèque Nationale, Sainte Geneviève, the Arsenal, and the Mazarine. Fully a quarter of the known production of early liturgical music printing was executed by printers in France.[1]

Attaingnant brought out a series of seven polyphonic Mass books in 1532, and in April, 1534 began issuing, monthly, a series of thirteen motet books.[2] The contents of the two series included works by distinguished composers of the time and slightly earlier. Among the older men were Divitis, Mouton, and Richafort.

Richafort and Some Lesser Men

The extant sacred works of Richafort comprise four Masses, at least eleven Magnificats, and some thirty-five motets.[3] One Mass is a Requiem,[4] through most of which the two tenors sing, as a *cantus firmus,* the Josquin *Circumdederunt me* canon (cf. pp. 255f) while the other voices weave their countermelodies. At times, the four old *Circumdederunt* phrases are repeated, subjected to variation, transposed. The *Virga tua* section opens *a 3,* half-way through it a fourth voice enters, and finally the remaining two sing in canon, there having been none thus far in this section; but now, instead of the *Circumdederunt,* they sing a short canon based on a phrase from Josquin's gay *Faulte d'argent,* however incongruous this may appear to be. The canon on the *Faulte d'argent* phrase recurs in the Offertory. In the chanson, this phrase is first sung to the words, *c'est douleur non pareille.* The symbolic

---

[1] Further about early French liturgical music prints, *see* MeN. Regarding Christophe van Remunde, the first producer of such prints in Antwerp, *see* BergT, 9ff.

[2] Modern ed. of the motet series now (1953) in course of publication in SmijT.

[3] Le Roy and Ballard printed 19 motets in *Joannes Richafort modulorum . . . Liber primus* (1556); *see* Catalogue X (1948) of A. Rosenthal, Ltd., p. 44. All but 3 appear in other sources also. The motet list in DoorR, 115ff (which does not cover the print just named), gives 57 numbered items, but does this by counting each *pars* separately and by including the Magnificats, from which, moreover, Nos. 13, 16, and 53 may be extracts.

[4] I am indebted to Dr. Ch. W. Fox for lending me the MS scores he has made of this Requiem and of those, presently to be mentioned, by Claudin and Certon.

meaning of the borrowing is therefore clear (as is that of the *Circumdederunt* melody). The superius sings the appropriate plainsong against the canon, but paraphrases it freely; there is much use of imitation. In view of the presence not only of the *Circumdederunt* canon but of a phrase from *Faulte d'argent,* it may well be that Richafort wrote this Requiem upon the death of Josquin.[4a] In the *Missa O Dei genitrix,*[5] Richafort, in the course of employing paired imitation, introduces double counterpoint on the words *Domine Deus rex coelestis.* The motet, *Misereatur mei,* seems to resort to symbolism such as we have found in the Requiem, for in this work, with a text recalling that of Josquin's *Miserere mei,* Richafort employs the same *cantus firmus* as did the older master.[5a] The superius of Richafort's *Sufficiebat* [5b] derives from the tenor of Hayne's *Mon souvenir.* The motet text is drawn from the speech made by the weeping mother, when Tobias is sent forth by his father to journey with the angel (Tobit V, 23–25). No doubt the quotation from Hayne is symbolically significant and is due to the line in the chanson that reads *"Sy sans cesser debvoye courir."* Richafort bases his *Gloria, laus et honor* on the chant setting. He lends variety to the latter's processional-hymn form (i.e., normal hymn-form, but with a refrain added at the opening and after each stanza) by giving a different paraphrase setting to each stanza that he treats (Nos. 1 to 3), the refrain of course remaining unaltered.[5c] Certain motets of Richafort's were frequently chosen as models for parody Masses. This type of Mass was generally preferred by composers throughout the 16th century. Josquin, Divitis, Mouton, Morales, and Palestrina are among those who based Masses on Richafort's *Quem dicunt homines,*[5d] probably his most famous work.

EXAMPLE 75. Opening of *Pars II* of *Quem dicunt homines*—Richafort (from Cambrai MS 124 f. 28ᵛ; transcr. by M. L. Versè).

[4a] Cf. p. 305 regarding Gombert's use of the *Circumdederunt* melody in a piece definitely composed on Josquin's death.

[5] Modern ed. in StnM, 508.   [5a] Cf. KillK, 61; LowBV, 195.   [5b] Pr. MaldR XVII, 33.

[5c] The motet pr. SmijT I, 25 (without indication regarding repetition of refrain); plainsong pr. Graduale (Ratisbon, 1877), 172. (Liber, 588, is less close to the version used by Richafort.) About the processional-hymn type, see WagE III, 479ff.

[5d] *Pars I* pr. HawkH II, 476, with wrong ascription to Willaert; *cf.* OH II, 110.

"Peter, lovest thou me? He answering said: Thou knowest, Lord, that I love thee." (After St. John XXI, 17)

Masses built on Richafort's *Philomena praevia* include one by Gombert and one variously ascribed in the sources to Claudin and Verdelot.[5e] *Christus resurgens,* undoubtedly by Richafort,[6] likewise served as a model for Masses. This motet and *Emendemus in melius* [6a] are both in the responsory form *aBcB,* which now assumes real importance in polyphonic writing.[7]

Another motet in this form by a composer of the time is *Beata es* by L'Héritier.[8] This, unlike the examples of the type thus far mentioned, is not divided into *partes;* in fact, there is polyphonic overlapping between the end of the first *B* and the opening of *c.* Moreover, the piece appends a coda after the second *B.* But the basic responsory form is unmistakably present.

One of the Masses on Richafort's *Christus resurgens* is a setting *a 4*[9] by Louis van Pulaer (born Cambrai, c. 1475; died there, 1528) who, after serving at Cambrai and Liége, directed the choir at Notre Dame in Paris from 1507 to 1527.[10] This Mass is his only known work. While he reminds one of the pre-existent motet often enough to justify entitling his composition after it, he uses the borrowed material with considerable liberty. He adds a voice for the final Agnus, but without introducing the canon that usually accompanies such a procedure.

In 1509, Richafort was succeeded as *maître de chapelle* at St. Rombaut in Malines by Noel Bauldeweyn (Baudouin, etc.; d. 1529), who in 1513 assumed a similar post at Our Lady in Antwerp, where he remained until 1517. Among the three motets ostensibly by him in Petrucci's *Motetti de la Corona,* Book IV (1519), is the *O pulcherrima mulierum* that bears an attribution to Févin in another source.[10a] One of the others is a *Quam pulchra es* (printed

[5e] *See also* SchmidtgG, 183.

[6] Pr. PubAPTM XVI, 243. It is ascribed to Richafort in the 4 sources listed in DoorR, 115f, 142, and in the print mentioned in fn. 3, but to Mouton in MS 18825 at the Nationalbibl., Vienna. (Cf. AmbG III, 285. PirH, 244, mentions, without further identification, a MS, copied by the scribe Alamire, that gives credit to Mouton. As is shown by *Die Österreichische Nationalbibliothek* [1948], 505, this is the same as Vienna 18825.) The piece is anon. in Cambrai 124.

[6a] Pr. MaldR XVII, 25.

[7] Further about Richafort, *see* DoorR. For other Richafort motets, *see* MaldR XVII, 23, 29; SmijT I, 34; II, 48, 110, 118. (The piece pr. in SmM, 117, credited to Richafort, is probably by the earlier J. Lupus, singled out on pp. 306, 341; cf. LowBV, 221.) *See also* p. 560, *infra.*

[8] Pr. SmijT I, 67; for other L'Héritier motets, *see* SmijT I, 44, 54; II, 67, 170.

[9] Pr. CPC, No. 29; Sanctus also in CouN, App., 1 (with composer's name given as Vaupullaire).

[10] Cf. *ibid.,* preface; PirB, 351f.

[10a] Cf. p. 279, fn. 540, *supra.*

without ascription [10b]), upon which Gombert was to build a Mass (cf. p. 347). Bauldeweyn's own works in this form include a Mass on the sequence *Inviolata integra* and a *Missa En douleur en tristesse,* based on a popular melody that appears in chanson settings by various composers, e.g., Willaert and Bauldeweyn himself.[10c]

Bauldeweyn was succeeded at Malines in 1513 by Jacques Champion of Liége, who held the post until 1519. Jacques's brother, Nicolas (d. 1533) accompanied Philip the Handsome to Spain, as a member of that prince's chapel. Both brothers eventually entered the service of Charles V. The name Champion appears in several forms—Campion, Sampion, etc.; it was sometimes replaced by "Liégeois." A few pieces survive clearly attributed to Nicolas; two are ascribed merely to "Champion" and may equally well be by either brother, since Jacques is referred to as a composer by Coclico (cf. p. 517).[10d]

Claudin de Sermisy and Certon; the French Mass Type

As we have seen in Chapter 6, many of the popular chanson composers held church posts and were active writers of sacred works. Claudin, as a member of the Sainte Chapelle, had ample reason to write music of this kind. In such a Mass as his *Domine quis habitavit* he followed the Netherlandish tradition.[11] But in a work like his *Missa plurium motettorum* [12] he helped to form a distinct French Mass-tradition. Compositions exemplifying this, to be sure, still reveal some Josquin traits—for instance, his voice-pairing. But, owing to the trend toward simplicity in French writing of the period, the voices in each pair often sound note against note and, at times, also in parallel motion. Occasionally, however, there is canon *a* 2 in the upper voices answered by such canon in the lower ones. Claudin likes to introduce passages varying the predominating four-part fabric. He favors chordal writing, in chanson style. The resulting clear text treatment is typical of him and of the French school. The melodies are short and smooth; large leaps found in the Josquin period are avoided. Ternary rhythm is no longer in fashion.[13] Many of the traits described are illustrated by Claudin's Requiem. Here the plainsong, which is in the third voice, is often shorn of melismas and even of initial or final notes of phrases, despite the effect that elimination of

---

[10b] Cf. Acta XX, 85; but the piece is credited to Bauldeweyn elsewhere.

[10c] For an article on him, *see* DoorB; *see also* MGG I, 1419f. For the first Kyries of his above-named Masses, in old notation, see RoediN, 2, 19, respectively; for a facsimile of the latter Kyrie I, after a Wolfenbüttel MS, see WolfMS, 84; MeK (transcr. *ibid.,* 74). About the *En douleur* melody, *see* GéroC, 11, 87f; ParisC, 87f (text section), 50 (music).

[10d] Further about the Champions, *see* esp. DoorCL. For the Kyrie I of Nicolas's *Missa super Maria Magdalena,* in old notation, *see* RoediN, 20. (The biographical notes in RoediT, 131, seem to be defective.)

[11] Cf. WagG, 250.

[12] Modern ed. in StnM, 1.

[13] Cf. *ibid.,* 16ff and *passim.*

the last note has on the mode of the chant: paraphrase consists of curtailment rather than of elaboration. The simple French style is present in Claudin's motets also, alongside Netherlandish traits. *Aspice Domine* [14] is in *aBcB* responsory form, with polyphonic overlapping between the end of the first *B* and the opening of *c*. In the two *partes* of the four-voiced *Clare sanctorum senate apostolorum,* Claudin presents, in points of imitation, fragments of the similarly named plainsong sequence, much admired at the time. [15] The original sequence is made the basis of a free variation chain. Book X of Attaingnant's motet series was devoted to Passions and contains one in four parts by Claudin. The text is founded on St. Matthew XXVI–XXVII. [16] Claudin builds his setting on the Passion Tones, which he treats as *cantus firmi,* with occasional melismatic elaboration. The composition is divided into forty little numbers. It is a dramatic-type Passion, but the words of an individual character are set polyphonically, and not always by the same combination of voices; thus Judas is represented twice by four-part music, thrice by a duo. Little attention is paid to verisimilitude, a passage for Pilate's wife being assigned to four men's voices. [17]

Certon, also a member of the Sainte Chapelle, wrote Masses, motets, etc. Settings by him of French metrical versions of the psalms by Marot survive only in transcriptions for voice and lute. [17a] In his sacred music, Certon retains the general style of his secular works. Like many of his contemporaries, he indulges in "peccadillos against decorum, against just Latin accentuation, even against music: and these defects made him perhaps more accessible to the general run of his auditors than the vigorous Claudin." [18] Masses of his were printed by several houses. An Attaingnant collection of 1540 is particularly interesting, since the three parody Masses it contains (two by Certon, one by Claudin) are accompanied by the motets on which they are based. [19] In another Mass, *Sur le pont d'Avignon,* [20] he treats the 15th-century tune (cf. p. 295), no doubt after some chanson setting. In this Mass and in the two bearing the titles *Adjuva me* and *Regnum mundi* [21]—all in four parts—he displays the customary imitation technique and usually has a section *a 2* at the middle of each movement. Passages in two parts are more common in Certon than in Claudin, and he tends to spin these out by loose imitation, apparently

---

[14] Pr. RoksT, 2, with attribution to Lafage, after Attaingnant's 11th motet book; but 3 sources give it to Claudin; cf. RubIL, 77. For a Lafage motet, *see* SmijT III, 72.

[15] Glareanus tells us that the melody was praised to him by Erasmus; GlarD, 135; PubAPTM XVI, 103. The motet pr. SmijT I, 1. For other motets employing imitation, *see* SmijT II, 80; III, 41, 140.

[16] An anon. St. John Passion from the same Attaingnant collection is described in KadP. 121ff.

[17] Cf. *ibid.,* 127ff.   [17a] Cf. p. 554 *infra;* also DouM I, 670.   [18] PirH, 320f.

[19] The relations between Certon's *Missa Dulcis amica* and its motet are discussed in WagG, 246ff, where Kyrie I is pr., preceded by one of the modern reprints of the motet (cf. p. 264).

[20] Pr. MMFTR II, 1.

[21] Pr. MMFTR II, 43, 81, respectively. Other exx. of Certon's sacred music pr. WagG, 248f; SmM, 120.

lacking the patience that prompted Claudin to work them out in canon. Certon's Requiem is like Claudin's in most respects. The cantus is frequently varied by being reduced to its bare skeleton rather than by the addition of notes. Often the texture is very plain and chordal.

Janequin; the "Wolf Pack" and Some Lesser Figures

Although Cléreau's choice of non-secular material as the basis for his parody Masses might lead one to expect works of a grave character, they are actually in the light terse French style. A Requiem of his is one of his better works.[22]

Janequin likewise made contributions to the literature of sacred polyphony. These include Masses, motets, and psalms. One of the Masses is based on his chanson, L'aveuglé dieu,[23] one on La Bataille de Marignan.[23a] In the latter Mass, Janequin concentrates on material from pars I of the celebrated chanson, reintroducing it from time to time. Pars II, with its attempts to duplicate the noises of battle, would have provided less suitable subject matter. While the new work, of course, differs considerably from its model structurally, Janequin seems less intent upon reworking the passages he has selected from this model than upon keeping them in a form easily recognizable by the listener. In 1533, Attaingnant published Janequin's Sacrae cantiones seu motectae quatuor vocum.[24] The psalms, of which there are two collections, survive in fragmentary form. Of the first, printed in 1549, only the superius, contratenor, and bassus are extant, but it is possible to supply the tenor, thanks to the phrase "sur le chant ja usité." The reference is to the tunes of the Calvinists (to which we shall return presently), and these can be made to fit the surviving parts. Of the second, printed in 1559, we have only the bassus. However, this fragment casts additional light on Janequin, since it contains a dedication written by him in verse, which reveals him as a poet of charm and ability.[25] In 1558, Le Roy and Ballard issued the Proverbes de Salomon set to music by Janequin; these too survive incomplete.

Benedictus Appenzeller, as master of the choirboys in the chapel of Mary of Hungary at Brussels, c. 1535 to 1551, had sufficient occasion to write sacred music.[26] His double canon, Sancta Maria, was embroidered on a tablecloth [27]

---

[22] Cf. WagG, 250ff.

[23] Cf. EitQ V, 274. For the chanson, see JanequinT, 82.

[23a] Pr. separately by Salabert, in 1947, as edited by Expert.

[24] FétB IV, 423, mentions this collection, but EitQ V, 274, declares its whereabouts no longer known. A single motet (Congregati sunt), however, does reach us; pr. by the Editions de l'Oiseau–Lyre (1950) as ed. by F. Lesure.

[25] Further about Janequin's psalms, see CauPJ, which prints one of them (p. 50) as well as the dedication (p. 52). For a chanson spirituelle of his, see DouM II, 78 (cf. ibid., 16).

[26] Note the sacred compositions named in columns 1 and 3 of the list of his works and those of Benedictus given in BarthaB, 14ff.

[27] Photograph in StraM VII, opp. p. 420.

offered to Mary in 1548. Each melody was, as usual with canons, presented once only (with a sign showing where the *comes* was to enter); and each was embroidered upside down with relation to the other, so that the piece could be easily rendered by performers sitting on two opposite sides of a table.

Pierre Cadéac, traceable in Attaingnant prints from 1538 on, calls himself master of the choirboys at Auch (west of Toulouse) in a Du Chemin print of 1556. His sacred music includes five Masses *a 4*. He uses French devices, but with somewhat more restraint than Claudin. In the *Missa Levavi oculos*,[28] there is much imitation. In the *Qui tollis*, this first exists in only three voices, while the fourth sings a countermelody that is later taken up by the other three; at *Et in Spiritum*, a theme is imitated in similar time-values in three voices and in augmentation in the remaining voice. Cadéac uses fewer chordal passages than Claudin, but balances this by often having passages of imitation in note-against-note writing. The Kyrie of the *Missa Ad placitum* is unusual in having the Kyrie I, *Christe*, and Kyrie II merged into a single movement without breaks.[29] The *Missa Ego sum panis* follows the plan, which we have found used in Obrecht's *Missa Libenter*, of setting the text of the Agnus to the music already employed for the three subsections of the Kyrie.[30]

A parody Mass on the Lupus or Cadéac setting of *Je suis desheritée* (cf. p. 307) is among the sacred works of Jean Maillard.[31] The chanson is closely followed in the Kyrie; the remaining movements are based on variations of the chanson melodies. Other contemporary Masses based on this model include works by Gombert, Jean Guyon of Chartres, and Nicolas de Marle.

It is possible to assign certain sacred compositions to one or another of the composers named Lupus or Lupi. For example, Petrucci printed, in 1519, a *Postquam consummati sunt*[32] which he ascribed to "Lupus" and which Rhaw reprinted in 1545 and credited to "Johannes Lupi". If the full name is correct, the composer must be the Johannes Lupi who preceded the Cambrai homonym, since in 1519, the latter would have been only about nine years old (cf. p. 306). Other sacred works by the earlier J. Lupi would necessarily include those contained in Bologna, Lic. Mus. Q 19, since the MS is dated 1518,[32a] and those contained in a MS at the Biblioteca Vallicelliana in Rome,[32b] also too early to represent the younger composer. This younger, Cambrai musician, however, is specifically named in an Attaingnant collection printed in 1542: *Jo. Lupi, Chori sacre Virginis Marie Cameracensis* [= of Cambrai] *Magistri Musice Cantiones*. If Cambrai is not specifically mentioned, as it is here, works

---

[28] Modern ed. in StnM, 34.   [29] Cf. StnT, 34.

[30] *Ibid.* The plan is applied also in Berchem's *Missa Mort e merci;* cf. SchmidtgG, 159. *See also* p. 348, *infra.*   [31] Modern ed. in StnM, 76.   [32] Pr. SmijT I, 183.

[32a] For one such motet, *see* MaldR XX, 25; cf. ReT, 108 (No. 439). The source of the "Lupus" motet pr. in MaldR XX, 22, is untraced; cf. ReT, 108 (No. 438).

[32b] Cf. LowBV, 177ff, 206, 212, 219, 221. *Pars I* of a motet appearing in this MS is pr. in SmM, 117, after a source crediting Richafort. Another motet in this Rome MS is the *In te Domine speravi*, listed (after Bk. 2 of Moderne's *Motetti del Fiore*) under No. 61 on p. 471, *infra.*

of late enough date to be by the younger J. Lupi may equally well, as far as chronological grounds are concerned, be by either. This would apply, for example, to a five-part *Missa super Veni sponsa Christi,* which a Scotus print of 1543 assigns to "Joannes Lupi".[32c]

Among the various sacred pieces bearing the name of Lupus Hellinck is a four-part motet, *Panis quem ego dabo,*[32d] upon which several Masses were based. The motet is in *aBcB* form, *a,* however, itself consisting of two sections. Several of the themes worked out in points of imitation are related to one another, so that a tightly knit composition results.

EXAMPLE 76. Five motifs from the motet *Panis quem ego dabo*—Lupus Hellinck (after SchmidtgM).

The Masses based on this motet include one [32e] credited by some historians to Hellinck himself. However, the source preserving this Mass—the fifth of the Mass books printed by Attaingnant in 1532—merely names "Lupus". In this composition, exact quotations from the motet seldom appear and then only briefly. Closely organized form is evident in the work. The texture is not as dominated by verticalism as is that of typical French Masses; it is more in the Netherlandish tradition. The *Osanna* and Agnus II are in ternary rhythm: the Netherlanders did not give up such rhythm to the same extent as did the French (cf. p. 338).[33]

Among the other Masses bearing only "Lupus" as the composer's name is a *Missa Hercules dux Ferrariae,* preserved in prints of 1532, 1539, and 1540. This is clearly modeled on Josquin's similarly named composition. But, whereas the Josquin Mass was dedicated to Hercules I, this one could have been intended only for his grandson, Hercules II. To be sure, the younger duke did not mount the throne until 1534, and the work, as already indicated,

---

[32c] The Benedictus is pr. CPC, No. 50. The *Quam pulchra es,* pr. in CPC, No. 28, falls into the previous category; although attributed merely to "Lupi" in the Cambrai MS followed in CPC, the piece is included in the print of 1542 mentioned at the bottom of p. 341 (checked by Dr. Lowinsky).

[32d] Pr. SchmidtgM, App. For another motet by Hellinck, *see* PubAPTM III, 291.

[32e] Modern ed. in StnM, 239.   [33] Further about this Mass, *see* StnT, 140ff; SchmidtgM, 85ff.

had appeared in print before that date. But conjecture has provided a likely explanation.[33a] The superius opens with a motto (head-motif) which, like Josquin's *cantus firmus,* is a *soggetto cavato dalle vocali: g′f′d′f′d′e′d′f′e′d′*. If we make allowance for mutation from the soft hexachord (used in notes 1, 2, and 4) to the natural hexachord (used in all the other notes), it will be clear that the vowels in the solmisation names of the first four notes (*re, ut, re, ut*) are the same as those in *"Hercules dux,"* and that the vowels in the names of the last four notes (*re, fa, mi, re*) correspond to those of *"Ferrariae"* (cf. p. 236). This leaves two notes (*re, mi*) in the middle, and these may well represent *"erit,"* so that the whole *soggetto,* as given in the motto, would signify "Hercules will be Duke of Ferrara." [33b] Lupus inserts an additional note in this motto to produce his *cantus firmus,* with the result that it seems to change its meaning to "Hercules shall shine forth, Renée live." [33c] The Renée in question is the daughter of Louis XII, whom Hercules married in 1528 and for whom Rore was apparently later to write *En vos adieux* (cf. p. 311). If, as seems likely, the Mass was written on the occasion of the marriage, it is of too early a date to be by the Cambrai composer. It would have to be the work either of the earlier J. Lupi or of Hellinck, and, since we have evidence of the former's presence in Italy but not of the latter's, the more likely ascription is to J. Lupi.

The three publications preserving the Hercules Mass, those of 1532 and 1540 being different printings of a collection issued by Moderne and edited by the younger Fr. Layolle, contain also the latter's *Missa Adieu mes amours.* The tenor of this work sings no less than eighty-eight times the notes for the first five syllables of the song, without proceeding further; only in the final Agnus [33d] is the entire melody presented. Though apparently liked, the composition was old-fashioned in plan and in choice of *cantus firmus;* and it is significant that it was printed in Lyons and Nuremberg and not in an up-to-date center like Paris.

Gombert

One of the three most important composers of sacred polyphony in the period between Josquin and Lassus was Gombert, the others being Clemens non Papa and Willaert. Gombert was affiliated in various capacities, as we have seen, with the Imperial Chapel of Charles V and subsequently with the cathedral chapters at Courtrai and Tournai. Although ten Masses of his

[33a] *See* ThürS, 192ff.
[33b] Other possible interpretations are given *ibid.*
[33c] For the explanation, *see* loc. cit.
[33d] Pr. BerH, 67. The pieces pr. in AmbG V, 201, 204, are also probably by this Layolle. They are taken from a *Contrapunctus* (Lyons, 1528), of interest in the history of polyphonic music for the Proper; *see* esp. EisZ, 75ff (with exx.); LippP, 45ff.

survive, most of his sacred music [34] is in the form of 169 motets (including eight Magnificats). Slightly over half of these motets are in two *partes:* the great majority are *a 4* or *a 5,* there being a small preference for writing *a 5.* On occasion, he knits his motets together by having a passage at the end of one *pars* repeated at the end of another, producing *aBcB* form (more rarely by having a repeated *cantus firmus* run through the whole work). As we have noted in his secular music (p. 304), Gombert likes to avoid literalness in repetitions, and this is true whether they are immediate or delayed. However, very nearly exact repetition may be seen in the endings of the two *partes* of *Angelus Domini ad pastores.*[35]

Pervading imitation, in its flower with Josquin, reaches full bloom with Gombert, of whose style it is a leading characteristic. He uses it much more consistently than does Josquin.[36] Hermann Finck, in his *Practica musica* (1556), states that in his time—by which he evidently means c. 1525 to c. 1555—Gombert, "pupil of Josquin of blessed memory," shows all musicians the way to write music consisting of a series of points of imitation.[36a] Gombert's predilection for imitation at close time-intervals is evident in his sacred music as in his chansons (cf. p. 304). Whereas it is characteristic of Josquin to work out a motif in imitation only once, Gombert may rework it several times before proceeding to a new motif. In doing this, he is very likely to avoid symmetry by having a different number of entries in the various parts; in its first entry the motif may even assume a form that presently proves not to be the basic one.[36b] The imitation is usually strict in writing *a 4.* But in writing *a 5* and *a 6* it is apt to be rather free, although the contour is generally retained. This feature is illustrated in Gombert's *In illo tempore loquente Jesu,*[37] upon which Monteverdi was to base a Mass *a 6,* printed in 1610 (cf. p. 500).

EXAMPLE 77. Extract from *In illo tempore loquente Jesu*—Gombert (from *Novum et insigne opus musicum,* Montanus and Neuber, 1558; transcr. by M. L. Versè).

[34] For a list, *see* SchmidtgG, 36off.
[35] SchmidtgG, App., 5.
[36] Cf. MerrM.
[36a] The orig. Latin is quoted in SchmidtgG, 127; *see also* BorIS, 17.
[36b] Cf. EppN, 52ff.
[37] Also in the *Ecce quia Dominus* passage in *Gaudeamus omnes; see* SchmidtgG, App., 38.

"[At that time] Jesus was speaking to the crowd . . ."

Departures from literal imitation sometimes take the form of tonal answers in the works of Gombert and his contemporaries, as in those of their predecessors, although real answers are still preferred.[38] In *Angelus Domini,* there is an example of paired imitation on two motifs, so handled that, in the first pair, the upper voice enters with its contrasting motif two time-units after the lower voice has entered with its own motif, whereas in the second pair the entries of the motifs occur in reverse order (cf. p. 231) and are separated by ten time-units. Despite his penchant for imitation, Gombert, in his sacred as in his secular music (cf. p. 304), shows no lasting interest in actual canon. In fact, as is indicated also by his infrequent application of the *cantus-firmus* principle, he tends strongly to avoid constructivist methods, his feeling for form being satisfied by the simple, flexible design resulting from a series of imitation-points. Such a design was to prove the preferred one of his contemporaries and successors, the constructivist methods of the past becoming more and more old-fashioned.

The employment of imitation sometimes causes a melodic idea, borrowed from the liturgical repertory, to permeate the polyphonic fabric, as in Gombert's *Pater noster.*[39] One of his best-known works, however, the Marian motet that bears the motto *Diversi diversa orant,*[40] is exceptional: the composition is formed, not by applying pervading imitation, but by drawing on seven different Marian plainsong melodies,[41] which are reshaped by rhythmic alterations, melodic interpolations, appendages, and pauses until they fit together, four melodies usually being sung at one time. More than a quarter of Gombert's motets are Marian compositions.[42]

As in his chansons, Gombert avoids clear-cut phrase divisions. His work

[38] Cf. *ibid.,* 132.   [39] Pr. MaldR XII, 115; plainsong in MissaleR, 346.
[40] Pr. MaldR II, 3, and SchmidtgG, App., p. 23.
[41] These are *Alma Redemptoris Mater,* Liber, 273; *Inviolata,* Liber, 1861; *Ave Regina,* Liber, 274; *Salve Regina,* Liber, 276; *Beata Mater,* Liber, 1681; *Ave Maria,* Liber, 1861; and *Hortus conclusus,* which is evidently not included in current plainsong books but may be found in Lucca Cod. 601 (*see* PM IX, p. 446 of facsimile).
[42] However, the *Dei Mater alma,* recorded on Lumen 32.013 (= Decca DX 120) and ascribed on the label to Gombert, is not by him. It is Costanzo Porta's setting of the *Ave maris stella,* beginning with line 2 (line 1 should be treated as a plainsong intonation), and is No. 14 in his *Hymnodia . . .* (1602); it is credited to Porta also in the Eler MS (a modern MS in score) at the Conservatoire, Paris. (The *Confitemini* on Lumen 32.021 [also = Decca DX 120] is *pars II* of Gombert's *Haec dies.*)

is generally marked by asymmetry, rather than by the symmetry familiar in Josquin. Indeed, his fondness for asymmetrical design is so strong that it leads him to set poetic texts as though they were prose, the symmetry that would otherwise result being thus avoided. The trait is an important component of his style. It is as though, in this respect at least, the mantle of Ockeghem had fallen upon his shoulders. In some works, such as *Super flumina Babylonis*,[43] he varies his voice groupings, proceeding somewhat like Ockeghem and Josquin, with their liking for contrast obtained through passages written for varying combinations of voices. Usually, however, his texture differs from theirs by being dense and uniform—this resulting from the fact that his smooth-flowing parts, once started, continue with infrequent and brief pauses. In the quotation from Finck mentioned above, the theorist states that Gombert likes to avoid cadences, rests, or anything of the kind that would halt the flow of the music. Finck's word *"pausas"* actually means more than mere rests; it includes "the alternating of paired voices which is characteristic of Josquin and his closest followers." [43a]

In keeping with the general pervading-imitation style, chordal writing seldom appears, but is occasionally used with expressive or formal significance, as in *Deus ultionum*.[44] It is sometimes employed to emphasize the close of a *pars* or to begin a second *pars*. Fauxbourdon-like chords occur in short passages, but without special emphasis.

Gombert's rhythmic structures are notable for their great plasticity and for the ingenious use of syncopation. This may be observed in *Super flumina*, in which the figure | ♩ ♩ ♩ | assumes such forms as | ♪ ♩ ♩ | or ♩♩♩ ♩ | or | ♫♩ ♩ |. The introduction of livelier motifs and shorter time-values toward the close of works occurs in this composer as in Ockeghem and Josquin.[45]

In all eight Magnificats preserved in a sumptuous MS at Madrid, Gombert follows the more common practice of setting the even-numbered verses, leaving the others to be performed in chant. The polyphonically reworked plainsong is handled variously: it may be given *cantus-firmus* treatment by being disposed in long notes, while the other voices move in imitation, or it may be bandied about from one part to another, etc. Each verse that Gombert sets turns into a little motet, each Magnificat into a motet cycle. In the Magnificat in Tones 3 and 8, the composer adds one voice in setting each successive even-numbered verse, there being three in verse 2 and the number growing until eight parts are present in verse 12.[46]

[43] Pr. HAM, 118.   [43a] GombertO I, 1.
[44] Pr. CommB VIII, 34 (cf. EppN, 81f, on the underlaying of the text).
[45] Further about the motets, *see* EppN; SchmidtgG, 195ff; PirH, 311ff. For additional motets, *see* AmbG V, 225; SchmidtgG, App., 16; SmijT I, 167; II, 147; MaldR XX, 15, 18. The piece ascribed to Gombert in MaldR XVI, 49, is spurious; cf. SchmidtgG, 358, 370; EppN, 85f.
[46] Further about the Magnificats, *see* esp. SchmidtgMG. For several complete verses, *see ibid.*, 307; KrV, 1, 4, 5, 16, 17, 41, 42, 43, 45, 51. The Madrid MS is described in detail in StraM VII, 344ff.

Only two of Gombert's Masses—the *Missa Tempore paschali* and *Missa Da pacem* [46a]—are based directly on plainsong. The rest are parody Masses and illustrate various aspects of the parody technique. Thus, the Mass *a 5* on Gombert's own *Media vita* [47] and the Mass *a 4* on his *Beati omnes* [47a] each reduce by one the number of voices employed in the model, while the Mass on Richafort's four-part *Philomena praevia* is among the examples that increase the original number of voices, being mostly *a 5* and adding a sixth voice in the Agnus (which consists of a single setting). The *Missa Quam pulchra es* [48] bears only a loose relation to Bauldeweyn's motet, many of the motifs being new, while the other Masses are usually rather faithful to the motivic material of their models, and generally rework it in the original order. (Retention of this order, however, is not a requisite of the technique.) As is common in parody Masses of the period, each of Gombert's contributions to the genre, whether loosely or closely related to a pre-existent work, begins every major movement with the initial material of that work, using it in the manner of a head-motif; the initial material of *pars II* of the model —or, if this composition is in one *pars,* then material taken from its middle portion—opens the Kyrie II, the *Qui tollis* in the Gloria, the *Et in Spiritum* in the Credo, the *Osanna,* and the final Agnus. Each individual movement also employs the close of the model. (Free parody Masses are characterized by the preservation of only the openings and closes of the model and by the filling in of the resulting framework with original material.)

Since, in Gombert's day, the handling of the Mass was in the main more conservative than that of the motet or of secular music, it is not surprising that *cantus-firmus* treatment, rare in Gombert's motets, is found in several Masses. It occurs in whole movements of his *Missa Je suis desheritée,* [48a] as also in his *Missa Forseulement,* which has the peculiarity of being built on two models —the anonymous *Forseulement* that may be by Josquin (cf. p. 234) and the setting by Pipelare. In both these Masses, however, the *cantus firmus* is assigned to the superius rather than to the tenor; the same thing happens in the final Agnus of the *Missa A la Incoronation* (composed on Richafort's *Sur tous regretz*) and *Missa Sancta Maria* (based on a motet by Verdelot). [48b] But in the seven-part Agnus of the mainly six-part *Missa Quam pulchra es,* the *cantus firmus* is assigned to the second tenor, which is the newly introduced voice. The *cantus firmus*—the antiphon, *Ecce sacerdos magnus*—is also newly introduced at this point. Gombert breaks up the plainsong into

---

[46a] Pr. GombertO I, 1.
[47] The final Agnus (*a 6*) of the *Missa Media vita* is pr. in ScherG, 97. The motet is itself based on the plainsong *Media vita* (which is not by Notker, as stated in SchmidtgG, 174; cf. ReMMA, 129).
[47a] Pr. GombertO I, 56.
[48] In modern notation in StnM, 377.
[48a] Pr. GombertO I, 81.
[48b] Pr. GombertO I, 30.

its component parts, which are sung in an unusual kind of canon at the octave by tenor II and the bass, the lower voice entering first. Tenor II sings each of the component parts twice, the time-values being halved in the repetitions. The bass sings each of these components once only, in the shorter time-values, the resulting gaps between the components being filled in with other material.

If here and there, as in the Agnus just described, Gombert in a discreet way lays aside his basic aversion for repetition, he does this more openly in the three subsections of the Agnus of the *Missa Forseulement,* which, like those of Cadéac's *Missa Ego sum panis,* use the music already employed for the three subsections of the Kyrie. Striking is his application of repetition in an independent Credo *a 8,* in which the symbolism characteristic of the period is carried beyond the time-honored introduction of passages that rise at *ascendit in coelum"* and fall at *"descendit de coelis"* (though Gombert's Credos contain such passages also): the words *"passus et sepultus est"* are set to the same music that had previously been used for *"et homo factus."*

Gombert's Masses, by never reducing the number of parts at such a common place for doing so as the *Christe,* show quite forcefully his general preference for maintaining a uniform texture. Even so, he does write an occasional subsection for a small number of voices, and in the Credo *a 8* he does vary the texture in another manner, to be discussed presently.[49]

As in the works of other composers of the time, the modes, in Gombert, frequently have the aura of modern major or minor, especially at cadences. Dorian characteristics, however, are rather common, Mixolydian features somewhat less so; the Phrygian mode is occasionally represented likewise.[50]

In his generally careful treatment of dissonance, Gombert anticipates Palestrina. However, the linear principle is still so strong that sometimes sharply dissonant passages occur even in note-against-note writing.

The position of Gombert as the greatest of his generation among the more than fifty composers represented in Attaingnant's motet series is unchallenged by any of them except Willaert. But, in addition to Cadéac, Lafage (cf. fn. 14), and several other composers already mentioned for their sacred music, the lesser musicians include many of considerable merit, such as Hesdin,[51] Guillaume Le Heurteur,[52] Matthieu Sohier,[53] Matthieu Gascongne,[54] and Rousée.

---

[49] Further about Gombert's Masses, *see* SchmidtgG, 157ff, to which the above section on these works is much indebted.

[50] Cf. EppN, 62.

[51] For motets by him, *see* SmijT III, 16, 151, 155. *See also* p. 371 *infra.*

[52] For a motet of his, *see* SmijT III, 104; for a Mass, StnM, 160.

[53] For works by him, *see* CPC, Nos. 51, 52.

[54] For motets by him, *see* RoksT, 12; SmijT I, 82, 92, 105; II, 57, 158; for a Mass, StnM, 196. About the composer, *see* RoksT, iii; also cf. p. 300 *supra.*

Some Writers of Polychoral Music; Crecquillon; Manchicourt; Minor Figures

In strong contrast to Gombert's usually uniform texture is that present in a work like Rousée's *Regina coeli,* written for two SATB choruses. In the first *pars*,[55] chorus I enters alone and is shortly joined by chorus II, then each chorus has a passage of its own, and finally both choruses unite for an eight-part *Alleluia*. Gombert did not have in mind two such sharply defined bodies when he wrote his Credo *a 8:* although SATB groups often answer one another, he seems intentionally to avoid making up his groups out of the same S, A, T, and B; the color remains more or less unchanged, but the personnel varies. Unlike the Rousée piece, Gombert's Credo would be unsuitable for performance by two groups each stationed in a different choir-loft. Polychoral part-music was, of course, not new; we have twice encountered it in 15th-century Italy (cf. pp. 28, 174). But it was destined to resume particular importance in the 16th century, especially in Venice. It is noteworthy that Rousée's piece was printed in 1535 (in Attaingnant's Book XII of motets), i.e., well before Willaert's famous antiphonal psalms of 1550. (The Gombert Credo was not printed until 1564.)

Another early 16th-century composer of music for double chorus is Dominique Phinot, who was active in southern France and northern Italy. Most of his approximately ninety motets are *a 5* and in pervading-imitation style. His music resembles Gombert's in that few rests are used, while those that do occur are brief, so that contrasts of high and low voices, or of a few voices with many, are rare. The five motets for two choruses *a 4,* published in 1548, are all the more remarkable in view of this usual liking for uniform texture and in view of Phinot's customary avoidance of anything of a sensational or striking nature. While these pieces form a small part of his total motet production, they are probably the works chiefly responsible for the renown he enjoyed. At any rate, they are the ones reprinted time after time in the miscellaneous collections of the 16th century. The setting of the Lamentations of Jeremiah[56] is an especially impressive example of writing for two choruses. Here, as in the Rousée piece, traits ordinarily associated with Willaert and Venice are found. There are four *partes* in all, the first being for two SATB choruses, which answer each other antiphonally in homophonic passages of ever decreasing duration, until the passages overlap, producing a *stretto*-like climax of tone and complexity. *Partes II* and *III*—each for four voices, *II* only for high voices, *III* only for low ones—are in imitative style. *Pars IV* ends the piece with music for eight real parts. Phinot's output

---

[55] Pr., with comments, in HertzM.
[56] Pr. CommB VIII, 49; 3 other two-chorus works of Phinot in CommB VIII, 59, 65; IX, 99.

includes also twenty-five chansons and two Masses. That he was admired in his day is proved by the high praise given him by his contemporaries. The highest praise comes from Cerone,[57] who calls Phinot one of the "first and best composers of the time" and further goes on to say that "if there had been no Phinot, . . . there would not have followed . . . Pedro Luys Prinestrina [Palestrina] who wrote in the style of Phinot." While this last statement seems a little over-enthusiastic, the fact remains that Phinot is an excellent composer.[58]

Cornelius Canis, who in 1542 succeeded Gombert as *magister puerorum* in the service of Charles V, has left us six Masses and many motets. He is one of the four musicians in service at the Spanish court, including Thomas Crecquillon, Nicolas Payen, and Jean Lestainnier, who, in 1548–49, jointly published a motet collection dedicated to their imperial patron.[59] Of these four, Crecquillon is the most important. His Masses include a *Missa D'ung petit mot sine pausa*.[60] The word *"pausa"* here has the meaning explained on p. 346; actually Crecquillon introduces no rests larger than a half-note (in the original time-values). Certain passages are reintroduced in a way characteristic of parody technique. However, the model of this Mass has not been identified. (It is not Crecquillon's own chanson, *D'ung petit mot*.) Like many Netherlandish Masses, this one is *a 5*, with a sixth voice added at the Agnus.

In such motets as his *Dum aurora finem daret* (to St. Cecilia) and *Super montem*, Crecquillon derives various themes from one root theme, in much the same manner that Hellinck followed in his *Panis quem ego dabo*.[61] He pays more than the usual amount of attention to text-expression and declamation. In his *Domine Deus conteris bella*, he uses numerous dissonances to depict the harshness of war.[62] A peak in his work is his six-part *Congregati sunt inimici nostri*, which combines *cantus-firmus* style, pervading imitation, and careful matching of sonority to word. The tenor sings the *Da pacem in diebus nostris* in *pars I* of this motet, while the second soprano has it, a fifth higher, in *pars II*.[63] In an *Ave Virgo*,[64] having a *pars II* beginning *Omnis sanctis*, all the voices enter the first point of imitation by descending a whole tone and rising a fifth; but, at the opening of *pars II*, the voices enter by upward leaps thus: S, a fourth; A II, a fifth; T, a fourth; A I, a fifth; B, a fifth. The leaps of a fifth are tonal answers to the leaps of a fourth. Tonal answers occur likewise in Crecquillon's *Carole, magnus erat* and *Quis te victorem*

[57] *El Melopeo y Maestro* (1613), 180.
[58] Further about Phinot, *see* esp. HansenP; HansenL; also Hansen in *Renaissance News*, III (1950), 35.
[59] For a motet by Canis, *see* CommB VIII, 28; *see also* AmbG III, 310. Concerning Payen, *see ibid.*, 309f; about Lestainnier, esp. DoorJ.
[60] Modern ed. in StnM, 295.
[61] Cf. LeiG, 76f. The motets are pr. in MaldR XII, 23, 32.
[62] Cf. LowL, 61.   [63] Cf. LowL, 62.   [64] Pr. MaldR XII, 27 (cf. ReT, 96, No. 202).

dicat, both of which are motets in praise of Charles V.[65] Musicians of the first half of the century, although they continued to use real answers, were increasingly attracted to tonal, or quasi-tonal, answers, the more they abandoned the relics of the modal system and veered toward major and minor.

Of many other instances of tonal answer in Franco-Netherlandish works of the time, attention may be directed to those in Couillart's *Viri Galilei*,[66] Du Lot's *Maria Magdalene*,[67] and Manchicourt's *Pater peccavi*,[68] dealing with the return of the Prodigal Son. Manchicourt served as *maestro* of the Flemish Chapel at Madrid. His *Missa Surge et illuminare*[69] reveals him as a composer in the Netherlandish rather than in the French tradition, as does another motet, *Ave virgo Cecilia*.[70] The latter, an unusual work, consists of five points, each involving paired imitation on two motifs: in all points except the second, each voice, after stating the first motif assigned to it, reworks the material originally stated by the voice that is paired with it; in the final point, the two upper voices, after reworking such material, enter for a third time, restating their original motifs. The paired imitation gives rise to several examples of double counterpoint.

Clemens non Papa; the Souterliedekens

The leading younger contemporary of Gombert making his career in the North was Clemens non Papa, whose sacred works, in addition to his *Souterliedekens* (cf. p. 355), include fifteen Masses, two Mass movements, and 231 motets. One of his Masses is a *Missa pro defunctis,* which, in the manner normal for its type, paraphrases the Chant in such movements as are set polyphonically; these do not include the *Dies irae.* All the other Masses use the parody technique. The ascendancy of this method and the decline of the *cantus-firmus* technique are emphasized by Clemens' avoidance of the old expression *"Missa super . . ."* and his adoption of *". . . ad imitationem moduli"* or *"cantilenae"*. Among his fourteen parody Masses are works based on chansons and motets by Clemens himself (*Miséricorde*,[71] *Languir my fault*—written on the same melody as is Claudin's chanson—*Ecce quam bonum, Pastores quidnam vidistis*), by Lupus (*Quam pulchra es, Spes salutis*), by Gombert (*En espoir*[71a]), by Claudin (*Or combien*), by Willaert (*A la fontaine du prez,* itself based on a folk song), by Manchicourt (*Caro mea* and probably *Jay veu le cerf*,[72] a setting by this composer of a

---

[65] Pr. *ibid.*, 15, 21. About another motet in praise of the Emperor, cf. LowL, 6of. For other Crecquillon motets, *see* CommB X, 80, 84; MaldR XII, 37; *see also* p. 591, fn. 112, *infra.* Further on Crecquillon, *see* PirH, 309f.

[66] Pr. SmijT I, 10; *see ibid.*, 13.   [67] Pr. SmijT II, 8.

[68] *Pars I* pr. StraM VIII, opp. p. 62; *see* the word *vocari.*   [69] Modern ed. in StnM, 468.

[70] Pr. CPC, No. 53. Further on Manchicourt, *see* StraM VIII, 6ff.

[71] Clemens wrote 2 *Miséricorde* chansons, and the Mass, pr. ClemensO I, 1, draws on both of them; cf. *ibid.*, ii.

[71a] Cf. SchmidtgG, 244; pr. MaldP XIV, 23.   [72] Modern ed. in StnM, 334.

popular drinking song), by Hellinck (*Panis quem ego dabo*), and by Lasson (*Virtute magna*[72a]).

As in Gombert's independent Credo, the symbolic repetition at *"passus et sepultus"* of the music already used at *"et homo factus"* occurs in Clemens' *Missa Caro mea* and *Missa Ecce quam bonum*.[73] In the latter Clemens Mass, the melodic material used at *descendit de caelis* is that to which the words *qui descendit in montem Syon* are sung in the model. In this Mass and in the *Missa Miséricorde, Missa Languir my fault* and *Missa Or combien*, repetition of the same melodic fragment (not necessarily in the same voice) is made to symbolize the thought in the words *Deum de Deo*. Clemens is among the composers who, somewhat strangely from the modern point of view, assign the *Crucifixus* to the upper voices.

In the Masses *Languir my fault* and *Panis quem ego dabo*, the same melodic passage is presented four times, with modification, at *"Laudamus te. Benedicimus te. Adoramus te. Glorificamus te."* Clemens sometimes shows particular skill in the way he reintroduces material, varying it artistically. He seldom quotes his model exactly. In the Kyrie of the *Missa Panis quem ego dabo*, in which Mass he supplies much of his own and usually draws upon only one pre-existent voice at a time, he nevertheless combines contrapuntally four borrowed melodic passages not presented simultaneously by Hellinck.

The *Missa A la fontaine* is a 6; of the other parody Masses, seven are a 4, six a 5. However, in the *Missa Virtute magna*, one of the works a 4, a second superius is added in the Sanctus, and to this combination a second bass is added in the Agnus. There is little writing in canon. While the texture is generally polyphonic in all the Masses, there is a good deal of chordal writing in the *Missa Or combien*. This Mass illustrates effectively Clemens' liking for prominent bass themes. An extremely bold example of dissonance treatment occurs in the *Missa Spes salutis*.[74] The *Missa Gaude lux Donatiane* (on an unidentified model) achieves the great length of 930 measures.[75]

Clemens was a prolific writer of motets.[76] There are 231 in three to eight voices, of which 120 are a 4, 88 a 5, and 16 a 6. By far the greater number are in two *partes*. The texts are usually short, often from the Bible. Most of the motets were written for the church. The subject of three of the secular ones is the praise of music, a subject that attracted many other composers of this and a slightly later period. Thus the text *Musica Dei donum* was set, not only by Clemens, but by several other musicians,[76a] including Lassus.

72a Although anon. in one source, credited to Verdelot in another, and to de Silva in still another (SchmidtgC II, 183), it is ascribed to Lasson in 4 sources (EitS, 658).

73 Cf. SchmidtgC I, 140.

74 Cf. *ibid*. II, 22.

75 Further about Clemens' Masses, *see* esp. SchmidtgC; also WagG, 189ff. The *Missa Panis* . . . is described also in SchmidtgM, 88f.

76 For a monograph on them, *see* KemJC.

76a Cf. Steinh V, 23f.

EXAMPLE 78. Opening of *Musica Dei donum*—Clemens non Papa (from *Liber tertius ecclesiasticarum cantionum quatuor vocum*, Susato, 1553).

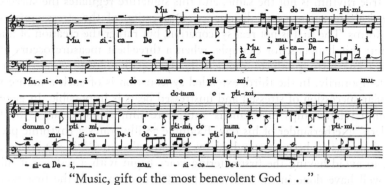

"Music, gift of the most benevolent God . . ."

It is noteworthy that Clemens' choice of texts was often shared by Crecquillon but not by Gombert. A few of the motets of Clemens are bi-textual: one of the voices sings its own words in longer notes as a commentary or a dramatic complement to the words sung by the other voices; thus the cry, *"Lazare veni foras"* is reiterated in the superius of the motet *Fremuit spiritu Jesus*,[77] which treats of the raising of Lazarus. This motet has been cited in support of the claim that Clemens, though seldom using notated accidentals, sometimes indicates the application of *musica ficta* in such a way as to produce elaborate chromaticism.[78] In general, however, Clemens conforms to the practice of his time in favoring diatonic progression.

Respond motets in the typical *aBcB* form are represented in Clemens' works, e.g., by *Angelus Domini, Jerusalem surge*,[79] etc. One of these, a setting *a 8* of the words of the Prodigal Son, *Pater peccavi* [80]—a motet in the Phrygian mode, but with Aeolian cadences (cf. p. 200)—is written for double chorus. Clemens' seven-voice *Ego flos campi* [80a] is likewise composed for alternating groups: a three-voice high one and a four-voice low one. Both of these works were printed in 1555, the *Pater peccavi* having previously been published in a version *a 4*.

Rhythmic movement in Clemens' music is mostly in minims (in the original notation) with few long notes or rapid melismas. The kind of free rhythm

[77] Pr. VNM XLIV, 13.

[78] The claim is set forth at length and with much brilliance in LowC, where it is stated that the chromaticism, alleged to be present in several Clemens motets and in certain others, had to be kept "secret" for religio-political reasons and was therefore expressed through the technique of *musica ficta* instead of being written out. Regardless of whether secrecy and such motives were involved, it does seem, on purely musical grounds, that chromaticism was implied in many of the examples presented in LowC. (For a criticism of LowC, *see* CreS.)

[79] Pr. CommB I, 8, and II, 9, respectively.   [80] Pr. *ibid.* I, 29.   [80a] *Ibid.* I, 23.

in which not all voices have their stressed beats at the same time was becoming increasingly common. However, in contrast to the practice often followed in the past, a single time-signature applies in all the voices even where their true rhythm is not the same, and this signature regulates the succession of vertical consonance and dissonance. Dislocation of the stress appears in three forms. The first is not real syncopation, but rather the creation of a new rhythm; this happens, for example, when a three-beat measure occurs in ¢. The second form produces momentary syncopation, displacing the stress only temporarily. In the third, extended syncopation is of such a nature that a regular succession of stressed and unstressed beats is impossible. In general, mensural relationships in Clemens' music are simple and clear, as befits a "modern" Netherlander of his day. Example 78 illustrates a rhythmic peculiarity that was to become standard by Palestrina's time,[81] if not sooner. In order to avoid having the first-entering voice begin with a rest—as it might very well have done in the 15th century—Clemens extends the first note of his tenor backward, so to speak, to fill the measure (in all the imitating voices, which obviously have the basic form of the motif, the first third of the tenor's ♩. is replaced by a rest).

During this period the use of freely invented motifs was becoming increasingly frequent. It has been held[82] that they were as common in the music of Clemens' contemporaries as were *cantus prius facti*. Certainly many of Clemens' motifs are original; he draws less on plainsong than does Gombert. Further comparison reveals that Gombert's motifs have more breadth and expression, more melismas and less tone repetition than those of Clemens. Whereas Gombert does not favor any one melody type, Clemens' melodies most often leap up and then return stepwise. With Gombert all the voices are melodically of equal interest; Clemens favors the superius. His motifs often derive their rhythms from the metrical accents of the words. This is especially true of the beginning sections of the motets, where the imitation is usually stricter than in the course of the composition. The types of motifs and the way Clemens uses them in imitation are characteristic of his time: (1) In motifs in two segments, whether separated by a short pause or not, the first segment may be imitated strictly, the second freely. (2) If motifs are rounded off by a melisma, this may differ at each statement. (3) Sometimes a motif is imitated by variants, the former never or hardly ever reappearing in its original shape. (4) There may be imitation of only the initial interval of a motif and even this may be free.[83] Clemens is among the composers who experiment in fashioning tonal answers—for example, in his *Super ripam Jordanis* and *Mane nobiscum*.[84] His counterpoint is generally of the note-against-note

[81] Cf. JepPS, 87.
[82] Cf. KemJC, 80.
[83] *Ibid.*, 63.
[84] Pr. CommB II, 17, and III, 20, respectively.

kind with much parallel motion, and includes archaic fauxbourdon-like writing. He resembles Gombert in making sparing use of both canon and of chordal writing. However, Clemens uses the authentic cadence with a greater effect of finality than had been customary in the past.

Most details of Palestrina's normal voice-relation technique are already present in Clemens. Among the exceptions,[84a] is the use of a tone that enters stepwise being approached as one kind of dissonance (auxiliary note or passing-note) and being quitted as another kind (suspension), provided the tone with which it clashes is stationary (cf. Ex. 68). Clemens rarely uses dissonance as an expressive device. For this purpose he employs other means, such as certain melodic intervals. Thus the plaintive connotation of the leap of a minor sixth is resorted to in the beautiful opening motif of *Vox in Rama.*[85] Like Josquin and Gombert, Clemens uses the minor second with words of pain or sorrow. Tender emotions are often expressed by a leap of a fourth or fifth downward followed by a whole step upward. In general, however, Clemens is not frequently given to word-painting. One of the most pleasing qualities of his style is his sonorous texture. Less favorable attributes are his frequently faulty text declamation [86] and a tendency toward lengthiness, brought about partly by his penchant for repetition, *ostinati,* and melodic sequences. It is noteworthy that his *ostinati* are often in the highest voice. Although his music occasionally seems to be written somewhat according to formula, Clemens is an expressive composer, particularly gifted in the delineation of tender and lyric moods.[87]

In 1556–1557, Susato published, in his *Musyck Boexken* ("Music Books"), IV–VII, Clemens' three-part *Souterliedekens* or "Little Psalter Songs." [88] (The books included also ten such pieces by Susato himself, written in Clemens' spirit.) These had been preceded by a volume of *Souterliedekens,* with monophonic settings, printed by Symon Cock at Antwerp in 1540. This book became popular immediately: at least 33 editions appeared between 1540 and 1613.[89] Clemens' *Souterliedekens* consist of part-settings of the texts and melodies in the Cock print. Jan Fruytiers used thirty-four of the same melodies for his rhymed version of *Ecclesiasticus* (1565).[90]

The collection of 1540 draws heavily upon folk or popular melodies, mainly

---

[84a] See KemJC, 75, and esp. the relevant exx. in the Appendix. Such exceptions, of course, are not peculiar to Clemens among pre-Palestrina composers. KemJC includes, among the exceptions, passing six-three chords in minims against a stationary voice; but see PalW V, 72.

[85] Pr. HAM, 134; ProsM, *Annus I,* II, 63.

[86] Less faulty, however, than it appears in CommB; cf. KemJC, 58ff. Further about text declamation in Clemens and other composers of the time, see LowA.

[87] See further, PirH, 262ff. For additional motets, see KemJC, App., 6; ProsM, *Annus I,* II, 320 (the eloquent *Tu es Petrus;* also in CommB III, 9; AV III, 166, and IV, 201 (*pars II*); BordA, *Motets,* I, 7); CommB I, 3, 14; II, 3; III (8 items, 2 of which appear also in BordA, *Motets,* II); V (5 items); VIII, 111; X (15 items, the last being the charming and jubilant *Ascendit Deus*); BordA, *Motets,* II, 76; MaldR XX, 6.

[88] Pr. CommB XI.   [89] Cf. ScheurS, 76.   [90] Republished with introduction, etc., in ScheurE.

Dutch,[91] current in the 16th century, but on rare occasion, also, upon art music. A few of the melodies are found in two 15th-century MSS [92] and in a MS written at Zutphen in 1537.[93] Cock had already printed twelve of the melodies (four of them with some variations) in 1539 in another book of sacred songs: *Een devoot ende profitelijck boecxken, inhoudende veel gheestelijcke Liedekens ende Leysenen.*[94] Four tunes are the same as, or at least recognizably related to, those of Claudin's *D'ou vient cela, Languir me fais,* and *Il me suffit* and Gombert's *Le bergier et la bergiere,* the tunes being applied, respectively, to Psalms LXXII, CIII, CXXVIII, and CXXXV (73, 104, 129, and 136). This, however, does not necessarily mean that the psalm melody was in every instance derived from the chanson named. It is likely that at least the Gombert piece and Psalm CXXXV (136) go back to a common source in folk or popular music.[95]

There are 159 texts in all. These are translations, into Dutch rhymed verse, of the 150 Psalms—Psalm CXVIII (119) being divided into four items—, the *Te Deum,* and five of the Canticles. The first words of the former folk or art text and those of the basic sacred text, in Latin (according to the Vulgate), are given in all instances, as is the Catholic number for each psalm. Luther's translation of the Psalms had been published at Antwerp in 1526, and there is some evidence [96] that it exerted an influence on the Dutch version.

All but twenty-five of the former secular texts have been recovered.[97] Just how the melodies should be accented in conjunction with the Dutch psalm texts has caused some difference of opinion.[98] The literary value of these translations has likewise been questioned, but their author showed sensitive musical feeling in fitting at least some of them to the melodies, e.g., in paralleling the latter's frequently complex musical structure.[99]

The *Souterliedekens* differ from the contents of the Genevan Psalter, to be

[91] About 12 French melodies are likewise included; also some German melodies and old Latin hymns.

[92] Described in BäumkN.

[93] About half the contents of the MS are pr. in FallerW; the rest, in MinU.

[94] Republished with introduction, etc., in ScheurD. The date is incorrectly given as 1538 in BergT, 10f; cf. ScheurD, [4]; W. Nijhoff, *L'Art typographique dans les Pays-Bas,* II (1926), 17 and Pl. VI, No. 21, in *Simon Cock* series. Nijhoff refers to the collection by its subtitle. *Gheestelijcke . . .* BergT, 12, fn. 1, recognizes that *Gheestelijcke . . .* and *Een devoot . . .* are the same thing, but Fig. 5 on that page refers to *Gheestelijcke . . .* as though it were a separate book; in the caption of that figure, incidentally, the correct date of 1539 is given.

[95] The relations existing in these 4 instances are pointed out in CommB XI, preface, 1. It is claimed there also that Psalms CXIII (114) and CXVII (118) are connected, respectively, with Richafort's *De mon triste deplaisir* and Arcadelt's *J'ay mis mon coeur.* The claim has been properly attacked in the last two cases in MinS (= MinZ), 288, 286. (MinS, 283, 291, also attacks, but without justification, the alleged relationship between *Le bergier . . .* and Psalm CXXXV [136] and *D'ou vient . . .* and Psalm LXXII [73].)

[96] *See* BruinS.

[97] *See* MinS.

[98] Cf. MinS; DuyNL; DuyL, *passim;* also the review of MinS in TVNM XII, 99.

[99] Cf. the 4 analyses in KemS.

discussed presently, in at least two respects: (1) The former were not used in the church service, but were designed to be sung in the home and at social gatherings, while the latter—in their purely melodic form—were prepared for use in the services of the Calvinists. (2) In the former, the words were fitted chiefly to folk or popular melodies, while in the latter the melodies were fitted by trained musicians to the words of a gifted poet and his successor.

The reputed and probable collector of the *Souterliedeken* melodies and translator of the psalms, etc., was Willem van Zuylen van Nyevelt, a nobleman of the province of Utrecht. He, or whoever the person in question may have been, undertook his task, according to the unsigned preface, "to give the young cause for liking to sing, in place of foolish fleshly songs, something good, by means of which God may be honored and they edified."

Clemens, in making his settings *a 3* of the *Souterliedekens* of 1540, called for twenty-six different combinations of voices, ranging (if we name the voices after the clefs) from TBarB to VSA.[99a] By far the most frequent grouping is STB. Next in order are TTB, SABar, and VABar. Apparently, in preparing the collection for social groups, Clemens (or Susato) planned it with a practical eye to providing material for as many different voice combinations as possible and to supplying the most common combinations with the most material. With respect to each setting, the Clemens collection indicates verbally which voice has the melody of the 1540 book. According to the information given, the melody appears in the upper voice in about a quarter of the 162 settings (Clemens sets Psalms XXXI–XXXIII [32–34] each twice). In at least one instance, however, the Clemens print is wrong:[100] the melody of *D'ou vient cela* is not in the tenor of Psalm LXXVII (78), as stated, but in the superius. Whenever Clemens places the melody in the middle voice, he tries to invent an equally expressive melody for the upper voice, which is always treated with especial affection.[100a] This is illustrated in the setting of Psalm LXV (66), the tenor melody of which— *Ick seg adieu*—enjoyed considerable popularity. It may be one of the tunes that entered the *Souterliedekens* of 1540 by way of *Een devoot ende profitelijck boecxken* (although the versions vary); it appeared, also in 1540, in a setting *a 4* in Georg Forster's *Der zweite Teil der kurtzweiligen guten frischen teutschen Liedlein* (cf. p. 706); among later settings is one by Episcopius in Phalèse's *Een duytsch musyck boeck* of 1572 (cf. p. 308).[100b]

[99a] CommB sometimes makes substitutions for the orig. clefs, but indicates what they were; the clef symbols given above are those used elsewhere in this book (e.g., on p. 249) rather than those employed in KemS.

[100] If the reprint in CommB is faithful to the orig.

[100a] Cf. KemS, 130.

[100b] About further uses, *see* MinS, 183 (where the Episcopius setting is wrongly attributed to Clemens; also there is room for doubt that René de Mel set this text—cf. ReT, 109, No. 462).

EXAMPLE 79. *Souterliedeken LXV* (66)—Clemens non Papa (after CommB XI, 50).

"Blissfully and blithely praise God, ye earthly hosts. Give him glory; set forth his praise. Say unto God, great and small: Wonderful are Thy excellent works in the world's plenitude. But this certainly do the godless deny."

(Transl. by Luise Haessler)

The Genevan Psalter; Bourgeois

Concurrently with the cultivation of early 16th-century Catholic music in France and the Low Countries, a form of Protestant music developed in French-speaking Switzerland. The year 1518 marked the definite rise in German-speaking Switzerland of a new religious movement, later known as Calvinism. First led by Zwingli, whose opposition to the Catholic church was based on both religious and political grounds, the movement soon took the form of a revolt. The ensuing civil war among the Swiss cantons cost Zwingli his life in 1531 and left Swiss Protestantism without vigorous leadership for several years. Although Zwingli was an amateur musician, no specific instance showing that he helped to establish congregational singing as a part of public worship is recorded (cf. p. 683).

When in 1541, however, the Frenchman, Jean Calvin, arrived in Geneva for the second time, Swiss Protestantism was provided with a leader well aware of the power of music *"d'esmouvoir & enflamber le coeur des hommes."* He lost no time in formulating a musical credo [101] in keeping with the austere simplicity of his religious views. St. Paul, who had advocated the singing as well

[101] Embodied in his preface (pr. in ExP iiiff) of the 1543 ed. of the Genevan Psalter; discussion in DouM I, 343ff.

as the reciting of the psalms, was his authority concerning appropriate texts for congregational singing, and he permitted no other texts to be used for this purpose. In keeping with his belief that the psalms should be understood by the congregation, he adopted the use of French translations, in verse. In a letter,[102] written from Strasbourg in 1538 during his temporary exile from Geneva, Calvin mentions his own translations of Psalms 25 (XXIV) and 46 (XLV).[102a] He found no objection to singing these and other psalm adaptations to German melodies borrowed from the Lutherans. His main stipulations in regard to a melody were that it should be the equal of the text in majesty and *"propre à chanter en l'Eglise."* [103] Throughout his leadership of almost thirty years during an era when polyphonic complexity and chordal innovation were prevalent, he remained hostile to part-singing and sanctioned only single-line melodies as psalm settings.

Calvin's first Psalter,[104] published at Strasbourg in 1539, contained eighteen psalms (six with texts of his own translation), the Song of Simeon, the Creed, and the Ten Commandments. The remaining twelve psalms used modified versions of texts by Marot, who, besides writing sprightly love poems, had since 1533 been supplying metrical psalm translations into French for the court of Francis I. Mention has been made [105] of the strange irony of "Metrical Psalmody beginning as the favourite recreation of a gay Catholic court and ending as the exclusive 'hall-mark' of the severest form of Protestantism." How Marot's texts came to be included in the Strasbourg Psalter is not clear. They had preceded him, apparently without his knowledge, in his flight from France, where the king was treating religious dissenters with such severity that before long Pope Paul III actually remonstrated.

Upon his arrival at Geneva, Marot became actively associated with Calvin, who had been recalled there in 1541. That Marot's urbane attitude proved incompatible with Calvin's rigid temperament is not surprising. Their relationship lasted less than two years. In spite of Calvin's reference to Marot as "a man in whom we take little interest although he has translated 50 Psalms which have edified 'good souls'," he showed a marked appreciation for Marot's texts, sacrificing his own in preference to them.

The poet who completed the translation of the Psalter was Théodore de Bèze or Beza (1519–1605), whom Calvin held in high esteem. Bèze's texts have been described as paraphrases, tending toward diffusion, and Marot's as translations of the greatest fidelity; [106] yet in many respects Bèze, though

---

[102] DouM II, 643, quotes this letter and one also dated 1538, from Jean Zwick to Bullinger, which states that Calvin preached 4 times a week at Strasbourg and that psalms were sung in the vernacular at these services.

[102a] References to Protestant psalm settings will give the Protestant number first in Arabic figures and then the Catholic number, if different, in parenthesis in Roman figures; cf. Chap. 2, fn. 282a.

[103] *See* ExP, vii.   [104] Facsimile in TerryP; DelétP.   [105] In TerryP, iii.

[106] DouM I, 593.

not as great a poetic genius, followed in Marot's footsteps. The general plan used by both poets in their translation of a psalm text is that of successive stanzas alike in structure. Great diversity of stanza form, however, is apparent throughout the complete Psalter. The average stanza contains six or eight lines, grouped in couplets, triolets, quatrains, or still longer metrical units. The length of lines varies between four and twelve or thirteen syllables, with an intermixture of masculine and feminine endings. Iambic rhythm is most frequent, but trochaic and also anapestic patterns occur.

The musician largely responsible for the melodic settings of the Psalter was Louis Bourgeois, who succeeded Guillaume Franc at Geneva (cf. p. 503) and remained there from 1541 to perhaps 1557.[106a] In addition to his connection with the Psalter, he is remembered for writing one of the first treatises to propose abandoning the method of learning music by the Guidonian hand in favor of learning it by solfeggio. (This means that he advocated, not abandoning the hexachord system for an octave system, but only the giving, in a consistent soft-natural-hard-hexachord order, of the solmisation syllables that follow the letter-name of a note. Thus G *sol re ut* would become G *re sol ut;* c *sol fa ut* would become c *sol ut fa,* etc.[107]) He also instituted the custom of suspending tablets in the churches to show the numbers of the psalms that were to be sung. Bourgeois, by composing, compiling, and editing, gave their final and accepted form to about eighty-five melodies of the Psalter. The remaining tunes were devised in the same manner though with less inspiration, by more than one of his minor successors.[108] The Psalter achieved its complete form in 1562.[109]

Secular melodies popular at the time were drawn upon to a much greater extent than was sacred music. Douen [110] has traced the origin of almost half the melodies of the complete Genevan Psalter: thirteen were taken from the Strasbourg Psalter of 1539, Psalms 36 (XXXV), 103 (CII), and 137 (CXXXVI) retaining their original melodies almost intact, while the others were modified; Psalm 125 (CXXIV) was originally a German canticle; Psalms 58 (LVII) and 105 (CIV) are composed of melodic fragments from other psalms; thirty-two have been identified as specific chansons, and four others appear to be based on chansons that have not been tracked down. The Genevan Psalter had many lesser counterparts, in two of which—the Flemish Psalter and the French Psalter of Antwerp—popular airs were used without any modification; unlike these psalters, that of Geneva contains melodies that frequently borrow only the first phrase of a chanson, then

---

[106a] *See* GaillB, 67, and esp. F. Lesure in RdM XXX (1948), 98.

[107] Cf. GaillB, 69ff; FétB II, 42; ReMMA, 151.   [108] Cf. GaillB, 88.

[109] This ed. reprinted in ExP, which includes Calvin's preface of 1543; this is given also, in facsimile, as presented in Goudimel's collection of 1565, in GoudP. For an English transl., *see* StrunkR, 349ff; for a discussion, GarsC.

[110] DouM I, 734f.

proceed independently. Bourgeois used several phrases of *Petite camusette* in setting Psalm 65 (LXIV). His successor commenced Psalm 48 (XLVII) with a fragment of Janequin's *Bataille*. Several instances of similarity to old Latin hymns have been pointed out.[111] The melody of Psalm 141 (CXL) is from *Conditor alme siderum;* that of Psalm 129 (CXXVIII), from *A Patri unigenitus.* The 13th-century *Exultet coelum laudibus* supplies the basis for the tune of Psalm 19 (XVIII); and a modification of the opening of *Victimae paschali* is used for Psalm 80 (LXXIX). The most famous of the Genevan melodies is that for Psalm 134 (CXXXIII) (*Or sus, serviteurs du Seigneur*), familiar throughout the English-speaking world as "Old Hundredth."

EXAMPLE 80. Psalm 134 (CXXXIII) (*Or sus, serviteurs du Seigneur*)
—Bourgeois (from ExP, 606).

Or sus, ser-vi-teurs du Sei - gneur,   Vous qui de maiden son hon - neur

De - dans sa mai-son le ser - vez,   Lou-ëz - le et son Nom. es - le - vez.

Ye servants of the Lord of might,
Who in his house do watch by night,
Attending there, your selves addres,
The Lord our God to praise and bles.

(From *All the French Psalm Tunes with English Words* . . . , 1632)

As translated, all the stanzas of a psalm have the same metrical form, and the music for stanza 1 is repeated for all the others. Poetically and musically, therefore, the results are actually hymns (and this is true of almost all Protestant "psalmody"). The old Catholic distinction between hymnody and psalmody, from the structural standpoint, no longer exists; the new pieces are psalms as to content, but no longer as to form. The texts are set, for the most part, one note to a syllable. The melodies, in which (in the original notation) breves and semibreves predominate, nevertheless display a wide variety of rhythmic patterns. Different combinations of long and short values are often used for lines of the same length and accentuation, even within the same tune.[112] The rhythm is binary. Syncopation occurs in nearly a third of the melodies and is characteristic of a certain melodic formula used for line-endings. The sounding of the initial note three times frequently occurs at line-openings. The general melodic contour is arched, and the motion is diatonic. Single phrases normally lie within a range of a fourth to a sixth, entire melodies may encompass an octave. Although all twelve modes are represented, there is a strong preference for those closest to our major and minor, the former predominating.

---

[111] WoodG, 174.   [112] Cf. PraM, 43ff, for analysis including tables.

In spite of Calvin's opposition to harmonization, four-part settings, which antedated those by Janequin mentioned on p. 340, were made by Bourgeois in 1547. These are mostly in chordal, syllabic style. His last known publication (1561) included settings *a 4, 5,* and *6*—described as suitable for instruments as well as for voices—of eighty-three of the melodies he had arranged at Geneva. While none of his harmonic versions found permanent acceptance, his melodic settings were perpetuated by the harmonizations of other composers, especially Goudimel.[113]

Rome: Costanzo Festa and Others

After the death of the music-loving Leo X in 1521, Adrian VI occupied the throne of St. Peter for less than two years. He, in turn, was succeeded by Clement VII, the former Giulio de' Medici, who was to be faced by the delicate problems resulting from Henry VIII's request for a divorce from Catherine of Aragon. Clement, like a true cousin of Leo, was a patron of music, as was his successor, Paul III.[114] Sacred music flourished in Rome—at the Papal Chapel, St. Peter's, St. John Lateran, and other houses of worship—as it did contemporaneously at Venice. But, whereas the Venetian development laid much stress on brilliance, Roman taste was more conservative and less given to sensuous display. The difference was to become more pronounced as the century progressed. Nevertheless, the churches of the Holy City, models for the Catholic world, resounded with some of the most splendid music the *cinquecento* produced.

Costanzo Festa remained in the papal service from his appointment in 1517 until his death in 1545.[115] His surviving sacred music consists of four Masses, more than forty motets, thirty Vesper hymns, thirteen Magnificats, and some Marian Litanies for two choruses *a 4.*[116] Many of Festa's works use pervading imitation in Franco-Netherlandish manner. But he is not absorbed by this technique as is Gombert: he writes chordally with equal readiness or merely suggests pervading imitation or employs non-imitative counterpoint. The music abounds in parallel thirds, sixths, and tenths. Festa's four-part *Te Deum,* long sung at the Vatican on occasions of great solemnity, is a chordal setting of the plainsong (simple Tone), discreetly paraphrased in the superius.[117]

The text of *Regem Regum*[118] incorporates part of the Litany of the Saints.

---

[113] Further about the Psalter, *see* BeM, esp. 16ff, 30ff; PraF; PraS; SchneiM; SchneiP; SchneiR. For harmonizations by Bourgeois, *see* PicM, 2431; DouM II, 83ff; GaillB, 126ff.

[114] For a list of musicians in the Papal Chapel from Paul III to Clement XI, *see* AdamiO, 159ff. For the *"Diarii Sistini"* beginning in the pontificate of Paul III, *see* CasS. *See also* CelaCP.

[115] HabR, 77, 82.   [116] For a list, *see* CamF, 11ff.

[117] Setting pr. in AlfiS VII, 400; BockM, VI, 31; opening section in TorA I, 55. For the plainsong, *see* Liber, 1834.

[118] Pr. MPI II, 48.

The petitions and acclamations throughout the work are each accorded special treatment: some are given duos of the upper and lower pairs, others are set chordally, still others are embellished with imitative polyphony. The entire motet, which is in two *partes,* is unified by a refrain which occurs first near the opening of *pars I,* again at its close, and finally at the end of *pars II.* The same contrast of textures is present in *Regem archangelorum,*[119] in which a striking feature is the appearance four times of the obsolescent under-third cadence. In the *Nunc dimittis,*[120] the melody to the words *"et in saecula saeculorum, Amen"* is first set in old fauxbourdon-like manner and is then immediately repeated in a more varied harmonization. The settings of the hymns *Veni Creator Spiritus* and *Vexilla Regis* [121] have alternate stanzas sung in polyphony and plainsong, recalling old practice; but, whereas in Dufay's hymns, for example, it was always the same polyphonic setting that alternated with the plainsong (with one exception, in which two polyphonic settings alternated with one another), in Festa's—as in hymns of later composers like Palestrina—each polyphonically sung stanza has a different setting (cf. p. 336, regarding Richafort's processional hymn). Festa sets the even-numbered stanzas for from three to five parts. The *Magnificat Sexti Toni,*[122] for from two to six parts, sets all the verses (except the opening word), the music being based on the plainsong. While, at this time, alternation of plainsong and polyphony is more common than the type setting all verses polyphonically, the latter is not infrequent. Festa's Magnificats include examples of the alternating kind also—both that in which the even-numbered verses are set and that in which the odd-numbered ones are set.[123] In the *Magnificat Sexti Toni,* perhaps the most interesting verse is No. 7, *Deposuit potentes,* set *a 5.* Four voices weave a web of imitation about the fifth, which sings the plainsong as *cantus firmus* in long notes. The imitation is based on a descriptive motif (found in its most complete form in bass I), not derived from the *cantus.*

EXAMPLE 81. Extract from *Magnificat Sexti Toni*—Festa (from MPI II, 99).

De - po - su- it   po - ten - tes   de se - des,   de se - des

"He hath put down the mighty from their seats . . ."

Verse 12 increases the number of parts to six. The four upper parts proceed in free, melismatic imitation, using a motif rather loosely based on the plainsong, while the two lower parts break the chant into its component elements

[119] Pr. TorA I, 49; MPI II, 45.   [120] *Ibid.* II, 35.   [121] *Ibid.* 78, 86, respectively.
[122] *Ibid.,* 91. For the plainsong, which differs from that in modern use, *see* IllM, 22
[123] Cf. IllM, 18f.

and progress in canon at the fifth, treating each element separately.[124]

Festa, when he joined the Papal Choir, was one of the few Italians in it; the singers were mostly French or Netherlandish. In the field of sacred composition, also, Franco-Netherlandish musicians predominated. Among them were Jean l'Héritier (cf. p. 285), who served as *maestro di cappella* at San Luigi de' Francesi and by whom we have motets, hymns, a Mass, and chansons, and Firmin le Bel (born at Noyon, near St. Quentin), who, when he was *maestro* of the Liberian chapel of Santa Maria Maggiore c. 1540, may have been a teacher of the boy Palestrina[125] (cf. pp. 455f). The greatest of the Netherlanders active in Rome at this time was Arcadelt (cf. p. 321). Several MSS in the Sistine archives[126] and a book of motets published at Venice in 1545 are probably among the works belonging to this period of his career.[127] Vicentino's *L'antica musica* . . . contains two motets[128] of his own, illustrating his theories of chromaticism; these motets probably date from his period at Rome, in view of the book's publication there in 1555. In 1538, i.e., a year before Arcadelt entered the Julian Chapel, Ghiselin Danckerts (born in Tholen, Zeeland) joined the singers of the Sistine Chapel, where he remained, under the pontificate of five popes, until 1565. Little of his music is left, but he must have been highly regarded, since he was appointed as one of the adjudicators of the celebrated dispute between Vicentino and Lusitano (cf. p. 329). He wrote a treatise to defend the decision. When the reform of the Papal Chapel took place according to the decree of the Council of Trent, Danckerts was dismissed, the entry in the records reading: "He is without voice, surpassingly rich, given to women, useless."[129]

Some Spaniards formed another group of non-Italians active in Rome at the time; the most important was the distinguished Cristóbal de Morales, who, during his Italian sojourn, produced some works of outstanding quality (cf. pp. 587ff).

Florence: Verdelot; Corteccia

At Florence, Verdelot and Corteccia produced sacred music as well as madrigals. Verdelot almost certainly sided with Savonarola in that high-minded Dominican's fatal struggles with the authorities. This appears partly from the composer's *Laetamini in Domino,* in which an *ostinato* to the words *Ecce quam bonum,* the motto of Savonarola's followers, undoubtedly presents the melody to which it was sung. The work is preserved in the large motet MS at the Biblioteca Vallicelliana in Rome (cf. p. 341), which shows con-

---

[124] Other sacred works by Festa pr. MPI II (13 items); BuH III, 245. The *Tu solus qui facis mirabilia* pr. BockM VI, 40, etc., as Festa's is actually a portion of Josquin's setting (cf. pp. 245, 258).   [125] *See* CasF; CamL. A motet of Le Bel's pr. CasR I, 21; CasF, 68.

[126] For a list, *see* EitQ I, 187.   [127] For a motet printed at Ferrara in 1539, *see* MaldR XX, 3.   [128] Pr. TorA I, 145, 147.   [129] Further about Danckerts, *see* esp. BruynD.

nections with the Savonarola movement in many other respects as well.[130]
The contemporary tendency to use tonal answers on occasion (cf. p. 351) appears in Verdelot. At the opening of his four-part *Ave sanctissima Maria,*[130a]
a-d′ in the altus is answered by d′-a′ in the superius and the tenor answers
the bass similarly. In *Gabriel archangelus,*[130b] however, Verdelot has each
voice enter with a descending leap of a fifth, producing real answers.

Corteccia's sacred works include several books of motets and a *Hymnarium.*
In the latter, Corteccia, like Festa, alternates stanzas of polyphony and plainsong, each polyphonically sung stanza having a different setting.[130c] Among
his compositions for the wedding of Cosimo I de' Medici and Eleonora of
Toledo (cf. p. 325) is a ceremonial motet *a 8* that opens with interesting examples of tonal answer.

EXAMPLE 82. Opening of *Ingredere foelicissimis auspiciis urbem tuam*
—Corteccia (from *Thesaurus musicus,* Montanus and Neuber,
1564; transcr. by I. L. Domingos).

"Enter, enter [thy town with the happiest omens.]"

---

[130] Cf. the stirring account in LowBV.

[130a] Pr. SmijT II, 182. The six-part *Ave sanctissima* pr. in SmijT III, 166 (= ScherG, 93) as
Verdelot's has been held in RubMM, 8, not to be his; but *see* p. 269 *supra.*

[130b] Pr. SmijT I, 99. Other motets *ibid.,* I, 143; II, 16, 25, 42 (= MaldR II, 35); III, 39; MaldR
XXIII, 26; XXVIII, 8.

[130c] Cf. HandMG, 228.

This work was "sung over the archway of the great door of the Porta al Prato with 24 voices on one side and on the other 4 trombones and 4 *cornetti* on the entrance of the most illustrious Duchess." [131]

Ferrara and Mantua: Jaquet of Mantua and Others

At Ferrara, Maistre Jhan composed a setting of the Passion according to St. Matthew that confines itself to Matthew XXVI and XXVII for its text and excludes the Seven Last Words from the Cross. These facts seem to give a Protestant cast to a piece composed for a Catholic court. Perhaps this is due to the Calvinist sympathies of Hercules' consort (cf. p. 311). The composer, in contrast to Claudin (cf. p. 339), represents the various dramatis personae by characteristic voice-combinations: Christ by TBB, the two maids by AAT, the *turba* by the full SAATBB complement, etc. Nevertheless, this Passion belongs for the most part to the motet type.[132] The organist at Ferrara during at least part of Maistre Jhan's tenure, Jachet Brumel, may have been a son of Antoine Brumel (cf. p. 260).[133] He should not, as has sometimes happened,[133a] be confused with Jachet Berchem.

Highly productive as a composer of sacred music was the Frenchman Jaquet (or Jachet, etc.) of Mantua (described in Latin as Jacobus Collebaudi de Vitre Rhedonensis, i.e., of Vitré, in the diocese of Rennes). Born probably c. 1495, in 1527 he was a singer, and in 1534 master of the choirboys in the Cardinal's chapel at Mantua. In 1539, while still in the Cardinal's service, he became *maestro di cappella* of the Mantuan Cathedral of St. Peter's. He probably died in 1559. Contemporary theorists refer to him with admiration. Jaquet composed many Masses, motets, Magnificats, hymns, etc., but apparently no secular works.[134] The motets include four on which Palestrina was to base Masses—*Aspice Domine* (upon which de Monte was also to model a Mass, and Vaet, to some extent, a new motet), *Salvum me fac,*[135] *Spem in alium,* and *Repleatur os meum.* The last of these consists of a canon *a 2* in the highest voices, the melody of which is imitated and freely elaborated by the three lower voices, at least one of which always anticipates the canonic pair.

---

[131] According to the print of 1539; transl. from Grove III, 277; *see* further, BorTM, 37. Other sacred works pr., LafC, 2, 4; TorA I, 121 (*Benedictus Dominus Deus Israel,* odd-numbered verses; based on the plainsong, Liber, 569).

[132] Further about this Passion, *see* KaP, 27ff (with exx.).

[133] BautJ, 103.

[133a] *E.g.,* in EitQ I, 452.

[134] Further data in Grove II, 747f; EitJ; KJ VI (1891), 115; HuD, 179ff; BautJ.

[135] *Aspice* is pr. MonteO, XXVI; *pars I* of *Salvum* in PalW XXXI, 58, both with wrong ascriptions to Berchem.

ISTITVTIONI
HARMONICHE
DEL REV. MESSERE
GIOSEFFO ZARLINO
DA CHIOGGIA,

Maestro di Capella della Serenissima Signoria di Venetia: di nuouo in molti luoghi migliorate, & di molti belli secreti nelle cose della Prattica ampliate.

Nelle quali; oltre le materie appartenenti alla Musica; si trouano dichiarati molti luoghi di Poeti, d'Historici, & di Filosofi; si come nel leggerle si potra chiaramente vedere.

Con due Tavole; l'vna che contiene le Materie principali: & l'altra le cose piu notabili, che nell'Opera si ritrouano

PER ME SI GODE IN CIELO
ET REGNA IN TERRA.

IN VENETIA,
Appresso Francesco dei Franceschi Senese.
M. D. LXXIII.

Autograph note written by Glareanus in the tenor part-book of Munich, Univ. Lib. MS 322–325, in which he praises the usefulness of singing sacred songs—as illustrated by many examples drawn from the Scriptures—but warns of perverted spirits who turn the best and most honorable pursuits into their very opposites

Title-page of Monteverdi's copy of Zarlino's Istitutioni harmoniche, bearing the composer's signature (from the Library of Dr. Dragan Plamenac)

PLATE IV

EXAMPLE 83. Extract from *Repleatur os meum*—Jaquet of Mantua (*Motetti del Frutto, Primus Liber cum quinque vocibus,* Gardane, 1538; Transcr. by M. L. Versè).

"Cast me not off in the time of old age." (Psalm LXX [71]:9)

In various works, in which he employs voice-pairing and tonal answer in the manner of the period, writes chordal passages with eloquent effect, and handles canon and conflict of accents with taste and skill, Jaquet reveals himself as a composer of more than ordinary excellence.[136]

[136] Additional motets pr. MaldR I, 12; XVII, 36, 40, 42, 47 (about these 5, *see* ReT, 93; about the last, *see also* RubIL, 83); LückS III, 65 (which survives in Jaquet's motet collection of 1545, as does MaldR XVII, 42). These are all wrongly ascribed to Berchem in the reprints cited. Jaquet's *Missa La fede non debbe esser corrotta* pr. 1892, by Reinbrecht, at Verden.—BautJ, 117, quite misunderstanding the bibliographical situation, doubts that the 5 motets in MaldR—all taken from Bologna, Lic. mus., Q 19—are by Jaquet of Mantua and makes three misstatements regarding ReT. It is not true, as implied in BautJ, that Q 19, in its ascription of the MaldR motets, includes the name of Mantua in the name of the composer. The pieces are attributed in this MS simply to "Jachet." Nor is it true that "none [of the Q 19 motets] appears in editions of motets of Jachet of Mantua or in other collections under his name." As pointed out above, one Q 19 piece is included in his motet collection of 1545. If the ascription to "Jachet" in Q 19 means Jaquet of Mantua in this one instance, it must mean that in the other four. BautJ further claims

Andreas de Silva, whom we have found in the service of the Duke of Mantua (cf. p. 326), is represented by one motet in Petrucci's *Motetti de la corona*, Book I, of 1514. Glareanus quotes the Kyrie and *Osanna* [137] of his *Missa Malheur me bat*, based on the chanson ascribed to Ockeghem. De Silva's four-part *O Regem coeli* [138] served Palestrina as the model for a Mass.

Milan

Werrecore's duties as *maestro di cappella* at the Milan Cathedral no doubt led to the writing of his sacred works, some of which appear in collections of compositions by various musicians; a publication devoted wholly to motets of his own appeared in Milan in 1555. His *O Crux, viride lignum*,[139] in two *partes*, reveals his Netherlandish origin. The ground-plan of each *pars* is the same: polyphony; chordal writing; polyphony (including an *Alleluia* section), the polyphonic portions being mostly imitative, but the repetition of texture not involving a repetition of content.

Treviso and Venice: Nasco; Willaert; Buus; Rore; Zarlino

At Treviso, a MS representing several composers preserves sixty-five sacred works by Nasco, mainly the fruit, no doubt, of his years as *maestro* at the Cathedral (c. 1551–1561). His widow in 1561 brought out a collection (later reprinted twice), containing four-part Lamentations by him, two Passions, etc.[140]

The great event in the domain of sacred music in contemporary Venice was the election, in 1527, with the support of the Doge Andrea Gritti, of Willaert as *maestro di cappella* of St. Mark's.[141] With the appointment of this foreign-born musician, Venetian sacred music acquired a leader destined to raise it to a position of loftiest eminence.

Willaert had already been in Italy several years when he was called to Venice. Zarlino reports [142] that, during the pontificate of Leo X, Willaert heard the Papal Choir sing his six-part *Verbum bonum et suave* under the impression that it was by Josquin.[143] As soon as the singers learned that it

---

that Jaquet would have been an adolescent in 1518, the date of Q 19. However, this statement is based on the assumption that Jaquet's age was the same as his wife's (!) and that he was therefore born c. 1500 (BautJ, 105). There is no evidence whatsoever that Jaquet may not have been older; indeed, the date of Q 19 would indicate the contrary. (Incidentally, BautJ is wrong in stating that ReT ascribes the chanson, *L'aultre jour*, to Jachet of Mantua; no such possibility is even hinted at.)   [137] Pr. PubAPTM XVI, 391f.

[138] Pr. KillK, 29. Another motet is pr. SmijT III, 115. The *Virtute magna*, pr. in KillK, 37, as Silva's, is really by Lasson; cf. fn. 72a. *See also* LowBV, 176.

[139] Pr. SmijT II, 125; another sacred work pr. HabW, App.

[140] Sacred exx. by Nasco pr. AV V, 105, 154, 202; VI, 13. *See also* AlesC, 159ff.

[141] For text of decree, *see* CafS I, 84f.   [142] ZarI, 428. Quoted in CafS I, 84; IMAMI I, xxviii.

[143] The date of this event must have been in or before 1519 since, in that year, Petrucci published the piece in the *Motetti de la corona*, Lib. IV, with attribution to Willaert.

was by the still comparatively uncelebrated Adriano, they lost interest in it and refused to execute it again. The piece is a variation-chain setting of the old sequence melody. (The *Motetti de la corona*, Lib. IV, contains, besides Willaert's setting, an anonymous one *a 5*, also a variation-chain composition.)

EXAMPLE 84. Openings of *pars I* and of the verses of the last pair of *pars II* of the six-part *Verbum bonum et suave*—Willaert (from *Motetti de la corona*, IV, 1519).

From Rome Willaert traveled to Ferrara, where he became attached to the court of the Este (1522–1525).[144] From there he sent Leo X the famous duo, *Quidnam* (properly *Quid non*) *ebrietas,* a setting of Horace's Epistle, Book I, 5; verse 16: "What a miracle cannot the wine-cup work!" On paper, at least, this secular Latin piece seems to end on the seventh, e-d'. In performance, however, the piece ended on an octave: at a given point in the

144 For details, *see* LenAW, 209ff.

lower voice, Willaert, needing a double flat at a time when the sign was not yet in existence, wrote certain notes a semitone higher than they were to be performed; at a later point he made a further such shift of a semitone, so that the written "e" actually sounded as "d." Spataro, in a letter to Aron, dated May 23, 1524, relates that the papal singers went astray when they tried to perform the duo; when the *violoni* attempted to play it, they were able to reach the end—*ma non troppo bene.* The piece is more interesting, perhaps, for its methodical use of modulation than for the little trick just described. The duo is probably a clever jest, by means of which Willaert was trying to tease and confuse musicians who were much occupied with the measuring of intervals ("tormented by the phantom of the 'major' and 'minor' semitone"[145]). The reference to Horace was undoubtedly intended to accuse the performers of being befuddled by what they saw because they had partaken too freely of the wine-cup.[146]

From 1525 to 1527, Willaert served Cardinal Ippolito d'Este at Milan. At some time during the latter year he became *cantor regis Ungariae.* This, however, does not mean that he spent time in Hungary (cf. p. 725). But it does help to show that his reputation had grown and to explain why he should have been made *maestro di cappella* at so great a house of worship as St. Mark's, regarded as the most important in Italy after St. Peter's. His fame spread all over Europe, and Susato, Attaingnant, and others published works of his even though he resided in Italy.

The thirty-five years that Willaert gave to St. Mark's (1527 to 1562, the year of his death) represent the best-known period of his life. The archives yield documents not only concerning his appointment but also regarding increases in salary, authorization to return to Flanders in 1542 and 1556, eight wills drawn from 1549 to 1562, etc. There is information about the hiring and discharging of singers, as in one source which states that a singer was dismissed for refusing to go to Willaert for lessons in counterpoint, "which is necessary in the choir and there is need for one to know it." Other documents deal with the reorganization, in 1562, of the choir into the *cappella grande* and the *cappella piccola,* an arrangement destined to continue until the regime of Zarlino, although originally intended to last only during what proved to be Willaert's final illness.[147]

As we have seen, numerous northern composers of earlier generations had previously been active in Italy; but, although they composed for Italian employers and absorbed Italian elements into their own music, they did not, to any marked degree, transmit Franco-Netherlandish technique to native

---

[145] AmbG III, 524.

[146] The piece is pr. and discussed at length in LeviA. *See also* LowC, 52ff.

[147] For the documents, *see* StraM VI, 191ff; ProdE, 31ff; LenC. For further factual data on Willaert at St. Mark's *see* esp. LenW.

composers. Willaert, however, by directing the music at St. Mark's and by functioning as a teacher as well as in other capacities, helped to establish what may legitimately be called a Venetian School. The effect of his residence in Venice is evident in the technical resources of sacred polyphony throughout Italy—including Palestrina's—during the whole of the century.

His fame as a composer of sacred music rests largely on his motets. Fewer than ten Masses have reached us. Five *a 4* appeared in a Venetian print of 1536.[147a] The first, constructed on Mouton's *Quaeramus cum pastoribus,* makes extensive use of the beginning of the model, quoting it almost literally in its own initial measures and skilfully varying it at later section-openings and at some other points. In the second Mass, Willaert freely expands or contracts phrases of Richafort's *Christus resurgens.* A frequently found touch of symbolism occurs in the *Crucifixus,* where writing *a 2* is replaced by writing *a 3* at *"tertia die."* This Mass, as well as the fourth one of the print, the *Missa Gaude Barbara,* survives likewise in Cambrai MS 124, which includes also the model of the last-named work, an anonymous motet *a 4.* Of the Masses *a 5* ascribed to Willaert, one [148] bears his name in two MSS, but Hesdin's in two others.[149] This composition belongs to a group of 16th-century Masses that apply the parody technique to Josquin's setting *a 6* of the sequence, *Benedicta es coelorum Regina* (cf. pp. 251f). Willaert himself wrote a motet setting of the sequence, but the basing of the Mass on Josquin's setting rather than on his own does not invalidate his claim to authorship: one source preserving this Mass—and also a five-part Willaert Mass without a title—dates from 1530–31, whereas Willaert's motet was not printed until 1539. For present purposes, the Mass will be considered his.[149a] Like the model, Kyrie I opens with the chant in canon between superius and tenor, but Willaert's rhythmic configuration is not the same as Josquin's and he ends his very first phrase at a different point; he soon abandons the canon and introduces melodic material of his own. His other three voices sing, in imitation, a revised version of the countermelody that Josquin had given, also in imitation, to his remaining four voices. The *Christe,* instead of opening with the Chant melody and the countermelody simultaneously (as do Kyrie I and the motet), presents the latter in two voices before the canonic treatment of the former begins. Kyrie II develops freely the few measures Josquin assigned to the words, *Te Deus Pater.* In the Gloria, Willaert adheres to Josquin's countermelody more closely than before. In the Credo, the *Et in Spiritum* treats *a 5* a portion of Josquin's two-part *Per illud Ave* passage, but in the Sanctus, the *Pleni* —itself a duo—incorporates part of the old duo bodily. The *Osanna* reworks the material used in Kyrie II. Each of the Agnus settings—*a 5, a 2,* and *a 6,* re-

[147a] Cf. HabMW. [148] Pr. VNM XXXV. [149] Cf. SmijMM, 15.

[149a] Since the above was written, AntonoB, which accepts the Mass as Willaert's on stylistic grounds, has come to our attention—too late, however, to be otherwise taken into account.

spectively—makes different use of material from the opening of the motet. The Masses *a 6* include a *Missa Mente tota* (apparently written c. 1515–1520),[149b] more complex than the Mass Févin had likewise based on *pars V* of Josquin's *Vultum tuum* (cf. p. 257): four of Willaert's voices are in canon throughout, except in the Benedictus and Agnus II, which are canonic duos. Another Mass *a 6*—*Mittit ad Virginem*—differs strikingly, being predominantly chordal; in the Agnus, however, there is a canon, the text of which, mentioning Alfonso II as Duke of Ferrara, shows that the work must date from 1559 or later.[150]

Willaert's three main contributions to sacred polyphony in Italy—the last two apparently made solely (aside from his activity as a teacher) through his motets, etc.—were (1) the establishment of Franco-Netherlandish technique as a part of the musical language of church music there; (2) the development of choral antiphony; and (3) the cultivation of a "modern" style emphasizing faultless declamation of the text.

Willaert's role as a bearer of the Josquin tradition is evident in his predilection for the variation-chain sequence. Among works of his printed in Italy, this type is represented not only by his setting of the *Verbum bonum et suave*, but by his settings of the *Benedicta es coelorum Regina; Salve, crux sancta; Inviolata, integra; Veni, Sancte Spiritus;* and *Victimae paschali laudes.*[151]

Franco-Netherlandish technical style is found also in Willaert's setting *a 4* of *Ave Regina coelorum, Mater Regis.*[152] The two upper voices are written in skilful canon at the fifth below, and the two lower voices at times share the thematic material of the canon, occasionally introducing it in anticipatory imitation. Willaert's setting, unlike Frye's and Obrecht's (cf. pp. 94f, 191), is continuous, no break occurring before the *Funde preces.*

Having the choir divided for the antiphonal singing of part-music was, as we have seen, a device known in the north; moreover, it was not new to Italian soil (cf. pp. 28, 174), but the old practice was to achieve new life at the hands of Willaert (who, however, is not credited with its invention by Zarlino, as is often claimed). No doubt inspired especially by the two choir-lofts at St. Mark's, one facing the other, Willaert wrote for two choirs singing alternately, each *a 4* and at times together *a 8*. A psalm collection of 1550 includes eight works by Willaert that require both kinds of singing, the writing *a 8* being confined to the *Gloria Patri*. These compositions are called *salmi spezzati* ("broken" psalms).[153] In another type—the *salmi a versi con le sue*

[149b] Described in LenMT.

[150] Cf. LenAW, 214f. Further about Willaert's Masses, *see* PirH, 240ff; WagG, 197f; SmijMM, 15 (about No. 2 in MS 72A).

[151] Pr. WillW I, 67 (= WillO I, 78), 70 (= WillO I, 83; SmijT I, 188), 80, (= WillO I, 95), 120, 146 (= HAM, 116), respectively.

[152] *Ibid.*, 114.

[153] They do not include the psalms pr. in CommB II, 60, 71. These, like the Magnificat pr. *ibid.* 47 (which is similarly in *coro spezzato* style), were pr. by Commer after the *Thesaurus musicus* of

risposte—each verse is a separate little piece *a 4,* there being no actual writing *a 8*. Such compositions—since they are not genuinely polychoral, as are the *salmi spezzati* by virtue of their passages *a 8*—could actually be sung by a single chorus *a 4*. In the collection of 1550, Willaert shared six psalms of this second type with Jaquet of Mantua, the odd-numbered verses being Jaquet's and the even-numbered ones Willaert's.[154] The book contains other psalms of type 2 by Jaquet alone, by Jaquet and Phinot jointly, and by an unknown composer. It includes also psalms in which verses of chant alternate with verses of polyphony. None of these are by Willaert, but examples of this type appear in his book of psalms of 1555. Polyphonic writing for alternating choirs made for color and brilliance and had an important effect upon the further history of polyphony.[155] In fact, the technique was more commonly used by some of Willaert's successors, e.g., the Gabrielis, than by him. Where music was composed for alternating choirs, it was—notwithstanding occasional polyphonic passages, especially at cadences—essentially in block-harmony style, thus giving expression to the Italian predilection for chordal writing.

EXAMPLE 85. Opening of *Domine probasti me*—Willaert (transcr. by H. Zenck).

* Asterisks indicate plainsong notes.

"O Lord, thou hast searched me and known me. Thou knowest my downsitting and my uprising, thou understandest my thought [afar off]." (Psalm CXXXVIII [139]:1, 2)

The "modern" style, illustrated in certain works by Willaert, in a sense the reverse of the old Franco-Netherlandish manner, clearly took form under

[154] The Willaert *Simulacra gentium* (pr. MaldR I, 19; MartiniE I, 211; ChorP V, *Livraison* 6, 106; ReissmA I, App.; GrégoL IV, 33 [of the second series of numbered pages]) is v. 12 of the *In exitu Israel* in this collection.
[155] Further about Willaert and the *coro spezzato, see* esp. ZenckSS; also AlesP.

the influence of humanistic culture, especially as it unfolded in Italy. The style is exemplified in Willaert's secular motet, *Dulces exuviae,* yet another setting of Dido's lament, described by Ambros as almost "a tragic monologue".[156] The rhythm, melody, and harmonic progressions are dictated solely by the words; pervading imitation is dispensed with, careful attention is given to text declamation, regard being paid to the accentuation of the Latin; the melodic line approximates the inflections of speech, the sonorities are built on the chord root, the bass carries the harmony.[157] A tendency toward dramatic expression, here evident, is revealed also in Willaert's setting, in three *partes,* of the story of Susanna.[158] His concern for correct declamation extends to works that treat words free of dramatic import, for example, his eloquent four-part *Pater noster,* which has, as *pars II,*[159] an *Ave Maria* whose text varies somewhat from the standard one. Each *pars* is an elaboration of the Gregorian melody for its text. The elaboration, though polyphonic, is sufficiently restrained not to interfere with good declamation. The contrast that results from the liturgical practice of having almost all of the Lord's Prayer chanted by the priest, but of having *"sed libera nos a malo"* treated as a choral response, is reflected in Willaert's setting by a full close before these words and by their being assigned the only highly chordal writing in the composition.[160]

Fastidious craftsmanship was markedly characteristic of Willaert. Zarlino says that "in the manner of a new Pythagoras examining minutely all the possibilities [in music] and discovering countless errors, he set out to correct them and to restore music to the honor and dignity it once possessed and logically should possess; and he revealed a rational method of composing each musical *cantilena* in elegant style and has given a most clear example thereof in his works." [161]

Willaert's Book I of motets *a 6* (1542) [161a] includes three pieces bearing the name of Jachet Berchem (also one credited merely to "Jachet"). Berchem may therefore have belonged in some way to Willaert's circle. His presence in Venice is at any rate attested to by the wording of the dedication of his madrigal collection of 1546. Although chiefly a composer of secular music, he produced not only some motets but a number of Masses.[161b]

The first organist at St. Mark's from 1541 to 1550, i.e., during part of Willaert's regime as *maestro,* was Jacques Buus (Bohusius, von Paus), prob-

---

[156] AmbG III, 523. Music pr. WillW I, 133.   [157] Cf. LowL, 54.

[158] Cf. AmbG III, 523; CafS I, 87; StraM VI, 249f. (Although excluded from the Protestant and Jewish Bibles and assigned to the Apocrypha, the story of Susanna forms Chap. XIII of the Book of Daniel in the Vulgate.)

[159] Complete work pr. WillW I, 97; AmbG V, 538. *Pater noster* only in SmijT II, 1; MaldR II, 25; ObrMT, 131; HAM, 80. (Wrong ascription to Obrecht in ObrMT and in the 1st ed. of HAM). *See* also ChilP.

[160] For motets now (1951) available, but not yet cited, *see* SmijT I, 73, 131; II, 93, 176; CommB I, 75; LückS IV, 128; MaldR II, 30, 32 (= WillW I, 37; WillO I, 36); XVI, 42; AV V, 129; VI, 135, 159; WillW I (which contains 45 pieces in addition to those already referred to, 27 of them appearing also in WillO I).   [161] ZarI, 2.   [161a] Pr. WillO IV.   [161b] The works ascribed to him in MaldR I and XVII, LückS III, and MonteO XXVI, however, are not his; cf. fn. 135, 136. *See also* fn. 30.

ably born at Ghent. In 1550, he obtained a leave of absence and went to Vienna, becoming organist at the imperial court in 1551. He may have died in that city c. 1564. Buus is important mainly as a composer of instrumental music (cf. pp. 529, 537), but a handful of secular vocal music survives as well as nineteen motets *a 4*, printed in 1549, and two others found in collections representing various composers. Buus based most of his texts on biblical passages, which he treated very freely. Musically, his motets proceed in Netherlandish through-imitation manner without clear-cut sections such as characterize Josquin, but with the asymmetrical overlapping that we have noted in Gombert. Still, one does find chordal passages and fauxbourdon-like writing. The themes stem from Gregorian Chant, although they, like the texts, are very freely handled. The six-part wedding motet, *Qui invenit mulierem bonam*,[162] is of special interest. The two tenors are assigned, in *pars I*, a canon at the unison, in which the *comes* sings in augmentation, and, in *pars II*, a mirror canon at the octave, with the *comes* again in augmentation. The canonic parts have a text different from that of the other four.[163]

Willaert, as we have seen, was succeeded as *maestro* in 1563 by Cipriano de Rore. Among the latter's pupils was Luzzasco Luzzaschi, who has left a document in which he mentions a *Miserere* composed by Rore as a youth in Flanders; but obviously most of Rore's music, sacred as well as secular, belongs to his Italian period.

Five Masses by Rore survive. Of these, a *Missa a note negre* derives its name from the short note-values that abound throughout the work (cf. p. 320). Two of the other Masses, obviously belonging to his Ferrarese period, were written in homage to Hercules II. One is *a 5*, the other *a 7*. In the former, a structurally old-fashioned *cantus-firmus* Mass, the tenor is assigned the words *"Vivat felix Hercules secundus, dux Ferrariae quartus"* and derives its melody from them, each text syllable being represented by the solmisation syllable that contains the same vowel: *mi, fa, re, mi, re, ut, re, re, ut, ut, ut* (Rore, confronted by *ut* thrice in a row, obtains variety by shifting from the soft to the natural hexachord for the first *ut*), *re, fa, mi, re, fa, ut*.[164] The *cantus firmus* of the other Mass of homage, the *Missa Praeter rerum seriem*—based on Josquin's similarly named motet—bears somewhat similar words: *"Hercules secundus, dux Ferrariae quartus, vivit et vivet*.[165] These two works were undoubtedly inspired by Josquin's Mass dedicated to Hercules I. In writing at least some of his Masses, Rore seems to have had no wish to be the pioneer he so notably was as a madrigalist.[166] However, it was his *Missa Praeter*

[162] Pr. CommB VIII, 76.

[163] For special study of Buus, *see* KrausB; *see also* MGG II, 542ff.

[164] Exx. pr. PirH, 254ff.   [165] Cf. MusiolR, 72ff.

[166] Further about Rore's Masses, see MusiolR, 70ff, where the composer is credited with 7 such compositions. It is clear, however, from the intensive investigation of Rore's Masses that is being undertaken by Mr. Alvin Johnson (cf. Chap. 5, fn. 348b), that the work discussed in WagG, 199ff (on the basis of a MS score by Thürlings), is not by Rore and that the Mass *a 4*, which EitQ VIII, 306, claims was included in La Hèle's Mass collection of 1578 (cf. p. 511) never existed.

rerum that Hercules II selected to send as a gift to Lassus' great patron, Albert V of Bavaria. The letter of thanks (dated April 25, 1557) [167] expresses warm admiration.

Rore's first motet book (Venice, 1544) contains seven works by him and sixteen by ten other men. His own pieces are mostly in the older Franco-Netherlandish style, but the occasional appearance of short passages of syllabic declamation, such as we have observed in his madrigals, shows the influence—which was to become increasingly evident—of Willaert's Italianate modern manner. Book II (1545) is devoted entirely to Rore. In this collection he pays more attention than he did in the earlier one to grouping the voices used in a single work in varying smaller combinations. In the *Beatus homo*, in three *partes*, he omits the superius throughout *pars II*, thus obtaining a striking contrast. In Book III (1549) there is some notably sensitive handling of text. This trait is impressively evident in the *Infelix ego*,[168] included in the second of two sets of *Sacrae cantiones* by Rore printed after his death, one in 1573 and one in 1595. Also in the second collection is an *Ad te levavi*, presenting some use of accidentalism of more than passing interest.[169] About 1565, Albert V had a great illuminated MS prepared at Munich, containing twenty-five motets by Rore and eighty-three miniatures—including a portrait of the composer [170]—by Hans Mielich, the court painter (cf. pp. 690f). Among the motets is a fine six-part *Hodie Christus natus est* (which was to be printed in the *Sacrae Cantiones* of 1595),[171] in which the altus II and tenor II sing a canon at the fifth against the free polyphony of the other parts. Also among the contents is *O altitudo divitiarum* (included in the collection of 1573),[172] a work of magnificent breadth and dignity.

In 1557, Rore's Passion according to St. John, which he had written for Hercules II, was published at Paris, together with other works. It is modeled after the St. Matthew Passion, composed earlier for Ferrara by Maistre Jhan. The writing is in two to six parts; the music for the Evangelist is *a 4*, that for the *turba* is *a 6*, and that for the other dramatis personae *a 2*—Christ's passages being set for the two lowest voices, the others for the two highest. Thus there is some attempt at characterization, though the Passion is mainly of the motet type.[173]

Rore was succeeded in 1565 as *maestro di cappella* at St. Mark's by another pupil of Willaert's—the celebrated Gioseffo Zarlino (1517–1590). He began to study for the Church at an early age. In 1541, he moved from his native Chioggia to Venice, where his studies with Willaert prepared him for his

---

[167] Pr. StraM VI, 136f.   [168] Pr. MusiolR, App., 25.   [169] *See ibid.*, 29.
[170] Reproduced as frontispiece to SCMA VI.   [171] Pr. DehnS, *Lieferung 5*, p. 2.
[172] Pr. MonteO IV, App. Other motets by Rore pr. AV V, 82, 177, 190; VI, 80, 185; MaldR I, 18 (= ReissmA I, App., 24); XII, 19. (All except AV V, 177, appear in the Munich MS.)
[173] For discussion of Rore's Passions, with exx., *see* KadP, 33ff.

career as a musician. His chief work is his *Istitutioni harmoniche* (1st ed., 1558), which soon achieved such fame as to be translated into French and German and reworked in Dutch.[174] Though, like Zarlino's other dissertations, it was printed in the second half of the century, it reflects in many ways the practice of the first half. The treatise is divided into four books. In the first Zarlino includes a general discussion of the excellence of music. In Book II he recognizes—like Lodovico Fogliano before him, but with a fuller understanding of just intonation—the correctness of Ptolemy's division of the tetrachord into a greater tone, a lesser tone, and a diatonic semitone. This brought upon him the wrath of Vincenzo Galilei. A former pupil of Zarlino's, Galilei nevertheless attacked the latter's view in his own *Dialogo della musica antica e della moderna* (1581) and again in his *Discorso intorno alle opere di messer Gioseffo Zarlino di Chioggia* (1589),[174a] in which he favored the Pythagorean division (rejected by modern theorists) into two greater tones and a limma. Book III of the *Istitutioni,* dealing mainly with the laws of counterpoint,[175] treats with special attention the problems of double counterpoint; with the exception of Vicentino, Zarlino is the earliest theorist to handle the subject fully. This Book is especially notable for a passage in Chapter 31. Like every well conducted theorist of his day, Zarlino discusses the intervals available between two voices; but here he goes further, pointing out, for the first time in theoretical writing, that the basic variety of all partmusic derives from the major and minor harmonies (actually he refers to the position of the major third within a fifth, i.e., to the position below or on top of the minor third, or within a fifth above an octave). Book IV is devoted chiefly to the modes. Like Glareanus, Zarlino lists twelve but, unlike him, places the Ionian and Hypoionian first and the Aeolian and Hypoaeolian last (cf. p. 185). He thus not only recognizes major and minor, like the Swiss theorist, but places them in positions of special prominence. He counterbalances his advanced attitude, however, by burdening his exposition of each mode with an outworn attribution of ethos.[176] In Chapter 32, he stresses the importance of expressing the mood of the words (*imitare le parole*).[177] In Chapter 33 he gives ten rules—intended to guide not only the composer but also the singer—for underlaying words to polyphonic music. These may be

---

[174] About the 2 French versions, *see* BrenZ; the German transl., by J. C. Trost, is lost. A. Werkmeister, in his *Harmonologia Musica* (1702), 110, mentions a Dutch transl., meaning perhaps the original form of Sweelinck's *Compositions-Regeln* (surviving today only in a German version), which treatise incorporates much material taken over from the *Istitutioni* (modern ed. of the *Regeln* in SweeW X). StrunkR, 229ff, gives a modern English transl. of several extracts.

[174a] For a facsimile ed. of the former, *see* GalD; of the latter, GalZ. Partial reprint of the former in GalDM.

[175] Discussed in detail in RobbinsB, 8ff.

[176] Cf. the criticism in WintG I, 104. Much of the explanation of the modes in polyphony, given in WoolS, is based on Zarlino.

[177] Cf. CaraC, *passim*.

summarized as follows (the note-values, it should be recalled, are usually halved in transcriptions into modern notation):

(1) Long and short syllables should be combined with notes or figures of corresponding value, "so that no barbarism be heard." (2) Only one syllable should be sung to a ligature. (3) A dot augmenting a note should not be given a new syllable. (4) A syllable is, as a rule, not to be assigned to a semiminim or to notes of smaller value or to a note immediately following. (5) Notes that immediately follow a dotted semibreve or minim and are of smaller value than the dots themselves—e.g., a semiminim after a dotted semibreve—are not usually given a syllable. (6) If a syllable has to be given to a semiminim, another syllable may also be given to the note following. (7) A syllable must be given to a note, whatever its value, at the beginning of a piece or of a passage after a rest. (8) In plainchant, neither words nor syllables should be repeated. In figurate music, repetitions of individual words or syllables are likewise forbidden, but, "when there are notes in such quantity that repetition is suitable," there may be repetitions of word-groups whose meaning is complete in themselves or "for the better expression of words that contain some important sentence, worthy of consideration." (9) At the close, the penultimate syllable may be combined with a number of notes, but only if it is long; combination of several notes with a short syllable would produce a barbarism. (10) The last syllable must coincide with the last note (cf. p. 35 regarding 15th-century practice as attested by the Canonici MS).

Zarlino's ten rules illustrate the concern over text treatment that proved one of the most important features of 16th-century composition, especially in the realms of sacred and Italian secular music. He reflects the taste of his time faithfully: there is a point beyond which he regards technical tours de force as producing examples of *arte sofistica,* even though, as an admirer of Willaert and an accomplished contrapuntist himself, he esteemed technical ability. He felt that antiquity had reached the *somma altezza* in music and that, during the Middle Ages, this had been followed by an *infima bassezza* which, thanks to the Almighty, had been overcome in his own time through the genius of Willaert.

In 1571, Zarlino's *Dimostrationi harmoniche* appeared. This is divided into five *Ragionamenti* and is written in the form of dialogues which, according to Zarlino, report the conversation of friends meeting in 1562 at the house of Willaert, who was ill with gout. The speakers are Willaert, his pupil Francesco Viola (*maestro di cappella* to Alfonso d'Este), Claudio Merulo, Zarlino, and a certain Desiderio of Pavia, a friend of Willaert's who, having read many Greek and Latin writers on music, wished to hear the discussion. The subjects treated include the proportions of intervals, the division of the monochord, the modes, etc. In 1588, Zarlino published his *Sopplimenti musicali,* partly in answer to Galilei's attacks. Of special interest is his exposition (in

Book IV, Chap. 27f) of the system of equal temperament as applied to the lute. In 1589, he brought out his collected writings in four volumes, which included, besides the treatises mentioned, several works not dealing with music. Zarlino's post presumably caused him to write many compositions; very few, however, survive. They reveal him as an estimable composer,[178] but he lives mainly as an outstanding theorist, representing a period when excellent theorists were numerous.[179]

[178] But cf. WintG I, 119. For 4 motets, *see* TorA I, 69, 79; AV V, 44; PaoluA II, 250 (a work *a 6,* parts 3–5 from the top being in canon and giving their melody—derived from the Gregorian *Virgo prudentissima*—direct, inverted, and direct, respectively). The statement, sometimes found, that Zarlino wrote music for an *Orpheo* is erroneous; cf. SolA I, 36.

[179] Further about Zarlino, *see* esp. ChierZ; HögZ; ZenckZ; RieG, 389ff; WoolT, 89ff.

Chapter 8: SECULAR VOCAL MUSIC OF THE LATE RENAISSANCE: Arcadelt, Le Jeune, Lassus, Sweelinck, and their Contemporaries as Writers of Polyphonic Chansons; Palestrina, Monte, Marenzio, Monteverdi, and their Contemporaries as Writers of Italian Madrigals

T
HE latter part of the 16th century saw Italian music come markedly to the fore. The Italians, in whatever degree they influenced the Franco-Netherlanders earlier, had clearly been of secondary importance. In the late *cinquecento,* however, they became definite rivals of their northern contemporaries and in some respects—for example, in the field of the polyphonic Mass—surpassed them. The overflowing genius of the Italian Renaissance, which was enriching the visual arts with many of their most brilliant masterpieces, expressed itself, at last, in the music of native Italians. At the same time, the state of Franco-Netherlandish music was affected by unfavorable political conditions in the Low Countries. If, in former days, Franco-Netherlanders frequently traveled abroad, more of them now left home without returning. The leading Franco-Netherlanders of the late 16th century—Lassus and Monte—settled in Central Europe and died there. But the prestige of French culture helped the chanson to maintain some autonomy on foreign soil. Moreover, in France itself, where political conditions were comparatively stable, the chanson enjoyed a new lease on life. Sacred music, however, declined there, while the sacred music of the *émigré* Netherlanders—partly owing to the use of Latin texts, having no national associations, and notwithstanding the marked characteristics of Franco-Netherlandish style—tended to become a part of the music of the country in which the composer had settled. That, from Dufay to Josquin, the Italians as a group produced music less great than that written by the Franco-Netherlanders, is beyond question; but it is clear that in the late *cinquecento* for every Lassus there was a Palestrina.

Arcadelt

It was probably c. 1553 that Arcadelt returned permanently from Italy to France, since it is in that year that the great chanson production distinguishing the final phase of his career began to appear from the presses of Le Roy and Ballard. A few chansons had been published by Attaingnant and Moderne between 1538 and 1543, but these years belong to what was primarily his madrigal period. In 1557 a book of Masses issued by Le Roy and Ballard bore a dedication to Charles de Guise, second Cardinal of Lorraine, whom Arcadelt served as *maître de chapelle*. He was also a musician to the king.[1]

The popularity of his chansons is attested by many reprints. These works are quite varied in style. In *Quand je vous ayme* [2] the characteristic repetition of the closing section (cf. pp. 294f) is less clearly marked, as a result of strongly overlapping cadences, than in the typical Claudin chanson. *Souvent amour ne sçay pourquoy* [3] is predominantly polyphonic, with short passages of imitation, while the very brief *Si c'est amour* [4] is strictly chordal throughout. In general, Arcadelt's chansons, despite occasional use of imitation, are predominantly chordal and dancelike; both opening and closing sections are almost invariably repeated, although at times with small differences. He likes to vary writing in binary rhythm with chordal passages in ternary meter. *Margot labourés les vignes* [5] is especially interesting, since it is a setting of a well-known folk tune, closely resembling the perhaps still better known *En passant par la Lorraine*.[6] The famous *Ave Maria*, attributed to Arcadelt and apparently first published in 1845, is in reality a modern adaptation of his lively three-part chanson, *Nous voyons que les hommes font tous vertu d'aimer,* whose text is scarcely suggestive of religious contemplation.[7] Gay texts, however, are the exception in Arcadelt's chansons, which tend to be on serious subjects.

The sixth book of chansons includes settings of five Latin poems by Vergil, Martial, and Horace. The Vergilian piece is a simple but highly dramatic setting of the scene of Dido's death (starting nine lines before *"Dulces exuviae"*). These five settings, while not strictly observing the Latin meter, treat the accents of individual words carefully. The representation of classical meters, however, was presently to become a major concern of French musicians, but not before the way had been prepared by certain developments in literary circles.

Humanism; the Académie; Claude Le Jeune

The popularity that Marot had enjoyed during the first half of the century did not go unchallenged. In 1549 appeared, in answer to Thomas Sibilet's *Art poétique* (1548) defending Marot, Joachim Du Bellay's *Deffense et*

---

[1] Cf. PirH, 257.   [2] Pr. ELAM XI, 42.   [3] Pr. SCMA V, 31.   [4] Pr. *ibid.,* 22.
[5] Pr. *ibid.,* 20; CauQ, 30.   [6] Cf. GéroC, 56, 97, 79.
[7] Cf. RdM, VIII (1927), 45; PirH, 260; BorFA, 12. For the chanson, *see* SCMA V, 23. For other Arcadelt chansons not yet cited, *see ibid.* (2 of these also in PubAPTM XXIII, 1, 4; 5 also in MaldP X, 46, 48, 49, 50, 51, but *a 3* instead of *a 4* [cf. ReT, 80, 92]); PubAPTM XXIII, 3, 7; CommB XII, 77; EinIM I, 268; MaldP X, 47 (cf. ReT, 80, 92).

Illustration de la langue françoise.[8] (*"Illustration"* here means "rendering illustrious.") Together with Ronsard's *Abrégé de l'art poétique françois*[9] (1565) it constitutes the manifesto of that group of poets known as the Pléiade. Fundamentally, the *Deffense* aimed at a new greatness in French literature: "Sing to me," wrote Du Bellay, "those odes, yet unknown to the French muse, on a lute well tuned to the sound of the Greek and Roman lyre. . . . Above all, take care that the type of poetry be far from the vulgar, enriched and made illustrious with proper words and vigorous epithets, adorned with grave sentences, and varied with all manner of colorful and poetic ornaments." While it urged the imitation of classical forms and meters, it specifically noted that the French language "has not long and short syllables."[10] Finally, Ronsard recommended that poets follow certain procedures which he felt would render their verses particularly suitable for musical setting, the literary result being what the Pléiade called *vers mesurés à la lyre.*[11]

This type of poetry is not to be confused with the *vers mesurés* advocated by Baïf, one of the Pléiade leaders. He sought to revive the lyricism of antiquity by writing what came to be called *"vers mesurés à l'antique,"* which followed the rules of classical prosody. This involved attributing long and short quantities to French syllables, contrary to the principles that had been enunciated by Du Bellay. Baïf was not, as he claimed, the first to essay such writing. As early as 1497, Michel de Boteauville had set up arbitrary rules for determining quantity in French syllables and produced a poem applying these rules. Similar attempts had likewise been made in Italy, and Baïf doubtless became acquainted with them on his visit there, c. 1563. In 1567 he began translating the Psalms into *vers mesurés* and produced, about this time, his *Chansonnettes mesurées.* As independent poems, these failed to become popular; it was only in association with music that they surmounted their rather precious pedantry.[12]

In 1570 Baïf, together with Joachim Thibaut (known as de Courville),[13] *joueur de lyre du roi,* founded the *Académie de poésie et musique* (consisting of *professionnels* and *auditeurs*) in order to establish a closer union between the two arts. Ronsard, too, was associated with it. Baïf's house became famous for the concerts he offered, at which Charles IX, a most active patron, was often present. The regulations governing the Académie included admonitions against talking or making any disturbance during performances; late-comers

[8] For abridged transl., *see The Great Critics,* James H. Smith and E. W. Parks, eds., 1939, p. 165.
[9] For abridged transl., *see ibid.,* 179.
[10] Quotations from *op. cit.,* 175f.
[11] Further about Ronsard and music, *see* ComteR, RMR, TierR, ExF, ThibaultB (a bibliography of Ronsard poems set to music in the 16th century, with 4 musical exx.), ThibaultA, DrozB.
[12] Further about Baïf and his predecessors, *see* MassonH, 1299f; YaF, *passim;* WalkM, *passim;* esp. about Baïf, *see* AugéB.
[13] About 4 chansons of his, *see* WalkB, 91. One is pr. LesAC, 107.

Tenor part of Kyrie II *of Gheerkin's* Missa Panis quem ego dabo *from the fancifully orna-mented MS Cambrai 124*

Superius of Arcadelt's Nous voyons que les hommes font tous vertu d'aimer, *reworked in the 19th century into the* Ave Maria *foisted upon the composer (from LeRoy & Ballard's* Chansons à quatre parties, *1554)*

PLATE V

were to be admited only at the conclusion of a chanson.[14] The special aims of
the Académie were the composition, performance, and teaching of *musique
mesurée,* music in which the long and short syllables of *vers mesurés* were
correspondingly set to notes of long and short values, the longs having generally twice the value of the shorts. Thus the text determined not only the
form but the rhythmic pattern of the music, and, since this uniformity was
imposed upon all the voices simultaneously, it resulted inevitably in a chordal
texture. Since such limitations on musical creativeness might have been
rather stultifying, it was fortunate that the Académie included such a brilliant artist as Claude Le Jeune. Born at Valenciennes c. 1525–1530, he settled
in Paris by 1564, where he was in touch with Huguenot circles. Late in life he
was *compositeur de la musique de la chambre* to Henry IV; he died in 1600.[15]
(His name has at times caused him to be confused with Claudin de Sermisy.)
The popularity he attained is attested by the fact that his *Mélanges,* first
published in 1585, was reprinted in 1586 and 1587.[15a] *Le Printemps,*[16] Le
Jeune's settings of thirty-nine chansonnettes by Baïf, of which thirty-three
are in *musique mesurée,* shows that the poet's emphasis on rhythmic formulas
by no means shackled the composer's extraordinary gift for graceful melodies
and original harmonies. These pieces illustrate how the strict formula,
whereby long note-values correspond to long syllables, could be varied by
the substitution of little melismatic figures that contribute both lightness
and expressiveness but are never developed to an extent that upsets equivalence
to the literary scansion. The quantitative meters that are read into the texts
sometimes produce extraordinary fluidity in the rhythm of the music; so much
so that transcriptions into modern notation seldom provide bar-lines, but
instead indicate the quantity-scansion, before each piece, by means of prosodic
symbols. If bars were added to the opening of *La bel'aronde,* the result would
be as follows:

EXAMPLE 86. Opening of *La bel'aronde*—Claude Le Jeune (after
MMRF XII, 28).

"The pretty swallow, messenger of the gay season . . ."

[14] Further about the *Académie's* concerts, *see* BrenFA, 29ff; WalkB; YaF.
[15] For further biographical data, *see* BoutE; WalkJ.
[15a] For 13 French pieces from the *Mélanges,* see MMRF XVI; 6 of these also in MaldP XXIX
(1 of these = ELAM IX, 14); 1 other of the 13 also in MMRFR I, 36.
[16] Pr. MMRF XII, XIII, XIV. Individual nos. also in MassonH, 1312 (= MMRFR I, 42), 1328,
1334; BordC, No. XXV. The set includes Janequin's *L'Alouette* and *Chant du rossignol* with both
a fifth voice and some new sections added by Le Jeune (*see* MMRF XII, 50, 92).

The texts of these chansons in *musique mesurée* consist of strophes, called "*chants,*" and refrains, called "*rechants*" and "*reprizes.*" The words of the refrains are, of course, invariable; those of the strophes vary, but the stanza structure almost always remains the same within a single piece, thus permitting re-use of the *chant* music without change. The refrain appears after every strophe and sometimes at the beginning also. There is no one stereotyped plan, though all the plans are closely akin. In the exquisite *chanson* quoted above, Le Jeune writes merely a *rechant a 6* (which, however, begins *a 4,* as our example shows) and a *chant a 4.* The *rechant* opens the piece, and then the *chant* and *rechant* alternate until all five strophes have been sung. On the other hand, in *Cigne je suis,*[17] the two strophes (there are no more) are of dissimilar length: the first has five lines; the second, seven. Le Jeune sets the first pair of each strophe to the same music, treats the last pair the same way, and gives the music of strophe 1, line 3 (somewhat altered), to the likewise central line of strophe 2; lines 3 and 5 of strophe 2 have new music. The *rechant* first appears *a 3* and immediately thereafter (renamed *reprize*) *a 5,* in which form it recurs after each strophe. The same top part (*dessus*) is used in both versions of the *rechant,* but the lower parts are different. Le Jeune frequently offers variety by thus providing two versions of his *rechant.* Also, he sometimes contrasts his *chants* more sharply than in *Cigne je suis.*

A different but no less interesting example of Le Jeune's experimental inclinations is the brief chanson, *Qu'est devenu ce bel oeil,*[18] which makes liberal use of degree-inflection; it illustrates the application of a rarely employed chromatic mode. Under Italian influence, chromaticism, from c. 1550, gained considerable favor among the French. Le Jeune's *Octonaires de la vanité et inconstance du monde* [19] gives further proof of his interest in technical problems. This collection is based on some moralistic texts by the Calvinist minister, Antoine Chandieu, each poem consisting of eight lines (whence the term *Octonaires*). The collection contains thirty-six pieces, three for each of the modes in the twelve-mode system. Each set of three comprises two pieces *a 4* and one piece *a 3.* It is noteworthy that Le Jeune follows a classification, used during the last third of the century, in which the Ionian rather than the Dorian is Mode I—the major mode is coming further to the fore. Le Jeune employs only numbers to indicate the modes, avoiding the use of the old names (cf. p. 377). He goes to some pains to illustrate the technical characteristics of each mode. Indeed, his designation of the Ionian as Mode I merely reflects general trends; his use of the modes is on the whole conservative. These chansons reveal, in their word-painting, the growing influence of the Italian madrigal.

Among Le Jeune's chansons there are some of grand proportions. *Mignonne je me plains* covers no less than sixty-three pages in MMRF XIII. *Du trist'*

[17] Pr. MMRF XIII, 79.   [18] Pr. ExR, 1287; MMRFO 3063.   [19] Pr. MMFTR I, VIII.

hyver, which covers thirty-nine, is a setting of a complete *sestina.* Le Jeune sets each of the six-line stanzas, and also the three-line *envoi,* as a separate *pars.* The anonymous text not only follows the normal procedure of using the same six line-ending words in all the stanzas, in varying order, but even makes them rhyme (three words to each of two rhymes). The *envoi,* however, reintroduces only four of the terminal words. The composition begins with the following impressive measures: [20]

EXAMPLE 87. Opening of *Du trist' hyver*—Claude Le Jeune (after MMRF XIV, 47).

"The rigid ice of sad winter gives way to the rays of the gracious sun."

Mauduit; Du Caurroy

The history of the Académie as founded by Baïf is somewhat confused after 1571. During the reign of Henry III, we learn of an *Académie du Palais,* which met at the Louvre and of which Guy Du Faur de Pibrac was the guiding spirit. Some historians have regarded this as replacing Baïf's Académie, but the new group seems, rather, to have been an extension of the old one and to have cultivated philosophical debate, while the parent body continued in the old manner.[21] The academicians were prevented, almost at the outset, from engaging in their activity undisturbed, owing to the religious and civil fighting that was eventually to cost Henry III his throne and life, and they disappear as an organized body after 1585. The early 17th-century scientist

[20] Further citations to Le Jeune chansons: ExFR VI, 1, 7, 11, 19; ExR, 1263, 1281; BuH III, 271; LesAC, 95, 112, 114, 123, 141, 144. *See also* Chap. 6, fn. 30.
[21] Cf. YaF, 31, 35.

and theorist, Marin Mersenne, in a somewhat fulsome *Eloge* [22] records that the composer Jacques Mauduit, during the fighting in Paris (in 1589?), saved for posterity certain works of Baïf and Le Jeune. Some of the compositions of Mauduit (1557–1627), such as *Vous me tuez si doucement,*[23] are quite charming. His *Vostre tarin je voudrois estre* illustrates gracefully the rhythmic fluidity that he, like Le Jeune, was able at times to achieve in setting *vers mesurés.*

EXAMPLE 88. Opening of *Vostre tarin je voudrois estre*—Mauduit (after MMRF X, 33).

"Your goldfinch I would be, in the emprisoning cage."

Mauduit was an important member in the later life of Baïf's Académie. In these closing years, the rather artificial equilibrium between poetry and music, which Baïf had sought to maintain, was no longer preserved. Music, possibly aided by the greater prominence now granted to instruments, gained the ascendency.[24]

After the disbanding of the academicians, Eustache Du Caurroy (1549–1609) was among those who still wrote *musique mesurée.* This composer, who entered the royal service about 1569, was the eventual recipient of many titles, among which were *sous maître* in the royal chapel and *compositeur de la musique de la chambre* to the king.[24a] His *Meslanges,*[25] published in 1610 by Pierre Ballard, son and successor of Robert, contains a variety of moralistic and general chansons, including some *noëls* and a sampling of pieces in *musique mesurée.* Having been hostile to such *musique,* he was inspired to attempt writing it as the result of a performance "by nearly a hundred voices" of a *psaume mesuré* by Le Jeune.[26] It is difficult to agree with Mersenne's claim that Du Caurroy outranks his great model, although a "measured" chanson like his *Deliette, mignonette*[27] is quite lovely. Such freer compositions as his *Noël, Un enfant du ciel nous est né*[28] show him as an amiable exponent of more traditional polyphony.

---

[22] Pr. in his *Harmonie Universelle,* Book VII; reprinted in BrenV, 201ff.

[23] Pr. MMRF X, 2; MMRFR I, 34; MassonH, 1337.

[24] Cf. BrenFA, 37. Further about Mauduit, *see* BrenV, 199ff. MMRF X contains 22 Mauduit chansons not yet cited; *see also* MMRFR I, 31; MassonH, 1339.

[24a] Cf. LesAC, *Notices,* No. 45. For further biographical information, *see* DufoDC.

[25] Portion pr. MMRF XVII.   [26] Cf. MassonH, 1306.   [27] Pr. MMRF XVII, 80; ExR, 1279.

[28] Pr. MMRFR I, 26; MMRF XVII, 26 (which vol. contains in all—besides 6 psalms [cf. Chap. 9]—14 Du Caurroy chansons, including 7 *noëls*); 2 more chansons in LesAC, 132, 135.

Despite its limited popularity, the type of chanson cultivated by the academicians was not, as we shall see later, without effect outside its own restricted circle.

Goudimel; Costeley; Some Lesser Figures

During the second half of the century, several fine chanson composers flourished who, unlike Du Caurroy, were not, so far as we know, turned into devotees of *musique mesurée*. These men, representing a variety of styles, are alike in their allegiance to the tradition of the freer chanson, some of them being markedly affected by their Italian colleagues.

Claude Goudimel was a native of Besançon. His birth is usually dated in the first decade of the 16th century but should probably be placed later, since the first known publication in which his music was represented is a book of chansons issued in 1549 by Du Chemin at Paris, where Goudimel was then probably living. His name reappears in many subsequent collections, in a few as publishing collaborator with Du Chemin.[28a] His conversion from Catholicism to Protestantism presumably occurred c. 1560. By 1565 he had taken up residence in Metz, but soon left with many other Huguenots, owing to the hostility of the new *commandant,* and went first to his native Besançon and then to Lyons. It was probably during the last year of his life, 1572, that he edited a selection of Arcadelt's chansons. In continuation of the St. Bartholomew's Day massacre at Paris on August 24 of that year, fanatics assailed the Huguenots at Lyons, and, between the 28th and 31st, Goudimel was among those killed.[29]

Although Goudimel's fame rests primarily upon his religious works, he was also an estimable chanson composer. When he set Ronsard's *Qui renforcera ma voix,*[30] he repeated both the text and the music of the last line, in time-honored fashion. In supplying music for Ronsard's "Pindaric" ode, *Errant par les champs,*[31] he put the strophe and antistrophe to the same music and wrote a separate setting for the epode. Similarly, for Ronsard's sonnet, *Quand j'apperçoy,*[32] he provided one section, to be repeated for each of the two quatrains, and a through-composed portion for the sestet. A certain number of syncopations liven the rhythm of these pieces, which are essentially chordal, though not infrequently decorated by melismas; imitation appears, but this often affects figures made up of chord-tones.[33]

[28a] Cf. LesG, but in the light of LesE, 275.

[29] Further biographical data, etc., in BrenG.

[30] Pr. TierR, 113; facsimile of orig. ed. in P. de Ronsard, *Oeuvres Complètes* (P. Laumonier, ed., 1932), 218.

[31] Pr. TierR, 105 (= ExF, 14); facsimile in Ronsard, *op. cit.,* 202.

[32] Pr. TierR, 110 (= ExF, 10; ELAM IX, 25); facsimile in Ronsard, *op. cit.,* 212.

[33] MaldP XI, 3, 4, 5, gives 3 of the original 4 voices of 3 pieces by Goudimel; cf. BrenG, 46ff; ReT, 99. For other chansons, *see* CauQ, 46; LesAC, 73, 85. For a list of Goudimel's works, *see* BrenG, 36ff.

Guillaume Costeley (c. 1531–1606), organist to Charles IX, was born in Normandy, it is thought. The claim that he was of Celtic origin is untenable, being based solely on the fact that an Irish family named Costello had migrated to France; there is no evidence that they changed their name to Costeley.[34] Costeley does not seem to have been greatly influenced by madrigal techniques. His *Las je n'yray plus* [35] is in a gay *parlando* style. A chordal chanson such as *J'ayme trop souffrir la mort,*[36] which repeats both opening and closing sections, recalls Claudin. His battle pieces, *Guerre de Calais* and *Prise du Havre,*[37] diverge from Janequin's methods in similar works, for Costeley is less interested in detailed programmatic effects than in creating broader musical contrasts between the several *partes* into which both these chansons are divided. His *Allon gay, gay, gay, bergères* [38] is one of the lively and thoroughly secular *noëls* in which this period was rich. Costeley's work is characterized by spontaneity and polish, of which a particularly beautiful example is his well-known setting of Ronsard's *Mignonne, allon voir.*[39]

EXAMPLE 89. Opening measures of *Mignonne, allon voir*—Costeley
(Complete piece in MMRF III, 75; ExF, 44; BordC, No. 4; ELAM VI, 28).

"Come, sweet, let us see if the rose, which this morning did unclose its purple mantle to the sun . . ."

[34] Cf. CauD. The *s* in the composer's name is silent.   [35] Pr. MMRF XVIII, 1; MMRFR I, 3.
[36] Pr. MMRF XVIII, 31.   [37] Pr. MMRF XIX, 12, 50, respectively.
[38] Pr. MMRF III, 65; BordC, No. VII.
[39] For Costeley chansons not yet cited, *see* MMRF III (26 items); XVIII (19 items); XIX (10 items); MMRFR I (6 items); ExF (5 items); ELAM VI, 20, 38; BordC, Nos. V, VI; CauQ, 48; ExR, 1276; LesAC, 76, 78. *See* further MGG II, 1704ff.

It was probably Costeley who in 1570 organized the Confraternity of St. Cecilia at Evreux, of which he was the first elected *"prince."* The Confraternity's Cecilian festival included services on the eve of the Saint's day, and High Mass and evening services on the day itself. The day following, a Requiem was sung.[40] Musical contests were added in 1575, and Costeley was among those who provided for continuing them in subsequent years. Prizes for compositions were musical instruments made of silver, an organ representing highest honors. The first year this prize was awarded to Lassus for his motet, *Domine Jesu Christe qui cognoscis.* Among other prize-winners were George de la Hèle (1576; cf. pp. 510f), Du Caurroy (1576, 1583), and Mauduit (1581).[41]

Anthoine de Bertrand, born c. 1545 at Fontanges, in Auvergne, delighted in experiment. His two volumes of four-part chansons setting Ronsard's *Amours* (1578) [42] contain some pieces in chromatic modes and enharmonic modes (involving quarter-tones) and one, *Je suis tellement amoureux,*[43] in which the last seventeen measures are "only chromatic and enharmonic, with no mixture of diatonicism except in an interval in the *bassecontre* and another in the *hautecontre,* made to express the word 'death'." [44] This is not a very successful work; Bertrand seems to have realized the difficulties of singing quarter-tones, for in a later edition (1587) he abandoned them. Indeed, he emphasizes in a preface that music should appeal to the senses and not be bound by mathematical subtleties.[45] Many of his works display imagination as well as skill, for example, his *Las je me plains.*[46] A third collection, drawing on various poets, appeared in 1587.[47]

The *Chansons de Pierre de Ronsard . . .* (1569)[48] by Nicolas de la Grotte, organist to Henry III, includes short chordal pieces in a gracefully simple style. The melody-bearing superius is here triumphant, and the other voices merely accompany; the same music serves for successive stanzas. This is the type of popular chanson that developed from the earlier *vaux-de-vire* (*voix-de-ville*).[48a] The term appears in the preface of Du Bellay's *Vers lyriques* (1549) and on the title-page of Le Roy's *Premier livre de chansons en forme de vau-de-ville* (1573); it was eventually to be replaced by the term *"air"* or *"air de cour."* [48b] Of de la Grotte's chansons written in this simple and chordal style, the charming *Quand ce beau printemps je voy* [49] is typical. *Je suis Amour* [50] is noteworthy for its flexible combination of duple and triple rhythms. Jehan Chardavoine, in his collection of

---

[40] For details, *see* SchlettM, 187.
[41] For a list of prize winners, *see ibid.,* 201f. *See also* BonninP. [42] Pr. MMFTR IV–VI.
[43] Pr. MMFTR VI, 27. [44] From Bertrand's *Advertissement,* reprinted in MMFTR VI.
[45] Cf. his *Au lecteur debonaire,* pr. MMFTR IV. [46] Pr. *ibid.,* 34.
[47] Pr. MMFTR VII. Further about Bertrand, *see* ThibaultAB; MGG I, 1813ff.
[48] For facsimile of superius of printing of 1575, *see* RochaC.
[48a] Cf. pp. 205f. [48b] Cf. MGG II, 1067f. [49] Pr. ExF, 60.
[50] Pr. *ibid.,* 62. Other chansons by de la Grotte, *ibid.,* 52–59; LesAC, 69. Further about him, *see* DrozC; RMR, 36f; LesAC, *Notices,* No. 25.

monophonic *"chansons en forme de voix de ville,"* drew heavily on the tunes used in the superius of de la Grotte's settings.[50a] Similar to those settings are the ones contained in Didier le Blanc's *Airs de plusieurs musiciens . . .* (1579; reprinted, 1582).[50b]

François Regnart (= Regnard), brother of the more famous Jacques (cf. p. 710), studied at the University of Douai and the Cathedral of Tournai. In 1575 his four- and five-part *Poésies de P. de Ronsard & autres Poëtes* appeared at Douai. His setting of Ronsard's *Petite nymphe folâtre*,[51] less airy than Janequin's earlier one, differs also by including the poet's *Responce.* The *Chansons, Odes, et Sonetz de Pierre Ronsard,* set *a 4, 5,* and *8* by the prolific Jean de Castro, appeared in 1576.[51a] Many additional Ronsard settings are included among his other works. The elegant poet continued to be a source of inspiration to a host of composers.

Paschal de l'Estocart, born at Noyon, in Picardy, c. 1540, resembles Le Jeune in having set Chandieu's *Octonaires*.[52] While, in the main, his writing is conventional, his rather frequent use of augmented-sixth chords is worth noting. Examples occur—as by-products of the polyphony, to be sure —in as early a composer as Machaut, and there are instances also in Costeley, Bertrand, and others. L'Estocart, however, employs them often enough to warrant the assumption that they are no mere by-products in his work, but are produced deliberately, with full awareness of "vertical" considerations.[53]

Lassus

Among the finest examples of the Renaissance chanson are those by the Walloon, Roland de Lassus—or, to use the better known Italian form of his name, Orlando di Lasso—although, of his total production of some 1,250 compositions, the 148 extant chansons [54] seem to constitute a fairly insignificant portion. They comprise sixty-nine four-part pieces, fifty-eight five-part, five eight-part, four six-part, and one three-part.

Lassus was born at Mons, probably in 1532,[55] and served his musical apprenticeship as choirboy in the church of St. Nicholas there. Such was the beauty of his voice that he was thrice kidnapped,[56] the last abduction resulting in his entering, at the age of twelve, the service of Ferdinand Gonzaga, Viceroy of Sicily. He thus became subjected, at an early age, to the Italian influences that were destined to have a marked effect on much of his music. In 1554 or 1555, Lassus returned from Italy to Antwerp and remained until 1556.

[50a] Cf. MGG II, 1101f; 6 melodies from Chardavoine's book are pr. ExF, 74ff.
[50b] Pr. MMFTR III.   [51] Pr. MMRF XV, 49; ExF, 65; ELAM X, 28.
[51a] Cf. ThibaultB, 54. *See* also MGG II, 904ff.
[52] Book I pr. MMFTR X.   [53] Cf. MlrS, 23ff.
[54] Of these, 11 survive incomplete. The 137 complete chansons are pr. in LassoW, XII, XIV, XVI (which includes an index to the 3 vols.), and Ser. II, I. About the 38 pieces pr. with French text in MaldP, *see* ReT, 104ff. (To the data there given may be added that ReT Nos. 350, 394 = LassoW VIII, 27, 84, respectively.)
[55] Cf. BorLN.   [56] Occurrences of the sort were not rare in those days; cf. PirH, 306.

The twenty-three-year-old composer saw his first published works appear in 1555, at both Antwerp and Venice, the Antwerp volume containing six chansons as well as madrigals, *villanesche,* and motets. Thereafter his compositions were printed and reprinted in these two cities, in Paris and Louvain, in Rome and Milan, in Nuremberg and Munich. The great European publishing houses entered into a veritable competition in the issuance of his music.

In 1564, Lassus being then in Munich, Le Roy and Ballard brought out their first publication devoted to him exclusively.[56a] When, in 1571, he visited Paris it was to Le Roy that he owed his introduction and warm acceptance at the French court. Charles IX, in 1574, offered him a munificent salary as chamber musician, but Charles died in the same year, and Lassus remained in his post at Munich. Friendly relations with Paris continued, however, and Henry III granted him, in 1575, a special privilege for the publication of his works, which was renewed in 1581 and 1582.[57]

The French verses chosen by Lassus reflect his wide catholicity of taste. While his favorite poet seems to have been Marot, his texts range from works by earlier poets such as Alain Chartier to the popular members of the Pléiade. Many poems that had already been treated by composers of the Attaingnant generation prompted him to test his own mettle.[58] He set the diverse texts with a strong regard for the mood and meaning of each.

The first chanson in the Antwerp collection of 1555, *Las voulez vous,*[59] already displays many features typical of Lassus' best work in this genre, in so far as anything can be called "typical" where the most distinguishing feature is great scope of expression achieved by means of an extraordinary variety of musical ideas. About half the chansons begin with imitation, but the motifs producing it are treated in many different ways, musical method sometimes being directly inspired by the literary content. For example, the opening measures of *J'ay cherché la science* [59a] playfully, but learnedly, reflect a "search for knowledge" by the way they employ exact inversions of the fugal theme. Similarly, in *Fuyons tous d'amour le jeu,*[60] two seven-note themes, treated in imitation, illustrate the flight from love. Strict treatment of such a relatively lengthy motif is rare in these works, fugal expositions more often being reserved for short motifs, as in *Le rossignol,*[61] in which only four notes are involved. The only chanson in the form of a canon is *Célébrons sans cesse.*[62]

[56a] The collection, however, consisted almost entirely of pieces known to have been previously printed elsewhere. Cf. BorR.

[57] For further biographical data, *see* esp. BorOL, 1ff; BorRL, 29ff; SandB I, 58ff; III, 308ff; and BoettL, the new (1958) and most comprehensive study of Lassus. Particularly regarding Lassus' sensitivity to the intellectual and spiritual currents of his time, *see* SandO.

[58] For a discussion of Lassus' French texts, *see* SandR, 386ff (SandR is the same as SandA I, 87ff, and is incorporated in LassoW XII, vff; XVI, vi).

[59] Pr. LassoW XII, 3; MMRF I, 1.   [59a] Pr. LassoW XII, 57.

[60] Pr. *ibid.* XII, 80; MaldP X, 13.

[61] Pr. LassoW XIV, 107.

[62] Pr. *ibid.* XVI, 162.

Of these chansons that do not commence in imitative style, about half open chordally, the others in non-imitative counterpoint. A light-hearted example of the former type may be found in *Margot labourez les vignes,*[63] which uses the same words, but not the same tune, as the Arcadelt setting (cf. p. 381). An example of the latter type is provided by *Las, voulez vous;* another, a particularly beautiful one, by *La nuict froide et sombre.*

EXAMPLE 90. Opening of *La nuict froide et sombre*—Lassus (complete piece in LassoW XII, 34; MMRF I, 61; CW XIII, 9).

"The night cold and sombre, covering the earth and heavens with dark shadow . . ."

This piece works up to a noble climax at the close, where Du Bellay's text describes how dawn carpets the great universe with variegated colors. The composition shows the mood and style of the Italian madrigal, as—among many others—does the sensitively harmonized and deeply moving *Toutes les nuitz.*[64] Its text is from a *rondeau,*[64a] but the setting, ending after the incipit of the medial refrain, ignores the *rondeau* form.

Sometimes Lassus employs a special integrative technique, a common one being the limitation of the bass part in one section of a work to a single motif repeated at various transpositions. This technique is of particular structural importance in many through-composed pieces, in which it is applied near the end to give clarity and pattern to a work whose careful reflection of literary meaning threatens to destroy the musical structure, e.g., *Le temps peut bien, A ce matin, Le vray amy* (both in measures 16–22 and near the end).[65] Frequently, the insistence on a single motif has a textual connotation, as in *A ce matin.* Here, after colorful declamatory passages in which we are told about some of the pleasures of good living that the poet wishes were his, we are rather abruptly brought to the point, which is that before they

[63] Pr. *ibid.,* XII, 102; MaldP X, 41.   [64] Pr. LassoW XIV, 130.
[64a] In JP I, fol. CXXX[v], as pointed out to me by Dr. Plamenac.
[65] Pr. *ibid.,* XII, 76 (= MaldP X, 25), 28 (= MMRF I, 50; MaldP IX, 25), and 62 (= MaldP X, 16 [with substitute text]), respectively.

can be had *"Le principal c'est d'avoir de l'argent."* To the free character of the preceding music a forthright down-to-earth little motif is counterposed, in which the bass stubbornly persists.

Textual structure and general meaning often suggest the basic musical scheme, melodic elements being derived more or less directly from specific literary ideas. This is true of the solmisation exercises of the amateur singer in *En m'oyant chanter;* [66] of the little melismas on the word *"chanter"* in *Las, voulez vous* and *Chanter je veux;* [67] and of the treatment of *"soupirer"* in both *En espoir vis* and *Le tems passé* [68] in exactly the same way, the singers being constrained in each instance to take a quick catch-breath on the brief rest that precedes the word.

Lassus often displays his delight in the mere sound of words, as in *Un jour vis un foulon qui fouloit,*[69] in which the syllable *foul* recurs repeatedly in different combinations. This chanson was several times reprinted with new texts and found its way into Shakespeare's *Henry IV, Part II,* Act V, Scene 3, becoming the "Samingo" song of the drunken Silence.[70] Lassus in his chansons, as also in his letters,[71] was a master of humor and burlesque. In *Il estoit une religieuse,*[72] the solemn, motet-like, perhaps sacrilegious setting of the words *"Pater"* and *"Ave Maria"* contrasts mockingly with the light-hearted tone of the rest of the piece. An amusing effect is produced in *Sçais tu dire l'Ave?* [73] by confining the bass part to a monotonous reiteration of three notes to the words *"Disoit-il."* Half-comic, half-tragic, is *Quand mon mari,*[74] a little piece in which a young wife complains that her jealous old husband beats her and throws the cooking spoon at her head. Musically, this chanson is one of those that show Lassus applying the technique of the Paris school, with respect to both chordal texture and form: the music for lines 1 and 2 is repeated for lines 3 and 4; the last two lines are repeated to the same music.

The six-part *Dessus le marché d'Arras* [75]—the last two lines of which are repeated to the same music, but with exchange between two pairs of voices —is based on a popular tune. The very famous *Susanne un jour* is likewise written on a pre-existent melody. In 1548, the *Premier livre de chansons spirituelles composées par Guillaume Guéroult et mises en musique à quatre parties par Didier Lupi second et autres* appeared at Lyons. Guéroult wrote the poems; there is no clue showing which settings are by Lupi and which by the *"autres."* [76] One of the poems is that of *Susanne un jour,* dealing with Susanna and the Elders, which gained wide circulation. Although of Calvinist

---

[66] Pr. *ibid.,* 106; ExFR II, 18; MaldP I, 1 (with substitute text).
[67] Pr. LassoW XIV, 50.
[68] Pr. LassoW XII, 52 (= MMRF I, 100), 49 (= MMRF I, 93; MaldP IX, 44), respectively: further about tone-painting in Lassus' chansons, *see ibid.,* xxxix.
[69] Pr. *ibid.,* 39; MMRF I, 72; ELAM II, 15; MaldP X, 30 (with substitute text).
[70] Cf. StainS.   [71] *See* SandB III, 247ff (52 letters).   [72] Pr. LassoW XII, 74.
[73] Pr. *ibid.,* 66; ExFR II, 4.
[74] Pr. LassoW XII, 23; MMRF I, 40; SquireM II, 39; MaldP IX, 33.
[75] Pr. LassoW XVI, 152.   [76] For a description of this print, with 2 pieces from it, *see* BeG.

inspiration, this poem enjoyed wide popularity among Catholic and Protestant composers alike.[77] The Lassus setting was clearly much the most famous.[78] He himself re-employed the musical material later (cf. pp. 696f, 709). It is not unlikely that many of the composers who treated this melody became acquainted with it through the Lassus' setting rather than through the Guéroult volume. When Bassano prepared his *Motetti, Madrigali et Canzoni francese . . . diminuti* (Venice, 1591), he included Lassus' chanson as one of his examples. The passive participle *"diminuti"* refers to the decorating of a melodic line by means of ornaments. The following shows the opening of the chanson superius as given by Bassano, together with the same measures in the original form:

EXAMPLE 91. Opening of Lassus' *Susanne un jour;* original and superius with Bassano's diminution (from HaasA, 117).

"Susanna one day, her love solicited, . . ."

It is not clear how widespread the practice of such diminution (*diminutio*) was, but it is plain that Renaissance compositions, as they come down to us in writing, are only the skeletons of the full bodies that were presented in at least some performances.[78a]

Some Lassus chansons are long enough to be divided into *partes*. In the four *partes* of *Pour courrir en poste,*[79] the music parallels the repetitions in Marot's comical text. Line 4 of each stanza, *"Frère Lubin le fera bien,"* is identically set throughout, except for exchange of music between quintus and tenor in *pars III* and initial elaboration in the last *pars*; line 8, *"Frère Lubin ne peut le faire,"* has the same music in *pars I* and *pars II*, again except for exchange between tenor and quintus. Allowing for the same exchange, and

[77] Among the reprints is that in the *Sommaire de tous les recueils de chansons,* 1579, and this source is indicated by the word, *"Sommaire,"* in the heading of Lassus' chanson in LassoW XIV, 29. This has been misunderstood by Osthoff, who in OsN, 151, gives "Sommaire" as the name of the poet.

[78] It even survives in a Spanish source with the text translated into Spanish; cf. BalT, 63. Settings (with the text in different middle Dutch paraphrases) by Episcopius and Turnhout (cf. p. 308), are pr. in VNM XXVI, 62 and 104, respectively. The openings of these settings are based on the same melodic material as is used by Lassus. See further BorQ, 77ff, and esp. LevyS, which presents the basic composition and a comprehensive study of the various vocal compositions based on it.

[78a] Further on vocal ornamentation, *see* esp. HorsE; BukR; KuV, esp. p. 5–49; GoldI, *passim;* LachOM.

[79] Pr. LassoW XVI, 61.

for additional chords to alter the tonality, *pars III* and *pars IV* end identically, with a phrase containing some figures also found at the end of the first two *partes*. In *Bonjour, et puis,*[80] the much repeated word, *"Bonjour,"* is set to the same music for about four measures at the end of each *pars*, except that in *pars I* two chords extend the cadence so as to avoid closing in F, the prevailing tonality. *Pars II* restores this tonality, in which, as expected, it closes. In the double choruses, *Un jour l'amant* and *Di moy, mon coeur,*[81] climax is achieved by increasing the overlapping of the two alternating choruses *a 4* until finally they sing extended phrases together. In each of these pieces, two such climaxes are formed; the first is approximately in the middle; the choruses then pull apart once more and the process is repeated, building up to a final climax even more impressive than the first one.

So popular were Lassus' chansons that some were reprinted by Huguenot publishers with moralistic texts replacing the amorous originals. Thus the five-part *Mon coeur se recommande à vous*[82] became *Mon coeur se rend à toy, Seigneur.*

Monte; Waelrant; Pevernage; Some Lesser Figures

Philippe de Monte, (b. Malines, 1521), destined to become a friend of Lassus, passed his early maturity in Naples. Subsequently he returned to the Netherlands and then journeyed to England. He was a member there of the choir of Philip II of Spain, during the first year or so (1554–1555) of the king's marriage to Queen Mary. It was reported, however, that he did not wish to remain in this choir because all of the other members were Spaniards. During his stay in England, he must have made the acquaintance of William Byrd (cf. p. 702). A letter written from Brussels about this time to Albert V of Bavaria by his Chancellor, Dr. Seld, gives a good idea of Monte's personality and qualifications; he is described as "a quiet, unassuming man, gentle as a girl," knowing Italian, Latin, French, and Flemish, and being "without any doubt the best composer in the whole country. . . ."[83] Monte did not, however, enter Albert's service, but shortly returned to Italy. He spent many years, nevertheless, in the employ of the imperial court, and died at Prague in 1603.[84]

Though Monte was a most prolific composer, the number of his chansons

---

[80] Pr. *ibid.*, 53. [81] Pr. LassoW XIV, 136, 150, respectively.
[82] Pr. LassoW XIV, 15. This chanson is not to be confused with the piece *a 4* of the same name (pr. ELAM II, 3; etc.), popularly attributed to Lassus, though without precise reference to a source. On grounds of style this attribution would seem to be incorrect, notwithstanding Lassus' stylistic diversity. For discussion and lists of substitute texts in Lassus chansons, *see* LassoW XII, xxiiiff; XVI, viiif, xixff.
[83] Seld, however, does not say that Monte sang bass, as stated in DoorPM, 6; cf. CreAC, 295. For the letter, *see ibid.*, SandB I, 55.
[84] Further biographical data in DoorPM; NuffM.

is small. The texture of such chansons as *Sortez regretz, Si par souffrir,* and *Secourez moy, Madame,*[85] is polyphonic, motet-like, and harmonically rich. Even the bass has an individual melodic character, without, however, forgoing its supporting function. These pieces open with imitation, but Monte, who seems to have made a deliberate attempt to avoid clichés generally, excludes one voice from the imitating group and gives it a markedly contrasting melody. A kind of free *Stimmtausch* sometimes (as on the words *"mort et mercy . . ."* in *Sortez regretz*) substitutes for an expected point of imitation. Monte's *Susanne un jour,*[86] in line with the prevailing character of his writing, avoids using the familiar melody literally, but does contain reminders of it at important points. In *O triste ennuy* and *La déesse Venus,*[87] the four stanzas of each text are set as separate but tonally related *partes.* These *partes* in the former end respectively with triads on A, E, C, and A; in the latter, with triads on G, D, G, G.[88]

Both Lassus and Monte, like many contemporary natives of the Low Countries, made their real careers abroad. In 1568, the repressive measures of Philip II precipitated the Eighty Years' War—partly religious, partly political—for freedom from Spain. While musical life in the Low Countries was by no means extinguished, Netherlandish musicians, having long been visitors in foreign countries, now tended, in greater number, to go abroad and not return. We shall meet several such musicians later in this book.

The musical activity of Hubert Waelrant (born c. 1517; died 1595 at Antwerp) besides publishing (cf. p. 290) and composing, included singing, teaching and work in theory. At Antwerp he founded a music school. Waelrant was one of the early musicians in the north to adopt a system of solmisation based on the octave rather than on the hexachord. The term "bocedisation" gained some currency with reference to this system. Solmisation based on the octave had already been proposed by the Spaniard Ramos (cf. p. 586). It is not clear whether the system was evolved independently in the north or to whom the term "bocedisation" is due.[89] Waelrant's chanson, *Musiciens qui chantez* [90]—in which the bass at one point ascends a major sixth and then descends a major seventh—contains some amusing, if obvious, bits of word-painting, as after the word *"taire,"* where all the voices rest.

[85] Pr. MonteO XX, 9, 13, 42, respectively. The music of the second was also used to set a Calvinist text, *L'Homme inconstant.*
[86] Pr. MonteO XX, 35.   [87] Pr. *ibid.,* 49, 66, respectively.
[88] 3 chansons not yet cited are pr. in MonteO XX. *Au feu d'amour,* p. 5, is a setting of the text also used by Pierre de la Rue (cf. p. 272). Other Monte chansons in MonteO IX, App.; XXV, 46, 59; lute transcriptions of the last 2 pieces in modern notation *ibid.,* 4, 12; the second is a setting of Ronsard's sonnet, *Que me servent mes vers,* with the same music for the two quatrains. About the 3 pieces with French texts, attributed to Monte in MaldP, *see* fn. 145.
[89] Further biographical data in the Belgian *Biographie nationale,* XXVII (1938), col. 14; BeW; BogaWA. About bocedisation, *see* esp. RieG, 428f; LangeZ, 573ff.
[90] SquireM II, 94. Another Waelrant piece pr. with French and Flemish texts in MaldP I, 8, is really a madrigal (cf. fn. 241).

Andries Pevernage (also Bevernage, Beveringen, etc.) was born in Harel-beke near Courtrai in 1543. In February, 1563, he became choir director at the Cathedral of St. Sauveur in Bruges, but a successor was in his place as early as the next September. From Bruges, Pevernage went to Courtrai, as-suming the post of choir director at Notre Dame there the following month. In 1564, he became chaplain and, in 1569, permanent vicar. At Courtrai, he joined the guild of St. Cecilia, and for it wrote some of his compositions. In the course of the war, the Protestants captured Courtrai (1578) and persecu-tion of the Catholics followed. The number of choirboys diminished to two. Pevernage left Courtrai for Antwerp the same year and is not again trace-able until 1584, though he probably lived in the latter city. He was allowed to resume his post at Courtrai in 1584 and stayed there briefly. The next year, Alexander Farnese recaptured Antwerp, and Catholicism was restored. Pevernage was appointed choir director at the cathedral, and reorganized the musical activities. He died in 1591.[91] Pevernage enjoyed considerable fame in his own time, and such musicians as Kerle and Monte sought his good offices in establishing contacts with publishers.

We possess about 115 sacred and 120 secular compositions by Pevernage, some of the latter including works with Latin texts. The approximately 80 chansons were published mainly in four collections,[92] 1589 to 1591. They are the work of a talented composer, a master of the technique of his time, who, if he does not belong in the highest rank, is nevertheless far above the fair-to-middling class. They are written mostly in one *pars* and *a 5*. Once a point of imitation has been started, Pevernage likes to keep all his voices busy. Imitation, while not rare, makes way frequently for chordal writing and free polyphony—the latter, however, often giving the impression of be-ing chordal writing with quasi-polyphonic decoration. Short, rapid melismas seem especially characteristic. *Parlando*-like passages occur. Pevernage is adept at shifting the rhythmic accent and at producing rhythmic flexibility generally, even where the texture is not especially complex. Among many chansons illustrating this point, *Fais que je vive* and *Recherche qui voudra* [93] may be singled out. The influence of *coro spezzato* writing is evident in a few pieces *a 7* and *a 8*. A setting of *Susanne un jour* [94] contains, as might be expected, reminders of the famous melody.

Corneille Verdonck (1563–1625), like Waelrant, his teacher in Antwerp, spent the greater part of his life in his native country. From 1579 until his

[91] Further biographical data in StellP, 7ff.

[92] MaldP reprints many pieces from Books I and III and all of Book II, but with frequent changes of text, etc.; cf. ReT, 111ff, or StellP, 65ff ("1869, 5" on p. 65, line 7, should be "1869, 4"; "1869, 9" on p. 65, line 15 from bottom, should be "1865, 9"; "1870, 3" on p. 66, line 7 from bottom, should probably be "1871, 3"; "1866, 6" on p. 67, last line, should be "1866, 4" and refers to MaldR—not to MaldP as do the other items); the StellP references are to the num-bers (not to the pages) in MaldP and MaldR. The chanson pr. as Pevernage's in MaldP II, 8, is not identified in StellP.

[93] Pr. MaldP VI, 21; VII, 32, respectively.   [94] **Pr. as** *Rachel pleurait* in MaldP V, 45.

death he was continuously in the service of wealthy burghers of the Low Countries. Verdonck, in the preface to his collection of chansons (1599), deplores the decline of music in his country, of which this art had once been the glory: "whether these sweet harmonies have been interrupted by the tempests of Mars, who has too long been master of these provinces, or whether it [music] has ceased to be esteemed by those who, filled with confusion . . . , cannot value what is full of agreement and harmony." [95]

Verdonck's *Le feu couvert,*[96] from the *Rossignol musical* (1597), is characterized by lively syncopation. A Latin occasional piece *a 6* of his [97] was written in 1599 for the entry into Antwerp of the Archduke Albert and Archduchess Isabella. According to Bochius, secretary to the town and author of the text of the composition, it was sung by six choirboys carried on the back of a huge elephant.

Among several other composers represented in the *Rossignol musical* were Noel Faignient [97a] and Severin Cornet (c. 1540–1582). The year 1581 saw the publication of Cornet's *Chansons françoises* at Antwerp, where, for some twelve years, until his death, he was *maître des enfants de choeur* at the Cathedral of Our Lady. He also composed motets, madrigals, etc.[98]

Sweelinck

Jan Pieterszoon Sweelinck (1562–1621) was born in Deventer and spent most of his life in Amsterdam, approximately his last forty years as organist at the Oude Kerk (Old Church). Mattheson, in his *Grundlage einer Ehren-Pforte* (1740), states that Sweelinck studied with Zarlino in Venice, but this seems to be an error.[99]

In some of his works (outside the scope of this study [100]) Sweelinck appears as a composer of the baroque period. His chansons, however, are mostly in the French Renaissance tradition, except perhaps with respect to tonality, which is often clearly defined according to modern feeling. These points are well illustrated in *Tu as tout seul* (published in the *Rossignol musical;* perhaps reprinted from one of two lost Sweelinck chanson collections),[101] a lively setting *a 5* of Marot's humorous text. Here the number of active voices varies constantly, and thematic fragments are exchanged among them; the key is plainly C major. His pieces in a 1584 volume of chansons *a 5* for instruments or voices,[102] which contains also some works by Verdonck, are

[95] BergCV, 125. Further biographical data in that article.   [96] Pr. MaldP XXVIII, 15.
[97] Pr. MaldP XII, 27. The ostensible chanson pr. in MaldP II, 38, is really an Italian madrigal; cf. fn. 240.
[97a] For 2 of his contributions, *see* MaldP XXVIII, 17, 19.
[98] For an article on him, *see* DoorSC.
[99] Cf. esp. MrS, 42ff. Fuller biographical data, *ibid.,* 16ff. For Sweelinck's will, *see* ScheurJS.
[100] But cf., e.g., BukMB, 74 ff.
[101] Pr. SweeW IX, 51; ELAM XI, 2. About the lost collections, *see* MrV, 12; SweeW IX, i.
[102] Which survives complete only in a 1594 reprint. Sweelinck's portion of this vol. pr. SweeW VII.

spirited and at the same time technically complex: in *Susanne un jour*,[103] the melody—a free version of that used also by Lassus—is disposed in six phrases (four with two repetitions); in each phrase there is fresh counterpoint derived from fragments of the tune in diminution. Eye-music appears in a passage in *Quand je vois ma maitresse*,[104] where the words *"ce m'est obscure nuit"* are set in "blackened" notes; this device had already been much used by the Italian madrigalists. In *Bref à vous*,[105] the first voice to enter sings the initial word on a breve. Descriptive melismas appear, such as those made up of the writhing dotted figures in all voices in *pars II* of *Vostre amour est vagabonde*[106] on the word *"lacx"* ("snares"). Structural relation of *partes* in this piece is achieved by the treatment of the words *"Non, non, je ne le feray pas,"* which serve as the final line of both stanzas: this line is set four times at the end of each stanza, the first three settings being common to both. The final phrases are altered so as to close in different tonalities: the first on a triad on G and the second on C. A Latin epithalamium *a 5* (1607)[107] relates its two *partes* by presenting a theme imitatively in several voices at the beginning of *pars I* and inverting this theme in the same four voices (but with the order of entry changed) at the opening of *pars II*.[108]

In the *Rimes françoises et italiennes* (1612),[109] the scoring is notably reduced. Of the French secular pieces six are *a 2*, five *a 3* and one *a 4*. The use of imitation is their most conspicuous technical characteristic. *Beaux yeux*, for its first twenty-five measures, might be called a tonal canon.

EXAMPLE 92. Extract from *Beaux yeux*—Sweelinck (after SweeW VIII, 9).

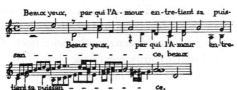

"Beautiful eyes through which love maintains its power."

All the French pieces in this book are in one or two *partes* except *Rozette*,[110] which is in four. Here the last phrase of *pars I* is identical with that of *pars III*, concluding on a G triad, and that of *pars II* with that of *pars IV*, concluding on a C triad. The Italian pieces will be discussed in due course.

[103] *Ibid.*, 35.   [104] *Ibid.*, 4.
[105] Pr. SweeW VII, 12 (*pars II* of *Elle est à vous*, p. 8).
[106] Pr. *ibid.*, 18; the melismas in question on pp. 23, 24.   [107] Pr. *ibid.* IX, 18.
[108] Other secular Latin pieces by Sweelinck *ibid.*, 27, 37 (*a 8*), 85.
[109] Pr. SweeW VIII.
[110] Pr. *ibid.*, 81. SweeW VII, VIII, and IX contains, respectively, 14, 11, and 2 of his chansons not yet cited. Further concerning the chansons, *see* esp. BorQ.

Actually, the chief difference is one of language, for the influence of the Italian madrigal was so strong during the late Renaissance that the French chanson nearly merged with it in matters of technical musical construction.

General Remarks on the Later Italian Madrigal

"The notes are the body of music, but the words are the soul." Thus the madrigalist Mazzone in the introduction to his Book I *a 4* in 1569 tersely stated the ruling principle of madrigal composition during the second half of the 16th century, when the search after expression led composers to the highest refinement and ultimate exhaustion of the madrigal form. The desire for ever more vivid expression brought about increased use of chromaticism; a trend away from constructivism toward free designs dependent upon the changing content of the text; and the suggestion of dramatic recitative. The last of these, with its approach to monody through the predominance of the top voice and, incidentally, to the major-minor system, thus went hand in hand with much the same kind of chordal writing and lightly imitative counterpoint that are found in other music of the period.

As the century progressed, although composers sometimes continued to try to capture the spirit of the text, as Rore had done, oftener they depicted the minutest word-images. Routine phrases of verse came to be matched by routine musical clichés, and the form finally wore itself out—though not before a vast and splendid literature had been created.

Petrarch continued to be set, as well as other poets who had inspired musicians earlier in the century, and Boccaccio increased in popularity. Although few works by Dante were used, one pasage from the *Inferno,* describing the shrieks of the damned (*Quivi sospiri*) was set to music by no less than seven composers,[111] presumably because it lent itself well to tone-painting. Sannazaro (cf. p. 139) became Marenzio's favorite poet, and Tasso's *Jerusalem Delivered* attracted many composers of the close of the century.[112] But besides such literary texts there was, late in the century, a great amount of *poesia per musica* also.

A social development contributed no small share in creating poetry for music, in setting musical and poetic standards, and in musical composition. Little groups—or academies, as they were called—of poets, musicians, artists, and amateurs met regularly to discuss intellectual and artistic subjects, to hear each other's works, and to witness musical performances.[113] The earliest academy to survive more than a brief existence and to be interested primarily in music seems to be the *Accademia Filarmonica* of Verona,[114] founded in 1543, which employed the composers Nasco and Ruffo, and for which

[111] For more details, *see* EinDM, 142f.   [112] For more details *see* EinI and KlefA, Chap. 2.
[113] *See* EinIM I, 192f.
[114] For its history, and a discussion of its old holdings, *see* TurrA.

many famous composers furnished music. The example of the Verona academy was followed throughout Italy, in large towns and in small.

The sheer quantity of madrigals written from c. 1550 to c. 1600 is bewildering. Of some 350 items listed in a surviving catalogue printed by Gardano in 1591, about 170 are madrigal collections; a catalogue produced by Vincenti the same year names approximately 225 items, and the number of such collections among them is about 100.[114a] The most distinguished musicians who produced madrigals include Palestrina, Lassus, Monte, Wert, Marenzio, Gesualdo, Striggio, Banchieri, Vecchi, Andrea and Giovanni Gabrieli, and Monteverdi. Lesser masters were legion. The gap in craftsmanship, moreover, between great and lesser composers is comparatively small; all shared a common approach, idiom, technique. Nevertheless, the madrigal changed complexion rapidly from decade to decade; novelty and modernity were prized. As early as 1544, the madrigals of Arcadelt, published only five or six years before, were already considered out of date by Antonfrancesco Doni (cf. p. 316), who in his *Dialogo della musica* remarks, "What do you want with such music? It is too old" and says also, "If Josquin were to come to life again, he would cross himself in wonder." (Nevertheless, Monteverdi was to feel it worth while in 1627 to bring out an edition of Arcadelt's madrigals *a 4*, as a means of teaching composition to beginners.)

Palestrina

Amid these trends, Palestrina's madrigals, although attractive and well written, are relatively unimportant. (His life was so inextricably bound up with ecclesiastical activity that biographical data will be reserved for the next chapter.) His Book I *a 4* (1555), his second published work, includes *Quai rime fur sì chiare*,[115] the text and music of which are Palestrina's tribute to Francesco Rosselli (François Roussel, one of Palestrina's predecessors at the Julian Chapel, with the title of *magister puerorum*, c. 1548, and at other times *maestro di cappella* at St. John Lateran and at S. Luigi dei Francesi): "What verse so bright . . . to be worthy of your melody, Rosselli?" This Book seems to stem directly from Arcadelt's madrigals *a 4* and appears old-fashioned by contemporary standards. The mood of a poem may be paralleled by means of discreet word-painting of the kind the early madrigalists employed (cf. pp. 318f), but there is no use of dramatic contrasts such as characterized the madrigal after Rore had set the example. The tone is frequently one of restrained sadness, from which excesses of feeling are excluded. It is almost as if Palestrina were modifying the idiom of sacred music and applying it to secular writing. The "rules" of dissonance treatment and melodic progression that govern his sacred style are, as a matter of fact, seldom transgressed in

---

[114a] The catalogues are reprinted in ThibaultD.   [115] Pr. PalW XXVIII, 50.

his madrigal style. Here, as there, it is his principle to exclude leaps greater than a minor sixth, except the octave, and all augmented and diminished leaps; and there are few deviations. Chromaticism is rare and never takes the form of genuine degree-inflection.[115a] Frequent repetition of a melody note is avoided in the interest of variety.

Book II *a 4* (1586), which includes the well-known *La cruda mia nemica* and *Alla riva del Tebro*,[116] despite such use of expressive dissonance as occurs on *"cruda"* in the former piece, is still essentially conservative, like its predecessor. But the quarter-note has replaced the half-note as the unit, and there is a more frequent use of accidentals. In *Morì quasi il mio core,* clashes between the macrorhythm and microrhythm produce conflicts in accentuation that are not only interesting but of great elegance and charm.

EXAMPLE 93. Excerpt from *Morì quasi il mio core*—Palestrina (complete piece in PalW XXVIII, 104; ELAM I, 3; CDMI, *quad. 83,* 3; accent signs added).

"What may the sweet fruit do, if now a fair flower has nearly destroyed my heart?"

Chordal writing is used more extensively than in the early book and text expression is more vivid, but the music does not yet quite attain real dramatic power. The limits of Palestrina's modernity as a madrigalist are marked, more or less, by such pieces as *Soave fia il morir,*[117] at the beginning of

115a Cf. JepPS, 32ff.
116 Pr. PalW XXVIII, 112 (= CDMI, *quad. 83,* 11) and 105 (= ELAM I, 17), respectively.
117 Pr. *ibid.,* 231; PalO IX, 152; CDMI, *quad. 84,* 12.

which word-painting is constant, albeit restrained: *"soave"* is depicted by long notes and pleasant harmonies, *"morir"* by an unexpected C-sharp, *"viver sempre"* is set by a repetition of a short motif consisting of quarter-notes, *"chiuder gli occhi"* ("closing the eyes") by a lessening of motion and a descent into the low register. In a later madrigal [118] on the great naval victory won by the Italians and Spaniards over the Turks in the Gulf of Lepanto in 1571, descending octave leaps in three voices illustrate the word, *"impallidir"*.

In one respect, Palestrina as madrigalist did set the pace. His *Vestiva i colli* [119] became the prototype, during the last third of the century, of hundreds of Italian narrative or descriptive pieces in the style of the narrative chanson of the Paris school (cf. pp. 292f). (The text of this piece is a sonnet, and is set in two *partes;* cf. Willaert's practice, p. 324.) The French style is applied to *pars I*, which opens in simple imitation, with the figure ♩ ♪♪, which, whatever its origin, had become associated with the French chanson.[120] The popularity of *Vestiva i colli* is attested by numerous early reprints. It is one of the pieces provided with ornaments by Bassano (cf. p. 394),[121] another being the also popular *Io son ferito*.[122] Both numbers, regardless of any question of venturesomeness, are highly ingratiating.

Like Rore, Palestrina set Petrarch's *Vergine,* though without the last two stanzas and *commiato*. Each of the eight stanzas that are set is treated as a separate piece. The rhythmic patterns that open the madrigals in this finely wrought cycle [123] divide it into parallel halves and help to unify it: Nos. 1 and 5 begin 𝅝 ♩ ♩; Nos. 2 and 6, 𝅝 ♩ ♩; Nos. 3 and 7, ♩. ♩; Nos. 4 and 8, 𝅝. ♩ (original values). (Here the first two patterns have no connection with narration.) Both word-painting and text expression are especially striking in No. 6, *Vergine chiara,* in which the words *"questo tempestoso mare"* are treated with syncopations and other unexpected rhythmic patterns; *"fidata"* is underscored by smooth scalewise ascending melismas; a figure consisting of a series of dotted quarters alternating with eighths is used in imitation to depict the storm at *"in che terribile procella";* a syncopated passage for all voices illustrates *"senza governo"*. This eight-section *canzone* appeared in Palestrina's Book I *a 5* (1581) together with a ten-section *canzone* and another one in eight sections. He showed a special proclivity for dealing with cycles and, as early as 1558, two especially fine ones—settings of Petrarch's *canzoni, Chiare, fresche e dolci acque* and *Voi mi poneste in foco* [124]—had been included in a collection of Antonio Barré's. Palestrina's Book II *a 5* (1594) is actually a canzone in thirty sections, each forming a *madrigale spirituale*.[125]

---

[118] Pr. PalW XXVIII, 183; PalO IX, 141. [119] Pr. PalW XXVIII, 239; PalO IX, 117.
[120] Cf. EinN, 478. [121] Ornamented cantus in PalW XXXIII, 60.
[122] Madrigal in PalW XXVIII, 179; PalO II, 161. Bassano ornamentation in PalW XXIII, 62; *see also ibid.,* 63. [123] Pr. PalW XXIX, 1ff; PalO IX, 1ff.
[124] Pr. PalW XXX, 48 (= PalO II, 107), 99 (= PalO II, 127), respectively.
[125] This book is pr. PalW XXIX, 97ff. Further concerning Palestrina's secular works, *see*

Lassus

Although more numerous and somewhat more "advanced" than Palestrina's, the madrigals of Lassus similarly play no outstanding role in the historical evolution of the type. But they are often of great intrinsic beauty. After ten years of his youth (1544–1554) passed in service at Sicily, Milan, Naples, and Rome, his first two publications appeared in 1555, one at Antwerp, the other at Venice, the former partly devoted to madrigals, the latter wholly so (cf. p. 391). Lassus' madrigal style, like his sacred style, is less reserved, seemingly more spontaneous than Palestrina's. His madrigals range from long, contrapuntal pieces to light, chordal ones reminiscent of the *villanella,* a form in which Lassus composed also (cf. p. 444). In mood, choice of text, and technique he grew more conservative as time went on, more serious. Petrarch's sonnets *In vita di Madonna Laura* gave way in the later period to the gently melancholy ones *In morte di Madonna Laura.* Many of his late works, moreover, are *madrigali spirituali.* Petrarch seems to have been Lassus' favorite source of madrigal texts. He set poems also by Ariosto, Tasso, Guidiccioni, Bembo, and Fiamma, among others.[126] The poetic forms that he selected included the *sestina,* represented by seven complete settings [127] as well as partial ones.

Chromaticism, present partly in the form of discreetly used degree-inflection in *Cantai,*[128] the very first madrigal in his Book I *a* 5 (the Venice publication of 1555), virtually disappeared subsequently. Early similar application of it that is even more effective, however, occurs in the setting of the Latin ode, *Alma Nemes* (first printed in the Antwerp publication of 1555).[129] This piece may be regarded as the equivalent in Lassus of *Calami sonum ferentes* in Rore (cf. p. 331), which unquestionably served as a model.[130] At the end of the ode, the words *"dulce novumque melos"* are set to a beautiful and bold series of transitions, which move from D major directly into F-sharp major and progress down the circle of fifths to B, E, A, D, and G, and from there to E, A, and A minor, to close in E.

Musical underscoring of words appears in Lassus' madrigals—there is, for example, the delightful insistence on the second word of *"i tuoi diletti"* in *Il grave de l'età,*[131] but he oftener prefers to depict the general mood of a

---

WagPK; WagMP; EinU; EinIM I, 321ff, 435ff; II, 623f, 658f. Practically complete ed. of them in PalW XXVIII–XXX; those in PalO are in Vols. II, IX; CDMI, *quad. 82–84,* contains 6 exx. not yet cited. On *madrigali spirituali* generally, *see* esp. EinIM I, 191.

[126] Cf. SandA, 68ff (= SandL, 426ff); EinCC, 76.

[127] The compositions labelled *"canzon"* in LassoW IV, 65, 128, are actually *sestine;* for the other 5, *see ibid.,* IV, 6; VI, 50, 70 (= MaldP XIII, 3); VIII, 3, 46.

[128] Pr. LassoW II, 1.

[129] Pr. MaldP III, 3; BuH III, 317; with substitute text (as in the *Magnum opus musicum*) in LassoW III, 169.

[130] Concerning the influence of Rore upon the writing of this ode, *see* MusiolR, 52.

[131] Pr. LassoW VI, 126.

poem. His use of imitation is comparatively sparing. Some of his madrigals or *partes* thereof begin with exact imitation, which, however, disintegrates after three or four notes. Points of imitation within the body of a piece are rare. In certain instances, the imitation is inexact, the deviations not being limited to such as produce tonal answers. *Quando'l voler* [132] illustrates a technique common to various composers and used conspicuously by Monte in his chansons (cf. p. 396): in the Lassus piece, four of the five voices begin with the same figure, but the superius, entering simultaneously with the first voice of the brief exposition, is in counterpoint with it and does not itself have the figure until five measures later. In contrast with these loose uses of imitation, *Come la cera* (*a 6*),[133] has the two uppermost voices in canon throughout.

Some of Lassus' madrigals are for as many as eight or more voices. Most of these are in dialogue or quasi-dialogue form. But in much of *Passan vostri triomphi* (*a 10*) all the parts are kept active together. Considerable independence of the voices is maintained and results in an unusual total range: cantus 1 and 2 ascend to a'' while the bass descends to great D.[134]

At some point in a madrigal in many parts, as in other multivoiced works, Lassus is very apt to introduce what may (with a little stretching of the meaning of "pedal") be termed a decorated inverted pedal, divided between the two highest parts, which cross and recross each other.

EXAMPLE 94. Excerpt from *Le voglie e l'opre mie*—Lassus (after LassoW VI, 18).

"Since my soul deprived within itself of thy favor [is not able] to gain so good a thing" (immortal honor)

---

[132] Pr. *ibid.* II, 17.   [133] Pr. *ibid.* VI, 66.

[134] For the madrigal, *see* LassoW X, 53. In the motet *a 8, Laudabit usque,* Lassus exceeds this total range, taking the bass down to great C.

As here, the decoration of the pivotal note is often accomplished with re-sourcefulness and imagination. Lassus's interest in such a note, frequently evident in less concentrated form, is one of several indications of his feeling for harmonic considerations. Palestrina has this kind of feeling also, but less pronouncedly, and his avoidance of frequent note-repetitions constitutes a mark of distinction from Lassus.

The *Lagrime di San Pietro*,[135] twenty *madrigali spirituali a 7* with a concluding motet, are Lassus' last work (his foreword is dated May 24, three weeks before his death) as well as his longest cycle. The text, consisting of poems by Luigi Tansillo (d. 1568), is set syllabically almost throughout—but nevertheless with very little block-chord writing—and the great wealth of Lassus' contrapuntal resources is drawn upon to heighten its expressiveness.[136]

Monte

A high point in the madrigal is reached in the works of Monte, the most prolific composer in this field. His long residence in Italy ended in 1554, when his first madrigal book (*a* 5), purely Italian in style, appeared at Rome, where he had gone after leaving his position with the Pinelli family in Naples (cf. p. 395). He continued to write Italian madrigals after removing to Germany, as, also, did Lassus. No less than thirty-six volumes of Monte's secular madrigals are known to us, besides five of *madrigali spirituali* and individual madrigals in collections drawing on various composers. The total of his compositions in this genre exceeds 1,100.

Monte's favorite poets in his madrigals are Petrarch, Bembo, and Sannazaro. Neither radical nor conservative, he used most of the devices of his time —melismatic word-painting, moderate accidentalism, contrast of registers, and rhythmic contrasts. Naïve eye-music is found in *Fa ch'io riveggia*,[137] on the words *"far di notte giorno,"* where, after a measure and a half of black notes, *"giorno"* is set with minims. That the madrigal was intended more for performers than for listeners is emphasized by the appearance of eye-music in innumerable compositions, especially in the latter part of the century.[137a] The device, however, is quite rare in Monte, who probably regarded it as frivolous. So serious was he in secular composition that he wrote nothing in the lighter forms of the day—the *villanella, canzonetta,* etc. Restraint without austerity and, as in the chansons, the avoidance of clichés are characteristic. He is important, however, not for innovations but for the quality of his ideas and technique. Technically, indeed, he ranks with Rore and Lassus. The basis

[135] Pr. CW XXXIV, XXXVII, XLI.
[136] Further on Lassus as a madrigalist, *see* esp. EinIM II, 477ff. Other madrigals by him pr. LassoW II, IV, VI, VIII, X (which contains an index to all 5 vols.), and Ser. II, I; 4 of these also pr. CW XIII; 7 pr. ELAM II; etc.
[137] Pr. MonteO XIX, 50.   [137a] Cf. EinIM I, 234ff, 243f.

of his writing is contrapuntal, somewhat like Rore's except that Monte seems to have a greater liking for contrasting chordal sections, as for example in *pars II* of *Mentre, fiamma d'orgoglio*,[138] where the values are greatly lengthened on the words *"misero e lasso."* Here all the voices sing in a low register, and a certain irregularity derived from dotted notes and slow syncopations might suggest sobbing.

In *Ahi chi mi rompe*[139] occurs a progression—common enough in music of the period—that sounds to our ears like V–IV not used in the manner that Classical practice was to establish as normal.[140] Scale passages, including examples in contrary motion, are frequent in Monte's writing, which tends to be of a "busy" nature. The contrary motion may involve corresponding note-values with syllabic setting of the text, or the scale passages may be rhythmically elaborated, as in *In qual parte del ciel,* where they constitute a polyphonic melisma on the word *"l'aura."* Rhythmic contrast is once more strikingly illustrated after this swift-moving passage in the simple but expressive one employing whole-notes and half-notes (in the original values) on the line *"la somma è di mia morte rea"* as the superius moves downward through a diminished octave to the accompaniment of descending outlines in most of the other voices:

EXAMPLE 95. Extracts from *In qual parte del ciel*—Monte (from MonteO XXV, 40f).

"... [tresses so] fine loosed to the breeze ... the sum [of her charms] is accountable for my death."

Many of Monte's madrigals begin in imitation—sometimes strict, sometimes with various modifications such as inversion, inexact statements, or other departures from normal imitation that illustrate his dislike of stereotyped procedures. Thus the six-part *In questo dì giocondo*[141] opens with a point of imitation in which the motif enunciated by the first voice to enter is rhythmically imitated by all the other voices but is exactly imitated intervallically only once; on the other hand, one of the modified versions derived from it is imitated twice. Unlike Lassus, Monte frequently begins phrases

---

[138] MonteO XIX, 80.

[139] *Ibid.* XXV, 51; *see* meas. 5. Instrumental transcr. *ibid.,* 7.

[140] I.e., with the highest voice rising from the fifth of V to the root of IV.

[141] Pr. MonteO VI, 180.

imitatively within a piece, subjecting such passages to variations comparable to those observed in his chansons. Imitation in pairs, not infrequent in Monte, appears in *Mentre sperai,*[142] the six voices of which form three pairs, the third pair imitating the first exactly at the octave, while in the second pair the entry of one of the subjects is delayed, giving rise to new contrapuntal relations. In *Mentre fiamma d'orgoglio* one pair of voices imitates the other at the lower seventh. In scoring *a 6* and *a 7,* Monte constantly varies the number of active voices, so that a suggestion of dialogue sometimes results, but without the opposition of defined groups seen in polychoral composition. In contrast with such contrapuntal writing, *Stella del nostro mar* [143] begins with the declamatory repetition of a single chord. In matters of form, as in details of composition, Monte apparently preferred not to follow a beaten path: the sonnet *Dimmi, lume del mondo* [144] is set in two *partes,* as had been done with sonnets since Willaert's time, but the division is between the first quatrain of the text, as *pars I,* and the rest of the poem, as *pars II.*[145]

Wert

Like Monte, Giaches de Wert (1535–1596) was another Netherlander who spent much of his life in Italy and whose main production was madrigalian. Wert served as a choirboy to the Marchesa of Padulla (in the region of Salerno) and later as court musician to the counts of Novellara. He was *maestro di cappella* at the court (including its Church of Santa Barbara) at Mantua [145a] from 1565 until his death in 1596. His service was interrupted by illness in 1583 and 1586; on each occasion his place was temporarily filled by Giovanni Giacomo Gastoldi (who may also have served as Wert's assistant), but there is no evidence that Gastoldi succeeded to the post.[145b] However, Wert's long absences at the closely related court of Ferrara made it impossible for him to perform his duties at the Mantuan court with any regularity. Wert's life had its full share of tragedy. He had married, at Novellara, a well-to-do woman who, after accompanying him to Mantua, entered into a

---

[142] *Ibid.,* 69.　　[143] *Ibid.,* 34.　　[144] *Ibid.,* 58.

[145] Further on Monte as a madrigalist, *see* esp. EinIM II, 498ff. MonteO VI, XIX, XXV, jointly pr. many madrigals not yet cited (one each of these also *ibid.* XIV, App., and EinGA, 40); other exx. in EinIM III, 297; DTO XLI, 1, 67, 75; MaldP II, 21 (cf. ReT, 110, No. 483), 25 (= HawkH II, 492), 28. The pieces pr. MaldP I, 5, 37, are Monte madrigals with substitute French texts; the piece pr. *ibid.,* 36, as Monte's is also a madrigal with substitute French text, but is actually anon. in the source; (cf. ReT, 110, Nos. 480–82.) *See also* fn. 152. Further on Monte madrigals, *see* EinPM.

[145a] Re-examination of the Mantuan archives leads to the conclusion, despite the contrary opinion of some historians, that the *cappella* served both the Church of Santa Barbara (which was the only ducal church during Wert's lifetime) and the court (as the *cappella di camera ducale*).

[145b] The assumption that he did so is based upon the fact that certain of his madrigal prints carry the title *Maestro di Cappella nella Chiesa Ducale di Santa Barbara,* but in none of the official lists that survive is he so named. He may have been permitted to use the title because of his periods of substitution, but it is noteworthy that Wert does not himself put it on his madrigal collections. The author is indebted to Mrs. Carol MacClintock, who has herself examined the Mantuan Archives, for the information in this fn. and the preceding one.

liaison with one of his subordinates. The ensuing scandal made Wert the butt of ridicule. His wife returned home and, after becoming engaged in a conspiracy against the court of Novellara, died in prison. Wert thereupon became engaged in protracted efforts, in part successful, to recover her property for his children. In 1583, Wert began his visits to Ferrara. Here he fell in love with Tarquinia Molza, who, with Laura Peperara and Lucrezia Bendidio, took part in celebrated concerts of women performers at the court of the Este. Tarquinia was composer, conductor, singer, and instrumentalist in the court, but her love affair with Wert put an end to her career. Her family refused to consent to their marriage; the Duchess dismissed her from her court post, and she was banished to Modena. Wert returned to Mantua.[146]

Wert wrote eleven books of madrigals *a* 5 and one *a* 4. His popularity among his contemporaries and immediate successors is revealed in a letter [147] written by Palestrina to Duke Guglielmo Gonzaga (cf. p. 457), mentioning Wert as a *"virtuoso così raro,"* and in references made to him by Zacconi and Monteverdi.

Wert was more of a modern—more of a successor to Rore—than Monte, employing, in his later works, writing characteristic of the Italian madrigal at the end of the century. The early *Chi salirà per me* (first printed in 1558),[148] however, is in the Franco-Netherlandish tradition of imitative counterpoint and of form dictated by musical principles rather than by textual content. The opening of this madrigal agrees almost exactly in all voices with that of Palestrina's *Morì quasi il mio core* (1586, also Franco-Netherlandish in style), the voices even entering at the same points. Wert's Book VII contains presumably the earliest settings of stanzas from the *Jerusalem Delivered* [148a] of Tasso, with whom Wert was acquainted. Book VIII (1586) contains settings of no less than twelve such stanzas, grouped according to the dramatic content of the text. The groups are, in fact, virtually secular cantatas in madrigalian form. This madrigal book, with its dedication to Alfonso II of Ferrara, contains also three pieces,[148b] each including parts for three high voices, evidently for Lucrezia, Laura, and Tarquinia, whom Wert refers to in the preface as *"Tre nobilissime giovani Dame."* At some points these three parts are definitely the main ones, the lower voices merely accompanying.[149] The activity of the three ladies appears to have given additional impetus to the development, in the madrigal, of the *concertante* style —actually, Josquin's old manner of contrasting one group of voices against another. This impetus, indeed, was felt not only in Ferrara, but throughout

---

[146] Further about Tarquinia, *see* RamazM; EinIM II, 512f and *passim;* DrinM, 220f. Further about Wert's biography, Santa Barbara and the ducal chapel (in Wert's time), etc., *see* esp. BogaW; BautW; EinIM II, 511ff. BertolM, 39ff; CanM, 704ff; *Enciclopedia italiana*, XXII, 173.
[147] Pr. BertolM, 47f.   [148] Pr. SquireM II, 102. Cf. BautW, 45.
[148a] Cf. EinIM II, 519.
[148b] One of these pr. *ibid.,* III, 306.
[149] Further about this book, *see* EinVK.

Italy. Another madrigal in Book VIII, *Io non son però morto,* is remarkable for its motivic working-out.[149a] *Ah dolente partita* (from Book XI *a 5*[150]) shows Wert writing in the newly favored Italian manner, in which native madrigalists approached the monodic style; this piece "almost provides us with an example of an aria in advance of its time, albeit an aria for five voices."[151] Wert's tonality, like Sweelinck's, is often clearly marked, as in much of the *canzone, O primavera.* His chromaticism (accidentalism), without being extreme, is sometimes quite striking, as in *Ah dolente.* This piece is ostensibly written in the Hypodorian mode once transposed, but F and E are respectively sharpened and flattened so that the tonality of G minor results. The trend toward modern tonal structure is seen in the presence of a completely chordal melody, used—in *pars II* of *Cruda Amarilli*—even as a subject of imitation, the subject being remarkable also for its exceptional range:

EXAMPLE 96. Extract from *Cruda Amarilli*—Wert (from *L'Undecimo Libro de madrigali,* Gardano, 1595; transcr. by A. Hartmann).

"But the shores and mountains will cry out through me . . ."

Amor io fallo opens with all five voices singing, in imitation, a subject containing a leap of a seventh.[151a] Unusual intervals imitated in other works include the tenth and the diminished fourth.[151b]

Like his contemporaries, Wert employs elaborate and detailed text illustration at times, as in *E s'altri non m'inganna,* where a long hold for all voices on the word *"fermar"* precedes long melismas on *"il pio fuga."* Dissonance is skilfully used to illustrate sorrow in the imitative passage that concludes *Ahi come soffri,* on the words *"lamenti, pianti e guai."* A striking descent to great E, in a passage spanning the range of a thirteenth in the bass, under-

149a EinIM II, 831; the piece pr. *ibid.* III, 301.

150 Mr. Arnold Hartmann has been so kind as to place at my disposal his transcript of this entire Book, which includes the remaining Wert madrigals mentioned above. *Ah dolente* pr. EinGA, 71.

151 EinGA, 94.   151a Cf. EinIM II, 517.

151b Cf. *ibid.,* II, 571, 573.

scores the invocation of the spirits of the lower world in *Udite lagrimosi spirti d'Averno.*[151c]

Luzzaschi and the Accompanied Madrigal for Solo Voices; Some Lesser Figures

Wert took part with other madrigalists in paying tribute to Laura Peperara, in the collection, *Il Lauro verde . . . a sei voci* (1583). These men included Monte,[152] Macque (*Io vidi,* cf. p. 430), the Netherlander Leonardo Meldert,[153] Marenzio, Luzzasco Luzzaschi, and Bartolomeo Roy (cf. pp. 425, 430).[154] Luzzaschi (d. 1607), a pupil of Rore's at Ferrara—himself the teacher of Girolamo Belli,[155] and eventually of Frescobaldi—became first organist there at the court chapel of Duke Alfonso II. He composed seven madrigal books *a 5.* On occasion he accompanied the Duke's court singers at the harpsichord, and his *Madrigali . . . per cantare, et sonare, a uno, e doi, e tre soprani . . .* (1601) was composed for Laura and her two companions. (Despite the late date of publication, Luzzaschi's madrigals were certainly composed prior to the death of Duke Alfonso II in 1597—perhaps as early as c. 1570. Their publication was delayed by the duke's wish to reserve the music for the use of the *Dame*). Luzzaschi's book contains five accompanied "madrigals" for three solo voices, four for two voices, and three for one. Performances of madrigals as solos with the remaining parts played on an instrument or instruments were, of course, not unknown. We have records of court entertainments including dramas in which they were so presented, and a number of pieces survive in this form for such use (cf. pp. 567f, 570). But the Luzzaschi book of 1601 is unique in providing the only extant specimen, from the period, of written-out accompaniments for keyboard (the Peerson book, mentioned on p. 836, being somewhat later). The voice parts are very highly ornamented. Although the accompaniments at first glance seem simply chordal and not unlike those of the 17th-century monodists, whom they may have influenced, closer examination shows them to be very much what one would expect a keyboard reduction of a madrigal of the chordal type to be: the basic material of the vocal line or lines, as the case may be, is incorporated in the accompaniment, but not the *fioriture.*[156]

[151c] Further on Wert as a madrigalist, *see* esp. *ibid.,* II, 511ff; 568ff; 831ff. Other Wert madrigals pr. *ibid.,* III, 208, 219, 221; MonteO XXI, App. (= HAM, 160).

[152] His piece pr. MaldP II, 30.

[153] His piece pr. *ibid.,* XI, 33.

[154] His piece pr. *ibid.,* II, 34.

[155] Whose publications included 12 madrigal books. *See* further TebAP, 27ff; EinIM I, 211; II, 754ff.

[156] Further concerning this book, *see* esp. KinL, which contains numerous excerpts; 3 complete pieces in KinO, 286ff; 1 more each in WolfME, 107; ScherG, 176; EinIM III, 310. *See also* facsimile *ibid.,* II, opp. 709.

EXAMPLE 97. Extract from *Ch'io non t'ami*—Luzzaschi (from KinO, 291).

"How can I leave thee and not die?"

(In the accompaniment, in both measures 1 and 5 above, nothing is provided on beat 3 for the alto and bass lines .This is true to the original print. Renaissance keyboard sources are eminently practical. In the alto, in each instance, there is really a unison with the tenor but, since the note cannot actually be played twice, it is printed only once [in the lower part]. In both measures the absence of a dot in the first bass note is probably connected with the fact that the string would continue to sound after the removal of the finger from the keyboard.)

The kind of elaborate ornamentation printed in this madrigal book was evidently improvised sometimes in performances of polyphonic music written down in simpler style—or the parts might be rewritten before performance. A large number of *cinquecento* manuals dealing with improvised and written-out embellishment include not only Bassano's book, mentioned on p. 394, but also the *Practica musica* (1556) of the German, Hermann Finck (cf. p. 344),[156a] Girolamo dalla Casa's *Il vero modo di diminuir* (1584),[156b] Lodovico Zacconi's *Prattica di musica* (1592),[157] Giovanni B. Bovicelli's *Madrigali e motetti passeggiati* (1594), and Giovanni Luca Conforto's *Breve . . . maniera . . . a far passaggi* (1593).[158] Finck recommends, among other things, that all the voices use embellishment, but in turn, so that it can be heard clearly. He warns against its use when there is more than one singer to a part, since each individual might apply it differently.

156a For a German transl. of the remarks about singing, *see* EitF.
156b Cf. HorsE, 14ff.
157 Cf. ChrysZ. Further about Zacconi, *see* esp. KretZ.
158 Facsimile ed. in ConfB.

Luzzaschi was among the seven composers who set the *Quivi sospiri* passage from the *Inferno* (cf. p. 400). His version,[159] from his Book II *a* 5 (1576), is highly chromatic for the time, containing many instances of expressive degree-inflection.

Another setting of *Quivi sospiri,* by Pietro Vinci,[160] although later (1584), is much more conservative, using degree-inflection quite sparingly. Vinci (b. Nicosia, Sicily, c. 1530–1540; d. 1584) was *maestro di cappella* at Santa Maria Maggiore at Bergamo, 1568 to 1580, and at the Cathedral in Nicosia, 1581 to 1584. He wrote nine madrigal books and a book of settings of *sonetti spirituali* (1580) by the celebrated Vittoria Colonna, Marchioness of Pescara, friend of Michelangelo and of Cardinal Bembo.[161]

Shift in Leadership from the Franco-Netherlandish Madrigalists to the Native Italians; Andrea Gabrieli

Monte and Wert virtually conclude the list—which had begun with such names as Arcadelt, Willaert, Rore, and Lassus—of Italianized Netherlanders who played a major part in shaping the course taken by the early and middle-period madrigal. During the last third of the century, the leadership passed into the hands of native Italians. Such brilliant composers as Marenzio, Gesualdo, Andrea and Giovanni Gabrieli, Vecchi, Banchieri, Striggio, and finally Monteverdi take over the madrigal, and in their hands it becomes more colorful, more concerned with delineating text than with the absolute values of polyphony. Music becomes more dramatic, and the desire to express personal emotions leads composers logically toward the monodic style. Before the "birth" of dramatic monody, however, we find the curious phenomenon, already manifest in the thoroughly Italianized Wert, of polyphonic music attempting to be monodic. Systematic imitation gives way, as there is a revival of the native Italian predilection for chordal writing in which the highest voice is the most important; changing effects inspired by the text follow one another rapidly; contrasts become sharper; harmonic and vocal color are exploited for dramatic ends.

One of the breakers of the new path was the Venetian, Andrea Gabrieli (c. 1520–1586). He is said to have begun his career as a singer at St. Mark's in 1536 and to have come under the influence of Willaert, but evidence on these points is lacking.[161a] In 1564, he became organist at the Cathedral and, in 1585, first organist.[162] During his youth, the player at the first organ was

---

[159] Pr. EinGA, 53; EinMD, 409. Other normal madrigals by Luzzaschi pr. EinIM III, 257, 262. For further data on him, *see* OrbaNL.

[160] Pr. MomV, 161. For still another setting, by Domenico Micheli, *see* EinMD, 412.

[161] Further concerning Vinci, *see* esp. MomV. 7 other madrigals by him *ibid.,* 114ff; 3 more in TorA I, 299ff.

[161a] Cf. CMI V, 91.

[162] These dates are incorrectly given in several places; *see* IMAMI I, lxxix, lxxiv.

Baldassare da Imola, from whom Andrea may have learned much as an organist. Later his own pupils included not only Italians, such as his brilliant nephew Giovanni Gabrieli and the theorist Zacconi, but also foreigners such as Hans Leo Hassler, who went to Venice to study with him. He, in turn, traveled north: in 1562 he journeyed with Lassus in Bavaria, Bohemia, and along the Rhine.[163]

Andrea's earliest published madrigal appeared in a collection of 1554, devoted primarily to Ruffo (cf. p. 416). The first volume devoted solely to Andrea, the *Sacrae Cantiones,* dedicated to Duke Albert of Bavaria, was printed in 1565. During the following years he composed madrigals, motets, Masses, instrumental *ricercari* and *canzoni francesi,* etc. That his gifts were recognized is attested by his having been asked to write music in celebration of the victory of Lepanto, as well as upon the occasion of the visit to Venice, in 1574, of Henry III of France. In 1585, he composed choruses for a presentation of *Oedipus Rex* at Vicenza.

Andrea's early madrigals, such as *Ecco l'aurora con l'aurata fronte* (1566),[164] continue the contrapuntal tradition and point only occasionally to the "Venetian" style, which he helped to mould. His late works show that style brought to full fruition, with their brilliant choral groupings and driving rhythm, their sonorous masses of chords, and use of *cori spezzati* and similar effects. In his harmony as well, Andrea reflects the significant changes that occurred in the two decades between 1565 and 1585. Having begun as a moderate, he writes in his last works passages such as this from his second setting of Petrarch's *I' vo piangendo* (a favorite text of the madrigalists):

Example 98. Extract from *I' vo piangendo*—Andrea Gabrieli (after EinSP, 89).

The dialogue, *A le guancie di rose,*[165] is a splendid specimen of Andrea's mature style. The eight voices are divided into two choruses, each having a fairly extended passage alone at the beginning; thereafter, the choruses answer each other and finally merge, the sound building up to a most effective

---

163 For further biographical data, *see* esp. CMI V, App.; IMAMI I, lxxivff. For a list of Andrea's works appearing in early prints, *see ibid.,* xcviii; corrections in ZfMW XV (1933), 238f.

164 Pr. EinGA, 32.   165 Pr. TorA II, 129.

climax. Much of this music is sheer choral recitative; save for a few pictorial melismas, such as those on *"riso"* and *"furore,"* the words are set syllabically. Dialogue treatment, which was to gain in popularity, eventually helped to bring about the dissolution of the madrigal. Guarini's *Tirsi morir volea,*[165a] set as a dialogue by Andrea, illustrates the relish for epigrammatic verse shown by the later madrigalists. The piece is in the pastoral style, for which they also revealed a strong liking and of which Andrea was one of the musical founders. Sannazaro's *Arcadia,* published as early as 1502, had set the tone of pastoral verse for the whole century. Later Guarini's *Pastor fido* became a favorite source of texts for madrigal composers. Nymphs and shepherds people innumerable madrigals, imparting the sadly playful tone of their joys and loves and heartbreaks. Of great brilliance is Andrea's eight-voice *Battaglia,*[166] modeled perhaps on Janequin's *La Guerre.* This *Battaglia,* like *I' vo piangendo, A le guancie,* and *Tirsi* is from a large collection, published by Gardano in 1587, containing madrigals and motets by both Andrea and Giovanni. The excessive concern with detail that was to become characteristic of the late madrigal is foreshadowed in Andrea's *La bella pargoletta,*[167] a moving setting of a lament by Tasso on the death of a girl, the music following the words so closely that, at points where her charms are recalled, it assumes an almost gay character.[168]

Lesser Madrigalists of the Venetian Orbit

Among the lesser madrigalists of the Venetian orbit are Annibale Padovano, Vincenzo Ruffo, Costanzo Porta, the brothers Francesco and Gioseffo (Giuseppe) Guami, Baldisserra Donato, and Francesco Portinaro. Ruffo and Porta made more important contributions in the field of sacred composition, Annibale in that of keyboard music. However, all seven wrote competently in the madrigal form.

Annibale (1527–1575) had preceded Andrea as second organist at St. Mark's, holding the post from 1552 to 1564, later entering the service of the Austrian Archduke Carl at Graz, where he died. That word-painting had not yet become a fetish in madrigal writing is illustrated by Annibale's treatment of the word *"Canto"* in two madrigals: in *Spirto real* it is set with elaborate melismas, but in *Cantai un tempo* it is sung to a V–I progression, unembellished save for a suspension of the leading-tone.[169]

[165a] Pr. EinIM III, 190.   [166] Pr. IMAMI I, 203; *pars I* in TorA II, 139.
[167] Pr. DTO XLI, 14; cf. EinIK, 9f.
[168] Further on Andrea as a madrigalist, *see* esp. EinIM II, 520ff. Other madrigals by him pr. DTO XLI, 9, 18; TorA II, 105, 201 (with *pars II* by Giovanni Gabrieli); EinIM III, 178, 182, 199, 248.
[169] These two pieces, resp., in TorA I, 239; DTO XLI, 27 (= ValleA, 81). Other madrigals by Annibale in ValleA (a monograph on him), 87, 94, 103; TorA I, 219, 235; DTO XLI, 22. Further on him as a madrigalist, *see* EinP.

Ruffo, of Veronese birth, comes to the fore at about the middle of the century, though a Magnificat printed in 1539 may be his and a book of motets *a* 5 by him appeared in 1542.[170] In the latter publication he is described as a *musico* in the service of Alfonso d'Avalos, Marquis of Vasto (near Ancona). Also in 1542 he is represented by a work in a book of Masses published by Scotto.[171] He taught at the Accademia Filarmonica in his native city in 1551–52 and began to serve as *maestro di cappella* at the Cathedral there in 1554 and at the Milan Cathedral in 1563. In 1574, he is found at the Cathedral at Pistoia and in 1580 at Sacile (near Treviso), where he died February 9, 1587. He was a prolific composer of Masses, motets, and madrigals. His five-voice *L'aquila è gita al ciel* reveals him as possessing adequate contrapuntal skill.[172]

The Franciscan monk, Costanzo Porta (born in Cremona, c. 1530), was another of the long list of Willaert's pupils at Venice to attain eminence both as composer and choirmaster. He directed the choir at the Cathedral of Osimo from 1552 to 1565;[173] at St. Anthony's, the great church of his order in Padua, from 1565 to 1567; and at the Cathedral of Ravenna, from 1567 to 1574. In 1575, he became *maestro di cappella* at the Santa Casa di Loreto.[174] After an interval following his departure from Loreto, he in 1595 resumed the post he had held at St. Anthony's in earlier years, a post he retained until his death in 1601.[175] He was evidently an excellent teacher; among his pupils were Viadana, Balbi,[176] and Diruta. His *Se le mie acerbe pene*[177] shows him employing Franco-Netherlandish contrapuntal and rhythmic intricacy. Porta wrote one of the twenty-eight settings of Guarini's *Ardo sì, ma non t'amo*,[178] which constitute the volume *Sdegnosi ardori* (1586).

The Guami brothers, born in Lucca and active there during part of their careers, were for a time court musicians at Munich. Francesco was, in 1593, *maestro di cappella* at San Marciliano in Venice; Gioseffo, the more important of the two, became first organist at St. Mark's in 1588.[179] Both published books of madrigals.[180]

Donato was placed in charge of the *cappella piccola* at St. Mark's when it was organized in 1562 (cf. p. 370). This composer, who had become a singer at the Cathedral in 1550 and who succeeded Zarlino as *maestro* in 1590, in-

---

[170] Cf. EitQ, VIII, 353.   [171] Cf. EitS, entry under 1542a.

[172] Pr. TorA I, 205. Other madrigals by him *ibid.*, 215; EinIM III, 160, 163, 164. Further data in ToR (including list of works); ValeR; EinVR.

[173] IMAMI VI, xxiii.   [174] *Ibid.*, xxiv.   [175] Further biographical data in TebAP, 6ff.

[176] Balbi, essentially a church composer (cf. p. 495), produced 2 madrigal books (1570, 1589), the later one consisting of settings *a* 5 of the superius parts of well-known pieces by such other masters as Arcadelt, Berchem, Rore, Marenzio, and others; cf. EinB, 1589⁴. See also TebAP, 10f.

[177] Pr. TorA I, 253.

[178] Porta's ex. in KiesS, 28; settings by 3 others in LassoW VIII, 144; DTO XLI, 54, 56. Another madrigal by Porta in EinGA, 59.

[179] Cf. IMAMI I, lxxiv.   [180] See further NeriS, 157ff, 194f.

cluded, among his publications, four books of madrigals.[181] Although Donato lived until 1603, his activity as a composer of secular music is confined to his youth.

Portinaro (born in Padua, c. 1517) was associated with local *accademie* and also for a time with the Este family. His publications include seven books of madrigals and three of motets.[181a]

Merulo

Claudio Merulo (b. Correggio, 1533; d. Parma, 1604) became a colleague of Annibale's and Donato's at St. Mark's, succeeding Parabosco as first organist in 1564. While still in his early twenties, he had served as organist at the Cathedral of Brescia. His tenure at St. Mark's ended in 1584, and two years later he assumed duties at the Church of the Steccata at Parma, where his salary was more than double that at Venice. In 1617, his nephew gave to a confraternity at Parma "an organ for the most part by the hand of the most excellent musician, Claudio Merulo of Correggio, uncle of the donor." Merulo, then, was something of an organ builder too. He had been active also as a music printer at Venice (in company with a partner), his first publication appearing in 1566. Zarlino presents Merulo as one of the interlocutors in his *Dimostrationi harmoniche*.[182]

Although Merulo's most original works are for keyboard (cf. pp. 540f), he was also a madrigal composer of merit. The above-mentioned 1566 print was a new edition of Verdelot's madrigals, distinguished by its unequivocal placing of accidentals before notes to be inflected.[183] Merulo brought out also, in 1568, a new edition of Festa's collection *a 3* of 1537. Merulo's own madrigals are mainly conservative. In *Madonna poi ch'uccidermi volete,*[184] chordal writing, resulting from the combination of one main melody with countermelodies moving primarily in the same rhythms, recalls Arcadelt. On the other hand, the recitative-like passages in *Da le perle e rubini*[185] are in the later style. Melodic curves outlining a seventh—no particular rarity in Merulo's day—seem to have been especially pleasing to him: the first time the word *"rubini"* occurs, it is set to the notes f', d', g—at the end, moreover, of a phrase. Such curves appear also in Merulo's setting of stanza 1 of the Petrarch *Vergini,*[186] in *Quand'io pens'al martire,*[187] and in *Vergine madre figlia del tuo figlio.*[188] In the latter, the bass and superius, in repeating the words *"via ch'al ciel,"* once outline a ninth and a seventh, respectively.

---

[181] For madrigals by him, *see* TorA I, 177, 185, 188; EinIM III, 155, 322.
[181a] A madrigal of his pr. DTO XLI, 4.
[182] Further biographical data in CatM; BariM; IMAMI I, xxxix, xliv. Incorrect dates concerning Merulo at St. Mark's are widely printed.
[183] For details of this ed., *see* EinC.   [184] Pr. TorA I, 367.   [185] Pr. *ibid.*, 387.
[186] Pr. *ibid.*, 371.   [187] Pr. EinGA, 21.   [188] Pr. TorA I, 380 (cf. EinIM I, 204).

Giovanni Gabrieli

With Giovanni Gabrieli (1557–1612), nephew and pupil of Andrea, the Venetian School reaches a peak in its development, and he is among the composers with whom it enters the realm of composition for voices with *basso continuo* (cf. pp. 488f), a characteristic of baroque music. Nonetheless, Giovanni wrote many works that continue the older Renaissance tradition. In 1576, he went with Lassus to the ducal court at Munich, where he remained until 1580.[189] For a few months in 1584 he filled the vacancy at the first organ at St. Mark's after the departure of Merulo and before the appointment of Andrea, but never was himself officially appointed first organist.[190] In 1585, however, he became second organist.[191] Although he evidently was not an extraordinary performer, his reputation as a composer drew to Venice, as pupils, both Michael Praetorius and Heinrich Schütz.

Giovanni's most characteristic madrigals are distinguished by brilliance of harmonic, vocal, and textural color; cogent rhythmic drive; and use of *cori spezzati*. A fine example of Gabrieli style is found in the eight-voice *Lieto godea*. The voices are divided into two groups of four; frequently one group gives out a short phrase and the other echoes it, while the first rests or has reduced motion; the two groups merge for intermediate and final cadences. Thus, though polyphony is lost, as often in polychoral writing, in the illustration printed opposite, a climactic effect and a feeling of breadth result. Equally typical is the predominance of the major mode and the simplicity and sonority of the harmonies. Gabrieli achieves an effect of brilliance and amplitude by creating vigorous melodic movement over static chords. He uses dominant and tonic with the enthusiasm of a child for a new-found toy, and possibly for that reason makes them sound fresh. The usual Gabrielian excursion into triple meter occurs, beginning with the words *"ogn'hor sospira,"* and the impressive final cadence is also typical. Throughout this piece g″ occurs repeatedly in both superius parts (also occasionally a″). Whereas many of Gabrieli's contemporaries viewed the melodic line in curves and undulations, taking care not to repeat notes of extreme register unduly, to him melodies were flat and panoramic, to be filled in with brilliant colors. This tendency is seen even in *Quand'io ero giovinetto,*[192] written when the composer was eighteen. *Sacri di Giove augei* [193] is an extraordinarily brilliant work *a 12,* not polychoral, but much of it in genuine twelve-part writing, maintaining exceptional independence of the voices. This, as well as *Lieto godea,* is from the Andrea-Giovanni collection of 1587.

[189] Cf. SandA, 12; IMAMI I, lxxix, lxxxiv.
[190] Cf. IMAMI I, lxxiiif, lxxx.   [191] *Ibid.,* lxxiv.
[192] Pr. EinGA, 44.   [193] Pr. TorA II, 159.

EXAMPLE 99. Extract from *Lieto godea*—Giovanni Gabrieli (complete piece in IMAMI I, 35; TorA II, 193).

"Sitting happily, I enjoyed the breeze that trembling sweetly whispers of April."

The Madrigal at Florence

Giovanni's *Sacro tempio d'honor* is included in a collection (1586) of twelve settings of rather inferior sonnets by G. B. Zuccarini, written in honor of Bianca Cappello, the beautiful Grand Duchess of Tuscany.[194] Among other composers represented were Palestrina,[195] Merulo, Andrea Gabrieli, Porta, Vincenzo Bell'Haver (a pupil of Andrea's and his successor as first organist at St. Mark's),[196] and Marenzio.[197] The *Trionfo di musica* of 1579, likewise dedicated to the Grand Duchess, had made available compositions performed at her wedding that year to the Grand Duke Francesco de' Medici. This print opens with an *Epitalamio,* consisting of a sonnet and a *sestina,* each stanza of the latter being by a different composer—Andrea Gabrieli,

194 Cf. EinB, under 1586⁴. *Pars I* of Giovanni's piece (covering the octet of the sonnet text) is pr. in TorA I, 149. Other madrigals by him in IMAMI I, 136, 164; TorA II, 155.

195 His piece pr. PalW XXVIII, 195.

196 His contribution and 2 other pieces by him pr. TorA I, 405, 399, 417; about Bell'Haver's succeeding Andrea, cf. IMAMI I, lxxiv.

197 Marenzio's piece pr. MarenW II, 22.

Bell'Haver, Merulo, Donato, Orazio Vecchi (cf. pp. 433ff), and Tiburtio Massaini (= Massaino).[198]

To Bianca Cappello was addressed also the dedication of the first madrigal book of Vincenzo Galilei (1520?-91), father of the astronomer. (Only one part-book survives.[198a]) Galilei was an influential member of the circle of Count Bardi, which, a few years after the composer's death, was to make Florence the birthplace of what are commonly considered the first operas. His Book II [199] contains pieces essentially in traditional madrigal style, though revealing imagination in the use of "modern" materials. Thus his solemn *Dura mia pietra viva* employs two subjects that incorporate degree-inflection, one being imitated in all five voices. Galilei is important not only as a composer but as a lutenist of note and as a theorist (cf. p. 377). It was he who, in his *Dialogo della musica antica e della moderna* (1581),[199a] first printed the so-called Hymns of Mesomedes, pagan Greek pieces dating from the early Christian era.[199b]

Marenzio

The perfection of the madrigal style is reached by Luca Marenzio (b. 1553 at Coccaglio, near Brescia; [200] d. 1599 at Rome), who combines the various trends in madrigal composition but adds the imprint of his own powerful musical personality. Marenzio is on occasion as brilliant as the Gabrielis, as simple as Arcadelt, as complex as Rore, as serious as Monte, as light-hearted as Nola. He may, as a boy, have studied with Giovanni Contino, *maestro di cappella* at the Brescia Cathedral. From 1579 to 1586 he served Cardinal Luigi d'Este at Rome, and later Cardinal Cinzio Aldobrandini, patron of the arts and protector of Tasso. For a few years he was in the employ of King Sigismund III of Poland,[201] and he had relations also with the court at Ferrara.

Except for externals, such as a preference for music *a 5*, it is almost impossible to discover a typical Marenzio style, since for the special problems of every madrigal he sought a special solution. He uses all the characteristic madrigalian devices, and is adept also in purely contrapuntal writing: *La bella man* [202] has its two uppermost voices in canon; four of the five voices of *Scaldava il sol* [203] open the piece with brief imitation in pairs—a device he

---

[198] Vecchi's stanza and a different madrigal of Massaino's, from the same collection, pr. GhiFM, 85, 79, respectively; *see also ibid.*, xxxviiiff.

[198a] One piece, however, was reprinted in Galilei's *Fronimo* (cf. p. 523); it is pr. in IMAMI IV, 21; ChilS, 31.

[199] Pr. IMAMI IV, 113ff; 1 piece also in EinIM III, 265.

[199a] Extract in English transl. in StrunkR, 302ff.

[199b] Cf. ReMMA, 49.   [200] Cf. BigM.

[201] Further biographical data in HabLM; Grove III, 321ff (both to be used in the light of BigM and OrbaN); EngB.

[202] Pr. TorA II, 224.   [203] Pr. SquireM II, 53; MarenW I, 126.

liked—and the second pair is an inversion of the first; passages containing typically madrigalian effects may be interspersed with normal free-flowing polyphony. Marenzio also composed in chordal and syllabic fashion, especially in his pieces in the "lesser" forms (cf. p. 443). Notwithstanding Zarlino's rule that individual syllables should not be set by values smaller than half-notes, Marenzio occasionally uses a syllabic style in conjunction with passages in eighth notes, as in the madrigal, *L'aura che'l verde lauro* [204] and the elegy, *Oimè il bel viso*.[204a] The declamatory lines of *Io piango* and of the polychoral *Se'l pensier* and *Cantiam* [205] disclose Marenzio master as well of an idiom not unlike the younger Gabrieli's. Although best known for his shorter works, he was quite capable of writing extended madrigal cycles, such as the complete setting of Sannazaro's *sestina* "Sola angioletta",[206] the *commiato* being combined, in *pars VI,* with the last stanza.

Most striking among Marenzio's traits is his highly detailed and literal painting of words that represent a visual object, a sound, an idea, or a mood. In some of the lesser madrigalists, such literal treatment yields sterile formulas and episodic structure. But Marenzio's musical concentration—resulting in part from the readiness with which he forgoes having each voice sing the full text—is great enough to preserve continuity, and his genius transforms the essentially naïve device of word-painting into a means of high artistic expression. The well-known setting of *Gia torna* [207] might be called a translation of the text into music. The opening motif turns from an ascending leap of a fifth to a descent of a minor third on *"torna";* the next phrase translates *"rallegrar"* into a joyous, swift-moving figure, then depicts air by three higher notes and earth by a descending leap. The light-hearted idea of "April, the youth" permeates the following phrase; after an incomplete cadence, the word *"mar"* is represented by waves in the melodic lines. The image in *"s'acqueta"* ("becomes calm") is pictured in three ways at once: the motion slackens; the superius leaps down an octave; and an unexpected chromatic change in harmony emphasizes the contrast between the sea moving and the sea at rest. Some measures later, a brief melisma suggests the singing of birds. Minute illustration of this sort continues throughout the remainder of the madrigal; sight, sound, and mood are all paralleled in the music.

Of the innumerable other examples of word-painting, a few of particular charm include, among those of the visual type, the lilting melisma, which, in *A cui giova,* paints a perfect picture of the movement of swans (on the word *"cigni"*), being at the same time luxuriously lovely as pure music.

[204] Pr. TorA II, 238.
[204a] Pr. MarenW I, 98.
[205] Pr. *ibid.* I, 74 (= EinSH, 286), 85; II, 137, respectively.
[206] *Ibid.* II, 47.   [207] *Ibid.* I, 82.

EXAMPLE 100. Extract from *A cui giova*—Marenzio (after MarenW II, 27).

The noble, six-part apostrophe to Rome, *Cedan l'antiche tue chiare vittorie,*[208] represents the arches of the great city by means of an ascending and descending melodic curve in several voices. Here, as in the treatment of the waves of the sea in *Gia torna,* the music delineates the text not only by means of sound but also graphically on paper. Marenzio, perhaps more than any of his contemporaries, employed another form of eye-music, in which blackened notation set words having to do with darkness or anything comprehensible as opposite to white. This is presumably the sole reason, in *Oimè, dov'è'l mio ben,*[209] for the change to triple meter on the word *"cieco."* Instances might be multiplied. Sound images add charm to Tasso's *O tu che fra le selve,*[210] in which the poet puns by means of echo effects. Thus, one line is *"Mi risponde, non son d'amante esempio?"* to which the echo answers, *"Empio."* Marenzio's obvious but inevitable procedure is to set the echoed syllables with identical echoing music.[211] It is the musician who puns in *Mi fa lasso languire;*[212] here Marenzio, like earlier composers, matches words with the solmisation syllables they suggest. The sound of a sob is heard in the rise and fall of a minor second in *Stillò l'anima.*[213] In *Ridean gia per le piagge,* the idea in the words *"Al tempo novo"* and *"novo tempo"* is represented literally by a change of meter.[214] *Oimè il bel viso* follows the thought and mood of almost every word in the description of the deceased, though without disrupting the unity of the whole. Marenzio's usually minute correlation of word and note in delineating mood—in contrast with the over-all type of expressive mood delineation generally found in Arcadelt or Palestrina—is illustrated in the sombre *Udite, lagrimosi spirti,*[215] where, for example, a diminished triad is used on the word *"crudel."* In other pieces,

---

[208] Pr. ELAM III, 2.

[209] The passage in question is in white notes in MarenW I, 4, meas. 53, because of the use of modern notation; however, in the original it is in blackened notation. Further about eye-music, *see* EinA.

[210] Setting pr. MarenW I, 33.

[211] For an article on echo effects and dialogue in old music (including this piece), *see* KrE.

[212] Pr. MarenW I, 80.   [213] *Ibid.,* II, 112.

[214] *Ibid.,* I, 118. Cf. *pars I,* meas. 48; *pars II,* meas. 94.   [215] Pr. MarenW II, 110.

similar expressive dissonance takes the form of a diminished-seventh chord.[216] In late works like *Udite,* however, Marenzio tended in the main to renounce such detailed symbolism.

Marenzio introduces chromaticism sparingly but with telling effect. Like some of his contemporaries, he frequently portrays grief or pain by chords whose roots progress a major third up or down in the bass while degree-inflection occurs in an upper part.

EXAMPLE 101. Extracts from *Io piango*—Marenzio (complete piece in MarenW I, 74; EinSH, 286).

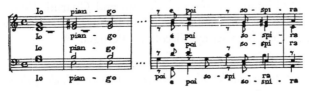

"I weep . . . and then [she] sighs . . ."

The striking *Solo e pensoso* [217] begins with a kind of chromatic *cantus firmus* in the superius, which ascends in whole notes, semitone by semitone, from g' to a", and then returns a fifth downward. This madrigal contains examples of a favorite idiom of Marenzio's, one that employs a scale-degree both in unaltered and in chromatically altered form, not consecutively, but in close proximity to each other, as in the following pattern of conjunct seconds: descending minor, ascending major, ascending minor.[218] Accidentalism in Marenzio sometimes suggests a remarkable number of tonalities in rapid succession.[219] *O voi che sospirate,* within a few measures, follows the circle of fifths downward from A-flat to E (with some interpolations).[220] This composition shows awareness of enharmonic equivalence in the modern sense (Marenzio combines G-sharp and A-flat, F-sharp and G-flat) and, to that extent, of equal temperament.[221]

At one point in *Solo e pensoso,* the bass leaps down a major ninth. Marenzio's basses at times exhibit exceptionally wide range, and may be as expressive as any higher part: in the rich setting of Tasso's *Giunto a la tomba,* the bass sings:

[216] Cf. EngM, 262. Further about dissonance in Marenzio, *see ibid.,* 264f.
[217] Pr. in TorA II, 228; *pars I* in ScherG, 174 (with values halved).
[218] The exx. of this type in *Solo e pensoso* are on *"deserti campi"* and *"genti, Perchè";* see also EinMD, 418f, meas. 20–23. For variants, *see* TorA II, 238, 1st system; MarenW, 69, meas. 20.
[219] Cf. MarenW II, 18, meas. 31–33; I, 107, meas. 6, 7.
[220] Cf. KrI, 135f; WintG II, 88. The piece is pr. in MarenW I, 69; WintG III, 156.
[221] Cf. EinIM II, 624.

EXAMPLE 102. Extract from *Giunto a la tomba*—Marenzio (after MarenW II, 3).

Pren-di, pren-di,pren-di   ch'io ba - gno di   do-glio · so hu-mo - re,

"Take [my sighs and kisses] that I bathe in grievous tears."

Marenzio gave the pastoral style its finest expression, his most celebrated madrigal in this vein being probably his setting of Guarini's *Tirsi morir volea*.[222] Fastidious in his choice of texts, he set poems by Petrarch, Ariosto, and Dante, in addition to Sannazaro, Tasso, and Guarini. Franco Sacchetti is represented by a setting of "Passando con pensier," the *caccia* which, during the *trecento*, had been set by Niccolo da Perugia.[223]

The Naninos; Giovanelli; the Anerios; Other Madrigalists at Rome

Marenzio, as well as the aging Palestrina and many of the less renowned composers who followed in his wake, were members of a society that eventually developed into the present-day *Accademia di Santa Cecilia*. The society, originally called the *Compagnia dei Musici di Roma*, was organized in 1584. (The *Nobil Accademia delli Pittori* was founded for painters at about the same time.) The membership included musicians of both sexes, active in the sacred and secular fields, vocal or instrumental; the organization existed more for the sake of mutual assistance than for artistic purposes. It enjoyed the patronage of Gregory XIII, but was at first opposed by the Papal Choir, which forbade its members to join. Later, however, the Choir gave its approval.

Giovanni Maria Nanino (c. 1543–1607), who became a tenor in the Choir in 1577, belonged to the *Compagnia*, along with his brother and pupil, Giovanni Bernardino (c. 1550–1623), whose publications include three madrigal collections. Giovanni Maria had served as choirboy in the Vallerano Cathedral, and it is fairly certain that he had studied in Rome with Palestrina, whom he succeeded in 1571 as *maestro di cappella* at Santa Maria Maggiore. He held the same post at San Luigi de' Francesi, 1575 to 1577. In 1604 he became director of the Sistine Chapel. While significant chiefly as a church composer, he was a prolific writer of secular works: the madrigals

---

[222] Pr. MarenW I, 12.

[223] Cf. ReMMA, 365. EinCC is an article on Marenzio's setting. Further concerning Marenzio's madrigals, *see* esp. EinIM II, 608ff; EngM; EngB; HeuW. MarenW I and II reprint complete the contents of Marenzio's Books I–VI *a 5*. Other madrigals pr. TorA II, 215; EinIM III, 233, 252; EinMD, 414; EinGA, 65; KiesS, 43 (= HawkH III, 198), 49; PistR, 27, 32, 36, 40; ELAM III, 16; SquireM II, 60; MartiniE II, 78, 82, 88, 95, 164, 229 (= ChorP VI, 212 [= BuH III, 205], 214, 216, 219, 225, 249).

of his, contained in two books of his own and in one written jointly with Annibale Stabile, are supplemented by many appearing in collections that represent various composers.[224]

The Naninos and the other composers, to be mentioned, who lived at Rome in the shadow of the great Palestrina employed much the same smooth contrapuntal writing and strict treatment of dissonance as he, but without imitating him slavishly. Marks of the later time, e.g., instances of recitative-like lines, syllabic setting of eighth-notes, and minute word-painting can be found in their madrigals. Other members of the *Compagnia* include Paolo Bellasio, Stabile, Giovanni Andrea Dragoni, Ruggiero Giovanelli, Annibale Zoilo, Cristofano Malvezzi, Paolo Quagliati (cf. pp. 442f), Bartolomeo Roy and Giovanni de Macque (both of whom we shall meet again in Naples), Francesco Soriano (or Suriano), and the brothers Felice and Giovanni Francesco Anerio.

The publications of Bellasio, active at Verona as well as Rome, include six madrigal books. Stabile (born in Rome, c. 1540; died c. 1595) is known to have been a pupil of Palestrina's, as is Dragoni (born Meldola, 1540; died Rome, 1598). Both served as *maestri* at St. John Lateran; Stabile also at the Collegium Germanicum and at Santa Maria Maggiore. Each of these men issued madrigals, etc., as well as sacred works.

Giovanelli (born in Velletri, near Rome, c. 1560; died in Rome, 1625)—having been *maestro di cappella* at San Luigi de' Francesi (1583-1591), following the two Naninos, and also at the Collegium Germanicum—succeeded Palestrina, after his death in 1594, as *maestro* at St. Peter's, where he remained until 1599, when he was elected singer in the Papal Chapel. He was also in the service of Cardinal Aldobrandini. Although, like several of his colleagues in the *Compagnia,* he is more distinguished as a composer of sacred music, Giovanelli was a prolific writer of madrigals; most of his six books of such pieces underwent numerous reprintings.[225]

Zoilo, who served as contralto in the choir from 1570 to 1577, after having been *maestro di cappella* at St. John Lateran, produced two madrigal collections.[226] Malvezzi (1547-1597), *maestro di cappella* to Francesco and Ferdinando de' Medici and author of three madrigal books, was the teacher of Jacopo Peri. Soriano (born in Suriano [Viterbo], 1549; died 1621) studied under Zoilo, Roy, G. B. Montanari, G. M. Nanino, and Palestrina. In his youth he was a contralto at St. John Lateran and, at various times from 1580 on, *maestro di cappella* at San Luigi de' Francesi, Santa Maria Maggiore, St.

---

[224] Further biographical data in HabN, CamD, RadN. Two madrigals by him pr. TorA II, 11, 25; another (*Vienn' Himeneo*) pr. separately in *Ausgewählte Madrigale*, No. 26 (Breitkopf & Härtel), W. Barclay Squire, ed.

[225] For madrigals by him, *see* TorA II, 419; ELAM VIII, 22. WinR is a monograph on him.

[226] For madrigals by Zoilo, *see* TorA I, 275, 281, 287, 293.

John Lateran, Tivoli Cathedral, and St. Peter's. He served also at Mantua, beginning c. 1581, being for a while *maestro* of the duke's private chapel. His works include three books of madrigals.[227]

G. F. Anerio, the younger of the brothers (born in Rome, c. 1567; died 1630 in Poland), was choirboy at St. Peter's under Palestrina, 1575–1579, and *maestro di cappella* at St. John Lateran, 1600–1603. He served at the court of King Sigismund III of Poland, c. 1609; at the Cathedral of Verona, 1610; and as prefect of the Roman Seminary of Jesuits, 1611. He served as *maestro di cappella* at Santa Maria dei Monti in Rome from 1613 to 1620.[228] Five of Giovanni Francesco's collections include madrigals. Felice Anerio (born in Rome, c. 1564; died 1614) served as choirboy at Santa Maria Maggiore from 1568 to 1574, learning the elements of counterpoint there from G. M. Nanino. From 1575, Anerio was soprano and, from 1577, contralto in the Julian Chapel, then under Palestrina's direction. He was, in 1579–80, contralto at San Luigi de' Francesi under Soriano. In 1585, he was appointed *maestro* at the Collegium Anglicum. Clement VIII called him (1594) to assume officially the post of composer to the Papal Chapel, which Palestrina had held *de facto*. Anerio enjoyed the patronage of Cardinal Aldobrandini.[229] His madrigal books are four in number. In 1589, he directed the musicians of the *Compagnia* and the same year published *Le Gioie,* a collection of madrigals *a* 5 by various members, including Marenzio and Palestrina.[230]

Seven Notable Anthologies; the Italian Madrigal Outside Italy

Another notable collection in which both Palestrina [231] and Marenzio were represented is *Il Trionfo di Dori* (1592), the model for the English *Triumphes of Oriana* (cf. p. 831). Other contributors include Vecchi,[232] Giovanni Matteo Asola,[233] Massaino,[234] Leone Leoni,[235] Striggio (cf. pp. 435f),[236] and Giovanni Giacomo Gastoldi. Asola (born in Verona, c. 1560; died in Venice, 1609) was appointed *maestro di cappella* of the cathedral at Treviso in 1578 and of the one at Vicenza in 1581. Although important chiefly as a composer of sacred music, he produced three madrigal books. One of these, the *Madrigali . . .* of 1584, is a curiosity in that it consists of canons *a* 2.[237] Gastoldi (c. 1550–1622), active as a madrigalist and especially noted for his work in a related lighter form (cf. pp. 445f), seems to have been Wert's assistant at the court

---

[227] For further data, *see* KinsS, 113; HabFS.

[228] Further biographical details in HabGA; FederhA; MGG I, 470ff.

[229] For further biographical data, *see* TorG; HabFA; MGG I, 470ff; for data on both Felice and his father, Maurizio, *see* CamM.

[230] The Palestrina piece pr. PalW XXX, 126.   [231] His piece pr. PalW, XXVIII, 246.

[232] Pr. TorA II, 283.   [233] *Ibid.,* 367.   [234] Pr. SmM, 143.

[235] 2 other madrigals of his pr. TorA II, 407, 411.

[236] Pr. TorA I, 357.

[237] 14 of them pr. BartC; a normal madrigal in TorA I, 367.

in Mantua (cf. p. 408). His *Al mormorar*,[238] from the *Trionfo di Dori*, is gay and gracious, if a bit conventional as regards word-painting devices. Like all the other pieces in this collection, Gastoldi's concludes with the exclamation, *"Viva la bella Dori!"*

A collection of 1598, *Pietosi affetti*, containing settings of poems by Padre Don Angelo Grillo, prior of San Giuliano at Genoa, includes "Monsig. Gio. Matteo Asola" and "Monsig. Gio. Giacomo Gastoldi" on its roster of *"diversi Reverendi & Eccellentissimi Autori."* Listed also, with fifteen other *Reverendi*, are Porta, Leoni, "Fra Lodovico Viadana," and a "Monsignor Incerto [*sic*]." Lodovico Grossi da Viadana (1564–1627), of outstanding importance in the early history of the *basso continuo*, nevertheless wrote in older style likewise, his production including two madrigal books and two books devoted to the "lighter" forms, as well as pieces in collections containing works by various composers. He was *maestro di cappella* at the Cathedral of St. Peter in Mantua during much of the time that Gastoldi was *maestro* at Santa Barbara.

Gastoldi, Marenzio, and Andrea Gabrieli are among the composers represented in at least three of the four Italian madrigal collections—*Harmonia celeste . . . raccolta per Andrea Pevernage* (1583); *Musica divina* (1583); *Symphonia angelica . . . raccolta per Huberto Waelrant* (1585); and *Melodia Olympica* (1591)—all brought out at Antwerp and all reprinted several times.[239] The prestige of the Italian madrigal was such that collections were published in various parts of Europe and works of the type were written by non-Italians not only in the peninsula but at home. The *Nervi d'Orfeo*, printed at Leyden in 1605, is noteworthy for its eight Italian madrigals by Claude Le Jeune. (His *Mélanges* of 1585 had included these eight together with no fewer than twenty-eight other Italian pieces.[239a]) Pevernage, who is not known to have visited Italy, included several of his own madrigals in the *Harmonia celeste*,[239b] and among the other northerners represented is Faignient.[239c] Both composers reappear in the *Musica divina*. The *Symphonia angelica* contains two pieces by Verdonck,[240] who likewise seems never to have visited Italy, as well as compositions by Waelrant[241] himself, Monte, Wert, and René de Mel (*see* be-

---

[238] Pr. TorA II, 93; SquireM II, 8.

[239] Gastoldi's piece in the third is published separately in *Ausgewählte Madrigale*, No. 38 (Breitkopf & Härtel), W. Barclay Squire, ed. The form is rather that of a *canzonetta* (cf. p. 446) than of a madrigal. Some of Marenzio's contributions to the first pr. in MarenW I, 12 (cf. fn. 222), 18, 93; some of those in the third, *ibid.*, 25, 53, 96; some of those in the fourth, *ibid.*, 5, 7, 43, 44, 46. For descriptions of all 4 prints *see* EinB, under 1583¹, 1583², 1585¹, and 1591¹.

[239a] 2 of these pr. SquireM II, 44, 49 (= MaldP XXIX, 23, 21, respectively).

[239b] 3 pr. MaldP II, 11, 15, 23 (cf. ReT, 111).   [239c] His 2 nos. pr. *ibid.*, XIII, 15, 18.

[240] One, *Donna bella*, is pr. *ibid.*, II, 38, but with a French text; cf. BergCV, 130; ReT, 116, No. 603.

[241] One Waelrant piece, *Vorria morire per uscir* (*a 4*), pr., with substitute Flemish and French texts, in MaldP I, 8; cf. BorFA, 15f; ReT, 117, No. 607.

low.) Verdonck is found also in the *Melodia Olympica,*[242] as is Pevernage.[243] The international character of the madrigal is emphasized by the title-page description of the *Symphonia angelica* as *"raccolta da Pietro Philippi Inglese"*; Philips (cf. pp. 793f) contributed five pieces of his own to this collection.[244] In his native country, the madrigal took such firm root that England, as we shall see, was second only to Italy in producing examples of the type. To be sure, most of these had English words, but even Englishmen set some Italian texts. For example, Byrd's *La Virginella*[245] is a setting of a stanza from *Orlando furioso,* and it even makes use of part of the Italian *Ruggiero* melody in its bass.[245a]

The dissemination of the madrigal in England was furthered not only by printed music but by the presence of Alfonso Ferrabosco—one of the sons of Domenico Ferabosco (cf. pp. 791, 821; Alfonso spelled his last name with "rr," whereas Domenico's is usually found with "r"). To the name of Alfonso (b. 1543 in Bologna; d. 1588 in Turin) the figure "I" is usually affixed nowadays to distinguish him from his similarly named son and grandson, who were born in England. We shall re-encounter Alfonso I in that country, which he left in 1578, entering c. 1582 the service of Duke Charles Emmanuel I of Savoy at Turin, but also spending a large part of his last years in Bologna.[246] Two madrigal books *a* 5 of his appeared at Venice in 1587—one dedicated to the Duke, the other to the Duchess. His madrigals selected from the first of these books and from other sources for the English publication, *Musica transalpina* (cf. p. 821), are dignified and motet-like, maintaining both clarity of chordal structure and independence of the voices, often by means of wide leaps in the inner parts.[247] Chromaticism and the detailed word-painting that are typical of the later madrigal have little place in his work. His *Gravi pene in amor*[247a] sets a stanza of *Orlando furioso,* incorporating a pre-existent melodic formula (other than the *Ruggiero*) in the manner of Corteccia and other Italian composers (cf. pp. 325f).

Three Late Franco-Netherlandish Madrigalists

René de Mel (Rinaldo del Mel, etc., born c. 1554; died c. 1598), mentioned

[242] One piece pr. MaldP II, 40.

[243] For 1 of his pieces in this collection, *see ibid.*, 18. Further on his madrigals, *see* StellP, 77ff.

[244] One pr. HawkH III, 328.

[245] Pr. EMS XIV, 124; ByrdW XII, 124. About a subsequent version with English text, *see* Chap. 16, fn. 11.

[245a] As pointed out to me by Dr. John Ward.

[246] About Alfonso I's biography, *see* esp. LiviF, 127ff; KermanMA, 222ff.

[247] 9 madrigals by him (and 2 chansons) pr. OEE XI (8 items), XII (3 items), after *Musica Transalpina,* and therefore only with English texts; the Italian (and French) titles, however, are indicated.

[247a] From the Sambrooke MS, New York Public Library (17th century). Cf. KermanMA, 230, and facsimile opp. p. 226.

above, entered the choir school of St. Rombaut, at Malines, his birthplace, in 1562. He served as *maestro di cappella* to two kings of Portugal, and later was in the service of Cardinal Paleotti at Rome. Sometime after July, 1587, he became director of the episcopal chapel at Liége. His publications include eight madrigal books, two books of *"madrigaletti"* and one of *"madrigaletti spirituali."* *Pars V* of his setting *a 6* of Petrarch's *sestina, Standomi un giorno,*[248] begins with the words, *"una strania fenice."* The voices, in entering, denote the strangeness of the phoenix by successively leaping a sixth, some upward, some downward, three of the intervals being major and one of these, a descending leap in the bass, being followed by a further descending step before a turn is made in the opposite direction.[249]

Striking proof that Italian music had come to the fore is the fact that, whereas Netherlanders had gone to Italy as mentors in the early part of the century, toward its end they journeyed there as students. When Cornelis Schuyt (1557–1616) visited Italy to perfect his skill, his native town of Leyden paid the expenses. In the preface to his Book I of madrigals *a 5* (1600), dedicated to Leyden officials, Schuyt eulogizes the Dutch city in a composition on the Italian text, *O Leyda gratiosa.*[250] His musical style, also, at times reveals his fidelity to the north,[251] notwithstanding his Italian tutelage and the aptitude he shows for the Italian manner.[252] If it is true that Sweelinck's alleged trip to Italy to study with Zarlino is apocryphal (cf. p. 398), he must at least be counted among the stay-at-homes who wrote Italian madrigals. The fifteen Italian pieces *a 2* and *a 3* in his *Rimes françoises et italiennes*[253] recall his chansons in their rhythmic decisiveness and lively mood. Detailed word-painting is negligible, and some lengthy melismas can hardly be justified except as being expressive of a general spirit of buoyancy. The madrigals *a 2* include a setting of Boccaccio's *Io mi son giovinetta,*[254] with quotations from the old version by Domenico Ferabosco; here Sweelinck's modal treatment is retrospective, though elsewhere among the madrigals, as among the chansons, there is occasional evidence of a strong feeling for major–minor tonality. Besides the Italian pieces in this book, Sweelinck wrote a few that appeared in collections drawing on various composers.[255]

---

[248] Sambrooke MS, 451ff.

[249] Two other voices, after leaping a sixth, skip an additional third in the same direction, but that, producing an outline of an octave, is less remarkable, from the standpoint of 16th-century technique, than the progression in the bass, producing an outline of a seventh. Further about Mel, *see* DoorRM.

[250] Pr. VNM XLV, 7.

[251] A facsimile of a puzzle canon by him, with Dutch text, pr. VNM XLV, 4; 2 resolutions *ibid.,* 5f; SeiffCS, 258f.

[252] 8 other Italian madrigals of his pr. *ibid.;* 3 in VNM V.

[253] Pr. SweeW VIII.

[254] Pr. *ibid.,* 22; DaA, 45.

[255] Other Sweelinck madrigals pr. SweeW IX, 61, 65, 68.

The Madrigal at Naples; Gesualdo

The diversity of idiom of the Late Renaissance, that could include the subtlety and elegance of Marenzio, the forthrightness of Sweelinck, and the declamatory writing of Wert, had room also for the striking dramatic directness and extreme chromaticism of Carlo Gesualdo, Prince of Venosa (ancient Venusia, the birthplace of Horace). This extraordinary nobleman, distinguished as a lutenist and patron of the arts and one of the virtuoso composers of the century, was born c. 1560 in Naples and died there in 1613. His father, Don Fabrizio, had established an academy and employed, among others, Giovanni de Macque and Bartolomec Roy, whom we have encountered in Rome, and Pomponio Nenna (born c. 1555; died c. 1617), to whom we shall return presently. Macque (born in Valenciennes, c. 1552; died in Naples, 1614), a pupil of Monte's, was appointed second organist in the Church of the Annunciation in Naples in 1590, the aged Nola (cf. p. 333) being still *maestro di cappella* there. Macque became very effectively tied to Naples in 1592, when he married a *"damigella"* whose parents stipulated, in the marriage contract, that he was not to leave the city without the lady's written consent, upon penalty of payment of 1,000 ducats.[256] His six-part madrigal, *Io vidi amor,*[257] presents points of imitation in rapid succession. Melismas paint the words *"acque"* and *"velo"* in his smooth setting of Petrarch's *Non al suo amante.*[258] Roy received the title of *maestro di cappella* from the Viceroy of Naples in 1585.[259]

When, in 1585, Carlo became the heir of the house of Gesualdo upon the death of his elder brother, he was obliged to marry to produce further heirs. His first cousin, who, at the age of 21, had already been married twice, became his ill-fated bride. After a few years, having discovered that she was unfaithful to him, he murdered her, her lover, and an infant whose paternity he doubted. After the tragedy, Gesualdo traveled through northern Italy; in 1594, he married Eleonora d'Este and settled for a time at the brilliant court of Ferrara. The death in 1597 of Alfonso II, last in his line, marked the end of this court, the cultural center of the Late Renaissance in Italy. After a few years, Gesualdo returned to Naples, where he died.[260]

Although Gesualdo knew Tasso, this did not develop in him a keen perception of literary values. Settings of verses by this poet share space, in the prince's collections, with settings of the merest doggerel.

Gesualdo's famous "modernism" constitutes a fascinating bypath in the

---

[256] For further biographical data, *see* ProtaN; MB IV, xxviff. The claim, occasionally made, that there were two Giovanni de Macques, father and son, appears to be wrong.

[257] Pr. MaldP IX, 3.

[258] Pr. *ibid.,* VII, 48. Another madrigal by him, *ibid.,* 51. The piece pr. *ibid.,* 46, with French text, is also a madrigal (from the *Melodia Olympica*); cf. ReT, 109.

[259] About a madrigal of his, cf. fn. 154.

[260] Further biographical data in GrayG (or, better, GrayV, a revision of the biographical portion thereof); VatP; DiseG.

history of music. Expression was his primary interest—emotional expression, not concerned with eye-music or musical description of individual words. To this end, he made novel use of chromaticism. His first book *a 5* (1594),[261] however, illustrates his technical proficiency in the established idiom rather than bold innovation. Thus, in *Tirsi morir volea*[262] accidentals are relatively rare. Degree-inflection is almost negligible throughout this book. In Book II *a 5* (1594),[263] however, the opening of *Sento che nel partire*[264] contains mild degree-inflection, and the last two notes of its altus form a descending leap of a diminished fourth.

Gesualdo's chromaticism is more often harmonic—resulting from the contrasting of block-chords belonging to distant tonalities as in *Io tacero* (from Book IV, 1596)[265]—than melodic; but chromatic scalar passages occur, as in *Moro lasso al mio duolo*[266] (from Book VI, 1611), and melodic and harmonic chromaticism sometimes blend, as in *Tu m'uccidi* (from Book V, 1611).

EXAMPLE 103. Extract from *Tu m'uccidi*—Gesualdo (from *Libro quinto de madrigali . . .* ; after score ed. by Molinaro, Pavoni, 1613; complete piece in CDMI, *quad. 62,* 10).

"*. . .* crying, alas that I die loving!"

This example shows that Gesualdo, like most skilful composers, tends to balance complexity in one element of composition with compensatory simplicity in another; his most intricate chromaticism occurs in slow, rhythmically simple passages, while chromatics are absent or rare where the rhythm is

[261] Pr. IISMM I, 1–67; duplications in CDMI, *quad. 59,* 3 (= HawkH III, 214); *quad. 60,* 3; NeyR V, 102, 108.
[262] Pr. IISMM I, 37 (= CDMI, *quad. 59,* 18).
[263] Pr. *ibid.,* 68ff. This is properly Book I; cf. EinIM II, 695.   [264] Pr. IISMM I, 101.
[265] Pr. GesualdoM 16; *pars I* in CDMI, *quad. 61,* 3.
[266] Pr. KrV, 33; BuH III, 223; GesualdoM, 30.

swift or comparatively involved. Especially unconventional passages are apt to be confirmed in one way or another. Thus the opening three measures of *Resta di darmi noia,* exhibiting a treatment of the second inversion and accidentals that shock even modern ears, are immediately repeated in sequence.

EXAMPLE 104. Opening of *Resta di darmi noia*—Gesualdo (from *Libro sesto de madrigali . . .* ; after score ed. by Molinaro, Pavoni, 1613; complete piece in CDMI, *quad. 62,* 18).

"Stay thee from giving me torment."

In Gesualdo's Books V and VI *a 5,* and in his imperfectly preserved, posthumously published Book *a 6,* the musical audacities—rhythmic, melodic, harmonic—spring from an approach to the text too individual to give rise to an enduring school. However, some contemporary musicians must at least have wished to emulate him, for, in 1613, a volume was published containing his six books in score, and the rare score-prints of the time seem to have been intended primarily for students of composition.[267] In fact, Gesualdo's boldness is not entirely without parallel. On the basis of certain similarities between his compositions and those of Nenna, it has been alleged that the latter was his teacher.[268] Nenna's *Ecco, o mia dolce pena,*[269] for example, contains unprepared dissonance, irregular resolutions, and degree-inflection, but compared with Gesualdo's extreme pieces it is tame enough. There is, actually, no conclusive proof that Carlo learned his daring idioms from this musician of his father's. As far away as Milan, Giuseppe Caimo, organist in the cathedral of that city (1580–1588), was engaging in comparable harmonic experiments: his *E ben ragion*[270] employs successively the chords of D minor, B-flat, E-flat, A-flat, D-flat, G-flat, B-flat, G and B.

The score-volume of Gesualdo was prepared by Simone Molinaro who, in 1605, succeeded his uncle and teacher, G. B. dalla Gostena, himself a

---

[267] Further about Gesualdo's music *see* EinIM II, 688ff; KeinM; KrI, *passim,* esp. 137ff. Other madrigals pr. TorA IV, 1 (= CDMI, *quad. 60,* 14), 5 (= GesualdoM, 26), 9 (= ScherG, 178; GesualdoM, 22), 13, 17 (= ChorP VI, 239; MartiniE II, 237—*a 6* though from Book III "*a 5*"); CDMI, *quad. 60,* 9, 19; *quad. 61,* 8, 16, 22; *quad. 62,* 2, 23; GesualdoM, 6, 11; HAM, 182; MartiniE II, 198 (= ChorP VI, 239; KiesS, 52).

[268] Cf. IMAMI V, lvii; but *see* contra IISMM II, ixf.

[269] Pr. *ibid.,* 104. This vol. contains 2 complete madrigal books by Nenna. Another madrigal pr. KrV, 28.

[270] Pr. WolfME, 87. Other madrigals pr. EinIM III, 214, 216. *See* also MGG II, 641ff.

madrigalist, as *maestro di cappella* of the Genoa Cathedral. Molinaro produced madrigals also, but is more important in other fields.

The "Choral Dramatists": Orazio Vecchi; Striggio; Croce; Banchieri

During the last quarter of the century, there is, in the works of certain composers, much reciprocal influence between the serious madrigal and the various "lighter" forms, the madrigal absorbing something of the gay style of the *villanesca* and of such of its companions as the *balletto* and *canzonetta* (cf. pp. 445f) and the lighter forms assuming certain features of the madrigal. This hybridization is reflected in the avoidance of the word "madrigal" in titles given to certain secular collections: *Li amorosi ardori di diversi eccellentissimi musici* (1583); *Armonia di scelti autori* (1586); and many others.

The late 16th century produced also a large body of "entertainment" music, with texts quasi-dramatic or otherwise suggested by action, though not intended for the stage. Its chief composers were Vecchi, Striggio, Croce, and Banchieri. Less important was Gasparo Torelli.[270a] In this music, especially, many of the traits of the light forms appear: simple technique and predominantly chordal texture; tuneful, catchy melodies; texts, often comic and dealing with themes of everyday life. While the more lofty madrigal continues to speak of hopeless love or of nymphs and shepherds, entertainment music furnishes a real picture of the people of 16th-century Italy.

The greatest of the "choral dramatists" was Orazio Vecchi (b. Modena, 1550; d. 1605). He served at the Cathedral of Correggio as canon (appointed in 1586) and archdeacon (appointed in 1591); he returned to Modena in 1593 to direct the singers in the cathedral. In 1604 the bishop dismissed him despite the protests of the parish. (It is said that a pupil desired to replace him.) He died four months later.[271]

Vecchi, who wrote many of his own texts, composed sacred music, numerous charming *canzonette* and fine madrigals. *Ahi tormento*,[272] in which imitation and chordal passages alternate, is a serious madrigal of the traditional type, as is the setting *a 5* of *Il bianco e dolce cigno*,[273] in which the alto at the beginning and the end quotes Arcadelt's superius. Many of Vecchi's pieces, however, represent the hybrid forms of the late madrigal period. Among his major madrigal collections are the *Selva di varia ricreatione* (1590)[274] and *Convito musicale* (1597).[275] But it is for his *L'Amfiparnaso* that Vecchi is most memorable.

L'Amfiparnaso, representing the type of quasi-drama, is a series of fifteen pieces (one *a 4*, the rest *a 5*), grouped into a prologue and three acts, these

[270a] For his *Fidi amanti, see* TorA IV, 73.
[271] Further about Vecchi, *see* HolHV, RoncOV, FratC.
[272] Pr. TorA II, 267. [273] Pr. SquireM II, 86.
[274] WeckC contains bibliographical description, with an ex., of the *Selva; see also* fn. 338 and p. 523. [275] An ex. pr. in EinGA, 76.

being divided into fourteen very loosely connected scenes. Gardano first issued this remarkable work in 1597, adorned with attractive cuts, one for each scene, illustrating characters or moments in the action.[276] Nevertheless, *L'Amfiparnaso* is not meant to be acted, as is clearly stated in the prologue, which (along with the rest of the text) was probably written by Vecchi himself: "This spectacle is observed with the mind, which it enters through the ears, not the eyes." Some of the characters are traditional ones of the old *commedia dell'arte*: Pantalone, the Venetian merchant; Gratiano, the Bolognese doctor, et al.; while others, such as the lovers Lucio and Isabella, are Vecchi's own. The lines of these dramatis personae, however, are sung throughout polyphonically, except at the very opening (after the prologue) where two characters are represented monophonically. The speech of various foreigners and provincials is represented—that of the Spanish captain, the Jewish moneylenders, the Bergamask servants, and others. The work is mainly comic, although serious portions are found, such as Isabella's lament on the supposed death of her lover, with its especially effective final portion. In Act I, scene 1, the courtesan Hortensia introduces herself in a *villanella*-like passage *a 3*, consecutive fifths being used in the old-fashioned manner. At the beginning of scene 2 of Act III, Dr. Gratiano sings a parody *a 4* of Rore's *Anchor che col partire* (cf. p. 332), incorporating Rore's superius, but with new parts for the three lower voices. The words play upon the original, the very first line being transformed into *Ancor ch'al parturire*. The varied musical techniques range from choral recitative to full-fledged polyphony.[276a]

EXAMPLE 105. Extracts from Act II, scenes 3 and 4 (Isabella's Lament) of *L'Amfiparnaso*—Orazio Vecchi (after facsimile in VecA).

"O here is the captain; here is my sweetheart and my hope."

[276] Pr. PubAPTM XXVI; TorA IV, 148ff; VecA (both facsimile of orig. ed. and transcription).
[276a] *See* further DentA; PerinA.

"Receive my hot blood and my sad soul."

(Note, in Ex. 105b, the two descending leaps of a
diminished fifth, the first—followed by a rise of a diminished fourth—in meas. 5–6, the second in meas. 7.)

Vecchi's *Veglie di Siena* (1604)[277] besides caricaturing a German, a Sicilian,
and others, contains a second section in which the "humors" expressible in
"modern music" are presented—among others, the gay, the sorrowful, the
courteous. The preface to this work, in answering attacks made on
L'Amfiparnaso, invokes the authority of Aristotle, Horace, Castiglione, and
Marini, and avows the purpose of writing dramatic poetry in order better
to imitate life. The *Seconda veglia* opens with a *caccia d'amore* which, in describing the hunt, simulates the barking of dogs. While not canonic like
early *caccie,* this piece contains much imitation. Here and in *"L'Umor allegro,"* the superius reaches b-flat". In *"L'Umor misto,"* Palestrina's *Vestiva i
colli* is briefly parodied, an augmented triad being outlined by one of the
lower voices.[278]

Orazio Vecchi is not to be confused with Orfeo Vecchi (born in Milan, c.
1550; died 1604), *maestro di cappella* (c. 1590) at Santa Maria della Scala
in Milan, after which the opera house La Scala was to be named. Essentially
a composer of church music, Orfeo also wrote *canzoni spirituali,* a set of
twelve (1611) being modeled after the instrumental *canzone francese,* itself
modeled especially on the narrative type of French chanson (cf. pp. 292, 295,
534ff, 538f, 550f).[279]

Well before *L'Amfiparnaso,* Alessandro Striggio had written a work that
may be considered the prototype of such quasi-dramatic compositions, *Il
cicalamento delle donne al bucato* ("The chattering of the women at the
laundry"; printed 1567),[280] representing comic and dramatic episodes, occurring at the public washing-place of an Italian village. Of the five *partes,*
the first is *a 4* and the others *a 7,* but the number of active voices varies con-

[277] Pr. CP II.
[278] Further about Vecchi's madrigals, *see* EinIM II, 772ff; HolA; HolH; HolS; HolV. Other
reprints in TorA, 247; SmM, 124, 130 (= ELAM III, 130). *See also* fns. 198, 232.
[279] Further about Orfeo Vecchi, *see* EinOV; HabOV; letters by him in GanL.
[280] Pr. CP IV; SolM; also published separately by La Zarliniana, Milan, Rome (ed. by C. Perinello), 1940.

siderably. Some genuine choral dialogue is present. At one point the melody of the *Romanesca* (cf. p. 524) is introduced.[280a] Dialogue figures also in *Al vag'e incerto gioco di primiera*,[280b] one of a number of madrigals that deal with *giocchi* (games), such as the card game of *primiera* involved here.[280c] Striggio's madrigal, *Chi fara fed'al cielo*,[281] is one of the earliest works to have been mechanically reproduced: Salomon de Caus's *Les Raisons des forces mouvantes avec diverses machines . . .* (Frankfurt, 1615) gives the music in score and states, in its account of *"La roue musicale (un orgue mécanique),"* that this is the *"pièce de musique qui est posée sur ladite roue."* Striggio (c. 1535–1587), a nobleman, was born and died in Mantua. For some years he was attached to the court of Cosimo de' Medici. He visited England and Paris in 1567. He is known to have been an excellent organist, lutenist, and violist, as well as the composer of music for a number of *intermedi* (cf. pp. 568f).

Giovanni Croce, best known for his sacred works, also composed music suggested by action, such as *Mascarate piacevoli et ridicolose* (1590) and *Triaca musicale* ("Musical Medication"; 1590), which includes a *gioco* piece on a game of dice.[282] Born in Chioggia, c. 1557, Croce sang in the choir at St. Mark's under Zarlino and presumably studied with that master. He became a priest, attached to Santa Maria Formosa at Venice. In 1593, he was appointed teacher of the choirboys at St. Mark's and, with the death of Donato in 1603, *maestro di cappella,* remaining in that post until his own death in 1609.[283]

Adriano Banchieri (1567–1634), important as a theorist, composer of sacred and secular vocal music and of instrumental music, like Orazio Vecchi wrote outstanding madrigal comedies. Born in Bologna, he studied with Gioseffo Guami, then was organist at his monastery of San Michele in Bosco near Bologna, and later (1601–1607) at Imola. Having returned to Bologna, he founded, in 1615, the *Accademia de' Floridi,* and in 1620 became abbot of San Michele. His theoretical works are of especial importance for the light they cast on instrumental practice. Banchieri's *La Pazzia senile* (1598),[284] probably modeled after *L'Amfiparnaso,* represents some of the same stock characters, such as Pantalone and Dr. Gratiano. Doralice's lament recalls that of Vecchi's Isabella. Gratiano sings (polyphonically) a parody of Palestrina's

[280a] Cf. EinIM II, 766f.

[280b] Pr. *ibid*. III, 285.

[280c] For details, *see ibid*. II, 767f.

[281] Pr. AMO X, 153. Other madrigals pr. TorA I (5 items); MonteO X, App.; HawkH II, 331; cf. fn. 236. Further about him, *see* EinIM II, 761ff; CanM, 725f; GanL.

[282] Pr. TorA II, 345; the whole *Triaca* in CP III. For the exact meaning of *"Triaca," see* EinIM II, 800.

[283] *See* further *ibid*. II, 798ff; HabGC; MGG II, 1791ff.

[284] Pr. TorA IV, 281ff (but *see* EinIM II, 803); excerpts in CDMI, *quad*. 2; 1 in BartC, 46.

Vestiva i colli. The scoring is *a 3,* SSB clef-combinations for the most part alternating with TTB combinations. Early examples of the dynamic directions "piano" and "forte" occur in this work (but *see,* in addition, pp. 521, 551). The *Festino nella sera del giovedi grasso* (1608),[285] similarly constructed though *a 5,* contains the madrigal [286] in which a cuckoo, owl, cat, and dog are represented improvising *"contrappunto bestiale"* against a mock liturgical *cantus firmus.* Other collections by Banchieri are the *Metamorfosi musicale* (1600); *Il Zabaione musicale* (1603); *Barca di Venezia* (1605); and *La Prudenza giovenile* (1607), which was reissued (1628) as *La Saviezza giovenile.*[287] In the *Gioco della passerina* [288] from *Il Zabaione musicale,* five persons eat a sparrow and, as each additional part is consumed, a new voice is added to the refrain. When the sparrow has been devoured, all conclude that a capon would have been preferable.[289]

Monteverdi

The Italian urge toward opera, evident in the madrigal comedies, as well as in the incidental music added to plays and in the *intermedi* presented between their acts (cf. pp. 171ff, 566ff), succeeded in producing actual opera at the turn of the century. The first unquestionably great composer in this new baroque genre was Claudio Monteverdi (b. Cremona, 1567). His predecessors, with the exception of Marco da Gagliano—an excellent composer both in the new idiom and in the older one of the madrigal [290]—had been no more than intelligent dilettanti. Though Monteverdi is best known for his baroque compositions, which lie outside the scope of this study, certain of his works are firmly rooted in the Renaissance tradition. Moreover, even in his most spectacular innovations the influence of the older chromaticists and writers of expressive dissonance is apparent. He had studied counterpoint, viol, voice, and probably organ with the *maestro di cappella* of the cathedral of his native city, Marc'Antonio Ingegneri (born in Verona, c. 1545-50), and refers to himself on the title page of his first four madrigal books as Ingegneri's pupil. Monteverdi's dependence on Rore may be traced through Ingegneri, who in the dedication of his own *Madrigali a sei voci* (1586) indicates that he had studied with the Netherlander. Ingegneri, a pupil of Vincenzo Ruffo's as well, c. 1563, may have settled at Cremona, the main

285 Pr. CP I.
286 Also pr. CDMI *quad. 1,* 17 (2 other pieces from the *Festino* on pp. 2, 10).
287 Excerpts in CDMI, *quad. 3.*   288 Pr. CDMI, *quad. 1,* 23.
289 Further about Banchieri, *see* esp. EinIM II, 802ff; also MGG I, 1206ff; further about the quasi-drama with special reference to Banchieri, *see* VatV.
290 For studies of him, *see* esp. EinIM II, 729ff; VogelG; madrigals, etc., in EinIM III, 267, 275; EinGA, 85; TorA IV, 23, 27 (cf. EinIM II, 729, 742).

scene of his activity, as early as c. 1568. In 1578, he became a singer at the Cremona Cathedral and is referred to, a few years later, as *"magistro musice capelle"* there. He died at Cremona in 1592.[291] He was a fine madrigalist, in the main conservative, though at times introducing mild chromaticism, including degree-inflection.[292]

Monteverdi, after spending some time at Milan, was called to Mantua in 1590 to serve as violist[293] to Duke Vincenzo I Gonzaga. There he married Claudia Cattaneo, daughter of another violist and herself a singer. In 1595, he accompanied the Duke to Hungary, whither an expedition set forth to fight the Turks. Although, during this trip, Monteverdi provisionally held the title of *maestro di cappella* to the duke, the official post was held by Wert, a year after whose death in 1596 it passed to the Cremonese, Benedetto Pallavicino,[294] much to Monteverdi's chagrin. In 1599, the composer again accompanied the Duke on a trip, this time to Flanders. After Pallavicino's death in 1601,[295] Monteverdi was finally appointed *maestro della musica,* one of his duties being the composition of operas. But the work was strenuous, the salary poor and the climate of Mantua unfavorable to his health. So, after Claudia's death in 1607, Monteverdi, grief-stricken and ill, asked for release from his court position. This was denied, but better conditions were granted. Upon Duke Vincenzo's death in 1612, the release was at last obtained and Monteverdi visited Milan and Cremona. From 1613 to his death in 1643, he was *maestro di cappella* at St. Mark's, having joined the priesthood in 1631.[296]

The twenty-year-old Monteverdi, in his Book I *a* 5 (1587),[297] shows himself master of older techniques. Contrapuntal skill combines with powerful and direct dramatic expression. *A che tormi il ben mio* illustrates his bold use of expressive dissonance (still rare) and, on the words *"Ahi mio tesoro,"* his power in building a climax in even a short passage. This piece, in its deliberate avoidance of stereotyped imitation, is most intricately planned, despite its deceptively simple appearance. Others had avoided stereotyped imitation also (cf. p. 407), but Monteverdi does this with singular inventiveness.

---

[291] Further biographical data in IMAMI VI, ixff; DohrnI, 7ff; SommiM, 15ff; HablI, 8off.

[292] E.g., IMAMI VI, 128, meas. 9f; 211, meas. 2f, 5, 7, 1of, 13, etc. 44 madrigals of his pr. this vol. (discussion on p. xliiff); another in WalM, 499; *see also ibid.,* 146ff.

[293] Not in 1589 and not as both violist and singer, as sometimes stated; cf. PaoM, 53f.

[294] The composer of 10 madrigal books and 1 motet collection. For 2 madrigals, *see* TorA II, 307, 315. (The *maestro* for the intervening year was Francesco Rovigo; cf. PruCM, 10, 208; PaoM, 78.)

[295] *See* PaoM, 77f; SartM, 407ff; the evidence marshaled in VfMW III, 323ff; VII, 282, aiming to show that Pallavicino lived beyond this date, is evidently based on posthumous publications.

[296] For further biographical data and documents, *see* esp. PaoM; PruCM; LunI; VogelM; MalCM; SartM; RedM; RedMLW.

[297] The madrigal books discussed above are pr. in MontevO I–VI; dedications to Books I and II in MontevO IX, 123, 125.

EXAMPLE 106. Opening of *A che tormi il ben mio*—Monteverdi (from *Primo Libro de madrigali . . .* ed. of 1621; complete piece in MontevO I, 8).

"Why take away my treasure, if I say that I am dying . . ."

The superius sings line 1 of the text once to theme 1, and line 2 once each to themes 2 and 3. Before theme 1 is imitated, the altus and tenor enter, singing line 2 to simultaneous, mostly note-against-note, statements of themes 2 and 3. Theme 1 is imitated by the quintus, which thereafter sings line 2 twice, but each time to theme 3; its first statement of this theme is sung while the superius has theme 2, but here the statements are not made note-against-note —the quintus enters a minim after the superius, preserving this distance for a few notes. In consequence, the superius and quintus give forth a modified paired imitation of the altus and tenor lines. The bass is the last voice to enter, singing theme 1 and then line 2 to theme 3 at the fifth below (all other imitations being at the unison or octave). The simultaneous introduction of themes 2 and 3 before theme 1 is imitated brings about the interlocking of two different points of imitation, the second being paired. (Still additional complexities reveal themselves upon close inspection; note, for example, the rhythmic treatment of theme 1 in meas. 11ff.) Such intricate manipulation of thematic material, though not limited to Book I, is especially characteristic of it.[298]

Book II *a 5* (1590) displays a surprising simplification in technique, at times recalling Arcadelt, as in the delightful *Non giacinti o narcisi*.[299]

[298] Comparably refined "mussing up" of imitation and irregular pairing of themes may be found in MontevO I, 29 (after the chordal introduction), 42, 61, 64, 67; II, 1 and 7f, 44; III, 19.

[299] *Ibid.*, II, 24.

Monteverdi clearly admired the older master (cf. p. 401). *Non si levava*[300] reintroduces, at the close, the musical material of the opening, but to new words. *Crudel perche mi fuggi*[301] repeats the last two lines of text to a varied repetition of the music, in contrast with *Dolcissimi legami,*[302] in which two closing lines, upon recurrence, repeat their music almost literally. In the latter piece, the word *"catene"* is illustrated by chains of syncopations (not, however, involving suspensions). The later Monteverdi is foreshadowed through the suggestion of rapid parlando style in *Mentre io mirava fiso*[303] and through occasional harmonic venturesomeness. Monteverdi prefers to set the mood of the poem, but instances of common word-painting devices are found, such as the elaborate melismas in *Cantai un tempo.*[304] Book II includes the lovely *Ecco mormorar l'onde,*[305] which opens with almost static melodic material and develops into a warmly colorful nature picture.

Book III *a* 5 (1592), despite increased use of recitative-like style, contains also polyphonic passages, such as one in *pars II* of *Vattene pur crudel,*[306] where a descending chromatic motif[307] is treated in imitation, with the resulting suggestion of modulation to remote tonalities.

In Book IV (1603), the *parlando* style emerges full-fledged: passages in actual *falsobordone* occur in *Sfogava con le stelle*[308] and elsewhere. The further increase in choral recitative reflects the tendency of the times to assure intelligibility of the text. This trend, emphasizing the growing importance of the listener in secular music, is found in both the madrigal and the new-born opera. Monteverdi, though not wholly abandoning the polyphonic technique, turned more and more to lucid chordal writing: even in polyphonic passages, he often truncated successive entries to permit all the active voices to sing the same text at more or less the same time. To be sure, truncation had been applied earlier, e.g., by Marenzio and even Palestrina, but in Monteverdi it became the characteristic (though not invariable) practice.

Book V (1605) introduces an element that helps to transform the madrigal into the cantata: a *continuo* part is provided for all pieces, being obligatory for the last six,[309] which are thus written in a baroque style. (The *continuo* is traceable earlier than this in the field of the motet; cf. p. 487. It should not be confused with a completely written-out accompaniment, tantamount to a reduction of the polyphony, such as Luzzaschi employed.)

[300] *Ibid.,* I.   [301] *Ibid.,* 83.   [302] *Ibid.,* 19.   [303] *Ibid.,* 58.   [304] *Ibid.,* 102.   [305] *Ibid.,* 68.
[306] *Ibid.,* III, 48.
[307] Not all the accidentals are given in the source, but it is clear that they are meant to be applied; cf. *ibid.,* 54, fn.
[308] *Ibid.* IV, 15.
[309] MontevO V omits this part from all but the 6 in question; cf. EinD, 111; BukMB, 35; PruCM, 41.

The first pieces in this collection are characterized by considerable use of choral recitative. A striking unprepared dissonance appears in *Cruda Amarilli:* [310] the superius enters, after a rest, with the ninth from the root and leaps down to the seventh, whereupon the chord (a dominant seventh) resolves. This is among various Monteverdi passages condemned by Artusi in his treatise attacking "the moderns," *L'Artusi overo delle imperfettioni della moderna musica.* [310a] The theorist had heard this piece before its publication. Monteverdi, referring to his own manner of writing as the *"seconda pratica, overo perfettione della moderna musica,"* in his foreword [311] to Book V mentions a reply he had written and threatens to publish it. [312]

Book VI (1614), though containing some of Monteverdi's finest madrigals in Renaissance style, includes also pieces definitely in baroque style, [312a] and is indeed the last of his secular collections to lie within the scope of this study. In Book VI is found the *sestina* setting *a 5, Lagrime d'amante al sepolcro dell'amata.* [313] The pieces in it are distinguished by simplicity and extensive use of choral recitative. *Pars VI,* comprising both the final stanza of the poem and the *commiato,* has a ten-measure introductory period in recitative style for all voices, repeated with changes, a fifth higher, in which the spacing produces a singularly rich sonority. Thereafter, following the words, *"Ecco l'afflitto Glauco fa risonar Corinna,"* superius and quintus take up the lament, *"Ahi Corinna,"* which they echo through ten measures while the other voices sing new text. A nine-measure passage in *Ohimè il bel viso* [314] employs six suspensions, of which one resolves normally, two on $\frac{6}{4}$ chords, and three on harmonies other than those against which the dissonance is sounded. Presumably, the success of Arianna's lament, *Lasciatemi morire*—in his opera *Arianna,* which had been produced at the court of Mantua in 1608— prompted Monteverdi to compose the very eloquent setting *a 5,* included in this Book. The madrigal version adds striking expressive dissonances, including the unprepared ones with which the altus and tenor begin and, later, the sharply dissonant *appoggiatura* on the word *"dura".* [315]

[310] Pr. MontevO V, I; *see* meas. 13.

[310a] The extract given in English transl. in StrunkR, 393ff, includes the criticism in question.

[311] Facsimile in MontevO V. Reprints in VogelM, 428; MalCM, 71f.

[312] The foreword was reprinted in Monteverdi's *Scherzi musicali* of 1607, accompanied by a declaration by his brother, Giulio Cesare. Facsimile in MontevO X, 69ff; English transl. in StrunkR, 405ff.

[312a] Monteverdi provides an instrumental bass-part for the whole Book, but MontevO VI retains it for only 6 numbers.

[313] *Ibid.,* 46ff.   [314] *Ibid.,* 70.

[315] Opinion differs whether there should be degree-inflection in meas. 4 of the monodic version as in Ex. 107; cf. MontevO XI, 16; but also ScherG, 201. However, the evidence of the madrigal version would seem to be conclusive. Further about Monteverdi's madrigals, *see* SchradeMM, 124ff, 135ff, 179ff, etc.; EinIM II, 717ff; 850ff; RedM; LeiM; PruCM, 27ff, 144ff; MalM.

EXAMPLE 107. Extracts from the monodic and polyphonic versions of
Lasciatemi morire—Monteverdi (from VogelM, 443; MontevO
VI, 1, 3).

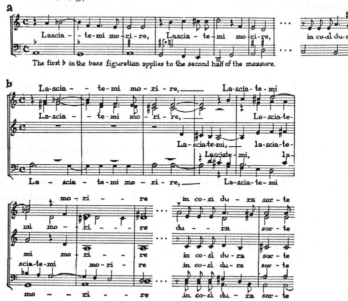

"Let me die . . . in such a grievous lot . . ."

Rossi; Quagliati

At the court of Mantua during part of Monteverdi's career there, we
find Salomone Rossi, Hebreo (born c. 1570; died c. 1628) and his sister,
Madama Europa, a celebrated singer and actress. Although Salomone was
essentially a baroque composer, his works belong partly to the Renaissance.
Some madrigals in his Book I *a* 5 (1600) are purely vocal, while others have
a *chittarone* accompaniment.[316]

An effort to bridge the gap between the new accompanied monody and
the old polyphonic madrigal is found in a publication of 1608, containing
music by Paolo Quagliati (d. 1630), organist from c. 1608 at Santa Maria
Maggiore in Rome and also a fine cembalist. The book in question was his
*Primo Libro de' madrigali a 4 concertati per cantar con l'instromento, con un
libro separato dove stà il Basso seguito per sonarli*. This publication appears
to be the only one of its kind; the pieces in it are given not only *a 4* but in a

[316] For 22 selections from his madrigal Books I and IV, *see* RossM. For some details concerning Rossi and other Jewish musicians at Mantua, *see* CanM, 701f; *see also* IdJ, 196ff;
GradenMI, 136ff.

version for solo voice with partially figured bass, these two parts drawing on more, respectively, than the superius and bass of the original. The experiment was not a complete artistic success.[317] Indeed, while examples of the old Italian madrigal continued to be reprinted and sung, the heyday of its creative life was over.

The heightened expression of pathos and passion, illustrated by such a work as *Lasciatemi morire,* helped to bring about the break-up of the madrigal. If music was to portray such strong emotions and was to do this on a grander scale, the small chamber-art of the madrigal had inevitably to be abandoned and to be replaced by the larger forms of the cantata and opera.

The "Lighter" Forms, Including the Villanella, Balletto, and Canzonetta

Lighter forms flourished beside the madrigal in the later part of the 16th century as in the earlier. These forms were neither the bourgeois counterpart of the aristocratic madrigal nor pieces composed by native Italians reacting against Franco-Netherlandish polyphony, but were by the same men and intended for the same audience as the more serious madrigal.[317a] As might be expected, these pieces were mostly chordal, strophic, and dance-like; but, just as they occasionally brought lightness to the madrigal, the latter occasionally lent a mildly polyphonic character to them.

The term *"villanesca"* continued in use only until c. 1570, when *"villanella,"* already current, superseded it. Among the later composers of *villanesche* was Donato, who brought out collections of them in 1550 and 1568. The earlier book contains the well known *Chi la gagliarda.*[318] The last two decades of the century witnessed a large production of prints including the word *"villanella"* in their titles. Many leading composers wrote *villanelle*: Lassus published some charming ones, as did Marenzio,[319] the latter's being models of elegance and grace. A theoretical distinction is sometimes made between *villanesca* and *villanella* on the basis of the rhyme scheme of the text (cf. pp. 332f), the two-line strophes of the *villanella* being described as couplets having a separate rhyme for each pair. However, this distinction is far from absolute: the first book of *Villanelle . . . a tre voci* (1574),[320] collected by Giovanni de Antiquis, contains twenty-two pieces by such composers as Nenna and Stefano Felis, not one of the texts answering to this description. Here the patterns vary, but the most usual one is *ab* + refrain-with-

---

[317] Further about this collection, *see* EinD.   [317a] Cf. EinIM I, 340.

[318] Pr. TorA I, 183; BuH III, 216. Other *villanesche* by him pr. TorA I, 175 (= WolfME, 104); EinIM I, 449.

[319] For 10 Marenzio *villanelle, see* MarenV; 3 more in EinIM II, 586, 588, 590; 2 more in ChilS, 26; VelA, Supp. IIb.

[320] Pr. IISMA I with the *Secondo Libro* of the same year.

rhyme-*b, ab* + refrain, *ab* + refrain, *ccc,* which is very close to the *villanesca* rhyme pattern. The relationship with this *strambotto*-like pattern, however, tends to weaken at this time, although the eleven-syllable line is retained. From the standpoint of musical structure, most of these Antiquis pieces consist of two sections, each immediately repeated to the same text. This repetition pattern is characteristic, though not invariable, in the light forms discussed here, except for the *villota.* Indeed, the general similarity of the light forms, despite the presence of some distinguishing features, is such that *cinquecento* prints themselves are not consistent in their terminology and many scholars now make no distinction at all with regard to several terms.[321] However one may designate the various types, they preserve among themselves certain musical traits of the *villanesca* that have been described in Chapter 6. Parallel fifths continue to be used in writing *a 3,* a conspicuous example being found in Nenna's *Signora, io penso.*[322] *Cantus prius facti,* both complete and fragmentary, are still employed, Palestrina's *Io son ferito* being a particular favorite.[323] In Lassus' *Sto core mio,* from his Book I of 1555, the superius and tenor of a pre-existent piece exchange roles and are combined with two new voices.[324] A second book in popular style appeared in 1581, containing *villanelle, moresche,* and *"altre canzoni,"* the last designation probably adopted because of the difficulty in classifying completely the wealth of light pieces that were being written. The *moresca,* in Neapolitan dialect, represents the dialogue of Negroes enslaved in Southern Italy. The 1581 book included six *moresche,*[325] half *a 4,* half *a 6,* dealing primarily with the same ribald characters: Giorgia, Lucia, and others.[325a] Of the "other songs," *Zanni*[326] might be regarded as akin to the polyphonic quasi-drama. It is a comic dialogue between Pantalone and his Bergamask servant, each character represented by a chorus *a 4.* ("*Zanni,*" the traditional name for a comic servant in the *commedia dell'arte,* is the source of the English word "zany.") Another of the *altre canzoni, O la, o che bon eccho,*[327] is a playful double chorus *a 8,* the second group repeating literally each phrase sung by the first. The 1581 set includes also the famous *Matona mia cara,*[328] a serenade by a German soldier, in Italian but with a characteristic accent (*Matona = Madonna*), recalling the *canti carnascialeschi* that poked fun at

[321] E.g., CorteS, 246; EngMV, 267; VatC, 618.   [322] Pr. IISMA I, 40.

[323] *See* the 8 citations in KiS, 58 (without mention of the Palestrina source; KiS lists also 3 pieces earlier than Palestrina's that begin with much the same melodic fragment but have different texts; these pieces no doubt merely use the same current melodic idiom). On the general subject of musical citation, *see* EinV.

[324] The piece pr. LassoW X, 69; MaldP X, 12. (In both places it is preceded by 5 additional *villanelle,* the first of which is also pr. in CW VIII, 22; the second likewise in ELAM II, 27.)

[325] Pr. LassoW X, 86, 97, 104, 112, 120, 125. About the *moresca* pr. *ibid.,* 70, cf. EinB, 1562⁵, fn.

[325a] For a *moresca,* perhaps by Nola, *see* EinIM III, 83.

[326] LassoW X, 135.   [327] *Ibid.,* 140.   [328] *Ibid.,* 93.

the Emperor's *lanzi*. Pieces mimicking a German accent in Italian were called *todesche* or *tedesche*.[329]

Dialect pieces became extremely popular, those of different regions of Italy naturally predominating; thus, there were *bergamasche, toscanelle, mantovane, ferrarese,* and *venetiane*. The word *"napolitana"* became practically synonymous with *"villanella"; "canzone alla napolitana"* was used as well as the simple term, *"canzone."* Among prolific writers of such compositions were Massimo Troiano,[330] Giovanni Leonardo Primavera,[330a] Girolamo Conversi—whose *Sola, soletta* [330b] was especially popular—and Giovanni Ferretti.[331] Some of the *villanelle* by Marenzio mentioned above are reworkings *a 3* of certain of Ferretti's five-part *canzoni alla napolitana*.[331a] The latter's *canzoni* have been characterized as retaining "the general form of the villanella . . . , while elaborating the individual lines *alla madrigalesca.*" [331b] Nola also contributed to the *villanella* literature.[332] Texts in dialects or a *mélange* of languages include poems by Antonio Molino, who introduced words of Renaissance Greek into Italian contexts. Settings of such poems are known as *greghesche*. Andrea Gabrieli brought out a collection of them in 1564. (A classical Greek text appears in a *"villanella greca"* in Wert's *Primo Libro delle Canzonette Vilanelle a cinque voci* of 1589. While this collection, of course, consists mostly of pieces with Italian text, it includes also three *villanelle francesi* and two *villanelle spagnuole*.[333]) Another class of regional piece was the Venetian *giustiniana*, usually representing three old men—not too old to be lustful—who stutter.[334]

The *villota*, with its street-song nucleus, still tends to use nonsense syllables, dancelike rhythmic patterns, and contrast of duple and triple meter. Azzaiolo's little song about the cricket, *Quando la sera*,[335] shows the three traits; the famous *Chi passa* (cf. pp. 691, 859) [335a] reveals two of them. *Villote*, too, appear with regional names: there are *villote alla paduana, alla veneziana,* etc.

The dancelike *balletto*, associated mainly with the name of Gastoldi, in its

[329] Further about the *tedesca*, see EngMV, 269.

[330] Further about this colorful figure, *see* EitQ, IX, 459; a *villanella* pr. EinIM III, 230. *See also* p. 691 *infra*.   [330a] A *napoletana* pr. VelA, Supp. IIa.

[330b] Pr. separately in *Ausgewählte Madrigale*, No. 47 (Breitkopf & Härtel), W. Barclay Squire, ed.; another piece pr. HolV, App., 10.

[331] Further on Ferretti, *see esp.* EinIM II, 593ff. Exx. by him pr. *ibid.* III, 234; ChilCP, 115; HolV, App., 4.

[331a] Cf. DartCL, 2.   [331b] EinIM II, 594.

[332] Exx. by him pr. KrV, 6; EinIM, III, 231 (cf. *ibid.* II, 583).

[333] Cf. VogelV II, 345. One of the *villanelle francesi* (*Un jour, je m'en allai*) is pr. separately in *Ausgewählte Madrigale*, No. 40 (Breitkopf & Härtel), W. Barclay Squire, ed.

[334] Further about these two forms, *see* EinGG; a *giustiniana* by A. Gabrieli pr. EinIM III, 177. This is a continuation of the older *giustiniana* (cf. p. 165) only in the sense that it is a burlesque of it.

[335] Pr. CorteS, 246; PistR, 44; AzzaiV, 21.

[335a] Pr. ChilJ, 90; BorLI, 117; AzzaiV, 4. Ten other Azzaiolo *villote* pr. AzzaiV (2 = PistR, 45, 46); another pr. EinIM III, 77. *See* further esp. VatV I, 23ff.

typical form is strophic and divided into two portions, each repeated and ending in a *fa-la-la* or similar refrain. It was to inspire the famous ballets of Thomas Morley. *Vezzosette ninfe belle* [336] illustrates the simplicity and regularity of construction of these pieces: the first section is made up rhythmically of the pattern, ♪ ♪ | ♩ ♩ ♩ ♩ | ♩ ♩, employed four times; the second uses the pattern ♩ | ♪ ♪ ♪ ♩ ♩ | ♩ ♩, twice literally, then elaborated. The *balletto,* being a dance form, presents a clear alternation of heavy and light beats. Such alternation, in fact, is common in the lighter forms generally. The following example is typical, with its lilting rhythm, regularity and clear definition of phrases, chordal construction, and general high spirits: [337]

EXAMPLE 108. Extract from *Lo schernito*—Gastoldi (from EinIM III, 246).

"If you see, my life, that I am languishing for your love, fa la . . ."

Of the light forms the *canzonetta,* sometimes called *"aria,"* was perhaps the most favored. This form avoided the crudities sometimes found in the *villanella* and was in effect a refinement of the latter or, perhaps better, a compromise between *villanella* and madrigal. The *canzonetta,* normally in the two-section repetition pattern and either *a 4* or *a 5,* is characterized by lightness of mood, clarity of texture, dance-like rhythm, a certain amount of word-painting (limited, of course, by the strophic form), and frequent use of simple figures of imitation.

Among *canzonetta* writers, Vecchi is outstanding. In his hands pieces of this type become more artistic than most *villanelle,* but are always in a light vein.[338] The pieces in Monteverdi's *canzonetta* collection of 1584 [339] are of high quality, and reveal complexities which, with respect to the *canzonetta*

---

[336] Pr. EinSH, 297.

[337] Further on Gastoldi's *balletti, see* esp. EinIM II, 602ff. Other *balletti* pr. GastB (15 items); EinIM III, 242; HAM, 179; WolfME, 105 (= TorA II, 103; BuH III, 231); BuH III, 232 (= WolfGM I, 92 [this became the chorale, *In dir ist Freude in allem Leide*]); PistR, 88 (= NefO, 116).

[338] *Canzonette* by him pr. EinIM III, 295 (2 items); TorA II, 253, 257, 259, 271; BartC, 91, 96; VelA, Supp. IV. ChilB V (7 *canzonette* from the *Selva;* an additional item from it on p. 20 [= ELAM III, 37], labeled *Aria,* is actually a *balletto;* a "capriccio" from it [*Margarita dai corai*] is pr. separately by Ricordi [V. Veneziani, ed.]).

[339] Pr. MontevO X, 2–24; IMAMI VI, 276ff; 3 also in KrV; 2 also in PistR.

generally, may be regarded as the equivalents of the intricacies found in his madrigals. Caimo's *canzonetta* print of the same year offers some examples [339a] of extraordinary charm. G. M. Nanino, also an elegant *canzonetta* writer, includes madrigalian melismas and occasional imitation in his *Primo Libro delle canzonette a tre voci* (1593).[340] Four *canzonette* in this book jointly set Petrarch's sonnet "Erano i capei d'or," one piece being provided for each quatrain and one for each tercet. The first of these is headed *"Aria di cantar sonnetti,"* the music being intended, like certain sonnet-settings of the *frottola* period (cf. p. 161), to serve in the rendition of any sonnets. At the very end is a *canzonetta* entitled *"Aria di cantar in ottava rima."*

There were some *canzonette* with religious texts. A collection of such pieces *a 3* and *a 4* (some in Latin, some in Italian) appeared at Rome in 1586 in two editions under the title *Diletto spirituale.* One edition was provided not only with the voice parts but with intabulation for lute and for *"cimbalo."* The other edition, purely vocal, was engraved by Martin van Buyten for Simone Verovio (who came from 's-Hertogenbosch and whose real name may have been Simon Werrewick), and the collection is the earliest known example of copperplate engraving applied to a music publication, although this method had been previously used for complete musical compositions reproduced within a few pictorial prints (cf. p. 517). The composers represented in the *Diletto* include Felice Anerio, Giovanelli, Marenzio, G. M. Nanino, Soriano, and Verovio himself.[341] Also in 1586 Verovio brought out the *Melodie spirituali* of Jacopo Peetrino (Jacob Pieters of Malines).[342] All the composers in the *Diletto* except Verovio are among those drawn upon in a purely secular *canzonetta* collection [343] printed by the same establishment in 1591. This, too, was provided with lute and *cembalo* intabulations, as were Verovio's *Ghirlanda di Fioretti Musicali* (1589) [344] and *Lodi della Musica a 3 voci* (1595).[345]

[339a] 2 of them pr. EinIM III, 237, 239.

[340] Pr. PV II; another *canzonetta* by him in BartC, 60.

[341] For description, *see* EinB, under 1586[10] and 1586[11]. For facsimile pages, *see* WolfH II, 256; PalW XXX, 1 and opp. 3; KinsP, 153. Three pieces by F. Anerio pr. KinO, 280, 281 (= AV II, 184); AV II, 186; 3 Palestrina exx. pr. PalW XXX, 3–5; 3 Giovanelli exx. pr. AV II, 187, 188, 190. The Verovio ex. pr. TebAP, 124; AV II, 194. About Verovio, *see* esp. CasSV.

[342] For an article on him, *see* DoorP; for a facsimile from the *Melodie,* KinsP, 153; 1 of the *Melodie* pr. StraM, VI, 518.

[343] Pr. WotC; individual pieces also in BartC, 82; PalW XXVIII, 137, 138 (= BruL I, 24); ELAM VIII, 18.

[344] Cf. EinB, under 1589[6]. Two Palestrina items pr. PalW XVIII, 135 (= DehnC, Supp. I), 136; exx. by Peetrino and Zucchelli in DehnC, Supp. III and II, respectively; 1 by Anerio pr. HAM, 181; another pr. TebAP, 124; 1 by Stabile pr. WeckC, 338.

[345] Cf. EinB, under 1595[3]. For other pieces in the light forms, *see* BartC, 48, 50, 52, 56, 58, 62, 68, 71, 74, 79, 82; PistR 3, 9, 47, 48, 86; KrV 3.

Chapter 9: SACRED VOCAL MUSIC OF THE LATE RENAISSANCE: Italian Composers, including Palestrina at Rome and the Gabrielis at Venice; French and Netherlandish Composers, including Goudimel in his Relation to the Genevan Psalter and Lassus at Antwerp

The Council of Trent

IN THE latter part of the 16th century, sacred music was profoundly influenced by the rising tide of Protestant thought and the far-reaching measures of the Counter-Reformation. The new Protestant attitudes resulted in a fresh corpus of music, and the Catholic repertory—especially in Italy and Spain—took on a new aspect in response to the Council of Trent's sweeping reforms and also to independently occurring changes in taste.

A generation before the Council met, Erasmus—commenting on a passage in I Corinthians, XIV, about intelligibility of speech in preaching—had voiced a feeling that was growing ever more widespread:

We have introduced an artificial and theatrical music into the church, a bawling and agitation of various voices, such as I believe had never been heard in the theatres of the Greeks and Romans. Horns, trumpets, pipes vie and sound along constantly with the voices. Amorous and lascivious melodies are heard such as elsewhere accompany only the dances of courtesans and clowns. The people run into the churches as if they were theatres, for the sake of the sensuous charm of the ear.[1]

The first concerted action, however, was taken by the Council of Trent (1545–1563), which considered, among other matters, the use of music in church, and by a Commission of Cardinals, which was appointed for further study of the problem and which sat in Rome (1564–1565).

The Council was held at Trent to satisfy the demand for a town of the Empire and yet have the meeting place be close to Rome to facilitate control by the pope. Indeed, the Italian prelates were constantly in the majority. The Council was convened to deal with abuses that were felt to have crept into various parts of the liturgy and only incidentally with music which, however, occupied a large portion of its attention for a little over a year. The final recommendations of the Council were negative rather than positive (thus

---

[1] Transl. from LeiE, 319. For the orig. Latin, *see* Desiderius Erasmus, *Opera Omnia*, VI (1705), col. 731 (at F).

contrasting with the Papal Encyclical of 1749 and the Motu Proprio of 1903, which made specific recommendations for improving church music). The Council of Trent simply forbade particular practices and insisted that certain results be obtained, without specifying the means. A committee of deputies on September 10, 1562, drew up a canon dealing with the music to be used at Mass.

All things should indeed be so ordered that the Masses, whether they be celebrated with or without singing, may reach tranquilly into the ears and hearts of those who hear them, when everything is executed clearly and at the right speed. In the case of those Masses which are celebrated with singing and with organ, let nothing profane be intermingled, but only hymns and divine praises. The whole plan of singing in musical modes should be constituted not to give empty pleasure to the ear, but in such a way that the words may be clearly understood by all, and thus the hearts of the listeners be drawn to the desire of heavenly harmonies, in the contemplation of the joys of the blessed. . . . They shall also banish from church all music that contains, whether in the singing or in the organ playing, things that are lascivious or impure.[2]

Approved four days later, this canon was sent to the entire body which, at the twenty-second general session (September 17), banned from church music all seductive or impure melodies, whether instrumental or vocal, all vain and worldly texts, all outcries and uproars, that "the House of God may in truth be called a House of prayer." Music came up again at the twenty-fourth general session (November 11, 1563). Two new cardinals who had been appointed in March, 1563, to fill vacancies caused by death—Giovanni Moroni, Bishop of Palestrina, and Bernardo Navagero—advocated monophonic music for the Mass and stronger prohibitions of "scandalous noises." At this new session, therefore, the whole question was reconsidered. The deliberations of the clerical body were transmitted to the lay deputies. One of the latter relayed the news to his sovereign, Emperor Ferdinand I, who, in turn, sent a letter to the cardinals warmly defending the retention of polyphonic music at Mass. As a result of this and other efforts toward the same goal, the Commission of Cardinals, consisting of Carlo Borromeo and Vitello Vitellozzo, was appointed to examine Masses written in the reformed manner and submitted to them at Rome for study. At the earlier sessions (1562) the frequent performances of Kerle's *Preces speciales pro salubri generalis concilii* had probably predisposed the delegates to look favorably on contrapuntal church music. Kerle, Palestrina, Animuccia, Lassus, and "Il Rosso" [2a] contributed to the investigation by composing contrapuntal Masses. Duke Albert V of Bavaria, who had just recently acquired Lassus as his *Kapellmeister* and who maintained the most brilliant musical establishment in Europe, exercised

---

[2] For the orig. Latin, *see* WeinK 3f; Augustin Theiner (ed.), *Acta genuina ss. Oecumenici Concilii Tridentini . . . ab Angelo Massarello . . . conscripta* (1874), II, 122.
[2a] Concerning this enigmatic figure, see MQ XLI, 385f.

considerable influence, as shown by extensive correspondence between him and Cardinal Vitellozzo, in bringing about the ultimate triumph of polyphonic music, pruned to accord with ecclesiastical and humanistic ideals.[3]

The final action of the Commission conformed with tendencies, already noted in Chapter 7, toward observing Latin accentuation and curtailing melismas purely on artistic and humanistic grounds, as, for example, in the "modern" style of Willaert, whose death (1562) occurred while the Council was in session. Both tendencies, naturally, helped to make for intelligibility of the text.

The Latin accentuation accorded with 16th-century rather than medieval principles, i.e., it regarded not merely the tonic accent but also the quantity of the syllables.[4] The Gregorian practice of normally setting the syllable with the tonic accent higher than the following syllable (and often higher than the preceding one),[5] but of not heeding quantity, seemed inadequate to the *cinquecento,* and the presence—far from rare in plainsong—of more notes on a short syllable than on a long one, seemed "barbarous" (cf. Zarlino's Rule 1 for underlaying words to polyphonic music, p. 378). Not comprehending the validity of the Gregorian principle, Late Renaissance musicians considered the plainsong MSS defective and sought to "correct" them—of which more will be said presently. The prestige of the Chant was in a state of decline.

The action taken by the Commission also coincided with other trends then current and associated with the decline of the Chant. The smaller churches —which had adhered to plainsong, since they were not equipped to execute the elaborate polyphonic Masses—preferred to discard the Chant and to emulate the larger churches so far as possible; they consequently called for Masses written as part-music, yet not too difficult. Moreover, even the greater churches did not put the elaborate and festive Masses to everyday use; having employed the Chant for such purposes, they wished for Masses that could be rendered with equal speed. In response to these two needs, there became common a shorter, simpler type of Mass that happened to conform to the requirements of the Commission—the *Missa brevis,*[6] as the Italians called it.

With the new disparaging attitude toward the Chant, the latter part of the century also saw, as might be expected, fewer plainsong renditions of the Proper and an increasing demand for polyphonic settings of it.[7] This attitude, it should be added, was not in the main directed against the Gregorian melodies as subjects for polyphonic setting, however critical it

---

[3] For a detailed study of the Council of Trent in its relation to music, *see* WeinK. *See also* LeiE and DTB XXVI, xliiff.

[4] About the treatment of the Latin accent in polyphony from Josquin on, *see* esp. PM VII, 37ff.

[5] Cf. Paolo Ferretti, *Estetica gregoriana* (1934), 16ff.

[6] Cf. WagG, 402f.   [7] Cf. WagG, 404, fn. 2.

may have been with respect to the treatment of accent. Some individual composers, to be sure, refrained from drawing upon plainsong to such an extent that one may conclude that they did not favor it; but many others did use it, with the offending "barbarisms" removed.

It has been implied that the Tridentine reforms affected Catholic music primarily in Italy and Spain and only secondarily in other Catholic regions. In France and the Low Countries, Mass composition had so declined that there was only limited occasion for the reforms to be heeded. Even had this not been so, the results in France would have been less readily evident, since, as we have seen in Chapter 7, the simpler style developed there in the first half of the century obviated the necessity for the cardinals' recommendation of greater intelligibility of the text. In Germany, especially, parody Masses continued to be based on compositions of the gayest sort. There are many instances in which the titles of the models are unhesitatingly given in the titles of the Masses. Possibly, however, some Masses are *sine nomine* or *sine titulo,* etc., to avoid calling undue attention to the presence of secular material.

The wishes of the Council and the Commission, if not in all respects fulfilled, yet influenced the sacred polyphony of every Catholic country to some extent, and are thus basic to a consideration of this music in the late 16th century. And, since it is Italy rather than the Franco-Netherlandish areas that reveals the effects of the reforms the more clearly, it is to the peninsula that we shall first direct our attention.

Kerle

Jacobus de Kerle (born in Ypres, c. 1532; died in Prague, 1591), whose *Preces speciales* has been mentioned, early went to Italy and in 1555 became *magister capellae* at the Cathedral of Orvieto (near Rome) and a few months later cathedral organist and town carillonneur. In 1558 his *Hymni totius anni* appeared at Rome, and in 1561 a set of Vesper Psalms and Magnificats at Venice which seem to anticipate the fully developed Roman polyphonic style.[8] In 1562, Kerle entered the service of Otto von Truchsess von Waldburg, Cardinal of Augsburg, then at Rome, whom he was eventually to accompany to Germany (cf. p. 698). The *Preces* (Venice, 1562),[9] commissioned by the cardinal, contains settings of ten Latin poems by Petrus de Soto, Professor of Theology at Dillingen. These works, devotional rather than liturgical, may have done much to influence the opinions of the Council regarding polyphonic music in the Church (cf. p. 449). Some historians,[9a] at any rate, feel that Kerle should share with Palestrina the title "saviour of church music" traditionally

[8] Cf. UrK, 183.
[9] Pr. in DTB XXVI, the preface of which includes full biographical data; English transl. of the orig. dedication is given in StrunkR, 355f. [9a] *See,* for example, LeiE, 320.

bestowed upon the latter composer as a result of his having written the *Missa Papae Marcelli* (cf. p. 480).

In each of the ten *Preces*, the main portion, which makes use of a corpus and three verses, is based on the familiar responsory pattern; a *Gloria Patri* and Kyrie appear at the end. The main portion of the third *Prex* has the form one would expect of a responsory with three verses: *aB-cBdBeB* (the letters before the hyphen jointly representing the corpus intact, in this pattern and in those that follow). In the other nine *Preces*, the refrain-like recurrences of parts of the corpus follow a slightly more intricate plan. In six, the pattern of the main portion is *aBCD-eBfCgD;* the following three patterns each occur once: *aBC-dBCeCfC, aBCD-eBCfBgC,* and *aBCD-eBCDfCgD* (the last appearances of *C* and *D* in this pattern being varied). The Netherlandish style of these pieces is combined with an Italian clarity and an avoidance of obtrusive details, with a sparing but effective use of such madrigalisms as tone-painting and chromaticism. The result is much closer to the lyric style of Palestrina than to the dramatic one that Lassus often employed in his church music.[10]

Also published in 1562 at Venice was a book of six Masses by Kerle, one a Requiem, another a *Missa de Beata Virgine,* based on the selection of Chant melodies normally followed by 16th-century composers—the same as Brumel had used, except that Sanctus XVII now replaced Sanctus IX—and incorporating the usual Marian tropes. After leaving Italy for the Empire, Kerle in 1582 issued this Mass again in a revision from which the tropes were removed.[11]

The Early Roman Background of Palestrina: the Laude; Animuccia

The Rome in which Kerle worked was deeply absorbed in furthering the Counter-Reformation. Active there was St. Philip Neri, who was responsible for the next important step in the history of the *laude spirituali* after the publication of the two Petrucci *lauda* collections of 1507–1508. Born in 1515 in Florence, Neri resided mainly at Rome, where he was ordained priest in 1551 and went to live with the priests of San Girolamo della Carità. In his room there he discussed ethical and other problems with his disciples. As his following grew, the room no longer sufficed as a meeting place. In 1554 he obtained from the deputies of San Girolamo a side of the church for the construction of an oratory in which to hold his discussions;[12] to these, sermons were added and then the singing of *laude spirituali.*

[10] *See* further DTB XXVI, preface; LeiE.

[11] The 6 Masses are pr. in MaldR XXII–XXVIII (1 also both in CasAP II, 207, and BordA, *Messes,* II, No. 12), the *Missa de Beata Virgine* being given in its earlier form.

[12] Most historians give 1558 as the date of the beginning of St. Philip's Oratory, this being the date of construction inscribed in the room itself, but there is evidence that the designation "oratory" (= "place of prayer"; for the technical meaning, *see* CE XI, 271) was assigned to a meeting place for orisons in the attics of the church in 1554, or the next year at the

Becoming also rector of San Giovanni dei Fiorentini in 1564, Neri, ten years later, transferred his exercises to the larger oratory there. The members of the community, however, resented being ousted to make room for the new-comers. Neri, therefore, tore down the small, dilapidated church of Santa Maria in Vallicella and on its site erected the Chiesa Nuova to answer the needs of his followers. With the authorization of Gregory XIII, he founded there, in 1575, the Congregation of secular priests called the Congregazione dell'Oratorio.[13]

Collections of *laude* sung by Neri's Congregation and by others appeared in print during his lifetime and continued to do so long after his death in 1595. Among the earliest of these was one (Venice, 1563) consisting of *laude* sung by Florentine groups and edited by Serafino Razzi, a Dominican friar. His *Libro Primo delle Laudi Spirituali* contains about seventy pieces for from one to four voices. Using texts from Petrarch, Savonarola, Lorenzo de' Medici, Feo Belcari, Lucrezia de' Medici, and others, Razzi had industriously evolved his *laude* from secular songs of the time. For example, he transformed *La pastorella si leva per tempo* into *Lo fraticello* [or, for nuns, *La verginella*] *si leva per tempo*.[14] Razzi was, of course, following a time-honored method. It was to remain in force: some *lauda* collections end with *tavole* which, for the benefit of those unable to read music but capable of singing a well-known tune, name the melodies after their original secular texts—folk or popular. (The contents of all known 16th-century collections, however, consist mainly or entirely of part-music settings.) In the dedication, Razzi states that the *laude* "are sung not only in monasteries and convents . . . but also at social gather-ings and in private homes."[15] He issued a further collection in 1609.

The same year as Razzi's first set appeared, 1563, another was published at Rome by the Florentine, Giovanni Animuccia (d. Rome, 1571).[16] The con-tents had been written for Neri's Congregation. Animuccia, besides serving as *maestro di cappella* at the Julian Chapel from 1555 on (succeeding Pale-strina in the post, after the latter's first tenure of it), became *maestro di cappella* of Neri's Oratory at San Girolamo in 1570. In that year, he issued his Book II of *laude,* which requires more highly trained singers than did the earlier collections. The book contains *"mottetti, salmi et altre diverse cose spirituali, vulgari et latine."* The dedication reads:

To the illustrious, excellent Abbot Podocataro, Gio. Animuccia. Some years have passed since, for the consolation of those who came to the Oratory of San Girolamo I brought out the Primo Libro delle Laudi, *in which I sought to pre-serve a certain simplicity that seemed fitting to the words themselves, to the nature*

---

latest. Cf. Louis Ponnelle and Louis Bordet, *S. Philip Neri and the Roman Society of His Times* (transl., 1932), 172.

[13] Cf. Ponnelle and Bordet, *op. cit.,* 310f; CE XI, 272; AlaS, 31ff.

[14] The pieces pr. with both secular and *lauda* texts, in AlaL, 33. Further discussion of *lauda* texts, *ibid.,* 14ff. For 6 other pieces from the 1563 collection, *see* DentL, 69ff.

[15] AlaL, 4. [16] For 2 of his *laude, see* ScherG, 119; DentL, 77.

of that place of prayer, and to my own aim, which was only to stimulate devotion. But the aforementioned Oratory having, by the grace of God, come to increase with the concourse of prelates and of chiefest men of quality, it has seemed to me also suitable in this Secondo Libro *to increase the harmony and the combinations of voices, varying the music in different ways, composing now to Latin words, now to words in the vernacular, both with many voices and with fewer, with rhyme of this kind or of that, committing myself as far as possible to an absence of canons and intricacies, so as not to obscure the meaning of the words, that with their effect, aided by the harmony, I might be able to penetrate more sweetly the heart of him who listens.*

The collection contains twenty-seven compositions with Latin text and eighteen *laude* for from two to eight voices.[17]

A third Roman book of *laude* was brought out in 1577 at the instance of the Fathers of the Congregazione dell'Oratorio, the music of which is in three parts throughout and, as indicated in the preface, is easier than that in the first two books "so that it can be sung by all." *Giù per la mala via,*[18] for example, is exceedingly simple, having a repeated rhythmic pattern, dictated by the accentuation of the text, and one chord to a syllable. This book was reprinted in 1583, with some alterations, to start a new series of five collections, edited by the Spaniard, Padre Francisco Soto de Langa (1539–1619), who had entered the Papal Choir as a singer in 1562 and still preserved his voice at the age of 80.[19] Also in 1583, Book II of that series was issued, containing twenty-eight three-part *laude* and nineteen *a 4;* four are from the 1577 book; six are in Spanish. Book III (1588) contains twenty-three three-part *laude* and twelve *a 4;* two are in Spanish. All three books were combined into one in a reprint of 1589, with some changes and additions, including a reduction to three voices of all pieces formerly for more. Two further collections by Soto followed in 1591 and 1598. Some of the melodies he used show the marks of a trained hand, others are folk tunes, of which many have been identified. Evidently, Soto had no objection to consecutive fifths.[20] In 1599, the last of the 16th-century *lauda* collections, the *Tempio armonico,* was produced by an ardent follower of Neri's, Padre Giovenale Ancina.[21]

Strangely enough, the *laude* seem never to have achieved the status of models for Masses, etc. There appears to have been no connection between them and music for actual liturgical use.[22]

Animuccia gained recognition as a composer not only of *laude* but of Masses. A collection appeared at Rome in 1567, containing four Masses *a 4,* one *a 5,* and one *a 6.* All are based on plainsong melodies and, to that extent,

[17] Cf. AlaS, 305f.   [18] Pr. *ibid.,* 88.   [19] Cf. *ibid.,* 58ff: Grove V, 82.
[20] For pieces in which such fifths are found, *see* AlaS, 89, 93.
[21] Cf. AlaS, 306ff. Typical exx. from the 1588, 1591, 1598, and 1599 collections are pr. *ibid.,* on pp. 89f, 90ff (1 with Latin text), 89 and 93ff, and 102ff respectively. Exx. in a more florid style, using imitation, etc., are given on p. 95ff, these being from the 1583, 1591, and 1598 collections.
[22] Cf. BesM, 291.

are in agreement with the Tridentine reforms. In his preface, Animuccia says that he has sought to escape the reproaches directed against those who obscure the text. But his music does not follow the syllabic, chordal style adopted, for example, in Ruffo's Masses of 1580 (cf. pp. 489f). In the Kyrie and Gloria [23] of Animuccia's four-part *Missa Conditor alme siderum,* his style is fairly ornate and makes considerable use of imitation. His paraphrasing of the hymn appears mainly in the highest voice and is especially well handled at the beginning of the Gloria. In the four-part *Missa Ave maris stella,*[24] the Gregorian melody is paraphrased with much freedom and imagination. At the beginning, it is sung, embellished, in free imitation by the tenor and superius. The other two voices open with a related melody, constructed so as to produce a touch of tonal imitation of the plainsong at the opening. After a few measures, they share in the singing of the decorated chant, fragments of which are frequently woven into the polyphony throughout this brilliant work, whose melismas and contrapuntal texture evidently reflect Franco-Netherlandish influence. In 1568, two *Missae de Beata Virgine* appeared from which the Marian tropes are omitted.[25] A *Magnificat Quinti Toni* (1568),[26] setting the odd-numbered verses, combines simple polyphony with brief chordal passages. Franco-Netherlandish texture, however, is evident not only in Animuccia's Masses but in such a little piece as the canon, *Sancta Maria,*[27] to a greater extent than one would expect in the work of a *lauda* composer.

Some historians have suggested [28]—though without direct documentary evidence—that after Animuccia's death in 1571, when Palestrina resumed the duties of *maestro di cappella* at the Julian Chapel, he also continued the work of Animuccia in Neri's Oratory.

Palestrina: Biography

Giovanni Pierluigi, who was to add the name of his native town—Palestrina—to his own surname, was born probably in 1524 or 1525. During the pontificate of Paul III, "Giannetto" was taken to Rome to study singing. A document of 1537 [29] lists him among the *pueri cantantes* of the Cappella Liberiana at Santa Maria Maggiore, but the date of his entry is unknown. Having begun his musical studies under the Frenchman, Robin Mallapert, choirmaster at the church in 1539, he may have continued them under

[23] Pr. TorA I, 159, 165, respectively. *See* comments in WagG, 420f.
[24] Pr. PV I.   [25] Cf. WagG, 421.   [26] Pr. TorA I, 149.
[27] Pr., with two resolutions, in LafE II, 103ff; for discussion, *see ibid.,* I, 372ff. For other music by Animuccia, *see* MartiniE I, 129, 181 (= ChorP V, *livraison 6,* 68, 97); AV VI, 39, 231; also fn. 16 *supra.* Further about him, *see* PirH, 289ff, MGG I, 483ff.
[28] Cf. CamP, 219f; CoatesP, 51.
[29] Pr. CasD, 33f; *see also* p. 8f. About another document bearing upon the year of birth, *see* CamN.

Firmin Le Bel, who became director in 1540 (cf. p. 364). It has been conjectured, however, that not Le Bel but Arcadelt became his master [30]—a possibility made all the more likely by striking stylistic resemblances in the music of the two men.

Palestrina was engaged, in 1544, as *"organista e cantore"* at the cathedral of his birthplace. The future Pope Julius III was then local bishop; during this period no doubt, he formed the high opinion of Palestrina that prompted him to call the musician to St. Peter's a few years later to direct the choir of the Julian Chapel.

While still at Palestrina the composer, in 1547, married Lucrezia Gori and with her received a considerable dowry. Two sons were born to them there —Rodolfo c. 1549 and Angelo c. 1551, shortly before the newly elected pope appointed Palestrina to the Julian Chapel. The composer was given the title of *maestro di cappella,* whereas his predecessors—such men as Arcadelt, Domenico Ferabosco, and Rosselli—were called merely masters of the boys.

Palestrina's Book I of Masses (1554) was dedicated to Julius III and opened with a Mass based on the Gregorian antiphon in commemoration of a pontiff-confessor, *Ecce sacerdos magnus.* At each entry of the subject, Palestrina had an engraving of Julius III's coat-of-arms inserted by the printer. To reward the composer, the pope appointed him a singer in the Pontifical Choir on January 13, 1555, although tradition says that his tenor voice was poor. The appointment was made, moreover, without either an examination by the other singers or their consent, both of which were normally considered necessary. The pope, however, who wished to obtain new works for the choir, was not exceeding his prerogative. Although Palestrina was later to assume the duties of composer to the Papal Chapel, there is no record of his official appointment to that position in the archives.[31] Upon accession to his official new post of singer, Palestrina relinquished his old one of *maestro* at the Julian Chapel, where, as already noted, he was followed by Animuccia.

On March 23, Julius died. His successor, Marcellus II, during a pontificate cut short by death after only three weeks, announced his intention of making reforms in church discipline and worship; he was much concerned, according to the notes of the papal secretary, that "the Passion and Death of the Saviour . . . be sung in a suitable manner, with properly modulated voices, . . . so that everything could be both heard and understood properly." [32]

Marcellus' successor, Paul IV, continued the reform work. He issued a *motu proprio* which, among other things, excluded married members from the Pontifical Choir. The three married members—Leonardo Barré, Domenico

---

[30] *See* Grove IV, 16f. Regarding the possibility that he studied with Rosselli (Roussel), *see* CasD, 7.
[31] *See* CamP, 104; TorG, 498; cf. also p. 426 *supra.*
[32] Transl. from CoatesP, 41.

Ferabosco, and Palestrina—were dismissed and were given a pension of six scudi a month. Palestrina's publication, in 1555, of his Book I of madrigals *a 4*, in the title of which he described himself as a singer in the Papal Chapel, was probably regarded as a further offence, for the pope had also objected to the publication of secular works by papal singers.

Lassus, who had been serving as *maestro di cappella* at St. John Lateran, left the post in 1554,[33] and about a year later Palestrina assumed it, his pension from the Pontifical Choir, however, being continued. But the years at the Lateran proved difficult; music here was affected by general economic conditions, the choir being limited in number, the salaries poor. Palestrina's period of employment, during which his third son Iginio was born (c. 1557), ended in 1560, the deliberations of a commission of canons, organized to reduce expenses, prompting his decision to leave.

In 1561, the former choirboy was appointed *maestro* of the Cappella Liberiana at Santa Maria Maggiore. His pension from the Pontifical Choir being endangered the same year by the addition of a new member, he forthwith wrote some works for the choir and secured the continuance of his pension and even its increase. The composer seems always to have maintained a satisfactory financial status, contrary to the romantic assertions of his earliest important biographer, Baini. While director of the Cappella Liberiana, Palestrina held for three months, in 1564, the post of *maestro* of the concerts given in the villa of his patron, Cardinal Ippolito d'Este at Tivoli. Then, abandoning both positions, he became, c. 1566, the first master of music in the Roman Seminary—recently founded as the result of a decision reached by the Council of Trent in 1563—in which the students were taught not only literary and ecclesiastical subjects but also music, especially Gregorian Chant.

Resuming his duties at the Villa d'Este in August, 1567, Palestrina was considered for the post of music director at Maximilian II's court in Vienna; but he demanded such a high salary that in May, 1568, Philippe de Monte was engaged instead. The year 1568 marks also both the fulfilment of a commission, from Duke Guglielmo Gonzaga of Mantua, for a Mass to be used at Santa Barbara and, as a result, the beginning of a long-lasting association between the two men. The duke was an amateur composer as well as a patron of music, and correspondence shows that he sent works of his own to Palestrina for criticism—a madrigal and a motet in 1570, a Mass in 1574.[34]

After a five-year absence from church posts, Palestrina, in 1571, regained the directorship of the Julian Chapel upon Animuccia's death and went to live near St. Peter's at the corner of a lane later known simply as "del Pelestrino".[35] Here he remained until his death.

[33] Cf. CasL.

[34] For 12 letters from Palestrina to the Duke, *see* BertolM, 47ff (German transl. of some in HabA, 35ff). *See also* CanM, 684ff; JepU. For the Kyrie I of a Mass by the duke, *see* CesB, 126.

[35] For a special article on Palestrina's homes in Rome, *see* CamC.

Between 1572 and 1580 an epidemic killed Palestrina's sons Rodolfo and Angelo, his brother Silla, and finally his wife. The composer had entertained high hopes for his sons, and had included works by them and by Silla in his motet book of 1572, dedicated to the Duke of Mantua; as a result, the duke had promised the post of organist at Santa Barbara to Rodolfo.[36] A decline in Palestrina's production is probably due to the deaths; while some music is attributable to this period, he published nothing from 1575 to 1581.

In 1577, Gregory XIII commissioned Palestrina and Annibale Zoilo[37] to examine the chant-books issued after publication of the Breviary and Missal ordered by the Council of Trent and to cleanse the plainsong of barbarisms and other defects accumulated through the mistakes of "composers, scribes, and printers."[38] Palestrina and Zoilo set out to fulfill their task, but never completed it. Years later, Palestrina's only surviving son, Iginio, attempting to obtain the money promised to his father, had the revision finished by other hands and offered the result as entirely genuine. Despite years of bickering, however, his ruse failed and the Graduale was rejected.[39]

After his wife's death, Palestrina thought of becoming a priest, and asked admission into the Minor Orders. However, he presently met Virginia Dormoli and married her hardly seven months after the death of Lucrezia. Virginia was the widow of a wealthy fur merchant who had become "furrier to the Pope" shortly after the election of Gregory XIII. The marriage made Palestrina the owner, among other things, of a fur shop with ermines, minks, and sables. He took another man into partnership and, later, his wife also. The profits were invested in the purchase of building lots.[40]

Artistic productivity returned. From 1581 to his death in 1594, Palestrina published four books of Masses, three each of motets and madrigals (two of the latter being devoted to *madrigali spirituali*), two each of offertories and litanies, and one each of hymns and Magnificats.

In 1583, the composer had another opportunity to leave Rome, this time to become musical director in the court of his patron, the Duke of Mantua. But again he requested too high a sum. Perhaps his exorbitant demands were prompted in part by a disinclination to quit the Eternal City. At any rate, he did not show himself to be mercenary when, shortly before his death, he planned to resume his modest early post at the cathedral of his birthplace.[41]

---

[36] Further about Palestrina's sons, *see* esp. CamPA.

[37] The composer of Masses, etc. 8 exx. are pr. in ProsM, *Annus I, IV.*

[38] An English transl. of the pope's brief is given in StrunkR, 358f.

[39] For full details about post-Tridentine reforms of the Chant, including the facts regarding Palestrina's commission, *see* MolT. A revised edition—the *Editio Medicaea*—not chargeable to Palestrina, finally appeared in 1614 (now superseded). This was prepared entirely or mainly by Felice Anerio and Soriano.

[40] Further about the fur business, *see* CamPC.

[41] Cf. CasMP. Biographical studies on Palestrina are numerous. *See* the bibliography in FellP, 183ff.

Palestrina's Historical Position; General Comments on His Style

The position of Palestrina in the history of music is in some ways anomalous. His sacred works have long been regarded as representing the ideal application of polyphony to music for the Catholic Church. Nevertheless, a slightly derogatory attitude has taken form in some quarters during the 20th century, as a reaction against romanticization of the composer in the 19th century, when he was often looked upon as a lonely figure without a flaw. The more recent view has replaced overevaluation with underevaluation. Actually, Palestrina, in his church music, reveals himself as one of the three greatest composers of the twilight period in Renaissance music, the other two being Lassus and Byrd. If Josquin is historically a greater composer, that is due not only to his extraordinary intrinsic genius but to his good fortune in having lived when Renaissance music was at its high noon. The spiritual quality of Palestrina's sacred compositions, even when they are based on secular prototypes, is not to be denied; his technical proficiency is such as to make the old legend of flawlessness almost credible.

Palestrina has sometimes been considered as too conservative for his period. It is correct to look upon him as in some ways a conservative, but not on the grounds usually advanced. In certain aspects of detail his technique was "modern"; in the larger aspects, it was conservative. Palestrina came to be viewed as the typical figure of his time to such an extent that his style has been the ostensible basis of the study of strict counterpoint at least since the time of J. J. Fux (d. 1749). As a result, those who proceed from a theoretical study of counterpoint to an actual examination of the music (i.e., those who place the cart before the horse, as happens too often in this field) find, in the music, what their training has led them to believe orthodox. Actually, Palestrina represents the last stage in the development of a style that systematized the handling of dissonance and the use of certain time-values in particular rhythmic contexts. That style, even if it avoided chromaticism, was one of the up-to-date modes of writing in its time. Dissonance treatment regarded as bold, such as is found, for example, in English Tudor music, is not so much actually daring as it is archaic; the older Franco-Netherlanders had written in much the same vein. Whether one manner of writing is better than another is, of course, irrelevant here; the point is that, in detail-technique, Palestrina's style should not be looked upon as actually reactionary in its day.

On the other hand, in some ways Palestrina ignores the "modern" manner of Willaert—though in certain ways the inescapable influence of Willaert (perhaps indirect) is evident. Of Palestrina's 105 surviving Masses, not one is known to be based on a work by the great Venetian—or on Gombert or on Clemens non Papa. Gombert's absorption in almost unrelieved polyphony was as foreign to Palestrina's nature as was the quasi-dramatic, declamatory quality of the Venetian "modern" style. Palestrina sought in all things perfect balance.

Reacting against the unbridled dynamism and the stress on polyphonic technique of the generation before, he resumed the Josquin style of 1500 with its predilection for symmetrical structure and quiet harmonies and gave it an austere serenity almost unique in post-medieval Christian art.[42]

What has been referred to as Palestrina's "detail-technique" has been handled in such exemplary fashion by Knud Jeppesen in *The Style of Palestrina and the Dissonance,* that there is no need to examine it in full at this point. Some aspects of dissonance treatment, however, will be mentioned here, while a few other phases of detail-technique will receive incidental attention in the discussion of individual works.

Palestrina, especially if compared with his Franco-Netherlandish predecessors and his successors, e.g., Monteverdi, applied dissonance as a technical device and as a means of emotional expression very circumspectly. Indeed, his use of it in the latter way is so rare that it may be dismissed. The following may be regarded as principles of prime importance in Palestrina's method of treating dissonance:

(1) The rules governing dissonance are not abstract, but are bound up with the practical consideration of time-values; the longer these are, the more careful the treatment. The dissonant note is never greater than a minim (the basic time-value) or preceded by a note of smaller value than itself. (References here are to original time-values which, the reader is reminded, are normally halved in the 16th-century examples in this book.) In a group of four minim beats, the first being at the beginning of a measure, the first and third must (unless a suspension is present) always be consonant. Quarter-notes are treated more freely; thus, in a descending group of four quarter-notes, the third, or the second and third, may be dissonances.

(2) With the longer values, Palestrina avoids dissonance in note-against-note writing, therefore at times altering notes in imitative entries. But he sometimes uses dissonance in such writing in quarter-note movement, each of the two clashing notes, however (which must appear in upper voices), being consonant with the bass. Josquin, and others, on the contrary, taking far more liberty, employed half-note dissonance in note-against-note writing, thus producing a greater amount of harmonic asperity than does Palestrina.

(3) Dissonances arise from melodic ornamental figures such as (a) the one employing a single auxiliary note, this being found almost exclusively in quarter-note or eighth-note figures and being more often a lower auxiliary; (b) the anticipation (= *portamento*), used by Palestrina only in conjunct

[42] SachsCA, 126.

descent, but by his predecessors both ascending and descending, by leaps of thirds and fifths as well as by seconds; (c) the *nota cambiata;* [43] etc.

(4) Palestrina prepares suspensions carefully, by introducing, on an unaccented beat and as a consonance, the note which, remaining stationary, is to become dissonant on the following accented beat, this in turn being succeeded by a resolution on a consonance reached by conjunct descent. By Dufay, Josquin, Arcadelt, and Clemens non Papa, however, the note that was to become a suspension, was sometimes introduced as a dissonance in the first place (cf. pp. 322, 355).

(5) Normally the fourth from the bass is regarded as a dissonance.[44]

In view of the strict regulation in Palestrina style of what may or may not be done on the first and third beats or on the second and fourth, one tends to feel that those investigators take an exaggerated position who claim that there was no regular accentuation in Renaissance polyphony. Although stresses may not have been as heavy in this period as later, there would have been no point in confining suspensions, for example, to the first and third beats in binary rhythm or to the first and second beats in ternary rhythm, etc., if there had been no such underlying accentuation. Certainly, the idea of regularly recurring accents had not been unknown to early medieval polyphony since, without such accents, there would have been no difference between the first and second rhythmic modes or between the third and fourth rhythmic modes, except one of presence or absence of up-beat.[44a] Moreover, it is conceded generally that recurrent accent did exist in Renaissance dance music. It would perhaps be closer to the truth to say that Renaissance polyphony was much more elastic in the regular recurrence of its accent than was the music of the baroque, classic, and romantic periods, but that this elasticity was made manifest with reference to a prevalent meter. The elasticity could result in two ways: (1) the composer could change the actual meter, through the sense of the music itself, without changing the time-signatures, as Obrecht did when he introduced quintuple meter by means of sequence patterns in the *Qui tollis* of his *Missa Je ne demande;* or, (2) as we have frequently pointed out, by an accent-producing long or high note at a normally unaccented point in the measure, thus causing a momentary conflict between the macrorhythm and microrhythm. In fact, there could be no such conflict in the absence of a marcrorhythm with regularly recurring accentuation.

Granted that Palestrina's Masses are, as a group, his greatest contribution, some of his finest compositions are nevertheless found among his motets and related works. We can easily recognize—in the clarity of the individual parts and the tendency toward note-against-note setting—the application of the

[43] About the 3 *cambiata* configurations standard with Palestrina, *see* JepPS, 211f. Cf. also p. 75 *supra.*
[44] About the exceptions, including the "relatively consonant" six-four, *see* JepPS, 232ff.
[44a] Cf. ReMMA, 272ff.

common-sense principles, enunciated by Palestrina in a letter to the Duke of Mantua,[45] that the music should "give a living spirit to the words" and, as desired by Marcellus II, that these words be heard and understood. Palestrina realized that his music was to be illustrative of the text, and not a demonstration of his ingenuity, though this might be present in abundance if not unduly conspicuous. Palestrina wrote whole books devoted to various sections of the service, occasioned at least in part, it would seem, by the requirements or needs of the church choir with which he happened at the time to be connected. His output embraces over 250 motets including settings of texts from the Song of Solomon, 68 Offertories, 45 hymns, at least 13 complete sets of Lamentations, 35 Magnificats, 20 psalms, 12 Litanies, *Improperia,* and other pieces.

Palestrina: Motets, etc.

Many motets are constructed on the familiar *aBcB* pattern. These include: *a 6,* the motets *Assumpta est Maria* (which opens with a paraphrase of the plainsong antiphon), *Tu es Petrus* (which bears no relation, in musical content or form, to the powerful setting *a 7*), *Tribularer si nescirem* (based on Josquin's *Miserere*), *Sancta et immaculata virginitas* (with different canons *a 2* in each of the two *partes*), and *Beata Barbara* (*B* is the final eight-measure cadence in each of the two *partes*); *a 5,* the motets *Fuit homo* (*B* is twice as long as either *a* or *c*), *Canite tuba,* and *Ascendo ad Patrem meum* (some of *B* is anticipated in the first *alleluia* passage).[46]

In the five-part *Corona aurea,*[47] the appearance of the passage on *expressa signo,* etc., in both *partes,* gives the motet an *aBcdBe* pattern. A varied refrain is met with in the five-part *Alleluia, tulerunt Dominum,*[48] in which, though the form is *AbAcAdAeA,* the *A* (the word *alleluia* with its music) is never twice quite the same.

The masterly four-part *Sicut cervus* demonstrates most clearly the famous Palestrina curve, which may be briefly defined as a gradual rise in the melodic line followed by a fall that balances it with almost mathematical exactness.

EXAMPLE 109. Opening of superius of *Sicut cervus*—Palestrina (complete piece in PalW V, 148; PalO XI, 42).

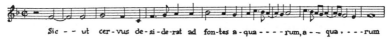

Sic - - ut cer-vus de-si-de-rat ad fon-tes a-qua - - - - rum,a - ~ qua . - - - rum

"As the hart panteth after the water brooks . . ." (Psalm XLI [42], 1)

---

[45] *See* BertolM, 49.

[46] These 8 motets pr. in PalW VI, 28; II, 121, 81, 109, 101; III, 39; II, 43, 33 (the last 7 also, respectively, in PalO VII, 162, 107, 146, 35; III, 46; VII, 56, 42). Other exx. in PalW II, 88; III, 9, 18 (= respectively, PalO VII, 117; VIII, 18, 23); IV, 121.

[47] PalW II, 12; PalO VII, 13.　　[48] PalW I, 30; PalO V, 35.

The bass of a four-part *Alma Redemptoris Mater*,[49] at *quae per via*, rises from f to f′ and takes about the same number of notes to return.[50]

Although most Palestrina motet themes are freely invented, some derive from plainsong. The *Alma Redemptoris Mater,* just mentioned, paraphrases the familiar antiphon, as do two settings,[51] *a 8*, for double choir. In one, the two choirs unite occasionally to produce eight-part writing; in the other, however, the combination of choirs finds the voices of the same register singing in unison, as happens in much English music written for the *decani* and *cantoris* sides of the choir (cf. p. 799). In the latter *Alma*, the paraphrasing consists mainly in retaining essential melodic leaps, as reminders of the plainsong, on which the composition is actually a free fantasy. Palestrina's various treatments of the *Salve Regina* supply further examples of his plainsong paraphrases.

With these might be included some of the settings of the great sequences. The two settings of *Veni Sancte Spiritus* (both *a 8*) differ sharply from each other. In one, in ternary rhythm,[52] the paired versicles have the same music; in the other, mostly in binary rhythm,[53] the variation-chain technique is applied with remarkable felicity. The three *Lauda Sion* settings [54]—none textually complete; two *a 8*, one *a 4*—follow the sequence melody closely, though not slavishly. In the piece *a 4*, which treats only versicles 1, 2, and 23, the music for 2 is a variation of that for 1, the two lower voices in the latter part of this variation presenting in double counterpoint the melodies they had sung in the corresponding part of 1. In one setting *a 8*, the paired versicles are musically the same almost throughout; in the other, the even-numbered versicles differ from their predecessors sharply. Of the four *Victimae paschali* settings (all *a 8*), only one,[55] which survives incomplete, draws considerably on the familiar chant. Another [56] has suggestions of the plainsong for the openings of verses 1 and 2 in the altus and cantus II respectively, but not elsewhere; no attempt to preserve the sequence form is evident, beyond the introduction of strong cadences at verse endings. The remaining two settings [57] have thematic material in common, but do not draw on the standard melody; perhaps they are based on a different common source, rather than one on the other. Here, too, sequence form is absent. Palestrina's celebrated, but somewhat overrated, *Stabat Mater* [58] shows no signs of sequence structure. This strongly chordal work attains a high degree of rhythmical elasticity

---

[49] PalW V, 156; PalO XI, 52.
[50] For other exx. of the curve, *see* the motets pr. in PalW V, 41, 60 (= PalO III, 49, 74, respectively). Other aspects of thematic construction in Palestrina's motet writing are discussed in RaheT.
[51] PalW VI, 159; VII, 73.
[52] PalW VII, 117.
[53] PalW III, 143.
[54] PalW III, 138 (= PalO VIII, 180); VII, 91; V, 36 (= PalO III, 42).
[55] PalW XXXII, 180; cf. viii.
[56] PalW VII, 105. [57] PalW VII, 112, 194.
[58] PalW VI, 96 (Richard Wagner issued an ed. replete with Wagnerian nuances).

through its mingling of groups of different metrical character, producing interesting conflicts between the microrhythm and macrorhythm.[59]

Palestrina's four settings of the *Ave Regina* [60] all paraphrase, in varying degrees, the somewhat sequence-like plainsong. In two, the even-numbered verses of the two double pairs vary the music of the odd-numbered verses; in the other two, variation is present only in the opening pair.

The standard procedure of having each text unit generate its own musical complement, usually employing imitation technique, frequently results, in Palestrina, in a form somewhat resembling a sequence: points of imitation (or, more rarely, chordal sections) are often immediately repeated, subtle variations being at times introduced. This procedure is exemplified in *Nos autem gloriari*,[61] which is in modified *AABBCCDD* form. In *Veni sponsa Christi*,[62] which is among the best of the early motets, the form is *AABB'CC'DD'*, sections *B'*, *C'*, and *D'* being upward transpositions of *B*, *C*, and *D*, the changes in *tessitura* in the repetitions adding an antiphonal effect to the piece. To this group belongs *Super flumina Babylonis*,[63] a masterpiece among Palestrina's shorter works, which has the design *aBB'CC'C"DD'EE'*. For all its succinctness, this setting of Psalm CXXXVI (137) vividly expresses the sadness of the Hebrew exiles.

A number of Palestrina motets apply the canonic devices more popular with an earlier generation of composers. Among these works are the six-part *Cum ortus fuerit* and *Columna es immobilis*,[64] in which the canon at the fifth, sung by two voices, is anticipated by the remaining four. *Accepit Jesus calicem* [65]—which, since it is depicted in the composer's hand in a Vatican portrait, was presumably a favorite of his—is a canon *a 3*, though not absolutely strict, with three additional free parts.

Of word-painting, the motets afford many examples: e.g. in one of the best early motets *a 4*, *Dies sanctificatus*,[66] the word *descendit* is set to a falling fifth; in the outstanding five-part *Peccantem me quotidie,* the change from the major form of a triad to its minor form at *timor mortis* is—in a texture as free from this sort of thing as Palestrina's—strikingly expressive of the fear of death; [67] in *Innocentes pro Christo*,[68] the little phrase on *ipso sequuntur* is canonically repeated eight times in five measures by the four voices. Of the seven motets beginning with some form of the word *"surgere,"*

---

[59] *See* the ed. of A. Schering (Eulenburg score, choral ser., No. 16).

[60] PalW III, 150; IV, 146 [*pars II,* 149]; V, 152 (= respectively, PalO VIII, 95; XII, 80 [*pars II,* 84]; XI, 46); VII, 124.

[61] PalW V, 66; PalO III, 82.   [62] PalW V, 105; PalO III, 132.

[63] PalW V, 125; PalO XI, 14; cf. FellP, 120ff.

[64] PalW III, 107, 116; PalO VIII, 140, 151.

[65] PalW III, 123; PalO VIII, 160.   [66] PalW V, 3; PalO VIII, 160.

[67] Degree-inflection, however, is not actually present, since there is a rest between the two chords. The motet is pr. in PalW II, 73, and in PalO VII, 98.

[68] PalW VII, 56.

all open with a conjunct or disjunct ascent of a fifth—except one,[69] which has an ascending leap of a fourth in the first and third voices to enter, answered, in the second and fourth voices to enter, by an ascending leap of a fifth. This composition, the four-part *Surge propera,* bears some resemblance here and there to the popular *Vestiva i colli* (cf. p. 403), but is not an adaptation of it. (Concerning an adaptation *a 5*—also a *Surge propera*—not by Palestrina himself, *see* p. 490.) In another motet, however, *Quam pulchri sunt gressus,* Palestrina does adapt material from a pre-existent work, the *Quam pulchra es* of J. Lupi.[70] The opening words of the *Quam pulchra* text occur in the course of the *Quam pulchri* text, and it is at this point that the paraphrase, appropriately, takes place. In Palestrina's five-part *Jubilate Deo omnis terra,*[71] the word *"exultatione"* is provided with ornate melismas. His *Exultate Deo*[72] underscores descriptively the names of instruments—*tympanum, psalterium, cythara, tuba,* and *buccina* (included in the imperative, *buccinate*). This joyous psalm setting is written with brilliant virtuosity.

The kind of ornamentation added by Bassano to *Vestiva i colli,* etc. (cf. pp. 394, 403), is applied by him also to several Palestrina motets.[73]

In 1584, Palestrina issued his Book IV of motets *a 5,* comprising twenty-nine pieces on verses from the Song of Solomon.[74] Though undoubtedly accepting the Church's allegorical interpretation of the text, he reveals more intensity here than usual, e.g., in *Vulnerasti, Introduxit me rex, Vox dilecti mei,* and *Veni, veni dilecte mi*—all of which illustrate Palestrina's customary skill in vocal "orchestration." Madrigalisms abound in Book IV—three of the above-mentioned examples of the word *"surgere"* occur in it. In *Vox dilecti mei,* the text *"saliens in montibus"* is underscored by leaps, including the leap of an octave (the widest one used in Palestrina style), and by high notes on the last word. A trait typical of Palestrina's fugal openings is strikingly illustrated by this set: rarely does he allow the highest voice to be the last one to enter. It is as though he wished to avoid the piling up of such a climactic effect as might result from having the top voice enter last. In spite of the nature of the texts in this set, Palestrina departs from his normal procedure only once (in No. 8).

The 68 Offertories[75] for the whole year, all *a 5,* issued in two books in 1593, are of historical importance. These works and the Offertories of Lassus are the first ones known to have been written in free motet style; the few earlier polyphonic examples (such as those in the Propers of the Trent

---

[69] PalW V, 47; PalO III, 57. For the other 6, *see* PalW III, 134; IV, 41, 44, 50, 130, 159 (= respectively, PalO VIII, 174; XI, 142, 146, 154; XII, 58, 100).
[70] For Palestrina's motet, *see* PalW V, 83; PalO III, 104; about Lupi's, *see* Chap. 7, fn. 32c. Lupi's work must have been a favorite of the Roman composer; cf. Mass 42 in the table on p. 471.
[71] PalW III, 69; PalO VIII, 208.   [72] PalW IV, 151; PalO XII, 88.
[73] Cf. PalW XXXIII, 45–59; BrenP, 126–8; FellP, 162f.
[74] PalW IV, 3–83; PalO XI, 89–200.   [75] PalW IX, PalO, XVII.

Codices) are settings of plainsong melodies. Palestrina's Offertories are mostly unadorned settings, with here and there a melisma or an ascending octave run. In *Si ambulavero*, at *extendes manum tuam*, etc., several octave leaps followed by the gradual descent of the superius effectively suggest God's hand extended down to earth.

EXAMPLE 110. Extract from Palestrina—*Si ambulavero* (after PalW, IX, 150).

". . . thou shalt stretch forth thine hand. . . ." (Psalm CXXXVII [138], 7)

The Offertories are rich in felicitous touches of many kinds. The note-group E-F-E, used in various ways, permeates so much of *Illumina oculos meos* that the work gives the impression of being evolved through the developmental technique usually associated by us with later periods. Several Offertories illustrate Palestrina's skill in handling varied repetition, e.g., in *Scapulis suis,* the form of which is *AA'bCC'C''*, the *C*'s are actually variants of *A,* so that the basic form is really *aba'*. The neatly varied repetition of the setting of *"ritribue servo"* in *Confitebor tibi* involves the presentation, at a time-interval of one measure, of two melodic fragments which, in their first presentation, had appeared simultaneously.[76] In *Bonum est,* the use of high notes at the two occurrences of *"altissime,"* though obvious in principle, is carried out with much charm. The setting of the words *"Domine, clamavi,"* in *Exaltabo te* is also uncommonly effective. Conflict of accents is handled deftly in *Laudate Dominum* (at *"psallite nomine"*) and *Improperium expectavit* (e.g., at meas. 14).

In the Offertories, as elsewhere, Palestrina differentiates himself from earlier masters such as Josquin (cf. p. 259) by his easily discernible sensitivity to tonality. For example, if one combines the initial notes sung by the various parts in an opening point of imitation, one will find that they normally form the final chord of the work (e.g., in *Laudate Dominum* and *Exaltabo te*) or its subdominant (*Jubilate Deo* and *Bonum est*) or its dominant (*In*

---

[76] For other Offertories that show Palestrina's skill in varying repetition, *see* PalW IX, 87, 164, 170 (= PalO XVII, 87, 164, 170, respectively).

te speravi and *Domine Deus*).[76a] A strong feeling for harmony, moreover, is evident in other ways throughout Palestrina's work: e.g., in a point of imi-tation, upon the third entry, the melody is sometimes slightly changed in one of the voices to produce a full triad;[77] and themes are at times based on broken chords. He is not, however, led by his predilection for full chords and chordal themes to go as far as does, for example, his younger contem-porary Victoria in the direction of major–minor tonality; the chords that he selects in a given piece hold close to those that belong to the mode in which he is writing.[78]

The forty-five *Hymni totius anni* [79] follow the common, but not invariable, 16th-century practice of providing each melody with different settings for the odd-numbered stanzas, the others—and also the incipit of stanza 1—re-maining unset, to be sung in plainsong. All forty-five begin *a 4*, but the number of voices (three to six) often varies in a single hymn, from one polyphonically treated stanza to another. The plainsong is usually para-phrased in the highest voice, but not always, and, though imitation is fairly frequent, canons are generally reserved for stanzas with the greater number of parts. Thus there are canons at the fifth in the final stanzas (*a 6*) of *Conditor alme siderum* and *Hostis Herodes impie*, at the lower octave in the final stanza (*a 5*) of *Deitatis aures*, and at the fourth below in the final stanza (*a 5*) of *Ut queant laxis*. Note-against-note writing, however, is also frequent, an extreme case occurring in the final stanza (*a 4*) of *Deus tuorum militum*, which is especially chordal, except at the middle and final ca-dences.

The Litanies [80] come to us in MSS, preserving shorter examples, and in two printed books, each containing one long work. The Litany of Book I has five *partes*, the form being $Ab\overparen{CAd}C\overparen{AdCAf}CAgC$. The Litany of Book II,

---

[76a] Further about the Offertories, *see* LippP, 55ff.

[77] Cf. JepPS, 88f.   [78] Cf. MayV, 135.

[79] PalW VIII; PalO XIV. CasC, App., includes different settings of strophes 1 and 3 of *Tibi Christe splendor Patris* and settings for the following strophes not provided with music in PalW and PalO: strophes 2 and 4 of *Conditor alme siderum* and *Hostis Herodes impie* and strophes 2, 4, and 6 of *Christe Redemptor . . . Ex Patre*. Like Dufay (cf. Chap. 2, fn. 238), Palestrina com-bines several melodies with texts somewhat or entirely different from those with which they are now associated in the Liber. Thus, he has the same text-melody combinations as Dufay for *Ad coenam Agni providi, Aurea luce, Christe Redemptor . . . Conserva, Christe Redemptor . . . Ex Patre, Conditor alme siderum, Hostis Herodes, Jesu nostra redemptio, O lux beata Trinitas,* and *Ut queant laxis.* Unlike Dufay, he uses for the *Sanctorum meritis* and *Iste confessor* texts the melodies that they have in the Liber; *see* Liber 1159, 1177. In several instances he combines texts and melo-dies otherwise than either Dufay or the Liber. Thus, melodically, his *Deus tuorum militum* (No. 28), *Jesu corona virginum* (No. 33), *Rex gloriose martyrum* and *Tristes erant apostoli* = the first *Nunc Sancte nobis Spiritus* in Liber, 808 (or *Aurora lucis rutilat* in AntiphonaleM, 455, or *Aurora coelum* in Antiphonale, 385; note that this is the same melody that Palestrina—and Dufay—used for *Ad coenam Agni;* about the *Tristes* text in relation to the greater text of which it is a part, cf. p. 604); *Doctor egregie* = *Egregie Doctor Paule* (Liber, 1349); *Exultet coelum laudibus* = *Ex-sultet orbis gaudiis* (Liber, 1115); *Jesu corona virginum* (No. 32) = the first *Fortem virili pectore* in Liber, 1234; *Quod cumque vinclis* = *Quod cumque in orbe* (Liber, 1334).

[80] PalW XXVI.

identical in structure except that *A* may be further subdivided into *abb,* is scored for ATTB with an indication that the altus may be omitted.

The various settings of the Lamentations [81] follow the standard tradition, presenting soaring, melismatic settings for the naming of the Hebrew letters and less elaborate music for the Latin text.

EXAMPLE 111. Melisma from the *Lamentations* for Holy Saturday (*Book III*)—Palestrina (after PalW XXV, 139; PalO XIII, 160).

A soaring melisma in Palestrina, however, does not have the wide expanse found in Josquin (cf. p. 238). Here there are no leaps of tenths; the range of a melisma is usually confined to a fifth, sixth, or seventh. In the Lamentations the music for the Latin text is sometimes so simple as to approximate *falsobordone.* Actual *falsibordoni* by Palestrina include his celebrated setting, for double choir, of the *Improperia* [82] for Good Friday. Although the simplicity of the means employed prevents the composition from being technically interesting, its moving character is not to be gainsaid. One of the sources preserving the *Improperia* (incomplete) is Codex 59 at St. John Lateran, the only known musical holograph of Palestrina. It contains also Lamentations and hymns. [83]

There are four series of Magnificats,[84] all four having a Magnificat for each of the eight Tones, and there are three additional settings, one each in Tones I, IV, and VI. The writing, varying from three-part to eight-part, is strictly modal and in contrapuntal style, at times introducing canons.[85] Two series provide polyphony for the even-numbered verses, one for the odd-numbered verses, and one for verse 1 plus the even-numbered verses (all settings of verse 1, of course, omit the word *"Magnificat"*). One of the extra settings (*a 8*)

---

[81] PalW XXV; XXXI, 16, 125, 130, 161 (all included in PalO XIII, which, on p. 252ff, prints a setting of *Lectio II* for Holy Saturday, not given in PalW; PalO rejects the remaining, dubious, settings printed in PalW). For a criticism of statements made by Baini with regard to the use of Palestrina's Lamentations in the Papal Chapel (BaiP II, 187ff), see Grove IV, 27, fn.

[82] Pr. after two sources, in PalW XXXI, 171, 175. Palestrina's *Improperia* provide no music for the text *Quia eduxi te per desertum . . . et lancea perforasti latus Salvatori tuo* (for the plainsong setting see Officium, 529ff). Evidently the omitted section was to be sung in plainsong.

[83] Two pages of facsimile of Codex 59 are pr. in PalW XXXI after p. 172. For a monograph on the MS., see CasC, which includes 10 pages of facsimile.

[84] PalW XXVII; PalO XVI.   [85] For one in contrary motion, see *ibid.*, 211.

provides polyphony for every verse; the other two, for the even-numbered verses. The *Gloria Patri* which closes the Magnificat in Tone III in the series setting the odd-numbered verses and which is occasionally printed separately in modern editions, is the source of the Protestant hymn, *The Strife Is O'er,* in which, however, various changes are made.

If *The Strife Is O'er* is not quite genuine Palestrina, some works current under his name are not his at all. An *Adoramus te* widely disseminated as his —beginning with a'—g-sharp'—a' in the superius—is actually derived from one by Rosselli.[86] A well-known *Tenebrae factae sunt* is still reprinted as Palestrina's, although it has long been known that the set of twenty-seven *Responsoria* to which it belongs (printed among the *opera dubia* in PalW XXXII) is in fact by Ingegneri (cf. p. 491). Of several *O bone Jesu* settings ascribed to Palestrina, a popular one "without doubt owes its origin to a later master." [87]

Palestrina: Masses

Although Palestrina was a good composer of madrigals and a superior one of motets, it is in his Masses that he particularly excels. They illustrate all the standard techniques. There are paraphrase, parody, and even archaic *cantus-firmus* Masses, as well as Masses that consist of canons and others that are freely composed. The following table (in which "tenor" equals *"cantus-firmus"*),[88] points out the type to which each of the 105 Masses belongs and also indicates, where known, the piece upon which each Mass written on pre-existent material is based.[89]

[86] Rosselli's motet, correctly attributed, is pr. ProsM, *Annus I,* IV, 307, and in WüllnC, *Stufe II,* 34. Another setting, with the identical superius but with 3 quite different lower parts, is pr. under Palestrina's name, in NeyR I, 144, and RochlS I, *Abt. 2,* 1. A less popular *Adoramus te,* beginning with a'-b-flat'-a' in the superius, is genuine Palestrina; it is pr. in PalW V, 176; PalO XI, 78; WüllnC *Stufe II,* 18 (transposed ed.); and (attributed to Felice Anerio) in NeyR VI, 203, and RochlS I, *Abt. 2,* 21.

[87] JepPS, 47; for the piece, *see* PalW XXXI, 145.

[88] The table in the text, compiled in the main by Oliver Strunk, is printed here by his permission. (Additional identifications for Nos. 7, 40, and 73 are given by Jeppesen in Acta XVIII–XIX [1946–47], 82, but have not been verified. About Nos. 7 and 40, *see* KillK, 62, 52, respectively.)

[89] Modern editions of these pieces (where known to be available) may be found as follows (the first number in each entry is that of the Mass in Table VI). (1) Liber, 1176; (2) KillK, 29; (3) *ibid.,* 37 (with misattribution to de Silva); (4) SmijT I, 99; (5) Liber, 808—the first of 2 settings with the text, *Nunc Sancte nobis Spiritus* (the text has been changed from *Ad coenam* . . .); (6) Liber, 40ff, 64, 61f; (7) Liber, 1861; (10) MonteO XXVI, App.; (11) *pars I* in PalW XXXI, 58; (14) EinlM, III, 56; (16) Liber, 63 (cf. WagE III, 456, fn. 3); (17) our Ex. 16; (19) = No. 6; (21) PalW V, 36; PalO III, 42; (23) Liber, 852—now *Salutis humanae Sator;* (24) our Ex. 16; (27) PalW I, 137; PalO V, 184; (28) PalW II, 132; PalO VII, 132; (29) PalW XIV, v; (30) Liber, 866; (31) SchmidtgM, App., 3; (32) Liber, 1177; (34) PalW I, 90; PalO V, 121; (37) Liber, 1807; (38) Liber, 46; (39) PalW V, 3; PalO III, 1; (41) *see* caption of Ex. 112; (42) CPC, No. 28; (44) Liber, 1861; (45) Liber, 1159; (47) Liber, 1173; (48) PalW VI, 21; XXXI, 63; (51) *pars I* in HawkH II, 476, with wrong ascription to Willaert (*see also* Ex. 75 *supra*); (52) Liber, 1181; (53) PalW I, 3; PalO V, 1; (54) PalW II, 7; PalO VII, 7; (55) PalW I, 111; PalO V, 149; (57) Liber, 274; (58) PalW V, 105; PalO III, 132; (59) PalW XXVIII, 239; PalO IX, 117; (62) Liber, 1834; (64) PalW XXVIII, 26; PalO II, 25; (65) PalW XXVIII, 179; PalO II, 161; (66) PalW II, 3; PalO VII, 1; (69) Liber, 275; (70) MonteO XXIII, App.; (71) Antiphonale, 641—now

Table VI

List of Palestrina Masses

Year of first publication	No.	Title	No. of parts	Type	Remarks, including comments about pre-existent material used by Palestrina
1554	1	Ecce sacerdos magnus	4	Tenor	Antiphon
	2	O Regem coeli	4	Parody	De Silva, 1532
	3	Virtute magna	4	Parody	Lasson, 1532
	4	Gabriel archangelus	4	Parody	Verdelot, 1532
	5	Ad coenam agni providi	5	Canonic	Hymn
1567	6	De Beata Virgine	4	Paraphrase	Mass IX, Credo I, Mass XVII
	7	Inviolata	4	Paraphrase	Sequence
	8	Sine nomine	4	Free	Original
	9	Ad fugam	4	Canonic	Original
	10	Aspice Domine	5	Parody	Jaquet, 1532
	11	Salvum me fac	5	Parody	Jaquet, 1538
	12	Papae Marcelli	6	Free	Original
1570	13	Spem in alium	4	Parody	Jaquet, 1539
	14	Io mi son giovinetta	4	Parody	Ferabosco, 1542
	15	Brevis	4	Free	Original
	16	De feria	4	Paraphrase	Mass XVIII (for Pal.'s Sanctus)
	17	L'Homme armé	5	Tenor	Popular song
	18	Repleatur os meum	5	Canonic	Jaquet, 1538
	19	De Beata Virgine	6	Paraphrase	Mass IX, Credo I, Mass XVII
	20	Ut re mi fa sol la	6	Tenor	Arbitrary
1582	21	Lauda Sion	4	Parody	Own motet, 1563
	22	Primi toni	4	Free	Original
	23	Jesu nostra redemptio	4	Paraphrase	Hymn
	24	L'Homme armé	4	Paraphrase	Popular song
	25	Eripe me	5	Parody	Maillard, 1559
	26	Secunda	5	Parody	Unidentified
	27	O magnum mysterium	5	Parody	Own motet, 1569
1585	28	Confitebor tibi	8	Parody	Own motet, 1572
1590	29	Aeterna Christi munera	4	Paraphrase	Hymn
	30	Jam Christus astra ascenderat	4	Paraphrase	Hymn
	31	Panis quem ego dabo	4	Parody	Lupus Hellinck, 1532
	32	Iste confessor	4	Paraphrase	Hymn
	33	Nigra sum	5	Parody	L'Héritier, 1532
	34	Sicut lilium inter spinas	5	Parody	Own motet, 1569
	35	Nasce la gioia mia	6	Parody	Primavera, 1565
	36	Sine nomine	6	Parody	Unidentified
1591	37	Pro defunctis	5	Paraphrase	Requiem Mass
1592	38	Dominicalis [90]	5	Paraphrase	Masses XI and XII and Credo peculiar to Mantuan use

Festivis resonent; (72) Liber, 273; (73) Liber, 275; (74) PalW V, 26; PalO III, 30; (75) PalW II, 33; PalO VII, 42; (76) MusiolR, App., 18; (77) Liber, 1515 (= 1578); (78) PalW I, 105; PalO V, 141; (79) PalW II, 164; PalO VII, 219; (80) PalW III, 155; PalO VIII, 203; (81) PalW VI, 6; (82) PalW VI, 28; (83) Liber, 19 and 21 (Kyrie, Sanctus), 81 (Gloria), 27 (Agnus), concerning Credo, *see* PalW XXIII, ii; (84) Liber, 25; (85) Liber, 1598; (86) ElúsA, 45; (87) Liber, 885; (88) MissaleR, 346; (89) = No. 88; (90) Liber, 276; (91) BesN, 14 (= VNM XXXVIII, Supp. II); (92) PalW II, 121; PalO VII, 162; (94) = No. 14; (105) PubAPTM VI, 243.

[90] About the disputed authenticity of this Mass, *see* JepPS, 215; JepMP; StrunkP.

Year of first publication	No.	Title	No. of parts	Type	Remarks, including comments about pre-existent material used by Palestrina
1593/4	39	Dies sanctificatus	4	Parody	Own motet, 1563
	40	In te Domine speravi	4	Parody	Unidentified
	41	Je suis desheritée	4	Parody	Lupus, 1533 (recte Cadéac?)
	42	Quam pulchra es	4	Parody	Lupi, 1532; cf. p. 342
	43	Dilexi quoniam	5	Parody	Maffoni [90a]
1594	44	Ave Maria	4	Paraphrase	Prayer [91]
	45	Sanctorum meritis	4	Paraphrase	Hymn
	46	Emendemus in melius	4	Parody	Unidentified [92]
	47	Sacerdos et pontifex	5	Paraphrase	Antiphon
	48	Tu es pastor ovium	5	Parody	Own motet (MS)
1595	49	Illumina oculos meos	6	Parody	De Silva (MS) [92a]
1596	50	Ave Maria	6	Tenor	Unidentified
1599	51	Quem dicunt homines	4	Parody	Richafort, 1532
	52	Dum esset summus pontifex	4	Paraphrase	Antiphon
	53	O admirabile commercium	5	Parody	Own motet, 1569
	54	Memor esto	5	Parody	Own motet, 1572
	55	Dum complerentur	6	Parody	Own motet, 1569
	56	Sacerdotes Domini	6	Canonic	Unidentified
1599	57	Ave Regina coelorum	4	Paraphrase	Antiphon
	58	Veni sponsa Christi	4	Parody	Own motet, 1563
	59	Vestiva i colli	5	Parody	Own madrigal, 1566
	60	Sine nomine	5	Canonic	Original
	61	In te Domine speravi	6	Parody	Lupus, 1532; cf. p. 341
	62	Te Deum laudamus	6	Paraphrase	Hymn
1600	63	In illo tempore	4	Parody	Moulu, 1518 [93]
	64	Già fu chi m'ebbe cara	4	Parody	Own madrigal, 1555
	65	Petra sancta	5	Parody	Own madrigal (Io son ferito), 1561
	66	O Virgo simul et Mater	5	Parody	Own motet, 1572
	67	Quinti toni	6	Free	Original
1600	68	Descendit angelus	4	Parody	Penet, 1532
	69	Regina coeli	5	Paraphrase	Antiphon
	70	Quando lieta sperai	5	Parody	Rore, 1552
	71	Octavi toni (Festum nunc celebre)	6	Tenor	Hymn
	72	Alma Redemptoris	6	Paraphrase	Antiphon
1601	73	Regina coeli	4	Paraphrase	Antiphon
	74	O Rex gloriae	4	Parody	Own motet, 1563
	75	Ascendo ad Patrem	5	Parody	Own motet, 1572
	76	Qual è il più grand'amor	5	Parody	Rore, 1550
	77	Tu es Petrus	6	Tenor	Antiphon
	78	Viri Galilei	6	Parody	Own motet, 1569

[90a] See Jeppesen in MQ XLI (1955), 471f.

[91] Jeppesen, in Acta XVIII–XIX (1946–47), 82, states that this is based on the *Ave Maria* of Fogliano (JepI, 163). Fogliano's setting is based on the plainsong, i.e., on the same melody as is employed by Palestrina. But Palestrina does not draw on any other material presented by Fogliano.

[92] Baini claimed this Mass to be based on the *Emendemus* of Calvez (cf. Jeppesen in Acta *loc. cit.*). Brit. Mus. Egerton 2461 includes a modern MS score, made by Santini, of an *Emendemus* purporting to be by Calvez; the Santini Collection at Münster has another such score. Examination of microfilm reproductions of the two scores shows that they both actually present the *Emendemus* by Richafort (cf. p. 337), which is not the model followed by Palestrina.

[92a] Cf. HabV, 167.   [93] Identified by Dr. Edward Lowinsky.

Table VI (continued)

List of Palestrina Masses

Year of first publication	No.	Title	No. of parts	Type	Remarks, including comments about pre-existent material used by Palestrina
1601	79	Laudate Dominum	8	Parody	Own motet, 1572
	80	Hodie Christus natus est	8	Parody	Own motet, 1575
	81	Fratres enim ego accepi	8	Parody	Own motet (MS)
No date	82	Assumpta est Maria	6	Parody	Own motet (MS)
1888	83	In majoribus duplicibus	4	Paraphrase	Mass II (for Pal.'s Kyrie & Sanctus), Gloria I *ad lib.*, Mass IX (for Pal.'s Agnus)
	84	In minoribus duplicibus	4	Paraphrase	Mass IV, Credo IV
	85	Beatus Laurentius	5	Paraphrase	Antiphon
	86	O sacrum convivium	5	Parody	Morales (MS)
	87	Veni Creator Spiritus	6	Tenor	Hymn
1887	88	Pater noster	4	Paraphrase	Prayer
	89	Panem nostrum	5	Tenor	Prayer
	90	Salve Regina	5	Paraphrase	Antiphon
	91	Benedicta es	6	Parody	Josquin, 1520
	92	Tu es Petrus	6	Parody	Own motet, 1572
	93	Ecce ego Joannes	6	Parody	Unidentified
1892	94	Io mi son giovinetta	6	Parody	Ferabosco, 1542
In MS 93a	95	Sine nomine ("*a voci mutate*")	4	Free	Original
	96	In duplicibus minoribus I	5	Paraphrase	
	97	In duplicibus minoribus II	5	Paraphrase	
	98	Beate Marie Virg. I	5	Paraphrase	
	99	Beate Marie Virg. II	5	Paraphrase	
	100	Beate Marie Virg. III	5	Paraphrase	See Jep MP, 46
	101	In festis Apostolorum I	5	Paraphrase	
	102	In festis Apostolorum II	5	Paraphrase	
	103	In semiduplicibus maioribus I	5	Paraphrase	
	104	In semiduplicibus maioribus II	5	Paraphrase	
	105	Christus resurgens [94]	4	Parody	Richafort, 1540

Totals according to types: Parody, 52; Paraphrase, 34; Tenor, 8; Canonic, 5; Free, 6.

To give some idea of the nature of these Masses, brief descriptions will be given here of a few typical ones.

The first published Mass,[94a] based on *Ecce sacerdos magnus* (cf. p. 456), employs the outmoded *cantus-firmus* technique. With few omissions, the plainsong recurs throughout the Mass, always with the original text. The other voices, singing the Ordinary, weave counterpoint based on new melodic material or on elements of the plainsong. In most sections, the *cantus firmus*

[93a] Masses 95-104, as edited by Knud Jeppesen,, are pr. in PalO XVIII, XIX.
[94] Discovered by R. Stevenson; *see Fontes artis musicae* II, 12.
[94a] PalW X, 3; PalO I, 1.

is in the tenor, but it is given occasionally to the superius, altus I, and altus II (in Agnus II, which is *a 5*). The *Pleni,* Benedictus, and *Osanna II* are without *cantus firmus*. In clever but old-fashioned manner, Palestrina in Agnus III uses three different types of measure simultaneously.[95]

In the Hexachord Mass,[96] Palestrina displays his great gift for building elaborate structures on the simplest material: superius II consists of only the ascending and descending *hexachordum durum*[97] (absent from no section), which, in varying rhythmic forms, serves as *cantus firmus*. This hexachord and also the *hexachordum naturale* appear at times in the other voices, but the *hexachordum molle* is never present. A seventh voice (altus III), added in the final Agnus, sings the *cantus firmus* in canon at the fifth below with superius II.

In the earlier of his two *L'Homme armé* Masses,[98] Palestrina places the *cantus firmus* in the quintus (tenor II) and presents it in the Mixolydian mode. At some points, elements of the melody appear also in the other voices.[99] In the later Mass, entitled merely *Missa quarta*[100] in Book IV of Masses, the old melody is given in the Dorian mode. Paraphrase technique is used in the main, but *cantus-firmus* style is occasionally resorted to.

In his two printed paraphrase Masses *de Beata Virgine,* Palestrina uses the same selection of plainsongs as did Kerle (cf. p. 452). The text of the Mass *a 6*[101] included the Marian tropes in the edition of 1570, but these were replaced in a later edition (1599) by repetitions of the liturgical words. The borrowed plainsong material permeates all six voices at various points throughout the Mass, the Gregorian Kyrie, for example, being sung in imitation by all voices at the opening. Word-painting is found in the Credo at *descendit* and at *Et resurrexit tertia die,* where only the three upper voices sing, in ternary rhythm (which contrasts with the preceding binary rhythm). Variety of treatment is obtained, in the Sanctus and Agnus, through a shift to the *cantus-firmus* technique, the plainsong melodies being assigned at different times to the tenor I, tenor II, and altus.

The four-part *Missa de Beata Virgine,* though printed three years before the first edition of the one *a 6,* appeared without the words of the Marian tropes. However, they must once have been included, since the trope melodies are plainly present [102]—together with repetitions of the liturgical words. The handling of the plainsongs in this Mass differs from that given them in the

---

[95] For a special article on the Credo of this Mass, *see* FellC, 44ff.
[96] PalW XII, 165; PalO VI, 216.
[97] Superius II does not, as stated in WagG, 439, have the *hexachordum naturale*.
[98] PalW XII, 75; PalO VI, 97.
[99] For special articles relating to this Mass, *see* AudaP, AudaT.
[100] PalW XIII, 45; PalO X, 60.
[101] PalW XII, 135; PalO VI, 175.
[102] As is shown by a comparison with WagG, 469, 472, etc. For the Mass, *see* PalW XI, 1; PalO IV, 1.

one *a 6. Cantus-firmus* technique is absent; also, paraphrasing is accomplished in other ways. Thus, in the Kyrie, Palestrina draws on more of the plainsong in the Mass *a 4* than in the Mass *a 6* (omitting, in the process, the melody for invocation III and making some changes in the original order of the melodies of the other invocations). In Agnus II, *a 5,* the added voice (tenor II) is in canon at the fifth with the alto, the melodic material being at first freely invented, the plainsong appearing for the first time in this section at *dona nobis pacem*.

The last nine Masses in Table VI are of special interest, partly because their Glorias and Credos alternate plainsong and polyphony. As was normal in alternation Masses of the period, the even-numbered verses [103] are set polyphonically. (Palestrina, however, in verse 2 of the Glorias in question, applies polyphony only to the words *"bonae voluntatis"*; in verse 2 of the Credo, he excludes the words *"Patrem omnipotentem"* from polyphonic treatment.) The other three sections of the Mass text are set complete, except for the end of the Agnus. The plainsongs which lie at the basis of these Masses, written for Mantua, are versions used at Santa Barbara, where Chant MSS according to the Mantuan use reposed until recently. The *Missa dominicalis,* No. 38 in Table VI,[104] is also an alternation Mass, and its melodies likewise conform with the Mantuan use, although only the Credo is peculiar to it. Whether the work is really Palestrina's has been questioned, but it may nevertheless be another genuine work written by him for Mantua.[104a] (It differs from the nine Masses mentioned above, however, in that verse 2 is set complete in both Gloria and Credo.) [105] In a letter of November 1, 1578, Palestrina, writing to Duke Guglielmo of Mantua about some revisions the duke had made in certain Chant melodies, pronounces the melodies "well-purged of barbarisms and wrong notes" and suggests that the amended versions be printed in the new edition of the Graduale (cf. p. 458, fn. 39). As to the form in which Masses should be sung at Santa Barbara, the letters seem concerned with pure plainsong only, but the principles enunciated are equally relevant to the shape of the plainsongs polyphonically set in these alternation Masses since, as has been stated, Palestrina follows the Mantuan versions. In the Kyrie, Gloria, and Sanctus of the *Missa dominicalis,* these are versions of the Gregorian melodies of Mass XI, while the Agnus is based on a version of the concluding chant of Mass XII. A comparison of the themes of this easily available alternation Mass with the versions in the Vatican Graduale [105a] suggests what the composer's methods would have been had he fulfilled the task assigned to him of revising the Graduale.[105b]

---

[103] Sometimes called the "second parts."   [104] PalW XXXIII, 1.   [104a] Cf. JepMP, 47.
[105] Further about these Masses, *see* JepMP and (on No. 38) StrunkP.
[105a] Or, as in StrunkP, 237f, with their forms in Lansdowne MS 462.
[105b] This is true even if this Mass should some day prove not to be Palestrina's, since it follows versions obtained by applying principles of which he approved.

Such a comparison reveals, among other things, a deep concern that the quantity of the syllables be observed: notes in melismas are sometimes redistributed among syllables so as to combine more notes with long than with short quantities. Zarlino had held views regarding the underlaying of text in plainsong that were similar to the duke's and Palestrina's—and to his own concerning the setting of words in polyphony (cf. p. 378).[106] As to plainsong, Palestrina shared the outlook of his own time, however misguided, and was in that respect a "modern."

Palestrina's Mass for the Dead [107] follows the normal practice of paraphrasing the plainsong. He sets the Kyrie, Offertory (in which the paraphrasing is rather free), Sanctus, and Agnus, leaving the Introit, Gradual, Tract, and Communion to be sung in plainsong.

Various archaic features [108] stamp Palestrina's parody Mass on *Benedicta es coelorum Regina* [108a] as an early work, but it is far from being without interest. The Kyrie I opens with the sequence melody (cf. pp. 251f) in canon between the two highest voices, with a countermelody, in imitation, reminiscent of Josquin's but so different from it that it can hardly be called a derivative. In the *Christe*, however, a bass figure used by Josquin (at the first full repetition of the words *"a quo illuminaris"*) is presented in imitation in several voices; also in the *Christe*, a figure treated by Josquin *a 3* (at the words *"te Deus Pater"*) is handled by Palestrina *a 5*. Kyrie II makes varied use of the material with which Josquin closes his *pars I* (on the words *"Ave plena gratia"*); at the very end Palestrina appropriates the motet superius and bass, embellishing them slightly and providing them with more complex countermelodies. At the Gloria opening, where the sequence again appears in canon, Josquin's initial countermelody is briefly introduced; the *Qui tollis* draws on the *tu praeclara maris* passage of the motet. A canon on the plainsong, in short time-values, begins the Credo. Josquin's *Per illud* duo is worked out *a 3* by Palestrina for his *Pleni*, and Josquin's *nunc mater exora natum* section is used in the *Osanna*. The sequence melody, in new rhythmic configurations, recurs in both settings of the Agnus. In general, Palestrina draws on Josquin's motet less than does the composer of the Mass variously ascribed to Willaert and Hesdin.

Palestrina's parody Mass *a 4* on the Lupus-Cadéac version of *Je suis desheritée* was printed as a *Missa sine nomine*. The form of the chanson—on which others had already written parody Masses (cf. p. 341)—is *ababcdeFF*. Palestrina shows his ingenuity at the very beginning. Here his superius is the same as that of *ab* of the chanson, and the tenor, which in the original had begun as the *dux* of a canon with the superius, also remains the same except at the cadence; Palestrina likewise has his bass duplicate that of the

---

[106] For English transl. of the relevant passage from the *Istitutioni harmoniche, see* StrunkP, 237f.
[107] PalW X, 138; PalO I, 164.   [108] Concerning which, *see* JepP, 35ff.   [108a] PalW XXIV, 72.

original in the first measures (except at the cadence); but he has discovered that by changing one part only—by replacing the old altus with a new one that imitates the bass—he can produce imitation in pairs (cf. Ex. 112*a*). In the *Christe,* the superius has *cde* of the chanson superius, but the altus is new except for a brief reminiscence at the opening, while the tenor begins as in the chanson, but changes its point of entry to one following rather than preceding the superius; the rest of the tenor is mostly free except for a short reminiscence toward the close; a new bass imitating the altus is provided, Palestrina again producing imitation in pairs where this did not exist before. In Kyrie II, the superius has the *FF* of the original; the altus, which in the chanson had entered simultaneously with the superius imitating that voice after four notes, is shorn of those notes by Palestrina in both statements, so that the imitation stands out more clearly; the tenor is new in the first statement, but reproduces the original (with a few interpolated notes) in the second statement; the bass, which, after three notes had previously accompanied the superius in tenths (except at the cadence), is, in the first statement, raised a third and made to enter two measures earlier than before, so that it now sings in anticipatory imitation of the superius; in the second statement, this voice returns mainly to its original function, but toward the cadence Palestrina makes a few changes to produce a better bass from the harmonic standpoint. In the rest of the Mass, Palestrina exhibits similar resourcefulness and imagination in writing a fantasy on the material offered by all the voices of his model.

The poem of Rore's four-part madrigal, *Qual'è il più grand', o Amor,* the model of another fine Palestrina parody Mass, has the following of its eight lines repeated: line 2, once; line 7, twice; line 8, three times—fourteen text units in all. There are corresponding musical repetitions, none exactly alike save the last pair, some variations being quite subtle: thus, in repetition 2 of line 7, the bass has the melody originally sung by the tenor, the superius has new material, and the inner voices have material that was new in repetition 1. The form of the madrigal is *aBB'cdefGHG'H'G''H''H''*. In building thereon his Mass *a* 5, Palestrina, in his Kyrie I, has the first four voices that enter draw on the tenor and bass of Rore's phrase *a* while the last—the altus—has the same melody it had in the original madrigal (cf. Ex. 112*b*). Most of the rest of Kyrie I reworks *a* 5 the three voices of Rore's *BB'*; the bass, near the end of the section, has the notes it had at the close of Rore's *H''*. This voice terminates with the same notes in several other sections of the Mass—the Gloria, Credo (at the close of *Et incarnatus* and *Et in Spiritum Sanctum*), Sanctus (at the close of the Benedictus), and Agnus; Palestrina uses a similar means of unification in many other Masses also. The *Christe* draws on all voices of Rore's *c* and *d,* the first reproduction of *c* being almost literal. This unit then seems to be avoided purposely until the

Et in Spiritum Sanctum of the Credo and then recurs only in modified form. The structure of Kyrie II resembles that of Kyrie I, the material, however, being drawn first from *e;* the conclusion reworks *a 5* the two-part writing in Rore's *f.* The various units of the madrigal are similarly manipulated throughout the Mass, but unit *G* appears only in its *G''* form and only near the conclusion of the Gloria. Agnus II, as though finally to recall the madrigal as a whole, presents elements both from its opening and its closing units (the material from the former being used not only in its original form but also inverted).

Palestrina's Mass [109] on Hellinck's celebrated *Panis quem ego dabo* incorporates a considerable amount of direct quotation and often presents the motifs in the order in which they appear in the model. Double counterpoint and imitation at close time-intervals exhibit Palestrina's technical skill, as does a canon in the final Agnus between the bass and an added voice.[110]

Palestrina's parody Masses include his only examples of Masses for antiphonal choirs. There are four such (Nos. 28, 79–81 in Table VI). Of these, the *Missa Hodie Christus* [111] is one of Palestrina's only two Masses that open with all the voices in block-chord harmony rather than in imitation.[111a]

Among Palestrina's parody Masses on his own motets, the very beautiful ones on *Assumpta est Maria* and *Ascendo ad Patrem* abound in felicitous details. One passage from each of these Masses, together with its model, is given in Example 112c and *d. Pars II* of the motet *Assumpta est* opens with a setting of *"quae est ista quae progreditur"* that is frequently manipulated in the Mass. The reworking at the opening of the Benedictus is simple but effective. Here, in the second statement, the first and third motet-voices change position and the other two voices reverse the direction of their leaps; in addition, the rising conjunct lines on *"quae progreditur"* are recast in a rhythmic form borrowed from a still later motif (not shown in our example) to set *"venit"* and to provide material for subsequent development. The *Missa Ascendo ad Patrem* contains several instances of changes in the order of voice entries. The order is the same at the opening of the Mass as at the opening of the motet but, as shown in Example 112d, it is completely changed at the beginning of the Sanctus. Still another order is used at the beginning of Agnus I. In this work—as, indeed, in many parody Masses, whether by Palestrina or others—individual motifs from the model are often made the subject of new developments in imitation that show at least as much skill and imagination as do the reworkings of polyphonic passages.

---

[109] PalW XIV, 34; PalO XV, 44.
[110] Further about this Mass, *see* SchmidtgM, 90ff.　　[111] PalW XXXI, 135.
[111a] The other is pr. PalO XIX, 168. The above statement about the special nature of the opening of the *Missa Hodie,* as well as the one appearing on p. 480 regarding the augmentation canon in the *Missa Repleatur,* is made without access to Mass 105 in Table VI.

EXAMPLE 112. Illustrations of Palestrina's parody Mass technique: (*a*)
Openings of *Je suis desheritée* (Lupus or Cadéac; complete
piece in CW XV, 6; ScherG, 115; PubAPTM XXIII, 20) and
of Palestrina's Mass on it (after PalW XV, 44), (*b*) Openings
of Rore's *Qual' è il più grand', o Amore* (after MusiolR, 18f)
and of Palestrina's Mass on it (after PalW XXI, 62), (*c*) Openings of *Pars II* of Palestrina's motet *Assumpta est Maria* (PalW
VI, 31) and of the Benedictus of his Mass on it (after PalW
XXIII, 115), (*d*) Openings of Palestrina's motet *Ascendo ad
Patrem* (PalW II, 33; PalO VII, 42) and of the Sanctus of his
Mass on it (PalW XXI, 53).

The movements of the *Missa Repleatur os meum* [112] present, from Kyrie to Agnus I, a cycle of canons at the octave, seventh, sixth, fifth, fourth, third, second, and unison, the progressive arrangement being the opposite of that followed in Ockeghem's *Missa Prolationum*. (Palestrina refrains from using canon only in the *Crucifixus* and Benedictus, each *a 3*). In addition, the composer, in the respective movements, has the time-interval between the entries of the *dux* and *comes* correspond to the pitch-interval of the canon: i.e., in the canon at the octave, the *comes* enters 8 semibreves after the *dux;* in the canon at the seventh, it enters 7 semibreves later, etc. The basic SATB vocal "orchestration" of the work is supplemented throughout by a quintus, which changes character from time to time, becoming successively a soprano II, mezzo-soprano, alto II, and tenor II; and the tenor I sings in canon with each of these in turn. (In the final Agnus, *a 6*, the quintus becomes a soprano II again and is joined by a sextus—a mezzo-soprano.) In nine out of the eleven divisions containing canon, the last of all the voices to enter is one

[112] PalW XII, 105; PalO VI, 136.

that participates in the canon; Palestrina generally has a *comes* enter last throughout his canonic Masses. Agnus I contains the only augmentation canon in Palestrina's Masses of any type. The final Agnus provides a climax in the form of a double canon, one canon being at the octave and one at the fourth. The work is named after, and borrows its basic canon material from the *Repleatur* motet by Jaquet of Mantua (cf. pp. 366f), in which, however, the canon has only one pitch- and one time-interval—a fifth below and two measures, respectively. At no time does Palestrina employ the same plan. His genius is revealed with particular clarity by his virtuosity in discovering in musical material interesting possibilities not worked out by the original composer, and this faculty is perhaps nowhere more brilliantly evident than here.

The "freely" composed *Missa Papae Marcelli*[112a] early won much favor, partly through its merit, partly through its special character. In it Palestrina plainly concentrated on clear text declamation and avoided such polyphonic elaboration as would interfere with it. As a result, the Mass conforms with the expressed wishes both of the Pope for whom it is named, who reigned briefly in 1555, and of the Council of Trent. Whether it dates from c. 1555 or from the latter days of the Council has been a subject of dispute.[113] The clarity in the treatment of the text results from the high percentage of note-against-note writing,[114] yet the departures from it and in particular the skilful handling of rhythmic variety[115] and vocal registration prevent the work from losing a true polyphonic character. The *Christe* bears a clear relationship to the Gloria of Palestrina's *Missa Benedicta es*,[116] but the Mass as a whole is based on no pre-existent model. A predominating motif, sung at the opening by the two basses, recurs at various points.

The theme appears at *deprecationem* in the Gloria, at *Patrem omnipotentem* (bass II) and *factorem coeli et terrae* (bass I) in the Credo—which closes with an Amen of extraordinary power, built on scale passages—, and in canon *a 3* in Agnus II. Derived themes occur at the opening of the Gloria, at *Dominus Deus Sabaoth* in the Sanctus, at the beginning of the *Osanna,* and at the beginning of Agnus I.

112a Pr. PalW XI, 128; PalO IV, 167.

113 In support of the former view, see HabK (which would accept a date even slightly earlier than 1555, but relies heavily on the wrong dating of a MS) and esp. WeinK. JepM presents a strong case for the latter view. If this is correct, the Mass would presumably have been named in memory of Pope Marcellus because it applied principles he had favored.

114 On this point, *see* JepPS, 41ff.

115 Cf. MorrC, Ex. 51; also the barring in the edition by A. Schering (Eulenburg score, choral series, No. 13).   116 Cf. JepM, 134ff; JepP, 24f.

Palestrina's Masses reveal masterly treatment of form. Nevertheless, he is less concerned than Josquin in preserving a balance between interesting structure and beautiful sonority.[117] Glareanus had regarded Josquin's music as an *"ars perfecta"*—an art to which nothing could be added, a classic art. Not only skillfully contrived form, but also the ideal of writing *a 4* characterized Josquin's classicism. Such writing strikes a balance between linear polyphony and harmony; more voices add nothing essential: sonority is increased but not basic substance. In Palestrina, linear polyphony is more subject than in Josquin to the law of the triad. The later master's handling of dissonance shows the tensions between line and harmony being resolved according to harmonic laws. Writing *a 5* and *a 6* lays emphasis on harmony, on the vertical mass of sound. To be sure, Josquin occasionally wrote in more than four parts also, but his concern for balancing structure and sonority is the outstanding trait of his classicism. While Palestrina's harmony is less rigid, sound and substance are no longer in perfect balance. Nevertheless, with all his liking for harmonic effect, Palestrina is still more interested in polyphony than is characteristic of Italian genius when not subjected to foreign influence. Indeed, it may be said that he is more Netherlandish than his chief contemporary, Lassus, and that Lassus, as we shall see, is more Italianate than Palestrina. The latter of these two great artistic figures is more intimately bound up than the former with a new phase of the history of the Roman church. He is essentially a man of the Counter-Reformation, and his works may be regarded as the classic musical expression of the new ecclesiasticism.[118]

In the field of sacred music, Palestrina quite overshadows the other members of the Roman School. His supremacy is most nearly challenged by the Spaniard, Tomás Luis de Victoria, who, however, returned to Spain and will be discussed in Chapter 11. In justice to Palestrina's remaining colleagues, it must be said that while, like Victoria, they were devoted admirers of the master, they were not slavish imitators. There are Masses and motets of great distinction among their productions.

Other Romans, including Marenzio, the Naninos, and the Anerios

Marenzio wrote excellent motets. These, as might be expected, exhibit madrigalian touches, but, while degree-inflection and word-painting are present, he appears to have deliberately used them in a more subdued way here than in his secular works. Nevertheless, the word *"serpente"* in *Estote fortes,*[119] is set to a writhing melisma. But, if in *O quam gloriosum,*[120] the

---

[117] Further about Palestrina's Masses, *see* KillK, 28ff; WagG, 432ff; PirH, 293ff; WidmaM; SamsP (to be used in the light of Acta, XVIII–XIX [1946–47], 80ff); HalbG, 33ff; MosVC, 132ff.
[118] Cf. BirtR.   [119] Pr. HabRMS II, fasc. 9–12, 97; CasR IV, 15.
[120] Pr. ProsM, *Annus I,* II, 410.

word *"sequuntur"* is descriptively treated (by repetitions and sequences)
Marenzio is restrained in his treatment of the same word in *Innocentes pro
Christo*,[121] where, however, the word *"lactentes"* ("sucklings") is underscored by light and delicate melismas. Degree-inflection is found in the *"Alleluia"* of *O Rex gloriae*,[122] the opening of which shows Marenzio's fondness
for imitation in pairs. In *Conceptio tua*,[123] as in several other motets, he repeats fragments of text to variations of the music previously heard; a delicate
touch is achieved here by ending a musical phrase (on the word *"Virgo"*)
with a short melismatic figure which then recurs as the opening of the next
melody that is subjected to imitation. The eight-part *Jubilate Deo* [124] is a brilliant example of writing for double chorus.

Among the numerous composers writing sacred music at Rome were the
Netherlander, J. Matelart,[124a] René de Mel,[125] Quagliati,[126] the two Naninos,
the two Anerios, Soriano, Stabile, Dragoni, and Giovanelli.

G. M. Nanino proves his mastery of contrapuntal technique by writing
thirty different canon settings (*a 3, a 4*, and *a 5*) of a single *cantus firmus* in
his *Motecta* of 1586. These apparently have a pedagogical purpose. Here the
composer disposes the *cantus* in long notes, in one voice or another, while the
remaining voices sing in canon at various intervals. Thus, in *Lapidabant
Stephanum*,[127] the *cantus firmus* is in the bass and the other two voices sing
in canon at the fifth above; in *Hic est beatissimus Evangelista* (*a 3*),[128] the
cantus is in the middle voice, the outer voices rendering a canon at the octave
below; in *Laetamini in Domino*,[129] the *cantus* is in the superius, the two
other voices executing a canon at the unison; in *Exultent et laetentur* (*a 3*),[130]
the *cantus* is in the bass, the remaining voices singing a canon at the sixth below; in *Cantate Domino*,[131] the *cantus* is in the middle voice, the other two
adding a mirror canon at the second; in *Qui vult venire post me* (*a 5*),[132]
the *cantus* is in the superius, three voices participate in a canon, and the
fifth part (marked *si placet*) is free. Nanino wrote also a series of 157 settings

---

[121] Pr. HabRMS II, fasc. 9–12, 5; CasR II, 17.

[122] Pr. CasR IV, 23; LückS III, 91; AV III, 81; ProsM, *Annus I*, II, 169.

[123] Pr. *ibid.*, 277; AV III, 117.

[124] CommM XVI, 55. 19 motets not yet cited are pr. in HabRMS II, fasc. 9–12 (1 also in CasR V, 7); 9 items in MarenM (1 also in CasR VI, 17); 12 more items in ProsM, *Annus I*, II (duplications in CommM XXV, 47 [= *ibid.*, XXVIII, 77]; XXVII, 3 [= LückS III, 23]; XXVIII, 79 [= AV IV, 195]; AV IV, 227).

[124a] This is the musician designated as Jean Matelart II in EitQ VI, 377. The title of a 1596 publication states that he was living in Rome and was *maestro di cappella* at San Lorenzo in Damaso. Part of his career was also spent as *Kapellmeister* at Bonn. For *exx., see* MaldR I, 20 (cf. ReT, 109, No. 452); Nos. 3 and 6 in the series, *Canticum vetus*, ed. by G. Fellerer (Schott, Mainz); KillK, 273.

[125] For exx., *see* MaldR XII, 6 (= ProsM, *Annus I*, III, 15; CommM XXVI, 44); CommM XX, 53; XXI, 72, 74; XXVI, 57, 59, 63, 65. The works ascribed to Mel in MaldR I, 25; XI, 40, 43, 44, 49; XII, 3, 4, are by an earlier Renaldo; cf. p. 220 *supra*.

[126] For exx. *see* KillK, 335, 352, both *a 8* with organ bass.

[127] Pr. ProsM, *Annus I*, II, 52.   [128] *Ibid.*, 57; AV VI, 103.   [129] Pr. ProsM, *Annus I*, II, 473.

[130] Pr. TorA II, 15.   [131] *Ibid.*, 18.   [132] *Ibid.*, 20.

(*a 2* to *a 11*) of a *cantus firmus* by Costanzo Festa. Although the *cantus-firmus* technique had become outmoded by this time in motet as well as in Mass writing, apparently it continued to be applied longer in the former type of composition than in the latter, especially if a teaching purpose was to be served.

Nanino further showed his predilection for canon when Clement VIII and Leo XI both died in 1605, by writing a canon *a 4* commemorating each. Both compositions bear verbal directions requiring complete repetitions, these to take place in the first piece at successively higher fourths, in the other at successively higher seconds. The directions accompanying the former canon include the words *"semp. ascendendo";* however, the force of *"semper"* here (and in the second composition, which is based on the Kyrie of Mass IX) naturally reaches its limits when the voices of the singers reach theirs. With the continuing repetitions, each canon *"ascendit in caelum"* (these words appear in connection with the second canon) like the soul of the departed pontiff.[133]

That Nanino was capable of writing effectively without indulging his predilection is shown by his lovely *Diffusa est gratia*,[134] making free use of imitation; his *Hodie Christus natus est*,[135] with its sparkling *"Noe"* passage in ternary meter, contrasting with the preceding binary meter; and his *Cantate Domino*,[136] for double chorus, in which alternation of the same two meters and fleeting conflicts between the macrorhythms and microrhythms prevent the rhythmic monotony that is often present in the chordal passages typical of double-chorus writing. A *Missa Vestiva i colli* of Nanino's is based both on Palestrina's famous madrigal and on the master's own Mass thereon.[137]

The fact that Giovanni Bernardino was younger than his brother, Giovanni Maria, is very clearly reflected in his production, for he was one of the first composers to abandon the old style of the Roman School for the new music with figured bass.[138]

Even though Felice Anerio, in his sacred music, is usually a close follower of Palestrina, he does at times resort to devices Palestrina would not have

[133] Further about these canons, *see* CamD.
[134] Pr. LückS IV, 110; BordA, *Motets*, I, 80.
[135] *Ibid.*, 17; ProsM, *Annus I*, II, 34; AV V, 51.
[136] Pr. CommM XXV, 1. Other works for double chorus *ibid.*, 6; TorA II, 1. Other reprints in ProsM, *Annus I*, IV, 210 *(falsobordone)*; RochlS I, 13, 14, 15; HabRMS I, fasc. 8 (Lamentations); AV IV, 86. For the facsimile of a composition by Nanino designed to present to students every possible variety of ligature used in his time, *see* KJ, XIII (1898), 30ff (with transcription).
[137] Cf. MosVC, 137ff. This Mass published, 1935, by the Verlag für musikalische Kultur und Wissenschaft, Wolfenbüttel, H. W. Frey, ed.
[138] For an example of such music by him, *see* KillK, 330. (Bernardino here has several instances of one auxiliary note leaping to another between 2 statements of a harmony note, a type of ornamental dissonance not belonging to Palestrina style; cf. JepPS, 221. Bernardino, however, restricts himself to having the upper auxiliary leap to the lower.) For other exx., *see* ProsM, *Annus I*, III, 151, 156, 164, 172.

used. Thus, in his *Missa octavi toni "Hor le tue forze adopra,"*[139] he lends a descriptive touch to the word *"suscipe"* in the Gloria through the use of degree-inflection. Such inflection reappears on the first *"dulce"* in Anerio's setting of the hymn *Crux fidelis*.[140] In his treatment of the odd-numbered stanzas of the hymn *Christe Redemptor . . . Ex Patre*,[141] Anerio paraphrases the plainsong with considerable liberty. He treats the Chant similarly in some of his settings *a 4* of the four Marian antiphons,[142] but adheres to it rather faithfully in others. The four-part *Vidi speciosam* and *Sicut cedrus*[143] illustrate his use of the *aBcB* responsory form, the *c* section being set *a 3*. In *Alleluia, Christus surrexit*,[144] a brilliant conclusion is achieved by presenting twice the *"Alleluia"* that is given once at the opening and by then developing the passage further. Literal repetition of the final section sometimes gives the impression, as in *Regnum mundi*,[145] of being an easy means of extending a composition. But the repetition of the second portion of Anerio's delightful *Factum est silentium*,[146] is amply justified by the literary content of the antiphon from which the words are taken and produces a fine, albeit madrigalian, result. The text states that there was silence in heaven when the dragon was about to begin the battle with Michael the archangel. It proceeds: "a voice was heard, thousands of thousands, saying, 'Salvation, honor, and strength, to the all-powerful God.' Thousands of thousands, ministered unto him [Michael] and ten times a hundred thousand attended upon him." Immediate repetitions of *"millia millium"* and *"decies centena millium,"* as well as repetition of the whole final section, help, through simple means, to produce a powerful climax. An impressive result is obtained also in the *Ave Regina coelorum* for two SATB choruses with organ.[147] Anerio wrote a varied assortment of works in the new style with organ bass.[148] Although his music was not strikingly original, its general excellence quite justified his appointment as official composer to the Papal Chapel. G. F. Anerio, like his brother, wrote a quantity of sacred music with organ bass.[149] His *Teatro armonico spirituale* (1619), consisting of dialogue *laude,* which employ chorus, soloists, and instruments, makes an important contribution toward the development

---

[139] Pr. ProsS I, 35. *See also* WagG, 430   [140] Pr. ProsM, *Annus I,* II, 379.
[141] *Ibid.,* III, 347.
[142] *Ibid.,* 453, 456, 458, 461, 502, 534 (the first and penultimate items being different settings of the *Alma;* the fourth and last, different settings of the *Salve*).
[143] *Ibid.,* II, 351, 354 (= AV IV, 179), respectively.
[144] *Ibid.,* 141.   [145] Pr. ProsM, *Annus I,* II, 516; AV III, 196.
[146] Pr. ProsM, *Annus I,* II, 385.   [147] Pr. NeyR VI, 183.
[148] For another ex., in 2 versions, *see* HabFA, 44, 45. For additional works, *see* ProsM, *Annus I,* II, 139 (= SchöbS II, 614; AV IV, 95; LückS, III, 74), 311 (= SchöbS II, 525), 464, 466, 545; III, 126ff (6 psalms), 318 (Magnificat); BordA, *Motets* I, 53 (= RochlS I, *Abt. 2,* 22; AlfiR, 42); II, 183; LückS III, 126; SchöbS III, 793. The *Adoramus* credited to Anerio in NeyR VI, 203, and RochlS I, *Abt. 2,* 21, is actually Palestrina's (cf. PalW V, 60). A so-called *Missa Vestiva i colli* that has come to be credited to Anerio is actually Palestrina's *Missa Laudate Dominum;* cf. MosVC, 376.
[149] For an ex., *see* HabGA, 61.

of the oratorio.[150] However, his *Missa brevis*[151] is in the style of Palestrina's short Masses. He is one of the composers who adapted the *Missa Papae Marcelli,* which he rearranged *a 4*[152] from its original form *a 6.* Paraphrase is used with most eloquent effect in the Introit of his *Missa pro defunctis.*[153]

Soriano, in his dramatic-type Passions according to Matthew,[154] Mark,[155] Luke,[156] and John,[157] sets the lines of the Synagoga polyphonically wherever these represent the words of a group—the disciples or the crowd, etc.—and in a few instances where they give the words of an individual. These instances include, in the St. Matthew Passion, the message of Pilate's wife, for which Soriano writes a *si placet* setting. Settings are provided also for several of the utterances of Christ in the Matthew, Luke, and John Passions. Characterization is attempted: the maids who speak to Peter (in the St. Matthew Passion) and Pilate's wife are represented by a trio of high voices. The music has restrained dramatic quality. Soriano's six-part *Missa super voces musicales*[158] is a hexachord Mass, drawing on the hard and natural hexachords. The final Agnus *a 8* incorporates a mirror canon *a 2* on the hard hexachord. Soriano based his four-part *Missa Nos autem gloriari*[159] on Palestrina's motet[160] of that name and made an arrangement *a 8*[161] of the *Missa Papae Marcelli.* He further contributed the *Christe* (*a 8*) and the *Et ascendit* (*a 4*) to the *Missa Cantantibus organis,*[162] based on Palestrina's similarly named motet,[163] a Mass (mostly *a 12*) that was a joint undertaking of Palestrina, Stabile,[164] Dragoni,[165] Giovanelli, Prospero Santini,[166] and Curzio Mancini. Giovanelli also based an entire Mass of his own, a work *a 8,* on another Palestrina model, the master's own Mass on *Vestiva i colli.*[167]

[150] *See* further AlaS, 165ff (music exx. *hors de texte*).   [151] Pr. HabRMS I, fasc. 1.

[152] Pr. ProsP, 53, without *continuo,* as in the edition of 1646; a *continuo* is included in the various other editions (1626–1689).

[153] Pr. ProsM, *Annus II,* I, No. 2 (*Dies irae* also in SchöbS III, 812; other portions of the Mass *ibid.,* 793, 806, 808, 954, with wrong attributions to Felice. The *Pie Jesu* extract from the *Dies irae* also wrongly attributed to Felice in BordA, *Motets,* III, 9). For other exx., *see* HabGA, 65; HabRMS I, fasc. 2, i, xxi; CasAP II, 183, 190, 200, 203, 205; AV IV, 148. A *Te Deum* pr. ProsM, *Annus I,* IV, 402, is wrongly attributed to Felice (cf. EitQ I, 147). Another *Te Deum* by G. F. Anerio is pr. LückS IV, 149.

[154] Pr. ProsM, *Annus I,* IV, 3; BordA, *Motets,* III, 20 (all but *si placet* sections also in HabRMS, II, fasc. 3, 1; 5 such sections in CasAP I, 171. 172, 175, 182, 183).

[155] Pr. ProsM, *Annus I,* IV, 19.

[156] *Ibid.,* 27 (5 *si placet* sections also in CasAP I, 38, 173, 174, 176, 184).

[157] Pr. ProsM I, *Annus I,* IV, 41; BordA, *Motets,* III, 36; HabRMS II, fasc. 3, 15 (2 *si placet* sections also in CasAP I, 181, 182).

[158] Pr. ProsS I, 205.   [159] *Ibid.,* II, 461; BordA, *Messes,* III, 1.

[160] Pr. PalW V, 66; PalO III, 82.   [161] Pr. ProsP, 77.

[162] Pr. MPI I. For other works by Soriano, *see* ProsM, *Annus I,* III, 225ff (= supplement to KJ, XIX [1905]; set of 8 Magnificats, 1 for each Tone; the first also in LückS IV, 125), 425, 443–453 (5 items; 1 also in AV III, 214, another in SeiffN II, 21); CasAP II, 198; CommM XXV, 11.

[163] Pr. PalW III, 9; PalO VIII, 10; MPI I, 87.

[164] Other exx. of sacred music pr. CommM XVI, 70; XXII, 44.

[165] 12 other exx. of sacred music pr. CasAP II.   [166] Another ex. pr. CommM XXV, 80.

[167] Cf. MosVC, 138ff. Giovanelli's Mass is pr. separately by Sulzbach-Verlag, Berlin, ed. by H. W. Frey. For other sacred works by Giovanelli, *see* CommM XXV, 17, 23, 29; XXVI, 1, 5, 15; ProsM, *Annus I,* III, 194; TorA II, 423, 433. *See* further LeiG, 189ff.

The Neapolitans

The only Italian rival that Rome had in the cultivation of sacred music late—as early—in the *cinquecento* was Venice. However, various other centers made noteworthy contributions also, among them Naples, where the Spanish Court fostered music for the church. The excellent Spanish composer and theorist, Diego Ortiz (cf. pp. 592, 625ff), summoned by the Duke of Alba, served as *maestro* of the Viceroyal Chapel, 1555 to 1570. His successors included Francisco Martinez di Loscos (1570–1583), Roy (1583–1598), Macque (1599–1614), and Macque's pupil, Giovanni Maria Trabaci (1614–1647).

Roy, c. 1590, added strings and reed instruments to the choir.[168] His *Missa Panis quem ego dabo,* based on Hellinck's motet, was printed at Venice, 1565, together with Palestrina's Mass on the same model. Like Clemens (cf. p. 352), Roy provides a considerable amount of original writing and draws on Hellinck's themes only at certain points. Textual recurrences bring about musical recurrences: thus the music that accompanies *"Jesu Christe"* in the Gloria sets the name of Jesus Christ also in the Credo; likewise the music for *"simul adoratur et conglorificatur"* is similar to that previously used for *"Adoramus te, glorificamus te."* [169]

Macque's Book I of motets *a 5, 6,* and *8* (1596) reveals not only his Netherlandish origin but also the Palestrinian influence that was evidently exerted upon him during his stay at Rome, before he finally settled at Naples in 1586.[170] Trabaci, unlike his predecessors, a native Italian, was a central figure in Neapolitan music of the late 16th century and the first decades of the 17th.[171]

Among other contributors to Neapolitan sacred music of the time were Pomponio Nenna; [172] the native Neapolitan, Gian Domenico Montella (b. 1570), who entered the Viceroyal Chapel as a lute-player in 1591; [173] the Calabrian, Rocco Rodio (cf. p. 532), whose five-part *Missa de Beata Virgine* may be rendered *a 4* by omitting the *Pars quinta,* or *a 3* either by omitting that voice and the superius or by having only the three top parts sung; [174] and Gesualdo, whose sacred works reveal the liking for chromaticism so conspicuous in his madrigals. Three voices produce degree-inflection toward the close of his five-part *Ave Regina.*[175] The device is used strikingly elsewhere also, e.g., in *Peccantem me quotidie* and *O vos omnes.*[176] In the

---

[168] Cf. ProtaN, 191.

[169] Further about this Mass, *see* SchmidtgM, 89f. For a motet by Roy, *see* CommM XXV, 35.

[170] For further information on this collection, with many short exx., *see* IMAMI V, xxxiiiff.

[171] 20 motets and 2 Masses of his are pr. in IMAMI V.

[172] For discussion of his sacred music, with many exx., *see* IMAMI V, liiiff; for another ex., *see* ProsM *Annus II,* II, fasc. 2, 37.

[173] A Mass and 6 motets of his pr. IMAMI V, 5ff.

[174] The Mass is described in AmbG IV, 91, where further information is given about Rodio.

[175] *Ibid.,* 221.

[176] *Ibid.,* 255 and 260, respectively. IMAMI V contains 11 other motets by Gesualdo; its preface provides a useful survey of Neapolitan sacred music of the time.

former, the composer resorts to madrigalian procedures also at the words *"timor [mortis]*," where each voice leaps down, and at *"salva me"* where the third of the chord is raised to make it major.

Sacred Polyphony at Florence, Bologna, Modena, and Ferrara

At Florence, interest was very clearly concentrated on secular music. Galilei is known to have written a setting of the Lamentations, but this does not survive. His Book II of madrigals includes two motets,[177] and in his *Fronimo* (cf. p. 523) there is a transcription for voice and lute of a part of his lost setting of *In exitu Israel*,[178] the voice being assigned the bass part. Striggio, though primarily a madrigalist, has left two Masses and a few motets. One of these, *Ecce beatam lucem*, is extraordinary in that it is a forty-part work, written for four choirs—one *a 8*, one *a 10*, one *a 16*, and one *a 6*. All parts are provided with words. Although a MS preserving the work dates from as early as 1587, the document includes an organ bass (which is additional to the forty voices).[179] The composition itself dates from not later than 1568 (and therefore must belong to Striggio's Florentine period), for Massimo Troiano tells us in his *Dialoghi* (1569) that it was performed that year at the marriage of Duke William of Bavaria and Renée of Lorraine. He states, moreover, that it was executed by eight *tromboni*, eight *viole da arco*, eight *flauti grossi*, one *instrumento da penna*, and one *liuto grosso*. Since by *"instrumento da penna"* is meant a *cembalo*, the bass part mentioned above was presumably worked out at this instrument.

At Bologna, the chief musician of the period was Banchieri. Although essentially a composer of secular music, his *Concerti ecclesiastici* of 1595, containing music for double chorus, has the distinction of being one of the oldest prints containing an organ part. (Concerning an earlier instance by Croce, *see* p. 500.) This, designated as a *spartitura*, gives the bass of the first chorus and also—evidently as an aid to the organist in determining the harmony—the superius. Barring is used. The terms *"a 4"* and *"a 8"* are inserted here and there to show whether only the first chorus is singing or both.[180] A note *A gli sig. organisti* tells the player that where *"a 8"* appears the superius and bass of the second chorus are to be added. Banchieri wrote also Masses, psalms, etc.

At Modena, as might be expected, Orazio Vecchi wrote sacred works much affected by secular traits. Thus, in *Velociter exaudi me* (Psalm CXLII [143], 7),[181] at *"defecit spiritus"* ("my spirit faileth"), rests, producing an ef-

[177] Pr. IMAMI IV, 157, 254.
[178] *Ibid.*, 25. The vocal version there given is the editor's reconstruction from the transcr. in *Fronimo*.
[179] For details, *see* SchneidA, 67; insert with 3 pp. of facsimile given opp. that page.
[180] Cf. ArndA, 7. [181] Pr. ProsM, *Annus I*, II, 559.

fect of gasping, are inserted in the course of the setting of each of these words, in several of their repetitions. Toward the end, all voices imitate a motif which is at first wholly conjunct but which, in the process of repetition, is varied by leaps, those in the lowest part converting it from a purely melodic voice into a genuinely harmonic bass. At the opening of the four-part *Cantabo Domino*,[182] Vecchi avoids the obviousness of ordinary imitation by having the tenor omit the first six notes of the motif; the treatment of imitation is somewhat similar at the beginning of *Erat Jesus*.[183] In his setting of the canticle, *Benedictus Dominus*,[184] Vecchi alternates verses *a 4* with verses in chant, the former being mostly in *falsobordone,* the monotony of this type of music, however, being relieved by the application, to some of the verses, of normal polyphony.

At nearby Ferrara, Luzzaschi produced a collection of motets *a 5* (printed 1598). Here, too, Paolo Isnardi, musician to the Duke and *maestro di cappella* at the Cathedral, composed Masses, motets, Lamentations, etc.[185]

Sacred Music at Mantua

At Mantua, Wert proved himself a worthy incumbent of the post of *maestro di cappella* of Santa Barbara by writing sacred music of high excellence. The fine motet *a 7, Egressus Jesus*,[186] a setting of the text from Matthew XV, 21–28, is dramatically powerful. The seven voices are grouped in different ways, though not consistently, to characterize Jesus, the woman of Canaan, and the disciples. Praetorius [187] describes a rendition of this work (presumably in Germany) by two theorbos, three lutes, two citterns, four *clavicembali* and spinets, seven *viole da gamba,* two transverse flutes, two boy singers, one alto singer, and one bass-viol. He says that the combination, which he designates as an "Englisch Consort [i.e., a broken one]" made "gar ein schoenen effectum." [188]

Gastoldi, Wert's probable assistant (cf. p. 408), published Masses, motets, vesper psalms, etc.,[189] while Pallavicino, Wert's successor as *maestro* to the duke, brought out a volume of motets *a 8, a 12,* and *a 16.* Girolamo Belli,[190] who sang in the duke's choir, printed volumes of *Sacrae cantiones,* etc. At the Cathedral of St. Peter's in Mantua, Viadana—who was *maestro* from 1594 to 1609—made an important early stride in the history of baroque music

---

[182] *Ibid.,* 556.   [183] *Ibid.,* 103.

[184] Pr. CommM XXVII, 14. Other sacred works in ProsM, *Annus I,* II, 103 (= AV IV, 32), 497; ProsS II, No. XVI; CommM XVI, 24; XXIII, 72 (= TorA II, 277); XXVII, 11, 19, 21; LückS III, 134; TorA II, 293; SchöbS II, 771; AV V, 175.

[185] Cf. EitQ V, 251f.

[186] Pr. CommB IV, 71, with wrong ascription to Vaet; CommM XXIII, 76.

[187] Cf. PraetoS III, 133f.

[188] For other sacred exx., *see* CommB II, 24 (with wrong ascription to Vaet); DehnS, *Lieferung* VI, 2; SmM, 92; AV VI, 151. *See also* BautW, 63f.

[189] A Magnificat pr. TorA II, 79.   [190] An ex. pr. KillK, 301.

with his *Cento concerti ecclesiastici* of 1602. This was published with organ bass. But, whereas earlier printed organ basses had been of the *basso seguente* type—in which the organ bass duplicates the melodic line of the vocal bass or of whatever part happens to be functioning as the lowest one at any given moment—Viadana provides a real *basso continuo*. This may at times duplicate the lowest given voice, at times differ from it. In many of the *concerti*, especially those for a small number of voices, it is an integral and indispensable part of a composition (the nature of the *basso seguente*, of course, having been such that it could be omitted without eliminating anything from the polyphonic web). In such a piece *a 4* as the *O sacrum convivium* [191] from the *Cento concerti*, however, the vocal parts make quite complete conservative polyphony by themselves.[192] Viadana's skill in writing Renaissance-type polyphony is shown not only by works like the *O sacrum convivium*, but by music conceived without an organ part in the first place.[193]

Mantua was the scene also of the composition of synagogue music. Salomone Rossi's collection, *Hashirim Asher Lishlomo*,[193a] was printed at Venice in 1622. It consists of settings of psalms, hymns, and prayers for sabbaths and other occasions. The music is in Italian Renaissance style, without any special Hebraic character. While the music reads, of course, from left to right, the Hebrew text runs from right to left.

Sacred Polyphony at Genoa and Milan

At Genoa, Simone Molinaro's activity included the composition of Masses, motets,[194] and Magnificats, some being provided with organ bass.

At Milan, Vincenzo Ruffo was the outstanding composer of sacred music, beginning in 1563, the year both of his appointment as *maestro* at the Cathedral and of the earliest sessions of the Council of Trent devoted to music. Strangely enough, in view of its late date, his Mass of 1542, a work in the Netherlandish style, seems to be the first polyphonic Mass by a native Italian to be printed.[195] It was followed in 1557 by a collection of four Masses *a 5* and these, in turn, in 1580, by a set of four more, *"novamente*

---

[191] Pr. with organ bass, in ArndA, 31; without organ bass, in LückS III, 143; BordA, *Motets,* II, 112.

[192] Similar exx. from this collection are the *Ave verum* (pr. with organ bass in SchneidA, 188; without organ bass, in CasAP I, 151); *Exultate justi* (pr. without organ bass in CasR IV, 1); *Cantate Domino* (pr. with organ bass in SchneidA, 191). Further about the *Cento concerti* and for other exx., see ArndA, 2ff, 9ff; SchneidA, 69ff, 172ff; WolfME, 117; ScherG, 181; BukMB, 27, 24f.

[193] I.e., his four-part *Missa sine nomine*, ed. by F. X. Haberl and published separately, 1883, by F. Pustet. For the *Missa Cantabo Domino*, see HabRMS I, fasc. 5. The Gradual and Tract of Viadana's *Officium defunctorum* (1600) pr. HabRMS I, fasc. 3, iv, vi. For *falsibordoni* by Viadana, see AV IV, 247; ProsM, *Annus I,* III, 48ff.

[193a] Pr. RossP; see further, IdJ, 198ff; GradenMI, 138ff.

[194] For exx., see CommM XV (7 motets), XVI (3 motets).

[195] Cf. WagG, 400.

composte seconda la forma del Concilio Tridentino." This collection, aiming to meet the wishes of the Council, avoids both secular models and technical display. Chordal writing, which is conspicuously present, allows the text to be heard with perfect clarity.[196]

EXAMPLE 113. Extract from the Credo of *Missa de Feria*—Ruffo (from TorA I, 197).

(Note the oblique cross-relation from the end of measure 6 to the beginning of measure 7)

The 1580 set contains a letter of dedication to Paolo Caymo, canon of the Milan Cathedral, in which the signer, Antonio Antoniano, states that Cardinal Borromeo "moved Vincenzo Ruffo to undertake this work, not, indeed, uselessly." The music shows that the Cardinal had reason to feel that the principles, in behalf of which he had labored, were being observed. In 1592, Ruffo brought out another collection of Masses, and these bore the significant title *Missae Borromeae.* Ruffo's *Adoramus te,*[197] a preponderantly chordal work, shows him applying the same style in the field of the motet. On the other hand, in his *In convertendo Dominus*[198] he seems intent upon adding, to a chordal basis, passages of some interest from the standpoint of polyphony; the contrapuntal technique of Ruffo the madrigalist is a little more in evidence. However, the more concise style was, in Italy, particularly characteristic of the north, though, owing to the pronouncements of the Council of Trent and to the decline in the use of plainsong, it was naturally applied in the south also. Perhaps the special tendency in northern Italy was a result of proximity to France.

The production of Masses, motets, Magnificats, etc., of the other notable composer active at Milan—Orfeo Vecchi—includes a collection entitled *Motetti di Orfeo Vecchi Maestro di Cappella di S. Maria della Scala e d'altri eccellentiss. Musici* (1598). Among the contents are a *Surge propera* and a *Quanti mercenarii* which are actually motet adaptations, by Orfeo, of Palestrina's *Vestiva i colli* and *Io son ferito.*[199] In 1604, a whole *Scielta* of his offered twenty-one similar adaptations, which drew on madrigals by Merulo, Ingegneri, Palestrina, Wert, G. M. Nanino, Orfeo himself, and others.[200]

[196] For a Gloria from the same collection, *see* TorA I, 193.
[197] Pr. CasAP I, 169; LückS, IV, 1; AV III, 63.
[198] Pr. TorA I, 209.
[199] The adaptations pr. PalW XXVIII, 239 and 179, respectively (after a print of 1605).
[200] For fuller data, *see* HabOV, 172f; EinB, 1604³.

Pre-eminently a church composer, Orfeo at the same time is clearly a member of a new generation: his Masses are provided with *basso continuo*.

Sacred Polyphony at Cremona, Bergamo, and Brescia

Ingegneri is the chief composer whose career ran its course at Cremona, the main events of Monteverdi's career having unfolded elsewhere. Ingegneri followed the course of his teacher Ruffo in writing Masses in simple style, but did not compose them to the exclusion of Masses making a greater use of polyphonic technique. Thus, at least one of the works [201] in his Book I of Masses for from five to eight voices (1573) reveals a tendency toward polyphonic elaboration, though not, to be sure, to the extent that this is found in the music of the older Netherlanders. This work shows that it is unwise to draw too sharp a line between the north Italian and Roman groups, imputing a strong tendency to the former to compose *Missae breves* and to the latter to write in a more polyphonic manner, though tendencies in these divergent directions clearly did exist in a general way. A second book of Ingegneri Masses (1587) contained four works *a 5* and one *a 8*, all on ecclesiastical themes. His output includes also a set of twenty-seven Responses for Holy Week (1588), once thought to be by Palestrina.[202] These mainly short compositions are in the familiar *aBcB* form or in *ABcBAB* form.[202a] They are *a 4*, but the *c* section in all but one is *a 3*, the exception consisting of a canon *a 2*. The writing is largely chordal and declamatory, but imitation occurs also, especially in the sections *a 3*, as in the *Tenebrae factae sunt*.[203] Degree-inflection is present, e.g., on the word *"quomodo"* in *Una hora* and at the opening of *Plange*.[204]

Massaini became *maestro di cappella* in Cremona in 1595, after having formerly served in the same capacity at Salò, Prague, and Salzburg, and later on at Piacenza and Lodi. He published Masses, motets, hymns, Lamentations, etc.

Born at Cremona, though active mainly in Germany, was Cesare Zacharia (Zachariis), who wrote motets, hymns, *falsibordoni*, etc. The *falsobordone* of his that follows may be taken as characteristic of the type generally. The fact that *cinquecento* musicians went so far as to print numerous *falsibordoni*—actually harmonizations of the Psalm Tones, Magnificat Tones, etc.—, these being intended to supply part-music to alternate with plainsong, provides additional evidence of the decline in prestige that unadorned plainsong had suffered.

---

201 The Kyrie and part of the Gloria pr. IMAMI VI, xxxi, xxxiv.

202 They are pr. in PalW XXXII, 93ff (1 also in WolfME, 93, with the *aB* portion of the next piece included, evidently in error). About the misattribution and its correction, *see* Habl, 78f.

202a This is the liturgical pattern for the last of each set of 3 responsories in Holy Week; *see*, for example, those for Good Friday in Officium, 458, 461, 463, 469, 471f, 479ff.

203 Often reprinted in popular-priced editions with the wrong ascription to Palestrina.

204 For other sacred works by Ingegneri, *see* CommM, XV, 69 (for double chorus); DehnS, *Lieferung 12*, 8; AV V, 38, 78; VI, 85, 191.

EXAMPLE 114. (a) No. 12 from the set of *falsibordoni* for Tone 8, from Zacharia's *Intonationes cum Psalmodiis* . . . , 1594[205] (after ProsM, *Annus I*, III, 44); (b) the same as applied to the even-numbered verses of Psalm CXIII (114), the odd-numbered verses being intended for performance in plainsong (after T. Schrems, *Falsobordonisätze für Vesperpsalmen* . . . , 41; for the plainsong, *see* Liber, 117).

At Bergamo, the Masses and motets of Pietro Vinci reveal him in a favorable light. His six-part hexachord Mass *La sol fa mi re ut* contains a fine Kyrie.[206] His moving motet, *O Crux benedicta*,[207] makes sparing but eloquent use of degree-inflection.

By Costanzo Antegnati (1557–c. 1620), outstanding in the musical life of Brescia, where he was born and where he served as cathedral organist, we have motets, psalms, two books of Masses, etc.[208] (*See* further p. 530.) Likewise born at Brescia, but more active at Trent, was Giovanni Contino (c. 1513–1574), perhaps Marenzio's teacher (cf. p. 420), *maestro di cappella* to the court of Mantua, 1561–1565. His surviving works—all printed in 1560–1561 —include a book of Masses, one of Lamentations, and two of motets, of

[205] This set, providing *falsibordoni* for all 8 Tones (with several settings of each Tone), pr. in ProsM, *Annus I*, III, 12ff. Other exx. of Zacharia appear in ProsM, *Annus I*, III, and *Annus II*, IV.
[206] Pr. TorA I, 317.
[207] Pr. BellerC, 419 (with wrong attribution to Goudimel; cf. JepPS, 47); KillK, 310. Other motets *ibid.*, 315; TorA I, 325, 328.
[208] Cf. EitQ I, 164f.

which one, containing Introit, Gradual, and Alleluia settings, testifies to the current interest in music for the Proper.[209]

Sacred Polyphony in Cities Near Venice

In the vicinity of Venice—and at times in the city itself—we find Asola at Treviso [209a] and Vicenza; and Porta, Balbi, and Giulio Belli (not to be confused with Girolamo Belli) at least on occasion at Padua.

Asola's large output included, in 1565, a collection of Introits and Alleluias, i.e., a collection of music for the Proper. A collection of *Falsi Bordoni per cantar Salmi* by Asola (1575) contains also examples by his teacher, Ruffo. In the *Nisi Dominus* [210] from his eight-part *Nova Vespertina . . . Psalmodia* (1587), Asola counterbalances the plainness of some of the writing by attractive clashes between the macrorhythm and microrhythm and by contrasts of timbre. Another piece *a 8, Quem vidistis pastores,*[211] is for two choirs ostensibly singing bodily in canon at the unison with one another; however, there is little *stretto.* Another collection of *Psalmodia vespertina,* which appeared in 1592, contained a dedication to Palestrina, written by Asola; the preparation of the collection was an act of homage, and among those who contributed were Asola himself, Croce, Gastoldi, Leoni—*maestro di cappella* at Vicenza late in the 16th century and early in the 17th [212]—and Porta. Asola's printed Masses, *a 3* to *a 8,* appeared between 1570 and 1591. That he had been Ruffo's pupil is at moments evident in them.[213] His *Missa pro defunctis* [214] illustrates the combination, characteristic of the north Italians at this period, of chordal writing (e.g., in the *Ingemisco*) with concise polyphony. The Gregorian melodies appear now in one voice, now in another. The alternation of plainsong and polyphony is treated with particular eloquence in the *Dies irae.* Asola's Passions, according to Matthew, Mark, and Luke,[215] leave the parts of Christ and the Evangelist to be intoned to the plainsong formulas. The other sections are mostly chordal. In the course of the 16th century, *falsobordone* style became increasingly prevalent in the setting of the Passion, so that little could be accomplished in the way of describing situations or characters.[216] Although in the main conservative, Asola is among the first to use a *basso continuo* for organ.[217]

---

[209] Further on Contino, *see* GuerrGC.

[209a] About the MSS of polyphonic music owned by the cathedral there in the late 16th century, *see* AlesM.

[210] Pr. TorA II, 373.

[211] Pr. CasAP II, 147. For other motets, *see ibid.,* 158, 162; ProsM, *Annus I,* II, 124 (= PaoluA I, 253; BordA, *Motets,* II, 22); CommM XXVII, 23; AV V, 66; VI, 227.

[212] For 2 other motets of his, *see* CommM XXII, 36, 40.

[213] For Asola's 4-part *Missa octavi toni, see* ProsM, *Annus II,* I, No. 1.

[214] Pr. ProsM, *Annus I,* I, 259; Kyrie in BockM XII, 43.

[215] Described, with exx., in KadP, 143ff.

[216] Cf. SchzI, 101, where the *Crucifige* in Asola's St. John Passion is cited as a modest exception.

[217] Cf. KinO, 204.

Porta, in the preface [218] to a Mass collection of 1578, dedicated to the arch-bishop of Ravenna, explained that he had striven to make the text intelligible; thus he aimed to conform with the requirements of the Council of Trent. But, in such a movement as the Sanctus [219] of a *Missa Mortuorum* of his, he did not hesitate to write imitative polyphony, though in a moderate style.

Porta's first contributions to the sacred repertory had issued from the press of Gardano: in 1555, his first book of motets *a 5* and, in 1559, his first book of motets *a 4*.[220] A collection of settings of plainsong Introits for Sundays and another collection of Introits for Saints' Days were among the earliest publications to come from the little music-printing office set up by Merulo in 1566.[221] In 1580, Porta brought out a book of fifty-two motets, which includes the antiphon *a 7, Diffusa est gratia*. In this work, four voices are in canon, two *"per motum rectum,"* and two *"per motum contrarium."* This motet has been described as uniting "in a peculiar way the highest learning of the Netherlands with a fine Italian feeling for sonority." [222] A collection of motets published at Nuremberg in 1583 includes three motets by Porta, among them the six-part *Oravi Dominum Deum*,[223] which opens with a passage containing some graceful clashes between macrorhythm and microrhythm. In 1585, there appeared a book of motets *a 6*, dedicated to Sixtus V, which contains an *Ecce sacerdos magnus* [224] that may have been written in special homage to him.

Striking evidence of Porta's skill in contrapuntal writing is furnished by the motet *a 4, Vobis datum est*,[225] printed at the end of Artusi's *Delle imperfettioni della moderna musica* (1600). This motet may be sung in two ways. Each voice is supplied with two clefs. The one nearer the notes is to be used in reading them in the normal way. The one nearer the margin is upside down and is to be used in reading the notes that way. (Once the page is inverted, one reads from right to left, from the original beginning of the piece). Porta has been credited with inventing this type of tour de force, called *contrappunto inverso*. The piece, while not Porta at his best, is nevertheless quite respectable. Posthumous publications of Porta's works include the four-part *Hymnodia sacra totius per anni circulum* (1602), containing forty-four pieces. No. 14 is a particularly fine setting of the *Ave maris stella*. Porta writes music for the odd-numbered stanzas, except for line 1 of stanza 1, which, together with the even-numbered stanzas, he leaves to be sung in plainsong.[225a] He treats stanza 5 freely, but paraphrases and imitates the chant in stanzas 1, 3, and 7. Example 115 gives corresponding portions of these three stanzas and shows some of the varied ways in which the chant is set.

[218] Quoted in HabK, 92.   [219] Pr. PaoluA II, 127.
[220] Motets from this book pr. ProsM, *Annus I*, II, 43, 281 (= AV III, 124), 403.
[221] The date of the first is given as 1556 in IMAMI VI, xxiv, but this is evidently an error; cf. BolC II, 130f.
[222] LeiG, 144. For the piece, *see* BuH III, 227; MartiniE II, 265; etc.
[223] Pr. DehnS, *Lieferung 4, 5*.   [224] Pr. ProsM, *Annus II*, II, No. 7.   [225] Pr. HawkH I, 112.
[225a] Cf. Chap. 7, fn. 42. The tritone on syllable 2 of *Solve*, on the record, is due to an error; note 1 of the interval should lie a third higher.

EXAMPLE 115. Extracts from *Ave maris stella*—Porta (from *Hymnodia sacra totius per anni circulum,* Gardano, 1602; transcr. by M. L. Versè).

The posthumous publications include in addition the eight-part *Psalmodia vespertina cum 4 canticis B.V.* (1605). In the *Lauda Deum tuum Syon* (Psalm CXLVII [148]),[226] from this collection, at the passage that includes *"velociter curit sermo eius"* ("his word runneth very swiftly") the note-values are greatly reduced; Porta's handling of the double-chorus technique produces a resounding composition.

By Balbi, who was *maestro di cappella* at San Antonio in Padua (1585–1591), we have Masses, motets, a volume of *Ecclesiastici concentus* with organ or other instruments (1606),[227] etc. Giulio Belli, who, besides being active there for a time, held posts also at Ferrara, Osimo, Forlì, and elsewhere, composed sacred compositions of the same kinds, his *Concerti ecclesiastici* including a number calling for two cornets (= zinks) with violins or *basso continuo.*[228]

---

[226] Pr. TorA I, 263. Other sacred works pr. *ibid.*, 245; ProsM, *Annus I*, III, 513, 526 (= AV VI, 51); LückS IV, 31; PaoluA I, 226 (= MartiniE, I, 164); III, 46; MartiniE I, 3, 18, 44, 68, 95, 116, 142, 217 (= ChorP V, *Part 6*, 3, 13, 24, 38, 49, 62, 78, 107, resp.); CommM XXVI, 80; AV V, 12, 16, 33, 185, 187, 214; VI, 59, 91, 205, 220.

[227] *See* further TebAP, 11f.

[228] For an article on Belli, *see* BrigiB.

Sacred Polyphony at Venice, including the Music of the Gabrielis and Monteverdi

At Venice, the line of great musicians that added still further luster to St. Mark's in the early part of the century maintained its high excellence toward the close. Strangely enough, the organists, on the whole, contributed more brilliantly to the repertory of vocal polyphony than did the *maestri di cappella*. This polyphony flourished with particular splendor. But it was to the motet rather than to the Mass that Venetian composers, as a group, dedicated their best effort.

The production of the versatile Merulo (first organist, 1557–1584) included Masses—one on Wert's *Cara la vita mia,* one on Andrea Gabrieli's *Benedicam Dominum,* etc.—, Magnificats, and numerous motets. Among the last, his six-part *In Deo speravit cor* [229] is noteworthy for a delightful clash between the macrorhythm and microrhythm on *"refloruit caro mea."* In his *Sancti et justi,*[230] at the words *"vos elegit Deus,"* the middle voice for three measures begins its real, accentual measure on beat 2 while the other voices for the most part begin it on beat 1. *Ave gratia plena* and *Mirabiles elationes* [231] show Merulo writing for two antiphonal choirs.

Andrea Gabrieli, succeeding Annibale Padovano at the second organ in 1564 and Merulo at the first organ in 1585—when he was himself succeeded at the second organ by Giovanni—produced sacred music of great distinction. His Masses include a four-part *Missa brevis* [232] in the normal style for this species, which, for him, is unusually simple. Andrea's earliest known sacred works survive in a volume of motets *a 5* devoted solely to him (1565). Its title includes the words *Motecta . . . tum viva voce, tum omnis generis Instrumentis cantatu commodissimae* ("Motets . . . most suitable to be performed, sometimes by the living voice, sometimes by all kinds of instruments"). The volume was reprinted several times. Andrea opens *Cor meum,*[233] one of the motets in it, with tonal imitation between the two lowest voices and shows madrigal influence by fanciful melismas on the word *"volabo."* In *Cantate Domino,*[234] he repeats a passage on the words *"Quoniam magnus Dominus,"* but with a contrast in color: the first time the soprano is omitted; the second time, the bass. A collection of 1576, *a 4,* includes the exquisite *Filiae Jerusalem.*[235] This opens with an old-fashioned point of real imitation at the fourth below, in which all the voices leap down a fifth; a

[229] Pr. TorA I, 393.   [230] Pr. CommM XXV, 44.

[231] Pr. *ibid.,* XXVII, 51, 56, respectively. Other Merulo motets, pr. *ibid.,* XVI, 65; XXVII, 25; XXVIII, 82.

[232] Pr. ProsM, *Annus I,* I, 165. The 6-part *Missa Pater peccavi* is pr. ProsS II, No. 7; 3 individual Mass movements are pr. in CMI V, 1, 17, 38. For a discussion of Andrea's Masses, *see* WagG, 408ff.

[233] Pr. TorA II, 111.

[234] Pr. IMAMI I, 1. Another 1565 motet pr. TorA II, 117.

[235] Pr. ProsM, *Annus I,* II, 475; BordA, *Motets,* II, 186; AV III, 180.

diminished fourth is outlined melodically in two passages. Motets,[236] treating of the unnamed fallen woman anointing Christ's feet and of Mary Magdalene and the "other Mary" visiting his tomb, have their dramatic touches: in the former, a descending melisma on one of the words illustrates the phrase, *"lacrymis coepit rigare pedes ejus"* ("began to wash his feet with tears"); in the latter, the first words of the angel, *"Jesus quem quaeritis,"* stand out from the preceding polyphonic texture by being set chordally.[237] The book of *Salmi Davidici* of 1583, like the 1565 collection, mentions instruments on the title page. In the dedication to Gregory XIII,[238] Andrea explains that he was inspired by the ancient Hebrew practice of having instruments participate in the rendition of the psalms. The presence at St. Mark's of instruments (in addition to the organs) and the wish to hear his motets executed by them undoubtedly had their share in prompting Andrea to indicate two manners of performance; very likely a third, the combination of voices and instruments, was resorted to also. The *Salmi* are works *a 6*. While a feeling for color is evident in Andrea's motets *a 4* or *a 5*, it becomes more so as the number of voices increases. In the *De profundis*,[239] the contrasting of groups with differing vocal timbres is most effective. At the opening, four of the voices underscore the words by leaping an octave from *De profundis* to *clamavi*. The *Beati quorum remissae sunt*[240] is a "noble piece, of wonderful sonority, [showing] those fine gradations of a basic hue, without violent contrast of color, that seem to be characteristic of Andrea."[241] The 1587 volume, containing compositions by both Andrea and Giovanni (cf. p. 415), includes a splendid seven-part *Angelus ad pastores ait* by Andrea, of which Schütz thought well enough to make a paraphrase for voices and instruments.[242] It included also a *Deus misereatur nostri*[243] for three choruses *a 4*—SSAT, SATB, TTTB—written in the antiphonal style of which Giovanni was an outstanding master; the work was no doubt composed under his influence. The three choruses sing contrasting passages; at one point a soprano part is added to the TTTB choir; at another, a fine passage *a 6* (where, moreover, the rhythm changes from binary to ternary), a new color is introduced by combining SS from choir 1 with AT from choir 2 and T³B from choir 3; at several points, including the close, all twelve voices unite. The work has something of the majesty of a canvas by Giovanni Bellini or Tintoretto.[244]

---

[236] Pr. ProsM, *Annus I*, II, 339 (= AV IV, 206), 146 (= AV IV, 99).

[237] Other 1576 motets pr. ProsM, *Annus I*, II, 193 (= AV III, 96; LückS III, 109), 207, 342 (= AV IV, 212), 399 (= BordA, *Motets*, I, 89), 450 (= AV IV, 233), 457 (= AV III, 175), 481 (= BordA, *Motets*, I, 188; LückS IV, 102), 513 (= AV IV, 242).

[238] Pr. IMAMI I, lxxx.

[239] Pr. IMAMI I, 13; ProsM *Annus II*, II, fasc. 3, 17.

[240] Pr. TorA II, 123. [241] LeiG, 220.

[242] The 2 versions are pr. in Heinrich Schütz, *Sämtliche Werke*, VIII, 191, 171.

[243] Pr. KillK, 277; CMI V, 71.

[244] A Magnificat from the 1587 vol. is pr. in CMI V, 71.

Among the sacred compositions of Giovanni Gabrieli are a Kyrie, Gloria, Sanctus, and Benedictus, all included in a print of 1597 and presumably belonging to a single Mass. The lower parts of the Kyrie *a 5* [245] appear to be instrumental, the highest for a vocal soloist. This part has *piano* and *forte* echo effects (cf. pp. 521, 551) and coloratura writing that requires a virtuoso performer. Another Benedictus [246]—from Book II of the *Sacrae symphoniae* of 1615 (cf. p. 552)—is for three choirs *a 4*, consisting of TrebleSST, SATB, and TTTB. At the beginning, these choirs twice follow each other in the order lowest-highest-middle and then gradually build up to a resounding *Osanna,* in which all twelve voices participate. However magnificent this Benedictus may be, it is nevertheless true that Mass composition was of secondary importance to Giovanni, as it was to most of his Venetian contemporaries. The golden age of the polyphonic Mass, indeed, was drawing to a close.[247] In Giovanni's motets, however, the Venetian style of polychoral composition attained its culmination. Motets of his began to appear in the 1587 volume representing him and Andrea jointly. Even in examples for a single chorus, he preferred writing for many voices, as in his six-part *Beata es Virgo, Miserere,* and *Timor et tremor;* [248] seven-part *Sancta Maria, Ego dixi,* and *Benedixisti;* [249] and eight-part *Jubilate Deo.*[250] Colorfulness and richness of sound are obtained by means of the spacing and of vocal registration. Little use is made of melismas, the few that appear being mostly brief scale passages filling in what would otherwise be leaps. In the *Miserere,* there are instances of degree-inflection. In *Timor et tremor,* the opening is illustrated in madrigalian fashion: "*timor*" is expressed by a rest between the two syllables; "*tremor,*" by eighth-note alternations of two pitches. The *Jubilate* is not antiphonal, but in genuine writing *a 8*. The polychoral motets and Magnificats include works for two choirs *a 4*: e.g., *Deus Deus meus, O Domine Jesu Christe, Anima mea Dominum, O quam suavis, O magnum mysterium, Hodie completi sunt, O Jesu mi dulcissime;* [251] two choirs *a 5*: *Domine exaudi;* [252] two choirs *a 6*: *Angelus ad pastores ait;* [253] three choirs *a 4*: *Magnificat sexti toni;* [254] three choirs *a 5*: *Salvator noster;* [255] and four choirs *a 4*: *Ascendit Deus.*[256] The various choirs in a single piece are differently constituted and are contrasted and united with one another so as to produce the greatest brilliance and power. The *O quam suavis* has effective degree-inflection on the word "*suavis.*" The

---

[245] Fragment pr. WintG III, 108; WagG, 414.   [246] Pr. WintG III, 42.
[247] Cf. WagG, 413ff.
[248] Pr. WintG III, 29, 55, and 133 (incomplete), respectively.
[249] Pr. *ibid.,* 24, 3, and CommM III, 62, respectively.
[250] Pr. WintG III, 32.
[251] Pr. *ibid.,* 7, 16 (= CW X, 42), 18, 58; EinSH, 290; CW X, 9, 21, respectively.
[252] Pr. WintG III, 15.   [253] Pr. TorA II, 177.
[254] Fragment in WintG III, 124. (For a Magnificat *a 8, see* ProsM, *Annus II,* IV, last no.)
[255] Fragment *ibid.,* 127.
[256] Fragment *ibid.,* 101.

same device is used with striking eloquence in Giovanni's *In ecclesiis*[257] on *Deus, Deus*. This piece—which juxtaposes passages for soprano (supported by the organ), for tenor (similarly supported), for each of these as well as for both of them with chorus *a 4*, for an instrumental group *a 6* (three *cornetti*, one *violino*, two trombones), for alto and tenor with the instrumental group, for this combination with chorus *a 4*, for soprano and tenor duet, and finally for the instrumental group with two choruses *a 4*—is a work of remarkable sumptuousness and opulence. "Giovanni Gabrieli is the musical Titian of Venice, as Palestrina is the musical Raphael of Rome."[258] With his compositions, however, we have definitely crossed the border into the domain of baroque music.

The motets of Gioseffo Guami, who became Giovanni's colleague by succeeding Bell'Haver at the first organ in 1588, include a five-part *In die tribulationis*[259] that opens with a point of imitation, in which all voices ascend a minor sixth chromatically; degree-inflection continues to play a role in the rest of this highly dramatic work.

In a publication of 1585, the Giovanni Bassano whose work dealing with ornamentation has been mentioned several times, names himself "*Musico dell'Illustr. Signoria di Venetia*"; in 1595, or earlier, he became *maestro* of music at the Seminary of St. Mark's and, by 1607, "*capo de' concerti*" at St. Mark's.[260] His varied production includes motets—some with organ bass.[261] When Bassano was appointed *maestro* at the Seminary, he succeeded Donato in the post, the Seminary having been moved to a distance from the cathedral in 1592 and Donato having succeeded Zarlino as *maestro di cappella* there in 1590. Though preponderantly a composer of secular works, Donato has left us a small quantity of sacred music.[262]

A number of Masses by Croce—Donato's successors as *maestro* in 1603—which appeared from 1596 to 1599, indicate that he was the chief representative of the *Missa brevis* in Italy. Their brevity can hardly be exceeded. The Benedictus of the five-part *Missa prima sexti toni*[263] comprises only eleven measures, the *Osanna* included. The writing of this work, however, is not perfunctory. The two Agnus settings present interestingly different treatment of the same melodic material and unifying relationships are worked out between the Kyrie I, Gloria, and Sanctus, between the Kyrie II and *Cum Sancto Spiritu*, etc. Croce's motets, if they reveal no striking personality, show skill in handling the style of the day. Latin accentuation is scrupulously ob-

[257] Pr. *ibid.*, 73; HAM, 175.   [258] AmbG III, 543.
[259] Pr. CommM XVII, 52; other motets *ibid.*, 49, 56, 61, 65, 70 (= DehnS, *Lieferung 10*, 7), 73; a Mass *ibid.*, XVIII, 18.
[260] Cf. CafS I, 44, 195, 207; EitQ I, 367.
[261] For 2 exx. of motets for double chorus, see CommM XXVII, 29, 35.
[262] For a motet, *see* CommM XXIV, 80.
[263] Pr. HabRMS I, fasc. 4; HabGC, Supp. Other short Masses by Croce in HabRMS I, fasc. 9; II, fasc. 8.

served. The ability to combine terseness with careful craftsmanship is again evident in such responsories as his *In Monte Oliveti* and *Tristis est anima mea*.[264] Word-painting—as on *"tremuit"* in *Velum templi* [265] and in the descending scale-passage on *"inclinato capite"* in the *Tenebrae* [266]—and degree-inflection—as in *Exaltabo te* [267]—are used with moderation. Writing for double chorus is managed smoothly and effectively. *Buccinate in neomenia tuba* [268] is a brilliant example, with passages, on the words *"in voce tubae corneae," "in chordis et organo,"* and *"in timpano,"* characteristically suggesting the instruments mentioned. In *Incipite Domino*,[269] also for double chorus, a ternary passage on the words *"Cantate Domino"* recurs as a refrain, contrasting with the binary rhythm of the rest of the piece. A collection of double-chorus motets by Croce, published in 1594, contains one of the earliest known examples of printed organ basses.[270] This, unlike the Banchieri *spartitura* of 1595, gives the bass parts of both choruses.

Monteverdi—succeeding Croce, in 1613, after the intervening incumbency of Martinengo—is the last of the *maestri* at St. Mark's belonging to our period. His production of sacred music was small before he assumed this post. His early *Sacrae cantiunculae* (printed in 1582, i.e., during his Cremonese period),[271] short compositions *a 3*—almost exercises in classic polyphonic writing—show how firmly he had been grounded in the traditional style by Ingegneri. Nearly all these little pieces open imitatively but, in some, literal imitation seems to be deliberately avoided. In his Mass printed in 1610,[272] Monteverdi again pays his respects to the past, but writes on a much grander scale. The composition—which is *a 6*, with a final Agnus *a 7* [273]—is an example of the parody Mass, by then almost obsolete, and is based on Gombert's *In illo tempore loquente Jesu*. The writing is full and rich, but archaic in manner for Monteverdi, who reworks, in traditional fashion, the ten motifs upon which Gombert had built his points of imitation. For instance, Monteverdi reworks, in Kyrie II and at *"Deum de Deo"* in the Credo, the motif Gombert applies to the words, *"loquente Jesu ad turbas"* (cf. Ex. 77 *supra*); he likewise introduces, in Kyrie II and at various other points, a sequential figure derived from the opening notes of this motif. A collection printed in 1641 and another printed in 1649 each contains a Mass *a 4*,[274] these also being in old

---

[264] Pr. AV III, 34, 37, respectively; less completely in ProsM, *Annus I*, IV, 105, 107.
[265] *Ibid.*, 123; AV III, 43.   [266] Pr. ProsM, *Annus I*, IV, 128; AV III, 46.
[267] Pr. ProsM, *Annus I*, II, 96; AV VI, 180.   [268] Pr. TorA II, 323.
[269] *Ibid.*, 335. Other motets pr. ProsM, *Annus I*, II, 158 (= AV IV, 107), 201 (= AV III, 102; LückS III, 140), 454 (= AV IV, 237; CasAP, 141), 562 (= CasAP, 145; LückS IV, 5), 563, 565 (= AV VI, 178; BordA, *Motets* III, 58), 567 (= AV VI, 118); IV, 114 (= AV III, 40), 149 (= AV III, 49); CommM XXIII, 31, 34; LückS IV, 21.
[270] Cf. KinO, 196; ArndA, 6f.
[271] Pr. IMAMI VI, 216ff; MontevO XIV, 1ff.   [272] *Ibid.*, 57.
[273] The *Crucifixus* is not *a 9*, as stated in PruCM, 114, but *a 4*. (The original French version of PruCM is correct.)
[274] Pr. MontevO, XV, 59 (= *Claudio Monteverde "Messa a quatro da cappella," mise en partition . . . par Antonio Tirabassi* [1914]); XVI, 1, respectively.

style. A *basso seguente* is provided for all three Masses. Monteverdi's most distinctive productions in the sacred field consist not so much of conservative, though admirable, works like these as they do of music combining voices and instruments and contributing to the development and establishment at St. Mark's of the blossoming baroque style.[275]

Sacred Music by Arcadelt Printed in France

In 1557, i.e., after the Council of Trent had opened but before it had taken its important action regarding music, Le Roy and Ballard printed a collection of three Masses by Arcadelt, the only ones by him known to survive. In these, although himself among the leading madrigal and chanson composers of the day, the *maître de chapelle* to the Cardinal of Lorraine did not offend against the proprieties by drawing on secular models. One is a parody Mass based on Mouton's motet, *Noe, Noe*.[276] Each movement of the Mass begins with the first motif of the model, with other motifs drawn upon in Mouton's order. In Kyrie I, Arcadelt follows also the order of voice entry set by Mouton; later he varies his treatment with regard to both plan of voice entry and rhythmic accent. Of the other two Masses, one is a *Missa de Beata Virgine*, while the other is based on Andreas de Silva's *Ave Regina*. Likewise in 1557, the same firm issued *Piissimae ac sanctissimae Lamentationes*, which included three sets of Lamentations by Arcadelt[277] (also sets by Carpentras, Festa, and others). The melodies are broad and flowing and are developed in freely treated through-imitation. The *Lamed* passage in the Lamentation for *Feria V, Lectio III*, is noteworthy in that the tenor sings the *cantus firmus* while the bass repeats a descending scale (f-F) three times, each time in a different rhythm, and the other three voices weave a contrapuntal web derived from the *ostinato*.[278]

Goudimel

Goudimel, whose sacred music is best known for its contributions to the Protestant repertory, composed works for Catholic use prior to his conversion, which seems to have occurred c. 1560.[279] The latter works include five Masses, three Magnificats, and several motets.[280] His four-part Masses

---

[275] Further about Monteverdi's sacred works in both the old and new styles, *see* RedR; PruCM, 109ff; PaoM, *passim;* BukMB, 65ff, 70.

[276] Pr. KillK, 205.   [277] A substantial extract from one of them, *ibid.*, 252ff.

[278] Further about Arcadelt's sacred music, *see* AmbG III, 593ff; PirH, 257ff. About the *Ave Maria* current under Arcadelt's name, *see* p. 381 *supra*. For an 8-part *Pater noster* (not for double chorus), *see* CommB VIII, 21.

[279] Correspondence between him and the anti-Protestant administrator of the Archbishop of Besançon shows Goudimel aiding in the persecution of a Protestant musician in 1554. Cf. BrenG, 20.

[280] A list *ibid.*, 36ff.

Audi filia, Tant plus ie metz, De mes ennuys, and *Le bien que j'ai* [281]—all fairly short and simple—are written in French style. Goudimel introduces duos and trios, but tends to do so more sparingly than does, for example, Certon. The *Audi filia* and *Tant plus ie metz* Masses add a fifth voice in the final Agnus. Once Goudimel opens a section chordally or in imitation, he generally maintains the style he has established. Despite the frequently chordal texture, phrases rarely end simultaneously in all parts. Such a motet as the predominantly contrapuntal *Domine, quid multiplicati sunt* [282] is much the same in technical detail as the Masses. The *Salve Regina* [283] for three SATB choruses, however, is unique in Goudimel. Sometimes all three choirs answer each other; at other times two groups unite to answer the third; at four points the three choirs are combined in writing *a 12.* The work opens with the first four notes of the plainsong sung by the superius of each of the three choirs in turn, in the manner of a threefold intonation; the rest of the piece bears no relation to the plainsong. A fine climax is built up on *O clemens, o pia, o dulcis Virgo Maria.* In this passage, transitions involving an instance of degree-inflection are made through several keys. At the close, all twelve voices join and return to the key of the opening.[284]

The most famous of Goudimel's sacred works are found among his psalm settings. There are some sixty of these in motet style, *a 3* to *a 6,* of which eight were published by Du Chemin in 1551 and the rest by Le Roy and Ballard from 1557 to 1566. At this time, Catholics and Protestants alike sang the Genevan melodies until the former were forbidden to do so by ecclesiastical authority. Goudimel's incorporation of these melodies into his earliest psalm settings, therefore, does not indicate that he had already abandoned Catholicism. Destined to achieve greater popularity than his motet-like psalms were his two collections of strophic settings *a 4* of the entire Genevan Psalter, published by Le Roy and Ballard in 1564 and 1565, by which time he must have changed faith. The 1564 collection [285] is in embellished chordal style, that of 1565 in note-against-note style. A Genevan edition of the latter set was published in 1565 also.[286] In the preface [286a] to this edition, Goudimel stresses that it is intended for home use rather than for the service—important, in view of Calvin's insistence that music in the church be restricted to monophony. Goudimel is credited with being the first to place the psalm melody in the superius, and he does so in all but fifteen of the psalms in the collection of 1564. In the 1565 collection, however, only seventeen psalms have the

---

[281] Pr. MMFTR IX, 1, 45, 80; BordA, *Messes* II, 42, respectively.
[282] Pr. BuH III, 267; MaldR III, 15; *see also* BrenG, 45.
[283] Pr. MaldR III, 3. (Cf. ReT, 99, No. 253.)
[284] An additional motet available in modern print under Goudimel's name—*O Crux benedicta*—is actually by Vinci; cf. p. 492.
[285] No copy of this edition survives. For a modern edition based on a reprint of 1580, *see* MMRF II, IV, VI.
[286] Facsimile edition in GoudP.
[286a] English transl. in StrunkR, 349.

given melody in the superius, the remainder having it in the tenor.[287] The frequent absence of the third of the chord when the text is grave is noteworthy. If the same melody is used several times, Goudimel harmonizes it differently each time.[288] His harmonizations continued to be republished in France and elsewhere in the early 19th century.

EXAMPLE 116. Psalm 134 (CXXXIII) (*Or sus, serviteurs du Seigneur*) —Goudimel (after facsimile in GoudP).

(This setting, with the melody in the tenor, is from the 1565 collection; for the 1564 setting, with the melody in the superius, *see* MMRF II, 98.)

In 1565 also, there was published the Lausanne Psalter. This was the most significant of the lesser contemporaries of the Genevan psalter. At Lausanne, the early tunes used for Marot's texts were preserved, but the texts of Bèze were sung to settings by Guillaume Franc, who had gone there from Geneva (cf. p. 360). Ultimately the Genevan Psalter was adopted by the church of Lausanne, as well as by the great majority of Reformed churches.[289]

Protestant and Catholic Psalm Settings by Le Jeune, Mauduit, and Others

Rivals of Goudimel's harmonizations of the Genevan melodies are the settings *a 4* of Claude Le Jeune. (A collection of ten *"en forme de motets"* [1564] is his first published psalm collection.) Here the psalm tune remains in the tenor, but a melody of equal significance is given to the superius. Le Jeune likewise set, *a 3* to *a 7*—here also using the Genevan melodies—, twelve psalms [290] according to the twelve modes, following Zarlino's order (cf. pp. 377, 384). These settings, some of which are of large dimensions, attain a

---

[287] 2 settings of *A toi, mon Dieu, mon coeur monte,* one (from the 1565 set) with the Genevan melody in the tenor, the other (from the 1580 [= 1564] set) with it in the superius, are pr. successively in ExR, 1270ff. [288] *See* esp. PicM, 2421ff.

[289] Further about developments at Lausanne, *see* DouM I, 613f.

[290] The first 3 are pr. in MMRF XI (No. 1 also in DouM II, 225). Other Le Jeune settings of Genevan psalm tunes pr. in DouM II, 250, 252, 256, 257; HaverH, 56 (= Grove IV, 271); MMRFE, Nos. 3069 (*Helas, Seigneur;* a very fine piece), 3492, 3493 (*Ainsi qu'on oit le cerf bruire,* the melody of which was later to serve for *Freu dich sehr, O meine Seele*); MMFTR VIII, 50; LejP (5 items).

grand and noble style. Particularly impressive is Psalm 35 (XXXIV), in thirteen *partes* (respectively *a 5, 5, 5, 5, 3, 3, 4, 4, 5, 5, 6, 6, 7*), which, in progressing from *pars* to *pars,* shifts the complete Genevan melody from one voice to another, each statement being made against fresh polyphony in the other voices. Jambe-de-Fer and many others harmonized Genevan psalm tunes also.[291]

Le Jeune drew not only on the Genevan texts and tunes but, when setting psalms in *vers mesuré*,[292] on Baïf as well. The *Pseaumes en vers mezurez mis en musique* of 1606 contains a few examples in Latin beside the main body in French. Pieces with Latin text—a Magnificat and three motets—are included also in the *Second Livre des meslanges.*[293]

Like Le Jeune, the Catholic Mauduit also drew on Baïf for *vers-mesuré* psalm versions. Of the texts, by this poet, of Mauduit's eight psalm settings [294] written in the *musique-mesurée* system and incorporated in Mersenne's *Quaestiones celeberrimae,* one of the pair in Latin and two of the six in French consist of Sapphics, the music, of course, reproducing the meter of the words.[294a] Especially attractive is another of the settings, *En son temple sacré* (Psalm CL),[295] with its naïve, but charming, tone-painting on *"fanfarans clairons et trombons . . . le fifr'et tambour,"* etc. Mauduit wrote a Requiem Mass on the death of Ronsard, and Mersenne, in his *Harmonie universelle,* printed from it the *Requiescat in pace,* the last sung portion of the Absolution (which liturgically follows the Mass for the Dead rather than actually belonging to it).[296] The *falsobordone*-like setting pays strict attention to the quantities of the Latin syllables.[297]

A Requiem Mass is included also among the sacred compositions of Eustache Du Caurroy. This work has special significance, owing to its having been sung at the funerals of the French kings at St. Denis until the 18th century. It includes the *Libera me,* the responsory for the Absolution; the following example gives the second versicle. The composer, as might be expected, paraphrases the Chant melody,[297a] which, like the text, resembles the *Dies irae* sequence. Indeed, it is as a trope to this responsory that the sequence undoubtedly came into existence.[297b]

---

[291] For a selection, *see* DouM II.

[292] For such settings by Le Jeune, *see* MMRF XX–XXII. For 2 additional psalms, *see* MMFTR VIII, 61, 70.

[293] One of these pr. MMRFR No. 3068.

[294] Pr. ExFR VII.

[294a] It is interesting to compare one of the French texts in Sapphics—*Sus: tous ses servants (ibid.,* 16)—with *Or sus, serviteurs du Seigneur,* since it is a different French metrical version of the same psalm.

[295] *Ibid.,* 1; ExR, 1294.   [296] Pr. TierR, 137. Cf. Liber, 1771, 1816 (top).

[297] Further about Mauduit's sacred music, *see* MassonM; BrenV, 233ff.

[297a] Pr. Liber, 1767.

[297b] It has been claimed that the *Dies irae* was composed as a sequence for the first Sunday in Advent. The evidence of both text and music, however, favors the derivation given above. *See also* Clemens Blume in Michael Buchberger, *Lexikon für Theologie und Kirche,* III (1931), 314.

EXAMPLE 117. *Dies illa* from the *Libera me* of Du Caurroy's *Missa pro defunctis* (after SchafferR, 165 [297c]).

Du Caurroy's surviving sacred music includes also two books of *Preces ecclesiasticae*. The *Harmonie universelle* of Mersenne preserves a *Pie Jesu* in the form of a canon *a 6*. In Du Caurroy's *Meslanges* (cf. p. 386) there are settings of seven *vers-mesuré* versions of the psalms, six in French,[297d] one in Latin.

Cornelis Boschop (Boscoop), who in 1573 succeeded Sweelinck's father as organist of the Oude Kerk at Amsterdam, published a collection of fifty psalm settings in 1568.[298] These have the usual Dutch texts; some paraphrase the *Souterliedeken* melodies, while others appear to be freely composed.

There is evidence that Waelrant harbored Protestant tendencies. As a printer, he brought out, in 1555, together with Laet, a book of fifty Marot psalm versions in settings by Jean Louys. During the same period, he and Laet printed a four-volume *Jardin musiqual* (*sic*)—one volume *a 3*, three *a 4*—and its varied contents included further French psalm settings. (The title page of Book II *a 4*, consisting of twenty-eight *chansons spirituelles,* names Jean Caulery, "*Maistre de chappelle de la Royne de France,*" as among the composers represented: thirteen of the twenty-eight pieces bear ascriptions to him, thirteen bear other attributions, and two are anonymous.[299] The remaining volumes, likewise devoted to various composers, name none of them in their titles.) Waelrant himself contributed to the *Jardin,* eight of his pieces being settings of Marot psalms.[300] The Inquisition at Mons, in 1568, confiscated two motet books printed by him.[301] There is some evidence that he

297c Certain portions of the Mass (not including the above) reach us in defective form. The work is reconstructed in complete form in SchafferR and also in the ed. of E. Martin and J. Burald, published by Rouart-Lerolle.
297d Pr. MMRF XVII, 56, 58 (the text is another French metrical equivalent of *Or sus, serviteurs du Seigneur;* cf. fn. 294a), 61, 67, 70, 73.
298 Pr. VNM XXII.
299 For further data on Caulery and for one of his pieces, *see* BeC.
300 For 1 of these, *see* BeW, 21.
301 Cf. BeW, 9; *see also* LowC, 126.

was affected by the teachings of the Anabaptists. This embraces his choice of words for motets, which excludes texts about the Virgin or the saints, but includes a whole cycle dealing with the life of Jesus: indeed, none of the motet texts selected by him shows clearly that he was writing for the Catholic liturgy, nor did he compose other works specifically related to it, such as Masses.[302] He at times employs chromaticism, including degree-inflection, and does not hesitate to use sharp dissonances and forbidden parallel intervals if he feels that the text warrants them.[303]

The Antwerp Motet Book of Lassus

In 1554 or 1555 Lassus came to Antwerp, where he remained until the end of 1556. During this period, his first publications appeared, among them a volume entitled, *Di Orlando di Lassus il primo libro de mottetti a cinque & a sei voci* . . . , printed by Waelrant and Laet in 1556. This "Antwerp Motet Book," as it has been called, contains eighteen motets, of which some perhaps had been composed while Lassus was still in Italy, though it is evidently at Antwerp that most of them were rewritten.[304] Collectively, the eighteen show that, despite his youth, Lassus had already developed his personal style to a remarkable degree.

Lassus' motets, together with Palestrina's Masses, are often regarded as representing the culmination of all the developments of polyphony in the preceding generations, though, in view of the climactic position of Josquin, "culmination" is probably a less suitable term to apply than "dénouement." It is in the motet, his favorite form, that Lassus reveals himself at his best. The many facets of his varied personality and a wide gamut of emotion found expression in his works in this form. This is already apparent in the Antwerp motets, which present a great diversity of subject matter. Besides settings of religious texts (mostly taken from those psalms that treat of the passionate struggle of man with himself and his God) there are political motets, such as *Heroum soboles,* in honor of Charles V; *Deliciae Phoebi,* a musical dedi-

---

[302] Cf. *ibid.,* 121ff.

[303] The App. to LowC prints substantial extracts from some more "modern" motets by Waelrant. For 2 complete motets of a conservative nature, *see* CommB I, 57, 63.

[304] For a special study of this work, *see* LowL, to which the discussion that follows above is much indebted. The 18 motets appear (scattered) in LassoW as follows (the citations adhering to the order of the original print): XI, 81 (= MaldP III, 9); VII, 100; XI, 44 (= MaldP IV, 6); VII, 152; IX, 6 (= CommM VIII, 11), 18, 150; V, 73, 18 (= CommM VIII, 7); III, 127 (= MaldP III, 32); IX, 34, 128; XV, 23; XI, 122 (= MaldP IV, 35), 118; XIII, 68, 74, 72. Except in Vol. XXI, the Latin works in LassoW have thus far all been republished from the *Magnum opus musicum,* 1604, which was "edited" by Lassus' sons, and not, where earlier prints or MSS exist, from such more authentic sources. This is particularly unfortunate from the scholarly standpoint because (1) among the changes made by the sons is the substitution, in some pieces, of religious for secular texts (the MaldP reprints follow source material earlier than the *Magnum* . . . ; cf. ReT, 78, 106f) and (2) the chronology of the Latin works is obscured, as is the form of the collections originally containing them.

cation to one of Charles' statesmen, Antonio Perenotto; *Te spectant,* a tribute to the English cardinal, Reginald Pole; and *Stet quicunque volet potens,* an idyll of the quiet life of the burgher, possibly written with the inhabitants of Antwerp in mind.[305]

From Lassus' vigorous and dramatic settings of these texts, it is evident that the ideal of evenness of mood and movement, evinced by Gombert's music, was not his ideal. Since Gombert, of course, a marked change of style had taken place, owing to the increasing attention given to the text. In moulding polyphonic motets, Lassus' northern predecessors had accorded the text only a subordinate role. The words could influence the melodic line and the choice of mode and of dissonances, but they could not interfere with the purely musical plan of the structure. The application of text to music had continued to be casual: it was not only the printer who did not care whether the words were under the right notes; the composer himself was apparently often uninterested (cf. p. 355). The trend fully evident in Zarlino's ten rules for handling the text had not yet gathered much force. We still find, in the works of these predecessors, long notes on short syllables and short notes on long ones; there are repetitions of single words and of fragments of sentences that make no sense by themselves. Since the melodies are still largely melismatic, it sometimes continues to be difficult for the listener to distinguish the text. The changes of style of 1540 to 1550 concentrated, as Italian influence became stronger, on making the text clearer and on expressing its emotional and pictorial content. Also, the text repertory now drew oftener on the more emotional and personal aspects of life and religion. In a number of scenic motets, tragic figures of the Bible were presented: Job, the Prodigal Son, Rachel mourning for her children. This development had been evident in the works of men like Clemens and Crecquillon. The ultimate result of the new text–music relationship in the Low Countries was a decline in the use of melismatic writing in favor of syllabic writing, a shift from a strictly polyphonic to a more chordal style that employs choir divisions and echo effects, and a change from modal counterpoint to a harmonic texture making more frequent use of chromatic tones producing organized modulatory effects.

Among the exponents of the new trends, one of the most progressive was apparently Waelrant. His significance has been underestimated, perhaps because he was not nearly as prolific as Clemens and Crecquillon, whom, however, he surpasses in his mastery of vivid text declamation.

These men, and others of smaller stature, helped to forge the style of which Lassus was the supreme master. In his texts we do not find the tranquillity typical of the text repertory of a Gombert or a Palestrina. Neither do we find this peace and balance in his music. His motifs and melodies abound in wide

---

[305] Pr. LassoW XI, 122 (= MaldP IV, 35), 81 (= MaldP III, 9); III, 127 (= MaldP III, 32); XI, 44 (= MaldP IV, 6), respectively.

leaps, sudden breaks, unexpected beginnings and endings. The rhythmic patterns are enlivened by syncopations. Very characteristic is the appearance of dotted rhythms. The lack of balance is conspicuous, the unexpected is the rule; there are frequent changes from quick to slow movement, from regular accents to strongly marked syncopations.

What seems arbitrary and inorganic, judged by the standards of music such as Gombert's, becomes meaningful and logical, considered in the light of the texts employed and of the way in which they and the music are fitted to each other. The rhythm and accent of the spoken word are carefully observed. Long syllables receive long notes, short syllables short ones; dotted rhythms have their origins in words like *culmine, lubrico, positus*. Sudden changes in movement are but means of expression. Slow and hesitant rhythms portray moods of mourning, despair, uncertainty, or fear of death. Movement in equal notes with emphasis on the strong beat is found on words of promise or cheer. Small intervals like the minor second appear, as one might expect, on words expressing humility and penitence, large intervals often represent strength and confidence. Even the speech melody is reflected in Lassus' themes: a question is set to an ascending melodic line. The curtailing of melismas goes hand in hand with the more frequent presence of tone repetitions, used sparingly by Gombert. What the melody may thereby lose in organic development, it gains in faithfulness to the text. Adoption of this word-generated style in Lassus' motets was no doubt prompted in large part by his residence in Italy and familiarity with the madrigal.

Lassus' polyphony is harmonically determined; the bass lines carry the harmony. Whereas Gombert's open sound-structure results from many melodic lines flowing freely and independently, the different voices in Lassus are set in such a way as to achieve sounds that are compact and full. He prefers the complete triad with the root in the bass and with the major third in the highest voice. It is rhythmic rather than melodic independence that he emphasizes. Often the writing is actually chordal but, by successive entrances on various members of a chord, an effect of polyphony is obtained.

Lassus is fond of modulatory transitions through the cycle of fifths, especially in setting words like *suavis, dulcis,* or *mirabilis.* The transitions and the full sound of four or five parts in triad structure are felt as "soft," "sweet," or "marvellous."

The contents of the Antwerp Motet Book show, in general, that the very free treatment of the technique of imitation characterizing Lassus' music in all fields, and applied by him with particular eloquence in his motets, was already in extensive use at this early stage of his career. To be sure, a work like *Domine non est* [306] is built, in standard old Netherlandish fashion, on the stricter kind of imitation, with a fair distance between the entries, and

[306] Pr. LassoW VII, 152.

this method is employed elsewhere in the Antwerp Motet Book also. But clearly in the ascendancy is imitation that merely gives a suggestion of the earlier type: only the contour of a motif is imitated, or only the rhythm, and the entries are close. Lassus, moved like his contemporaries in Italy by a strong harmonic tendency, ventured much farther than had Gombert or Clemens upon changes in the art of imitation; and this is the variation of it that was adopted by his personal style and developed with singular brilliance and imagination. The following, from No. 7 in the Antwerp Book, shows three successive points of pseudo-imitation with close entries.

EXAMPLE 118. Extract from *pars II* of *Ad te levavi*—Lassus (after LassoW IX, 153).

". . . teach me thy paths, Lead me in thy truth, and teach me. . . ." (Psalm XXIV [25], 4, 5)

However predominant free imitation may be in the Antwerp collection, this publication presents considerable variety. In several of its motets, Lassus makes striking use of chordal writing, notably in the splendid *Heroum soboles*. He produces quite as readily a setting of a Gregorian *cantus firmus* in a *Da pacem*,[307] a canon *a 2* within the framework of his *Creator omnium Deus*,[308] and an *ostinato* with independent text in *Si qua tibi* and *Fremuit spiritu Jesus*.[309] The last-named motet was composed in imitation of Clemens' setting of the same text (cf. p. 353). Lassus takes from Clemens the treatment *a 6*, division of the text into two *partes,* and the *ostinato.* The younger master surpasses the older in technical perfection and dramatic expression, while Clemens excels in the intimacy and warmth of his lyricism. The *Creator omnium Deus* is also derived, being based on Willaert's motet of the same name. From it, Lassus took the canon, though not literally throughout, and adapted it to another scheme, changing the distance between the *dux* and *comes* of Willaert's canon from four measures to one. Again Lassus surpasses his model. He does so in concentration of form, plasticity of themes, expressiveness and richness of harmonic color.[310] The Willaert and Clemens motets had been published at Antwerp by Phalèse, an indication that Lassus' settings of the same texts are probably not among the pieces he wrote in Italy. The Italian influence, particularly that of the Venetian School, exerted itself not only on Lassus, but also, through the printing of works by Willaert and Rore in Antwerp, on other Netherlandish composers publishing in the north. The efforts of the Netherlandish publishers had been most laudable as regards both quality and quantity: Susato, Phalèse, and Waelrant, gave their public no less than 551 works in 33 motet books, mostly between 1546 and 1556. (Waelrant had proved himself especially progressive in his choice of material.)

It was in the latter year that Lassus was called to enter the court *Kapelle* at Munich, in the employ of which he was to remain for the rest of his life. As a young man, he had already demonstrated, in his first motet publication, his mastery of all the technical means within the Netherlandish tradition.

George de la Hèle; Monte's Direct Contact with Sacred Music in the West

George de la Hèle (or Helle; b. 1547, Antwerp; d. 1587, Madrid) was, like Lassus (cf. p. 389), a prize winner at Evreux. In fact, in 1576 he won two prizes—a silver harp for the second best motet *a 5* and a silver lute for the best chanson, likewise *a 5.* He had probably been among the boys Manchicourt brought from the Low Countries to Madrid when he reorganized the Royal Chapel in 1560. He was enrolled among the students at the University of Louvain in 1571, it being noted that he was under royal protection. In 1572, he was appointed *maître de chapelle* at St. Rombaut, Malines. There he remained until 1574, when he went to the Tournai Cathedral in a similar ca-

---

[307] *Ibid.,* XIII, 74 (plainsong in Liber, 1867).   [308] *Ibid.,* XIII, 68.
[309] *Ibid.,* XI, 118; XV, 23, respectively.   [310] Cf. LowL, 95.

pacity. In 1578 he received a demi-prebendary at Tournai, resigning on his departure for Madrid in 1581. He spent the rest of his life there, directing the music in the chapel of Philip II. In addition to the two works that won prizes at Evreux, only another motet and eight Masses have survived. All the Mass compositions, beautifully printed by Plantin[310a] at Antwerp in 1578, are parody Masses, the models being indicated in the table of contents. These models include Josquin's *Benedicta es* and *Praeter rerum seriem,* Rore's *In convertendo,* Crecquillon's *Nigra sum sed formosa,* and four motets by Lassus.[311] (Continuing admiration for Josquin's *Benedicta es* is shown not only by the first of these Masses but by the setting for two choruses, printed in 1568, in which Guyot [Castileti] added six parts to the original six of Josquin.)

While a publisher could easily dispose of antiphonaries and missals, it was more difficult to find purchasers of new works by living composers, and la Hèle had to give Plantin a guarantee to buy forty copies of his book of Masses at sixteen florins each (the regular price was eighteen florins). Plantin required even so distinguished a composer as Philippe de Monte to contribute 135 florins toward the cost of printing this musician's first book of Masses (1587).[312]

Monte, at the time this book of Masses appeared, was in the employ of Emperor Rudolph II. His sojourns in his native land during his maturity were, indeed, too brief for him to make any marked impression, through personal contact, on the development of sacred music there. His visit north from Italy, from 1554 to perhaps 1557, included his stay in England; in 1570, he made a brief trip to the Low Countries to engage musicians to serve the emperor. In this year, Phalèse and Bellère published a collection of chansons devoted to Lassus, Rore, and Monte, but one of the Monte pieces—*Donnés au Seigneur gloire*—is actually a setting of Marot's version of Psalm CVI (107); although a Catholic composer at a Catholic court, Monte elaborates in the tenor the melody sung to this psalm at Geneva.[313]

Musica reservata

It was during Monte's earlier visit that Dr. Seld sent to Albert V of Bavaria the letter (dated September 22, 1555) mentioned on p. 395. In the same letter, Seld described Monte as "the best composer in the entire country, particularly in the new manner and *musica reservata."*

[310a] About the musical significance of the catalogues and inventories of the Plantin archive, *see* StellM. For bibliographical information about Plantin's musical prints, *see* StellBP.
[311] The Mass on his *Gustate et videte* has been separately pr. by Schwann in Düsseldorf, 1950. Further about la Hèle, *see* esp. DoorH; facsimile of *Christe* from *Missa In convertendo* in BergT, 23.
[312] BergT, 25 (where the date of the Monte vol. is wrongly given as 1578).
[313] For the melody, *see* ExP, 491; for the setting, MonteO XX, 23.

The expression *"musica reservata"* has become one of the problems of music history. The term appears, or supposed equivalents of it appear, in several sources dating from between 1552 and 1610 or 1611.

(1) and (2): In 1552 there were printed at Nuremberg two publications by the Fleming, Adrianus Petit Coclico (c. 1500–1563). One of these was a collection of forty-one motets entitled *Musica reservata Consolationes piae ex Psalmis Davidicis . . .* ; the other was the treatise, *Compendium musices descriptum ab Adriano Petit Coclico discipulo Josquini de Pres.*[313a] (Besides declaring himself in this title to have been a pupil of Josquin's, Coclico alleges elsewhere that he has served the pope as *musicus primus* and has been Bishop of Ducatum—additional claims which, together with some others, can be disproved; in fact, Ducatum appears to exist only in the realm of fiction. Coclico says that he has been not only in Italy, but also in France and Spain. Converted to Protestantism, he was employed in various German cities, being forced to quit at least one of them. This fantastic creature—a portrait of him,[314] printed in both the *Musica reservata* and the *Compendium,* reveals a gnomelike figure adorned by a beard of prodigious length—was evidently something of an impostor.) [315] Coclico states, in the preface of the *Compendium,* that he has written the treatise "in order now to call back to light again that music which they ordinarily refer to as *reservata."* [316]

(3) and (4): *Musica reservata* is mentioned by Dr. Seld not only in his letter of September 22, 1555, but also in a prior one of April 28, 1555. In this earlier letter, he writes from Brussels, to Duke Albert V of Bavaria, concerning an alto singer, Egidius Fux:

To gratify me, the choirmaster here [Cornelius Canis] had him sing two duos in the Imperial Chapel. He pleases me very much and has a good straightforward voice, particularly in church. Afterward I took him and others of our group to my home. As we sang all sorts of Reservata *and music unknown to him, I consider that he is certain enough in all of them so that he, as all the others say, can compare favorably with any alto of the Imperial Chapel.*

Further on in the same letter Dr. Seld again refers to *musica reservata,* this time in connection with the fact that Nicolas Payen is to succeed Cornelius Canis as choirmaster in Brussels. He states:

And so musica reservata *will become still more the fashion than heretofore, inasmuch as Cornelius Canis could not well reconcile himself to it.*[317]

(5) The preface of Lassus' *Il primo libro dove si contengono Madrigali, Vilanesche, Canzon francesi, e Motetti . . .* (1555) is addressed to a certain

---

[313a] The former pr. EDMR XLII; the latter pr. in facs. in CocliC.
[314] Reproduced in KinsP, 84; CreAC, 273.
[315] *See* further esp. *ibid.,* 33ff.   [316] For the orig. Latin, *see ibid.,* 241.
[317] For the orig. German, *see* SandB III, 300ff; CreAC, 294.

Signor Stefano and states that he, "being enamoured of the kind of music that is called *osservata,* wishes that it were known to all and were pleasing to all." It has been held [318] that *osservata* is equivalent to *reservata,* a claim which, if correct, would mean that Lassus' collection probably includes some examples of the type in question. However, the claim has been disputed.[319]

(6) Vicentino's *L'antica musica ridotta alla moderna prattica* (1555) contains a passage that may be translated:

. . . they understand that (as the ancient authors prove) the chromatic and enharmonic music was fittingly reserved [reservata] for another purpose than [was] the diatonic, for the latter was sung, for the benefit of ordinary ears, at public festivals in places for the community: the former was used, for the benefit of trained ears, at private entertainments of lords and princes, in praising great personages and heroes.[320]

(7) A madrigal collection of Ruffo's, dated 1556, is entitled *Opera nuova di musica intitolata armonia celeste nella quale si contengono 25 Madrigali, pieni d'ogni dolcezza, et soavità musicale. Composti con dotta arte et reservato ordine dallo Eccellente Musico Vincenzo Ruffo.* It has been held that *reservato ordine* refers to *musica reservata;* [321] but, if it does, the collection features no technical trait in such a way as to elucidate the term.[321a]

(8) The most famous reference to *musica reservata* was written by the physician and humanist Samuel Quickelberg, a native of Antwerp, who, like Seld, was a member of Albert V's court at Munich. The reference occurs in Quickelberg's commentary on the miniatures contained in the beautifully ornamented MS of Lassus' Penitential Psalms, composed c. 1560 (cf. p. 695f). It reads:

He expressed [the content] so aptly with lamenting and plaintive melody, adapting where it was necessary [the music] to the subject and the words, expressing the power of the different emotions, presenting the subject as if acted before the eyes, that one cannot know whether the sweetness of the emotions more adorns the plaintive melodies or the plaintive melodies the sweetness of the emotions. This kind of music they call musica reservata, *and in it Orlandus proved the excellence of his genius to posterity just as marvellously as in his other works, which are almost innumerable.[322]*

(9) An anonymous treatise of 1571 at Besançon instructs the student as follows, with regard to contrapuntal writing:

So let it tend that the voices, in progressing in various and contrary movements

[318] SandB I, 110.
[319] *See* CreAC, 301ff.
[320] For the orig. Italian and a somewhat different transl., *see* LowC, 90. Chapter VII of LowC provides a particularly important discussion of *musica reservata.*
[321] Cf. OsN, 274; CreAC, 299; LowC, 94.   [321a] Cf. Ein VR.
[322] For the orig. Latin, *see* CreAC, 300.

(as much as possible), come together at last in perfect consonances and present the final of some mode. In continuous rhythm, however, avoid the clausula, so that what they call musica reservata *results.*[323]

(10) A petition, presented by Raimundo Ballestra, in 1610 or early in January 1611, to the Austrian Archduke Ferdinand, asked for funds to further the publication of a collection that included "some *reservata*." The request was granted.[323a]

Of the ten sources, the ninth is the only one specifically mentioning *musica reservata* that discusses it in technical language. But the passage, by itself, can hardly be described as crystal clear.

It would appear from these sources that the *musica reservata* concept was known at least in the Netherlands, Italy, France, and Germany. As for the sources associated with Germany, to the extent that they are musical, theoretical, or esthetic, they are by Netherlanders (Coclico and Quickelberg); such source material as does come from a German (Seld) is only in the form of general comment.

The meaning of the term *"musica reservata"* has been the subject of much debate, but the findings have been inconclusive and often at variance with each other. Among the theories advanced are those defining *musica reservata* as (1) music expressive of the emotions delineated by the text,[324] (2) music reserved in expression,[325] (3) music with improvised ornamentation,[326] (4) music characterized by reserve in the use of figuration,[327] and (5) music reserved for the elite, a sort of vocal chamber music.[328] Of these views, only the first can claim really direct support from one of the sources—Quickelberg's statement. Unquestionably, Quickelberg held expressiveness, as he conceived it, to be an integral part of that music which "they call *musica reservata.*" However, he did not touch on the question of what its technical nature might be. The almost complete silence on this point in all the sources of the period has opened the way for the application by some modern scholars [329] of the term *"musica reservata"* to all music (regardless of period or nationality) in which an "expressive" style or even good text declamation is involved. Moreover, such scholars sometimes tend, in discussing a work by a composer associated with *musica reservata,* to regard it as an example of the type, whether there is clear evidence linking that particular work with *musica reservata* or not. It is plain, however—for example, in the close of our

---

[323] For a chapter of the treatise, in Latin with German transl. (including above passage), *see* BäumkUK.

[323a] *See* FederhQ.   [324] In SandB I, 110; LowC, 109; LeiMR; etc.

[325] KemJC, 77.   [326] HuI, Chap. III.   [327] UrVG, 368.

[328] LowC, 90f; HuI, 109ff. All of these views are discussed in CreAC, 293ff, 320f. It should be noted that the pertinence of some of the evidence cited by the modern writers to support their views is doubtful.

[329] Cf. KrMR, 142; LeiMR.

quotation from Quickelberg—, that the 16th century was itself prepared to differentiate, in the production of a single composer, between works written in *musica-reservata* style and works written in other styles.

The theory that *musica reservata* has to do with ornamentation derives from a letter of Seld's, dated July 1, 1555, in which he comments upon coloratura passages improvised by Netherlandish singers,[330] and from Coclico's treatment of improvised embellishments in his *Compendium*. However, Coclico does not specifically state that the embellishments are related to *musica reservata*. Furthermore, as has been convincingly pointed out,[331] the addition of improvised embellishments would be in conflict with the very essence of what Quickelberg states *musica reservata* to be: the expression of words in tone.

Quickelberg's statement, however, is consistent with the view that *musica reservata* is vocal chamber music for the elite, a view suggested by the passage from Vicentino.[332] This passage also shows that some examples of *musica reservata* employ the chromatic or enharmonic genus (though not necessarily to the exclusion of the diatonic). *"Musica reservata,"* then, may not be a technical term at all, but quite possibly one referring to the social function the music was meant to serve. Vicentino's own chromatic and enharmonic madrigals (cf. pp. 328f) are probably examples of one kind of *musica reservata*. The madrigal, indeed, obsessed as it is with word-painting, would seem to be the medium through which *musica reservata* found its most characteristic outlet. The concept may well have originated in the north and have reached Italy through Willaert, to attain its fullest development in the peninsula.[333] It is only in the sacred field, however, i.e., in the collection of forty-one motets by Coclico, that one finds the term used as the actual title for a substantial body of music.

An examination of the forty-one motets is disappointing in that it reveals a composer characterized as much by inexpertness as by anything else. In determining what light they can throw on the question of *musica reservata,* one must give more consideration to such of Coclico's intentions as are clearly indicated than to his actual achievements. The music is sprinkled with consecutive octaves, fifths, and other crudities, but the desire to express the text in tone is sometimes unmistakably present. Dissonances musically unjustifiable according to the standards of the period are occasionally warranted by the text. Unfortunately, dissonances of this kind also appear at times without such justification. The following illustrate (a) word-painting and (b) textually unwarranted dissonance.

---

[330] *See* SandB I, 53f; CreAC, 297.
[331] In LowC, 97ff; EinIM I, 227.
[332] Cf. LowC, 90f.
[333] Cf. EinIM I, 224.

EXAMPLE 119. Extracts from (a) *Afflictus sum* and (b) *Non salvatur rex*—Coclico (from *Musica reservata,* Montanus and Neuber, 1552; transcr. by M. L. Versè).

(a) "I roared with the groaning of my heart." (Psalm XXXVII:9 [38:8])
(b) "Neither shall he deliver any by his great strength." (Psalm XXXII [33], 17)

In *Vidi impium* (Psalm XXXVI [37]: 35, 36) [334] the composer treats the text in a manner that is at the same time naïve and bizarre. In the lines *"et transivi, et ecce non erat; et quaesivi eum, et non est inventus locus ejus"* ("Yet he passed away and, lo, he was not; yea, I sought him, but he could not be found"), the last syllables of *"erat"* and *"ejus"* are omitted to illustrate the idea of disappearance. In *Non derelinquet Dominus,* Coclico introduces accidentals which, in turn, require the insertion of numerous other accidentals, through the operation of the laws of *musica ficta,* thus producing rather elaborate chromaticism (accidentalism).[335] In several motets, the polyphonic flow is re-placed often enough by passages in which all the parts begin and end together for this trait to be noteworthy. Perhaps Coclico derived this feature from the study of compositions by his putative master. (The same feature is strikingly present also in the Penitential Psalms of Lassus; cf. pp. 695f.) Likewise note-worthy is the fact that, while Coclico employs suspensions in the body of his motets, he avoids them at his final cadences with only three exceptions.[336]

If Quickelberg and Vicentino seem to support the view that *musica reservata* was music reserved for the élite, there appears to be evidence that applica-tion of the term *"reservata"* also sometimes included a type of music revived from the past. It is possible to interpret Seld's statement that Monte was adept "particularly in the new manner and *musica reservata"* as implying that *musica reservata,* as he understood it, was something not belonging to the new man-ner. Moreover, Coclico himself, in the chapter on ornamentation to be applied

[334] Pr. CreAC, 424; for a facsimile of another piece, *see ibid.,* 274; for a transcr. of still another, *see* KadAC, 26.
[335] For an extract from this motet, *see* CreAC, 281.   [336] Motets Nos. 24–26.

in singing, uses the passive verbal form of the same root to mean "preserved":

There lived among them many princes of musicians, Josquin des Prez, Pierre de la Rue, Jacobus Scampion [probably Jacques Champion; cf. p. 338], and others, who used admirable and most sweet embellishments of clausulae; *the fragrant memory left by these men is still preserved* [reservatur] . . .[337]

Franco-Netherlandish "Picture Motets"; Sweelinck

In the latter part of the century, the visual arts regarded with special interest the representing of actual pieces of music in paintings and drawings. In 1584, a group of copper engravers, following the lead of Johannes Sadeler, began engraving copperplate reproductions of pre-existent art works, among these being many that incorporated within them complete musical compositions.[338] One of the composers honored was Pevernage, there being pictorial engravings that preserve his *Laude pia Dominum, Osculetur me, Gloria in excelsis,* and *Dignus es.*[339] His *Nata et grata polo* adorns the title page of the *Encomium musices,*[340] published c. 1590. Pevernage's sacred music comprises also six Masses and many additional motets.[341] The latter are mostly in two *partes,* but these seldom employ identical endings; plainsong is rarely drawn upon; a predilection is shown for inverting themes.[342]

Verdonck,[343] Schuyt,[344] and Lassus [345] are among other composers whose motets grace pictorial engravings.

Sweelinck's sacred works in Renaissance style include his four books of settings of French psalms.[346] *Or sus, serviteurs du Seigneur* [347] moved him to produce a particularly fine six-part work: the superius has the famous melody, successive fragments being preceded and followed by derived melodic material—a result made possible by word repetition. The melody permeates other voices also. The four-part *Il faut que de tous mes esprits* (Psalm 138

---

[337] The orig. Latin is reprinted in CreAC, 325. It should be added that the Italian verb *riserbare* or *riservare* has at times had the secondary meaning "to conserve." Cf. *Vocabolario della Lingua Italiana già compilato dagli Accademici della Crusca,* G. Manuzzi, ed., III (1863), 871.

[338] Cf. BöttcM, 121f; SeiffBZ, 52.

[339] Pr. SeiffN I, 5 (= MaldR II, 39, with 1 voice missing), 13, 21 (= MaldR II, 21); II, 9 (= MaldR XVI, 51), respectively. The pieces are accompanied by reproductions of the engravings in SeiffN; reproductions also in SeiffBZ, 59, 58, 56 (= StellP, opp. p. 91), 57.

[340] Complete facsimile in HR VI; the title page also in BergT, 27; SeiffBZ, 64. The motet is reprinted in MaldR II, 3.

[341] Other motets pr. CommB VIII, 40; MaldR II, 17 (the work ascribed to Pevernage *ibid.,* 11, 6, is actually anon.; cf. StellP, 98).

[342] Cf. StellP, 101ff.

[343] For 2 motets (with the pictures), *see* SeiffN I, 16 (music also in MaldR II, 41; picture also in SeiffBZ, 55); II, 4 (music also in CommM XXI, 87; ProsM, *Annus II,* II, No. 12; MaldR I, 13; picture also in SeiffBZ, 54).

[344] Motet (with picture) in SeiffN II, 17 (picture also in SeiffBZ, 62).

[345] Motet (with picture) in SeiffN I, 9 (music also in CommM IX, 51; LassoW III, 58; MaldR XVI, 52; picture also in SeiffBZ, 60).

[346] Pr. SweeW II–V.　　[347] *Ibid.,* II, 207; VNM VI, 53.

[CXXXVII]) [348] is especially attractive. The four-part *On a beau sa maison bastir* (Psalm 127 [CXXVI]),[349] in three *partes,* uses the Genevan melody unembellished in old *cantus-firmus* fashion, twice in the superius, once in the bass, and twice in the tenor (in that order). Sweelinck's book of *Cantiones sacrae* (1619), though the words *"Cum Basso Continuo ad Organum"* appear on its title page, reveals many features of standard polyphonic writing. The *De profundis* [350] in it makes use of degree-inflection. Probably the most famous piece in the collection is the *Hodie Christus natus est,*[351] in which unity is obtained through the use of a theme and its inversion twice each in the course of the composition. The bright *Noe* and *Alleluia* passages make this one of the most joyous of Christmas motets.

With Sweelinck, the great production of the Netherlanders in the field of vocal polyphony comes to an end. It does not wane ignominiously, however, but closes in a brilliant and noble sunset.

[348] SweeW, II, 22; VNM XII, 71; for the Genevan melody, *see* ExP, 622.
[349] SweeW III, 9; Genevan melody in ExP, 586.
[350] Pr. CW XIV, 16; SweeW VI, 100.
[351] *Ibid.,* 69.

Chapter 10: INSTRUMENTAL MUSIC OF THE 16TH CENTURY: The Italian Production, including the Lute-Books Printed by Petrucci and those Written by Francesco da Milano, Galilei, and Molinaro, the Keyboard Works of the Cavazzonis, Merulo, and Andrea Gabrieli, and the Ensemble Compositions of Giovanni Gabrieli; the French and Netherlandish Production, including the Lute-Books of Le Roy and Besard and the Keyboard and Ensemble Collections Printed by Attaingnant; Music in the 16th-Century Theater

Music MSS and prints as well as literary sources are far more informative about Italian instrumental music of the *cinquecento* than about that of the *quattrocento*. To be sure, technical information about the structure of musical instruments of the time comes mostly from German authors. And Spanish and German writers of textbooks on the performance of specific instruments make an especially brilliant showing. Nevertheless, Italy has left us one of the most important bodies of instrumental music produced by the Renaissance. In fact, although at least in the first half of the *cinquecento* Franco-Netherlandish vocal music excelled that of Italy—the traditional land of song—the northerners were outstripped by the Italians, throughout the entire century, in the field of instrumental music. Important as such music was to the Italians early in the century, it became even more so later; as word setting received increased attention in vocal music, the "absolute" character of most instrumental music, as though by way of compensation, received increased attention also.

Early Appearances of Some Italian Terms

If, in the title of a collection, the words *"da sonar"* appeared, rather than *"da cantar,"* instrumental performance was indicated (cf. the Antico print of 1517 mentioned on p. 161). Some other expressions that indicated types of composition for instrumental performance are first found comparatively late, perhaps owing to the loss of source material. The earliest dated appearance of the term *"ricercare"* (which is spelled in many ways) occurs in Spinaccino's

Intabolatura de Lauto, 1507. Its first known use in connection with organ music, as well as that of the term *canzone* in connection with instrumental music of any kind, takes place in Marco Antonio Cavazzoni's *Recerchari, motetti, canzoni* of 1523. In 1536, a piece by Francesco da Milano is called a *tochata* (= toccata) and one by Marco d'Aquila is named a *fantasia*.[1] The earliest surviving work designated as a *sonata* is one by Gorzanis published in 1561.[2] The term, however, comes to us in literary sources from as far back as 1486.[3] Lodovico Balbi uses the designation *capriccio* in a print of 1586.

Some Lutemakers in Italy; Italian Tablature

The lute was the most widely used instrument in 16th-century Italy; it was played by both courtier and burgher. Spreading from Spain all over Europe during the 15th century, the art of lutemaking found its earliest masters north of the Pyrenees in the Tyrol and Bavaria, whence they made their way to all countries. It was a German, Laux Maler (d. 1528), who established at Bologna a reputation for his lutes similar to that later earned by Stradivari at Cremona for his violins. Also early in the *cinquecento* the Tieffenbrucker family becomes traceable—a family which, later in the century, produced famous instrument makers active at Padua, Venice, and Lyons.[4]

From c. 1450, lutes normally had eleven strings, all but the highest pitched forming double-strings or courses; since the two strings of a course were tuned to the same pitch, it is usual to speak of a six-stringed lute. The "six" strings were commonly tuned *Adgbe'a'* or *Gcfad'g'* in the *cinquecento,* the pitch-levels, however, being relative.[5] The instruments were fretted, and lute music was written in tablature—in a notation that indicates finger placement on the frets rather than pitches in a strictly tonal sense. Tablatures varied; there were Italian, French, and German types. The Italian type had six lines, each representing a string (or course), the highest line standing for the lowest-sounding string, etc. Figures from 0 to 9 were placed on the lines, 0 calling for the open string, 1 for use of the first fret, etc. Since the frets divided the fingerboard into semitones, the tablatures *ipso facto* indicated all chromatic inflections, and no problems arose concerning the application of *musica ficta*. Time-values were expressed by different kinds of stems, placed above the top line in a single row; their absence implied repetition of the last time-value graphically indicated. This system applied primarily to the moving part. What was to be done rhythmically to the other parts has given rise to two

---

[1] *See* WolfH II, 55; ScherG, 89.   [2] Cf. ChilS, 17.   [3] Cf. NeS.

[4] Further about Maler and the Tieffenbruckers, *see* LütgG II, 313, 515ff; ZuthH, 185, 273.

[5] Nevertheless, it is not superfluous, especially when transcribing from tablatures, to think in terms of these 2 different tunings in order to avoid keys that would not have been within the contemplation of a 16th-century musician.

schools of thought among transcribers into modern notation, some of whom transcribe literally, while others aim to "restore" the part-writing.[6]

EXAMPLE 120. Opening of Palestrina's *Angelus ad pastores* [7] as intabulated for lute by Terzi (*Intavolatura di liutto, Libro primo* . . . , Amadino, 1593; transcr. by E. Lawry according to two methods).

Lute-tablature—whether of the Italian, French, or German type—reaches us in such an advanced stage that it must have had a prior history. However, the earliest surviving examples, which are Italian, come to us only from the beginning of the 16th century.[8]

Lute Music Printed by Petrucci; the Capirola MS

The long list of Italian lute-books assignable to specific years begins with the four-volume *Intabolatura de Lauto*, printed by Petrucci. (No copy of Book III survives.) To this group should be added the undated but slightly later MS lute-book of Vincenzo Capirola at the Newberry Library, Chicago, which provides "the earliest occurrence of legato and non-legato, of two kinds of trills, and of dynamic indication."[9] Petrucci's Books I and II, by Francesco Spinaccino,[10] appeared in 1507. More than one-third of the contents of Book I consists of transcriptions of pieces from the *Odhecaton* series. The Books include transcriptions of two anonymous pieces having as a ground the early *bassadanza* melody, *La Spagna*. This melody, which in Chapter 4 (cf. p. 177) we have found serving as the *cantus firmus* of a 15th-century piece, recurs in several 16th-century compositions from various countries, appearing in the highest voice only rarely.[11] Book IV, by Joan Ambrosio Dalza,[12] includes

[6] About the 2 views, *see* articles by O. Gombosi and L. Schrade in ZfMW XIV (1931–32), 185, 357: ApelN, 59ff.
[7] Original apparently lost; not given in PalW or thus far (up to Vol. XVII) in PalO.
[8] Further about Italian lute tablature, *see* esp. ApelN, 56ff; WolfH II, 51ff.
[9] *See* O. Gombosi in JAMS, I (Spring, 1948), 58. A full study of this MS, by Dr. Gombosi, is in preparation.
[10] Pieces by him pr. in BruL I, 17; EnI, App., 7; ApelN, 63 (facsimile); ScherG, 62, 63; KörL, 129.
[11] Cf. GomH, 59; BukMR, 207.
[12] Pieces by him pr. in KörL, 132 (= HAM, 101), 148 (a section also in ApelM, 20); KoczLO, 398; TapS, 4; WasG, App., 3 (= BruS, 23), 20; BruS, 75; *see also* fn. 16.

frottola transcriptions. But the original compositions for lute, present in the works of both men, are of more historic importance. Among them are short, quasi-improvisational pieces, called *"ricercari,"* that consist of chords and running passages and are therefore quite different from what the term *"ricercare"* came to signify only a few years later. They were evidently designed to be played as preludes or postludes, or both, in connection with vocal works or transcriptions of them for voice and lute or for lute alone. The Capirola MS, which contains transcriptions of works by Brumel and Obrecht, among others, includes thirteen *ricercari,* one of which is *nel ton de Sta. trinitas,* the last two words alluding to Févin's motet, which is among the compositions transcribed. With four of his pieces, Dalza uses the expression *"Tastar de corde con li soi recercar dietro"* ("Touching of the strings with the *ricercare* afterward"), *"Tastar de corde"* referring to an opening section, which no doubt represents a formal crystallization of the process of "warming up." The lute repertory of the time also includes dances—*pavane, saltarelli,* etc.—to which we shall return later.

In 1509 and 1511, Petrucci brought out two books of *Tenori e contrabassi intabulati col sopran in canto figurato per cantar e sonar col lauto* by Franciscus Bossinensis (= of Bosnia).[13] In the main, these offer transcriptions of vocal works. The highest voice remains in mensural notation and the tenor and bass are intabulated, as the title indicates; the alto, the last part written and therefore the least organic (cf. p. 181), is simply omitted. Bossinensis' voice and lute parts are not always printed in the same keys, and when this happens he states that the voice part is to be transposed.[14] Each book concludes with a group of *ricercari.* A transcription of one of Cara's *frottole,* with a *ricercare* written for it by Bossinensis, is given in Example 33*b.*[15] Dalza, in transcribing a *frottola,* not for voice and lute like Bossinensis, but for lute alone, preserves the outer parts and fills them in by drawing sometimes on the alto, sometimes on the tenor.[16]

Later Italian Transcriptions, Dances, Ricercari, Fantasie, and Duets for Lute

The first high point in the literature for the lute comes with Francesco Canova da Milano (1497–1543) and the many mid-century works produced by his pupil, Perino Fiorentino, and by Melchiore de Barberiis, Domenico Bianchini, Giov. Maria da Crema, Marcantonio del Pifaro, Antonio Rotta, Vindella, Pietro P. Borrono, Antonio Casteliono, and others. Among a vast number of later lute-books, especially outstanding are the published ones by

[13] Cf. pp. 161, 163f. Their contents are listed in SartFB, 242ff.   [14] Cf. FerandH, 320.

[15] Other Bossinensis exx. pr. ScherG, 70; ApelM, 21; BruL I, 18; WasG, App., 20 (= BruS, 23); TapS, 6 (= BruS, 122). *See also* fn. 16.

[16] *See* Chap. 4, fn. 51, about a Tromboncino *frottola* that survives *a 4* and also in transcriptions by Bossinensis and Dalza. Regarding a lute-book devoted entirely to transcriptions from Tromboncino and Cara, *see* WolfEA; for an ex. from it, *see* BruS, 15.

Jean Matelart (1559),[16a] Giacomo [de] Gorzanis (1561–1571), Vincenzo Galilei (1563–1568), Giulio Cesare Barbetta (1569–1603), Fabritio Caroso (c. 1577), Gabriele Fallamero (1584), Orazio Vecchi (1590), Gastoldi (1604), Giovanni Terzi (1593–1599), Simone Molinaro (1599), and Cesare Negri (1602–1604). To these should be added three MSS (two dated; 1590 and 1620), including pieces by Santino Garsi. It will be simpler to deal with this huge mass of material by types rather than by individual composers.

Lute transcriptions of vocal polyphony became more numerous as the century progressed. In 1536, Willaert brought out a volume devoted entirely to transcriptions for voice and lute of twenty-two madrigals by Verdelot, one being the exquisite *Con lagrime e sospir*.[17] Later important prints containing voice-and-lute transcriptions include the books listed above by Fallamero and Vecchi, the latter's being the *Selva di varia ricreatione* (cf. p. 433), which presents some pieces in alternative versions for three or more voices or for one voice with lute. The earliest of Galilei's lute-books (1563) is devoted mainly to transcriptions of polyphonic works for lute alone; further examples occur in his famous *Fronimo* (1st ed., 1568).[18]

Dance pieces, mostly simple, occupy an important place in the lute repertory. The earliest known examples of the *pavana,* which superseded the 15th-century *bassadanza,* are contained in the Dalza collection previously mentioned. Here, too, are *saltarelli*—which contrast, by means of their ternary rhythm, with the binary-measured *pavane*—some of which perpetuate the *quattrocento* tradition for this dance by beginning on the upbeat; others, however, begin on the downbeat. The latter, in reality, represent a new though similar dance, the *gagliarda.*

While dance pieces of more than one type had appeared in the Capirola and Spinaccino books, it seems that it remained for Dalza to combine three dances into *pavana–saltarello–piva* suites. He makes some use of variation technique in deriving dances 2 and 3 from dance 1.[19] Casteliono's *Intabolatura de leuto* (1536) presents suites consisting of a *pavana,* three *saltarelli,* and a *tochata.* In these, *saltarello* 1 is a variation of the *pavana,* the other numbers being freely invented, but in the same key.[20] Borrono, represented in the Casteliono book as well as by a collection dated 1546, omits the *tochata.* He was undoubtedly the inventor of the suite consisting of a *pavana* with three *saltarelli,* concerning which he says that, where no *saltarelli* 2 and 3 are given, they may be taken over from other suites.[21] But the most popular combination

[16a] This is the musician designated as Joannes Matelart I in EitQ VI, 376.

[17] Pr. TapS, 18; EinIM III, 319; BruL I, 20; another ex. pr. TagA I, 1.

[18] Exx. of transcriptions by Fallamero pr. ChilLS, 84, 86; ChilS, 33f; by Vecchi: ChilB V; by Galilei: IMAMI IV, 10 items (3 = ChilLS, 58, 88, 90; 1 = ChilS, 31); ChilLS, 56, 60, 92; ChilS, 28; ChilLV, 756 (Arcadelt, not Verdelot should be named as the original composer). About those vocal pieces transcribed with great frequency, *see* WardU. In Italy, transcriptions of vocal polyphony were usually purely instrumental; voice-and-lute arrangements were rare.

[19] Cf. NorG, 174.   [20] *Ibid.,* 174f; EnI, 18f; ex. of a *saltarello* of his in TapS, 20.

[21] Exx. of his *saltarelli* pr. ScherG, 90; ChilLI, 260f. On early lute suites, *see also* DoL, 132f; also p. 671 *infra.*

of melodically related dances, in instrumental music generally, was to be found in the *pavana-gagliarda* pairs.

The middle of the century marks the disappearance in Italy of the *pavana* in favor of its less solemn equivalent, the *passamezzo* (= *passo e mezzo*, i.e., "a step and a half," referring to the choreography).[22] The music of this dance is normally, but not always, composed over one of two *ostinato* basses—the *passamezzo antico* or the *passamezzo moderno* (or *comune*). These basses also appear later in pieces that are not *passamezzi*. Related to the *passamezzo antico* formula are the *romanesca* and the *folia*, each of which often, but by no means always, appears with a standard discant of its own. On rare occasions, these discants appear without the bass melody.[22a]

EXAMPLE 121. The *Passamezzo antico, Romanesca, Folia,* and *Passamezzo moderno* basses (from BukMB, 41).

(The earliest example of the *folia* is of Spanish origin, but this bass was known in Italy too, though its appearance was more frequent there in the 17th century than in the 16th.) This group, together with the *passamezzo moderno* and also the *Ruggiero* (cf. Ex. 70*b*), provides a repertory of five stock basses, commonly used in some schematic fashion. For instance, a breve, as given in Ex. 121, might be represented by a shorter note at the beginning of a two-measure unit and a semibreve by a shorter note at the beginning of a single measure, with free material filling in the gaps. Moreover, the direction of a melodic leap might be changed, i.e., a descending fourth could be replaced by an ascending fifth (cf. Ex. 210). Each procedure, obviously, tended to obscure the melodic character of the basses, so that, in effect, they often operated chiefly as generators of harmonic formulas. Briefer than the *basse-danse cantus firmi,* these basses represent a younger tradition which, however, derives from the old one. Found in lute music, the basses are by no means confined to it.[23]

Passamezzi are included in Rotta's lute-book of 1546, which contains also an early instance of the substitution of the *gagliarda* for the *saltarello* and of the introduction of the *padovana* (which may or may not have a connection

[22] Cf. SachsW, 357. It should be noted, however, that investigators have proposed additional interpretations of the term.

[22a] WardV, 334f.

[23] Further about these stock basses, *see* esp. GomI, GomF, and GomCF. For other anonymous pieces using either of the 2 *passamezzo* basses, *see* SchraTI, 451ff.

with the old *pavana;* this problem still awaits a satisfactory solution).
Similar to his *passamezzo–gagliarda–padovana* suites [24] is the *passamezzo–
padovana–saltarello* combination used in Bianchini's lute collection of the
same date.[25] Each composer is known to have based a suite on a single motif,
varied from dance to dance.[26] But it is a suite by Gorzanis, consisting of a
passo e mezzo and *padovana* (1561), that for the first time, in extant material,
bears the title *sonata* (cf. p. 520).[27] His normal type, like that of Bianchini,
comprises a *passamezzo, padovana,* and *saltarello,* all derived from the same
melody.[28] The plan of his pieces is often broadened by variations that form
part II of a dance. An undated Gorzanis MS at Munich contains, to use
modern terminology, a cycle of 24 *passamezzo–saltarello* suites that go through
all the major and minor keys in ascending chromatic succession.[29] Earlier
departures from strictly modal writing had been apparent in works by Spinaccino and Dalza, whose use of accidentals, though often obscure in purpose
(if judged by modern standards with regard to the effect on tonality), at times
brought about clear modulations.[30]

Of simple structure are the suites by the dancing master Fabritio Caroso,
contained in his dance manual *Il Ballarino* (1581; reissued in 1600, in an enlarged edition, as *Nobiltà di dame* [31]). In the 16th century, as in the 15th,
dance manuals enrich the repertory of instrumental music. Caroso generally
follows the practice of having the later dances in a suite built on the material
of the first one. (Their number, however, and their order within a suite
vary.) But he often departs from the earlier procedure by composing the
last dance on a melodic or chordal plan of its own. Although divers names
are given to the pieces, they are, nevertheless, closely related to the old dance
forms. A tune included in this book, the *Pavaniglia,*[31a] survives also in several
keyboard transcriptions (cf. pp. 628, 865f). In Caroso, as elsewhere, the tune
is associated with the *folia* bass.[31b] Negri further increased the repertory of
practical dance music with *Le gratie d'amore* (1602) [32] and *Nuove Inventioni di Balli.*[33] Among his pieces is an example of the *brando,* the Italian
counterpart of the *branle.*

Giovanni Maria Radino's *Balli per sonar di liuto* (1592) [34] is noteworthy
for dance pieces containing frequent modulations. A *chiarenzana* (a slightly

[24] Fragment pr. NorG, 176; a *padoana* pr. BruS, 81.   [25] Ex. pr. ChilLI, 53f.

[26] Further about the Dalza, Borrono, Rotta, and Bianchini suites, *see* EnI, 18f. About the
dance aspects, *see* SachsW, 323f, 355ff.

[27] Pr. ChilS, 17.

[28] Exx. pr. ChilLS, 26ff; other dance pieces pr. BruL I, 23; ChilN, 656. (Another piece, a
villanella, pr. ChilV.)

[29] Further about Gorzanis, *see* HalbH; ChilJ; OsG, 7.   [30] Cf. KörL, 82ff.

[31] Pr. ChilB I (after 1605 reprint); exx. also pr. ChilLS, 82f; ChilN, 659f; BruS, 13, 19, 32;
BruL II, 11.

[31a] As pointed out by Mr. John Ward in *Italian Popular Music and English Broadside Ballads,*
a paper read before the Michigan Folklore Society at East Lansing, Mich., March 24, 1951.

[31b] Pr. AmbG II, 535 (after *Ballarino*); ChilB I, 21 (after *Nobiltà*).

[32] Pr. ChilB I; exx. also pr. ChilLS, 187; ChilN, 661; BruL II, 10.

[33] Ex. pr. TapS, 59.   [34] Pr. RadiL; 1 ex. pr. ChilN, 664.

faster *passamezzo*) by Marcantonio del Pifaro,[35] a *pavana et saltarello* by Barberiis, and a *passamezzo* by Barbetta are all based on Janequin's *Bataille de Marignan*. The same chanson was also transcribed for lute by Francesco da Milano, though not as a dance piece.[36] Vincenzo Galilei says in his *Fronimo*, which treats especially of lute-tablature, that he composed more than 500 *romanesche*, 300 *passamezzi*, and 100 *gagliarde*, all different, as well as numerous other works. A few dance pieces are printed in the *Fronimo*.[37] Garsi's [38] works, entirely devoted to dance compositions, include numerous *gagliarde* [39] containing syncopations, complex rhythms, and echo effects.

The peak of structural achievement attained in dance pieces was the variation suite, of which Terzi [40] and Molinaro [41] were the outstanding composers. Their suites comprise a *passamezzo* and a *gagliarda*, each of which consists of several sections, all sections of both movements having the same underlying chordal succession. Melodically, the first section of a *gagliarda* is usually a compressed derivative of the first section of its preceding *passamezzo*. The melodies of the subsequent sections of both movements develop freely. A gradual increase in motion, from quarter-notes to eighth-notes, etc., is the basis of Terzi's plan of variation. Molinaro used the same technique, but with greater flexibility. Terzi's style tends to be contrapuntal; that of Molinaro is more chordal, with a predilection for successive thirds and sixths. Although three sections to a movement is the norm for many of these suites, a *passamezzo* by Molinaro contains ten sections and its *gagliarda* six.

Ricercari continued to be of a decidedly instrumental character. Pieces of this type were sometimes called *fantasie*.[42] These two names seem to have been used interchangeably, even after imitation became important in the structure of the pieces themselves. The number of motifs within a piece and the degree of freedom with which they were developed did not, as sometimes stated, determine the choice of title. The name *ricercare*, however, was commoner in the earlier lute collections, *fantasia* in the later ones. The composer of the first known imitative *ricercare* for lute and also the person through whom this type of composition reached its artistic zenith in lute music was Francesco Canova da Milano, sometimes called *"il divino"* by his admirers. Born in 1497, he was at Mantua in 1510, where he studied with Gian Angelo Testagrossa (1470–1530), a favorite of Beatrice and Isabella d'Este.

[35] Pr., with other pieces by him, in ChilLI, 234ff; cf. also ChilN, 651.   [36] Pr. ChilS, 37.
[37] Cf. IMAMI IV, 97ff; ex. of a *gagliarda* in ChilN, 657; 12 additional exx. in ChilG.
[38] For a monograph on him, *see* OsG; his *Battaglia* pr. TapS, 69.
[39] Exx. pr. OsG, 123ff. About a *gagliarda*, surviving in 1 of the Garsi sources (and elsewhere) but perhaps by Rore, *see ibid.*, 145 (including music); SchraG; about the possibility, however, that it is not by him but is a *gagliarda* from Cyprus, *see* ZfMW XI (1929), 444ff.
[40] 2 variation suites are included among his pieces in ChilLS; a *passamezzo* by him is pr. in ChilN, 665.
[41] His lute-book pr. MolinL (many of these pieces also pr. ChilLS 136ff; 1 in BruS, 66); for a study of the book, *see* DartM; *see also* RoncM.
[42] Cf. OpieR.

From 1535 he is traceable at Rome in the service of Paul III, whose nephew he instructed in performing on the lute. Here, in 1538, Salinas heard him improvise on a *gagliarda* tune as tenor, yet no dance pieces appear among his published works. He also accompanied the pope to the Council of Nice in 1538, where he captivated Francis I of France with his playing. He died only five years later.[43] Francesco's original compositions (he also transcribed numerous motets and chansons) include pieces in free style, imitative *ricercari* or *fantasie,* and others in which toccata-like sections, with rapid scale-passages, trills, and turns, alternate with contrapuntal sections. The latter type is particularly suited to the lute, upon which, obviously, a complex polyphonic structure cannot always be made evident. But part-writing is so clear in some of his pieces that they might be transcribed for string trio or quartet with little adjustment.[44]

EXAMPLE 122. Close of *Fantesia* [*sic*] 6 from Francesco da Milano's *Intabolatura de lauto . . . Libro II . . . ,* Gardano, 1546 (from NewmM, 68).

Another lutenist described as *"il divino"* is Laurencinus Romanus, given the appellation by Besard (cf. pp. 554f), who included in his *Thesaurus harmonicus* more *fantasie* by this musician [44a] than by any other. Apparently this is the *"Lorenzini del liuto"* who was in the service of Cardinal Ippolito d'Este in 1570.

Bianchini, in 1546, is likewise among the earliest composers of imitative *ricercari.*[45] We have both imitative and non-imitative *ricercari,* dating from 1546, by Giov. Maria da Crema.[46] A *fantasia* by Perino Fiorentino consists of embellishments of a chordal structure.[47] Embellishment rather than imitation is likewise used by Julio Abondante in a *fantasia* published in 1548.[48]

[43] Further biographical data in NewmM; DorezM, 108ff; MercF.
[44] Pieces by him are available in NewmM (1 also in BruS, 96 [tablature, 181]; 2 also in ChilCI, 65f; 3 also in ChilF, 392 [= ScherG, 114], 393f; 3 also in ChilLI, 40ff). Others in BruL I, 19 (= WasG, App., 21), 22 (= ChilF, 387; ChilLI, 48); BruS, 25 (= WolfH II, 55); ChilCI, 67; ChilF, 388ff, 396ff; ChilLS, 53 (= ChilB VIII, 3; ChilN, 646); ChilS, 37.
[44a] A *passamezzo* (written on the *antico* bass) by him pr. ChilLS, 198.
[45] Ex. pr. ChilLI, 51.
[46] Exx. pr. ChilLI, 253ff; ChilN, 652; chanson transcr. pr. ChilCI, 203ff.
[47] Pr. ChilLI, 44.   [48] *Ibid.,* 247.

Galilei wrote *ricercari* in the old prelude or postlude style as well as in the imitative vein.[49] An imitative *fantasia* by Giovanni Battista dalla Gostena is interesting because of its degree-inflection.[50] Terzi is known to have composed six *fantasie*. Of fifteen *fantasie* by Molinaro, all begin with imitation except one, which opens with a free section in chordal style.[51]

Among these and other lute compositions, there are a few for two lutes, the earliest by Spinaccino. Although no such works by Francesco da Milano are known, a second lute part was added to some of his *ricercari* by Matelart.[52] In the performance of these pieces, the accompanying lute was often tuned a degree higher than the first lute, to gain greater sonority through an increase in the total number of open strings. Book X of Barberiis contains *Fantasie per sonar a due laute*. Galilei's *Fuga a l'unisono* for two lutes and his *Contrappunto,* in which the second lute supplies a chordal accompaniment to the eighth-note motion of the first lute, survive in the *Fronimo*.[53] Terzi's *Intavolatura di liutto* (1593) contains eight transcriptions for two lutes of madrigals and chansons.

Soon after 1600, the lute lost its importance in Italy. Vincenzo Giustiniani informs us in 1628 that it was no longer in use. Since the violin was fast becoming the vehicle of virtuoso performance, the easier Spanish guitar and the theorbo were preferred to the lute for *dilettante* use. In the 16th century, on the other hand, the guitar had had little importance in Italy. But toward the middle of the century a seven-string guitar was in use (having three courses of two strings, plus a single string). Four compositions for it survive in the appendix to Barberiis' *Intabolatura di lauto* (1549), entitled *Fantasie per sonar sopra la chitara da sette corde*.[54]

Methods Used by the Italians in Notating Keyboard Music; Some Data on Construction of their Keyboard Instruments

Italian compositions for keyboard begin to reach us both in quantity and in a steady flow only from the comparatively late date of 1517, when Antico's *Frottole intabulate da sonare organi*[54a] appeared at Rome (cf. p. 161). The usual Italian "tablature" for keyboard is actually a form of ordinary mensural notation, coming very close to the kind of notation now in use.[55] Normally, the Italians employed two staves regardless of the number of parts, the upper staff having either five or six lines, the lower ranging from five to

[49] Exx. pr. IMAMI IV, 8ff; WasG, App., 22; KinO, 283ff.
[50] Pr. ChilN, 667 (= ChilLS, 174). Gostena's whole book pr. GostL.
[51] Cf. MolinL, 73ff; ChilLS, 170.   [52] Ex. pr. ChilF, 400. (*See also* p. 588, fn. 97c.)
[53] Cf. IMAMI IV, 12ff.   [54] Pr. KoczM, 16f.
[54a] Facs. of title-page and colophon printed in SartMS, opposite p. 1. This work provides bibliographical details concerning Italian instrumental music—with the exception of tablatures for plucked instruments—printed in Italy before 1700.
[55] For a description, *see* ApelN, 3ff; WolfH II, 249ff. About a keyboard tablature, sometimes used by the Italians, that indicates finger placement (a requisite, according to some modern writers, of genuine tablature), *see* ApelN, 48f; WolfH II, 266.

eight. Open scores, using a separate staff for each part, reappear c. 1575, with Gardano's publication of a book of keyboard arrangements of French chansons (cf. p. 538). It is curious that the return of open-score notation, after only sporadic use since the days of the conductus and organum, should have been associated with music for a solo instrument, as is shown by such expressions as *"per sonar d'instromento perfetto,"* rather than with ensemble music. (*"I[n]- stromento perfetto"* applies to any kind of keyboard instrument.[56])

Keyboard players had to be acquainted not only with the "tablature" and open-score methods, but with two other types. In 1549, Gardano issued, in part-books, a collection of *ricercari* by Buus (cf. p. 537) that bore in its title the words: *"da cantare et sonare d'organo e altri stromenti,"* showing that the contents were for any performing medium, including the organ, that could encompass them. Since a keyboard player could not play from several part-books at once, they must have served his solo performances mainly as a source from which to prepare a score or an arrangement. That part-book publications were intended primarily for ensemble performance is reasonably clear; otherwise Gardano would hardly, in the same year, have brought out in keyboard tablature four of the Buus pieces that appeared also in part-book form.[57] On the other hand, there is evidence that in accompanying vocal music organists on occasion played from a bass part-book alone. When they did this, it would seem that they improvised the upper parts, probably after having already formed some acquaintance with the complete composition; or else they "added notations to the bass part—those notations that later developed into the figured bass."[58] There is also evidence that accompanying organists sometimes played from choir-books.[59] Obviously, they could make arrangements or scores from such sources as readily as from part-books.

Basically, Italian organs retained their 15th-century structure, though more registers began to be added c. 1530 and reeds were introduced c. 1540. Pedals were used to some extent, but not all organs had them.[60] As a rule, only one solo stop, the flute, was provided. Chamber organs, known in Italy as *organino, organetto,* or *organo di legno,* continued in favor and were often preferred to stringed keyboard-instruments, which were incapable of sustaining sounds. Nevertheless, Italy figured prominently in the construction of stringed keyboard-instruments.[61] Both the earliest surviving clavichord (1537) [62] and the earliest known perfect example of one (1543) [63] are of Italian origin. The

[56] Cf. ApelN, 19.

[57] Cf. KinO, 141; SutherR, 449. Similarly, there would have been no point in the issuance of lute intabulations of some of the Padovano music mentioned on p. 537 if the part-book versions were wholly sufficient for the lutenist.   [58] MendP, 338.

[59] Cf. KinO, 20, 98f, 190ff; ArndA, 6ff. Cf. also p. 594 *infra.* There is parallel evidence with regard to lutenists. Cf. DiseL.   [60] JepO, 39, 45.

[61] According to an announcement made at Padua as early as 1397, a certain Hermann Poll of Vienna claimed to have invented a keyboard instrument that he called a *clavicembalum* (PirP. 51).

[62] Now in the Metropolitan Museum of Art, New York. Cf. Pl. XII in JasE, 93.

[63] Picture in KinsP, 122.

oldest existing harpsichord is the work of Geronimo di Bologna, Rome, 1521.[64] In fact, the majority of 16th-century harpsichords were made in Italy, Venice being the center. Their outer cases were often inlaid with precious materials and were further decorated with carving and, in some instances, with paintings. A spinet made by Rosso of Milan, 1577, is said to have been ornamented with nearly 2,000 precious and semi-precious stones.[65] Three sizes of spinets were made, pitched respectively at the usual eight-foot tone, a fifth higher, and an octave higher than the first size, for purposes of tonal variety. Stops occasionally added to harpsichords made possible either a change in timbre or in intensity of tone. An instrument with three stops, described in the 1576 inventory of the Fugger collection, Augsburg, as having a powerful tone, was made in Venice by Franco Ungaro. A 16th-century Este inventory that includes an *instromento piano e forte* may well refer to another harpsichord provided with dynamic contrast by means of stops.[66] Organists, too, sought variety by combining registers, a practice later described by Costanzo Antegnati, last of a famous family of organ builders, in his *L'arte organica* (1608).[67] The sound of the flute stop was admired for its similarity to the tone of the flute itself. Yet Galilei rightly found these early keyboard instruments inadequate for producing tonal nuance and acclaimed the superiority of the lute in this respect.[68]

Problems of Pitch, especially with regard to Keyboard Instruments

Interest centred on the tuning of keyboard instruments. In 1523, Aron first explained mean-tone tuning, with pure thirds and the fifths flattened by one quarter of a comma. Inspired by the mid-16th-century experiments in chromatic and enharmonic music, organ builders made provision for the execution on their instruments of various intervals smaller than the semitone. In 1548 Zarlino had a clavicembalo constructed having two sizes each of all major and minor semitones. In 1555, Vicentino described his *arcicembalo* and in 1561 his *arciorgano,* each with six manuals containing thirty-one keys to the octave. Luzzaschi mastered both instruments, and Rome and Milan could each boast an *arciorgano.*

Since there was no international pitch—diverse interpretations of pitch existed side by side in each region, town, even church—different organs were tuned at varying pitch-levels.[68a] This made it necessary for organists to be able to transpose, for they were often called upon to accompany singers or to perform antiphonally with them. Certain mechanical aids seem to have been available for the less expert. For example, double keyboards, pitched at dif-

[64] Cf. Pl. XXXIV in JasE, 114.   [65] Picture in KinsP, 123; JasE, 100.
[66] Further about keyboard instruments *see* SachsHI, esp. 307, 332, 339ff; KrebsK. 91–127.
[67] Modern ed. (with German transl.) in AnteO.   [68] Cf. KinO, 138f.
[68a] For a thorough study of organ-pitch, *see* MendP.

ferent levels, may have made it possible to transpose while playing on keys that, visually at least, represented the original pitches.[68b] (The use of mixtures may actually have produced more than two different pitch-levels from the two keyboards.) As a general problem, the prevalence of mean-tone tuning, and the consequent presence of semitones of two different sizes, of course eliminated the possibility of transposition into certain keys that were to become available, much later, when equal temperament was eventually adopted for keyboard instruments. Aron, Zarlino, and the Spaniard Bermudo are among theorists who gave instruction about the art of transposition, and they regarded it as an important part of an organist's equipment.[69]

Another factor making it important for accompanying organists to be fluent in transposing was the use, in vocal music, of transposed clefs—*chiavi trasportati,* or *chiavette* as they later came to be called, in contrast to the *chiavi naturali,* SATB. Actually, although adopted for the benefit of singers and applied to vocal music, the *chiavette,* as will presently be seen, had a greater bearing on the tasks of instrumentalists than of vocalists: the organist had to transpose consciously, whether at the keyboard or on paper, deriving his part through one of the several procedures described on pp. 532f, whereas the singers found significance in the staff-degrees less with regard to fixed pitch than with regard to relative pitch.

Early writing *a 3* had often been notated with only two different clefs, and early writing *a 4* with three-clef combinations. As was shown in Chapter 3, the parts crossed one another less in writing *a 3* as the range was extended downward. But, as writing *a 4* became the norm, the additional voice at first caused congestion to reappear, especially within the area of the inner voices. In time, however, the inner parts became increasingly differentiated in range, crossing less frequently, and it became customary to use a different clef for each part. The use of many clefs (the Renaissance musician knew nine) had as its purpose the avoidance of leger lines, notation employing more than one such line being a rarity. While many clef combinations were used, the group SATB became a more or less standard set, as did also, to a lesser extent, the groups VMABar (Bar sometimes being replaced by T), later called the "high" *chiavette,* and MTBarSub (Sub sometimes being replaced by B), later called the "low" *chiavette.*[69a] Both of the latter groups appear either with a signature of one flat or with no signature.

The purpose behind the use of these two clef combinations has been a subject of controversy among historians. All three combinations have the same intervallic structure—fifth-third-fifth—and the VMABar set stands a third lower on the staves than the SATB, while the MTBarSub stands a third higher. To the modern musician, reading from score (a rare procedure before 1600), these facts make the use of such clef combinations a handy expedient for

[68b] Cf. MendD.   [69] KinO, 127ff.   [69a] About these symbols, cf. Chap. 5, fn. 338.

transposing by a third. If SATB is taken as the standard combination, it is easy to read music notated in VMABar a third lower than actually notated and music written in MTBarSub a third higher, by imagining that the clefs are replaced by the familiar SATB, and that three or four sharps or flats are added to or subtracted from the signature, according to whether the transposition is to be a major or minor third upward or downward.

However, not a single reference to the use of *chiavette* for transposition by a third has been discovered in the literature dating from before 1847, and the theory that the *chiavette* were a signal for such transposition, though widely held, must be abandoned.[69b] But there is considerable evidence that the use of the baritone or tenor clef for the lowest voice was a signal for transposition down a fourth or a fifth—i.e., a signal to the choirmaster to give the pitch a fourth or fifth lower than he would if the lowest voice were written in bass clef, and to the keyboard accompanist, if any, to transpose accordingly. The earliest explicit references to such signals so far uncovered date from the very end of the 16th and beginning of the 17th century. Examples illustrating the practice are not lacking in 16th-century keyboard reductions of vocal music. Morley, in his *Plaine and Easie Introduction to Practicall Musicke* (1597) seems to protest against transposing music written in the *chiavette* from the pitch-level of the actual notation.[70] Rocco Rodio (*Regole di musica,* 1609), the earliest authority ever cited for the supposed practice of transposition down a third, does not in fact discuss it. Caspar Vincentius, in 1611,[71] refers explicitly to transposition down a fourth or a fifth, of pieces in which the lowest part is notated in tenor clef, as possible to "anyone at his pleasure." Praetorius, in Book III, Part II, Chapter 9, of his *Syntagma musicum* (1619), gives it as a rule that "every piece that is written in high clefs [i.e., as he explains, in

[69b] The theory, of the high *chiavette,* succinctly explained in JepCP, 58, is generally credited to Kiesewetter (KiesC) and Bellermann (BellerC, 70ff), though it was not advanced by them. These men suggested transposition up or down a third as a convenience to the modern musician (as indeed it is), but did not attribute it to 16th-century practice, except indirectly in Kiesewetter's misreading of Rocco Rodio. It was so attributed, however, by Riemann (RieG, 387f; RieL, 305f; RieH II[1], 259f), and the attribution has been widely accepted. Arthur Mendel's excellent account of the whole question and its history—including Ehrmann's attack on the third-transposition theory (EhrS), Kroyer's defense of it (KrZC), Schering's rebuttal (ZfMW, XIII, 493), and Kroyer's sur-rebuttal (ZfMW, XIII, 494)—together with items of evidence for and against the connection between clefs and transposition from Josquin, Carpentras, Aron, Glareanus, Ancrio, Palestrina, Morley, Cerone, Schütz, Samber, Paolucci, and G. B. Martini, in addition to most of those mentioned here, will be found in MendP, 336–357 and 575–578. The discussion here summarizes that account, with Prof. Mendel's permission. The Schonsleder passage was communicated to the present writer by Prof. Mendel after publication of the latter's study, in which bibliographical data for all the other sources will be found.

[70] *See* MorlP, 165f (= MorlPE, 274ff). He accompanies his remarks by clef combinations, which make it clear that by the low key he means the one indicated by the *chiavi naturali,* not the one indicated by the low *chiavette*. However, he prints the low *chiavette* too (but with the alto clef replacing the mezzo) and says that they are used in "compositions for men onely to sing." This statement, showing that Morley associates these *chiavette* with music on a generally still lower pitch-level than that of his low key, is consistent with his adverse view regarding transposition.

[71] In his *Bassus generalis* part to Schadaeus' *Promptuarium musicum* (Strasbourg), Part II, preface.

which the bass is written in tenor or baritone clef] must be transposed when it is put into tablature or score for players of the organ, the lute, and any other foundation instruments, as follows: if it has a flat in the signature, down a fourth, canceling the flat; if it has no flat in the signature, down a fifth, adding a flat. . . ." (He later explains how the organist can transpose by imagining—or, if necessary, by pasting into his music—a new clef at the beginning of each line.) He also contemplates the possibility of transposing down a fourth even where there is no flat in the signature. This involves imagining a signature of one sharp—an innovation, and one for which the tuning of many organs was ill suited. One of the *Psalmen Davids* of Heinrich Schütz, published the same year as Praetorius' *Syntagma,* made use of such a signature in its organ part. By 1631, Wolfgang Schonsleder, who wrote under the pseudonym of Volupius Decorus, in his *Architectonice musices* treated the one-sharp transposition as a regular alternative. And his discussion is the earliest so far known that explicitly gives all four clefs in the VMABar combination as the "higher clefs," in which he says he is "amazed to see the majority of musicians customarily writing many of their songs, although they know that if anyone wishes to sing them they will have to be transposed downward." In the high-clef notation, he says, such pieces are better adapted to instruments than to voices. (Praetorius had connected various specifically named clef-combinations with particular combinations of instruments.) Schonsleder's remark points to one of the characteristics of the emerging instrumental styles: exploitation of the extremes of range. Morley, by urging that pieces be sung where they are written, illustrates within the domain of vocal music itself the continuing Renaissance tendency to extend the limits of the pitch range, already referred to.[72] He also shows, by his very remonstrance, that transposition was in fact applied to the *chiavette* in his day, so that it is fair to assume that the observations of the somewhat later theorists cited are in the main applicable generally to the practice in western Europe in his time.

For Organ or for Stringed Keyboard?

The same music could be and evidently was performed on all types of keyboard instruments. The presence of sustained time-values did not necessarily limit the medium of performance to the organ. Works containing sustained notes, ineffective on instruments of the stringed type could nevertheless be performed on them with the interpolation of any of a number of ornaments, probably borrowed from vocal music; these gave the illusion of prolonging the essential note. But their esthetic value was appreciated likewise; and they were used in organ music as well, where they were not needed. Dance music,

[72] For a full discussion of this tendency, *see* LowMS.

however, was not considered appropriate for the organ, which is noticeably absent from the list of instruments in a collection published by Gardano in 1551, entitled *Intabolatura nova di varie sorte de Balli da sonare per arpichordi, Clavicembali, Spinette, & Manichordi, Raccolta de diversi excellentissimi Autori.*[73] Another collection of dance music, *Il primo libro di Balli d'Arpicordo* (1592) [73a] was put out by the same Radino whose collection of dances for lute has previously been cited.

The Earliest Italian Keyboard Prints, including the Collections of Girolamo Cavazzoni

The pieces in the first major source of Italian keyboard music after the Faenza MS noted in Chapter 4—Antico's print of 1517 (cf. pp. 161, 528), with its twenty-six transcriptions of *frottole,* all but one of which survive also in their vocal form—are definitely instrumental in style, though some rhythmic and melodic elements are derived from contemporary vocal music. Mordents, inverted mordents, turns, trills, and trills-plus-turns appear in the upper parts, while the bass of the original remains almost unaltered. Broken chords are not yet in evidence. Dissonances are more freely handled than in vocal compositions: a striking cross-relation—F-sharp above a sustained F—occurs several times in one of these pieces.[74] The structure of the original is faithfully preserved, except for the occasional elimination or addition of a measure or the variation of repeated passages.[75]

The next volume of Italian keyboard music to reach us is much more significant. The composer, Marco Antonio Cavazzoni was born in Bologna c. 1490, but left that city before 1512, spending some time at Urbino. (He is called *"da Bologna, detto d'Urbino."*) He appears to have known Bembo at Urbino and to have followed him to Rome in 1513. He is traceable in 1517 at Venice, where he entered the employment of Francesco Cornaro, nephew of the Queen of Cyprus. In 1520–1521, he served Leo X and from 1522 to 1524 and from 1528 to 1531 was again at Venice. In 1536–1537 he was active as an organist at Chioggia, and thereafter returned to Venice where he served as a singer at St. Mark's, 1545–1559. In 1565 he was organist at Santa Barbara in Mantua. He was still alive in 1569. A friend of Spataro, Aron, and Willaert, he was a recognized master.[76]

Marco Antonio's *Recerchari, motetti, canzoni, Libro I* (1523) [77] consists of two *recerchari,* two transcriptions of motets and four of chansons. The

[73] Exx. pr. ApelM, 23; WasG, App., 88.   [73a] Pr. RadiA.   [74] Cf. JepO, 10*.
[75] For a study of these pieces and reprints of 6 of them, *see* JepO, 56ff, 3*ff; facsimiles, *ibid.,* 7ff.
[76] For further biographical data, *see* CMI I, 89; JepO, 89ff.
[77] Pr. CMI I, 1ff; JepO, 35*ff; pages of facsimile in ApelN, 5; JepO, 10ff.

first-named are quasi-improvisational pieces, like the earlier keyboard *preambula,* etc., of Ileborgh and Paumann (cf. pp. 657f) and like the also earlier *ricercari* in Petrucci's lute-books (cf. p. 522). They differ, however, by developing, in modest fashion, not only passage-work groups but also characteristic motifs; and they seem to be the earliest originally instrumental works to do so. There are even some fragments of imitation, but the improvisational character predominates. These *recerchari* bear melodic resemblances to the two motets and were clearly intended as preludes to them. The motets, whose vocal originals are unknown and may have been by Marco Antonio himself, employ some imitative writing. The four *canzoni* are generally similar in style, but their forms are repetitive: *aba* (two exx.); *aab* (*b* incorporating some *a*); *aaba.* The presence of such repetition schemes, to be sure, is due to the form of the original vocal *canzoni francesi;* but, as we shall see, the adoption of schemes of the sort was to have an important effect on the development of purely instrumental *canzoni.* In all these pieces the writing is basically chordal, but passing-notes and other non-chordal notes impart a semipolyphonic aspect to it. The latter occasionally give rise to sharp dissonances, which sometimes are not resolved if a consonance occurs on the next strong beat.[78] There are many cross-relations in Marco Antonio's works. Some are in close oblique position,[79] the second *recerchare* containing examples from which one of the clashing voices moves in an unexpected direction.[80] Elsewhere F-natural as the upper note of a trill is sounded simultaneously above an F-sharp in an ascending scale.[81]

Marco Antonio's son, Girolamo Cavazzoni, a pupil of Willaert's, wrote the next known extensive collection of Italian keyboard music, the *Intavolatura cioè Recercari, Canzoni, Hinni, Magnificati* of 1542.[82] Our only biographical data on the composer is found in the dedication,[82a] which names Bembo as his godfather and indicates that he was born while his father was in Bembo's service; since Girolamo refers to himself as a youth, he was probably born c. 1520. The four *ricercari* contained in this print differ in texture from earlier pieces so designated; they resemble the motet by being genuinely polyphonic, but go somewhat farther than the average motet in the extent to which the imitation reworks motivic material.[82b] In other words, the term *"ricercare"* here assumes the meaning that became standard. The *ricercari* in Girolamo's

---

[78] Further about Marco Antonio's music, *see* CMI I, 90ff; JepO, 100ff. About 2 other works that may be his, *see* CMI I, 70, 93; JepO, 95ff, 26*.

[79] Cf. JepO, 36*, 46*.   [80] *Ibid.,* 51*.

[81] *Ibid.,* 62*. For a vocal polyphonic piece probably by Marco Antonio, from another source, *see ibid.,* 26*; for discussion, *ibid.,* 95ff.

[82] Pr. CDMI, *quad. 23–24; 25,* 12–28; *26,* 9–20. A large selection pr. TorA III, 1–44; individual pieces pr. TagA I, 32ff; HAM, 121; ScherG, 99. About the date, usually given as 1542, *see* SartC, 363f.

[82a] Pr. in SartMS, 9f.   [82b] Cf. ApelOR, 141f.

Intavolatura employ pervading imitation and expand upon normal motet practice by lengthening individual points of imitation through numerous re-iterations of the subject.[83] Girolamo's music for the Magnificat (Tones 1, 4, 6, and 8) consists of different settings for odd-numbered verses, the others being sung as pure chant. Despite the alternation, Magnificat settings are unlike organ-Masses structurally. In the latter, the melodic material changes contin-uously; in the former, the same melodic material recurs for each verse, so that, as in analogous vocal examples, a variation-chain results. Each Cavazzoni variation may be regarded as a little *ricercare* on a liturgical formula. No voice is excluded from carrying the plainsong, but the superius and tenor are preferred. Much the same general texture is found in the hymn settings, but the plainsong is sometimes disposed in long notes in old *cantus-firmus* style. A single setting is provided for each hymn, to alternate with stanzas of vocally executed plainsong. The *canzoni* may be described as free para-phrases on the themes of Josquin's *Faulte d'argent* and Passereau's *Il est bel et bon*. Except that these *canzoni* retain the repetition schemes of the originals, they are technically in the same general *ricercare* style as Girolamo's other pieces. The Passereau transcription is naturally rather sprightly in character.[83a] In the main, the 16th-century *ricercari* tend to be of a serious cast; *canzoni*, more lively. In 1543, Girolamo brought out another book,[84] similar in style, which contained not only hymns and Magnificats for organ but also three complete organ-Masses (cf. pp. 174f). As may be expected, the Masses, which include a *Missa de Beata Virgine*, alternate sung plainsong and organ para-phrases.[85]

> EXAMPLE 123. The setting of the melody of the *Mariam gubernans* trope to Gloria IX, included in Girolamo Cavazzoni's *Missa de Beata Virgine* for organ, preceded by the plainsong itself for compari-son (after CDMI, *quad. 23–24, 57*).

In the paraphrases, the Gregorian melody sometimes wanders from one voice to another. Banchieri, in his *L'organo suonarino* (1605) draws on Cavazzoni in his description of the organ-Mass.[86] (He provides data about alternation

---

[83] Further about these pieces, *see* IMAMI I, lxxxvii.
[83a] On the *canzone francese* and its vocal models generally, *see* KnappC.
[84] Pr. CDMI, *quad*. 25, 2–11; 26, 2–8, 21–27; 27. A Kyrie also pr. HAM, 123; ApelMK, 52.
[85] Cf. HAM, 229.
[86] Asola included a description also in a treatise of 1605; about both tracts, *see* ScherZ, 20ff. Here, by way of sample, is the standard plan of alternation used in Credos: (1) *Credo in unum*

of plainsong and organ in his *Conclusioni nel suono dell'organo* of 1608 also.[86a])

Ricercari, Canzoni, Toccate, Fantasie, and related Italian Works for Keyboard, including those of the Gabrielis and Merulo

Cavazzoni is represented by a *ricercare* [87] in *Musica nova* (1540), containing twenty other *ricercari* by Giulio Segni (13), Willaert (3), Parabosco (2), and others. Four *ricercari* by Jacobo (Giacomo) Fogliano,[88] which may be earlier than Cavazzoni's, seem to represent a transitional stage between the old and new *ricercare* types.

The further development of the *ricercare* and of other forms used in keyboard music was largely in the hands of five organists at St. Mark's: Buus (organ 1, 1541–1551); Annibale Padovano (organ 2, 1552–1564); Merulo (organ 1, 1557–1585); Andrea Gabrieli (organ 2, 1564–1585; organ 1, 1585–1586); Giovanni Gabrieli (organ 2, 1585–1612).

A set of Buus *ricercari* appeared in part-books two years before those of 1549, mentioned on p. 529. Among the long, strictly four-part pieces, characteristic of Buus' collections, is found the first monothematic *ricercare*.[89] But the motet-like, multi-motivic type, with points of imitation on different motifs sometimes numbering up to 20 or more, continued to prevail for several decades. Among the traits differentiating Buus' works from vocal motets is a larger range in individual parts. His melodies occasionally are rather angular, but at times reveal a bold sweep. Where a *ricercare* is available both in keyboard score and in part-book form (cf. p. 529), the keyboard version contrasts with the other one through its considerable use of ornamentation.[90]

In 1556, a set of four-part *ricercari* [91] by Annibale Padovano appeared in part-books. Since Annibale was outstandingly active as an organist, it is probable that these pieces, like those of Buus, were occasionally adapted for rendition at the organ, however much the form of publication may indicate that ensemble performance was primarily intended. (The title and dedication do not mention a medium of performance.) [91a] Annibale's *Toccate e Ricer-*

Deum (intoned by the celebrant); (2) *Patrem omnipotentem* (organ); (3) *Et in unum Dominum* (choir); (4) *Et ex patre* (organ); (5) *Deum de Deo* (choir); (6) *Genitum* (organ); (7) *Qui propter nos,* and (8) *Et incarnatus est* (choir); (9) *Crucifixus* (organ); and so on, the alternation continuing until No. 19, which is an elaboration for the organ on the Amen.

[86a] Cf. BanchC, 22ff.

[87] About what may be still another, cf. FrotO, 184.

[88] Pr. CMI I, 59ff; further about these pieces, *see ibid.,* 90, 93.

[89] Pr. WasG, App., 30; RieM, 70.

[90] *See* the ex. in KinO, 245, and the comments, *ibid.,* 141. Further on Buus' *ricercari, see* esp. KrausB, 81ff; SutherR.

[91] Pr. PadovanoR. The reference in fn. 57 applies to music in this set.

[91a] Further about the occasional impossibility of distinguishing between instrumental solo and ensemble music in the 16th century, *see* KentonN.

cari,[92] which reaches us in a posthumous publication of 1604, was, on the other hand, printed in organ score. (Concerning the *toccate,* see p. 540.)

With Andrea Gabrieli, Italian keyboard music of the Renaissance rises toward a climax. Six prints published between 1587 and 1605, preserve thirty-three *ricercari* of his. Four of these prints include in the title *"tabulati per ogni sorte di stromento di tasti"* ("intabulated for all kinds of keyboard instruments") or similar words, the exceptions being sets of part-books. Andrea shows that composers felt a need for the closer knitting of the *ricercare* form. One solution, perhaps suggested by the *canzone,* is illustrated by a *ricercare a 8,*[93] in which, after six different points of imitation, Andrea reintroduces the first. In a *ricercare* that employs as much repetition as does one on Tone 12,[94] the border line between *ricercare* and *canzone* practically disappears. The distinction vanishes also with respect to the spirit of the music; Andrea wrote *ricercari* as jolly as any *canzoni.* But he also wrote standard *ricercari.* He even composed some monothematic examples.[95] In these, to avoid the sameness that would result from adherence to a single theme, he introduced quasi-improvisational interludes. Ornamentation, as might be expected, is at times present in greater profusion in the intabulated pieces [96] than in those printed in part-books.[97]

Andrea's *canzoni francesi* provide transcriptions of some famous chansons, including Lassus' *Susanne un jour* [98] and Crecquillon's *Ung gay bergier.*[99] He drew on madrigals also, as in his transcription of Rore's *Anchor che col partire.*[100] Much ornamentation is applied to the originals. The pattern ♩ ♩ ♩ | ♩ (or ♩ or ♪) is fairly common at the opening, as in a *Canzon ariosa* of 1596,[101] but that, of course, is due to its presence in the prototype. So far as is known, all *canzoni* up to Andrea are arrangements of pre-existent works [102] —e.g., the pieces printed in the Gardano tablature, the second edition of which appeared in 1577. (The first edition, not known to survive, seems to have been the earliest publication—apart from theoretical treatises—to print music in open score.[103]) Perhaps original compositions in *canzone* style were often included under the term *"ricercare"* in Andrea's day because *"canzone"* had come to imply an arrangement of a pre-existent work. Some of Andrea's *ricercari* are companion pieces to *canzoni,* just as the original

---

[92] For a study of this print, *see* ValleA, 41ff; the 2 *ricercari* in it are pr. in TorA III, 79, 85 (= TagA I, 94; RieM, 94).

[93] Pr. IMAMI I, 25. About the degree to which this piece is adaptable for performance on 2 organs, *see* FrotO I, 196f.

[94] Pr. *ibid.,* 86; HAM, 147; GabriR, 9.　　[95] E.g., the ones pr. IMAMI I, 45, 68, 81.

[96] E.g. in TagA I, 73; but *see* TorA III, 61; WasG, App., 43.

[97] *Ricercari* not yet cited pr. IMAMI I, 54, 64, 74; GabriR, 4, 7.

[98] Pr. KinO, 264, with the original.

[99] Pr. WasG, App., 66. *See also* RieH II¹, 464ff; OH III, 67. Other chanson transcrs. pr. IMAMI II, lxx, lxxiii (incomplete); WolfME, 130 (= ParrishM, 66 [with model]).

[100] Pr., with the original, TagA I, 65, 67.　　[101] *Ibid.,* 70; BonnO I, 10; WasG, App., 57.

[102] Cf. FischerI, 390.

[103] Cf. EinB, entry under 1577⁴. About the use of score in a treatise pr. in 1537, *see* LowSS.

ricercari were introductory pieces; thus, he wrote not only *canzoni* on Jane-quin's *Martin menoit,* and on Giaches de Ponte's *Con lei foss'io,*[104] but also a *ricercare* on each. Sometimes the original is not named and the piece is merely called a *ricercare arioso.*

The 1596 print containing the *Canzon ariosa* includes also a *Fantasia allegra.* The background of the *fantasia* is clear when we learn that at the examinations of prospective organists at St. Mark's the applicant was given a theme on which to improvise an example of the type. It is therefore not surprising that written-out *fantasie* appear late, the earliest known keyboard example being the one in Antonio Valente's *Intavolatura de cimbalo* (1576). When the *fantasia* emerges with Andrea and, in 1593, with Orazio Vecchi,[105] it is highly developed, based on one theme, which is modified by ornamenta-tion, inversion, and other devices. (This description, however, does not fit all *fantasie;* cf. p. 526.) Its style is much like that of a keyboard *ricercare,* but more fanciful.[106] Andrea's piece seems to be based on three themes, but "theme 2," usually presented in abbreviated form, is a decorated inversion of "theme 1" and "theme 3" is a variant of "theme 2."

EXAMPLE 124. Extracts from Andrea Gabrieli's *Fantasia allegra* (com-plete piece in TagA I, 77; TorA III, 67; RitZ II, 3; WasG, App., 53).

Included also among Andrea's compositions is a *Pass'e mezzo* in five sec-tions, which is one of the earliest examples in Italy of keyboard variations on a ground.[107]

In 1593, a volume appeared containing *intonazioni;* eight are ascribed to Andrea, eleven to Giovanni.[108] These are little, quasi-improvisational preludes

---

[104] The first chanson, with fragments of its treatment as a *canzone* and as a *ricercare,* is pr. in FrotO, 200. The *ricercare* on the second chanson is pr., in WasG, App., 60; the madrigal is pr. in MaldP, 10 (with substitute text; cf. ReT, 114).

[105] Pr. WasG, App., 73; RieM, 107.   [106] Further concerning the *fantasia,* see DeffÜ.

[107] Pr. TorA III, 71.

[108] When these were reprinted in B. Schmid's *Tabulaturbuch* (1607), they were all ascribed to Andrea; cf. IMAMI I, cxxvf.

for liturgical use, intended to give the pitch to the officiant or choir. They begin with sustained chords, proceed with passage-work in alternating hands, and end with a written-out trill, beginning on the upper note.[109] Expanded in length, the *intonazione* becomes Andrea's normal type of toccata. Examples of this differ from Annibale's toccatas, in that the latter open with a section in ordinary toccata style, proceed with a polyphonic section, and either end there or close with another section in toccata style.[110] However, the type with a contrasting polyphonic section is not unknown to Andrea.[111]

Merulo produced a large quantity of music definitely for keyboard: *ricercari*,[112] *canzoni*, etc. His *Canzoni d'intavolatura d'Organo . . . Lib. 1.* (1592) includes four pieces which, like the four Buus *ricercari* mentioned on p. 529, reach us both in keyboard tablature and, separately, in part-book form. Two of the four bear dissimilar titles in the different forms; since these titles involve names of families or individuals to whom the pieces are dedicated— *La Zerata, La Jussona*, etc.—, the change takes on significance; evidently Merulo regarded each version as a sufficiently individual work to be variously dedicated.[113]

EXAMPLE 125. Opening of Merulo's *La Zambeccara* in both the part-book version (complete in DiseM, 318) and the keyboard version (complete in KinO, 296; MeruC, 8).

But his most important contribution is in the field of the toccata. He goes beyond Andrea and even beyond Annibale. (In connection with the latter, it should be recalled that, although his *toccate* survive in a print of 1604, he had died c. 1575; Merulo's *Toccate . . . Lib. I* is dated 1598.) Merulo likes toccatas with a substantial polyphonic, *ricercare*-like middle section between two brilliant sections in toccata style,[114] and sometimes expands the scheme

---

[109] The exx. ascribed to Andrea pr. AMO X, 3ff; also HAM, 146 (= ApelMK, 54); WasG, App. 79; EinSH, 300. The exx. ascribed to Giovanni pr. TorA III, 131ff; also ApelM I, 24; TagA II, 7f; WasG, App., 80; RitZ II, 17.

[110] Exx. pr. TagA I, 99; KinO, 301.

[111] An ex. pr. WasG. App., 81. An ex. of the normal type pr. TorA III, 77.

[112] Exx. pr. EinSH, 301; TagA II, 17.

[113] *Lib. I* pr. MeruC; No. 6 also in WolfME, 96 (*see*, in addition, caption of Ex. 125); cf. further DiseM. Another *canzone* in RieM, 98.

[114] Exx. pr. HAM, 168 (= ApelMK, 57); AMO X, 53, 61, 116; WintG III, 362; TorA III, 91, 99; TagA II, 11.

to include a fourth section in *ricercare* style, and a fifth one in toccata style.[115] He occasionally introduces a *ricercare* theme in the course of the opening toccata section and recalls it in the last one. A further refinement sometimes present in Merulo's *ricercari* and *ricercare* sections is the working out, in a later point of imitation, of a theme first introduced as a countermelody in an earlier point.[116] Merulo's passage-work and harmonic treatment reveal much imagination and daring.[117]

Giovanni Gabrieli, too, has left us *ricercari, fantasie, toccate,* and *canzoni.* Florid passages of varying length frequently conclude these compositions. One of his *ricercari* [118] is devoted to the simultaneous development of three motifs. Another [119] opens with a long, toccata-like subject worked out in points of imitation which are later alternated with sections devoted to sequences of a short new motif; this *ricercare,* as far as internal structure is concerned, is a fugue. The theme of a third *ricercare* [120] consists, in part, of sequences of a three-note pattern. The countersubject of a *Fuga del IX tono* [121] is especially prominent; this and the opening subject are treated in *ricercare* fashion. His *Fantasia del IV tono* [122] also is similar to a *ricercare.* The *Fantasia del VI tono,*[123] however, is in three sections, the last of which is in toccata style. Giovanni writes toccatas [124] consisting entirely of brilliant passage-work, or containing a contrapuntal middle section. Since the majority of his *canzoni* were composed for a group of instruments, they will be discussed in the section devoted to ensemble music.

A definite sense of structure, but the absence of fixed forms, may be discerned likewise in the *ricercari,* toccatas, and *canzoni* of other 16th-century composers.[125] A number of *ricercari,* such as those by Luzzaschi, Giovanni Cavaccio (1556–1626), Girolamo Diruta (1557–1612), Gian Paolo Cima (born c. 1570), Gabriele Fattorini,[126] and Antonio Valente [127] (fl. c. 1575), and eight attributed to Palestrina [128] display a highly developed technique

---

[115] Exx. pr. RitZ II, 8; TorA III, 109, 123; ScherG, 151; TagA II, 5; CommM I, 6.

[116] Cf. Vicentino's recommendations of such a procedure (to spare the composer the task of creating a new theme!); *L'antica musica* . . . , *Lib. IV, cap.* 36, quoted in KinO, 144.

[117] Merulo toccatas in the Gabrieli style pr. AMO X, 49; TagA II, 1. Merulo organ music for the Mass pr. MeruO. Further about Merulo's keyboard music, *see* CatM, 43ff, *passim.* For a discussion of his toccatas, *see* ValentinT, 33ff, but esp. 38ff. Further about the history of the toccata, *see* GomVT; SchraB.

[118] Pr. TagA II, 70; FosA, 7; RitZ II, 18; HilleR, 6 (here called a *canzon*).

[119] Pr. TagA II, 76; RieM, 100; WasG, App., 48.

[120] Pr. TagA II, 90. Another *ricercare* by him pr. HilleR, 4.

[121] Pr. TagA II, 93. *Fuga,* in standard 16th-century practice, still denoted a canon, of which this piece is not an ex. But c. 1600 the Germans used the term as a synonym for *canzona francese* or *ricercare.* The source used by TagA is apparently of Northern origin.

[122] *Ibid.,* 81.   [123] *Ibid.,* 86.   [124] *Ibid.,* 73 (= TorA III, 137), 83.   [125] Discussed in TorM.

[126] Exx. by these 5 men pr. TorA III (1 by Luzzaschi also pr. TagA II, 27). Another ex. by Diruta pr. KrebsD, 388.

[127] A fragment of a *ricercare* by him in a tablature that he devised himself is pr. in facsimile, with transcr., in CaravI, 506f.

[128] FrotO, 223, accepts their authenticity but considers them inferior to Palestrina's vocal works; RitR, 135, says that if they are not by Palestrina, then we have another excellent composer. Pr. PalW XXXII, 80–92; PalR; RitR, after 146; one pr. RitZ II, 6 (= FosA, 1).

of thematic imitation. In some of these *ricercari,* the initial entries follow one another at close time-intervals; in others, the entrances are more widely spaced, in the way that Pietro Ponzio recommends in his *Raggionamento di musica* (1588). More numerous free passages occur in the *ricercari* of Antegnati,[129] and his imitation is not always strict. Sperindio Bertoldo (c. 1530–1570) alternates binary with ternary rhythm in one of his *ricercari,*[130] which he concludes with a flourish. Two of Valente's *Versi per organo*[131] are imitative *ricercari,* another is more like a toccata.

Toccatas by Bertoldo, one of which has an imitative introduction, lack the florid passages typical of such works. Bell'Haver, in one instance,[132] places a more contrapuntal section between two sections in toccata style. Imitation introduces an example by Gioseffo Guami,[133] which then proceeds with extended scale patterns. In a toccata by Luzzaschi,[134] motifs wander successively through all the parts but are not used in *stretto.* A toccata by Cavaccio[135] is indistinguishable from a *ricercare,* but examples by Diruta[136] consist mainly of scale embellishments of a chordal structure.

As pointed out on p. 295, even the Italians found the French chanson, with its clear-cut musical forms, preferable to the madrigal, with its concentration on expression of the text—often at the expense of the form—, as material for instrumental transcription. That point has by now been made amply clear. The process of chanson transcription led eventually to the writing of instrumental *canzoni* that were original, but generally similar to the chanson in style. Incidental mention has been made of some such works for keyboard. Further consideration will show that, as a type of composition, the instrumental *canzone* proves to be a study in the fitting together of musical sections—a study in structure—, just as the *ricercare* is a study in the exploitation of contrapuntal resources. In many ways, the experiments with contrasting sections and with repetitions remind one of the rather similar, brilliantly successful attempts, made by the Franco-Netherlanders late in the 15th century, in the field of vocal secular polyphony. To obtain an idea of the nature of the new *canzone* it is necessary to give some attention to the sectional organization of representative examples.

Luzzaschi achieves unity in one of his *canzoni*[137] by basing all of its three sections on the same short ascending scale-pattern, rhythmically altered for each section. Of three imitative sections in a work by Giacomo Brignoli (born c. 1550),[138] sections 1 and 3 are based on the same theme, but 2 has a new theme. *La serpentina* (1591),[139] a *canzone* by Vincenzo Pellegrini, consists of five sections, of which 1, 3, and 5 (a repetition of 3) use imitation,

129 Pr. TorA III, 153.   130 *Ibid.,* 55; for another *ricercare* by him, *see ibid.,* 58.
131 *Ibid.,* 45ff.   132 *Ibid.,* 179.   133 *Ibid.,* 183.
134 *Ibid.,* 151 (= TagA II, 28; RitZ II, 14; FosA, 3).   135 *Ibid.,* 191.
136 *Ibid.,* 165, 167 (= KrebsD, 383, 386); another toccata by him pr. KrebsD, 384.
137 *Ibid.,* 3; TagA II, 25; RieM, 131.   138 Pr. RitZ II, 16.   139 Pr. TorA III, 49.

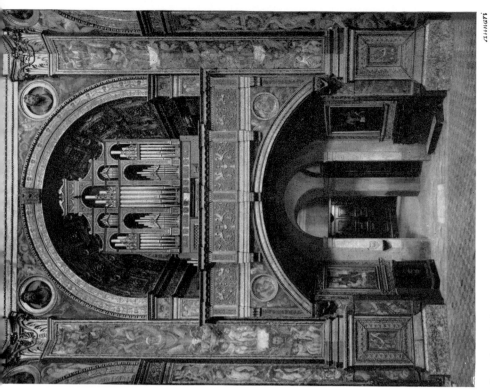

Interior of the Church of the Incoronata at Lodi, the birthplace of Gafori, with organ altered by Giovanni Battista Antegnati in 1544

annari

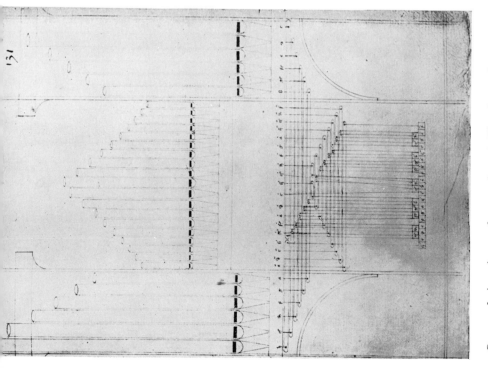

Organ design from the treatise of Henricus Arnaut of Zwolle (d. 1466) (after Cerf, Plate XIII)

PLATE VI

and 4 is an embellishment of the four-measure chordal section 2. His *La capricciosa* [140] develops a motif of three descending notes through sequence and free imitation in section 1; section 2 is chordal; and section 3 resembles a toccata. Included among a group of brief, imitative pieces *a 4* by Banchieri are several *suonate,* a toccata, and a *canzone italiana,* all of which, regardless of title, are similar in style.[141] Theme fragments are developed in *canzoni* of Guami [142] and Cristofano Malvezzi (born c. 1560).[143]

Contrapuntal resourcefulness characterizes the keyboard music of Giovanni de Macque.[144] In his *Capriccio sopra un Sogetto,* each half of the theme is developed separately in imitation *a 4*. Near the middle of the piece, imitation *a 4* of the first half of the theme appears in augmentation, with a slight rhythmic change. The same fragment in normal time-values is next coupled with its inversion, then wanders up and down through all four parts in a section that concludes the piece.

EXAMPLE 126. Extracts from *Capriccio sopra un Sogetto*—Macque (from MB IV, 39f).

Extract 1: Opening. *Extract 2:* Imitation based on second member of motif presented in Extract 1. *Extract 3:* Imitation based on first member, coupled with its inversion.

All the themes of his *Capriccio sopra tre Sogetti* are introduced at the opening of the work. Their subsequent treatment includes diminution of the time-values. Extensive use of arpeggio figures outlining in turn the chords of F, C, G, and D gives descriptive quality to his *Toccata a modo di Trombette.* Sixteen successive sequences of a motif in the *Capriccio sopra re, fa, mi, sol,* however, become monotonous. Macque's *Partite sopra Ruggiero* spins toccata-like passages, first in a single line and later in two voices in contrary motion, above the stock melody in the bass. When florid passages occur in the bass, it is the upper parts, instead, that suggest the *Ruggiero* melody. Numerous *canzoni* in the style of the period as well as toccata-like *stravaganze* are included among his ingenious works.

Of interest in the history of Italian keyboard music are Simone Verovio's

[140] *Ibid.,* 51.   [141] *Ibid.,* 354ff.   [142] Ex. pr. FosA, 5; RitZ II, 15.   [143] Ex. pr. FosA, 11.
[144] Exx. pr. MB IV, 33–69; EinSH, 311; HAM, 200.

publications (1586–1595) of vocal pieces together with their keyboard and lute transcriptions in tablature (cf. p. 447). The voice parts appear on the left-hand pages, one voice after the other, the tablatures on the opposite right-hand pages.[145] Verovio also brought out (1607) a purely instrumental publication consisting of sixteen *gagliarde* by G. F. Anerio, intabulated both for *cembalo* and for lute.[146] Dance pieces of various kinds form an attractive aspect of *cinquecento* keyboard music.[147]

Some Aspects of Italian Performance Practice at the Keyboard

The fact that improvisation was an important phase of organ playing may account, in part, for the absence of works by many famous organists of the time. An increased—perhaps excessive—appreciation of performance is shown by a Venetian decree of 1546, providing that no canons or priests should interrupt performing organists, but should remain quiet and patiently await the end of a piece.[148] Mention is made of performances on two organs by Annibale Padovano with Parabosco or Merulo, also by Merulo with Andrea Gabrieli.[149]

The virtuoso character of 16th-century keyboard music required considerable skill on the part of the player. Ten or twelve years was the period that Cardinal Bembo considered necessary for acquiring proficiency, when he refused his daughter Elena's request for *monacordo* lessons and advised her to content herself with the *essercitio delle lettere*—and with sewing.[150] Although the study of keyboard instruments was widely cultivated in Italy throughout the century, a method was not published there until the close of the *cinquecento*, when Part I of Diruta's *Il Transilvano* appeared in 1593. Part II followed in 1608.[151] This treatise is a synthesis of previous practice, and especially of Merulo's teachings, rather than an attempt to formulate new theories, and is significant for its treatment of the esthetic as well as the technical aspect of performance. Hand position and fingering are discussed; the manner of playing the organ is contrasted with that of playing other keyboard instruments. Numerous musical examples include works by Merulo, the Gabrielis, Luzzaschi, Bell'Haver, and Gioseffo Guami, as well as some of Diruta's compositions, which, since they were composed to illustrate various problems of performance, appear to be our earliest keyboard etudes. Diminution (ornamentation), which Diruta regards Merulo as having used with particular skill, is treated at length. Ornaments are described, including trill

---

[145] Described in KinO, 126; facsimiles in KinsP, 153; PalW XXX, opp. p. 3 (facsimile of title page, *ibid.*, xix); WolfH II, Pl. I after p. 256.

[146] About this set, *see* BecherA; for a page of facsimile, *see ibid.*, opp. p. 161 (= WolfH II, Pl. II after p. 256); for a transcr., *see* ScherG, 211.

[147] Regarding an anon. collection of *passamezzi*, etc. (1551), *see* SchraTI (with 6 exx.).

[148] Cf. CafS I, 31.   [149] Cf. FrotO I, 196.   [150] Cf. CafS I, 95.

[151] For a monograph on *Il Transilvano, see* KrebsD; described also in HaraD; FrotO, 228ff; HäfnE, 49ff; SeiffG, 41f, 44ff.

variants (such as the *tremolo, tremoletto,* and *groppo*); the *minuta,* a free dissolution of the melody into passage-work; the *trillo,* an accelerated repetition of a tone; etc. Ornamentation, Diruta contends, should be used sparingly, if at all, in points of imitation. He considers it unsuited also to pieces originally in notes of short time-values such as Giovanni Gabrieli's *La Spiritata,* a composition for ensemble—cf. p. 551—, but one evidently familiar in keyboard adaptation. He recommends, however, that ornamentation be used for pieces with less motion, like Antonio Mortaro's *canzone, L'Albergona.*[152] Part II of *Il Transilvano* is devoted to composition, improvisation, transposition, and accompanying.

Notable as early examples of completely written-out independent keyboard accompaniments, are those in Luzzaschi's collection of 1601 (cf. pp. 411f). But toward the end of the *cinquecento* organ basses to both sacred and secular music had begun to appear, called *"partitura," "basso generale," "basso principale,"* or *"basso per l'organo."* Vincenti and the Milan firm of Tini and Besozzi were among the earliest to publish these, which appear in works by Croce, Lucretio Quintiani, and Bassano. In 1602, Viadana, in his *Cento concerti ecclesiastici,* gives rules [153] (presumably influenced by earlier practice) for playing such basses, the forerunners of the figured-bass parts which were to constitute an essential factor in the music of the next 150 years.

The Use of Wind and Bowed Stringed Instruments in Italy

In addition to keyboard instruments and lutes, the profusion of musical instruments used in the *quattrocento* attained increasing prominence during the *cinquecento* at public functions and private gatherings in all strata of society throughout Italy.[154] The principal courts vied with one another and even resorted to intrigue in securing the most skilled players, who were often expected to know how to play more than one instrument and also to sing. Members of city bands of *pifare,* trombones, and trumpets acquired artistic reputation as well as ample remuneration by playing at frequent affairs of state and at festivities of prominent families. Benvenuto Cellini, at the age of thirteen, became a member of such a band in 1513 at Florence, where his father played *pifara.*[155] Though a skilled player of flute and cornet (*zink*), Benvenuto, to his father's chagrin, expressed a strong aversion to music. Nevertheless, he later participated with seven other instrumentalists in the performance of some motets, which he regarded as "of great beauty," at Clem-

[152] Pr. RitZ II, 22, unembellished, and both with and without ornaments in KrebsD, 379.
[153] Further about his rules, *see* ArndA, 9ff; FrotO, 240f. An ex. with an organ bass pr. WolfME, 117.
[154] For a monograph on the use of various instruments in secular music of the 16th century, *see* ElsU.
[155] The official record of his employment is reprinted in GaspI, 634.

ent VII's *Ferragosto* (August festival), playing the soprano part on the cornet so creditably that he was prevailed upon to become one of the pope's musicians.[156]

Various instrumental groups are portrayed in the paintings of Montagna, Luca Peni,[157] Tintoretto,[158] Gentile Bellini,[159] Gaudenzio Ferrari,[160] and others. Purely instrumental performances, as well as those of vocal and mixed ensembles, are mentioned in accounts of banquets. During the fifth course of a wedding banquet at the court of Ferrara, 1529, music was played on five trombones and a cornet. Two *dolzaine,* one *storta,* one *cornetto grosso,* and one *trombone* were heard at the seventh course; and for the eighth, the ensemble consisted of five viols, one *strumento di penna* (cf. p. 487), one *flauto grosso,* one *lira,* one *trombone,* and one *flauto d'Alemana.*[161] Occasional reference to instrumental music, without the customary collaboration of voices, occurs also in connection with *intermedi* (cf. pp. 173, 567ff). Enjoyed by the Florentine nobility, according to accounts of 1586, were frequent performances by the children of the orphanage, who played *"cornetto, traversa, viola o trombone."* These children traveled also to Ferrara, Pistoia, and Lucca. Their leader, Franciosio, founded a school for instruction in playing wind and stringed instruments.[162]

Contemporary treatises name many instrumentalists and praise their skill. According to Bartoli's *Ragionamenti* (1567), Chapter 3 [163] of which is devoted to instrumentalists from the time of Leo X to c. 1545, Striggio amazed listeners by the agility and artistry of his viol playing. Antonio da Luca excelled in playing the lute, viol, and cornet; and Lorenzo da Lucca played the lute and viol *"con una grazia maravigliosa."* A number of players, some of whom are mentioned by Doni in his *Dialogo della Musica* (1544) and by Luigi Dentice in his *Dialoghi* (1553), used the name of their instrument as a surname, e.g., Antonio da Cornetto, Bartolomeo Trombone, Ascanio and Girolamo Trombetti, and many others. Perhaps the most famous violist to do this was Alfonso della Viola (cf. pp. 324f, 568).[164]

From Bottrigari's *Il Desiderio* (1594) [165] we learn of the excellent musical performances—for which all sorts of instrumental combinations were used—that took place among the various *Accademie,* etc., and also of the instrument collection and concerts at the court of Ferrara. Particularly vivid is his description of the concerts of an ensemble of ladies playing wind and stringed instruments. After the performers had silently assembled at a long table, the *maestra del concerto* (possibly Tarquinia Molza) entered and, with a long polished

---

[156] *See* the *Autobiography of Benvenuto Cellini* (transl. by John Addington Symonds; Modern Library ed.), 42.
[157] Reproduced in KinsP, 111.   [158] Cf. *ibid.,* 113; BesM, 296.
[159] Reproduced in IMAMI I, frontispieces, and opposite xlvi.
[160] Reproduced in BesM, 243.   [161] For further details, *see* ScherA, 67f.
[162] Cf. CanM, 741f; ElsU, 18.   [163] Reprinted in IMAMI I, livf.   [164] *Ibid.,* lvi.
[165] Reprinted, with introduction, in BottrigD. *See* MGG II, 154ff.

stick, gave the signal to begin, whereupon the group played with marvelous unanimity.[166] *Il Desiderio,* however, is chiefly concerned with the question of combining keyboard, wind, and stringed instruments, among which a variance in tuning exists. Bottrigari divides instruments into three groups: (1) stable-tuned—keyboard instruments and harps; (2) stable-tuned but alterable—lutes, viols, flutes, and cornets (upon which the performer may make slight adjustments in the pitches fixed by the frets or finger holes); (3) completely alterable—trombones, *ribechini,* and *lire* (which have no finger holes or frets). To combine all these instruments in a performance that would sound in tune, he says, is extremely difficult if not impossible. However, the addition of the voice, which easily accommodates itself to all kinds of *armonia,* serves, in his opinion, as an equalizer. But, like Ramos, Aron, and Lanfranco, he recommends that, in combining instruments, those of the same tuning classification be used together wherever possible. At all events, not more than two of the three differently tuned groups should be used simultaneously. The carrying out of this advice was facilitated by the increasing tendency in the 16th century to construct instruments in families, usually of three ranges—soprano, alto-tenor, and bass. Perhaps the emergence of such consorts was, like that of imitation, related to the Late Renaissance expansion of the tonal range: it was no longer necessary to differentiate frequently crossing parts by means of markedly contrasting timbres.

For chamber music, then in high favor, viols were especially preferred, and wind instruments were generally considered inappropriate. To honor Ferdinand of Bavaria, visiting in Ferrara in 1566, cornets and trombones were played—but in the adjoining room.[167] The Duke of Mantua liked only *gli strumenti delicati,*[168] and the Duke of Milan, in 1544, had music played to him morning and evening on four viols.[169] Earlier, Castiglione, in the *Cortegiano,* had described music played on four *viole da arco* as *"soavissima e artificiosa."* Chamber music was by no means restricted to court performances: people visited each other purposely to make music together. On one such occasion Buus played *violone il soprano* and Doni *viola* with five other musicians.[170]

Viols of the *gamba* type were used for chamber music, viols of the *braccio* variety being considered street instruments.[171] This differentiation, expressed by Zacconi in his *Prattica di musica,*[172] was maintained throughout and well beyond the 16th century. Likewise excluded from intimate ensembles was the violin, which began to develop from the *braccio* family during the latter half of the century. To the lute and viol center of Brescia belongs the distinction of producing some of the earliest violins—the work of Gasparo

[166] Cf. BottrigD, 48; KinO, 159; DrinM, 221.   [167] SandB, 353.   [168] CanM, 691f.
[169] ElsU, 63.   [170] *Ibid.,* 19.
[171] For a comparison of the two types of viols, *see* SachsHI, 347.   [172] Cf. GreuB, 16.

Bertolotti da Salò (c. 1542–1609).[173] At this time, too, the famous Amati dynasty was founded at Cremona by Andrea Amati (c. 1535–after 1611), to be continued by his sons Antonio (c. 1555–after 1640) and Hieronymus (c. 1556–1630). But its culmination was not reached until the next century, with the fine instruments made by Nicola (1596–1684), son of Hieronymus.

Methods of instruction for flute and viol, unlike those for lute and keyboard, antedate any surviving music that we can say, with certainty, was composed specifically for the instruments discussed. The earliest known flute method, Silvestro di Ganassi's *Fontegara* (1535),[174] contains a diagram,[175] in which the way to produce a scalar succession of pitches is shown by various combinations of blackened, partially blackened, and empty circles representing finger holes. The corresponding staff notation is given, thus enabling the flutist to adapt to his instrument any mensural music of appropriate range.

Ganassi was likewise the author of one of the earliest viol methods, the two-volume *Regola Rubertina* (1542–1543).[176] One chapter explains how to transfer mensural music to viol tablature—additional evidence that any composition was the common property of all media by which it could be performed. Italian viol-tablature[177] was so similar to Italian lute-tablature that, in the main, either lute or viol could be used in playing from it. This was possible because, as Lanfranco pointed out in his *Scintille di musica* (1533),[178] the tuning of the *violone* was identical with that of the lute (actually it is the tenor-alto viol which is tuned like the lute), but the former had single strings instead of courses. The discant viol was tuned a fourth higher and the bass a fifth or a fourth deeper, but in all sizes the intervallic relationship of the six strings was the same.[178a] In addition to tablature, Ganassi's comprehensive treatise deals with transposition, diminution, and the art of accompanying a song, as well as such basic matters as the correct way to hold the instrument, tuning, and placement of the frets. Fretless playing was sanctioned only when the range of the music exceeded that of the fifteenth fret. Especially significant are the chapters on bowing and fingering. As many as six different ways of fingering a given passage are shown. The bow was held between the thumb and middle finger, with the hand turned palm upward and outward, the index finger regulating the pressure. In general, Ganassi recommends drawing the bow *"con lo braccio pronto e mano leggiadra e ferma,"* midway between the bridge and the fingerboard. But he is aware of the harsher

---

[173] Further about the early history and structure of the violin, *see* PeluzV; StraeV I, 35ff.
[174] Facsimile edition in GanaF.   [175] Reproduced also in WolfH II, 242.
[176] Facs. edition in GanaR; discussed also in GreuB; MoserGV, 25ff; AlbiV, 84.
[177] Not to be confused with violin tablature, concerning which *see* esp. PlamV.
[178] Quoted in GreuB, 13.
[178a] About high and low tunings of the viols as a body (rather than with respect to one another) and the relation of these tunings to organ pitch, *see* BessarA, 367ff.

sound produced by bowing near the bridge and the *mesto* quality that results from bowing near the fingerboard, though he does not use the terms
"sul ponticello" or *"sul tastiera."* The use of *"tremar"* is applied not only to
the left hand but to the bow arm as well. Additional advice is given on various
ways of using the bow in order to attain effects appropriate to different types
of pieces. All this signifies a highly developed technique of viol playing and
the recognized obligations of the player as an interpreter. Four-stringed and
three-stringed viols (the latter tuned in fifths) and the *lira* are dealt with in
Book II of the *Regola Rubertina*. Both volumes contain *ricercari* in tablature,
a version in ten-line mensural notation being included also for those in Book
I. All these pieces are for solo viol and are in the early prelude style, with
generous use of double stops and some genuine writing *a 2*. These *ricercari*, together with a few examples in Scipione Ceretto's *Della Prattica Musica vocale
e strumentale* (1601) are the only extant evidence of Italian viol-tablature.
Ganassi's pieces, moreover, are among the earliest known compositions written specifically for the viol.[179]

Instrumental Ensemble Music in Italy, including that of Giovanni Gabrieli

Various instrumental *bicinia*, definable as imitative *ricercari a 2*, have come
down to us. Four by Bernardino Lupachino and one by Joan Maria Tasso
are from a collection repeatedly reprinted between c. 1559 and 1701. A highly
imitative *fantasia* by Giovanni de Antiquis bears the date 1584. Of the same
date are twenty-nine two-part *Contrapunti* in *ricercare* style by Galilei.[180]
Still later are five refreshing *bicinia* by Gastoldi (1598), which make use of
thematic inversion, echo effects, and the patter of repeated notes.[181] *Bicinia*
were often intended for purposes of instruction.[182]

Various three-part *ricercari* survive by Willaert [183] and Rore, all of which
come to us in part-books. Both men are represented in a print of 1549, which
contains also many *ricercari* by the violist Tiburtino—perhaps evidence, additional to that of the part-book format, that the pieces are for instrumental
ensemble.[184] Moreover, a keyboard instrument is never named in any of the

[179] 5 of these *ricercari* (Vol. I, Nos. 2–4; Vol. II, Nos. 1, 2) pr. BachV; Vol. I, No. 1, pr. HAM,
127, and WolfH II, 225; Vol. II, No. 1, pr. TapS, 22; Vol. II, No. 2, pr. HAM, 127.

[180] Pr. SCMA VIII.

[181] The pieces mentioned in this paragraph, except Galilei's, are pr. in DoflS. For a special
Gastoldi collection, *see* GastS.

[182] Cf. EinVG.

[183] Exx. pr. WillR (1 also pr. Ham, 120; WasG, App., 27; another also in RieM, 78; TagA
I, 4); ScherG, 102.

[184] Further *ricercari* by Willaert were pr. in 1552 and 1559. *See* IMAMI I, lxxxvii; SutherR,
449.

titles of Willaert's compositions.[185] Likewise in part-books were three *fantasie* [186] by Willaert, printed in 1559 together with other numbers.

Two of three *fantasie a 4* by Julius de Modena (= Giulio Segni; cf. p. 627) open with the same motif, which appears in imitation in all four parts but does not recur thereafter. The third *fantasia* uses this motif also, but not until the eleventh measure.[187] Giovanni Bassano's seven *Fantasie a tre voci per cantar e sonar con ogni sorte d'Istrumenti* (1585) [188] show pervading imitation among the three parts but lack thematic repetition or development. A *fantasia* (1603) [189] by Banchieri has the form *abab*. His *Fantasia in Eco movendo un Registro* (1603) [190] is in *aba* form with coda. Section *b* is chordal, with alternating indications of *forte* and *piano*. Likewise in *aba* form is his *Sinfonia d'Istromenti senza voci* (1607),[191] but the brief section *b* is a triple-time treatment of the duple-time theme of section *a*.

Annibale Padovano and Andrea Gabrieli each wrote an eight-part *Battaglia per strumenti da fiato*,[192] paraphrases, in a sense, of Janequin's *Bataille* and also elaborations of Werrecore's *Bataglia Taliana*. In fact, an entire section of Werrecore's *Bataglia* is recognizable in the pieces by Annibale and Andrea,[193] which are genuinely descriptive, especially in their second *partes*, where there are representations of the trotting of horses and of the conflict and cries of battle. In spite of the specification *"strumenti da fiato,"* Annibale's piece was performed, at least on one occasion, with eight *tromboni*, eight *viole da arco*, eight *grandi flauti*, one *strumento da penna*, one *laute*, and voices, making an ensemble of forty.[194]

The *canzone da sonar*, however, was the type that was most favored in works for instrumental ensemble. Here Italian composers exercised a high degree of ingenuity in organizing sections of contrast and repetition into a unified whole. One of the first men to write instrumental-ensemble *canzoni* of this chain type was Fiorenzo Maschera. Earlier than his collection of 1584, nevertheless, are a few extant works, including an imitative five-part *canzone da sonare, La Bella* (1572), by Vicentino [195] and two *Arie di canzon francese per sonar* for four instruments by Ingegneri. The structural plan of the first *canzone* is *aba*, that of the second is *abcd*.[196] As for Maschera's

185 Cf. FrotO, 191.
186 Pr. as Nos. 19 and 38 of *Blätter der Sackpfeife*, publ. by Nagel [1932–33].
187 All 3 *fantasie* pr. as No. 6 of same series.
188 Pr. BassaT.
189 Pr. WasI, 12. Further about Banchieri's instrumental music, *see* VatS, esp. 121f.
190 Pr. WasI, 10.   191 Pr. RieM, 114; ScherG, 155.
192 Pr. IMAMI I, 93, 177; commentary *ibid.,* xciiff.
193 Compare IMAMI I, 122ff, 196 (from meas. 3)f, with Tirabassi's edition (1931) of Werrecore's *Bataglia*, xxiiff (or Ochsenkhun's transcription in DTO XVIII, 49, meas. 26–62).
194 Cf. IMAMI I, lxiii.   195 Pr. *ibid.,* II, xlvi.
196 The pieces pr. *ibid.,* II, l, lii. The form of the first *canzone* is incorrectly described on the earlier of these cited pages.

twenty-one *canzoni,* a few are in two sections, either or both being repeated, with coda;[197] but the majority contain three or more sections, with coda.[198] Only one of these pieces is homophonic in texture, with double-chorus effect suggestive of the *canzoni* of Giovanni Gabrieli.

In his period, Giovanni was undoubtedly the most prolific and ingenious composer for instrumental ensemble. Included in a collection of works by various composers printed in 1608, are four of his early *canzoni a 4.*[199] All except the first of them, *La Spiritata* (cf. p. 545), conclude with a return to the opening theme, followed by a brief coda. A *canzone* of his *a 8,* in the same collection, is noteworthy for its *ostinato* bass figure, the recurrences of which are widely separated by rests.[200] Many innovations occur in the fourteen *canzoni* and two *sonate* of his first book of *Sacrae Symphoniae* (1597).[201] One of the *sonate,* the famous *Sonata pian e forte,*[202] has the distinction of being the earliest known ensemble work to indicate dynamic contrasts (cf. p. 521). It is also among the first to designate precise instrumentation. In 1580, Galilei had composed specifically for tenor voice and viols, a setting *a 5* of Count Ugolino's lament in the *Divine Comedy.*[203] Giovanni shows a decided preference for cornets and trombones, a choice no doubt influenced by the fact that these instruments were used at St. Mark's, having been commonly included in performance there after Zarlino became *maestro di cappella* in 1565. With these instruments, Giovanni uses the *violino* (similar in range to our viola), but never the delicate-sounding viol. In fact, his instrumental specifications are confined exclusively to cornets, trombones, and *violini.* Structurally, the *sonate* contain sections unrelated thematically, but these sections are not as distinctly separated as are those of the *canzoni,* in which a long succession of brief, contrasting sections is linked together in chain fashion. In some of these chain *canzoni,* each section differs thematically from the rest; in others, a recapitulation of one or more of the sections takes place. The most frequent repetition of a single section occurs in the rondo-like *canzone a 10* having the form *abacadaeafag.* The *a* sections of this work (one of three compositions for single choir) are chordal. The contrasting sections are mostly for two high solo parts with bass or scant chordal accompaniment, suggesting the later trio-sonata. The work as a whole, with its contrast of large and small instrumental groups, anticipates the *concerto grosso.*

[197] Exx. pr. *ibid.,* lxix (= WasI, 1); HAM, 201.
[198] Ex. pr. WasI, 2; RieM, 92. For a thematic index of the 21 *canzoni, see* IMAMI II, lviff; for an outline of their form, *see ibid.,* lv; for Terzi's lute transcr. of No. 11, *see* ChilLS, 108.
[199] Pr. GabrC. No. 1 also (in keyboard score) in PirAO, 1191; TagA II, 67.
[200] We are indebted to Dr. Hans David for access to his MS score of this work.
[201] All pr. in IMAMI II; analyzed *ibid.,* lxiiiff. Single *canzoni* in WasI, 4; WintG III, 119.
[202] Pr. HAM, 198; ScherG, 148; WasI, 7.
[203] Cf. SolO, 145, 210; ScherA, 79.

EXAMPLE 127. Opening of *Canzone IX* from Giovanni Gabrieli's *Sacrae symphoniae* of 1597 (after IMAMI II, 118).[204]

The extensively developed motifs [motif] and [motif] in another *canzone a 10* for single choir have—inevitably—been compared to the similar ones in Beethoven's Fifth Symphony.[205]

The motet *Surrexit Christus*,[206] like *In ecclesiis* (cf. p. 499)—both pieces are from the second book of *Sacrae symphoniae*—, contains short instrumental *sinfonie* scored for cornets, trombones, and *violini*. A collection of Giovanni's *canzoni e sonate* (1615), in from three to twenty-two voices, includes an apparently early *canzone a 5*[207] in *aba* form and a *canzone a 6*[208] with the structure $aba^1ba^2ba^3bba^4$ plus a coda.[208a] In the *Sonata con tre violini* from the same collection, the three *violini* maintain the structural unity of the piece through thematic imitation, but function in various other ways also, above an organ bass, to which a stringed bass may be added if desired.[209] The bass line, though retaining a melodic character, has little thematic material and often moves in notes of longer time-values than those of the upper parts, foreshadowing 17th-century practice.

In brief, one recognizes in the works of Giovanni Gabrieli, both the full flowering of Late Renaissance music and the budding of baroque style.

Lute Music in France

In France as in Italy, the lute was a favorite Renaissance instrument. Actual names of French lutenists begin to reach us from as far back as 1396,

---

204 The parts for 2 organs given in IMAMI II are by the ed.; cf. *ibid.*, lxxxii.
205 *Ibid.*, 75; lxxvi.   206 Pr. WintG III, 66.
207 We are indebted to Dr. Hans David for access to his MS score of this work.
208 Pr. WasI, 15; OH II, 431.
208a Further on Italian *canzoni* for instrumental ensemble, *see* CrockerC.
209 Cf. preface of *Sonata con tre violini*, Werner Danckert, ed., Kassel, 1934. For other editions, *see* FiscS, 5; WasI, 13; WintG III, 118. Further about Giovanni's instrumental works, *see* BedbG; CoopI; KretS, 4ff.

when Henri de Ganiere, *"joueur de viele et de lus"* was presented with a gift by Duke Louis of Orleans.[210] The earliest publication of French lute music, however, dates only from 1529, when Attaingnant published his *Dix-huit* [actually 19] [211] *basses dances . . . avec dixneuf Branles. . . .*[212] Dances were often grouped to form a *basse dance–recoupe–tourdion* set (cf. the Italian *pavana–saltarello-piva* set). This combination was gradually replaced during the 16th century by the *pavane–gaillarde* pair. Titles affixed to many pieces in the *Dix-huit basses dances . . .* seem to indicate a derivation from popular songs. The melody is sometimes written out in mensural notes above the tablature and designated as the *subjectum*. With one exception, it is in the superius, and there is a striking feeling for major and minor. Some of the pieces bear the initials "P. B.," the only indication of an arranger's or editor's name. Technically, these pieces are rather easy; strict counterpoint is not maintained. The collection is unusual in its inclusion of a number of compositions *a 2*.

Later in 1529, Attaingnant printed his *Tres breve et familiere introduction . . .* , obviously intended as an instruction book, since it contains a detailed explanation of lute tuning and tablature. The French tablature of Attaingnant's day, as distinguished from the Italian (cf. pp. 520f), usually employed a five-line staff, in which the highest line represented the string highest in pitch. The lowest course was represented, when necessary, by a leger line. The eight fingerboard frets were designated in the tablature by the letters *b* to *i*, with *a* indicating an open string. (The *Introduction* uses capital letters, but this practice was not followed in other publications.) Time-values were indicated as in the Italian system.[213]

Among the Italian musicians serving Francis I (cf. p. 291) were two Mantuan lutenists, Albert Trame and Albert de Ripe (Alberto da Ripa). De Ripe's fame brought tributes, on his death in 1551, from Baïf, Ronsard, and others. Le Roy and Ballard dedicated a book of lute music to his memory. His pupil, Guillaume Morlaye (a slave trader), collected six volumes of his works, which were published between 1553 and 1558. The contract entered into by Morlaye and the printer Fezandat, on April 19, 1552, with respect to the first book, calls for an edition of 1,500 copies, which indicates that there was no lack of amateur lutenists in France. Some towns actually organized lute-

---

[210] About early French lutenists, see BrenN, 643ff.

[211] Cf. BlumeS, 138f.

[212] Dances from this vol. pr. BruA, 28 items (1 also in TapS, 13; 2 also in BlumeS, App., 24 [= KörL, 150; ScherG, 85], 35); BruD (2nd ed., 1927), 17; BruL I, 30 (= BlumeS, App., 33; WasG, App., 6); KörL, 151 (fragment in BruS, 124); WolfH II, 75 (with facsimile), 79ff; ApelN, 68 (= BlumeS, App., 45; facsimile in Wolf MS, 68)); BlumeS, App., 40; BruS, 12 (= TapS, 12), 17.

[213] For the text-matter that opens the book, see WolfH II, 72f (abstract in ApelN, 64). Solo pieces from the book pr. BruA, 16, 23 (= BruL, 28), 24 (= BruL, 30); KörL, 133, 135, 153.

schools for children: in 1545, the town council of Marseilles rented a house to the lutenist Barthélemy de la Croix for such a school. Morlaye himself, while not ranking with his master, produced three volumes of original works and transcriptions, the latter including pieces by Janequin and Arcadelt and the first book of *Psaumes* by Certon, the original of which is lost. The Certon psalms, printed in Morlaye's voice-and-lute transcriptions in 1554, had already appeared in transcription two years earlier in Le Roy's *Tiers Livre de tablature de luth*.[214]

France was host to lutenists from other countries also—to the celebrated Hungarian, Bakfark (cf. pp. 719f), by whom a lute-book was printed at Lyons in 1552, and to the Polish lutenist, Jacob (cf. pp. 755f).

A later counterpart of Attaingnant's *Tres breve . . . introduction* was written and published by Le Roy, himself a famous player, in the form of an *Instruction de partir toute musique facilement en tabulature de luth* (1557). It survives, however, only in two English translations (London, 1568 and 1574). Here, as presumably in the original, Le Roy's work is divided into three parts. The first gives extensive instruction in the setting (or intabulation) of vocal works for the lute, with a discussion of the eight modes and how they are best handled on the instrument. For musical examples, Le Roy introduces several chansons by Lassus, the first of which he sets part by part in order to show the student those difficulties that may arise in transferring four vocal lines to the lute and how it is often necessary to "edit" the original. The second part of the work contains an explanation of the tablature and rules for playing the lute. The third part consists of "diverse Psalmes, and many fine excellente Tunes." The "Tunes" are to be found also in the *Livre d'Airs de Cour miz sur le Luth*, printed by Le Roy in 1571 (cf. p. 557). The psalms are mixed in with the chansons toward the end.

The popularity of the lute continued and even increased as the century drew to a close. An important collection, published in 1600, was the *Trésor d'Orphée*[215] of Antoine Francisque (c. 1570–1605). It contains seventy-one pieces—preludes, *fantaisies, passemèses*, pavanes, *gaillardes, branles,* gavottes, *courantes, voltes,* and a ballet. The collection opens and closes with two transcriptions—of Lassus' ever popular *Susanne un jour* and of *La Cassandre* from Arbeau's *Orchésographie* (cf. p. 564).[216]

Another large collection of this period is the *Thesaurus harmonicus* of Jean-Baptiste Besard (born c. 1567), published at Cologne in 1603. Besard's tastes were truly international, ranging from Dowland's *Lachrymae* (cf. pp. 840f) to fantasies by Lorenzini (cf. p. 527), whom he had known while at Rome. The collection contains dances, preludes, *airs de cour,* etc. In 1617, appeared Besard's

214 Cf. SmithL, 31; DouM II, 513, No. 43. For 1 of the Certon–Morlaye Psalms, *see* BruS, 94. Further about de Ripe and Morlaye, *see* LiuO, 81ff; ProdM; LauLL, 51, 54; BrenN, 646.
215 Pr. in a piano version, in QuitT.
216 Further about Francisque, *see* LauL; LauLL, 93f.

Novus Partus sive Concertationes Musicae, including transcriptions for three lutes. Besard was also the author of two lute instruction books.[217]

In the latter part of the century, the guitar became popular in France, and Le Roy and Ballard brought out music for it.[217a]

Lute Music in the Low Countries

In the Low Countries, the lute was similarly popular, and from the early part of the 16th century the fame of Belgian and Dutch lutenists led to the importation of several into England. In the same year as the two Attaingnant lute-books appeared (1529) an anonymous instruction book for *"Manicordion* [clavichord] *Luc et Flutes"* was published in Antwerp, the *Livre plaisant et tres utile. . . .* This is a free translation of the second part of Virdung's *Musica getutscht* (cf. p. 656), but describes French rather than German tablature—the former was used in the Low Countries—and substitutes *Een vroylic wesen* for the German religious song used as an illustration by Virdung. The *Livre plaisant* is interesting both as the oldest example of French lute-tablature, after Attaingnant's *Dix-huit . . . ,* and as the first such example to use six lines rather than five.[218]

The most famous publisher of lute music in the Low Countries was Phalèse, whose lute publications, dating from 1545 on, included foreign as well as native productions. Part I (1552) of his best-known collection, the *Hortus musarum,* includes fantasies by Francesco da Milano, Rotta, and Gintzler (cf. p. 669) and some pieces for two lutes, among which are one transcribed from Appenzeller and one from Gombert. The music is divided between the two instruments in various ways: sometimes the voice-parts shift from one lute to the other; one lute may perform the piece in simple form, while the second plays it in ornamented form; or, in *airs de dance* especially, the second lute may reinforce the first an octave lower. Pieces for two lutes could be played either on two equal lutes, or on one ordinary instrument and one large instrument tuned a fourth or fifth lower. Lute duets appeared also in Phalèse's *Luculentum theatrum musicum* (1568). He continued to issue lute collections until as late as 1579.[219]

Two-, and even three- and four-lute pieces are included in the *Novum pratum musicum* (1584) of Emanuel Adriansen (Hadrianus) of Antwerp.[220]

---

[217] Further about Besard, *see* ChilGB; ChilS, 9f; ChilN, 669f; LauLL, 94ff; LauL. Pieces for lute alone from Besard collections pr. in ChilLS (21 items: 18 for 1 lute, 1 for 2 lutes, 2 for 3 lutes with soprano and bass); ChilB IX (24 items; some duplications of ChilLS); ChilN, 671f (2 items; 1 = BruL II, 13); ChilGB (7 items; some duplications of ChilLS and ChilB IX); ChilS, 32 (2 items), 34; BruS, 61 (= ChilLS, 188; ChilB IX, 4; ChilGB, 11), 66, 92, 97 (= ChilLS, 203; ChilB IX, 19), 121 (= ChilLS, 204).

[217a] Cf. LesGF.

[218] Further about the *Livre plaisant, see* FoxP; NijM.

[219] Further about Phalèse collections, *see* QuitM, 261ff; LauC, xviiiff, xliv.

[220] Cf. LauLL, 62. For a study of the fantasies in this book (with 3 complete exx.), *see* HambF.

The following example gives excerpts from a *gaillarde* that Adriansen presents first in a plain version, then in an embellished one. When two forms of a piece thus occur in a lute tablature they are no doubt intended as alternatives rather than as versions to be played successively. Nevertheless, the practice in a way foreshadows the *doubles* of the 17th century.

EXAMPLE 128. Extracts from (*a*) the straightforward and (*b*) the ornamented version of the same *Gaillarde*—Adriansen (the former complete in BruL, 38; WasG, App., 23; the latter complete *ibid.*, 24).

This collection is apparently the first example of French tablature after the *Livre plaisant* to use a six-line staff, which became standard in the 17th century.

The close musical interrelationship of European countries during the Renaissance is well illustrated by a MS collection made in Leyden c. 1600 and known as the Thysius Lute-Book [221] after its owner, the Thysius Library at Leyden, although its probable compiler and first possessor was a Rotterdam pastor named Adriaan Joriszoon Smout. It contains numerous lute dances, fantasies, and transcriptions of sacred and secular vocal works representing composers of Italy, England, and France, as well as of the Low Countries. The collection includes a short composition for four lutes.[222] Among the many English works are the famous *Greensleeves,* and a number of melodies, such as *Goe from my window,* that appear in the Fitzwilliam Virginal Book (cf. pp. 851, 861).

Several lute collections by Joachim van den Hove, among them his *Delitiae musicae* (1612),[223] were brought out at Utrecht. A collection of 1615, the *Secretum musarum,* published in Amsterdam by the Frenchman Nicolas Vallet, contains mainly preludes and fantasies, but also dances and a few tran-

[221] Described in LandT, which prints many exx. Exx. also pr. BruS, 28, 36, 37, 58, 110 (some being duplicated in LandT).
[222] Pr. LandT II, 333.   [223] Ex. in BruS, 18.

scribed chansons, including Le Jeune's *Quand on arrestera*. As in the Thysius book, many of the dance themes are melodies already used by the English virginalists. The *Secretum* reappeared in a two-volume French edition (1618–1619), the second half including works for several lutes.[224]

A taste for the guitar spread to the Low Countries, as to France, and music for the instrument appeared from the presses of Phalèse.[224a]

Lute Songs in France and the Low Countries

Attaingnant's *Tres breve . . . introduction* and Phalèse's *Hortus musarum* contain, besides the purely instrumental music already discussed, songs for voice and lute. Le Roy and Ballard's *Livre d'Airs de Cour miz sur le Luth* (1571) was devoted entirely to such music. In each of these books,[225] the vocal part is in ordinary notation, the instrumental part in tablature. Attaingnant adopts the convenient modern method of setting each line of accompaniment directly below its corresponding line of melody and text, but Le Roy prints the vocal and instrumental parts on opposite pages, while Phalèse prints the whole vocal part at the top of the page and the whole instrumental part at the bottom. All three collections give bar-lines in the lute part, but only Attaingnant has them in the vocal part as well.[226]

Attaingnant's collection contains twenty-four *chansons au luth* transcribed by an anonymous musician from contemporary chansons. The only originals that have been identified are eight by Claudin, seven of which had appeared in the *Chansons nouvelles* of 1528. These originals are little altered in the transcriptions except for the occasional addition of slight figuration in one part or another, or, as in *Jouissance vous donneray* (which is otherwise an almost literal reproduction),[227] the omission of an inner voice. A piece is sometimes transposed.

Part II (1553) of the *Hortus musarum* contains, besides a Spanish chanson and five religious pieces, twenty lute chansons—including nine after Crecquillon [228] and five after Clemens non Papa—most of which are not found in vocal part-settings until a later date. On the whole, these transcriptions, like Attaingnant's, correspond fairly literally with their vocal counterparts. The anonymous *Incessament mon povre coeur* [229] proves to be an arrangement of Pierre de la Rue's composition (cf. p. 273), which must have been a great favorite if it could achieve inclusion in spite of its outmoded *rondeau* form. (*Incessament* appears also among the transcriptions for solo lute in Part I.)

Le Roy and Ballard's *Livre d'Airs de Cour* is important as presenting the first use of the term *air de cour*.[230] In his dedication to the Countess de Retz, a talented member of the *Académie du Palais,* Le Roy explains the character

224 Cf. LauLL, 100ff.   224a Cf. LesGF.   225 For facsimile pages, *see* LauC, xxxiv, xlvi, liv.
226 The French chansons from all 3 pr. *ibid.*   227 Pr. *ibid.*, 44.
228 1 pr. *ibid.*, 61; BruS, 104.   229 Pr. LauC, 128 (full text on p. lii).
230 Cf. LauC, xxvf; DoA, 1135.

and purpose of this type of chanson. Part of his earlier *Instruction . . .* was based on the chansons of Lassus, but these, he says, are difficult to play; therefore, he now offers a collection of much lighter chansons in the style once called *voix-de-ville,* but now *airs de cour.*[231] The majority of these are actually lute-song versions of the chansons arranged for lute solo in Part III of the *Instruction.* The *air de cour* is simple and strophic. It could be sung by a single voice with or without instrumental accompaniment. *Musique mesurée* seems to have had some influence on it.[232] The designation *"air de cour"* was also applied, though less frequently, to chansons for several voices and to pieces for lute alone.

Le Roy, who himself made the transcriptions, offers several pairs that give the chanson first in a close reproduction of the original, then in a version marked *"autrement,"* in which the first version is *"plus finement traitée."* In one version so marked (*Has tu point veu*) there is some added figuration; in another (*Tant que j'estoys*) [233] the piece is transposed (there being some other changes also). Likewise of particular interest is the transcription of la Grotte's lovely *Je suis Amour* (cf. p. 389),[234] since it may have been sung as part of one of the *intermèdes* during the court *fêtes* of 1565 at Fontainebleau.[235] Although, like Attaingnant and Phalèse, Le Roy drew predominantly on chordal chansons, which could be transcribed almost literally, he makes a somewhat greater effort to write a truly instrumental accompaniment, the lute part supporting the vocal line with relatively greater freedom.[236]

Airs de cours are included also by Besard in his *Thesaurus harmonicus.*[237] Between 1608 and 1618 appeared eight books of *Airs de differents autheurs,* a collection of melodies to which the French court-lutenist, Gabriel Bataille, had supplied lute accompaniments.[238]

Keyboard Music in France, including the Attaingnant Prints and Titelouze

Early in 1531, Attaingnant printed seven books containing music for *"Orgues Espinettes et Manicordions"* [239] ("Organs, Spinets, and Clavi-

---

[231] Le Roy's dedication pr. LauC, xxvf.   [232] Cf. WalkI.

[233] The compositions pr. LauC, 150, 165, respectively.

[234] Pr. LauC, 167; RMR, 36 (transposed).   [235] Cf. RMR, 34ff.

[236] 2 Psalms from Le Roy's *Tiers livre de tablature de luth,* which also illustrate this point, pr. BruS, 46, 145.

[237] 11 of them (plus a *villanella*) pr. ChilB VII (9 of these and 1 additional ex. pr. ChilCB; 1 also pr. BruS, 56; ChilN, 670). Other exx. pr. BruS, 66 (plus 2 *villanelle, ibid.,* 55, 74; another pr. ChilS, 26); ChilGB, 14; ChilLS, 189.

[238] Exx. in BruL II, 12; BruS, 34, 85.

[239] Several dated January–March, 1530 (= 1531, new style); cf. p. 290. Nos. 1–4—*Dixneuf chansons musicales . . . , Vingt et cinq chansons . . . , Vingt et six chansons . . . ,* and *Quatorze Gaillardes neuf Pavennes sept Branles et deux Basses Dances*—are pr. in facsimile in AttainC I–IV. Nos. 5 and 6—*Tabulature pour le jeu d'orgues Espinetes et Manicordions sur le plain chant de Cunctipotens et Kyrie fons* and *Magnificat sur les huit tons avec Te deum laudamus et deux Preludes*—are pr. in RoksO. No. 7—*Treze Motetz musicaulx avec ung Prelude . . .* —is pr. in RoksT, with the original motets (in all cases except 1, which is a reconstruction by

chords")—which implies that in France, as in Italy, no marked difference existed between music for organ and for stringed keyboard instruments. Again as normally in Italy, the "tablature" consisted of ordinary mensural notation; it differed from its Italian equivalent, however, in having only five lines in each of the two staves. But this more modern arrangement was not commonly adopted until about a century later. Bar-lines were used; chromatic alteration was indicated by flats and sharps or, more often, by dots. Smaller values are employed by Attaingnant than by Marco Antonio Cavazzoni (and therefore do not call for reduction in transcriptions into modern notation).[240]

Of the seven Attaingnant books—the first keyboard publications in France —three (Nos. 5–7 in order of publication) are devoted mostly to motet transcriptions and liturgical compositions and four to dance and chanson transcriptions.

Some of the works chosen for transcription in the *Treze Motetz,* one of the books in the group of three, are by well-known composers who were to be represented in Attaingnant's motet series of 1534–1535 (cf. p. 335). The works include compositions by Févin (*Benedictus* from the *Missa Ave Maria* and *Sancta Trinitas*), Compère (*O vos omnes*), Claudin, Brumel (*Sicut lilium*), Moulu, Obrecht (*Parce Domine*), Gascogne, Prioris (*Consummo*), and Busnois (*Fortuna desperata*).

The authorship of these transcriptions has not been traced, but the disparity of talent shown suggests the work of an *atelier,* probably Parisian, rather than of any single artist. A definite effort is made to realize the special capabilities of keyboard instruments, particularly of the organ. The pieces are not mere literal reproductions with the addition of clustered decorations; the opening of the especially fine *Sancta Trinitas* transcription suggests the chorale fantasias of a much later day.

EXAMPLE 129. Opening of Févin's *Sancta Trinitas* with the keyboard transcription of it, printed in 1531 (from RoksT, 28).

the ed.). Individual reprints: from No. 2, ScherG, 87; from No. 3, KinO, 260; from No. 4, ScherG, 86f (2 items; 1 = EitT, 83); EitT, 78ff (12 items; item on p. 81 = BlumeS, App., 35; BesM, 275); HalbK, 7f (2 items; 1 = EitT, 86). Nos. 1–4 discussed in AttainC V; Nos. 5–7, in RoksMO, 211ff.

[240] *See* further ApelN, 4ff.

The transcription here suggests the organ's dual capacity for massive sustained chords and for virtuosic scale-passages. As in many other pieces, a balance in texture is achieved between the two registers (compare meas. 1–2 with meas. 3–4). A strong general tendency to use four-measure sections sometimes causes a distortion of the original motet form. "Busy" figuration does not always allow the original thematic contours to stand out as clearly as they do, for example, in the embellished adaptation of Claudin's *Aspice Domine*.[241]

One Attaingnant book, devoted to organ-Masses (cf. pp. 174f, 536), mentions in its title *"le plain chant de Cunctipotens et Kyrie fons. Avec leur Et in terra, Patrem, Sanctus et Agnus dei."* But, in view of the custom of piecing together an Ordinary out of individual chants, it is not to be expected that the Masses named in the title necessarily conform to the present-day plainsong *Missa Fons bonitatis* and *Missa Cunctipotens* (Masses II and IV). Attaingnant's *Missa Cunctipotens*[242] does conform, but the other,[243] from the Gloria on, does not; indeed, the rest of this Mass is written on the same melodies as form the basis of the Gloria, Sanctus, and Agnus of the *Missa Cunctipotens*, adding to them the melody of Credo I. Attaingnant's print provides no Credo for the *Missa Cunctipotens;* perhaps the one given with the Mass *Kyrie fons* was to serve in both. Occasionally a verse is provided with an introduction or coda.

In the book containing settings for alternate verses of the *Te Deum* and of the Magnificat in the eight Tones, the plainsong is assigned to an upper voice. The Magnificat organ-verses present contrast within themselves; here, not only introductions and codas, such as are found in the Mass book, but also interludes contrast with passages based on the Chant. In both the Magnificats[244] and the *Te Deum*,[245] especially the latter, the *cantus* is less rigidly treated than in the Mass book. This greater flexibility at times results in pieces that may be described as free fantasias. For each of six Magnificats only two verse settings are provided; there are four for Tone 8 and five for Tone 4. In some ways a few of the pieces in this book betray their vocal antecedents much more clearly than do the contents of the Mass book. In fact, verse 2 of the Magnificat in Tone 8 is modeled on the *Et exultavit* of a Magnificat by Richafort.[246] This book includes also two independent preludes. The second, called *Prélude sur chacun ton*, derives its name from its use of melodic motifs that are repeated sequentially on all the degrees of the scale. Another brief prelude appears in the *Treze Motetz*.[247]

Interestingly enough, the keyboard books of 1531 that are devoted to chanson transcriptions include arrangements of seven chansons from Attaingnant's first book (1528) that were drawn upon also for the *Tres breve . . .*

[241] Pr. RoksT, 2. Cf. p. 339 *supra.*   [242] Pr. RoksO, 19.   [243] Pr. *ibid.*, 1.
[244] Pr. *ibid.*, 34–50.   [245] Pr. *ibid.*, 51.   [246] Cf. RoksF; RoksMO, 260.
[247] The 3 preludes pr. RoksO, 29, 31; RoksT, 1.

introduction for lute. In comparison with the lute versions, those for keyboard reveal but minor changes in the figuration and disposition of the voices. Selections by Claudin printed in the *Trente et une chansons musicales* of 1529 are also included in the 1531 keyboard books. The volume devoted to dance pieces contains keyboard transcriptions of fourteen *gaillardes,* nine *pavanes,* seven *branles,* and two *basses dances.*

One wonders whether these keyboard books came into the hands of Eleanor, who had married Francis I in 1530 and who, like her brother Charles V and her sisters, had been instructed in playing at the keyboard by Herry Bredemers (1472–1522). This famous organist had, in the service of Charles and his father, traveled to Spain, Germany, and England, and had great influence not only on contemporary musicians, but also on the taste of his high-born pupils.[248]

The wide diffusion of French organ makers indicates that their instruments were highly favored.[249] The making of stringed keyboard-instruments, too, flourished in the north, the most prominent name in this connection being that of the Ruckers family in Antwerp.[250] At this period, it should be remembered, the organ was by no means exclusively a church instrument, and we have evidence of its use in court festivities and domestic entertainments. On the other hand, sacred music could be played on a stringed keyboard-instrument as well as at the organ. Marot, for example, speaks of *"saintes chansonnettes"* played on the *espinettes.* Eustorg de Beaulieu mentions *"chansons divines"* played on the *"jeu de manichorde,"* and, as we have noted, Attaingnant's titles all cite *"Orgues, Espinettes et Manicordions."*

Curiously, there is little if any evidence that the Attaingnant collections of 1531 stimulated the further writing of keyboard music in France. While we know the names of organists and *clavecinistes* of the time,[251] their works (if these men were composers also) seem on the whole to have disappeared. We do possess a *Fantazie sus orgue ou espinette* by Costeley, who, as has been noted in Chapter 8, was organist to Charles IX; also there exists a tablature by D. Megnier. Undoubtedly, works were played at the keyboard that were not intended primarily for it. But it would seem that there was a period of comparative sterility in the production of music specifically for keyboard instruments.

The first collection of French keyboard music after Attaingnant, a *Premier livre de tablature d'Espinette, chansons, madrigales et gaillardes,* came, in 1560, from the shop of Simon Gorlier, musician and printer of Lyons. In 1610, Ballard printed Charles Guillet's *Vingt-quatre Fantasies à quatre parties*

---

[248] For an article on Bredemers, *see* DoorHB.
[249] About the organs and organ makers, *see* RoksMO, 379ff; DufoE, 125ff; DufoD.
[250] Cf. StellB, 85ff; Grove IV, 469ff. About 16th-century organs in the Low Countries generally, *see* esp. VenteB.
[251] About organists, *see* RoksMO, 369ff; about clavecinists, PirC, 25.

disposées suivant l'ordre des douze modes,[252] comprising a series of pieces in the twelve modes untransposed and another series in the modes transposed. The composer (who later wrote a theoretical work, *Institution harmonique*) cites Zarlino in justifying his modal arrangement. Musically, the *fantaisies* follow Zarlino's disposition of the twelve modes, with their finals from C to A. But Guillet's nomenclature is different. The C modes are Dorian, the D modes Phrygian, the E modes Lydian, the F modes Mixolydian, the G modes Ionian, the A modes Aeolian. The order is almost like that of Glareanus, but only "Aeolian" is used by both men in connection with the same final. In Guillet again there is a hint of the growing importance of the major mode (cf. pp. 377, 384). His foreword to the publication specifically states that the *fantaisies* may be performed on either organ or clavier. This is especially significant, since the collection was printed in part-books (cf. p. 529). As might be expected in view of the format, these compositions offer nothing striking with regard to idiomatic keyboard style.

With the advent of Jean Titelouze (1563–1633), the French organ school reasserts itself. Born at Saint-Omer, where many emigrants from England had settled, among them his own family, he may well have been affected directly by English musical influence. He was distinguished not only for his organ improvisations, but for his knowledge of organ construction. In the preface to his *Hymnes de l'Église* (1623) he expressed his desire to supply France with organ tablatures, the printing of which was *"hors de la souvenance des hommes."* The Attaingnant prints of 1531 had evidently been forgotten. In addition, Titelouze wished to utilize the technical advantages of the organ with two manuals and pedal keyboard. In his collection, he provides each hymn melody with a series of different settings, to alternate with stanzas of vocally rendered chant, the resulting variation-chains revealing much ingenuity and imagination. The *Ave maris stella* is particularly attractive. The polyphony is rather retrospective but of excellent quality. A later volume, *Le Magnificat . . . suivant les huits tons . . .* (1626) contains music similar in style, but much easier to play.[253]

Keyboard Music in the Low Countries

Contemporaries of Titelouze, born in the Low Countries, include Charles Luython and Simon Lohet, who, however, were active mainly abroad and will be discussed elsewhere.

In Sweelinck we find the diversity of English variation technique (cf. pp. 862f) and the brilliance of Italian toccata style combining with the ingenuity

[252] 12 of these pieces pr. MB IV, 4ff.
[253] AMO I is a complete edition of Titelouze. Further about him, *see* PirT (an expansion of the pref. of AMO I).

of Netherlandish polyphony to establish the beginnings of the great schools of 17th-century organ music. As organist of the Oude Kerk in Amsterdam, Sweelinck gained fame for his virtuosity, though, strangely enough, only his vocal compositions were published during his life. Whereas some of his chansons remained within the bounds of Renaissance style, the baroque manner is more evident in his organ pieces, mainly fantasies, toccatas, and variations on religious and secular vocal compositions. In these last works he helped to develop variation technique. A similarity is apparent to some of the variations of John Bull (cf. p. 862), who had settled on the Continent in 1613 and who seems to have formed a close friendship with Sweelinck.[254] Color contrast appears strikingly in Sweelinck's fantasies *"op de manier van een echo,"* [255] in which melodic figures are reiterated with contrast of dynamics, sometimes of registration, and frequently of both. In his more fugue-like fantasies, e.g., his brilliant *Fantasia chromatica,*[256] the opening theme is used as the basis of the entire work, appearing in imitation, augmentation, etc., new thematic material being supplied by countersubjects. One is reminded of the monothematic *ricercari.*

The fantasies of Pieter Cornet (1593–1626), organist to the Infanta Clara Eugenia at Brussels, show indebtedness to the *ricercare,* but also to the English tendency to work out motivic figures (cf. p. 863) and to Sweelinck's proclivity for cohesive design.[257] The influence of Sweelinck as a keyboard composer, however, did not have its greatest effect in his own country, but in northern Germany, where it helped to pave the way for the keyboard works of Johann Sebastian Bach.

Instrumental Ensemble Music in France and the Low Countries

Although Italian composers travelled and even settled in France in the 16th century, they seem not to have aroused in their hosts any strong desire to emulate them by composing in such standard Italian instrumental ensemble-music forms as the *ricercare* and *canzone a sonar.* Aside from dances, all we have in France at this time, by way of instrumental ensemble music are *fantaisies,* preserved in a small body of early 17th-century part-books.

In 1530, Attaingnant printed, also in part-books, two volumes containing *basses dances, branles, pavanes,* and *gaillardes.*[258] Between c. 1547 and 1557,

---

[254] Variations by Sweelinck pr. SweeW I, 121ff.

[255] An echo fantasy pr. SweeW I, 75 (= HAM, 209). SweeW I and XI constitute a complete edition of Sweelinck's keyboard works.

[256] Pr. *ibid.,* I, 1 (= ScherG, 163). Further about Sweelinck's instrumental music, *see* esp. MrS; GomSF; BorO, 132ff.

[257] Organ works by Cornet pr. in AMO X, 181ff; RitZ II, 60ff. Further about his keyboard music, *see* BorO, 175ff.

[258] One of these books pr. GiesA (which also includes 6 galliards and 6 pavans that Attaingnant had included in a chanson collection of 1529); part of the contents also pr. EitT, 78ff; 7 more pieces in BlumeS, App. B; 2 more in OppelF, 214f.

he brought out, in similar form, a series of ten further volumes of dances, composed or edited by Claude Gervaise, Etienne du Tertre, and anonymi.[259] The *danceries* in these books include examples of the same types. The tunes are simple, the treatment chordal. The music is suitable for dancing. *Pavane-gaillarde* pairs show the normal melodic relationship (cf. p. 523f). The ubiquitous *passamezzo antico* bass is incorporated in a *Pavane passemaize* by Gervaise.[260] Moderne, in his undated *Musique de Joye*,[261] brought out a generally similar collection of 29 *basses dances, tordions, pavanes, gaillardes,* and *branles. Il me suffit* reappears in it as a *Moytié de Basse dance.* The *Orchésographie* (1588),[262] a manual by Thoinot Arbeau (1519-1595; real name Jehan Tabourot), has detailed descriptions and many pictorial illustrations, from which the choreography of the French versions of the various dances may be reconstructed. He includes a description of the *courante,* the first mention of which occurs in Marot's *Epitre des dames de Paris* (1515) and of which the earliest known musical example is the *saltarello*-like *Corante du roy*[263] preserved in the tablature (1577) of the German, Bernhard Schmid the Elder. The *Orchésographie* contains, in addition to monophonic melodies a four-part *Pavane avec les mesures et battemens du tambour.* Arbeau mentions that the *basse dance* was going out of fashion and had been doing so for forty or fifty years. In view of the date of his book, this means that a decline in the popularity of the dance had already set in when Attaingnant's examples were printed.

Nevertheless, *basses dances* were published not only in France but in the Low Countries. Susato's *Het derde musyck boexcken . . .* (1551)[264] contains examples of them as well as of other dances. Although Attaingnant offers more pieces, Susato compensates for this by the superior musicianship evident in the arrangements he prints, which are no doubt his own. His settings are more polyphonic and make a more knowing use of dissonance. The *boexcken* includes thirteen *basse danssen* (Nos. 1-3 with *reprise*), nine *ronden,* one *saltarello,* six *branlen,* eight *allemanden* (No. 1 with one *recoupe,* No. 8 with two), seven *pavanen,* and fifteen *gaillarden.* These dances fall into three categories: (1) adaptations of chansons, such as *Le cueur est bon,*[265] serving as *reprise* for *basse dance* No. 3, or *Dont vient cela* (*basse dance* No. 1) and *C'est une dure départie,* both by Claudin; (2) popular songs; (3) popular

[259] Selections pr. in MMRF XXIII. Du Tertre was also a chanson composer; for exx., *see* CauQ, 28; PubAPTM XXIII, 1, 16.

[260] Pr. MMRF XXIII, 28.

[261] Pr. ModF. Other surviving dance music of the time for instrumental ensemble includes the *Danceries* of Jean d'Estrées (cf. EitQ III, 358) and some exx. copied by André Danican Philidor (d. 1730); cf. VfMW, I (1885), 531ff.

[262] Modern editions in ArbOF, ArbOB, ArbOE. *See also* MaryO; BarkT.

[263] Pr. MerT, 112.

[264] SusaD. 16 of the dances also pr. EitT; 5 pr. BlumeS, App. B; 7 pr. MohrA; 2 pr. ScherG, 119; 1 pr. OppelF, 217.

[265] An anon. piece; *see* MMRFBT VIII, 12.

dance tunes, such as *Hoboecken dans*.[266] The melody of one of the *gaillarden* (*Ghequetst ben ick*) had been drawn on for a *Souterliedeken* (Psalm CI [102]). Some of these Susato dance tunes appear also in other contemporary collections, such as Attaingnant's first and third dance-books, Phalèse's *Liber primus* (1571) [267] and *Chorearum molliorum collectanea* (1583),[268] and Arbeau's *Orchésographie*. A *Pass'e mezzo d'Italia* in the Phalèse book of 1583 contains a striking example of a chord of the augmented sixth.[269]

Le Jeune and Du Caurroy were the chief composers of French instrumental ensemble music. By the former we have three *fantaisies,* one *a 5* and two *a 4*. All are fairly extended works. Each of the pieces *a 4* [270] opens with a long motet-like section in binary rhythm and ends with a shorter dance-like one in ternary rhythm. The two sections are thematically independent. The *fantaisie a 5* is based on *Benedicta es coelorum Regina*. Le Jeune constructs points of imitation on three phrases of the plainsong. At the opening, he combines Josquin's countermelody with the first phrase, and the two melodies then recur in imitation in pairs. Josquin had begun with such imitation also, but Le Jeune makes subtle and ingenious changes with regard to both rhythm and the point of entrance. His borrowings elsewhere, however, are in the main fragmentary, and the work is literally a fantasy on them.[271]

By Du Caurroy we have about forty *fantaisies,*[272] *a 3* to *a 6*. Many are in tenor-motet style, the *cantus firmi* being partly of sacred, partly of secular origin. Thus, Fantasy X is on *Requiem aeternam,* XIV and XV on *Ave maris stella;* XIX and XXV on *Conditor alme siderum*. Nos. XVIII and XXV have the titles of two *chansons spirituelles;* five pieces in a row have as theme *Une jeune fillette;* and the last piece of the book is composed on *Je suis deshéritée*. (The *Jeune fillette* melody later became associated with the text *Von Gott will ich nicht lassen* and as such was set as a chorale by Bach.[273]) There is a noticeable difference in the treatment of sacred and secular tenors. While the former furnish the entire thematic substance of a fantasy, the latter are combined with a motley array of material.[274]

In view of the form in which the Guillet *fantaisies* were printed, they must be counted among the works produced by the French for ensemble performance, notwithstanding the prefatory statement that they might be played on the organ or clavier (cf. p. 562). Among the musical examples in Mer-

---

[266] OppelF, 220, having in mind Hoboken, New Jersey, thought that this dance may have been the earliest ex. of American music to appear in a European document (!); however, Hoboken, a suburb of Antwerp, was in existence in the 16th century.

[267] Described (with list of contents) in OppelF, 220ff; 6 exx. in BlumeS, App. B (2 also in Wolf ME).

[268] Several exx. in BlumeS, App. B.   [269] *Ibid.,* 50, system 2, meas. 3.   [270] One pr. ExCL I.

[271] Further about the Le Jeune pieces, *see* MeyeM, 49f.   [272] 5 *fantaisies* pr. ExCL II–VI.

[273] For the basic French melody, *see* MGG II, 1102. For a Du Caurroy setting, *see* BonnA, 7 (pr. as an organ piece).

[274] Further about the Du Caurroy pieces, *see* PirAO, 1263ff; MeyeM, 48f; BrenFA, 35f; QuitI, 1214ff.

senne's *Harmonicorum instrumentorum libri IV* (1636) is a fantasy *a* 5 by a certain Henri Le Jeune, concerning whom nothing is known. It is supplied with an extra version of the superius, which shows how that part might be *diminuta* ("diminished," i.e., embellished).[275]

Music such as these *fantaisies*—perhaps some of these actual pieces—may well have been performed in the concerts of the *Académie*. Apparently the combinations of instruments employed by that organization were at times most haphazard. In a contemporary letter, d'Aubigné—friend of Henry IV, poet, historian, and grandfather of Mme. de Maintenon—writes of having heard "an excellent concert of guitars, twelve viols, four spinets, four lutes, two pandoras, and two theorbos." [276] The main part of the program consisted of pieces *a* 6 and *a* 7. By enumerating twenty-four musicians (not counting the guitarists), d'Aubigné, therefore, seems to imply that there was more than one player to a part. However, it is not clear in how much of the program doubling of parts took place. (As we have seen [cf. p. 488], Praetorius mentions with praise a rendition of a motet *a* 7 by Wert, in which doubling also took place, three voices being joined by two theorbos, three lutes, two citterns, four stringed keyboard-instruments, eight viols, and two flutes.)

Such intensive cultivation of instrumental music at Paris must have had counterparts, even if on a more modest scale, in other centers. At any rate, instrumentalists were sufficiently active in the provinces to chafe under the direct authority of the *rois* of the Confraternity at Paris (cf. p. 7). Virtual branches of the organization had consequently been set up as early as 1461 at Amiens and in 1508 at Tours; another followed at Orleans in 1560, and further branches were to be established in the next century at Abbéville, Bordeaux, and Blois.[277] It is the Parisian body, however, that was to last long enough to cross swords with Lully in the 17th century and with Couperin in the 18th.

Music in Dramatic Presentations in Italy

In providing music for use in connection with dramatic or semi-dramatic productions, instruments, in the 16th century as in earlier days, co-operated with voices. The *sacre rappresentazioni,* drawing upon both, continued to be performed in Rome and Florence, but began, even at the opening of the century, to decline in popularity. Nevertheless, the type clung tenaciously to life. Here is a description of the prologue of Giovanmaria Cecchi's play, *Esaltazione della Croce,* performed at Florence as late as 1589:

> *When the curtains arose for the first time, Jacob was seen in a meadow asleep. . . .*
> *While he slept, heaven opened, and seven angels appeared, seated upon clouds, and*

---

[275] For the piece with the *pars . . . diminuta, see* QuitI, 1254ff.   [276] QuitI, 1217.
[277] Cf. BernhM, 534f (in Vol. IV). As this book goes to press, LesC has appeared, a new study on the organization of French instrumentalists in the 16th century.

making a most pleasant noise with horns, greater and less viols, lutes and organ. . . . The music of this and all the other interludes was the composition of Luca Bati, a man in this art most excellent. When they had played and sung, the cloud disclosed, and showed a second heaven, where sat God the Father. All the angels worshipped Him, and heaven increased in splendor. Then a ladder was let down, and God, leaning upon it, turned to Jacob and sang majestically to the sound of many instruments in a sonorous bass voice. Thereupon angels descended and ascended the ladder, singing a hymn in honor of the Cross; and at last the clouds closed around, heaven disappeared, and Jacob awoke from sleep.[278]

It was inevitable that the *sacre rappresentazioni* should lose favor. Their essentially medieval spirit was not in harmony with the new humanism. Lorenzo de' Medici's influence, leading to the introduction of pagan themes into the *trionfi* and *sacre rappresentazioni,* and the creation of Politian's *Orfeo* had already shown the direction of the newer trends in the late 15th century, as did, in 1502, the revival of Plautus' *Asinaria* with interpolated music by Tromboncino (cf. pp. 158, 173). The taste for the revival of Latin plays and for Italian plays in the classic style increased during the *cinquecento.* At Rome, Venice, Urbino, Mantua, and especially Ferrara, such plays flourished. If the emphasis on music was not quite as great as in the *rappresentazioni,* it was sufficient, in combination with stress on dance and *mise en scène,* to operate at the expense of dramatic unity.

In 1513, Cardinal Bibbiena's comedy, *Calandria,* was given at Urbino with magnificently mounted *intermedi.* The *brando* and *moresca* were danced. In conclusion four voices, accompanied by four viols, sang a prayer to Love. Ariosto's *I Suppositi* was presented before Leo X in 1518 with *intermedi* that called for pipes, *cornetti,* viols, lutes, organ, voices, etc. Raphael designed the scenery.[279] Playwrights, fearing that interest would be detracted from their plays, naturally protested against the interpolation of so much music.

The high point of the festivities at the wedding of Cosimo de' Medici and Eleonora of Toledo at Florence in 1539 (cf. p. 325) was the performance of a comedy, *Il Commodo,* by Antonio Landi, with *intermedi* that included madrigals supplied with texts by Giovambattista Strozzi and music by Corteccia. To begin the comedy, Aurora sang accompanied by a harpsichord and by little organs with various stops (*organetti a varii registri*). In the execution of most of the madrigals, the costumed singers had the support of instrumental accompaniment. The six-part *Guardan almo pastore* [280] was sung at the end of Act I by six shepherds and then repeated with six other shepherds doubling the voices on cromornes. (The four-part *Hor chi mai,*[281] sung at the

---

[278] John Addington Symonds, *The Renaissance in Italy,* II, 55f (Modern Library ed.).
[279] Further about *La Calandria* and *I Suppositi,* see SolP, 212; PruB, 31f; RollM, 37f (also available in an English edition); QuitI, 1200.
[280] Pr. GhiFM, 49.
[281] *Ibid.,* 58.

end of Act IV by eight huntress nymphs, is the only madrigal written for these *intermedi* that lacks directions for instrumental accompaniment.) Other instruments used in the accompaniment of the madrigals included flutes, lutes, sackbuts, and a viol.[282] On the viol, Silenus apparently rendered chordally all four parts of the madrigal *O begli anni dell'oro* as he sang the superius.[283] The comedy was brought to an end by a *Ballo di Satiri et Baccante,* sung and danced by four satyrs and four bacchantes, "with various instruments all at once, which nimbly, after nightfall, was the end of the comedy." [283a]

The sack of Rome by the followers of Charles V in 1527 and the fall of Florence in 1530 to the powers seeking to restore the Medici, who had been expelled three years before, had left behind political conditions that interfered with freedom of expression. This had been present in the new pseudo-classical drama which, under the circumstances, was not encouraged. Performances continued, however, throughout the century, but with an apparent attempt to center the interest of the audience on elaborate production. The place of the pseudo-classical drama as the main type was taken by the *favola pastorale,* whose uncontroversial, soothing nature was welcomed by churchmen and princes alike. The coming of the pastoral fable had already been indicated by Sannazaro's *Arcadia* and by Politian. The type provided an opportunity to focus attention less on possibly debatable content than on lyric poetry, opulent settings, and music.[284]

Beccari's *Sacrifizio,* produced at Ferrara in 1554 with music by Alfonso della Viola, marks the arrival of the new type. A musical number for solo and chorus and the *canzone finale* have been preserved.[285] A recitative-like melodic line, with many repeated notes, is sung by a priest (Alfonso's brother, Andrea, in the original performance), who carries a *"lira"* (probably the same as *lira da braccio*). It is likely that this was more than a stage prop and that the priest accompanied himself on it. The priest's melody, which strikingly foreshadows the *stile recitativo* of fifty years later, is thrice repeated to different words. The repetitions are separated by choral responses *a 4,* whose text is constant but whose music changes with each occurrence. Della Viola wrote music, now lost, for other plays: Cinzio's *Orbecche* (1541), Lollio's *Aretusa* (1563), and Argenti's *Lo Sfortunato* (1567).

In 1565, Corteccia and Striggio provided music for *intermedi* by Giovanni Battista Cini, based upon Apuleius' tale of Cupid and Psyche, given between the acts of d'Ambra's *La Cofanaria,* a comedy performed at the marriage of Francesco de' Medici and Johanna of Austria. There was an attempt to

[282] Cf. GhiFM, xxif; AmbG III, 607; Grove III, 277.

[283] Cf. ScherZG, 190ff; FerandM, 350; HaasA, 131. For the music, *see* ScherG, 95; KiesS, App., 65.

[283a] Transl. from E. J. Dent in Grove III, 277.   [284] Cf. RollM, 41f.

[285] Both pr. in SolA I, after p. 12; SolP, 217ff; the priest's part in ScherZG, 193. (About flaws in Solerti's reprints, *see* EinIM I, 301.)

relate the subject of the *intermedi* to that of the comedy. A great many instruments were used since "the hall . . . was of a singular magnitude and altitude" and it was therefore "necessary to make the Concerts of Musick very full." The vocal music had instrumental accompaniment, sometimes from behind the scenes. There was a piece of instrumental program music, representing heavenly harmonies. It called for four harpsichords, four viols, two sackbuts, two lutes, two tenor recorders, a flute and a cornet ($= zink$) and had the practical purpose of filling the time during which stage machinery was being manipulated.[286]

Merulo wrote music for Lodovico Dolce's *Troiane* (1566) and for a *pasticcio*, called *Tragedia*—which, however, was more a cantata than a dramatic presentation[287]—performed in 1574 before Henry III of France at Venice. In 1585, Andrea Gabrieli (as noted in Chap. 8) supplied music for Giustiniani's translation of the *Oedipus Rex* of Sophocles.

Tasso, who had seen *Lo Sfortunato* at Ferrara, published his famous pastoral, *Aminta,* in 1573. This, for years, provided musicians with the occasion to write incidental music. Between 1581 and 1590, Tasso's fellow-poet and friend, Guarini, wrote his *Il Pastor fido.* The work of della Viola, Tasso, and Guarini at Ferrara gave this city singular importance in the development of musico-dramatic forms. After *Aminta* and *Il Pastor fido,* the vogue of the pastoral with music became enormous, and there were many imitations. Tasso, like Baïf and the Pléiade in France, advocated the union of music and poetry.[288] A frequenter of Gesualdo's academy (cf. p. 430), he admired the high emotional quality of the prince's music. His acquaintances included Marenzio, Rinuccini, Cavalieri, and Laura Guidiccioni (who wrote the dramatic poems set by Cavalieri at Florence and perhaps also the text of his *Rappresentazione di Anima e di Corpo,* important in the history of baroque music). The last two supervised a production of *Aminta* with music by Cavalieri at Florence in 1590. Rinuccini, when he later became the first opera librettist, merely continued in the tradition of the Tasso pastoral. An interlude that he wrote for a comedy presented at Florence in 1589, in honor of the marriage of Ferdinand de' Medici and Christine of Lorraine, had as its subject the combat between Apollo and the dragon. In this interlude, for which Marenzio provided the music, is to be found the kernel from which the *Dafne* libretto of 1594 evolved, the libretto that was set by Peri and, later, by Marco da Gagliano and Heinrich Schütz. This Rinuccini–Marenzio interlude was the third of six. Marenzio provided music also for *intermedio* 2, while Malvezzi composed *intermedi* 1, 4, 5, and 6, but with one contribution in each respectively by Antonio

---

[286] For a full account of these *intermedi,* see SonA or SonM. (The orig. Italian of Lasca's *Descrizione,* pr. in SonA, is replaced by an English transl. in SonM.) Cf. also KinO, 168ff; IMAMI I, lxi; ElsU, 54.

[287] See CatM, 24.   [288] Further about Tasso and the pastoral, see RollM, 44f.

Archilei, Peri, Bardi, and Cavalieri, the last three men destined to become leaders in the monodic experiments of the coming century. Among the performers were Striggio, Caccini, and the celebrated virtuoso singer Vittoria Archilei, wife of Antonio. Malvezzi's *Intermedii et Concerti* (fourteen part-books, 1591) preserves the music and gives an account of the performance. The first madrigal in *intermedio* 1, *Dalle più alte sfere,* Malvezzi says, "was sung as a solo by Vittoria, the wife of Antonio Archilei . . . she playing a large lute, accompanied by two chitarrones, one played by her husband and the other by Antonio Naldi . . ." One part-book gives this piece (as well as two others) in four-part score, the version being the one played by the instruments; the highest part recurs in another part-book, greatly elaborated with difficult coloratura passages (cf. Ex. 97), this being the version sung by Vittoria. Malvezzi's *Io che l'onde raffreno* (printed in five part-books, all provided with text) "was wonderfully sung by Vittoria Archilei alone, to the accompaniment of a lute, a chitarrone, and an *arciviolata lira* played by the masterly hand of the famous Alessandro Striggio." [289]

Music in Dramatic Presentations in France

Although 15th-century Franco-Burgundian court banquets were accompanied by elaborate diversions in which pantomime, music, etc., were included (cf. pp. 57ff), these entertainments, notwithstanding a slight trend toward dramatic unity, lacked the coherence that the further growth of humanism was to provide. A spectacle more unified than these *entremets* was presented by the old Franco-Burgundian tournament, thanks to the plot of the championed lady, round which its action revolved. The court entertainments and tournaments, between them, possessed *ballet-de-cour* elements, which the combined influence of the *canti, trionfi,* and *intermedi* transformed by contributing choruses that comment on the action, figured dances, and pantomime enacted to music. Modification of traditional forms, caused by the growing enthusiasm for Italian importations, is found in both indoor and outdoor spectacles of the reigns of Francis I, Henry II, and Charles IX. But it was only in the indoor type, the *mascarade de palais,* that poetry, music, and dance could compete with the customarily elaborate décor.[290]

In 1554, the Marshal de Brissac brought to the French Court the Milanese dancing master, Pompeo Diobono; and with him, or a little later, there came a large band of players on instruments of the violin family, headed by Baldassare da Belgioioso, who eventually changed his name to Balthasar de Beaujoyeulx.[291]

---

[289] Further about the *intermedi* of 1589, *see* SolA II, 19f; AmbG IV, 254f; SchneidA, 53ff. 11 compositions from the *intermedi* pr. *ibid.,* 116ff; 1 of these pr. also in KiesS, 70; KinO, 306; 2 of the 11 pr. also in KiesS, 67 and 69; 2 additional items pr. KiesS, 49; KinO, 312.
[290] Cf. PruB, 9ff.   [291] Cf. PruB, 52, 78; EmC, 511.

The arrival of additional Milanese dancing masters at the French court intensified the vogue of Italian figured dances, which culminated in the choreographic complexities of *Le Ballet des Polonais* (1573). This entertainment, in which instruments of the violin family participated, was tendered by Catherine de' Medici to the Polish embassy that had chosen her son Henry as king of their land. Lassus was commissioned to write part of the music, if not all. One selection, a dialogue *a 8* with Latin text, seems to survive, with dramatis personae and text altered, in a volume of 1573, dedicated to the Fuggers of Augsburg. Three of the parts were originally sung by personifications of France, Peace, and Prosperity, while the rest were played on instruments.[292]

The environment in which the court ballet evolved was pervaded by the humanistic concepts of the Pléiade and the Académie. Baïf had formulated a principle of equal duration of steps and notes. The resulting *danse mesurée* was a fitting complement to *musique mesurée;* and Baïf and his followers believed that, with the union of their kind of dance, poetry, and music, they were reviving the tradition of the ancient drama. Poets like Jodelle, Ronsard, and Baïf supervised the court entertainments, and those traits of unity and relevancy of the parts emerged that found full expression in the *Ballet comique de la royne* of 1581 and make it the first genuine *ballet de cour*. The *Ballet comique de la royne* presents an amalgamation of earlier *mascarade* forms with traits of the Italian pastoral. Chorus, declamation, air, and dance are all relevant to the action. The co-ordinator of these hitherto unrelated elements was Beaujoyeulx, and under his supervision were conceived the verse by the Sieur de la Chesnaye, the decorations by Patin, and the music by Lambert de Beaulieu (celebrated for his bass voice), Jacques Salmon, and other court musicians. Variety is provided by choruses with echo responses, examples of air and dialogue for soloists, an overture for various instruments, and, to accompany the dances, pieces for a violin-family orchestra. Portions of the music were evidently improvised; only the two outer parts of the instrumentally accompanied *Chant des quatre vertus,* for example, are supplied, and it is likely that these were filled out by means of extemporization.[293]

The wars of religion and an impoverished exchequer reduced the scale of such magnificent festivities in France. It was rather the English masque that carried on the tradition of the grand *ballet de cour*.[294]

[292] Cf. Grove III, 103; LassoW XII, xviif; EmC, 511. For the piece in question, *see* LassoW XIX, 138.

[293] For the surviving music of the ballet (the overture and probably other portions are lost), *see* WeckB (with added piano accompaniments). *See also* PruB, 82ff; QuitI, 1208f; AmbG IV, 170ff; FerandM, 324; HaasM, 117.

[294] Further about music in Italian and French Renaissance drama, *see* RollH, SolA, BrooD, ElsU.

Part Two: THE DIFFUSION AND DEVELOP-
MENT OF THE MUSICAL LAN-
GUAGE OF THE RENAISSANCE IN
THE HISPANIC PENINSULA, GER-
MANY, EASTERN EUROPE, AND
ENGLAND

Chapter 11: SPAIN AND PORTUGAL: The Musicians of the 15th Century, including those of Ferdinand and Isabella; the 16th-Century Polyphonists, including Morales, Guerrero, and Victoria; the Writers of 16th-Century Instrumental Music, including the Six Great *Vihuelistas* and Cabezón

The Early 15th Century: French Influences; the Spanish Outpost at Naples; Spanish Theorists at Home

SPANISH music, in the 15th century, as in the two preceding centuries,[1] continued to be affected by outside influences. Of these, the strongest was exerted by France, which, in addition to dominating European music generally throughout the later Middle Ages, had special relations with Spain through several prominent French families and the Papal Chapel at Avignon. King John I of Aragon (1350–1396),[2] twice allied to the French reigning house by marriage, established a Chapel Royal that was like the Papal Chapel at Avignon, in both its repertory and its Franco-Netherlandish personnel.[3] To the court of John I and his successors came such musicians as Jacques de Selesses,[4] Jean Trebor,[5] and Gacian Reyneau of Tours [6]—all three of whom have compositions, with French text, in MS Chantilly 1047 (it is quite possible that the noble French family, at whose court this MS was written, had close ties with Spain).[7] John I himself composed, to French words.[8] Another of John I's singers, sometime member of the Burgundian chapel, was Colinet Forestier. A colleague of Forestier's in Spain was Jean (Johannes) Martini of Noyen (near Le Mans; he should not be confused with the later Martini of Armentières).[9] That these foreigners on Spanish soil did not forget the art of their native land is indicated by a notarized docu-

---

[1] Cf. ReMMA, 373ff.   [2] Cf. *ibid.*, 375f, 384.   [3] For further details, *see* MME I, 14 (text).

[4] Three Jacomís, who were musicians, were in Spain during this period. One who was in the service of John I in 1377, was ordered to show his *"chansons nouvelles"* to the court minstrels (*see* PedJ, 240). BesS I, 200, fn. 4, points out that the name Jacomi appears in the Chantilly MS (*see* WolfG I, 331), where it is identified with Jacob (= Jacques) de Senleches. AngG, 64, considers the identification "highly probable." For a full discussion, *see* AngJ. Cf. p. 12 *supra*.

[5] *See* MassonB, 117. It should be noted that WolfG I, 331, fn. 3, is in error in considering "Trebor" merely an anagram for "Robert."

[6] *See* AngG.   [7] For details of this family connection, *see* MME I, 15 (text).

[8] *See* PedJ, 240; ReMMA, 375.

[9] For quotations from documents relating to foreign musicians in Spain from the 14th to the 16th centuries, see AngCO; StraM VII–VIII (subtitled *Les Musiciens néerlandais en Espagne*); and PedJ, 229ff.

ment [10] of 1408, in which Reyneau and Martini established their legal rights as Forestier's heirs to a volume called *De Motets e de Ballades,* which Forestier had lent to the monastery of Poblet, in Tarragona, but which the abbot had been reluctant to give back. Records show that Trebor was still serving at the court of Aragon under Martin I, in 1409, and that Reyneau continued on into Alfonso V's reign (1416–1458), during which—after more than thirty years' service at the Aragonese court—he died, in 1429.

From Italy there came persistent and increasing cultural influence, through both ecclesiastical and political channels: in 1443, Alfonso V ("el Magnánimo") became King of Naples and set up a court that cultivated music and literature (cf. p. 139). One of the composers there was Johannes Cornago, evidently identical with the Franciscan who was sent to Rome by the king in 1455 and, Alfonso having died in 1458, was chief almoner to his son and successor, Ferrante in 1466.[11] Cornago's largest surviving work, a *Missa de la mapa mundi* (in Trent MS 88),[12] may reflect the growing Italo-Spanish interest in exploration and its connection with religious fervor. In 1480, the King furnished a painter, Giovanni di Giusto, with enough Holland linen to trace a map of the world. This is possibly the map referred to in the Italian text (*Ayo* [= *aggio*] *visto lo mappamundo*) belonging to the *cantus firmus* and written under the tenor of the Gloria and Credo of Cornago's Mass.[13] Twelve or thirteen shorter extant pieces of his are to vernacular texts—Spanish or Italian—and one to Latin.[14] The last of these texts, *Patres nostri peccaverunt,* is from Lamentations (being part of Lesson III for Holy Saturday); the piece, which is *a 4,* appears to be one of the earliest polyphonic settings of a passage from that source.[15] It is preserved in MS Monte Cassino 871 N, which contains also two anonymous Lamentation settings *a 3.*[16] A late 15th-century MS, apparently Spanish, contains still another such setting.[17]

Of Cornago's compositions with Spanish words, three (all originally *a 3*) appear in a late 15th-century collection that will be considered as a whole presently, the *Cancionero de Palacio* or Barbieri *Cancionero* (so named after its 19th-century editor).[18] The first, *Pues que Dios,* with its merely supporting

---

[10] Text in AngG, 69f.

[11] Biographical data in Camillo Minieri Riccio, "Alcuni fatti di Alfonso I. di Aragonia dal 15 Aprile 1437 al 31 di Maggio 1458," in *Archivio per le province napoletane,* VI (1881), 437; Nicola Barone, "Le cedole di tesoreria dell'archivio di stato di Napoli dell'anno 1460 al 1504," in same *Archivio* . . . , IX (1884), 209; PirH, 157 fn.   [12] For incipits, *see* DTO VII, 43.

[13] *See* PirMC, 206; N. Barone, *op. cit.,* 406; and especially GhiSL, 61f.

[14] *See* the lists in MME I, 95f, 104f, 117 (text). One of the pieces is Cornago's 3-part *Qu'es mi vida?,* reworked as a 4-part piece by Ockeghem (cf. p. 119). *See also* fn. 18.

[15] Aside from such a setting as Dufay's Lament on the fall of Constantinople, with its inclusion of a passage from Lamentations (together with its Gregorian melody) merely as a motet tenor.

[16] PirMC, 206.   [17] *See also* MME I, 117 (text), item 9; GasBC, 4ff.

[18] Barbieri prepared his edition from a copy now in the Bibl. Nac., Madrid; a new 3-vol. ed., following the orig. MS is now (1951) in course of publication, Vols. I and II having appeared as MME V and X. The 3 Cornago pieces in question pr. BarbiC, 234, 268 (the fourth part [contralto] is the addition of a later hand), 286, 2nd piece (anon. in this *Cancionero,* but ascribed to Cornago elsewhere); these 3 citations = , respectively, MME V, 2, 51, and 72

lower lines, is soon followed in the collection by another, probably later, version, credited to a composer named Madrid, who employs the same superius and tenor, but provides a third voice that is more flowing and has more melodic independence. The two other Cornago pieces in the *Cancionero*— *Gentil dama* and *Señor, cual soy venido*—are, like the first, Spanish *villancicos* (cf. pp. 581ff). At Alfonso's Neapolitan court at least two national strains mingled—the Spanish and the Italian. Cornago apparently belonged to the Spanish strain.[19]

Native Spanish names are numerous among early 15th-century musicians in the Iberian homeland. One of the highly individual manifestations of the native impulse took the form of musical treatises in the vernacular. In 1410, Fernando Estéban, sacristan of the Chapel of St. Clement in Seville, wrote a book *Reglas de canto plano é de contrapunto é de canto de órgano*. The last three words constitute the Spanish term for "mensural music." Estéban had some fantastic ideas of music history: he thought, for instance, that St. Gregory invented the note-symbols GABCD etc., beginning them with G because it was the first letter of his own name, and that Boethius lived after St. Gregory. But he was better informed about more recent music: he mentions, for example, Vitri and Machaut. Later in the century, other theoretical works, which still survive, were written by Spaniards. An anonymous treatise written in Spanish, c. 1480, mentions—among others—Dunstable, Dufay, and Ockeghem. Guillermo Despuig (= Guillermus de Podio) brought out an *Ars musicorum* at Valencia in 1495—an example of a Spanish *incunabulum* containing a musical illustration [20] for which the staves were printed, the notes, etc., being inserted by hand. Later he wrote an *Enchiridion,* which is preserved in MS, along with a Spanish treatise and some musical compositions also probably by him. Much of the theoretical work written or copied in Spain during the 15th century was based on convention or ignorance; but it was destined to have its fruition, toward the end of the century, in the brilliant and revolutionary treatise of Ramos de Pareja, which will be considered later, and, during the next century, in that of Salinas.[21]

The Latter Half of the 15th Century: Anchieta; Peñalosa

The second half of the 15th century was more productive for Spain than the first in the field of composition. The anonymous four-part *Lealtat! O lealtat!* (c. 1465) [22] may be taken as representative of a body of occasional court music,

---

[19] MitM, 1957, refers to him as an Italian; but cf. MME I, 24f (text). Further about Cornago, *see* MGG II, 1680ff.   [20] Facsimile in AngME, Pl. 38.

[21] For a fuller discussion of Spanish theorists in the early 15th century, *see* MitM, 1949ff; AngLME, 364ff.

[22] Facsimile in CarrH, opp. p. 288. Pr. BarbiC, 605; MitM, 1947f. The piece is preserved (probably not very accurately) on a separate sheet bound in with the *Crónica del Condestable Miguel Lucas de Iranzo*, attributed variously to Juan de Olid, Diego de Gamez, or, more probably, Pedro de Escavias. Since this sheet is bound in at the material for the year 1466, that date

now lost. This artistically unpretentious piece lauds Miguel Lucas de Iranzo, Constable under Henry IV of Castile (reigned 1453–1474). Iranzo's defence of Jaén, in 1465, and his loyalty at other times, had saved Henry his crown. The composition reminds the king of this fact, and urges him not to forget his friends. In view of its early date, this almost entirely chordal piece is interesting for its considerable use of progressions capable of being analyzed as V-I.[23]

The greater abundance of Spanish musical MSS in the late 15th century is due partly to the more stable political conditions that prevailed after the union of Castile and Aragon in 1474 under Ferdinand and Isabella (*"los Reyes Católicos"*). Their ability to finance Columbus' expedition is but one indication of the stability of their reign; in 1492, moreover, by the conquest of Granada, they drove the last of the Moors from Spanish soil. Isabella, in particular, fostered music, employing some forty singers at a time, not to mention instrumentalists; the son of the monarchs, John, so enjoyed singing that instead of taking a siesta he would customarily meet at the palace with his *maestro de capilla,* Juan de Anchieta, and four or five choirboys, "and the Prince sang with them two hours, or as long as he pleased, and provided them a tenor, and he was indeed good in the art." [24]

The court of *los Reyes Católicos* particularly favored sacred music.[25] Spanish historians sometimes call the period from 1474 to the death of Ferdinand in 1516 (Isabella died in 1504) *el siglo de oro,* "the golden age."

Juan de Anchieta was one of the leading Spanish sacred composers of his day. Born c. 1462, in the Basque town of Azpeitia of the same noble family as St. Ignatius Loyola, he became chaplain and *cantor* to Ferdinand and Isabella in 1489 and in 1493 *maestro de capilla* to John. In 1519, being "already old," he was pensioned and excused from further service at court by Charles V. Retiring to his native town, Anchieta died in 1523. In a codicil to his will, there is an implication that he had once been in the Low Countries.[26]

Anchieta's sacred music makes considerable use of Gregorian melody. The Gloria of a Mass [27] (whose other sections are not known to draw upon the Chant) is based on the Gloria of Gregorian Mass XV.[28] In the *Missa de*

---

has usually been assigned to the piece. The composition, however, has no integral relation to the text of the chronicle; and CarrH suggests that it illustrates better some of the material under the preceding year.

[23] Cf. BushC.

[24] Gonzalo Fernandez de Oviedo, *Libro de la Cámara,* quoted in BarbiC, 12f.

[25] Among exx. of the period available in print are 9 motets from MS 5–5–20 in the Biblioteca Colombina (pr. ElúsA; *see also* AngS; this early 16th-century MS was once owned by the son of Christopher Columbus; it includes a work by a Juan Ponce, who ElúsA thinks was related to Ponce de Leon) and 6 Masses from MS No. 3 at the cathedral at Tarazona, near Saragossa (MME I).

[26] Further biographical data in CosterA; BarbiC, 20ff; ElúsA, xxxiiif; MME I, 6; MGG I, 454f.

[27] Pr. MME I, 1 (music).

[28] In the Credo there may be a reminiscence of a popular Spanish tune *Ea judíos,* sung in

Nuestra Señora [29]—with Sanctus and Agnus by Pedro (?) de Escobar (*see below*), the rest being by Anchieta—, the Kyrie, which includes the trope *Rex virginum,* is based on the Kyrie of Mass IV. The Gloria, as might be expected of a Mass to the Virgin, is provided with the usual Marian tropes and draws on the chant of Mass IX. (Escobar employs the Sanctus of Mass VIII and the Agnus of Mass IX.) Anchieta's *Salve Regina* [30] breaks up into ten sections, of which the odd-numbered ones are in chant, while all but the last of the even-numbered ones are in polyphony *a 4,* the last being *a 5.* In the polyphonic sections, the superius paraphrases the plainsong. At the close of the first and last polyphonic sections, Anchieta suddenly introduces additional voices, in the manner of his Northern French forerunners. Sustained chordal effects appear occasionally in this work, as they do also in Anchieta's *Domine Jesu* and *Virgo et Mater* [31]—chordal passages being interspersed among passages of imitation (sparingly used) and free polyphony. Like his northern contemporaries, he shows a fondness for passages *a 2* in which the voices move in tenths. In addition to sacred works, we have examples by Anchieta of the *villancico,*[32] which will be discussed presently.

The Pedro de Escobar who may have written two movements of the *Missa de Nuestra Señora* flourished between 1507 and 1514. There was also a Cristóbal de Escobar, known as the writer of a *Tratado de canto llano.*[33] (*Canto llano* = plainsong; but cf. p. 585.) Since several compositions bear merely an ascription to "Escobar," there is obviously some difficulty in making attributions.[34]

Even more highly regarded in his day than Anchieta, apparently, was Francisco de Peñalosa; in the art of music he was said to surpass "Apollo, its inventor." [35] Born c. 1470, perhaps in Toledo, he became a singer of Ferdinand's in 1498 and continued in the Chapel Royal until 1516. Whereas Anchieta was the son's *maestro de capilla,* Peñalosa was that of a grandson also named Ferdinand. On King Ferdinand's death, in 1516, another grandson—the future emperor, Charles V—came from the Low Countries and took over the rule, bringing with him Netherlandish customs and an entire *capilla*

---

derision of the Jews on their expulsion from Spain in 1492. The tune is given in BarbiC, 21. If Anglès (in AngP, 69) is right in suggesting that this relationship exists, this particular Mass may be the one of Anchieta's referred to by Salinas in his *De musica* (1592), p. 312. The relationship between the tune and the Mass, however, is not very close; and in MME I, 52 (text), Anglès does not consider the Mass mentioned by Salinas as having been found.

[29] Pr. MME I, 35 (music).   [30] Pr. ElúsA, 8.   [31] Pr. *ibid.,* 1, 5, respectively.

[32] Exx. in BarbiC, 346 (= MME V, 206), 414, 474 (= MME X, 97, 158, respectively); there is a *romance* on p. 499 (= MME V, 155). MME I, 107ff, lists about 10 additional sacred works that bear Anchieta's name. *See* further CohenA (which includes, in modern notation, 5 exx. not thus available elsewhere).

[33] Pr. WolfCE. *See also* RiaC, 72ff.

[34] *See* further MME I, 7 (text). Biographical data on Pedro de Escobar in ElúsA, xlviiiff; for a motet, *see ibid.,* 33. Some secular pieces credited to "Escobar" will be mentioned presently.

[35] Cristobal de Villalón, *Ingeniosa Comparación* . . . (1539), quoted in ElúsA, xliii.

flamenca and reigning as King of Spain. (The *capilla flamenca,* as it was called in Spain, was actually the continuation of the old Burgundian chapel choir, which travelled with Charles as he went from place to place.) Even before Ferdinand's death, however, Franco-Netherlandish composers, as we have seen, had been in Spain, notably Ockeghem, Agricola, and la Rue. The intensification of Netherlandish influence after Ferdinand's death may have been responsible for Peñalosa's leaving Spain, or the Italy of the Medici may have attracted him more; at all events, in 1517 he was mentioned in letters written by Leo X as a member of his chapel in Rome, an active chorister, exercising his art "with great prudence and probity." Peñalosa was awarded various preferments, returned to Spain by 1525, and died at Seville in 1528.[36]

Peñalosa apparently profited by his association with the highly trained musicians at Rome. In the opening of his *Missa Ave Maria,*[37] portions of the Gregorian *Ave Maria* are first assigned to the tenor (at times transposed up a fourth) and the opening fragment is finally assigned to all voices in imitation. The next movements are based on the Gloria of Mass XV and on Credo IV. The Sanctus and Agnus employ phrases of the *Salve Regina.* In Agnus III, the *Vita dulcedo* phrase is in the superius, while the tenor sings, in retrograde motion, the tenor of Hayne's *De tous biens plaine,* the symbolical significance being that with which we are already familiar (cf. p. 227). Peñalosa's *Missa Nunca fué pena mayor*[38] is based on the superius of a secular piece to which we shall presently return. The borrowed melody appears in the top voice. A striking example of Peñalosa's virtuosity appears in a six-voice *ensalada* or quodlibet, *Por las sierras,*[39] in which four *villancicos* are sung simultaneously and are linked together harmonically by free outer parts, the bottom one being to the words *"Loquebantur variis linguis magnalia dei"* ("They spoke in various tongues the wonderful works of God").[40] This piece survives in the *Cancionero de Palacio,* as do eight other more conventional examples of Peñalosa's *villancico* writing.[41] The inclusion of nine pieces of his in such a MS and the considerable quantity of sacred music ascribed to him show that his work was well liked at the time of *los Reyes Católicos.*[42]

[36] Further biographical data in BarbiC, 41f; ElúsA, xxxvff; MME I, 7 (text); MitN, 129.
[37] Pr. MME I, 62 (music).
[38] Pr. MME I, 99 (music).   [39] Pr. BarbiC, 585; MME X, 75.
[40] Perhaps a paraphrase of Acts II, 11.
[41] Pr. BarbiC, 304 (= MME V, 101), 328 (2 items [= MME V, 150, 153]), 394, 400, 403, 428, 438 (= MME X, 58, 72, 78, 122, 139, respectively). Another piece pr. *ibid.,* 599; MME X, 195.
[42] MME I, 113ff (text), lists some 50 further compositions that bear the name Peñalosa. Of these EsL prints 6 motets (1 = ElúsA, 16). Grove IV, 99, suggests that these motets (it gives their number wrongly as 8) and 1 of the unprinted Masses are by a later Juan Peñalosa (fl. 1549–1566), partly because one of the motets, *Memorare,* "is dated 1549" in the Toledo MS from which Eslava transcribed. However, that seems to be the date of the MS (cf. MME I, 130 [text]); at any rate, the piece exists also in 2 earlier MSS (cf. *ibid.,* 114, 121).

The Latter Half of the 15th Century: the Cancioneros; Encina

Nunca fué pena mayor [43] was a famous piece of the time, a *villancico* composed by the Fleming, Johannes Wreede (= Urrede, etc.) of Bruges, in the service of the Duke of Alba. In 1476, the Duke granted Wreede a sum of money for teaching singing to three Negro boys.[44] Wreede's composition opens the *Cancionero de Palacio,* probably because the text is by the Duke himself; the piece thus gives the keynote to the whole collection, which represents the domestic repertory of the House of Alba. This *villancico* recurs in thirteen other MS sources, and is referred to by the fine Portuguese dramatist Gil Vicente (c. 1465-1536?) in his tragi-comedies, *Cortes de Jupiter* and *Faragoa de Amor.*[45] Wreede's *villancico* appears also in the *Odhecaton.* It is well to bear in mind that, according to his surname, Petrus Castellanus, the editor of this collection was a Castilian—a fact that may have influenced his choice. Other compositions by Wreede are extant.[46] One that long remained popular in Spain is his setting, preserved in the Segovia MS, of the traditional Spanish melody for the *Pange lingua.* More than once his work served as the basis for *glosas* or variations, and as late as 1669 a Spanish composer made it the basis of a Mass.[47] The melody itself, which was to be set by many composers and is still in use beside the standard one of the Roman Church, is definitely traceable no further back than the 15th century but may date from the 13th or 14th.[48]

The normal form of the *villancico* in the Middle Ages had been *ABccabAB;* thus it was clearly the Spanish equivalent of the French *virelai,* the Italian *ballata,* and the Arab *zajal.* Which of these came first and influenced the others, need not here be investigated.[49] The standard name for the refrain was *estribillo;* for the strophe proper, *copla.* Of the *copla,* the *cc* group was called the *mudanza* (= the *piedi* of the *ballata*) while the *ab* group constituted the *vuelta* (= the *volta* of the *ballata*). (But it should be stressed that these terms were not applied consistently.) The relative conservatism of Spanish secular music is shown by the retention of the old form—sometimes with an

[43] Pr. BarbiC, 233; MME V, 1; HewO, 226; StraM VIII, opp. p. 454; facsimile in StaE I, 104, after MS Ashmole 831.

[44] Further biographical data in MME I, 126 (text); MitN, 131. MME also presents evidence that a Johannes Ureda served under Ferdinand from 1477 on, but suggests that this may be another person.

[45] Complete list of MSS and prints in HewO, 130.   [46] MME I, 95ff, lists works in 7 MSS.

[47] MME II, 175, has notes on the *glosas,* prints one set, p. 119; MME I, 127, gives details about the Mass.

[48] For the Spanish melody in one version, see *Cantus ad processiones et benedictiones* (1920), 89; TreM, 197; a variant version in Liber, 1852; Vesperale, 90*; SuñPL, 215, 258. The former version appears in numerous polyphonic settings. For an article on this melody, see SuñPL, which includes a discussion of the several variants in the sources.

[49] For the history and theories of *villancico* origins, see AmoS. About the influence of one old form on another, cf. ReMMA, 245f.

interesting change, however—while Italy had practically abandoned the *ballata* in favor of the newer *frottola*. The change consisted in the absorption of the *estribillo*, after its first enunciation, into the *copla*, or, to word it differently, in a "telescoping" of the small *ab* and the subsequent *AB*. This was accomplished by having the last *B* section of the *estribillo* serve as the *b* section of the *vuelta* and by eliminating *bA;* complete repetition of the *estribillo* after the various *coplas* was then apparently given up (only the *B* section of the *estribillo*, consequently, continuing to perform the function of a refrain). The process that resulted in the new *aBccaB* pattern (subject to variation, particularly with regard to the number of lines involved [50]), calls to mind the one, in the realm of sacred music, that yielded the modified responsory form (cf. p. 94).

There are four noteworthy *cancioneros* of the late 15th and early 16th centuries that give us a good idea of the *villancico* repertory. The one whose contents date farthest back is MS 7-1-28 at the Biblioteca Colombina in Seville.[51] Ferdinand Columbus, son of the explorer, acquired this MS for his library in 1534. In all, it contains ninety-five pieces, of which twenty also appear—some with added parts—in the *Cancionero de Palacio*. The composer's name occurring most frequently in the Seville *Cancionero* is Triana. Two settings of the "Song of the Sibyl" are included—one by him.[52] A "Song of the Sibyl," by Alonso de Córdoba, is found also in the *Cancionero de Palacio*.[53] Triana's setting has the old melody in the altus. Two drinking songs that reappear in the *Cancionero de Palacio* as anonymous are also his.[54] In general, the Seville *Cancionero* is much like that of the Palace: most of the pieces are *a 3*, and the texts are in various languages—twelve in Latin, two in French, and the rest in Castilian.

The *Cancionero de Palacio* contains 463 pieces,[55] mostly *villancicos* with the main melody in the superius. Usually the voices begin together, but occasionally there are brief initial points of imitation—sometimes, in pieces *a 3*, in two parts [56] or in all three.[57] In compositions *a 4*, not only does imitation occur in two and three parts, but sometimes in all four—either in normal manner or

---

[50] For a discussion of the variants of the *villancico* form, see MitU, 15ff, esp. 35.
[51] The contents of the MS are listed in MME I, 104 (text). For a facsimile page, see AngME, Pl. 20. Cf. also AngS, 66f.
[52] Pr. AngL, opp. p. 298. For further data on the "Song of the Sibyl," see ReMMA, 195, 199.
[53] Pr. BarbiC, 434; AngL, opp. p. 298; MME X, 134.
[54] Pr. BarbiC, 573, 575 (= MME X, 9, 16, respectively).
[55] In addition, the MS originally contained 92 pieces on sheets that have been lost. The titles of these pieces are given in MME V, 35f (text) (BarbiC, 49ff omits 1 item); 3 of the compositions may be preserved in the Upsala *Cancionero* and 3 more in a Portuguese *cancionero*, both presently to be discussed (for further data, see MitU, 64, 66, 70; JoaC, 127, 129, 136).
[56] Exx. in BarbiC, 262, 301 (imitation in inversion), 340, 450, 451, 516, 575 (= MME V, 42, 92, 186; X, 199 [system 4ff], 200; V, 98; X, 16, respectively), etc.
[57] Exx. BarbiC, 291 (= MME V, 80), 349 (2 pieces = MME V, 214; MME X, 61), 373 (2 pieces = MME X, 3, 4), 377 (2 pieces = MME X, 10, 11), 392 (= MME X, 55), 455 (2 pieces; the 2nd = MME X, 207), 548 (= MME X, 85), 563 (2 pieces = MME V, 159, MME X, 121).

pairwise.[58] *A los baños* employs canon.[59] In *Al alba venid*,[60] there are *fermata*-marked block-chords. Despite the brief points of imitation, the music in this *Cancionero* is mainly chordal in an Early Renaissance manner. Most of the texts are in Castilian, but some are in Italian, Latin, Portuguese, broken French, and even Basque. Among the Italian songs are four found also in Petrucci's *frottola* books, including Josquin's macaronic *In te Domine.*

The composer most evident in the *Cancionero* is Juan del Encina, with more than three times as many *villancicos* to his credit as anyone else.[61] Encina was born in or near Salamanca in 1468 or 1469. The son of a shoemaker,[62] he yet made his way rapidly in the courtly world, becoming master of cere-monies at the palace of the Duke of Alba. There, in 1492, he wrote and di-rected a Christmas eclogue on the theme of the Nativity. Pastoral plays of this type, deriving ultimately from Vergil, offered the occasion for some of Encina's activity as a composer; for he produced many examples of the *quatro de empezar* ("quartet for beginning"), sung by way of an overture, or as a clos-ing number. So essential was the singing of these frequently four-part pieces that in Encina's *Auto del Repelón,* where there are only three characters until almost the end, a fourth is finally added in order to round out the musical ensemble. Three of Encina's compositions [63] in the *Cancionero* are traceable to known eclogues. According to Encina himself, most of his musical and poetic work was written before he was twenty-five; consequently, this period of his life as a courtier—gallant, clever, worldly—is to be understood as the background of his contribution to the *Cancionero*. Some of his *villancicos* may be occasional pieces, one evidently on the death of Prince John, another on the death of Isabella.[64] The majority of his compositions, however, are love songs.

EXAMPLE 130. *Un' amiga tengo, hermano*—Encina (after MME X, 54).

[58] Exx. of ordinary 4-part imitation, *ibid.*, 250, 325, 387, 420, 533 (= MME V, 137, 145; X, 42, 104; V, 239, respectively); of imitation in pairs, 552 (2 pieces), 565, 581, 596 (= MME X, 130 and 142; V, 188; X, 24, 131, respectively).

[59] Pr., without canon, *ibid.*, 337; with it, MME V, 174.

[60] Pr. BarbiC, 241; MME V, 10.

[61] 62 pieces pr. BarbiC with ascriptions to Encina. All attributions have been retained in MME V, X, except the one for BarbiC, No. 35, which is anon. in MME V, No. 45. Some additional items, not certainly by Encina, have been omitted from the above figure of 62.

[62] The father's name was Juan de Fermoselle; Cotarelo (in EncC, 8) says that the Fermoselle named as composer of a *villancico* (pr. BarbiC, 314; MME V, 113) was Juan del Encina's brother, Diego de Fermoselle, who taught music at Salamanca University, 1478–1522.

[63] Pr. BarbiC, 527, 528, 529 (= MME V, 196, 198, 203, respectively).

[64] Pr., respectively, BarbiC, 508 (= MME X, 87), 487 (= MME V, 109; facsimile in AngME [facs. 19]).

"*I have a sweetheart, brother, gracious and of great value. I swear ten times that she is mine.* I swear to you by San Gil that, if you should know her, you certainly would not speak of having another more elegant. There cannot be among a thousand another of more gentility. I swear ten times that she is mine. . . . *I have a sweetheart, brother, gracious and of great value. I swear ten times that she is mine.*" (This is stanza 1; for the full text, *see* BarbiC, 190ff.)

Encina is as definitely a composer of secular music as Anchieta is of sacred. Also, he broke new ground for the Spanish secular drama [65] and united in his work both popular and art elements. His *romance* based on the popular ballad *Conde Claros,* for instance, uses a variant of the old text, but changes the melody to one of his own contriving.[66]

The first volume of Encina's poetic works, containing eight plays, appeared in 1496. Angered at his failure to secure the post of choirmaster of Salamanca Cathedral, he went to Rome to enlist the aid of the Spanish pope of the house of Borgia (Borja), Alexander VI. Most of the rest of his life was spent at Rome. In 1519 he was ordained, made a pilgrimage to the Holy Land, and celebrated his first Mass at Jerusalem, and on his return to Rome published an account of his journey. In 1523 he was in residence at León as prior, and presumably died there in 1529 or 1530.[67]

Though none of the sixty-five compositions now in *O Cancioneiro Musical* in the Biblioteca Públia Hortênsia, in the Portuguese town of Elvas, bears an indication of its authorship, four are essentially the same as pieces by Encina in the *Cancionero de Palacio.*[68] The only other composer known to be represented in both is "Escobar," [69] though to a lesser extent. The general style of the Portuguese *cancioneiro* is much like that of the Spanish collections, only somewhat simpler and more homogeneous: all the numbers are brief, all are for three voices or fewer, and the great majority are chordal throughout.

[65] Further on his musical contributions to the Spanish theater, *see* ChaseO, 292ff; SalaM, 97ff; LivS, 141f.

[66] Pr. BarbiC, 501; MME V, 158. For the traditional melody, *see* TreM, 225 (cf. 104); for *glosas* on it, *see* MME II, 185.

[67] Further biographical and bibliographical data in ChaseJ; SubM, 9ff.

[68] Cf., respectively, JoaC, 80, 81, 84, 91, and BarbiC, 541, 322 (= MME X, 54 [= our Ex. 130], 53, respectively), 342 (= MME V, 193), 432 (= MME X, 130). Variants are noted in JoaC, 128f, 131, 136.

[69] Cf., respectively, JoaC, 37, 43, 92, and BarbiC, 359, 368, 415 (= MME V, 229, 243; X, 99, respectively). Textual and melodic similarities also exist between JoaC, 39, 89, 95, and BarbiC, 248 (= MME V, 21), first piece on 565 (= MME V, 184), and 433 (2 pieces based on the same melody, = MME X, 133, 156).

Though not named, Encina is represented also in the *Cancionero de Upsala* —among whose 54 *villancicos,* however, there are pieces dating from later than the *Cancionero de Palacio*—, printed at Venice in 1556. The first twelve pieces are *a 2,* fourteen are *a 3,* twenty-two *a 4,* and the last six *a 5.* It is a more varied and orderly collection than the rest. The texts are mostly Castilian, but four are in Catalan and two in Gallego-Portuguese. The music employs conspicuously more imitation than does that of the *Cancionero de Palacio,* often in all parts.[70] The only composer actually named in the Upsala *Cancionero* is Gombert, who is represented by one of the compositions *a 5.*[71] This piece incorporates the melody of *El cantollano del Cavallero* (cf. p. 628; the meaning of the term *"canto llano"* came to be incorrectly extended to include *cantus firmus,* obviously because a *cantus firmus* was so often a piece of plainsong). It will be recalled that Gombert was active in Spain in the service of Charles V (cf. p. 303). Could the greater amount of imitation throughout this *Cancionero* perhaps show his strong Late Renaissance influence?

While each of the *cancioneros* has its distinct character, there are many points of contact among them. In addition to some composers already named, the following are represented in more than one of the collections: Enrique, Borote (or Torote), J. de León, Madrid, Moxica, Lagarto, Gijón, F. de la Torre, Gabriel, and Aldomar. The *villancico* is shown in various aspects. Most of the pieces are quite short,[72] but such an example as *Que farem del pobre Joan!* occupies eight pages in MitU. The texts are varied also, some being amatory, historical, or elegiac, while others are obviously connected with dancing, religious as well as secular.[73] Many are associated with festivals of the church year—especially Easter and Christmas.[74] In the course of the 17th century, the *villancicos de Navidad* pre-empted the field, and the *villancico*— like the carol in England—became a predominantly religious form associated with the Christmas season.[75]

Within the framework of the Spanish secular drama with which it had early been associated, moreover, the *villancico* underwent further development along secular lines. Among the imitators of Encina was Lucas Fernández (b. Salamanca, 1474; d. there, 1542), Encina's successful rival for the post of choirmaster at Salamanca Cathedral,[76] who wrote one play that not only con-

[70] Exx. in MitU, 1–24 (*a 2*); 25, 31, 39, 43 (*a 3*); 58, 70, 91 (*a 4*); 125, 130, 148 (*a 5*).
[71] Pr. MitU, 125. On stylistic grounds, one might suspect the following piece also to be his.
[72] For the ways in which these may have been expanded in performance, *see* SalaP, 5.
[73] GeiB, 78, discusses the various types. A notable *villancico,* apparently accompanying a dance before the Virgin, is pr. in MitU, 116. For religious dancing in Spain, *see* SachsW, 335; ReMMA, 110; also p. 597 *infra.*
[74] Exx. of Christmas *villancicos* in BarbiC, 476 (= MME X, 164); MitU, 100; of Easter *villancicos* in BarbiC, 468 (2 pieces; = MME X, 2, 48).
[75] A table of the relative frequency of Christmas and other types of *villancicos* from 1450 to 1617 is given in AmoS, 116. Further about the *villancico, see* PopeV, GeiB.
[76] Further biographical and bibliographical data in ChaseO, 296f; SalaM, 101; HerrT, 75ff; FernanF.

cludes with a *villancico* [77] but also has songs alternating with spoken text and another that was sung throughout.[78] Other followers of Encina were Fernán Lopez de Yanguas and Bartolomé de Torres Naharro. Gil Vicente made considerable use of choral song throughout his plays: one calls for an anvil chorus, another for a concluding *ensalada*.[79]

Ramos de Pareja

Still within the flowering period of the early *villancico,* the Spaniards made important contributions as musical theorists. Bartolomé Ramos (= Ramis) de Pareja was born c. 1440, at Baeza (near Jaén), studied under Joannes de Monte, and lectured on Boethius at Salamanca. Rather early in his career, Ramos wrote a vernacular musical treatise, which is lost. By 1472 he had left Salamanca; and in 1482 he published his *Musica practica* at Bologna, where he was giving public lectures. Later he went to Rome,[80] and was apparently still living there in 1491. In addition to his work on musical theory, he wrote several sacred compositions, no longer extant.[81]

Ramos' *Musica practica* is significant not only as one of the oldest incunabula on music; it was revolutionary in its day, breaking sharply with convention and arousing a storm of controversy. Ramos wished to replace the solmisation syllables based on the Guidonian hexachord with a set of syllables *psal-li-tur per vo-ces is-tas,* based on the octave.[82] He declared the major and minor thirds consonant, and, while remaining within the general framework of the Pythagorean theory of tuning, approached just intonation when he revised the older system to achieve the ratios of 4:5 and 5:6 for the major and minor third, respectively.[83] Also, he built a twelve-tone scale, thus anticipating by about seventy years the somewhat similar and better known efforts of Vicentino (cf. p. 328). Ramos, in addition, gave a clear explanation of the nature of pervading imitation at a time when it was still new. He used for "imitation" the old term for canon, *"fuga,"* though he made it clear he would admit liberties that do not exist in true canon.[84] Instruments, *musica ficta,* the solving of enigmas propounded by verbal canons, etc., are likewise among his topics.

A storm of protest and defence ensued at Bologna upon the publication of the *Musica practica.* Some Italian theorists whom we have already en-

---

[77] An anon. setting pr. BarbiC, 480 (= MME X, 169).
[78] A setting (by Badajoz) of the tune to which it was sung pr. BarbiC, 531; MME V, 218.
[79] Cf. ChaseO, 298; SalaM, 102f.
[80] He may have been a singer at the Vatican in 1447; cf. AngLME, 364.
[81] Further bio-bibliographical data in RamosM, xiff; SorbM, 104. RamosM is a modern edition of the *Musica practica;* StrunkR, 201ff, gives an extract in English.
[82] Exposition of system, RamosM, 19, 27.
[83] For Ramos' explanation of thirds, *see* RamosM, 63, 98 (= StrunkR, 203); for its relation to Pythagorean tuning, *see* BarbP, 297f.
[84] RamosM, 68.

countered became violently partisan in print. Burzio in his *Musices opusculum* (1487) protested the slur upon the memory of Guido. Ramos' pupil, Spataro, countered with an *Honesta defensio* (1491). Gafori renewed the attack in his *Practica musicae* (1496). These pieces of incunabula, together with Gafori's *Apologia* of 1520 and Spataro's *Dilucide . . . demonstratione* of 1521—cf. p. 180—show how hard it was for most theorists to bring theory in line with practice. The controversy may also have been motivated by academic jealousy: the chair of music had been created at Bologna in 1450, through the influence of Nicholas V and despite the mathematical faculty's protest that music belonged in its field. Ramos apparently came to Bologna with some expectation of being appointed to the new chair, but left because he had no regularly paid appointment at the University.[85]

In Spain, also, Ramos' theories became a focal point of controversy. Gonzalo Martinez de Bizcargui in his *Arte de canto llano,* published at Burgos in 1511, followed Ramos. Juan de Espinosa, however, launched an attack in his *Retractiones de los errores,* published at Toledo in 1514.[86]

Morales and Some Other Late Renaissance Polyphonists

Flourishing shortly after Ramos were not only some composers already named, but also Antonio de Ribera, who was in the Papal Choir, 1514-1522, and to whom we shall return presently in connection with the *Mystery of Elche;* Martin de Rivaflecha or Rivafrecha (d. 1528); [87] Fernando de Contreras (born c. 1470; died 1548); [88] Juan Escribano (d. 1558), who was in the Papal Choir, 1507–1539; [89] Pedro de Escobar's successor as *magister puerorum* at the Seville Cathedral, Pedro Fernandez de Castilleja. The last of these, who served at the Cathedral for sixty years (1514–1574), may well have exerted a direct influence on Morales [89a] and on Francisco Guerrero, who called him *"maestro de los maestros de España."* A *Salve Regina* of Castilleja's and some hymns and motets that survive incomplete indicate that he was an able composer, but lacking in imagination.[90]

Cristóbal de Morales (born in Seville c. 1500; died 1553) held the position of *maestro de capilla* at the Cathedral of Ávila from 1526 to 1530. In 1535 he is found at Rome, where he was admitted as a singer in the Papal Chapel under Paul III. He obtained leave to return to Spain in 1540 and again in 1545, in the fall of which year he became *maestro de capilla* at Toledo. The rest of his

[85] For further data on the controversy, *see* SorbM, 106ff; RamosM, xiv, 105ff; RieG, 330ff; HawkH II, 336ff; SpataroD, 5ff.
[86] These and other Spanish theorists of the period are mentioned in AngLME, 364ff.
[87] Biographical data, ElúsA, xlivff; exx. *ibid.,* 23, 26, 28.
[88] About him, *see* MitE, 59ff.
[89] About him, *see* AngLME, 374; Grove II, 177.   [89a] But see StevnsnC, 10.
[90] Cf. TreCM, 21; motets in ColM, 258; EsL, *Ser. I,* I, 157, 161.

career was divided between that city, Marchena (near Seville), and Málaga.[91]

Morales—the first great Spanish master of the Late Renaissance—is one of the finest composers of the generation of Gombert, Clemens, and Willaert. Unlike them, however, he seems to have written very little secular music: only a handful of pieces with Italian and Spanish text survives.[92]

His twenty-two known Masses [92a] (sixteen printed in 1544) are mostly written on motets and Gregorian melodies, the eight exceptions including two composed on Spanish songs, *Tristezas me matan* and *De silde al cavallero*,[93] two *L'Homme armé* Masses, one *a 4*, one *a 5*,[94] and a six-part *Missa Mille regretz*,[95] based on Josquin's four-part chanson. In the first of these, the voice with the *Tristezas* tune has the Spanish words while the others sing the liturgical text. Some other Morales Masses also incorporate extraneous texts in the way followed by certain composers from Dufay on. The four-part *Missa L'Homme armé* shows the composer in retrospective vein in that he here retains the form of the old *cantus firmus* intact. In the other *L'Homme armé* Mass, however, Morales is "progressive" to the extent that he allows the *cantus firmus* to permeate all the voices.[96] In the *Missa Mille regretz*, the superius, perhaps symbolically, begins the *Crucifixus* at the point in the chanson melody that has the words *"j'ay si grand dueil et paine."* The three other works belonging to this group of eight are a Hexachord Mass, a *Missa Cortilla* (also called *Missa super Fa re ut fa sol la*), and a *Missa Caça*.[96a]

Among the Masses built on motets, *Quaeramus cum pastoribus* [97] and *Benedicta es coelorum Regina* [97a] draw on Mouton, while *Aspice Domine*,[97b] *Si bona suscepimus*,[97c] *Quem dicunt homines,* and *Vulnerasti cor meum* [97d] are based, respectively, on Gombert, Verdelot, Richafort, and an anonymous motet, preserved in Petrucci's *Motetti de la Corona,* Book I, and in other places.[98] In the Kyrie of the five-part *Missa Quaeramus,* the two highest voices begin like those of the motet (the opening of the motet introduces each movement of the Mass), while the three lowest ones have the theme of the motet bass; themes from the bass and tenor are used at still other points. The *Missa Benedicta es,* although constructed mainly on Mouton's motet, at times quotes that of Josquin, notably in the Benedictus.

---

[91] Further biographical data in StevnsnC; TreCM; ElúsA, xlixff; PiqM, 75ff; MitE, 183ff.

[92] For an Italian madrigal, *see* SmM, 110; for a Spanish piece (in *vihuela* transcription), MorL I, xli; II, 196; StevnsnC, 40.

[92a] But see pp. 27ff of MoralesO III (publ. since the present book first appeared) regarding the possibility that the anon. Requiem *a 4* thought to be by Morales is not actually his.

[93] The song and portion of the Kyrie of the former printed in TreCM, 34; *see also* MitE, 223. Concerning the latter, *see* M&L XXXVI (1955), 289.   [94] Pr. MoralesO I, 193.

[95] Pr. *ibid.*, 238, I am indebted to Dr. C. W. Fox for having loaned me, prior to the appearance of MoralesO I, the MS scores he had made, in whole or in part, of this and several other Morales Masses. Mr. Niles Saxton has also placed me in his debt by lending me his score of the *Missa Benedicta es* (since publ. in MoralesO III).   [96] Cf. WagC, 418.

[96a] At least, to judge from its title. About these 3 works, *see* MoralesO (text), 58f; StevnsnS, 54.

[97] Pr. MoralesO I, 148; BordA, *Messes* II, 62.

[97a] Matelart's lute intabulation of the *Osanna* is pr. ChilN, 655.

[97b] Pr. MoralesO I, 35.   [97c] Pr. *ibid.*, 274.   [97d] Pr. MoralesO I, 70.

[98] Cf. MoralesO I, 52ff, and PirH, 285 (which, however, contains some errors).

The Masses written on Gregorian melodies include a four-part and a five part *Missa de Beata Virgine*. The former [99] paraphrases the usual material (cf. p. 452). The three Kyrie sections are each built on the plainsong and a free countermelody; Kyrie I uses the two themes imitatively in pairs. The superius paraphrases the chant in the Gloria (which includes the Marian tropes), and the other voices employ the same material in imitation. The plan of the Credo is similar, except that the chant is in the tenor; the *Crucifixus* is for the three lower voices only. A fifth voice is added for *Osanna I;* the two upper voices sing in canon at the fifth, the underlying material being taken from four neumes [100] of the plainsong. In *Osanna II,* the bass reiterates, at different tone-levels, a motif derived from the first two of these neumes. The chant, in Agnus I, appears first in the highest voice; in Agnus II, it is in the lowest. Agnus III is *a 5*. The plainsong is not clearly defined in any voice until the words *"dona nobis pacem"* are reached, at which point the tenor has the plainsong theme, which it retains to the end. Generally, with regard both to this Mass and to other works that borrow from plainsong, it may be said that Morales treats Gregorian melodies with an almost severe regard for the preservation of their essential contours: he embellishes sparingly and applies his ingenuity instead to providing the melodies with a setting that his rather grave artistic personality considers suitable. While the five-part *Missa de Beata Virgine* is naturally based at least in part on plainsong Mass IX (as the title implies), its Credo is erected not on Credo I, in the usual way, but on the *Ave Maria* antiphon.[101] A tenor Mass *a 4* built directly on the antiphon adds two extra voices for the Agnus III, which presents the *cantus firmus* in canon.

EXAMPLE 131. Opening of the *Agnus Dei III* from the *Missa Ave Maria* —Morales (from *Christofori Moralis Hyspalensis Missarum Liber II,* Moder, 1551; transcr. C. W. Fox; Mass pr. almost complete by Annie Bank, Amsterdam, 1950).

Canon figures also in the five-part *Missa Ave maris stella*.[101a] Kyrie I opens with the chant in the superius while the next two voices form a canon at the fourth on another theme. The fourth voice and the bass, which enter before the voices already mentioned, sing in anticipatory imitation of the plainsong and of the canon, respectively. Later in this portion of the Kyrie, the two voices

---

[99] Pr. WagG, 457; MoralesO I, 1.   [100] Nos. 1, 2, 5, and 6.
[101] Cf. WagG, 418.   [101a] Pr. MoralesO I, 104.

incorporating the plainsong abandon it and join in imitating the canon. In the Sanctus there is again a canon at the fourth—this time based on the Gregorian theme and sung by the second highest and second lowest voices. The canon embraces all the phrases of the chant, repeating the last. Unity of form is aided by the presence, in the bass of the Sanctus, of the theme found in the canon of the Kyrie. Reappearance of themes from one movement to another takes place also in Morales' Requiem *a* 5. This work adheres more closely to the plainsong melodies than do a number of contemporary French Requiems. Morales uses as his Gradual the *Requiem aeternam* rather than the *Si ambulem*. The chant, throughout, is nearly always in long notes and is little varied. Occasionally, a Gregorian melisma is omitted—further indication of the sobriety of Morales' style. Unlike some Frenchmen of the time (cf. pp. 339f), he nearly always ends his theme on the same note as does the Gregorian version. The other voices often imitate the plainsong, usually in anticipatory fashion, the bass sometimes holding aloof from the imitation and proceeding largely in fourths and fifths. In the Gradual, the voices move in pairs, two having the Gregorian theme, two a theme of their own. The Sanctus is rather chordal. The various manners of writing are usually clearly marked from one another in the several movements, but sometimes sections or even phrases differ from one another stylistically in a single movement.[102]

Morales' setting *a* 4 of the Office of the Dead,[103] in which plainsong alternates with polyphony, is written in restrained and sober style, with sparing elaboration of the Gregorian melody (usually in the superius of the polyphonic sections) and frequent tendency to chordal writing. In the *Parce mihi, Domine,* a general pause of a measure before and after the word *"peccavi"* offers a striking use of silence for expressive purposes. In the *Ne recorderis* we see, from a passage several times repeated, that Morales did not refuse to employ consecutive fifths when one of them resulted from the presence of a passing-note.

The alternation of plainsong and polyphony often present in settings of the Magnificat is found in a volume published in 1545 at Venice, consisting of sixteen Morales settings—eight with the odd- and eight with the even-numbered verses written in polyphony fundamentally *a* 4. In the last of these settings,[104] Tone 8 appears successively in the superius, bass, alto, tenor, and superius again; then, in the last verse, two additional voices are introduced, singing Tone 8 in canon.

Plainsong again alternates with polyphony in Morales' *Salve Regina*,[105] which is developed by means of imitation in pairs. In an early work, a cere-

---

[102] Further about some of the Masses, *see* FoxM. About another Requiem, *see* StevnsnC, 38.
[103] Pr. PedH I, 1; but *see* StevnsnC, 12.
[104] Pr. PedH I, 20; ProsM, *Annus I*, III, 298. For the *Sicut erat* of the Magnificats in Tones 2, 3, and 5 from the series of even-verse settings, *see* MartiniE I, 38, 63, 110 (or ChorP V, *livraison* 6, 21, 35, 56, respectively.) Five Magnificats of the 1545 set had already been printed in 1542 with all the verses set; *see* IllM, p. 11 at back.   [105] Pr. ElúsA, 73.

monial motet, *a 6, Jubilate Deo*,[106] written for the peace conference arranged by Paul III and held in 1538 between Charles V and Francis I, the quintus appropriately sings *Gaudeamus* over and over to the notes of the Gregorian Introit, *Gaudeamus omnes*. One part again comments on the text of the other parts in another ceremonial motet, celebrating the elevation of Ippolito d'Este to the cardinalate in 1539.[107] Morales appears to have liked having one voice sing a text different from but relevant to that given to the others. In his six-part *Pater peccavi*,[108] tenor II sings the Lord's Prayer in long notes while the other voices proceed with the words of the Prodigal Son. At the beginning of *Hoc est praeceptum meum*,[109] which is mainly a motet *a 4*, a fifth voice twice invokes a saint to "pray for us." The most striking example of the type is probably the *Emendemus in melius*,[110] in which Morales combines in a single composition the Ash Wednesday response *Emendemus* and the words the priest utters during its rendition, these words—"Remember, man, that thou art dust, and into dust thou shalt return"—being assigned to the tenor, which sounds them six times. The melody of the plainsong response, present during part of the composition, is shorn of some of its melismas. The piece is starkly powerful. Another example of simultaneous use of two texts is *Andreas, Christi famulus*, in which superius II has an *ostinato* on the words *Sancte Andrea, ora pro nobis*.[111] However, it is a work with the same text in all five voices—*Lamentabatur Jacob* [111a]—that is his most celebrated motet.

Morales has a point of contact with Gombert in that his first published motets appeared, in 1541, in volumes devoted primarily to Gombert's works. However, Morales' tendency to have the voices sing fairly often in pairs and other smaller groups, rather than to keep all of them occupied most of the time, allies him more with the Josquin than with the Gombert tradition.

Morales was joined at the Papal Chapel in 1536 by Bartolomé Escobedo (born in Zamora, between 1510 and 1520; died in Segovia, c. 1563), who acted as one of the judges in the controversy between Vicentino and Lusitano (cf. p. 329). In 1554, he returned to Spain permanently (having revisited it in 1541) and became *maestro de capilla* at Segovia. Motets, Magnificats, and two Masses of his survive.[112] Other Spaniards of this period who wrote sacred music and spent time at the Holy See include Pedro Ordoñez (born in Palencia, c. 1500; died in Rome, 1550), who entered the Papal Choir in 1539; Melchor Robledo, who returned to Spain in 1569, became choirmaster at the older of the two cathedrals at Saragossa, and died in 1587; [113] and Francisco

---

[106] Opening of *pars II* pr. MitM, 1976   [107] Cf. MitE, 197f; PirH, 283.   [108] Pr. ElúsA, 52.
[109] Pr. *ibid.*, 41.   [110] Pr. HAM, 138; PedH I, 29; EsL, *Ser. I*, I, 109.
[111] See fragment in TreCM, 33.

[111a] Pr. AraH, 243; EsL, *Ser. I*, I, 119; etc.; *cf.* StevnsnC, 6, about PedH I, 40. For other works by Morales, see PedH I, 47 (= EsL, *Ser. I*, I, 127), 51 (= EsL, *Ser. I*, I, 131; BordA, *Motets* III, 80); ElúsA, 37, 45, 64, 69; MitM, 1979; AmbG V, 595; OH II, 152 (= RieM, 62). The *O vos omnes* ascribed to Morales in PedH I, 36; EsL *Ser. I*, I, 116, is by Victoria.

[112] Further on Escobedo, see ChaseM, 85; AnglLME, 357f; Grove II, 176; for exx., see AmbG V, 584; EsL, *Ser. I*, I (3 items bear his name, but 1 is by Crecquillon; see RdM XXXVI [1954], 84).   [113] Cf. ElúsA, lxxxii. 4 exx. in EsL, *Ser. I*, I; 1 in AraH, 263; 1 in ElúsA, 130.

Soto de Langa, already mentioned in Chapter 9 in connection with the five collections of *laude spirituali* edited by him in Rome. While the texts of most of these *laude* are in Italian, a few are in Spanish,[114] some of the music being by Francisco Guerrero (cf. p. 596). At Naples, Diego Ortiz (b. Toledo) was *maestro de capilla*, 1555–1570, to the viceroy, the Duke of Alba. Although more important historically in the field of instrumental music, Ortiz wrote estimable sacred music also.[115]

In 1556, when Charles V abdicated, making over the ancestral Hapsburg possessions to his brother Ferdinand I and the Spanish holdings and Burgundian inheritance to his son Philip II, the *capilla flamenca* naturally fell to the lot of the latter. While this group of singers had been attached to the person of the emperor and accompanied him regularly on his journeys, the *capilla española,* established in 1526 by his consort, Isabel of Portugal, remained permanently at Madrid. Both chapel choirs were taken over, substantially as they stood, into the household of the new king. The old prestige of the Flemish chapel continued. Among the musicians who held the post of its *maestro* and presided over the destinies of the Spanish chapel also, we find distinguished men such as Pierre de Manchicourt and George de la Hèle. Eventually, under Philip III, the Spanish chapel was united with the Flemish chapel to form the royal chapel in 1636.[115a]

Among Spanish composers who flourished about the middle of the 16th century, but who are not known to have pursued their careers in Italy, are Andres Torrentes (d. 1580 [116]), who was *maestro de capilla* at Toledo before Morales obtained the post in 1545; Bernal, a shadowy figure; [117] Rodrigo Ceballos (= Cevallos) who, ordained a priest in 1556, became *maestro* first at Cordova and, in 1561, at Granada; [118] Francisco Ceballos (brother of Rodrigo?), who was *maestro* at the Burgos Cathedral from 1535 to 1571 or 1572, when he died, and who is sometimes credited with works that seem to be Rodrigo's; [119] Andrés de Villalar, who, after an unsatisfactory intermediate incumbent, succeeded Rodrigo at Cordova, was appointed *maestro* there in 1563 and held a similar post at Zamora in 1593; [120] Bernardino de Ribera, *maestro* at Toledo in 1563; [121] Francisco de Montanos, *maestro* at Valladolid, 1547–1579, and author of the *Arte de música teórica y práctica*

---

[114] Cf. AlaS, 307ff.

[115] Exx. pr. ProsM, *Annus I*, III (10 items); IV, 283, 412; EsL, *Ser. I*, II, 191; MartiniE, 73 (= ChorP V, *livraison 6*, 40). The dates when Ortiz was *maestro* are often given otherwise than as above; but cf. IMAMI V, xv.   [115a] Cf. Pope S.

[116] This date given in AngLME, 376 (OH II, 149, gives it as 1544); a *Sanctorum meritis* pr. KrV, 22; a Magnificat pr. EsL, *Ser. I*, I, 87.

[117] Conflicting data summarized in MME VIII, 22f (text); exx. *ibid.*, 74; MorL II, 197 (cf. RieMF, 88); perhaps also EsL, *Ser. I*, I, 167.

[118] *See* further, MME VIII, 23f. Exx. of his sacred music pr. ElúsA, 138, 141 (= AraH, 266; EsL, *Ser. I*, I, 102), 144 (= EsL, *Ser. I*, I, 96), 147, 150, 154; EsL, *Ser. I*, I, 106 (cf. MME VIII, 23 [text]). For secular exx., *see* fn. 222.

[119] Ex. apparently Francisco's pr. MitM, 1975.   [120] Ex. pr. ElúsA, 134.

[121] 3 exx. pr. EsL, *Ser. I*, I.

(1587), which was regarded in Spain as the best and only complete treatise on musical composition and went through more than twelve editions by the 18th century; [122] and Juan Navarro (born in the province of Seville; died in Palencia, 1580), who in 1554, competed unsuccessfully against Francisco Guerrero for the post of *maestro* at Malaga, but held such a post successively at Salamanca, Ciudad Rodrigo, and Palencia.[123]

Spaniards in the New World

This Navarro has been confused with a homonym, born at Cadiz, who migrated to Mexico and was responsible for one of the earlier music prints brought out in the New World—a plainsong *Liber in quo quatuor Passiones Christi Domini continentur* (Mexico, 1604)—the first print, likewise a chant-book produced in Mexico, having appeared in 1556.[124] (Among the interesting contents of this publication, an Augustinian *Ordinarium,* is the no longer current *Ite missa est* that had served as the *cantus firmus* of the last section of Machaut's Mass.[124a])

The "earliest composer of church polyphony in the Western Hemisphere about whom we have definite information" is Fernando Franco, who was born near Alcántara, a few miles from the Portuguese border. He seems to have arrived in the New World c. 1554 and was active both in Guatemala and—from 1575 until his death in 1585—as *maestro de capilla* of the Cathedral in Mexico City. His surviving works include seven Magnificats and two *Salve* settings, as well as miscellaneous psalms, hymns, and responsories.[124b] Some of his music,[124c] used by missionaries in training the Indians, has text in the Nahuatl language and is the only surviving early polyphony in one of the native tongues.

Francisco Guerrero and Some Minor Figures

Back in Spain, musical activity was intense, especially, as is made clear by some of the place names mentioned, in Andalusia.

[122] Exx. pr. ElúsA, 100, 104; JulbeM, 58.
[123] Exx. pr. ElúsA, 108, 116, 119, 124; EsL, *Ser. I,* II (5 items); MartiniE I, 149, 204 (= ChorP V, *livraison 6,* 82, 104, respectively); MME VIII, 53, 83 (= PedCP III, 184), 106, 128.
[124] On the problem of identity, *see* ChaseN. (Still another Navarro—Francisco Navarro, died c. 1660—is the composer of the charming madrigal, *Enojado esta el Abril,* pr. PedCP III, 217.) About the earliest music prints in America, *see* SpellF; StevnsnMM, 70ff; about music at the Cathedral of Mexico in the 16th century, *see* SpellM.
[124a] Communication of Mrs. Péguy Lyder. The melody opens the current *O quam suavis* for Corpus Christi and Sanctus VIII.
[124b] Cf. StevnsnMM, 103; further on him, see, *ibid.,* 104ff, which includes several compositions and sections of compositions.
[124c] E.g., that pr. *ibid.,* 119, 120 (texts on 121). Several additional pieces by Franco, transcribed by S. Barwick (from whose prefatory note the opening quotation is made), have been published separately by Peer International Corporation, New York, 1952; also a piece by Franco's contemporary, Fructus del Castillo. For lists of works by other early Hispanic composers in the New World, *see* StevnsnMM, 103ff; RayJP, 113f. *See also* BarwickS.

The painter Luis de Vargas (b. Seville, 1502; d. there, 1568) was also a musician. In 1561, six years after a twenty-eight year absence in Italy, he painted, in a chapel at the Seville Cathedral, his *Retablo de la Gamba,* in two panels of which he presented angelic musicians performing a four-part *Tota pulchra es,* which is probably his own composition. In one panel, four angels are shown singing from a choir-book; in the other, one angel is represented, also provided with a choir-book, playing—presumably from the bass part (cf. p. 529)—at the organ. Vargas was a friend of Guerrero's.[125]

Francisco Guerrero was born in 1528 in Seville. He received his first instruction in music from his brother Pedro, and later was a pupil of Morales. Vincenzo Galilei, in his *Fronimo,* praises Pedro; Fuenllana published some of his music, transcribed for *vihuela,* in the *Orphénica Lyra* (cf. pp. 623f).[126] Francisco, when scarcely 15, became a choirboy at Seville under Pedro Fernandez de Castilleja. In 1546, he was appointed *maestro de capilla* at Jaén; in 1550, a singer at Seville; and, in 1554, *maestro de capilla* at Malaga, whence he returned to Seville. He spent the rest of his life in the service of its Cathedral, eventually becoming Castilleja's successor. Both by training and scene of activity, Guerrero was a more completely Spanish composer than either Morales or Victoria. Guerrero's first collection was printed in 1555 at Seville; nine more were published during his life, all containing religious works. In addition, some of his secular pieces were printed in instrumental transcriptions by Fuenllana, Daza, and Mudarra, as well as in purely vocal form. In 1556, Guerrero visited Lisbon, to present his first book of Masses to John III of Portugal. The composer's major periods of absence from Seville, on leave, were occasioned by a trip to Rome (1581–1584) and a pilgrimage to the Holy Land (1588–1589)—the latter described in his travel-book *Viaje de Jerúsalem* (1596). He died at Seville in 1599.[127]

Guerrero has been called *el cantor de María*—justifiably, since Marian compositions figure prominently among his works. His style is more tender and graceful than that of the dour Morales, but has less character. Guerrero's volume of Magnificat settings (1563) contains one in each of the eight Tones, with the even-numbered verses written in polyphony fundamentally *a 4* Unlike Morales' setting in Tone 8, Guerrero's in Tone 1 [127a] first presents

[125] Further on Vargas, *see* esp. MitE, 97ff (the motet is on p. 123f). August L. Mayer, *Die sevillaner Malerschule* (1911), Pl. 15, provides a better reproduction of the panel showing the organist-angel than appears in MitE (which includes reproductions of both panels and of the central picture); Valerian von Loga, *Die Malerei in Spanien von 14. bis 18. Jahrhundert* (1923), 99, presents a better reproduction of the panel showing the four singers.

[126] Further data in TreM, 128f; Grove II, 477; MME VIII, 25f; MitG, 22, fn.; MitM, 1980, fn.; ElúsA, liii. Two motets pr. ElúsA, 80, 83 (erroneously ascribed to Francisco on p. xxiii), 86 (erroneously ascribed to Francisco on p. xxiii and in the index). Two madrigals pr. MME VIII, 100, 112 (also pr. MorL II, 222, in Fuenllana's transcription for voice and *vihuela*).

[127] Further biographical data in MitG; MME VIII, 26ff. About early Guerrero prints, *see* PedH II, xxixff.

[127a] Pr. *ibid.,* 1.

the psalmodic formula divided among the voices. In Verses 4, 6, 8, and 10, the Tone appears in S, B, T, and A, respectively; in Verse 12, an alto II is added and sings the Tone in canon at the unison with alto I. Guerrero allows himself a certain degree of harmonic freedom: at measure 21, for example, he introduces a chord of the augmented fifth, the dissonant note entering as resolution of a suspension.

Other Marian works also show Guerrero's gentle lyricism. The text of the five-part *Ave, Virgo sanctissima* (printed, 1570) [128] is a cento, drawing on familiar songs to the Virgin. Where the words *"maris stella"* occur, a musical figure reminiscent of the *Ave maris stella* appears. At the word *"salve,"* the opening motif of the *Salve Regina* is repeated in each voice, the figure having been twice incorporated in melismas near the beginning, evidently by way of intentional preparation. There is considerable use of imitation in the piece, and the upper voices form a canon at the unison. Guerrero's *Trahe me post te, Virgo Maria* (printed, 1589) [129] opens with extensive imitation, which gradually subsides to the following calm and beautiful passage of a comparatively chordal nature:

EXAMPLE 132. Extract from *Trahe me post te, Virgo Maria*—F. Guerrero (after PedH II, 20).

This, in turn, leads into further imitation. [130]

Guerrero published during his lifetime eighteen Masses, [131] of which two are based on secular models (Janequin's *Bataille de Marignan* and Verdelot's *Dormend'un giorn'a Bai*), [131a] five on Marian themes. In a *Missa de Beata Virgine* there are—following old Seville custom—textual insertions that introduce the name of Mary into all three sections of the Kyrie. Also, Guerrero dedicated his Book II of Masses (1582) to the Virgin. Among his printed non-Marian works are two Masses for the Dead, the calm gravity of which contrasts strikingly with the somber terror of Morales' Requiem. (These Guer-

---

[128] Pr. *ibid.*, 13; ElúsA, 89; BordA, *Motets* III, 1; MitG, App.; EsL, *Ser. I*, II, 99; AraH, 273.

[129] Pr. PedH II, 18; EsL *Ser. I*, II, 105.

[130] Additional motets, etc., in VicO I, 142 (cf. fn. 149 *infra*); JulbeM (6 items; 1 = CommM XXVII, 9); PedH II, 48 (= HAM, 150; ElúsA, 94 [this is Guerrero's *Salve Regina*, a fine piece]); VI, 16; ElúsA, 86.

[131] One pr. BordA, *Messes* II, 159; another pr. EsL, *Ser. I*, II, 111. [131a] Cf. Saxton V.

rero settings contain some material in common.) An Office for the Dead [132] followed in the motet book of 1589.

Guerrero's dramatic-type Passions (printed in 1585), one each according to Matthew and John,[133] consist of somewhat chordal settings for various combinations, a 2 to a 6. In the St. Matthew Passion, one passage, which seems to be an addition to the official text—though, again, not without precedent—depicts the remorse of Peter after hearing the third cockcrow. In the passages provided for the *turba,* Guerrero introduces dissonance for expressive purposes—for example, in the one that contains the cry "Barrabas." [134]

A minor but interesting part of Guerrero's work is somewhat or completely secular. In 1589, he published a collection of *Canciones y villanescas espirituales* to Spanish texts, some of which, according to the preface, are religious parodies.[135] *Ojos claros y serenos* [135a] and *Pan divino, gracioso, sacrosancto* [135b] (originally *Prado verde y florido* [135c]) illustrate Guerrero's ability to achieve elegance with unpretentious means. Among the other pieces in this collection, *Esclarecida madre,*[135d] a version *a lo divino* of *Esclarecida Juana* (No. 163 in Medinaceli 13230; cf. p. 616), appeared also among Soto de Langa's *laude spirituali* (cf. p. 454), as did a setting [135e] of Lope de Vega's "Si tus penas no pruebo," the music of which survives likewise with the text, "Tu dorado cabello" (No. 80 in the Medinaceli MS).[136]

The Seises

One of the posts that Guerrero occupied at Seville—one in which he succeeded Castilleja—was that of *maestro de los moços* ("master of the boys"). The group of boys popularly known as the *seises* (from the Spanish word for six, *seis*), officially designated as *niños cantorcicos* ("boy choristers"), was organized at Seville in the 15th century as a result of steps taken by the dean and chapter of the cathedral, confirmed and sanctioned by Pope Eugene IV in 1439. This innovation provided for a group of six boys, under ten years of

[132] Pr. PedH II, 8. The 2 Masses are described in MitG, 69.
[133] The former pr. PedH II, 24; EsL, *Ser. I,* II, 77; the latter, *ibid.,* 90.
[134] Further about these Passions, *see* KadP, 153ff.
[135] Description and list of contents in TreBM, 521ff; pref. in PedH II, xlif.
[135a] Sacred version pr. MME VIII, 57 (text); secular version *ibid.,* 1 (music).
[135b] Pr. JulbeM, p. (9).
[135c] Pr. PedCP III, 71; MME VIII, 104 (cf. *ibid.,* 48 [text]); also, in Daza's voice and *vihuela* transcr., in MorL II, 242; MitG, 88; MitM, 2004.
[135d] *Ibid.,* 1987. [135e] Pr. BalT, 15; PedCP III, 74.
[136] Other pieces pr. *ibid.,* 77; JulbeM (9 compositions); MorL II, 246 (in Daza's voice and *vihuela* transcr.; cf. TreBM, 526). 4 secular pieces, unassociated with the *Canciones . . . espirituales* and ascribed in Medinaceli 13230 to "Guerrero" (Francisco? Pedro?) are pr. MME VIII, 25, 27, 29, 31. Another madrigal by Francisco, in Mudarra's voice and *vihuela* transcr., pr. MorL II, 114; MME VII, 94 (cf. MME VIII, 34 [text]; MorL II, xlviii).

age, to be set apart from the main body of choristers, with the duty of reciting and singing certain prayers for the Divine Office. They also performed ceremonial dances on particular feast days, notably that of Corpus Christi.

The Master of the Boys had the responsibility of lodging the *seises* in his home, of educating them and instructing them in music, as well as of feeding and clothing them. This last was a rather troublesome and expensive item, for the *seises* wore elaborate costumes, which had to be frequently altered or renovated. Guerrero gave much of his money away to the poor, hence there were complaints that he did not spend enough to keep the *seises* dressed properly.[137]

It is difficult to determine exactly at what date the dances of the *seises* were introduced. The dances are first mentioned in writing in the cathedral archives under date of 1508, but they are then referred to as an established practice. The custom of religious dancing was very prevalent in Spain (cf. p. 585), and particularly at Seville. In 1264, a bull of Urban IV authorized the celebration of Corpus Christi "with songs and other demonstrations of joyfulness," and in Seville this was taken to justify all kinds of elaborate processions, masques, and dances, in which the religious guilds of the city took part. In 1487, there is mention of sword dances as figuring in the celebration of Corpus Christi in Seville. The dances of the *seises* undoubtedly developed from this popular tradition, but it is to be noted that from the beginning the boys danced without masks and without the accompaniment of popular instruments such as the *tamboril* (side drum). Thus the more solemn religious character of their dancing was stressed from the outset. It is curious that the number of dancers is not known ever to have actually been six. At first there were eight, then eleven, twelve, and sixteen, until 1565, when the number was fixed at ten. The dances—which appear to have originated prior to 1439—were performed before the Blessed Sacrament. The dancing of the *seises* was reformed by Cardinal Palafox in 1699, and suppressed in 1780, but later restored.

Toledo had antedated Seville by centuries in instituting a group of *seises*. Here their history apparently goes back to Visigothic times, and it is undoubtedly Toledo that set the precedent for other places to follow. In the Mozarabic rite, the role of the boys was an active one, including the performance of the Song and Dance of the Sybil and the Dance of the Shepherds; and the efforts of Cardinal Ximenez de Cisneros to revive the old rite late in the 15th century [137a] paved the way for the establishment of a school for the Toledan *seises* by Cardinal Silíceo in 1545.[138]

[137] For a detailed list of the duties assigned to Guerrero as master of the *seises*, see RosaS, 82.
[137a] Cf. ReMMA, 112.

[138] Further about the *seises* at Toledo, particularly in recent times, see MoraledaS (photographs of dancers, facing pp. 28, 30; Mozarabic dance figures, p. 72). About the *seises*, see also the article by Juan José Bueno in *La Illustración Católica* (Madrid, Feb. 28, 1880).

Portuguese Polyphony

John III of Portugal, whom we have found Guerrero visiting in 1556, was a liberal patron of music, and the art prospered during his reign (1521–1557). The cosmopolitan Portuguese nobleman, friend of Erasmus, Damião de Góis (Goes; 1502–1574), composed sufficiently well to be represented by a motet in the *Dodecachordon*.[139] Lusitano—who, to be sure, is best known for his career at Rome—was not only a theorist (cf. p. 329), but a composer. André de Escobar,[140] who emigrated to the Indies in 1550, wrote a method for the shawm. Heliodoro de Paiva (d. 1552), a canon at the Monastery of Santa Cruz in the university town of Coimbra, has left us Masses, motets, and Magnificats.[141] Music was intensively cultivated at the monastery, and a "school" of composition may be said to have existed there.[141a] Such a "school" flourished, on a larger scale, in the province of Alentejo, its headspring being at Evora, which city soon exerted its influence on Elvas and Portalegre and later, outside the province, on Lisbon. Villaviciosa, near Evora, was also a productive center, but showed a certain independence. Gines de Morata, by whom we have sacred works and some excellent secular ones,[141b] is the earliest known director of music there in the chapel of the Dukes of Braganza.[141c] Antonio Pinheiro (d. 1617), a pupil of Guerrero's, was a later director. At Evora,[142] the leading early figure is Manuel Mendes (d. 1605),[142a] whose pupils included Felipe de Magalhães[143] and Duarte Lôbo (born c. 1560–1565; died 1646).[144] They, in turn, taught many musicians—Magalhães, for example, was the principal instructor of the Spanish-born Estêvão Lopes Morago, choirmaster of the Cathedral of Viseu (northeast of Coimbra) from 1599 to 1628.[144a] The activity of several of these younger men takes us well into the latter part of the 17th century. A focal point for the launching of this activity was the court of the music-loving king, John IV (1604–1656), who wrote music himself, defended Palestrina in print, and assembled a remarkable library (destroyed in the Lisbon earthquake of 1755).[145] Among the promi-

[139] Pr. PubAPTM XVI, 211; HawkH II, 438. For biographical data, *see* SampaA II; LupP, 101.
[140] For biographical data, *see* VasM I, 95f.   [141] Cf. LupP, 103f; MME I, 119f (text).
[141a] Cf. SampaC; LupP, 103ff.   [141b] Exx. in MME VIII, 57, 63, 66, 72, 78, 91, 117.
[141c] Cf. JoaP, 73; MME VIII, 25 (text).
[142] For a discussion of its school as a whole, *see* FreitC.
[142a] Biographical data, etc., in LupP, 106; VieiM II, 82f; VasM I, 266; Mendes' *Missa de Feria*, published by Manuel Joaquim, 1942; his five-part *Asperges* pr. by Joaquim (with 3 added parts by Manuel Soares [d. 1756], undistinguished from the original 5) as a supplement in *Música* (*Revista dos Alunos do Conservatório de Música do Pôrto*) for Jan. 1945.
[143] Biographical data, etc., in LupP, 108; VieiM II, 57ff; VasM I, 220ff.
[144] A motet and 2 Masses pr. SanP I, 38, 40, 57; 16 Magnificats in LôboC I. Biographical data in LupP, 106f; VieiM II, 39ff; VasM I, 199ff. (Lôbo did not, as sometimes claimed, live to the age of 103.)
[144a] Biographical data, etc., in JoaM, which includes the motet *Intellige;* 3 other motets pr. JoaN, App.; a *Te Deum* pr. JoaU, Supp.
[145] His *Crux fidelis* pr. LückS II, 45; SanP I, 35; etc.; *Adjuva nos* pr. *ibid.*, 33. His tract defending Palestrina's *Missa Panis quem ego dabo* was pr. at Lisbon in 1654. The first part of a

nent composers at his court was Manuel Cardoso (c. 1569–1650),[146] who was born near Elvas, studied at Evora, but made his career at Lisbon. His works include a *Tantum ergo* that is a setting in *cantus-firmus* style of the Spanish *Pange lingua;* the melody is in the superius, but the altus is the highest-sounding voice most of the time.[147] The influence of Palestrina exerted itself upon these later Portuguese musicians—who, in the mid-17th century still wrote in 16th-century style—as it had done upon the greatest of the Iberian composers of the Renaissance, Victoria.

Victoria

Born at or near Ávila in 1548,[147a] Tomás Luis de Victoria (Italian form, Vittoria) probably studied under Escobedo at Segovia. In 1565, Victoria received a grant from Philip II, apparently for further study at Rome. There he entered the Jesuit Collegium Germanicum, a seminary founded by St. Ignatius Loyola to combat Lutheranism, and perhaps studied under Palestrina, who was *maestro di cappella* at the nearby Roman Seminary. In 1564, Victoria left the Collegium Germanicum to become choirmaster and organist at other churches in Rome, succeeding Palestrina in his post at the Collegium Romanum in 1571. Victoria's first collection of printed works, including most of his motet production, appeared at Venice in 1572, with a dedication to Cardinal Otto von Truchsess von Waldburg (cf. p. 451). For a time the German and Roman seminaries were joined, but in 1573 Gregory XIII reorganized the Collegium Germanicum as a separate institution, with Victoria as *maestro di cappella.* For the ceremony of separation, Victoria wrote a setting of *Super flumina,*[148] for two antiphonal choruses *a 4* and organ; and it was performed, by torchlight, with the collaboration of singers from the Sistine Chapel. In 1575, Victoria was ordained a priest. The following year, he published his second collection. He resigned from the German seminary in 1578 and became a resident priest at the Church of San Girolamo della Carità (cf. p. 452). Two new collections of his works were published in 1581, one in 1583, two in 1585, and one each in 1592, 1600 (in part a reprint), and 1605, the last two at Madrid, the others at Rome. One of the 1585 prints, the *Motecta festorum totius anni,* includes two pieces by Guerrero and one by Soriano.[149]

---

catalogue of the library was pr. at Lisbon in 1649, and has been reprinted in VasJ. For further biographical data, *see* VasE.

[146] Biographical data in LupP, 107f; VasM I, 35ff.

[147] Pr. SanP I, 77. Other works by Cardoso pr. ProsM, *Annus I,* II, 12, 98 (= BordA, Motets, III, 187; SanP I, 75); SanP I, 78, 96 (a *Missa Filipina, a 4* in which one voice or another sings "*Philippus quartus*" all the way through, the work having been written for Philip IV of Spain). Further about Portuguese polyphony of the period, *see* pref. of SanP I (in Portuguese, French, and German); LupP.   [147a] *See* HernánV.

[148] Pr. VicO VII, 53; cf. VIII, xix; ColV, 57ff.

[149] One of the Guerrero pieces is pr. as Victoria's in VicO I, 142. I am indebted to Mr. Niles Saxton for calling this to my attention.

Highly regarded in Italy, Victoria, like Morales, undoubtedly might have remained there had he so chosen. It is interesting, however, that, unlike such masters as Willaert and Lassus, the two great Spaniards wished to return to their native soil. With such a purpose, Victoria entered the service of the Empress Maria, sister of Philip II and widow of Maximilian II, and accompanied her to Madrid, where in 1584 she and her daughter Margaret entered the convent of Descalzas Reales. Serving at various times as priest, choirmaster, and organist at the convent, Victoria remained there from 1586 to his death in 1611.[150]

Ancina (cf. p. 454) in some complimentary epigrams appended to the 1585 motet collection says that Victoria was known "even to the Indies," a statement that is no mere rhetorical flourish. At any rate, the composer did have a debtor in Lima, Peru.[151] His works were printed over a wide area during his lifetime: in Italy, Germany, and Spain.[152]

Although Victoria—unlike most of his fellow members of the Roman school, including Palestrina—wrote no madrigals, his motets show traces of madrigalism. In *Quam pulchri sunt* the word *"gressus,"* [153] referring to the dainty steps of the Virgin, is set (in the original time-values) to quarternotes. In *Ascendens Christus in altum* the opening theme ascends through the compass of an octave, and in *Descendit angelus domini* [154] it descends slowly by thirds. In *Nigra sum sed formosa* two voices have a remarkable ascending scale-passage covering a ninth on the plea to the beloved to rise up, *"surge."* [155] Wherever the text introduces the idea of concerted action, e.g., at the word *"omnes"* in *Ecce Dominus veniet,*[156] all the parts usually move in uniform rhythm. In the six-part *Benedicta sit sancta Trinitas,*[157] the idea of the Trinity is first presented by three parts only and that of unity by basically chordal writing. In *Vere languores,*[158] Victoria sets the word *"dolores"* four times to a melodic interval of a minor second, and once to a broken minor triad descending; a descending triad (usually, in Victoria, a symbol of pain) appears on the word *"portavit,"* referring to Christ's bearing the sorrows of the world. The motet *Cum beatus Ignatius* [159] is even more remarkably descriptive, with its representation of the martyr being rent by wild beasts.

Gregorian Chant is made to serve the purposes of text delineation in

---

[150] For further biographical data, see VicO VIII; CasV; ColV; MitE, 229ff; MarieV; TreV; PedT; ChaseM, 79ff; Grove V, 495ff.

[151] See VicO VIII, lxxxv.

[152] Victoria's contract with his printer in Madrid for a collection that appeared in 1600 provided, among other things, for a regular edition of 200 copies; the printer might prepare 100 more and sell them at a later date; the composer was to pay 2,500 reales; cf. VicO VIII, lxxxv.

[153] Pr. VicO I, 6; cf. MayV, 45. VicO, the complete edition of Victoria, is widely available, and all citations here will refer only to it. Attention, however, is called to the numerous reprints of Victoria in ProsM, EsL, CasR, JulbeM, etc.

[154] Pr. VicO I, 53, 77, respectively.   [155] Ibid., 138.   [156] Ibid., 67; cf. MayV, 124f.

[157] Pr. VicO I, 118; cf. LeiG, 374; MayV, 118, 125.

[158] Pr. VicO I, 24; cf. LeiG, 374; MayV, 42ff, 138.   [159] Pr. VicO I, 72; cf. MayV, 57.

Iste Sanctus,[160] in which the tenor, after participating in the free polyphony of the opening, quotes plainsong on the Latin for the words: "for he was founded upon a sure rock," the plainsong being written out in long, sustained notes, with the Gregorian "barbarism" on *"erat"* eliminated. Victoria, however, makes only occasional use of the Chant in his motets: there is but a suggestion of the plainsong in *Ecce sacerdos* and in the settings *a 8* and *a 4* of the *Ave Maria.*[161]

In addition to melodic curves and leaps characteristic of the Gregorian and Palestrina styles, more abrupt and vigorous lines, with leaps that neither of those styles would allow, make their appearance in Victoria, particularly in his early works.[162] For example, the leap of a major sixth occurs in the motet, *Vadam et circuibo.*[163] By using it, the composer simultaneously avoids parallel octaves and fifths and delineates the term of endearment *"dilectum meum."* Also he occasionally employs the ascending diminished fourth, e.g., at the words asking comfort for those who grieve, *"refove flebiles,"* in the motet, *Sancta Maria, succurre* (*see* Ex. 133*a;* note also the oblique cross-relation). As with Palestrina and other composers, the octave leap is used not only in the course of normal melodic writing, but to heighten a special effect. At the opening of *Veni, sponsa Christi,* for instance, the upward leaps of an octave in two voices are undoubtedly occasioned by the vocative, *"sponsa"* (see Ex. 133*b*).[164] Like some of Victoria's other motets, this one begins with imitation in pairs, such as the composer applied more extensively in his Masses. The superius enters first with a theme reminiscent of the plainsong; the altus then enters with a different one, and the pair of themes is imitated in the other two voices. The words and plainsong return at the end of the piece, all voices making the octave leap on the final *"veni, sponsa."*

EXAMPLE 133. (*a*) Extract from *Sancta Maria, succurre*—Victoria (VicO I, 19), and (*b*) Opening and close of *Veni, sponsa Christi*—Victoria (VicO I, 50f).

---

160 Pr. VicO I, 43; cf. LeiG, 375f; ColV, 181.
161 Pr., respectively, in VicO I, 46, 146; VIII, 4. The basis on which the 4-part *Ave Maria* is attributed to Victoria, while not conclusive, is fairly reliable; cf. VicO VIII, xcvii. The *Jesu dulcis memoria* and *Missa dominicalis,* however, current under Victoria's name, are almost certainly not his; cf. MayV, 144ff; CasMD.
162 Statistics and exx. (based mainly on the Masses) in MayV, 15f, 19f.
163 Pr. VicO I, 97; cf. MayV, 12f.
164 Further on Victoria's use of the octave leap, *see ibid.,* 19ff, 71ff.

This dramatic *Veni, sponsa Christi* contrasts strikingly with Palestrina's, in which all the voices have the same theme and in which the mood is one of quiet exaltation. The microrhythms in Victoria's motet are flexible and varied, combining duple, triple, and compound groups within the prevailing macrorhythm.[165] Successive and contrapuntal rhythmic combinations lend elasticity and interest also to the setting of the words *"et admirabile sacramentum"* in the exquisite Christmas motet, *O magnum mysterium*.[166]

When opening with imitation, Victoria, like Palestrina, usually contrived, after enough voices had entered, to have them form a full triad, even renouncing the imitation in a voice, if necessary, to secure completeness, e.g., in the motet *Resplenduit facies eius*.[167] In a few motets (e.g., *Doctor bonus* and *Ecce sacerdos* [168]), the third voice enters against a suspension in one or both of the upper voices to form a $^6_4$ chord. As in Palestrina, it is common for the first note in each voice to be a tone that will appear in the final chord; thus, in *Ecce sacerdos*, the voices enter and conclude on either G or D.

Of Victoria's motets *a 5*, three employ canon at the unison in the two topmost voices. Among the twelve motets *a 6*, moreover, *Trahe me post te* [169] (the text of which suggests that one voice should draw the others after it) has strict double canon throughout.

In *Domine, non sum dignus*,[170] a setting of words that paraphrase those of the Centurion who entreated Jesus to heal his ailing servant—words that are uttered by the Priest before receiving Communion and again before distributing it—Victoria repeats the Latin for "that thou shouldst enter under my roof." The music for the repetition is a harmonic sequence, a third lower, of the first presentation. But, while Victoria retains the outer parts in the se-

---

[165] Further about this motet, *see* MayV, 103f; LeiG, 373; AmbG IV, 81.
[166] Pr. VicO I, 11.
[167] *Ibid.*, 88; cf. MayV, 106, 119.
[168] Pr. VicO I, 3, 46, respectively.
[169] *Ibid.*, 140.
[170] *Ibid.*, 39; cf. MayV, 69f.

quential repetition, he writes new inner voices within the limits of the harmonic framework.

The four-part *Duo Seraphim* [171]—with its *pars II* beginning *Tres sunt*—is remarkable for both text delineation and formal plan. As the first words of each part suggest, the opening of *pars I* is sung by two voices, that of *pars II* by three. Toward the end of the latter passage, at the words affirming the unity of the Trinity, the meter changes for four measures from duple to triple. The concluding *"Sanctus"* portion is again in duple meter, and *a 4*. It repeats, with some changes, the material of the corresponding portion of *pars I*, but with an exchange of melodic lines among the voices—a procedure that is often adopted by Victoria where there is repetition at the ends of *partes*.

The eighteen responsories *a 4* [172] from Victoria's Office for Holy Week are, of course, in either *aBcB* or *ABcBAB* form (cf. p. 491). He consistently reduces the number of voices in section *c*. While, in each piece, the cadences of the four sections are either all on the final, or some on the final and some on the dominant or subdominant, he obtains variety by giving certain cadences a Phrygian structure, although the prevailing mode is not Phrygian. Thus, the Dorian mode being transposed, *Judas mercator* has a normal D-cadence for section *a*, a normal G-cadence for *B*, and a Phrygian cadence on D for *c*. The powerful *Caligaverunt oculi mei* employs the same cadence material, but reverses the positions of the G- and D-cadences. The sorrow voiced in the text is expressed by numerous minor seconds and even by degree-inflection, rare in Victoria. In *Tamquam ad latronem*, the composer has the Phrygian cadence on D in section *c*, but the G-cadence in both *a* and *B*. On the words *"ad crucifigendum,"* the altus descends a ninth scalewise. (Word-painting in *Unus ex discipulis* takes the conventional form of having the first word sung by a single part; the other voices join in only on *"ex."*) The *Tenebrae factae sunt* has Phrygian D-cadences in both *a* and *c*, with a G-cadence on *B*. The highly dramatic character of this responsory is partly due to the rising leap of a minor sixth—still rare at this time—present in three voices in the opening point of imitation. Minor seconds are again expressive of grief, as they are in *O vos omnes*. A presumably earlier setting [173] of this text, sometimes ascribed to Morales (cf. p. 591, fn. 111) but included in Victoria's book of 1572, is composed *a 4* throughout. Here the music—which may be described as a veritable fantasy on the minor second—provides the words of Jeremiah with a setting steeped in the mood of lamentation. The *Sepulto Domino* ends its *B* section with a plagal extension of a polyphonically veiled perfect cadence, the third of the subdominant being lowered. (Since the minor third of the triad on the final is to be raised after the plagal cadence, Victoria does not raise it after the perfect cadence.) Plagal extensions at the close, with and without

---

[171] Pr. VicO I, 36; cf. MayV, 126.   [172] Pr. VicO V, 135ff, 160ff, 188ff.   [173] *Ibid.*, I, 27.

the lowered third, are so common in Victoria that they constitute an important feature of his style.

Also in the Office for Holy Week are Victoria's two Passions, both of the dramatic type. Performed in the Sistine Chapel during Holy Week for well over three hundred years, these Passions have probably achieved greater distinction than any other polyphonic settings of the Latin words. Included in the Office likewise is a setting of the *Improperia* for Good Friday,[174] which, unlike that of Palestrina, is to be performed with alternation of plainsong and polyphony.

In the thirty-two hymns *a 4* in the *Hymni totius anni* (1581),[175] Victoria varies the settings from one polyphonically treated stanza to another, but, unlike Palestrina, he allows the odd-numbered stanzas to be sung in plainsong and writes polyphony for the even-numbered ones. His music is of a more intimate character than Palestrina's, no stanza being set for a larger number of parts than four. Wherever the alternation permits three or more stanzas to be clothed in a polyphonic dress, Victoria varies the predominantly four-part writing by setting one of the central stanzas *a 3*. (For the central stanza of *Christe Redemptor . . . Ex Patre* he provides alternative settings *a 3* and *a 4*.) *Ad coenam Agni providi* and *Tristes erant apostoli* are written on the same plainsong,[175a] and Victoria uses the same setting for the closing *Gloria tibi* stanza, which is common to both texts. (The stanzas of *Tristes* constitute a portion of the hymn text, *Aurora lucis rutilat*. The complete hymn is divisible either into three *partes* or—in English practice—into two. In the former division, *pars II* opens with *Tristes;* in the latter division, with the next stanza, which begins with the words *"Sermone blando."* [175b]) The poem of the *Pange lingua* is supplied with two settings, one based on the familiar melody of the Roman rite and the other—a splendid piece, which includes the words *"More Hispano"* in its title—on the local Spanish melody.[176] The refinement of Victoria's art is favorably shown in the different settings he evolves for a single melody.

Victoria's output includes various works for two or three four-part antiphonal choruses with organ and one for antiphonal four- and five-part choruses with organ.[177] The instrument is always assigned a reduction of the music sung by chorus I and is silent when that chorus rests. Possibly chorus II or III was accompanied by other instrumental resources, but, in conjecturing on the

---

[174] Pr. *ibid.*, V, 113, 170, 174, respectively. About the Passions, *see* KadP, 151ff.

[175] All pr. VicO V.

[175a] Cf. Chap. 9, fn. 79.

[175b] Cf. Ancient & Modern, 198 (the melody on p. 197 is the variant English form). The *Aurora lucis* in AntiphonaleM, 455, is *pars I* in the tripartite division.

[176] The music of the last stanza is widely known in a strophic adaptation that sets to it the penultimate stanza (*Tantum ergo*) as well as the last one.

[177] Pr. VicO I, 146, 153; III, 81, 95; IV, 72, 99; VI, 1, 26, 59; most of VII.

subject, one should remember that the actual prints provide music only for the single organ, as described.[178] Victoria's antiphonal choruses are often both SATB groups; where there is contrast, it is never violent. (Varied groupings include SSAB with SATB; SSABar with SATB; etc.) Each of the four great Marian antiphons is represented by a setting for antiphonal choirs—as well as by settings *a 5*, the *Salve Regina* by two of them and also by a setting *a 6*. One of the settings *a 5* is antiphonal also in the sense that it alternates polyphony and plainsong. Of the three sequences that Victoria set antiphonally, the *Veni, Sancte Spiritus* may be singled out as a felicitous example of variation-chain writing.

Among Victoria's compositions for antiphonal choruses and organ are two settings of the Magnificat published in 1600—one *Primi toni* for two, the other *Sexti toni* for three choruses *a 4*. Both settings include all verses, and differentiate sharply among the sonorities for each verse.

In addition to these two pieces, Victoria wrote sixteen Magnificat settings [179]—eight beginning with *Anima mea* and including only the odd-numbered verses, eight beginning with *Et exsultavit* and including only the even-numbered ones. Of these sixteen, six were in print by 1576, and the rest by 1581. There is considerable variety among the verses within any one of these settings: the Tone may appear in any voice, or it may be modified. The number of parts changes for various verses: the first few are *a 4*, a verse toward the middle of the work is usually *a 3*, and the last verse is often *a 5* or *a 6*, with extensive use of canon. The *Magnificat quinti toni* beginning *Et exsultavit* opens with imitation in pairs: the superius and tenor sing the Tone, while the altus and bass sing a countertheme containing an exultant run of a seventh in quarter-notes (original values). Verse 4 opens with imitation of the first three notes of the Tone in all voices—an ascending broken major triad, which in Victoria (as elsewhere) usually connotes joy. For the last verse, this melodic figure is set for six voices related to each other in two groups of three: the two cantus sing the Tone in canon, imitated by the tenor, while the two alti and bass sing a countertheme derived by diminution from the opening of the other three voices.

We have twenty Masses by Victoria, of which eleven are parody Masses on motets of his own. Composing on a secular model is almost completely avoided. There is not even a *L'Homme armé* Mass.

Of Victoria's Masses based on plainsong, the *Missa Ave maris stella* would seem, on the basis of internal evidence, to be the earliest: stylistically, it is in spots rather archaic for a work printed in 1576.[180] The *Missa de Beata Virgine* [181] is, like Morales', based on the normal selection of plainsong melodies;

[178] *See* further about the instrumental accompaniment *ibid.*, I, ixff; VIII, lif; KinO, 201.
[179] All pr. VicO III.   [180] Cf. WagG, 422ff; the Mass pr. VicO II, 1.   [181] Pr. *ibid.*, 93.

but, dating as it does from after the Council of Trent, it omits the old Marian tropes in the Gloria.

Among the parody Masses on Victoria's own works, the *Missa O magnum mysterium* [182] borrows sparingly from its prototype: it draws on the beginning of the Christmas motet for the opening of the Kyrie and incorporates, in Kyrie II and Gloria, the motif from the motet for the text unit *"jacentem in praesepio."* The Credo, at the words *"Et resurrexit tertia die,"* illustrates the presence of madrigalian touches in Victoria's Masses: at this point the meter suddenly becomes ternary and only three of the four voices sing *"tertia die."* The Sanctus begins with material from the opening of the motet neatly reworked. In the motet all four voices use the same melody in imitation, but in the Sanctus changes are made that produce paired imitation on two themes. After the first two notes (those of the motet theme in diminution), the upper voices of the two pairs imitate a fragment drawn from the free counterpoint of the motet superius. The lower voices of the pairs begin with an exact quotation from the motet theme, but go on with notes from measure 15f of the motet bass. The time-intervals are reduced in the Sanctus, both between the voices of each pair and between the pairs themselves (*see* Ex. 134*a*). A fifth voice, in canon with the superius, is added in the Agnus, for which portion of the Mass, however, only one setting is provided. The whole work is concise and avoids elaboration; no doubt it shows Victoria influenced by the French Mass style. It is among his best works, as is the four-part *Missa O quam gloriosum*,[183] in which the parodying of the motet is almost as interesting for what it omits as for what it appropriates. The motet opens with a simple but powerful "written-in" *crescendo*, but this fine passage is not drawn upon in the larger work, apparently because Victoria's deeply devotional spirit regarded it as too striking to be suitable for the Mass. However, he reworks other portions of the motet in what is by no means a perfunctory transfer of material from one composition to another.[184] The six-part *Missa Vidi speciosam*,[185] also one of Victoria's best, is a notable illustration of his free handling of motet themes in Masses. Among the many felicitous passages is the opening of the *Hosanna*, where the four-part music for *"Et sicut dies verni"* in the motet is presented twice, each time in a different vocal "orchestration" (neither being quite the same as that of the model), and where a related passage *a 6* follows, introducing a snatch of diminution in the bass, and various other kinds of alterations—rhythmic and intervallic—, although the basic resemblance remains quite easily perceptible.

[182] Pr. *ibid.*, 69.
[183] Pr. *ibid.*, 56.
[184] For an analysis, *see* MayV, 82f. *See also* EB XV, 24f, 851f.
[185] Pr. VicO IV, 56.

EXAMPLE 134. Illustrations of Victoria's parody Mass technique: (*a*) Openings of his motet *O magnum mysterium* and of the *Sanctus* of the Mass based on it (after VicO I, 11, and II, 77), (*b*) Extract from the motet *Vidi speciosam* and opening of the *Hosanna* of the Mass based on it (after VicO I, 113, and IV, 70).

The Masses *Salve Regina, Alma Redemptoris Mater,* and *Ave Regina,*[186] all for two four-part choruses with organ, are not based directly on the simi-

[186] Pr. *ibid.,* IV, 72, 99, and VI, 1, respectively.

larly named plainsong melodies, but mainly on Victoria's own organ-accom-
panied antiphon settings *a 8,*[187] in which the themes derive from those of the
Chant; in addition, each Mass, in its sections for fewer voices (e.g., the *Christe*
and *Benedictus*), draws upon one of the settings he had made for a smaller
combination.[188] The four-part *Missa Quam pulchri sunt* [189] adds a tenor II
for the Agnus I (= II)—which sings in canon with the tenor I—and a sixth
voice for the Agnus III; the five-part *Missa Trahe me post te* [190] adds one
voice for its single Agnus. Both six-part sections contain double canons *a 2,*
that in the latter Mass being substantially the same as the one in the model.
The five-part *Missa Ascendens Christus,*[191] still another Mass based on a
Victoria motet, also has only one Agnus, again *a 6,* but this one embodies a
single canon *a 3.* Victoria, however, usually writes his canons discreetly, "without any parade of unnecessary ingenuity. They are mostly canons in unison or
at the octave." [192] The *Missa quarti toni* [193] incorporates some material from
Victoria's motet *Senex puerum portabat* [194] but, if it is to be regarded as a
parody Mass at all, may be termed only a very free one.[194a]

Victoria's reverence for Palestrina is reflected in his *Missa Surge propera,*[195]
since this is a parody of the Roman master's similarly entitled motet *a 4* (cf.
p. 465). The *Missa Simile est regnum coelorum* [196] is based on Guerrero's
motet of like name, contained in that composer's collection of 1570. This Mass
a 4 introduces four additional voices in the final Agnus—a quadruple canon.
For his brilliant six-part *Missa Gaudeamus,* Victoria draws on Morales'
Jubilate Deo, the title of the Mass deriving from the plainsong *ostinato* in
Morales' quintus (cf. p. 591).[197] The *Missa pro victoria* (1600),[198] *a 9* (two
SATB choirs with an additional S) and organ, is of special interest in view
of the composer's usual avoidance of secular music, since it is based on Janequin's *La Guerre.*[198a] The Mass is in the baroque style that was taking form
in Venice. Victoria, however, does not write as convincingly in the new style
as do the Venetians or as he himself composes in his earlier Roman manner.
The tendency, already present in his previous works, to write chordally, with
many repeated notes and short time-values,[199] is here very much in evidence,
undoubtedly owing in part to the nature of the model. The quality of mysti-
cism which some writers find particularly typical of Victoria [200] is conspicuously absent from this Mass. The title suggests that it commemorates an actual

[187] Of his 4 *Salve Regina* settings, the one *a 8* is pr. *ibid.,* VII, 120. The other antiphon settings
are pr. *ibid.,* 73, 85.   [188] Those used are pr. *ibid.,* VII, 112, 68, 81, respectively.
   [189] Pr. *ibid.,* II, 38.   [190] II, 145.   [191] II, 162.   [192] Grove V, 498.
   [193] Pr. VicO II, 81.   [194] Pr. *ibid.,* I, 17; cf. MayV, 84f.
   [194a] The remaining true parody Masses on Victoria's own motets are those on *Dum complerentur* (model: VicO I, 59; Mass: IV, 29) and *Laetatus sum* (model: *ibid.,* VII, 27; Mass: VI,
59). Further about this group of Masses, *see* SaxtonV; MayV, 82ff; WagG, 427f.
   [195] Pr. VicO II, 119.   [196] *Ibid.,* 21.
   [197] *Ibid.,* IV, 1. (The portion of the motet pr. MitM, 1976, is reworked in the *Et incarnatus.*)
The relationship between this Mass and its model, as well as that between the *Missa Simile* and
the Guerrero motet, is pointed out in SaxtonV.   [198] Pr. VicO VI, 26.
   [198a] As pointed out to me by Mr. Arnold Hartmann.
   [199] Cf. MayV, 46.   [200] *See* esp. ColM.

military victory; but Philip III, to whom it was dedicated, achieved few victories, and on the basis of certain portions of the text especially stressed in this setting, it has been suggested [201] that the work was a prayer *for* victory.

Victoria's "swan song," as he himself termed it, was his six-voice *Officium defunctorum,*[202] written for the funeral of the Empress Maria in 1603 and published at Madrid in 1605, with a dedication to the Princess Margaret. In 1583, he had published a four-voice *Missa pro defunctis* (including the Responsory for the Absolution, *Libera me*) [203] with the plainsong in the superius. For the *Officium,* he eliminated some of the melismas from the plainsong and assigned it to superius II throughout. Several sections of the later work draw on the corresponding portions of the earlier one. In the *Libera me,* the section *a 3, Tremens factus sum,* is a literal quotation. At the words *"Requiem aeternam"* in the newer *Libera,* the long-sustained chords, held by all voices, delineate eternal rest more clearly than does the imitative introduction of that passage in the earlier work. The ensuing Lesson is strictly chordal and written *a 4,* bringing the whole composition to a tranquil close. This is among the finest of Victoria's works.

Though, compared to a universal genius like Lassus, Victoria seems to have few strings to his lyre, he works with such perfection within his limited range that he must be considered one of the great masters of the Late Renaissance.

Contemporaries of Victoria in the Field of Sacred Polyphony

Contemporary with Victoria, also a priest and active at Rome, was Fernando de las Infantas (born in Cordova, 1534; died c. 1608). He early devoted himself to sacred music under the protection of Charles V, on whose death he wrote a funeral motet. About 1571, he went to Italy to secure publication of his works, apparently with a subvention from Philip II. Learning of the revision of the Gradual that had been commissioned, Infantas protested to Philip II and Gregory XIII against the proposed alteration of the Chant; [204] the Pope recalled the commission. In 1578–1579, Scotto, in Venice, published four collections by Infantas. The composer returned to Spain c. 1597.[205]

Of Infantas' 189 published pieces, most are based on the Chant. On the victory of Lepanto he composed a *Cantemus Domino,* in which the plainsong is repeated throughout in the antiquated tenor-motet manner.[206] A commenting tenor is to be found in his motet in honor of the victory over the Turks at Melilla in 1565. In the six-voice *Victimae paschali,*[207] the plainsong permeates all the parts; the lower voices ask the question *"Dic nobis . . . ?"* and Mary's reply is given by the higher ones. Like earlier Netherlandish composers, Infantas used canon extensively. In his six-part *Domine ostende nobis*

---

[201] In Grove V, 500.   [202] Pr. VicO VI, 124.
[203] Pr. *ibid.,* VI, 102.   [204] Letters pr. in MitI, 46ff; MolT I, 277ff.
[205] Further biographical data in MitI, 13ff.
[206] Of his 88 motets in the first 3 collections, no fewer than 10 are tenor motets; cf. MitI, 64f, 69, 73ff.   [207] Pr. EsL, *Ser. I,* II, 175; DehnS, *Lieferung 5,* 6.

Patrem,[208] he has canon *a 2*, evidently for symbolic reasons, at the words *"Qui ego in Patre et Pater in me."* His real canonic tour de force appears in his *Plura modulatione genera* (1579), a volume of 100 contrapuntal compositions on the plainsong *Laudate Dominum*, for two to eight voices.[209] One of the pieces *a 2*, a puzzle canon, shows skilful use of inversion.

EXAMPLE 135. Opening of Mirror Canon on *Laudate Dominum*—Las Infantas (from MitI, 124).

Some of the conservative tendencies noted in Infantas are present also in Juan de Esquivel, *maestro* at Salamanca. Canon appears often in his Masses (1608), which make much use of the old *cantus-firmus* technique. In two, based on plainsong, the original text appears in one or more of the voices in certain movements. His hexachord Mass *a 8* recalls Palestrina's *a 6*, and his *Batalla* Mass *a 6* seems, like Victoria's *Missa pro victoria*, to be related to Janequin's *La Guerre*.[209a] Unusual treatment is accorded the Agnus, which opens *a 3*, is *a 8* or *a 9* by the middle of the movement, and *a 12* at the end. Esquivel's motets, *a 4* to *a 8* were published at Salamanca in 1612; he also wrote hymns and Magnificat settings.[210]

Also primarily a composer of church music, Juan Ginés Perez (b. Orihuela, 1548; d. there, 1612) was for a time *maestro* at Valencia. His works show a fondness for alternating unison or solo with polyphonic sections; in his *Benedictus Dominus Deus Israel*[211] he wrote a bassoon part to accompany the solo passages. He also is credited with some of the music sung at the annual performance of the *Mystery of Elche,* a religious drama on the death and assumption of the Virgin Mary, which has been given annually in Spain since 1603.[212] According to local legend, an ark containing a miraculous image of the Virgin—and also the words and music for this ceremonial—drifted to the Spanish coast at Elche in the 13th or 14th century. The existing text is dated 1639, and the oldest existing copy of the music 1709, though both undoubtedly go back to earlier MSS. The music of Part II is not so ancient as that of Part I, and Antonio de Ribera (cf. p. 587) and Lluis Vich, besides Perez, are supposed to have contributed to the score.[213]

[208] Cf. MitI, 74.   [209] Cf. *ibid.*, 81ff.

[209a] At least, the extracts in GeiE, 151ff, so indicate, though the author tries to make a case for derivation from a *villancico.*

[210] Further biographical data and stylistic analysis in GeiE, 138ff.

[211] Pr. PedH V, 1. (PedH V is devoted entirely to Perez; for another ex., *see* JulbeM, 51).

[212] Cf. ReMMA, 195. For a description of a performance in 1900, with the music, *see* PedE, 203ff.

[213] PedE, 218ff. Further about this Mystery, *see* TreME. About another Mystery with music, performed during the Renaissance but having a prior history (the "Mystery of Sybil Cassandra"), *see* TreSC.

Juan Pablo Pujol (b. Barcelona, 1573; d. there, 1626), priest, *maestro* successively at Tarragona, Saragossa, and Barcelona, is also connected with a local festival in Spain—though in Catalonia rather than Valencia. Many of his works were written for the festival of St. George, the Catalan patron saint.[214] The compositions are mostly based on Gregorian Chant. The psalms *a 4* employ writing in *falsobordone* style.[215] A *Missa pro defunctis*,[216] also *a 4*, follows the plainsong faithfully, presenting it as a *cantus firmus*, mostly in long notes, in the superius or altus. Few things could illustrate the transition from the more youthful to the mature and even senescent stages of Renaissance music than a comparison between an early masterpiece like the Requiem of Pierre de la Rue and Pujol's staid, formal setting. In other of his psalm and Mass settings,[217] Pujol uses two choirs skilfully, combining them sometimes homophonically, sometimes contrapuntally. Though fundamentally a composer of church music, he is also credited with some secular settings of Spanish texts.[218]

Other Spanish writers of sacred polyphony in Late Renaissance Spain include also the anonymous composer of a *Nobis datus* (preserved in a MS at Toledo), having a one-flat signature in the three upper voices—the tenor sings the Spanish *Pange lingua*—while the bass has a signature of two sharps; [219] Alfonso Lobo (born in Borja, c. 1555; died after 1610), who was active at Lisbon, Toledo (where he was elected *maestro* in 1593), and Seville; [220] Philippe Rogier (born in Arras, c. 1562), a composer of Masses and motets, who was in Spain as a choirboy in 1572, later became a member of the *capilla flamenca* and eventually its *maestro* and died in 1596; [220a] and Juan Bautista Comes (b. Valencia, 1568; d. there, 1643), who served at Lérida (Catalonia), Valencia, and Madrid. Comes' music includes polychoral works, e.g., a twelve-part *Hodie Christus natus est* for three choruses. More than 200 compositions of his survive, some being religious works in secular forms—*romances, villancicos, folias,* etc.—in which a few voices render the verse, while the chorus is sung in six or more parts by the choir.[221]

---

[214] Further data on the St. George festivals in PujO I, xxxviiff.

[215] Pr. *ibid.*, 1ff; the volumes in print are only 2 of a projected 8.

[216] Pr. *ibid.*, 159.   [217] Pr. *ibid.* II, 1ff.

[218] For list of works, *see ibid.*, I, viiff; Grove IV, 285; AngLME, 398, 406. *See also* UrL, 98f.

[219] Pr. KrZC, 114 (with facsimile opposite); KrV, 19. (*Nobis datus* is stanza 2 of the *Pange lingua.*) This motet, having the clefs SAAB (constituting neither the *chiavi naturali* nor the *chiavette*) is cited by Kroyer to support the mistaken view that the *chiavette* called for a transposition a major or minor third up or down (cf. pp. 531f *supra*). He is no doubt right in believing that the clefs and signatures show that the piece may be performed at either the level indicated by the flat or the one indicated by the two sharps; but this very fact may attest that a means other than the use of the *chiavette* existed to indicate a transposition at the distance of a third, and may therefore run directly counter to his argument. (For further controversy about this motet, which, however, has no bearing on the foregoing point, *see* ZfMW XIII [1931], 493–500.)

[220] 4 exx. pr. EsL, *Ser. II*, I; 1 of them pr. AraH, 297.

[220a] A Mass of his pr. MaldR XXI, 3.

[221] Cf. Grove I, 687. A selection of Comes' works pr. ComesO. The *Hodie* pr. EsL, *Ser. II*, I, 1; another ex. pr. AraH, 310 (= JulbeM, 47). About Comes' polychoral music, *see also* VicO I, xi.

Secular Polyphony: Vasquez; Brudieu; the Medinaceli and Sablonara Cancioneros

The production of true secular vocal music had, of course, continued, some of it being written by composers like Rodrigo Ceballos,[222] best known for their sacred music. A few examples by Morales and Guerrero have been mentioned in passing. Secular song in 16th-century Spain, however, presents several new names. It includes, as in other countries, not only vocal polyphony but vocal melodies accompanied by plucked stringed instruments. We shall mention the latter type in passing here and turn to it in more detail presently.

Although the Spaniards wrote madrigals in Italian style, the type never flourished in their country as it did, for example, in England. The *villancico*, however, continued to exert its influence, and in Juan Vasquez found a distinguished exponent. Vasquez, born in Badajoz, entered the service of Don Antonio de Zúñiga, in the Andalusian area, probably before 1551. If the composer is the same Juan Vasquez whose name appears at the end of the license in Fuenllana's *vihuela* book of 1554 (cf. pp. 623f),[223] he was for a time in the employ of the king. By 1556 he had become a priest and was in the service of a certain Juan Bravo, perhaps identical with Count Juan of Urueña (in the province of Salamanca), called "el Santo." Vasquez was living in Seville in 1560. His *Villancicos y canciones . . . a tres y a cuatro* was printed in 1551; his *Recopilación de sonetos y villancicos a quatro y a cinco*, in 1560; his *Agenda defunctorum* (dedicated to Juan Bravo), in 1561.[224]

Vasquez's secular music is of excellent quality. It includes full-fledged madrigals—settings of sonnets and other poems by Boscán, Garcilaso, etc.—employing points of imitation and chordal passages such as are found in madrigals elsewhere. But, however fine such examples as No. 6 (*a 4*) and Nos. 1–7, 9, 14, and 18–20 (*a 5*) in the *Recopilación* may be, such more typically Spanish compositions in it as the many *villancicos* and the *romance, Los braços traygo*,[225] are of greater historical interest. The Spaniards had evidently tired of the large amount of repetition called for in the old *villancico* pattern; at this period, the *villancico* is often merely a form in which the refrain occurs at both the beginning and the end. Vasquez frequently treats the recurrence of the refrain with considerable ingenuity, as, for example, in *Agora que soy niña*.[226] Mere perfunctory reiteration does not satisfy him. The modifications in his *villancicos* are sometimes rhythmic, sometimes melodic. In *Ojos morenos*,[227] the refrain text recurs to music which, though related to that of the opening, presents so many changes as to be substantially new. The text lines

---

[222] Exx. pr. MME VIII, 125, and probably 22 and 89 (cf. *ibid.*, Introduction, 24); very likely also MorL II, 244, 251 (voice and *vihuela* versions by Daza).
[223] ". . . *Yo el principe. Por mandado de sua alteza Juan Vasquez.*"
[224] For a description of the 1551 print, *see* TreBM, 535ff; the *Recopilación* is reprinted complete in MME IV; for fuller bio-bibliographical data, *see ibid.*, *Texto*, 9ff.
[225] *Ibid.*, 193 (cf. *Texto*, 42).   [226] *Ibid.*, 150.   [227] *Ibid.*, 102.

that return may be not only a group that includes the first, but lines 2 and 3 or 3 and 4 or line 2 alone. (Occasionally the wording of the lines is slightly varied upon their reappearance.) *Vos me matastes,* an especially lovely *villancico,* illustrates a variant of the type that reintroduces lines 2 and 3: here, when the music of the refrain returns, the first few words are different. There is fascinating use of rhythmic conflict between the voices.

EXAMPLE 136. *Vos me matastes*—Vasquez (after MME IV, 82; accent signs added).

"You have killed me, little one, in your tresses . . ."

This is one of several Vasquez pieces that were transcribed for voice with an accompanying instrument by the *vihuelistas* (cf. Ex. 139*b*), the men who in Spain corresponded to the lutenists in other countries (except that their instrument was not the same). In some instances, the *vihuelistas* use the same melodic material with so much apparent freedom that their pieces may be not so much transcriptions from Vasquez as arrangements of melodies, arranged also by him, from folk or other popular sources. It is clear that Vasquez sometimes drew on pre-existent material: the *romance* mentioned above plainly has in its altus an earlier melody, used also, as the vocal soloist's part, by one of the *vihuelistas* in a print of 1547.[228] Another piece in the *Recopilación, Dizen a mi,* while a different composition from the similarly named *villancico* in the *Cancionero de Upsala* (printed four years earlier) [229] has not only the same text but the same basic melody. It is highly probable that Vasquez's *Con qué la lavaré?* [230] is based on a *cantus prius factus,* since the same text and tune underlie *villancicos* in the *Cancionero de Upsala* and in the books of four different *vihuelistas;* most of these versions vary to such a degree that it is not likely that all are based on the same standard art version.[231] A melody that Vasquez set differently in both the 1551 and the 1560 books—*De los álamos vengo, madre* [232]—gives strongly the impression of being a folk tune. It is

---

[228] Cf. MME IV, 193, with MorL II, 163 (Valderrábano). For another treatment of the text, *see* BarbiC, 514; MME X, 194.

[229] Cf. MitU, 130, and MME IV, 118. [230] Pr. *ibid.,* 209; MitM, 2010.

[231] Cf. MitU, 65 (Upsala version); MME III, 79 (version of Narváez); MorL II, 148 (Valderrábano), 183 (Pisador), 200 (Fuenllana). The last is closest to Vasquez, whose name, indeed, appears opposite the title in Fuenllana's table of contents.

[232] For a voice and *vihuela* transcr. of the 1551 version, *see* PedCP III, 154 (= MorL II, 210). For the 1560 version, *see* MME IV, 153. The tune has been used by de Falla in the first movement of his Harpsichord Concerto.

plain that Vasquez's compositions hold the mirror up to activity in the field of Spanish secular music in his day, by virtue both of their embodiment of popular melodies and of their finding sufficient favor themselves to be transcribed for performance by vocal soloists with *vihuela* accompaniment.[233]

Another 16th-century madrigalist, who also wrote a Requiem Mass, was Joan Brudieu (d. 1591), by birth a Frenchman from the diocese of Limoges. In 1538, he and four other French singers participated in the Christmas festivities at the Catalonian town of Urgell, in the Pyrenees. As musician and churchman, he spent the rest of his long life there, except for three absences of a few years each—in 1543, apparently to study for the priesthood; in 1576, to go to Balaguer; and in 1578, to serve as *maestro* and organist at Barcelona. The see of Urgell subsidized the publication of his *Madrigales* (1585), dedicated to the Duke of Savoy, Philip II's new son-in-law; no doubt some of the pieces were sung to honor the wedding-party as it proceeded through northern Spain.[234]

Of the sixteen madrigals in the collection (the great majority of which are for SSAT), five are to Catalan texts. The collection opens with the Catalan *Gosos de nuestra Señora* ("Seven Joys of Mary"),[235] in nine sections: introduction, seven "joys," and conclusion. All the sections use the same melodic material, with modifications, in an upper voice, to fresh accompaniment in the other voices. Six sections are *a 4,* the third joy is *a 3,* the seventh *a 5,* and the ending *a 6.* The meter is exclusively binary until the sixth joy is reached: here, while the other parts continue in simple binary rhythm, the altus sings in $\frac{6}{2}$ (original time-values). In the seventh joy, finally, the rhythm of all the voices is ternary and dancelike; while the conclusion, again in binary rhythm, provides a majestic ending to the entire work.

The second piece in the collection [236] expresses the general rejoicing over the victory of Lepanto, using a style more light and nimble than do the imposing compositions of Palestrina and Infantas celebrating the same event (cf. pp. 403, 609). The fifth piece, *Las Cañas* ("The Lances"),[237] depicts an allegorical tournament between Love and Majesty, with voices representing drums and trumpets in a way that calls to mind Janequin's descriptive compositions. Nos. 6 and 7 in the collection have the same text and an initially similar melody (one in binary, the other in ternary rhythm); likewise, Nos.

---

[233] For *vihuela* pieces, not yet mentioned, that are transcriptions of Vasquez compositions in the *Recopilación,* or are based on related material, *see* MorL II, 122, 146, 166, 233, 239 (cf., MME IV, 198, 207, 76, 125, 107, respectively. For transcr. related to Vasquez pieces not in the *Recopilación, see* PedC II, 132, 135, 139, 141, 143 (= PedCP III, 160 [= MorL II, 201], 165, 171 [= MorL II, 206], 171, 174, 151); MorL II, 213, 216, 219.

[234] Further biographical data in PedF, text, 7; BorJB, 208; SnB, 288; UrJ; BrudieuM; AnglME, 387; PedM.

[235] Pr. BrudieuM 1 (music); note that Brudieu's tune is not the same as that of the 14th-century Catalan song similarly entitled; cf. ReMMA, 374.

[236] Pr. BrudieuM, 22 (music).

[237] Pr. *ibid.,* 55–108; a German transl. of the Catalan text is given in UrJ, 190.

8 and 9 provide a single text with two settings (respectively in binary and ternary rhythm), employing material that is related (though rather loosely).[238] In some of his madrigals, Brudieu makes rather liberal use of dissonance: in No. 8, for instance, three seconds occur in succession.[239] Harmonic liberties appear also in the Requiem Mass.[240] Brudieu follows the chant fairly closely in the superius, but he often varies it in a way that a stricter composer like Victoria would not have thought of doing.[241]

Pedro Alberch Vila (b. Vich, near Barcelona, 1517; d. Barcelona, 1582) had the reputation of being one of the very finest Spanish musicians of his time. Unfortunately, only the altus of his *Odarum quas vulgo madrigales appellamus . . . lib. I* (1561) survives. This collection presents texts in Spanish, Catalan, Italian, and French. He was already organist of the Barcelona Cathedral in 1538 and later became a canon there. His *Libro de Tientos* for organ has been lost, only two pieces by him for the instrument being preserved.[242] Some other works are extant in MS.[243]

Among the other Spanish madrigalists, using the term in a broad sense, are Mateo Flecha the Elder (b. Prades, Tarragona, perhaps in 1481; d. Poblet, Catalonia, aged seventy-two) and Mateo Flecha the Younger, his nephew (b. Prades, c. 1520–30; d. 1604). The uncle, who in 1523 became a singer and later *maestro* at the Lérida Cathedral and subsequently *maestro* to the Infantas of Castile, composed *ensaladas* collected by the nephew and published by him at Prague in 1581 together with *ensaladas* by himself and by *"otros authores."* Only one voice-part survives, but a number of the pieces—which have earned the elder Flecha some fame—are preserved in other sources. The nephew entered the service of Maria, before she married Maximilian II. He became a Carmelite, and in 1564 was in Italy, later following Maria, now Empress, to Vienna and Prague. Maximilian made him *Hofkaplan*. In 1568, he was named abbot of Tihany in Hungary and in 1599 abbot of the Monastery of La Portella (Catalonia), where he died. A madrigal collection of his, mainly *a 4* and *a 5*, with one text in Spanish and the rest in Italian, appeared at Venice in 1568. An instrumental five-part *Harmonia* of his, dedicated to Maximilian, is also extant—to which, of course, must be added some of the *ensaladas* (the problems of attribution, however, are difficult)—but other

[238] UrJ, 181, suggests that in each instance the dancelike ternary version is the later one and illustrates Brudieu's development in the direction of the *volksmässig*.
[239] *See* BrudieuM, 215 (music). About the actual appearance of these seconds in the original print, *see* TreSM, 23; however, the manner in which they are used (involving passing-notes) is not as unusual as the author of TreSM would seem to believe. It is clear from the musical context that the intervals do not result from the printer's having placed a group of notes a third too high or too low.
[240] Pr. BrudieuM, 215 (music); analyzed in BrudieuM, 91ff (text).
[241] Cf. the comparative table, *ibid.*, 121.
[242] Pr. MME II, 43, 45. The *tiento* attributed to him in PedAO I, 37; MusetS, 12, is by Cabezón (cf. MME II, 172 [text], 31 [music]).
[243] *See* further esp. *ibid.*, 172f (text); AngLME, 386f; KastnCE, 162f.

works that he is known to have written are either partly or entirely lost.[244]

Additional madrigalists, who, like the younger Flecha, spent much time abroad, include Pedro Valenzuela (or Valenzola), Sebastian Raval, and Pedro Ruimonte (Rimonte). Gardano published a book of Valenzuela's madrigals at Venice in 1578.[245] Raval, the composer of two collections of madrigals and one of *canzonette,* was active at Urbino, Rome, and Palermo. He was skilled in extemporizing counterpoints, but not sufficiently to avoid defeat in a contest with G. M. Nanino and Soriano; he won a later contest with Achille Falcone, but only upon reconsideration by the judges.[246] Both Valenzuela and Raval wrote to Italian texts. Ruimonte, however, composed to Spanish texts; and his madrigals printed in 1614 are "the only examples of the later chromatic madrigal with Spanish words." [247] He was *maestro músico de camera* at the archducal court at Brussels, 1603 to 1605, received money to return to Spain in 1614, but seems to have been in Brussels again in 1618. To the group of wayfarers probably belongs also José de Puente, who published a book of madrigals at Naples in 1606.[248]

Most of the remaining madrigalists, including anonymi, are represented in one or more of a few noteworthy miscellaneous collections: Medinaceli Library, Madrid, MSS 13230 (already referred to) and 13231 (= *Tonos castellanos A* and *B*) [249] dating, respectively, from the late 16th and early 17th centuries; the *Cancionero* of Turin, which preserves *canciones* and *villancicos* of the late 16th century; [250] *Romances y letras de a tres vozes,* a MS from the first half of the 17th century at the Biblioteca Nacional, Madrid; [251] and the *Cancionero* of the scribe Claudio de la Sablonara, of the same date.[252] Among the men in question are Juan Blas de Castro (c. 1560–1631),[253] Gabriel Diaz (c. 1590–1631),[254] Pujol (cf. p. 611), Manuel Machado (still living in 1639),[255] Alvare de los Rios (d. 1623),[256] and Mateo Romero ("Maestro

---

[244] Further about the Flechas, see esp. AngLME, 380f, 388; EinIK, 14ff (about the younger Flecha). There are wide discrepancies in the various biographical accounts (cf. HaraF and RieL I, 515, and the works there cited; also Grove II, 253). For exx., see AngME, facsimile 24 (sacred); PedCP III, 54, 177 (= PedC II, 145; after Fuenllana); PedC II, 161 (facsimile on 160), 163; DTO XLI, 30, 32 (Italian madrigals).

[245] One of them pr. separately in *Ausgewählte Madrigale,* No. 36 (W. Barclay Squire, ed.), Breitkopf & Härtel; another pr. TurrA, Pl. 26f.

[246] See esp. RadS; TibyR.

[247] J. B. Trend in Grove IV, 487. For a non-chromatic madrigal of his, see BalT, 81.

[248] Cf. EitQ VIII, 81.

[249] Both described in TreBM, 489ff; MS 13230 also in MME VIII, which prints 51 pieces from this source (MME will publish the remaining contents in due course); TreM includes extracts from the MS and, on p. 232, 1 complete piece (= MME VIII, 52). One composition from the MS (Lassus' *Susanne un jour* with Spanish text) and 4 from MS 13231 are pr. BalT (which credits the Spanish *Susanne* . . . to MS 13231; but see MME VIII, 21 [text], No. 172).

[250] 1 piece in WolfME, 100; 7 in BalT.

[251] 7 pieces *ibid.*

[252] Pr. ArocaC; for studies of the MS, see MitC, 14, 233; SmithD, 168ff.

[253] 20 exx. pr. ArocaC; 1 each also pr. BalT, 1, and PedCP III, 189.

[254] 8 exx. pr. ArocaC; 2 also pr. PedCP III, 199, 204.

[255] 4 exx. pr. ArocaC; 1 other pr. PedCP III, 213.

[256] 9 exx. pr. ArocaC; 1 also pr. PedCP III, 207.

Capitán": d. 1647).[257] Blas de Castro, a friend of Lope de Vega, was introduced by the dramatist as a character in several plays and is mentioned by him in a number of poems. He became *músico privado* to the Duke of Alba at Salamanca, apparently c. 1594, and was in the service of Philip III in 1605. His works, generally, give the impression of being intended for use in plays.[258] Diaz—to whom Lope de Vega dedicated a poem—was a composer also of church music,[258a] and included among his posts that of *maestro* at the convent of the Descalzas Reales, Madrid, formerly held by Victoria.[259] Romero, who enjoyed a high reputation in the Peninsula, was born in Flanders (his name, at first, may have been "Rosmarin"). He arrived in Spain in 1586, entering the *capilla flamenca* of the royal palace as *cantorcillo,* was in 1594 named a *cantor* of the *capilla* and in 1598 its *maestro.* He was a pupil of Rogier (cf. p. 611). Romero's pieces in the *Cancionero de Sablonara* include settings of Lope de Vega, whose poems were favored by many composers.[260] The writing of more or less similar music continued far into the century.

Salinas and Cerone

The cross-fertilization between musical life in Italy and Spain that produced the madrigal also bore fruit in the field of Spanish musical theory. More specifically, Zarlino gave the impetus to two important syntheses of Renaissance musical theory and practice: those of Salinas and Cerone.

Francisco Salinas (b. Burgos, 1513; d. there, 1590), blind from infancy, attended the University of Salamanca. Later he entered the service of the Archbishop of Compostela, who, when elevated to the cardinalship, took Salinas with him to Rome. During twenty-three years in Italy, Salinas increased his musical knowledge, both by study of Greek MSS and by observation of the rich musical life about him. Sometime between 1553 and 1557, Salinas served as organist at the palace of the Duke of Alba in Naples, and in 1561 returned to Spain. Five years later he was elected to the chair of music at Salamanca, and for twenty-one years he taught there.[261]

His great theoretical work, the *De musica libri septem* (Salamanca, 1577) restates in Latin many of the doctrines that his friend Zarlino had enunciated in Italian. Though, to be sure, Zarlino preceded Salinas in print with an account of ⅓-comma mean-tone temperament, Salinas is usually credited with having invented it.[262] His own words are that it "has been proposed by no-

---

[257] 22 exx. pr. ArocaC; 3 also pr. BalT, 7, 32, 50; 2 also pr. PedCP III, 193, 197. A motet pr. EsL, *Ser. II,* I, 101.

[258] Cf. MitC, 248ff; Grove I, 389.

[258a] Some exx., apparently unique, survive at Puebla, Mexico, where music by various other Spaniards of the period is also to be found; cf. RayJP.

[259] Cf. esp. MitC, 255ff.

[260] Further about Romero, *see* esp. BalT, 103; MitC, 241ff. BalT contains numerous Lope de Vega settings. Further about the Spanish madrigalists, *see* esp. TreN (substantially the same as TreS), TreSM.

[261] Further biographical data in TreC; SaliM, *Praefatio;* HawkH III, 123; SubM, 27, 36ff.

[262] E.g., by BarbT, 33, and A. J. Ellis in HelmhS, 547; cf. SaliM, 140, 143ff.

body, so far as I know." [263] In his exposition of the methods of mean-tone tuning, Salinas worked out for the first time the details of the relationship between ⅓-, ²⁄₇-, and ¼-comma tuning.[264] The last part of Salinas' work deals with rhythm, and contains illustrations from Classical verse as well as from folk songs of Salinas' own day, heard in Italy and Spain. Though Salinas did not set out to deal with folk song for its own sake, he gave posterity a unique record of at least scraps of popular rhythm and melody as heard in the 16th century.[265]

Domenico Pietro Cerone (b. Bergamo, 1566), sometime singer in the Cathedral of Oristano in Sardinia, was admitted to the chapel of Philip II in 1592, continued to serve under Philip III, and was transferred in 1608 to the Royal Chapel at Naples. There he wrote, in Spanish, his 1160-page *El Melopeo y Maestro* (*The Art of Music and Instructor*), published at Naples in 1613.[266]

The treatise contains some misinformation, but also offers much of value. An interesting feature is the author's opinion of other musicians. Although often old-fashioned, Cerone is a child of his time in looking upon Josquin's music as a strange mixture of good and bad. Guerrero and Victoria, he says,

have composed a music plain, grave, and very devout. . . . Whoever wishes to know great variety and differentiation in counterpoint and to pass the time in observing spicy bits of music . . . should see the hundred counterpoints of Don Ferdinando de las Infantas, . . . worthy to be known by all contrapuntists but not all meriting emulation by good composers.[267]

Cerone recognizes the supreme position of Palestrina during this period, and devotes one entire book (of the twenty-two books into which the extensive treatise is divided) to a study of Palestrina's *Missa L'Homme armé* (1570).[268]

In dealing with interval progressions, Cerone says, ". . . two fifths separated by a sixth may be used freely by any who profess to follow the art of music; but the other fifths, only by the great masters and eminent composers." [269] At one point, he gives examples of admissible progressions in which a bass note reached in normal course remains stationary, while the upper voices form a $^6_4$ chord [270] with it, and is succeeded by another note a scale-degree away.[271]

Books IX to XV [271a] deal with counterpoint and composition in a manner

---

[263] SaliM, 164.

[264] Further on Salinas' contribution to musical theory, *see* RieG, 394ff. About other early theorists and mean-tone tuning, *see* esp. BarbT, 25ff.

[265] Transcr. in TreC, 14ff; PedF, 372; cf. ReMMA, 374f.

[266] Further biographical data in Grove I, 593; MME II, 44ff (text); AngLME, 412; MGG II, 969ff.

[267] CeroM I, 89f.   [268] *Ibid*. II, 1028–36.   [269] *Ibid*. II, 664. Transl. from HanC, 414.

[270] Cerone's actual words deal with the eleventh from the bass (cf. CeroM II, 660).

[271] For further discussion of Cerone's harmony, *see* HanC, 413ff.

[271a] StrunkR, 263ff, gives part of Book XII in English transl.

free from the pedantry of the Five Species.[272] The approach is gradual, from simple counterpoint to the composition of Masses and motets. Cerone also gives a great body of beginnings and endings that might be used by a composer. He likewise discusses plainsong, the way in which one should make *glosas* or variations, the proportional system,[273] and the solution of musical enigmas. In explaining the keyboard instruments, he speaks of an instrument of fifty keys, instead of the more usual forty-two, thus indicating that in Spain and Italy the enlarged range for keyboard instruments, extending lower in the bass register, was taken for granted.[274]

Instrumental Music in the 15th Century

Though 15th-century Spanish literary sources abound in references to instruments, their makers, and performers, little instrumental music survives. Cathedral and court archives preserve the names of German, French, Italian, and Spanish organists and organ builders.[275] Chronicles include accounts of festivities and ceremonies in which instrumentalists played an important part.[276] In the *Ordenanzas de Sevilla* (1502), details of a compulsory examination for all instrument makers are recorded.[277] But of the music-books copied out for organists there is no trace.

That Spanish 15th-century instrumental ensemble-music should have included settings of the *Spagna* melody—itself, as already stated, probably of Spanish origin—is obvious. The setting *a 2,* mentioned on p. 177, may be Spanish; a three-part *Alta* (= *saltarello*) by F. de la Torre (which has the tune in the tenor),[278] one of the few pieces without text in the *Cancionero de Palacio,* certainly is.[279] The various settings from other countries—e.g., the four in a German source (cf. p. 665)—very likely provide at least an echo of old Spanish court music also.

The Vihuelistas of the 16th Century, including Milán and Fuenllana

In the 15th and 16th centuries, organs and instruments called *"vihuelas"* are frequently mentioned. The term *vihuela* served both the viol and guitar

[272] HanA, 75f, points out some of the superiorities of Cerone over Fux.
[273] Further on Cerone's use of proportions, *see* HanE, 9.
[274] Cf. KinO, 66. For a general article on Spanish 16th-century theorists, *see* ColE. A late 16th-century treatise, outstanding for its comprehensive treatment of *canto de órgano* (cf. p. 577), is pr. in ColT.
[275] Cf. AngO, 12ff; AngCO, 49; HillM, 487.
[276] Anglés, in MME I, cites many documents.
[277] Quoted in PedO, 90f. For part of the examination given instrument makers, quoted from the *Ordenanzas de Granada* (1552), *see* ChavM, 82.
[278] BarbiC, 585; MME X, 84; also pr. HAM, 103, as "Keyboard Dance," though hardly with historical basis for the appellation. *See also* MME I, 71 (text); MGG I, 378f; BesCC, 97ff.
[279] Spanish directions for dancing both the *alta* and the *baxa* (= *basse danse*) are given in a 16th-century MS quoted, in part, in E. Cotarelo y Mori, *Colección de entremeses, loas, bailes, jácaras y mojinganzas,* I (1911), ccxxxiiif.

families; but for the 16th-century tablatures the *vihuela de mano* or *vihuela commun* is specified. There can be little doubt that this vihuela was a six-course guitar tuned like the lute.[280] The theorist, Fray Juan Bermudo, makes this clear: ". . . if you wish to make the *vihuela* into a guitar *a los nuevos* [i.e., with four strings tuned a fourth, a third, and a fourth apart], take off the first and sixth [strings], and the four strings that are left are those of the guitar. And if you wish to make the guitar into a *vihuela,* put on the sixth and the first [strings]."[281] There is evidence that the four- and six-course guitars had well-defined functions, the former as a popular instrument of city and country, the latter as the instrument of courts and art musicians. But why the Spaniards, after transmitting the lute from the Arabic world to Europe, chose to develop the guitar while the rest of the Continent favored the lute, is not clear. The surviving documents do not help, since they contain few references to the lute and lutenists, nor is Spanish music calling specifically for lute preserved.[281a]

As if to compensate for the lack of 15th-century monuments, the 16th century has left us voluminous instrumental tablatures for both the *vihuela* and the organ. The first known work is Luis Milán's *Libro de Música de Vihuela de Mano intitulado El Maestro* (Valencia, 1536).[282] Its notation, as well as that of the other six preserved *vihuela* books, is the lute tablature which appeared earlier in Italy, though there are some uniquely Spanish characteristics, such as the use of red ciphers to indicate the part to be sung.[283] Not only does the title, *El Maestro* ("The Instructor"), indicate a didactic purpose, but Milán states in his preface that the book is primarily for beginners, and the music is so presented that the student may progress from simple to more difficult pieces. The elegance of Milán's music is in keeping with his accomplishments as courtier, author of a treatise [284] on court life modelled after Castiglione's *Il Cortegiano,* and arranger of court entertainments at Valencia. His book contains instrumental compositions—*fantasias, tientos, pavanas*— and songs, early surviving examples of accompanied monody—*villancicos, sonetos, romances. Fantasias* form the bulk of the music. These are simple in texture, unpretentious in their formal structure, quite often developing by means of short sequences or the repetition of a phrase in different registers of the instrument. A freer treatment of form is found in the four *tientos* [285] (Milán uses the Portuguese term *tento*), which, though richer in texture and longer, are similar to the *ricercari* of the Italian lutenists Spinaccino and

280 Cf. ChaseG; SalaL; SalaE I, 388ff; WardV.   281 BermuD, fol. xcvi.
281a On the little that is known about the lute in Spain, *see* WardL.
282 Pr. MilánM; for critical comment, *see* Gombosi's review in ZfMW, XIV (1933), 185. Excerpts from all the *vihuela* tablatures appear in MorL (in extremely poor transcriptions). Transcribed excerpts from Milán's and other tablatures will be found in TapS (with facsimiles), TagA (only the first version of each piece should be consulted), ApelM II, ScherG, and BalR (with "improved" transcriptions).
283 According to BalF, these red ciphers were also played on the *vihuela.*
284 Pr. MilánL. *See* TreL, 69ff.   285 Pr. MilánM, 131ff. *See* KastnCE, 145ff; SalaE I, 404.

Dalza. Their looseness of structure suggests improvisation, as do Milán's double settings of *villancicos,* in which the second setting is a free embellishment of the first, the vocal line remaining the same in both versions. It is possible that the double *villancico* settings, *tientos,* and many of the *fantasias* are a noting down of older improvisational performance techniques. The very polish of Milán's music, especially that of the six *pavanas*[286] and of such song settings as that for the *romance, Durandarte,*[287] implies an extensive instrumental development in Spain, an implication borne out by the 15th-century literary references. (Successive cross-relations, illustrated in Ex. 137, occur frequently in the *vihuela* sources.[287a])

EXAMPLE 137. Opening measures of *Durandarte*—Milán (complete piece in ScherG, 91, BalR, 14; MilánM, 77; MorL II, 41).

"Durandarte, Durandarte [= Roland], good, proven knight."

Technical finish is found also in the second published tablature, Luis de Narváez's *Los seys libros del Delphin de música* (Valladolid, 1538).[288] However, instead of alternating sections of chords and simple polyphony with passages of figuration, Narváez integrates the two, creating a smoother texture than does Milán. Narváez's skill is best observed in his *diferencias* (variations). Here, with one of the first full-fledged appearances of the instrumental theme-and-variation form in Western music, we find an exhaustive probing into the variation idea. For example: on the melody of the hymn, *O gloriosa Domina,* Narváez creates a series of short *fantasias,* each complete in itself, yet all of them related by the appearance of the hymn melody in each variation (cf. p. 628).[289] With the famous *Conde Claros* as theme, Narváez exploits the full technical resources of the instrument in twenty-two brief *dife-*

---

[286] Pr. MilánM, 65ff.

[287] Another version of the same *romance,* set *a 4,* pr. BarbiC, 513; HAM, 100.

[287a] But this is not true of simultaneous cross-relations. Cf. WardV, 255.

[288] The whole tablature pr. MME III. An earlier partial transcr. is given in TornC; however, there are editorial "improvements." Two motets by Narváez were pr. in 16th-century collections; see EitS, 73, 128.

[289] Pr. HAM, 130 (with errors); MME III, 44 (music).

rencias,[289a] often suggesting the theme by implication through its harmonic outline rather than by melodic variation. On the equally famous theme *Guárdame las vacas,* he writes seven variations,[290] each a short character piece.[291] Elements of a technique that foreshadows the chorale prelude are found in the *diferencias* on the *villancico, Si tantos halcones la garça combaten,* the following fragment of which will suggest something of Narváez's treatment of this technique.

EXAMPLE 138. Extract from the third *diferencia* on *Si tantos halcones la garça combaten*—Narváez (from *Los Seys libros* . . . , Valladolid, 1538; transcr. by J. Ward).

In the Milán and Narváez tablatures we find some of the earliest known indications of tempo (*tiempo*). Milán suggests tempos for most of his compositions: one *fantasia* should be played "with a beaten or hurried measure" (*batido o apressurado*), another "neither too fast nor too slow, but with a measured beat" (*un compas bien mensurado*), and in another *fantasia* the consonances must be played slowly and the *redobles* (ornaments) rapidly. Narváez provides signs for two different tempos (Φ for *apriessa,* "hurried", and ₡ for *muy de espacio,* "very slowly") ; Milán had used the terms, but not the signs.[291a]

The third published tablature is Alonso de Mudarra's *Tres libros de música en cifra* . . . (Seville, 1546).[292] Its contents are similar to those of the first two books: intabulations of motets and chansons (Narváez had been the first to include such transcriptions), *villancicos, sonetos,* and *canciones, pavanas, gallardas,* and six pieces for the four-course guitar. Like most of the tablatures, Mudarra's includes *diferencias* on a ground—there are four sets on *Guárdame las vacas*—as well as several settings of *romances* for voice and *vihuela.* The grounds, or *bassi ostinati,* and *romance* tunes belonged to popular tradition, and most 16th-century Spanish composers employed fragments of them in

---

[289a] Pr. *ibid.,* 82 (music).   [290] Pr. *ibid.,* 85 (music); and in part in ApelM II, 14.
[291] The first 4 variations are based on the first part of the melody, which is actually the *romanesca* (cf. GomCF, 88f); the last 3, on the second part, which is the *passamezzo antico.*
[291a] Further about tempo indications in the *vihuela* books, *see* WardV, 74.
[292] Pr. MME VII. *La mañana de San Juan,* ascribed to Mudarra in MorL II, 112, is by Pisador (cf. MME VII, 77 [text] ; PedCP III, 146).

their works. Salinas printed many of the *romance* melodies in the latter part of his treatise,[293] while Morales used one in a Mass (cf. p. 588). In instances where two or more versions of the same *romance* melody are preserved, such as *Paseábase el rey moro,* which was set by Narváez, Pisador, and Fuenllana,[294] their melodic disagreements point to an ultimate source in oral tradition.

After Mudarra, the tablatures progressively contain more intabulations of music by Flemish, French, Italian, and Spanish composers. Enriquez de Valderrábano's *Libro de música de vihuela intitulado Silva de Sirenas . . .* (Valladolid, 1547)[295] contains pages of motets and chansons by Gombert, Willaert, Josquin, Verdelot, Mouton, and Morales, arranged either for one *vihuela* or for two. The duets are printed in such a way that two performers can read from the same book while sitting opposite each other. In addition to arrangements of music by *"famosos auctores,"* Valderrábano includes his 120 variations on *Guárdame las vacas* and 33 *fantasias,*[296] music of real invention and skill.

Diego Pisador's *Libro de música de vihuela* (Salamanca, 1552)[297] continues the intabulation fashion with arrangements of eight Masses by Josquin, and motets, chansons, *villancicos,* etc., by other composers. While the inclusion of so many intabulations deprives us of original works by Valderrábano and Pisador, they provide valuable clues to Renaissance performance practice. *Vihuela* notation, being almost identical with one of the lute notations, indicates exact pitches, since here, too, each symbol refers to a fret on the instrument. Consequently a comparison of a vocal polyphonic work that survives with few or no accidentals with its *vihuela* intabulation gives us clues to the application of *musica ficta* in 16th-century Spain. The *vihuelistas* show a marked tendency to apply sharps.[298]

One of the richest *vihuela* tablatures is that of Miguel de Fuenllana, blind musician of the court of Philip II. His *Orphénica Lyra* (Seville, 1554)[299] contains numerous intabulations, which Fuenllana often pairs with *fantasias* of his own writing (cf. Ex. 139a). These *fantasias,* less overtly instrumental in style than Narváez's, are products of a mature polyphonic skill, rich in musical ideas artistically worked out. Considerable variety is found in Fuenllana's treatment of the form. There are *fantasias a 2, a 3,* and *a 4,* on several themes and on one; the fullness of the polyphonic texture is astonishing in view of the

---

[293] He includes versions of *Conde Claros,* p. 342, and *Guárdame las vacas,* p. 348.

[294] Narváez's setting pr. MME III, 60; Pisador's, in MorL II, after 179; Fuenllana's, in WolfH II, 161 (with facsimile of the original); MorL II, 198; PedCP III, 148.

[295] AngLME, 393, cites another work by Valderrábano, *Tratado de cifra nueva para tecla, arpa y vihuela, canto llano de órgano y contrapunto* (Alcalá de Henares, 1557), which is apparently lost.

[296] A *fantasia* pr. ApelM II, 15, and a few *diferencias* on *Guárdame las vacas* in HAM, 133. *See also* ApelSM, 299ff.

[297] Cf. HutchV; CortP. (*See* fn. 294 *supra.*)

[298] Cf. FoxA. For details about particular intabulations by several *vihuelistas, see* WardU.

[299] Cf. KoczD; RieMF (includes list of contents); AngMF; BalF; PedC I, 125.

technical limitations of the *vihuela,* while the use of *falsas* (dissonances) is liberal. Among the transcriptions for voice and vihuela is one of Vasquez's *Vos me matastes* (Ex. 139*b;* cf. Ex. 136). Like its model, the accompanied song has a ternary time-signature which, however, now seems inappropriate, since the rhythmically conflicting parts that justified the signature have been replaced by an accompaniment that agrees with the underlying duple rhythm of the basic melody. In reworking the material, however, Fuenllana has produced a real gem. (The large number of transcriptions which, like this one, retain their texts in the *vihuela* books distinguishes these sources from the lute books of Italy [cf. p. 523, fn. 18] and other countries, in which the arrangements of vocal music are most often purely instrumental.[299a])

EXAMPLE 139. (*a*) Extract from a *Fantasia*—Fuenllana (*Orphénica Lyra;* transcr. by J. Ward), (*b*) Opening of Fuenllana's voice-and-vihuela transcription of Vasquez's *Vos me matastes* (complete piece in MorL II, 204; PedC II, 137; PedCP III, 169).

The *Fantasia sobre una passado forçado* [300] is remarkable for the way in which the theme is introduced twenty-nine times, sometimes in augmentation, sometimes in diminution, in the midst of a continuous flow of excellent counterpoint. This complex music fully substantiates the reports that Fuenllana was a *consumado tañedor,* a consummate player of the *vihuela.* The last part of his book is a miscellany, containing intabulated *ensaladas* by the Flechas, *fantasias,* and *tientos,* for the five-course *vihuela* and for that with four courses, called *guitara.* The latter instrument, according to Bermudo, was associated with popular performance of the *romances,* and apparently Fuenllana was acknowledging this tradition when he set *Paseábase el rey moro,* one of the loveliest of 16th-century songs, for this instrument.

The last publication for the six-course *vihuela* is Esteban Daza's *El Parnaso* (Valladolid, 1576).[301] Its contents are much the same as those in the other tablatures—*fantasias* ("on each of the eight *tonos*"), intabulated motets, chan-

---

[299a] Cf. WardV, 285.   [300] Pr. RieM, 76.

[301] A stipulation in the royal license for the printing of Daza's tablature demands that the price of the book appear on each copy sold. At the bottom of the title-page of the Biblioteca Nacional copy is pr. *"Esta tassado en 130. Marauedis."*

sons (several to be *"tañidas sin cantar,"* i.e., played without singing), *villa-nescas* and *villancicos. El Parnaso* marks the end of a tradition; after its pub-lication the *vihuela* is rarely mentioned; its place is taken by the so-called "Spanish" guitar. Bermudo describes this five-course guitar as rare in 1555, though, as we have seen, Fuenllana wrote music for this instrument. That it had grown in popular esteem is evidenced by the publication of Juan Carlos Amat's treatise *Guitarra española* (Barcelona, 1586? [302]), though no collec-tion of music for the instrument appeared until the beginning of the 17th century.

In addition to the *vihuela* music in the seven tablatures, some is included in Bermudo's treatise and in the organ tablature of Venegas de Henestrosa, while the music of Cabezón was published for "keyboard, harp, and *vi-huela"* [303]—words which suggest that *vihuelistas* "reduced" keyboard as well as vocal music for their instrument. A certain Guzman is mentioned not only as a gifted performer on the seven-course *vihuela,* but also as a composer, though none of his music survives. The name *"vihuela"* occurs occasionally until the beginning of the 18th century, but the last music for it is a 17th-century MS of Antonio de Santa Cruz, containing *pasacalles, fantasias,* etc. [304]

Music for Strings: Ortiz

There are many literary references to other stringed instruments in 16th-century Spain, but little music for them remains. The single work devoted to the viol is Diego Ortiz's celebrated *Tratado de glosas sobre cláusulas . . .* (Rome, 1553), [305] a text-book giving the general rules of instrumental impro-visation, ornamentation, and of what the English came to call "divisions on a ground." Most of the *Tratado* is devoted to music examples: pages of ca-dential variation, exercises in the free ornamentation of previously composed music, and models for improvisation over *bassi ostinati.* These latter Ortiz calls "Italian tenors," and they include the *folia, romanesca, Ruggiero, pas-samezzo antico,* and *passamezzo moderno.* [306]

Music for Keyboard, notably that of Cabezón

Though no Spanish music specifically calls for harpsichord, it is safe to assume that this instrument was used in Spain: the Spanish word *tecla* means simply "keyboard", and it is probable that music composed by Cabezón and other organists was played on any keyboard instrument. Certainly vocal music

[302] The problems of dating this work are dealt with in PedC I, 181. *See also* PedA.

[303] Hayes' conjectures (HayesM II, 92) that *"vihuela"* in this instance means "viol" and thus that Cabezón's music was intended in part for "consort viols," is unfounded.

[304] Cf. AngCM, 341f.

[305] Pr. OrtizT. An edition with Italian text appeared in Rome, probably also in 1553; cf. SubM, 34.

[306] Cf. GomF.

was so performed. Ortiz includes two "reductions" of madrigals for harpsichord in his *Tratado* and suggests that the harpsichordist arrange other vocal works "as he is ordinarily accustomed to doing." Other instruments are mentioned by Bermudo: *banduria* and *rabel* (both discussed in the book devoted to the *vihuela*) and *harpa*. No specific music for these instruments survives; however, in the preface to the works of Cabezón there is the following note: "The harp is so like the *tecla* that all music played on the *tecla* can be played on the harp without much difficulty." In his treatise, Bermudo devotes a few chapters to the harp and cites Ludovico as a famous performer on the instrument, and in the tablature of Mudarra one piece is titled *Otra fantasia que contra haze la harpa en la manera de luduvico.*[307]

Ensemble music, in addition to that for two *vihuelas,* is much discussed in the various treatises.[307a] Bermudo wrote at length about the possibilities of *música en concierto,* giving lists of various instrumental combinations, together with the necessary tunings, and suggesting the last book of Masses by Morales as suitable music for adaptation. Ortiz mentions viol ensembles, while Henestrosa printed a *fuga* in forty parts[308] that could be performed by ten instruments. There are also references to *bandas de trompetas,* which were connected with the various courts, though no music for them survives.

The remaining instrumental music of Renaissance Spain is for the organ. Time has left us only two printed collections and a few MSS. Part of the loss is due to the desire of Spanish organists to keep their works for their own use, a practice that Bermudo deplored. Especially serious has been the loss of such printed books and MSS as the *Libro de Tientos* of Vila (cf. p. 615) and six MS books that Henestrosa claims to have prepared for printing. Unlike the *vihuela* books, the two surviving organ prints are in a tablature unique to Spain:[309] whereas each of the six lines of *vihuela* notation represents a course of the instrument, each line in the organ notation represents a polyphonic line. The first book to employ such a tablature is the *Libro de Cifra Nueva para tecla, harpa y vihuela* (Alcalá de Henares, 1557),[310] compiled by Venegas de Henestrosa. This work is particularly noteworthy as an anthology of mid-16th-century Spanish and Italian instrumental music. Many famous organists of the time are represented, among them, Francisco Perez Palero, organist of the Royal Chapel at Granada; Pedro Vila, organist of the Barcelona Cathedral; the royal organist Pedro de Soto; Antonio [de Cabezón];

[307] Pr. MorL II, 103.
[307a] Cf. also the *Harmonia* and the *Alta* mentioned, respectively, on pp. 615, 619, *supra.*
[308] Pr. MME II, 163.   [309] Cf. KinO, 20ff; WolfH II, 264ff; ApelN, 47ff.
[310] The whole tablature pr. MME II. Excerpts pr. PedAO I and, evidently after it, in MusetS, 1, 3, 12 (cf. fn. 242), 27 (the rhythm seems to be wrong in MusetS, 27 [= PedAO I, 57]; cf. MME II, 76). Pedrell ascribed to Cabezón, in PedH VIII, all the pieces labelled "Antonio" in Henestrosa's book, and his conjecture has been accepted in MME II, 69 (text). *See also* KastnM.

Julius de Modena (= Giulio Segni). Henestrosa also included *vihuela* and lute pieces, translating them into his *cifra nueva*. The nineteen anonymous *fantasias de vihuela* in the *Libro* are, in fact, compositions from the tablatures of Narváez, Mudarra, Valderrábano, and Francesco da Milano. Comparing these *fantasias de vihuela* with their sources shows that Henestrosa left some originals unaltered, but completely recast others.[310a]

Besides *fantasias, tientos, fabordones, himnos, villancicos, salmos, romances,* and *canciones,* Henestrosa includes a type of intabulation known in Spain as *glosa*. Rare in *vihuela* literature, it occurs in profusion in keyboard sources. A typical example is Palero's *glosa* of Verdelot's motet *Si bona suscepimus*.[310b] Though the original voice-complex is preserved, individual voice-parts, particularly the highest, are frequently transformed by elaboration. The *glosa* was the despair of many 16th-century musicians, who felt that it corrupted music; Diego Ortiz, as has been indicated, wrote a treatise on the subject, and numerous *glosas* were composed by Cabezón, the greatest of Spanish Renaissance organists.

Antonio de Cabezón (= Cabeçón; born c. 1510 in Castrojeriz, near Burgos; died, 1566, in Madrid) was the composer of what is by far the most important organ tablature, the *Obras de música para tecla, arpa y vihuela* (Madrid, 1578).[311] Blind, like Salinas and Fuenllana, Cabezón was chamber musician to the courts of Charles V and Philip II, and accompanied the latter on his brief nuptial interlude in England. Cabezón's music, printed twelve years after his death, was put into tablature and published by his son Hernando. The contract [311a] for the printing of this work called for an edition of 1,200 copies and stipulated that Henestrosa's collection be used as a model. The contents of Cabezón's *Obras* resemble those of the earlier tablature, but the quality is of a different order. Cabezón's mastery is everywhere apparent. Within a miniature frame it is found in the *versillos*—brief settings of the psalm-tones —each of which is a perfect gem. In one such set, the *Versillos del primer tono,*[312] the plainchant appears successively in the soprano, alto, tenor, and bass, accompanied each time by new polyphony. Formal balance on a grander scale is found in the *tientos* (i.e., *fantasias*), which, in breadth and invention, surpass all other Spanish essays in this form. In richness of texture they are comparable to the *fantasias* of Fuenllana; the resources of the keyboard, however, allow a greater polyphonic unfolding than is possible on the technically more limited *vihuela*.[312a] Still another aspect of Cabezón's art is

[310a] *See* WardVH.   [310b] Pr. MME II, 175.
[311] Reprinted in part in PedH III, IV, VII, VIII; most of the intabulations are omitted. The prefaces to III and VIII contain biographical details and documents; *see also* KastnC, 227ff; Anglés in MGG II, 595ff; M&L XXXVI (1955), 203.
[311a] Partially reprinted in PedH VIII, xvi; reprinted entire in PaL.   [312] Pr. PedH III, 21.
[312a] For a particularly brilliant *tiento,* see the *Fuga al contrario* pr. PedH IV, 59; ScherG, 112.

found in the *diferencias,* which were evidently an outgrowth of the older examples for *vihuela.* Equal in variety and freshness to those of Narváez, the *diferencias* of Cabezón are further unified by one variation's proceeding without break to the next, thereby creating continuous music.[312b] An excellent example of this point is the set of *diferencias* on *El cantollano del Cavallero.*[312c] The theme of another set, *El pavana italiana,*[313] which had been used also—rather freely—by Mudarra,[313a] is the *Pavaniglia* melody found in Caroso (cf. p. 525).[314] This melody is here combined with the *folia* bass (cf. p. 524). Cabezón's settings of plainsong hymns are of great eloquence. The *Ave maris stella* in the *Obras* provides music for four stanzas,[315] in which the modifications to which the contrapuntal material is subjected reveal a truly superior imagination. Of the several settings of the Spanish *Pange lingua,* one of the pair whose titles refer to Wreede's piece (cf. p. 581) is fairly close to the model, while the other constitutes a most resourceful application of the parody technique on a small scale.[315a] In his intabulations, Cabezón generally treats an original with more freedom than did the *vihuelistas;* a *glosa* such as he writes on Crecquillon's *Ung gay bergier* is a free keyboard translation, quite unlike the anonymous literal one in the Henestrosa book.[315b] The frequent comparison of the music of Cabezón and Bach by modern scholars is suggested, no doubt, by the organ background and the high seriousness of purpose which these two masters have in common.

EXAMPLE 140. Fourth *Versillo del primer tono*—Cabezón (after PedH III, 22; plainsong in bass), (*b*) Third verse provided by Cabezón for one of his organ settings of *Ave maris stella* (after PedH III, 49).

[312b] *See* further NelsV, 29.

[312c] Pr. PedH VIII, 3; HAM, 145. For an analysis, *see* NelsV, 131. *See also* p. 585 *supra.*

[313] Pr. PedH VII, 73. *See* KastnCE, 105.

[313a] Piece pr. MME VII, 22; MorL II, 100.

[314] As pointed out by John Ward in *Italian Popular Music and English Broadside Ballads;* cf. Chap. 10, fn. 31a. Another, similarly entitled set of *diferencias* by Cabezón (pr. PedH VIII, 6), uses the *folia* bass, like the *Pavana* mentioned above, but not the *Pavaniglia.*

[315] Pr. PedH III, 48 (cf. our Ex. 140*b*); stanza 4 = MME II, 127, after Henestrosa (cf. WardVH, 110). MME II, 121, 122, 123, 125, 130, are different settings.

[315a] For the two, *see* MME II, 119; PedH III, 65. The other settings are pr. MME II, 1, 111, 113, 115 (= PedH III, 17), 117.

[315b] Pr. MME II, 199. For some details on Cabezón's arrangement technique, *see* WardU.

Compositions by Hernando de Cabezón, as well as a *Glosado* by Antonio's younger brother Juan, are included in the *Obras*. Other organ works of the 16th century appear as examples in the treatises of Bermudo [316] and Sancta Maria,[317] and there are still others by Francisco de Paraza and Bernardo de Clavijo, which are preserved in MS, and seventeen by the Aragonese organist Sebastián de Aguilera de Heredia (d. 1570), among which is a *batalla*. Several of the works of Victoria, printed with organ parts written out (cf. pp. 604f, 607f), reflect another aspect of the organist's profession and preserve important evidence concerning Renaissance musical practice.[318]

A fairly large repertory of keyboard music is preserved in two Portuguese MSS at the Biblioteca General of the University of Coimbra. One of these, MS Mus. 43, contains intabulations of motets and other works by Clemens non Papa, Cadéac, Canis, Crecquillon, Gombert, Arcadelt, Willaert, Josquin, Verdelot, Claudin, Richafort, Buus, Mouton, and Janequin, among others. Iberian names include Soto, Antonio de Ribera, Morales, and some that are less well-known. The other MS contains more compositions of a purely instrumental character, though arrangements of motets and chansons still occur. Some Portuguese composers are present, e.g., Heliodoro de Paiva (cf. p. 598), Macedo, and Carreira. Among the more famous names that appear are those of Crecquillon, Hesdin, Manchicourt, Lassus, Clemens non Papa, Castileti, Mouton, Janequin, and Bermudo.[318a] A volume of keyboard works was the earliest instrumental music printed in the country. This was the *Flores de Musica para o Instrumento de Tecla, & Harpa* by Manuel Rodrigues Coelho (born before 1583; died c. 1623), published in 1620 at Lisbon. Coelho was renowned as

---

[316] Several exx. pr. KinO, 227ff.

[317] Several exx. pr. *ibid.*, 236ff; MusetS, 8. (About the Sancta Maria *falsibordoni* pr. as vocal pieces in PedH VI, *see* KinO, 25, fn.)

[318] Cf. VicO IV and VI; also TreV. Works by Paraza and Clavijo pr. PedAO I, 54 (= MusetS, 17), 77, respectively; by Heredia, *ibid.*, 64, 65, 74 (= MusetS, 22). About Clavijo, *see* MGG II, 1473ff.

[318a] Further on these MSS, *see* KastnMM.

both organist and harpist. In 1603, he entered the Chapel Royal, where he remained for twenty years, holding the post of *Capellão e Tangedor de Tecla de Sua Magestade* ("Chaplain and Player on Keyboard Instruments to His Majesty"). The *Flores* consists of twenty-four *tentos,* four *glosas* on *Susanne un jour,* and various pieces based on plainsong.[319]

Bermudo and Tomás de Sancta Maria [320] brilliantly illuminate the Spanish instrumental scene in their treatises. Bermudo's *Declaración de Instrumentos Musicales* (Osuna, 1549, 1555),[321] is a book for students who wished to learn to play an instrument. In it theory is treated in detail, since a good instrumentalist must be well grounded in the rudiments of music; instruments are carefully considered, most of the possible tunings analyzed and evaluated, technical problems discussed, suitable repertory suggested, and contemporary musicians who best exemplify musical practice cited so that the student may follow good models. Bermudo does not confine himself to contemporary Spanish practice: he suggests new accordaturas (including Italian) for instruments and urges the revival of old instruments and the invention of new.

The *Libro llamado Arte de tañer fantasia assí para tecla como para vihuela* . . . (Valladolid, 1565) [322] of Sancta Maria is devoted to the study of instrumental technique and music, particularly to that of the clavichord (*monachordio*). Musical examples, including original compositions by Sancta Maria, illustrate each point of the text. His rules for "beautiful playing" include playing cleanly, in good time, and with taste, and he suggests different fingerings for different tempos. His directions for learning to play *fantasia* constitute one of the really important documents of the period.[323] Milán's *fantasias, tientos,* and double settings of *villancicos,* Narváez's *diferencias,* as well as those of the other *vihuelistas,* imply an improvisational basis, while the *recercadas* of Ortiz openly own it. Sancta Maria analyzes the practice of improvisation and thereby reveals some of the inner workings of instrumental style in an important period of gestation.

Music in the Theater

As for instrumental music in the theater, Cervantes (1547–1616) makes considerable use of it in his plays. In *Rufián Viudo,* a group of musicians appears at first without their guitars, which they have left at the barber's; when

---

[319] Further about Coelho, *see* CoelhoT; for 6 of his *tentos, see* CoelhoT (5 items); KastnCP, 6.
[320] Biographical data in *Enciclopedia Universal Ilustrado,* LIV (1927), 190f.
[321] Pr. in facs. in BermuD. Bermudo intended the 1555 edition to be the second volume of his treatise; instead, the chapters of new material on instruments are interlaced with the material of Vol. I. For a discussion of the work, *see* KinO, 9ff. Cf. also MGG I, 1764f.
[322] Partial German transl. in SaV. *See also* KinO, 25ff; HarZ.
[323] Cf. DeffÜ, 15; KinO, 132ff. The *arte de tañer fantasia* is not to be confused with that of the *glosa.* The art of the *fantasia,* though rooted in formulas, was creative and often original, whereas the *glosa* was fundamentally a parasitic form.

the instruments are brought, the men perform several pieces. In *Pedro de Urdemalas,* there is, for atmosphere, "every kind of music, and the bagpipes of Zamora." The North African scenes in *Los Baños de Argel* and *La Gran Sultana* are particularly colorful, and depend much on the introduction of Moorish music for their effectiveness.[324]

Earlier, the dramatist Diego Sanchez de Badajoz, some of whose poems were set by the madrigalists, in *La Farsa del Juego de Cañas* (c. 1550) had prescribed something approaching recitative for one of the characters, the Sybil, and the singing and dancing of a *folía.*[325] Many of the pieces by the madrigalists (e.g., some of those in the *Cancionero de Sablonara*) were evidently intended for use in theatrical entertainments. At the same time as Lope de Vega was secretary to the Duke of Alba, Blas de Castro was serving the Duke as musician (cf. p. 616) and undoubtedly wrote music for some of Lope's plays.[326]

Lope himself describes thus the use of musical instruments in one of his plays: "The instruments occupied the front part of the theatre, without being seen, and to their harmony the actors sang the verses; all the effects, such as surprise, lamentation, love, anger, being expressed in the composition of the music itself." [327] Instrumental ensembles frequently crowded out the formal prologue and substituted a merry ballad, or *jácara.* In a comedy, at the first intermission a *baile* was sung and danced, to the accompaniment of *vihuela,* harp, etc. The *entremes,* originally placed in the first intermission, was now shifted to the second.[328]

Combinations of music and drama, such as we find in Sanchez de Badajoz, Cervantes, and Lope, pave the way for the *zarzuela,* the Spanish national theatrical form, which, in the 17th century, was established by the greatly gifted poet, Calderón.[329]

[324] For comprehensive studies on music in Cervantes, *see* QuerC, SalaC. *See also* LivS, 144ff.
[325] ChaseO, 299; SalaM, 101; SachsW, 413.
[326] Cf. AngLME, 405.
[327] Transl. from ChaseM, 97; original Spanish in Emilio Cotarelo y Mori, *Historia de la Zarzuela* (1934), 36.
[328] Cf. AngLME, 414.
[329] For further data on music in the Late Renaissance theater in Spain *see* ChaseM, 90ff; ChaseO, 301ff; LivS.

Chapter 12: GERMANY: Pre-Reformation Vocal Polyphony, including the *Lochamer, Glogauer,* and other Miscellaneous *Liederbücher,* the Franco-Netherlandish Element as Represented by Isaac, and the Music of Heinrich Finck; Monophony—The Meistersinger; Instrumental Music through the 16th Century, including the Keyboard Works of Paumann, Schlick, and Hofhaimer and the Lute Pieces of the Newsidlers

ALL through the 13th and 14th centuries the German-speaking countries had occupied a peripheral position in relation to the main stream of musical development, and they remained in that position throughout the 15th century. Just as the early Minnesinger had been influenced by the troubadours and trouvères, and just as such a later figure as Oswald von Wolkenstein (c. 1377–1445) adapted several French works to German texts,[1] so his immediate successors were strongly influenced by the music of their western neighbors, and we find many compositions from France and the Low Countries reproduced in 15th-century German MSS—often in garbled and anonymous versions and sometimes with German texts replacing the originals.

Oswald's polyphonic pieces, as well as those of the Münch von Salzburg (fl. second half of the 14th century), primitive as they are, represent the beginnings of a tradition that was to govern German secular vocal music for more than a century: they are the earliest examples that have come down to us of polyphonic settings of German lieder.

Early Renaissance Secular Lieder, notably those in the Lochamer, Schedel, and Glogau Song-Books

Some works of this type have been transmitted to us through MSS Strasbourg 222 C.22 and Munich, Staatsbibl. 3232a, both of which we have already encountered. Only three of the former's polyphonic pieces with German text were copied out by Coussemaker before its loss: *Min herz* and *Min frow* by Alanus and *Wie lieflich is der mai* by Egidius de Rhenis. Nothing definite is known about these composers.[2] Whatever their nationality, the musical style of these pieces indicates at least a north French influence; moreover, characteristic Flemish spellings are applied to the German texts.[3] Only four of the 276 numbers in the Munich MS have German texts; and in one of these four

---

[1] See ReMMA, 231, 379.

[2] There is some possibility that Alanus was the Alain mentioned on p. 22 and not a German. The 2 Alanus pieces are pr. RosenU, App. 1 (= CW XLV, 9), 3; *Wie lieflich* pr. CW XLV, 10. Among the Italian pieces in this MS is Zacharia's *Cacciando per gustar* (cf. p. 32), now transformed into a motet to the Virgin. [3] *See* OsN, 23.

the German words *"Nu pitten wir"* appear only in the superius of a piece *a 3,* each of the other voices having its own Latin text, in the manner of a 13th-century motet. The other three compositions are all settings *a 3* of the famous tune *Christ ist erstanden.* Musically, these settings show little that is typically German; one, in fact, is by the westerner, Brassart (cf. p. 38), who in 1443 was *cantor principalis* to Emperor Frederick III.[4] This piece is the earliest known polyphonic treatment of a German lied by a foreigner, and its style is that of Dufay.[5] Textually, however, all four pieces show a trait, besides the linguistic one, that reveals their national origin, for they belong to the literature of the *leisen,* a German species [5a] marked by the concluding cry *Kyrioleis* (or some variant; in a number of reworkings, *Alleluia* is substituted). The oldest known monophonic example, *Christ ist erstanden,*[5b] dates from c. 1350; the oldest polyphonic one [5c] from c. 1394. These, and two other early monophonic examples, reveal no melody that was as yet standard. But eventually there were to be eleven such melodies, *Christ ist erstanden* being the most important. None of the eleven, strangely enough, seems to derive from a Kyrie of the Ordinary, but some are traceable to Kyries of Litanies.[5d]

Settings of *Christ ist erstanden,* one *a 4* and three *a 3,* appear also in the Trent Codices.[6] Although these MSS are so often cited in connection with French and other non-German music, one should not lose sight of the fact that the MSS themselves come down to us from a region which, though inhabited by Italians, was a part of the Empire and subjected to strong German influence. But just as the Strasbourg MS shows the degree to which French music was current along the western imperial border, and just as a MS at Breslau,[6a] dating from c. 1375, shows how far it had penetrated into the Empire's eastern area,[7] so the Trent MSS show the extent to which it was current along its southern border. In all four settings of *Christ ist erstanden,* the borrowed melody is in the top voice—not a German trait, as we shall see, but a western one; and their general style is that of Dufay's hymns. There are ten other pieces with German text in the Trent MSS. These reveal a more advanced stage of development than does contemporary music of unquestionably German origin, and it is likely that at least some of them are western pieces supplied with German words. This is definitely true, for example, of the one piece for which a composer is named: *So lang sie mir in meinem sinn* ascribed to Pullois,[8] which occurs in Escorial MS IV. a. 24 with a Flemish text and an attribution to "W. Braxatoris." [8a]

---

[4] PirP, 51.   [5] For a discussion of 2 of these settings, *see* TeuC, which is a study of 54 polyphonic pieces based on the tune up to 1600. The Brassart composition pr. OsN, 525; DèzE, 77.

[5a] Its origin has given rise to a controversy, summarized in RiedelL, Chap. 1.

[5b] In the version that is pr. BöhA, 658.   [5c] The *Willekommen, herre Christ* pr. CW XLV, 5.

[5d] For the most comprehensive study of the *leisen, see* RiedelL.

[6] DTO VII, 260–264. (DTO VII, 262 = CW XLV, 5.)   [6a] Now Wroclaw in Poland.

[7] This MS contains several French *ars-nova* pieces, including a motet by Philippe de Vitri. *See* FeldM, 126.

[8] Pr. DTO XI¹, 117; CW XLV, 12. Cf. OsN, 37.   [8a] Communication from Dr. Plamenac.

Three large collections of German polyphonic music have come down to us from the latter portion of the 15th century: the Lochamer, Schedel, and Glogau song-books. The first (sometimes referred to as the *Älteres Nürnberger Liederbuch* [8b]) is in a MS written by various hands in or near Nuremberg between 1455 and 1460. Once in the Library at Wernigerode, the source eventually became Berlin, Öff. wiss. Bibl., MS 40613. The song-book contains forty-seven anonymous pieces with music, of which forty-four are lieder—seven *a 3,* two *a 2,* and thirty-five *a 1* (one of these appears again as the tenor of one of the pieces *a 3;* the Münch von Salzburg's *Benedicite, Almechtiger got* [9] and Oswald's *Wach auf, mein hort* [10] are also among these one-line lieder)—and three are monophonic compositions with Latin texts.[11] Of the monophonic lieder, eight are marked "Tenor" or "Discant," an indication, of course, that they are voices taken from polyphonic pieces. It is believed that most of the other one-line melodies are also extracted from such pieces,[12] but that they may well have been performed monophonically, nevertheless.[13] (Cf. p. 206 regarding the Tournai Chansonnier and the collection of tenors in Paris, Bibl. nat., n. a. fr. 4379.) A Flemish text—*Ein vrouleen edel von naturen*—appears in one of the pieces *a 3.* One of the Latin songs (*Ave dulce tu frumentum*) is marked *"Geloymors"* and corresponds to the tenor of Binchois's *ballade, Je loe amours.*[14] The first part of another (*Virginalis flos vernalis*) is taken from the *basse dance, Languir en mille distresse,* found in the great *basse dance* MS at Brussels (cf. p. 36). The melody of the German lied, *Ach meyden,* also comes from a piece in that source, *Une fois.*[15]

Most of the *Schedelsches Liederbuch* (Munich, Staatsbibl. 3232), also known as the *Münchener* or *Waltersches* or *Jüngeres Nürnberger Liederbuch,* was written down during the 1460's in the hand of the doctor and historian, Hartmann Schedel (b. Nuremberg, 1440; d. 1514), during his student days in Leipzig, Padua, and perhaps also Nuremberg. Of its 128 pieces with music, 68 are polyphonic lieder, two monophonic lieder, twenty chansons, eighteen Latin pieces, two Italian, and eighteen without text.[16] Foreign composers repre-

[8b] Also by incorrect variants of Lochamer.

[9] Cf. ArL, 139; RosenU, App., No. 4.

[10] Cf. ArL, 94, and ReMMA, 379; also RosenU, App., No. 5.

[11] Facsimile of the complete MS in AmeL; of 1 page in WolfMS, 90. Transcrs., almost complete (but faulty) in ArL; the 9 polyphonic pieces pr. AmeD (1 = ScherG, 40); 18 of the monophonic lieder pr. RosenL (1 = ScherG, 41); etc. Commentary and analysis may be found in RosenL, RosenU, MülleL, and UrV III. For a philological study of the texts, *see* Karl Hoeber, "Beiträge zur Kenntnis des Sprachgebrauchs im Volksliede des XIV. und XV. Jahrhunderts," in *Acta Germanica,* VII (1908), 1, *passim,* but esp. 111ff.—Since the above was written SalmL, a style-critical study of the *Lochamer Liederbuch* (including transcrs. of 7 monophonic pieces), has been published.

[12] MosG I, 334; UrV III, 320; GeutU, 341. But OsN, 28f, points out that until reliable material for comparison, in the form of older polyphonic versions, turns up, it will be difficult to determine the true state of affairs. The present writer has expressed elsewhere his misgivings regarding the frequently shown tendency to leap to the conclusion that 15th-century melodies preserved in monophonic form must perforce be extracts from polyphonic works.

[13] Cf. RosenL, 80.   [14] Cf. BesM, 225; FunC.   [15] Cf. OsN, 29f.

[16] For a list of contents of the MS, *see* MaiM, 125ff. Transcrs. of the 70 lieder pr. EitD II, 43-166 (not wholly reliable); 16 of the lieder pr. RosenS; 2 of the instrumental pieces pr. EitT.

sented in this collection include Dufay, Ockeghem, Busnois, Pullois, Morton, Touront, Dunstable, Walter Frye, and Bedingham.

The extensive *Glogauer* (or *Berliner*) *Liederbuch* (Berlin, Öff. wiss. Bibl. 40098), a MS in three volumes marked "Discantus," "Tenores," and "Contratenores," was probably written c. 1477–1488 and may therefore be the earliest known example of writing in part-books. Its 294 pieces, mostly *a 3* and the rest *a 2* or *a 4*, are even more varied than the contents of the other two *Liederbücher;* it includes 158 Latin pieces (16 of which appear also, anonymously, in the Trent Codices), 70 lieder, 61 pieces apparently intended for instrumental performance, three quodlibets (the earliest German examples of this curious form), one Italian song, and one Slavic song.[17] Many of the instrumental pieces and some of the Latin ones have been identified as works, originally with French texts, by Dufay, Ghizeghem, Ockeghem, Tinctoris, Busnois, Caron, Vincenet, and Brolo.[18] Most of the Latin pieces, however, are hymns, sequences, responsories, and antiphons. The Latin texts are usually given in full, but most of the German ones are represented only by their first words.

Though all three of these *Liederbücher* include such generous quantities of foreign music, and though, as we shall see, foreign traits may be found in much of the German music, it must not be thought that the German pieces are all mere imitations of popular western counterparts. Few of the composers of these German pieces are named; none in the *Lochamer Liederbuch;* Paumann, Xilobalsamus, Walterus de salice, Walterus Scam or Seam, Wenzel Nodler, and W. Ruslein in the *Schedelsches Liederbuch;* and Attamasch, Bebrleyn, Paulus de Broda, and Rubinus in the *Glogauer Liederbuch.* Of these only Paumann is a figure of some eminence (cf. p. 658). Broda may be the Paulus de Rhoda represented in a MS at Rome and another at Leipzig; and Rubinus may be the Guillaume Ruby listed among the musicians employed at the Burgundian Court in 1415.[19] Very little is known of the others, and it is not even certain that they were Germans. Nevertheless, the German pieces in all three MSS have enough in common to warrant the conclusion that a national Early Renaissance style was taking shape, strongly influenced by French and Netherlandish techniques, but adding something of its own.

This German quality is in part an outgrowth of the Minnesinger tradition. The songs used in these polyphonic settings are descendants of the courtly Minnelieder. Some of them are *Hofweisen* ("court tunes"), but most of them are addressed to a wider audience than were their prototypes; hence the

---

[17] Transcrs. of all the lieder and instrumental pieces in EDMR IV and of 45 of the Latin pieces in EDMR VIII; 15 of the lieder in both RingA and EitD II (1 = LiliD, 205); 2 more in RingA; 3 more (quodlibets) in EitD I, 1ff (1 = HAM, 85); 47 more in EitD II, mostly 168ff; 10 of the instrumental pieces in EitT (1 = HAM, No. 83b); 2 others in ScherG, 43, and HAM, No. 83a. Commentary and analysis in RingG.

[18] *See* GomQ; EDMR IV, 55ff; BukU, 47f.

[19] Cf. pp. 43; 48, fn. 80; 92f *supra. See also* OsN, 43, for the theory that Rubinus may be the Rubino who sang at St. Peter's in Rome c. 1447 or the Rubinet of Florence, Bibl. naz. centr., Banco rari 229.

designation *"Gesellschaftslieder"* ("social songs"), songs for the educated classes—the nobility, the clergy, and members of the learned professions. The great majority of the pieces are love songs, and, as regards form, they fall into two main classes: the *Bar* form type (*Stollen, Stollen, Abgesang*) and the through-composed type.

It is very likely that in these pieces only the tenor was sung—to which part the borrowed melody was usually given—and that the other parts were performed on instruments. The technical skill shown in these settings varies greatly, even within a single collection. Thus the *Lochamer Liederbuch* contains both the two-part *Kan ich nit über werden*,[20] which, except for the fact that the parts do not cross, is hardly more than a primitive gymel (with the stereotyped unisons at all the phrase endings) and the three-part *Mein traut gesell* (Ex. 141*a*), in which the parts are all independent and some effort is made to give the superius a smooth and songlike character.[21]

This example reveals traits common to many of the best German pieces in all three *Liederbücher*. Western influence is apparent in the frequent use of the under-third cadence, in the care given to make an independent countermelody out of the discant, and in the fact that discant and tenor form a unity in themselves while the contratenor is merely a filling-in part. But instead of the continuous flow of the contemporary Franco-Netherlandish style we here have a more or less clear-cut division into sections of uneven length. This may be due to an adherence to older models of the Dufay–Binchois period or it may be a native trait, all the more so since the divisions are even more marked than in the earlier western music.

Some of the pieces *a 3* in these collections have the *cantus firmus* in the middle voice (cf. p. 59).[22] Imitation, which in the *Lochamer Liederbuch* appears only in an instrumental piece [23] and *Ein vrouleen edel von naturen,* is frequently employed in both of the later collections, perhaps reflecting the influence of such a composer as Busnois.[24] The Glogau MS also contains polyphonic lieder in which the pre-existent melody is in the superius, including some, quite chordal in style, that bear every indication of being settings of popular tunes.

[20] AmeD, 20.

[21] Ameln, in fact, prints the text under the superius, indicating his belief that the pre-existent melody is in the discant. It is much more likely, however, to be in the tenor, not only because it was the almost invariable German custom during the period in question to put it there but because the tenor part of this setting shows every sign of being a self-sufficient melody, the clinching evidence being that its cadences are "primary," i.e., they move from the second scale-degree down to the first, a characteristic of practically all the *cantus firmi* in German polyphonic lieder of this period. *See* OsN, 34; MosPH, 77; RosenU, 8f.

[22] E.g., *Der winter will hin weichen, Möcht ich dein begeren, Der wald hat sich entlaubet,* in AmeD, 12, 26, 24, respectively. The texts of the first 2 lieder should properly appear under the tenor. *See* fn. 21.

[23] *Der summer* (AmeD, 18).

[24] Concerning the frequency with which imitation appears in the *Schedelsches Liederbuch, see* OsN, 41. Some exx. from both: RosenS, 30; RingA, 18, 20, 30.

EXAMPLE 141. (*a*) Extract from *Mein traut gesell* (after AmeD, 10; ArL, 148), (*b*) *Es leit ein Schloss in Österreich* (after EDMR IV, 16).

a

"My beloved friend, my chiefest refuge, know that my words wish for thee on the day on which the year begins that everything conceivable for thy happiness be always granted to thee; and that whatever displeases thee pass thee by. Then would my heart leap for joy."

b

"There is a castle in Austria which is quite finely constructed of cinnamon and cloves. Where can one find such walls, yes walls?"

Such melodies as the one in the superius of Example 141*b* are often referred to as folk tunes by some writers, but it has been claimed [25] that not a single folk song has come down to us in authentic form, the surviving versions being altered ones made by various composers to fit polyphonic settings. Moreover, it might be better to refer to these tunes as "popular" than as "folk" material.

[25] GeutU, 342, 344.

In the music of these *Liederbücher* may be found the basic elements of the German secular polyphonic music of a good part of the 16th century. Such masters as Heinrich Finck, Paul Hofhaimer, Heinrich Isaac, and Ludwig Senfl developed this music further, but they built on the foundations established here, even using some of these melodies for their own settings.[26]

Polyphonic Lieder at the Turn of the Century, notably those of Heinrich Finck, Hofhaimer, and Isaac

After the Glogau Book we find no large collections of German secular polyphony until the second decade of the 16th century. Three such sources (now commonly named after their printers) reach us from that decade. The *Liederbuch* printed from movable type by Erhard Öglin in 1512 is probably the earliest German music so produced and the first German collection wholly *a 4*. It contains forty-three German secular and sacred lieder and seven pieces, including Marian hymns, with Latin texts. All are anonymous; and the texts appear only in the tenor-book, at the end of each piece.[27] Similarly, in Peter Schöffer's *Liederbuch,* published the following year, the complete text of all the lieder (except the last, in which only the words *"Christ ist erstanden"* appear) is given solely in the tenor-book, though the words of one appear in the discant-book also. This collection comprises sixty-two German lieder, some of whose composers are named.[28] Schöffer was the son of Gutenberg's similarly named associate (cf. p. 154). Another *Liederbuch* printed in four part-books is that of Arnt von Aich (Arnt of Aachen), of uncertain date but in any case published during the decade in question, containing seventy-five anonymous lieder.[29]

The composers named in Schöffer's *Liederbuch* are Jörg Schönfelder, Malchinger (Malchier), Jo. Fuchswild, Jo. Sies, Jörg Brack, Andreas Graw (Hraw), M. Wolff, H. Eytelwein, and Se. Virdung. Of these, Malchinger is represented by one piece in the Öglin collection also, and Brack by a piece in Arnt von Aich's *Liederbuch.* Several of these composers were attached to the court of Duke Ulrich of Württemberg at Stuttgart; Johannes Sies, an Aus-

---

[26] Some of these melodies have been productive in modern times. From the *Lochamer Liederbuch* Brahms chose *All mein Gedanken* (No. 30 of the *Deutsche Volkslieder* for voice and piano) and *Ich fahr dahin* (No. 9 of the *Deutsche Volkslieder* for mixed chorus). The *Schedelsches Liederbuch* has supplied *Es taget vor dem Walde,* arranged by Robert Franz for mixed chorus (Op. 49, No. 2), as well as *Herzlieblich Lieb, durch Scheiden, Mein Herz in steten Treuen,* and *Mein Herz ist mir gemenget,* arranged by Arnold Schoenberg, the first for mixed chorus and the other two for voice and piano. The Schoenberg versions are published in *Volksliederbuch für die Jugend,* 1930, which contains some arrangements of melodies from the other two *Liederbücher* also.

[27] Pr. PubAPTM IX, where the text is applied to all 4 voices of each piece; 1 sacred lied also in JödeC I, 82, and LiliD 421.

[28] Facsimiles of the 4 part-books in SchöfL; 15 of the lieder in CW XXIX (1 = JödeC III, 168); 1 in JödeC VI, 51; 1 piece in ScherG, 71.

[29] Pr. MosL. *See also* MGG I, 175ff. One of these lieder, *Ich schell mein Horn,* was arranged by Brahms for voice and piano (Op. 43, No. 3) and for chorus of men's voices (Op. 41, No. 1).

trian by birth, is one of the better composers in this group; [30] and Brack was highly regarded by the theorist Andreas Ornithoparchus (= Vogelmaier or Vogelsang), who dedicated to him the second book of his *Micrologus* [31] (Leipzig, 1516). None of the others is of such importance except Virdung, whose fame rests not on his music but on a treatise (*see* p. 656). Of the three leading masters of the early German polyphonic lied—Hofhaimer, Isaac, and Finck— the other two *Liederbücher* contain pieces by the first two, as well as by such lesser composers as Adam von Fulda (cf. p. 35).

Adam, born in Fulda c. 1445, is best known for his treatise, *De musica,*[32] written in 1490, but one of his polyphonic lieder, *Ach hülf mich leid,* seems to have achieved considerable popularity in the 16th century, to judge by the comment of Glareanus who, in his *Dodecachordon,* states that it is *"per totam Germaniam cantatissima"* and who prints it there with a sacred Latin text.[33] The chief point of interest in the other two secular pieces that have survived— *Ach Jupiter* and *Apollo aller Kunst*—is the choice of texts, which shows Adam's humanistic leanings. All three lieder appear in Arnt von Aich's collection.[34] Also represented in it is Adam Rener (cf. p. 649), who is sometimes confused with Adam von Fulda. His four-part lied, *Mein höchste frucht,*[35] is particularly lovely.

Although Heinrich Finck is not represented in any of these early collections, his output dates almost entirely from the pre-Reformation period, and we shall therefore consider his secular works here. He was born c. 1445, probably in Bamberg or Transylvania, and spent considerable time, interrupted by a journey through Hungary, Austria, and Germany, at the Polish Court in Cracow. From c. 1509 to 1513 he was employed by Duke Ulrich at Stuttgart. Later he served for a while as *Kapellmeister* at the Salzburg Cathedral, and toward the end of his life became musical director at the imperial court at Vienna, where he died in 1527.[36] In 1536, a collection was printed, devoted mainly to him; in it he appears as a secular composer, except for three pieces, which include his fine setting of *Christ ist erstanden.*[36a]

Finck's secular works reveal him as a composer of skill and resourcefulness. Most of these pieces [37] are based on melodies believed to be of his own inven-

---

[30] 4 of his pieces pr. DTO XXXVII[2], 63ff.

[31] An English transl. of the *Micrologus,* by John Dowland, was published at London in 1609.

[32] GerS III, 329.   [33] Pr. GlarD, 262; PubAPTM XVI, 208.

[34] MosL, 44, 74, 124. MosLL, 19ff, prints these lieder together with contemporary arrangements. The biographical material in MosLL should be read in the light of GurL.

[35] Pr. MosL, 38; PubAPTM IX, 34; another lied pr. *ibid.,* 45. Further data on Adam in MGG I, 79ff.

[36] For additional biographical data and some letters by Finck, *see* MosPH, 58, 193f.

[36a] Pr. PubAPTM VIII, 1. The 37 compositions by Heinrich Finck in this vol. include 26 other pieces from the 1536 collection.

[37] There are 26 lieder *a* 4 and 1 *a* 5 in PubAPTM VIII (2 = JödeC III, 17, 19; 1 = ScherG, 33); 3 other lieder and 2 instrumental pieces in DTO XXXVII[2], 20ff; 4 others in LiliD; 1 more in JödeC I, 49.

tion, which are allotted to the tenor part. The other parts are not mere accompanying voices; there is a considerable amount of imitation, especially at the beginning of a work (more of his pieces begin with imitation than do not); and the top voice is often so constructed as to have the character of an independent melody, equal in importance to the tenor. The bass almost attains the same status. Both these points are illustrated in the following passage:

EXAMPLE 142. From *Ich stund an einem morgen*—Heinrich Finck (from DTO XXXVII², 22).

"[. . . I heard many dolorous words] from a lass who was pretty and charming, who told her love [that they must part]."

This example shows also Finck's tendency, shared by other German composers of the period, to group two of the voices together (discant and bass in meas. 27–29 and 33; alto and bass in meas. 31). The dissonances in measures 31, 32, and 37 are characteristic of German music of the time. It was probably such passages that caused Finck's great-nephew Hermann Finck to say of him (1556) that "he excels not only in talent but also in learning, but his style is hard." Several of Finck's songs contain refrains; in some,[38] the last line of both text and music of the first strophe is repeated at the end of the other strophes; in others, however, the procedure is somewhat less simple: in *Wer hat gemeint,*[39] for example, line 6 of the text is repeated twice after line 8, the second time a third lower. The best of Finck's pieces, especially the love songs, are markedly superior in both workmanship and expressiveness to the secular polyphonic pieces in the 15th-century *Liederbücher.*

The Öglin and Arnt von Aich collections contain lieder that have been identified as compositions by Paul Hofhaimer. This important figure, who was regarded as the greatest organist of his time, seems to have been one of

---

[38] E.g., *Anders kein freud* and *Kurzweil ich hab,* in PubAPTM VIII, 53, 56.
[39] *Ibid.,* 26.

the very few German composers of the period known outside of the German-speaking countries. Another is Erasmus Lapicida (Steinschneider?), a rather shadowy figure some of whose compositions were published by Petrucci (cf. pp. 159, 165) and who can be traced in Austria, old and ill, as late as 1544, through payments made to him by Ferdinand I.[40] Hofhaimer was born in Radstadt, near Salzburg, in 1459. At the age of twenty he became court organist to Archbishop Sigmund at Innsbruck; when Emperor Maximilian I took over the Archbishop's musical establishment in 1490, Hofhaimer passed into the imperial service, where he remained for many years. In their course he seems to have been "loaned out" occasionally to various courts. During the festivities celebrating the double wedding of Maximilian's grandson and granddaughter to the daughter and son of King Wladislaus II of Hungary at Vienna in 1515,[41] Hofhaimer was knighted by the King and raised to the nobility by the Emperor. After Maximilian's death in 1519, Hofhaimer became organist in the Cathedral at Salzburg, in which city he died in 1537.[42]

In many ways, Hofhaimer's style is very similar to Finck's. In Hofhaimer's lieder [43] we find the warm lyricism, the clear though sometimes rather stiff construction, and the approach to equal importance of all the parts that characterize the works of his eminent contemporary. Most of Hofhaimer's best pieces are believed to have been written between 1490 and 1510,[44] and many of them in fact look backward to the earlier century rather than forward to the later. Thus, some of these pieces,[45] like those in the 15th-century *Liederbücher,* are constructed in sections marked by simultaneous cadences in all the voices, rather than in the smoothly flowing, unified manner characteristic of the Franco-Netherlandish style. As with Finck, the main melody is almost always in the tenor; an exception to this rule is *On freyd verzer ich,*[46] where it is in the discant. This piece *a 3* was long regarded by scholars as an organ work, but Moser has shown that it is a song for solo voice with instrumental accompaniment.

That Hofhaimer was not without humor is shown by his *Greyner zanner;* [47]

---

[40] 7 polyphonic lieder and an instrumental piece pr. DTO XXXVII², 46ff. Further about Lapicida, *see* esp. MosPH, 76f, 199ff; FederhB, 38; LunT, 47f.

[41] For a summary, with quotations, of contemporary accounts of the music performed on this occasion, *see* NowakZ, 71ff.

[42] For a detailed study of Hofhaimer's life and works, *see* MosPH and its Suppl. in ZfMW, XV (1933), 127, 138. The spelling of his name used here is the one he himself seems to have preferred (cf. MosPH, 3).

[43] His complete works, including 24 lieder and instrumental pieces, pr. MosPH; 16 lieder and 5 instrumental pieces pr. DTO XXXVII², 31ff (2 = AmbG V, 301, 303, and JödeC III, 45, 48, respectively; 2 = JödeC III, 42, 50; 1 = AmbG V, 299; 1 = WolfME, 64).

[44] MosPH, 120.

[45] E.g., *Ach edler hort, Ach lieb mit leyd, Ich hab heimlich ergeben mich* (pr. MosPH, App. II, 24, 26, 56 (= respectively DTO XXXVII², 31, 31 [= AmbG V, 299], 39 [= JödeC III, 45; AmbG V, 301]).

[46] Pr. MosPH, App. II, 78; DTO XXXVII², 42.

[47] Pr. MosPH, App. II, 48; DTO XXXVII², 37.

and that he was capable of attaining unusual intensity of feeling is shown by his piece, *Meins traurens ist.*

EXAMPLE 143. Opening of *Meins traurens ist*—Hofhaimer (complete piece in DTO XXXVII², 41; HAM, 96)

"My sorrow is caused by a malady of which I dare not complain to anyone. For thy sake alone, my shining light, I must endure my pain."

Melismas such as those in the alto in measures 11 to 14 and in the bass in measures 10 and 11 appear much more frequently in Hofhaimer than in Finck. We shall observe a similar device in the music of the Meistersinger (cf. p. 654). Characteristic of much German music of the time is the growing feeling for harmony. To be sure, the roots of chords tend, at cadences, to progress in thirds rather than fifths; but sometimes in a piece in *Bar* form the *Stollen* end on the dominant and the *Abgesang* ends on the tonic.[48]

Though Finck and Hofhaimer sum up the best qualities of the lieder of this period composed by native Germans, pre-Reformation secular polyphony in the country was carried to a still higher peak through the activities of a non-German composer—Isaac. Isaac and Hofhaimer probably knew each other well. In 1484, Isaac stayed for a few months in Innsbruck, where Hofhaimer was court organist; thirteen years later, having returned to Innsbruck from Italy, Isaac was appointed court composer to Emperor Maximilian, in whose service he remained until his death in 1517, although for much of the time he lived in Italy (cf. pp. 169f). Hofhaimer often set his pupils to making organ arrangements of Isaac's works; and Hofhaimer's younger friend Ludwig Senfl was one of Isaac's favorite pupils.

[48] E.g., Hofhaimer's *Einr junckfrau zart* and *Herzliebstes bild* (pr. MosPH, App. II, 38, 52 (= respectively DTO XXXVII², 34, 38 [= JödeC III, 42]).

As we have seen, one of Isaac's outstanding qualities was his extraordinary versatility. His chansons are different from his *frottole,* and both differ from his lieder. Many of his lieder,[49] in which the main melody is usually in the tenor, are settings similar to Finck's and Hofhaimer's. But his Netherlandish origin reveals itself in the fact that he almost always strives to achieve a continuous flow. The notable exception to this rule is his second and more famous setting of *Isbruck, ich muss dich lassen,*[50] which in its division into short sections separated by pauses anticipates the form of a Bach chorale.[51] It is exceptional in other ways also: the melody, which, it has been suggested,[52] may be a borrowed one and may date from before the middle of the 15th century, is in the discant, the other voices being subordinated to this one; and the setting is predominantly homophonic. These traits may point to the influence of the Italian *frottola.*[53] Without the altus, the piece would be entirely non-quartal (cf. pp. 103f). With it, a succession of parallel fourths appears on the word *"elend"* ("miserable"). These have been regarded as having a "threnodic" significance, but the interpretation is questionable.[54] In the earlier setting of *Isbruck,*[55] which is probably intended for instruments, the main melody appears in canon in the tenor and alto.

While *Isbruck* stands alone among the lieder of the time, Isaac's other German works are by no means stereotyped imitations of the German style. These pieces range from settings [56] that incorporate canon based on a scarcely altered borrowed melody, with the tenor functioning as one of the canon voices, to more freely written settings [57] in which the borrowed melody, again assigned to the tenor but imitated by the other voices, is modified—rhythmically and melodically—far more than was customary with German composers of the time. Unlike those composers, Isaac allows the alto to participate as an equal partner in passages of imitation. A remarkable piece which, like *Isbruck,* has no counterpart among surviving contemporary lieder, is the humorous *Es het*

---

[49] There are 22 in DTO XIV¹ (11 = PubAPTM I, 5, 9, 14 [= LiliD, 284], 43 [= JödeC IV, 20], 90, 106 [= LiliD, 259]; II, 118, 121, 196, 199 [= SmijO, 189; JödeC III, 53; LiliD, 343]; IX, 5 [= HAM, 91; LiliD, 254]; 4 = JödeC I, 33 [2 items]; III, 56 [= VI, 87], 58 [= LiliD, 349; Grove II, 741; SmijO, 190]; 1 = AdlerH I, 321). A facsimile of Isaac's *In Gottes namen fahre wyr* in his autograph in AdlerH I, 320; DTO XIV¹, frontispiece.

[50] Pr. LiliD, 349; Grove II, 741; SmijO, 190; DTO XIV¹, 15; and many other places. For a detailed study, *see* RietschI.

[51] The melody was actually used by Bach. In 1598 a hymn text by Johann Hesse, *O Welt ich muss dich lassen,* founded upon the original secular words, was fitted to Isaac's music, and it is by this title that it is found in Bach. (Brahms wrote two organ *Choralvorspiele* on this version, Op. 122, Nos. 3 and 11.) In 1633 still another text, *Nun ruhen alle Wälder,* was set to the melody, and in this form it is still used in Lutheran churches.

[52] OsN, 69.

[53] For a study of the relation between the *frottola* and the German lied of the period, *see* RosenF.

[54] As pointed out in FoxNQ, 51.   [55] Pr. DTO XIV¹, 83; RietschI, 38; JödeC VI, 87.

[56] E.g., *Zwischen perg und tieffe tal* (DTO XIV¹, 26; LiliD, 254; PubAPTM IX, 5).

[57] E.g., *Mein Müterlein.* Compare Isaac's tenor (DTO XIV¹, 18) with the reconstruction of the original in BaumD, *Melodien der Lieder,* No. 61.

ein Baur ein Töchterlein,[58] a work in which real polyphony—the main melody wanders through all the voices—alternates with occasional passages of homophony.[59] In his four-part *Ain frelich wesen,* Isaac placed the bass melody of Barbireau's three-part *Een vroylic wesen* in his altus and added three voices of his own.[60]

The characteristic traits of the German polyphonic lied style, evolved between c. 1450 and the Reformation, may be summed up as follows: (1) the settings are usually *a 3,* but toward the end of the period frequently *a 4,* and are based on a pre-existent tune—most often a *Gesellschaftslied,* but sometimes a *Hofweise* or a folk song, which is almost always in the tenor; (2) where the setting is *a 4,* the fourth part (alto) often merely fills in; (3) there is a tendency toward sectional structure; and (4) there is generous borrowing of technical devices from the western music of the Dufay–Binchois and Busnois–Ockeghem generations. Isaac adopts all these traits but usually avoids sectional structure, gives the alto an equal share in the polyphony, and, in one version of *Isbruck,* places the borrowed melody in the discant.

Sacred Polyphony at the Turn of the Century, notably that of Heinrich Finck and Isaac

Germany's peripheral status in relation to the main stream of musical development during the 15th century is even more plainly evident in the sacred polyphonic music produced by German composers in that period than in the secular music. The sacred music with Latin text shows, on the whole, extreme conservatism, and it yielded no product with such specifically German traits as did the polyphonic lied.

The backwardness indicated by some German pieces is astounding. Thus, in a MS dating from about 1500 (Breslau, Univ.-Libr. I.F. 391), we find passages of organum *a 2* that could have been written five or more centuries earlier, characterized as they are by progressions of parallel fifths, with occasional contrary motion employing only the unison, octave, and third.[61] Most of the German sacred music, however, has the same general character as its western counterpart and leans even more heavily than does the secular music upon Franco-Netherlandish precept. Perhaps the tendency to follow foreign models was intensified as a result of the first and only visit to Germany of the Papal Choir, during the Council of Constance (1414–1418; it is just possible that Dufay and Dunstable [62] attended also); in any case,

---

[58] DTO XIV[1], 7.   [59] For a detailed study of Isaac's lieder, *see* OsN, 49–84.
[60] Pr. DTO XIV[1], 62.

[61] *See* FeldQ. For exx. of similarly primitive organum from a German MS of about the same date, *see* WolfDQ, 42; from German MSS that are only a century older, *see* WolfQ and WolfME, 1. Other relatively late German MSS (mostly dating from the 14th century) that contain pieces in this style are listed in SchraO, 468, fn. 11.

[62] Cf. NedQ, 48, 51. For indications of a possible English influence on music in a Zwickau MS of c. 1500, *see* ZfMW XIII (1931), 562.

German composers appear to have approached the task of setting sacred Latin words to music in an impersonal spirit. This seems to be true, for example, of the Mass fragments in the Strasbourg MS 222 C.22 by German composers—Zeltenpferd, whose Gloria *a 3* is cited by Anonymus X to illustrate certain details of notation, Henricus Hesseman de Argentorato (= Strasbourg), and Heinricus de Libero Castro (Liberum Castrum = Freiburg im Breisgau; this Heinrich may not, as was once thought, be Heinrich Louffenberg.)[63]

An exception to the general conservatism may be the eight-part double motet *Ave mundi spes Maria—In gotes namen faren wir* in the Trent Codices.[64] Like most of the pieces with German text in this collection (cf. p. 633), its technique is more advanced than is that of unquestionably German music of the time: it is the only piece in the whole collection that is written in more than four real parts.[65] The claim that it is German rests principally on its use of the old German pilgrims' *leise, In gotes namen,* a reason that is not very convincing—Obrecht is not known to have worked in Germany, but he chose the German lied, *Maria zart,* as the *cantus firmus* of one of his Masses (cf. pp. 193f; also p. 256 regarding Josquin's use of a German tune). Somewhat stronger evidence has been adduced in support of the claim that a four-part *Salve Regina* in the Trent Codices, attributed in another MS to Dufay, is actually by a German.[66] The composer appears to have been thoroughly familiar with the Ockeghem style, but the emotional intensity of some of this music, the tendency to fall into closed, uneven periods, as opposed to the smooth, unceasing flow of Franco-Netherlandish music, the continuous activity of all four voices, as opposed to the western preference for varying the texture by means of passages for two or three voices, and awkwardness in the treatment of rhythm, all point away from France and the Netherlands and toward Germany.

The last three features just mentioned characterize most of the German sacred polyphony to about 1500. The chief sources of this music are the MSS: Berlin, Öff. wiss. Bibl. 40021;[67] Leipzig, Univ.-Bibl. 1494 (a MS bound in 1504 at the expense of Magister Nikolaus Apel in Leipzig);[68] Munich, Staatsbibl. 3154;[69] and Breslau, Mus. Inst. at the Univ., Mf. 2016.[70] All of these MSS contain, besides the usual share of western pieces, works by specific German composers, as well as many that are regarded as German on the basis of internal evidence.

[63] These pieces are discussed in BorB, 239ff. Louffenberg (c. 1385–1460) was an important writer of religious poems (*see* VogQ, 106ff). A motet *a 3* ascribed to Heinricus de Libero Castro, with two "tuba" parts, is pr. BorM, 98. *See also* MGG VIII, col. 325.
[64] DTO VII, 266; MosK, 2.   [65] Cf. OsN, 36.
[66] Pr. DTO VII, 178. *See* DèzS for a detailed analysis.
[67] List of contents in MfMG XXI (1889), 95. Facsimile of 2 pages in WolfMS, 6, 7.
[68] 1 piece pr. ScherG, 53. Description and list of contents in RieNA. On the hymns in this MS, *see* GeH.
[69] Description and partial list of contents in MaiM, 19.
[70] Analysis in FeldC I; transcrs. of 2 Masses, an Agnus, and 25 motets in FeldC II.

Found in all four of these MSS, as well as in Regensburg, Bibl. Proske, B 216–219, is a Mass, called *"Officium Auleni"* in three of them and untitled in the others. It is thought to be by a Johannes Aulen, who is otherwise unknown except for a motet published by Petrucci in 1505. The Mass,[71] which probably dates from the last third of the 15th century, is *a 3* throughout, except in the *Pleni,* during most of which the lowest voice is silent. There is apparently no *cantus firmus;* and the same head-motif opens each of the principal movements. While there is some imitation, there is a considerable amount of chordal writing, and the style as a whole is very similar to that of the old conductus (cf. p. 17). An interesting feature is the occasional use of melodic sequences, sometimes in one voice, sometimes in all three. The rather wide distance between the top voice and the others, the "lively" bass (i.e., a bass not less lively than the other two parts), and the "rich, very definite" harmony are regarded as German traits by some writers.[72]

The Breslau MS contains two anonymous Masses that share some of the traits of Aulen's composition. The first of these Masses [73] has an unusually long head-motif (six measures in some movements, twelve in others); only the Benedictus employs a borrowed melody; and while there are only three parts (a sign of conservatism) there is much use of imitation. A Mass *a 4* by Adam von Fulda in the Berlin MS employs a tenor *cantus firmus* that bears a general resemblance to the tenors of two chansons by Dufay and the superius of one by Binchois. There is little of special interest in this work, which "in many ways seems like a copy of Dufay." [74]

Unlike the *Officium Auleni,* the three known Masses by Heinrich Finck employ borrowed melodies. The three-part *Missa de Beata Virgine* uses the first invocation of the Kyrie of plainsong Mass IX as a head-motif in one or more voices at the beginning of most of the sections of the Mass; in the Christe the lowest voice begins with what seems to be a free paraphrase of the Christe of Mass IX.[75] Finck's work contains a great deal of imitation, some $\frac{6}{3}$ writing, many passages in parallel thirds, and occasional use of melodic sequences. The following passage illustrates the last two features:

EXAMPLE 144. Extract from Gloria of *Missa de Beata Virgine*—Finck (after AmbG V, 254).

[71] Pr. CW XXXI.   [72] E.g., RieH II¹, 186.
[73] Pr. FeldC II, 1.
[74] WagG, 269. The Kyrie of this Mass pr. EhmA, App. 2; NieS, 35. NieS contains 15 pieces with Latin text by Adam. EhmA is a monograph on Adam's sacred music. According to EhmA, 35, one of the pieces pr. by Niemann, *Namque triumphanti,* is not by Adam.
[75] Pr. AmbG V, 247.

The Agnus II, *a 2,* bears the direction, *"Agnus secundum quaere in Basso";* it is a mensuration canon, the values in the upper voice being halved in the lower voice. A work predominantly *a 6* [76] by Finck is the most brilliant and imposing pre-Reformation Mass, by a German composer, known to the writer. It was probably composed for the musical establishment of Duke Ulrich of Württemberg, by whom, as we have seen, Finck was employed from c. 1509 to 1513. Only the *Pleni* is in less than six parts and the Credo is *a 7.* Some Late Renaissance traits appear. There is a great deal of imitation, with occasional chordal passages, especially in the Credo. Both this Mass and Finck's four-part *Missa dominicalis* employ borrowed liturgical melodies. [77]

A four-part *Missa carminum* by Isaac [78] is of special interest here because it was apparently intended not for liturgical use but for school and private groups [79] and it employs melodies borrowed not from the Chant but from German lieder. Thus, the *Christe secundum* is almost precisely the same as the setting of *Isbruck, ich muss dich lassen* that incorporates canon (cf. p. 643); and in the *Qui sedes* the bass employs the complete tune *Die brünlein die do fliessen.* This Mass is relatively short and simple; only three parts are used in the *Qui tollis, Pleni,* Benedictus, and Agnus II. There are occasional passages of $^6_3$ writing, and others in which one pair of voices is juxtaposed against the other. More elaborate is a *Missa paschalis* [80] preserved in *Chorbuch 36* at Jena; it is also one of eight Masses *a 5* by Isaac preserved in a MS at Munich. The Sanctus is divided into short sections, each bearing a rubric calling for canon between two voices, e.g., in the *Pleni,* between vagans and discantus (at the eleventh). There is alternation between plainsong and polyphony. Throughout most of the latter the Gregorian melody (from Mass XVII) proceeds calmly in the discantus while fragments of it appear in the other parts. In the Benedictus, however, the borrowed melody is shifted to the bass and there is no canon, though there are lively bits of imitation here and there. The *Osanna,* with the chant (marked by asterisks) now in the tenor, is as follows:

EXAMPLE 145. *Osanna* from *Missa paschalis*—Isaac (Transcr. by L. Berberich).

[76] Pr. CW XXI. The title there given it, *Missa in summis,* was added by the editor. The Kyrie pr. MosK, 4.

[77] Further on the *Missa de Beata Virgine* and the *Missa dominicalis, see* WagG, 273ff.

[78] Pr. CW VII; Kyrie I in old notation in RoediN, 178.

[79] Pr. CW VII, 3. RietschI, 36, conjectures that the Mass may have been written for a monastery in the Tyrol, to which Isaac was admitted as a lay member in 1506.

[80] For the Kyrie and Sanctus through *Osanna I, see* WagG, 296ff. Kyrie I in old notation in RoediN, 178f.

Another Mass of Isaac's based, like the *Missa carminum,* on secular material, and dating (to judge from the source in which it survives) from his German period, is the one *a 4* built on his four-part lied, *Ain frelich wesen* (cf. p. 644).[81] The Mass is based primarily on the superius of the Isaac lied but draws on Barbireau too, and not only on his bass—e.g., the superius of the Credo incorporates almost all of Barbireau's superius.[82] The *Missa O praeclara* was published by Petreius at Nuremberg in 1539.[83] It is possible that Isaac's motet *Rogamus te* (cf. p. 215) was a preliminary study for this Mass, which is built on the same four-note motif. In the Credo, the music of the motet appears note for note, the first half at *Patrem omnipotentem* and the second at *Et unam sanctam,* so that the work plays a role in the formative stage of the history of the parody Mass. Between the two halves new material is inserted, beginning with *Et resurrexit.* Throughout the Mass, as in the motet, the basic motif is used in a great variety of melodic, rhythmic, and harmonic contexts.[84]

The most imposing musical creation of the entire pre-Reformation period in Germany is Isaac's *Choralis Constantinus* (discussed in Chap. 5). This huge cycle, providing settings of parts of the Proprium Missae for Sundays (and some feast and saints' days) throughout the entire church year, was published in three volumes by Hieronymus Formschneider at Nuremberg, the first in 1550 and the other two in 1555. Its publication reflects the growing wish in Germany, as well as elsewhere, for polyphonic settings of music for the Proper (cf. pp. 216; 343, fn. 33d; 450). A truly German touch was given by Isaac to at least one portion of the cycle, the introit *Resurrexi.*[85] Here the liturgical *cantus firmus* in the discant is combined with the tune of *Christ*

---

[81] Kyrie pr. ScherG, 50; analysis of the whole work in FoxF, 65ff.
[82] *See* SaarB, 126.
[83] Complete Kyrie pr. WagG, 286ff; discussion of the Mass *ibid.,* 282ff.
[84] Cf. AmbG III, 394.   [85] Pr. DTO XVI¹, 39.

ist erstanden, sung to its Latin words, *Christus surrexit,* in the lower voices.

In a four-part *Salve Regina* by Isaac at Munich, the *cantus firmus* is in the tenor, while the discant uses several German tunes as well as *Le serviteur* and *J'ay pris amours.*[86] Two motets by Isaac—the four-part *Imperii proceres* and the six-part *Virgo prudentissima*—are addressed to Maximilian I. The former, with its many passages of block-chords, followed by thin-textured counterpoint with occasional bits of imitation, is not especially noteworthy; but the latter is a brilliant work, full of contrasts: between upper voices and middle, middle and low, and between a pair of voices and the full choir. The voices are independent almost throughout, chord passages appearing only in *pars II.* In 1538, the motet reappeared with another text, *Christus filius Dei,* a prayer for Charles V. A six-part *Missa Virgo prudentissima* is based on this motet.[87]

Masses and motets reach us also by Adam Rener (born c. 1485), another Franco-Netherlander imported into Germany, whom we have found represented in the Arnt von Aich *Liederbuch.* He was one of Maximilian I's choirboys in 1498 and returned west in 1500. From 1507 until his death in 1520, he was in the service of the Elector of Saxony, Frederick the Wise—who in 1521 was to give Luther asylum at the Wartburg. Rhaw (cf. p. 678) published various works of Rener's including, in 1541 and 1545, five Masses. Eight Magnificats by him were printed in 1544.[88]

Hymn writing flourished in Germany, at a time when the Franco-Netherlanders had begun to abandon this type of composition. In many of the German hymns a slow, sustained *cantus firmus* in the discant is accompanied by lively and probably instrumental lower voices.[89] Some have a second borrowed melody, constructed like and sounding simultaneously with the first, and having a different, though related, text.[90] Another type is that in which the borrowed melody, again in long notes, is allotted to the tenor part of a setting *a 4* or *a 5.*[91] As a rule, only one strophe is set to music, which

---

[86] OsN, 81f.

[87] *Imperii proceres* pr. DTO XIV[1], 53; *Christus filius Dei* pr. AmbG V, 314. In a setting *a 4* of *Virgo prudentissima* (pr. AmbG V, 337) Isaac sets the last 2 words of the phrase *"pulchra ut luna et electa ut sol"* on the tones *ut, sol* (here G, D). According to AmbG III, 396, he does the same in the setting *a 6.* For Kyrie I of the Mass in old notation, *see* RoediN, 175f. For other Latin pieces by Isaac, not yet mentioned, *see* AmbG V, 305, 341, 349f; PubAPTM XVI, 215, 272, 290, 309, 414.

[88] About them, *see* WernM; IllM, Part I, also pp. 8, 11, at back. For the opening Kyries of 5 Rener Masses and extracts from motets and sequences (all in old notation), *see* RoediN, 89, 91, 96, 101, 107f, 176ff; a motet is pr. EisZ, 150. Cf. also LippP, 34. For biographical data, *see* GurJ, 19f; GurL, 127f.

[89] E.g., the 3-part *Conscendit iubilans* (by Florigal) and *Urbs beata Jerusalem* (anon.) pr. CW XXXII, 10, 11, respectively.

[90] E.g., an anon. *Christe qui lux es* pr. FeldC II, 61; Finck's *Veni Creator Spiritus* (combined with *Veni, Sancte Spiritus*) pr. CW XXXII, 19; and Adam von Fulda's *Nuntius celso veniens* pr. CW XXXII, 21; NieS, 11.

[91] E.g., Finck's *Festum nunc celebre* and the anon. *Qui paraclitus* pr. CW XXXII, 14, 23, respectively.

presumably served for alternate stanzas, the others being sung in plainsong.[92] Canon is found occasionally. e.g., in Adam von Fulda's *Nuntius celso veniens*,[93] the tenor follows the discant in strict canon at the octave throughout, and in a *Dies est laetitiae* attributed to Finck [94] the tenor follows the bass, and the discant the alto, in double canon at the fourth.

German polyphonic music was to draw inspiration for the next phase of its development from the native lieder, secular as well as sacred, as Isaac had already done from time to time, e.g., in his *Missa Carminum* and in the *Resurrexi* of the *Choralis Constantinus*.

Monophony: The Meistersinger

German monophony of the 15th and 16th centuries is divided into three main classes: (1) liturgical music; (2) secular music; and (3) an intermediate category in which the music resembles secular music in style but the text is religious.

The first class comprises a group with Latin text, and one with German. The music of the former group is neither abundant nor very important, though Germany, like the other Christian European countries during this period, offered its own contributions to the musical repertory of the Catholic Church. The earliest German version of the Gregorian Passion with "divided roles" supplied with all the necessary music appears in a Silesian MS (Breslau, Univ. Lib., I F 459) dating from before 1340. In some surviving fragments of an Alsatian MS, dating from the end of the 15th century and containing principally sections of the Ordinary of the Mass,[95] one Lasarus Prussz is named as the composer of Sanctus and Agnus melodies. The music in this MS is markedly inferior to that of the classic Chant. The melodies are characterized not by flowing lines but by broken chords; there is much use of the major and minor modes; and there are frequent series of leaps of a third in the same direction, along with an occasional use of scalelike passages. The same melodies are often used for both a Sanctus and an Agnus, and sometimes a whole Sanctus and Agnus are constructed out of the same few phrases. St. Gall Cod. 546, dating from before 1510 and containing principally music for the Ordinary of the Mass and sequences, also shows a definite deterioration from the high estate of Gregorian Chant at its best.[96]

An offshoot of this group is formed by pieces with Latin texts, religious

---

[92] However, p. 2 of CW IX (which volume contains 8 hymns by Finck) suggests—since the polyphonically set stanza is not always the first or second—that perhaps only 1 stanza was set polyphonically. The music, pr. *ibid.*, 4, 13, and 20, provides settings for stanzas 4, 6, and 4 of the respective hymns. The stanza 6 in question, belonging to the *Pange lingua*, might readily have been detached from the complete hymn together with stanza 5 (*Tantum ergo*), which would then be sung in plainsong. It is less easy to account for the other 2 items.
[93] See fn. 89.   [94] Pr. PubAPTM VIII, 79.   [95] *See* WolfDQ.
[96] The MS is described, and much of its music pr., in MarxC.

in nature but not strictly liturgical. Such are the *cantiones* in a MS from Neumarkt, near Breslau, dating from c. 1480 and probably intended for use in a school. A *Liber generationis* in this codex, largely monophonic but containing passages in organum *a 3*, bears markings requiring that the one-line sections be divided among the tenor, "*medius*," and discantus, according to the register of those sections.[97] That a similar method of performance was applied to wholly monophonic melodies of wide range is substantiated in one of several MSS from Rebdorf containing eleven sacred pieces, with Latin text, that were employed in private devotions. Here, at the end of a one-line *In Christi Jesu thalamo*, dated 1523, appears an inscription directing that the lowest portions of the melody be sung by a bass, the middle portions by an alto, and the highest by a tenor.[98]

The first Catholic collection of liturgical monophony with German text is Michael Vehe's *Ein new Gesangbuechlin geystlicher Lieder*, published at Leipzig in 1537 and containing fifty-two songs. This was followed by numerous others, of which perhaps the most noteworthy is the large collection of *Geistliche Lieder und Psalmen* published by Johann Leisentritt in 1567 (2nd ed., 1573; 3rd, enlarged ed., 1584).[99] Partly based on Vehe's collection, as well as on Protestant sources, is a curious MS compiled by Johann Braittenstein, a Bavarian parish priest, for his own private use. The book, the last entry in which is dated 1565, contains all sorts of pieces for the Mass and Office with Latin, Greek, and German texts; there are even attempts at translations into Hebrew and Aramaic.[100]

Protestant liturgical melodies will be discussed in the next chapter. There is little to be said here of the other two main groups—secular and religious, but non-liturgical, German music—except as they are represented in the Meistersinger repertory. While monophonic pieces belonging to these groups outside of that repertory were published as broadsides during the 16th century, there are few collections; many of the most important melodies are known only in polyphonic settings,[101] of which some have been mentioned earlier in this chapter and others will be treated in the next.[102] The only considerable collection of monophonic secular pieces is the *Rostocker Liederbuch*, written during the last quarter of the 15th century.[103] There are twenty-seven monophonic pieces and two *a 2*. Seven of the pieces have Latin texts, and six of the

[97] *See* SchzC, 388.   [98] GmelchU, 71.

[99] Further on German Catholic monophony of the 15th and 16th centuries, *see* BäumkK I and II, an important compilation of texts and music; the contents of the Vehe and later collections are described and listed in I, 124ff; *see also* UrK, 98ff.

[100] *See* BecL and StäbK. Stäblein prints the melodies with German text that are not in BäumkK or are not taken from Protestant sources.

[101] BaumD is an attempt to establish the basic form of 73 songs from an analysis and comparison of the melodies as they appear in various polyphonic vocal and instrumental settings.

[102] A few secular monophonic songs from the 14th and 15th centuries pr. WolfTL and WolfDL.

[103] *See* RanR.

German lieder appear also in the *Lochamer Liederbuch*. Evidence of both western influence and characteristic conservatism is furnished by the presence at the end of the MS of the tenor and *motetus* of a motet *a 3* from the 14th-century *Roman de Fauvel,* one of the motets that may be by Philippe de Vitri.[104] By far the largest body of German monophony in the 15th and 16th centuries is the music of the Meistersinger.

Probably the first important Meistersinger was Michel Behaim of Heidelberg (1416–1474) whose journeys found him active as soldier and singer in the service of German, Danish, and Hungarian princes; [105] the last was Adam Puschmann (1532–1600), a pupil of Hans Sachs. In the period from 1450 to 1600 Meistersinger guilds flourished in all the important German towns. The singers considered themselves musical and poetic heirs of the Minnesinger. But there is a fundamental sociological difference between Minnesinger and Meistersinger, as well as a qualitative difference in their musical products. The Minnesinger were professional musicians, often of noble birth; most of the Meistersinger, on the other hand, were musical amateurs who earned their living as tradespeople. As a result, the compositions of the Meistersinger lack the plasticity and warmth of the Minnesinger melodies; and their art, like most organized amateur activities, was overburdened by an intricate system of rules.

The Meistersinger attributed their origin to twelve great masters who supposedly were contemporaries under Emperor Otto I (912–973) and sang for him and Pope Leo VIII. Actually, however, these masters [106] were Minnesinger who lived between the 12th and 14th centuries. It was not until the 15th century that musicians called themselves Meistersinger or were described as such; and even some of these—for example, Behaim, Rosenplüt, Veit Weber —still spent much of their time traveling from one place to another specifically as minstrels.

Schools were established wherever there were Meistersinger guilds; the oldest school was that at Mainz. Each school had its *Tabulatur* or list of rules.[107] The customs prevailing in the contests held at the schools are faithfully depicted in Wagner's *Die Meistersinger*. There were normally not one but three or four *Merker* (markers), whose duty it was to listen for infractions of the rules and mark the contestant accordingly. Penalties for such infractions

---

[104] Cf. ReMMA, 337.

[105] His 11 surviving melodies pr. MünzerS; *see also* KühnR; MGG I, 1570ff.

[106] They vary in different accounts. According to Wagenseil (WagenM, 503) they were Frauenlob, Mögeling (Müglin, Mügling, Mügeln), Klingsohr, "der starke Poppo," Walter von der Vogelweide, Wolfgang Rohn (Wolfram von Eschenbach), Marner, Regenbogen, Sigmar der Weise (Reimar von Zweter), Geiger (Konrad von Würzburg), Cantzler, and Stoll. Klingsohr or Klingsor (who is replaced in some lists by Heinrich von Ofterdingen) is a semi-legendary character who was credited by the Meistersinger with magical powers. He was supposed to have vanquished, with the aid of the devil, 52 other masters, but his infernal ally could not prevail against the pious Wolfram von Eschenbach.

[107] For the Mainz *Tabulatur see* RthG, 271ff; the Nuremberg rules are printed in WagenM, 521ff, MünzerS, 85ff, and NagSM, 53ff; and extracts from the Augsburg rules, *ibid.*, 137ff.

were painstakingly listed in the *Tabulatur*. The members of the Nuremberg school were divided according to their accomplishments as follows: a *Schüler* or apprentice was one who had not yet learned the *Tabulatur;* when he had, he became a *Schulfreund;* a member who knew well four to six "tones" was a *Sänger;* one who wrote songs to existing "tones" was a *Dichter;* and the inventor of a "tone" was a *Meister*.[108]

There is some confusion about the exact meaning of the word *"Ton"* and the distinction between it and *Weise* (tune). *Ton* seems to have meant usually the verse and rhyme scheme of the poem or that scheme together with the melody; *Weise,* the melody alone. But the two words were frequently used interchangeably.[109] The Meistersinger had a large supply of "tones" [110] —many of them borrowed more or less accurately from the Minnesinger— which had individual and sometimes fantastic names, e.g., "the tone of the proud miller's daughter," "the ape-tune," and "the tone of the red bat." The four most important ones, called the "crowned tones," were by Mügling, Frauenlob, Marner, and Regenbogen.[111] The Meistersinger, it seems, frequently employed the melodies of the old "tones" and created new texts in the same metrical and rhyme patterns that governed the original texts. But the number of old melodies used was strictly limited by the *Tabulatur,* for example in Nuremberg to three or four, in Colmar to seven. The rules required that no melody for a new *Meisterton* should remind one of the melody of an old *Meisterton*. Consequently, the Meistersinger strove for melodic originality at all costs, with results that seem somewhat labored.

The Bible was the chief source of the texts, which often included a reference to the chapter and verse on which they were based. More attention seems to have been paid to the choice of the text and especially to its versification than to the melody: Meistersinger who visited neighboring guilds more frequently wrote down the words of new songs than the music; and most of the penalties listed in the *Tabulaturen* apply to improper versification, false rhymes, and the like. Since each verse or line had to be sung in one breath, it was ruled that no verse could exceed thirteen syllables in length. But there seems to have been no limit to the number of lines allowed in one strophe; and we find Puschmann remarking that a strophe of 100 lines is really long enough.[112]

Most of the songs were cast in the old *Bar*-form of the Minnesinger. The *Abgesang* frequently included a repetition of the *Stollen* melody. The music

---

[108] The Colmar school introduced a further refinement to distinguish among *Meister*. They were divided into *Singermeister, Singermeistermeister,* and *Singermeistermeistermeister,* according to the number of new songs they composed.

[109] For modern interpretations, *see* EberM, 15; MeyMM, 17; RunS, xix; Grove V, 63, fn. (apparently wrong); MosG I, 321f.

[110] Puschmann speaks of 400 "tones" and reports that in the 6 years of his stay in Nuremberg he learned more than 250 of them (GoetM, 65).

[111] Pr. WagenM, after 554, and, according to Puschmann, in RunS, 138, 68, 120, 116.

[112] MünzerS, 91.

in most Meistersinger MSS is written in some form of *Hufnagel* notation.[113] The notes are all of equal length. It is only in a few of the later MSS that attempts were made to employ mensural notation.[114] The influence of plainsong is noticeable in many of the melodies, in which the ecclesiastical modes govern the melodic structure. Other songs, however, betray an affinity to folk song and an approach to major and minor tonalities. On the whole, it may be said that the melodic structure of the Meistersinger tunes represents a transitional stage between the church modes and the major and minor scales.

Characteristic of the master-songs are the melismas, called *"Blumen,"* by the Meistersinger, on a word or syllable, usually at the beginning of a line or at an important caesura. The position of these melismas has given rise to the theory that they replaced instrumental preludes, interludes, and postludes performed in conjunction with Minnesinger pieces. (Instruments were not employed by the Meistersinger.) The *Blumen* may be divided into two types: those that are freely interpolated cadenzas; and those that may be considered elaborations of the basic melody.[115]

The most famous of all Meistersinger is Hans Sachs, the cobbler-poet of Nuremberg (1494–1576). He was extraordinarily prolific, his extant works numbering more than 6,000, of which two-thirds are master-songs.[116] Here is his *Klingende Ton,* written in 1532. The text is based on 1 Samuel, XIX, 1–3.

EXAMPLE 146. *Klingende Ton*—Hans Sachs (after MünzerS, 80).

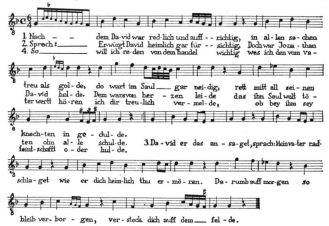

---

[113] Cf. ReMMA, 138.

[114] For a discussion of the rhythmic interpretation of Meistersinger melodies, *see* MosG I, 307ff.

[115] MosG I, 310. An ex. is given of each type.

[116] Sachs's *Silberweise* pr. LudG, 206; ScherG, 75; his *Güldenton,* in HAM, 21. The *Kettenton* of Hans Folz (c. 1560) appears in ScherG, 75; MosG I, 328. For a song by Puschmann in conjunction with one by Behaim, *see* LudG, 206. Additional master-songs, by Sachs and other Meistersinger, are reproduced in MünzerS and some early ones in RunS.

The characteristic thing about this text is the syllable and rhyme pattern, obvious in the German. No attempt has been made to retain it in the following translation.

"According as David was honest and upright, in all things true as gold, so Saul became envious of him, spoke to all his servants in private. He said: Choke David secretly and very carefully. But Jonathan was fond of David. He sorrowed in his heart that Saul wished to kill him free of all guilt. He spoke to David, said: My father ponders how he can kill thee secretly. Therefore till the morrow remain in hiding, conceal thyself in the fields. I will speak about the important matter, what I hear from my father will I faithfully report to thee, whether there be in him enmity or grace."

The Meistersinger made a sincere effort to perpetuate the musical treasure of the Minnesinger, but their stifling pedantry, their isolation from the main currents of contemporary musical life,[117] rendered their compositions, in comparison with the older German monophony, forced and stuffy. Nevertheless, the Meistersinger made an important contribution to the history of music. All countries had church music, and other countries had court music, but only in Germany was there such intensive musical activity among the *bourgeoisie*. The Meistersinger were instrumental in bringing music into the middle-class home; and they may have laid the foundations for the widespread love of music among all classes that helped in making possible the preeminent German musical productivity of later centuries.

Instrumental Music, including the Treatises of Virdung and Agricola

Although the Meistersinger did not employ instruments, ample evidence exists of their widespread and intensive use throughout the German-speaking countries during the 15th and 16th centuries. Wandering players had begun to settle down in many communities as early as the 13th century; later, they acquired official recognition as *Stadtpfeiffer* (town-pipers) and performed at municipal ceremonies of various kinds. On the third day of the wedding festivities of John the Steadfast (later elector of Saxony) at Torgau in 1500 the choir, under the direction of Adam von Fulda, sang two Masses accompanied by an organ, three trombones, a zink, and four cromornes.[118] The great woodcuts made by Hans Burgkmair and others, including probably Dürer, of the triumphal procession of Maximilian I show the importance attached to instruments by the music-loving emperor: there are several wagons

---

[117] Ambrosius Metzger is the only Meistersinger known to have written art music (his 4- and 5-part *Venusblümlein* appeared in Nuremberg, 1611–12). The guilds had rules to the effect that no popular song was to be introduced in the school; and that no unpublished master-song was to be sung outside the school. An exception to the latter rule seems to have been made in the public theatrical performances sometimes given in the 16th century by the Meistersinger, in which master-songs were sung as musical entr'actes.

[118] AberP, 81.

full of musicians playing their instruments, including one devoted to *"die suess Meledey"*—five string-players (*ain quintern, ain grosse lauten, ain Rybeben, ain Fydel, ain harpfen*) and three wind-players, one with tabor (*ain tämerlin, ain klein Rauschpfeiffen; ain grosse Rauschpfeiffen*); there are cavalcades of trumpeters and of other wind-players (*Burgundisch pfeiffer*); and Hofhaimer is represented in another wagon seated at an organ.[119] The thousands of pilgrims who came to Cologne annually from all along the Rhine early in the 16th century included musicians who played their instruments as the others sang a religious song, while many drummers beat out the rhythm of the processional march. Among the several female singers named in contemporary records are some who also played instruments.[120]

Among the musicians represented in Burgkmair's woodcuts is the trombone maker Hans Neuschel of Nuremberg (d. 1533), who was called to Rome by Leo X and rewarded for the silver trombones he had made for the pontiff. Of Neuschel a contemporary reported that he not only knew how to make the best trombones, but was also skilful in "blowing, muting, and tuning the same." [121] The Germans were excellent wind-instrument makers and many went abroad. The services of German players were sought in foreign lands, and we hear of German instrumentalists in the 15th century at the courts of Burgundy and Ferrara and at Lyons and Venice.[122]

Instruments are illustrated in a 15th-century "Dance of Death" print,[123] as well as in the earliest printed treatise on them—Sebastian Virdung's *Musica getutscht* (*getutscht* = "rendered into German"), published at Basle in 1511.[124] This work, cast in the form of a dialogue, is mainly devoted to describing the various types of instruments and to teaching the student how to transcribe vocal music for the organ, the lute, and the flute. The text is embellished with woodcuts showing many varieties of aerophones, chordophones, and membranophones. Virdung's treatise was translated into Latin by the German composer Luscinius (Ottmar Nachtgall) at the request of a Milanese bookdealer, and French and Flemish versions were made also.[125] Based on *Musica getutscht,* but written in the form of rhymed verse, is Martin Agricola's *Musica instrumentalis deudsch,* published in 1528 and reprinted in several editions during the next two decades.[126]

[119] These woodcuts are reproduced in *Jahrbuch des Kunsthistorischen Sammlungen des Allerhöchsten Kaiserhauses. Triumph des Kaisers Maximilian I. Tafeln,* 1883–84, Pls. 3, 18, 20, 22, 24, 26, 77–79, 115–117.

[120] There is a large special literature devoted to musical activities, including the use of instruments, in various German localities. *See* the bibliography in BesM, 323, to which may be added KoczA, MosM, MyG, NefB, RattM, RiessM, SandB, ScP, SpieT, and WaldN. *See also* FrotV.

[121] JahD, 29. "Dämpfen," in the original may mean either muting with a sordino or softening the tone to establish a balance within the ensemble.

[122] PirH, 154.   [123] *See* WalB.   [124] Pr. PubAPTM XI; VirdungM (facsimile).

[125] Further about Virdung, *see* NefV; WalS.

[126] The 1528 and 1545 editions pr. PubAPTM XX. *See also* MGG I, 163ff. Paul Hindemith's cantata, *Mahnung an die Jugend* (1932), is based on a text from Agricola's work.

While Virdung and Agricola confine themselves to the discussion of transcriptions of vocal music and do not mention composing original music for any instrument, a MS found in the Thomasschule at Leipzig and dated 1542 contains "26 canons in the 8 modes . . . of which the first 17 are in 3 parts and the other 9 in 2 . . . for all equal-voiced instruments and especially zinks . . ." Johann Walter (*see* p. 677) is named as the composer.[127] These are not the earliest pieces written in Germany expressly for instruments. We possess a great deal of detailed information concerning such music, composed for the organ.

Although there is no actual musical evidence for the use of the organ in Germany earlier than the 15th century, we find literary reports referring to its employment there as early as the 12th.[128] Ecclesiastical documents indicate its use for liturgical purposes: one, from Wernigerode, dates from c. 1330; another, recording the foundation of the chapter house of St. Stephen at Vienna in 1365, orders that on all the main festivals the whole Office is to be sung by the professors and students of the University, accompanied on the organ. We know that in 1384 Margrave William established weekly performances of a Marian Mass, with organ, in Leipzig. It is also stated that when the Emperor Sigismund attended the Council of Constance in 1417 a Te Deum was performed with organ accompaniment. From then on references to the organ are frequent; it is at about that time, too, that the first musical sources appear.[129]

Keyboard Music, including that of Paumann, Schlick, Hofhaimer, and the "Paulomimes"

The earliest sources of German organ music are a Sagan MS of c. 1425 and a MS by Ludolf Wilkin of Winsem (c. 1430). The first includes parts of an incomplete Gloria, and the second a *Summum Sanctus* and a Credo (incomplete) as well as some arrangements of a German lied.[130] Another important MS, dating from 1448 and now owned by the Curtis Institute of Music in Philadelphia, is that of Adam Ileborgh, who lived in Stendal in northwest Germany. The MS contains five preambles and three *"mensura"*, the latter all based on the tenor *Frowe all myn hoffen*. While half of the pieces, like all of those in the earlier MSS, are *a 2*, two preambles and two *mensura* are *a 3;* the Ileborgh MS is thus the earliest organ tablature to contain three-part pieces. The earliest known indication of the use of the pedal is represented by the

[127] *See* ZIM, XIII (1911), 275. One of the pieces *a 3* pr. ScherG, 77.
[128] *See* FrotO, 47.
[129] For a comprehensive survey of organs and organists in various German communities during the 15th century, *see* MosPH, 83–99.
[130] The Sagan MS is described in FeldM, 116ff (transcr. of the Gloria in App. II, 1); the Winsem in SchraI, 87ff. About the contents of both, *see* SchraO. Facsimile of a piece from Winsem in WolfMS, 32f; transcrs. of the Sanctus and Credo pr. SchraM, 150.

remark *"pedale seu manuale."* A noteworthy feature is the unusually wide range of this music. Schlick (cf. pp. 661f) requires a keyboard extending from F to a″ and German organ music was content to remain within these limits until well into the 16th century; but though Ileborgh does not venture above f″, he goes down as far as B-flat.[131]

One of the most celebrated of these early documents is the *Fundamentum organisandi*[132] of Conrad Paumann, who was born at Nuremberg in 1410 and became organist of the Church of St. Sebaldus in that town; he was later appointed organist at the court of Albert III of Bavaria in Munich, where he died in 1473 and was buried in the Frauenkirche. Paumann, who was blind, achieved widespread fame as an organist; during a sojourn in Mantua he is said to have refused an invitation to Milan, for fear that envious Italian organists would poison him.[133] Besides the organ, he played lute, fiddle, flute, and trumpet. His *Fundamentum organisandi* is handed down to us in the same Berlin MS 40613 that contains the *Lochamer Liederbuch* (cf. p. 634), with which it has much in common, for all of the German lieder employed as tenors of organ pieces in the *Fundamentum* are represented in the *Liederbuch* also. The *Fundamentum* is a manual of composing for the organ. It demonstrates how to write a lively counterpoint to a generally slow-moving tenor that proceeds upward or downward in conjunct progression (*simplex*) or by thirds, fourths, fifths, or sixths. There are also examples for treating cadences (*pausae*) and repeated notes (*voces redeuntes*). These examples are followed by pieces employing a German lied as tenor (one of these, *Mein Hercz jn hohen frewden ist,* is marked *"per me Georgium de Putenheim"*) as well as some miscellaneous compositions including a *Magnificat sexti toni,* a piece based on the tenor *"En avois"* (*recte: Une fois;* cf. p. 634),[133a] one attributed to Wilhelmus (Guillaume) Legrant and another to Paumgartner, and, finally, three preambles.

The most comprehensive 15th-century German collection of organ music is the *Buxheimer Orgelbuch* (Munich, Staatsbibl. Cim. 352b), dating from about 1460 and containing more than 250 pieces. About fifteen of these are preambles; the rest are all arrangements of vocal compositions, including some that appear also in the *Lochamer Liederbuch-Fundamentum organisandi* MS, some in the *Schedelsches Liederbuch,* some that have been identified as pieces by Dunstable, Binchois (there are no fewer than seven arrangements of *Je loe amours* in the MS), Dufay, Bedingham, Pullois, Brolo, Franchois, and Frye, and others that are specifically ascribed to Legrant, Jacobus Viletti, and Joh. Touront and the Germans Baumgartner (Paumgartner) and Götz. Four *Fundamenta* similar to the *Fundamentum organisandi* are in-

---

[131] Further about this MS, *see* ApelT, in which the 5 preambles are transcribed (1 = ApelN, 43; ApelK, 213; HAM, No. 84a; another = HAM, No. 84b). Facsimiles of the first 2 pp. appear in WolfH II, 11, and of p. 1 in ApelK, opp. p. 210, and ApelN, 41.

[132] Complete facsimile in AmeL; 2 pp. in ApelN, 45; 4 others in WolfH II, 14, 16; ApelK, opp. p. 211; WolfMS, 96; Latin text with German transl. and transcrs., in ArL, 178ff; 2 transcrs. also in ScherS, 31, 37 (= HAM, 85); another in ScherG, 42.

[133] SchraI, 37f.   [133a] *See* MülleI.

corporated in the MS; two of these are anonymous, but the other two are actually ascribed to Paumann.[134]

The notation of all these 15th-century German tablatures is in principle the same as in the earlier Robertsbridge MS (cf. p. 849). The top voice (the pieces in these German MSS are mostly *a 2*, except in the *Buxheimer Orgelbuch*, where they are mostly *a 3*) is written in mensural notation on a staff that usually consists of seven lines, while the lower voice or voices are indicated by letters. Except for the Robertsbridge MS, this scheme was used for keyboard music in Germany only, and was retained there throughout the 15th century and most of the 16th. Thus, whereas the normal keyboard tablature of Italy and France was entirely a mensural system and that of Spain was a finger-placement system, the method employed by the Germans was a combination of both. The stems of the notes in the top voice always point upward, an added descending stem indicating sharpening or flattening, except in the Ileborgh MS, where it indicates sharpening only. Sometimes, as in the *Fundamentum* of Berlin 40613, a descending stem crossed by a small diagonal line is used to indicate chromatic alteration. The form ♩ , which appears in both the *Fundamentum* and the *Buxheimer Orgelbuch*, probably indicates an ornament. The letters, *a* to *h*, have the same significance as they do today (*h*, of course, being the symbol for B-natural and *b* for B-flat, as in modern German); if a lower voice proceeds from one octave to the next higher one, notes in the higher octave are indicated usually by a small dash above the letters; chromatic tones are shown by a small loop attached to the letter (these alterations are almost always sharpenings, E-flat, for example, being indicated by a *d* with a loop). Metrical values are shown by dots over the letters, for the larger values, and stems, for the smaller ones (in the *Fundamentum*, metrical values, in doubtful places, are shown by red mensural notes).[135]

The organ-Mass sections in the Sagan and Winsem MSS are additional evidence of the backwardness of German composers of this period. A slow-moving tenor, based on a Gregorian melody, is set against a lively upper part. The result is hardly more than an instrumental adaptation of the style of the 12th-century St. Martial sustained-tone organa.[136] The Mass sections in the *Buxheimer Orgelbuch* reveal a quite different style. We still find pieces in sustained-tone organum style, though the tenor has now acquired rhythmic organization; but the chief trait in most of these pieces is the influence of the polyphonic conductus, shown especially in the frequent successions of chords.

---

[134] Buxheim is pr. complete in facs. in BuxO and in a modern ed. in EDMR XXXVII–XXXVIII. It is described, and about 50 pieces, including 2 of the *Fundamenta*, are transcribed in whole or in part, in EitB (2 also pr. HAM, 88 [1 = ApelK, 227]; another also pr. ApelM, 4); transcrs. not in EitB: 8 Mass sections in SchraM, 152ff; 1 piece in ScherS, 163. Facsimiles of individual pages in ScherS, 149–52; WolfH II, opp. p. 18; ApelN, 25; WolfMS, 97; MGG II, 545. The word "*Portigaler*," which appears in connection with one piece (pr. EitB, 83), is not the name of a composer, as EitB, 9, and MosG I, 342, assume, but the title of the Dufay composition mentioned on p. 51 *supra*, which the *Orgelbuch* gives in elaborated form. Further about the MS, *see* SchnoB and MGG, col. 544ff.

[135] Further on German organ tablature, *see* ApelN, 22–47.   [136] *See* ReMMA, 265f.

Sometimes the two styles—sustained-tone organum and conductus—alternate in the same piece;[137] in one passage *a 3*[138] they appear simultaneously: the two lower voices (the lower of these is doubled in the pedal) move in block-chords while the top voice has lively instrumental figurations. The *cantus firmus* is usually divided between the two low voices.[139]

Something of the sustained-tone organum style survives also in Paumann's organ pieces based on lieder; but, though the upper voice is in general much livelier than the lower, the latter has achieved some animation and, not infrequently, a note-against-note relation with the upper voice. Two methods of handling the lied melody are illustrated in the *Fundamentum* of Berlin MS 40613. In one, by far the more frequent, the melody lies, more or less intact, in the tenor, while the upper voice weaves a free counterpoint over it, as in Example 147*a*. There the two upper staves give the setting transcribed from the Berlin MS 40613; in staff 3 the melody with stems pointed upward represents the monophonic version in the *Lochamer Liederbuch,* while that with stems pointed downward represents the tenor of the organ arrangement in the *Buxheimer Orgelbuch.* In the other method (*see* Ex. 147*b*), the melody, freely paraphrased, "migrates" from one voice to another.

EXAMPLE 147. Openings of (*a*) *Des kleffers neyden* according to Paumann, the *Lochamer Liederbuch* and the *Buxheimer Orgelbuch,* (*b*) *Mit ganczen willen* according to the *Lochamer Liederbuch* and Paumann (after ScherS, 17, 24, 37).

[137] E.g., the *Cum Sancto Spiritu* (SchraM, 159f).
[138] First half of a *Christe* (SchraM, 153).
[139] Further on the early German organ-Mass, *see* SchraO, SchraM.

The second of these types is found frequently in the *Buxheimer Orgelbuch*. This MS bears the following notice at the beginning: "Mark well that where the contratenor lies above the tenor, the tenor is to be played on the pedal. If, however, the contratenor is set beneath the tenor, then play the tenor above [i.e., *manualiter*] and the contratenor below." The use of the pedal indicated here and in the Ileborgh MS places this German music in the class of true organ music, as opposed to the contemporary English, Italian, and French keyboard music, which could be played on any clavier.

The organ music we have discussed thus far is all based on material borrowed from vocal music, the *Buxheimer Orgelbuch* repertory being particularly dependent on such music, since much of it consists of mere transcriptions of polyphonic vocal pieces. However, the preambles in this MS, as well as in the Ileborgh and Berlin 40613 MSS, represent old keyboard music that is completely free of vocal antecedents. In style, to be sure, these preambles are hardly more specifically instrumental than the other organ pieces. Like the Mass sections in the Sagan and Winsem MSS, the five Ileborgh preambles consist mostly of a sustained lower voice or voices set against an upper voice full of elaborate figurations. In three of these pieces there are passages in which the lower voice becomes more animated and the upper voice less so, with resulting note-against-note progressions. This is true also of the style of the preambles in the two later MSS, though the figurations here are less extravagant than in the Ileborgh MS and the bottom voice is livelier.

No German organ tablatures have survived from the period between c. 1460 and the second decade of the 16th century. After the *Buxheimer Orgelbuch,* the next important collection of instrumental music is Arnolt Schlick's *Tabulaturen etlicher lobgesang und lidlein uff die orgeln und lauten ("Tablature of some songs of praise and little songs for the organ and lute")* published in 1512 by Peter Schöffer at Mainz.[140] Schlick, who, like Paumann, was blind, at least toward the end of his life, is also the author of a *Spiegel der Orgelmacher und Organisten* (1511), the first printed work in German on organ construction. "Many of Schlick's recommendations are being carried out by the best organ-builders today; some builders would find it difficult to meet all his requirements." [141] His tablature, the earliest printed collection of keyboard music, contains fourteen organ pieces, twelve songs with lute accompaniment, and three pieces for lute alone. Almost all of the organ pieces are based on melodies borrowed from Gregorian Chant. Although these melodies still often appear in the form of sustained notes allotted to the tenor, the style of these pieces is wholly instrumental. A recent element in organ music

---

[140] Transcribed complete in SchlickT; most of the pieces transcribed in MfMG, I (1869), App. to 115ff (2 = HAM, 101f; 1 = BruL, 2; DTO XXXVII², 82; 1 = BruL, 4; 1 = DTO XIV¹, 159; 2 = TapS, 8, 10; 2 of the songs with lute accompaniment in KörL, 154f); 1 p. of facsimile in ApelN, 27.

[141] GleS. The book is reprinted in SchlickS and MfMG I (1869), 77 (faulty). *See* MendP, 32ff and KenN for a discussion of Schlick's method of tuning the organ.

is the appearance of passages in imitation—e.g., in the piece based on the *Maria zart* melody,[142] where a fragment of this lied, before or after it appears in the tenor, is imitated in the other voices.[142a]

We have only one true organ composition by Isaac, a *ricercare,* which, according to the inscription it bears, was written for an organist at Constance.[143] This work is *a 4* and contains much imitation. Only a few keyboard works by Hofhaimer have survived, in spite of his fame as an organist. These include a transcription of Barbireau's *Een vroylic wesen* that "sounds —and even looks—like nothing but keyboard music," [144] a *Recordare,*[144a] and a *Salve Regina.* The last of these is an extended piece in five sections, setting the odd-numbered verses of the Chant melody and leaving the others to be sung in plainsong. Another polyphonic section, interpolated by one of his pupils, is a setting of *Nobis post hoc,* the latter part of verse 6.

EXAMPLE 148. The *O clemens* verse of Hofhaimer's *Salve Regina* (complete piece in MosPH, App., 8; MosF, 16).

Though we have so little of Hofhaimer's organ music, a large quantity by his German pupils (the so-called "Paulomimes") and followers survives in MS. The most important sources are the collections made by Hans Buchner ("Hans of Constance"), Kotter (the composer of the *Nobis post hoc* setting mentioned above), Fridolin Sicher, and Leonhard Kleber. The MS by Buchner (born in Ravensburg, near Lake Constance, 1483; organist at Constance, 1504; died c. 1538), called a *Fundamentum,* comprises a Latin treatise on playing the organ and writing for it and thirty-five pieces (many consisting of two or more sections) based on sacred melodies, most of them borrowed from the Mass.[145] Kotter was born in Strasbourg c. 1485, became organist at Freiburg in Switzerland, whence he was banished as a Protestant in 1530; he died at Berne in 1541. His collection—dated 1513 on the title page, though the last piece is dated 1532—contains a total of sixty-seven pieces including, besides some of his own, works by Isaac, Josquin, Martini, Barbireau, Moulu, and such Germans as Hofhaimer, Buchner, and Dietrich.[146] This MS of Kotter's once

---

[142] Pr. HAM, 102; etc. *See* further OH II, 385ff.
[142a] For details about Schlick's relations to Trent, *see* LunT, 48ff.
[143] Pr. DTO XVI¹, 229.
[144] Quotation from FoxF, 69. The piece is pr. MosPH, App., 34; MosF, 48; DTO XXXVII², 91.
[144a] Pr. MosPH, App., 17; MosF, 9.
[145] The treatise is pr., and 18 of the pieces transcribed, in PäslC; 1 also in ScherG, 78. 4 pieces by Buchner from other sources pr. MosF. *See also* MGG II, 418ff, and especially LenzB.
[146] Facsimile in ApelN, 29. Transcrs. in MerO; 20 pieces in MerT, 44ff (2 = DTO XXXVII²,

belonged to the celebrated humanist Bonifacius Amerbach, and was apparently used by him for performance at home. Sicher (1490–1546), organist at Bischofszell and St. Gall, was a pupil of Buchner. His tablature (St. Gall 530, probably written over a period of years, from c. 1503 to c. 1531) is the most comprehensive of this whole group; it contains 176 pieces, including, besides one piece by Sicher himself, transcriptions of works by Isaac, Josquin, Obrecht, Agricola, Pierre de la Rue, Mouton, Japart, Busnois, Pipelare, Loyset Compère, Craen, Stokhem, Weerbecke, and Brumel, as well as the Germans Hofhaimer, Senfl, Buchner, Kotter, Grefinger, and Fuchswild.[147] Kleber (b. Gröppingen, Württemberg, c. 1490; d. Pforzheim, 1556) was probably a pupil of Schlick and seems not to have been a "Paulomime," though his tablature, dated 1524, includes pieces by Hofhaimer. Other composers represented in this collection (which contains 112 pieces) are Isaac, Josquin, Obrecht, Brumel, and, among the Germans, Buchner, Nachtgall (Luscinius), Finck, and Senfl.[148] Finally, a MS at Trent contains four anonymous organ pieces that in style and notation seem to stem from the Hofhaimer school.[149] The Hofhaimer influence is present not only so near Italy but within Italy itself: one of the German master's pupils was Dionisio Memmo, organist at St. Mark's in Venice. Also, compositions by Hofhaimer are found in Polish tablatures.

The notation in these collections is fundamentally the same as that in the 15th-century German tablatures, except that Schlick and Kotter employ six lines while Buchner, Sicher, and Kleber use five. In pieces *a 4*, Kotter and Kleber write the lowest part as the highest row of letters, so that this order results: discant, bass, alto, tenor—an order that Buchner, too, recommends but does not ordinarily follow in his compositions. Buchner is the first German to give rules for fingering. He designates the thumb as 5 and the index finger as 1, thus: left hand, 4, 3, 2, 1, 5; right hand, 5, 1, 2, 3, 4. The following are some sample fingerings, in modern terms, for rapid passages. (To illustrate his system he marks the fingering for a whole piece.[150])

82, 89; 2 = MosF, 57, 58; 2 = ApelM, 6, 7 [= HAM, 89]; 1 = HalbK, 5 [= HAM, 104]); 9 in DTO XIV¹; 4 more in DTO XXXVII² (2 = MosF, 50, 52); 2 more in MosF, 22, and ScherG, 78. One of the Isaac pieces and 1 anon. piece are settings of *Fortuna desperata,* the former being different from the *Fortuna* settings by Isaac mentioned on p. 214 *supra.* For a special study of this tablature, *see* GurK.

[147] NfO is a detailed study of this MS and includes a thematic index of all the pieces. One facsimile in ApelN, 31; 14 pieces in MosF (to be used in the light of the corrections in NfO; 1 piece = MosPH, App., 8); 2 other pieces in DTO XXXVII².

[148] *See* LöK. Facsimiles of individual pages in WolfMS, 16; WolfH II, 26; ApelK, opp. p. 226. Transcrs. of 18 pieces in EitB, 96ff (2 = HAM, Nos. 84e, f); 12 in MosF (2 = DTO XXXVII², 91, 92 [the altus given for this last piece in MosF does not apply to the Kleber version]); 7 more in DTO XXXVII²; 8 in DTO XIV¹; 2 in ApelM, 7 (= ApelK, 228), 8. There are 5 transcrs. of *Fortuna desperata,* including 1 each by Luscinius and Buchner.

[149] They are described in MosO.   [150] PäslC, 31f (facsimile); 71ff (transcr.).

The practice of imitation, which, as we have seen, is exemplified in Schlick's collection, is given theoretical recognition in the last part of Buchner's treatise, where we find a table showing various ways of using it. The type of setting most frequently found here is that in which the borrowed melody appears in a single voice—which may be any voice except the alto—while the other voices have more or less lively counterpoint. In another type (called *permutatio* by Buchner) the *cantus firmus* is begun in one voice and continued in another. In a third type the *cantus firmus* is introduced in fugal exposition, the melody being sounded in several voices at a close time-interval. Thus it may be seen that several pieces in Buchner's collection contain a considerable amount of imitation, also frequent in Sicher's and Kleber's tablatures. Most of the pieces based on vocal models in Kotter and Kleber are similar in technique to such pieces in the *Buxheimer Orgelbuch.* Kotter, who is rather conservative, usually intabulates only three parts of a four-part original, omitting the alto. Coloration is employed deliberately: this is a form of elaboration consisting of more or less stereotyped, repeated figures. Buchner mentions it; and Kleber marks a transcription of a Latin vocal composition *a 3 "non colloratum"* and then gives the same piece in a transcription *a 4,* colored. Kotter applies coloration, when he does use it, only to those voices that do not have the *cantus firmus.* Most of the pieces in Sicher are transcriptions of polyphonic vocal and instrumental works, often merely intabulated note for note, and seldom altered to suit the organ.

The preambles found in Kotter and Kleber are similar to those in the *Fundamentum* of Berlin MS 40613 and the *Buxheimer Orgelbuch,* though more skilfully and clearly constructed, especially in Kleber. Like those earlier pieces, they are apparently freely invented. A favorite device is to alternate chordal passages with runs, as in this preamble by Kleber:

EXAMPLE 149. Praeambulum—Leonhard Kleber (From FrotO, 115).

Here, in embryo, is the toccata. Among the Kotter pieces is a *fantasia,* perhaps the oldest work so named for clavier or organ, though the title is not rare in lute music. It is in Kotter, too, that we find dances, for the first time in a German tablature. Some of them have traits in common with the *bassedanze* of Petrucci's lute tablatures. Additional evidence of foreign influence is the presence of four *Spagna* settings (cf. p. 619). Two of these are abnormal: in one, by Jo. Weck,[151] the old melody, elaborated, lies in the superius; in the other—*Spaniol Kochersperg* [152]—it is given in octaves. The latter piece shows the organum character mentioned on p. 38. Some dances have a *Nachtanz* (after-dance) in a different rhythm. The style of all these dances seems to point to a stringed keyboard instrument, rather than to the organ. Indeed, it is claimed that they are probably "the oldest known original compositions [specifically] for the clavier, and thus the first indication of a dichotomy, existing as early as the beginning of the 16th century though not yet very pronounced, between clavier and organ style." [153]

In the German organ tablatures of the second half of the 16th century coloration is applied so copiously and unimaginatively that much of the music in these collections suffers by comparison not only with contemporary English, Spanish, and Italian keyboard works but even with such earlier German products as Schlick's pieces and the preambles of Kleber. German organists, wrote Heinrich Finck's great-nephew, Hermann, in 1556, produce

"empty noise wholly devoid of charm. In order the more easily to cajole the ears of untrained listeners and to arouse admiration for their own digital skill, they sometimes permit their fingers to run up and down the keys for half an hour at a time and hope in this manner, by means of such an agreeable din, with God's help to move mountains, but bring forth only a ridiculous mouse. They pay no heed to the requirements of Master Mensura, Master Taktus, Master Tonus, and especially Master Bona fantasia." [154]

The most prominent intabulators of this period, often known collectively as the "Colorists," are Elias Nicolaus Ammerbach, Bernhard Schmid the Elder, Jakob Paix, Christoph Löffelholtz, Augustus Nörmiger, and Bernhard Schmid the Younger. Perhaps the most striking feature of their tablatures is the change in notation. Mensural notes disappear entirely and all the parts are written in letters—a type of notation, called "the new German organ tablature," that lasted in Germany until the middle of the 18th century.

These tablatures, like all tablatures, indicate the application of sharps and flats clearly. An effort has been made to deduce rules [155] for the use of *musica ficta* from these tablatures alone and to apply these rules to all music of the time. While the tablatures do show a certain amount of uniformity in the

---

[151] Pr. MerT, 48; HAM, 104.
[152] Pr. MerT, 46. The other 2 *Spagna* settings are pr. *ibid.*, 44, 50.
[153] MerO, 91.
[154] Quoted in FrotO, 141. About Hermann Finck's remarks on ornamentation in singing, *see* p. 412, *supra*. See also p. 344.
[155] *See* ApelAT.

application of sharps and flats, it would be hazardous to assume that such rules are valid for non-German music or for music other than for the organ (cf. p. 623): the sharps and flats in the German tablatures may be a result merely of local practice or of defects in the structure of the organ at the time or of both.

Ammerbach (b. Naumburg c. 1530; d. 1597) was organist at the Thomaskirche in Leipzig for many years. He published three tablatures—in 1571, 1575, and 1583—the third being a considerably revised edition of the first. The first contains transcriptions of pieces by Isaac, Hofhaimer, Senfl, Lassus, Scandellus, Malchinger, Le Maistre, Ivo de Vento, and Regnart, and the third omits some of the older men and adds Crecquillon, Godard, Rore, Arcadelt, and others—in short, the two editions offer works by many of the "celebrated authors" of the time, as well as dances. The 1575 tablature comprises transcriptions, *auffs beste colorirt* ("colored in the best possible manner"), of sacred Latin and German pieces, almost half of which are by Lassus, the rest being by Crecquillon, Ivo de Vento, Clemens non Papa, and others.[156] The elder Schmid (c. 1520–c. 1596) was organist at Strasbourg, where his *Zwey Bücher einer neuen künstlichen Tabulatur . . .* were published in 1577. He was strongly influenced by the Netherlanders, especially Lassus, whose works predominate in his tablature. Also his tablature contains (like Ammerbach's of 1583) some music based on the same material as are certain dances in Phalèse's collection of 1571. Schmid's pieces are set *a 4* to *a 6,* and the bars are marked by a gap between the groups of notes.[157] Paix was born in Augsburg in 1556, became organist at Lauingen in Swabia, and died c. 1617. His tablature, which appeared in 1583, comprises motets, songs, and dances. Among the composers represented are Lassus, Janequin (the *Bataille*), Josquin, Senfl, Hofhaimer, Philippe de Monte, Ingegneri, and many others.[158] In his introduction *an den Käuffer* ("to the purchaser") Paix advises him to make more use of the thumb. The tablature by Löffelholtz, a MS dated 1585, contains forty-eight pieces, mostly dances. The composers named include Rore, Regnart, Lassus, Striggio, and Lechner.[159] Nörmiger, court organist at Dresden, wrote his tablature in 1598 for Duchess Sophia of Saxony. It is di-

[156] For biographical data on Ammerbach, *see* WustmannA or WustM, 186. 4 pieces in DTO XXXVII², a preamble and several dances in WustM, 220, 239 (= BöhT, 67; MerT, 177), 241, 251, 252 (= HAM, 171); 4 more dances in MerT, 76ff (= BöhT, 68f; 2 in HalbK, 9; 1 in HalbK, 10; ScherG, 136); 2 others in HalbK, 9, 10; 1 in DTO XIV¹, 15.

[157] Biographical data and a description and list of contents of the tablature in VogQ, 333. A thematic index and 16 pieces in MerT, 82ff (5 = EitT, 104, 105 [= BöhT II, 73], 106 [= TapS, 42], 107 [= BöhT II, 75; incomplete in MerT], 108 [= BöhT II, 71]; 1 = BöhT II, 76; 1 = ScherG, 137); other pieces in EitT, 103 (= BöhT II, 72); HalbK, 12.

[158] Partly thematic index and 20 pieces (all dances but one) in MerT, 116 (3 = EitT, 109 [= BöhT II, 77], 111, 115; 1 = DTO XXXVII², 90); other pieces in EitT, 109 (= HalbK, 19), 113; HalbK, 20.

[159] Thematic index and 22 pieces in MerT, 167ff (1 = SmnP, 138; 1 = HalbK, 21 [less complete in MerT]); other pieces in HalbK, 22 (2 items).

vided into two parts: Part I contains seventy-seven sacred Protestant songs; Part II, thirty-nine songs, mostly secular, and ninety-four German and foreign dances.[160] The younger Schmid, son of the Elder, was born in Strasbourg in 1548. His tablature, dated 1607, contains principally Italian pieces, by Andrea and Giovanni Gabrieli, Marenzio, Rore, and others, as well as works by Aichinger, Hassler, and Erbach.[161]

Almost all of these tablatures, according to their titles, were written *auff Orgel und Instrument,* the latter term apparently referring to any stringed member of the clavier family. The virginal was among the stringed keyboard instruments known in Germany. Virdung uses the name, describes the instrument, and illustrates it with a woodcut. Before him, Paulus Paulirinus of Prague, in his *Tractatus de musica,* c. 1460, says: "The virginal is an instrument with the form of a clavichord, having metal strings which make it sound like a *clavicembalo.* It has 32 courses of strings set in action by striking the fingers on projecting keys, sounding sweetly in both tones and semitones. It is called a virginal because, like a virgin, it sounds with a sweet and tranquil voice." [162] However, a derivation from *virga,* the Latin name for the jack (part of the string-plucking mechanism) seems more logical.[162a] An unusually interesting clavier is that reputed to have been invented by Buus and constructed at Vienna; it was later owned by Luython and described by Praetorius in his *Syntagma musicum.* This instrument had seventy-seven keys, within four octaves, arranged in three rows. One row provided the diatonic degrees, a second, the sharpened degrees, and a third the flattened ones (each whole tone, therefore, being divided into three parts); this arrangement provided for insertions between E and F and between B and C in each octave, so that performance was possible in the diatonic, chromatic, and enharmonic genera.[163]

Not all of the transcriptions are overburdened with "color." In Ammerbach's collection of 1583 and in the sacred songs of the Nörmiger MS, for example, embellishments are either very moderately applied or lacking altogether. In some of the tablatures, however, it seems to be assumed that the player will, on his own initiative, add "color" to uncolored or sparsely colored pieces, according to his skill and taste. Ammerbach (1583) and the younger Schmid extend the upper limit of the compass to c'''. Though, as we have seen, the earlier intabulators sometimes omitted one voice of the original, in order

---

[160] List of contents, partial thematic index, and 69 pieces in MerT, 220 (4 also in ApelM; 2 = HalbK, 28 [2 items]); other pieces in HalbK, 27; SmnP, 140 (2 items). 1 p. of facsimile in ApelK (transcr. on p. 237 = TapS, 52; this is part of HalbK, 28 [2nd item]).

[161] Description and list of contents in VogQ, 437; list of contents and 1 piece in MerT, 259; 3 pieces in ScherG, 137; 1 in EitT; facsimile in ApelN, 35.

[162] For the original Latin, *see* ReissP, 263.

[162a] Cf. SachsHI, 335.

[163] *See* KoczG; PraetoS II, 63f; PubAPTM XIII, 75.

to facilitate playing the polyphony clearly, the Colorists occasionally add a voice and stress the chordal element instead. These settings contain many parallel fifths and octaves.

If the transcriptions of vocal pieces are usually empty and mechanical, the dances in these tablatures offer much of interest. They are often homophonic in style, with a melodious right-hand part and chords in the left hand. There are strongly marked rhythms—another indication that these pieces were planned for the clavier rather than the organ. A piece in the Löffelholtz MS called *Die kleine Schlacht* [164] is probably the earliest German example of program music for a keyboard instrument; and in some of the dances in the Nörmiger MS we find one of the earliest German attempts to combine several keyboard pieces to form what was later to be known as a suite. The first known allemande for clavier appears in the elder Schmid's tablature (pieces thus named are found in earlier French and other lute collections, and it is thought that Schmid merely borrowed one of those pieces).[165] Some pieces by Simon Lohet (d. 1611), a Belgian organist active at Stuttgart, were printed in Woltz's *Tabulatur-Buch* (1617). They include a setting of the plainsong *Media vita*, the borrowed melody being in the bass throughout.[166]

Music for Lute and for Other Instruments, including that of Gerle and the Newsidlers

The lute was the favorite instrument in German homes during the 16th century; and most of the writers of lute-tablatures attempted to couch their explanations in a form easy enough for use in self-instruction. No German lute music has survived earlier than that in Schlick's *Tabulaturen* (cf. p. 661), but many collections follow it. Among the most important of these are the tablatures by Hans Judenkünig (published at Vienna, 1523); [167] Hans Gerle (Nuremberg, 1532, 1537, 1546, 1552); [168] Hans Newsidler (Nuremberg, 1536 [2 parts], 1540, 1544 [2 different books]); [169] Rudolf Wyssenbach (Zürich,

[164] Pr. MerT, 190.
[165] MohrA I, 14; the allemande pr. *ibid.*, 15. Further about the tablatures of the Colorists, *see* FrotO, 140–170, and MerT, 21ff. *See* DietG, 14ff, about an anon. tablature, dating from shortly after 1565 and containing sacred compositions for the organ.
[166] This piece and 3 others pr. RitZ.
[167] Biographical data and list of contents of his tablature, also of his treatise, *Utilis . . . introductio* (Vienna, c. 1515–1519), in DTO XVIII², xviiff. *See also* KoczJ. Facsimile in ApelN, 79; DTO XVIII², vi; 5 excerpts from the treatise and 16 pieces from the tablature *ibid*. (1 from treatise also in ApelM, 6; 1 of the 16 also in WasG, App., 4); 3 pieces in DTO XXXVII² (1 = BruD, 16); another pr. TapS, 11 (= BruL, 6).
[168] Biographical data and description of all 4 books in TapL. List of contents of the 1532 book in MfMG III (1871), 211; of the 1546 and 1552 books in IV (1872), 38. Facsimile in WolfH II, 47; 7 pieces in DTO XXXVII²; 6 in WasG (1 = EitT, 101; 1 = WolfME, 77); 3 more in EitT, 100 (2 items), 102; 2 in KörL, 145, 152 (= BruL, 8); 2 in TapS.
[169] Biographical data and list of contents of all 4 tablatures in DTO XVIII², xxiiiff. The 2 parts of the 1536 print and one of the 1544 books are described, and their contents listed, in MfMG III (1871), 152, 210. Facsimiles in WolfH II, 43; DTO XVIII², vii (= ApelN, 81); 35 pieces *ibid*

1550); [170] Hans Jacob Wecker (Basle, 1552); Wolf Heckel (Strasbourg, 1556); [171] Sebastian Ochsenkhun (Heidelberg, 1558); [172] Matthäus Waissel or Waisselius (Frankfurt on the Oder, 1573, 1591, 1592 [2 books]); [173] Melchior Newsidler (Strasbourg, 1574); [174] and Sixt Kargel (Strasbourg, 1586). [175]

Most of these collections employ a special notation, the invention of which is ascribed by Judenkünig to an unnamed contemporary and by Virdung and Martin Agricola to Conrad Paumann. This is a rather complicated affair, in which the "strings" (five at first and six later, one less than the full number being double strings in each instance) are numbered and the frets indicated by letters running across the fingerboard. Rhythmical values are shown by stems, usually united into groups, i.e., two semiminims are indicated by ⧻, four fusae by ⧻⧻. Some writers, e.g., Schlick and Judenkünig, like the Italians, place the time-signature before each piece; others, e.g., Gerle, H. Newsidler, Ochsenkhun, omit them altogether or insert them only at a change of meter. A few Germans, including Simon Gintzler (Venice, 1547), [176] Melchior Newsidler (Venice, 1566; 2 books), [177] and Kargel (1574), produced tablatures in Italian notation also. [178]

All of these tablatures contain principally lute transcriptions of polyphonic vocal pieces and instrumental preambles, etc., and dances. The vocal pieces, like those in the organ tablatures, include sacred and secular compositions drawn from foreign as well as domestic sources. A characteristic title is that of Melchior Newsidler's collection—*Teutsch Lautenbuch darinnen kunst-*

(4 = ChilL, 3, 4, 10 [= HAM, 107], 12 [= WolfME, 73]; 2 = KörL, 137 [= ScherG, 88; BruL, 6], 138; 2 = ApelM, 9, 10 [= HAM, 108]; 1 = TapS, 21; 1 = BruL, 7 [= WasG, App., 12]; 1 = SmnP, 137); 27 more pr. DTO XXXVII² (1 = ChilL, 1; RaL, 333); 3 more pr. ChilL, 2, 6, 8; 4 pr. DTO XIV¹, 138, 151 (= BruD, 22), 161 (= BruD, 18), 166; 2 more pr. BruD, 20, 21; 1 pr. TapS, 24.

[170] Facsimile in WolfMS, 59.

[171] Brief description in VogQ, 290. Three pieces pr. DTO XXXVII² (1 = RaL, 335); 2 more pr. DTO XIV¹; 1 each pr. TapS, 35; EnI, App., 11; BruD, 5.

[172] Description and list of contents in MfMG IV (1872), 52. Facsimile in WolfH II, 45; 7 pieces pr. DTO XXXVII² (1 = RaL, 334; 1 = KörL 162; TapS, 34; WolfME, 79); 3 more pr. BruL, 8ff; 2 pr. DTO XIV¹; 1 pr. WolfH II, 44.

[173] 4 pieces pr. EnI (1 = TapS, 51); other pieces pr. BruL, 15 (= TapS, 49); RaL, 336; TapS, 50.

[174] Biographical data and list of contents in VogQ, 324. 2 pieces pr. BöhT; 1 each pr. DTO XXXVII², 88; TapS, 40 (= BruL, 14).

[175] Brief description in VogQ, 352. One piece each pr. EnI, App., 12 (= BruL, 14); ScherG, 138.

[176] 7 pieces pr. DTO XVIII² (2 = ChilL, 18 [= EnI, App., 8], 20; 1 = WolfME, 77).

[177] See MfMG III (1871), 154f. KosackL, 102ff, gives a thematic index of Benedikt de Drusina's collection of 1573, which is actually a transcr. of these Newsidler prints into German tablature; a thematic index of Drusina's own book of 1556 is given *ibid.*, 100ff.

[178] 11 pieces from tablatures not yet mentioned, including that of Philipp Hainhofer (1604), pr. BruD. About an anon. tablature dating from 1537–1544 and containing 26 pieces in Italian notation and 59 in German, see SchneidL. Further about the German notation, see ApelN, 72–80; KörL, 3–44; WolfH II, 38–50, which also lists 30 important printed tablatures and a number in MS. Fuhrmann's lute book (1605) is in French tablature, as is a German MS dating from c. 1580–1590, now in the Newberry Library, Chicago.

liche Mutetē, liebliche Italiänische, Frantzösische, Teütsche Stuck, fröliche Teutsche Täntz, Passoemezzo, Saltarelle, und drei Fantaseien Alles mit fleiss aussgesetzt, auch artlich und zierlich Colorirt . . . ("German Lute-Book, containing artistic Motets, pleasing Italian, French, and German Pieces, gay German Dances, Passamezzi, Saltarelli, and three Fantasies, all carefully set and cleverly and gracefully Colored . . ."). The Ochsenkhun differs from the others in being entirely devoted to transcriptions of vocal pieces, these including Févin's *Sancta Trinitas* and Claudin's *Si bona suscepimus.* Transcriptions of vocal works were very popular in Germany. Monte's works were among the favorite sources drawn upon.[179] The Wecker and Heckel are probably the first German tablatures for two lutes; Heckel includes a number of chansons borrowed from Attaingnant.

Schlick's songs with lute accompaniment are transcriptions of originals *a 4;* the voice sings the top part (given in mensural notation), the alto is omitted, and the tenor becomes the upper voice in the two-part lute accompaniment. Coloration is used in varying degrees: Judenkünig, for example, employs it in moderation, while Hans Newsidler distinguishes between colored pieces (with *scharpffen laiflein*) and uncolored:

EXAMPLE 150. Openings of uncolored and colored lute transcriptions of Hofhaimer's *Nach willen dein*—Hans Newsidler (from DTO XXXVII², 84).

The German lutenists, unlike the Italian and unlike their own organ-playing compatriots, on the whole employed embellishment discreetly, possibly because most of their tablatures, as we have seen, were intended for amateurs. The style of these transcriptions is largely chordal, with much passage-work, and only occasional attempts at polyphony, usually in the form of imitation at the introduction of motifs.[180]

The numerous dances in these tablatures represent only a few forms. One of the most common is the *passamezzo,* usually followed by a *saltarello.* Other

---

[179] 8 transcrs. from German sources (with the models) in MonteO XXV.

[180] For a list of 451 German secular lieder based on 313 different melodies, transcribed in 16 printed and 8 MS lute-tablatures, *see* RaL, 318–32. For a comparison of various 16th-century lute transcrs. of Hofhaimer's *Nach willen dein, see* NowakH.

Players on the oliphant, fife and drum, and trumpet. Detail from The Feast of Herodias *by Israel van Meckenem* (d. 1509)

Singers, with open choir-book (the man appears to be beating the tactus), and harpist. Detail from Danaë and the Shower of Gold, *16th-century tapestry* (School of Philip van Orley and Jan van Roome)

A trumpeter, two shawm players, and two cromorne players. From the woodcut series, Triumph des Kaisers Maximilian I, *by Hans Burgkmair and other artists of Augsburg and Nuremberg*

PLATE VII

types are the *pavane, gaillarde,* and *padoana.* All of these, of course, are based on foreign importations, and we find instances of actual borrowing—Juden-künig, for example, reproduces more or less intact two dances from Dalza's *Intabolatura de Lauto.* The German contribution is the *Tantz,* generally in duple time, with its *Nachtantz* (among whose other names are *Hupff auff, Auff und nider, Tripla, Proportz, Sprung,* and *Gassenhawer,* as well as *saltarello*), which is usually a repetition, sometimes elaborated, in triple time, of the material in the *Tantz.* Here is a fairly typical example:

EXAMPLE 151. Openings of *Der Nunnen tantz* and its *Hupff auff*—
   H. Newsidler (after DTO XVIII², 38).

About the mid-century, the Italian device of grouping several dances into a suite begins to appear in German tablatures—Wecker, for example, has suites consisting of a *passamezzo,* a *gaillarde,* and a *padoana,* while Waissel has several suites, some consisting of as many as four movements.[181]

It was probably shortly before 1500 that the principle of the lute fingerboard was adopted by the makers of viols. The first German to provide music specifically for *Gross-Geigen* (viole da gamba) was Hans Gerle, whose lute tablatures contain pieces for the bowed instruments also.[182] It is quite conceivable, however, that the compositions that have come down to us without text—such as Isaac's charming *Der Hund,*[183] the popular *T'Andernaken,*[184] and pieces of this sort in the Schedel and Glogau song-books and Fridolin Sicher's MS part-book collection (St. Gall MS 461) [185]—may have been meant for, and were perhaps performed on, viols. As elsewhere, however, the lute was by far the more popular of the two instruments; and it is not until the first decade of the 17th century that we find any considerable quantity of German music composed for viols. The dances and other instrumental pieces by such

[181] *See* the first and fourth of the 5 thematic indexes of Waissel collections, given in KosackL, 104ff. Further on the dances in German lute-tablatures, *see* DieL, which contains a detailed listing of all the dances found in 23 prints and 21 MSS. About the Polish dances in such tablatures, cf. p. 755.

[182] They are listed in EinZ, 5.

[183] Pr. MosC, 7; DTO XXXVII², 75; fragment in DTO XVI¹, 225.

[184] Various versions in DTO XXXVII², 52, 91–94; etc.

[185] Pr. GiesS. So many pieces in this MS are also in the *Odhecaton* series that Sicher very likely copied many of them from Petrucci's prints.

composers as Melchior Franck (c. 1573–1639) and Valentin Haussmann (fl. c. 1600) were usually published, according to their titles, "for all kinds of instruments," but some of these titles add "especially for viols."[186] Undoubtedly meant for any kinds of instrument that could perform them were the twelve textless pieces *a 2* by Lassus first published in 1577. Of these, the second, with its very tricky rhythms, is especially delightful.

Probably intended for zinks and trombones are the twenty-eight intradas *a 5* and *a 6* by Alexander Orologio, zink player at Dresden. These pieces (published in 1597) together with the ten intradas in Hans Leo Hassler's *Lustgarten* (1601; cf. p. 711) are harbingers of the great upsurge of instrumental ensemble music in Germany at the beginning of the 17th century.[187]

[186] DDT XVI contains music by both; 1 piece by Haussmann reappears in ScherG, 159.
[187] *See* NefI, which reprints 1 of Orologio's intradas *a 5*.

Chapter 13: GERMANY: Music of the Reformation, including the Collections of Walter, Rhaw (1544), and Eccard; 16th-Century Catholic Polyphony from about 1520, including the Music of Senfl and the Franco-Netherlandish Influence as Represented by Lassus and Monte; Secular Polyphony, including the Ott and Forster *Liederbücher* and the Collections of Hassler

The Earliest Music of the Lutherans; the Role of Luther; Walter

JUST as German vocal polyphony up to the Reformation leaned heavily upon French and Netherlandish music, so German composition of the last three quarters of the 16th century continued to be strongly influenced by foreign models: Franco-Netherlandish at first; Franco-Netherlandish and Italian toward the end. The Reformation caused a powerful and widespread upheaval in German religious, social, and political life; but its effect on German music, while profound and enduring, was neither early nor, when it came, sudden. The Reformation itself was the result of forces that had been tugging at the foundations of the Church for many years before Luther's time; and the use of music in the Lutheran Church represented in some ways an official recognition and intensification of practices that had begun spontaneously in many sections of Germany long before Luther, in 1517, nailed his 95 theses on the church door at Wittenberg. And, as we shall see, during the years of Luther's revolutionary activity, and for a whole generation after his death, his radical alterations in the liturgy and in the kind of music used in it produced little that may be regarded as constituting a specifically Protestant musical style. That was still to come.

Luther (1483–1546) was a lover of music: he had some skill on the lute and the flute and is reported to have sung the alto part in performances of polyphonic music at his home; he was a competent enough musician to compose melodies and at least one short motet—the four-part *Non moriar sed vivam*—and perhaps another.[1] He was convinced that music had the power to elevate the minds and stir the hearts of the people, and neglected no opportunity to

---

[1] *Höre Gott meine Stimm' in meiner Klage* (*see* MosZL). Both pr. LuthW; the beginning of *Non moriar* pr. MosG I, 362.

stress its importance. As far as church music was concerned, he insisted that the texts be in the vernacular, so that the congregation could understand them and partake in their performance, but he did not object to retaining Latin for pedagogical purposes. His favorite composer was Josquin, of whom he said: "Josquin is a master of the notes, which must express what he desires; on the other hand, other choral composers must do what the notes dictate"; [2] but he also had a high regard for such men as Senfl, la Rue, and Heinrich Finck.

At first, the music for the Lutheran Church was derived from two main sources: the chants of the Catholic Church and the pre-Reformation, predominantly German, religious songs. In the first group belong hymns and other chants whose texts (translated into German, sometimes by Luther) and melodies were taken over bodily and incorporated into the Protestant liturgy. Thus, to mention three hymns translated by Luther, *Veni Redemptor gentium* became *Nun komm, der Heiden Heiland; A solis ortus cardine* became *Christum wir sollen loben schon;* and *Veni Creator Spiritus* became *Komm Gott Schöpfer, heiliger Geist.* Sometimes only the old text was used and a new melody supplied (or the old one so altered as to become unrecognizable), as with the sequence *Media vita in morte sumus,* which in Luther's magnificent translation became *Mitten wir im Leben sind.*

The second group is much larger and falls into several classes. One consists of non-liturgical pieces in Latin or a mixture of Latin and German, some of them already centuries old in Luther's time. In the early days of Lutheranism they were frequently sung in German, but just as often in Latin. Such are *Dies est laetitiae (Der Tag der ist so freudenreich), Puer natus in Bethlehem (Ein Kind geborn zu Bethlehem), Resonet in laudibus (Singet frisch und wohlgemut;* this appears as *Joseph, lieber Joseph mein* in Johann Walter's *Gesangbuch,* 1544, in which version it is still popular),[3] and *In dulci jubilo, nun singet und seid froh.* Another class is formed by the wholly German religious songs that came into existence during the three or four centuries preceding the Reformation. Among the oldest of these are the three *leisen, Nun bitten wir den heiligen Geist, In Gottes Namen fahren wir,* and the glorious Easter song, *Christ ist erstanden.*[3a] These songs had been used in many churches since the days of the *Geissler* (1349),[4] although they were not officially admitted as part of the liturgy.[5] A third class consists of songs in which the melodies of the old pieces were retained, but the texts rewritten to suit Protestant ideas—in short, *contrafacta.* As earlier, the distinction between secular and sacred music was so vague in the first decades of the Reformation that no hesitation was felt in adapting sacred texts to secular melo-

---

[2] BuszL, 91. A selection of Luther's remarks about music may be found in that article.

[3] It was used, for example, by Brahms in his *Geistliches Wiegenlied,* Op. 91, No. 2, and by Max Reger in his *Mariä Wiegenlied,* Op. 76, No. 52.

[3a] With Lutherans as well as Catholics singing *leisen,* it is not always clear in which camp a particular *leise* originated; cf. RiedelL.   [4] *See* ReMMA, 238f.

[5] For a study of 13th- to 16th-century German religious songs, *see* PflU.

dies, just as the Catholics did not hesitate to write Masses based on secular tunes. A famous example of this class is Luther's Christmas song for children, *Vom Himmel hoch, da komm ich her,* based on the secular song *Aus fremden Landen komm ich her.* The Lutheran Church produced or adopted 174 *contrafacta* in the 16th century, as compared with forty-two taken up by German Catholicism during the same period—figures that reflect the great need of the new Church for suitable material.[6] To these three classes was added a fourth, the most important one, comprising songs especially written for the Lutherans. The songs with texts by Luther—some original with him, some translations from the Latin, and some "parodies" of older texts—form the core of this group. There are thirty-six of these song texts, and approximately fifty melodies survive to which they were set during Luther's lifetime. Of these fifty melodies, about twenty can be traced to pre-Reformation sources, another twenty seem to have originated in or near Luther's seat at Wittenberg, and the remaining ten are first encountered elsewhere, especially in Strasbourg. The composers of the Wittenberg melodies, which include *Ein feste Burg* and *Aus tiefer Not,* are not known; it is not impossible that Luther himself wrote at least some of them. The difficulty of attempting to determine the extent of his contribution, however, may be illustrated by an examination of *Aus tiefer Not.* This song (the text of which is based on Psalm 130 [CXXIX]) is printed with a Phrygian melody in the Erfurt *Enchiridion* (1514) and an Ionian melody in the Strasbourg *Teutsch Kirchenamt* (1525); both are still in use today.[7] Compare the beginning of the Phrygian melody with part of a Marian song by the Minnesinger Frauenlob (d. 1318),[8] the bass part of Ockeghem's *Mi-Mi* Mass, and the tenor of Josquin's *Petre tu pastor omnium:*

EXAMPLE 152. Opening of *Aus tiefer Not* compared with that of three earlier melodies.

As this example shows, the early Lutheran melodies employed turns of phrase that were the common property of the time, a fact that accounts for the similarity of many Protestant tunes.[9]

[6] BlumeE, 14f. For a list of secular melodies to which religious texts were adapted, *see* BöhA, 810.

[7] Facsimiles of both early prints in BlumeE, 18f.   [8] *See* ReMMA, 232f.

[9] For a detailed study of the texts and tunes of Luther's lieder, *see* LuthW, which contains also all of his forewords to published collections of music. *See also* BlumeE, 19f. AmeK is a set of about 100 polyphonic settings of Luther's songs by various 16th-century composers.

In Luther's *Formula Missae et Communionis* (1523) he prescribed a form of Latin Mass that differed from that of the Catholic Mass only in a few essential points.[10] But two years later he summoned Conrad Rupsch (c. 1475–1530) [11] and Johann Walter (to whom we shall return presently) to Wittenberg and with their aid produced a German Mass, which differed radically from his Latin Mass as well as from the Catholic. In this *"Deudsche Messe"* (first published in 1526) [12] the entire text is in German, the Gloria is lacking, the Epistle is followed by a German song, such as *Nun bitten wir den heiligen Geist,* instead of the Gradual, and the Gospel by the German Credo, *Wir glauben all an einen Gott.* The Offertory is omitted, and, in place of the Sanctus, Luther's *Jesaja dem Propheten das geschah* is sung. There is no Communion. If many communicants are present, other German songs, such as *Jesus Christus unser Heiland,* are added. Finally, there is a German Agnus, such as *Christe du Lamm Gottes.* Neither Luther's Latin Mass nor his German one was adopted intact. Instead, they formed the basis from which all sorts of combinations were made in the various Protestant regions for almost two centuries. The elasticity of the Lutheran liturgy was such that the following main possibilities were offered:

(*1*) *Every service may be held entirely in Latin. . . .* (*2*) *Every service may be held entirely in German. . . .* (*3*) *For any portion of the Latin text a German prose translation may be substituted.* (*4*) *For any Latin or German prose text a German lied may be substituted.* (*5*) *A German lied may be added to any Latin or German prose text.* (*6*) *At certain places (before and after the sermon, during the Communion) German lieder may be freely added.*[13]

Two of the chief aims of Luther's German Mass were to render the text understandable to the congregation and to encourage it to participate in performing the musical portions of the service. Just how the congregation did participate is not clear. It seems likely that it sang in unison and unaccompanied (the use of the organ was limited to supplying the intonation, playing postludes, and so on; the instrument was not employed in support of congregational singing until the 17th century).[14] The polyphonic lieder were sung by children, who were taught to do so in school, and by adults of the

---

[10] *See* BlumeE, 28f.   [11] For biographical data, *see* GurJ, 17ff.

[12] Reprinted in facsimile in LuthD. The "German Sanctus" pr. ScherG, 75.

[13] BlumeE, 34. Further on the musical changes made by Luther in the Catholic Mass, *see* WolfL and SchremG, 4–20; for details about the music of the early Lutheran liturgy in various regions, *see* SchremG, 58–83.

[14] However, an account of 1581 mentions congregational singing accompanied by a zink and three trombones in Berne (BlumeE, 74). How did the congregation learn the new tunes and texts? The following account, despite its date, may indicate one way: "A wandering beggar sold several songs by Martin [Luther] in the market-place at Magdeburg and sang them in public wherever he went, and taught men and women, as well as girls and boys, so many and the German lieder and psalms became so well known that the people thereafter sang them daily and openly in all the churches, before the sermons began, and still do so." (Quoted in FunA, 31, from J. Vulpius, *Magnificentia Parthenopolitana,* 1702).

educated classes who formed singing societies for the purpose of performing choral music. To guide such groups many choral collections were published, of which the first was Walter's *Geystliche Gesangk Buchleyn,* printed at Wittenberg in 1524, reprints following in 1525, 1537, 1544, and 1551, with changes and additions in each.[15]

Johann Walter was born in 1496 in a village near Jena. From 1517 to 1526 he sang in the court choir of Frederick the Wise of Saxony. In 1526 he became municipal Cantor in Torgau, where he built up a chorus consisting of students at the Latin school (at that time attended by 170 boys), members of the clergy, teachers, and other interested citizens. This group furnished the music for school festivities, including Latin and German comedies and tragedies, and important religious and civic events. At various times during Walter's long stay in Torgau, his chorus included one of Luther's sons as well as Georgius Otto (teacher of Heinrich Schütz) and the fathers of two composers who were to achieve considerable eminence in Germany—Leonhart Schröter and Michael Praetorius. In 1548, two years after Luther's death, Walter was called, upon Melanchthon's recommendation, to Dresden, to organize and direct the court *Kapelle* of the Elector of Saxony. There he stayed until a new Elector dismissed him with a pension in 1554, whereupon *"der alte Kapellmeister"* returned to Torgau, where he died in 1570.[16]

Walter's *Geystliche gesangk Buchleyn* is expressly intended, as Luther's foreword [17] shows, for youthful singers. The first edition contains forty-three pieces, of which five are Latin motets; twenty-nine are *a 4,* twelve *a 5,* and two *a 3.* The thirty-eight German lieder, twenty-three of which employ texts by Luther, are all *cantus-firmus* pieces; in thirty-six of them the principal melody is in the tenor, and in the other two it is in the discantus. As regards style, all these songs fall into two main and approximately equal-sized groups, both marked by traits we have found characteristic of the polyphonic lieder of Hofhaimer, Finck, and Isaac. In the first group, the tenor proceeds in long notes which are occasionally broken up into short figures, while the other voices move freely, in livelier fashion, above and below it.[18] There are occasional essays at imitation, usually at the beginning of a section, but the imitation is short-breathed and has no constructive significance. Sometimes, in the five-

---

[15] For a comparative table of contents of all these editions, *see* PubAPTM VII, 18, which volume gives the pieces contained in the first edition. 13 of these pieces also pr. AmeK (1 = JödeC I, 30; ScherG, 76); 3 more pr. JödeC I, 54, 88, 102; 1 in II, 47; 1 in IV, 17; 1 in V, 39; 1 pr. AmeH III², 19; 1 pr. HAM, 115; 7 later pieces pr. AmeH I² (1 = JödeC I, 31), 1 in II, 2 in III (1 = WintK I, App., No. II); 2 pr. AmbG V, 404, 419 (= WolfME, 81; LippGZ, 116; JödeC III, 171); 16 pr. AmeK (1 = WintK I, App., II²); etc.

[16] For further biographical data, *see* GurJ; AberP, 85–100; MichW. *See also* SchröW; GerhW.

[17] English transl. in BuszL, 87f; StrunkR, 341. A transl. of Walther's foreword to the rev. ed. of 1537 (which served also as the foreword of later eds.) is given *ibid.,* 343f. PubAPTM VII includes the German of both forewords.

[18] It was apparently because of the relative simplicity of the tenor parts in much German music that the *Tenoristen* of the Königsberg court choir in 1543–44 received only 12 marks annually, while the other singers were paid 20 (FedM, 16).

part lieder, a second voice bears the *cantus firmus* in canon with the tenor. As in many of Isaac's lieder, the free voices maintain a continuous flow, bridging over the caesuras in the main melody. The second group represents a type of setting that, though not new with Walter, was, because of his use of it, to have important consequences in the development of Protestant music. In this type, the voices proceed more or less chordally, with no imitation, and with clear-cut caesuras and a definite cadence in all the parts at the end of each line. The harmonic function of the bass here is plainly audible. Only one more step was needed to make of this type of setting essentially the Protestant chorale as we known it today, but that step—the shifting of the main melody to the top voice—was destined not to be taken in a decisive way for another sixty years (cf. p. 684).

Walter's music is not as skilfully written as the lieder of his predecessors, and it is somewhat simpler. But its position as forming the first Lutheran collection, and the powerful influence exerted by its intimate association with the Reformer himself, established Walter as an important figure and gave rise to other collections written along the same lines and, in part, based on the same material.[19]

Other Members of the First Generation of Protestant Composers

Perhaps the most important of these is the *Newe deudsche geistliche Gesenge . . . für die gemeinen Schulen,* published by Georg Rhaw (Rhau) in 1544.[20] Rhaw (1488–1548), a friend of Luther's, printer, composer, and at one time teacher in the University of Leipzig and Cantor at the Thomasschule, established a publishing business at Wittenberg in 1524 and set himself the task of providing the Lutheran churches, choruses, and schools with a comprehensive repertory for their musical needs. Of his activities as a composer we know nothing definite, except that he wrote a Mass *a 12* to introduce the famous debate between Luther and Eck at Leipzig in 1519.[21] The *Newe . . . Gesenge* offers a comprehensive view of the variety of early Protestant styles. There are 123 pieces, including thirty by Balthasar Resinarius, seventeen by Arnoldus de Bruck (c. 1500–1554), eleven by Senfl, eleven by Lupus Hellinck,

---

[19] Many Protestant song-books, containing texts and one-line melodies, appeared in various German cities, beginning in 1524. A large selection of pieces from these books in AmeH, I¹ and III¹. For a list of the books, *see* BöhA. BraunV lists 1,020 such lieder that were published in Nuremberg alone, between 1525 and 1570.

[20] Pr. DDT, XXXIV. 15 pieces also pr. AmeK; 6 pr. AmbG V, 232ff; 5 pr. WintK I, App.; etc. About an interesting collection by Johann (Hans) Kugelmann (*Concentus novi,* 1540; 3 pieces pr. WintK I, App., Nos. 22 [= JödeC I, 137; ScherG, 107], 23 [= AmeH I², 23], 24 [= AmeK, 109]; 4 more pr. AmeK; 6 pr. AmeH I² [1 = WolfME, 74]; 1 in II; 2 pr. JödeC V), *see* BlumeE, 53f. Biographical data on Kugelmann in FedM, *passim.*

[21] For biographical data, *see* GossR, 73ff. On Rhaw's other Protestant publications, *see* BlumeE, 62ff. For a collection of the German pieces *a 2* from the *Bicinia Gallica, Latina et Germanica . . .* published by Rhaw in 1545, *see* ReichB (1 piece in WolfME, 76; 2 in JödeC III).

ten by Benedictus Ducis (d. 1544), eight by Sixtus Dietrich (1492–1548), five by Stephan Mahu, four by Thomas Stoltzer (= Stolzer; c. 1450–1526), three by Martin Agricola, two by Georg Forster (c. 1510–1568), one each by Isaac (attributed here to Stoltzer) [22] and Johannes Weinmann (d. 1542), and twelve anonymous. It is interesting to note that at least five of these composers (besides, of course, Isaac) were definitely or probably Catholics: Arnoldus de Bruck, Hellinck, Mahu,[23] Senfl, and Stoltzer.

The pieces by the composer most generously represented in the collection— Resinarius (real name, Harzer), a pupil of Isaac and later Bishop of Leipa in Bohemia—are quite conservative. Most of them are in the first of the two styles we have found in Walter's collection (though with a greater use of imitation and more importance granted to the discantus), and Resinarius, like the composers in the 15th-century *Liederbücher,* still employs the under-third cadence. In his *Mitten wir im Leben sind,* however, he displays a nice sense of form, though in the main he follows that of the pre-existent Lutheran melody (which underlies his work [24]), by building to a climax through setting reiterations of the closing words, *"Kyrie eleison,"* to previously stated musical elements. Worthy of note also, in view of later developments, is his *Te Deum* for double chorus; [25] the two choruses *a 4* sing mostly in alternation. More interesting, though in some ways old-fashioned, are the pieces by Stoltzer (to whom we shall return in Chap. 14) and some of the anonymous lieder, which here and there achieve a high degree of expressiveness. A most dramatic composition bearing Senfl's name is *Da Jakob nun das Kleid ansah,*[26] which, with its striking contrasts between writing *a 2* and *a 4,* and between polyphony and chordal passages, employs the expressive means of a Josquin motet. In Senfl's fine *Christ ist erstanden,* the famous melody is woven together in counterpoint with *Christ der ist erstanden* (a different chorale tune) and *Jesus ist ein süsser Nam'.*[26a] Another representative of the older German style is Ducis, who differs, however, from his colleagues in the freedom with which he sometimes handles the *cantus firmus.* Ducis, first traceable in 1532, was a Protestant pastor at Ulm, negligent of his duties and given to beating his wife, but a friend of humanism.[26b] Unusual

---

[22] *Christ ist erstanden. See* ZfMW, XIV (1932), 223. It appears under Stoltzer's name in HAM, 112.

[23] 2 Magnificats pr. CommM XVIII, 1ff; Lamentations pr. XXVII, 1ff. For some biographical data, *see* FederhB, 42ff.

[24] Pr. DDT XXXIV, 138. The melody is one of the standard *leisen;* cf. RiedelL.

[25] Pr. DDT XXXIV, 183. 6 pieces by Resinarius pr. JödeC I; 1 in II.

[26] DDT XXXIV, 180; HAM, 114. GeerV, 173, claims that this piece is not by Senfl but by his compatriot Cosmas Alder (d. 1550; 5 other pieces in GeerP; 1 in BerH, 79; further on Alder, *see* MGG I, 308f).

[26a] The piece pr. DDT XXXIV, 27; PubAPTM III, 339; WintK I, App., No. 6; MeistK I, App. 2, No. 8; JödeC I, 27; *see* analysis in TeuC, 45. For the *Christ der ist . . .* melody, *see* No. 259 in BäumkK I, 533; for *Jesus . . . , ibid.,* 377. All 3 melodies are *leisen;* cf. RiedelL.

[26b] Efforts to identify him with Benedictus Appenzeller and Benedictus de Opitiis are no longer given credence; cf. MGG I, 567.

among his pieces is *Nun freut euch, lieben Christen gmein*,[27] in which each line of the text is first sung by the tenor (solo?) and then repeated by the chorus. Perhaps the most "advanced" of all the pieces in the collection are those by Dietrich, who is the only one to follow more or less consistently the second of the two styles in Walter's *Gesangbuch*.

EXAMPLE 153. Opening of *Aus tiefer Not*—Dietrich (after DDT XXXIV, 109).

"Out of the depths have I cried unto thee, O Lord. Lord hear my voice." (Psalm 130 [CXXIX]:1, 2)

In some respects, Dietrich anticipates such later masters as Hassler, Eccard, and Michael Praetorius. Thus, in his *Vater unser*,[28] in six sections, the entire melody (not the normal Lutheran one [28a]) appears as *cantus firmus* in the tenor of each section, but the bass repeats a single line of text and music (the latter varied in repetition) throughout a section—a device that was adopted by Praetorius in Part IX of his *Musae Sioniae* (1610). Arnoldus de Bruck, whose origin is unknown [29] but who served from 1541 to 1545 as chief *Kapellmeister* at Vienna, like Ducis, treats the *cantus firmus* freely, but employs imitation throughout in several of his pieces. The Hellinck compositions, in the comparative smoothness and elegance of their polyphony, are the least characteristic of all the lieder in the collection.[30]

Among the Protestant composers of the Rhaw collection, Dietrich is of special interest. He was a friend of the humanist Bonifacius Amerbach, some of whose verses he set to music. He was also intimately acquainted with Glareanus and supplied him with five examples [31] for the *Dodecachordon*. His chief compositions, aside from the pieces in Rhaw, are his antiphons (1541) and hymns (1545). The chordal style of his Rhaw lieder is exceptional; most of his sacred works are tenor *cantus-firmus* pieces in the polyphonic style of the contemporary Franco-Netherlandish composers, although

[27] Pr. DDT XXXIV, 133; AmeK, 156. Of the 9 other Ducis pieces from the Rhaw collection pr. DDT XXXIV, 6 are pr. in AmbG V, 232ff; 1 other piece pr. AmeK, 128.
[28] DDT XXXIV, 76.   [28a] Pr. ZahnM II, 141.
[29] It has been conjectured (HirzD, 155) that his name may indicate that he came from Bruges, but, according to BlumeE, 52, the Vienna archives offer evidence to the contrary. Bruck added two voices to Févin's 4-part *Sancta Trinitas;* the arrangement was printed in a collection published at Nuremberg in 1555. Of the 17 sacred songs pr. DDT XXXIV, 3 = JödeC I, 37 (= ScherG, 108), 85 (= LiliD, 236); HAM, 115. Other sacred songs pr. JödeC I, 114; 2 pr. V, 84, 95; 3 secular pieces pr. JödeC III, 14; 2 in IV, 41 (= AmbG V, 382), 100; 2 pr. AmbG V, 369, 377; 1 pr. LiliD, 17. *See* further MGG I, 66off.
[30] Further about the Hellinck lieder, *see* OsN, 89–98; 2 pr. JödeC I. For a study of the whole Rhaw collection, *see* GossR. 2 of the anon. pieces from it pr. JödeC I.
[31] Pr. PubAPTM XVI, 228, 288ff, 303ff.

he sometimes places the borrowed melody in the discantus or bass, or even in the alto. In one of his hymns he combines two modes: the discantus, alto, and bass, with a signature of one flat, are in Mode 6, while the tenor, without the flat, is in Mode 3.[32] Three of Dietrich's sacred pieces appear in Kriesstein's *Selectissimae . . . cantiones* (1540), which important collection contains also works by Josquin, Gombert, Andreas de Silva, Senfl, and others. Another composer who contributed pieces to the *Dodecachordon* is Gregor Meyer (d. 1576), a Swiss Catholic who served as organist at Solothurn and later in the Reformed Church at Basle.[33]

A close friend of Rhaw, who published all his works—strangely enough, there are none in the *Newe deudsche geistliche Gesenge*—was Joh. Hähnel (called Galliculus and Alectorius; born c. 1490). Of his relatively small output, which includes a theory handbook that reached six printings by 1553,[34] the most widely disseminated was an Easter Mass *a 4* based partly on *Christ ist erstanden* (1539).[35] Most of the sections—the work contains music for both the Ordinary and the Proper—employ Gregorian melodies; and the old *leise* is worked into the texture in three different ways: as a normal tenor *cantus firmus* (in the first part of the *Victimae paschali,* a setting which, alternating plainsong and polyphony, begins at *Agnus redemit oves*); as an *ostinato* bass (in the second part of the same sequence); and as a motif woven into all four parts of a motet-like structure (in the Agnus). The influence of Isaac and his German successors is evident in the general character of the polyphony. The Mass was included in the *Officia paschalia,* printed by Rhaw in 1539. This collection, containing compositions for the Proper and the Ordinary, illustrates, like its successor, the *Officia de Nativitate . . .* of 1545, the gradual nature of the departure of the Lutheran liturgy from that of the Catholic Church. However, the series that had undoubtedly been planned was never continued, owing to the break that finally came.[35a]

The first generation of German Protestant composers—Walter, Resinarius, Dietrich, Hähnel, and others—includes also Leonhard Paminger (1495–1567) and Caspar Othmayr (1515–1553). The former's *Opus musicum,* published posthumously in four volumes (1573–1580) and originally planned to comprise works for the whole ecclesiastical year, contains motets, some of which are in *cantus-firmus* style with considerable imitation, while others are in a more chordal style. Paminger was a cultured humanist who produced a number of literary works, and a friend of Luther and Melanchthon.[36] Oth-

---

[32] ZenkS, 66. For further details about Dietrich and for 13 of his Latin pieces, *see ibid.,* 109ff; 8 duplicated in EDMR XXIII, which contains 69 of the 122 pieces in Dietrich's hymn collection of 1545; another Latin piece in WalM, 495. 1 religious song in JödeC I; 1 in V.

[33] Biographical data in MerM; NefB, 548ff; and MerG, which prints several of his Latin pieces. 6 canons *a 2,* excerpts from 11 Kyries, and 3 motets pr. PubAPTM XVI.

[34] For a study of musical theory as taught in Wittenberg about this time, *see* AberW.

[35] Pr. CW XLIV. A religious lied in AmeH III[2], 68.   [35a] *See* further LippP, 47ff.

[36] For further information about Paminger, *see* RothP. 1 religious lied pr. AmeH I[2]; 4 in II; 1 in III[2]; 1 pr. AmeK, 143; 1 pr. JödeC I, 103; a *Pater noster* pr. ProsM, *Annus I,* III.

mayr represented these two leaders of the new faith in his *Symbola* (1547),[36a] a collection of motets whose texts feature the heraldic mottoes, or *symbola*, of thirty-four illustrious men of the day. The work was printed by Montanus and Neuber, and the motto of Montanus is one of those included. Among Othmayr's other works are German religious lieder and psalms.[37] Like Paminger, a friend of Melanchthon—but presumably on a less lofty plane—was Coclico, (cf. p. 512), who, having turned Protestant, pursued his restless career in Wittenberg (1545), Frankfurt on the Oder (1546), Königsberg (1547), Nuremberg (c. 1551–1552), and other German cities.

The Protestant Transition Period of the 1560's and 1570's

The 1560's and 1570's seem to be a transition period in the development of Protestant music. Complaints appear about the waning of interest in congregational singing and about the emphasis on art music; Latin, never wholly ousted by the vernacular, begins in some degree to regain its old place. In Matthaeus Le Maistre's *Schöne und auserlesene teutsche und lateinische geistliche Gesänge zu 3 Stimmen* (1577), for example, there is a free polyphonic setting of a Latin translation of stanza 3 of Luther's *Ein feste Burg*. It was not until the end of the century that German gained the upper hand in Protestant liturgical music; even then Latin was retained for the Ordinary of the Mass and in some communities survived for about another century alongside German in connection with other portions of the service. Le Maistre (d. 1557) was a Netherlander who succeeded Walter as *Kapellmeister* to the Elector of Saxony in 1554. Although his religious songs[38] reveal individuality and skill, they contain little, stylistically, not already found in the collections of Rhaw and Walter. Other Lutheran composers of this transitional period include Jobst vom Brandt (1517–1570),[39] Leonhart Schröter (1532–1601),[40] Gallus Dressler (1533–c. 1585),[41] and Jacob Meiland.[42]

[36a] Pr. EDMR XVI.

[37] 12 religious pieces pr. AmeK; 1 pr. AmeH I²; 3 in II; 13 secular ones in JödeC III (8 of them pr. LiliD, 130 [= LippGZ, 114], 210 [= LippGZ, 70], 211, 277, 338, 351, 355 [= LippGZ, 89], 411); 1 in IV; 3 more pr. LippGZ.

[38] KadM reprints 20 sacred and secular pieces or sections of pieces (6 = MaldP I, 21 [= ScherG, 124], 32 [= MaldP XII, 42]; XII, 40, 43, 45, 49 [cf. ReT, 108]; others = JödeC V, 119; SchöbS II, 969, 970; the 2 pieces with Italian texts in KadM are by Werrecore; cf. p. 333, fn. 180); 6 pieces pr. AmeK (1 = JödeC V, 20); 8 pr. AmeH I²; 4 in II; 1 in III²; 2 pr. OsN, 538ff; 2 pr. CW XXX; 1 pr. BockM XI; 1 each pr. JödeC II, VI; 1 pr. ScherG, 123 (= SchöbS II, 891); 2 pr. AmbG V, 421ff; 1 Latin motet pr. CommB VIII, 72. About Le Maistre's lieder, see OsN, 97–137.

[39] 1 religious lied in AmeH I², 199; 4 secular lieder in LiliD, 12 (= JödeC III, 6; LippGZ, 118), 325, 388, 404 (= JödeC III, 11). See AlbD.

[40] 11 pieces in SchöbS II (5 = BockM V, 72 [= JödeC I, 4], 74; VI, 61 [= WintK I, App., No. 41; AmeH III², 80]; XI, 67, 69 [= JödeC I, 129]; 2 = JödeC I, 35, 79; 1 = WintK I, App., No. 42); others pr. WintK I, App., No. 40; JödeC I, 75; V, 8; 2 pr. AmeH I², 24; II, 337. See HofL; HofS.

[41] For this fn., see next page. [42] For this fn., see next page.

Zwingli and Music; Reciprocal Musical Effects of Swiss and German Protestantism; Lutheran Psalm Collections

While Luther, as we have seen, encouraged the performance of music in the church, the Swiss reformer, Zwingli (cf. p. 358), frowned upon it and was instrumental in having the organs destroyed in Swiss churches. Zwingli was nevertheless himself a cultured musician, perhaps even a composer,[43] and numbered among his friends the Swiss composer Johannes Wannenmacher (d. 1551). Of Wannenmacher's twenty-seven surviving works, his motet *An Wasserflüssen Babylon*[44] is perhaps the most important. This piece, which is in five sections, reveals its composer's liking for contrast: the first section is *a 4*, the second *a 2*, the third *a 5*, the fourth *a 2*, and the last *a 6*. In this last section the *cantus firmus* appears unchanged in the tenor but embellished in the discantus.[45]

It was at Strasbourg in 1538 that Calvin became acquainted with congregational psalm-singing in German. Here Matthias Greitter, who was the principal singer at the Cathedral—which at that time was in the possession of the Protestants—, had composed some original melodies for the purpose.[46] Calvin adapted several of Greitter's, and other German, melodies to French psalm texts (cf. p. 359). Complete Protestant psalters, with one-line melodies, began to appear in Germany during the 1530's and 1540's; the first polyphonic setting of the complete psalter in German was the four-part *Der gantz Psalter Davids* of Sigmund Hemmel (d. 1565), published in 1569.[47] But it was the Goudimel Psalter of 1565 that made the greatest impression in Germany, as in other Protestant regions. In the translation by Ambrosius Lobwasser, this work began to appear in 1573 and ran through more than 50 printings in the next five years.

[41] 12 pieces in BockM XI, of which *Lobet den Herren, alle Heiden* is a particularly attractive one (10 of them are also pr. SchöbS III, of these, 1 = CW XXVIII, 17; 3 = AmeH, II, 116, 119, 132); other pieces pr. SchöbS III, 783; CW XXVIII, 4, 11, 15, 19; AmeH II, 113; JödeC II, 79, 126. See WernH, 683ff and esp. LuD.

[42] 1 piece pr. SchöbS II, 853 (= WintK I, App., No. 44); 1 in III, 888; 1 in WintK I, App., No. 43; 1 in JödeC II, 131; 6 Latin motets pr. CommM XIX, 43ff. See OppelJ.

[43] 3 songs whose texts, and possibly whose melodies also, are by Zwingli were published as part of a collection printed at Zürich in 1570; cf. GeerV, 46f.

[44] Pr. PubAPTM III, 300. Two Latin psalms *a 4* by him in GeerP; 2 other pieces in MerG.

[45] Further on Wannenmacher and other Swiss composers of the Reformation, see GeerV. About the Netherlander Samuel Mareschall (1554–1640), who was active as composer and organist at Basle for many years, see KenM, LdnL.

[46] One of them, for Psalm 119 (CXVIII), *Es sind noch selig*, was soon applied to the text *O Mensch, bewein dein' Sünde gross*, in which combination it was to be used in several works by Bach. On the history of this melody, see MacmE. For a piece by Greitter that employs the first notes of *Fortuna* as a *pes*, see PirH, 275f. 1 secular song pr. AmbG V, 361 (= MosGR, 13); 2 in LiliD, 189 (= JödeC III, 39; LippGZ, 106), 304. About early Protestant music at Strasbourg, see GéroP, GéroS.

[47] 2 of Hemmel's psalms are pr. NedP, 313ff. About a Mass by him, see MarquS, 72f.

The simple chordal style present in the Goudimel collection marks also the *50 geistliche Lieder und Psalmen* published by the Lutheran Lucas Osiander in 1586; [48] but in these pieces *a 4* the principal melody is in the top voice. We have already encountered German works of this general type in Walter and Rhaw (and even earlier in a secular composition like Isaac's *Isbruck*), but they were comparatively few and scattered and were intended for trained singers, while Osiander's entire collection is deliberately written in this style "so that a whole Christian congregation may sing along throughout." Osiander's publication was soon followed by many similar ones, written by some of the most eminent composers in Protestant Germany, including Andreas Raselius (1588), Rogier Michael (1593),[49] Bartholomäus Gesius (1594),[50] Seth Calvisius (1597),[51] Melchior Franck (1602),[52] Melchior Vulpius (1604),[53] and Hans Leo Hassler (1608).[54] (Hassler's 1608 collection was preceded in 1607 by one [54a] that treated twenty-five of the same melodies—*Es spricht* twice and *Aus tiefer Noth* three times—with greater polyphonic elaboration; thus the two collections bear somewhat the same relation to each other as do Goudimel's two complete psalters.) While most of the pieces in these collections are based on the old Lutheran lieder, Michael Praetorius, in Parts V to VIII of his *Musae Sioniae* (published 1607 to 1610) adds a great many new songs.[55] As a composer, Praetorius belongs essentially to the history of baroque music; but his treatise, *Syntagma musicum,* published in three books (1615–1620) is full of valuable data about Late Renaissance music. Book II—*De organographia* [56]—is devoted to detailed descriptions of the structure and properties of instruments.

[48] Pr. OsiaG. 12 of these pieces also pr. WintK I, App., Nos. 50–54 (Nos. 52, 53 = SchöbS III, 336; I, 220); SchöbS II, 19; III, 494; 1 pr. ScherG, 142; 3 pr. AmeH I², 1 pr. III².

[49] 1 piece pr. AmbG V, 463.

[50] 8 later religious pieces pr. SchöbS I (3 = AmeH I², 283 [2 items]; III², 7), 24 in II (1 = AmeH I², 209; 1 = WintK I, App., No. 60); 31 in III (1 = AmeH II, 209; 1 = JödeC I, 113; 1 = WintK I, App., No. 65); 5 more pr. AmeH I²; 1 in III²; 4 pr. WintK I, App., Nos. 61–64; 1 pr. JödeC I, 44.

[51] 5 pieces from the collection of this date pr. WintK I, App.; 2 pr. AmeH I²; 1 pr. SchöbS II, 74; 1 in III, 542. *See* WustM, 351ff.

[52] 2 later religious pieces are pr. SchöbS I; 7 in II; 73 in III (4 of these 82 = AmeH II, 142, 177, 179, 193); 10 more pr. AmeH II; 5 motets pr. CW XXIV; 1 piece pr. EitD, 272; 1 pr. JödeC I; 4 pr. II.

[53] 19 pieces from this collection among the 49 pr. SchöbS (1 of the 19 = JödeC I, 130); another from it pr. AmeH I², 53. His *Hinunter ist der Sonnenschein* (SchöbS III, 686) is an unusually attractive work.

[54] All the pieces in this collection except 2 *a 8* are pr. HasK; 1 of those *a 8* is pr. AmbG V, 552; 40 of the others are among the 47 Hassler pieces pr. SchöbS (these figures recognize that SchöbS II, 790 = III, 733); of the 40, 6 = WintK I, App., Nos. 72, 74–76, 78, 79; 1 = AmeH I², 100; other duplications of pieces in HasK are pr. in WintK I, App., Nos. 73, 77 (= AmeH I², 25).

[54a] Pr. HasPG; 8 pieces also pr. HasP.

[55] For a comparison of the beginning of 9 versions of *Ein feste Burg,* from Hemmel (1569) to Michael Praetorius (1610), *see* BlumeE, 76.

[56] Reprinted in PubAPTM XIII; PraetoS II is a facsimile ed. of this Book. Book III has been reprinted in PraetoS III. An English translation of the First and Second Parts of Book II is available in BlumenS.

Motet-like Polyphony among the Protestants; Eccard and Some Lesser Figures

The other composers mentioned did not restrict themselves, of course, to writing simple settings for congregational use. They also produced many elaborate motet-like pieces based on the same or similar religious lieder; and in these works the influence of two foreign styles is apparent—the Franco-Netherlandish (with its admixture of Italian elements) as exemplified in the works of Lassus, and the Venetian (with its strong Franco-Netherlandish components) as exemplified in the works of the Gabrielis. Lassus, though a Catholic, and connected with the Catholic court at Munich, exerted so powerful an influence that it affected the whole field of German music, including the Protestant. Works of his written in Germany will be discussed presently; suffice it to say here that certain aspects of his style are reflected in much of the music of his Protestant admirers.

There was, in fact, little difference in style between Protestant and Catholic motets written in 16th-century Germany. As we have seen, in Luther's time Protestant collections included works by Catholics; such differences of style as existed were the result of personal factors rather than of the distinction between faiths. In the latter half of the century, Protestants still wrote many motets with Latin texts and some Catholics (including Lassus himself) set Lutheran texts.

Protestant motet-like works based on religious lieder represent both the chordal and the richer polyphonic types. But most of these works are written in the restrained polyphonic manner that had been gaining ground ever since the French style won favor early in the century. A fine example is Johann Eccard's *Komm, heiliger Geist,* from his *Geistliche Lieder auf dem Choral . . .* (published in two parts in 1597).

EXAMPLE 154. Opening of *Komm, heiliger Geist*—Eccard (from EccG I, 32).

The borrowed melody is in the highest voice. While the music has the visual aspect of polyphonic writing, its homophonic basis becomes sufficiently clear upon closer examination. Without such lieder "Bach is unthinkable."[57]

Eccard was born in Mühlhausen, Thuringia, in 1553, studied with Lassus in Munich, became in 1580 vice-*Kapellmeister* and in 1604 first *Kapellmeister* at Königsberg. In 1608 he moved to Berlin, where he died in 1611. Like Joachim a Burck (real name, Moller, 1546–1610),[58] with whom he was associated early in his career, he set to music many of the religious poems of Ludwig Hembold (1532–1598). His *Newe Lieder* (1589), *a 4* and *a 5*, include twelve religious and thirteen secular pieces. Among the latter are one in French and three predominantly in Latin, as well as an Italian piece apparently representing a scene for characters from the *commedia dell'arte* and very likely composed in imitation of such pieces by Lassus. The best known collection in which his music appears is probably the *Preussische Festlieder,* written jointly by Eccard and his pupil, Johann Stobäus (1580–1646). Stobäus published it in two parts in 1642 and 1644, after his teacher's death. Eccard is one of the most gifted of Lassus' German followers and one of the most important Lutheran composers of the Renaissance.[59]

Equally gifted is Leonhard Lechner, who was born in 1553 in the Tyrol and brought up as a Catholic; he studied under Lassus as a choirboy in Munich, and after some wandering turned Protestant and eventually became court *Kapellmeister* at Stuttgart, where he died in 1606. Much of Lechner's music, and particularly his settings of German religious texts, is marked by unusual intensity of feeling, striking contrasts, and a dramatic power that is rare in the music of his German contemporaries and points toward the baroque. The first of these qualities is especially evident in his *Neue teutsche*

[57] BlumeE, 85.
[58] For a collection of Burck's compositions, *see* PubAPTM XXII (of these, 5 = SchöbS II, 604 [= WintK I, App., No. 103], 792 [= BockM XI, 80], 919 [= BockM XI, 86]; III, 559, 776; 1 = WintK I, App., No. 102; 1 = BockM III, 3 [= JödeC I, 118]); 13 other religious works pr. SchöbS II (1 = BockM XI, 78; 1 = WintK I, App., No. 105); 11 more pr. SchöbS III (1 = JödeC I, 70; 1 = LippGZ, 56); others pr. WintK I, App., No. 104; LippGZ, 53; BockM XI, 81, 83, 87; JödeC II, 145; AmeH II, 35. About his life and compositions, *see* BirtP; MGG II, 471ff.
[59] The 52 five-part *Geistliche Lieder* pr. EccG; Part I also in EccGL; other duplications: 11 in WintK I, App., Nos. 121–126, 129, 131, 135, 136, 153 (= respectively, SchöbS II, 137, 123, 508 [= BockM VI, 67]; I, 423 [= BockM V, 77]; JödeC I, 20]; II, 505, 585; III, 490, 345; II, 893; III, 613 [= BockM VI, 70], 973); 16 more in SchöbS II, 582, 929, 931, 934, 985; III, 335, 338, 427, 437, 480, 482, 763, 769, 838, 943, 993; others in WintK I, App., Nos. 118–120, 127, 134, 137; JödeC I, 73, 122; AmeH I², 203. The *Newe Lieder* pr. PubAPTM XXI (4 also in JödeC II, 121; V, 5; VI, 53, 131; 2 more in WintK I, App., Nos. 115, 116). The *Preussische Festlieder* pr. EccP; 11 of Eccard's pieces also in SchöbS II, 206, 302, 591, 607, 793, 812, 833 (= respectively, WintK I, App., Nos. 150, 140, 146, 147, 142, 141 [= BockM XI, 76], 149), 605, 687, 734; III, 1004 (= WintK I, App., No. 145; BockM VI, 65); others also in ScherG, 167; BockM V, 24 (= AmeH III², 84; WintK I, App., No. 143); WintK I, App., Nos. 148, 151. Other German religious pieces pr. WintK I, App., Nos. 110–114, 134, 138, 144 (= respectively, SchöbS III, 531, 714, 723; II, 590 [= BockM VI, 74], 728 [= BockM VI, 76], 232 [= BockM VI, 69]; III, 526 [= JödeC I, 122]; II, 271 [= BockM VI, 76]), also 132 (= BockM VI, 68); SchöbS II, 685, 862, 990; III, 341, 716, 799; AmeH I², 151, 213. 2 Latin pieces pr. WintK I, App., Nos. 117, 139. A secular lied pr. LippGZ, 22.

Lieder (1582),[60] a collection of twenty-four sacred and secular pieces; while all three qualities may be found in the six motets on lines from the Song of Solomon [61] and in the *Sprüche von Leben und Tod*.[62] This last is a cycle of fifteen pieces varying in style from free polyphony (No. 10) to a purely chordal setting (No. 5) but bound together not only by the underlying idea of the texts but by a common tonality, all the pieces but one ending either on the tonic, G, or the dominant.[63]

Calvisius (real name, Kalwitz; 1556–1615) became cantor of St. Thomas' at Leipzig in 1594. He was highly regarded not only as a composer (his *Joseph, lieber Joseph mein* [64] is a particularly lovely piece) but as a teacher and theorist. His four treatises, of which the *Exercitationes Musicae duae* (Leipzig, 1600) is the most important, are based on Zarlino and served to introduce that writer's theories into Germany. It was Calvisius who, in discussing fugal writing and in translating Zarlino's terms *"guida"* and *"consequente"* into Latin, introduced the nomenclature, *dux* and *comes*.[65]

Larger Sacred Works of Hassler; Sacred Polychoral Music

Perhaps the most important of all the Germanic composers of this period, probably the only one besides Senfl who can be ranked with the great Franco-Netherlanders of the 16th century, is Hans Leo Hassler (1564–1612). Born the son of an organist at Nuremberg, he went to Venice at the age of twenty and studied with Andrea Gabrieli; Giovanni became his friend and colleague. Fifteen months after going to Venice, Hassler was appointed organist to Octavian II Fugger, of the great Augsburg banking family. His fame spread rapidly; in 1602 he returned to Nuremberg as chief *Kapellmeister* of the town and with the reputation of a composer "whose like has not been found among the Germans up to this time." Six years later he became chamber organist and music librarian to the Elector of Saxony.[66]

Though Hassler seems to have been a Protestant, he directed the music for Catholic services in Augsburg and wrote a number of Masses. Some of the texts of his Latin motets are of a Catholic, some of a Protestant, nature, while many were usable by both faiths. His early works show the influence of Lassus, and his later ones reveal the deep impression made upon him by his studies in Italy. In the Masses and motets of his maturity, his natural propensity for

[60] Pr. LechnerTL; 1 piece also pr. JödeC II; 2 in V; 2 in CommM XVIII, 81ff (1 = BraunfA, 21), 2 in XIX, 17ff. 2 other sacred German pieces by Lechner pr. AmeH I[2]; 2 in II.

[61] Pr. LechnerH.   [62] Pr. LechnerD.

[63] For biographical data, *see* SchreiL. On his works, *see* AbertS, 101ff, and SchreiA. A sacred Latin motet pr. DehnS, *Lieferung* VIII; a secular one pr. WernH, 715ff.

[64] ELAM XII, 12; etc.

[65] Further on Calvisius, *see* BenndC; WustM, *passim;* RobbB, 72ff; MGG II, 674ff.

[66] For complete biographical data, *see* DTB V[1]. An index of Hassler's printed works is given in EitHL. About a lawsuit brought by Hassler in connection with some mechanical organs made for him, *see* Leichtentritt in MQ, XX (1934), 19.

writing light, almost popular, melodies and for very careful workmanship is coupled with a grace and fluidity derived from the madrigalian dance songs and a fondness for polychoral structures. The result is a sacred style that makes up in charm and sonority for what it lacks in profundity.[67] We have encountered polychoral writing in Germany as early as 1544 (cf. p. 679), and it appears sporadically after that; [68] by the end of the century writing for double and even triple choruses is common there, and unlike the earlier pieces the later ones clearly attempt, sometimes successfully, to capture the splendor and richness of the Venetian style. The Protestant composers who wrote in this German-Venetian manner include—besides Hassler—Eccard, Hieronymus Praetorius (1560–1629),[69] Georgius Otto (c. 1550–1618),[70] Andreas Raselius (c. 1563–1602),[71] Adam Gumpelzhaimer (1559–1625),[72] and Philippus Dulichius (1562–1631).[73]

German Passions

Many polyphonic settings of the Passion appeared in Germany during the Reformation. The Passion was first sung in German at Strasbourg in 1531,[74] but a few Protestant composers continued to employ the Latin text. Probably the first of these was Galliculus, whose Passion was published by Rhaw in 1538; [75] Gesius produced one as late as 1613.[76] The Galliculus work, based on St. Mark, belongs (as does the Gesius) to the motet type of Passion. Other compositions of this type, but with German texts, were produced by Joachim a Burck (after John, 1568),[77] Johannes Heroldt (after Matthew, 1594),[77a] and Lechner (after John, 1594),[78] his being perhaps the finest of all the German Passions written in the 16th century. The dramatic type

---

[67] Motets, etc., by Hassler pr. DDT II, XXIV, XXV (6 also pr. ProsM, *Annus I*, II, 284 [= HAM, 186], 307, 335, 549, 552, 553; others also pr. CW XIV, 21; JödeC II, 4; V, 121); ProsM, *Annus I*, III, 426. 8 Masses pr. DDT VII (3 = ProsM, *Annus I*, I, 185; ProsS, *Annus I*, I, No. 8; *Annus II*, I, No. 3). About the motets, *see* LeiG, 297–307; AbertS, 119–37; the Masses are discussed in WagG, 342–49.

[68] E.g., in Walter (1566; AmbG V, 404) and Schröter (1571; *ibid.*, 465). An ex. by Paminger (1556) is mentioned in OsN, 239, fn.

[69] 16 pieces (including 2 for quadruple chorus) pr. DDT XXIII (2 also pr. CW XIV, 10, 12); exx. also pr. SchöbS I, 249; II, 225, 937; III, 525 (= WintK I, App., No. 66); WintK I, App., Nos. 67, 68; 2 in DehnS, *Lieferung* VII. *See also* FrieV.

[70] 8 pieces (1 *a 8*) in BlumeG; biography and style study in GrösG.

[71] 22 pieces pr. DTB XXIX–XXX. 2 lieder pr. SchöbS I; 3 pr. III; 1 pr. AmeH I[2]; 3 pr. II; 3 pr. III[2].

[72] *See* DTB X (1 = SchöbS I, 92 [= WintK I, App., No. 156]; 2 = SchöbS III, 565 [BockM XI, 93], 903; 1 = BockM XII, 53; 1 = JödeC I, 15; 7 = JödeC V, 14, 16, 17, 57, 67, 91, 114); other pieces pr. SchöbS III, 621 [= BockM XI, 95], 825 [= BockM XI, 97; JödeC I, 57]; WintK I, App., Nos. 154, 155; BockM II, 82; XI, 87, 90; JödeC V, 113; VI, 13, 17, 32; AmeH I[2], 248 [2 items], 263, 264; II, 3, 4; III[2], 14; LippGZ, 15. CaP is principally a study of modulation in Gumpelzhaimer's polychoral motets.

[73] Latin and German sacred pieces in DDT XXXI and XLI. Biography and style study in Introduction to the former.

[74] VogQ, 227.   [75] *See* KadP, 18ff. Among Rhaw's publications was also a Latin Passion by Resinarius, pr. CW XLVII.

[76] *See* KadP, 64ff. A German Passion by Gesius is reprinted in SchöbS II, 412ff.

[77] Pr. PubAPTM XXII.   [77a] For discussion of this work, with exx., *see* MosLC, 15ff.

[78] Pr. LechnerL; AmeH I[4], 153.

of Passion is represented in works with German text by Walter (after Matthew, c. 1550) [79] and others. A mixture of these two types may be seen in the German St. John Passion of Antonio Scandello (c. 1561),[80] in which the words of the Evangelist are set *a 1,* those of the "damsel that kept the door," Peter, Pilate (usually), and others *a 3,* of Jesus *a 4,* of an officer and occasionally Pilate *a 2,* and of the crowd *a 5.*[81]

Catholic Polyphony: Senfl

Those sections of the German-speaking countries that retained the old faith produced few important native composers during the 16th century, and these few contributed no essentially new elements to the music of the Catholic Church, but they include the great figure of Ludwig Senfl. Senfl was born at Zürich, c. 1490, and became a pupil of Isaac. He sang in the court choir of Maximilian I and then was appointed chamber composer. In 1520 Senfl appeared in Augsburg, where he completed Isaac's *Choralis Constantinus.* From 1523 to some time in the 1540's he was associated with the musical establishment of the Bavarian court at Munich, but then his trail disappears, and the date of his death is unknown, though he seems to have died before or during 1556.[82]

That Senfl was the pupil of Isaac may be clearly seen in the mastery of Franco-Netherlandish counterpoint displayed in his seven *cantus-firmus* and parody Masses.[83] The Kyrie of a *Missa dominicalis* [84] is of particular interest, in that it begins with the liturgical melody in long notes in the discantus while an instrumental figure in *tuba* style (cf. p. 21, etc.) is bandied about among the other three voices. Perhaps the most noteworthy of these works is the four-part *Missa dominicalis super L'Homme armé,*[85] in which the chanson tune, in one voice, is combined with plainsong in another. This combination is the more remarkable in that it appears throughout the Mass, whereas such composers as Josquin, Obrecht, and Compère, when employing a double *cantus firmus* in a Mass, usually restricted it to the Credo. The plainsong Kyrie is based on that of Mass XV,[85a] the Gloria on that of Mass XII, the Credo on Credo I; the source of the plainsongs used in the Sanctus

[79] Pr. KadP, 274, where it is incorrectly dated 1530. *See also* HaasZ.

[80] Pr. KadP, 306.

[81] For further details about German 16th-century Passions, *see* KadP. The music of 13 Passions and other sacred *Historien* of this period pr. in AmeH I[3] and I[4]. On a MS at Vienna, containing the *turbae* only of a German St. Matthew Passion of 1559, *see* AdlerM. For a type of monophonic Passion described by Martin Agricola, which differs from the Catholic Passion based on the Gregorian recitation-tone by being more liedlike, thus inviting participation by the congregation, *see* FunA, 73.

[82] Further biographical data in DTB III[2], xvff; *see also* KoczA, 537ff.

[83] Pr. SenflW I (= EDMR V). Analyses in LöhM, BirtS, and WagG, 317ff.

[84] Pr. SenflW I (= EDMR V), 27.   [85] *Ibid.,* 3.

[85a] The version used by Senfl is closer to the one that appears in the *Ordinarium* pr. in Mexico in 1556 (cf. p. 593) than to the one pr. in Liber, 56.

and Agnus is unknown. In some passages, Senfl treats one or the other borrowed melody freely, making interpolations and other digressions. The popular tune is in the tenor (except in the Benedictus, where it does not appear at
all) and the plainsong in the discantus, except in the Agnus, where the two
cantus exchange positions. The two free voices sometimes imitate phrases from
one cantus or the other. Equally interesting are Senfl's motets, in which his
skill in counterpoint and variation is supplemented by the frequent warmth
and lyricism of his own melodies. A particularly fine motet is the *Ave rosa
sine spinis*,[86] which is based on the tenor of *Comme femme* (cf. p. 87), undoubtedly via Josquin's *Stabat Mater*.[87]

About the middle of the 16th century, various European rulers began to
"raid" the Netherlands for composers and singers to enrich their musical es-
tablishments. Just as the taste of Charles V led to the activity in Madrid
of the musicians of his Netherlandish chapel choir and the tastes of Margaret of Parma and Duke Hercules II caused them to enlist Franco-Netherlanders for their courts at Brussels and Ferrara, so the desire of the German
princes to improve their musical forces resulted in the presence of Franco-
Netherlanders in Vienna, Dresden, Prague, and other capitals. The organization of the various *Kapellen* included also the hiring of Italian performers,
and resulted in a change in German instrumental practice from the hitherto
customary preference for wind instruments and lutes to the predominance
of strings characteristic of the Italian taste.[88]

Catholic Polyphony: Lassus

The prize Franco-Netherlander, however, was won by Duke Albert V of
Bavaria, whose emissary persuaded Lassus to go from Antwerp to Munich
as a singer in 1556.[88a] A few years later Lassus became *Kapellmeister,* succeeding Ludwig Daser.[89] In 1558, he married Regina Wäckinger, daughter
of a maid of honor to the Duchess; and twelve years later he was knighted by
Maximilian II. The miniatures in Munich, Staatsbibl., Mus. MS A, by the court

---

[86] Pr. AmbG V, 385. 14 other motets pr. SenflW III (= EDMR XIII); 3 of these = DTB III²,
118, 125, 163 [= MerG, 15; CommM XVIII, 12]; 1 = ScherG, 72; 1 = MosK, 14; 9 more
motets (1 = HAM, 113) and 8 Magnificats pr. DTB III²; other motets pr. WintK I, App., Nos.
10, 11; EisZ, 155, 160; KrV, 14; MerG, 22; etc. *See also* fn. 87.

[87] Another link with Josquin is found in Senfl's *Ave Maria . . . virgo serena* (JosqMT, I,
157), in which Senfl reworks the thematic material used by Josquin in his setting of the same
text (cf. pp. 253, 256).

[88] For a study of the Italians and Italianized Netherlanders at Vienna, Innsbruck, and Graz,
c. 1564–1625, *see* EinIK. For a description and discussion of 16 pictures of German court and
other choirs (1488–1575), *see* EhmM.

[88a] Albert's patronage of the arts was so extensive that he left a great burden of debt upon his
death in 1579. About his role and that of Johann Jakob Fugger in founding what is now the
Staatsbibliothek at Munich, *see* WalH. An inventory of instruments in the possession of the
Bavarian court in 1571 (i.e., during Albert's reign) is pr. in Wall.

[89] About Daser and his music, *see* SandB, 37ff; KelM.

painter, Hans Mielich, which contain valuable evidence of contemporary *Auf-führungspraxis*,[90] include likenesses of Lassus. Mielich executed also a portrait of Rore (cf. p. 376); the latter probably sat for this when he passed through Munich in 1558, at which time he and Lassus undoubtedly met. That Lassus' relations with Albert's son, William V, were particularly friendly is shown by his letters to William, written in a cheerful mixture of languages, e.g., Italian, Latin, French, and German mingling in a single letter.[91] When William married Renée of Lorraine in 1568, Lassus, who had charge of the music at the festivities, composed a special motet, *Quid trepidas*[92] for the occasion and, among other things, sang Azzaiolo's celebrated *Chi passa* to his own lute accompaniment.[92a] A description of the music-making at the event is included in the account that comes down to us by Massimo Troiano (cf. p. 445).[93] Lassus remained at the Bavarian court, except for occasional trips abroad, until his death in 1594.[94]

In 1604 Lassus' sons, Rudolph and Ferdinand, published at Munich, under the title *Magnum opus musicum*,[95] a collection of 516 motets, in from two to twelve parts, by their father, some previously published and others newly printed from MSS. Most of the motets date from the Bavarian period. The twenty-four pieces *a 2*,[96] of which twelve have text and twelve seem intended for instruments (cf. p. 672), were originally printed in 1577 and probably written as exercises for the younger members of the Bavarian chapel. They appear ideal for this purpose, not only because of the technical problems presented to the performers, such as, in the vocal pieces, lengthy melismas, wide leaps, and scale passages, but because of their charm and fine construction. Most of the pieces *a 3* are contrapuntal throughout, but those in four or

[90] *See* the reproductions in HaasA, opp. p. 112, and UrK, opp. p. 208. Further on Mielich, *see* B. H. Roettger, *Der Maler Hans Mielich*, 1925.

[91] 48 letters from Lassus to William V among the 52 pr. in SandB III, 247ff. About William's relation to music, *see* esp. WalU.

[92] Pr. LassoW XI, 111.   [92a] Cf. BorLI, 117.

[93] For this description, *see* Massimo Troiano, *Discorsi delli triumphi . . . fatte nelle . . . nozze, dell'Illustr. . . . Duca Guglielmo . . .*, Munich, 1568; German transl. by F. Wirthmann, *Die Vermählungsfeier des Herzogs Wilhelm V . . .*, Munich, 1842 (extracts in MfMG VI, 109). Extract from the original in CorteA, 156; English transl. of a portion in K. M. Lea, *Italian Popular Comedy*, 2 vols. (1934), I, 7ff. Especially about the instruments used at this wedding, *see* BorLI, 114ff. A contemporary engraving of the wedding scene, showing the *Hofkapelle* under Lassus, is reproduced in BesM, 230.

[94] Further biographical data, for Lassus' German period, in SandA; BorOL; PirH, 306ff. Munich offers an extreme example of the influx of foreigners: in 1544 one of 13 musicians was a foreigner; 32 years later, only one of 54 musicians was a German (MosG I, 456).

[95] Pr. LassoW, odd-numbered vols. from I to XXI. (20 motets also pr. ProsM, *Annus I*, II; 3 in *Annus II*, II; 1 in JödeC II; 4 in V; 30 motets and other Latin pieces also pr. MaldR III, XII, XVI, XXIV, and MaldP III–V; on text discrepancies between LassoW and MaldP, *see* ReT, 104ff, Nos. 343, 351, 352, 399, 403, 408. There are many other reprints.) Since the editing by Lassus' sons is unsatisfactory in some respects, it is a pity that the *Magnum opus musicum* was made one of the bases of the *Gesamtausgabe*, even where earlier prints existed and might have been used as a basis instead. (Some pieces included in the *Magnum opus* have, of course, been cited already in Chaps. 8 and 9.)

[96] Pr. LassoW I.

more parts contain a considerable amount of chordal writing, judiciously mingled with the polyphony—the breakdown of pervading imitation (cf. pp. 508f) is well under way. A feeling for harmonic propriety is made evident by the many chord roots that progress by leaps of fourths and fifths, in contrast to the many that proceed by step in Palestrina. Moreover, Lassus omits the third or fifth of a chord much less often than does the Roman master. The latter, however, is apt to change chord with considerably greater frequency; for example, a comparison of one of his *Surrexit pastor bonus* settings with Lassus' *Videntes stellam* or of one of his *Fuit homo missus* settings with Lassus' *Te merito* [96a]—each pair consisting of works of approximately equal length—shows about 30% fewer changes of chord on the part of the Netherlander in the first pair and about 15% fewer in the second. These comparisons may present extreme cases, but they are in keeping with a general trend.[96b] Palestrina's more frequent change of harmony, however, is probably less the result of a strong interest in chordal variety for its own sake than a by-product of his greater emphasis on flowing polyphony. Lassus at times shows a strong liking for the "irregular" harmonic "V–IV" progression, already encountered in Monte (cf. p. 407), and uses it eloquently in the following passage from his five-part *Tristis est anima mea,* a composition in which Lassus provides a moving setting for Christ's words in the Garden of Gethsemane.

EXAMPLE 155. Excerpt from *Tristis est anima mea*—Lassus (complete piece in LassoW V, 49; ParrishM, 80).

Palestrina's stronger emphasis on polyphony is responsible not only for the difference from Lassus credited to him above, but also for the Roman's more liberal use of suspensions and his greater expansiveness. When the two men set the same text, Lassus is likely to prove the briefer. Thus, a *Tribus miraculis* setting by Palestrina has 106 measures while that of Lassus has 76; [96c] the above-mentioned *Surrexit pastor bonus* of the former has 75 measures, while the latter's setting [96d] has 66; etc.[96e] The attitude toward polyphony naturally

---

[96a] The 4 pieces are pr. PalW V, 177 (= PalO XI, 79); LassoW V, 22; PalW V, 38 (= PalO III, 46); LassoW V, 160, respectively.

[96b] So far as can be judged with the collected edition of Lassus still incomplete. (This reservation applies to some of the other conclusions presented here also.)

[96c] Pr. PalW V, 14 (= PalO III, 15); LassoW V, 25.   [96d] Pr. *ibid.,* V, 57.

[96e] To be sure, both men make 42-measure madrigal settings of *La ver l'aurora* (PalW XXVIII, 17 [= PalO II, 16]; LassoW IV, 65), and Palestrina's setting of *Nessun visse giammai* (PalW XXVIII, 15 [= PalO II, 15]) is actually shorter than that of Lassus (LassoW VIII, 137); but such instances seem not to be typical.

affects the melodic writing of the two composers also: Palestrina's lines are usually longer and more melismatic than those of Lassus. They are likewise more conjunct. On the other hand, as though by way of compensation, a melodic phrase by Lassus is very apt, in spite of its larger number of leaps, to span a smaller total range. Palestrina's lines have greater elegance and grace; those of Lassus have more rugged power and unusual movement. Lassus' concentration on melodic pivotal notes, as, for instance, in his examples of the decorated inverted pedal divided between the two highest parts of multivoiced compositions (cf. pp. 405f), is beautifully illustrated in certain motets. Notably fine applications of the technique occur in the six-part Song of Solomon motet, *Quam pulchra es*,[96f] especially at the point in *pars II* where the *sponsa* interrupts the *sponsus*: " 'Thy throat is like the best wine . . .' 'worthy for my beloved to drink.' " Here the two superius parts twine about a fairly high reiterated note (c''), successively ascend to a higher note (e'') on the important word *"meo,"* and then continue the original decorated pedal for the rest of the passage.

Lassus sometimes draws upon a plainsong melody (cf. pp. 509f), but in the main is considerably less interested in reworking pre-existent material than is Palestrina. For example, whereas Palestrina's hymns—like those of Festa and Victoria, among others—present virtual variation-chains consisting of different settings of a Chant melody, not one of the compositions on hymn texts contained in the *Magnum opus musicum* is based on plainsong at all. Not only does Lassus exclude plainsong from the polyphonic complex in these works; he makes no provision, as do the other composers mentioned, for the singing of stanzas alternately in polyphony and in monophonic chant: in most compositions on hymn texts he provides settings of his own for all stanzas.[96g]

The magnificent hymn, *Aurora lucis rutilat,* contains a striking oblique cross-relation at the expression *"gemens infernus ululat."* [96h] Examples of this kind of clash, avoided by Palestrina, occur from time to time in Lassus, both as bits of word-painting,[96i] as in the instance just mentioned, and without illustrative purpose. There is a striking instance of the purely musical sort in the setting of the Offertory, *Improperium expectavit cor meum.*[96j]

96f Pr. LassoW XIII, 149. (For other Song of Solomon motets, *see ibid.,* I, 96, 99; V, 120, 124; IX, 42; XIII, 154, 158; XXI, 9.)

96g E.g., in those pr. *ibid.,* V, 171; XI, 172; XIII, 18, 43, 139, 174; XV, 3; XXI, 119. Only the last stanza and *Amen* are wanting in the hymn setting pr. *ibid.,* VII, 86. The 4 other pieces incorporating texts from hymns are not true hymn compositions: *Ut queant laxis* (*ibid.,* V, 152), which sets stanza 1 of the text, is a pleasantry on the Guidonian solmisation syllables; *O salutaris hostia* (*ibid.,* V, 79), which of course sets stanza 5 of *Verbum supernum,* is undoubtedly a Sacrament motet; the 2 settings of *Verbum caro* (*ibid.,* I, 58, 111), which is stanza 4 of *Pange lingua . . . corporis,* may be such motets also.

96h *Ibid.,* XXI, 120, meas. 2f.

96i *See,* for example, *ibid.,* VII, 93, meas. 11f; 115, meas. 2 from end; XXI, 49, meas. 9f; 128, meas. 2; 129, meas. 4f; etc.

96j *See ibid.,* III, 22, meas. 16. For other exx., *see ibid.,* I, 60, meas. 7; XXI, 47, meas. 3 from end; etc.

Lassus, like Palestrina, was a pioneer in the writing of Offertories in motet style (cf. p. 465).[97]

In the domain of form, Lassus shows no liking for the *aBcB* responsory pattern or the variation-chain sequence—no doubt in part because in the structural field also he prefers the evolving of something new to the reworking of something old, and in part because he is less interested than Palestrina in symmetry and balance for their own sake. The form of each motet is likely to be determined by the nature of the text and of the motivic content, without much reference to established patterns. As in *Nos qui sumus in hoc mundo,*[97a] a section of a motet appearing in a new meter toward the end, and seeming at first acquaintance to have its *raison d'être* in the contrast it provides, may actually be based on motivic material taken from the early part of the composition, recast in a new rhythmic mold. Unification is much more likely to result from such less obvious means than from literal or near-literal repetition.

The principle of rhythmic contrast plays a large role in Lassus. Whereas Palestrina is apt to maintain homogeneous rhythmic activity for a considerable time—even throughout a whole work—the Netherlander is often inclined to break up a composition into fairly small sections with markedly different rhythmic patterns. To be sure, this may on occasion result from a madrigalian attitude toward the text rather than from purely musical considerations. The descriptive passages that imitate instruments in the six-part *In hora ultima* [97b] illustrate this point most attractively. On a grander scale it is illustrated in the eight-part *Omnia tempus habent.*[98] Lassus takes the magnificent lines that open Ecclesiastes III, "To every thing there is a season . . . : A time to be born, and a time to die; . . . A time to kill, and a time to heal . . ." and, through much of the motet, sets them antiphonally, there being a SAAT choir and an ATTB choir, the brighter-voiced choir often having just the more joyous verbal phrase in each pair and the darker-voiced choir only the sadder phrase. But it would not be true to Lassus' nature for him to follow so

---

[97] LassoW III, xxi, is of course incorrect in stating that no other 16th-century composers set Offertories. Lassus' cycle of Offertories was divided between the *Sacrae cantiones* of 1582 (*a 5*) and 1585 (*a 4*). Unfortunately these collections are not reproduced intact in LassoW (cf. Chap. 9, fn. 304). However, all but one of the pieces in the 1585 publication were included in the *Magnum opus musicum* and, since that old edition is reprinted whole in LassoW, it is possible (most conveniently by consulting EitHL) for one to reconstruct from the modern edition at least the 1585 print, almost complete and in its original order, as follows: LassoW III, 16 (= ProsM, *Annus I*, II, 115), 17 (= ProsM, *Annus I*, II, 240), 19, 20, 21 (= ProsM, *Annus I*, II, 120); I, 150 (= ProsM, *Annus I*, II, 111); III, 62 (= ProsM, *Annus I*, II, 80), 63, 65, 66, 23, 67, 25 (= ProsM, *Annus I*, II, 261), 70 85 (= ProsM, *Annus I*, II, 539), 86, 88, 89, 91, 92 (= ProsM, *Annus I*, II, 258): I, 152, 90; III, 31 (this is the very eloquent *Miserere*, which has gained a certain currency—especially through a phonograph recording—in another version [pr. as No. 2 in Carl Thiel, *Auswahl hervorragender Meisterwerke des a-cappella Stils* . . . , Sulzbach, Berlin]; however, the version pr. in LassoW, after the *Magnum op. mus.*, agrees with that of the 1585 print), 32, 33, 72 (= ProsM, *Annus I*, II, 255), 49 (= ProsM, *Annus I*, II, 93), 73 (= ProsM, *Annus I*, II, 250); I, 155 (= ProsM, *Annus I*, II, 243), 157 (= ProsM, *Annus I*, II, 167), 158 (= ProsM, *Annus I*, II, 82). The piece from the 1585 print that is missing in the *Magnum opus musicum* (and therefore from LassoW) is the *Stabat Mater*, the last item in the original publication; it is pr. CommB XII, 68. Further about the Offertories of Lassus, *see* especially LippP, 6off.

[97a] Pr. LassoW I, 139.   [97b] Pr. *ibid.*, XV, 151.   [98] Pr. *ibid.*, XXI, 77.

obvious a plan all through. Among the departures are the settings of the words that have to do with embracing and love, which the composer distributes, undoubtedly with poetic intent, among both choirs. In the motets, as elsewhere, Lassus' treatment of text abounds in felicities.[99] To the influence of the madrigal is due also the considerable use of degree-inflection in such motets as *Christe, Dei soboles*[100] and *Timor et tremor,*[101] a device which, however, as has already been noted (p. 404), is not typical of Lassus generally. The motets for eight or more parts contain passages in which, as in *Omnia tempus habent,* one chorus is pitted against another antiphonally, although as a rule Lassus prefers to merge the choruses, as in the very brilliant *Tui sunt coeli,*[102] which leaves no doubt that the heavens are indeed the Lord's, and the resplendent *Laudate Dominum,*[103] suitably chosen as the work with which to close the *Magnum opus.*

In surveying the motets as a whole, we find a wide range of mood, from majestic splendor, as in *Tibi laus, tibi gloria,*[104] to—in some of the secular pieces—frothy comedy, as in the eight-part *Jam lucis orto sidere,*[105] from religious fervor expressed with great intensity, as in *Quis mihi det lacrimus gemitus*[106] or *In monte Oliveti,*[107] to pastoral charm, as in the secular *Dulci sub umbra.*[108] The secular motets include two on texts by Vergil, one being, as might be expected, *Dulces exuviae.*[109] In all these works, clear-cut motifs or melodies, a free flow of varied and contrasting rhythms, and richly expressive combinations of polyphony and chordal writing convey the general mood of the text.

The individual motets are the high point of Lassus' output. Worthy of being ranked with them are such cycles as the seven *Psalmi Davidis poenitentiales* (which were completed in 1560, copied into the above-mentioned Munich Mus. MS A, and published in 1584)[110] and the twelve *Prophetiae Sibyllarum* (composed c. 1560, published in 1600).[111] In the sixth of the Penitential Psalms (*De profundis*) psalm-tone 6 appears as *cantus firmus* in one voice or another in each of the ten sections. In section 2 it is the subject of a

---

[99] Various technical and rhetorical devices used by Lassus (and other 16th-century composers) were codified as *figurae* by Joachim Burmeister in treatises published in 1599, 1601, and 1606. This "*Figurenlehre*" was to lead to the "*Affektenlehre*" of the 18th century. *See* BrS.

[100] LassoW III, 95; CW XIV, 4.

[101] LassoW, XIX, 6; CW XIV, 6; CommB VIII, 108.

[102] LassoW XXI, 5; several other polychoral works *ibid.*

[103] Pr. *ibid.,* XXI, 152.

[104] *Ibid.,* III, 130; CommB X, 93.

[105] LassoW XXI, 84; CommB VIII, 3; MaldP IV, 44.

[106] LassoW V, 44.

[107] *Ibid.,* XI, 187; CommB VII, 11.   [108] LassoW XI, 49.

[109] *Ibid.,* XI, 57; the other is *Tityre, tu patulae* (beginning of the first Eclogue), *ibid.,* XIX, 68; MaldP IV, 38.

[110] Pr. LassoS; also published separately by Annie Bank, Amsterdam (Nos. GW 94–100); analyses in BäuM; *see also* BezL, 52ff. Part of 1 psalm in HAM, 157. The psalms are Nos. VI, XXXI, XXXVII, L, CI, CXXIX, CXLII (= 6, 32, 38, 51, 102, 130, 143).

[111] Pr. CW XLVIII. About the date of this cycle, *see* LowC, 92f.

canon at the fifth between the altus and tenor II, and in section 3 there is another canon between the same voices, but this time at the fourth and with the subject inverted in the altus. In keeping with his tendency to relinquish pervading imitation, however, Lassus does not often employ strict contrapuntal devices of this sort. The Prophecies of the Sibyls, settings of Latin verses by an anonymous poet, are unusually chromatic.[111a]

Fifty-three Masses survive.[112] Unlike Senfl, Lassus employs Gregorian chants in very few of his works in this form. The great majority of them are parodies of chansons, motets, madrigals, and other Masses, by himself as well as by other composers. (The Masses based on chansons and madrigals illustrate the less strict compliance with the wishes of the Council of Trent shown by music in Germany as compared with the greater respect that prevailed in Italy.) To the first category belong the Masses on his own *Susanne un jour,* on Sandrin's *Douce memoire,*[113] Clemens non Papa's *Entre vous filles,*[114] Gombert's *Le bergier et la bergiere,* the Cadéac-Lupus *Je suis desheritée,* and others; to the second, those on his own *Sidus ex claro,*[115] *Credidi propter, Dixit Joseph,*[116] *Deus in adjutorium meum,*[117] *Vinum bonum,*[118] on an *In die tribulationis* probably by Jaquet of Mantua, and others; to the third, those on Arcadelt's *Quand' io penso,* Palestrina's *Io son ferito,*[118a] and Rore's *Ite, rime dolenti, Qual donna attende,*[119] and *Scarco di doglia,* and others; and to the last, those on Daser's *Missa Ecce nunc benedicite* and Fossa's *Missa super carmen italicum* (*Amor ecco colei*). Two Masses employ German sacred lieder: *Beschaffenes Glück*[120] and *Jesus ist ein süsser Nam'.* In his Masses, just as in his secular music, Lassus is the "most international" master of his time.[121]

His parody technique, as shown for example in four of the Masses based on his own motets, reveals few unusual traits. Each of the five sections of the

[111a] Further about Lassus' motets, *see* BorOL, 57ff; BalmO; AbertS, 72ff; LeiG, 96ff; BezL, 52ff.

[112] Modern reprints include 6 in CommM V; 2 in VII; 2 in VIII; 1 in IX; 2 in X; 1 in XII; 1 in ProsS I; 1 in II; 2 in ProsM, *Annus I,* I; first movement of a *Missa pro defunctis* in HAM, 156; etc.

[113] The Mass pr. CommM VII, 103; BordA, *Messes* I, 99.

[114] The chanson and the complete Kyrie pr. WagG, 359ff.

[115] Motet pr. LassoW III, 153; Mass in CommM X, 64.

[116] Motet pr. LassoW XV, 76; CommB VIII, 103; Mass pr. CommM VIII, 65.

[117] Motet pr. LassoW XVII, 160; Mass pr. CommM V, 79.

[118] Motet pr. LassoW XXI, 91; Mass pr. CommM V, 92.

[118a] HuschL, 177, states that the model of this Mass is by Nola. Mr. J. D. Volante has made modern scores of Nola's composition and of the Mass, and from these it is clear that this madrigal is not the model. The Mass, however, is so closely related to Palestrina's composition that there can be no doubt that Lassus based his own work on it.

[119] The Mass pr. ProsS I, No. 3.

[120] This is the melody, *Il me suffit,* probably written by Claudin (cf. p. 295) and reset by others. It has survived in the German chorale *Was mein Gott will, das gscheh' allzeit* (a setting *a* 5 by Eccard in WintK I, App., 136). About Lassus' Mass, *see* WagG, 375ff.

[121] WagG, 397. Concerning a Mass by Lassus that may be composed on a *canzonetta, see* BorMC.

Mass usually opens with material borrowed from the model, bodily in the first Kyrie and more freely in the other movements. Sometimes the beginning of a subdivision of a Mass section also leans on the motet (e.g., the *Et incarnatus* of the six-part *Deus in adjutorium meum intende*). In the six-part *Dixit Joseph* and the five-part *Sidus ex claro*, Kyrie II opens with the beginning of *pars II* of the motet. The *Osanna* of *Dixit Joseph* also employs the opening of *pars II*, the third voice of the model being now allotted to the second of the Mass and the meter changed from $\frac{4}{2}$ to $\frac{3}{2}$. The borrowed material here seems far better suited to its new use (in the motet it represents the jubilant announcement to Jacob that his son Joseph lives) than is that in some of Lassus' chanson and madrigal Masses. The end of the *Et in Spiritum* of *Sidus ex claro* employs material from the beginning of *pars II* of the motet. Motifs and sometimes whole brief passages from the motet may appear in the course of a movement (as in the Gloria and Sanctus of the eight-part *Vinum bonum*, Kyrie and Gloria of *Sidus ex claro*, Credo of *Dixit Joseph*). The relations with the model are most tenuous in those sections of the Mass that employ fewer voices (the four-part *Christe, Crucifixus,* and Benedictus of *Vinum bonum,* the four-part *Crucifixus* and three-part Benedictus of *Dixit Joseph,* the three-part Benedictus of *Sidus ex claro,* and the four-part Benedictus of *Deus in adjutorium*). The Mass on *Deus in adjutorium* is the freest of the four: aside from the beginning of the *Et incarnatus,* already mentioned, the opening of the Credo proper, and the first measures of the Gloria, where only the four lowest voices are based on the model, little resemblance to that model is discernible. The Masses as a whole are often written with Lassus' wonted skill, and contain many passages of unusual interest and effectiveness, but, especially in the short Masses, written for minor occasions, a perfunctory attitude is sometimes evident: the unchanging text of the Ordinary does not seem to have stirred the composer's imagination as profoundly as the varying texts of the motets (cf. p. 246). However extraordinary he may be as a motet composer, he is not on a level as a Mass composer with either Josquin or Palestrina.[122]

The *Patrocinium musices,* a twelve-volume collection of works by five composers, printed at Munich (1573–1598) by Adam Berg, contains twenty-three Magnificats by Lassus, as well as his five-part Passion after St. Matthew.[123] In 1619, Rudolph Lassus published a collection of one hundred Magnificats by his father.[124] About half of these are composed on Gregorian material, and most of the others, like most of the Masses, are parodies of chansons, madrigals, or motets, by Lassus (*Susanne un jour, Dessus le*

---

[122] Further on Lassus' Masses, *see* WagG, 349ff; BorOL, 127ff; HuschL.

[123] CommM VI, 18. Vols. I–V, VII, and VIII of the *Patrocinium* are devoted to Lassus. Among the works of his included are 11 of the Masses. For list of contents, *see* 2nd ed. of Grove I, 307.

[124] 9 Magnificats pr. ProsM, *Annus I,* III; 22 (of which 8 are also in ProsM) pr. CommM, X and XI.

marché, Deus in adjutorium, etc.), Rore (*Anchor che col partire, Vergine bella*), and others. Both types are further examples of the practice of setting alternate verses (here, the even-numbered ones) in polyphony.[125] In the Magnificats based on the Chant, the borrowed melody is treated rather freely and is not confined to a particular voice. It usually appears, however, in each of the polyphonic verses.

The complete set of nine Lamentations, published in 1585,[126] reveals Lassus in his best form. The second Lamentation for Holy Saturday is particularly fine, with its vigorous use of conflicting accents.

The Counter Reformation is responsible for the *Teutsche geistliche Psalmen* (1588), fifty settings *a 3* (half by Lassus [127] and half by his son Rudolph) of a German psalter published with one-line melodies by Caspar Ulenberg in 1582, a psalter written to combat the popular Lutheran psalm-lieder. On the whole, however, the musical reforms decreed by the Council of Trent were more effective in Italy than in Germany or France.

Catholic Polyphony: Kerle; Aichinger; Amon

Kerle—who, as we have seen, helped turn the tide when it seemed as though polyphony in the Church was endangered at the Council of Trent (cf. p. 451) —after accompanying Cardinal Truchsess von Waldburg on a trip to Spain in 1563, went with him to Dillingen, 1564–1565. Thereafter the composer was active at Ypres, Rome, Augsburg (where he served as organist, 1568–1575), etc., finally becoming, from 1582 to his death in 1591, imperial court chaplain to Rudolph II at Prague. Kerle's years in Germany and Bohemia were productive, especially of motets, collections of which appeared from 1571 on, at Nuremberg, Munich, etc. His works were instrumental in spreading the influence of the Roman School in the Empire. Of two *Te Deum* settings (1571 and 1575), the earlier—a composition *a 5,* mainly chordal, designed to alternate part-music and monophonic chant, the plainsong for the Simple Tone being assigned, in the part-music passages, to tenor I—exists in several sources and was evidently much favored.[128] Chordal writing, such as prevails here, however, is infrequently found in complete works by Kerle or in lengthy sections.

[125] Lassus sets the entire text in one Magnificat. In this piece for double chorus, one chorus performs the odd-numbered verses and the other the even-numbered, the two choirs merging near the middle and at the end (BorOL, 152f).

[126] Pr. CommM XII. Other sacred pieces by Lassus include *Lectiones* after Job (1 in CommM VII, 47; 1 in VI, 40); Litanies (1 CommM XII, 79, 2 in ProsM, *Annus I,* IV; 1 in *Annus II,* III).

[127] Pr. LassoW XX.

[128] This setting pr. MaldR I, 1, with the plainsong for the Solemn Tone drawn on (evidently by Maldeghem, in error) for the intonation. Other motets from the German period pr. *ibid.,* I, 7; XVII, 3, 7, 12, 16, 20 (all 6 from the *Selectae . . . cantiones* of 1571); ProsM, *Annus I,* II, 88 (from the *Liber Modulorum* of 1573; *pars II* also pr. HAM, 163). Further on this period, *see* esp. DTB XXVI, xxviff.

Notable among the native German composers influenced by the Roman School is Gregor Aichinger (1564–1628), a priest who served as organist for the Fuggers in Augsburg and later visited Italy. His motets show, besides evidence of a careful study of Lassus, the clarity of structure, careful voice-leading, and concern for beauty of sound that are among the traits of the Roman style. His six-part *Intonuit de coelo* is a brilliant piece, based on a short motif. The opening shows Aichinger's use of a tonal answer, a strong domi-nant-tonic feeling, lively rhythm, and skill in maintaining a varied and flow-ing polyphony without chromaticism.

EXAMPLE 156. Opening of *Intonuit de coelo*—Aichinger (after CommM, XXVIII, 1).

"The Lord also thundered in the heavens . . ." (Psalm XVII [18], 13)

An expressive composition in a different vein is his five-part *Maria uns tröst,* one of a set of thirty-three pieces based on the same musical theme, which Bernhard Klingenstein (1545–1614), *Kapellmeister* of the cathedral at Augs-burg, invited as many composers to write, each setting one verse of a poem in praise of Mary (Aichinger chose Verse 16). The collection was published in 1604 under the title, *Rosetum Marianum.*[128a]

The effect of Venetian influence on the Catholic polyphonists of Germany is shown in the music of Blasius Amon (c. 1560–1590). The first German composer to adopt the double-choir technique, he may in his youth have been a pupil of Andrea Gabrieli. He seems to have composed no secular music, but has left us two books of motets for from four to eight voices and a book of Masses *a 4,* all printed before his death, and three books of motets, *a 4, a 5,* and *a 6,* issued after his death, as well as some works in MS.[128b]

[128a] *Maria uns tröst* pr. separately in the series *Musica orans* (Heft 24), Volksvereinsverlag, München-Gladbach. Biographical data and 16 sacred pieces in DTB X¹; 6 motets in ProsM, *Annus I,* I, II (1 = HAM, 188); 3 settings each of *Alma Redemptoris, Ave Regina,* and *Salve Regina,* and 2 of *Regina coeli* in III (the *Salve Regina* and *Regina coeli* on pp. 537 and 472, re-spectively, being the famous ones—not actually exx. of Aichinger at his best; the *Salve* on p. 492 = DTB X¹, 109; the *Ave* on p. 486 = JödeC V, 92; DTB X¹, 53); a litany *a 3* and a *Stabat Mater* in IV; 1 motet in *Annus II,* II. Aichinger was one of the first German composers to publish motets with a *basso continuo* (1607). See further MGG I, 177ff.

[128b] About Amon, see HuigA, MGG I, 429f. 71 compositions of his pr. DTO XXXVIII¹ (of these, 6 also pr. CommM XXI); 3 additional pieces pr. CommM XXI.

Sacred Polyphony at the Imperial Court, notably that of Monte

Kerle was one of a large number of Netherlandish and other foreign musicians to hold important posts at the Hapsburg court during the latter half of the 16th century.[129] Among the Netherlanders, Petrus Maessens was chief *Kapellmeister* in Vienna from 1546 to 1560, Jacob Vaet from 1564 to 1567, and Philippe de Monte from 1568 to 1603; Jacques Buus was organist there from 1551 to 1564 (cf. p. 374); Jacques Regnart (to whom we shall return) held various posts at different times; Christian Hollander sang in the choir, as did Johannes de Cleve (1553-1564; active in Graz also and later in Augsburg); Carl Luython (c. 1556-1620), a pupil of Monte's, and Franciscus Sale [129a] were both active in Vienna and Prague, the latter having become tenor in the Imperial Chapel under Monte in 1589; [129b] and Lambert de Sayve, another pupil of Monte's, succeeded his master as Imperial *Kapellmeister*. As we have seen, Mateo Flecha the younger came to Vienna in 1568 and stayed for some years before he returned to Spain. Jakob Handl (Gallus) worked in Prague, after having sung in the court choir at Vienna. (Whether the Hapsburg court was held in Vienna or Prague, it was still a Germanic court, even though Prague was a Czech city. Nevertheless, since Handl was a Slav and was active mostly in Bohemia, though not born there, he will be treated in the Bohemian part of Chap. 14.) Elsewhere in Austria were the Netherlander, Alexander Utendal (d. 1581), *Kapellmeister* at Innsbruck, and the Italian, Annibale Padovano, *Kapellmeister* at Graz. For the wedding of William V of Bavaria, Annibale wrote a Mass *a 24,* an eight-part *Battaglia* (cf. p. 550), and pieces for an ensemble of six viols, a zink, and five trombones, with organ.

Vaet, whose nenia on the death of Clemens non Papa has helped to establish the death date of that composer and who was himself the subject of a funeral song by Regnart, has left us three chansons, nine Masses, eight Magnificats, and seventy-six motets. The motets, mostly *a 5* or *a 6,* show the same attitude toward imitation as a constructive force that is evident in Lassus. Often imitation is restricted to some of the voices only or to a very few notes; occasionally, just the rhythmic outline is retained. Vaet's free treatment of imitation, including the reworking of motifs in individual voices, may be illustrated by the *et cum eo* passage of *Ecce apparebit Dominus,* a passage noteworthy also for its use of a simultaneous cross-relation. The clash, which is established beyond question in a keyboard tablature version of the motet, is a natural concomitant of the curves of each of the two lines.

---

[129] For data on musicians at the imperial court, 1543-1619, *see* SmijKH.

[129a] Vols. IX and XII of the *Patrocinium musices,* pr. by Adam Berg, are devoted entirely to Sale. Vol. XII is reprinted complete in MaldR IV, 3-35; Vol. IX almost complete in MaldR I, 14-17; IV, 36-50; V, 3-50; VI, 3-31; cf. ReT, 78, 115f.

[129b] For special articles on the Imperial Chapel under Monte in 1582 and 1594, see, respectively, DoorMR and DoorC.

EXAMPLE 157. Extract from the motet, *Ecce apparebit Dominus*—Vaet (from SteinhV, 121f).

"[Behold, the Lord shall appear] upon a white cloud and with him thousands of saints, and he shall have [upon his thigh the writing: King of kings and Lord of lords.]"

Although cross-relations in Renaissance music are certainly not confined to Vaet (cf. pp. 297, 535, 783), they take on special interest in his work. More frequent than simultaneous examples and equally demonstrable, are oblique ones.[129c] The dissonances in Vaet include also the augmented sixth. A few Vaet motets are among the pieces of evidence showing that the standard practice of raising a minor third from the bass in a final chord was by no means universal. That *Postquam consummati essent* is meant to end on a G-minor chord is shown by the treatment of b-flat, first established as a held note in an inner voice and reaffirmed by its presentation as part of an *ostinato* figure in the superius. In *Stat felix domus Austriae* an *ostinato* figure is actually a *soggetto* derived from the vowels of the title words of the motet.[130]

This *soggetto* was also used by Cleve in his motet in praise of the Archduke Charles, *Carole sceptrigeri patris*. This work and another that incorporates a *soggetto*, *Forti qui celebres*, written in praise of the Emperor Ferdinand I, were printed in Cleve's *Cantiones sacrae . . . Lib. I* (1559).[131] For a collection of rhymed Gospel sermons in German prepared c. 1569 by the rector at Graz, Andreas Gigler, and designed to compete with similar Protestant

[129c] SteinhV, 48ff; 82f.
[130] Biographical data in SteinhV, 1ff; CW II; CreC, 183ff. Facsimile of a motet in HaasA, 129; a Requiem Mass in CommM XXII, 62; 20 motets, etc. in CommB II, IV, V, IX (3 = CW II, 5, 23, 36; 1 = MaldP XIII, 20); 6 more pr. SteinhV, 110, 120, 129; CW II, 11, 14, 31.
[131] Cf. ThürS, 186f. The pieces pr. MaldP I, 23, 28. Cleve's *Cantiones sacrae . . . Lib. I* and *II* are included complete in MaldR I, XII–XVI; MaldP I, IX, XII (cf. ReT, 94ff).

publications, de Cleve set ten melodies of Protestant lieder and ten by Gigler, all *a 4*. These are old-fashioned tenor *cantus-firmus* settings.[131a] Hollander, highly regarded as a composer by his imperial employers, wrote many motets and lieder which reveal him as a skillful craftsman in the late Netherlandish style.[132] Luython, who, like Aichinger, contributed to Klingenstein's *Rosetum Marianum,* produced a number of motets, mostly *a 6,* and Masses in the style of the late Netherlanders.[133] Lambert de Sayve, another contributor to Klingenstein's cycle, published in 1612–1613 a set of 141 motets for from four to sixteen voices, including one written for the wedding of Sigismund III Vasa of Poland and Constance of Austria (1605), another for that of Matthew of Austria and Anna of Styria (1611), and a third for the coronation of Matthew as emperor (1612). He also produced a set of twenty-four four-part *Teutsche Liedlein* in the style of *canzonette,* published at Vienna in 1604 and reprinted by Michael Praetorius in 1611.[134] Utendal published Penitential Psalms and *Orationes* (1570), three Masses and a Magnificat (1573), and three books of motets (1571, 1573, 1577), as well as some lieder.[135]

The most important of the composers at the imperial court was Monte, whose work is sometimes ranked with that of Lassus with respect to quality as well as quantity. The greatness of Lassus' motets makes this estimate questionable on the score of quality, but Monte's music does represent the dissemination of Franco-Netherlandish technique through one of its chief native-born, Late Renaissance exponents. Despite his thirty-five year stay in Austria, Monte seems never to have published any lieder, although he produced many chansons and madrigals. All the motet collections devoted solely to him, while printed in Italy, date from his German period; many motets of his appeared likewise during these years in collections drawing on various composers and printed mostly in Germany. Still other motets survive in MS. Monte, who had visited England in 1554–1555 as a singer in the retinue of Philip II, had formed a friendship with Thomas Byrd, the father of William Byrd, then a boy of about thirteen years. British Museum MS Add. 23624 contains an eight-part *Super flumina Babylonis* [136] by Monte, bearing the inscription "Sent by him to Mr Wm Bird, 1583," and also a *Quomodo cantabimus,* likewise *a 8,* marked "Made by Mr Wm Byrd to send in to Mr Phillip de Monte, 1584" (cf. p. 788).[137]

131a See OsN, 325ff; MosJC.
132 Biographical data and style study of the lieder in OsN, 208–41; 25 motets in CommB; 1 lied in OsN, 559; 1 in CW XXX, 13.
133 1 Mass in CommM XVII; 2 in XVIII; 1 in XIX; 1 in XXVII; Lamentations in XX; other sacred pieces in XXII; the Marian lied—*Maria, ein reisz des paradeisz,* in BurbL, 24ff; 8 *ricercare, fantasie,* etc. in MB IV, 73ff. About Luython's motets, see SmijL.
134 The Praetorius reprint in CW LI; 2 of the lieder in OsN, 600ff; 1 in JödeC VI. About these, see OsN, 422–46. See also BragL, which reprints 1 motet.
135 1 lied in CW XXX, 16; 1 in OsN, 583; 1 in KrV, 11. See OsN, 333–43.
136 Pr. MonteO XV, 57.
137 Other Monte motets pr. DehnS, *Lieferung IV,* 2; MonteO I, App.; II; XV; XVII; XXII (51 items in these 4 vols.; XXII, 1 = CommB VI, 72); XXIV, App.; 8 Magnificats in XII.

Of Monte's forty-eight Masses,[138] one is a Requiem [139] that includes the *Si ambulem* removed by the Council of Trent and six are settings of the Ordinary that are based on liturgical melodies and thus probably represent an attempt to meet the Council's requirements. Of the remaining seventeen that are available in modern print, four are *sine nomine* and the rest are parody Masses based on madrigals by Rore (*Anchor che col partire, Quando lieta sperai*), Giaches de Wert (*Cara la vita mia*), Striggio (*Nasce la pena mia*), Palestrina (*Vestiva i colli*), Verdelot (*Ultimi miei sospiri*), and Monte himself (*La dolce vista*), a chanson (Monte's *Reviens vers moy*),[140] and motets by Jaquet of Mantua (*Aspice Domine*),[141] Josquin (*Benedicta es coelorum Regina*), Rore (*O altitudo divitiarum*),[142] Lassus (*Confitebor tibi*),[143] and Monte (*Cum sit omnipotens rector Olympi,*[144] *Inclina cor meum* [145]). All of these Masses reveal a style that is on the whole less bold and dramatic than that of Lassus' motets, but richer and more moving than that of Lassus' Masses. The style is predominantly contrapuntal (only one of the Masses is largely chordal); [146] the voices are often of equal importance, with few "instrumentalisms." A predilection for scale-passages, and an occasional filling-in of leaps present in the originals that Monte is parodying, sometimes bring about a decline in melodic character. On the other hand, the chords resulting from the confluence of the melodic lines are more varied than in Lassus' Masses, Monte being less prone to writing such chords in root position. His Masses are *a 4* to *a 8*, the number of voices established in the Kyrie usually remaining constant throughout each Mass, except in the Benedictus and *Crucifixus*, which, in accordance with normal practice, usually call for fewer voices. Only rarely is a voice or two omitted from the *Christe* or *Et resurrexit*. When the Benedictus is for fewer voices than the rest of a Mass, the normal complement usually returns for the *Hosanna,* as customary; and sometimes this *Hosanna* calls for more voices than the rest of the Mass.[147] In such Masses *a 8* as *La dolce vista* and *Confitebor tibi,* there is a division occasionally into two choirs *a 4* but as a rule the entire chorus is treated as a unit.

With Monte the parody technique is often subtle and almost never as perfunctory as it sometimes is with Lassus. In the Kyrie, Monte nearly always alters the borrowed material, either rhythmically, or by changing the order of

---

[138] 17 in MonteO (1 = MaldR VIII–IX; another = CommM XXIV); 7 more in MaldR VI–X (X, 5 = VNM XXXVIII). The conclusions here tentatively offered are based on these 24 works—half of the composer's production in the field of the Mass.

[139] Pr. MonteO XIII.

[140] These 8 Masses and their models pr. respectively, *ibid.,* VIII, XXIII, XXI, X, XVIII, V, XIV, IX; Wert's *Cara la vita* and the Sanctus from Monte's Mass in HAM, 160f.

[141] Not Berchem as stated in MonteO XXVI, which reprints Mass and model (cf. p. 366 *supra*).   [142] Mass in MonteO IV.

[143] Mass pr. MaldR IX, 24; X, 3; model pr. LassoW XXI, 56. Identification by I. L. Domingos.

[144] Mass and model pr. MonteO, XXIV; Mass in MaldR VIII, 47; IX, 3.

[145] Mass and model pr. MonteO I.   [146] *Sine nomine, a 6, ibid.,* VII.

[147] E.g., *O altitudo divitiarum* (*a 5;* the *Hosanna* is *a 8*); *Sine nomine* (*a 4,* in MonteO III; the *Hosanna* is *a 5*).

the voices, or by varying the inner parts; and even on the rare occasions when the borrowed material is taken over note for note at the beginning of the Kyrie, he likes to change it in the other movements. The Masses based on madrigals retain a brightness of harmonic complexion and a sophistication of melodic line derived from their models. This madrigalian atmosphere is heightened through the use of adroitly planned and skilfully executed changes of key within a movement, as for example at the words *"gratias agimus tibi"* in *La dolce vista.* This splendid Mass *a 8* treats the borrowed material very freely throughout. The *Missa Vestiva i colli* appears *sine nomine* in a Nuremberg MS. Like the madrigal, it is based largely on one motif and a principal variant, one form or another appearing fifteen times in the Mass. The high-water mark of this work is the *Osanna,* which features an ingenious variation of imitation in pairs. In *Anchor che col partire,* Monte follows a progressive plan of borrowing, drawing each of the motifs from the madrigal into his Mass in the same order in which they succeed each other in the model. Kyrie I introduces the first motif; *Christe,* the second; Kyrie II, the third; the Gloria uses all these in order and adds three more. The Benedictus *a 3* is based entirely on freely composed material. The *Qui tollis* of *Cara la vita mia* opens with the first theme of the madrigal in retrograde motion in the superius, followed immediately by the second theme in diminution. In measures 1 to 5 of the Sanctus, the first theme (now in its normal form, but augmented), in tenor II, is surrounded by figures based on itself in the other voices, in shorter note-values, starting on various scale-degrees, and inverted as well as in normal form. The six-part *Benedicta es* makes unusually abundant use of the model, especially of its superius and bass. Kyrie I is derived mainly from the opening phrase of the sequence and Josquin's countermelody to it (cf. Example 158).

EXAMPLE 158. Opening of *Missa Benedicta es*—Monte (complete work in VNM XXXVIII; MaldR X, 5).

The *Christe, a 3,* is modelled after the duo section, *Per illud,* while Kyrie II, again *a 6,* follows the *Nunc mater* section. This rotation of divisions of the motet on which the Mass sections are patterned continues throughout, with several changes in the number of parts. Neither the *Pleni* nor *Hosanna I* is included in this Mass; instead there are two settings of the first part of the Sanctus. Both Sanctus II and Agnus II are *a 8*. In the former, a *Fuga prior in diapason, altera verò in diapente,* the tenor II follows superius I at the octave below in canon at a distance of three measures and the altus II follows superius I similarly at the fifth below at a distance of eight measures; and in the latter, a *Fuga prior in diapente, altera verò in diapason,* altus II and tenor II exchange roles, at a distance of one and three measures, respectively. Both *fugae* are built chiefly on the four-note phrase, g, a, b, g, which is derived from the sequence, and on Josquin's countermelodies. Among the Masses *sine nomine* one finds the same kind of technique as in the parody Masses, and they are probably based on as yet unidentified models.

Secular Polyphony, including the Ott and Forster Song-Books and the Collections of Hassler

Humanism was introduced into Germany toward the end of the 15th century, one of its chief founders there being the poet Konrad Celtes. To help his pupils learn the nineteen meters of Horace's odes and epodes and other Latin metrical patterns, Celtes had one of his students, Petrus Tritonius (= Peter Treibenreif), set representative Latin poems to music. This was written in four parts, moving in block-chords, the note-values of the chords faithfully reflecting the longs and shorts of the text meters—a type of writing which, in principle though not in quality, anticipates French settings of *vers mesurés* by about seventy-five years. Tritonius' odes were published by Öglin in 1507. Similar settings were composed by Senfl, who retained Tritonius' tenors, and also, toward the end of his life, by Hofhaimer.[148] Reuchlin employed the same method in teaching Hebrew accents.[149] The odes were taken up in the Latin school-dramas that were presented throughout the German-speaking countries during the 16th century, and it has been conjectured [150] that they may have served, by way of these dramas, as the connecting link between the polyphonic songs of the beginning of the century and the chordal pieces (such as Osiander's) of the end. Even psalms employing Horatian meters were set to music in this manner, by Statius Olthoff, and published in 1585 and 1619.[151]

We have seen humanism reflected in the texts of lieder by Adam von Fulda

---

[148] 19 odes, each separately set by Tritonius, Senfl, and Hofhaimer pr. LiliH, 49–91 (1 Tritonius ex. = ScherG, 70); 35 settings by Hofhaimer (including those in LiliH) pr. MosPH, App., 112ff. *See also* SternR, 106ff; StrunkV, 488ff.

[149] In his *De accentibus et orthographia linguae hebraicae,* 1518 (PirH, 126, note). Facsimile of a page from this work in *Musikbibliothek Dr. Werner Wolffheim* (1929), II, 34. (For a study of German elements in the music of the early German Synagogue, *see* IdD.)

[150] In LiliC, 309–13. This work lists 124 plays appearing between 1497 and 1620 and contains a discussion and exx. of the music employed. For a study of 8 plays performed in Basle, 1532–71, and their music, *see* RefM. 2 pieces *a 4* that probably come from a Basle play in BerH, 108f. About the music of a Passion play given at Lucerne in 1583 and 1597, *see* ArltL; M. B. Evans, *The Passion Play of Lucerne,* 1943.   [151] Discussion and 30 exx. in WidmK.

(cf. p. 639); it continued to influence the words of German secular songs during the 16th century. Collections of predominantly secular lieder began to appear, after a hiatus of some fifteen or twenty years (Arnt von Aich's collection being the last previous one), with Johann Ott's compilation of *121 neue Lieder,* published by Formschneider at Nuremberg in 1534.[152] (Nuremberg about this time became the center of a flourishing German music-publishing industry. It is here that not only Formschneider was active, but also Johann Petreius, Johann vom Berg [Montanus] and Ulrich Neuber, and subsequently Dietrich Gerlach and Paul Kaufmann, among others.) This was followed the next year by the *Gassenhawerlin und Reutterliedlin,* issued from the press of Christian Egenolff at Frankfurt on the Main.[153] Other important collections include the *Fünff und sechzig teütscher Lieder* printed by Schöffer and Apiarius at Strasbourg in 1536, the five parts of the *Frische teutsche Liedlein* brought out from 1539 to 1556 by Georg Forster, doctor and composer,[154] and a second set, containing 115 pieces, published by Ott, in 1544.[155]

Ott's first collection is unusual in that all its contents, save for a few anonymous pieces, are attributed to three composers—Senfl,[155a] Arnoldus de Bruck,[155b] and Wilhelm Breitengraser (d. 1535), the "most humanistic"[156] of the German lieder composers. It contains several pieces that employ *Fortuna desperata* as a *cantus firmus,* either alone or in combination with *Pange lingua* or a favorite lied.[157] Ott's second set includes, besides works in French, Latin, and Italian (by such composers as Crecquillon, Gombert, Richafort, Hellinck, Andreas de Silva, and Verdelot), German lieder by Senfl, Isaac, Stoltzer, Breitengraser, Bruck, Dietrich, Hellinck, Mahu, Paminger, and others. Among the predominantly secular contents are a few religious pieces, such as Senfl's noble setting of the old Easter melody, *Also heilig ist der Tag.*[157a] Many of the composers in Ott's book are represented in Forster also,

---

[152] *See* MosH.   [153] Facsimile edition (with missing discant from a later ed. of the work) in MosGR; 8 tenor melodies, with text, in MosDK.

[154] Part 1 pr. EDMR XX; Part 2 pr. PubAPTM XXIX. For studies of the song-texts in Forster's collection, *see* MarriF and KalG, 2 pieces by Forster in LiliD, 135 (= PubAPTM XXIX, 80; JödeC III, 21), 180 (= JödeC I, 14; AmeK, 12); 2 more pr. JödeC IV, 97; AmeK, 124; 8 anon. pieces from his collection pr. JödeC III, 1 pr. IV, 2 pr. ScherG, 84.

[155] Pr. PubAPTM I–III (there are many other reprints of individual pieces; cf. fn. 162); commentary in IV.

[155a] 2 of the pieces ascribed to Senfl are attributed to Wolfgang Grefinger by Forster and are among the 8 lieder pr. under his name in DTO XXXVII², 25ff (1 of the other 6 = MosL, 89). The 2 pieces, however, are pr. under Senfl's name in SenflW IV (= EDMR XV), 59, 135 (*see ibid.,* 149, 154, about all sources), which volume is devoted to his pieces in this Ott book.

[155b] 11 of the 19 lieder by Bruck pr. DTO XXXVII² are from this Ott book.

[156] MosH, 3. The Bruck songs are discussed *ibid.*

[157] 4 such pieces by Senfl pr. BerH, 38ff (= SenflW IV [= EDMR XV], 12, 18, 20 [= ScherG, 81; PubAPTM XVI, 108], 132). An anon. setting of *Fortuna* from MS St. Gall 462 (1510–16) pr. BerH, 36.

[157a] Pr. BäumK I, 524. Senfl's piece pr. PubAPTM III, 339; JödeC I, 27; WintK I, App., No. 5.

as are the members of the so-called "Heidelberg School" of lied composers—
Lorenz Lemlin (born c. 1495) and his pupils: Forster himself, Othmayr, Jobst
vom Brandt, and Stephan Zirler (d. before 1576).[158] In Ott (1534) and Egenolff the text is supplied only for those parts that are presumably meant to
be sung, but in Forster all the parts are furnished with text; in Forster's last
book, writing *a 5* becomes the norm.[159] Another publication that may be mentioned here is Wolfgang Schmeltzl's *Liederbuch* (1544), the first considerable
collection of quodlibets in Germany.[160]

Generally speaking, the secular lieder by all the German composers represented in these publications continue the tradition established by Hofhaimer,
Finck, and Isaac. The overwhelming majority of the songs are *cantus-firmus*
pieces often indistinguishable in style and idiom from the Protestant lieder
written during the same period and by many of the same composers. More
advanced than most in some respects are the songs of Othmayr, perhaps the
first composer to publish a complete cycle of songs as an independent work.[161]
Noteworthy among the secular lieder are those by Senfl.[162] Like his sacred
pieces, they show mastery of Franco-Netherlandish contrapuntal style, combined with a gift for warm, flowing melody. The text of the four-part *Lust
hab ich ghabt zuer Musica*[163] mentions Isaac and contains "Ludwig S" as
an acrostic. In one of Senfl's settings *a 4* of *Ich stund an einem Morgen*[164] he
employs the unusual device of allotting the melody to both outer voices, in
tenths, while simultaneously it is syncopated and abbreviated in the tenor. His
six-part *Das gleut zu Speier,* constructed entirely out of three chords (it "belongs to the strongest dominant-tonic monuments of the 16th century"[165]),
paints a delightful picture of merrily pealing bells, and is thus a forerunner of

---

[158] For a special study of this group, with biographical data, *see* ReinhH. The tenor of
Lemlin's *Der Gutzgauch* (EinW, 377; JödeC III, 65; LiliD, 251; LippGZ, 74) is the subject
of a *fugato* in Hindemith's *Der Schwanendreher.*

[159] In Forster I, a song by Lapicida and another by Hofhaimer contain added (alto) parts by
Virdung.

[160] It contains other pieces also. Most of the quodlibets are pr. EitD (1 = ScherG, 110). *See*
BienS. According to VelA, 19, Bienenfeld seems to be mistaken in her claim that one of
the pieces in Schmeltzl's collection is a madrigal by Verdelot with a German text substituted
for the original Italian.

[161] *See* OthmayrR.

[162] 154 lieder, sacred and secular, pr. SenflW II, IV (= EDMR X, XV); duplications in
AmbG V, 398, 400; JödeC III, 152; IV, 29 (*a 4; a 5* in SenflW II [= EDMR X], 89; KrV, 18;
LiliD, 9 (*a 4; a 7* in SenflW IV [= EDMR XV], 44; BerH, 73), 145, 206 (= ScherG, 80;
PubAPTM I, 45), 272, 288, 365; LippGZ, 30, 86 (= JödeC III, 118); WolfME, 72. 68
other lieder in PubAPTM I–III (duplications in JödeC III, 120, 122 [= LiliD, 150], 129, 132
[= LiliD, 202], 139 [= LippGZ, 108], 142, 145, 148 [= LiliD, 191]; IV, 19; LippGZ, 98);
LiliD, 28 (= LippGZ, 48); 313 (= JödeC III, 125; PubAPTM XXIX, 81), 359 (= JödeC
III, 133). 4 instrumental pieces are pr. MosC. See also fns. 155a, 163, 165, 167. (Since the
foregoing was written, SenflW V, also devoted to German lieder, has appeared.)

[163] Pr. SenflW II (= EDMR X), 56; MosI, 132.

[164] Cf. BaumD, 78f, or OsN, 75.

[165] MosI, 124. The title of the piece is given as it appears in Schmeltzl's *Liederbuch;* in Ott
1534 it is *Trink lang.*

such later lieder in which bell sounds are imitated as the *Wohlauf, ihr lieben Gäste* [166] of Thomas Sartorius (which incorporates a night-watchman's call that reminds one of Wagner's *Meistersinger*). One of the Senfl settings (*a 4*) of *Wol kumpt der May* [167] has the main melody, in the tenor, anticipated a fifth lower in the bass; fragments of the tune appear in the other voices, and toward the end there is a melisma much like the *"Blume"* of a mastersong. In several pieces, he combines two or three tunes with their texts.[168] One of his loveliest songs is *Geduld umb Huld*.[169]

EXAMPLE 159. Opening of *Geduld umb Huld*—Senfl (after SenflW II [= EDMR X], 11).

"Patience and favor shall I have . . ."

With Senfl the first flowering of the German polyphonic lied, after a century of development, reached its highest point and its end. No secular lied publications of any importance appeared from 1556, the date of the fifth part of Forster's collection, until 1566. In that year there was printed at Nuremberg *Il primo libro delle Canzone Napoletane* by Antonio Scandello (1517–1580),[170] a member of the *Kapelle* at Dresden, the first exclusively Italian vocal collection published in Germany. During the same year Le Maistre's

[166] Pr. separately in the *Auswahl hervorragender Meisterwerke des a-cappella-Stils* (Bd. III, No. 7), Sulzbach, Berlin.

[167] Pr. SenflW IV (= EDMR XV), 58; EinSH, 275.

[168] Both Arnold von Bruck and Stephen Mahu combine two pre-existent melodies in a song, and the former composer unites three in his 6-part *Ich stund an einem Morgen* (DTO XXXVII², 10).

[169] For a comparison of Senfl's *Mein herz in hohen freuden stet* with versions from the *Lochamer Liederbuch*, the *Fundamentum organisandi* of Berlin MS 40613, *Schedelsches Liederbuch*, *Buxheimer Orgelbuch*, Trent Codices, and by Isaac, etc., *see* MosH, 8ff.

[170] Excerpts from a Mass, 2 lieder, and a *canzone napolitana* in AmbG V, 428ff (1 lied = AmeK, 3); 2 lieder in CommM XIX, 65ff; 3 in AmeH II (1 = BockM XI, 5); 3 in SchöbS III (2 = BockM VII, 47; XI, 10); 2 in WintK I, App., 49; 1 in JödeC VI, 108. Biographical study in KadeS. About his 4 pieces published in the *Thesaurus musicus* of 1564—2 sacred motets, a secular one, and a Magnificat—*see* BorTM, 45f.

Geistliche und Weltliche Teutsche Geseng[171] appeared, and the following year saw the publication of Lassus' first German contribution, the *Newe Teutsche Liedlein mit fünff Stimmen,* comprising twelve secular and three religious lieder. In the secular songs of both of these collections, the influence of the madrigal and *villanella* and, in the case of Lassus, of the chanson is unmistakable. Other German lieder by Lassus appeared in collections published in 1572, 1573, 1576, 1583, and 1590.[172] (During his Munich period, of course, he continued to write chansons and madrigals also.) Some of the texts of these German songs come from the Ott and Forster compilations; and one is a poem by Hans Sachs.[173] Some of the lieder are written in motet style, and in the religious ones Lassus sometimes uses borrowed melodies; but in the secular pieces as a rule the melodies are freely invented and short, and wander from voice to voice instead of remaining in the tenor, text phrases are often repeated, and there is a considerable amount of chromaticism and tone-painting—all traits of the madrigal; the quasi-parlando style of some passages stems from the chanson; while the influence of the *villanella* is seen in the increase in the homophonic element. Lassus sets German words as carefully and naturally as any of the native composers. *Susannen frumb,*[174] published in 1576, though not the same as the chanson, *Susanne un jour,* of 1560, is based on it as regards both text and music. The secular pieces include reflective or devotional songs, drinking and other humorous songs, and love songs. Among the first group is *Die gnad kombt oben her,*[175] whose twelve sections all end with a refrain, sometimes slightly varied as to text and every time somewhat varied as to music. Another religious piece is the five-part *Vater unser,*[176] based on the melody associated with Luther's text (cf. p. 680). Lassus assigns the melody—slightly ornamented and with free material after some phrases —to the tenor at the beginning and end, but to other voices in between, and allows it to permeate the texture through imitation. Many of the songs, both sacred and secular, are in *Bar* form, the first *Stollen* usually leading directly into the second without any caesura. Among Lassus' lighter pieces, *Ich weiss mir ein meidlein* illustrates the success with which he could enter into the spirit of German humor.[176a]

[171] 2 songs in AmbG V, 421ff; 1 in OsN, 544.

[172] Lassus' German songs pr. LassoW XVIII, XX; 2 also in JödeC I; 2 in II (1 = BraunfA, 32; 1 = LippGZ, 46); 2 in IV (1 incomplete); 5 in V; 1 in ScherG, 124; 2 in BraunfA, 29, 38; 2 in LippGZ, 39, 129; 2 in OsN, 548ff; etc. The 5-part lieder of 1567 were freely arranged *a 3* in 1581 by Anton Gosswin (c. 1540–94), a Belgian who was Lassus' first pupil at Munich (3 of Gosswin's own lieder in JödeC VI; 1 motet in DehnS, *Lieferung IV,* 8; *see* HirzG and OsN, 276ff).

[173] *Ein körbelmacher in eim dorff* (LassoW XX, 124). The text of *Tritt auff den rigel von der thür* (ibid., XVIII, 35) is very similar to the one that was to serve for Brahms' *Vergebliches Ständchen.*

[174] *Ibid.,* XVIII, 109. [175] *Ibid.,* XX, 4. [176] *Ibid.,* XVIII, 1.

[176a] All of Lassus' lied publications, by the way, are marked "to sing and to use on all sorts of instruments." Further concerning his lieder, *see* BehrD; BorOL, 220ff; OsN, 139ff; Introduction to LassoW XX (reprinted in SandA, 139ff).

EXAMPLE 160. Beginning and end of *Ich weiss mir ein meidlein*—Lassus (after LassoW XX, 28).

"I know a maiden both fair and fine, watch out, she may be both false and friendly . . . Watch out, do not trust her, she's fool-fool-fool-fool-fooling you!"

Italianate characteristics are present in the lieder brought out by Scandello in 1568 and by Ivo de Vento (c. 1540–1575; a compatriot and colleague of Lassus' at Munich) in 1569; [177] and the shift to the Italian style is openly announced in the title of the *Kurtzweilige teutsche Lieder zu dreyen stimmen nach art der Neapolitanen oder Welschen Villanellen* by Jakob (Jacques) Regnart (died c. 1600), a Netherlander active at various German courts. This work was published in three parts (1576, 1577, 1579; complete edition [sixty-seven *lieder*], 1583).[178] Regnart's pieces were the most popular of all the German lied publications between 1570 and 1600. In 1579, Lechner published arrangements *a* 5 of twenty-one of Regnart's pieces *a* 3,[179] in which he dras-

[177] Perhaps the most prolific composer of lieder, except Senfl, in the 16th century. 3 lieder in OsN, 566ff; 2 in CW XXX; 1 in JödeC II, 23 (= BockM XI, 12; SchöbS III, 102); 2 in V; 2 in VI; etc. About his life and works, *see* HuI; his lieder are given special consideration in OsN, 242ff.

[178] For a study of the Italian influence upon the texts of German lieder from c. 1570 to c. 1610, *see* VelA.

[179] Regnart's 67 songs and Lechner's 21 arrangements pr. PubAPTM XIX; of the 67 lieder, 18 also pr. RegnT (2 = JödeC VI, 73, 95); 5 more in JödeC VI (1 = OsN, 589); 2 in ScherG, Nos. 139a (= OsN, 587), 139b. 2 of the arrangements pr. JödeC IV. Five pieces *a* 5 from Regnart's *Newe kurtzweilige Lieder* (1580) in RegnD; 1 in OsN, 591; 2 later pieces in SchöbS

tically altered Regnart's chordal settings into polished songs of a madrigalian nature.

While Regnart's three-part lieder are almost wholly Italian in texture, the German songs of Ivo de Vento and Lechner (who sang in Vento's choir as a youth) are Italian mainly in their structure; in spirit, in their homely sentiment and often crude humor, they are characteristically German.[180]

The Italian and German qualities are most successfully synthetized in the lieder of Hans Leo Hassler. His first publication was a set of twenty-four four-part *canzonette* (1590),[181] and in 1596 he brought out a collection of Italian madrigals [182] that rank with the finest written in the 16th century. In 1596, too, appeared the *Neüe teütsche Gesang nach art der welschen Madrigalien und Canzonetten*,[183] twenty-four pieces *a 4* to *a 8*. These songs are rather more simply constructed than madrigals; [184] they are prevailingly chordal and divide into short, well-defined sections. Especially charming in its tender feeling and gentle humor is the four-part, wholly chordal *Junckfraw, dein schöne gstalt*.[185] Although Hassler wrote that he composed the words as well as the music of these pieces, the texts seem to be based on Italian models. His best-known collection of lieder is the *Lustgarten neuer teutscher Gesäng, Balletti, Galliarden und Intraden* (1601),[186] which contains thirty-nine vocal and eleven instrumental pieces. The *balletti* of the title are usually called *Tantz* inside the collection; they have all the characteristic traits, including the "falas" and after-dance. The *balletti* of Gastoldi, as we have seen, were popular in Germany, as were Morley's (his *First Booke of Balletts to 5 voyces* was reprinted in a German translation at Nuremberg in 1609; cf. p. 824).[187] Among Hassler's pieces is the five-part *Mein gmüth ist mir verwirret*, the superius of which was supplied with a religious text—*Herzlich thut mich verlangen*—as early as 1613 and was used by Bach, with Paul Gerhardt's words, *O Haupt voll Blut und Wunden*, in the St. Matthew Passion. Here are the first lines of Hassler's lied, showing its interesting use of hemiola, removed in the later versions:

III; 1 in CW XXX, 25; 1 in JödeC VI, 98. A study of his style in OsN, 343ff. On his music for a play (1584) by Archduke Ferdinand II of the Tyrol, the first drama written in German prose, *see* OsU. 1 secular piece by Lechner pr. JödeC IV, 12; 11 in VI (1 = LippGZ, 34; 1 = WolfME, 95); 4 more (and 1 religious one) in LippGZ.

[180] For a comprehensive list of compositions with German text by Netherlandish composers from c. 1430 to 1640, *see* OsN, 470ff.

[181] Pr. DTB V[2].

[182] Pr. *ibid.*, XI[1]. See EinH.

[183] Pr. *ibid.*, V[2]. 3 pieces also pr. JödeC IV, 65, 69; 1 in HAM, 187.

[184] "The Germans never assimilated the madrigal; it was unsuited to their temperament and still more unsuited to their language. The German composers who wrote real madrigals (such as Hassler) wrote them to Italian words." (DentB, 25.)

[185] DTB V[2], 72; MosG I, 497f.

[186] Pr. PubAPTM XV; 2 pieces also pr. ScherG, 155ff; 3 pr. JödeC IV; etc.

[187] For a detailed study of the Italian influence on Hassler, *see* SchwartzH.

EXAMPLE 161. Opening of *Mein gmüth ist mir verwirret*—Hassler (after PubAPTM XV, 24).

"My mind is troubled, the cause is a gentle maiden; I am gone utterly astray, my heart is full of grief."

In both of Hassler's collections, the main melody is usually in the top voice. His style profoundly influenced his younger German colleagues and is clearly evident in the lieder of such men as Melchior Franck, Valentin Haussmann, Christoph Demantius (b. 1567), Johann Staden (1581–1634), and Hermann Schein (1586–1630). These last two men, however, belong more to the history of baroque music than to that of the Renaissance.

Music in Scandinavia

We know little about music in the Scandinavian countries in the 16th century. The rulers of Sweden, from Gustav Vasa (reigned 1523–1560) to Sigismund of Poland (reigned over Sweden, 1594–1598), were all fond of music, and musicians' names appear in the court records from 1526 on. The *Piae Cantiones,* published in 1582 by Theodoricus Petri at Greifswald in western Pomerania, then part of Sweden, is a collection of anonymous school and religious songs in from one to four parts which, according to the introduction, were much used in Sweden and Finland.[188] They all have Latin texts except *In dulci jubilo,* which is partly in Latin and partly in Swedish. Some of the pieces (e.g., *Ad cantus laetitiae* [189]) date as far back as the 13th century, while others stem from German Lutheran collections (Petri's Protestantism is apparent also in the transformation of some of the texts from praises of the Virgin to praises of Jesus).[190] From the surviving MSS and other prints we find that the composers most frequently performed in Sweden were, up to c. 1560, Gombert, Janequin, Crecquillon, and Clemens non Papa; after 1560, Lassus, then Protestant composers such as Meiland. A copy of one of Newsidler's lute-books has been found. About 1600 Giovanni Gabrieli and Hassler seem to have been the most favored composers in Sweden.[191] Concerning Denmark we know that the court choir comprised eighteen singers in 1519 and that its repertory about the middle of the century—as is shown by

---

[188] Pr. WoodP.
[189] *See* ReMMA, 395, where it is cited as an early example of *Stimmtausch* technique.
[190] For further details, *see* NorS. [191] *See* NorS and NorH.

two surviving MS collections, one of 1541 and the other of 1556—drew upon much the same composers as did the Swedish, as well as upon Senfl and Heinrich Finck. Two settings of *Christ ist erstanden* survive by a Netherlander, Franciscus Marcellus Amsfortius, who served as *Kapellmeister* at Copenhagen from 1557 to 1571; and we have a *Das alte Jahr vergangen ist* by his successor from 1571 to 1586, Arnoldus de Fine. Coclico served the court as *musicus* and singer from 1556 to 1562 and probably ended his days in Copenhagen. John Dowland was appointed lutenist to the music-loving Christian IV in 1598 and retained that post until 1606 (cf. p. 810). In 1599 Christian dispatched five musicians—including the composer Mogens Pedersøn—to Italy, to receive instruction from the younger Gabrieli; and in 1611 Pedersøn and three others went to England, to study music there. In 1608 Pedersøn brought out a madrigal collection and in 1620 a *Pratum spirituale*.[192] When Christian's youngest brother, Hans, set off for Russia in 1601 to marry a daughter of the Czar, his entourage of 342 persons included 18 musicians.[193]

[192] For compositions from these collections, *see* PederV; 3 madrigals by Pedersön and 3 by his compatriot Hans Nielsen in CW XXXV.

[193] SeiffM, 293. For further details, *see* HammN and EllgM. For a facsimile of a Danish Lutheran Gradual (1573), containing one-line melodies, some with Danish text and others with Latin, *see* JespG.

Chapter 14: MUSIC IN HUNGARY, BOHEMIA, POLAND, AND THE ADRIATIC COASTAL AREAS OF THE SOUTHERN SLAVS

MUSIC IN HUNGARY
BY OTTO GOMBOSI

Medieval Antecedents

THE history of music in Hungary begins with folk song. When, at the end of the 9th century, the confederation of Finno-Ugrian and Turkish tribes of Central Asiatic origin occupied the Middle Danube Basin, they brought with them their folk music, elements of which can be reconstructed by comparative study. Pentatonic melodic structure and the repetition of phrases at the fifth or lower fourth are common characteristics both of the oldest stratum of Hungarian folk song and of that of some Finno-Ugrian and Turkish tribes in Southern Russia (Tcheremis) and Anatolia,[1] the relationship being, in some instances, so close that there are actually examples of identical melodies. Another old group of songs, including children's songs, laments, carolling of the litany type, etc., seems to be the last remnant of pre-Christian rituals, and is related to similar songs of Finnish tribes.[2]

Songs and singing of the early Hungarians elicited comment from several contemporaries. Theophilactus (7th century) mentioned their hymns to the Earth; Nestor's Chronicle describes their singing at Kiev in 885; Heribald, the monk of St. Gall, was thoroughly shocked by their "shouting to their gods" (926). In the anti-Christian rebellion of 1061, the pagan shamans by means of the old songs exhorted their people to murder the bishops and priests of the new, officially introduced, religion. With the general acceptance of Christianity most of the old pagan customs and cults were suppressed. However, some of them, together with their musical features, escaped extinction by being transformed into semi-religious functions and were preserved in folk customs such as carolling, the singing of laments, midsummer-night celebrations—all belonging to the litany type.

Closely connected with this type of ritual singing must have been the musical style of the epic and satirical songs performed at court, at residences, and at public gatherings. The "storytellers" were the principal preservers

---

[1] Cf. BartókF, 346. [2] KodS; SzabE.

of the nation's historical tradition. During the 12th and 13th centuries, at least, they formed an officially recognized group, supported by royal donations; but, from the 14th century on, their role changed rapidly to that of mere entertainers and instrumental musicians (*joculatores*), without, however, their altogether giving up their old functions (cf. below). *"Kürt"* (horn) and *"síp"* (pipe) were, from the early 12th century on, used as or incorporated in the names of towns. The royal trombonists (*buccinatores*) are first mentioned in a document dating from 1257. Royal musicians of obviously the same category (*trumbatores domini regis*) were the owners of the village Gajdosbogdány (earliest record, 1272), named after the instrument *gajd* (oboe, perhaps also horn). The documentary evidence concerning stringed instruments is somewhat less old. The short-necked lute, *koboz,* is first mentioned in 1326, the fiddle in 1358, although this instrument is represented in one of the 11th-century statues of the cathedral of Pécs.[3]

No MSS or detailed descriptions of the singing and playing of these entertainers and musicians of medieval Hungary are extant. Folk song, however, is the subject of the charming anecdote preserved in the anonymous *Vita major* (variously dated from the 11th century to the 14th) of St. Gellért, apostle of Hungary, bishop of Csanád, and close adviser of King St. Stephen. Once the bishop traveled with Walter, the *magister* and cantor of the school of Csanád, and spent the night in a farmhouse. About midnight they were awakened by the singing of a maid who was making flour on a primitive hand mill. The bishop, fascinated by the strange tune, asked his expert companion: *"Audis symphoniam Ungarorum?"* ("Do you hear the symphony of the Hungarians?"), and later, jokingly using technical terms, *"Quis istius melodiae cantus sit?"* ("What kind of song is this melody?"). And Walter answered: *"Ista modulacio carminis est"* ("It is the singing of a [secular, i.e., folk] song"). No traces of secular music, however, have been preserved.

Gregorian Chant was generally accepted in Hungary in the 11th and 12th centuries.[3a] Monastery and cathedral schools were the centers of its dissemination. But local production seems to have impaired the purity of the Gregorian tradition rather early. The singing of unauthorized chants had to be prohibited by the synod of Esztergom in 1112. Tropes and sequences made their imprint on the Gregorian material, while the influence of Latin hymns upon the development of early poetry in the vernacular was especially important. Obviously of Hungarian origin is one of the most interesting examples of *Laudes Regiae*, from the Dalmatian city of Zara, dating from c. 1107–1109.[4] Toward the end of the 14th century, the hymn *Gaude felix Ungaria,* written in honor of St. Elizabeth of Hungary by a Dominican of Kassa, used the troped melody of a Gregorian antiphon. Similar appropriation of Gregorian melodies oc-

[3] SzabS, 159; FarkU.   [3a] About early Chant MSS in Hungary, *see* esp. TellerM.
[4] BukML, 191, 204.

curs in the 15th-century mystery plays with mixed Latin and German texts, preserved in the archiepiscopal library of Eger. The first Gregorian tunes with Hungarian texts can be found in the Nádor Codex of 1508.

Foreign Secular Influences

Foreign musical influences other than Gregorian Chant certainly reached Hungary rather early. The court of the kings of the House of Árpád (1001–1301) was connected by ties of blood and marriage with Byzantine, Polish, German, Italian, French, and even English courts. With the brides, the music and musicians of their respective countries found their way to Hungary. This influence must have become even stronger with the ascent to the throne of the Neapolitan Anjous, followed by the Polish Jagiełłos, Bohemian Luxemburgs, and Austrian Hapsburgs. Documentary evidence, however, is almost entirely lacking. But it exists for Peire Vidal's sojourn at the court of King Emeric (c. 1200) and for Oswald von Wolkenstein's and Michel Behaim's later travels to Hungary. On the other hand, Hungarian clerics visited foreign schools and certainly brought home more than an improved knowledge of the pure Gregorian tradition. A certain Elvinus, who was sent to Paris by King Béla III in 1192 *"ad discendam melodiam"* ("to learn music"), must have been attracted by the art of Perotin and his predecessors. Again, the meager remnants of written music show no evidence of any indigenous development of the higher forms. The first monuments of Hungarian music come from a quite different domain.

Dance Music

Tunes closely related to the present-day "Swineherd's Dance" of some rural districts of Hungary have been preserved in 16th-century sources and are variously called *Ungaresca, Ungarischer Tanz* or *Ungarischer Aufzug,* and *Heyducken Tantz* ("Foot-Soldier's Dance").[5] This intricate and strenuous sword dance, which in 1572 was demonstrated at the imperial court by the great lyric poet Valentin Balassi (1551–1594), himself no mean soldier, had been popular among soldiers for a century before its first surviving tune was written down. The short, repeated motifs of these dance tunes show a tendency toward ending each phrase on the tonic and are often supported by one or two root-fifth-octave organ-points, reminiscent of the drone of the bagpipe.[6]

[5] Jan of Lublin's organ book, Cracow, Academy (*Hayduczky*); lute MS, Breslau, Mus. Inst. of the University, dating from 1544 (*Ungrisch Tantzl*); Wolf Heckel's Lute-Book (1556, 1562) (*Ein Ungarischer Tantz*); *Chorearum molliorum collectanea,* Phalèse, 1583, and Jakob Paix's organ book, 1583 (*Ungarescha*); Cister MS, Dresden J. 307m, and lute MS, Leipzig, Stadtbibl., ii. 6. 15 (*Heyducken Tantz*), also in August Nörmiger's keyboard book, Berlin, Öff. wiss. Bibl., MS Mus. 40089 (*Ungrischer Aufzug*). Another *Ungrischer Aufzug* in Nörmiger's MS is a Polish dance. The last 3 pr. MolnM.

[6] To a higher stratum belong the 2 Hungarian dances (pr. ChilB II), in Giovanni Picchi's *Balli d'arpicordo* (1621), and the *Passemezzo Ungaro* in B. Jobin's lute book (1573), as well as that of B. Schmid the Elder (1577), one of the *passamezzi* that do not use either of the two *passamezzo* grounds.

EXAMPLE 162. *Ungarescha*—Jakob Paix (after MerT, 149; EitT, 111).

The vogue for such exotic dances spread all over Europe with the political and military upheavals of the 16th century. An early example is the *Zeuner Tantz* ("Gipsy Dance"), preserved by Hans Newsidler,[7] which was danced by royal guests at the wedding of Matthias Corvinus and Beatrice of Aragon at Buda, 1476. In 1483, there is mention of Beatrice's gipsy musicians *"qualli sonano di lauto"* ("who played the lute"). They played the *"cithara"* at court in 1525. Although the gipsies had not yet gained special prominence in Hungarian musical life, they were among the carriers of lower-class dance music. Subsequently, documents mention gipsy fiddlers (1543) who, strangely enough, beat their instruments in the manner in which the dulcimer is beaten and, at the same time, sang. Gipsy fiddler-singers are mentioned later too: in 1584, some gipsies were captured as they were coming from the residence of a Turkish official in the occupied parts of Hungary, and their singing and instruments—a two-stringed fiddle (rebec) and a psaltery plucked by the fingers, "with which the students make music at the Mass"—were duly admired.[8]

Music Performed on the Lute or Fiddle; Secular Monophony

Ordinarily, however, neither the itinerant nor the resident musician of the time was a gipsy. Both types of musician performed on either a lute or a fiddle of some variety—the latter being either plucked or played with a bow. The itinerant musicians sang in taverns, at forts, and in castles, about the heroic deeds of past generations. Sometimes their versions were at variance with those of the official chroniclers. This epic singing reached all social strata. Galeotto Marzio heard it at the court of Matthias Corvinus in 1485, where, at table, *"musici et citharoedi"* sang in the vernacular, *"in lyra"* (i.e., with lute accompaniment), the deeds of national heroes. As for the texts, fragments have been preserved in MSS that date back to 1463. By 1538, the printing press began to be utilized. The rapidly progressing Reformation was responsible for much of the turning to the Bible for subject matter, but borrowings from Italian *novelle* or classical mythology and literature are not uncommon. While in the printed sources most of the tunes are indicated merely by title or *incipit,* forty-odd tunes are preserved, most of them in the two main sources, both

---

[7] DTO XVIII², 39.

[8] Present-day Hungarian-Gipsy musicians are usually instrumentalists. Gipsy folk song, however, is sung by gipsies who are not specifically musicians.

from the Hofgreff press in Kolozsvár (= Cluj): the fragmentary anthology of mostly biblical songs (1552 or 1553) with seventeen tunes and the *Cronica* of Sebastian Tinódi "the Lutenist" (1554), by far the most important poet-musician of the time, with twenty-three tunes.[9]

These tunes are syllabic; some of them show the influence of humanistic scansion, others point toward the religious songs of the Moravians, especially in their verse form and meter. But Tinódi (1505/10–1556), whose songs became the ringing voice of national pride and despair, created his tunes under the deep influence of what must have been the folk song of his day. This is, of course, hard to prove, since the only surviving folk-song document is a short, two-line fragment notated c. 1520 by the Minorite Father, Philip Pominoczky, on the inner side of the cover of his *Manuale*.[10] At any rate, Tinódi's melodies left a significant imprint on Hungarian song: some survived in song-books, both Catholic and Protestant, of the 17th, 18th, and early 19th centuries, while others still live in Hungarian peasant singing. Tinódi undoubtedly was the composer and performer of his tunes; his patent of nobility (1553) emphasized his *"ars canendi historiarumque . . . in rhythmos elegans compositio"* ("art of singing and the elegant writing of historical poems in [varied] rhythms").

EXAMPLE 163. *Emperor Soliman's Fight with Kazul Pasha* (1546)— Tinódi (after SzabTS).

Sok ki-rál-ról, csá-szár-ról em-lé-kaz-tem,   Csuda hada-kat rólok be-szé-löt-tem,

De te-rek nemzetröl nem el-mél-köd-tem,   Meg-hall-já-tok mit fe-lö-lök ér-töt-tem.

"Many a king and emperor have I remembered. I have told of their wonderful campaigns, but I have not pondered on the Turkish nation; you shall hear what I have learned about them."

What is the background of this biblical, epic, satiric poetry and its music? In some respects the Meistersinger seem to have exercised their influence; at least, the treatment of biblical subjects is not without parallel. Michel Behaim (1416–1474), the Meistersinger adventurer, was for a while in the service of Hungarian lords and also at the court of Ladislaus V, the second Hapsburg on the Hungarian throne.[11] *Meistergesang* undoubtedly was known in the German cities forming "islands" in the west, north, and south of Hungary. But the melodic style of the Hungarian tunes shows no sign of either the peculiar strophic structure or the mannered ornamentation of the *Meister-*

[9] SzabU, 649; SzabTS; SzabM.
[10] Batthyányi Library in Gyulafehérvár (= Alba Julia); reproduced in SzabL II, opp. p. 73.
[11] BleyB, 25, *passim*.

gesang. Somewhat closer in style are the tunes of German historical songs in broadside prints of the 16th century.[12] Surviving epic poetry of eastern Europe, and especially folk ballads, show highly developed improvisatory ornamentation, and it is to be assumed that in actual performance the simple syllabic tunes of Tinódi and of his contemporaries were subjected to similar embellishments. Nothing, however, is known about the role, extent, and style of instrumental accompaniment. Parallels may be drawn with the somewhat similar Spanish practice of the 16th (and evidently also the 15th) century, but it may be rather far-fetched to claim a relationship, although the practice may have been known at the court of the Hispano-Neapolitan wife of Matthias Corvinus.

Fiddle and lute are the instruments of the storyteller and the poet. The instruments figure in documents dating from 1394 and 1427. Both as accompanying and as solo instrument, the lute became increasingly popular. At court, the most famous 15th-century lutenist, Pietro Bono, attached to the court of Ferrara, was sent to Buda by Queen Beatrice's sister Eleonora, wife of Hercules I, in order that his music might aid the queen's recovery from illness.[13] Other famous players of stringed instruments made similar journeys from Italy to the Hungarian court. About 1520, both Queen Mary, a pupil of the famous organist Bredemers, and King Louis II were proficient instrumentalists, she on the virginals and he on the lute. Mary in 1518 sent four lute players [14] to the wedding of the king's uncle, Sigismund I of Poland, to Bona Sforza. The lutenist who served John Szapolyai—governor of Transylvania and, after 1526, king of Hungary—but whose name has not been preserved,[15] was capable of educating in Buda one of the great players and composers of lute music of all times, Valentin Bakfark.

The Lute Music of Bakfark

Born in Brassó (= Braşov in Roumania), 1507, Bakfark [16] became court lutenist to John Szapolyai, after whose death (1540) he visited Italy and France and served for a while Count Tournon, minister and archbishop of Béthune and later of Lyons. Lutenist of the king of Poland from 1547 to 1566, Bakfark took a leave of absence (1522–1554) to renew former connections with Prince Albert of Prussia, to travel through Germany, France, and Italy, and to publish his first lute book in Lyons (1553). The second book, dedicated to Sigismund II of Poland, was published in Cracow, 1565. By this time, however, some political machinations of Bakfark's miscarried and he

---

[12] LiliV IV. [13] GomV, 112f. [14] HaraM, 180.

[15] There is no evidence for his being identical with Sigismund, the king's lutenist, as Haraszti assumes in HaraL, 162.

[16] 11 compositions in DTO XVIII², 68–95; for special monograph, *see* GomVB (with bibliography and App., containing 10 fantasies); *see also* MGG, II, 1092ff.

escaped via Breslau to Vienna to become court lutenist to the Emperor. Two years later, he returned to his native Transylvania, where he received an estate from Prince John Sigismund. After the prince's death (1571), Bakfark retired to Padua. Prince Stephen Báthori of Transylvania desired his services and, when Bakfark declined, confiscated his estate. Bakfark died in Padua, a victim of the plague, August 15 or 22, 1576. On his deathbed, he burned his available MSS, stating that only he could play his music to his satisfaction. His surviving works consist of a *Passamezzo,* two Polish song transcriptions, lute-intabulations of chansons, madrigals, and motets (Josquin, Gombert, Clemens, Lasso, and others), and ten fantasies. His transcriptions are amazingly faithful to the polyphony of the originals and show much taste and restraint in ornamentation. Their technical requirements are exceptional. His fantasies may be termed instrumental motets in the international Franco-Netherlandish style, especially that of Gombert and Clemens. Their delicate *fioriture,* noble melodic material, fine contrapuntal texture, and beautiful form make them outstanding representatives of the strictly polyphonic lute music of the 16th century.

EXAMPLE 164. Opening of a Fantasy for lute—Bakfark (from GomVB, App., 15).

While Bakfark came from the southeast of the country, Pozsony (= Brati-slava) in the northwest was the home of the outstanding Newsidler brothers, Melchior (1507–1590) and Hans (1508?–1563).[17] Both worked in Nuremberg, the former also in Italy (Venice), Augsburg, and Innsbruck. (Cf. Chap. 12.)

Before Bakfark retired to Padua, another Hungarian lutenist, Andrew Fekete, made a living there, c. 1560, by instructing members of the Hungarian nobility who studied at the University. Lute playing became the pastime of princes and nobility. John Sigismund, who had Valentin Bakfark and his brother Michael[18] in his employ, was a lute player himself, as was also Prince Sigismund Báthori (1572–1613; reigned 1588–1598). The latter's cousin, Cardinal and later Prince Andrew Báthori (d. 1599), showed more proficiency on the virginals.[19]

Other Instrumental Music

There is confusion in the early nomenclature, not only of stringed instruments but also of wind instruments. A performer's function is not always clear from the term applied to him. *Sipos* (*fistulator,* "piper") includes every player from the wandering *joculator,* against whom the church issued one edict after another, to the military piper and to the members of organized pipe-bands of cities, lords, and kings. The martial military oboe is mentioned as the "Turkish pipe" in 1544, but was also known under its local name *tárogató* (1572). The royal pipers obviously played the cornet (zink), the cromorne (cf. below), and the trombone, as did also the city musicians and the pipe-bands of the aristocrats and high officials of state and church.

The Turkish influence on military music soon led to the acceptance of giant kettledrums by the trumpet corps. They were introduced into western Europe through Hungary. German and French sources mention the impression these drums made when, in 1451, the ambassadors of Ladislaus V visited Germany and France with trumpet corps in their retinue. The number of trumpeters at court varied between six and twelve, according to the ups and downs of the finances. The tradition was maintained at the court of the princes of Transylvania. At the opening of the parliament of Medgyes, 1585, while the prince was on his way to attend a Te Deum, eight trumpeters and the kettledrum player, posted in front of the city hall, alternated with the city trombonist

---

[17] Music by Hans in DTO XVIII[2], 15–59.

[18] He served Queen Isabella during John Sigismund's minority, according to a letter of Valentin Bakfark to Prince Albert of Prussia, 1555.

[19] About Sigismund Báthori and music, *see infra.* Andrew Báthori visited Rome, 1583–84, and became cardinal in 1584. During his stay he befriended Palestrina, who dedicated to him and to Báthori's more famous uncle Stephen the fifth book of motets *a 5,* containing those written in their honor (1584). Cf. GárB and HaraS, 212.

standing on the church steeple. During the following banquet, which lasted from 1:30 to 10:00 p.m., the trumpeters played in front of the hall.[20]

While pipers and trumpeters took care of secular instrumental music, although their co-operation in church music on festive occasions is well known, the organ was primarily, but not exclusively, an instrument of the church. Organ music flourished in Hungary from the first half of the 15th century. Surviving documents cover only a few cities, cathedrals, and monasteries, but it can safely be assumed that similar conditions prevailed all over the country. Organs were used in the Coronation Cathedral in Székesfehérvár (Alba Regia) and in Lőcse (= Levoča) during the first half of the century. The organ of the cathedral of Pécs is first mentioned in 1437. Felsőbánya received its organ as a gift of Governor John Hunyadi in 1452. Körmöczbánya (= Kremnica; Kremnitz) had a church organ at least from 1464.[21] Gallus, organ builder in Kassa, is mentioned in 1519. About the turn of the century, Pozsony, Buda, Bártfa (1517), Kassa (= Košice), Brassó, and Kisszeben (1502), and the great cathedrals of Esztergom and Eger also had organs. The *Ordinaria* of these cathedrals, printed at this time but obviously based on older usage, contain some quite precise references to the role of the organ in the liturgy. Magnificent organs with silver pipes, played by Magister Daniel and by the Italian Stefano da Salerno, were admired at the residences of King Matthias Corvinus in Visegrád and Buda.[22] The organists of Esztergom, Brassó—Valentin Klein—and the court—Grimpeck—were famous at the beginning of the 16th century. Grimpeck's successor seems to have been Wolfgang Grefinger, one of the outstanding pupils of Paul Hofhaimer.[23] Hofhaimer's connection with the Hungarian Jagiełło kings is known: it was at the double wedding ceremony of the future Ferdinand I with Anna of Hungary and of the future Louis II with Mary of Hapsburg, later known as Mary of Hungary, that Wladislaus II knighted him.

Visitation reports from small monasteries testify to the presence of organists among the monks—and of more than sufficient liquid inspiration at their disposal.

Toward the end of the 16th century the court of Transylvania and the cathedral of the residence in Gyulafehérvár (Alba Julia) were famous for their organ music. While Prince John Sigismund (1540–1571) neglected the organ, owing to certain Protestant scruples toward which he had leanings, the Báthori princes (1571–1599) did their best for the old faith; Sigismund, in particular, for whom Diruta wrote his *Transilvano*,[24] was interested in the instrument and rebuilt the cathedral organ, which had been destroyed in

---

[20] GárB; HaraS, 200. Cf. Christoph Demantius' six-part *Tympanum Militare Ungerische Heerdrummel und Feldgeschrey, neben andern auch Ungerischen Schlachten und Victorien Liedern*, 1600: a collection of programmatic "battle music" in which the Hungarian and Transylvanian kettledrums play a significant role; cf. also BleyD.
[21] IsozK.   [22] GomV; CsánM; FökM, 12.   [23] GomWG, 54.   [24] HaraD, 75f.

1565. The organist was Antonio Romanini who is represented in the *Transilvano* by a toccata.[25] Two more organists, one Italian, the other French, are listed among the court musicians. A mid-16th-century MS, from the collection of St. Egidi in Bártfa (now in the National Museum in Budapest), containing Introits, etc., by Isaac, Stoltzer, and others, indicates the alternation of the organ with plainchant and vocal polyphony.

The Royal Chapel; Stoltzer

Part-singing is mentioned in various documents from the time that the Royal Chapel of King Matthias set the pattern.[26] The bishop of Castella, papal envoy at court, in 1483 mentions the king's singers with great admiration and rates them higher than those of the Papal Chapel. The master of the choir at this time was Johannes Stokhem. Besides the king's chapel, a similar but separate organization seems to have existed for the personal service of Queen Beatrice. Her connection with Tinctoris, who probably had some role in her musical education at Naples, is evidenced by the dedication to her of the *Terminorum musicae diffinitorium* (1475), written one year before Beatrice left Naples for Hungary.[27]

After Matthias's death (1490), the Royal Chapel was disbanded, obviously because his successor, Wladislaus II Jagiełło, then already king of Bohemia, brought his own musicians to Buda. Some of Matthias' singers, like Cornuel (Verjust),[28] retired to their respective prebends, others like Johannes Bisth joined the reorganized Burgundian chapel of Maximilian.[29] Whether Barbireau—who visited Buda in 1490 as Maximilian's special envoy and was received with all the homage due his importance as a composer[30]—had any role in initiating this migration, is not known.

Although financial difficulties limited the court personnel during the reign of the last two Jagiełło kings (1490–1526) and the splendor of one of the greatest Renaissance courts was suddenly ended, music remained an essential part of court life.[31] The chapel had at least one important member—Thomas Stoltzer—from 1490 (first documents, 1492) and up to the tragic end at the battlefield of Mohács (1526), where both the young King Louis II and Stoltzer met their death.

Stoltzer, born c. 1470 in Schweidnitz (Silesia), was one of the most out-

[25] GárB. HaraS, 203, cannot find Antonio's name in the list of musicians as given by the contemporary chronicler Szamosközi, although he reprints it in his article. The Italian mentioned in the next sentence above is "Antonio Venetus, organista."
[26] CsánM; FökM; GomV.
[27] MS VI. E. 40 of the National Library at Naples, containing six *L'Homme armé* Masses, is dedicated to Beatrice.
[28] PirJC, 201.   [29] Cf. several lists of chapel singers published by StraM.
[30] GomV; GomJ, 379.
[31] FrakL; FogL. About life at court, especially after Mary's arrival in Buda, cf. HaraM, 180f.

standing and prolific German masters of his time. His works were not included in printed collections until 1532, but gained dominating importance
in Rhaw's publications and in a group of MSS presumably from Saxony. A
total of about 150 compositions (plus about 60 fragments) are preserved: Latin
hymns and psalms,[32] Masses, introits, responsories, antiphons, a *Liber generationis,* eleven German songs, and nine German psalms and hymns. Stoltzer's
style is an outgrowth of German 15th-century style. His voices paraphrase
liturgical *cantus firmi* with great rhythmical freedom and are rich in expressive quality and ornamental design. His liturgical music is stylistically akin
to Isaac's (*Choralis Constantinus*) and Finck's (hymns); his German songs
recall Hofhaimer. Toward the end of his life, when he wrote some of the
greatest of his Latin motets and his German psalms and hymns (several on
Luther texts),[33] the style changed abruptly to humanistic treatment of the
declamation, regular imitation, balance of the several parts, clear harmonic
conception, and monumentality of form, indicative of the shadow of Josquin.
One of the German psalms, *Erzürne dich nicht,*[34] composed at the request
of Queen Mary in 1526 and sent with a personal letter to Prince Albert of
Prussia, is a massive work in seven *partes.* It is based on the German form of
psalm-tone 6 and is therefore an early Protestant outgrowth of the psalmody
of the Office.[34a]

EXAMPLE 165. Extract from *Erzürne dich nicht* (Psalm 37 [XXXVI])
    —Stoltzer (from CW VI).

"Rest in the Lord, and wait patiently for him: fret not thyself . . ." (*from
verse 7*)

[32] DDT LXV.   [33] Reprints in DDT XXXIV and in AmbG V, 280–298.   [34] CW VI.
[34a] Cf. MosTS.

Of particular importance is Stoltzer's indication, in the letter to the prince, that he has written the psalm with the idea of *ad libitum* instrumental performance on cromornes. Whether a similar wind ensemble or a group of viols was supposed to play his *Octo tonorum melodiae*,[35] a collection of eight fantasies *a* 5 (one in each of the eight ecclesiastical modes), is not known. At any rate, the work is the earliest preserved example of a cycle of instrumental pieces in the literature of music.

Willaert, another great master of the time, has often been mentioned as a member of the Royal Chapel of Hungary. This, however, seems to be a mistake. There is no trace of Willaert in any of the surviving documents. The source of the error is Jacques de Meyere's *Rerum Flandriacum tomi X* (1531), which calls Willaert *"cantor regis Hungariae."* The king of Hungary at that time, however, was Ferdinand I of Hapsburg, the later emperor, brother of Charles V and of Mary of Hungary. De Meyere obviously referred to Ferdinand by his then highest title. Willaert seems to have been connected with Ferdinand's Imperial Chapel, the personnel of which is not yet exactly known.[36]

Music-Making at Other Centers, including the Transylvanian Court

While the Royal Chapel and its repertory, at least as far as Stoltzer's works are concerned, are not entirely unknown, very little is preserved belonging to similar organizations in cities, cathedrals, and castles. The singers of the Cathedral of Buda, singing *figuraliter,* are mentioned in the accounts of the court. The *Ordinarium* of Eger, referred to above, prescribes the performance of the responsory *Ascendit* on Ascension Day by a five-part "figural" chorus, indicating a standing choral organization at this cathedral that certainly was duplicated at the other nine sees, some of them occupied by the greatest humanists of Hungary. The rich cities, especially the German settlements of the north and of Transylvania, were similarly provided. At the parliament of Medgyes (cf. p. 721), the opening church service consisted of a motet sung *"figuraliter"* by the singers with the assistance of a trombone player and an Italian violinist in the service of Stephen Báthori, King of Poland. The following *Te Deum* was sung in plainchant (*"simpliciter"*). The service was concluded with another motet sung by the choir. At Prince Sigismund's wedding, the vespers on the eve of the ceremony were performed by singers and instrumentalists. The same group of Italian musicians sang and played Mass on the field the day after the battle in which the Imperial General Basta captured them (1601).[37] Remnants of the church-music libraries of Bártfa,[38] Lőcse, and Brassó [39] testify to extensive musical life. Singing was an important part of the school curriculum. About 1500, the school children of Buda

[35] Pr. StoltzerO; EDMR XX, 69ff. (EDMR XX contains 21 additional works by Stoltzer.)
[36] Cf. GomW, 54.   [37] HaraS, 206.   [38] GomA, 41f; GomMB, 338.   [39] MüllerM.

sang at court on the principal holidays. Provisions for the musical and humanistic education of school children were made by the Lutheran reformer of Transylvanian Germans, Johann Honterus, who published his collections of twenty-one metric *Odae cum harmoniis*—partly taken from Tritonius—in Brassó (1548; 2nd ed., 1562).[40] This was the first music printed in Hungary.

While especially the Lutheran cities of the periphery continued—in spite of adverse internal political conditions, wars, and religious troubles—to maintain high standards throughout the 16th and 17th centuries, the Turkish occupation of the central part of the country and the Calvinist movement eradicated the vestiges of the musical past in other places. The episcopal library of Szombathely has preserved, among other material, some Masses by Josquin.[41]

We are somewhat better informed about the music of the Transylvanian court toward the end of the 16th century. Ever since the days of Prince John Sigismund, the court's cultural and artistic orientation had been mainly Italian. The Báthori princes, like most members of the great families, were educated in Italy. Stephen Báthori's Polish court was well staffed with musicians. His nephew Sigismund, himself a composer, surrounded himself with Italians and kept a group of musicians, mostly Italian, under the direction of Giovanni Battista Mosto of Udine, a pupil of Claudio Merulo's. Mosto, after having been active at the Cathedral of Padua, went with some other singers (among them Matteo Foresto—who was at the Cathedral of Mantua in 1587, and in Cologne in 1591—and Pietro Busto or Busti—who has left an interesting account of the conditions at court) through Cracow to Gyulafehérvár in 1591, where he died in 1597. He was succeeded by a certain Francesco d'Ancona. Mosto composed several books of madrigals. His only book of madrigals *a 6* (Venice, 1595), evidently the fruit of his first years in Transylvania, is dedicated to Prince Sigismund. Mosto was highly esteemed by Philippe de Monte, who, obviously upon Mosto's initiative, dedicated his seventeenth book of madrigals *a 5* (Venice, 1595) to Sigismund.[42]

The members of the chapel, other than the three organists mentioned above, one *cantor,* and one dancer, were designated as *musici.* They were, evidently, singers as well as instrumentalists, mainly violists. With a member of the Venetian school at the head of the chapel, the music at court evidently included the best of the madrigal literature of the time.

The musical taste, however, must have been rather catholic throughout the country among the educated classes, to judge, for instance, by the tune references added to the poems of Valentin Balassi. His preferred stanza seems to have been influenced by French models (he knew and used Marot's and Bèze's psalms). Hungarian tunes are referred to in the company of Rumanian, Turkish, Slovenian, Polish, and Croatian tunes and Latin, Italian, and German songs (e.g., Jakob Regnart's *villanella, Ich hab vermeint,* 1576).[43]

[40] SzabO, 338f.   [41] WerR, 90ff.   [42] GárB; HaraS, 210.   [43] EckB; WaA; KastH.

Besides Stoltzer's and Mosto's works, very little is known of choral music composed in Hungary or by Hungarian composers during the 16th century.[44] A Thelamonius Hungarus is represented in Rhaw's *Tricinia* (1542). A Moravian pupil of Stoltzer's, Anselmus of Brno, has a fragmentary responsory in MS Zwickau 16. Georg Ostermayer of Brassó, who worked in different southern German cities, has left a fragmentary motet (composed in Heilbronn, 1569) in a Heilbronn MS. The Ostermayer family of Brassó had other musical members: Hieronymus Ostermayer was organist of the city of his birth in 1544 and left a valuable chronicle;[45] another Ostermayer is represented in the Fitzwilliam Virginal Book. A Petrus Siculus (the composer of a *Salve Regina,* written before 1574, preserved in Liegnitz MS 18) may have been of Transylvanian origin. ("Siculus" means "of the Székely tribe" as well as "Sicilian.") Finally, a setting *a 6* of Psalm CXXXIII (134) by Anton Jung of Kolozsvár (= Cluj), minister in Szászorbó, written in 1577, is to be found in the library of Brassó.[46]

Theorists

This meager list of the surviving music can be supplemented by two theoretical works. One is the *Epithoma utriusque musices practice* (Cracow, c. 1517) by Stephanus Monetarius of Körmöczbánya (= Kremnica; cf. p. 746).[47] The work is based on Tinctoris, Gafori, and Anselmo da Parma. The other work consists of notes on plainsong theory taken by Ladislaus Szalkai—later Archbishop of Esztergom and Primate of Hungary (d. 1526, at the battle of Mohács)—while studying at the Augustinian monastery at Sárospatak, 1490. The MS is preserved in the archiepiscopal library at Esztergom. The course of study is based chiefly on Anonymus XI (CouS III, 416), but it also utilizes Pseudo-Aristotle (Lambertus), Simon Tunstede, and Pseudo-Vitri's *Liber musicalium*. It complements the borrowed text with practical, explanatory passages, obviously originating from the pen of the master of the monastery school, John of Kisvárda.[48]

The Hungarian Renaissance reveals a highly diversified musical life, reaching from courtly splendor and humanistic culture shown in the patronizing of great international art, to the rudiments of local art forms based on indigenous tradition. The vicissitudes of a century full of trouble cut off its nourishing roots and almost entirely eradicated its monuments. The 17th century inherited material for its flourishing religious folk music, but otherwise had to start afresh in developing its monophonic song literature and dance music.

[44] GomU, 84.   [45] HajM, 13.   [46] MüllerM, 88.
[47] The work is dedicated to George Thurzó, head of one of the great families, patron of humanists, and business partner of the Fuggers in the exploitation of northern Hungarian mines.
[48] BarthaS, 2.

MUSIC IN BOHEMIA
BY RITA PETSCHEK KAFKA

Bohemia, situated in the heart of Europe, has nurtured so many heterogeneous cultural elements that its history reveals periods in which no one type of music can be singled out as especially characteristic. Such periods will figure in parts of this section. Foreign influences, easily assimilated by the Bohemians, have helped to mould the culture of their country; the final result is a combination of the cultural elements of foreign influences and those of the various indigenous national groups.

The Renaissance offers a somewhat different aspect in Bohemia from the one it presents in other countries. The Middle Ages and the Reformation were more closely linked together here, and the Renaissance itself is hardly perceptible; although, to be sure, the Reformation is itself one phase of the Renaissance. But in Bohemia the Reformation took on an attitude unfriendly to music, as well as to painting and sculpture, and the flowering of the arts found elsewhere in the Renaissance was here nipped in the bud. Nevertheless, music was cultivated in Bohemia in the 15th and 16th centuries, although its development was, in a sense, somewhat one-sided. The music of this period is strongly national; yet it does not reject the tradition of earlier times.

Medieval Antecedents

The liturgy of the Eastern Church had been brought to Bohemia by the missionaries Cyril and Methodius in the 9th century and was not replaced by that of Rome until the 12th century. The only song in the Czech language that we have from these early days is the famous and popular *Hospodine pomiluj ny* ("Lord have mercy on us"),[1] popularly attributed to Adalbert, second bishop of Prague (10th century; but the piece may well be later).[2] The bishop was eventually canonized as St. Vojtěch. The song ends with a *Kyrie eleison* (which in the mouths of the people became simply the disyllable, *Krles*), sung thrice. This plainchant melody was sung not only at Mass but, apart from the liturgy, in times of national crisis.

The 12th and 13th centuries in Bohemia were periods of great upheaval. During the famous Czech dynasty of the Přemyslids,[3] many German colonists were called into the country and German cultural influence became widespread. Minnesinger and trouvères brought their music to the court at Prague, among them the famous Heinrich Frauenlob and Tannhäuser.[4] Heinrich von

---

[1] Pr. BatG, 15; NejC, App., p. i; for a facs. *see* MGG II, 22.   [2] *See* BatG, 12ff.

[3] For the history of their period, *see* S. H. Thomson, *Czechoslovakia in European History*, Chap. 2.

[4] About these men, *see* ReMMA, 232f, 376.

Mügling [5] is known to have been the last Minnesinger in Prague. He left there in 1358, when the first period of German influence in Bohemia may be said to end. The Bohemian composers took over the German Minnelied without greatly changing it. Only one name of a Bohemian Minnesinger has come down to us: that of Mülich of Prague, who belongs to the time of the transition from the Minnelied to the Meisterlied. We do not have much information about him, but we know that he lived at the beginning of the 14th century. His music is found in the 15th-century Colmar MS. Two tones [6] and four poems are recorded there. His tones comprise the Long Tone, for which he is most famous, and one *Reige*.[7] All the texts are in German.

There was much musical activity in Bohemia besides that of the Minnesinger. In 1255, a new organ was installed in the Cathedral at Prague, and a choir of twelve boys (*bonifantes*) was established there in 1259. Instrumental music flourished at the court and at the castles of the nobles. According to the chronicle of Königssaal, the following types of instruments were among those used at the coronation of Wenceslaus II in 1297: *tympana, nabla, tuba, sambuci, rota, figella, lira*.[8]

Tropes, mostly to the Kyrie, Sanctus, and Agnus were very popular in Bohemia. The first MS in Bohemian notation [9] is a troparium of the year 1235. The influence of folk music on tropes was so great that Huss later claimed they were more an inducement to dancing than to worship.

The next century was a period of great prosperity and cultural development. The dynasty of the Luxemburgs came to the throne in 1310, and under John of Luxemburg (1310–1340) and especially his son, Emperor Charles IV, Prague became the cultural center of the Holy Roman Empire.

John was a true representative of the age of chivalry, but he was more a man of war than of art. Unfortunately, his many travels abroad and his cultural contacts with foreign nations, especially France, never greatly benefitted his kingdom, because he seldom stayed in Bohemia for more than a few months at a time. Although Guillaume de Machaut spent many years as secretary to King John,[10] French influence became widespread only under Charles, who was educated in France. French music theory became widely known. When Charles founded the first university of Central Europe in Prague in 1348, musical mensural theory and the principles of consonance were taught there after the doctrine of Jean de Muris. Early in the 15th century, Wenceslaus of Prachatitz prepared a compendium of Muris's writings.

A famous song, *Svátý Václave* ("St. Wenceslaus"),[11] probably dates from the beginning of the 14th century. It is an invocation of the patron saint, Wen-

---

[5] Cf. Chap. 12, fn. 106 and p. 653.   [6] Cf. p. 653.   [7] These 2 pieces pr. BatL, 44.
[8] *See* BatG, 65, fn. 9.
[9] For a description of this variant, *see* HuttC, 150; for a facsimile ex., *see ibid.*, Supp., III.
[10] Cf. ReMMA, 347.   [11] Pr. BerthaA, 2598; BatG, 60.

ceslaus, and became a national song similar to the *Hospodine pomiluj ny*. During the Hussite Wars, it was used as a battle song of the Catholic side.

The development of the first Bohemian school of composition takes place during this century. The external circumstances were conducive to such a development, since Charles IV greatly furthered all artistic activity.

Four factors influenced this school of composition: the art music of France, that of Germany, native secular folk music, and, underlying these three factors, the potent influence of the liturgical folk song (based on Gregorian Chant), which was the spontaneous expression of a religious people.[12]

The first composer of this school, known by name, was Magister Záviš, who was probably its founder. He was a poet as well as a musician. Not much is known about his life. In 1379, he acquired the degree of Bachelor of Arts at the University of Prague; in 1382, he became Master of Arts, and was then made professor at the University. He spent the years 1396 to 1398 in Rome and died soon after 1410.

We have five compositions bearing his name: two Kyries, one Gloria, one Alleluia, and one love song. All of these, including the love song, are musically liturgical in character; they are monophonic and show the influence of Gregorian Chant. His actually liturgical works all start with the same motive in different variations.[13] Záviš's compositions were later taken over into the Hussite song-books and were still performed in the Hussite churches, in Czech, at the end of the 16th century.

Záviš was influenced not only by Gregorian Chant, but by the Minnelied. His Alleluia [14] is written mainly in double versicles, but is less close in structure to a liturgical sequence than to a *Leich;* this secular form had been brought to Bohemia in the 13th century by the German Minnesinger. Záviš's originality lies in his treatment of the melodic line. It is restless, abounding in skips and "forbidden" intervals. Throughout, he adheres strictly to the Phrygian mode. At times he writes the arpeggio of a major chord. The following, a part of the love song, is an example of Záviš's melodic line.

EXAMPLE 166. Extract from *Jižt mne vše radost ostává* ("My joy is waning")—Záviš (From NejZ, 60).

"Her gaze shoots through my eye, straight to my heart . . .
Yearning for thy love, although it may be given me."

[12] Cf. NejZ, 56.   [13] Pr. NejP, 129.   [14] For transcr., *see* NejZ, 58f.

Another composer of the school of Záviš is Jan of Jenštejn, archbishop of Prague from 1380 to 1396. His compositions show considerable French influence, since he studied in Paris and there became familiar with the *ars nova* movement. He is the first Bohemian composer of mensural music known by name. (It would seem, however, that the earliest known Czech song in mensural notation is actually a somewhat earlier anonymous sacred song, the *Buoh všemohúcí* ["Almighty God"] [15] which has an appended *Kyrie eleison*.) Although Gregorian Chant is still a basis for his works, they are nearer to folk music than Záviš's. Jan's monodic *Decet huius cunctis horis,*[16] from the office for the Feast of the Visitation, is a liturgical sequence. The archbishop, fired with zeal for this Feast, offered Pope Urban VI the text for this office, and it was accepted and introduced in Prague, Mainz, and other cities. The archbishop adapted old melodies for the service, but used also some new ones, which may be his own. The *Decet* belongs to the latter group.

An anonymous love song from the beginning of the 15th century, *Otep myrrhy* ("A bouquet of myrrh"),[17] may also be included as a product of this school of composition. Most of its motives are clearly taken from Frauenlob's paraphrase on the Song of Solomon, which survives in the Colmar MS; but, through secularization and use of the folk style, they become much more lively and flexible than they are in Frauenlob's strict composition. The love song is in the form of a *Leich*. It consists of six strophes, set to three tunes, each of which in turn consists of four phrases. An interesting feature is that the last phrase is the same in each of the three tunes, a feature that reminds one somewhat of the medieval *estampie*. (The third tune repeats the last two phrases of the first.) Thus the plan is: *a (tuvu)* :||: *b (vwxu)* :||: *c (yzvu)*. This song was found in a MS dated 1410; the piece is one of the oldest Bohemian examples of monodic mensural music.

During the reign of Charles IV, liturgical music in Bohemia displayed much variety and richness. The use of the Ambrosian liturgy and of one of the Slav liturgies [18] was permitted in certain churches. The choir in the cathedral was greatly enlarged: in addition to the *bonifantes* there were twenty-four mansionaries with a precentor at their head.[19]

A type of song used at this time was the *koleda*. It had been sung in Bohemia since the early Middle Ages. At first, it was an incantation song but, by the 14th century, it had become more of a beggar's song—students went about the streets singing for money. There were *koledy* for all feasts—Christmas, Easter, etc.; they may be compared to western carols.

[15] Pr. NejC, App., p. i. [16] Pr. NejZ, 65. [17] Pr. NejZ, 68.
[18] The Slav liturgy was used only in the Emmaus Church in Prague.
[19] "Mansionary" came (1) from *manere* ("to remain"), and differentiated a singer so named from the *bonifantes*, who quit at the age of 16, and (2) from *mansio*, the common house in which the mansionaries lived together from 1350 on.

Easter dramas were very popular at this time. At first they were strictly liturgical; later they became mostly secular, with Czech texts replacing the Latin.[20]

It is recorded in the chronicle of the town of Königssaal [21] (c. 1338) that the people everywhere, not only the accomplished musicians, sang polyphonically in sixths, thus somewhat approximating fauxbourdon practice.[22]

The next two centuries, the 15th and 16th, show a new trend in Bohemian music, but much was nevertheless taken over from preceding centuries.

Jan Huss' Pre-Reformation Movement

With the coming of Huss (1373–1415) a new era starts in Czech history in general, and also in the history of Czech music. The pre-Reformation, with Huss at its head, sought to abolish the alleged abuses of the Church and to recapture the simplicity and sincerity of early Christianity. The futility of worldly life was at first a leading tenet of the Hussites and therefore all the pleasures of the world and the luxuries of life were automatically banned. In the history of Czech music, Huss was a "historical catastrophe." [23] "Through the Czech Reformation, the Middle Ages of music were extended to the 17th century." [24]

Huss' antiartistic tendencies were based on purely religious grounds. Too much luxury had brought about those conditions in the Church of which the Hussites complained, and therefore they declared that art had to be banned, because in a way it was a luxury too. The use of instruments in Church was forbidden; organs were destroyed, and only bells were retained. In 1435, musicians, looked upon as ungodly people, were denied the right to take Communion. All music was banned in the 15th century, except monophonic song, which was the typical art of the Hussites. Huss believed in the devotional value of singing and, driven by the burning ardor of religion, the whole of Bohemia sang.

This Hussite song was neither secular nor liturgical. The life of the people was permeated by one religious idea, and the barriers between secular and liturgical music fell, a development that had, in fact, already started in pre-Hussite times. "It was the song of life turned toward God." [25] The Hussite song was human and simple, national and social and, we might say, democratic. Folk song and liturgical song form its basis; many songs were derived from Gregorian sources.

Since the Hussites were against all embellishments, polyphony, which

---

[20] The most famous of the Easter Plays was the so-called *Mastičkář,* which contained a humorous song on the medical profession (pr. NejZ, 46).

[21] *De novitatibus morum,* Chap. XXIII, Book II.   [22] For more information *see* BatG, 153ff.

[23] NejC, 18.   [24] NejC, 19.   [25] NejH, 2.

they considered one, was absolutely forbidden, except in the *koledy,* which were sometimes even accompanied by instruments. In Huss' day, the singing of these songs, which was restricted to Christmas time, was permitted in polyphony *a* 2. However, the Hussites generally considered monophony more effective and more powerful, since, as they said, unison makes all men equal in their worship. They also returned to the early policy of the Church in pointing out that the words are more important than the music and that polyphonic singing obscures the words. Jakoubek of Stříbra, a radical Hussite, said that breaking of voices also breaks the heart. (The reference is to polyphony—*cantus fractus,* i.e., "broken song".) Thus, polyphonic song became an exception and a sign of conservatism. A great battle was fought over the admission of polyphony into the Church throughout the 15th and 16th centuries until polyphony emerged victorious.

There were two main parties among the Hussites: the radical reformers called the Taborites, and the conservative ones called the Utraquists [26] (also called the Prague Party).

Huss had made no change in the liturgy, but the Taborites introduced new forms. They proceeded to burn all liturgical song-books because they considered them to be evil and insincere. They opposed ritualism because it was of human invention. Their liturgy was strict and simple. The Mass was considerably shortened, and it was rendered in Czech. It consisted of only three parts: the Lord's Prayer, Consecration, and the Eucharist. Mass could be held anywhere, not only in church, and all ceremonial of the Roman liturgy was rejected. Properly speaking, there was no *cantus ecclesiasticus* at all, since so many portions of the Mass were eliminated. During the few that remained, there was at first no singing; but Czech songs were admitted later. The people were allowed to sing anything, according to their mood, so that religious folksong began to replace the liturgical chant. Only syllabic pieces were permitted; ornamentation was still strictly forbidden. The Lord's Prayer thus became one of the most important Taborite songs.

At first the songs of the Taborites had been polemic in character, defending their radical views. Later the songs became mainly didactic, the texts being scriptural paraphrases. These compositions show a remarkably hard and steady rhythm, usually ♩♪ ♩♪ ♩♪, etc., with a sharp accentuation of the short note. There were no regular measures (unless these two-note groups are regarded as such). The repeating of notes on the same pitch is another characteristic element of these as well as of most other old Czech songs. The melody usually moves stepwise or in thirds.

The Taborites also had songs for penitence, for the Holiness of the Altar, for Communion of the children (all Hussites lay much stress on children's song), etc. In addition, they had a great love for hymns; these were translated

[26] Utraquism: receiving communion in both kinds (*sub utraque specie*).

into Czech from the Latin. The funeral songs of the Taborites were gay, because any person was deemed happy who had left this world.

By far the most famous pieces were the Taborite battle songs; the best known of these is the anonymous *Ktož jsú boží bojovníci* ("Ye, who are champions of God"). The oldest copy of this composition survives in the contemporary Cantionale of Jistebnice, which, in fact, contains most of the old Taborite songs that are preserved. This battle song consists of three stanzas, each made up of three sections (almost all Taborite songs have three-section stanzas). The music of the first section, marked $\mathbb{V}$ is repeated for the second section, while the third section marked R° [27] has a new poetic form and a new melody (so that what we have is an application of the *Bar* form). In this song, the R° contains only four phrases, while the $\mathbb{V}$ contains five. Eventually, the piece was changed into a strophic song; the music of the R° was discarded, its words being adapted to fit the melody of the $\mathbb{V}$.

EXAMPLE 167. *Ktož jsú boží bojovníci*—Anon. (from NejC, 257).

Section I $\mathbb{V}$ "Ye who are champions of God and of his law, pray for God's help and have faith in Him that, in the end, ye shall always be victorious with His aid.

Section II $\mathbb{V}$ Christ repays a hundredfold the losses ye have sustained; whosoever lays down his life for him shall live eternally. Happy is he who perishes in the cause of righteousness.

Section III   R°   For the Lord bids us not be afraid of bodily afflictions. He commands us to lay down our lives for the love of our fellowmen."

(For the other two stanzas, as well as the original notation, see NejC, 910.)

Smetana used this melody in his symphonic poems, *Tábor* and *Blaník* in the cycle "My Country"; [28] and Dvořák used it in the overture "Husitska".

[27] R° stands for Repetitio; it was rather illogically identified with the third section, which was not repeated. For a discussion, *see* Analecta I, 9ff.

[28] Nejedlý points out that Smetana employs $\frac{3}{2}$ time instead of $\frac{6}{4}$, thus making the rhythmical pattern ♩♩♩♩ instead of ♩♩♩♩; Smetana's version has become the generally accepted one, although it coincides neither with the earliest one in the *Cantionale* of Jistebnice nor with the later one in a printed book of 1530 at Mladá Boleslav. Nejedlý considers the pattern ♩♩♩♩ typical of most Taborite songs.

The music of the Utraquists was more varied and less strict. After 1422, Mass was held in Czech in Prague, but, in contrast with the practice of the Taborites, all portions were retained. Notwithstanding this, the Utraquist Mass became strongly differentiated from the Roman. The translation of the Latin text into the vernacular was a step in the process of making the Mass more folklike. The melody had to be changed quite often to enable it to fit the language, and thus new rhythmic and melodic structures resulted. The music of the Mass was rendered either by recitation on a psalm-tone or by the singing of a Chant melody. The only way the Hussite Mass assigned different music to different groups of people was in distributing portions of the chant among various singers (as, for example, in traditional responsorial singing); it never made such an assignment for purposes of polyphony.

It is interesting to note that the Kyrie of the Hussite Mass became very similar to a folk song. Actually, the Kyrie proper was omitted; instead the people sang tropes to the Kyrie, and in so doing used Czech words. The Credo, sung by the people, also in Czech, became a real religious folk song.[29]

The Czech Brethren and Their Song Books; the Czech Rorate Chants

After the Hussites, the Czech Brethren, founded by Peter of Chelčic, further developed religious song all through the 16th century. The Czech Brethren compiled many hymn books and published them, beautifully illustrated.[30] The most important one was published by Bishop Jan Blahoslav, in 1561.[31] The tunes of the Czech Brethren either were taken from Gregorian Chant or were borrowed from the music of other nations, often from secular songs. Many melodies of the French Calvinists were adopted in the four-part settings of Goudimel.

Persecuted first in Bohemia and Moravia, and later in Germany, the Czech Brethren—or Moravian Brethren, as they were later called—came to America in the early 18th century. They arrived in Georgia in 1735, and later settled in Pennsylvania.[32] By that time many of the original chorales had been translated first into German and then into English, and the melodies had been transcribed into mensural notation and harmonized, so that some of the hymns sung in the Moravian Church today bear only a faint resemblance to the original chorales of the Brethren.[33]

[29] For a Credo of this type, see NejH, 476.

[30] A copy of the beautiful hymnal published in Kralic in 1615 may be found in the Archives of the Moravian College and Theological Seminary in Bethlehem, Pa.

[31] This bishop wrote the first Czech printed book on musical theory, published in 1558. For a facsimile of the title page of his hymn book of 1561 and of that of an earlier edition of 1541, see MGG II, Pl. 2.

[32] One of the first communities settled by the Moravians was Bethlehem, today still one of the headquarters of the Moravian Church.

[33] For more details, see ScotM, 51ff, and JulD, 153ff.

The 16th century [34] saw the development of the Czech Rorate chants and songs. The former were used at Advent and received their name from the *Rorate coeli,* the Introit of the Mass for that festival. They consisted of tropes, with Czech texts, to the Kyrie and various other parts of the Mass. These chants, in turn, gave rise to the Rorate songs, which likewise had Czech texts. Some of these texts were translations from the Latin, while others were new. It was the characteristic feature of the Rorate song that its melody—which was a composite—was taken in part from the Chant, in part from folk song. The folk-derived section, which consisted of mensural music, was appended to the Chant-derived section.[35]

Songs in the Czech language had become so popular that, in spite of the ban decreed on them by the Council of Basle in 1435, the Catholic clergy introduced them again at the end of the 16th century.

Vocal Polyphony of the Counter-Reformation Period: Gallus and Some Lesser Figures

The unfavorable attitude of the Hussites toward polyphonic music neutralized influences from abroad, and Bohemia benefitted only in part from the great development of polyphony in the Low Countries, Italy, France, and England. Nevertheless, we have some motets with Czech texts, and usually for three voices, by the early 16th-century composers Gontrášek and Tomek.

If the Hussites, in their reformative zeal, rejected polyphony and instrumental music, the Jesuits, leaders of the Counter-Reformation, encouraged polyphonic writing and also the use of instruments.

The most famous musician serving the Counter-Reformation in Bohemia, a great friend of the Jesuits, was the composer called, in the Latin form of his name, Jacobus Gallus, or, in the Germanized form, Jakob Handl. His real name was probably Jakob Petelin.[36] Gallus was not a native Bohemian, having been born in Carniola, probably at Ribnica in 1550. Some modern writers include him when discussing German music. Since, however, Carniola (now part of Yugoslavia) is a Slovene area, and since Gallus spent most of his life and wrote his chief works in Bohemia and Moravia, this is unjustified. We know that Gallus was a devout Catholic, and he may have received his earliest musical education in the Cistercian Monastery at Sittich, which took a leading part in the Counter-Reformation. Although his music shows great affinity with the Venetian School, it is not certain whether he ever went to Venice. It is probable that he traveled to Fiume or Trieste, where Venetian influence was very strong.[37] We know definitely that he was a member of the choir at

---

[34] Not the 14th century, as often claimed; cf. NejP, 282ff.
[35] Further on the Rorate chants and songs, *see* OrelR; Analecta I, 25ff; NejP, 282ff; PachtaP.
[36] *See* DTO VI[1], xiif.   [37] Cf. DTO VI[1], xi.

the Vienna Court Chapel in 1574. From 1575 to 1578, he seems to have wandered about Bohemia, Moravia, and Silesia, and spent much time at Prague and Breslau. After that he was for a while in the service of the bishop of Olomouc (Olmütz), Jan Pavlovský. During his stay there, he finished his Masses and started on his greatest work, the *Opus musicum*. Prague, at that time, was the capital of the Hapsburg Empire, and the brilliant court of Rudolph II attracted many famous composers—among them Philippe de Monte, Jakob Regnart, and also Gallus. He must have lived there from at least the year 1586, for the preface to Book I of his *Opus musicum* was dated in Prague in that year. The only official position that he is known to have had in the Bohemian capital was that of cantor at St. John's Church. He died in Prague in 1591.

Gallus cannot be placed within any school of composition. "His technique of composition shows a wholly individual fusion of the Netherlands and Venetian styles."[38] He is close to the Venetian style in his use of double choruses for tonal effect; but, in his works for less than six parts, he shows a mastery of the contrapuntal imitative style of the Netherlanders. Nevertheless, it is clear, from a statement he wrote in his own defense, that some of his contemporaries regarded his compositions as chaotic. He tries to free himself from traditional formulas and often indulges in rhythmic intricacies. Strikingly colorful effects are obtained by his use of chromaticism. He likes harmonic progressions in which the roots move a third and in which the second root supports a chord that lies outside the scale of the preceding chord. The following passage illustrates the impact of his harmonic progressions.

EXAMPLE 168. Extract from the motet, *Mirabile mysterium*—Gallus (from DTO VI^1, 162).

[38] DTO XLII^1, iv.

The *Opus musicum*,[39] in which the *Mirabile mysterium* was published, is a collection of motets for the whole liturgical year, printed in four books, one in 1586, two in 1587, and the last in 1591. The first, dedicated to Gallus' three patrons, the Archbishop of Prague and the Bishops of Olomouc and Breslau, contains motets for the period from the first Sunday in Advent to Holy Week. The second provides for the period from Holy Week to Pentecost, and the third completes the cycle for the Proper of the Season. Book IV contains motets for the Proper of the Saints. These motets, *a 4* to *a 24,* show a remarkably varied technique. Gallus exploits nearly all the possibilities of different voice combinations. For example, in the two motets *a 12,* one, *Cantate Domino*,[40] has a double chorus in which the first group is predominantly treble and the second predominantly bass, whereas the other, *Tribus miraculis*,[41] uses three equal choruses. Gallus shows great ability in handling up to four choruses, mostly homophonically and antiphonally—in *Dum vagus* and *Nympha, refer quae sit vox*,[42] he uses echo choruses—but sometimes also in contrapuntal imitation. On the other hand, such imitation underlies almost all of the motets *a 4* and *a 5.* An exception is the simple and very eloquent four-part *Ecce quomodo moritur justus*,[43] his best-known work. It is a strictly homophonic composition, in *aBcB* form. G. F. Händel incorporated it in his "Funeral Anthem." Madrigalian pictorial writing abounds in the *Opus musicum;* [44] e.g., there are descriptive melismas on the words *"aquae quae fluunt impetu de Libano"* in the motet, *Ego flos campi.*[45] Gallus closed the collection with two psalms *a 24,* which he called "triumphal psalms."

In addition to the *Opus musicum,* Gallus wrote nineteen Masses, sixteen of them printed in Prague in 1580; almost all of them are parody Masses.[46] For models, Gallus used principally motets, either of his own composition (from the *Opus musicum*) or by such famous contemporaries as Clemens non Papa, Vaet, and Hollander. Three Masses are based on German lieder (including one on Lassus' *Im Mayen*), one on a French chanson (Crecquillon's ubiquitous *Ung gay bergier*), and three on Latin and Italian secular pieces. Sometimes, Gallus is almost entirely faithful to his model, e.g., in the Kyrie of the *Missa Ung gay bergier.* At other times, he may restrict himself to small changes in rhythm and in the number of voices active in a particular passage, to inserting or omitting, to repeating notes, etc. But more often Gallus goes further. He uses melodic variation (expansion, simplification, successive juxtaposition of motives separated from one another in the model, superimposition of figuration, insertion of embellishing notes, etc.) or rhythmic variation (the *Osanna* is usually in triple rhythm even if the model was binary), harmonic changes,

[39] Pr. DTO VI¹, XII¹, XV¹, XX¹, XXIV, XXVI.   [40] Pr. DTO VI¹, 97.
[41] *Ibid.,* 110.   [42] Pr. DTO XXIV, 83, 87, respectively.
[43] Pr. DTO XII¹, 171; ScherG, 133; etc.   [44] Discussed in NayH.
[45] PR. DTO XXIV, 18.
[46] 6 of these Masses (including those to be discussed in the text) pr. DTO XLII¹.

and changes made for contrapuntal purposes (inversions, diminutions, augmentations, strettos). Passages originally polyphonic may become homophonic and vice versa. In some cases, passages set for only a few voices in the model are set for double chorus in the Mass. On occasion there is a different distribution of voices within the choruses: e.g., there are two equal choruses in the *Missa Elisabethae impletum est tempus,* whereas in the model Chorus I is set for treble voices and Chorus II for bass. Sometimes Gallus only alludes to his model. The Benedictus is usually freely invented.[47]

In 1590, Gallus completed a collection of simple madrigals *a 4* (called *Moralia*) by means of which he tried to appease his critics. He stated that he chose Latin texts partly because Latin was the language most neglected in madrigal composition. These madrigals were to be free of all "offense and ambiguity." In his effort to avoid the frivolity of the current madrigal, he chose didactic texts mainly, a good many of them dull and unpoetic.

In addition to these, he wrote a funeral song *a 8* for his patron, Abbot Caspar of Zabrdovice; a part-song *a 4* on a German text; and forty-seven additional *moralia* in five, six, and eight parts on Latin texts by his friends, e.g., a song in praise of music.

Another Catholic musician, a contemporary of Gallus, was Jan Trajan Turnovský, parish priest of Netvoř and Sepekov. Some of his works have been preserved in a MS from the town of Benešov, now in the Library of the Prague Conservatory. One historian has gone so far as to call Turnovský the "Bohemian Palestrina."[48] This composer wrote motets for from three to six voices, mostly for choirs consisting wholly of tenors and basses, a procedure extremely rare in his time. He was very skillful in combining parts, either in homophony or polyphonic imitation, and he did not shrink from using audacious dissonances.[49]

The Protestant nobleman, Christof Harant of Polžic and Bezdružic (1564–1621), was a musician and author who wrote a motet *Qui confidunt* for six voices and a Mass for five voices. His technique was that of the late Franco-Netherlandish School.

Musical Societies; the Speciálník MS; Music in Rural Districts

Polyphonic music was further cultivated at the court and at the castles of the nobles, and especially in the literary societies (or fraternities). These were widely spread over the country in the 16th century,[50] so that most Czech towns had their societies, organized by townsmen. The members

[47] Further about the Masses, *see* PiskP.   [48] *See* BraM, 14.   [49] Cf. BraM, 11.
[50] It has often been claimed that the literary fraternities were first organized in the 14th century in connection with the performance of the Rorate songs. This belief is unfounded, since the Rorate songs originated much later. Cf. fn. 34.

were the first citizens of the community. They were zealous performers of the best polyphonic music of their time. Every fraternity, organized like a guild, had its own song-book. The scribe's charges were paid by the fraternity, and the book was likely to be beautifully illustrated. These collections contained monophonic and polyphonic compositions with Latin and Czech texts.

The most famous of these societies was founded in 1616 and bore the name Collegium Musicum. It had an international membership of twelve men who met once every fortnight to study and perform polyphonic secular music, especially madrigals.

Although Nejedlý maintains that the *socii* were not creative artists, Orel is inclined to attribute to them some compositions found in the *Speciálník,* a manuscript of Hradec Králové,[51] containing, for the most part, 15th-century Mass sections and motets on Latin texts for from three to five voices *ad aequales*. The *Speciálník* contains 300 polyphonic compositions in all styles. Only two Czech composers are named—the early 16th-century Gontrášek and Tomek. However, there are many pieces with Czech texts or at least Czech titles. The *cantus firmus* is usually a Hussite chorale, or a Czech mensural song. Foreign composers are also represented in the MS, among them Alexander Agricola, Tinctoris, Lannoy, and Pullois. The 15th-century contents include likewise an anonymous *Náš milý Svatý Václave* ("Our beloved St. Wenceslaus") which is the oldest polyphonic setting that is known of the song *Svatý Václave*.[52]

Since Prague was an international center, the national character manifested itself more clearly in the polyphonic music of the rural districts. We have a few examples of such music—Mass sections and motets, based on Bohemian religious folk songs. These works are simple and relatively free of foreign influence. They are folklike, with a strong emphasis on harmonic formulas, and are mostly in a major key (C or F). One voice is sometimes replaced by an instrument, usually the four-stringed, guitar-like *chiterna,* which had been popular in Bohemia since the 14th century. Independent instrumental music existed only in dance forms.[53]

There was a great deal of musical activity in Bohemia in the 15th and 16th centuries. A fusion of the religious genius of the people and the art of the professional musicians could have brought about the development of a great Bohemian national school.[54] But by the time the Hussites had relaxed their strictures against polyphonic and instrumental music—in other words, by the time such a fusion would have been possible—the defeat of the Protestants

---

[51] OrelP, 163f.
[52] For more information on the music in the *Speciálník see* OrelP, 149ff.
[53] Further about this music of the rural districts, *see* OrelP, 212f, and OrelS, 89f.
[54] Cf. BerthaA, 2601.

on the White Mountain in 1620 [55] ruined all national cultural developments in Bohemia. The best-educated men were sent into exile, some of them were murdered (including Christof Harant), Bohemia was Germanized, and almost everything Czech and national was suppressed. Many Czech musicians left Bohemia, since there was no fertile soil for their activities at home, and became famous in other countries. Czech culture thus merged with general Western culture, and it was impossible for any national school to develop until the 19th century.

MUSIC IN POLAND *

1. THE FIFTEENTH CENTURY [1]
BY Franciszka Merlan

Medieval Antecedents

When, late in the 10th century, Poland accepted Christianity in its Western rather than Eastern form, she was opened to all the influences of Western civilization, including that of its music. As it survives, Polish music in its first period, i.e., roughly up to the beginning of the 15th century, is essentially a branch of Gregorian Chant; there are no remnants of pre-Christian music. It is probable, because only natural, that the path through which Western influences mainly entered Poland lay through the German countries.[2]

The oldest MS in Poland that contains music is Gniezno Cathedral, No. 149 (11th century). It is a plainsong MS, employing staffless neumes, some

[55] For historic background, *see* S. H. Thomson, *Czechoslovakia in European History*, 48ff.

* Dr. Dragan Plamenac has been most kind and generous in helping in the preparation of the sections on Poland.

[1] This section has been written with the following limitations: Not all items listed in the bibliography could be consulted. However, they have been cited to the extent that the writer felt reports on their content are dependable. Moreover, practically no effects of World War II, such as loss or transfer of MSS, destruction of libraries, changes of frontiers, etc., have been taken into consideration. Original sources and often even some secondary sources being inaccessible, it will at times be impossible here to make definitive statements concerning the character of Poland's medieval and Early Renaissance music. Much of it, unfortunately, has either not been published at all or has been published in a form not meeting the standards of modern musicology. Probably there are still some unknown or unexplored MSS.

[2] Silesia would have been the most likely gateway. On the controversial question of cultural relations between Silesia and Poland, *see* e.g., H. Barycz, *Ślązacy na Uniwersytecie Jagiellońskim od XV–XVIII w.*, 1935, and J. Skoczek, *Stosunki kulturalne Śląska ze Lwowem w wiekach średnich*, 1937; on the specifically musical relations, *see* FeldM; also the review thereof by Pietzsch in AfMF, III (1938), 488. On German influence on music and musical instruction (theory), *see* ChybP; ChybD; WagT I, vii. The presence of German Chant dialect (cf. ReMMA, 122) in Polish MSS (*see* PuliP, 12; SzczepN, 38) and the frequent use of Gothic notation (*Hufnagelschrift*) in the latter part of the 15th century (*see* SzczepH, 287; PietzschD, 169) are perhaps indicative.

of them heighted.[3] Some other remnants, dating from before the 15th century,[4] are Offices with music, one in honor of St. Adalbert, another in honor of St. Stanislaus; sequences,[5] five of which are to St. Stanislaus,[6] one (*Grates nunc omnes*) with a Polish translation of the text;[7] one in honor of both St. Adalbert and St. Stanislaus; one to the Virgin (*Salve salutis ianua*),[8] the MS of which gives what may be the name of its composer, the bishop Jan Kempa (d. 1346), who thus would be the oldest Polish composer known by name; two Easter songs;[9] one song of the Annunciation;[10] a piece in honor of St. Stanislaus (*Gaude mater Polonia*);[11] and another to St. John Kanty.[12] All these compositions are monophonic; some—notably the sequence to St. Adalbert and St. Stanislaus and one of the St. Stanislaus sequences (*Ihesu Criste rex superne*)—are extant also in Czech MSS,[13] thus belonging to the musical tradition of two countries.

The remnant of early Polish music that is most celebrated is the monophonic composition *Bogurodzica* ("Mother of God"), whose opening melody is the same as that of a Kyrie from a 12th-century Litany to All Saints (Graz, Universitätsbibl., MS 807).[13a] The oldest source for this piece (Jagiellońska Library MS 1619, dating from 1408) contains only a pair of stanzas, each with different music, which may possibly be by two different composers. Two sections were added later. The piece is of the *lai* type. Originating not earlier than the 14th century, the piece is said to have been sung as a battle hymn at the crucial battle of Tannenberg (1410). It became a national anthem and has come down to us with its original text, which is the oldest surviving specimen of Polish poetry.[14]

Early 15th-Century Sources

Passing to the 15th century, we find the Church continuing to foster instruction in sacred music. The University of Cracow, which had been founded in 1364, became a prominent center of musical studies.[15] The 15th century produced also the earliest known musical treatise of Polish origin: the *Musica*

---

[3] Cf. JachH, 1. 2 facsimiles in TrzK. For many descriptions (some with facsimiles) of neumatic notation in other Polish MSS, *see* ThibML. GiebG, 51ff, lists liturgical MSS in the archives of the Cathedrals of Gniezno and Cracow. The two 16th-century graduals analyzed in GiebG, 74ff, use Gothic neumes; liquescent neumes and some of the decorative neumes are virtually never used.   [4] Selected from the ones enumerated in JachH, 9ff; JachMPJ, 531ff.

[5] On the presence of Polish sequences in Sweden, *see* MobergU, Index, under "Poland."

[6] A facsimile of 1 in JachMPJ, 539; transcr. in JachH, 10.   [7] Pr. JachH, 12; JachMPJ, 532.

[8] Pr. SurzB, App., No. 4; another (partial) transcr. in JachMPJ, 532.

[9] Cf. PolD, 34f; partial facsimile of 1, *ibid.*, 37.   [10] Facsimile in PolD, 34; JachH, 18.

[11] Facsimile in JachMPJ, 533; pr. *ibid.*, 531.   [12] Partial transcr. in JachMPJ, 532.

[13] Cf. Analecta IX, 249ff; OrelH, 227ff.

[13a] Kyrie pr. WagE III, 262. Concerning the relationship, cf. *Pamiętnik literacki* XLIII (1952), 352.

[14] Further about this composition, *see* ChybW, where the claims for an origin earlier than the 14th century are disproved, and JachZ, where particularly the stanzas added later are discussed. Cf. also JachMPJ, 532f.

[15] For details on musical instruction, the role of Cracow, etc., in the 15th century, *see* PietzschP, 424ff; WagZ, 5; GiebM, 183ff; GiebG, 11ff; ReissK; ChybK.

of Magister Szydłovita,[16] a compilation comparable to Szalkai's treatise (cf. p. 727) particularly in that both have among their sources the otherwise little known Hollandrinus (Olendrinus, Valendrinus).[17]

Our knowledge of Polish music of the first half of the century is based mainly on three MSS: MS 52 in the Krasiński Library, Warsaw;[18] MS 2464 of the Jagiellońska Library, Cracow; and the MS formerly known as F.I.378 of the Imperial Library in St. Petersburg, transferred in 1921 to the Warsaw University Library.[19] MS 52 [20] contains some thirty-five compositions and MS 378 [21] contains eighteen, seven of which occur also in MS 52. Some of the pieces in this repertory are definitely non-Polish; others are anonymous or, in three instances, bear names which may not be those of the composers (see below); nine are by Nicholas of Radom (Mikołaj z Radomia). The first group, comprising works by Zacharia, Ciconia, Grossin, and Egardus, is indicative of the speed with which Poland assimilated foreign influences.[22] Of the compositions belonging to the second group, one (*Ave Mater* in MS 52) occurs also in Bologna, Bibl. Univ. 2216 (No. 57) and Venice, Bibl. Marc., ital. IX, 145, two others (Sanctus and Kyrie) in Munich, Staatsbibl. 3232a (f.70[v] and 73[r]).[23] Claims to Polish origin for any of these pieces must thus be viewed with caution. One of them, however, *Cracovia civitas*,[24] in praise of Cracow, because of its text, seems more likely than the others to be a native Polish work. Three names appear on the pages of this second group, though not in the usual position of a composer's name: N. de Ostrorog (in *Pastor gregis,* a motet *a 3,* in treble-dominated style, in honor of St. Stanis-

---

[16] Edited and commented upon in GiebM and GiebG.

[17] About him, *see* FeldM, 100ff and App. I, containing the text of his treatise.

[18] Cf LudD, 422ff; JachMPH, 49ff.

[19] About 2 additional MSS in Lwów, reported by Chybiński, *see* MachM II, 34*. The Musicological Institute of the University of Lwów is supposed to have possessed, before World War II, a comprehensive collection of photographic reproductions of Polish polyphonic music of the entire 15th century (SzczepW, 2).

[20] Catalogued in JachM (should be used in connection with Chybiński's review in *Kwartalnik Muzyczny,* No. 9 [1930], 75ff; No. 10–11 [1931], 328ff; No. 12–13 [1931], 463ff).

[21] Described in SzczepN; cf. LudD, 430; LudQ, 220. A facsimile in ThibL, Pl. xvii.

[22] Traditionally, the humanist, Gregory of Sanok (Grzegorz z Sanoka), used to be credited with having opened Poland to Italian influence after his return from Italy in 1439, on the basis of the biography by his contemporary, Filippo Buonaccorsi (*Philippi Buonaccorsi Callimachi vita et mores Gregorii Sanocei,* Chap. 6, f. XI; ed. by Miodoński). If, however, all or most of the compositions in MS 52 were written down before that year, no such credit should be given to Gregory, and this, indeed, seems to be the opinion of many Polish scholars. However, if the Italian influence previous to 1439 came via Germany, in spite of her apparently not having herself been greatly affected by Italian music, the tradition could be maintained, though in a somewhat modified sense. Gregory, then, would have been the first to open Poland to *direct* Italian influence. Cf. DèzM, 72. The connection presently to be shown between the Bologna, Bibl. Univ., MS 2216, the Munich MS 3232a, and our MSS 52 and 378 clearly establishes the possibility of the route, Italy–Germany–Poland.

[23] Cf. SzczepN, 50. *Ave Mater* (*a 3*) has a fourth voice in the Bologna MS, a different contratenor in the Venice MS. For Oswald von Wolkenstein's adaptation, *see* DTO IX[1], 205.

[24] Pr. OpieP, App., vii. There is no conclusive evidence to support the tentative ascription to Nicholas of Radom there made.

laus);[25] Ewarger or Ewargeris (*tenor huius Ewargeris*), and Duchna Jankowska, a woman's name.[26] Six of the pieces in this group are polyphonic works to the Virgin. They show French influence inasmuch as they use French notation; moreover, five of them are in French treble-dominated style (the other two are in conductus style), and hocket appears also. On the other hand, melodic sequences and bits of imitation are among the traits that may show the presence of Italian influence. Generally, the writing is chordal—cadences using the $\frac{6}{3}$ technique are included—with some polyphonic elements.[27] This anonymous group includes also a setting *a 3* of the Magnificat, in which the lowest voice (containing the *cantus firmus*) is combined with more melismatic upper voices.[28] Particularly interesting is the third group, consisting of works of the earliest Polish composer of rank, Nicholas of Radom.[29] It comprises the following compositions *a 3:* a Magnificat in simple style, for some portions of which only two voices are notated, with the instruction that the third is to be added in fauxbourdon;[30] a textless composition in three distinct sections, the first of which is provided with two closes (and is therefore to be repeated);[31] a troped Gloria, starting with imitation and employing hocket;[32] a Credo which, opening with imitation, continues in conductus style;[33] a Gloria in treble-dominated style;[34] a Credo and a Gloria not yet analyzed;[35] *Hystorigraphi aciem,* a motet;[36] and another Credo (in MS 378) showing such great similarities with a Credo by Zacharia, present in the same MS, that we must infer that Nicholas of Radom was strongly influenced by Zacharia.[37]

Nicholas of Radom is familiar with the most recent techniques of his time. His music is another example of the influence of 14th-century forms (*ballade* and madrigal) on early 15th-century sacred music.[38] His works and possibly some other compositions in MSS 52 and 378 are indicative of the range of influence of Machaut and later western composers[39] and of the survival of earlier forms and techniques side by side with the most recent ones.[40]

---

[25] Analyzed in SzczepZ; facsimile in JachMPJ, 540.

[26] *See* SzczepN, 19, for a discussion of the slight possibility of her being the composer of some of the music in MS 378.

[27] The whole group, together with 3 pieces from MS 2464 (*see* below), is analyzed in SzczepW; for a summary, *see ibid.*, 342ff.

[28] Analyzed in SzczepM.

[29] About him, *see* SzczepU. For a list of non-Polish literature on the composer and on MSS 52 and 378, *see ibid.*, 94. Particularly important are LudD and MachM II.

[30] Cf. JachH, 27f; JachMPJ, 536; but *see* Chybiński's review (cf. fn. 20), in *Kwartalnik Muzyczny* No. 9, p. 80.

[31] *See* JachMPJ, 536, with transcr. of section 1; complete facsimile on p. 537. Jachimecki's assertion that this is a purely instrumental composition, because it is textless, is dubious in view of the *ballade*-like nature of the form (section 3 has the appearance of being a refrain).

[32] Cf. LudD, 430.   [33] LudD, 430; JachMPJ, 538.   [34] LudD, 430.   [35] *See* SzczepU, 91ff.

[36] Partial transcr. in JachMPJ, 536.   [37] *See* SzczepN, 53f.   [38] Cf. LudD, 430.

[39] Cf. MachM II, 34*.

[40] GrafcP, 164, seems to characterize Nicholas of Radom as combining the belated influence of the Florentine school and the most recent influence of the Dunstable–Dufay school.

In addition to *Cracovia civitas*, MS 52 contains other anonymous secular compositions,[41] some written to celebrate the birth of sons to King Jagiełło.[42]

Of the compositions in MS 2464, three are polyphonic pieces in praise of the Virgin—two *a 2* and one with only a single voice preserved. The former two both seem to show Italian influence, although one is in *ballade* form.[43]

Late 15th-Century Sources

On the whole, Poland in the first half of the century was abreast of musical developments in the west. For the second half of the century we have no sources comparable to MSS 52 or 378.[44] The survivals include the monophonic religious song, *Jezusa Judasz przedał*, with words by Władysław of Gielniów (1488);[45] two pieces *a 3*, one to St. Stanislaus and one to St. John Capistranus;[46] and a work *a 2* in honor of the Virgin (*O najdroższy kwiatku*),[47] the latter employing imitation. The pieces to St. Stanislaus and to the Virgin are important as the earliest known examples of sacred polyphony with Polish texts.

We have, further, from the latter part of the century, Lamentations *a 3*[48] and six *Libri generationis*. Five of these *Libri* survive in two MSS in the archives of the Wawel Cathedral in Cracow (one of 1489, one from the beginning of the 16th century) and in the 15th-century MS 2216 of the Library of the Academy of Fine Arts there. Two of these five *Libri* are *a 3*, three *a 4*. These pieces reveal a wide technical disparity. The settings *a 3* contain remnants of the old organum technique; in one, such remnants and the discant technique are present side by side. We find also melodic exchange (*Stimmtausch*); and the $\frac{6}{3}$ technique is applied in some passages *a 3* in the settings *a 4*, at least one of which is composed in the full-fledged later 15th-century style for point-against-point writing.[49] The sixth *Liber generationis* is preserved in a Polish MS (finished in 1525 and apparently written by a German), now Dresden MS A 52. It has sections *a 2*, *a 3*, and *a 4*, and is another example of the late survival of polyphony in organum style.[50] All six settings of the *Liber generationis* (it is remarkable that so many settings of it should be found in Poland) are notated in a decadent form of *Hufnagelschrift*. In the five earlier *Libri*, monophonic and polyphonic passages alternate, while the *Liber* in the 16th-century Wawel MS is *a 4* throughout. In the two set-

---

[41] The interpretation of the text of one secular piece, *Breve regnum*, has been the subject of controversy. *See*, for example, SzczepP.

[42] By his wife Zofja, whom he married in 1422. This helps to date the pieces.

[43] Analyzed in SzczepW. Cf. fn. 27.   [44] Cf. JachH, 33.

[45] JachH, 20f; JachMPJ, 534 (with partial transcr.).

[46] The former pr. JachMPJ, 541; facsimile of the latter, *ibid.*, 542. About both, *see* ReissL (with transcrs.).

[47] Analyzed in SzczepD; a facsimile in PolD, 35.   [48] Analyzed in SzczepL.

[49] Analyzed, with brief exx., in SzczepH.   [50] Analyzed in PietzschD.

tings *a 3* of the five earlier pieces, the *cantus firmus* is at different times assigned to all three parts; in the settings *a 4,* it is in the tenor, except for one section where it is shifted (in each instance) to the superius. In the Dresden MS, the *cantus firmus* is in the tenor throughout. All six settings have the same *cantus firmus,* which we find also in Cod. Vaticanus Pal. lat. 457 (originally a Heidelberg MS).[51] The few late 15th-century polyphonic compositions mentioned provide a link between the more productive first half of the 15th century and the brilliant 16th.[52]

2. THE SIXTEENTH CENTURY
BY ROMAN TOTENBERG AND GUSTAVE REESE

At the end of the 15th century, Cracow became the center of musical activities in Poland. Italian influences penetrated the country more and more, and Italian musicians were invited to the royal court. Plainsong according to the Cracow tradition set the example for all Poland. In 1492, Clemens of Piotrków, canon of the Cathedral at Gniezno, formed the plan of compiling a new antiphonary at Cracow, and he was supported in this undertaking by Cardinal Jagiełło, son of King Casimir IV. The seven-volume antiphonary was completed in 1506, four volumes still being preserved at Gniezno (MS 94–7 Gniezno Cathedral Library). In 1512, the singers at the Poznań Cathedral were ordered to adopt the Cracow tradition.[53]

16th-Century Treatises

In 1514, theoretical treatises began to appear in print in Poland, when the *Algorithmus Proportionum* by Henricus Scriptor (Schreiber) of Erfurt was published at Cracow. Then came two important mensural treatises, brought out c. 1519, also at Cracow, the *Opusculum musices* [54] of Sebastian de Felstin (Felsztyn), and the *Epithoma utriusque musices practice* of Stephanus Monetarius (Münzer) of Kremnica (in Slovakia).[54a] Monetarius' treatise relies heavily on Gafori's *Practica musicae,* while Felstin's seems more original in approach. Felstin produced another treatise, *Directiones musicae ad cathedralis ecclesiae Premisliensis usum* (1544), and an edition of St. Augustine's *De Musica.* These works, however, were apparently surpassed in popularity by the *Opusculum,* which underwent a number of reprintings, the 1534 and

---

[51] *See* BohH, 124 (No. 118); MosV, 10. Cf. also SchzC, 388, and FeldM, 111f, on Silesian MSS (58 of the Breslau Diocesan Archive and I.F.386 of the Breslau University Library) containing the *Liber generationis* in settings similar to the ones at Cracow.
[52] For a summary characterizing Polish music at the turn of the 15th century, *see* ChybM 38f.
[53] Cf. GiebM, 193f.   [54] *See* facsimile pages in JachMWP, 541f.
[54a] Facsimile pages in ReissK, Pl. I–VII.

1539 prints being combined with another tract, *De Musica Figurata* by Martin Kromer of Biecz. Both Kromer and Felstin omitted the section on counterpoint usually included by western theorists. Their treatises, of a rather simple character, are generally considered to have been written for the use of singers.[55]

Humanist Currents; Felstin and Some Lesser Figures

Western cultural currents that found their way into Poland at this period included humanism, introduced possibly by Konrad Celtes (cf. p. 705), who is known to have lived for a time in Cracow, or perhaps brought back by Polish students who in considerable numbers went to Germany to attend the University of Ingolstadt. In the University Library at Cracow is to be found an anonymous *Carmen saphicum* dating from before 1530, which attempts, in the manner of Tritonius (cf. p. 705), Celtes' pupil at Ingolstadt, to provide music in which the time-values are determined by the scansion of the Latin text.[56]

Among composers of the period we re-encounter Felstin. Born c. 1480, he enrolled in 1507 as a student of liberal arts in the University of Cracow. Later he became chaplain in his native Felstin, and finally provost at Sanok. He is known to have been alive as late as 1544.[57] Felstin's sequence, *Virgini Mariae laudes*,[58] and his two Alleluias, *Ave Maria* and *Felix es, Virgo Maria*, all preserved in MSS at the Wawel Cathedral, have Gregorian melodies in the tenor, entirely disposed in semibreves. The writing is primarily note-against-note, interspersed with short passages in imitation. Some melismas appear in the Alleluias, but few in *Virgini Mariae*. This sequence is in the pattern *abbccdd*, all repetitions being literal, i.e., the setting presents no variation-chain. All these compositions are examples of writing *a 4*, which was still rare in Poland. Felstin's historical position as a composer rests upon this fact and on his having assimilated Netherlands influences and brought them to bear upon Polish music. His compositions, however, are marked by rigidity, unresourcefulness, and even technical flaws.[59]

Polish composers active during the early and middle 16th century include a group known to us only by initials. Prominent are N. C.,[60] J. S., and M. H.[61] A piece by the last is so simple in its structure that it would not be surprising if it reflected folk influence.

---

[55] Further on these treatises, *see* ChybT; ChybP, 469f; JachH, 41f; JachMPH, 89ff; ReissK, Pl. VIII.

[56] Cf. ChybP, 471f; JachH, 47f.   [57] Further biographical data in ChybS.

[58] Pr. MMSP II, 23.

[59] Further on his extant compositions, *see* LobS.

[60] Interpreted as "Nicolaus Cracoviensis." Cf. p. 754 *infra*.

[61] Cf. ChybU, 344f; ChybP, 504.

EXAMPLE 169. *Bóg wieczny a wszechmocny*—Song initialed M. H. (after ChybU, 346).

"God eternal and omnipotent, the Lord of the Polish people, deigned to imbue mankind with His most holy, godly might, so that mankind should live for His eternal glory."

Vocal Polyphony of the "Golden Age": Szamotułczyk; Leopolita; Gomółka

The period, considered by many musicologists as the Golden Age of Polish music, was influenced considerably by the foundation of the *Collegium Rorantistarum,* in 1543, at the chapel in Cracow of King Sigismund the Elder (reigned 1506–1548). The *Collegium* consisted of a provost, nine singers, and a cleric. Although it was required that all members be Poles, foreign influence was acknowledged in the dedication of their repertory—which was sacred—"to the noble Italian art." [62] Sigismund Augustus (reigned 1548–1572), successor to Sigismund the Elder, enlisted for his court chapel the service of a brilliant group of musicians, including Bakfark and some major native Polish musicians. The tradition of maintaining the court music at a high level was continued, after the extinction of the Jagiełło dynasty, by King Stephen Báthori (1576–1586) and by Sigismund III (1587–1632), who had Luca Marenzio at his court from 1596 to 1598.

The musicians of Sigismund Augustus included the most significant Polish composers of the century, Szamotułczyk, Lwowczyk, and Gomółka.

The few surviving compositions of Wacław Szamotułczyk (Wacław of Szamotuł, Szamotulinus, Samotulinus—incorrectly, Szamotulski [63]), justify the high esteem in which he was held by his contemporaries.[64] Born probably c. 1520, Szamotułczyk studied first at the Collegium Lubrańskich in Poznań and in 1538 at the University of Cracow. In 1547, he was appointed composer to the King, a position he held until his death in 1572.[65] Szamotułczyk was known outside Poland. Compositions of his may be found in collections of

---

[62] Further on the Rorantists, *see* RybP, 2572; OpieP, 39f; and esp. ChybR.
[63] Cf. ChybB.   [64] Cf. OpieP, 40.   [65] For further biographical data, *see* ChybB.

Montanus and Neuber in Nuremberg (1554 and 1564). Since he was the first to introduce double-choir writing into Poland, it is especially unfortunate that his two-choir Mass has been lost. Other lost works of his include Passions, Offices, and Lamentations.[66] His style may be observed, however, in his two extant motets, *Ego sum pastor bonus*[67] and the impressive *In te Domine speravi,* and some fifteen other sacred pieces, including psalms.[68] In these works, the constant overlapping of phrases and full-fledged imitative style reveal Franco-Netherlandish influence, perhaps that of Gombert or of Clemens non Papa. Conflict of accents is felicitously illustrated in the *In te Domine:*

EXAMPLE 170. Excerpt from *In te Domine speravi*—Szamotułczyk (after WDMP IX, 15; accent signs added).

"Thou hast redeemed me, Lord God of truth."

The sacred songs and psalms, as distinguished from the motets, present two types: one generally in motet style except that it does not contain imitation; the other more folklike in character, with chordal harmonization. In the first group, the *cantus firmus,* for the most part in equal long notes, is in the tenor. In the second, the *cantus prius factus* nearly always appears in the superius and is rhythmically varied. The music of the second type is usually strophic, and the form is songlike, suggesting light pieces by Senfl and his contemporaries.[69]

The compositions of Marcin Lwowczyk (Martin of Lwów), better known by the Latin form of his name, Leopolita (1540–1589), said to have been a pupil of Felstin's,[70] reveal the influence of the Roman and the Franco-Netherlandish schools. He was predisposed to draw upon non-liturgical sacred songs used in congregational singing, reworking them in a contrapuntal-imitative texture which, however, is basically harmonic, in the late 16th-century manner. Of Leopolita's compositions there are extant: three Masses; a motet *a 5, Resurgente,* to be found in a tablature at Breslau;[71] an Introit for Whit-

[66] Cf. ChybP, 505; WDMP IX, pref.   [67] Pr. MMSP II, 14.

[68] Further concerning these pieces, *see* ChybU, 344f.

[69] Further about Szamotułczyk, *see* PolD, 73ff. Other pieces by him pr. OpieP, App. x, xiv, xv; partial facsimile in PolD, 77; CPM, 2.

[70] Cf. PolD, 78; JachMPH, 124ff.

[71] Partial facsimile in JachMPR, 532, also JachMPH, 127; beginning of same work pr. JachMPR, 531.

suntide; two other Introits, *Mihi autem* [72] and *Cibavit eos.*[73] A group of some forty anonymous motets preserved in a tablature in the archives of the Warsaw Musical Society, it has been suggested, may be arrangements of motets by Leopolita that are mentioned in documents, but are lost.[74] Leopolita's Masses furnish the only surviving Polish examples of the time of writing *a 6,*[75] episodes for six voices being found in all three. The *Missa Paschalis*[76] is in binary meter throughout except for fourteen measures in the Gloria. The counterpoint is primarily note-against-note, often forming successions of $\frac{6}{3}$ chords. Imitation is usually at the fifth or the octave, but short passages at other intervals occur. The Mass is based on four Easter plainsong melodies (Ex. 171a) that appear also in a plainsong *Credo Paschale* in the Cracow Gradual of 1740.[77] The composer uses melody 1 either in whole or in part in every section of the Mass. At times the melodies are combined, as in the Gloria, where, after giving a complete statement and partial repetition of melody 1, the superius (as shown in Ex. 171b) continues with melody 3 in counterpoint against melody 1 in the second tenor.

EXAMPLE 171. (*a*) Four Easter melodies (after FeiM, 122; MMSP III, Pref.), (*b*) Extract from *Missa Paschalis—*Leopolita (after MMSP III, 7).

(1) "Christ the Lord has risen; he has won the victory, for he has destroyed bitter death through his own precious death. Alleluia. Kyrie eleison."

(2) "Christ is risen. He is given us as a sign that we too shall arise to reign with the Lord God. Alleluia."

(3) "Lord Christ has now risen from the dead. He has tenderly made joyous his folk. Let us praise God. Alleluia."

(4) "The joyous time has come when the Lord Christ triumphed and rose on the third day."

[72] Facsimile *ibid.*, 535.   [73] Pr. *ibid.*, 532; partial facsimile in PolD, 81.
[74] About the group of motets in the Warsaw tablature, cf. JachMPH, 128f.
[75] In the Lwów archives, notes are to be found about compositions *a 12* of that time; cf. FeiM, 118.
[76] Pr. MMSP III, 1.   [77] Cf. *ibid.*, iv; FeiM, 124.

This third melody, which seems to have been extremely popular at the time (it appears in seven German collections), is similar to the Easter song, *Christ der ist erstanden,* which opens Senfl's motet *a 6* (cf. p. 679). As we have seen, this is not the same as *Christ ist erstanden,* which is Leopolita's melody No. 2. His No. 4 seems to be an old version of the tune that is recorded with the German text, *Also heilig ist der Tag* (cf. p. 706).

The birthplace of Nicholas (Mikołaj) Gomółka (born c. 1539) was probably Cracow, and it is known that he was a pupil of Hans Claus, a member of the Royal Chapel. Later, Gomółka himself was in the employ of the Royal Chapel, but left this position in 1563. His further life is for the most part shrouded in mystery. At the turn of the century he is known to have been in the service of Chancellor Jan Zamojski. The place and year of his death are still unknown.[78]

Gomółka's psalms, *a 4,* set metrical translations of high literary value by the Polish poet, Jan Kochanowski, and are dedicated to Bishop Peter Myszkowski but have a eulogistic Latin introduction by Andreas Trzycielski, leader of

[78] The tombstone at Jazłowiec, reproduced in PolD, 92, and JachH, 68, hitherto supposed to mark the resting place of the composer, is now believed to have been erected over the grave of his son, who was also a musician. Cf. JachMPH, 136.

the dissidents in Poland, similar to the dedication of Goudimel's psalms of 1565. Kochanowski's numbering of the psalms is the Hebrew (= Protestant), not the Catholic. In the original edition of Gomółka's work (Cracow, 1580) all 150 psalms are represented; each of the four parts is printed across two pages in the manner of a score but without the use of bar-lines.[79] Gomółka's own words, in his dedication, "to be performed by plain home-folk," are indicative of the rhythmic simplicity of these psalms. Gomółka's settings display mainly note-against-note writing but are distinguished from those of Goudimel and Gomółka's other contemporaries by liberal use of dissonance. In Psalm XXV, a C-natural is sounded in the descending superius against a C-sharp in the ascending altus.

EXAMPLE 172. Psalm XXV—Gomółka (after facsimile in JachMPH, 139).

(The text is based on the first two verses of the psalm.)

A harmonic diminished seventh appears in Psalm XVI. Other points of interest are unprepared sevenths and augmented sixth chords.[80] Degree-inflection is found in Psalm LV. At the same time, the crudities of parallel fifths and octaves are to be observed in some of these psalms.[81]

Influence of the Roman School; Transition to the Baroque: Zieleński

During the last decades of the century, the influence of the Roman School increased substantially in Poland, and its imprint on Polish church music

[79] See facsimiles of various psalm settings by Gomółka in JachMWP, 547; JachH, 65; JachMPR, 537; JachMPH, 139.

[80] Cf. ReissG, 253f. The author's statement, *ibid.*, 254, that the diminished seventh in Psalm XVI is followed by a melodic augmented second (f-sharp, e-flat) is not supported by his own MS copy of the Gomółka original at the New York Public Library. Reiss has introduced a flat into the passage in question either to prevent a false relation between superius and altus or because a flat appears before an E 7 notes earlier. Similar observations apply to the augmented second between C-sharp and B-flat, alleged *ibid.* in Psalm XXV.

[81] Psalms IV, VI, VII, LXXVII, CL, pr. SowinP, 223, 225, 228, 231 (= OpieP, App., XX), 233, respectively; Psalms XIII, XL, CXLII in OpieP, App., xiii (= CPM, 1), xix, xxi, respectively; Psalm XX in JachMPR, 536.

may be traced until approximately 1750. One of the first composers to reflect this influence was Thomas Szadek (b. 1550), Chaplain of the Rorantists, c. 1580,[82] whose works include a Mass, composed in 1578 and incompletely preserved, based on *Dies est laetitiae,* and another,[83] of 1580, that employs the melody *Pis ne me peult venir,* on which Crecquillon wrote a Mass also. Szadek's work shows talent for melodic line, but his polyphonic technique is unresourceful. Like Christopher Borek, second leader of the Rorantists,[84] Paligonius, Jan Brandt,[85] and others who were to follow, he often wrote in a chordal style.

In the period of transition to the baroque era, Italian models continued to serve Polish composers. Nicholas Zieleński, organist at Gniezno c. 1611,[86] published that year in Venice a volume of *Offertoria* for one to eight voices, this being supplied with an organ score.[87] The collection contains also a Magnificat *a 12* for three choruses.[88] Zieleński's writing reveals especially the influence of Giovanni Gabrieli and other Venetians, and of Viadana.[89] His use of the organ with antiphonal choruses represents the emerging baroque idiom. On the other hand, his *In Monte Oliveti,*[90] from the second part of the same work printed under the special title *Communiones totius anni,* is a skilful contrapuntal composition in true Late Renaissance style.

Instrument Makers; Keyboard Music, including that of the Jan of Lublin and Cracow Tablatures

Poland's activities in the vocal field were matched by her achievements both in the production of instruments and in instrumental writing and performance. The lutemaker, Matthaeus Dobrucki, Martin Groblicz, maker of lutes and viols, and Bartholomaeus Kicher (Kiejcher), who produced wood winds and instruments of other types,[91] were all active in Cracow but famous in Germany as well as in their own country. At the same time, the contemporary instrumental music of western Europe had found its way into Poland, as is attested by two voluminous organ tablatures: that of Jan of Lublin (1537–1548) and the Cracow Tablature (1548). The notation of both is similar to German tablature of the period, except that it contains verti-

---

[82] For biographical data on him, *see* ChybTP, 94ff. See also PolD, 82f.

[83] Pr. MMSP I, 1, as *Missa in melodiam moteti Pisneme.* Further on Szadek, *see* PolD, 82; JachH, 63.

[84] Further about Borek, *see* JachH, 62. [85] For data on Brandt, *see* PolD, 83f.

[86] Further biographical data in DuZ, 95ff.

[87] Facsimile of title page in JachMWP, 548, and PolD, 85; facsimile of 2 pages of the music in JachMPR, 544; partial facsimile of 1 page in JachMPH, 170.

[88] Facsimile of beginning in JachMWP, 550. Further on this piece, *see* SzczepZ.

[89] Cf. ChybU, 348.

[90] Pr. OpieP, App., xxii; MMSP II, 38. For other pieces by him, *see* MMSP I, 30; II, 19, 27; WDMP, XII.

[91] Further about Kicher, *see* TomkoH, 202ff; about the others, LütgG II, 106, 181.

cal lines running from the top to the bottom of each page. The Cracow Tablature [92] contains reductions into tablature of works by Josquin, Tromboncino, Janequin, Verdelot, Gombert, Senfl, and others not known to have lived in Poland; both MSS contain the name of Heinrich Finck (cf. p. 639), who was at the Cracow court from 1492 to 1506.[93] Both tablatures, moreover, contain pieces by composers represented only by initials. N. C. (= Nicolaus Cracoviensis; cf. p. 747), represented in both tablatures, was much predisposed toward pervading imitation and appears to have been an important composer. The issue of his identification with the composer appearing in the Lublin Tablature under the initials N. Ch., which have been interpreted as Nicolaus Chrzanowita, has not yet been settled.[94] In both tablatures is found an *Infunde unctionem* based on a theme used also by Hans Buchner in his *Fundamentbuch*. Each collection includes a title which, by mentioning the pedal, clearly refers to the organ: in the Lublin Tablature, *Preambulum pedale;* in that of Cracow, *Preambulum N.C. pro introductionis peduum applicare* [*sic*]. The Lublin Tablature contains not only music, but several sets of rules amounting virtually to a condensed treatise on composition. Curiously, Jan of Lublin includes, as perfect consonances, the third and tenth and their compounds (he seems not to have recognized imperfect consonances). His tablature is probably the only one of the period (1500–1550) to provide rules for the treatment of imitation. It is interesting that one of the rules formulates as an available procedure the common practice of having the *cantus firmus* enter after the other voices.[95] In the Cracow Tablature, a piece with a *cantus firmus* based on a Polish song, *Przez thwe szwyęte szmarthwywstanije* ("Through Thy holy resurrection"), illustrates this familiar procedure.[96]

Like the Cracow Tablature, that of Jan of Lublin contains as *cantus prius facti* not only plainsong melodies but tunes with Polish titles. As to foreign compositions, there are to be found in the Lublin Tablature transcriptions of vocal works by Costanzo and Sebastiano Festa, Verdelot, Janequin, Sandrin, and Sermisy, as well as pieces originally for keyboard by Cavazzoni. Other such pieces, as distinguished from arrangements, are found in the 21 four-part *preambula*. The writing in these *preambula* is basically note-against-note, ornamented by stereotyped diminution which is incidental except at the close of a piece, where a coloratura-like passage may succeed the cadence proper. A balance between chordal construction and independence of contrapuntal line is maintained throughout, with incidental introduction of skilful double counterpoint. The general style recalls that of Kleber and Kotter.

---

[92] For table of contents, *see* JachP, 207ff; thematic index, with commentary, in JachT.

[93] His name appears as "phynk" in the Lublin Tablature. Cf. ChybP, 482, 484f.

[94] Cf. ChybU, 344; ChybP, 504; JachMPJ, 550; JachMPH, 109. Various compositions and facsimiles of pieces preserved under the initials N. C. pr. in JachMPJ, 544ff.

[95] These rules pr. ChybP, 486ff.

[96] A different piece on the same *cantus firmus* is found in the Lublin Tablature; cf. JachT, 8. Further on the Cracow Tablature, *see* JachP, GleC.

Of thirty-four dances found in the Lublin Tablature, four are clearly of German origin, though, except for *Conradus,* the melody of which recalls one used in two pieces by Isaac,[96a] they seem to have no kindred in contemporary Renaissance collections. The occasional absence of titles makes impossible a clear distinction between pieces of Polish origin and those of German or perhaps Italian origin. None of them is actually labelled "Polish dance." [97] This designation does, however, appear somewhat later associated with a type that quickly assumed importance in Polish instrumental music and was to be found abroad, e.g., in Germany and Sweden. Normally, the Polish dance form seems to have followed the old precedent of combining a fore-dance and an after-dance, although in many sources only the fore-dance appears; it is possible that in these instances the after-dance was improvised, the musician merely adapting the melodic material of the fore-dance to the rhythmic pattern of the after-dance. The fore-dance usually consisted of two or three phrases, each being four or eight measures in length; common rhythmic patterns were: $\frac{2}{4}$ ♫♫, ♪♫, ♫♫, ♪♩ The after-dance was frequently characterized by the pattern, $\frac{3}{4}$ ♩. ♪ ♩, with a melodic quality suggesting a gliding motion rather than the leaping that was typical of after-dances. The Polish dance, designated as such, makes an early appearance in Löffelholtz's *Klavierbuch* (1585; cf. p. 666) and in the collection of Nörmiger (1598; cf. pp. 666f).[98]

Lute Music; Other Instrumental Music

As early as 1544, Hans Newsidler's tablature, *Ein new künstlich Lautten Buch* (cf. p. 668) had presented a piece entitled *Der Polnisch Tantz,*[99] the rhythmic character of which, however, is markedly different from the type, just described, which became established as the Polish dance. There are forty-eight Polish dances in Waissel's tablature books of 1592 (cf. p. 669).[100] In Besard's *Thesaurus* (1603) are to be found eight pieces, six of them *villanellas,* by Albert (Adalbert, Wojciech) Długoraj, lutenist to King Stephen Báthori—a musician who marred his good name by disloyalty to one of his patrons. Two Polish dances for lute by Długoraj occur in a lute tablature of the Stadtbibliothek in Leipzig (1619).[101] Another lutenist, who emerges upon the scene in France but was clearly a Pole, is Jacob Polonais (c. 1545-

---

[96a] I.e., in *Frater Conradus,* pr. DTO XIV¹, 145, and in *Fortuna—Bruder Conrat* (cf. p. 214 supra).

[97] Further on the Lublin Tablature, see ChybJL; ChybP, 476ff, which includes a table of contents and also one complete and several incomplete exx. A selection of exx. pr. WDMP XX; 1 ex. in OpieP, App., lxi.

[98] 1 ex. from the first pr. SmnP, 138; 2 from the second, *ibid.,* 140. Another Polish dance for keyboard pr. HalbK, 23.   [99] Pr. DTO XVIII², 53; SmnP, 137.

[100] Ex. pr. OpieP, App., lxii. Thematic index of all 48 in KosackL, 108f, 115f.

[101] 3 *villanelle* of his from the *Thesaurus* pr. OpieP, App., lxxii (= TapS, 57); lxxiii (= ChilLS, 188, top); lxxiv; ChilLS, 188, bottom; a fantasy pr. ScherG, 154. Further about Długoraj, see PolD, 103; JachMPH, 150ff (where 13 pieces are credited to Długoraj, but the *Thesaurus* is wrongly said to contain 9).

1605); [102] a third, Valentin Greff Bakfark (cf. p. 719), the most romantic and perhaps the most infamous musician of this period, was the highly gifted Transylvanian, who, after living in Poland for eighteen years, was deported as a spy.[103] The fact that he was Długoraj's teacher added to his influence on Polish music. The Italian-born Diomedes Cato received his education in Poland, achieving fame as both lutenist and composer. Among the eight *Choreae polonicae* in the *Thesaurus* of 1603, Besard attributes four to this musician. Several Polish dances, designated with the Polish word, *"tanietz,"* have been copied in by hand, in a copy of Kerle's *Selectae . . . cantiones* to be found in Stockholm; some of these dances are by Cato.[104] The following is an example of a Polish dance for lute from a late 16th-century MS.

EXAMPLE 173. Polish dance—Anon. (from ChilL, 46).

A textless piece *a 4* that may well be intended for instrumental ensemble— at least the three lower lines are rather instrumental in character, though the superius is vocal enough—is found in a Polish MS of 1589, which consists otherwise of anonymous works with Latin texts. This textless piece bears, at the end, the words, *"Finitur Duma."* [105] It is marked throughout by lively rhythm. (See the example on the opposite page.)

The instrumental works of Christoph Demantius (cf. p. 712) include his *Sieben und siebentzig newe auszerlesene liebliche, zierliche, polnischer und teutscher Art Täntze* for four and five parts (1601), *Conviviorum deliciae* (1608), containing among other works *"Fröliche polnische Täntze,"* and *Fasciculus chorodiarum* (1613), consisting of dances *a 4* and *a 5*, with a sec-

---

[102] Cf. OpieJ, which contains a discussion of the possible identification of Jacob Polonais with Jacobus Reys of Augsburg. *See also* JachMPH, 152f. 2 pieces ascribed to "Signor Jacob . . . il Polonese" in Besard's *Novus partus* pr. OpieP, App., lxxv (= ChilLS, 224); 1 ascribed to "Jacques Pollonois" in van den Hove's *Delitiae* pr. *ibid.*, lxxix.

[103] For a study of him in Polish, *see* OpieS.

[104] 2 galliards and a *passamezzo* by him pr. ChilL, 7, 8, 32; the Polish dance ascribed to him in ChilN, 671, is actually one of the anon. exx. in Besard's *Thesaurus*. Further about the above-mentioned lutenists, *see* LauLL, 47ff; JachMPH, 148ff. Other Polish dances for lute, etc. pr. ChilL, 15, 34; BöhT, 62; OpieP, App., lxiii (= JachMPR, 538ff).

[105] Further on this piece, *see* WDMP VIII, preface.—Since this book was first published, a text has been found. See Jozef M. Chomiński and Zofia Lissa, *Music of the Polish Renaissance*, 1955, 41, 197.

EXAMPLE 174. Extracts from *Duma*—Anon. (from WDMP VIII).

tion entitled *Polnische Art Täntze*.[106] The title of the *Venusgarten* (1602) by Valentin Haussmann (cf. p. 672) includes the words: *Darinnen hundert ausserlesene gantz liebliche mehrteils polnische Täntze*. In 1603, this composer published *Rest von polnischen und andern Täntzen*.[107]

The Poles seem to have been particularly predisposed toward the bowed stringed instruments, which presumably often participated in executing ensemble music of the kind just described. Agricola, in his *Musica instrumentalis deudsch* (1528, 1545), mentions *"Polische Geigen"* as a special kind of instrument evidently of the rebec type.[108] Sostrow, burgomaster of Stralsund, mentions the appearance of four *polnische Geiger* in his city in 1555.[109] The special proclivity of the Poles for the bowed stringed-instrument type is further indicated by their having apparently adopted the violin, after its invention, more generally than did their neighbors, and by the fact that the name *"polische Geige"* was transferred from the older instrument to the newer one.[110]

MUSIC IN THE ADRIATIC COASTAL AREAS OF THE SOUTHERN SLAVS *
BY DRAGAN PLAMENAC

Music in old Dalmatia occupied an honorable position beside the other arts. It is true that research in this field is of very recent date; yet, although it

[106] Polish dances from the second pr. BöhT, 100, 101; 2 from the *Fasciculus* pr. SmnP, 141, and KadeC, 542; *see* KadeC, 484ff, for further comment on Demantius' Polish dances.
[107] Selections from both pr. DDT XVI, 123–128 and 129–137, resp.; another ex. from latter pr. WolfME, 123. Full titles, dedications, etc. *ibid.*, viii. Further on the Polish dance, *see* NorT.
[108] Cf. PubAPTM XX, 189, 210.   [109] Cf. KretM, 127.   [110] Cf. LütgG I, 314f.

* Much of this section is condensed from PlamD and is printed here, with some additions, by permission of the American Musicological Society.

is not possible to give a comprehensive exposition of the development at this juncture, we can discern its general outline, thanks to the discovery of some isolated artistic facts.

Slavic Folk Song and Foreign-Influenced Art Music

During the Renaissance, as subsequently, there existed in Dalmatia two parallel lines of musical evolution, two separated musical worlds, produced by political and social conditions: the traditional and ancient folk music of the Slavic population and the art music in the towns and ports open to influences from across the Adriatic. The oldest musical notation of Dalmatian folk songs in the Serbo-Croatian language goes as far back as the 16th century, when some of them appear in the idyllic epic poem *Ribanje i ribarsko prigovaranje* ("The Fishing Trip") by Petar Hektorović of Hvar. As to secular music of urban type, it cannot be doubted that in all centers of feudal Venetian Dalmatia it was under the strong influence of Italian music. There was such a vogue for amorous songs accompanied on the lute that the Dalmatian moralists, headed by Marko Marulić, and the archbishops of Split in their statutes, were obliged during the 15th and 16th centuries to take action against ecclesiastics who, by night, changed clothes and wandered through the dark streets singing love songs, accompanying themselves on the lute or some other instrument.[1] At this point, it is fitting to mention the music that is suggested to us by the most ancient examples of the literary humanism of Dubrovnik (= Ragusa), beginning with the end of the 15th century: the lyric poetry of Šiško Menčetić, Džore Držić, and their comrades. This poetry can hardly be conceived without a musical complement. Like the Italian *strambotti* and other forms of Italian lyric poetry of the time, these pieces were often sung to the accompaniment of the lute, which is frequently invoked and apostrophized in the text. It is unfortunate that we do not possess even the smallest fragment of the music that accompanied the verses of these old Ragusan poets. To form an idea of what this music might have been, we are obliged to refer to analogous Italian works of the period.

Instrumental Music

The archives provide some items of information regarding 15th-century instrumental music in Dubrovnik.[2] Only in 1425 did the authorities do away with the old custom whereby, on the eve of the feast of St. Blaise, the patron of the city, men and women danced in the cathedral, accompanied by *fistulatores* (pipers). The records from 1379 to 1456 show that the city engaged (besides natives) Greeks, Germans, Italians, and Albanians to play

[1] Cf. *Stari pisci hrvatski* I, 118; Farlati, *Illyrici sacri Tomus III* (Venice, 1765), 444.
[2] Cf. JirS, 58f.

bagpipes, trumpets, etc. The 16th-century poet Mavro Vetranović, in a carnival song, still mentions the *"trumbetari"* and *"pifari"* from *"Alamannia."* Among the native instrumentalists serving the city there were Serbs, like the *"trumbeta"* Dragan from Prizren, and Croats from Senj or Zagreb, like the *tubicen* Nicolaus de Zagabria (1411–1414), among others. Instrumentalists in the service of princely courts are frequently mentioned; for example, the pipers, bagpipers, drummers, and especially lute-players (from 1450 on) of the King of Bosnia, a Southern-Slav province. It may well be that one of the musicians belonging to that group was a man who holds a modest but well-defined place in the development of Italian secular music of the early 16th century. We refer to Franciscus Bossinensis (i.e., "from Bosnia") whose two books of *frottole* by Cara, Tromboncino, and others, transcribed for one voice with lute and supplied with short preludes for the lute, called *recercari*, were published by Petrucci in 1509 and 1511.[3]

Social Background of Musical Activity

If the Italian 16th-century madrigal produced a lively repercussion in all countries of the European west and north and if Italian music after the invention of monody and opera reinforced its supremacy in the cultural centers of Europe, it can hardly be expected that Dalmatia, geographically and politically situated as she was, could escape the dominant Italian influence. The Slavic character of the country was not yet able to find expression in an artistic musical language of its own. In literature, thanks above all to the national tongue, it was easier to move toward emancipation from the Italian pattern than in the visual arts and in music.

Living conditions were very precarious for musicians in Dalmatia. Here there were no opulent patrons, such as existed in Italy; besides, the Turks made frequent incursions and the towns on the coast were constantly threatened. Consequently, there were only two ways for a musician to organize his life in the modest and provincial frame of the country: either to devote himself to his art in the calm of a monastery or else to find employment as choir director or organist at one of the cathedrals in the episcopal centers. The old Dalmatian organists and choir directors may be classified into two groups: those of Dalmatian birth and origin, and those who had migrated from abroad, principally from Italy. That country, at the time, had a great abundance of musicians of somewhat inferior but still very respectable talent who, after having finished their studies, looked about for employment; on the other hand, the Dalmatian chapters could find capable organists and choir directors among these Italian musicians more easily than among Dalmatian-born musicians. The musicians coming from Italy brought with them the artistic customs and musical technique of their own land. Their

---

[3] *Tenori e Contrabassi intabulati.* . . . Cf. pp. 163, 522, *supra.*

activity is significant from our point of view as it proves that the Dalmatian milieu was sufficiently developed to retain, occasionally, Italian musicians of some importance, including a number who passed their whole life there, like Tomaso Cecchini of Verona, in the early 17th century. It is unlikely that these artists would have been willing to pass their lives in a foreign country if it had been musically altogether uncultured. Moreover, we find interesting evidence concerning the position held by music in the intellectual and artistic life at least of Split (Spalato), at the beginning of the 17th century, in the dedication of Cecchini's printed Opus 7; there Split is mentioned as a city in which *"quest'Arte liberalissima, con applauso di mille orecchi, faccia prova di se stessa."* The fact that music was not neglected in other Dalmatian cities either is illustrated by the testimony we find in the diary, for the year 1575, of the Venetian ambassador, Jacopo Sorranzo. The author relates that he heard at Dubrovnik *"molti ottimi musici,"* thus showing that the cultivation of instrumental music in that city continued unabated.[4]

Madrigals

As to vocal polyphony, we possess documents that prove the Italian 16th-century madrigal to have been cultivated in the Dalmatian towns by the upper classes. We might here point to four madrigals *a 4* composed by Andrea Patricio, of the island of Cres (Cherso), which survive in a contemporary collection by Antonino Barges, *Il primo libro de villote,* Gardano, 1550.[5] Patricio belonged to a noble family, whose real name was Petris and whose descendants are still living today. He was certainly closely related to his contemporary, Francesco Patricio, also of Cres, the well known neo-Platonic philosopher, who occupied himself also with ancient Greek music.

Another work that is perhaps of still greater importance in establishing the cultivation of madrigal singing in Dalmatia during the 16th century is a collection of madrigals *a 4* and *a 5,* composed by Giulio Schiavetto, a musician attached to the service of Girolamo Savorgnano, Bishop of Šibenik from 1557 to 1573. This work, published in 1563 by Scotto in Venice, is dedicated to the Bishop; but we cannot form an adequate idea of it, the sole surviving copy, which belongs to the Accademia Filarmonica in Verona, being defective.

Sacred Polyphony

The center of gravity of musical activity in old Dalmatia must, however, be looked for first of all in the sphere of sacred music. This is quite natural, since, in default of princely courts and circles of wealthy amateurs, the development of secular music, which their opulence favored in 16th- and 17th-century Italy, could spread to the opposite shore of the Adriatic only in

---

[4] Cf. J. Sorranzo, *Diario* (Matković, ed.), published by the Yugoslav Academy, *Rad 124,* 20 (Zagreb, 1895). [5] One of these pieces, *Son quest'i bei crin d'oro,* pr. PlamD, 28.

very attenuated form. The principal patron of music in Dalmatia at this time is the Church, and the musical centers are the cathedrals in the episcopal seats, particularly those at Šibenik, Split, and Hvar. This flowering of sacred music in Dalmatia is reflected clearly in the works of Schiavetto, Lukačić, and Cecchini. Besides the incomplete copy of Schiavetto's madrigal collection of 1563, a collection of motets of his survives, dating from 1564, likewise dedicated to Bishop Savorgnano.[6] This proves that vocal polyphony of elevated style played a conspicuous role in Dalmatian churches in the mid-16th century, long before elements of monody (in the 17th-century meaning) had been introduced into religious music. Schiavetto (or Schiavetti) seems to have belonged to a family of old Šibenik extraction. His motets are frequently built over fixed *cantus firmi* which, in two inner parts, are elaborated in canon, entirely in the tradition of the old Netherlands masters. This late medieval ideal of musical structure, which composers of the Palestrinian period had taken over from their Franco-Netherlandish predecessors, appears in full clearness in Schiavetto's powerful six-part motet, *Pater noster*.[7] This piece features the *cantus firmus,* which is a slightly paraphrased version of the Gregorian melody for the *Pater noster,*[8] in canon in tenors I and II. It is remarkable for its severe and logical construction and its steady building up to a climax, reached only in the final chord. Comparison of Schiavetto's composition with Willaert's older setting *a 4* of the same melody, first published by Attaingnant in 1534, is instructive, as the latter piece was very likely known to the Dalmatian composer. Another example of the traditional aspect of Schiavetto's art is furnished by his five-part motet, *Asperges me, Domine,* in which the Gregorian *cantus firmus,*[9] in the tenor and bass I, is elaborated in what is in effect a mensuration canon at the fifth. The two parts, while beginning together, sing their initial series of semibreves, the one in imperfect, the other in perfect note-values. As a result, of course, bass I moves more slowly than the tenor. Thus, a distance is established between the two parts, preparing the way for what, in most of the rest of the piece, is a normal canon.

EXAMPLE 175. Opening of *Asperges me*—Schiavetto (*Motetti a 5 voci et a 6 voci,* Scotto, 1564; transcr. by D. Plamenac).

[6] Copy formerly in the Berlin State Library.
[7] Pr. PlamD, 35.
[8] Pr. MissaleR, 346.   [9] Cf. Liber, 11.

The new monodic style of c. 1600 was soon introduced into Dalmatia. Of course, the larger forms that the new conception prompted, primarily the opera, had to be neglected because of general and economic reasons. But in Dalmatian sacred music the new principles were introduced only a few years after the publication of Viadana's *Concerti ecclesiastici;* the new manner is applied in Dalmatia particularly in the works of Ivan Lukačić (d. 1648), and Tomaso Cecchini (d. 1644). The works of these men, who passed their lives near each other, one at Split and the other at Hvar, represent the climax of musical activity in Dalmatia during the early 17th century. These compositions prove that Dalmatian music of the time followed step by step the evolution of music in the west. This is the more remarkable, as one might suppose that the music of 17th-century "bourgeois" Dalmatia—the artistic expression of a peripheral civilization—would have lagged in introducing new esthetic principles. But these works, especially the motets of Lukačić,[10] may be placed on a level with respectable productions of contemporary composers in western Europe.

[10] A selection of 11 of them pr. LukO; about Cecchini, *see* PlamC.

Chapter 15

ENGLAND: Music from c. 1450 to c. 1535, including the Carols and the Works of Fayrfax and Taverner; the Composers of Sacred Music with Latin Text from c. 1535 to c. 1635, including Tallis, Byrd, and Philips; Sacred Music with English Text from c. 1535 to c. 1635, including the *Booke of Common Praier noted,* the Early Psalters, and the Anthems of Tomkins and Gibbons

The Conservatism of English Music after Dunstable

As the 1400's reached midpoint, England was one of the leading musical nations, owing largely to insular traits best exemplified in the music of Dunstable, who himself introduced them to the continent.[1] Somewhat later, composers of English birth—e.g., Morton—were active in the music-making of the Burgundian court (cf. pp. 98f). However, English composers on the continent represented but one aspect of 15th-century English music. Their works survive chiefly in continental MSS, while few of their names appear in the largest early 15th-century source of native English music, the Old Hall MS.[2] Moreover, while a man like Morton was to become rather French in outlook, the composers not known to have left England seem to have been little affected by musical developments across the Channel. Instead of following the "modern" styles of Ockeghem or Busnois, the English after the mid-century tended increasingly toward an insular conservatism, remaining less touched than continental musicians by the forces that were preparing for the appearance of a composer of the stature of Josquin. That this situation was recognized in the 15th century itself is evidenced by the writings of Tinctoris, who regarded Dunstable, Dufay, and Binchois as the teachers of the Ockeghem generation and who regretted that, while much that was new was being discovered, the English "continue to use one and the same style of composition, which shows a wretched poverty of invention."[3] The gradual decline of the prestige of English music abroad is borne out by the contents of the Trent Codices:

[1] Cf. ReMMA, 424. (For a discussion of Dunstable, *see ibid.,* 412ff; a complete ed. of his works by Dr. Bukofzer, constituting Vol. VIII of *Musica Britannica,* has been published as this book goes to press.)

[2] Cf. *ibid.,* 410f; *see* esp. BukMR, 34ff.   [3] CouS IV, 154 (transl., StrunkR, 195).

English music is well represented in the earlier MSS (those from c. 1420–1440), while less and less appears for the middle decades of the century, and for the period c. 1460–1480 no English works seem to be included at all. The conclusions suggested by this evidence have often been questioned. But investigation has not yet revealed a "missing link" that will provide really great music for the period between Dunstable and Fayrfax. English music isolated itself from the trends of late 15th-century Europe, developing an estimable—sometimes a highly estimable—but conservative school of composers. The persistence of conservatism in Late Renaissance English music, though with certain notable exceptions, will necessitate our proceeding further chronologically in England than on the continent to cover comparable developments. Fortunately, this persistence did not in the least prevent the production—mainly, to be sure, by the exceptional composers—of music that provides the Late Renaissance with some of its crowning glories.

MS Egerton 3307 and Music c. 1450; the Carols

Our knowledge of English music—as compared, for example, with that of Franco-Netherlandish music—is fairly sketchy from approximately 1450 to the closing years of the century, when the first sources of Tudor music begin to appear. However, Egerton 3307,[4] probably dating from c. 1450 or a little earlier, is one of the sources affording some idea of developments at about this time. Copied out at Meaux Abbey, Yorkshire,[4a] especially known for interest in the arts, the MS contains sixteen hymns and versicles, a Mass, two settings of the Passions, twelve carols, twenty-two Latin *cantilenae,* and a drinking song. The last of these, a setting of the goliard poem, "O potores exquisiti," [5] employs the isorhythmic technique, apparently in a spirit of travesty. Of great interest historically are the two Passions—the earliest polyphonic settings known. The *Passio domini . . . secundum Mattheum* is imperfect at the end, the MS having lost several leaves; the *Passio Domini . . . secundum Lucam* survives complete.[6] Both are set *a 3.* Neither the text nor the music for Christ and the Evangelist is included in the setting, since these portions were sung in chant, in alternation with the polyphonic utterances of the words of other individuals and of the *turba.* The St. Luke Passion is in triple measure throughout, the voices moving almost note-against-note in a style recalling the conductus, though the upper voice is slightly florid. The setting consists of small sections, all beginning in substantially the same way and giving the impression—whatever new motifs may be introduced in the course of a section—that the composer has applied polyphonic

---

[4] Described in SchofN, 525; BukMR, 113ff.
[4a] About the place of origin, *see* BukMR, 114; MusB IV, 125. About the date, *see* BukMR, 114; G. S. McPeek in JAMS III (1950), 156f.
[5] Facsimile in BukMR, opp. p. 129.   [6] Pr. SchofN, 43 (transcr Bukofzer).

treatment to a reiterated recitation formula, original with himself or derived from an unidentified plainsong.

The Mass of Egerton 3307 consists of a Kyrie (imperfect in the MS), a Sanctus, Benedictus, and Agnus Dei.[7] The presenting of this Ordinary as a unit differs from the Old Hall procedure of grouping together pieces having the same liturgical function, and a polyphonic setting of the Kyrie is unusual for English music even as late as the early Tudor period.[8] The Egerton Mass, omitting the Gloria and Credo, is the earliest known English *Missa brevis*. Identified plainsongs paraphrased in it show that it belongs to a feria in Holy Week. The Mass is set *a 3* and *a 4,* the fourth voice entering either above or below the bass as if to give an occasional fullness to the "harmony," then dropping out.

With the carols of Egerton 3307, we approach the popular realm of English music, although such pieces could be inserted in the liturgy.[9] In order of age, the group of carols in this MS is probably third among the repertories preserved in the four large early sources of English polyphonic carols, the examples in MSS Cambridge, Trinity O.3.58 and Oxford, Selden B 26 [9a] being apparently older, those in Brit. Mus. Add. 5665 (the Ritson MS) being later.[10] Pieces of the type in question are peculiar to England. Nevertheless, the English did not confine the texts of the carols to their own language. Included in the Egerton MS, for example, are carols with completely English texts, with English stanzas and Latin burden, with macaronic texts of English, Latin, and French, and with entirely Latin texts, pieces of the last type being usually called *cantilenae*. In his definitive work on English carol texts,[11] R. L. Greene defines the carol before 1550 as "a song on any subject,[12] composed of uniform stanzas and provided with a burden," [13] emphasizing that "the burden makes and marks the carol." [14] To the extent that the burden is meant to be sung after each stanza, it is a refrain. Sometimes, however, a refrain has already appeared at the end of the stanzas, as an integral part of them. The burden, on the other hand, is "a self-contained

---

[7] Pr. *ibid.,* 39.

[8] The custom of omitting the Kyrie from polyphonic settings of the Ordinary is traceable to the existence of many troped Kyries in the Sarum usage. Since these were suitable only for certain days, to set them polyphonically would limit the use of the whole Mass; hence a plainsong Kyrie was usually combined with a polyphonic setting of the rest of the Ordinary. *See* CollL I, 56f; StevT, 171.

[9] Cf. MllrC; BukMR, 148.   [9a] MSS mentioned in ReMMA.

[10] Cf. BukMR, 165. Complete exx. (from Egerton) pr. *ibid.,* 161, and in Fayrfax Ser., No. 14 (separate publication by Stainer & Bell, ed. by Dom A. Hughes) and (from Ritson) in SmM, 21, 22, 24; MllrC, 62 (cf. BukFR, 32); OH II, 340. The Ritson MS has been reproduced photographically in MLAC; copies are in the Library of Congress and the New York Public Library. (Since the foregoing was written, MusB IV, containing all extant English Carols of c. 1400–1500, has appeared.)

[11] GreC.

[12] Not until after c. 1550 did the carol become the form par excellence for Christmas songs: cf. p. 585 about the *villancico*.

[13] GreC, xxiii.   [14] *Ibid.,* cxxxiii.

formal and metrical unit." For ease of reference, therefore, it is better to limit the term "refrain" to the material recurring at stanza-closes. The term "chorus" sometimes appears in the MSS, applied to second settings of the burden "(and certain parts of the stanza also)." Apparently, if nothing was indicated to the contrary, a polyphonic carol was to be sung by a group of soloists. Consequently, if a second setting was provided with the indication "chorus," the first setting, sung by a group of soloists, was presumably followed by the second setting, sung by a choral group.[15]

To differentiate the carol from the ballad, the other English literary-musical form employing a refrain, Greene points out, among other things, the dependence of the popular ballad on oral tradition for its transmission and the essentially narrative character of its texts. Both ballad and carol derive ultimately from the dance, as may be seen in their alternation of stanza and burden. However, about 1400 the carol ceased to be danced, at least in cultivated society, and became a simple polyphonic form. The ballad, however, remained a popular form, essentially monophonic, though undoubtedly at times associated with improvised instrumental accompaniment.[16]

The popular nature of the carol (popular "by destination" rather than "by origin") [17] is suggested by several facts. The basic form of the carol (though it is more a type than a form)—ABcdeb (or a)AB—is related to other "popular" forms found on the continent at the same time: the *lauda, ballata, villancico,* forms derived ultimately from medieval dance, from solo-chorus performance,[18] and in the Renaissance associated with the social life of court and town and with religious groups. The carol structure is intimately related also to the processional hymn with its *repetenda* (cf. p. 336). It is significant that the Franciscans, who had utilized the primitive *lauda* in order to further their essentially folklike religious ideas, were among the best-known English authors of 15th- and 16th-century carol texts.[18a] These religious men made deliberate use of the popular carol to spread their teachings, and this use may in turn have shaped and developed the carol itself (especially in regard to text): five of every six surviving carol texts are of a religious or moralistic character and many carol texts incorporate fragments of religious verse (both liturgical and non-liturgical), often using the original melody, in an ornamented form, in one of the parts.

The carol before 1480 is set in triple measure, *a 2* or (less expertly) *a 3,* the

---

[15] "Burden" and "chorus" are therefore not synonymous. The former has to do with structure, the latter with method of performance. The above discussion follows BukMR, 148ff, from which the quoted passages are taken.

[16] In Robert Laneham's letter describing part of Queen Elizabeth's entertainment at Kenilworth Castle in 1575, we find a lengthy description of an "auncient Menstrell" with "hiz harp . . . dependaunt before him," who, "after a littl warbling on hiz harp for a prelude, came foorth with a sollum song," a ballad of King Arthur, *As it befell vpon a Penticost day.* See *Robert Laneham's Letter,* F. J. Furnivall, ed., 1907, 36ff.

[17] GreC, xciii.   [18] Cf. SachsW, 269ff.   [18a] Cf. GreC, cxxiff.

parts often moving in parallel thirds or sixths, recalling the earlier gymels. Either superius or tenor may be the leading voice or the parts may be of equal importance. After 1480 there is a tendency to add variety to the musical texture of the carol, and, in the early 16th-century Eton MS, carols with smooth-flowing polyphony in duple measure and with pairing of the voices show the influence of the Tudor motet style. About 1515, carols written in imitative counterpoint appear in the works of Richard Pygott [18b] and others, a style that leads directly to the carol motets of Byrd.

Like other forms of popular art, the carol is found current in higher social levels. Court records give us an occasional glimpse of court entertainments, such as that on Twelfth Night, 1488, when "at the Table in the Medell of the Hall sat the Deane and thoos of the kings Chapell, whiche incontynently after the Kings furst Course sange a Carall." [19] Under the Tudor monarchs such holidays were to be the occasion for dramatic entertainments by the Chapel choir.

The Masters of the Children; the Secular Part-Songs, including those of Cornysh and Henry VIII

There is mention of the Chapel Royal as early as 1135 in the *Red Book of the Exchequer,* though the first reference to choristers comes during the reign of Henry V. The chapel post of Master of the Children was created by Henry VI and, in 1444, John Plummer—presumably the Polumier by whom there are some motets in Modena, Bibl. Estense, a.X.I, 11—became the first Master appointed by royal patent. A commission was given him "to take throughout England such and so many boys as he or his deputies shall see to be fit and able to serve God and the King in the said Chapel Royal." [20] (John Pyamour, represented by a motet in the same Modena MS, who in 1420 had been commissioned to impress boys for the Chapel Royal, had, for all practical purposes, been a Master of the Children more than twenty years earlier.[21]) Plummer was succeeded, 1455 to 1478, by Henry Abyngdon (born c. 1418; died 1497),[22] who was the earliest to receive the Mus. Bac. from Cambridge (1463). (*See* further, p. 850.) There followed in succession Gilbert Banastre, 1478–1486; Laurence Squire, 1486–1493; William Newark, 1493–1509, who, during the

[18b] An ex. pr. Fayrfax Ser., No. 13 (ed., with misleading comment, by C. F. Simkins).

[19] *Joannis Lelandi . . . Collectanea,* ed. 1770, IV, 237, from British Museum, Cotton MS Julius B. xii, f. 43b. Quoted in SchofN, 523.

[20] Cf. ArkC; FloodCR; RimbC; for later exx. of such warrants, *see* C. C. Stopes, *William Hunnis and the Revels of the Chapel Royal* (1910), 296; Malone Society *Collections,* Vol. I, parts IV & V (1911), 359ff.

[21] Cf. FloodCR, 88.

[22] Cf. PulB, 4ff. Abyngdon's tenure is there (and elsewhere) said to have begun in 1465; but *see* FloodR, 230. For further biographical data on composers mentioned in this section, *see* PulB; FloodE; FloodC.

last three years of his tenure, had the additional duty of superintending and devising musical entertainments for Christmas festivities at court; and William Cornysh, 1509–1523, composer, poet, and writer of such "disguisings" as *The Garden of Esperance,* presented in 1517 and described in Hall's *Chronicle.*[23] With the court's growing taste for plays and pageants, the window toward the continent again opened, as may be seen in the secular songs (including secular carols) of the period from c. 1480 to 1520 that have been preserved in five sources.[24] These are Add. MS 5465, of c. 1503—the Fairfax Book, in which there are several works by the fine composer Robert Fayrfax (cf. pp. 774ff), but which derives its name from one of its former owners, whose family seems to have had no connection with that of the composer—,[25] Add. MS 5665 (Ritson),[26] Add. MS 31922,[27] Royal Appendix 58 (into which keyboard and lute pieces were copied some years later than the songs [28]), and a printed collection dating from 1530 (*In this boke ar cōteynyd xx sōges, ix of iiii ptes and xi of thre ptes*), one of the earliest examples of music printing in England, which was formerly considered to be a product of the press of Wynken de Worde.[29] During the period from Abyngdon to Newark, the style of the English part-song, or chanson—for such, despite linguistic confusion, it surely is—seems much like that of Ockeghem. This may be seen, for example, in the long melismatic cadences of Sheryngham's *My woful hart in paynful weryness* [30] and Edmond Turges' lovely *Alas! it*

---

[23] HallC, 585f.   [24] Cf. VoE.

[25] Of its 49 compositions (listed in BM I, 131f, and BM II, 124f), exx. by Newark are pr. BuH II, 541; SmC, 50 (anon. in BM II), 62 (= PeaM, No. 4); Fayrfax Ser., No. 8 (= PeaC, Pt. II, 19); by Cornysh: HawkH III, 3 (portion in RimbA, No. XII), 9 (= PeaC, Pt. II, 1); by Fayrfax: SmC, 4, 42 (= PeaC, Pt. II, 23), 46, 48, 53 (anon. in BM II); BuH II, 546; by Turges: SmC, 26, 31 (= PeaM, No. 3); BuH II, 548; by Sheryngham: SmC, 34; BuH II, 544; by Browne: PeaC, Pt. II, 5; by Philips: SmC, 14 (= PeaC, Pt. II, 27 [portion in RimbA, No. XI]); anon.: SmC, 8 (= PeaC, Pt. II, 15), 39 (portion in RimbA, No. X, with unjustified attribution to Fayrfax; see also fn. 32), 58; PeaM, No. 5. These transcrs. vary in dependability. Smith's orig. MS for SmC, including several songs not printed, is in the New York Public Library, Drexel 4030. Several texts pr. RimbS. (A complete modern ed. of the Fairfax MS will be included in *Early Tudor Songbooks,* in course of preparation by John Stevens. Further on the MS, *see* HughIF, 85f, 91.)

[26] An anon. secular ex. pr. PeaM, No. 2. *See also* fns. 10, 35.

[27] 29 pieces by Henry VIII are pr. HenryS (for duplications, see fns. 35, 36; Chap. 16, fn. 257a; others in PeaC, Pt. II, 31; NaySM, 64). For other exx. of English works in the MS, see 1 anon. piece in NaySM, 59; 1 piece by Cooper in HAM, 90; and 5 by Cornysh in ChappP I, 36 (= NaySM, 63), 40; Fayrfax Ser., Nos. 3 (= OH II, 351; HAM 90) and 4; and our Ex. 176 (= NaySM, 25); see also fns. 18b, 31e, 33. Further on this MS, see ChappS. (A complete modern ed. of the MS will be included in *Early Tudor Songbooks;* cf. fn. 25.)

[28] Cf. WardD, 112. A monophonic song from the MS is pr. ChappP I, 37; 5 more are pr. PeaC, Pt. I (with modern accompaniments added!); the first of the 5 is a version of the piece *a 3* in Add. 31922, pr. Fayrfax Ser., No. 4.

[29] It is unfortunate that only the bassus part survives. Composers represented include Cornysh, Pygott, Ashwell, Taverner, Gwynneth, Fayrfax, Cowper (= Cooper), Jones. Facsimiles of the bassus part may be seen in SteeleE, Fig. 6; E. B. Reed, *Christmas Carols Printed in the 16th Century,* 1932, 4ff.

[30] Pr. BuH II, 544.

is I that wote nott what to say [31] and in the absence of imitation from the latter piece. Stylistically this music belongs to the Early Renaissance.

In the following period, in which Henry VIII himself figured as an active composer, the influence, on the one hand, of popular music (including the carol and the ballad) and that, on the other hand, of Italian and French music, produced a different style. Pieces of popular music, or at least of music in the popular vein, undoubtedly included the "freemen's songs." The origin of their name has never been satisfactorily explained: it may go back to an Anglo-Saxon word, "fréoman," or it may be a corruption of "three men" (see below). In *The Lyffe of Sir Peter Carewe,* such songs are mentioned in connection with Henry VIII.

For the Kynge hime self beinge miche delited to synge, and Sir Peter Carewe havinge a pleasaunte voyce, the Kynge woulde very often use hyme to synge with hime certeyne songes they called *fremen* songs, as namely, "By the bancke as I lay," and "As I walked the wode so wylde," &c.[31a]

The fact that two singers are here specified would seem inconsistent with a derivation from "three men" unless a third part was played on an instrument. Michael Drayton, in his "Legend of Thomas Cromwell" (printed in 1609) mentions the introduction of "Freemen's Catches" into Italy on the occasion of a presentation before the pope; but John Foxe, in describing the same event in his "Actes and Monuments" (first printed in 1554) refers to the singing of "a three-man's song (as we call it) in the English tongue, and all after the English fashion." [31b] In 1609, Ravenscroft printed in *Deuteromelia* (cf. pp. 833f) pieces entitled *K.H. [King Henry's] Mirth, or Freeman's Songs* and, in spite of the print's late date, this material may be authentic and may, in part, even date from as far back as the reign of Henry VII. *Hey, Robyn, Joly Robyn,* from Add. MS 31922, illustrates the merging of popular elements with artistic ones not only in its music, by Cornysh, but also in its text, by Sir Thomas Wyatt. So far as the words are concerned, the refrain seems to be taken from a popular song, but the stanzas proper, which present a dialogue, appear to be Wyatt's own. In the composition, a round *a 2,* sung by the lower voices to refrain text, forms a *pes* over which two different stanza-melodies are sung alternately between renditions of a refrain melody. Part of the song is quoted in "Twelfth Night." In Act IV, scene 2, the clown sings "Hey Robin, jolly Robin, Tell me how thy lady does." (These words vary in some respects from those that appear with Cornysh's music in Add. MS 31922, but agree with those in Add. MS 17492, a literary source.) Probably the melody that Shakespeare wished the clown to sing is one of those that set the words in Cornysh's piece.

[31] Pr. *ibid.,* 548.   [31a] *Archaeologia,* XXVIII (1840), 113.   [31b] Cf. ChappP I, 52.

EXAMPLE 176. *Hey, Robyn, Joly Robyn*—Cornysh (transcr. from a facsimile of 2 pages of Add. MS 31922 in *The Poems of Sir
Thomas Wiatt*, ed. by A. K. Foxwell, 2 vols., 1913, but with text
chiefly from Add. MS 17492).

A complete performance of the piece would follow this plan (read from the bottom
line; the figures after the d's and e's indicate the stanza numbers; for the complete
text, *see* Foxwell): [31c]

Singer 3: – – C d[1] C e[2] C d[3] C e[4] C d[5] C e[6] C
Singer 2: – A B A B A B A B A B A B A B
Singer 1: A B A B A B A B A B A B A B A

This is one of no less than twelve pieces in Add. MS 31922 that contain rounds,
some of the others being by Henry VIII,[31d] by far the most liberally represented composer in the MS, Thomas Fardyng, who has three examples, and
Robert Cooper, who took his Mus. Doc. at Cambridge in 1502.[31e] Sometimes
in the songs by Henry and his contemporaries we approach the kind of chanson

[31c] The modern ed. in NaySM, 25, gives the piece with partial text from Add. MS 31922.
StR, 33f, disagrees with the 3-part resolution given there, claiming that the piece is *a 4*, with
the music of our phrases d and C (sung simultaneously) alternating with that of e and C (also
sung simultaneously) over the round in the lower voices. However, the very defects to which
StR directs attention—e.g., the consecutive unisons—, as well as at least one more example of
inept writing, disappear in the 3-part interpretation which, moreover, is consistent with the
layout in the MS, as well as the dialogue character of the poem (*see* the division of the lines
between the *Plaintif* and *Response* in Foxwell).
[31d] His round is pr. HenryS, 25.
[31e] StR is a study of the rounds in this MS. See *ibid.*, 36, regarding the defective eds. of 1
round each by Cooper and Fardyng in PeaC, Pt. I, 3, 6. (A Gloria by Cooper, ed. by H. B. Collins,
is pr. separately by J. & W. Chester, Ltd.) Further on the early Tudor court songs and carols,
see StC.

first printed by Attaingnant in 1528. This is particularly true, for example, in such part-songs as the anonymous *Who shall have my fayre lady*,[32] Cornysh's *Trolly lolly lolly lo* [33] and *Hoyda, hoyda, joly rutterkyn*,[34] or Henry's well-known *Pastyme with good companye*.[35] The texture is strongly homophonic with a dance-like rhythm and emphasis on the discant melody; in *Pastyme*, the music for lines 1–2 recurs for lines 3–4, while in Henry's *Helas, madame*,[36] the last line is repeated to a variation of the same music. (In *Gentil prince*, however, ascribed to Henry in Add. MS 31922, he turns to earlier days: actually, only the altus can be by him, since the other three parts are the anonymous piece of this title that had been printed in the *Odhecaton* and therefore date back too far to be his.[36a])

Foreign Musicians at Court; the Native Waits in the Towns

An explanation of the change to a more modern style may be found in the chronicles and records of the time. Hall writes of events in 1513: "On the daie of the Epiphanie at night, the kyng with a. xi. other were disguised, after the maner of Italie, called a maske, a thyng not seen afore in Englande. . . ." [37] At the same time, royal account books begin to list many foreign musicians who were engaged to play at court. There are numerous references to Philip van Wilder, lutenist, composer, and keeper of the instruments to Henry VIII; [38] Ambrose Lupo ("Lupus Italus"), "viall" player; Domynyk and Andryan, trumpeters; Guillam Troche and Piero Guye, flutists; Hans Aseneste, violist; Marc Antony, Gasper, Batist, "Musicians"; Benedictus de Opitiis (cf. pp. 265f; traceable in England, 1516–1518) and Dionisio Memo (Memmo), organists to the king.[39] Such an influx of continental musicians, and we have by no means exhausted the list, certainly affected musical composition in England. Undoubtedly many European musicians came to England for religious reasons. But one must also take into account the musical activities of Henry VIII, instrumentalist and composer of Masses, motets, and part-songs. The day-book of Sagudino, secretary of

[32] Pr. *Oxford Choral Songs from the Old Masters*, No. 1456, P. Warlock, ed., 1929; SmC, 39. In the song-book of 1530 (cf. p. 768), a song with this title is attributed to Jones.
[33] Pr. *Oxford Choral Songs from the Old Masters*, No. 1432, P. Warlock, ed., 1929.
[34] Pr. HawkH III, 9; PeaC, Pt. II, 1. BorMB is of the opinion that part of the text of this song is in Flemish.
[35] Pr. several places, e.g., HenryT, 13; HenryS, 1; PeaM, No. 6. The piece is preserved in both the Ritson MS and Add. 31922.
[36] Pr. HenryT, 11; etc.
36a Cf. HewO, 166, 209; the piece pr. HenryS, 18.   [37] HallC, 526.
[38] An inventory of Henry VIII's instruments, dated 1547, is pr. in GalpO, 292ff; HenryS, xxiiiff. A poem on Van Wilder's death, published in Tottel's *Miscellany* (1557), appears in H. E. Rollins' reprint of the work (1929), I, 162. For miscellaneous lists of payments made to musicians during Henry's reign, *see* StokesL, last installment.
[39] Cf. LafonK, 2ff; NagA; BorMB.

the Venetian embassy, contains an account of Henry's having listened for four hours to the playing of Memo.[40]

As distinguished from the royal players, there were town musicians—called waits—paid by cities to play at public performances. The name "waits" was originally applied to watchers at the gates, who used reed instruments in giving established signals regarding the town's safety. By the 15th century their function had become more musical, and they came to use ensembles of various instruments and to sing as well. Titles of pieces such as *London Waits* and *Oxford Waits* refer to compositions said to have been performed by them in the places named. (No specimens, however, are known to survive in prints earlier than the 17th century.) In the 16th century, since only London was able to support a formally organized company of independent musicians for any length of time, there was a strong tendency for musicians to secure a respectable status and regular pay by joining the waits. To be sure, other cities tried to form regular musicians' companies—some with temporary success—but only that of London can be traced back as far as 1500.[41]

Sacred Polyphony at the Turn of the Century, as Represented by the Composers in the Eton MS

Many of the early Tudor composers are represented in the great Eton MS, dating from the turn into the 16th century. Its four-, five-, and six-voice motets, Magnificats, etc., represent the style of English sacred polyphony after Egerton 3307. According to a contemporary list of contents,[42] the Eton MS contained ninety-seven works; but it has suffered seriously, and of the fifty-four pieces remaining, only forty-three are perfect. Of the original ninety-seven, no less than twenty-four were Magnificats (of which four remain). This large number shows the great interest of English composers in the Magnificat —an interest that can be traced back at least to the 14th-century English MS which contains the earliest known polyphonic setting of the canticle.[43] There is a great preponderance, in the Eton MS, of texts dedicated to Mary (even without counting the Magnificats), and the 15th-century statutes of Eton College ordering the scholars to sing an antiphon to her before leaving school in the afternoon and, toward evening, to say the Lord's Prayer in church and to sing an antiphon before the Virgin's image, help to explain this.

The usual Eton MS composition, outside of the Magnificats, is a long motet or motet-like piece *a* 5 or *a* 6 in well defined sections—often six or

---

[40] Cf. NagA, 3f. About this organist, *see also* p. 663 *supra*.
[41] Further on the waits, *see* BridgeT, HadlW, StpnW; about the companies, *see* WoodfillM.
[42] Pr. JamesC.
[43] Cf. Handschin in RB I (1947), 98; DaveyH, 27; FrereB, No. 864.

more—for varying groups of three or more voices with an occasional *tutti*. Imitation is rare, the voices in the main spinning out long melodies freely. Not until we come to a motet by Richard Sampson, *Quam pulchra es*,[44] preserved in Roy. MS II E. 11 where it bears the date 1516, is there extensive use of imitation (cf. p. 778), together with a clear feeling for harmonic propriety, elements of which Taverner was the first great English exponent. A *Salve Regina* by Richard Hygons, in the Eton MS, adds another composition incorporating the *Caput* melody to the Masses on it by Dufay, Ockeghem, and Obrecht.[44a] Richard Davy's four-voice *Passio Domini* for Palm Sunday, with text from St. Matthew, is unfortunately one of the imperfectly preserved pieces. However, those portions that remain display contrapuntal skill and a feeling for the dramatic possibilities of the text.[45] (An anonymous Passion, also based on St. Matthew and evidently only a little later, survives in Brit. Mus. Add. MSS 17802–5.[46]) The term *"gemell"* (= gymel) occurs in the Eton MS—not in the medieval sense, however, but to mark the division of a single part temporarily into two. The word *"semel"* is used to indicate a return to unison. Among other composers represented in the MS are Banastre, Cornysh, and Fayrfax.[46a]

Banastre appears with motets also in Cambridge MS Pepys 1236, in the company of several little-known composers.[46b] An anonymous piece *a 3*,[47] having the *Veni Creator Spiritus* melody in its tenor, sets the text *Adesto nunc*, i.e., stanza 2 of the *Salvator mundi* poem, which is associated with the melody at Compline on Christmas in the Sarum use.[48] The music was evidently intended for the even-numbered stanzas of the hymn.

The Sacred Polyphony of Fayrfax and of Some of His Other Contemporaries and Early Successors

The English Masses of the pre-Reformation era may be divided, for convenience, into two types corresponding to the Great and Short Services of Anglican Church music at a later date.[49] (There was, of course, nothing peculiarly English about such a division; cf. p. 450.) The Great type was usually for ceremonial occasions; the Short type, for ordinary purposes. The former is often *a 5* or *a 6* with a *cantus firmus* in the tenor. Great Services are extremely long, even when the Kyrie and portions of the Credo text are omitted.

---

[44] Excerpts pr. OH II (1st ed. only), 323. *See* fragment of a hymn by Cornysh from Eton MS in OH II, 161.

[44a] *See* HarrnC.   [45] Extract pr. OH II, 159. Further about Davy *see* FloodE, 6off.

[46] Cf. AdamsP, 260.   [46a] Further about the Eton MS, cf. SquireS; HughEM; and esp. HarrnE. The MS, ed. by F. L. Harrison, is in course of publication in MusB.

[46b] Cf. DaveyH, 81. FloodB constitutes a somewhat different treatment of the facts about Banastre given in FloodE, 13ff.

[47] Pr. Ancient & Modern, xxxvi.   [48] Cf. *ibid.*, 90; HMS xix, 3 (No. 8).

[49] Cf. pref. to TCM I, xxiii.

Where the Kyrie is not set polyphonically, it is sung in plainsong. Excisions in the Credo (cf. p. 69) are particularly numerous in English Masses.[50]

An example of the Great-Service type of Mass is John Lloyd's five-part *O quam suavis,* c. 1500.[51] It spells out, in long notes in the tenor, an unusually long chant that belongs to the Sarum tradition.[52] In the whole Mass the full melody appears (sectionally) only twice: the first statement embraces the Gloria and Credo; the second, the Sanctus and Agnus Dei. In addition to the *cantus firmus,* the Mass employs a three-part head-motif. There is occasional imitation.

The Short-Service type is of smaller dimensions, for fewer voices, and in a simpler style than the other. Diversity might be considered its chief trait: there are Masses of the genre that are written on a *cantus firmus* or are built on a special plan or are freely composed. Some omit the Kyrie and have the incomplete Credo, others are complete. Examples of Masses of this kind that are built on a special plan are the seven [53] Masses *a 3* (in Brit. Mus., Royal App. 45–48), one for each day of the week, by Nicholas Ludford (died c. 1540). In all seven, monophony and polyphony alternate. The initial section of a Mass movement constructed in this manner is stated by one part; this is followed by polyphony, utilizing the musical material of the first section either as *cantus firmus* or as thematic material to be imitated by all the voices. This technique is repeated throughout the movement, so that we have a type of variation-chain. And, since the same monophonic material is used in each of the movements so constructed, a larger unity is given to the whole Mass. We have seven additional Masses by Ludford, a Magnificat, and five motets.[54]

Among the older contemporaries of Ludford, Robert Fayrfax (born c. 1460; died 1521, the year of Josquin's death), is perhaps the most representative of early Tudor composers. He is first mentioned, in 1496, as Gentleman of the Chapel Royal, and later as organist of St. Alban's Abbey. In 1504, Fayrfax took his degree of Doctor of Music at Cambridge; in 1511, he "incorporated" at Oxford, receiving the earliest recorded degree of Doctor of Music there.[55] (John Dygon, by whom a motet *a 3* [56] reaches us, was awarded the degree of Bachelor of Music there the next year). The name Fayrfax

---

[50] On the English tradition of omitting a portion of the Credo text, *see* HughS, 335; CollL I, 57; CollM, xxxiiiff; OEE X, 7f. HanMC, the chief study of the whole subject, naturally treats of the English aspect also. One of the 3 anon. Masses on *O rosa bella,* mentioned in the text and first fn. on p. 93 (i.e., the one pr. DTO XI¹, 1), not only being based on a piece by an English composer, but also having excisions in the Credo, it is possible that the combination of circumstances indicates that the Mass is itself of English origin.

[51] Pr. CollM. The composer's identity has been established by Thurston Dart; *see The Listener* LIII (1955), 497.   [52] The plainsong pr. CollM, xii.

[53] Not 6, as stated in some reference books. The works are described in CollL II, 107ff.

[54] Further about Ludford. *see* FloodE, 72ff; Grove III, 243. On Mass fragments in a MS at Zwickau, *see* ZfMW XIII (1931), 562.   [55] Cf. WmsH, 16, 66, 120, 154.

[56] Pr. HawkH II, 519: for biographical data, *see* FloodE, 104ff.

heads the list of the Singing Men of the Chapel at the Field of the Cloth of Gold, June, 1520. His works include six Masses, twelve motets, two Magnificats, and a handful of secular songs, two of which were included in the printed song-book of 1530, seven others occurring in the Fairfax MS (regarding both, cf. p. 768).[57]

The motet *Ave Dei Patris filia,*[58] over 300 measures long, is preserved in more sources than is any other work by Fayrfax. Like many English motets of the period, it consists of several well-defined sections, assigned to variously constituted vocal groups. In this respect the style makes one think of Josquin, especially his Masses. But it would seem that Fayrfax, relying heavily on pure counterpoint, was much less interested than Josquin in exploring the possibilities of imitation and was stylistically, therefore, more an Early Renaissance figure. Frequent changes in the vocal groupings are found also in Fayrfax's *Regali* Magnificat,[59] based on Tone 6, in which the even-numbered verses, *a 5,* are set polyphonically. Actually, the full vocal resources are utilized only in verse 2, at the opening and closing of verse 6, and at the conclusion of the piece.

In the five-part *Missa Albanus,* a work of the Great-Service type, named after the patron saint of the abbey in which Fayrfax served, the subsections are more extensive than they usually are in Josquin. The Englishman often spins out lengthy passages on single words.[60] All the movements of this Mass (which does not include a Kyrie) begin with a long head-motif section *a 3;* smaller groups, in varying voice-combinations, replace the full complement of five voices at other points also. The nine-note *cantus firmus* is drawn from a hymn to St. Alban, *Albanus Domini laudans mirabile nomen,* used by Dunstable as the tenor of one of his motets.[61] It is sometimes absent for a considerable period; when present, it may shift from one voice to another. In Agnus III, for example, the melody does not appear in the setting *a 3* of the first two words—a setting extending over as many as 43 measures. However, when the writing *a 5* begins at *"qui tollis"* (*see* Ex. 177) the tenor has three inverted statements of it in augmented time-values at successively lower pitch-levels. At *"dona nobis"* there are consecutive appearances of it, one in each of the five voices, at various pitch-levels and in normal time-values. From *"pacem"* [62] to the end the tenor presents the melody on successively lower pitch-levels five times.[62a]

[57] Cf. HughRF, HughIF. For further biographical data, *see* ibid.; FloodE, 37ff; also pref. to TCM I, xxiff. For a discussion of Fayrfax's sacred music, *see* CollL II, 98ff.

[58] Extract pr. HawkH II, 516.

[59] Published separately, ed. by Dom A. Hughes, by Stainer & Bell (Fayrfax Ser., No. 1).

[60] *See* the extract from the Gloria pr. BuH II, 561; another extract from it pr. *ibid.,* 563.

[61] Pr. DTO XL, 32. Cf. CollM, x; HughIF, 99.

[62] This much, which immediately follows the extract given in Ex. 177, is pr. OH II (1st ed.), 320 (but without the time-values halved as in our ex.).

[62a] Further on the treatment of the *cantus firmus, see* HughIF, 103f.

EXAMPLE 177. *Missa Albanus*—Extract from Agnus III—Fayrfax (Cambridge, Gonville and Caius College MS 667).

The *Missa Regali,* which has no musical connection with the Magnificat, is based on the plainsong antiphon, *Regali ex progenie.*[62b] Fayrfax manipulates complicated rhythmic schemes in the *Missa O quam glorifica,* which was written as his "exercise" for the Oxford degree. In the Sanctus of this Mass, at the words *"Gloria tua,"* the upper voice sings groups of four dotted half-notes (original time-values) against the normal whole-note measure of the lower parts, while the proportional device of *sesquialtera* is used with skill, being further complicated by syncopations and cross-accents. It is possible that

[62b] Pr. Liber, 1626; cf. HughIF, 100. Opening of Fayrfax's Credo pr. OH II, 163; an extract from the Sanctus is pr. BuH II, 564, without identification of the Mass.

Fayrfax's *Missa O bone Jesu* is the earliest English example of the parody Mass.[62c]

The many other names occurring in MSS of the period include those of Pasche, Aston, Redford, Dygon, Whytbroke, Carver, Robert Johnson, Sampson, and Taverner. William Pasche (fl. late 15th, early 16th century) is represented by a *Christus resurgens* Mass, written on a Sarum chant,[62d] two Magnificats, and a motet, *Sancta Maria*.[63] By Hugh Aston, one of the brightest of the lesser lights, we have a *Missa Te Deum*,[64] based on three fragments of the plainsong (simple form): the opening phrase, the passage on *Tu ad liberandum . . . hominem,* and most of that on *Sanctus . . . Sabaoth.* The fragments at times are paraphrased, at other times are used as *cantus firmi,* the third fragment appropriately being employed as *cantus firmus* of the Mass Sanctus. The *Missa Videte manus meas (a 6)*,[65] like the Fayrfax *Missa Albanus,* illustrates the early Tudor predilection for dividing the movements into small sections and for occasionally changing the vocal registration.

The chief claim to notice of John Redford (c. 1486–c. 1545) is in the field of organ music. He was organist and almoner of old St. Paul's Cathedral. A motet *a 4* of his, *Christus resurgens*[66] is written in *cantus-firmus* style.

William Whytbroke was a contemporary of Taverner's at Cardinal College, Oxford, in 1525, and was ordained to the priesthood in 1529. His surviving music includes a four-part Mass *apon ye Square* (cf. pp. 786f), a Magnificat *a 6,* and a motet *Sancte Deus.* We have also a *Pars ad placitum W. Whitbroke fecit* to Taverner's motet *Audivi media nocte*.[67]

The extant music of Robert Carver (born c. 1491)—a Scottish monk at Scone Abbey—comes to us in a MS in the National Library of Scotland. This music includes a Mass on *L'Homme armé*—on which no similar composition attributed to a British musician is known—and an *O bone Jesu* (written c. 1546)[68] in no less than nineteen voice-parts. The motet is divided into eight sections for varying combinations of voices, most sections ending with the word *"Jesu"* set in *fermata*-marked block-chords for all of the nineteen voices.[69]

Robert Johnson (b. c. 1470; d. 1554), also Scottish, was a priest who ac-

---

[62c] Cf. HughIF, 91. Further about Fayrfax, see ShoreF. Too late to be consulted for the purposes of this book, I learn of a University of Michigan Ph.D. dissertation on *The Masses of Robert Fayrfax* by E. B. Warren.

[62d] *See* facsimile in FrereA, 241; part of Pasche's Sanctus pr. FloodE, insert between pp. 80 and 81.

[63] Further on Pasche, *see* FloodE, 79ff.   [64] Pr. TCM X, 1.

[65] Pr. *ibid.*, 39. This volume contains also 5 motets by Aston and, on p. xiiiff, biographical data. *See also* MGG I, 756f.

[66] Pr. PfatJ (which contains biographical data and some 70 compositions), music section, 89. See also StevM, 51.

[67] *See* further esp. FloodE, 89ff.

[68] Pr. CarvO.

[69] *See* further FullerS (some corrections in Grove I, 574; CarvO, pref. note); FarmS, 108f.

cording to an old account fled to England "lang before Reformation . . . for accusation of heresy." Here he is said to have acted as chaplain to Anne Boleyn, though evidence is lacking. His *Defyled is my name* [70] is a setting of the poem alleged to be her "complaint." He has left sacred compositions, some with English text, some with Latin. Of those with Latin, the Responsory, *Dum transisset,*[71] in *aBcB* form, is written in old-fashioned *cantus-firmus* style. The first two words are sung in plainsong; the rest of section *a* and all of section *B* are set in polyphony *a 5*, with the chant disposed in long notes in the tenor. Johnson does not set *c*, which is presumably to be sung in plainsong. The *Domine in virtute tua (a 5)* [72] is a tentative work in the more modern imitative style, which the British seem to have been slow in adopting.[72a]

Richard Sampson (d. 1554), Bishop of Chichester, Coventry, and Lichfield, has left two motets in a MS dating from c. 1517–1520: a four-part *Psallite felices,* believed to have been written in honor of Henry VIII, and a five-part *Quam pulchra es* (cf. p. 773).[73] The latter, like Johnson's *Domine in virtute tua,* is noteworthy for its considerable use, early for England, of imitation technique. The English were in no haste to adopt the main musical characteristic of the Late Renaissance.

Taverner

The greatest composer of this period is John Taverner (born c. 1495; died 1545). He was a boy chorister at Collegiate Church at Tattershall (near Lincoln) and in 1524 became Master of the Choristers. He held the post of organist of Wolsey's Cardinal College (now Christ Church, Oxford), from 1525 to 1530 and had relations with Cromwell in 1538–1539. His extant works include Latin motets and Masses. Of his eight Masses, two scored *a 5—Small Devotion* and *Mater Christi*—now lack the tenor.[74] The other six—*The Western Wynde, Playn Song, Sine Nomine, Gloria tibi Trinitas, Corona spinea,* and *O Michael*—appear complete in various MSS.[75] The polyphonic lines in Taverner's Masses show greater freedom and complexity as com-

[70] Pr. HawkH V, 433; MusB I, 59 (cf. StevM, 59f).

[71] Pr. BuH II, 593. (The text is *Cum transisset* in current liturgical practice [cf. Liber, 775]; for the plainsong in the early English form, *see* FrereA, 236.) This setting (from a MS at Christ Church, Oxford) is *a 5*. Another, but similarly constructed setting by Johnson, *a 4* (from Add. MSS 17802–5), is pr. separately in an ed. by Collins (publ. by Chester).

[72] Described ArkT, 42f; CollL II, 110.

[72a] *See* further FarmS, 109ff. The *Ave Dei Patris filia,* there (and in some other historical writings) ascribed to Johnson, is actually the Fayrfax motet, which survives with conflicting ascriptions.

[73] Opening pr. OH II (1st ed.), 323. Further on Sampson, *see* esp. FloodE, 83ff.

[74] Pr. TCM I, 70, 99, respectively; *see also* FRCMA, 14f. In *Small Devotion* the missing part has been supplied by the editors; *Mater Christi* is a parody on a motet of Taverner's (pr. TCM III, 92; *see also* TCMA, 18) found complete in several MSS, which has naturally simplified the task of supplying the missing voice.

[75] All pr. TCM I; *see also* TCMA, 13ff. The Benedictus of *The Western Wynde* pr. HAM, 115.

pared, for example, with those of Aston's, yet many of the same technical features are evident—frequent changes of vocal registration, repetitions of melodic fragments by varying voice-groups, and instances of *fermata*-marked block-chords.

Playn Song and *The Western Wynde* are *a 4*. The former, written almost throughout in point-against-point technique, is simple in outline yet strongly contrapuntal in content. The melody on which *The Western Wynde* Mass is based is of historical significance, since we have Masses composed on it by Tye and Shepherd also (cf. pp. 782, 784).

EXAMPLE 178. Melody of *The Western Wynde* (after ChappP I, 38).

Taverner's Mass consists of thirty-six variations—nine in each of the four movements (no Kyrie being provided). These are grouped in such a way that parallel structure results in the Gloria and Credo and also in the Sanctus and Agnus. Many different variation techniques appear.[76] *Corona spinea O Michael,* and *Gloria tibi Trinitas* are *a 6*. *O Michael* is of interest for its use of two-part canon: at the unison in the Gloria (the second *Qui tollis*), Sanctus, Benedictus, and Agnus III, and at the second in the Credo (*Filium Dei*), each time with a free third voice participating. *Gloria tibi Trinitas* is based on the Gregorian antiphon of that name.[77] The plainsong is sung as *cantus firmus* in the alto and is often imitated by the other voices. This Mass has historical importance because a whole species of compositions stems from it. There are, as we shall see, many instrumental *cantus-firmus* compositions, called *In nomine,* that are based on the *Gloria tibi Trinitas* antiphon. Since the words *In nomine* do not appear in that antiphon, the question of how the pieces got their name has long occupied investigators. The clue is to be found in the fact that at least those instrumental compositions entitled *In nomine* that bear Taverner's name are faithful transcriptions of the passage in the Benedictus of his *Missa Gloria tibi Trinitas* that sets the words *In nomine Domini*.[78] The whole *cantus firmus* appears in this passage, and other composers were moved by Taverner's example to write pieces on it also (several of these will be discussed in Chap. 16). The custom took root of designating these pieces by the same name as was applied to the transcriptions of Taverner's basic vocal music, which begins as follows:

[76] A detailed analysis of this and other Taverner Masses—and of much other English sacred music of the time—is given in Frank Ll. Harrison's *Music in Medieval Britain,* which appeared shortly before the fourth printing of the present book went to press.

[77] Given in FrereA, 286; ReIN, 8, in the form used by Taverner (cf. Liber, 914). For an analysis of the application of the chant in the Mass, *see* DonIN, 102ff.

[78] Further on this point, *see* ReIN, DonIN.

EXAMPLE 179. Opening of the *In nomine* passage of the *Missa Gloria tibi Trinitas*—Taverner (after TCM I, 148).

In all these Taverner Masses, the Kyrie is omitted and the text of the Credo is incomplete (cf. pp. 773f). The excisions in the Credo follow different plans. The one usually adopted omits the clauses from *Et in Spiritum* to *Et exspecto*. In his *Missa sine nomine,* however, Taverner omits the text from *Et iterum* to *Et exspecto,* and in the *Missa O Michael* there are three cuts: *Deum de Deo* to *genitum, Et iterum* to *cujus regni,* and *Et in Spiritum* to *Et vitam.* In the last two, there is no break in the music that would permit the insertion of plainsong.[78a]

Taverner's music to Latin text includes also three Magnificats,[79] one each *a 4, a 5,* and *a 6,* in which polyphonic settings of odd-numbered verses alternate with the chant. The setting *a 4* is based on Tone 6; the setting *a 6,* based on Tone 1, is considerably more florid, illustrating Taverner's liking for long melismas, which, in fact, are a marked trait of his style. In the five-part *Te Deum,*[80] Taverner similarly supplies polyphony to alternate with chant, but in this instance sets the even-numbered verses. The motet *Ave Dei Patris filia* [81] opens with the theme of the *Te Deum,* fragments of which are later employed in the tenor as a *cantus firmus.* There are two distinct settings of the *Dum transisset,*[82] both in *cantus-firmus* style with the chant in the tenor. The lovely responsory, *Audivi,*[83] for four equal voices, places the *cantus firmus* alternately in the triplex and contratenor. This piece strongly underscores the text in the closing section, on the words *"sponsus venit."* Only the first word of section *a* and all of section *c* are set polyphonically, the rest of *a* and all of *B* remaining to be sung in plainsong. *Christe Jesu (a 5)* [84] is written chiefly in point-against-point style; it makes considerable use of antiphonal writing, one group repeating the text previously sung by the other, the whole choir

[78a] *See* TCM I, 209, system 3; 210, systems 2–3. Further on Taverner's Masses, *see* CollT.
[79] Pr. TCM III, 3, 9, 17.   [80] Pr. *ibid.,* 26.   [81] Pr. *ibid.,* 61.
[82] Pr. *ibid.,* 37 (= BuH II, 557; alternative version in TCM III, 40), 43.
[83] Pr. *ibid.,* 35. For the underlying plainsong, *see* FrereA, 567, 576; *Processionale,* 236.
[84] Pr. *ibid.,* 73; *see also* TCMA, 18; TCMO No. 84. TCM III contains various other motets by Taverner, as well as individual Mass movements; see also TCMA, 17ff.

being employed at various points, including the close. The text of this motet contains a prayer for Henry VIII.

The Break with Rome; the Continued Use of Latin alongside with English

The formal break between England and the papacy came in 1534. An English Bible was set up in all churches in 1536. The dissolution and plundering of the monasteries occurred that year and in 1539. From then through the reigns of Edward VI and Mary to the ascent of Elizabeth in 1558 there was a period of uncertainty and confusion for composers of church music. Notwithstanding Henry's violent procedure, the Six Articles, enacted in 1539, reaffirmed the main points of Catholic doctrine. Henry was opposed to Lutheranism, and England continued to have a form of Catholicism, but without the pope. In 1539 or 1540, Myles Coverdale published *Goostly psalmes and spirituall songs* after Luther with fifty-one tunes, but Henry's anti-Lutheranism resulted in the book's being banned. The psalms in it are probably the earliest metrical ones in English to be printed with melodies. The music drew on Gregorian Chant and German chorales.[85] The destruction of the monasteries brought about the disbanding of the choirs and singing schools attached to them, and many trained musicians who had been choirmasters were thus left without posts. Extremists wished to have no music in the churches at all. One of the basic principles of the reform was that the service should be understandable: in 1542, it was ordered that a chapter of the English Bible of 1536 be read after the Te Deum and Magnificat. However, English did not become the official language of the service until later. As a result, it is not always possible to tell whether a piece of Tudor church music with Latin text was intended for the Roman Catholic service or the Anglican, in its earlier stages. In the interest of simplicity, we shall, from this point on, first treat of English sacred music having Latin text, without always regarding the faith for which it was written, and then discuss church music having English text.

Sacred Polyphony, with Latin Text, by Merbecke, Tye, White, Tallis, and Others

John Merbecke (or Marbeck, etc.; died c. 1585) has left two motets—*Ave Dei Matris* and *Domine Jesu Christe*—and a *Missa Per arma justitiae*,[86] his most important Latin work. He is traceable at St. George's, Windsor, in

---

[85] For English version of *Ein feste Burg,* see BoydE, 39; further on Coverdale's book, see LivingS, 9.
[86] All pr. TCM X. The Mass is based on the antiphon pr. Antiphonale, 81.

1531 and was organist there apparently from 1541 to his death. He was arrested in 1543, when a search of his lodgings brought to light writings that revealed Calvinist tendencies—Henry's regime was anti-Calvinist as well as anti-Lutheran—and narrowly escaped execution in 1544. After forming Protestant sympathies, Merbecke wrote no more Latin Church music—in fact, very little music of any kind—and devoted himself to his *Booke of Common Praier noted* (cf. pp. 796f) and to theological works. He is the author of the earliest Concordance to the whole English Bible. In the dedication to Edward VI, he mentions "the study of Musike and plaiyng Organs, wherein I consumed vainly the greatest part of my life."

More productive are such important composers as Christopher Tye, Robert White, John Shepherd, and Thomas Tallis.

Tye, born c. 1500, was, as a boy and young man, a singer at King's College, Cambridge. In 1541, he was appointed Master of the Choristers at Ely Cathedral, where he served, possibly not continuously, until 1561. In later life he took orders in the Reformed Church. He died in 1573 as rector of Doddington on the Isle of Ely. In Rowley's play, *When You See Me You Know Me* (1605), Edward VI is made to address Tye thus:

> *Doctor, I thank you and commend your cunning.*
> *I oft have heard my Father merrily speake*
> *In your hye praise and thus his Highnesse sayth,*
> *England one God, one truth, one Doctor hath*
> *For Musicks Art and that is Doctor Tye.*

The composer may have been the prince's music master.

It is presumed that Tye's Latin compositions were written early in his career, during Henry's reign. His works reveal him as a skilful technician, yet his chief aims seem to have included simplicity of harmonic and contrapuntal effect. Some twenty Latin motets survive and four Masses, including *The Western Wynde* [87] and a six-voice *Euge bone*.[88] The former work—"perhaps the best of the three" [89] Masses based on the old tune—has the melody repeated in the alto twenty-nine times, but with elaborations and changes in the time-values. In the *Missa Euge bone* the Sanctus opens with *fermata*-marked block-chords on the repeated word *"Sanctus."* At the words *"Pleni sunt caeli et terra,"* the highest part divides into a gymel and the three lowest voices are silent. There are four Agnus settings, three to the text ending with *"miserere nobis."* (Presumably the choir director chose two of these three.) In Agnus III, each of the two highest parts divides into a "gimel," the only other active voice being the tenor. This is one of the many Masses without Kyrie and with cuts in the Credo.

[87] Extract from the Gloria pr. OH II (1st ed.), 326.   [88] Pr. OEE X.
[89] CollL I, 59.

Among Tye's motets, his *Miserere* [90] is notable for the interplay of g and g-sharp, clearly meant to produce a brightening of the mood before the words *"quoniam in te confidit anima mea"* ("for my soul trusteth in thee"). The jubilant motet *Omnes gentes* [91] contains a striking example of cross relation. This feature, which we have found in continental music also, persisted longer in conservative England than across the Channel.

EXAMPLE 180. Extract from *Omnes gentes*—Tye (after Collins).

Robert White married an Ellen Tye, who was probably the daughter of the composer.[92] It is therefore likely that the older man influenced the younger one. White received the Mus. Bac. degree at Cambridge in 1560, and in 1561 or 1562 succeeded Tye as Master of the Choristers at Ely Cathedral. About 1570 he became organist of Westminster Abbey. He died in 1574. His works are almost all sacred and are, in the main, in Latin. They include a Magnificat, two Lamentations (one *a 5,* one *a 6*), twenty motets, and four anthems, not counting some fragments and *opera dubia*. The Magnificat,[93] in Tone 1, sets the even-numbered verses for varying groups of from three to six voices. One of the cadences in the Lamentations *a 5* contains this effective instance of rhythmical displacement (compare the figures in measure 4, voices 1 and 3, with earlier appearances of the same figures).

EXAMPLE 181. Extract from five-part *Lamentations*—White (from TCM V, 17).

[90] Extract pr. WalkerH, 54.
[91] Pr. separately, like Tye's *Rubum quem viderat Moyses,* by J. & W. Chester, Ltd. (H. B. Collins, ed.).
[92] Cf. TCM V, xiii.
[93] This, and the other works by White here cited, pr. TCM V; *see also* TCMA, 21f, 42.

(Ingenious use of such displacement occurs also at the end of *Porcio mea, Domine.*) This setting of the Lamentations is powerful, richly melismatic, and characterized by cadences in which White appears always to have sought some touch of the unusual. Of three settings *a 6* of *Domine quis habitabit,* one in particular makes elaborate and brilliant use of imitation. White's general employment of this device shows the technique firmly planted in England. We have no fewer than four settings by him of the lovely plainsong melody, *Christe qui lux es et dies.*[94] Each embraces stanzas 2 (*Precamur*), 4, and 6, the odd-numbered stanzas being left for performance in plainsong. One setting is almost entirely in point-against-point writing; the melody is in the superius in stanzas 2 and 6, in the alto in stanza 4. Two settings treat different material in imitation below the chant, which is in the superius throughout. The fourth setting keeps the melody in the tenor. In addition, White has left a textless (instrumental?) setting, with the title *Christe qui lux es et dies,* in which the plainsong, in the superius, is decorated. White is one of the best English composers of his time.

John Shepherd (probably born c. 1520–1525; died c. 1563) was a chorister at St. Paul's Cathedral under Thomas Mulliner (cf. p. 851). From 1542 to 1547, with interruptions, he was organist at Magdalen College, Oxford, and Fellow there from 1549 to 1551. During Mary's reign, he was a member of the Chapel Royal. Most of his works are set to Latin texts, among them being four Masses. These include the *Playnsong Mass for a Mene,* in which polyphony alternates with plainsong, and a Mass based on *The Western Wynde.* In this, Shepherd follows the same general structural plan as Taverner, but repeats the melody only twenty-three times, with a resulting overcrowding of the text in the longer movements. But the "counterpoint is freer and more vigorous as well as more ingenious than Taverner's."[95] The title of the *French Mass,*[96] a predominantly polyphonic work, possibly refers to the Franco-Netherlandish character of the writing. The composition is unified by a head-motif, treated in imitation. A setting of the *Haec dies* has, in the tenor, the chant version found in the Sarum Gradual. In one of the MSS preserving this piece, one part bears the words "a good songe, an excellent good songe"; and another the words "the best songe in England."[97]

Born c. 1505, Thomas Tallis was organist at Waltham Abbey for some years before its dissolution in 1540; beginning in that year, or earlier, he served as a Gentleman of the Chapel Royal until his death in 1585. In 1575, Elizabeth granted Tallis and Byrd jointly a 21-year monopoly for printing music and music paper, the Letters Patent that she issued being the earliest English

[94] Pr. HMS, 4 (No. 12).   [95] CollL I, 58f.
[96] Pr. separately by J. & W. Chester, Ltd. (H. B. Collins, ed.).
[97] About other Latin works by Shepherd, *see* CollL I, 6of. For 1 verse from a 5-part Magnificat, *see* BuH II, 587.

examples of the kind known. In the same year he and Byrd published the *Cantiones sacrae,* each contributing seventeen of its thirty-four motets. His life spans the entire period from Fayrfax to Orlando Gibbons, and he is generally regarded as the greatest Elizabethan composer older than Byrd. His output of Latin music includes two Masses, two Magnificats, two Lamentations, Office hymns, and some thirty motets.[98]

Four Marian motets, *Gaude gloriosa, Salve intemerata, Ave Dei Patris filia,* and *Ave rosa sine spinis* are structurally comparable to the works of early composers such as Fayrfax, having, as they do, numerous divisions and frequent changes in vocal registration; yet the contrapuntal technique is indicative of Taverner's period. *Miserere nostri* (*a 7*) is a technical triumph. Six voices engage in canon, the tenor providing an added free part. The two highest voices sing in canon at the unison; the next two voices also form a pair, the lower one singing in double augmentation of the higher; the two basses treat still another melody similarly (but with some rhythmical liberties in the treatment of repeated notes, due to the underlaying of the text).

EXAMPLE 182. Opening of *Miserere nostri*—Tallis (after TCM VI, 207).

The tremendous forty-part *Spem in alium* opens with a section in which twenty voices enter successively with the same theme in imitation. Thereafter the remaining twenty enter with fresh material, involving some imitation, small groups taken from the first twenty voices occasionally adding to the polyphony. Then all forty sing briefly. The rest of the piece, in the course of which a new theme is sung in imitation by twenty-eight parts, consists of passages for varying numbers of voices, the ending, of course, engaging all forty of them.

There are several responsories in from four to seven parts. One of the finest is *Dum transisset,* the text of which, as already noted, was set by Taverner and Johnson. In Tallis' version, in which the polyphony begins at the word

---

[98] Almost all Tallis' Latin works are pr. in TCM VI, which contains each number discussed above; *see also* TCMA, 22ff, 43, 49.

"*Sabbatum,*" the chant is given to the superius, the other voices singing the theme for that word in anticipatory imitation. Another responsory is a setting of the *Audivi,* in which Tallis applies plainsong and polyphony to the text in the same way as Taverner had done. All Tallis' Office hymns, in which the even-numbered stanzas are polyphonically set, are in *cantus-firmus* style. The chant is given to the superius, the other voices developing their lines in free imitation. *Procul recedant* (stanza 1: *Te lucis*) is set twice, once to the Festal Tone, once in chordal style to the Ferial Tone. In *Illae dum pergunt* (stanza 1: *Sermone blando;* cf. p. 604) the settings of stanzas 2 and 4 are alike except for an interchange of parts between discantus and contratenor; in stanzas 6 and 8, the same kind of interchange occurs, applied, however, to fresh music.[98a] *Adesto nunc,* as might be expected (cf. p. 773), is based on the melody usually—though it seems not originally [98b]—associated with *Veni Creator Spiritus.*

The Fayrfax-like technique present in the four Marian motets is employed in the five-part *Missa Salve intemerata,* a parody Mass on one of those motets. Each movement begins with the opening theme of the motet, sung by contratenor and bass. A nameless Mass *a 4,* chordal in style, introduces each movement with the same motif and harmonic progressions, the recurrence being exact in the Gloria and Credo, and only slightly altered in the Sanctus and Agnus. The Magnificat *a 4* and the Magnificat and *Nunc Dimittis,* mainly *a 5,* treat the even-numbered verses polyphonically and are written in imitative style. To Tallis' latest period must be assigned the two Lamentations, one of which is of great interest harmonically, by virtue of its frequent use of modulation.[99]

About Osbert Parsley (Persleye, etc.; 1511–1585), a contemporary of Tallis, very little is known. He was a Singing Man at Norwich Cathedral and the composer of sacred [100] and instrumental music. Another contemporary, Thomas Wright, was a Gentleman of the Chapel Royal c. 1552.[101] Robert Parsons (d. 1570, apparently at an early age) was appointed a Gentleman of the Chapel Royal in 1563. Sacred and secular vocal works of his survive, as well as instrumental music.[102]

William Mundy (died c. 1591) was vicar choral of St. Paul's and in 1564 became a Gentleman of the Chapel Royal. Several motets of his and two four-part Masses *Upon the Square* come down to us. H. B. Collins [102a] has

---

[98a] The piece uses the Sarum form of the melody, pr. Ancient & Modern, 197, not the continental form (cf. Chap. 9, fn. 79; Chap. 11, fn. 175b).

[98b] Cf. ReMMA, 106.

[99] Further on Tallis' Latin church music, *see* esp. CollTT.

[100] 2 Latin exx. pr. TCM X, 237, 247; *see also* TCMA 32, 55.

[101] His *Nesciens mater* pr. separately by J. & W. Chester, Ltd. (H. B. Collins, ed.).

[102] Latin works of his pr. TCM IX, 241, 303 (with misattributions to Byrd; cf. ByrdW VIII, vi). A 5-part *Ave Maria,* ed. by Sir R. R. Terry, was pr. separately in 1907.

[102a] In CollL I, 66.

suggested the following explanation of the title, based on a direct knowledge of the Masses.

Each movement is divided into short sections separated by full closes, these sections being sung by three of the voices only, the four being only employed together (as a rule) in the concluding section of each movement. It is obvious that if each of the four voices takes its turn to rest there are four possible combinations of the remaining three voices. Expressed in figures the combinations will be 1 2 3, 1 2 4, 1 3 4, and 2 3 4. I suggest that the four combinations are the four sides of the square.

Sacred Polyphony, with Latin Text, by Byrd

William Byrd (1543–1623), whose career, in its earlier stages, is in several ways intertwined with that of Tallis, was certainly the finest Elizabethan composer of Latin church music and one of the most versatile among the Late Renaissance masters anywhere. He was referred to in his own day, by Thomas Morley, as "never without reverence to be named of the musicians" and, by another writer,[103] as "the most celebrated musician and organist of the English nation." Byrd remained loyal to the Catholic faith, but was not seriously molested; in fact, he was both permitted and willing to hold positions in the Anglican Church from early in life to his death. He was organist of Lincoln Cathedral from 1563 to 1572, and in 1570 succeeded Robert Parsons as a Gentleman of the Chapel Royal, beginning in 1572 to share the duties of organist there with Tallis. On the latter's death in 1585, Byrd became sole owner of the printing monopoly that had been granted to the two jointly; and at some time thereafter he assigned his license to Thomas East (Este), whose first publication as assignee was entered at Stationers Hall in 1587. Byrd's works with Latin text [104] include his portion of the *Cantiones sacrae* of 1575, published by him together with Tallis, two other books devoted to *Cantiones sacrae* by himself alone (1589, 1591), two books of *Gradualia* (1605, 1607), three Masses, and numerous smaller works in MS.

The Masses (one each *a 3, a 4*, and *a 5* [104a]) are all complete settings. Each uses the old head-motif technique. In the Mass *a 3*, all movements except the Sanctus are affected by it; in the Mass *a 4*, all but the Credo, the other movements having two closely related head-motifs (or perhaps one should say a single motif in two forms); in the Mass *a 5*, the Kyrie, Gloria, and Credo have a freely handled head-motif, while the Benedictus (but not the opening of the Sanctus) and the Agnus have another. All three works appear to be freely composed. The Mass *a 3* opens with a Kyrie, simple to the

---

103 Father William Weston; cf. FelWB, 42.

104 Pr. ByrdW I–IX; many works also in TCM VII, IX (but *see* TCMA, 27ff, 50ff), etc.

104a Pr., respectively, in ByrdW I, 1 (= TCM IX, 3), 30 (= TCM IX, 17), 68 (= TCM IX, 36; MAS I).

point of dullness, in which each invocation—set once only—is evidently meant to be sung three times. Elsewhere in his Mass music, however, Byrd creates rich and brilliant polyphony, especially in the compositions *a 4* and *a 5*.

Examples of various styles appear in the *Cantiones sacrae* of 1575. The *Diliges Dominum* [105] for SSAATTBB is a crab canon. The eight voices present their individual lines up to the middle of the motet, at which point the voices of the same type exchange parts and repeat each other's melodies backwards. The setting *a 5* of a responsory for the Burial Service, *Libera me*,[106] is written in *cantus-firmus* style. The chant is given to the superius, the other voices entering in anticipatory imitation. Byrd provides a complete setting of the three sections—*Libera me, Quando caeli,* and *Dum veneris*—that constitute the corpus, which precedes verse 1 in the liturgy. Each of the three verses is therefore presumably to be sung in plainsong, *Quando caeli* being repeated after Verse 1, *Dum veneris* after Verse 2, and the entire *corpus* after Verse 3, according to liturgical use. Partly in *cantus-firmus* style is a setting *a 6* of the Compline antiphon, *Miserere mihi, Domine.*[107] This opens with the chant presented successively in the superius, tenor, and bass. The text is then repeated complete, this time with the chant melody slightly embroidered and sung by the two highest voices in canon at the fourth; the two lowest voices are also in canon at the fourth, while the two middle voices move freely.

The *Quomodo cantabimus*,[108] found in MS, is datable 1583. This is the setting of verses 4 to 7 of the psalm, *Super flumina,* that Byrd sent to Philippe de Monte in answer to the setting of the opening verses that Monte had sent to him (cf. p. 702); Byrd's work, a masterpiece of technical writing, is, like Monte's, *a 8.* It is written in two *partes.* The first contains a canon, at the octave, between bass I and alto I, alto II following in mirror canon. The other voices develop the opening subject by imitation in inversion. *Pars II* is also a complicated web of contrapuntal writing.

The contents of the *Lib. I Sacrarum cantionum* (1589), all *a 5,* reveal a liking for large dimensions: six motets consist of a single *pars,* but 8 are in two *partes,* one is in three *partes,* and one in four. The writing is almost entirely in imitation. There is but one example of *cantus-firmus* technique, *Aspice Domine.*[109] As is true of most of Byrd's vocal work, individual words are carefully treated in this book; but there seems to be a strong tendency to repeat them excessively. *Vigilate* [110] is notable for its madrigalisms: there

[105] Pr. ByrdW I, 232; TCM IX, 149.   [106] Pr. ByrdW I, 275; TCM IX, 81.
[107] Pr. ByrdW I, 240; TCM IX, 129.
[108] Pr. ByrdW IX, 99. The transcr. in TCM IX, 283, is defective; cf. FelWB, 106; TCMA, 31.
[109] ByrdW II, 139; MAS VI, 83.   [110] Pr. ByrdW II, 120; MAS VI, 73.

are series of descending scale passages over the repeated word *sero* ("at night"); at *an galli cantu* ("or at the cock-crowing"), bass II leaps up a major sixth and, as the words are repeated, several voices sing elaborate descriptive melismas; at *repente* ("suddenly") short time-values predominate; descending lines with dotted rhythms underscore *dormiente* ("sleeping"). *Ne irascaris* and *Civitas sancti tui* (especially the latter),[111] two *partes* of one motet, are known in English as well as in the original Latin. As *O Lord turn thy wrath* and *Bow thine ear,* they were included in the collections of Barnard, Boyce, and Tudway (cf. p. 798). In both *partes* Byrd makes colorful use of vocal registration. In *pars II,* on the word *"deserta,"* a major seventh, introduced as a suspension, resolves onto an augmented sixth. Such a sixth also occurs as an essential interval in the motet *Tristitia,*[112] likewise in the collection of 1589, and twice in the motet *Domine exaudi,*[113] in the collection of 1591. The latter publication, *Lib. II Sacrarum cantionum,* contains thirteen motets *a 5*—six having one *pars,* a like number having two, and one having three—and six motets *a 6,* of which two are in two *partes* and one in three. The general style is much like that of the previous publication. Here again only one number uses the *cantus-firmus* technique, the six-part *Descendit de coelis.*[114] The technique is seen declining in England—but later than on the continent. The powerful *Exsurge Domine* takes full advantage of the possibilities offered by the word *exsurge,* repeating it often and handling it with striking effect. (Note the leap of a minor ninth in meas. 7, middle voice.)

EXAMPLE 183. Extract from *Exsurge Domine*—Byrd (after ByrdW III, 132).

---

[111] ByrdW II, 151; MAS VI, 90.   [112] ByrdW II, 46; MAS VI, 29.
[113] ByrdW III, 71, 78; cf. FelWB, 70.   [114] ByrdW III, 150.

The closing number, a *Haec dies*,[115] contains some highly felicitous examples of hemiola, both successive and simultaneous. The piece, joyful in character, concludes with a series of brilliant Alleluias based on a phrase repeated in sequence in the bass.

The two books of *Gradualia* (various settings for the Mass and Office, not merely Graduals) contain thirteen mostly complete settings of the Proper, several being for Masses of the Blessed Virgin, one for Easter, one for Christmas (third Mass), etc. The works in the main are on an elaborate scale and intricately polyphonic. The Introit settings invariably employ one or two voices less in the setting of the verse than in that of the corpus, while all voices enter chordally for the *Gloria Patri*. The handling of the Gradual and Alleluia reveals certain peculiarities: sometimes these two divisions of the Proper are merged into one composition; elsewhere the word *"Alleluia"* that liturgically belongs at the opening of the Alleluia movement appears instead at the end of the preceding Gradual. There are other irregularities also. In the numerous settings of the *Gloria Patri* and of the word *"Alleluia,"* Byrd provides a variety of treatment and an artistic interpretation related to the setting and spirit of the text with which each is associated.

In the *Gradualia*, Book I, several pieces call for comment besides those for the Mass. The well-known, beautiful *Ave verum* is included in this collection, as is a fine four-part *Salve Regina*[116] not based on plainsong. The four-part, chordal *Laetania*[117] provides first a setting for the opening portion of the Litany of the Saints (through *"Sancta Trinitas . . . miserere nobis"*); the numerous invocations of the central portion are left to be chanted in plainsong, but Byrd provides settings for their responses;[118] then a continuous setting follows for the close. Byrd paraphrases the chant mostly in the tenor, but sometimes in the soprano and once in the alto. The *Turbarum voces*,[119] for three equal voices, is a very dramatic setting of the responses of the crowd in the Passion according to St. John. This opens in chordal style, but polyphonic writing, obviously intended to express the crowd's excitement, occurs at several points, e.g., at *"Non hunc,"* at *"Ave, Rex Judaeorum,"* and at the repeated cries *"Crucifige."*

In the *Gradualia*, Book II, there are striking examples of word-painting, such as the rapid repetition of the leap of a minor third over *"tremuit"* in the Offertory, *Terra tremuit*[120] and the suggestion, in *Solve jubente Deo*,[121] over the repeated word *catenas*, of the rattle of St. Peter's chains, by

---

[115] *Ibid.*, 228.
[116] These 2 works pr. ByrdW V, 27 (= TCM VII, 127), 84 (= TCM VII, 151), respectively.
[117] ByrdW V, 118; TCM VII, 166.
[118] For the way in which the plainsong and polyphony fit each other, cf. Liber, 835ff.
[119] ByrdW V, 198; TCM VII, 202.   [120] ByrdW VI, 150; TCM VII, 277.
[121] ByrdW VII, 90; TCM VII, 332.

means of a rhythmic figure of quarter- and eighth-notes (original values). In the effective *Tu es Petrus*,[122] *a 6,* a slow-moving phrase sung by the bass several times in melodic sequence to the words *"et super hanc petram,"* suggests the rock upon which the Church was to be founded; and the word *"aedificabo"* is underscored by rising scale-lines, sung in imitation by all voices. *O quam suavis*,[123] a lovely motet of devotional character, is notable for the degree-inflection present in the opening measure of the superius.

The *Quomodo cantabimus* is one of about twenty-five motets and motet-like works by Byrd that survive only in MS. Among them is a setting, *a 5,*[124] of the melody to the hymn *Christe qui lux es et dies,* which proved so attractive to White (cf. p. 784). Byrd provides stanzas 2 to 6 each with a separate setting; presumably stanzas 1 and 7 are to be sung in plainsong, stanza 7 being followed by Byrd's simple polyphonic Amen. The chant is given first to the bass and rises one voice in each successive polyphonically set stanza, finally appearing in the superius. The voices not having the plainsong supply every stanza with new countermelodies; the style is quite chordal. Another composition, *a 4* and bearing the first word of stanza 2 (*Precamur*) as its title, comprises four settings of the melody, which is placed in the superius throughout.[125]

Sacred Polyphony, with Latin Text, by A. Ferrabosco I, Morley, Deering, and Philips

Alfonso Ferrabosco I (cf. p. 428), who was to become a friend of Byrd's, arrived in England before 1562, when he was awarded a pension payable during the Queen's pleasure. In 1567 he fell into disfavor, being accused of the murder of a foreign musician. Alfonso claimed he was innocent; by 1569 the affair was settled and he bound himself to Elizabeth's service for life, being granted a pension once more. The same year he went to Italy to settle his affairs there and was back in England by 1572. But he broke his pledges to the queen in 1578, left his two children in the care of a court musician, and returned to Italy. His music was highly esteemed by his English contemporaries, and his surviving sacred works, consisting almost entirely of Latin motets, are preserved mostly in MSS in England.[126]

Undoubtedly one of the children left in England by Alfonso I is the com-

---

[122] ByrdW VII, 97; TCM VII, 336.   [123] ByrdW VI, 101; TCM VII, 253.
[124] ByrdW VIII, 63.
[125] The piece pr. ByrdW VIII, 34; 3 of the settings pr. TCM IX, 306. The composition is without text in the sources, but *see* ByrdW VIII, vi. Further on Byrd's Latin church music, *see* FelWB, 47ff; CollB. FelWB and HowesB are full-length books on Byrd. *See also* MGG II, 571 ff.
[126] Further about Alfonso I in England, *see* Grove II, 216f; ArkI; ArkM; ArkF, 223ff, 42ff, including a list of sacred works. For 2 motets, *see* CommM XXV, 40; DehnS, *Lieferung IX,* 3.

poser known as Alfonso Ferrabosco II (b. at Greenwich; d. 1628). He held several court posts and was music master to Prince Henry and, on the prince's death in 1612, to the future Charles I. It is sometimes difficult to know to which Alfonso a particular work should be credited.[127] The careers of Alfonso III and Henry Ferrabosco (instrumentalists, by whom no compositions are known), sons of Alfonso II, and of John (a composer), who may likewise have been a son, fall outside the scope of this book.

Thomas Morley (1557–1603) and John Wilbye (1573–1638), known chiefly as madrigal composers, have nevertheless left us some Latin works. Wilbye's six-part motet *Homo natus de muliere*,[128] in imitation style, employs a madrigalian running passage over the word *"fugit"*; his five-part *Ne reminiscaris* [129] assigns the superius to treble voices, but the other parts to viols.

Morley, Byrd's famous pupil, took the degree of Mus. Bac. at Oxford in 1588, perhaps while organist at St. Giles, Cripplegate, London. Later he became organist of old St. Paul's Cathedral, continuing in this post after his appointment as Gentleman of the Chapel Royal in 1592. In 1598, he was granted, for twenty-one years, the printing license previously held by Tallis and Byrd. He made assignments under this license, at various times, to Thomas East (Byrd's old assignee) and to William Barley, who was himself to hold the license after Morley's death (and was likewise to assign to East). Morley's *Plaine and Easie Introduction to Practicall Musicke* (1597) [130] is the most celebrated English treatise of the Renaissance. A passage in Shakespeare's *Taming of the Shrew* is very likely based on one in this work,[131] but the claim that Morley was acquainted with the poet rests on rather slim evidence.[131a] Morley composed several Latin motets and incorporated five of them into *Plaine and Easie*, e.g., *Eheu, sustulerunt Dominum meum, Domine fac mecum,* and *Agnus Dei.*[132] These are characterized by short restatements of each text phrase, generally by the development of melodic patterns either in exact sequence or in imitation, and by effective use of descending scales. The Easter motet, *Eheu, sustulerunt,* opens with the repeated exclamation, *Eheu,* the sigh of despair of the Magdalene, taken up by all voices, and thereafter is based chiefly on a series of descending passages in the superius, notably over the concluding words, *"nescio ubi"* ("I know not where"). *Domine fac mecum* is of a brighter color; in triple meter, it changes momentarily and effectively to binary rhythm toward the end. The *Agnus Dei,* in the Dorian

---

[127] About Alfonso II, *see* esp. ArkAF; ArkF, 48ff, including a list of sacred works. 1 such motet pr. *ibid.,* 50.

[128] Pr. OEE XXI, 24.   [129] *Ibid.,* 31.

[130] Facsimile ed. in MorlP; modern ed. in MorlPE. (For an essay on Morley's treatment of mode, *see* StevnsnP.)

[131] Cf. LongS, 22.   [131a] Cf. GordM.

[132] Reprinted together in *Thomas Morley: Three Motets in Four Parts,* H. T. David, ed. (Music Press No. 53).

mode transposed, may be described as a study in the use of the sixth scale-degree, both lowered and unlowered.

Richard Deering (died c. 1630) and Peter Philips (c. 1560–c. 1633), both Catholics—the former apparently by conversion and the latter by birth—spent important parts of their lives abroad, where most of their published works appeared. They were therefore not very well known in their own country, although Deering's works were admired by Cromwell, and Peacham says, "Nor must I here forget our rare Countreyman, Peter Phillips, . . . now one of the greatest Masters of Musicke in Europe." Deering spent some time in Italy and, by 1617, had become organist for a community of English nuns in Brussels; in 1625 he was court organist in England to Queen Henrietta Maria.[132a] Four sets of *Cantiones sacrae* by him were published during his life by Phalèse. To the extent that Deering made use of *basso continuo*, he may be classified as a baroque composer; but he is also the writer of music illustrative of Late Renaissance style. The five-part *Jesu dulcis memoria*,[133] which sets stanzas 1 and 2 of the hymn text in motet fashion, incorporates in its smooth and expert polyphony some effective examples of degree-inflection. There are still more of them in the six-part *O vos omnes*, where they add poignancy to the singing of the word *"dolor."* In this motet, too, there are instances of the descending leap of a diminished fifth, followed by a turn in the opposite direction. Degree-inflection occurs in *Vox in Rama* also; a descending leap of a diminished fourth is resolved in the normal way. This is a singularly powerful and dramatic work, probably affected by the influence of the opera, to which Deering must have been exposed during his Italian sojourn. A descending leap of a diminished fourth is present likewise in *Factum est silentium,* but the resolution is delayed. *Jesus, dulcedo cordium* reveals Deering in a more conservative mood.

From the dedication date of a collection of madrigals by Philips, it is known that he was definitely established at Antwerp in 1590. Some years later he served as organist at Brussels to Albert and Isabella of Austria. In 1610 he became canon at Soignies, and in 1621 at Tirlemont. His first set of *Cantiones sacrae* (*a 5*) was printed by Phalèse in 1612, followed, in 1613, by a second set for double chorus. Later publications containing sacred works *a 2* and *a 3*, as well as some for solo with *basso continuo*, and a set of Litanies to the Blessed Virgin, *a 4* to *a 9*, appeared from 1613 to 1633. *Les Rossignols spirituels,* an arrangement of popular melodies adapted to sacred texts, was brought out in 1616.[134]

[132a] For further biographical data, *see* esp. PlattD.

[133] This motet, and the others by Deering presently to be mentioned, are all published singly by Bosworth & Co., Sir Frederick Bridge, ed.

[134] It is believed that a volume of Masses and psalms, once in the library of John IV of Portugal, was destroyed in the earthquake of 1755.

The *Cantiones* of 1612 shows that Philips used the imitative technique in a great variety of ways. He handles it with considerable freedom, modifying and combining different forms of it with imagination and skill. Like Lassus, he often imitates merely a rhythmic pattern or a melodic contour. The *Alma Redemptoris Mater,* a richly polyphonic work, opens with a motif imitated in its normal form by three voices and in inversion by the other two; after each voice has sung the motif once, it presents that motif in a form not assigned to it before. In *Elegi abjectus esse,*[135] three voices sing the opening motif in real imitation, while a fourth makes a tonal answer; the alto is free. The motif is presented without interruption by the tenor, but is broken by a caesura in the other three voices. Characteristic of Philips' work is the "relatively consonant" six-four chord; it appears in this piece both as a preparation for a suspension and in the double role of a resolution from one suspension and a preparation for another. Also in this set is an *Ascendit Deus* [136] of simpler design, with broken major triads on *in voce tubae,* short, bright melismas on *jubilatione,* and a rousing chordal *alleluia* section. The setting of the words *"et Dominus"* presents a combination of imitative techniques—real answer, tonal answer, imitation by inversion, and imitation of rhythmic patterns. Philips draws on chant for his *Pater noster,* which is in old *cantus-firmus* style, and for his *Ave Maria,*[137] *Regina coeli,*[138] and *Salve Regina,*[139] which use the paraphrase technique. An interesting combination of degree-inflection and cross relation appears in the *Pater noster* on the word *"libera",* and a strong indication of the composer's madrigalistic background is shown in the *Salve Regina* by the insertion of a rest before the final syllable of *suspiramus.* In the dramatic five-part *Surge Petre*—a responsory in *aBcB* form, but with the two highest voices exchanging their former parts in the second *B*—the command *"Surge,"* addressed to St. Peter by the angel delivering him from prison (cf. Acts of the Apostles XII), is set to an ascending leap of a fifth, sung in exact imitation by three voices, the other two voices rising a fourth; repeated, the command is emphasized by an octave leap. Later, on the words *"Surge velociter,"* the bass sings the same fourth in augmentation while the upper voices, presenting the former leap of a fifth in imitation, fill it in with short notes, in anticipation of the word *velociter.*

[135] This motet and the *Alma* pr. separately, ed. by H. B. Collins.

[136] Pr. TCMO No. 6.

[137] This motet, the *Pater noster,* and 22 other motets appear in modern notation in LyderP.

[138] Pr. separately in editions by R. R. Terry (in the series, *Downside Motets,* published by Cary & Co.) and H. B. Collins (published by Chester).

[139] Pr. separately, ed. by R. R. Terry. Also separately available are the *Ave Regina* (as ed. by both Terry and Collins), *Ave verum* (Terry), *O virum mirabilem* (Collins), *Ego sum panis vivus* (W. B. Squire, ed.; published by J. Williams) and *Hodie sanctus Benedictus* (W. B. Squire, ed.; published by Novello). Other items: *O pastor aeterne* (*a 8*), in A. H. Jewell, *Madrigal and Motett Book,* No. 2 (1856); *Veni Creator* (*a 4*), in C. T. Gatty, *Arundel Hymns* (1905). (All *a 5* unless otherwise stated.) Further about Philips, *see* LyderP; HughesP; BergO.

EXAMPLE 184. Extracts from *Surge Petre*—Philips (Sambrooke MS, New York Public Library, fol. 44ᵛ; transcr. by P. Lyder).

"Arise, Peter, and put on [thy garments]. . . . Arise quickly."

Philips is one of the finest English composers of the period, excellent in the field of sacred music, but by no means limited to it.

The Adoption of English in the Anglican Church; Merbecke's "Booke of Common Praier noted"; Early English Psalters; Day's "Certaine notes"

Having discussed the English sacred music of the period that has Latin text, we shall now, as planned on p. 781, turn back and treat that with English text. In 1544 Archbishop Cranmer (perhaps in collaboration with Merbecke [139a]) issued the Litany in English,[140] set to the traditional chant, but modified so that there was only one note to a syllable, and in the same year a setting harmonized *a* 5 was printed, "according to the notes used in the Kynges Chapel." [141] In a letter of 1545 [142] to the King, Cranmer, discussing English translations he had made of certain processionals, stated that, if music was to be set to them, there should be just one note to a syllable.

Under Edward VI (reigned 1547–1553), not only Lutheranism but also

[139a] Cf. MerbO, 9.
[140] Facsimile ed. with comment in HunC. The *Portiforium secundum usum Sarum* of c. 1400 had already offered the Litany and 11 other items in English; cf. *New Schaff-Herzog Encyclopedia of Religious Knowledge,* III (1909), 177.
[141] DaveyH, 108; FelEE, 25; *see also* HunC, 22, fn.   [142] Pr. StrunkR, 350f.

Calvinism was tolerated, and the Anglican Church became Protestant. That the need was felt for musical settings of portions of the service in English is shown by the Wanley MS at the Bodleian Library, generally thought to date from 1546–47. This MS—originally a set of four part-books, one now missing —contains eighty to ninety compositions in English, "including the Morning and Evening Canticles, two harmonized settings of the plainsong of the Litany . . . and, what is still more remarkable, ten English settings of the Office for the Holy Communion, complete with Kyrie, Credo, Gloria in excelsis, Sanctus, Benedictus, and Agnus Dei." [143] The MS gives no ascriptions to composers, but two of Taverner's Masses are recognizable, adapted to English words.[144] Other identifiable composers are Okeland, Robert Johnson, Caustun, Shepherd, Tallis, and Whytbroke.[145]

The Royal Injunction of April 14, 1548, delivered to the Dean and Chapter of Lincoln Minster, ordered that "they shall from hensforthe synge or say no Anthemes off our lady or other saynts but onely of our lorde And them not in laten but choseyng owte the best and moste soundyng to cristen religion they shall turne the same into Englishe settyng therunto a playn and distincte note, for every sillable one, they shall singe them and none other." [145a]

The continuing growth of Protestantism eventually gave Britain equivalents of the Genevan Psalter. The publication that first led in this direction—a book without music and without date, but apparently printed c. 1548—contained nineteen psalm translations in verse, by Thomas Sternhold who, until his death in 1549, was Groom of the Robes to Henry VIII and Edward VI. Sternhold's psalms, like Marot's, were originally intended for court circles, but are by no means comparable in poetic quality. In 1549, a second book reprinted Sternhold's nineteen psalms, adding eighteen more of his as well as seven by John Hopkins; [146] again there was no music. But the same year *The Psalter of David . . .* , with translations by Robert Crowley, offered a single setting *a 4* [147] applicable to all 150 psalms. It is the Sternhold-Hopkins psalms, however, rather than Crowley's, that were destined to live.

The Act of Uniformity of January 21, 1549, directed that after June 9 the first book of Common Prayer be used, and none other. In 1550, there appeared Merbecke's *Booke of Common Praier noted,*[148] whose monophonic settings are partly adaptations from the traditional chant, partly the original work of

---

[143] FelEE, 8f.   [144] These versions pr. TCM III, 143, 169.

[145] Further about this MS, *see* FelEE, 39ff. For an anon. piece from it (with missing part restored) *see* TCMO, No. 83. About a MS of 1547–48 containing English church music, *see* FelEE, 36.

[145a] Henry Bradshaw and Chr. Wordsworth, *Statutes of Lincoln Cathedral,* II (1897), 592.

[146] Biographical data on Sternhold and Hopkins in JulD, 860f; LivingS, 25.

[147] Pr. Grove IV, 268. The year 1549 saw the publication of still another psalter without music, that of William Hunnis.

[148] Facsimile ed. with comment in HunC; scholarly ed. in MerbO. (Despite statements to the contrary, there was but one printing in 1550. Cf. MerbO, 12, 19). *See also* StevnsnM; TerryM, 77ff (= TerryF, 57ff); Grove III, 438f.

Merbecke. They are not, strictly speaking, plainsong, as the notation gives rhythmic indications, nor are they mensural, as the shape of the semibreve is sometimes used in recitation passages where it was unnecessary to indicate strict time-values. The result is a compromise between mensural music and plainsong. Merbecke reveals much skill in adjusting time-values to the normal accentuation of English. His "noting" of the Versicles and Responses forms the basis of almost all subsequent harmonizations of them. But this book as a whole seems never to have been very popular, and with the issuance of the second book of Common Prayer in 1552 it became obsolete.[149]

In 1553, the Sternhold-Hopkins collection was augmented by seven psalms by Whittingham, music still being absent, and a psalter by Francys Seager was printed, containing nineteen versified psalms and two settings *a 4*, one serving for twelve psalms, one for two. The Sternhold-Hopkins collection was carried to Frankfort and Geneva by Protestants leaving the England of Queen Mary. During their exile, the Anglo-Genevan Psalter was developed, with an altered version of the forty-four psalms of 1549 as its basis. First printed with music at Geneva in 1556, as a collection of fifty-one psalms with a tune for each, this psalter had expanded—through other editions—to eighty-seven psalms set to sixty tunes by 1561, when it reached its final edition, also printed at Geneva, although Elizabeth had meanwhile come to the throne and an edition had appeared in England in 1560. With respect to both texts and tunes the Anglo-Genevan Psalter, to which Kethe and Wittingham contributed translations, was heavily indebted to the French Psalter of 1551–1554. Who prepared the music, is unknown.

All six composers represented in the Wanley MS are among those drawn on in *Certaine notes set forthe in foure and three partes,* printed by John Day in 1560 but containing at least some works that we know date from before Mary's reign, since a number of them had been included in Wanley. Caustun, the most liberally represented, is an earnest but amateurish composer.[150] An English-anthem adaptation of Taverner's *In nomine* passage (cf. pp. 779f) is included with the text, *In trouble and adversitye*.[150a] A Communion Service by John Heath is among the Wanley works reappearing in Day's publication. But, meanwhile, religious controversy had resulted in the elimination of the Benedictus and Agnus Dei, and Day therefore omitted Heath's settings of them.[151] However, the Gloria, which was soon to be discarded also, is still present in Day.

[149] Some of Merbecke's music has again become current in the Anglican Church, however, as an incidental result of the activities begun by the Oxford Movement in 1833.

[150] Cf. FelEE, 42ff; for Caustun's Morning and Evening Service from the Day collection, *see* TCMO, Nos. 94 and 95.

[150a] Pr. TCM III, 199. Another English anthem arrangement *O geve thankes unto the Lord,* appearing in Br. Mus. 30480–3, is evidently somewhat later.

[151] After the adoption of the final *Book of Common Praier,* composers setting the Communion Service usually provided music only for the Kyrie, as a response to the commandments,

English Church Music of Tye and Tallis

Besides Merbecke, the chief composers to make important early contributions to English church music were Tye and Tallis. Merbecke, after the *Booke of Common Praier noted,* produced no more music. Tye and Tallis, however, continued to compose into the reign of Elizabeth. The temporary halt in the growth of a specifically English church music, in Mary's reign, ended, of course, with the accession of Elizabeth, who liked an elaborate service and opposed those extremists who wanted nothing more sung in church than psalms. Nevertheless, the writing of church music did not really flourish until the general cultural revival that took place in the latter half of Elizabeth's reign.

There are fourteen extant anthems by Tye. In the anthem of this period, the style is generally polyphonic, based on free imitation interspersed with chordal passages. In other words, a 16th-century anthem is simply a motet with English text. A fine example is Tye's *I will exalt thee,*[152] which reaches us in two famous old collections of English sacred music: John Barnard's *The First Book of Selected Church Musick . . .* (1641; part-books only) and William Boyce's *Cathedral Music* (3 vols., 1760–1778). These are important sources of early Anglican polyphony, since they preserve some pieces that do not survive elsewhere. (The MS collection of Tudway is another old repository of such polyphony.[152a]) Striking contrast is obtained in *pars II* of *I will exalt thee* where, after *pars I* has presented a constant flow of polyphony using much imitation, Tye resorts to clear-cut sections, at the ends of which all the voices not only reach their cadences together, but sustain rests together. In *Prayse ye the Lord, ye children,*[153] Tye shows a sensitive feeling for harmonic color. In 1553, appeared his *The Actes of the Apostles, translated into Englishe metre, and dedicated to the Kynges most excellent Maiestye, by Christopher Tye, Doctor in Musyke, and one of the Gentylmen of hys Graces moste honourable Chappell, with notes to eche Chapter to synge and also to play upon the Lute, very necessary for students after theyr studye, to fyle their wyttes, and also for all Christians that cannot synge, to read the good and godlye storyes of the lyves of Christ hys Apostles.* Tye himself wrote the versified text, which is of poor quality; but the music of Chapter 3 has been the source of such a well-known hymn tune as *Windsor.* The hymnlike nature of the music ("hymnlike" in the sense of more recent

---

and for the Creed. The Gloria, Benedictus, and Agnus Dei were entirely discarded, and the Sanctus was seldom set. The Canticles in the Morning Service to which music might be set were the *Venite, Te Deum, Benedictus Dominus Deus Isreal,* with the alternative *Jubilate.* The Canticles for the Evening Service were the *Magnificat* and *Nunc dimittis.* To each of these, except the *Te Deum,* a *Gloria Patri* was appended.

[152] Pr. BoyceC II, 10; TCMO, No. 59.   [152a] *See* Grove V, 401ff.

[153] Pr. TCMO, No. 58; other Tye anthems in TCMO, Nos. 57, 73 (early printings bear misattribution to Tallis).

centuries)—also the immature character of the verse—may be illustrated by
Chapter 10.

EXAMPLE 185. Chapter 10 of *The Actes of the Apostles*—Tye (after the
print of 1553).

In setting Chapter 14 (the last that he published, owing, perhaps, to a want of
success),[154] Tye writes in double canon, but in such a way as to create the
impression of great simplicity. The two *duces* begin together at the opening,
and there is much point-against-point writing.

That Tallis was represented in the Wanley MS and in Day's *Certaine
Notes* has been mentioned. His three anthems in the Wanley MS recur in
several other sources and must have been highly favored. Of these the four-
part *Heare the voyce and prayer* [155] is notable for an opening point of imitation in which an ascending leap of a diminished fourth figures prominently.
Another of the group, the four-part *If ye love mee*,[156] illustrates the common Anglican practice of having the *decani* and *cantoris* sides of the choir
(cf. p. 118, fn. 125) sing at times antiphonally, at times jointly. The method
is different from that of standard Italian polychoral practice, for in English
music the basic number of parts is not usually increased when the choir sings
"full" (i.e., when the sides unite). The two sides are similarly constituted
(e.g., they are both SATB groups) and ordinarily, in full passages, the voices
of the same type merely sing the same notes. But there are exceptions.
Toward the end of *If ye love mee,* the trebles of both the *decani* and *cantoris*
sides momentarily sing different notes at the same time, though owing to the

[154] Pr. HawkH III, 256; for the first 8 chapters *see* TyeA; Chap. 3 also in Grove V, 740.
[155] Pr. BuH III, 27.   [156] Pr. TCMO, No. 69.

disposition of rests genuine writing *a 5* is never actually heard. In these pieces, Tallis, though he does not depart far from the syllabic style advocated by Cranmer, contrives not to be shackled by it; melismas, if quite brief, nevertheless help to give the music some of the flow typical of the great polyphonic tradition. This tradition is in full evidence in *Blessed be Thy name,* but the work is an early adaptation of a Latin motet to English words.[157] In *Purge me, O Lord,*[158] the triad is used without third, not only at the end, but also at the opening and at the medial cadence, giving the piece an archaic touch. In all, we have seventeen anthems by Tallis.[159]

Tallis' Dorian Service[160] *a 4* is probably an early work, assignable to the reign of Edward VI. It embraces music for the Morning, Communion, and Evening Services, and the second of these includes a setting of the Gloria— contributory evidence of the work's early date. Since, in the Anglican service, the congregation remains standing after "Who for us men, and for our salvation, came down from Heaven," there is no occasion, after this point in the Credo, for a break in the music, such as has for some time been desirable after *descendit de coelis* in the Roman service, to correspond to the kneeling of the congregation before the *Et incarnatus* (cf. p. 125, fn. 154); Tallis, who starts a slightly free canon at "Begotten not made," therefore finds it possible to continue it, without a break, through "Who for us men, . . . came down from Heaven, And was incarnate by the Holy Ghost of the Virgin Mary." [161] Tallis writes a canon in the *Nunc dimittis* also, but in the main the writing is chordal and syllabic. A *Benedictus Dominus* for four men's voices survives in a MS dating from Edward's reign. But Tallis' Preces and Responses, Litany, five-part full Service and five-part *Te Deum* [162] probably belong to the Elizabethan period. Much of his English music has been lost.

Psalters of the 1560's

In 1567 or 1568, *The whole Psalter translated into English metre* by Archbishop Matthew Parker was printed, but the work was never placed on sale. It contains eight "tunes"—actually settings *a 4* by Tallis—set to psalm translations by the Archbishop and a ninth tune set to his translation of the *Veni Creator.*[163] The withholding of Parker's psalter from normal publication has been deplored [164] because it entailed the suppression of Tallis' tunes,

---

[157] For the English version, *see* TCMO, No. 75; for the Latin, TCM VI, 204.

[158] Pr. TCMO, No. 67.   [159] For anthems not yet cited, *see* TCMO, Nos. 68, 70.

[160] The edition in BoyceC I, 1, substitutes an anon. chant (known as the "Christ Church Tune") for Tallis' *Venite;* cf. FelEE, 48. An edition by C. H. Kitson of the *Te Deum, Benedictus,* Magnificat, and *Nunc dimittis* ("Morning and Evening Service in the Dorian Mode") was pr., 1917, by Bayley & Ferguson.

[161] Cf. PrenT.   [162] Surviving incomplete; reconstruction in TCMO, No. 72.

[163] All the tunes pr. EllinT, 197ff; the first 8 pr. BoydE, 45ff No. 3 is the tune on which Vaughan Williams has based his *Fantasia on a Theme by Tallis,* for string orchestra; No. 9 appears in a number of modern hymn-books with the title "Tallis's Ordinal" or simply "Tallis."

[164] By Wooldridge in Grove IV, 271.

"broad, simple and effective, . . . and, from the technical point of view, finer than anything of the kind that has been done since."

Meanwhile, in 1562, the history of the English Psalter, i.e., of the one containing the Sternhold and Hopkins translations, had progressed a step farther. That year, *The Whole Book of Psalms* was published at London by John Day. In this complete edition, fifty-three of the new translations were by Hopkins; there were sixty-five tunes (some being duplicates), of which thirty had appeared in one or another of the earlier editions. Who prepared the music is again unknown. From now on, changes were to be gradual. Comparison of this more or less definitive edition with the French Psalter shows, among the English, a predilection for common meter,[165] for musical line-patterns enclosing a series of short notes between two longs, for skips of fourths or fifths, and for the major mode and those modes most resembling minor.[166]

Day, in 1563, brought out *The Whole Psalmes . . .* , containing these sixty-five tunes and thirty additional ones in settings *a 4* by Caustun and some otherwise unknown composers, among them William Parsons (not to be confused with Robert Parsons), whose eighty-one contributions included a setting of Old Hundredth.[167] Often two, sometimes three or four settings, are provided for a single tune, the total number of compositions—"generally respectable and sometimes excellent" [168]—being 141. A few miscellaneous pieces at the end of the book include compositions by Tallis and Edwards, among others.

The Scottish Psalter, completed in 1564, shared a common development with the English Psalter, during the Anglo-Genevan period. But instead of adopting the English modifications, John Knox, as principal editor of the complete edition, retained the eighty-seven psalms of Geneva (cf. p. 797). Their metrical variety was apparently preferred, for it was emulated in twenty-one new texts supplied by two Scots, Craig and Pont. The remaining forty-two psalms needed to complete the collection were chosen from the English Psalter of 1562.[169] The settings in this early Scottish Psalter were all monophonic, a polyphonic version of the collection not being printed until 1635.

English Church Music of Byrd, Weelkes, and Some Other Composers

Among the composers of pieces in the appendix to Day's *The Whole Psalmes* is John Shepherd. His works to English text include also a Service, described as his "First" Service in the early MSS, and 2 settings of the *Te*

---

[165] ◡ — ◡ — ◡ — ◡ — | ◡ — ◡ — ◡ — | twice.

[166] Cf. PraM, 75f.   [167] Pr. HaverH, 53. Another psalm of his in Grove IV, 274.
[168] Grove IV, 273.   [169] Cf. LivingS, 10ff, 32; PraM, 72. *See also* TerryF, 1ff.

Deum and Magnificat. His neatly constructed anthem, *Haste thee, O God,*[170] consists of ten short chordal and imitative passages, five of the latter being based on descending themes that seem to have been deliberately related to one another. Robert Parsons has likewise left a service and anthem.[171]

By Robert White we have only seven works with English text—all anthems.[172] Here, as in his Latin church music, White proves himself to be a composer of superior quality, the rhythmical fluidity already noted on p. 783 being again in evidence.

Richard Farrant was attached to the Chapel Royal, though not continuously, from the reign of Edward VI until he died in 1580. In 1564, he was appointed Master of the Choristers and organist at St. George's Chapel. His Morning, Communion, and Evening Service (*a 4*) in A minor survives also, in some later MSS, in G minor.[173] The service is interesting for the way in which it uses voices from the *decani* and *cantoris* sides simultaneously for purposes of tone color, without, however, increasing the actual number of parts. Thus, there are occasional passages for two altos with two basses or for two trebles with two tenors. The fine short anthems, *Call to remembrance* and *Hide not thou thy face,*[174] help to give Farrant a place in the musical history of the period out of proportion to his small output. *Lord, for thy tender mercies' sake,* sometimes ascribed to Farrant, is more likely by Tye [175] or the elder John Hilton (d. 1608).[176] This last composer was a lay-clerk and member of the choir at Lincoln Cathedral in 1584 and became assistant organist there before he left in 1594 to be organist at Trinity College, Cambridge. Like Farrant, he wrote a *Call to remembrance.*[177]

In the generation following Richard Farrant, two Farrants, or possibly three, were active in English music, confusion in at least some attributions inevitably resulting. One man—a John Farrant—was organist, at various times from 1571 on, at Ely, Bristol, Salisbury, and Hereford cathedrals. A service, apparently his,[178] rich in chromatic alteration, contains examples of degree-inflection and false relation. Conflicting ascriptions have been made also with regard to *O Lord, the maker of all thing,* credit being given to Henry VIII, John Shepherd, and William Mundy—correctly, it would seem, with regard to the last.[179] Mundy is among the composers to whom the excellent anthem, *Rejoice in the Lord alway,*[180] anonymous in the source, is attributed by mod-

---

[170] Pr. TCMO, No. 77. For another anthem, *see* HawkH II, 523.   [171] *See* esp. PulB, 351f.

[172] Pr. TCM V, 192ff. Reprints also in BuH III, 67; OEE XXI, 1, 19; ScoE VIII, 2 (cf. TCM V, xxvif).

[173] So printed (with some errors; cf. Grove II, 204; FelEE, 63) in BoyceC I, 53. The Morning and Evening Canticles pr. in A minor in TCMO, Nos. 62 and 33.

[174] Pr. together in TCMO, No. 60.   [175] Cf. ArkA. The work pr. *ibid.,* 578; etc.

[176] Cf. FelEE, 63.   [177] Pr. TCMO, No. 97.

[178] Pr. TCMO, No. 54. See further, FelEE, 64f.

[179] Further on Mundy, see PulB, 337f; for the anthem, see BoyceC II, 1; HenryS, 63.

[180] Pr. TCMO, No. 55; HawkH V, 458.

ern writers, the others being Tye, Caustun, and, most frequently, Redford—but all without adequate evidence.[181]

An Evening Service,[182] attributed to Tye in some sources and to Parsley in others, appears to be by the latter, since the *Gloria Patri* in its *Nunc dimittis* is identical with that of the *Benedictus Dominus Deus* in a Morning Service [183] ascribed to Parsley only; moreover, much of the melodic material in the two services is similar.[184] This music avoids melismas, but is in a vigorous contrapuntal style.

Although Byrd remained faithful to the Catholic faith, he produced excellent music for Anglican use. Four services of his survive practically intact.[185] The Short Service is written in simple style, mainly note-against-note. But the rhythm is most flexible and enhances both the intelligibility of the text and the musical interest. The work comprises a *Venite, Te Deum, Benedictus Dominus Deus,* Kyrie, Credo, Sanctus,[186] Magnificat, and *Nunc dimittis.* Except for the Sanctus, these are the numbers usually set for a complete Service in Byrd's time, a *Jubilate* sometimes replacing the *Benedictus Dominus* (cf. fn. 151). The second Service introduces, it seems for the first time, the distinguishing feature of the "Verse" Service, i.e., passages written for solo voice with instrumental accompaniment, in this case organ.[187] This composition includes only the Magnificat and *Nunc dimittis,* as does the "Third" Service. The latter work, being mostly in triple meter, is called by Barnard "Master Bird's Three Minnoms." The Great Service, which, except that it omits the Sanctus, sets the same texts as the Short one, is an elaborate and lengthy composition: in TCM II it occupies about 100 pages. This is one of Byrd's masterpieces. Basically *a 5,* it is sometimes for as many as eight voices, since groups from the *decani* and *cantoris* sides occasionally unite to attain that number. The work thus differs from the pieces (already mentioned on pp. 799f, 802), in which some voices from the two sides unite without doubling but also without increasing the total number of parts, owing to the silence of other voices. Byrd obtains varied color effects by drawing on the two sides; thus the opening of the *Te Deum* is for SSTT and is immediately followed by writing for SAATB. The lesser doxologies that close the *Venite, Benedictus Dominus,* Magnificat, and *Nunc dimittis* all begin chordally; the one after the *Venite* ends rather simply also, but the last two in particular are very elaborate and resort to much text repetition—Byrd appears to have

[181] Cf. FelEE, 66; NagG, 51; PfatJ, 67; StevM, 50f.

[182] Pr. (with ascription to Tye) in RimbCS, 1; *see also* TCM X, 290 (organ part); TCMA, 32.

[183] Pr. TCM X, 271. For another Morning Service, *see ibid.,* 256.

[184] Cf. FelEE, 61.   [185] All pr. ByrdW X; TCM II; *see also* TCMA, 16f, 33.

[186] Against the authenticity of this Sanctus, *see* TCM II, xxxii; but cf. FelEE, 75; FelWB, 123; TCMA, 16.

[187] Cf. FelWB, 129; FelEE, 77.

found the words "world without end" particularly inspiring (*see* Ex. 186). There are many additional chordal passages elsewhere, but the style is generally polyphonic and the counterpoint of rhythms [188] is quite complex and of extraordinary brilliance.

EXAMPLE 186. Conclusion of the Great Service—Byrd (complete work in ByrdW X, 136; TCM II, 123).

Byrd's *Teach me, O Lord*,[189] a setting of part of Psalm 118 (CXVII), is an example of the Anglican *Psalmi Festivales,* as they are called in the early MSS. These pieces may have some connection with Anglican chanting, which was to be developed in the 17th and 18th centuries; but a more direct connection perhaps exists between such chanting and the Italian *falsobordone* treatment of the eight Gregorian Tones.[190] Byrd's setting, which alternates verses for solo voice and verses for full choir, has the solo passages accom-

---

[188] About this phase of the work, *see* esp. WhitB, 480ff.
[189] Pr. ByrdW X, 46; TCM II, 30.   [190] Cf. FelEE, 19f.

panied by an independent organ part. The choral passages approximate *falsobordone*.

Among Byrd's full anthems, *Arise, O Lord*,[191] with its *pars I* for five voices and *pars II* for six, is rich in texture and flexible in rhythm. *Alacke when I look back*,[192] a verse anthem, is written for contratenor and organ, these being joined in four passages (including the close) by chorus *a 4;* hemiola and false-relation are felicitously used. *Behold, O God*[193] is an example of a verse anthem containing passages for two solo voices in combination as well as alone. Some fine psalm settings and additional religious compositions were included by Byrd in three miscellaneous collections which are often referred to roughly as sets of madrigals.[194]

Of the four Services known to have been written by Morley, the one mostly *a 5*, entitled "First"[195] by Barnard, is a verse Service and includes the seven numbers usual in complete settings of the period. Morley here treats the verse technique more elaborately than does Byrd in his Second Service, for the work includes passages not only for a single soloist but for soloists *a 3* and *a 4*. This work is distinguished by flexible rhythms, combining, with perfect ease, measures that may be described as in $\frac{4}{4}$, $\frac{3}{2}$, and $\frac{6}{4}$. The same rhythmical fluidity is present in the fine anthems, *Nolo mortem peccatoris* (which mingles Latin and English) and *Out of the deepe*.[196] Morley has left also several *Psalmi Festivales* and settings of the Preces and Responses, as well as of the Burial Service in the English Prayer Book,[197] this last being the earliest example of its kind.

Thomas Weelkes (born c. 1575), still greater than Morley as a madrigalist, was organist of Winchester College from c. 1598 and became organist of Chichester Cathedral in 1602, retaining the post until his death in 1623. Only one madrigal collection of his appeared after his transfer to Chichester, and it would seem that he devoted his last years to sacred music. While Weelkes' church music is more conservative than his madrigals, making notably less use of chromaticism (cf. pp. 827f), it displays the same skill in handling six or more voices.

"Weelkes wrote more Services than any of the Tudor composers; as many as ten are known, but . . . not one of these has survived . . . complete. It has been found possible to reconstruct three . . . and the surviving text of the remaining seven is enough to demonstrate that Weelkes was the most original and perhaps

---

[191] Pr. ByrdW XI, 64; TCM II, 227.   [192] Pr. ByrdW XI, 98; TCM II, 223.
[193] Pr. ByrdW XI, 103; TCM II, 233.
[194] A complete ed. of Byrd's English church music pr. ByrdW X, XI. A large part of this music pr. TCM II; other pieces in EMS XIV (= ByrdW XII), 2, 10, 14, 20, 26, 32, 38, 44, 49, 53, 143, 159; XV (= ByrdW XIII), 1, 7, 14, 20, 27, 32, 38, 121, 135, 145, 225, 265, 280; XVI (= ByrdW XIV) 24, 31, 75, 88, 106, 143, 154, 178, 189, 199, 211. *See also* fn. 217.
[195] Pr. separately in TCMO, No. 64.   [196] Pr. TCMO Nos. 13, 71, respectively.
[197] Pr. BoyceC I, 43.

the greatest of all the English Service-writers in the Golden Age with the exception of Byrd." [198]

The reconstructions have been made possible by the Organ Book of Adrian Batten (d. 1637), a MS (Tenbury 791) [199] which contains a quantity of 16th-century church music compressed into organ score, some works surviving only here. Batten was an estimable composer in his own right.[200] Of Weelkes' ten Services, the one described as "for two trebles" is an elaborate work apparently written for large chorus and for some special occasion. It comprises a *Te Deum,* Magnificat, and *Nunc dimittis.*[201] There are passages for two solo trebles (whence the name) and others for two choirs, each *a 5.* The two other reconstructed works are Short Services, one *a 4*—simple but attractive—, one *a 5.*[202] The latter uses imitation in almost every phrase, including the one that sets the text "he hath put down the mighty." Here a descending leap of a seventh underscores the words "put down," the interval, moreover, being a major one in the alto II and bass. Another Weelkes Service is described as *"in medio chori."* The meaning of this term, which is applied to Services by some other composers also, is unknown, but it has been conjectured [203] that a small group of soloists may have been placed "beyond the choir-stalls in the centre of the space nearer to the sanctuary."

Of Weelkes' more than forty anthems, his settings of *Hosanna to the Son of David* and David's Lament on the death of Absalom [204] provide interesting bases of comparison with settings by other composers, Orlando Gibbons having likewise written music for the text of the former and Thomas Tomkins for that of the latter. Weelkes' *Hosanna* is *a 6,* and his facility in the handling of many voices helps to produce a work of great brilliance. The Lament, *a 7,* is an eloquent expression of deep sorrow.

Later Psalters

Several madrigalists—not, however, including Morley and Weelkes—are among the men who contributed settings *a 4* to East's *The whole Booke of Psalmes,* the first edition of which was printed in 1592.[205] Between the publication of Day's psalter in 1563 and East's in 1592, several psalters of lesser

[198] FelEE, 94. For details on the MS sources, *see ibid.,* 94f. The "restorations" are the work of Canon Fellowes.

[199] Described in FelCT, 159ff (including a page of facsimile); TCM II, xxvif.

[200] List of works in Grove I, 245. Exx. pr. BoyceC II, 75, 80, 82 (the last 2 also in TCMO No. 56); TCMO Nos. 76 (2 items), 78.

[201] The last 2 published by Stainer & Bell (Church Services, No. 276, E. H. Fellowes, ed.).

[202] The first pr. by Stainer & Bell (Church Services, Nos. 277–279, E. H. Fellowes, ed.); Magnificat and *Nunc dimittis* from the second pr. TCMO No. 96.

[203] FelEE, 97.

[204] Pr. TCMO No. 9; MAS XIV, 135, respectively. Other anthems by Weelkes in TCMO Nos. 17, 35, 45, 63, 88–90; MAS XIV, 70.

[205] Pr. MAS XI; preface also in StrunkR, 352ff.

importance had appeared in England: one by William Daman (Damon) in 1579; *Seven Sobs of a Sorrowful Soule for Sinne*, 1585, said to be a second edition of *VII Steppes to Heaven, alias the VII* [penitential] *Psalmes reduced into meter by Will Hunnys*, 1581; others by John Cosyn (1585) and Henrie Denham (1588); and two more by Daman (both printed in 1591, after his death). The Daman book of 1579 contained fourteen tunes not given by Day, including four later to become popular under the names *Cambridge, Oxford, Canterbury,* and *Southwell.* In one book of Daman's posthumous pair, the church tunes were given to the tenor, in the other, to the superius; the settings in both books are in motet style. Daman, apparently born at Liége, one of Queen Elizabeth's musicians, has left us also a few motets, an anthem, and instrumental music.[206] The contributors to East's psalter were John Farmer, George Kirbye,[207] Richard Alison, Giles Farnaby, Edward Blancks, John Dowland, William Cobbold, Edmund Hooper,[208] Edward Johnson, and Michael Cavendish, to several of whom we shall return. The style of the settings varies from simple point-against-point writing to quite elaborate counterpoint, and the general level of excellence is high. East appropriates five of Daman's new tunes and adds four more. He calls for the singing of many different texts to each of three melodies: those later called *Old Dutch* (thirty-three texts; setting by Blancks), *Cambridge* (twenty-nine texts; setting by Hooper), and *Oxford* (twenty-six texts; six to the setting by Kirbye, twenty to that by Dowland). The coupling of different texts with a single tune is restricted almost entirely to these three melodies. To three of East's four new tunes, names, for the first time, are assigned—*Glassenburie, Kentish* (afterward called *Rochester*), and *Cheshire.* Farmer's handling of the last of these produces one of the more attractive settings in East's *Booke.*

EXAMPLE 187. *Cheshire:* Psalm 146—Farmer (after *Whole Booke of Psalmes,* East, ed. of 1594).

---

[206] A motet pr. OEE XXI, 35. *See* further, PulB, 131f.

[207] For an anthem by Kirbye (whom we shall meet again, as a madrigalist), *see* TCMO No. 18.

[208] An anthem of his, *Teach me Thy way, O Lord* (from the Barnard Collection) is reprinted by Novello & Co. (J. E. West, ed.).

A much admired psalter containing music only by Alison was published in 1599: *The Psalmes of David in Meter. The plaine song beeing the commun tunne to be sung and plaide upon the Lute, Orpharyon, Citterne or Base Violl, severally or altogether, the singing part to be either Tenor or Treble to the Instrument, according to the nature of the voyce or for fowre voyces.* The tune is written in the superius throughout, but is omitted from the instrumental accompaniment (separate tablatures are provided for lute and cittern) so that an instrument was clearly meant to accompany only when the melody alone was sung. The words "the singing part to be either Tenor or Treble to the instrument" therefore indicate that the tune might be sung by the tenor an octave lower than written, not that the tenor part of the setting *a 4* might be sung to the given lute music.[209] Farnaby likewise prepared a psalter of his own and provided instrumental accompaniment: *The Psalmes of David to fower parts for viols and voyce;* only the superius, containing a dedication datable 1625 or later, comes down to us (in MS).[210] Farnaby had appeared also in *The whole Booke of Psalmes* brought out by Barley some time between 1604 and 1614; others represented included Morley and John Bennet (cf. p. 823), but this was for the most part an inferior production. However, *The whole Booke of Psalmes with the Hymnes Evangelicall and Songs Spirituall* (1621)[211] of Thomas Ravenscroft again made an important addition to the list of psalters. With its 105 harmonizations (of which twenty-eight appeared before and fifty-one are by Ravenscroft) this had more pieces in it than any other psalter except Day's, and added some new tunes to the repertory. The composers drawn on for the other settings include Alison, Blancks, Bennet, Cavendish, Dowland, Farnaby, Farmer, Kirbye, John Milton—father of the poet—,[212] Morley, Martin Peerson, Tallis, Thomas Tomkins, John Ward, and others. In the main, a trend is evident toward modern tonality and a favoring of harmonic considerations in the part-writing. In conjunction with these features, however, goes a decline in quality and style, at least so far as the work of certain of the newer men is concerned. Ravenscroft was a figure of some consequence in the field of secular music also.

Another English verse translation of the psalter was prepared by Henry Ainsworth and was published in 1612 with melodies only, at Amsterdam, for the use of English "Separatists" who had settled there. It was the Ainsworth Psalter, derived from both the English Psalter of 1562 and the Dutch Psalter (musically identical with the French[213]), that was brought to America by the Pilgrims in 1620.[214] Another psalter, the *Bay Psalm Book,* printed in

---

[209] For 1 of the Alison psalms, *see* BoydE, 55; for other Alison sacred exx., *see* EMS XXXIII, 104, 116, 129.

[210] See O. E. Albrecht in MQ, XXXI (1945), 498; BoydE, 60.

[211] A quasi-reprint in RavenB.

[212] For a monograph on him with music exx., *see* BrennM; 6 anthems in OEE XXII.

[213] PraM, 72f, prints a table showing the comparative indebtedness of the English, Scottish, and Ainsworth Psalters to French tunes.   [214] Pr. SmithP; *see also* SmithA.

Massachusetts by Stephen Daye (first edition, 1640),[215] contained texts only; but its *Admonition to the Reader* stated that some of the psalms were to be sung to music from the Ravenscroft Psalter and others to melodies in the English Psalter.

Among the contributors of verse to Alison's psalter of 1599 was William Leighton (d. before 1617), who was knighted perhaps c. 1603. While incarcerated for debt he compiled, in 1613, *The Teares or Lamentacions of a Sorrowfull Soule* (published 1614), consisting of fifty-four psalms and hymns. Of these, eighteen (called consort songs in the print) are *a 4*, the vocal parts being reinforced by treble viol, bass viol, flute (= recorder), lute, cittern, and pandore; thirteen more *a 4* and twenty-four *a 5* are without accompaniment. Eight of the group of seventeen have music by Leighton himself, and the remaining nineteen composers include John Bull, Byrd,[216] John Dowland, Alfonso Ferrabosco II,[217] Coperario, Thomas Ford, Orlando Gibbons, Milton, Ward, Weelkes, Wilbye,[218] Pilkington, Nathaniel Giles,[219] and others. This list includes men distinguished in various fields of music, e.g., Bull, important mainly for his keyboard works, and Dowland, mainly for his compositions for lute.[219a]

English Church Music of Bull, Tomkins, Gibbons, and Some Other Composers

Bull (b. 1563; d. Antwerp, 1628) was appointed organist of Hereford Cathedral in 1582. Early in 1585 he became a member of the Chapel Royal and, on the death of his former teacher William Blitheman in 1591, succeeded him as organist there. From Oxford, Bull received the degree of Mus. Bac. in 1586 and of Mus. Doc. in 1592, having previously taken the latter degree at Cambridge. Upon the queen's recommendation, he was appointed the first Music Professor at Gresham College in 1596, the requirement, previously adopted, that the lectures on theory be given in Latin being waived in his behalf, since he was unable to speak the language. He traveled, in 1601, in the Low Countries, France, and Germany, and was so admired that Elizabeth ordered him home lest some foreign court engage him. But in 1613 he left England without license and went to Brussels where, despite the English ambassador's assertion that Bull had fled to avoid just punishment for crimes, he was employed as organist by Archduke Albert. He became organist of the Antwerp Cathedral in 1617. While Bull's keyboard music is designed chiefly for the display of virtuosity, his few remaining sacred vocal works are of

[215] Facsimile ed., with introduction by Wilberforce Eames, 1905, Dodd, Mead & Co., N.Y.
[216] Byrd's contributions to *Teares* pr. ByrdW XI, 1, 5, 8, 20.
[217] 1 of his 3 contributions pr. DaA, 84.
[218] Wilbye's contributions to *Teares* pr. EMS VI, 173, 176.
[219] About Giles, *see* esp. AtkO, 26ff; also PulB, 208ff. His *Lesson of Descant* . . . pr. HawkH, III, 462.
[219a] Further about the psalters, *see* Grove IV, 267ff; BoydE, 40ff; Ancient & Modern, xxxvii–lx.

a more restrained nature. His verse anthem, *Almighty God, who by the lead-ing of a star* (described in early MSS as the "Starre Anthem"),[220] however, at one point has an upward leap from b to b-flat in the altus.

Dowland (1563–1626) was, in 1580, at Paris in the service of the am-bassador Sir Henry Cobham and while there became a Catholic. Within two years he returned to England. In 1588 he was awarded a Mus. Bac. degree by Oxford, in company with Morley, and he may have received such a degree from Cambridge also. In 1594, his application for a court post having been refused because of his faith, he went to Germany, first to the court of the Duke of Brunswick, then to that of the Landgrave of Hesse where he met Alexander Orologio (cf. p. 672). At both places he was well received and presented with offers for his services. He proceeded, however, to Italy, in-tending to study with Marenzio at Rome. At Venice he became a friend of Croce's. But he never went to Rome, although he was promised (so he states) "a large pension of the Pope," for at Florence he fell in with a group of English recusants, who, according to his own account, so shocked him by their plotting against Queen Elizabeth, that he turned about and went to Nuremberg. From there he sent, in November 1595, a long autobiographical letter (containing the account in question) to Sir Robert Cecil, who had helped him obtain a license to travel in Europe. In the letter he says he has given up the Catholic faith. Perhaps this facilitated his going back to England, to which he had returned by 1597. In that year he published his *First Booke of Songes*. In 1598, he was appointed lutenist to Christian IV of Denmark at a high salary. Dowland received many favors at Elsinore and in 1601 was sent to England to purchase musical instruments. He was there again in 1603 and seems to have remained through some time in 1605. His long ab-sences, also his becoming involved in financial difficulties, led to dissatisfaction at the Danish court, and in February 1606, in Christian's absence, Dowland was dismissed and returned home. That year he published at London an English translation of Ornithoparchus' *Micrologus*. In the preface of his last work, *A Pilgrimes Solace*, 1612, he is described as lutenist to Lord Walden. In October of that year he finally obtained the long-desired appointment as lutenist to the king, and he retained the post until his death.[221] Besides his contributions to Leighton's *Teares*, to East's psalter of 1592, and to Ravens-croft's, the small output of sacred music by Dowland includes a set of seven psalms, written for the funeral of Henry Noel, an Elizabethan courtier.[222]

[220] Pr. TCMO, No. 91. For a list of other vocal church music by Bull, *see* Grove I, 495. For Anthony Wood's biographical notes on Bull, *see* BoydE, 318f. (The writings of the antiquary, Wood [1632–95], contain comments on various musicians; BoydE prints a selection of them. Wood's diaries and other papers are drawn upon in *The Life and Times of Anthony Wood . . .*, Andrew Clark, ed. [Oxford Historical Society Publications XIX, XXI, XXVI, XXX, XL 1891–1900.])

[221] Further biographical data in WarA, 21ff; RavnE; FloodI; MannL; etc.

[222] Pr. TCMO Nos. 79, 80. Dowland's psalm settings for the East and Ravenscroft psalters are, of course, included in MAS XI and RavenB respectively; the settings he made of *Old 100th* for these psalters are also in HaverH, 54, 55.

The composer appearing in *Teares* as Coperario was John Cooper (born c. 1570; died 1627), who before 1604 visited Italy and adopted the name Giovanni Coperario, which he kept after returning home. He was a prominent writer of instrumental ensemble music and has left us a treatise entitled *Rules how to compose*.[222a] Thomas Ford (born c. 1580; died 1648) was in the service of Prince Henry in 1611 and, from 1625 until the civil war, was one of the king's musicians; he is of significance mainly as a composer of ayres (cf. p. 838).[223] Francis Pilkington (born c. 1562–1565; died 1638) received the Mus. Bac. degree from Oxford in 1595. He became a Singing Man at Chester Cathedral in 1602, a minor canon in 1614, and precentor of the cathedral in 1623. Though connected with the church, he is mainly a composer of secular music.[224]

Among the numerous other writers of English church music of the period, Thomas Bateson,[225] Michael East,[226] Thomas Hunt,[227] John Mundy (son of William Mundy),[228] and Richard Nicholson[229] should at least be mentioned; all were active madrigalists, Bateson being the most significant. Thomas Tomkins and Orlando Gibbons, who have been listed as contributors to the Ravenscroft Psalter and to Leighton's *Teares*, respectively, require fuller discussion.

Tomkins (b. 1571 or 1572; d. 1656), who came from a musical family, was like Morley a pupil of Byrd's. He became organist at Worcester Cathedral c. 1596, in succession to Nathaniel Patrick, a gifted composer who had been appointed Master of the Children in 1590 or 1591 and died, apparently young, in 1595.[230] Tomkins in 1621 became a member of the Chapel Royal, but continued to hold his post at Worcester until 1646, when services in the cathedral were suspended because of the civil war.[231]

"Although Tomkins lived till the middle of the 17th century, he adhered for the most part to the polyphonic style, and he must be regarded as belonging to the great group of English composers who flourished at the close of the 16th century: and it is a fact that much of his work was written before the close of the first two decades of the 17th century." [232]

The bulk of Tomkins' sacred compositions are contained in *Musica Deo Sacra*, printed twelve years after his death, only a few other such works surviving in MS, in his printed collection (mainly of secular material) of

---

[222a] Facsimile with commentary in CoperarioR.   [223] For an anthem, *see* MAS XIV, 61.
[224] 2 sacred exx. pr. EMS XXVI, 111, 177.   [225] An anthem pr. MAS XIV, 142.
[226] 8 anthems *ibid*. He should not be confused with Thomas East, known only as a printer.
[227] Morning and Evening Services pr. TCMO Nos. 65 and 66, respectively.
[228] An anthem pr. TCMO No. 92.   [229] An anthem pr. TCMO No. 48.
[230] Further biographical data in AtkO, 31ff. From a Service of his *a 4*, the Kyrie and Creed are included in *Short Communion Service . . . Completed under the Editorship of Ivor Atkins*; the *Te Deum* and *Benedictus Dominus* are pr. separately, the Magnificat and *Nunc dimittis* together (all ed. by Atkins; Oxford University Press).
[231] Further biographical data esp. in AtkO, 37ff; *see also* FelEE, 87f.
[232] E. H. Fellowes in Grove V, 354.

1622, and, of course, in the Ravenscroft Psalter. A *Pars Organica* was provided for *Musica Deo Sacra,* including both accompaniments to the vocal
solos and an outline score of the whole (cf. Batten's organ-book). Among the
contents of the collection are five Services.[233] Two of them, *a 4,* are of the
short type. A third, more elaborate in style, has several sections written for
as many as ten independent voices; the skilful handling of numerous parts
is characteristic of this composer. The remaining Services, of the verse type,
frequently suffer from a too elaborate organ accompaniment, and in one
of them the great number of verse passages leads to a disjointed effect. *Musica
Deo Sacra* preserves also a setting of the Preces and Responses, a portion of
the Burial Service, and ninety-three anthems. Of the last-named group, no
fewer than forty-one are verse anthems, but Tomkins is at his best in the older,
more polyphonic style. *Praise the Lord, O my soul* contains the following
felicitous counterpoint of conflicting accents.

EXAMPLE 188. Extract from *Praise the Lord, O my soul*—Tomkins
(after TCMO No. 49).

In the four-part *O give thanks unto the Lord,*[234] the words "O let your songs
be of him and praise him" are set to three successive points of imitation which,
if no great technical feats, are nevertheless effective: three voices take part
in each point, two singing in thirds (the pairing being changed each time)
and the third voice imitating the lower voice of the pair at the fifth above.
O pray for the peace of Jerusalem [235] ends with a noteworthy cadence, which
includes a diminished triad in root position. *When David heard that Absalom
was slain* (from the 1622 collection) [236] is a most dramatic setting of 2 Samuel
XVIII, 33; the old custom of resorting frequently to the minor second in
laments is here movingly continued. *Musica Deo Sacra* contains a twelve-
part *O praise the Lord, all ye heathen* [237] that is a tour-de-force in brilliant
and resourceful part-writing; the piece is not composed for antiphonal choirs,
but for twelve real parts. Notwithstanding his mannerism of repeating words

---

[233] All pr. TCM VIII.   [234] Pr. TCMO No. 19.
[235] Pr. TCMO No. 11.
[236] EMS XVIII, 112; HAM, 191.
[237] Pr. TCMO No. 100. For other Tomkins anthems, see TCMO, Nos. 98, 99; EMS XVIII,
199.

at the ends of phrases to a disconcerting extent, Tomkins is one of the finest early composers of English church music.

A supplementary page in one copy of the organ part of *Musica Deo Sacra* offers some statements of interest in the field of musical performance. We are told that a semibreve should equal two beats of the human pulse or of a pendulum 2′ long; also, that f is the pitch produced by an open pipe 2½′ long. While the latter item of information is of no great moment in view of the undependability of pipe measurements as indications of pitch,[238] the former item provides welcome confirmation of the fact (obvious, to be sure) that the minim had replaced the semibreve as the normal time-unit (cf. p. 188).

Orlando Gibbons (b. Oxford, 1583; d. 1625) came of a musical family, like Tomkins. His father William (c. 1540–1595) was appointed one of the waits at Cambridge in 1567, a fact which, at this time, would indicate that he was a singer or instrumentalist, or both. Orlando's brothers Edward (c. 1570–c. 1650) and Ellis (1573–1603) are each represented by a small number of surviving works. Christopher (1615–1676), his son, was to achieve an estimable position as a composer of the baroque period. As might be expected, some confusion in attributions has resulted from the fact that several members of the family composed.[239] Orlando, in 1596, entered the choir at King's College, Cambridge. He became organist of the Chapel Royal in 1605, and in 1606 took the degree of Mus. Bac. at Cambridge. On May 17, 1622, the Chair of History at Oxford was founded by William Camden (1551–1623), the antiquary and historian, and at his request the degree of Mus. Doc. was conferred upon Gibbons on this occasion. In 1623, Gibbons became organist of Westminster Abbey, and as such he officiated at James I's funeral in 1625. Soon thereafter he himself died suddenly at Canterbury where, with the rest of the Chapel Royal, he had gone in attendance upon Charles I; the new king was waiting there to leave for Dover and meet his bride Henrietta Maria upon her arrival from France.

Though Gibbons was an excellent composer of vocal and instrumental secular music, his reputation rests largely on his works for the Anglican Church. Of some forty anthems of his (several surviving incomplete), only fifteen are full, the rest being verse anthems. Yet, like Tomkins, Gibbons is as a rule much less successful with the newer verse type. Such full anthems as the magnificent six-part *Hosanna to the Son of David* and eight-part *O clap your hands* (with its *pars II: God is gone up*) [240] far surpass any of the verse anthems. Gibbons seems to lead the old polyphonic style to the last high point it was to reach in England.

[238] Cf. MendP, 588.

[239] Thus, *Sing we merrily*, ascribed to Orlando in TCM IV, 340, seems actually to be by Christopher; cf. Grove II, 381, col. 1.

[240] These and the other Gibbons works to be mentioned above are all pr. TCM IV; *see also* TCMA, 19f, 38ff.

EXAMPLE 189. Extract from *Hosanna to the Son of David*—Gibbons (after TCM IV, 208).

This composer's music is not very melismatic, but at times it is nevertheless polyphonically quite complex. That he could be eloquent also in simpler compositions is attested by the lovely *O Lord, increase my faith.* Of Gibbons' verse anthems, *This is the record of John* is probably the best. The text of each narrative verse section is repeated, in whole or in part, by the full chorus, but always to new music. Often in Gibbons' verse anthems, however, the solo passages are marred by a too "busy" accompaniment, and even in the full sections of the works a decline in style is noticeable.

Two Services by Gibbons are known: a Short Service *a 4* for full chorus, and a verse Service *a 5*. The former, a fine work including the seven numbers customary at the time, is more polyphonic than the usual Short Service. The latter, comprising only a *Te Deum, Jubilate,* Magnificat, and *Nunc dimittis,* is of lesser quality.[241]

"Orlando Gibbons . . . was . . . the last of the great Elizabethans. It used to be said that this famous School of composers came to an end at his death in 1625. In a general way this is true, although some notable English musicians did in fact survive him. . . . Tompkins and some of the lesser Church musicians lived for several years after this date, but the great wave of composition in the poly-phonic manner had spent its force. . . . England was shortly to be harassed with Civil warfare. . . . Until the coming of Henry Purcell and the Restoration School of composers English Church music languished sadly from 1625 onwards." [242]

[241] Further about the Services, cf. FelOG, 66ff.

[242] FelEE, 99. Notwithstanding their occasional lapses, much of this chapter (as of the next) is greatly indebted to the editions and writings of Canon Fellowes.

Chapter 16: ENGLAND (c. 1535 to c. 1635): The Madrigals, including those of Morley, Weelkes, and Wilbye; the Ayre; Instrumental Music, including the Lute Works of Dowland, the Keyboard Works of Byrd, Bull, and Farnaby, and the Ensemble Compositions of Tye, Morley, and Gibbons; Music in the Theater

As we have seen, English music flourished under Henry VIII, owing in no small measure to his interest in it, and also under Edward VI and Mary, to reach, at the end of Elizabeth's reign, a level rarely approached thereafter. As the English grew in riches and power and acquired an increasing knowledge of the art products of the continent through the importation of foreign talent and through travel, they abandoned their temporary insularity in cultural matters and eagerly assimilated, though at a late date, the ideas and ideals of the Italian Renaissance. Tudor church music was remarkable, but it is the secular forms of English music—the madrigal, lute ayre, virginal music, and fancies for viols—that embody most richly the spirit and power of the English Renaissance. The same accumulation of intellectual and artistic force that produced Sidney, Shakespeare, Bacon, Donne, and Inigo Jones also produced Morley, Weelkes, Dowland, and Orlando Gibbons.

The Continuing Tradition of the English Part-Song; the Contrapuntally Accompanied Solo Song; Byrd

The most brilliant variety of English secular vocal music is the Elizabethan madrigal,[1] but this bold nationalization of an Italian style did not take place in a void. The native tradition, stemming from the part-song described in Chapter 15, maintained its independence throughout the vogue for Italianate music. The alternation of several points of imitation with chordal passages

[1] The standard critical work on Elizabethan secular vocal music is FelE; a more comparative approach to the English madrigal is employed in HelmI and KermanM. *See also* DentB and PatMP. Valuable research aids are SteeleE and RimbB, which give the contents of all secular sets known in 1847 and a first-line index of all the songs they contain. FelV, OberM, and BolleE are useful reprints of poetic texts. Fellowes also edited EMS, a 36-volume series including the almost complete writings of the English madrigal composers; this is so widely available that citations of its contents will not be duplicated by references to other modern editions (except ByrdW). Attention, however, is called to these additional reprint sources: 17 of the 25 vols. of OEE; SquireM I, III; ELAM IV, V, VII; MAS II, III, V, VIII, XIII, XV–XVII; and very many in octavo editions.

in Richard Edwards' *In goinge to my naked bedde* (c. 1550–1560) [2] shows
the effect of continental influence, though not yet on a large scale, on English
secular music before the English madrigal proper was born. The melodic
idiom suggests the early Italian madrigal rather than the Franco-Netherlandish
chanson; e.g., the words "The fallyng out of faithful frends" are set to the
same stock idiom that ends Arcadelt's *Il bianco e dolce cigno*. Edwards (d.
1566) was a poet, playwright, musician, and Master of the Children in the
Chapel Royal.[2a]

Thomas Whythorne's seventy-six *Songes to three, fower, and five voyces*
(1571),[3] the only English secular set printed between 1530 and 1588,[4] shows
a slight foreign influence. In the preface, in doggerel verse,[5] Whythorne casts
light on the state of secular music in England. He reports that he has been
to Italy, mentioning "Musick . . . that called is Napolitane (a prety mery
one)"; and a piece like *The doutfull state that I posses* [6] may be regarded
as an English adaptation of the *villanella alla napolitana*. But Whythorne's
compositions are more in the tradition of the older English part-song. Archaic
by continental standards and sometimes technically unresourceful, though
not unattractive, they reveal the hand of a "Gentleman," as Whythorne styles
himself, and we could wish for a group of songs from this time by a more
knowing musician. The polyphony of *Geve not thy minde to heavines,*
though flowing, has a dense quality caused by the total lack of rests in the
five voices, and there are few clear cadences. In contrast, *Though choler
cleapt the hart about* is chordal, with clean-cut phrases. The imperviousness
of the composer to the true madrigal is shown in *It doth me good when
Zeph'rus rains,* where he sets the words "The birdes with gladsom tunes"
without the slightest attempt at word-painting.

[2] Pr. HawkH V, 453; EMS XXXVI, last number. The piece survives anon. and textless in a
keyboard arrangement in the Mulliner Organ Book (cf. p. 851), while the poem comes down,
attributed to Edwards, in *The Paradyse of Daynty Devises* (1576). Hawkins recovered the part-
song by drawing on both sources and, since Edwards was a composer, deduced that not only
the text but also the music was his. The historian likewise reconstructed from the same sources
When grypinge griefes (pr. HawkH V, 444), attributed to Edwards on the same grounds, as
well as *O the syllye man* (= *By painted words;* pr. HawkH V, 446), this being actually attributed to Edwards in the Mulliner MS, and *Lyke as the dolefull dove* by Tallis (pr. HawkH V,
450). By drawing on literary sources and the Mulliner arrangements, it is possible to recover
still other secular part-songs, e.g., the anon. *My frindes* and *I smyle to see howe yow devyse.* A
part-song by Shepherd, *O happye dames,* reduced for keyboard in Mulliner, survives elsewhere
with both text and music; this is true also of Tallis' *When shall my sorowfull sygheinge* (pr.
Oxford Choral Songs, No. 351). Tallis' *Fonde youthe is a bubble* in Mulliner, for which we
have no text, is musically the same as his *Purge me, O Lord* (cf. p. 800). The Mulliner keyboard
versions of all these pieces are pr. MusB I. For fuller information, *see* StevM, 55ff.

[2a] Further on Edwards, *see* esp. BoydE, 95ff.

[3] The poetic text, etc., and a copy of the music of the tenor part only is given in ImelS.

[4] A MS source, c. 1540–1550, unfortunately incomplete, is described in StevP.

[5] Reprinted ImelS and BoydE, 281ff.

[6] 12 of Whythorne's *Songes* are pr. separately in *Oxford Choral Songs from the Old Masters,*
Nos. 354–365, ed. by P. Warlock, 1927, and 3 more in a group ed. by M. Bukofzer, 1947, Music
Press, No. 90). *The doutfull state* is pr. as No. 361 in the Oxford set; the other pieces to be men-
tioned in the above text are pr. as Nos. 364, 354, and 360, respectively.

Some Whythorne pieces, though all the parts have words, belong stylistically to the important repertory of the Elizabethan strophic solo song with accompaniment of viols (usually four).[7] In this type, which may be called the contrapuntally accompanied solo song, the upper voice generally carries a syllabic setting of the poem, while the lower voices, faster moving and noticeably less melodic, weave an amorphous polyphonic texture below the tune, and fill in gaps between its phrases. Like the lute ayres, to which their kinship is apparent, these songs cover a surprisingly wide range of expression—from the humorous folklike pieces of Nicholson and Wigthorpe to the tragic songs of Farrant and Parsons, evidently used in early Elizabethan plays. A strong dramatic impression is made by the anonymous *Come tread the paths,*[8] lamenting a slain husband, with its repeated cries of "Guichiardo!" and "I dy, I dy." William Byrd, the master of the contrapuntally accompanied solo song, wrote many to religious texts, often psalm paraphrases, probably for private devotional use. His accompanying voices are often complex and ingeniously written, and his melodies show a subtle feeling for proportion and rhythmic variety. Among the loveliest of over thirty songs, preserved in MSS, are *My little sweete darling*[9] and *Blame I confes.*

EXAMPLE 190. Extract from *Blame I confes*—Byrd (from Oxford, Christ Church MS 984–8, No. 129; complete piece in ByrdW XV, 84).

*The note, g′, is correct, not a′ as pr. in ByrdW XV.

Byrd selected what he no doubt thought the best of such songs for his first secular publication, the *Psalmes, Sonets, & songs of sadnes and pietie* (1588).[10] This began a wave of publications lasting from c. 1590 to 1630.

---

[7] 22 Elizabethan songs for one voice and four stringed instruments pr. WarES. Two previously pr. ArkE. Byrd's songs pr. ByrdW XV.
[8] Pr. WarES III, 10; ByrdW XV, 89, with a doubtful ascription to Byrd.
[9] ByrdW XV, 105; WarES I, 14.
[10] EMS XIV; ByrdW XII.

Though words are supplied to all the parts, Byrd carefully explains in his preface: "heere are divers songs, . . . originally made for Instruments to express the harmonie, and one voyce to pronounce the dittie [i.e., the words], . . . now framed in all parts for voyces to sing the same." In most of the songs one voice, obviously quite distinct from the others, is called "the first singing part"; strophic songs predominate. The set is divided into three sections: "Psalmes"; "Songes of sadnes and pietie," related to the serious type of accompanied song; and "Sonets and Pastorales," gay folklike compositions; and all show even greater care than most of Byrd's MS songs in the imitative treatment of the lower voices. One piece in Italian, set to a favorite stanza of Ariosto's, "La virginella" (cf. p. 428),[11] has more note-against-note writing and clearer cadences than most of the others, but is still a contrapuntally accompanied solo song, far removed from the Italian style in texture,[12] despite the presence of the *Ruggiero* melody in the bass.

Byrd's *Songs of Sundrie Natures* (1589),[13] though "lately made and composed into Musicke," also resist Italian influence. Dent observes that the pieces *a 3* and *a 4* are more Netherlandish than Italian; the counterpoint is rather stiff and learned, the harmonic idiom severe, word-painting rare. The songs *a 5* and *a 6* in this set, as in Byrd's last publication, *Psalmes, Songs, and Sonnets* (1611),[14] show an interesting transition from the accompanied-solo style of 1588 to writing (sometimes madrigalian) more in the *a cappella* manner. But even the most Italianate pieces of the 1611 set, e.g., *Come wofull Orpheus*, with its elaborate chromatic illustration of the line "Of sowrest sharps and uncouth flats, make choise," still retain a strong native cast. This half-old, half-new style has a charm, power, and individuality of its own. Byrd seems to have considered the Italian style too frivolous for his own secular compositions, though he easily mastered it; as early as 1590, when Thomas Watson asked for a piece "after the Italian vaine" for his *Italian Madrigalls Englished*, Byrd responded magnificently with *This sweet and merry month of May*,[15] *a 6*, one of the greatest, though most Italianate of all English madrigals. His usually serious, conservative attitude [15a] is made clear by the inclusion of so many sacred compositions in the sets often regarded, though not quite accurately, as "madrigalian."

It must be remembered that Byrd, at forty-five, was already the most re-

[11] It was at once translated and reprinted in *Musica transalpina*, 1588, together with a second stanza. This version pr. EMS XIV, 216, 223 (= ByrdW XVI, 1, 8). Cf. Chap. 9, fn. 245. *See also* EinEM, 66ff.

[12] DentB is important to an understanding of Byrd's secular music. *See also* WestrB.

[13] EMS XV; ByrdW XIII.   [14] EMS XVI; ByrdW XIV.

[15] EMS XVI, 216; ByrdW XVI, 15. The fragmentation of the text, the changes of meter, the brief use of choral recitative broken by rests, the melismatic figure on "sing" and the syncopation on "play" are among the Italianate features in this composition, which are rare in Byrd's work elsewhere.

[15a] About the conservative nature of Byrd's music (which, of course, has nothing to do with its intrinsic value, *see* HandWB.

spected of English composers when *Musica transalpina,* in 1588, intensified the madrigal vogue. Several younger men followed him in spirit, if not always in technique, preferring old native features to those of the more elegant madrigal. John Mundy's *Songs and Psalmes* (1594), Richard Carlton's so-called *Madrigals* (1601), and Richard Alison's *An Howre's Recreation in Musicke* (1606),[16] present a rather amateurish, technically unskilful and confused mixture of compositions. Orlando Gibbons, whose single secular set (1612) was misnamed *Madrigals and Motetts,*[17] developed a rich and unique personal idiom within the general scope of the accompanied solo song. The style is clearly present in the popular *The silver swan* and *Ah dear heart,* and is suggested in the masterly setting of Sir Walter Ralegh's *What is our life?* The pieces that are more truly in the *a cappella* style employ a kind of abstract polyphony, closer to English instrumental writing than to the madrigal style of Morley, Weelkes, and Wilbye. Word-painting, sectional treatment of text, and other typically Italianate devices are entirely secondary in Gibbons' music, which is on a plane of high seriousness reflected by the choice of texts, largely of an ethical or philosophical nature. This is one of the most impressive of all secular publications of the time, and shows the continued vigor of the old style, crossed with the new, in the hands of an original and capable musician.

The Enormous Vogue of the Italian Madrigal

In the last decades of the sixteenth century, however, most English composers seem to have become fascinated by the knowingness and wealth of Italian music. The rise of the madrigal in England is a complete musical expression of one characteristic aspect of Elizabethan life, its eager emulation and appropriation of foreign culture. It parallels in time the literary Italianization that led to the "New Poetry" of Sidney, Spenser, and the sonneteers, c. 1580 to 1600, a period of enthusiastic translation, adaptation, imitation, and plagiarism of everything French, classical, and especially Italian.[18] Like this movement, the madrigal was a sudden growth for which models had been available for decades, a belated extension of a current already past its prime on the continent. In fact, about seventy English madrigals are set to translations of Italian madrigal texts.[18a] But like all pertinent manifestations of this general cultural tendency, the madrigal in England was more than a simple importation of an Italian ideal, as it was in Germany and the Netherlands; it was a unique nationalization of it, a relatively small but brilliant aftermath

---

[16] EMS XXXV (incomplete), XXVII, and XXXIII, respectively.
[17] EMS V.
[18] On the relation of Elizabethan poetry and music, *see* PatMP; PatLM; KermanM, Ch. 2.
[18a] Cf. OberM.

of the great madrigal tradition. Never before and perhaps never afterward have English musicians adopted a foreign style with such whole-heartedness and intelligence, and at the same time added so much of their own and produced so distinguished a native repertory.

Although the madrigal in England grew in the same cultural climate as the great school of Elizabethan poetry, much of its individuality stems from the fact that, unlike the Italian madrigal, it was not a literary development. English madrigal verse is much admired, but madrigal composition in England conspicuously lacks the strong tradition of setting serious poetry—works like those of Petrarch, Ariosto, Bembo, and Tasso—that practically determined the whole progress of the Italian music. In England, the real madrigalists rarely selected the accepted "great poetry" of the day for their music; they set very little by Sidney and next to nothing by Spenser, Shakespeare, Daniel, or Drayton. Indeed, other varieties of Elizabethan secular music were more consciously literary: the old-fashioned abstract music of Byrd was set to the distinguished native poetry of the time before the Petrarchan influence, and the lute ayre of Dowland to the poetry of reaction that sprang up at the turn of the century, with the poems of John Donne. English madrigalists generally chose light verses, *poesia per musica* often in the Italian manner, and consequently the English madrigal as a whole became lighter than the greatest Italian music. Moreover, in England there was little incentive for repeated settings of famous poems, whereby Italian madrigalists consciously vied with their greatest predecessors and their contemporary rivals, and maintained the most elevated esthetic tone in their work.

In every way the English madrigal was a less esoteric and more popular movement. There is no evidence of professional madrigal singers employed by the nobility, as in Italy; madrigals were designed more for the private use of the new gentry and the rising middle class. Perhaps most significant, England never imitated the important Italian madrigal academies (cf. p. 400), through which literary amateurs exerted a powerful control over the course of musical composition. While the Italian composers' instincts were often literary and dramatic, the Englishmen's were more purely musical—we shall mention specific features in the work of Morley, Weelkes, and Wilbye. They could not tolerate the sophisticated bare simplicity of the *villanella,* the *balletto,* and the *canzonetta;* on the other hand, they showed little sympathy for extreme dramatic features, such as choral recitative (cf. p. 415, etc.) and chromaticism. Most of their madrigals are diatonic in harmony and melodic line, and when they use chromaticism it is within a solid tonal structure. Though all Elizabethan madrigalists use word-painting, it rarely creates the form of their pieces; it is, rather, contained *within* the form. A typical English madrigal is more objectively constructed than an Italian piece; it is more a unified whole, with a prevailing mood and movement, than a constantly varying series of contrasting episodes. Perhaps the trait that distinguishes it most strongly is what we might call its "songfulness"—a tendency toward melodic writing that has some vague affinity with English folk song. Even in the most Italianate of English madrigals (for example, many by Weelkes), in which all the voices are equal in activity and in melodic importance, the preponderant effect is more "songful" than in a corresponding madrigal by Marenzio. And in a fair proportion of English madrigals, the top voice appears to carry the chief melodic content, one might say, the *principal* tune, since all the voices are to varying degrees tuneful. In many cases, one can trace the direct intrusion of the different song styles of Byrd or Dowland.

The number of Italian madrigals preserved in Elizabethan MSS, some from as early as the 1560's and 1570's,[19] shows that an enormous amount of Italian music circulated in England before native composers begin to write in the new style. Finally, in 1588, it became profitable to publish a large anthology of Italian madrigals with fairly efficient translations, under the title *Musica transalpina*.[20] In the very interesting preface,[21] the editor, Nicholas Yonge, explains that he headed a sort of singing society attended by "a great number of Gentlemen and merchants of good accompt (as well of this realme as of forreine nations)," and that he regularly imported music for them from Italy.[22] On the whole, their taste was relatively serious, up-to-date, but conservative; the man represented by the largest number of madrigals (and by two chansons) is Alfonso Ferrabosco I,[23] who emigrated to Elizabeth's court c. 1560 (cf. p. 791). His departure from England took place before the vogue for madrigals to English words began, and no such original settings from his pen are known. Though his style was old-fashioned and austere and though he seems to have had no great effect on the main stream of musical activity on the continent, "Master Alfonso" built up a great reputation as a madrigalist in England and did much to interest Elizabethan musicians in Italian music.[23a] But by this time they were concerned also with more brilliant and modern composers, particularly with Marenzio, who has the second largest number of madrigals in *Musica transalpina* and the lion's share of the next madrigal anthology, the *Italian Madrigalls Englished* (1590) by the influential translator and sonneteer Thomas Watson.[24] Within a few years,

---

[19] FelE, 38, mentions part-books at Winchester College dated 1564; *see also* OberV.

[20] The English poetic texts, with their Italian originals, are reprinted in OberM, 207ff. On the 5 Italian anthologies mentioned in the above paragraph, *see* EinEM, KermanA.

[21] Reprinted in OberM, 209ff, and in OEE XI.

[22] "Yeerely sent me out of Italy and other places." The "other places" must include the Low Countries, for *Musica transalpina* was modeled on the madrigal anthologies of Phalèse, notably *Musica divina,* 1583 (cf. p. 427).

[23] The 9 madrigals (3 having second *partes*) and 2 chansons pr. OEE XI, XII. Cf. Chap. 8, fn. 247.

[23a] *See* further KermanMA.

[24] The poetic texts, with their Italian originals, etc., are reprinted in OberM, 259ff. In an elaborate Latin hexameter poem praising Marenzio, Watson says: "The sweet power of your

there were actually three more of these anthologies printed, emphasizing the
lighter Italian music: a second book of *Musica transalpina* (1597), Thomas
Morley's *Canzonets. Or Little Short Songs to Foure Voyces: Celected out
of the best and approved Italian Authors* (1597), and *Madrigals to five voyces.
Celected* . . . (1598).[25]

Morley

Though these collections by no means introduced the madrigal into England, their effect in spurring interest in it was evidently very great. The first
two of them immediately preceded the publication of English madrigals, and
it is striking that English composers reset more poems from the anthologies
than from any native source—at times borrowing not only words but music
also. It is significant that two of the anthologies were issued by Morley, who
was the founder of the English school and its most prolific, popular, and influential, as well as most Italianate master. Born in 1557, he was exactly of the
generation to be most impressed by the culture of Italy, which captivated the
England of the 1570's; his historic role was to assimilate the Italian style and
present it to his countrymen in a somewhat popularized form. His five
madrigalian sets were published before almost any other English madrigals
went to print, and were practically the only English madrigal sets to require
reprinting at the time.[26] His influence is apparent in the work of every subsequent madrigalist of his country.

Morley's first set, the *Canzonets. Or Little Short Songs to Three Voyces*
(1593),[27] really consists of little madrigals, not canzonets. Here the true English madrigal style at once enters into its own—a highly successful combination
of native feeling with foreign idioms and techniques. Most of the pieces are
very light in tone, tripping along gaily, as does the passage in Example 191*a*.
In these Morley skilfully rearranges features from Marenzio and especially
from the Italian *canzonetta,* e.g., the disposition of the voices; the sudden
alternation of quick and slow sections; the tossing about of short motifs
from one voice to another; and the general lightness and delicacy of melody,
texture, and spirit. On the other hand, the set includes half a dozen compositions that are by no means little in scope or in expression. *Deepe lamenting,*

music stabs me; so may I die often, for in your song is life. When you sing, I dream it is the music
of the spheres, the harmony of the Muses." Morley suggests the following models for madrigal
composition in MorlP: "*Alfonso ferrabosco* for deepe skill, *Luca Marenzo* for good ayre and fine
invention"; and his words are echoed in Henry Peacham's *The Compleat Gentleman,* 1622.

[25] The English poetic texts, etc., of these 3 anthologies are given, with their Italian originals,
in OberM, 287ff, 333ff, 311ff, respectively.

[26] There are 4 contemporary eds. of Morley's 1593 *Canzonets,* and two each of his 1594
Madrigals and 1595 *Canzonets* and *Ballets.* The only other madrigalian sets reprinted at the time
are Weelkes' *Ballets* (1598) and, rather unaccountably, East's *Fourth Set* (c. 1618).

[27] EMS I.

Farewell disdainfull, and *Cease mine eyes* are among the first English serious madrigals, and contain passages such as the one in Example 191*b*.

EXAMPLE 191. (*a*) Opening of *What ayles my darling?*—Morley and
(*b*) Extract from *Now must I dye recurelesse*—Morley (both from *Canzonets* . . . , East, 1593; complete pieces in EMS I, 92, 66, respectively).

Arise gett upp my deere, the most elaborate piece in the set, is the first example of Morley's narrative madrigal, perhaps his most attractive and individual genre. The poem is about a rustic wedding, and Morley, in rapid succession, uses every resource of his style to paint all the vivid details that the text presents.[28] The success of this set evidently led to the publication of Morley's *Madrigalls to Foure Voyces* [29] in the following year, 1594. It is practically a replica of the *Canzonets,* with about the same number of serious pieces and a few more narrative madrigals. The new set is perhaps even more pleasing than the other, and the impression that it made at the time is shown by the publication within the next few years of three more sets of madrigals *a 4* by Giles Farnaby (1598), John Bennet (1599), and John Farmer (1599).[30] Though not of the first rank, they include many charming compositions.[31]

[28] The piece is pr. in EMS I, Part II, 101.   [29] EMS II.
[30] EMS XX, XXIII, and VIII, respectively.
[31] Farnaby's *Susanna faire* is of particular interest. He took the poem from *Musica transalpina,* 1588, where it accompanies Lassus' well-known chanson *Susanne un jour* (cf. pp. 393f); Farnaby's superius uses the famous tune as it appears in Lassus' superius, but the lower parts are new and seem instrumental in conception.

Two sets published by Morley in 1595, *Balletts to Five Voyces* and *Canzonets to Two Voyces,* allow us to follow very closely the growth of the English style from its Italian antecedents. Both were issued in alternate Italian and English editions,[32] most of the English poems being translations from Italian *poesia per musica* and much of the music being modeled on specific Italian compositions. This shocked some Victorian commentators,[33] but we have had many occasions to observe the attitude of a Renaissance composer in reworking the material of other musicians; rather than "plagiarism," this, in England as elsewhere, was a sort of compliment to pre-existent compositions, as well as a polite demonstration of how the composer thought they could be improved. The madrigals of Weelkes and Wilbye would have been impossible if Morley had not conscientiously moulded the Italian style to suit English needs.[34]

Many of Morley's best-known works appeared in the *First Booke of Balletts:* [35] *Now is the month of Maying, Sing we and chaunt it, Fyer, fyer, my hart!* Though the set is modeled closely on the famous *balletti* of Gastoldi (cf. pp. 445f), Morley's expansion of the form is striking. In the verse sections of the ballet he often follows Gastoldi quite literally, but in the "fa la" refrains he proceeds quite differently. With Gastoldi the refrain is very short and generally in the same simple style as the rest of the ballet; with Morley it is a long, contrapuntal interlude, instrumental in character, the most brilliant section of the whole composition. Moreover, in several pieces [36] Morley was dissatisfied with the simple chordal declamation of the Italian ballet, and wrote throughout in the more complex polyphonic style of the canzonet. In all, a more interesting and purely musical result is obtained, and the later English ballet writers—Weelkes, Youll, Pilkington, Tomkins, and Hilton—followed Morley's example. Morley also shows a more modern harmonic sense than Gastoldi. The following comparison [36a] between a favorite ballet of Morley's and its model shows that Morley had a clearer conception of tonality, which is typical of the English school as a whole.

[32] *See* PatP, 410f; PatMP, 98. OberM, 346ff, 373ff, gives the English poetic texts with their Italian originals.

[33] For different reactions to this procedure, cf. OliM, 93; DartCL, 2.

[34] It may be added that Morley's great *Plaine and Easie* . . . , the standard English didactic work for years, is saturated with Italian ideas and shows acquaintance with a wide variety of madrigal literature. It is interesting that Morley considers double counterpoint specifically Italian (p. 105) and also that he several times (pp. 96, 154, 163f) harangues against the well-known archaic procedure favored by the English—though not, of course, followed only by them (cf. pp. 297, 700f)—of employing cross relation in such a way that what we would call the raised and lowered forms of the seventh degree of the scale are heard in close conjunction, if not actually simultaneously (*see also* p. 535). This is a feature of Byrd's style, but is avoided by Morley and the more urbane madrigalists. Weelkes, however, occasionally uses it for a beautiful expressive effect (as in *Cease sorrowes now* and *O care*).

[35] EMS IV. The last 6 numbers are not ballets at all, but canzonets and madrigals. Similarly, there are several compositions in Gastoldi's set that are not *balletti.*

[36] Nos. 5, 8, 12, 14. No. 15 is on the border line between the two styles.

[36a] Taken from KermanM, Chap. 6.

Table VII

Gastoldi, *Viver lieto voglio* (see TorA II, 103; BuH III, 231)				Morley, *Shoote false love* (see EMS V, 4)			
line	cadences on			line	cadences on		
1		G (tonal center)		1		G (tonal center)	
2	C			2		D	
fa la		G		fa la	G		
3	C			3	C		
4	C			4		D	
5			D	5	G		
6	C			6		D	
7		G		7			A
8		G		8		D	
fa la		G		fa la	G		

Morley's knack of reaching in a very sure fashion for both the dominant and the "dominant of the dominant" gives him the "fresh" quality that has endeared him to modern madrigal singers. Examples may be multiplied in which Morley also takes care to exploit the mediant relationships in a modern way. If at one time the Italians outstripped the Franco-Netherlanders in chordal writing, they were in turn to be outstripped by the English in developing a feeling for harmonic propriety.

In the *Canzonets to Two Voyces*,[37] Morley reduced *canzonette a 4*, mostly by Felice Anerio, into *bicinia*, and this naturally gave him less scope for individuality than he had in his ballets. *Flora, wilt thou torment mee*, for instance, follows Anerio's *Flori morir debb'io*[38] very exactly throughout, as the following comparison indicates, but, even here, Morley moves to the dominant at the end of the tiny first phrase.

EXAMPLE 192. Extracts from (*a*) *Flori morir debb'io*—Anerio and (*b*) *Flora, wilt thou torment mee*—Morley (from KermanM, Ex. 53).

a

Flori mo- rir debb'i - o? Flo-ri dol - ce hen mi - o.

Flora fair love I languish, For love, Flo - ra, for an - guish.

b

Flo-ra, wilt thou torment mee, And yet must— I con-tent mee

[37] EMS I.
[38] Morley reprinted Anerio's canzonet with practically the same translation in his Italian selected *Canzonets* of 1597.

Morley's approach to the *canzonetta* type can be seen more clearly in his *Canzonets or Little Short Aers to Five and Six Voices* (1597).[39] Though the specific style features are all entirely Italianate, Morley's canzonets as a rule are much longer, more complex, more polyphonic, and more madrigalian than the concise compositions of Vecchi, Croce, and Anerio. The extended imitation at the opening of *Adiew, you kind and cruel,* for example, would be impossible at the opening of an Italian *canzonetta.* It is significant that no English canzonets were provided with extra stanzas, like the Italian compositions, which were designed to be sung through rapidly three or four times. This practically forced Morley to expand and complicate his simple Italian models; and again later English composers all profited from his experiments.

As we have seen, Morley's energies were devoted mainly to the lighter forms of Italianate music, the ballet and the canzonet. Most of his madrigals are of the lightest kind, and his serious efforts are not always his most successful; indeed, Morley wrote very few actual madrigals for the standard texture of five or six voices. It remained for younger composers to come to grips with the serious madrigal, and the climax of the English development is undoubtedly to be found in their works.

Weelkes

Thomas Weelkes [40] is the boldest and most individual of the English madrigal composers, even though, like Morley, he was strongly influenced by the Italians and in particular by Marenzio. But Weelkes was able to capture the most impressive qualities of Marenzio, which escaped Morley— the ability to paint and design on the grand scale, giving to some of his works the broad, Tintoretto-like strokes that distinguish the late Italian madrigal. His first books are relatively light in tone. The *Madrigals to 3. 4. 5. & 6. voyces,*[41] published in 1597 when Weelkes was about twenty-one years old, shows immediately a master hand. Although in the dedication Weelkes refers to his music as "the first fruicts of my barren ground, unripe, in regard of time, unsavorie, in respect of others," the madrigals *a 3* and *a 4* in particular, such as *My flocks feed not, Cease sorrowes now,* and *Three virgin Nimphes,* are excellently composed and full of character. Unquestionably his later works are even better. The *Balletts and Madrigals to five voyces* (1598),[42] which includes the charming *On the plains fairy trains,*[43] extends and exaggerates every tendency of Morley's *Balletts.* The rhythmic brilliance

---

[39] EMS III. The set includes 17 canzonets, 3 genuine madrigals, and a concluding Elegy.
[40] *See* FelTW; ArldW.   [41] EMS IX.   [42] EMS X.
[43] About the presence of both the *passamezzo antico* and *passamezzo moderno* basses in this piece, *see* GomE, 19.

that Weelkes achieves in them frequently stems from his scrupulous and yet imaginative scanning of the text, resulting in a single voices's having a rhythmic pattern quite at variance with the regular rhythm produced by the harmonic movement:

EXAMPLE 193. Extract from *Come, clap thy hands*—Weelkes (from *Balletts and Madrigals . . .* , East, 1598; complete piece in EMS X, 87).

The youthful enthusiasm and vivid imagination in all Weelkes' work counterbalance a certain roughness of style. His *Madrigals of 5. and 6. parts, apt for the viols and voices* (1600) [44] is one of the greatest and most serious of the English publications. The expression, "apt for the viols and voices," first appears in print in the title of this set, and something of the same nature was thereafter included in the title of almost every madrigal collection. The madrigals of 1600 reveal Weelkes' grand manner in such examples *a* 6 as *Thule the period of Cosmographie,* remarkable for its length, brilliance, and powerful text-delineation; *Like two proud armies,* containing melismatic passages such as are not found earlier in English secular music; and *Mars in a furie,* which can serve as an example of his dramatic expression. The extraordinary madrigal *O care thou wilt dispatch mee* [45] represents the extreme in harmonic experimentation in the English madrigal and, though the work is not a ballet, makes wonderful use of the conventional "fa la" refrain. The pathetic quality of the text is mirrored by accidentalism, a touch of degree-inflection, and impressive chord relationships, as in the following:

[44] EMS XI, XII.   [45] *See* FelE, 198; FelTW, 129.

EXAMPLE 194. Beginning of *pars II* of *O care thou wilt dispatch mee*—
Weelkes (from *Madrigals of 5. and 6. parts* . . . , East, 1600;
complete piece in EMS XI, 19).

This passage provides evidence of the ripe understanding of tonal principles
already suggested in connection with Morley. As a whole, this madrigal
illustrates a characteristic (and most un-Italian) tendency of Weelkes, that
of organizing compositions by means of free or strict recapitulations.[46] It is
to be regretted that Weelkes never published a sequel to this magnificent set;
he seems to have devoted himself henceforth mainly to the writing of sacred
music (cf. pp. 805f). The delightful *Ayres or Phantasticke Spirites for three
voices* [47] of 1608 does not make up for the absence of another set of genuine
madrigals.

Wilbye

Among the great English composers, John Wilbye (1574–1638), though
one of the least prolific, is the finest madrigalist. His musical ability having attracted attention even during his childhood, he early entered Hengrave Hall, a manor house near Bury St. Edmunds, as household musician to
the noble Kytson family. In 1613 he was granted a lease on some excellent
pasture land, from the proceeds of which he became a wealthy property owner.
His musical output seems to have suffered from his agricultural interests,
for from 1614 until his death twenty-four years later he published no more
music.[48] Wilbye's two madrigal sets,[49] printed in 1597 and 1609, reveal a
subtle stylist within a relatively restrained idiom. He is perhaps the only
Elizabethan composer who had the sensibility to comprehend fully the work
of Marenzio, several of whose texts in translation he reset in his first collection; but Wilbye has a very clear musical personality of his own—melancholy,
poetic, and extremely sensitive. He is equally adept at light madrigals and
canzonets, which overshadow Morley's, and serious compositions, which stand

[46] *See also* 1597, Nos. 2–4, 9; 1598, Nos. 19, 20; and 1600, No. 8 *a 5* and Nos. 3, 4, 7, and 8
a 6.
[47] EMS XIII.   [48] For further biographical data, *see* FelE, 209ff; FelJW.   [49] EMS VI, VII.

beside Weelkes'. With Wilbye the best of the Italian style was assimilated and reorganized into a thoroughly individual form of musical expression.

Wilbye is unrivaled in the setting of English texts. His rhythmic and melodic rendition of the prosody is invariably just as regards accent and quantity, and also highly imaginative and alive; his musical translation of the meaning and imagery of the poem is endlessly resourceful. Word-painting with him is never naïve, as it sometimes is with Morley and Weelkes, but always mature and more than superficially apposite.

EXAMPLE 195. Extract from *Alas what hope of speeding*—Wilbye (from *First Set of English Madrigals* . . . , East, 1598; complete piece in EMS VI, 36).

The point of this extract is best seen by comparing it with the setting of the same poem by George Kirbye, whose *English Madrigalls, to 4. 5. & 6. voyces* [50] appeared in 1597—a workmanlike and maturely conceived book. Both men use the same conventional devices; [51] the difference is between a competent imitator of the Italian style and a musician of high sensitivity and inspiration.

EXAMPLE 196. Extract from *Alas what hope of speeding*—Kirbye (from *First Set of English Madrigals* . . . , East, 1597; complete piece in EMS XXIV, 5).

The basis of Wilbye's writing is of course imitation, sometimes of a learned, sometimes of an easy, light nature, but contrapuntal devices never obscure the meaning of the text or become a mere decoration in the music.[52] Wilbye

[50] EMS XXIV.   [51] As pointed out in HeuW, 74f.
[52] For exx. of the lighter kind, *see* EMS VI, 6f, 44, 120; VII, 7, 123, etc.; for more complex ones, EMS VII, 54f; VI, 28, where pedantic counterpoint illustrates "What needeth all this travayle and turmoyling."

is particularly happy in choosing places in which to interpolate passages in block harmony to break the polyphonic texture.[53]

In his own way, Wilbye, too, exhibits the general English tendency toward purely musical organization, however intimately his music seems to be bound to the poetry that it sets. Most noticeable is his excellent use of sequences in ways that give further evidence of the growing understanding of tonality in England at this time. An especially impressive method employed in the *Second Set* (1609) involves a series of long pedal-notes in the bass [54] which move in a circle of fifths, while two upper voices (generally) move up the scale and down again in thirds. As in the following example, this device is always employed for textual reasons.

EXAMPLE 197. Extract from *Happy O happy he*—Wilbye (from *Second Set of Madrigals* . . . , East, 1609; complete piece in EMS VII, 82).

Many of Wilbye's madrigals deliberately incorporate solo-song features similar to those of the lute ayre; examples occur in sections of *Adiew, sweet Amarillis, Lady your words doe spite mee, Love me not for comely grace, Weepe, weepe mine eyes,* and others.[55] It is noteworthy that Wilbye sets some of the most serious poems of his choice, such as *When shall my wretched life* and *Where most my thoughts,* in an abstract idiom that cannot fairly be called madrigalian at all. These pieces are not composed sectionally according to the text, but establish an over-all somber mood, and move almost entirely in long notes. The rigorous organization of *O wretched man* is purely musical.

---

[53] *See,* for example, the alternation of contrapuntal and harmonic writing in EMS VII, 138ff and 236ff.

[54] More than other English madrigalists, Wilbye uses the bass as a cohesive element, employing longer notes than in the upper parts. *See* EMS VI, 122, 124f; VII, 97, 150f, 156f.

[55] This characteristic is also seen in the madrigals of Farmer (1599) and Pilkington (1613, 1624), and to a lesser degree in many of the later madrigalists.

The Lesser Madrigalists; the Decline

It is in the hands of Morley, and especially in those of Weelkes and Wilbye, that the importation of the madrigal into England finds its full justification. Many other Englishmen wrote madrigals,[56] though few published more than single sets; these contain many attractive pieces, but the standard as a whole is certainly no higher than with the average Italian madrigalists of the end of the century—men almost unknown today, such as Orologio, Eremita, Massaino, Baccusi, and dozens more. The universal acceptance of the Italian style in England is shown by the publication of *Madrigales The Triumphes of Oriana* (1601),[57] an ambitious anthology modeled on *Il Trionfo di Dori* (cf. pp. 426f), but issued in praise of Queen Elizabeth. Morley, the editor,[57a] was able to assemble twenty-four composers to write madrigals, though to be sure one or two of them are unknown except for their contributions to this set. On the whole, the music is more remarkable for good intentions than for a sustained level of high quality.

Although one of the finest English composers of the time, Peter Philips cannot be considered a member of the English school, for he wrote to Italian words and his style is Italian through and through.[58] By English standards, at least, he was a fairly prolific composer of madrigals: two sets *a 6* (1596 and 1603) and one *a 8* (1598) were published in Antwerp. They are very well composed, but offer nothing remarkable in comparison with the leading Italian madrigalists of the end of the *cinquecento*. Of the lesser English madrigalists, the most serious and literary-minded is John Ward. His single set of *English Madrigals to 3. 4. 5. & 6. parts* (1613) [59] shows a strong Italian influence, suggesting Monteverdi, in the breadth of his writing, the constant pictorialism, and a predilection for large masses of sound. The broad canvas of *If the deepe sighs,*[60] set in two *partes* to a poem by Drayton, represents a high point of the English madrigal. In his compositions *a 5* and *a 6*, Ward stands close to Weelkes in quality; in his madrigals for fewer voices, however, he is plainly Weelkes' inferior.

In general, the madrigal style is diluted in the work of the later English

---

[56] For further biographical information, etc., on the English madrigal composers, *see* FelE and the prefaces to the various volumes of EMS.   [57] EMS XXXII.

[57a] About the manner in which he based *Hard by a crystal fountain,* one of his 2 contributions to the *Triumphes,* on a madrigal by Croce, *see* KermanMT.

[58] *See* HughesP. Peacham (*Compleat Gentleman,* 1622) says of Philips: "He hath sent us over many excellent songs, as well motets as madrigals: he affecteth altogether the Italian veine." But only one of his madrigals was pr. in England: *The Nightingale,* to a transl. of Petrarch's *Quel rossignuol,* in Morley's selected Italian *Madrigals,* 1598. This too is entirely Italianate, even though it seems to have been written to the English words (*see* EinEM, 75). The piece is reprinted in ScoE XV, 2.   [59] EMS XIX.

[60] The 2 *partes* together cover 33 pages in EMS XIX. Note the rich use of suspensions and double-suspensions, the rapid parlando style (pp. 173–175), the poignant harmony (e.g., the A-flat in meas. 7 on p. 163), the constant word-painting, and the dramatic power.

composers. They incorporated many disparate elements into their writing—from native lute ayres and instrumental music, from the late Italian madrigal, and even from the *stile rappresentativo*—but achieved no synthesis comparable to that of the earlier masters whom we have discussed above. Thomas Vautor and Thomas Tomkins reveal some originality; they entitled their single publications of 1619 and 1622, respectively, *Songs* [61] rather than "madrigals," indicating the rather incongruous mixture to be found within their pages. Belatedly, the true baroque style broke through the English madrigal in the works of such a composer as Walter Porter (*Madrigales and Ayres,* 1632), a pupil of Monteverdi.[62]

The English madrigal began its long decline at the turn of the century; after 1613 the printed output fell off sharply, and it ended with John Hilton's *Ayres, or, Fa las for Three Voyces* [63] in 1627. Only six new sets appeared between these two dates, whereas five had been printed in the single year 1597. Even more significant is the fact that from 1600 to 1610 more lute ayre folios were published than madrigal books; it seems that fashions changed with the appearance of Dowland's popular *First Booke of Songes or Ayres* in 1597, the madrigal suffering from the competition of the less artificial, more native monody of the lutenists. This new music was accompanied by a new trend in poetry, a revulsion from the Italianate conceits of the "New Poets" of the 1580's and the sonneteers who followed them. Even Morley, the foremost English madrigalist, understood the change well enough; his *Canzonets or little Short Aers* (1597) include an alternate lute accompaniment part, and the last set of his own music consisted of lute ayres (1600). From its start, the English madrigal development was something of an anachronism, for by 1599 and the death of Marenzio—certainly after 1614 and the publication of Monteverdi's *Sesto Libro*—the madrigal on the continent was essentially a thing of the past. In this context, the achievements of Morley, Weelkes, and Wilbye seem even more astonishing. But even in their hands, the English madrigal could not long survive the termination of the brilliant age of Elizabeth, and the advent of the troubled and insecure reign of James I.

Compositions based on Street Cries; Ravenscroft's Collections of Popular Music

Weelkes and Gibbons are among those who applied their expert skill in writing vocal polyphony not only to the madrigal and its related forms, but to extended fantasies for voices and instruments incorporating nearly 150

---

[61] EMS XXXIV and XVIII, respectively. Notice Vautor's occasional use of "choral recitative."
[62] *See* ArkP; HughesPPM.
[63] MAS XIII. This set is excluded from EMS because of its poor quality.

cries and songs of itinerant vendors. These two men and Deering have each left us a composition *a 5,*[64] in which the text consists exclusively of the words of London street cries (except for the repeated *"alleluia"* that ends the piece by Weelkes), concerned with such matters as "New oysters, new walfleet oysters, New mussels, my lillye-whyte mussels, New cockles, new great cockles, . . . Hott mutton pyes, hott . . . Apples fyne . . . cherye rype, Rype, strawberye rype . . . Broome, broome, broome . . . Boots or buskins for new broome." The authentic music of the cries seems to make its appearance in all of these compositions, since some of the words recur, from piece to piece, with the same tunes. The Gibbons composition uses the *Gloria tibi Trinitas* melody as a *cantus firmus,* making the piece a vocal *In nomine* (cf. pp. 779f, 845f, 857, 868f). Deering's work is noteworthy for the many tradesmen's songs it preserves along with the cries. By this composer we have also a *Country Cryes,* which includes the song *Harvest home.* At one point, dealing with the humming of the bees, the bass is directed to sing "Buzz, buzz" for twenty measures, on one note, and the bass-viol player to drum with the back of his bow.[65]

The real popular music of Renaissance England, as distinguished from art music with popular elements, was performed by balladmongers, minstrels, and waits, by fiddlers and others who played music for dancing, and by tinkers and tailors who—not skilled enough for madrigals or consorts—were apt for catches and ballads. Great quantities of ballad texts were printed as broadsides,[66] usually with the direction "to be sung to the tune of" a current ballad air, such as *Greensleeves.*[67]

The largest collection of popular vocal music is preserved in Ravenscroft's three printed catch books: *Pammelia* (1609), *Deuteromelia* (1609), and *Melismata* (1611).[68] Everything about Ravenscroft's catch books calls to mind a "lay" public—the punning prefaces ("either *commend* me or *come* an *mend* me"), the type of audience addressed ("To the Well Disposed to Reade, And to the merry disposed to Sing"), and the helter-skelter mixing of sacred and secular, ribald and ballad texts. This impression is furthered by the fact that there are few catches or rounds attributable to Elizabethan composers of repute—Byrd's *Hey ho to the Greenwood* [69] is a notable exception—and

---

[64] Pr. separately, in the editions of Sir Frederick Bridge, by Novello: Nos. 1343 (Weelkes), 1345 (Gibbons), and 1346 (Deering). The Gibbons, ed. by H. Just, is pr. also by Schott (No. 1628).

[65] Further on the cries, *see* BdgC.

[66] Cf. H. E. Rollins, *An Analytical Index to the Ballad entries (1557–1709) in the Registers of the Company of Stationers of London, 1924.*

[67] Cf. LamE.

[68] All of the catches pr. RavenP. Other pieces from the 3 books pr. in the *Euterpe* octavo series (not the same as ScoE), Nos. 39–44, ed. by C. K. Scott (Oxford University Press).

[69] Cf. FelWB, 177ff, where the catch is pr.; also in ByrdW XVI, 120; RavenP, 1 (without ascription to Byrd); ScoER, 8.

by the fact that there was occasion to pass laws forbidding the singing of popular music by tradesmen, in order to protect professional musicians and actors.

For Ravenscroft, the terms "canon," "catch," and "round" are synonymous. After referring to a composition as "A catch or round" he labels the piece "Canon a 4 Voc." Morley [70] mentions the catch as a simple form of canon, a popular imitation of the more learned variety. Perhaps the best description of the form was to be given in Christopher Simpson's *A Compendium of Practical Musick* (1667), p. 174:

I must not omit another sort of Canon, in more request and common use (though of less dignity) . . . and that is, a Catch or Round: Some call it a Canon in Unison; . . . The contrivance whereof is not intricate: for, if you compose any short strain, of three or four Parts, setting them all within the ordinary compass of a Voyce; and then place one Part at the end of another, in what order you please, so as they may aptly make one continued Tune; you have finished a Catch.

Ravenscroft subtitled his *Deuteromelia* "*Qui canere potest canat. Catch, that catch can*" and some writers have defined the catch as a musical play upon words which becomes evident to the listener only when the several parts are sung simultaneously. However, the use of double meanings in the catch is more correctly associated with the mid-17th century catch than with the less sophisticated pieces of Ravenscroft.

In the preface to *Pammelia,* Ravenscroft writes: "what seems old, is at least renewed, Art having reformed what pleasing tunes injurious time and ignorance had deformed." These words and the fact that several texts found in the catch books are mentioned in earlier sources suggest that Ravenscroft included popular music from the mid-16th century and perhaps earlier. Whether or not he acquired the melodies and texts from oral tradition, several of the ballads found in *Melismata* are still current in Anglo-American folk tradition—e.g., *The Three Ravens, The Marriage of the Frogge and the Mouse,*[71] etc. It is noteworthy that one of the basic musical possessions of Anglo-American tradition, *Three Blind Mice,* first appeared in print in *Deuteromelia.* In *Pammelia* there is *A Round of three Country dances in one* for four voices.[72] To a simple bass melody, the upper parts sing the following Elizabethan dance tunes: *The crampe,*[73] *Tomboy,* and *Robin*

[70] MorlP, 177; MorlPE, 290.

[71] Cf. C. J. Sharp and Maud Karpeles, *English Folk Songs from the Southern Appalachians,* I (1932), No. 11 (*The Three Ravens*); II, Nos. 220, 221 (*A Frog He Went A-courting*), for American variants, and *The English and Scottish Popular Ballads,* ed. from the collection of Francis James Child by H. C. Sargent and G. L. Kittridge (1904), No. 26, and *Journal of the Folk-Song Society,* II (1906), 226, for English variants of the same two ballads.

[72] Pr. RavenP, 18.

[73] MeyeE, 162, relates this tune to the Dutch melody *De Rommelpot,* which occurs in a fantasia of Orlando Gibbons.

Hood. This is really not a round at all, but a quodlibet, in which each voice sings an independent melody without any interchange between voices.

Other non-imitative forms included by Ravenscroft are the "Countrie and Citie Conceits." These are unpretentious little part-songs, almost entirely homophonic, sometimes crude in the contriving, but pleasant sounding. The term "conceit" is related to "toy" (cf. p. 867, including fn. 255).

To what extent the music published by Ravenscroft appealed to the same people as took an interest in the madrigal is open to question. Perhaps the printing of this popular and semipopular music shows that publishers were trying to reach a public new to them. But whether or not the kind of people who had favored the madrigal found the Ravenscroft books to their liking, they did develop, as has already been mentioned, a preference for simpler music that prompted them to cultivate the ayre.

The Ayre, notably the Collections of Campion and Dowland

Although the preface to Byrd's *Psalmes, Sonets, and Songs of sadnes and pietie* indicates that ayres were being composed as early as 1588, none were published before 1597, when not only Dowland's *First Booke* appeared, but also an arrangement for voice and lute of fifteen of Morley's canzonets *a 5*. Morley's first and only *Booke of Ayres, or Little Short Songs,*[74] which includes the famous *It was a lover and his lass,* and the first collection of ayres by Jones were both published in 1600. The ayre continued to flourish throughout the first two decades of the century.

In the ayre, the highest part was the main one, as in the old English part-song of the time of Cornysh and Newark and in the contrapuntally accompanied solo song. Usually the ayre was deliberately planned for alternative methods of performance, in which either all the parts were sung or the highest part was sung and the lower ones were turned into an instrumental accompaniment. To be sure, both methods had long since been applied to vocal secular music on the continent. One need only recall the chansons published by Attaingnant *a 4* and as lute songs, or such early songlike madrigals as Verdelot's *Con lagrime e sospir,* printed in part-form and in Willaert's arrangement for solo voice and lute. But the typical ayre, as a genre, explicitly provides for both polyphonic and accompanied-solo performance. Although it was contemporary with the first operatic experiments in Italy, the ayre represents, formally and stylistically, an older type of song than was being developed at the same time in Florence.[75]

[74] EL, *Ser. I,* XVI.
[75] It is noteworthy, however, that Robert Dowland's *Musicall Banquet* (1610) contains, in addition to ayres by English composers, songs by Domenico Megli, Tessier, and two from Caccini's *Le Nuove Musiche* (1602)—*Amarilli* and *Dovro dunque morire*—with the figured bass fully realized in a harmonic accompaniment for the lute.

A completely worked-out instrumental accompaniment was always supplied by the composer; usually he provided also an arrangement for an ensemble of from two to five voices. In the latter event, the treble voice-part and the instrumental tablature were printed on the same page, with the lower vocal parts so disposed on the opposite page that all the performers could gather comfortably round one book. There was little consistency, apparently, in the accompaniment of the ayre. The lute, orpharion, and viola da gamba were usually mentioned in the titles of the song-books, but in various combinations. Thomas Campion (1567–1620), who had achieved recognition as a poet as early as 1593, throws some light upon the practice of the times in the preface to his first book of ayres (c. 1613) : [76]

> These Ayres were for the most part framed at first for one voyce with the Lute, or Violl, but upon occasion, they have since beene filled with more parts, which who so please may use, who like not may leave. Yet doe wee daily observe, that when any shall sing a Treble to an Instrument, the standers by will be offring at an inward part out of their owne nature; and true or false, out it must, though to the perverting of the whole harmonie. . . .

The lute seems to have been the standard instrument of accompaniment, while the bass viol was normally used in conjunction with it, to double the vocal bass part. Martin Peerson's *Private Musicke* . . . (1620) [77] suggests, for the first time, the use of the virginals to accompany voices. Part of the title page states that the songs "for want of Viols . . . may be performed to either the virginal or Lute."

In the accompaniment, the bass is usually the most interesting part melodically. Even where its role is primarily harmonic, it is frequently embellished by scale fragments and, in more contrapuntal passages, it often moves in melodic interplay, or in parallel tenths or thirteenths, with the principal voice. Dowland and Campion [78] make much of the inner parts also. But most other composers cut down both the range and the melodic interest of these parts, except where an ayre is imitative or otherwise madrigal-like.

Ayres are of several types: serious, emotional songs, which are often through-composed, with broad, asymmetric phrasing and no little individuality in the part-writing; simple metrical songs, usually strophic, with chordal accompaniment; and light, frequently gay ayres, relying for their effect upon rhythmic and imitative subtleties.

In serious songs, the rhythm and speech-melody of the text usually determine the treatment of the vocal line. The melody at times sweeps through a

wide range. Bold harmonies occur oftener in this type than elsewhere, and
the contrapuntal texture is likely to be enriched by many syncopations and
suspensions. Where imitation is used to any extent, it is found mainly near
the end of a song, rarely, if ever, at the beginning. The melodies of most of
the lighter ayres are based upon one or more phrase patterns. Usually only
the rhythm of the pattern recurs, each time underlying a different pitch-series;
occasionally, with the rhythm or instead of it, another element of the pattern,
such as its general melodic contour, is retained. Often, such patterns are made
up, in turn, of short recurrent motifs.

EXAMPLE 198. *Faire, if you expect admiring* (voice part only)—Campion (from Rosseter's *Booke of Ayres,* Short, 1601; complete
piece in EL [*Ser. I*] XIII, No. 11).

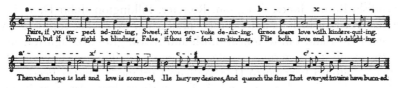

Dependence upon repetitive patterns tended to give the ayre a more regular
rhythmic outline than existed in the madrigal.

In the ayre, as elsewhere (cf. p. 692), the rhythmic progression of chords
is usually more rapid and crowded than in later music, but tonic, dominant,
and subdominant chords are employed with considerable feeling for their
functional value. In the application of a harmonic idiom using chords primarily for such a value and in the development of melodies based upon and
unified by one or two motifs, the English ayre quite outstripped its continental contemporaries.

The structural device most favored in the ayres is immediate repetition of
musical sections to either the same words or new ones. As a rule, the last
strain is repeated, even if the ayre is otherwise through-composed; in three-
section songs, repetition is common at both the beginning and the end, but
rare in the middle section. Songs in two sections outnumber those in three,
aBB being the preferred repetition scheme. In the ayre, as in the madrigal, the
musical form is usually adapted with care to that of the poetry, but with a
difference. The English madrigal, to be sure, was not so episodic as the Italian.
But, even so, it did often single out less than a line of text and base a point of
imitation or other short musical section on it; and to this extent it was more
episodic than the ayre. A musical phrase in the ayre, as in the French chanson, corresponds as a rule to a full line of the poetry, sometimes to more.

If word-painting is rarer in the English than in the Italian madrigal, it is
still less in evidence in the avre. The imitation of birdcalls appears, however,

in the works of John Bartlet [79] and Robert Jones; [80] the occasional descriptive treatment of a word connoting movement or direction is incorporated without special emphasis into the melody. A syllabic style prevails, even restrained melismas being reserved for the expressive treatment of a word here and there.

On the whole, the art of the lutenist song writers is a decorative and dispassionate one. Their songs are written with a nice concern for form, balance, and elegance of expression, and usually—like the contemporary madrigals and lyric poetry of England—without much display of personal or romantic feelings. Some of them, however, particularly those of Dowland and a few by Campion, are tinged with an intensity of emotion that reminds one of Gesualdo and Monteverdi.

Only Dowland's ayres reveal a marked individuality. Nevertheless, Michael Cavendish, Robert Jones, Campion, Rosseter, Pilkington, John Danyel, and Thomas Ford all include among their production ayres that compare favorably with Dowland's in technical finish and lyrical grace, though few are as moving as his more serious works. The ayres of Thomas Greaves, John Bartlet,[81] Alfonso Ferrabosco II,[82] William Corkine,[83] Martin Peerson, and John Attey,[84] although on the whole less distinguished, also contain much delightful music. A representative sampling of forms and styles is afforded by the eleven ayres that precede the instrumental dances in Ford's *Musicke of Sundrie Kindes* (1607); [85] of these ayres, *Since first I saw your face* [85a] is justly famous.

The ayres of Cavendish (1598) [86] and of Danyel (1606) [87] fuse textual and musical rhythms with great skill. Danyel's serious songs are perhaps second only to Dowland's. Like Dowland, Danyel and Jones often surprise by their expressive use of sudden rhythmic change and dissonance. Five collections of songs and duets by Jones appeared between 1600 and 1610.[88] They include some of the most lilting and tuneful of the ayres: *Farewell. deere love; Sweete, come away, my darling; What if I seeke for love of thee? Think'st thou, Kate, to put me down?* Most of his ayres are unpretentious, clear in texture, neat in form. Short, madrigal-like motifs are often treated in imitation, usually alternating with simple chordal passages.[89]

Rosseter's songs (1601) [90] are akin to those of Jones. They develop rhythmic motifs with much skill. The lute part is light and, though usually polyphonic, never obtrusively so. His songs, lively rather than profound, say little but say it perfectly. Only one [91] is serious in theme. All twenty-two of his examples

---

[79] E.g., EL, *Ser. II*, III, Nos. 19–21.   [80] E.g., EL, *Ser. II*, IV, No. 16.
[81] EL, *Ser. II*, III.   [82] EL, *Ser. II*, XVI.   [83] EL, *Ser. II*, XII, XIII.   [84] EL, *Ser. II*, IX.
[85] EL, *Ser. I*, III.   [85a] Pr. *ibid.*, No. 8.   [86] EL, *Ser. II*, VII. *See* further MGG II, 937f.
[87] El, *Ser. II*, VIII. *See* further MGG II, 1892f.
[88] EL, *Ser. II*, IV–VI, XIV–XV.   [89] E.g., in EL, *Ser. II*, XV, Nos. 4, 5, 7, 8, 10, 17.
[90] EL, *Ser. I*, VIII–IX.   [91] *Ibid.*, No. 3.

survive in a volume, the authorship of which he shared with Campion.[92]

Campion's works include, in addition, songs for five masques and four other volumes of ayres, two of which are believed to have been published c. 1613, two c. 1617.[93] His light songs—in general, more effective than the grave ones—are almost epigrammatic in the conciseness of their form, delicately balanced in their texture, often dancelike in their brisk movement. Campion's excellence in the literary field has unfortunately obscured his musical achievements, and his songs have received less attention than they deserve, musicographers being perhaps too severe in charging them with superficiality.[94] Such a criticism might be levelled with equal or greater justification against a large part of the ayre literature. While it is true that some of Campion's more serious works are among the dullest of the ayres, he did produce a number of fine serious examples, at least one of which, *Author of light*,[95] in its vivid religious fervor, in its long, powerful phrases, and in its expressive use of degree-inflection and modulation, is quite imposing.

Presumably, Campion wrote the texts of all his ayres. That he, with his poetic background, should have wished at least once to set syllables according to the principles of quantity, is not surprising, but he lacked Le Jeune's gift for such composition, and the piece is hardly a success.[96] His treatise on quantitative meter in English (1602) reveals an interest in Baïf and the Pléiade. This had little lasting influence. But another treatise, *New Way of Making Fowre Parts in Counterpoint*, is a different matter. Being attuned to the shift in taste toward the kind of writing the ayre composers represented, the book is more concerned with the chordal aspect of music than with the older conception of counterpoint. Indeed, in one passage it surprisingly foreshadowed Rameau's theory that a triad in root position and in its two inversions are all different forms of the same chord.[96a] *New Way* was reprinted several times in the 17th century. Morley's magnificent *Plaine and Easie . . .* had only one reprinting in that century (1608) and achieved no further publication until 1771. The days of the polyphonic period were numbered.

However, the contents of Pilkington's single volume of ayres (1605) [97] are still polyphonically conceived, in the madrigal tradition. His broad melodies often span a tenth. Some of his ayres are among the most imaginative ones, others among the most abstruse, lacking harmonic and rhythmic clarity. His seems to be a great lyrical talent obstructed by inadequate understanding of the solo medium; at times, the accompaniment is too intricate and heavy to provide proper support for the flow of the melody.[97a]

Dowland, whose qualities as a lute-player were highly esteemed in his day,

[92] Campion's songs from this collection pr. EL, *Ser. I*, IV, XIII.
[93] These 4 books pr. EL, *Ser. II*, I, II, X, XI.   [94] Cf. WarA, 98ff; BoydE, 131ff.
[95] EL, *Ser. II*, I, No. 1.   [96] Cf. PatMP, 130f.   [96a] *See* CoperarioR, 19.
[97] EL, *Ser. I*, VII, XV.   [97a] *See* further KastenC.

is the greatest of the ayre composers, partly because he alone fully realized the expressive potentialities of the solo medium. The concentrated, often passionate nature of his songs gives them a personal quality very different from the decorative suavity typical of most other ayres, a suavity of which his lighter pieces, however, show him to have been equally a master. His chief works include four volumes of ayres (1597, 1600, 1603, 1612) [98] and three songs contained in the anthology, *A Musicall Banquet* (1610),[99] compiled by his son, Robert Dowland. The records of a lawsuit involving the *Second Booke of Ayres* show that an edition of 1,023 copies was printed, and thus provide us with an informative hint regarding the degree to which ayres were disseminated.[100]

As varied as the moods of Dowland's ayres are the technical resources with which he depicts them. Although he is not known to have written madrigals, he makes extensive use of imitation and textual illustration. Not infrequently, the contrapuntal movement is interrupted by the dramatic interpolation of declamatory, recitative-like passages.

EXAMPLE 199. Extract from *In darknesse let mee dwell*—Dowland (from *Musical Banquet* . . . , Lowndes, 1610; complete piece in EL [*Ser. I*] XIV, No. 10).

Dowland's moving *Flow, my teares* (*Lachrimae*) [101] was so popular that it became a household word in England for years, as the references to it in contemporary literature show. The following extract from Massinger's *The Maid of Honour* (1621) is only one of several such passages: [102]

> *Or with the hilts, thunder about your ears*
> *Such music as will make your worships dance*
> *To the doleful tune of* Lachrymae.

---

[98] EL, *Ser. I*, I, II (= MAS XII), V, VI, X–XII, XIV.
[99] EL, *Ser. I*, XIV, Nos. 8–10. Discussed in ArkR.
[100] Cf. DowlgP.   [101] EL, *Ser. I*, VI, No. 2.   [102] *See* BoydE, 167f; WarA, 35f.

The song is trisectional, following the pattern *aabbCC* and is therefore easily adaptable as an instrumental pavan. As we shall see, the music exists in this form also. The words and music are matched with great artistry.

EXAMPLE 200. Last strain of *Flow, my teares*—Dowland (from *Second Booke of Songes or Ayres* . . . , East, 1600; complete piece in EL [*Ser. I*] V, No. 2).

Harke you sha-dowes that in darcke-nesse dwell, learne to contemne light,

Hap-pie,hap-pie they that in hell feele not the world's de-spite.

A group of anonymous ayres in MS includes the touching "Willow Song," which Shakespeare was to have Desdemona sing in Act IV of *Othello*.[103] The poem of another piece in this category, "O death, rock me asleep," [104] is said without much authority to have been written in prison, while awaiting execution, by either Anne Boleyn or her brother; but it is more probable that the lines are simply those of another of the "death songs" that appear in Elizabethan and Jacobean plays. *O death* is referred to by both Shakespeare (in *The Second Part of King Henry IV*) and Thomas Nashe (in the *Choice of Valentines*). Still another anonymous ayre in MS is a setting of Ben Jonson's lovely poem, "Have you seen but a whyte lillie grow." [105] The music shows the influence of the new Italian style that was being developed by Caccini.[106]

Nearly thirty volumes of ayres had been printed when Attey's collection appeared in 1622 and the output of such pieces virtually came to an end. The type experienced no important stylistic changes during its history. It appears to have emerged, full-grown, in the first works of Dowland and to have departed, unaged and unaltered, after twenty-five years.[107]

103 Pr. WarEA I, 19; PatMP, 169. Facsimile, after Brit. Mus. Add. MS 15117, in WarA, 127; Frank Hunter Potter, *Reliquary of English Song* (1915), opp. p. ix. This MS dates from after 1614. For a study of the "Willow Song," see CuttsR. A piece, *All a green willow*, appearing in Folger MS 4448.16, which dates from c. 1559–1571 (cf. p. 842) is a different composition.

104 Pr. in modernized editions in ChappP I, 111; DolS II, 1. The poem was also set, to quite different music, for solo voice and four instruments; this setting, an ex. of the contrapuntally accompanied solo song (cf. p. 817), pr. WarES III, 1.

105 Facsimile, after Brit. Mus. Add. MS 15117, in Potter, *op. cit.,* opp. p. x. Concerning the possibility that the piece is by Robert Johnson, see M&L XXXVI (1955), 124.

106 Further about the ayres in MS, see WarA, 125ff.

107 For further data about the ayre and its composers, see PatMP, 113ff; WarA; BoydE, 127–152; FelE, 304–331; BontC, 648ff.

Music for Lute and Related Instruments

As for surviving English works for solo lute, none can be dated with assurance earlier than the mid-century. Indeed, England was late also in producing great performers on the instrument. While the continent could boast of a Francesco da Milano and a Valentin Bakfark, comparable Englishmen began to appear only in the middle years of Elizabeth's reign. Not that there was a lack of lute-playing in the first half of the century. Henry VIII played "well on the lute," as did his three children. There were twenty-six lutes in Henry's collection of instruments and a good supply of performers, among whom the king especially liked to have Italians.[108]

The English lute music mentioned above includes seven short anonymous compositions that appear in Royal Appendix 58 (cf. p. 768). Brit. Mus., Stowe 389, contains a few pieces "written by one Raphe Bowle to learne to playe on his Lutte in anno 1558." [109] The most important lute MS of about this time is in the Folger Shakespeare Library, Washington. This is a commonplace book, tentatively dated 1559–1571, which belonged to several owners, three of whom contributed to a small section of lute-tablature at the front of the book. The earliest hand wrote in dances, song arrangements, and little descriptive pieces (e.g., *The Bagpipes*), as well as the play *July and Julian,* which occupies the last part of the MS. Both the lack of skill in notation and the crude contriving of the music itself make the first section of music the poorest. The second and third hands show a marked improvement: the tablature is more complete, especially with regard to rhythmic indications, the pieces (dances and songs) are longer, and the themes more skilfully worked out.

The first tablature printed in England is Le Roy's *Instruction de partir toute musique facilement en tabulature de luth,* which appeared in two (possibly three) different translations (cf. p. 554). The first edition, printed in 1563, is lost. The second (1568) was "englished by J. Alford Londenor," and the third (1574) was translated by "F. Ke. Gentleman." Whereas Le Roy employs a tablature of five rather than six lines, this practice was not adopted by the English in their own lute music, for all of which they used six lines. However, the basic system of tablature they followed was the French one.

The popularity of Le Roy's tablature in England did not end after the appearance of the third English edition. In 1596, William Barley printed *A new Booke of Tabliture* for the lute, orpharion, and bandora (= pandore), of which the text of the lute section was a new, partial translation of Part II of Le Roy's work. The pieces offered by Barley include examples by Francis Cutting,[110] I. D. (= John Dowland), P. R. (= Philip Rosseter), etc. Among

---

[108] Cf. NagA, 3f.   [109] This entry appears on fol. 120.
[110] For one of these, *see* HughesL, 30.

the Dowland pieces there appears, under the title *Lachrimae,* a lute transcription of *Flow, my teares,* the music thus becoming available in print in Barley's book before its publication in any form by Dowland himself.[111] *"Quadro pavan"* is an English name for *"passamezzo moderno,"* [112] and one of the pieces printed by Barley bears this title. Some of the other compositions set popular tunes of the day—such as *Goe from my window* and *Fortune my foe.* The English *Fortune* tune begins in the same way as the tenor of Busnois's *Fortuna desperata* and may have taken the earlier composition as its point of departure. (That the Busnois piece was known in England is shown by the inclusion, in Brit. Mus. Add. 31922 [cf. p. 768] [112a] of an anonymous version with an added part.) The similar openings have caused some historians to fall into the error of completely equating the two melodies and of concluding that *Fortuna desperata* is of English origin.[113] The *Fortune* tune was a great favorite among English lutenists.[114] The demands made by Barley's book on the player's technique are of an elementary nature; the publication was evidently intended as a self-instructor.[115] Before its appearance, two other works for lute had been licensed for printing: a *Scyence of Lutynge* in 1565 and an *Exhortation to all Kynde of Men how they shulde learn to play of the Lute* in 1567. Neither survives; perhaps they remained unprinted despite the licensing.

Continuing a survey of the sources, before discussing a few of the lutenists individually, we find, as the next printed work for the lute, Thomas Robinson's *Schoole of Musicke* (1603). The familiar device of the dialogue is employed, in this instance "betwixt a Knight, (who hath children to be taught) and *Timotheus,* that should teach them." Rules are given for the care of the instrument, for the position of the body when playing, for the fingers of each

---

[111] One of the MS sources in which it exists, William Ballet's lute-book, is sometimes dated still earlier than Barley's Book—1594—but the correct date may well be a little later. *See* NewL, 71.

[112] This was "called in Elizabethan England the *Quadro* or *Quadran Pavan* because it was in the major mode using B-natural (. . . 'b quadratum'), whereas the . . . *passamezzo antico* was in minor and used the B-flat . . ." (Gombosi in MQ XXX [1944], 145.)

[112a] Pr. JosqMS I, 107.

[113] *See,* for example, AmbG III, 58 (which is wrong in some other respects also). Ambros cites, in support of his theory, the keyboard variations by Scheidt, entitled *Fortunae cantilena anglica.* Scheidt does indeed employ the English tune (used also in keyboard pieces by Byrd and Sweelinck), but this melody is quite distinct from that of *Fortuna desperata,* except for the resemblance, noted above, in the openings. The English tune consists of 4 symmetrical phrases, all displaying approximately the same rhythmical configuration, and is clearly minor in tonality. Its symmetry, clarity of structure, and musical simplicity contrast with the more subtle nature of the *Fortuna desperata* melody, whose phrases are irregular in length and structure and in which any restatement of elements is accomplished with an avoidance of the obvious. While challenging Ambros' ascription of an English origin to the *Fortuna* melody, DiseV, 457, apparently accepts the premise of the identity of the two tunes. (The text of the ballad, "Titus Andronicus's Complaint," which begins with the words "Ye noble minds" [pr. in Thomas Percy, *Reliques of Ancient English Poetry,* I, 204]—the source of Shakespeare's *Titus Andronicus*—was written to the *Fortune* tune. Cf. BuH III, 87, 118; ChappP I, 76ff.)

[114] The sources listed in ChappP I, 76, include no fewer than 5 English lute-books.

[115] Cf. HughesL.

hand, for the tablature, the "relish" or ornament, etc. The text is followed by thirty-four lute solos and duets, mostly by Robinson.[116]

Pieces for solo lute are included in several of the song-books;[117] and lute parts, which often are actually reductions of the whole score, are normal in broken-consort books, such as will be discussed later. Finally, in 1610, Robert Dowland, together with his father, published *Varietie of Lute Lessons,* a collection of lute pieces prefaced by "Necessarie Observations Belonging to the Lute, and Lute-playing," a translation from Besard's *Isagoge in artem testudinariam,* followed by "Other Necessary Observations belonging to the Lute, by Iohn Douland, Batcheler of Musicke." The latter has special interest as the only original theoretical writing of the greatest English lutenist. Unfortunately, Dowland's "Observations" concern such secondary (though important) subjects as the art of choosing good lute strings and placing them on the lute, etc.[118] The composers represented in the *Varietie* include several continental masters, e.g., Diomedes of Venice (cf. p. 756), Jacobus Reys (cf. p. 756, fn. 102), and Laurencini (= Lorenzini) of Rome (cf. p. 527). Also included are several famous English lutenist composers, Daniell Batcheler, Anthony Holborne, Morley, and, of course, John Dowland.[119]

Compositions by English composers appear in several European lute-books, often without crediting the author, as in Besard's *Thesaurus harmonicus* (1603), Van den Hove's *Delitiae musicae* (1612), and Fuhrmann's *Testudo gallo-germanica* (1615). Aside from these few printed sources, the major part of English lute music exists in MS. Most important are (1) a group of related MSS in Cambridge University Library (Dd. 2.11,[119a] Dd. 5.78, Dd. 9.33, and Nn. 6.36), containing well over 500 compositions; (2) a MS in Archbishop Marsh's Library, Dublin, containing many anonymous pieces and a few attributed to John Johnson, who died in 1594; (3) the MSS of William Ballet and Thomas Dallis, at Trinity College, Dublin; (4) MSS in the British Museum, including *Jane Pickering's Book,* dated 1616; (5) MS 1610.1 of the Folger Shakespeare Library, probably owned by John Dowland, sold to Folger by distant heirs of the composer, and containing at least one autograph page in his hand.[120] This by no means exhausts the list, but gives some idea of the extent of the material.

Most of the music consists of dance compositions—pavans, galliards

[116] *See* further KinR; BoydE, 155ff.

[117] Dowland's song-books, 1597, 1600, 1612; Pilkington's, 1605; Danyel's, 1606; Robert Dowland's *Musicall Banquet,* 1610; Maynard's, 1611.

[118] In the preface to his transl. of Ornithoparchus' *Micrologus,* Dowland writes that he is at work on a treatise on lute playing. Nothing further is known of the work (unless he was referring to the *Observations*).

[119] *See* NewL, 69, on the question whether the pieces ascribed to Robert are really his or John's. *See also* pp. 79 and 81f, *ibid.,* regarding Batcheler and Holborne.

[119a] 4 pieces pr. NaySM, xi (facsimile on p. x), 28, 30, 52.

[120] For further discussion of the MS sources, *see* NewL.

corantos, almans [121]—either constructed on the pattern *aa′bb′*, etc., or writ-ten over a ground, e.g., pavan and galliard pairs that are actually *passamezzo* settings. These dance pieces may be simple, songlike in character, or more developed and polyphonic. With some composers, the texture is quite full, with others there are many written-out "relishes" and figurations. Quite often, popular tunes are used as the basis for variations. Or melodies that appear in lute songs may turn up also in dance measure [122] (e.g., *Now, O now, I needs must part = The Frog's Galliard*). The fantasias, or fancies, like those in other countries, are written in free imitative counterpoint and are mainly vehicles for the display of contrapuntal skill.

Certain vocal melodies each produced a special genre of English instrumen-tal music. Thus, there is a body of compositions, including some for lute, that bears the designation *Browning* and derives from a tune known also as *The leaves be greene.*[122a]

EXAMPLE 201. *Browning Madame,* in the form of a vocal canon (after Ravenscroft, *Deuteromelia: or the Second Part of Musicks Melodie* . . . , London, 1609).

Brown-ing   Madame,   brown-ing   Madame,   so   mar- ri-ly wee sing browning Ma-dame. The

fayr - est flower   in.   garden. greene, is   in   my loves breast full. comely seene, And

with all   others com - pare she can, there- fore now let us sing Browning Ma- dame.

Of greater importance are the approximately 150 *In nomine* compositions (about 100 dating from the 16th century) [123] for varying media of per-formance. The examples for lute and for keyboard instruments are greatly outnumbered by those for instrumental ensemble. The earliest specimens of the type date from 1530 to 1550 and are instrumental arrangements of the *In nomine* passage in the Benedictus of Taverner's *Missa Gloria tibi Trinitas*. As we have seen on pp. 779f, it is from the vocal polyphonic source, by way of these early specimens, that the whole genre derives its name; and it is because of this source, again through the arrangement in question, that all genuine *In nomine* pieces employ the *Gloria tibi Trinitas* antiphon as *cantus firmus*. Among the instrumental arrangements of Taverner's *In nomine* passage is a lute version contained in Brit. Mus. MS Add. 29246. Since the highest part of

[121] The English used many variant spellings of these terms.
[122] Which does not necessarily mean that the song came first.
[122a] Cf. ChappP I, 154.
[123] *In nomine* pieces continued to be written into the time of Purcell.

the original is omitted, it was obviously intended to be sung, the lute transcription being meant to serve as an accompaniment.[124] The same MS contains six other *In nomine pieces,* of which three, including the following (apparently not a mere accompaniment), are by White.

EXAMPLE 202. Opening and close of *In nomine* for lute—White (from Brit. Mus. MS Add. 29246; transcr. by Th. Karp).

Pieces entitled *Miserere* constitute a third group of instrumental settings based on vocal material. This type will be treated more fully in connection with keyboard music, although there are also *Miserere* pieces for lute.

Intabulated vocal polyphony which forms so important a part of the continental repertory is much less conspicuous in that of England. The largest single corpus of such material (Add. MSS 29246 and 29247) contains 106 works by many Tudor masters, from Fayrfax to Byrd, presenting whole Masses, motets, etc. Tenbury MS 340 also contains a large number of intabulations. Add. MS 31992 includes a great many intabulations of works by Byrd.[124a]

In turning from the larger canvas to individual figures, we find that three or four lutenist-composers stand out in particular, and none so much as John Dowland. He published no collection of solo music for the lute, but, as has been noted, a few of his pieces for the instrument were included in Barley's tablature and in Robert's *Varietie.* If John was somewhat disinclined to publish his lute music, others were not, and in the preface to his collection of seven *Lachrimae* pieces, etc. (1605; cf. pp. 873f), he writes with some bitterness: "Having in forren parts met divers Lute-lessons of my composition, publisht by strangers without my name or approbation; I thought it much more convenient, that my labours should passe forth under mine owne allowance, receiving from me their last foile and polishment. . . ." However, the *Lachrimae* collection, as we shall see, does not contain solo lute music. If we wish to judge such music by Dowland we must in the main look to the MSS, which are full of it.

---

[124] Cf. ReIN, 13.
[124a] The contents of these sources are listed, respectively, in BM III, 59ff; FelCT, 55; BM III, 63ff.

John Dowland's Autograph of His Late Piece, My
Lady Hunsdon's Allmande,* from MS 1610.1 at the
Folger Shakespeare Library, Washington

* Cf. the autograph in KinsP, 100, No. 3. The same composition as
My Lady Hunsdon's Puffe, printed in modern notation after Brit.
Mus. Add. 6402, in DowlLM, 28.

Page from Fuenllana's Orphenica Lyra, showing vihuela
transcriptions of vocal music by two of his fellow Spaniards

PLATE VIII

Dowland's lute pieces range from sprightly dances—such as the one from which Ex. 203 is taken—to compositions steeped in profound melancholy.

EXAMPLE 203. Extract from *The Right Honourable Ferdinando Earle of Darby, his Galliard*—John Dowland (from Robert Dowland's *Varietie of Lute Lessons;* transcr. by Suzanne Bloch).

In his almans, galliards, and toys,[125] crisp harmonies support typical dance tunes, only an occasional sudden shift of tonality suggesting that the composer made a journey to Italy during the last decades of the 16th century. Lovely as these light dances are, Dowland is most impressive in his serious works: pavans, fantasias, "funerals," etc. Here his genius for exquisite melody is most apparent; the emphasis is on long lines, with dramatic use of the leap of a fifth or sixth. Imitation is extensively employed, and on occasion free reign is given to the composer's bent toward degree-inflection. It is from the use of the latter device that the effect of melancholy sometimes results, as in the eloquent fancy, *Forlorne hope*.[126] This piece, which makes exacting demands on the performer, is built on a six-note descending chromatic scale, introduced no less than seventeen times. The same figure appears fourteen times in Dowland's *Farewell*[127] (here, however, in ascending form) and twenty-seven times in a fantasia of his in *Jane Pickering's Book*.[128] A cross between a fantasia and a pavan is found in the transcription of *Lachrimae* (*Flow, my teares*) that is printed in Besard's *Thesaurus* (1603).[129] Each of

---

[125] A toy (toye) was a short, light genre piece.
[126] Pr. DowlLM, 2 (for corrections, *see* NewL, 84).
[127] Pr. DowlLM, 20.   [128] Cf. NewL, 83.
[129] The transcr. in question is not the same as the one that appears in Barley's book. Further regarding lute transcrs. of *Lachrimae, see* MiesL, 63f. For other Dowland lute pieces from the *Thesaurus, see* ChilLS, 203 (= BruS, 97); BruJD, 3 (2 items). For such pieces from Van den Hove's *Delitiae musicae, see ibid.,* 6 (2 items), 8, 9 (but cf. NewL, 70). DowlLM contains 3 exx. from the *Varietie,* the *Invention for two to play upon one lute* (*My Lord Chamberlaine his Galliard*) from the *First Booke of Songs or Ayres* (printed also in BruL I, 37; MAS XII, 91), *Dowland's Adew* from the *Second Booke . . . ,* and 8 exx., not yet cited, from English MS sources. For an *Allemande* in the Thysius MS lute-book, *see* LandT II, 287 (*see also ibid.* I. 210f; II, 340f, 344). The *Galliarda* in BruS, 157, may likewise be Dowland's.

the three strains is varied on its second appearance, as is common in English pavans, whether for the lute or for virginals.

EXAMPLE 204. Extracts from *Fantasia on Dowland's Lachrimae* (from BruJD, 4).

To compare Dowland with Frescobaldi and thus consider him a man of the Baroque, would not agree with the opinion of his contemporaries. When, after long absences from England, he finally returned to stay in 1606, he found that "simple Cantors, or vocal singers" and "professors of the lute" found his music "after the old manner."

The number of composers for the lute is large; many wrote for no other instrument. Francis Cutting, several of whose pieces we have found in Barley's tablature, is best known for his ornate style, which he shares with Alfonso Ferrabosco II, whose *Miserere* is less a liturgically inspired work than a showpiece for dexterous fingers. Others, like Robinson in his *Schoole*, write in a simple vein. Especially interesting, because of the inclusion of many ballad and dance tunes, are the MSS of Dallis and Ballet, both dating from the end of the century.[130] These "collectors" have preserved versions of many standard Elizabethan popular songs, e.g., *The Shaking of the Sheets, Staynes Moris*, etc., some of which occur in no other contemporary source. One of the three sections of the Ballet MS presents music for the lyra viol.[131]

Apart from the publications for lute, there are text-books and a quantity of music for cittern, pandore, and orphorion. The cittern, flat-backed, strung with four wire strings, and played with a plectrum or a quill or the fingers, was standard barber-shop furniture in 16th-century London, a toy with which the waiting customer could amuse himself. The *accordatura* of the instrument

---

[130] For an article on these MSS, with 2 pp. of facsimile from each, *see* FitzL. For 2 other facsimiles from the Ballet MS (reproducing a *Ruggiero* and *Greensleeves*), *see* BontC, Pl. IV.

[131] Music for strings was sometimes written in tablature in England, as on the continent (cf. p. 548). This fact has occasionally caused viol pieces to be mistaken, by modern investigators, for lute pieces. Cf. NewL, *passim*.

involved tuning the string that was lowest in position higher than the next highest in position: thus the bass and tenor strings were reversed. The medieval form of the cittern, the citole, had been popular in England, and Galilei suggests that the type may have originated there; however, there is conflicting evidence on this subject.[132] The earliest known examples of cittern tablature appear in the *Mulliner Book,* mainly a keyboard MS (cf. p. 851).[133] Another MS source is Dd. 4.23,[133a] a book of solos at the University Library, Cambridge. Holborne published a *Cittharn Schoole* in 1597, including thirty-three compositions for solo cittern [134] and twenty-five other pieces (cf. p. 873). In 1609, Robinson published *New Citharen Lessons.* Music for the cittern is mostly of small esthetic value. Much of it is composed almost entirely in block-chords and is of a curiously monotonous nature. This may be due, in part, to the technical limitations of the instrument, which may be responsible also for its use mainly in ensemble music, in which its normal function was that of a *continuo* instrument.

The second part of Barley's *A New Booke of Tabliture* is for the orpharion. This instrument, a larger form of cittern, had eight double strings of wire. In his introduction, Barley cautions the reader that, while the music for lute may be played on the orpharion, and vice versa "the Orpharion doth necessarilie require a more gentle & drawing stroke than the Lute" because of its wire strings. The third part of Barley's tablature is for the pandore (also related to the cittern and a little larger than the orpharion) with six double strings.

Keyboard Music, notably that of Byrd, Bull, Farnaby, and Gibbons

England had known stringed keyboard-instruments from at least the 14th century,[135] and the Robertsbridge MS, containing music suitable either for such instruments or for organ, would seem at any rate to be a continental source from that period left behind by some foreign visitor, if it is not of English provenance.[135a] But sources of music, dating from the 15th century and associated with England, that are known to be for keyboard instruments are wholly lacking,[136] although there is ample evidence that the

---

[132] Cf. DartC, 50.   [133] All exx. pr. at end of StevM; 1 ex. pr. also in DartC, 57.
[133a] 1 piece pr. NaySM, 42.
[134] For facsimile and transcr. of one of them, *see* WolfH II, 134ff. (About earlier, lost cittern prints, *see* DartC, 51f.)
[135] Cf. ReMMA, 383f.
[135a] Cf. StevM, 12. ApelN, 384, doubts the English origin of this MS, partly because of the alleged presence of the name Petrone. The word, however, is *Retrove.* Cf. Gombosi in *Notes,* VII (1950), 284; WolfH II, 9; HandU, 9, 16; facsimiles in EEH I, Pl. 43; ApelN, 38. On the other hand, the argument against an English origin, advanced in ApelN on the basis of the notation, is stronger, as is the argument advanced in StevM on the basis of the repertory.
[136] GlynE, 1, is a piece by Dunstable (preserved in a 16th-century MS), alleged to be for organ. While this may be correct, there is no conclusive proof.

organ was in wide use.[137] Henry Abyngdon (cf. p. 767), who became known as a singer and organist about the time Paumann was writing his *Fundamentum organisandi,* was, upon his death, styled *"optimus orgaquenista"* by Sir Thomas More; [138] but we have no music by him.

An Edward Stanley, in 1502, sang and accompanied himself upon the virginal before the King of Scotland.[139] Virginal music was much favored at the court of Henry VII, and Henry VIII, himself a skilled performer, employed John Heywood (1497–1587) [140] as court virginalist. Edward VI retained Heywood and added, also as virginalists, Robert Bowman and Anthony Chounter. All three remained under Mary, but Heywood resigned upon the accession of Elizabeth, during whose reign virginal music reached its apex.

From the time of Henry VII to the Restoration, the English called all quilled keyboard-instruments "virginals," the square (spinet) type being the most common. In the early 16th century, the usual range was F to a″, at the height of the virginal period, it was A_1 to c‴.[141] In earlier instruments a short bass octave was common,[142] but with the growing employment of chromatic tones the missing notes were often added.[143] Most virginals probably used mean-tone tuning, like the organ, but equal temperament may sometimes have been applied or approximated.[144] Stops never occurred on the spinet type; indeed, they found little favor, even on the harpsichord type, until the 18th century. Double keyboards [145] had nothing to do with changes of tone color, but were used for transposition. No dynamic or accentual gradations were possible; [146] as on the continent, composers implied them through differences in fulness of the chords and complexity of the embellishments.

The sources of English keyboard music that come down to us—whether for organs or for stringed keyboard-instruments—are mostly MSS. The most com-

---

[137] E.g., there is extant a record of the cost of building an organ at Ely Cathedral in 1407; in 1450, Whethamstede, Abbot of St. Albans, gave to his church an organ costing the then enormous sum of £50, said to have been "superior to everything of the kind then in England in size, tone, and workmanship." Cf. Grove III, 747.

[138] PulB, 5.   [139] Cf. PirC, 37.

[140] Cf. Grove II, 626; ChamM II, 203, 443f; PulB, 234.

[141] Cf. PfatJ, 36, for a table of ranges in the various periods. Cf. also BorK, 359ff.

[142] Cf. JasE, 27f; BorK, 362f; GalpO, 124; SachsHI, 332f; also Philips' *Pavana dolorosa* (FullerF I, 321), where the final cadence would be unplayable without it.

[143] Cf. Tomkins' *Pavan* (FullerF II, 51), in which the bass descends by half-steps from A to E.

[144] For varying opinions, *see* SachsHI, 332; BorK, 328, 365f; GlynV, 90f; AndN, xxxiii, xl; GlynN, 48f. *See also* p. 861 *infra.*

[145] "Double virginal" probably meant an instrument whose compass embraced the pitches with double-letter names (according to the second system of nomenclature presented in ApelH, 586: the reader is reminded that elsewhere in this book the first system is used). Cf. GalpO, 290ff; SachsHI, 308 (which, however, concerns the regal). Other interpretations, given elsewhere, are less well founded.

[146] Further about the instrument, *see* Grove V, 543ff, and Supp., 651; SachsHI, 334ff; SachsMI, 142ff; SachsR, 416; RimbP, 48ff; JasE, 21ff; CerfI, 3ff, and Pl. VI. *See also* p. 667 *supra.* About virginal makers, *see* esp. JasE, *passim.*

prehensive is one of the latest, the *Fitzwilliam Virginal Book,*[147] long mistakenly known as *Queen Elizabeth's Virginal Book.* Written out by Francis Tregian [148] (d. 1619), apparently while in prison for politico-religious reasons, it contains nearly 300 pieces and includes practically all the major English keyboard composers and types of music they wrote from c. 1562 to at least c. 1612, the first and last dates specifically mentioned in it.[149] Among its contents are over 130 dances, forty-six arrangements of forty songs and nine of madrigals, twenty-two fantasias, nineteen preludes, six sets of hexachord variations, etc. The *Mulliner Book* (Brit. Mus. Add. MS 30513), compiled by Thomas Mulliner from c. 1545 to c. 1585,[150] is one of the oldest and most important of the keyboard sources. It includes dances, transcriptions of secular songs and anthems, as well as settings of psalm tunes and chant melodies. These are primarily for organ, but a few pieces seem to have been meant for the virginal. There is also some music for cittern (as already pointed out) and gittern. The MS preserves twenty-six or more pieces by Redford, eighteen by Tallis, fifteen by Blitheman, eight by Shepherd, five by Alwood, three each by Edwards and Robert Johnson, along with works by Taverner, Tye, Wm. Mundy, and others. The most carefully and beautifully written virginal MS is *My Ladye Nevell's Booke,*[151] copied out by John Baldwin (Baldwyne) [151a] and dated September 11, 1591. Devoted wholly to Byrd, it numbers among its forty-two pieces examples of nearly every kind of keyboard music he wrote. *Benjamin Cosyn's Virginal Book* (c. 1605–1622) [152] contains ninety-eight works credited to Cosyn, Gibbons, Bull, Tallis, Byrd, Bevin, Strogers, and Weelkes. *Will. Forster's Virginal Book,*[153] dated January 31, 1624, contains seventy-eight pieces by Byrd, Morley, Ward, Englitt, and Bull. Another probably important MS, the *Earl of Leicester's Virginal Book,*

147 Modern ed. in FullerF. Contents listed in Grove V, 547ff. Cf. also J. A. Fuller Maitland and A. H. Mann, *Catalogue of Music in the Fitzwilliam Museum,* Cambridge, 1893, p. 104ff, and BorK, 32ff, for more details, including its apparently close connection with the English Catholic refugee group on the continent. NayE is a description and critical analysis of this collection; BorK and NeuV also treat it in detail.

148 Cf. ColeT. About Tregian's role as scribe of 2 other MSS, *see* SchofT. He was the son of a famous Catholic exile of the same name, who died in 1608.

149 Grove V, 545f, points out that the MS contains a piece by Bull that is dated 1621 in another source. The conflict between this date and that of Tregian's death remains to be reconciled.

150 Modern ed. in MusB I (which appeared too late for systematic account to be taken of its contents in this book in making references to duplicate reprints). GlynE contains many pieces from it; 12 pieces pr. EKMV II; Grove, Supp., 651f, lists additional reprints (the references to HawkH are to the 1853 ed., not, as stated, to that of 1776). For commentary on the MS, *see* StevM.

151 Modern ed. in AndN. Cf. its preface—also AndE—for details. Contents listed in Grove V, 550; BM III, 104ff. GlynNV thinks there are Byrd autograph corrections in the MS. Lady Nevell may have been Byrd's pupil.

151a Who was also a composer; cf. BrennS.

152 No complete modern ed. Description and list of contents in Grove V, 551f. For a partial list of modern prints, *see* FullerBC; GibT. Cf. also GlynN, 41ff; BorK, 36f.

153 No modern ed. Description and list of contents in Grove V, 550f. Cf. also BorK, 36.

has disappeared.[154] One of the last collections of real virginal music is *Eliza-beth Rogers hir Virginall Booke* (Brit. Mus. Add. MS 10337) [155] dated February 17, 1656. There are four virginal MSS (not all dating within our period) in the Paris Conservatory,[156] and others of lesser importance are scattered about England and the continent.[157] The New York Public Library owns three virginal MSS: Drexel 5609, 5611, and 5612.[158] The most impor-tant of these, 5612, is thought to include a Gibbons autograph; [159] it contains music by Blitheman, Byrd, Bull, Dowland, Farnaby, Gibbons, Weelkes, and others. Drexel 5611 is a smaller, less interesting collection of works by Bull, O. and Chr. Gibbons, Tomkins, and fourteen others. Both of these MSS are unusual in that their contents are grouped by key ("Lessons in Gam UT," "Lessons in A re," etc.). Pages 1 to 48 of Drexel 5609, a later MS in modern notation, contain all but six pieces of the *Rogers Virginal Book;* [160] pages 57 to 156 correspond to a large part of one of the Paris sources mentioned above (MS Rés. 1186).

Although titles of Attaingnant keyboard prints had mentioned *espinettes* as early as 1531 (cf. p. 558), it is not until 1612 or 1613 that we find pub-lished in England *Parthenia, or the Maydenhead of the First Musicke that ever was printed for the Virginalls*. This collection, produced from en-graved plates, contains twenty-one pieces by Byrd, Bull, and Gibbons.[161] Five of these are pavans, ten are galliards. There are also a set of variations, a fancy, and some preludes. A companion volume, *Parthenia In-violata . . . ,*[162] appeared c. 1614. From the facts that *parthenos* is the Greek word for "virgin" and that in the new book a viol reinforces the bass of the keyboard part (as in Ortiz's *Tratado*), it soon becomes obvious that both titles are puns. The later English book, of which the New York Public Library possesses the unique copy, contains twenty anonymous song tran-

---

[154] Cf. GlynV, 37, 99.

[155] No modern ed. 15 pieces pr. EKMV V. Description and partial list of contents in Grove, Supp., 652. Full list in BM III, 107f.

[156] No modern ed. Description and partial list of contents in PerL, which, like Grove, Supp., 653, and GlynV, 127, uses accession numbers. The MS call numbers are as follows: For 18546, Rés. 1186; for 18547, Rés. 1122; for 18548, Rés. 1184 and 1185; for 18570, Rés. 1186 *bis*. Cf. ByrdF, first plate, where the accession number is shown stamped on the MS and the call number is used in the caption of the plate.

[157] Cf. Grove, Supp., 653, about English and other MSS; cf. also WolfH II, 278; DaveyA; DaveyH, 121ff. NieV, 12, mentions MSS in Berlin, Paris, Vienna, and Liége.

[158] No modern ed. Some pieces from them included in ByrdF; ByrdOB; FarnSP; GibC; GlynVP; WeelP. Cf. also Grove, Supp., 652f; MarkG; GlynF; GlynT.

[159] Cf. GlynF; GlynT.

[160] Nos. 34–38, 45, 69, all of which contain words. Cf. BM III, 107f.

[161] At least 6 issues were printed from the same music plates by 1659, several after the death of all 3 composers. Such a record was unusual and shows the book's great popularity. HR III is a facs. ed.; see its pref. concerning the date of the first issue. There have been modern eds. by Rimbault, Farrenc, Pauer, Glyn, and Stone. Of these StoneP is the best; Rimbault, in MAS XVIII, mistakes the text and Pauer copies him. Cf. ByrdF, xi.

[162] . . . *or Mayden-Musicke for the Virginalls and Bass-Viol, selected out of the compositions of the most famous in that Arte by Robert Hole . . .* For details, *see* BrennP.

scriptions and dances. In view of the many virginal pieces surviving in MS, their scarcity in print is surprising, especially when one considers the amount of other kinds of music that the English printed.

Virginal notation uses two staves, ordinarily of six or eight lines each, though occasionally a great staff of twelve or thirteen lines is employed.[163] Blackening of notes not only may indicate hemiola, but also may mark off the *cantus firmus* or the meane,[164] the latter being an inner part (in a piece *a 3*) that characteristically wanders from hand to hand. Little attention is paid to the vertical alignment of simultaneously sounded notes. The placing of accidentals is inconsistent and confusing, the clarity found in *My Ladye Nevelles Booke* being exceptional.

While most early English keyboard music might well be described as apt for virginal or for organ, a tendency to differentiate between styles suitable for each becomes increasingly apparent. Although Italy yielded keyboard music in quantity sooner than did England, a similar differentiation is less evident there. The claim of a pioneer character, made by English scholars, for the virginal music of their country is justified. It is reasonable to suppose that the English knew Italian keyboard music as they knew Italian madrigals, and were affected by it. But, if they were, they built something new on the old foundation. In the process, however, they may well have been influenced by Cabezón—a point to which we shall return.

Forerunners of the later virginal style are a *Hornpype* by Aston,[165] *My Lady Carey's Dompe*,[166] and the *Short measure off My Lady Wynkfyld's Rownde* (the last two anonymous, but sometimes conjecturally assigned to Aston), all in the part of Brit. Mus., Roy. App. 58, that dates from c. 1530–1535.[167] Portions of the *Hornepype* provide variations on a ground, as does all of *My Lady Carey's Dompe*.[167a] (The extent of Aston's reputation is indicated by the fact that several later composers, including Byrd, based works of their own on a "ground" of his.[167b]) The *Lady Carey* piece is the oldest known dump, all 16th-century examples of which are variation sets. One may therefore "date the use of variation technique by English instrumental composers before 1550"; moreover, these men wrote variations on a bass tune before they did so on a discant tune. The reason for the odd name "dump" has prompted many conjectures. There is no basis for believing the species to

---

[163] Cf. ApelN, 8ff, esp. fn. 1, p. 8.   [164] Cf. StevM, 21; MusB I, xiv.

[165] Pr. EKMV I, 4; SmM I, 82; WolfME, 57; ApelM II, 5; ApelMK, 62. Cf. BorK, 23ff; NieV, 10f, for a discussion of this piece and a comparison of its style with the less advanced keyboard technique of Schlick, Aston's German contemporary.

[166] Pr. EKMV I, 10; SmM I, 42; HAM, 105; NaySM, 7.

[167] The 7 other keyboard pieces from this MS are also pr. EKMV I. (The tentative ascriptions of the *Dompe* and the *Rownde* to Aston have been made on the rather unsafe ground that the compositions follow the *Hornepype* in the MS.)

[167a] The latter fact has been made the basis of the obviously exaggerated claim that the composer of this piece "invented" the variation form.

[167b] Cf. AndN, 194. In FullerF I, 226, it is called *"Treg[ian's] Ground."*

have been a dance form. There is agreement, however, on one point—the pathetic connotation of "dump"—and it is likely that the term is the equivalent of *déploration*.[168] The three pieces in Roy. App. 58 display a remarkable grasp of keyboard technique, using broken chords, scale passages, and recurrent rhythmic patterns in a manner typical of later virginal music. The composer of the *Rownde,* despite its advanced character,[168a] is old-fashioned in his use of conflicting signatures.

EXAMPLE 205. Extract from *Short measure off My Lady Wynkfyld's Rownde*—Anon. (complete piece in SmM I, 39; EKMV I, 12).[169]

The next important keyboard composer after Aston was Redford, whose organ pieces survive mainly in the *Mulliner Book.*[170] Some of these may be reductions of Latin motets. At any rate, the style (as also in such other works from *Mulliner* as Blitheman's *Meane,*[171] Alwood's *Voluntary,*[172] etc.) is often that of vocal polyphony without instrumental figuration.[173] However, there are also Redford pieces in a definitely instrumental style, among them *O Lux. on the faburden.*[174] Besides instrumental figuration, this piece illustrates a special kind of keyboard hymn-setting. In writing a work of this kind, one added a tenor in a mixture of sixths and octaves below the chant, as would have been customary in old-type fauxbourdon. (If necessary, in order to provide room for the insertion of the tenor, the plainsong was transposed up an octave.) When the composer had derived the tenor, which was called the faburden, from the plainsong, he discarded the latter and used the faburden as a *cantus firmus.* The setting he then wrote on it was intended, like normal settings of actual Chant melodies, to alternate with stanzas sung in plainsong. Organ compositions of Redford's, such as his *Veni Redemptor* and *Verbum supernum,*[174a] each consist of a group of hymn-melody settings

---

[168] For a study of the dump, *see* WardD.

[168a] About the phrase structure of this piece, *see* GomE, 18.

[169] This example, like the others in the section on virginal music, retains the original note-values of its source.

[170] Most pr. PfatJ, which also contains Redford exx. from other MSS. Cf. *ibid.,* 36f, for reasons why the music is assigned to organ rather than virginal. 2 of these pieces duplicated in HAM, 128; 1 in EKMV II, 11; 8 in GlynE, which also contains a *Meane* here ascribed to Redford, but not given in PfatJ. All Redford's Mulliner pieces are, of course, pr. MusB I.

[171] Pr. MusB I, 26; HawkH V, 464.

[172] Pr. MusB I, 13; EKMV II, 12; HawkH V, 467; WestO, 24. GlynE, 20ff, contains 4 other exx. by Alwood. Cf. Grove I, 76, on this composer.

[173] Cf. PfatJ, 34ff, for a discussion of this point.   [174] Pr. *ibid.,* music section, 50.

[174a] Pr. *ibid.,* 59, 63, respectively.

of the normal type. Among other English works of the time that alternate organ and sung chant is a *Te Deum* setting by Blitheman in the *Mulliner Book*.

A whole group of twenty anonymous, undated organ settings contained in Brit. Mus. Add. MS 29996 (fol. 158–178b) belongs to the type of hymn-setting using as a *cantus firmus* a faburden derived from a plainsong melody.[175]

Also based on a *cantus firmus,* here used normally, are the *Pretty Wayes: for young beginners to looke on,* contained in the same MS. These keyboard pieces *a 2* and *a 3,* which seem to date from c. 1600, illustrate various types of contrapuntal writing.[176] A particular feature of the MS is its inclusion of the sole surviving reasonably complete example of the organ-Mass in England, a work of the Welshman, Philip ap Rhys "off Saynt Poulles, in London." [176a] The earliest known duets at a keyboard (one each by N. Carleton and T. Tomkins) are likewise in this MS.[177] There is a piece "for two virginals" by G. Farnaby in the *Fitzwilliam Virginal Book*.[178]

Most of the Renaissance writers of keyboard music were organists and wrote on Gregorian melodies.[178a] Toward the mid-century, a body of music arose, based on the *Felix namque,* etc.—pieces which, in view of their *cantus firmi,* one would expect to be for organ, but whose content gives the impression that they are for virginal, though the medium for which they were intended is not stated. A type of contrapuntal accompaniment appears that makes free use of virginal keyboard figures and results in an expanded and more brilliant treatment of the kind of material that Redford handles simply in his organ music. (Variation form was emerging simultaneously. But it was not suitable for application to longer plainsong melodies, such as the *Felix namque:* English instrumental music generally used sacred *cantus firmi* intact, and the repetition inseparable from variation form, if applied to such material, would obviously have led to inordinate length; moreover, composers favored adherence to one type of figuration, more or less, throughout a single variation, and such adherence in the setting of a long *cantus firmus* would have produced monotony. Not until shorter and more metrical popular songs and dance tunes were drawn upon were composers free to use variation technique with the brilliant variety that led virginal music to achieve its full individuality.) As in earlier times, plainsong *cantus firmi* were

---

[175] Cf. MillS (but in the light of BukFR, 30f).

[176] Cf. MillP, which transcribes the *Wayes.* Concerning the possibility that these pieces are by Tomkins, *see ibid.,* 554.

[176a] Cf. StevT; StevO, 7.

[177] Cf. MillD, which includes transcrs. The MS is actually a composite consisting of several MSS (once the property of T. Tomkins) bound together. For 8 additional keyboard pieces from it, *see* EKMV IV, two—perhaps three—being T. Tomkins compositions.

[178] Pr. FullerF I, 202.

[178a] E.g., the 31 Chant melodies or sections (many of them set by more than one composer) used in *Mulliner;* cf. the list in StevM, 76f.

used in any voice, but, if they were assigned to an inner part, the uniform tone color of the virginal made them especially hard to follow. Owing to the natural predominance of the top and bottom voices, melodic variation (with the thematic material in the superius) and harmonic variation (with the thematic material in the bass) soon came into general use. A combination of the two, in which the superius carries the melody over strong harmonic support in the bass, with comparatively unimportant inner voices, was shortly found to be the ideal medium for the virginal and was the one most often favored by later composers.[179] An anonymous setting of *Aurora lucis rutilat* (cf. p. 604) is a good illustration.[180]

Typical of virginal music using plainsong *cantus firmi* in the older style are the two Tallis pieces of 1562 and 1564, based on *Felix namque* [181]—the oldest dated English plainsong settings of this kind. Each presents the plainsong once, the second decorating it to a greater extent. The first starts with the plainsong cantus in the tenor, accompanied by a simple, slightly ornamented melody in the superius, which is imitated in the bass and alto, forming a brief introductory section. From this simple beginning, the writing increases in complexity and in its demands on the player, using almost every form of figuration known to virginal technique— $\frac{6}{3}$ writing, hocket, broken chords, sequences, etc.—and ending with an elaborate cadence.

EXAMPLE 206. Nine extracts from *Felix namque*—Tallis (from FullerF 1, 427ff).

[179] Cf. BukMB, 11. *See* BorK, 347ff, for a discussion (to which the present one is much indebted) of the various basic types of writing used by the virginalists.

[180] Pr. PirAO, 1239. The Sarum form of the melody is used (cf. Chap. 15, fn. 98a). A Redford setting of that form is pr. in PfatJ, 29.

[181] Pr. FullerF I, 427; II, 1, respectively. For a list of some 16th- and 17th-century settings, *see* BorK, 166, fn. 15. For the complete plainsong, *see* FrereG, Pl. r. (near back); Liber, 1271, gives a large part of it. 13 other pieces by Tallis and 1 attributed to him pr. GlynE (1 of the 13 = EKMV II, 12).

(Ornamentation signs of the kind here employed will be discussed presently.) The chief point of interest of the second *Felix namque* is the ending, with its toccata-like figuration; no earlier dated example of such figuration is known to survive from any country.[182] Despite great beauty of detail the general effect is one of overornamentation and monotony. It is an open question whether Tallis originated the type of figuration used in these two pieces. There is some similarity between his work and that of Cabezón (known to have been in England in 1554—cf. p. 627), but whether there was any direct influence one way or the other is unknown. It is quite possible that English keyboard figuration had developed gradually from what seem to be its beginnings in Aston's music, several decades earlier, to reach its climax later in the work of Bull.

Another Chant melody drawn on by the virginalists, e.g., Byrd, was that of the *Veni Creator Spiritus*.[183] Since this melody served also the words of *Salvator mundi* (cf. p. 773), some settings bear this title.[184]

The *In nomine* naturally lent itself to providing the keyboard repertory with pieces written on a *cantus firmus*. The keyboard transcription *a 4*[185] of Taverner's *In nomine* passage (preserved in the *Mulliner Book*) is faithful to the Mass, which, in these measures, reveals little permeation of the polyphonic texture by the chant except in the imitation at the beginning. In an *In nomine* by Blitheman, dating from before 1591, occurs the earliest known example of triplet figuration in virginal music, the entire piece containing it.[186] A piece by Gibbons, entitled *In nomine,* has a different *cantus firmus;* [187] by his late day, the Gregorian tradition and its derivatives were so under a cloud in England that *"In nomine"* at times merely indicated some sort of connection with church music.[188]

The title *Gloria tibi Trinitas* appears on a number of settings of the antiphon melody, and among them are some that weave this melody into the contrapuntal texture instead of treating it as a *cantus firmus* in long notes.[189] Bull's *Gloria tibi*,[190] which does use the melody as a *cantus firmus,* perhaps represents the height of virginal figuration. Blitheman, in addition to his several settings entitled *In nomine,* has left six settings entitled *Gloria tibi Trinitas*.[191]

There are several *Miserere* settings based on the melody printed in the

---

[182] Cf. BorK, 163. [183] For 2 exx., *see* ByrdW XX, 142, 144 (= ByrdF, 8, 10, respectively). [184] For one by Bull, *see* FullerF I, 163. [185] Pr. GlynE, 14.
[186] Pr. FullerF I, 181.
[187] The piece pr. FullerBC, 40 (with ornaments); GibC IV, 19 (without them). Gibbons, however, did know the normal *cantus firmus,* as is shown by his 4 *In nomine* settings (for instrumental ensemble) in Oxford, Bodleian Lib., Music School MSS 26356–60 (D 212–16).
[188] Cf. BorK, 162, fn. 12, for later meanings of the term.
[189] E.g., GlynE, 12 (Tallis); ByrdF, 6 (= ByrdW XX, 135). [190] Pr. FullerF I, 160.
[191] Pr. MusB I, 67 (= EKMV II, 14), 68 (= RimbP, 237), 69, 70 (2 pieces), 72.

Liber usualis, 266. Among them are a charming one *a 3* by Byrd [192] and a learned and rather uninteresting one by Bull.[193] Another melody underlies two Byrd pieces entitled *Miserere* in the *Fitzwilliam Virginal Book,*[194] one *a 3,* one *a 4.* This melody is the *Clarifica me Pater,*[194a] which is closely related to the *Gloria tibi Trinitas*—a fact that may explain why one of the pieces is called *In nomine* in another source. Since the word *"Miserere"* does not occur in the *Clarifica me* text, it may be that we have here examples of a family of instrumental *Miserere* settings [194b] stemming from the Gloria or Agnus of an unknown *Missa Clarifica me Pater* in much the same way as the family of *In nomine* settings arose from a Benedictus.[195]

Still other plainsong melodies were occasionally used, but the manner of writing varies little. Related to the plainsong settings is a fantasia by Bull on the Dutch sacred melody *Laet ons met herten reyne* (which is preceded by a brief prelude), a piece that is remarkable for its inclusion of what are probably the oldest directions for organ registration.[196]

There are not many accidentals in the earlier virginal MSS, but the principles of *musica ficta* were undoubtedly applied. On the whole, virginal music employed a scale which, in spite of frequent inflections (especially of the third, sixth, and seventh degrees) is generally major in ascending and minor in descending passages.[197] The tonal system that results is something between the old modes and the major and minor of later music, never including, however, the augmented second of the modern harmonic minor scale. False-relations, such as we have found common in other English music, are particularly evident in pieces for virginal. For example, a chord with a major third often accompanies a melody in which the minor third occurs in a descending scale-passage. Melodic false-relations, like the one in the following example (notable likewise for its skilful use of suspensions) are also frequent.

EXAMPLE 207. Extract from *In nomine*—Bull (from FullerF II, 35).

---

[192] Pr. ByrdW XX, 139; ByrdF, 12.   [193] Pr. FullerF II, 442.

[194] Pr. FullerF II, 230, 232 (= ByrdW XX, 140, 137, respectively).

[194a] Pr. Liber, 1101.

[194b] *See,* for example, the Tallis pieces based on this melody (but untitled in the Mulliner MS), pr. MusB I, 74, 75, 76. *See also* StevM, 38.

[195] Of course, it is also possible that the title in *Fitzwilliam* is simply a mistake.

[196] Pr. WestO, No. 25b; BonnO I, 26. The music is contained in a Netherlands MS, Brit. Mus. Add. MS 23623 (the so-called "Tablature of 1629"), almost all of whose 63 pieces are by Bull. Further on this MS, which also contains virginal music, *see* Grove, Supp., 652; MillB; BM III, 82.

[197] Cf. *ibid.,* 18f; *see,* in addition, ByrdF, xiif, on the scale system; also BukMB, 12.

Still allied with vocal music are the many transcriptions of motets and secular pieces by Philips, Byrd, G. Farnaby, and others, which employ much figuration such as was used in France c. 1530 (cf. pp. 559f). In England, the figuration seems particularly germane to the keyboard. Most effective is a Lassus chanson transcription by Philips, dating from 1605.

EXAMPLE 208. Extracts from *Margot labourez les vignes* by Lassus (after LassoW XII, 103) and from Philips' transcription of it (after FullerF I, 333).

In a transcription[198] of Striggio's madrigal *Chi fara fed'al cielo* (cf. p. 436), Philips contrives to keep the original easily recognizable in spite of very lavish ornamentation. Byrd's *Qui passe*[198a] makes much freer use of Azzaiolo's *Chi passa* (cf. pp. 445, 691). (The Forster MS calls Byrd's piece *Kapassa;*[198b] the many instrumental transcriptions of the old *villota* that appear under variants of the title, e.g., *Kypassa, Kypascie,* etc., as well as its frequent mention in English literature, show how popular it was.)[198c] On the whole, Farnaby's transcriptions stay closer to their models. In his reworking of his own canzonet *Ay me, poore heart,*[199] for instance, the tune is used

[198] Pr. after 2 sources (together with the madrigal) in AMO X, 153 (pr. after 1 of these sources also in FullerF I, 312); *see also ibid.,* 83. Another Philips madrigal transcription pr. ScherG, 196 (the madrigal, *ibid.,* 193).
[198a] Pr. ByrdW XVIII, 69; AndN, 9.   [198b] Cf. *ibid.,* xxxix (No. 2).
[198c] The derivation from Azzaiolo has been pointed out by John Ward in *Italian Popular Music and English Broadside Ballads;* cf. p. 525, fn. 31a.
[199] Pr. FullerF II, 330. For the canzonet, *see* EMS XX, 65.

prominently and simply at the opening and remains on top most of the time, so that the figuration never obscures it.

Ornaments pose an intricate problem, since there are instances of various MSS applying ornamentation differently to a single piece.[200] The signs most frequently encountered are ‡ and ‡, commonly thought to mean (in reduced values)

respectively.[201] Unfortunately, we have no contemporary explanation. Certain investigators [202] feel that, in view of the MS discrepancies, the ornaments are not a real part of the melodic line and may be omitted; others,[203] who are probably right, think that ornamentation (though not necessarily specific ornaments in specific places) is an integral part of the virginal style, and should by all means be included.

Close to the types based on borrowed material is the music which, though clearly intended for the keyboard, is still written in the old polyphonic tradition, e.g., the fantasias, preludes, voluntaries, toccatas, etc. Of these, the voluntaries [204] make least use of ornamentation and figuration. Freest in structure are the toccatas and preludes. Originally, the English keyboard prelude, like the Italian *intonazione,* was a short organ piece combining chord progressions with some figuration, and its primary purpose was to give the pitch and mode to the choir or officiant in church. Later, however, when taken over by the virginalists, it strayed from pure modal writing and used more figuration. A Byrd *Praeludium* in *Parthenia* (No. IV) illustrates both points: it is definitely in C major and, throughout, figured writing appears in the left hand against sustained chords in the right, or the procedure is reversed. Among the many preludes for virginal, eight by Bull are notable for their demands on virtuosity. The few toccatas in English collections either are by Italians or show strong Italian influence.[205] The fantasia, too, recalls Italian keyboard models. It ranges from scholastic exercises to flights of fancy bordering on improvisation. There is some tendency to develop one subject extensively [206]—several, however, are often used—and to become more chordal toward the end, although many fantasias close in brilliant toccata fashion. The single subject of a fine

[200] Cf. esp. FelWB, 210.

[201] Cf. *ibid.,* 209; but *see also* ByrdF, xiiiff. There are other conflicting views on this subject. Cf. also BorK, 145ff.

[202] E.g., GlynV, 57ff; BorK, 148; AndN, xxxiif.   [203] E.g., S. Tuttle in ByrdF, xivf.

[204] For exx., *see,* by Redford: PfatJ, *passim;* by Gibbons: GibT, 27; WestO, 14, 31a, 31b (= GibC V, 16); GibC IV, 3, 15; by Weelkes: WeelP, 2, perhaps 4 (ascribed to Weelkes in WeelP, but anon. in source); by Byrd: AndN, 140, 243 (= ByrdW XVIII, 45, 44); 2 anon. exx: PirAO, 1241ff. Cf. also fn. 172 *supra.* For the original meaning of the term, *see* Grove V, 570f.

[205] About Italian influence on English keyboard music in general, cf. BorK, 138ff.

[206] For an extreme example, *see* a Philips *Fantasia* (FullerF I, 335), which employs the same subject 39 times.

fantasia by G. Farnaby,[207] who particularly excelled in the genre, is freely imitated and gracefully figured in writing *a 3* and *a 4*, with frequent use of sequences, broken chords, wide skips, passages in thirds, and much ornamentation in true virginal style. There is a striking modulation in it,[208] also an exceptional double appoggiatura at the final cadence. A descriptive fantasia by John Mundy,[209] effective despite the limited resources of the virginal, deals recurrently with "faire wether" and lightning-and-thunder, and ends with "a cleare day." The fantasia type includes sets of variations on the hexachord, the six degrees of which serve as a basis for learned counterpoint. There is usually little of esthetic interest. The theme, however, is sometimes used as a point of departure for arresting changes of key, as in Bull's *Ut, re, mi, fa, sol, la*.[210] The tonics of the keys in which the subject appears represent every degree of the chromatic scale, the order of the transpositions being such that the successive tonics form two whole-tone series (one on G, one on A-flat) with a final return to the opening key. All the settings of the subject are fairly major in tonality, though not entirely free of modal influences. The presence in a single composition of both C-sharp and D-flat, G-sharp and A-flat, as in the following example, suggests that the piece may well have been written for some instrument like the *arcicembalo*,[211] or for one whose temperament was equal or almost so (cf. p. 850).

EXAMPLE 209. Extract from *Ut, re, mi* . . . —Bull (from FullerF I, 183).

The type of virginal music most often encountered in collections from after the mid-century consists of variations that have folk songs and dance tunes as their basis.[212] *Goe from my window*,[213] *O Mistress Mine*,[214] *The*

---

[207] Pr. FullerF II, 270.   [208] *See* meas. 15–18; cf. FullerF I, xiv.

[209] Pr. TagA III, 28; FullerF I, 23. Other exx. by Mundy, *ibid.*, 19, 66; II, 449. Cf. also fn. 213 *infra*.

[210] Pr. FullerF I, 183. Analysis in BorK, 321ff.   [211] Cf. ApelH, 47; also pp. 530, 667, *supra*.

[212] For special treatment of this type, *see* esp. NeuV; BorK, Chap. V, pt. 6; NelsV, Chaps. 1–3.

[213] Byrd's setting pr. ByrdW XX, 20; ByrdF, 113; FullerC, 14. A setting having 7 variations is ascribed to Morley in Fitzwilliam (pr. FullerF I, 42) and reappears there later, with an eighth variation added, attributed to John Mundy (pr. *ibid.*, I, 153; HAM, 204; TagA III, 33). For 5 keyboard pieces ascribed to Morley without conflicting attributions, *see* FullerF. Cf. also ChappP I, 146.

[214] Byrd's setting pr. ByrdW XX, 41; FullerF I, 258. Cf. also ChappP I, 103.

Carman's Whistle,[215] *Wolsey's Wild,*[216] *Tower Hill,*[216a] and *Callino Castu-rame* (mentioned in *Henry V*, Act IV, scene 4) [217] are only a few of the many folk melodies drawn upon. Whether the popularity of variation form at that time is in some way connected with Cabezón's *diferencias* and his visit to England, is not clear, but the possibility exists. The unique contribution of English keyboard composers to the form is their treatment of the theme and first variation as a unit, no simple preliminary statement of the theme being given. Thus, in a melody consisting of two eight-measure strains, *a* and *b,* the initial statement would be *aa'bb',* and then this thirty-two meas-ure statement would be varied one or more times. Farnaby's *Why aske you?* [218] is a good example of this variation-of-a-variation type. Full cadences were not required after each variation, but a double bar often shows where the cadence has vanished into the continuous flow. Successive variations usu-ally increase in brilliance, frequently ending with a broad statement of the subject—sometimes the only clearly defined one. Such writing often loses touch with old-style polyphony and adopts the new harmonic style of ac-companied melody. Where present, counterpoint may not be strict, the voices entering or leaving at will, the insertion of rests, however, being rare.

There are four clearly defined variation techniques.[219] The first approxi-mates the old *cantus-firmus* technique, but is freer. It allows the melodic sub-ject, in a simple form, to pass from one voice to another while the other voices provide counterpoint against it. The best-known work of this type is Byrd's *Walsingham* variations, dating from before 1591,[220] and consisting of twenty-two short variations and a postlude. The writing is mostly *a 3* and *a 4,* but there is no consistency in the number of voices used. On the whole, the tonality is G minor, but, in accord with the modulation implied in the tune, nearly every section ends in G major, and the entire postlude is in that key.

In type 2 the theme appears in the superius throughout the work, either in its original form or somewhat figured. Using the same theme as Byrd, Bull gives us, in his *Walsingham* variations,[221] a superb example of this kind of writing. He takes full advantage of the implied modulation and creates a set of twenty-nine variations that use every resource of virginal figuration [222] and weave a contrapuntal fabric of great variety. The music increases mark-edly in complexity toward the end and requires a virtuoso performer.

In type 3 the bass remains constant while the other voices change. Grounds,

---

[215] Byrd's setting pr. ByrdW XX, 7; FullerF I, 214; ApelMK, 66; AndN, 189. Cf. also ChappP I, 253.   [216] Byrd's setting pr. ByrdW XX, 57; FullerF II, 184. Cf. also ChappP I, 267.
[216a] Farnaby's setting pr. FullerF II, 371. A slightly different anon. version from Brit. Mus. Add. MS 30486 pr. EKMV III, 3 (which vol. also prints 6 other keyboard pieces from this MS).
[217] Pr. FullerF I, 186. Cf. also ChappP I, 84f.   [218] Pr. FullerF II, 462.
[219] Discussed at length in BorK, 201ff, from which the classification is borrowed.
[220] Pr. ByrdW XX, 24; FullerF I, 267; AndN, 173. Cf. ChappP I, 69, for the original tune and information about the shrine of Walsingham. Cf. also WhitW.
[221] Pr. FullerF I, 1. BorK, 223f, dates this work tentatively c. 1610–15.
[222] Note also in variation 28 (FullerF I, 17) the crossing of hands that was to be so typical of D. Scarlatti a century later. Cf. BorK, 150f.

numerous in virginal music, characterize this type. Among the oldest pieces incorporating them is *My Ladye Nevels Grownde*.[223] Upon a systematically constructed, very harmonic bass line, Byrd erects six variations, increasing the complexity of the writing as he proceeds and concluding with a three-measure *codetta*.

Van den Borren calls type 4 the "melodico-harmonic" variation and describes it thus: "bass and superius form in each variation a harmonic and melodic extreme which cannot be exceeded, while in between is elaborated a different figuration in each variation".[224] Among the numerous examples of this kind (it became the standard variation type) may be mentioned Byrd's *Fortune*.[225] From variation 2 on, the bass and superius, as a rule, alternate in assuming the figuration against simple part-writing.

Much of the folk-song material on which virginal music is based is in the Ionian mode, with occasional modulation to the dominant. There are also modulations from minor to tonic major, and up or down a whole tone.[226] Different keys are often juxtaposed without any modulatory "pivot."

The frequent drawing on folk and dance tunes, with their metric nature, gives virginal music a rhythmic impetus lacking in purely contrapuntal writing—"rhythmic" in the later, accentual, sense, even though stress accents could not actually be produced on the instrument (cf. p. 850). While the rhythmic structure of the music is sometimes simple, the metric quality referred to did not necessarily lead to "squareness": a gem-like galliard by Philips [227] mingles what we would call $\frac{6}{8}$ and $\frac{3}{4}$ groups with exquisite skill. To be sure, especially in pieces based on songs rather than on dances, polyphonic overlapping is found, but clear-cut phrases are more characteristic. Sequential repetitions are frequent. Figuration patterns,[228] including ternary note-groups probably suggested by the old *tempus perfectum,* provided the virginalists with their structurally most important means of embellishment. This figuration is sometimes developed at considerable length over a solid harmonic base, and, having been passed on by the English to the Netherlanders of the Sweelinck generation, and by them to other nations, eventually proved to be the origin of our modern western keyboard style.

Among the dance forms—well represented in almost all later virginal books —the most plentiful are pavans and galliards, allemandes and courantes,[229] although minor forms such as jigs, brawls (i.e., *branles*), lavoltas, masks,

[223] Dating at least before 1591 (the date of the MS); pr. AndN, 1; ByrdW XX, 58.
[224] BorK, 208.
[225] Pr. ByrdW XX, 11; FullerF I, 254. Cf. BorK, 234ff, regarding use of the theme by Sweelinck and Scheidt, and for comments on Byrd's piece.
[226] E.g., Byrd's *The woods so wilde* (FullerF I, 263), which wavers repeatedly between F and G. Cf. GlynV, 18; ChappP I, 119.
[227] Pr. FullerF I, 351; TagA II, 102; SachsPM, 20. For 12 keyboard pieces by Philips not yet cited, *see* FullerF (1 = TagA II, 99).
[228] For a full analysis of these, with exx., cf. BorK, Chap. IV.
[229] For a detailed discussion of various treatments of these forms, *see* BorK, 251ff.

spagniolettas, morescas (morrisses), rounds, etc., also occur frequently.[230] In the minor forms the real dance character is kept; in the others, sometimes only the name remains and the musical import far exceeds that of the original dance. In all of these dance forms, the harmonic and rhythmic elements predominate, even where there is elaborate contrapuntal treatment. Scarcely a trace of the church modes remains. The normal *aabbcc* form of the pavan is often changed in English keyboard examples to *aa′bb′cc′*. Sometimes, as on the continent, the melodic material, presented in binary rhythm in the pavan, is varied in ternary rhythm in the galliard. The term *"passamezzo"* is occasionally combined with "pavan" or "galliard," but the so-called *"passamezzo* pavans," instead of following the usual English keyboard pavan form, are built on a single strain followed by variations. One of Byrd's eight pavan-galliard pairs in *My Ladye Nevell's Booke*[231] includes such a pavan, presents the same melodic material in the superius of the two dances, and uses the *passamezzo antico* formula (cf. Ex. 121) in the bass of each, letting the breves of the melody be represented by two-measure units and the whole notes by single measures. In the following example the beginning of the stock formula is marked by asterisks in each dance.

EXAMPLE 210. Opening measures of *The Passinge Mesures: the Nynthe Pavian* and of *The Galliarde to the Nynthe Pavian*—Byrd (complete pieces in AndN, 125, 133; ByrdW XIX, 36, 42; FullerF I, 203, 209).

[230] Cf. BorK, 304ff.

[231] All pr. AndN and ByrdW XIX. There are actually 10 "pavians," but Nos. 7 and 8 lack galliards. Pairs 1–3 and pavan No. 7 are also pr. FullerF II, 204, 207; 398, 400; 384, 387; and 427, respectively; pair 9 is likewise pr. FullerF (see Ex. 210); pair 10 is also pr. GlynP, 1 (bottom), 4; StoneP, 2, 6.

It is to such *passamezzo* pavans that Shakespeare refers when, in the fourth act of *Twelfth Night*,[232] he mentions a "passy-measure pavin." Philips' *Passamezzo Pavana* and *Galiarda Passamezzo* [232a] are also constructed on the *passamezzo antico* bass, whereas it is the *passamezzo moderno* (cf. Ex. 121) that appears in the *Quadran Paven* and *Galiard* pairs composed by Byrd [233] and Bull.[234]

Occasionally still other borrowed material appears in keyboard pavans. Byrd's *Pavana Lachrymae*,[235] Farnaby's *Lachrimae pavana*,[236] and a *Pavana* by Morley [237] are all based on Dowland's *Flow, my tears*.[238] At times dances are called after an individual, e.g., the pavan-galiard pairs, one by Byrd and one by Gibbons, named after the Earl of Salisbury,[239] or the titles are descriptive, as in Philips' *Pavana dolorosa Treg(ian)* and *Galiarda dolorosa*,[240] Tisdall's *Pavana chromatica*,[241] Tomkins' *Hunting Galliard*,[241a] or Bull's *Spanish Paven*.[242] The theme on which Bull writes his piece is the old *Pavaniglia* (cf. p. 525) which, as noted in Chapter 11, was reworked also by

[232] Scene 1, line 209.

[232a] Pr. FullerF I, 299, 306.

[233] Pr. *ibid*. II, 111 (= ByrdW XIX, 70), 103 (= ByrdW XIX, 64), respectively. Concerning the meaning of "Quadran," see fn. 112 *supra*.

[234] Pr. *ibid*. I, 99, 117. For another *Quadran Paven* by Bull, see *ibid*., 107.

[235] Pr. ByrdW XIX, 150; FullerF II, 42.

[236] Pr. *ibid*., 472.

[237] Pr. *ibid*., 173.

[238] Another keyboard setting, which should probably be regarded as anon., although it is attributed to Dowland himself in 1 source, is pr. GlynVP, 4.

[239] Byrd's pair pr. ByrdW XIX, 58 (= GlynP, 8; StoneP, 12, 13); pavan only, ApelMK, 68. Gibbons' pair pr. GibC III, 4; GlynP, 24; StoneP, 42, 32; HAM, 206. GibC contains 49 pieces by Gibbons not yet cited. Of these, 6 appear also in GibMG (cf. comment at end of this note), 6 in FullerBC and GibT, 4 more in FullerBC, 2 in GlynP (or StoneP) and TagA III, 2 in GibMG and FullerBC, 1 in GlynP (or StoneP) and SmM, 1 in TagA III and FullerF II, 1 each in GlynP (or StoneP), EKMV IV, V (*see* p. 8), and WestO. 12 other uncited pieces in GibMG, 9–16; 3 in FullerBC, 39 (= GibT, 16), 54, 55; 2 in WestO, 14a, 31a; 1 in FullerF II, 479 (= TagA III, 100); 1 in GibT, 21. Of the 21 pieces in GibMG, only 9 are ascribed to Gibbons in the sources; the other ascriptions rest on Glyn's opinion. She does not specify which 9 are so ascribed.

[240] Pr. FullerF I, 321, 327, respectively.

[241] Pr. *ibid*. II, 278. This piece has the subtitle, *Mrs. Katherin Tregians Paven*. Other pieces by Tisdall pr. *ibid*., 276, 306, 307, 486.

[241a] Pr. FullerF II, 100. That vol. contains 3 other Tomkins pieces (1 = GlynVP, 10, bottom). Another piece pr. GlynVP, 12; the piece *ibid*., 10, top, is attributed to Tomkins in both Drexel 5612 and Oxford, Ch. Ch., 1113, but to Farnaby in FullerF II, 421. Cf. also fns. 176 and 177 *supra*. MusB V, a complete ed. of Tomkins' keyboard music is announced.

[242] Pr. FullerF II, 131; ScherG, 146; cf. BorK, 239ff.

Cabezón and Mudarra. Perhaps the use of the tune by Spaniards led the English to call it Spanish—not only in their music, but in references in their literature [243]—even though its origin seems to have been Italian. The theme was again to be drawn upon in a set of variations written partly by Sweelinck and partly by Scheidt.[244] Besides the pavans and galliards already referred to, many additional ones are preserved in the Forster MS and in Drexel 5612.

After pavans and galliards, almans and corantos (as they are often called in the sources) are the dance forms most frequently found, and they are often paired also. Drexel 5611 and 5612 are especially rich in such pairs.[245] Unlike the early courante mentioned on p. 564, the examples here involved are typical of the real courante style in their light, flowing figuration. One *Coranto* by Byrd is based on the pavan *Belle qui tiens ma vie* that Arbeau had included in his *Orchésographie*.[246]

The jig, of English origin, has the basic plan *ab* or *abc,* and is usually in the equivalent of a lively $\frac{6}{8}$ or $\frac{12}{8}$ meter. An entertaining example is provided by *A Gigge. Dr. Bull's Myselfe*.[247] *The Nobodyes Gigge* by Farnaby [248] appears to refer to a comic character whose breeches reached to his shoulders and who is mentioned in *The Tempest*.[249]

Of a somewhat different type, yet belonging roughly to the "dance" category, are the pieces that are among the earliest examples of the march as an art form. Though not of great musical interest, the marches in Byrd's *Battell* [250] show a strong rhythmical sense, and an observant distinction is made between the heavy $\frac{4}{2}$ tread of the *Marche of Footemen,* the $\frac{3}{2}$ of the *Marche of Horsemen,* the $\frac{4}{2}$ (subdivided into triplets) of the *Irish March,* and the double $\frac{3}{2}$ measures of the *Marche to the fighte,* which builds up to bugle calls and *The battels be joyned.*

The descriptive *King's Hunt,*[251] ascribed to Bull in the *Fitzwilliam Virginal Book,* may actually be by Cosyn.[252] Among the descriptive compositions

---

[243] As pointed out by J. Ward in *Italian Music and English Broadside Ballads* (cf. Chap. 10, fn. 31a).   [244] Pr. SchweiB, 8; SweeW I, 128; cf. BorK, 240f.

[245] Many are also in Cosyn, Forster, Fitzwilliam, and Drexel MS 5609.

[246] For Byrd's piece, *see* ByrdW XVIII, 98; ByrdP, 34; FullerF II, 305; cf. *ibid.,* viii.

[247] Pr. *ibid.,* 257; ApelM II, 8; SachsPM, 17. Among pieces not yet cited that are attributed to Bull in at least one source, FullerF contains 36. Of these, 4 appear also in TagA, III, 3 in BullMG, 2 in FullerBC, and 1 each in RimbP, GlynP (or StoneP), HalbK. Other uncited Bull pieces in BullMG, 3, 4, 5 (= FullerBC, 10), 8, 10, 12, 13 (= GlynP, 10; StoneP, 16), 14 (= GlynP, 11; StoneP, 18); GlynP, 12, 15, 16 (= StoneP, 21, 26, 28); FullerBC, 1 (= GlynP, 9; StoneP, 15; TagA III, 38), 5, 8; TagA III, 55; RimbP, 248; WestO, 25a.

[248] Pr. FullerF II, 162.   [249] Act III, scene 2, line 136. Cf. PirD, 15.

[250] The piece, as preserved in the Nevell MS, pr. AndN, 20 (= ByrdW, 109), where it is preceded by *The Marche before the Battell* (= ByrdW, 105; FullerF II, 402 [with a different title]). 3 possibly later additions, preserved elsewhere, pr. AndN, 38; 2 pieces on 39 (= ByrdW, 123, 2 pieces on 126, respectively). Cf. AndN, xxxix.

[251] Pr. FullerF II, 116; RimbP, 245; TagA III, 39, 42 (2 versions).

[252] Cf. GlynV, 44. For exx. by Cosyn, *see* FullerBC, 22, 25, 27; GlynVP, 23, 24 (2 exx.), 26. The pieces pr. with attribution to W. Lawes, *ibid.,* 21, 22, are ascribed to Cosyn in Drexel 5611.

of Byrd is the exquisite *The Bells*.[253] Several sections of this piece are based on only two alternating chords, others on only three chords. But the undoubtedly deliberate harmonic paucity is completely counterbalanced by the imaginatively varied figuration, the effect of change-ringing being skilfully conveyed. Among other early examples of program music are Peerson's lovely *Fall of the Leafe*,[254] in almost pure D minor; the little autobiographical set of pieces, *Giles Farnaby's Dreame, His Rest*, and *His Humor,* to which might be added *Farnabye's Conceit*,[255] and the delightful anonymous pieces, the *Nightingall* and the *Mock-Nightingall*.[256]

Music for Instrumental Ensemble, notably that of Tye, Byrd, Morley, Gibbons, and Weelkes

Instrumental-ensemble music represents another peak in English composition of the 16th and 17th centuries. The vastness of Henry VIII's instrument collection (cf. p. 771, fn. 38) attests to the variety of instruments popular in his day. In 1526, Henry had in active use at court three lutes, fifteen trumpets, three rebecs, three taborets, a harp, two viols, four drums, a fife, and ten sackbuts; [257] these resources must have prompted considerable playing of chamber music. Wealthy citizens, in town and country, with their liking for instrumental music generally, cultivated music for ensemble, as well as for soloists.

The dance exerted a particularly strong influence on English chamber music from about 1500 to shortly before 1560. Binary rhythm and square-cut phrases were favored, as in a dance tune by Henry VIII in Brit. Mus. MS Add.

---

253 Pr. ByrdW XX, 96; FullerF I, 274. Cf. BorK, 337ff; NayE, 97f. ByrdW XVIII–XX gives a complete modern ed. of Byrd's keyboard works, but in "practical" versions that sometimes depart considerably from the originals. More dependable reprints of works not yet cited (to which the rest of this fn. is restricted) include 53 in FullerF. 10 of these compositions are also pr. AndN, which gives 16 additional Byrd pieces. Other duplications: ByrdF, 89, 127, 131 (= FullerF I, 263 [= AndN, 144]; II, 169, 135, respectively); GlynP, 5 (= StoneP, 8; FullerF I, 83); ApelM II, 9 (= FullerF II, 237). 35 more pieces are pr. ByrdF, 3 in GlynP (or StoneP). ByrdW omits the piece pr. in FullerF II, 209 (= ByrdF, 134), ascribed to Morley in Fitzwilliam; the piece pr. ByrdF, 80, anon. in the source; the pieces pr. ByrdF, 130, 139, ascribed, respectively, to Gibbons and to Farnaby and Bull in various sources. Cf. ByrdF, xxiiif.

254 Pr. GlynVP, 6, top; FullerF II, 423. Other Peerson exx. in FullerF I, 359 (= GlynVP, 6, bottom); II, 238, 422.

255 Pr. respectively, *ibid.*, II, 260, 261, 262, 424 (= FarnSP, 2, top, 2, bottom, 3, 1, respectively). Among pieces not yet cited that are attributed to Farnaby in at least 1 source, FullerF contains 42. Of these, 12 appear also in FarnSP, 2 in GlynVP, and 1 each in TagA III, SachsPM, HalbK; another piece, FarnSP, 5, is attributed to "Gorge" Farnaby. A *Toye,* attributed to Farnaby in FarnSP, 4, without mention of source, is anon. in FullerF II, 418.

256 Each preserved, in variant versions, in MS Drexel 5609 (after Rogers Virginal Book), and MS Drexel 5612. The 2 pieces pr., after the Rogers MS, in EKMV V, 3, 10. Further on English keyboard music through the Renaissance, *see,* in addition to material above cited, BedbK, BorVA, FelOG, FelSG, HäfnE, MaddV, SumnO, WestC, WestE.

257 Cf. PulV, 3. For data on instrumentalists in the royal courts, *see* esp. NagA; LafonK.

31922.[257a] Among the many other instrumental pieces in the same MS, there are some thirty *a 3* or *a 4* by Fayrfax, Cornysh, Fardyng, and others. The kinds of dance represented in the instrumental-ensemble sources include hornpipes, jigs, and foreign types, such as occur in Attaingnant's collections: branles, pavans, galliards, allemandes.[258]

Ensemble groups—or "consorts"—were of two types: the "whole consort" and the "broken consort." The former consisted of members of a single instrumental family, e.g., viols or recorders; the latter, of members of different families. Consorts of viols became increasingly popular and remained in favor until the mid-17th century. A complete consort of viols, rarely required, consisted of eight instruments: a high descant, treble, alto, small tenor, true tenor, small bass, full consort bass, and violone (seldom used). A normal chest of viols included two trebles, two tenors, and two basses.[259]

Especially in their *In nomine* settings, composers of instrumental-ensemble music made more ambitious attempts than in their dances. There are many more *In nomine* settings for ensemble than for keyboard or lute. The two chief sources of these settings are Brit. Mus. MS Add. 31390, which includes forty-two *In nomine* settings, and Music School MSS 26356–60 (D 212–216), a set of part-books at the Bodleian Library at Oxford, which contains seventy-three settings.[260] At least two of the *In nomine* pieces in the former source and at least ten in the latter make a bow to Taverner by beginning in essentially the same way as does his composition, before they proceed independently.[261] His own composition appears in a version *a 4* in the Bodleian MS and with a fifth voice added in the Brit. Mus. MS. Among writers of *In nomine* settings for ensemble are Whytbroke, White, Tye (one of the chief *In nomine* composers), Tallis, Robert Parsons, Brewster, Byrd, both Alfonso Ferraboscos, Weelkes, Orlando Gibbons, and a host of others. Eighteen settings by Tye in the Brit. Mus. MS have subtitles, such as *Howld fast, Free from all, Trust,*[262] etc. The title of the first of these may be related to the fact that the piece has longer time-values toward the end than at the beginning. (The slackening has nothing to do with the *In nomine* type as such: an *In nomine* by Parsons,[263] *a 5*, and another by Brewster [264] have the smaller time-values at the end; still other settings are unmarked by rhythmic contrast of either kind between the earlier and later portions.) A five-part *In nomine* by

[257a] Pr. MeyeE, 68; HenryS, 38.

[258] Cf. MeyeE, 69ff. The statement there made that dumps appear to have been performed more by instrumental ensembles than at the keyboard seems not to be borne out by the evidence.

[259] Further about consorts, *see* GalpO 270ff; HayesM II, 36ff; MGG II, 1635ff.

[260] The 64 items listed in MeyeM, 13f, are supplemented in the MS by a separately numbered series of 9 *In nomine* settings. Nos. 1–3 are by A. Ferrabosco II; Nos. 4–5 by O. Gibbons; Nos. 6–9, anon.

[261] Further on this point, *see* ReIN, 11.

[262] About subtitles in *In nomine* pieces, *see* ReIN, 21.

[263] Pr. EIM II (1st. ed.), 4.   [264] *Ibid.,* 11.

Byrd,[265] in five sections, is based partly on reiterated rhythmic patterns in the voices not bearing the *cantus firmus*. Reminiful of the *Qui tollis* of Obrecht's *Missa Je ne demande* is Tye's *In nomine,* with the subtitle *Trust,* which, regardless of its time-signature, organizes its notes into five-beat groups.[266]

EXAMPLE 211. Opening of *In nomine: Trust*—Tye (from Brit. Mus. Add. MS 31390; transcr. by Th. Karp).

An *In nomine* by Picforth is unusual in that each instrumental part consists of notes of only one time-value throughout, the values differing in each of the five parts. Although pedantic in principle, the piece is surprisingly satisfactory from the standpoint of sound.[267] It may help to illustrate Roger North's statement (*Memoirs,* 1728 [267a]) that the *In nomine* became a test piece, in which composers displayed their skill as contrapuntists. Although at first stylistically and rhythmically dependent on vocal polyphony, the *In nomine* evolved into a purely instrumental form and thus contributed to the development of a specifically instrumental style, especially in the field of ensemble music.[268]

Pieces entitled *Miserere* are likewise represented in the literature for instrumental ensemble. There are examples by Tye, Thomas Lupo, and others.[268a] Those by Byrd [269] and Alfonso Ferrabosco I included the forty settings, with "2 partes in one upon the playne songe *Miserere,*" that each wrote in the course of a friendly competition. East may have printed the result in 1603 under the title *Medulla,* but no copy survives. However, the nineteen canonic settings that survive in MS [269a] quite possibly represent Byrd's contribution.

Hymn melodies underlie several instrumental-ensemble pieces by Byrd.

265 *Ibid.,* 1; about 2 other *In nomine* pieces by Byrd, *see* FelWB, 192f.
266 The Bodleian *In nomine* settings include one by Nicholas Strogers that does this also.
267 Cf. ReIN, 22.
267a Modern ed. in NorthM; modern ed. of the same writer's *Musicall Gramarian* in NorthG.
268 For other *In nomine* compositions for consorts, *see* TerryC IV (an ex. *a 4* by Parsons); TerryC V (an ex. *a 4* by Persleye [Parsley]); EIM II (1st. ed.), 7 (an ex. *a 5* by A. Ferrabosco I); HAM, 202 (an ex. *a 3* by Tomkins). Further on the *In nomine, see* MeyeE, 83ff; MeyeN; MeyeM, 13f, 133ff.
268a Further on this subject, *see* MeyeE, 83.
269 For 2 fantasy-type exx., *see* ByrdW XVII, 108, 109 (= TCM IX, 305; 2 exx.). These are based on the melody pr. Liber, 266.
269a Pr. ByrdW XVII, 78ff. *See also* the 2 rounds *ibid.,* 104.

The chant associated with the *Christe qui lux es* text (stanza 2: *Precamur;* cf. pp. 784, 791) is the basis of a composition [269b] entitled *Te lucis.* These two words do not occur in the *Christe qui lux es* text, but, of the various *Te lucis* settings in plainsong, the one used on the first Sunday in Lent has the *Christe qui lux es* melody.[269c] On the other hand, a different *Te lucis* melody is set by Byrd and given the title *Precamur.*[269d] A partly parallel situation is produced by settings of two other hymn melodies: Byrd has left us a pair of compositions named *Sermone blando* that are settings of the usual melody (cf. pp. 604, 786),[269e] but he applies this chant also to a piece entitled *Salvator mundi,*[269f] instead of employing the *Veni Creator Spiritus* melody, as one would expect.

On the Browning tune (cf. Ex. 201), composers wrote "complicated and artistic variations . . . , weaving contrapuntal nets in all instrumental parts, including very lively passages and all kinds of polyphonic tricks. Among the composers of Brownings were John Baldwyne, Elvay Bevin, William Byrd, Robert Parsons, Henry Stoninge and Clement Woodcocke." [270] Byrd's five-part *Browning,*[271] consists of twenty polyphonic variations on the theme, which, at different times, is entrusted to each of the five instruments.

There is a large literature of ensemble music belonging to the category of fancies or fantasias and dating from the earliest examples in Brit. Mus. MS Add. 36526 (mid-16th century) until as late as Purcell. Byrd's fantasias are perhaps his best instrumental-ensemble pieces, and one *a 6* [272]—included in his *Psalmes, Songs and Sonnets* of 1611—is among the finest. The work is in three large sections, which, however, are not divided by full closes. The first section includes an imitative, twenty-measure opening, built on a single phrase; a rhythmically contrasted passage, one of whose two themes is related to the opening theme; a brief working-out of a third theme by all the voices; and a closing portion in which the highest and lowest voice pairs are in double canon, with varying time-intervals, while the freer middle voices have occasional snatches of canon of their own. Section 2, written in the equivalent of $\frac{6}{8}$ time, provides a second movement, in which the opening theme is interestingly derived, with rhythmic modifications, from theme 3 of section 1. Section 3 foreshadows the 18th-century minuet. Another fantasia *a 6,*[273] in two sections, introduces some well known melodies, such as *Walsingham* and *Greensleeves.*[274]

Morley's fantasias include fifteen examples *a 2.*[275] These are marked by clear cadences between sections, as distinguished from cadences with over-

---

[269b] Pr. ByrdW XVII, 116; TCM IX, 311.   [269c] Cf. Liber, 540. The differences are minor.
[269d] Pr. ByrdW XVII, 110; TCM IX, 308; for the melody, *see* HMS, 4, No. 14.
[269e] The piece pr. ByrdW XVII, 112; TCM IX, 309. Byrd, of course, uses the Sarum form, like Tallis (cf. Chap. 15, fn. 98a).
[269f] The setting pr. ByrdW XVII, 103; TCM IX, 309.   [270] MeyeE, 112.
[271] Pr. ByrdW XVII, 30; TerryC I.   [272] Pr. ByrdW XIV, 71; EMS XVI, 166.
[273] Pr. ByrdW XVII, 81.   [274] Further about Byrd's fantasias, *see* FelWB, 187ff.
[275] 9 of these pr. MorlF; 5 of the 9 also in DoflS.

lapping. *Bicinia* had been produced likewise by Whythorne, whose *Duos or Songs* (1590) constituted the earliest English printed collection of instrumental music. Morley has left us also fantasias *a 3* and *a 4*.

We have some forty fantasias by Alfonso Ferrabosco II.[276] A number of Bull's short works of this type are "miniature one-theme fugues." [277] The fantasias of Cooper, on the other hand, are usually more sectionalized than those of many of his contemporaries. He was a prolific composer of fantasias, some ninety in from three to six parts being extant.[278] Four suites [279] *a 3* with organ (the music for the organ is merely a reduction of that allotted to the other three instruments) each consists of a *Fancy,* an *Almane,* and a *Galliard.* Some pieces by Cooper for two bass viols and organ contain interesting chromatic figurations.[280]

Orlando Gibbons, "the greatest master of the fantasia of the period," [281] has left us numerous examples of the type. Some of these are quite long and break up into many small sections in the manner of the Italian chain-*canzona.* In content, however, his fantasias show little sign of Italian influence. The partitioning of the long pieces is accomplished by contrasts in both rhythmic and melodic material. Gibbons' "development of form shows the greatest advance among the English composers of *Fantasias.*" [282] He makes much use of imitation; his treatment of rhythm is markedly free.

EXAMPLE 212. Extract from *Fantasia a 3*—Gibbons (complete piece in MeyeS, 14; accent signs added).

In several of his string fantasias, Gibbons calls specifically for the use of the "greate dooble base" (that is, for the violone, which has contra-A

---

[276] For exx., *see* WalkerO, 70 (based on the hexachord); MeyeE, 257. *See* further, *ibid.,* 137f.

[277] MeyeE, 157. For a fantasia attributed to Bull in New York Pub. Lib. MS Drexel 4180–85, but to Cooper elsewhere, *see* EIM II (2nd. ed.), 5; MeyeE, 262.

[278] For fantasias by Cooper, *see* MangF, No. 1; *Blätter der Sackpfeife,* No. 25 (A. Nagel, 1933). *See* also fn. 277.

[279] Pr. EIM VII (1st ed.).

[280] Cf. NagG, 163. Further about Cooper's fantasias, *see* MeyeM, 135f; MeyeE, 148; WalkerO, 66f.

[281] MeyeE, 153.

[282] MeyeF, 52.

as the lowest string). The number of voices ranges from three to six. A set of nine fantasias *a 3* (c. 1610) constitutes Gibbons' first published work; it is also the earliest music to be engraved on copper in England, preceding *Parthenia* by perhaps a year.[283]

A Weelkes composition which, in the MS, bears merely the superscription "For 2 Basses Tho. Welkes," has with good reason been called a fantasia.[284] It is a singularly eloquent and stately composition.

EXAMPLE 213. *For 2 Basses*—Weelkes (Brit. Mus. Add. MS 17786-91).

* Observe that this b produces, if flat, an augmented second with the next note or, if natural, a cross-relation with the note above it. The latter is more likely to be the result intended. (It should also be considered, however, that the sharp before the c may be an error in the source.)

The source, apparently through error, has g' as the last note in the top part, meas. 4 from the end.

By Deering we have eleven fantasias, eight *a 5* and three *a 6* (one being incomplete). They consist, typically, of a long fugal section, a chordal section employing fewer instruments, and a polyphonic conclusion, in which the full

[283] Further about Gibbons' fantasias, *see* MeyeE, 153ff; MeyeM, 139; FelOG, 95ff. For printed exx., *see* MeyeS, 8; GibF (= MAS IX); *Fantazias for String Quartet*, Nos. 1 and 2, E. H. Fellowes, ed. (Stainer & Bell, Nos. 3197a, 3198a).

[284] By Arnold Dolmetsch; cf. the recording in the Columbia History of Music.

instrumentation returns. In his handling of melody, Deering shows less interest in variety. His style is generally conservative.[285]

Other noteworthy composers of fantasias of this period include Thomas Lupo,[286] John Ward,[287] and Thomas Tomkins.

The dance inspired instrumental-ensemble pieces in the second half of the century as it had in the first. Of numerous examples, attention might be called to pavan and galliard pairs *a 6* by Byrd and Gibbons, a galliard by Parsons, almaines by Deering, Cranford, and Ford, and pavans by Deering.[288]

Some pieces have descriptive titles. For instance, one of the examples *a 2* by Morley is called *La Caccia*.[289] Other works with fanciful titles include *A Knell* by Robert Johnson, *Perslis Clocke* by Parsley, and Woodcocke's *Hackney*.[290] The tenor of *Perslis Clocke* consists of an ascending and descending hexachordal scale. Ensemble works based on solmisation formulas are plentiful.

From 1597 on, a number of collections appeared containing pieces specifically for broken consorts. Holborne's *Cittharn Schoole* presents not only pieces for cittern alone, but also twenty-three compositions for cittern with bass viol and two for which a cittern part is provided as well as three staff-notation parts more suitable for recorders than for viols (no specific instruments are indicated).[291] Later publications include Morley's *First Booke of Consort Lessons made by divers exquisite Authors* (1599) for treble and bass viols, cittern, pandore, flute (= recorder), and lute; [292] John Dowland's *Lachrimae or Seaven Teares figured in Seaven Passionate Pavans, with divers other Pavans, Galiards, and Almands* (1605) [293] for five viols and lute; Captain Tobias Hume's *Poeticall Musicke* (1607), mostly for groups of bass viols, but partly for two lutes with bass viol, or for two orpharions and bass viol, or for other combinations; Rosseter's *Lessons for Consort: Made by sundry Excellent Authors* (1609) [294] for treble and bass viol, treble lute, pandore, cittern, and "flute"; and John Adson's *Courtly Masquing Ayres Composed to 5. and 6. Parts, for Violins, Consorts and Cornets* [zinks] (1621).

Hume, a rather eccentric composer, was nevertheless one of the greatest

[285] Further about Deering's fantasias, *see* HughesD; MeyeM, 137; MeyeE, 168f.—Since the above was written, SchofT has been published, reporting the discovery of 6 more Deering fantasies.   [286] For exx., *see* MeyeE, 144; MeyeS, 6.   [287] For ex., *see* MangF, No. 3.

[288] For a description of the Byrd pair, *see* FelWB, 183; for the music of the Gibbons pair, *see* *Pavan and Galliard*, E. H. Fellowes, ed. (Stainer & Bell, No. 3199a); for the Parsons *Galliard*, WarC II; for the Deering pieces, TerryC II, III; for those by Cranford and Ford, TerryC VI and VII.   [289] Pr. MorlF, 6; DoflS, 15.

[290] These 3 pieces pr. WarC I, IV, V, respectively. According to M&L XXXV (1954), 99, the *Je file* pr. WarC III is actually a chanson by Philip van Wilder, publ. after a viol source in which it is misattributed to Parsons; *see also* JAMS VIII (1955), 131.

[291] Cf. DartC, 52.

[292] All of the part-books except that for lute survive in either this ed. or in that of 1611. The missing lute part for about a third of the pieces survives in MS. Cf. DartCL, 3f.

[293] Pr. DowlL.   [294] Only 2 part-books and a fragment of a third survive; cf. DartCL, 7.

English bass-viol players of his time.[295] Adson played both the recorder and the zink.

In his *Booke of Consort Lessons,* which contains twenty-five pieces, Morley appears as editor rather than as composer. The contents include such varied items as a *Quadro Pavane and Galliard,* based on the traditional *passamezzo moderno* ground; an arrangement of Conversi's *Sola soletta* (the vocal version had been included in Watson's collection of 1590); an arrangement [296] of the same *O Mistress Mine* tune that Byrd set for virginals; dances by Dowland, Philips, and Byrd; and elaborate variations by Richard Alison on *Goe from my window.* The melody of the last of these and an example of Alison's use of it follow on pp. 875f.

Morley's *Booke* has special value partly because of its precise instrumentation: this is no collection adaptable for alternative media, but one calling for a particular instrument on each part.[297] The specified combination became quite popular: the above list shows that Rosseter's *Lessons for Consort* was written for it, and the eighteen consort songs in Leighton's *Teares or Lamentacions* (cf. p. 809) reinforce the voices with it. This type of ensemble must have been heard in households like Hengrave Hall, where we have found Wilbye. It is known to have flourished also in the theater.

Of the many reworkings of Dowland's *Flow, my teares,* the set of "Seven Passionate Pavans" that opens his *Lachrimae* of 1605 is the largest in scope. The first of the seven, a polyphonic elaboration of the whole song, evidently owes its title, *Lachrimae antiquae,* to the presence of old material throughout. The other six pieces, which have fanciful titles such as *Lachrimae gementes, Lachrimae tristes, Lachrimae amantis,* etc., draw upon the song only sparingly. All of these begin with the first notes of the melody in one of the voices; in several pieces the opening of the old bass is presented likewise, sometimes paraphrased; in one, the first measure quotes the song in four voices. The beginning of section 3, in some cases, also recalls the song; occasional fleeting resemblances at other points may be fortuitous. There is some charming degree-inflection in *Lachrimae amantis.* The writing for the strings, with its leading melody and freely contrapuntal supporting parts, reminds one of the contrapuntally accompanied solo song. The lute part is an approximate short-score of the five viol parts. The collection contains fourteen pieces besides the *Lachrimae.* The names of nine include "galiard"; those of two, "almand"; that of one, "pavan." The structure of the other two pieces, *Semper Dowland semper dolens* and *Sir Henry Umpton's Funerall,* shows that they are likewise pavans. One of the galliards, *Captaine Digorie Piper His*

---

[295] Cf. PulV, 11. His *Musicall Humors,* mostly for viola da gamba or for various combinations of strings, appeared in 1605.

[296] For description, *see* GordM, 123f.

[297] Further on Morley's *Lessons, see* DartCL.

EXAMPLE 214. *Goe from my window* (after ChappP I, 146) and an extract from Alison's setting of it in Morley's *Consort Lessons* (1599) (transcr. by S. Beck).

Galiard,[297a] has the same melody as *If my complaints,* and its full title explains why the tune is sometimes called *Piper's Galliard.* Another galliard,[298] while not the same as one by Dowland printed in the *Ausserlesener Paduanen und Galliarden Erster Theil . . . zu fünff Stimmen auff allerley Instrumenten und insonderheit auff Fiolen zu gebrauchen* of Füllsack and Hildebrand (1607),[299] is very closely related to it. The same collection contains two pavan and galliard pairs by Holborne,[300] one of which is of particular interest since, although its title does not so indicate, the pavan belongs to the family of *Lachrimae* pieces. The paired Pavan and Galliard by Peter Philips[301] in this collection are members of that family also.

In taking account of instrumental ensemble music in Renaissance England, one should not overlook that much primarily vocal music was designated as "apt for voices or for viols" and that collections such as Alison's Psalter of 1599 assigned to ensemble players an important supporting role. Also, the demand for incidental music in the theater produced a whole special body of instrumental-ensemble literature.

Music in the Theater; the Masques

From ritualistic beginnings in the medieval Church,[302] both religious and secular dramatic forms in the vernacular had developed in England by the

---

[297a] Pr. DowlL, 33.   [298] *Ibid.,* 34.   [299] The piece is reprinted in EngelkeM, 112.
[300] *Ibid.,* 105, 113.   [301] *Ibid.,* 71, 72.
[302] Cf. ReMMA, 193ff; ChamM I. The above section on music on the Elizabethan stage is, in effect, a summary of WardT.

late 14th century. The inherent popular appeal of the plays and the problems connected with their performance led to the transfer of control over them from the Church to the guilds, the former, however, retaining the role of adviser and possibly that of script provider. Each guild prepared a play (e.g., *The Fall of Lucifer, Noah's Flood, Doomsday,* etc.) and mounted it on a pageant, or wagon; at Corpus Christi veritable dramatic parades of such wagons moved through certain English towns. The resulting cycles of mystery and miracle plays, first mentioned toward the end of the 14th century, were presented as late as c. 1580. A few cycles survive in MS, and in many of the plays references are made to music, usually to interpolations of plainsong and songs in the vernacular. Thus, there are stage directions both in the Coventry play, *The Temptation* ("*Hic venient angeli cantantes et ministrantes ei:* 'Gloria tibi, Domine!' "[303]) and in the Vintners' play of *The Three Kings* in the Chester cycle ("Heare the messinger goeth to the kinge, and the mynstrilles muste plaie"[304]), while in a 15th-century MS of the York cycle five short pieces are preserved from the Weavers' play, *The Appearance of Our Lady to Thomas.*[305] These are simple compositions *a 2,* in a gymel style, with Latin texts.

Late 15th-century religious drama produced the morality play with its allegorical personification of good and evil, while the traditional art of the minstrels, the dramatic May games and sword dances of the folk, together with their bourgeois counterparts, the Feast of Fools and that of the Boy Bishop, produced the interlude. Thus play-acting had moved from Church to market place, banqueting-hall, and court. The interlude was a short dramatic episode, often farcical in character, of which one of the first masters, John Heywood (whom we have encountered as court virginalist), was both a musician and writer.[306] While only one of his songs survives, he may have written both text and music for those of his plays that were presented at court by the Children of the Chapel. Among the interlude writers was John Redford, whose *Wyt and Science,*[307] presented at court between 1538 and 1546, includes three songs; for one there is the stage direction: "Here cometh in four with viols and sing. . . ." During Sebastian Westcote's term as master of the Children of Paul's, the famous *Tragedie of Gorboduc*[308] was acted in the Hall of the Inner Temple on Twelfth Night, 1562, with the assistance of violins, cornets, flutes, hautboys, and drums. In Gascoigne's translation of

---

[303] *Ludus Coventriae,* J. O. Halliwell, ed. (1841), 211.

[304] *The Chester Plays,* T. Wright, ed. (1843), I, 152.

[305] *York Plays,* L. T. Smith, ed. (1885), 480. 3 of the pieces are transcr., 517ff, and 3 reproduced in facsimile. *See also* ChamM II, 140ff. In 1561, the *Herod* play of the York cycle was prepared by the Minstrels.

[306] For Heywood's 5 extant dramatic works, *see Tudor Facsimile Texts* series, J. S. Farmer, ed. (1907–13).

[307] Pr. *ibid.*

[308] Pr. *ibid.* About Westcote, *see* FloodS.

Euripides' *Jocasta*,[309] acted at Gray's Inn, 1566, there are five "dumb shows" that were accompanied by rather elaborate music (e.g., "Firste, before the beginning of the first Acte, did sounde a dolefull & straunge noyse of violles, Cythren, Bandurion, and such like, . . ."). In *A New Interlude and Mery of the Nature of iiij Elements* (1539?),[310] the direction, "Then the daunsers with out the hall syng this wyse and they with in answer or ellys they may say it for nede," is followed by this song:

EXAMPLE 215. *Tyme to pas with goodly sport,* from *A New Interlude and Mery of the Nature of iiij Elements*—Anon. (Transcr. after *Tudor Facsimile Texts*).

* About the trisyllabic pronunciation proposed above, cf. the claim that "good" was sometimes a disyllable in Elizabethan English, expressed in E. A. Abbott, *A Shakespearian Grammar* (ed. of 1876), 377 (comments), 380f (exx.). To be sure, an adverse view regarding the claim is expressed in A. J. Ellis, *Early English Pronunciation*, III (*Chaucer Society Publications, Ser. 2,* V [1871]), 947, but the above music tends to uphold it.

About the mid-century the ancestor of ballad opera appears in *The Commodye of pacient and meeke Grissill*,[311] with songs to be sung "to the tune of Damon and Pithias" or to that of the "latter Almain," etc.[312] In an Act of Common Council,[313] 1553: "Tayllors, Showmakers & such" who absent themselves from their labors and "doo cosenly use nowe A dayes to singe songes called thre mens songes in the Tavernes, Alehouses, Innes & suche" are forbidden such pastime, saving only "the poore felowship of the mynstrelles" or unless they "be songe in A comen playe or enterlude. . . ." Nor was the academic drama of the period without its music. In the Steward's Book of Trinity College, Cambridge,[314] there is the following entry for Christmas, 1552–53: "Item, gyven unto ye Wayttes upon our feast day when ye shew

[309] Pr. in *The Complete Works of George Gascoigne,* J. W. Cunliffe, ed. (1907–10), I, 244.
[310] Pr. in *Tudor Facsimile Texts.* About the date, *see* Grove IV, 254; also SteeleE, 5, 36.
[311] Pr. by the Malone Society, 1909.
[312] For information on ballad tunes in the plays, *see* ChappP I; LamE; Otto Gombosi in MQ, XXX (1944), esp. p. 142.
[313] Pr. in Malone Society, *Collections,* II, Part III (1931), 294f.
[314] Pr. *ibid.,* II, Part II (1923), 156.

was played cawled Anglia deformata and Anglia Restituta . . . ij^s vj^d."

The building of the earliest London playhouse in 1576—called, appropriately enough, simply the Theatre—gave English actors their first permanent home. And with the advent of John Lyly, in whose plays the classic elements of the university drama were mixed with those of court interludes and masques, the great age of English drama begins. Theatrical activity of the late 16th century is divisible into: (1) court-inspired drama, acted by boys in private, enclosed theaters, and patronized by the nobility and *bourgeoisie,* and (2) the plays presented in the public, open-air theaters, which shared their audiences and reputation with the neighboring bear-baiting pits.

The Theatre and its sisters of the Bankside were repertory theaters, producing a different play each acting day. In a typical two-week schedule for February, 1596, the Admiral's men presented ten plays on twelve acting days, two of them twice and one a new play.[315] Each play probably employed from ten to twenty separate musical effects. In such public theaters, the type with which Shakespeare was mostly associated, music was very likely regarded as a stage property, much as were costumes and machines. Play texts, both printed and MS, substantiate this assumption; e.g., when a king entered or left the stage, trumpets made a "noise," playing a flourish or a sennet. During banquet scenes "hoboyes" sounded and a drum beaten either on- or off-stage denoted a marching army. For each phase of a battle there was special music —"Alarum," "Parley," "Retreat," etc.—played by trumpet and drum, sometimes flute. Thus, certain dramatic situations had corresponding musical formulas. And it is quite evident that these were taken from contemporary real-life practices in Elizabethan England. Trumpets and kettledrums, for example, were the signs apparent of Elizabeth and her nobility, heralding the monarch on all state and public occasions. They were also part of the equipment of the armed forces, and the technical terms for trumpet and drum usage found in the military treatises of the period were also theater terms. Stage realism was carried to the point of differentiating between the drum for foot soldiers and the trumpet for cavalry.[316] For playing this music each theater had a band of musicians of indeterminate number who seem to have provided traditional military music or to have improvised to fit the stage action.[317] Many actors were also musicians, and it may be assumed that, besides singing, they accompanied themselves on the lute or viol.[318] Where the musicians of the early English stage were placed is not clear: it seems that the Elizabethan theater allowed them to roam the stage, while the Stuart

[315] Cf. *Henslowe's Diary,* W. W. Greg, ed. (1904), I, fol. 14^v.

[316] For further evidence on the use of music in the Elizabethan theatre, *see* CowM; FitzI; LawrM; NayM; NaySM; WardT; WardTT.

[317] *See* T. W. Baldwin, *The Organization and Personnel of the Shakespearean Company,* 1927.

[318] For evidence, *see* G. F. Warner, *Catalogue of the MS and Muniments of Alleyn's College of God's Gift at Dulwich* (1881–1903), I, 165ff; E. K. Chambers, *The Elizabethan Stage,* (1923), II, 333f.

theater gave them a place in the "tiring room," which was then often called the "musique room." [319]

It has been repeated to a tiresome extent that the Tudor age was a musical one, that everyone sang and played a musical instrument.[320] One need only look at the courts and cities of Renaissance Italy, France, and Spain to find similar outbursts of musical activity (often at an earlier date). However, exaggerate the fact as some writers may, the English theater was musical partly because the audience was more or less musically literate. If actors were singers, instrumentalists, and dancers, it was because the better class of spectator was himself all of these things or wished he were.[321] The musical accomplishment of many Elizabethan actors may also be due, in part, to the break-up of the monasteries under Henry VIII, which forced singing boys and men, well trained in music, into other employments.[322]

If, for lack of documents, we are rarely able to gauge the degree of musicianship of the adult actors, there can be no question about the skill of the Children of Blackfriars and Paul's, since they were taken from the two great London Chapels. The Children of the Chapel Royal took part in the court "disguisings," etc., at least by the time of Henry VIII (cf. p. 768), and such activity continued throughout the century.[323] For a few years before 1590, Lyly managed a group of boy actors at Blackfriars. This old monastery, situated in a fashionable residential quarter of London, had been converted into a private theater by Richard Farrant.[324] In 1600, Nathaniel Giles, then Master of the Chapel Royal, organized another company of child actors, leased Blackfriars, and, with Ben Jonson, competed with the other London acting companies.[325] Encouraged by Giles' success, the Earl of Derby revived the acting company of the Children of Paul's. Trained more as musicians than as actors, the children offered plays filled with songs, dancing, and instrumental interludes. Whereas the public theaters prefaced performances by three trumpet blasts, the private theaters seem to have begun with short concerts. In John Marston's *The Wonder of Women* (1605),[326] played by the Children

---

[319] On this point, *see* W J. Lawrence, *The Physical Conditions of the Elizabethan Public Playhouse* (1927), 83ff. Cf. also J. C. Adams, *The Globe Playhouse* (1942), 322ff.

[320] Cf. the oft-cited passage in MorlP, 1f; MorlPE, 9f.

[321] Cf. ArbOB, 17f, for an example of the sort of social pressure exerted on the ambitious bourgeois of the mid-16th century.

[322] Cf. FelEE, 7.

[323] Cf. ArkC; Mrs. C. C. Stopes, *William Hunnis and the Revels of the Chapel Royal* (1910); A. Feuillerat, *The Revels at Court under Edward VI and Mary* (1914); A. Feuillerat, *Documents of the Office of the Revels under Elizabeth* (1908).

[324] Blackfriars documents, including Farrant's lease, are pr. in Malone Society *Collections*, II, Part I (1913). Later, in 1610, Robert Jones and Philip Rosseter were given license "to practice and ex'cise in the quality of playing, by the name of Children of the Revells to the Queene within the white ffryers." *See* documents in Malone Society *Collections*, I, Part III (1909), 271f, and Part V (1911), 373f.

[325] *See* C. W. Wallace, *The Children of the Chapel of Blackfriars* (1906); J. Issacs, *Production and Stage-Management at the Blackfriars Theater* (1933).

[326] Pr. in *The Works of John Marston*, A. H. Bullen, ed., (1885), II, 231.

of the Queen's Revels (formerly called the Boys of the Chapel Royal), stage directions for entr'acte music include "cornets and organs playing loud full music for the Act" and "A Base Lute and a Treble Violl play for the Act." [327]

There was musical entertainment in the public theater, too, but this was presented after the play. Paul Hentzner, a Brandenburg jurist, wrote of his visit to London in 1598, "Without the city are some *Theatres* where English actors represent almost every day tragedies and comedies to very numerous Audiences; these are concluded with Music, variety of Dances and the excessive applause of those that are present." [328] Shakespeare's fellow actor, Will Kemp, was famous for his end-piece "jigs" which were part dance, part pantomime, part song—rude, slapstick affairs, accompanied by pipe and tabor.[329] It is worth noting that Kemp was one of the many English actors who went to the continent, where he served for a while at the Danish court.[330] The influence of touring actors, often driven from London and England by outbreaks of the plague which closed the theaters, spread to the continent.[331] Many imitations [332] of English plays and "jigs" appeared in Germany, and numerous English ballad and dance tunes may be found in European lute and virginal books as well as in works like Samuel Scheidt's *Canzon à 5 voc. super O nachbar Roland,* a tune known in Byrd's setting as *Lord Willobies Welcome Home.*[333]

Elements of the court masque first appear in the plays of the children's companies. Public theaters, in their rude conventions and taste for realism, had little room for such frills. By 1600, however, the masque's influence shows in such plays as *Twelfth Night,* with its songs and catches and its love-sick Duke who is pursued by the sound of music. To Heywood's play *The Rape of Lucrece* (1607),[334] originally including twelve songs and a catch, seven more were added, two by "the stranger that lately acted *Valerius* his part." Later, in the plays of Heywood, Beaumont and Fletcher, Middleton, and finally Shirley, the earlier musical formulas of the theater take on new and fantastic

[327] For evidence of act divisions in the plays of the boy actors and their absence in those of the adult companies, *see* W. W. Greg, "Act-Divisions in Shakespeare," in *Review of English Studies,* IV (1928), esp. 150; T. S. Graves, "The 'Act Time' in Elizabethan Theatres," in *Studies in Philology* (University of North Carolina) XII (1915), 117.

[328] Quoted from p. 27f of the partial English transl. of Hentzner's *Itinerarium Germaniae, Galliae, Angliae, et Italiae* (1612), ed. by Horace Walpole as *A Journey into England* (1881).

[329] Cf. BasE, which deals solely with the stage variety of jig.

[330] Cf. RavnE, 11. Kemp's own account of his dancing the morris from London to Norwich is contained in *Kemps Nine Daies Wonder,* A. Dyce, ed. (1840). One of the Cambridge lute MSS contains a jig named after Kemp; cf. NewL, 72, where there is mention of still other lute pieces named after actors of the time.

[331] *See* Albert Cohn, *Shakespeare in Germany in the 16th and 17th Centuries* (1865); BasE; Johannes Bolte, *Die Singspiele der englischen Komödianten und ihrer Nachfolger in Deutschland, Holland und Skandinavien* (1893).

[332] Pr. Cohn, *op. cit.;* BasE.

[333] Scheidt's "Canzon" pr. in *Werke,* Band II/III (1923–28), 47ff; for Byrd's setting, *see* ByrdW, XX, 45; AndN, 186. Other continental settings of the same tune occur in Nicolas Vallet, *Secretum musarum* (1615), 47, and in Thysius' lute-book (*see* LandT, 223).

[334] Pr. in *The Dramatic Works of Thomas Heywood,* J. Pearson, ed. (1874), V, 161.

forms. In *The Maids Tragedy* (1610) of Beaumont and Fletcher,[335] not trumpets but "Hautboys play within" to announce the king, and in the first act there is a masque of Hymen, with three songs and dances. In Middleton's play *The Witch* (1615),[336] there is a "Song above" by Hecate and a brood of fantastic creatures who, later in the play, sing "A Charm-Song about a Vessel," which ends in a dance. Music for this play survives attributed to Robert Johnson (d. 1634), composer and lutenist to the king (not to be confused with the Robert Johnson mentioned hitherto).[337] Strangely enough, the earliest known settings of a song from a Shakespeare play, Morley's *It was a lover and his lass,* has never been definitely connected with a performance of the play.[338] Not until the reign of James I are there documents showing the actual inclusion, in a play production, of an extant art setting of a song text contained in the play, i.e., an art setting as distinguished from a ballad.[339] There is some possibility, however, that a few surviving art settings did achieve performance in connection with plays. This is true of a number of contrapuntally accompanied solo songs, several of which have been mentioned on p. 817.

From the time when Henry VIII introduced a mask "after the maner of Italie" to the English court, the originally nebulous idea grew in scope. But it is in the masques of the extravagant Stuarts that the rise, climax, and fall of the masque occurs. Drawing ideas from the *ballet de cour* and the Italian *intermezzi* and *trionfi,* Ben Jonson [340] and the architect-designer Inigo Jones [341] almost paralleled the creators of the Florentine opera, but Jonson's predominantly literary interest seems to have been responsible for the English masque's remaining a poetic spectacle with music and dance. The basic form of these court entertainments included a prologue in verse, usually with songs and changes of scene; the "first entry" or dance; then, after an interruption by the actors, the "main dance," usually a measure, and the revels, in which the maskers invited the spectators to dance corantos and almans with them; and an epilogue followed by "the dance for going out." [342] That masques were

---

[335] Pr. in *The Works of Francis Beaumont and John Fletcher,* A. Glover and A. R. Waller, eds. (1906), I, 1.

[336] Pr. in *The Works of Thomas Middleton,* A. H. Bullen, ed. (1887), V, 351.

[337] One of the songs pr. RimbA I. A Johnson song for Fletcher's *Valentinian* and 1 for his *Lover's Progress* pr. LewisS, 7, 13, respectively. (*See also* next fn.)

[338] The song pr. EL (*Ser. I*), XVI, 26. On its relationship to the play, etc. *see* GordM and the literature there cited. For settings, by Robert Johnson, of *Full fathom five* and *Where the bee sucks, see* LewisS, 1, 4.

[339] For material on this subject, *see* LindM; LindS; FelS.   [340] *See* EvJ.

[341] Exx. of Jones' stage designs may be seen in P. Simpson and C. F. Bell, *Designs by Inigo Jones for Masques and Plays at Court* (1924).

[342] Early English sources on the dances of the period are printed in *Robert Laneham's Letter,* ed. by F. J. Furnivall (1871; reprinted 1890, 1907), clxff (the source is *The Maner of dauncynge of bace daunces,* translated by Robert Coplande from an unspecified French original and printed in 1521 at the end of Alexander Barclay's *The Introductory to Wryte and to Pronounce Frenche;* for a pseudo-facsimile of the Coplande item, see CopM); J. P. Collier, *"The passing measure Pavin,"* in *Papers of the Shakespeare Society,* I (1844), 24.

lavishly mounted may be inferred from the fact that it cost over £21,000 to produce Shirley's *Triumph of Peace* [343] at the Inns of Court, 1634. For the masque in honor of the marriage of Lord "Hayes" (= Hay), Campion, who wrote the poetry and some of the music, required the following orchestras about the dancing area: "on the right hand . . ten musicians, with Basse and Meane Lutes, a Bandora, a double Sack-bott, and an Harpsichord, with two treble Violins; on the other side . . . 9 violins and three Lutes, and to answere both the Consorts . . . sixe Cornets, and sixe Chappell voyces. . . ." [344] In a masque of 1609, Jonson introduced the "antimasque," in which acrobats, buffoons, and, most important for the Baroque, "country dances," contrasted with the preceding elegance by their lack or lampooning of it. Of *Lovers made Men* (1617),[345] Jonson writes: ". . . the whole Maske was sung (after the Italian manner) *Stylo recitativo.*" England was to come no nearer to opera until after the Civil War.

With the closing of the theaters in 1642, all of this dramatic activity was stilled. In *The Actors Remonstrance,*[346] an anonymous tract, printed January 24, 1644, the effect of this act on the lives of stage musicians is described by the author. "Our Musicke that was held so delectable and precious, that they scorned to come to a Taverne under twentie shillings salary for two houres, now wander with their Instruments under their cloaks, I meane such as have any, into all houses of good fellowship, saluting every roome where there is company, with *Will you have any musicke Gentlemen?*"

[343] Pr. in *The Dramatic Works and Poems of James Shirley,* A. Dyce, ed. (1833), VI, 253. One fragment of William Lawes' music for this masque pr. in E. J. Dent, *Foundations of English Opera* (1928), 30ff.

[344] The text of the masque pr. in *Campion's Works,* P. Vivian, ed. (1909), 57; the music provided by Campion, Thomas Giles, and Thomas Lupo pr. OEE I. On a large collection of masque music in the Brit. Mus., Add. MS 10444, *see* LawrMM.

[345] Pr. in *The Works of Ben Jonson,* C. H. Herford and P. Simpson, eds. (1925–41), VII, 449. On the presentation of masques, *see* MarkJ; ReyM; GomE; A. Nicoll, *Stuart Masques and the Renaissance Stage* (1938); E. Welsford, *The Court Masque* (1927).

[346] Pr. in E. W. Ashbee, *Occasional Facsimile Reprints of Rare and Curious Tracts* (1868-72), No. 4.

Bibliography

This bibliography lists the sources referred to by symbol and also a few that are not referred to but may prove useful to the reader. Those materials, mostly primary sources, that are referred to in the book without symbol are omitted.

AberP   Aber, A. *Die Pflege der Musik unter den Wettinern und wettinischen Ernestinern*, 1921.

W   Aber, A. *Das musikalische Studienheft des Wittenberger Studenten Georg Donat (um 1543)*, in SIM XV (1913), 68.

AbertS   Abert, A. *Die stilistischen Voraussetzungen der "Cantiones Sacrae" von Heinrich Schütz*, 1935.

Acta   *Acta Musicologica*. Quarterly Magazine of the International Musicological Society (formerly International Society for Musical Research). 1928–

AdamiO   Adami da Bolsena,*Osservazioni per ben regolare il Coro dei Cantori della Cappella Pontificia*, 1711.

AdamsP   Adams, H. *Passion Music before 1724*, in M&L VII (1926), 258.

AdlerF   *Studien zur Musikgeschichte. Festschrift für Guido Adler zum 75. Geburtstag*, 1930.

H   Adler, G. *Handbuch der Musikgeschichte*, 1st ed., 1924; 2nd ed. (2 vols.), 1929. Written by Adler with collaboration of outstanding specialists. References are to 2nd ed.

M   Adler, G. *Die Turbae einer deutschen Matthaeuspassion von 1559*, in *Festschrift [für]* . . . *Rochus Freiherrn von Liliencron* (1910), 17.

T   Adler, G. *Über Textlegung in den Trienter Codices*, in RieF (1909), 51.

AfMF   *Archiv für Musikforschung*. 1936–43.

AfMW   *Archiv für Musikwissenschaft*. Oct. 1918–Sept. 1927. Revived 1952.

AlaL   Alaleona, D. *Le Laudi spirituali italiane nei secoli XVIe XVIIe il loro rapporto coi canti profani*, in RMI XVI (1909), 1.

S   Alaleona, D. *Studi su la Storia dell'Oratorio musicale in Italia*, 1908. Republished in 1945 as *Storia . . . Italia*. References in this book are to the 1908 ed.

AlbD   Albrecht, H. *Die deutschen Psalmen und Kirchengesänge des Jobst vom Brandt*, in AfMF VII (1942), 218.

H   Albrecht, H. *Lupus Hellinck und Johannes Lupi*, in Acta VI (1934), 54.

AlbiV   Albini, E. *La Viola da gamba in Italia*, in RMI XXVIII (1921), 82.

AlesC   Alessi, G. d'. *Maestri e Cantori fiamminghi nella Cappella musicale del Duomo di Treviso* (Italia) (1411–1561), in TVNM XV (1938), 147.

L   Alessi, G. d'. *Il Tipografico fiammingo Gerardo de Lisa* . . . , 1925.

M   Alessi, G. d'. *I Manoscritti musicali del XVI° secolo del Duomo di Treviso*, in Acta III (1931), 148.

O   Alessi, G. d'. *Organo e Organisti della Cattedrale di Treviso (1361–1642)*, 1929.

P   Alessi, G. d'. *Precursors of Adriano Willaert in the Practice of Coro Spezzato*, in JAMS V (1952), 187.

——   Alessi, G. d'. *Zanin Bisan (1473?–1554)*, in NA VIII (1931), 21.

AlfiR   Alfieri, P. (ed.). *Raccolta di Motetti* [Palestrina, Victoria, F. Anerio], 1841.

S   Alfieri, P. (ed.). *Raccolta di Musica sacra*. 7 vols., 1841–46.

AM   *Annales musicologiques*. Publ. of the *Societé de musique d'autrefois*, 1953– .

AmbG   Ambros, A. W. *Geschichte der Musik*. 5 vols. (1st ed. 1862–78, 1882). Completed by H. Leichtentritt. Vol. 5 consists of Kade's supplement of musical examples. References are to the 3rd ed., 1887–1911.

AmeD   Ameln, K. (ed.). *Das Lochheimer Liederbuch. Teil I: Die mehrstimmigen Sätze*, 1925.

H   Ameln, K., C. Mahrenholz, W. Thomas, *et al.* (eds.). *Handbuch der deutschen evangelischen Kirchenmusik*. 3 vols., 1933–40.

K   Ameln, K. (ed.). *Luthers Kirchenlieder in Tonsätzen seiner Zeit*, 1934.

AmeL	Ameln, K. (ed.). *Locheimer Liederbuch und Fundamentum organisandi des Conrad Paumann.* Facsimile with supplementary comment, 1925.
AMO	*Archives des maîtres de l'orgue.* Ed. by A. Guilmant. 10 vols., 1898–1910.
AmoS	St. Amour, Sister M. P. *A study of the Villancico up to Lope de Vega,* in Catholic University of America. *Studies in Romance Language and Literature* XX, 1940.
Analecta	*Analecta hymnica medii aevi.* 55 vols. (G. M. Dreves in collaboration with C. Blume and H. M. Bannister), 1886–1922.
Ancient & Modern	*Hymns Ancient and Modern: Historical Edition,* 1909.
AncoO	Ancona, A. d'. *Origini del Teatro italiano.* 2 vols. (2nd ed., 1891).
S	Ancona, A. d'. *Sacre Rappresentazioni dei secoli XIV, XV, e XVI,* 1872.
AndE	Andrews, H. *Elizabethan Keyboard Music,* in MQ XVI (1930), 59.
N	Andrews, H. (ed.). *My Ladye Nevells Booke,* 1926.
Ang	Anglès, H. in Catalan; Anglés, H. in Castilian.
CF	Anglès, H. *El Chansonnier français de la Colombina de Sevilla,* in *Estudis Universitaris Catalans* XIV (1929), 227.
CM	Anglés, H. and J. Subirá. *Catálogo musical de la Biblioteca Nacional de Madrid. I Manuscritos,* 1946. (Vol. I of the series *Catálogos de la Música antigua conservada en España.*)
CO	Anglès, H. *Els cantors i organistes Franco-Flamencs i Alemanys a Catalunya els segles XIV–XVI,* in *Gedenkboek aangeboden aan Dr. D. F. Scheurleer* (1925), 49.
G	Anglès, H. *Gacian Reyneau am Königshof zu Barcelona in der Zeit von 139 . . bis 1429,* in AdlerF (1930), 64.
I	Anglès, H. *Un Manuscrit inconnu avec polyphonie du XVᵉ siècle conservé à la Cathédrale de Ségovie,* in Acta VIII (1936), 6.
J	Anglès, H. *El músic Jacomé al servei de Joan I i Martí I durant els anys 1372–1404,* in *Homenatge a Antoni Rubió i Lluch* (1936) I, 613.
L	Anglés, H. *La Música a Catalunya fins al segle XIII,* 1935.
LME	Anglés, H. *La Música en España,* in J. Wolf, *Historia de la Música . . .* (Spanish transl. of WolfGM; 1944), 335.
ME	Anglés, H. *La Música española . . . Catálogo de la Exposición histórica . . . ,* 1941.
MF	Anglès, H. *Dades desconegudes sobre Miguel de Fuenllana, vihuelista,* in *Revista Musical Catalana* XXXIII (1936), 140.
O	Anglès, H. *Orgelmusik der Schola Hispanica,* in *Peter Wagner-Festschrift* (1926), 11.
P	Anglès, H. *La Polyphonie religieuse péninsulaire antérieure à la venue des musiciens flamands en Espagne,* in *International Society for Musical Research, First Congress, Liége, September 1–6, 1930, Report,* 67.
S	Anglès, H. *Die spanische Liedkunst im 15. und am Anfang des 16. Jahrhunderts,* in *Theodor Kroyer-Festschrift* (1933), 62.
AnteO	*Konstanz Antegnati: Die Orgelkunst (L'Arte organica) . . . , 1608.* German transl. by P. Smets; ed. by R. Lunelli, 1938.
AnthA	Anthon, C. *Some aspects of the Social Status of Italian Musicians during the Sixteenth Century,* in JRB I (1946), 111, 222.
Antiphonale	*Antiphonale . . . pro diurnis horis,* 1912. (Typis Polyglottis Vaticanis)
AntiphonaleM	*Antiphonale Monasticum pro diurnis horis,* 1934.
AntonoB	Antonowytsch, M. *Die Motette Benedicta es von Josquin des Prez und die Messen super Benedicta von Willaert, Palestrina, de la Hêle und de Monte,* 1951.
ApelAT	Apel, W. *Accidentien und Tonalität in den Musikdenkmälern des 15. und 16. Jahrhunderts,* 1937.
F	Apel, W. *French Secular Music after Machaut,* in Acta XVIII–XIX (1946–47), 17.
FM	Apel, W. (ed.). *French Secular Music of the Late Fourteenth Century,* 1950.
H	Apel, W. *Harvard Dictionary of Music,* 1944.
K	Apel, W. *Early German Keyboard Music,* in MQ XXIII (1937), 210.
M	Apel, W. (ed.). *Musik aus früher Zeit.* 2 vols., 1934.
MK	Apel, W. *Masters of the Keyboard,* 1947.
N	Apel, W. *The Notation of Polyphonic Music 900–1600,* 1942.
OR	Apel, W. *The Early Development of the Organ Ricercar,* in MD III (1949), 139.
P	Apel, W. *The Partial Signatures in the Sources up to 1450,* in Acta X (1938), 1; XI (1939), 40.

ApelR   Apel, W. *A Remark about the Basse Danse*, in JRB I (1946), 139.
    SM   Apel, W. *Early Spanish Music for Lute and Keyboard Instruments*, in MQ XX (1934), 289.
    T   Apel, W. *Die Tabulatur des Adam Ileborgh*, in ZfMW XVI (1934), 193.
ArL   Arnold, F. W. *Das Locheimer Liederbuch nebst der Ars Organisandi von Conrad Paumann*, in *Jahrbuch für Musikalische Wissenschaft* II (1867), 1. Reprinted 1926.
AraH   Araiz Martínez, A. *Historia de la Música religiosa en España*, 1942.
ArbOB   *Thoinot Arbeau: Orchesography (1588)*. English transl. by C. W. Beaumont, 1925.
    OE   *Thoinot Arbeau: Orchésographie, et Traicté en Forme de Dialogue (1588)*. English transl. by M. S. Evans, 1948.
    OF   *Thoinot Arbeau: Orchésographie (1588)*. Ed. by L. Fonta, 1888.
ArkA   Arkwright, G. E. P. *The Authorship of the Anthem "Lord for Thy Tender Mercy's Sake,"* in SIM VII (1906), 563.
    AF   Arkwright, G. E. P. *Alfonso Ferrabosco the Younger*, in R. Grey, *Studies in Music* (1901), 199.
    C   Arkwright, G. E. P. *Elizabethan Choirboy Plays and their Music*, in PMA XL (1914), 117.
    E   Arkwright, G. E. P. *Early Elizabethan Stage Music*, in MAn I (1909), 30; IV (1913), 112.
    F   Arkwright, G. E. P. *The Ferrabosco Family*, in MAn III (1912), 220; IV (1912), 42.
    I   Arkwright, G. E. P. *Un Compositore italiano alla Corte di Elisabetta*, in RMI IV (1897), 1.
    M   Arkwright, G. E. P. *"Master Alfonso" and Queen Elizabeth*, in ZIM VIII (1907), 271.
    P   Arkwright, G. E. P. *An English Pupil of Monteverdi*, in MAn IV (1912), 236.
    R   Arkwright, G. E. P. *Robert Douland's Musicall Banquet, 1610*, in MAn I (1909), 45.
    T   Arkwright, G. E. P. *Some Early Scottish Composers*, in MAn II (1910), 42.
ArldW   Arnold, D. M. *Thomas Weelkes and the Madrigal*, in M&L XXXI (1950), 1.
ArltL   Arlt, G. O. *The Vocal Music of the Lucerne Passion Play*, abstract in BAMS, No. 8 (1945), 24.
ArndA   Arnold, F. T. *The Art of Accompaniment from a Thorough-Bass*, 1931.
ArocaC   Aroca, D. J. (ed.). *Cancionero musical y poético del siglo XVII recogido por Claudio de la Sablonara*, 1918.
AronT   *Pietro Aron: Il Toscanello in Musica*, ed. of 1523.
AtkO   Atkins, Sir Ivor. *The Early Occupants of the Office of Organist and Master of the Choristers of the Cathedral Church . . . , Worcester*, 1918.
AttainC   *Pierre Attaingnant: Chansons und Tänze. Pariser Tabulaturdrucke aus dem Jahr 1530 von Pierre Attaingnant*. Facsimile ed. with commentary by E. Bernoulli, 1914.
─────   Attaingnant, P. *See also* GiesA, RoksO, RoksT, and SmijT.
AuI   Aubry, P. *Iter hispanicum II*, in SIM VIII (1907), 517.
    P   Aubry, P. (ed.). *Les plus anciens monuments de la musique française*, 1903.
AudaL   Auda, A. *La Musique et les Musiciens de l'ancien pays de Liége*, 1930.
    P   Auda, A. *La Mesure dans la Messe "L'Homme armé" de Palestrina*, in Acta XIII (1941), 39.
    T   Auda, A. *Le "Tactus" dans la Messe "L'Homme armé" de Palestrina*, in Acta XIV (1942), 27.
AugéB   Augé-Chiquet, M. *La Vie, les idées et l'oeuvre d'Antoine de Baïf*, 1909.
AV   *Anthologia vocalis*, 6 vols. Ed. by F. Hamma, O. Ravanello, *et al.*, 1921–28.
AzzaiV   *Azzaiolo, Filippo: Villotte del fiore*. Ed. by F. Vatielli, 1921.
BachV   Bacher, J. *Die Viola da gamba*, 1932.
BaiP   Baini, G. *Memorie storico-critiche della Vita e dell'Opere di Giovanni P. da Palestrina*. 2 vols., 1828.
BainesT   Baines, A. *Fifteenth-century Instruments in Tinctoris' "De inventione et usu musicae,"* in *The Galpin Society Journal* III (1950), 19.
BaixC   Baix, F. *La Carrière "bénéficiale" de Guillaume Dufay*, in *Bulletin de l'Institut historique belge de Rome* VIII (1928), 265.
BalF   Bal y Gay, J. *Fuenllana and the Transcription of Spanish Lute-Music*, in Acta XI (1939), 16.
    R   Bal y Gay, J. (ed.). *Romances y Villancicos españoles del siglo XVI*, 1939. (Modern arrangements with piano accompaniment.)

BalT   Bal y Gay, J. (ed.). *Treinta Canciones de Lope de Vega puestas en Música*, 1935.

BalmO   Balmer, L. *Orlando di Lassos Motetten. Eine stilgeschichtliche Studie*, 1938.

T   Balmer, L. *Tonsystem und Kirchentöne bei Johannes Tinctoris*, 1935.

BaloT   Balogh, L. *The Musical Dictionary of Johannes Tinctoris.* Master's thesis, Western Reserve University, Cleveland, O., 1940, unpublished.

BAMS   *Bulletin of the American Musicological Society*, 1936–45.

BanchC   Banchieri, A. *Conclusioni nel suono dell'organo*, 1608. Facsimile ed., 1934.

BannM   Bannister, H. M. *Monumenti Vaticani di Paleografia musicale latina*, 1913.

BarbP   Barbour, J. M. *The Persistence of the Pythagorean Tuning System*, in *Scripta Mathematica* I (1933), 286.

T   Barbour, J. M. *Tuning and Temperament*, 1951.

BarbiC   Barbieri, F. A. (ed.). *Cancionero musical de los siglos XV y XVI*, 1890.

BarbirO   *Jacobi Barbireau: Opera omnia.* Ed. by B. Meier. Vol. I, 1954; Vol. II, 1957.

BariM   Barilli, A. *Claudio Merulo e Ottavio Farnese*, in RMI XII (1905), 623.

BarkT   Barker, E. P. *Master Thoinot's Fancy*, in M&L XI (1930), 383.

——   Barreda, E. M. (ed.). *Clásicos españoles de la Música*, 1938–39. (Contains "practical" transcriptions; should be used with care.)

——   Barreda, E. M. *Música española de los siglos XIII al XVIII*, 1942.

BartC   Bartoli, R. (ed.). *Composizioni vocali polifoniche*, 1917.

BarthaB   Bartha, D. von. *Benedictus Ducis und Appenzeller*, 1930.

N   Bartha, D. von. *Bibliographische Notizen zum Repertoire der Handschrift Cambrai 124 (125–128)*, in ZfMW XIII (1931), 564.

P   Bartha, D. von. *Probleme der Chansongeschichte im 16. Jahrhundert*, in ZfMW XIII (1931), 507.

S   Bartha, D. von. *Szalkai érsek zenei jegyzetei monostor-iskolai diák korából (1490)* (*Das Musiklehrbuch einer ungarischen Klosterschule in der Handschrift von Fürstprimas Szalkai [1490]*) (Introduction in Hungarian and German) (Vol. I of *Musicologia Hungarica*), 1934.

BartókF   Bartók, B. *Collecting Folksongs in Anatolia*, in *The Hungarian Quarterly* III (1937), 337.

BarwickS   Barwick, S. *Sacred Vocal Polyphony in Early Colonial Mexico.* Ph.D. dissertation. Harvard University, 1949, unpublished.

BasE   Baskervill, C. R. *The Elizabethan Jig and Related Song Drama*, 1929.

BassaT   *Giovanni Bassano: Sieben Trios für Geige, Bratsche und Gamba oder andere Melodieninstrumente aller Art.* Ed. by E. Kiwi, 1933.

BatG   Batka, R. *Geschichte der Musik in Böhmen* I, 1906.

L   Batka, R. and P. Runge. *Die Lieder Muelichs von Prag*, 1905.

BäuM   Bäuerle, H. *Musikphilologische Studie über die "Sieben Busspsalmen" . . . des Orlando di Lasso*, 1906.

BaumD   Baumann, O. A. *Das deutsche Lied und seine Bearbeitungen in den frühen Orgeltabulaturen*, 1934.

BäumkK   Bäumker, W. (ed.). *Das katholische deutsche Kirchenlied in seinen Singweisen von den frühesten Zeiten bis gegen Ende des 17. Jahrhunderts.* 3 vols., 1883–91.

N   Bäumker, W. *Niederländische geistliche Lieder nebst ihren Singweisen aus Handschriften des 15. Jahrhunderts*, in VfMW IV (1888), 153, 287.

UK   Bäumker, W. *Über den Kontrapunkt. Eine kurze Anweisung aus dem XVI. Jahrhundert*, in MfMG X (1878), 63.

BautJ   Bautier-Regnier, A.-M. *Jachet de Mantoue (Jacobus Collebaudi), v. 1500–1559*, in RB VI (1952), 101.

W   Bautier-Regnier, A.-M. *Jacques de Wert (1535–96)*, in RB IV (1950), 40.

BdgC   Bridge, Sir Frederick. *Old Cryes of London*, 1921.

BeB   Becker, G. *Eustorg de Beaulieu: poète et musicien. Notice biographique et bibliographique*, 1880.

C   Becker, G. *Jean Caulery et ses chansons spirituelles*, 1880.

G   Becker, G. *Guillaume Guéroult et ses chansons spirituelles . . .* , 1880.

M   Becker, G. *La Musique en Suisse depuis les temps les plus reculés jusqu'à la fin du dix-huitième siècle*, 1923.

W   Becker, G. *Hubert Waelrant et ses psaumes . . .* , 1881.

BecL   Becker, A. *Die Berliner liturgische Handschrift Mus. ms. Z. 95 und ihre deutschen Lieder*, in ZfMW I (1919), 633.

BecherA   Becherini, B. *Giovanni Francesco Anerio ed alcune sue Gagliarde per Cembalo*, in *La Bibliofilia* XLI (1939), 159.

D   Becherini, B. *Due Canzoni di Dufay del Codice fiorentino 2794*, in *La Bibliofilia* XLIII (1941), 124.

BedbG   Bedbrook, G. S. *The Genius of Giovanni Gabrieli (1557–1612)*, in *The Music Review* VIII (1947), 91.

K   Bedbrook, G. S. *Keyboard Music from the Middle Ages to the Beginnings of the Baroque*, 1949.

BehrD   Behr, L. *Die deutschen Gesänge Orlando di Lassos*, 1935.

BellerC   Bellermann, H. *Der Contrapunct*, 1877. References in this book are to the 1887 ed.

M   Bellermann, H. *Die Mensuralnoten und Taktzeichen im 15. und 16. Jahrhundert*, 1858; 2nd ed., 1906. References in this book are to the 2nd ed.

T   Bellermann, H. *Joannis Tinctoris Terminorum musicae diffinitorium* in *Jahrbücher für musikalische Wissenschaft* I (1863), 55.

BenndC   Benndorf, K. *Sethus Calvisius als Musiktheoretiker*, in VfMW X (1894), 411.

BerH   Bernoulli, E. *Aus Liederbüchern der Humanistenzeit*, 1910.

BergCV   Bergmans, P. *La Biographie du compositeur Corneille Verdonck (1563–1625)*, in *Bulletin de la Classe des beaux-arts de l'Académie royale de Belgique*, 1919, p. 125.

O   Bergmans, P. *L'Organiste des archiducs Albert et Isabelle, Peter Philips*, in *Bulletin de l'Académie royale d'archéologie et d'histoire de l'art de Belgique* for 1902 (1903), 575.

S   Bergmans, P. *Un Imprimeur-musicien: Tielman Susato*, in *De Gulden Passer (Le Compas d'or)*, n. s. I (1923), 45.

T   Bergmans, P. *La Typographie musicale en Belgique au XVIe siècle*, 1930.

VM   Bergmans, P. *Variétés musicologiques . . . Ser. III*, in *Annales de l'Académie royale d'archéologie de Belgique* LXVII (Ser. 6, VII; 1919), 147.

BermuD   Bermudo, F. J. *Declaración de Instrumentos musicales*, 1555. Facs., ed. by M. S. Kastner (in *Documenta musicologica*), 1957.

BernhM   Bernhard, B. *Recherches sur l'histoire de la corporation des ménétriers ou* Ser. 1, III (1842), 377; IV (1843), 525; V (1843), 254 (1844), 339.

BerthaA   Bertha, A. de. *Autriche-Hongrie*, in EC, Partie I, V, p. 2597.

BertolM   Bertolotti, A. *Musici alla Corte dei Gonzaga in Mantova dal secolo XIV al secolo XVIII*, 1890.

BesBF   Besseler, H. *Bourdon und Fauxbourdon*, 1950.

BU   Besseler, H. *The Manuscript Bologna Biblioteca Universitaria 2216*, in MD VI (1952), 39.

C   Besseler, H. (ed.). *Capella. Meisterwerke mittelalterlicher Musik*, I, 1950.

CC   Besseler, H. *La cobla catalana y el conjunto instrumental de danza "alta,"* in *Anuario musical* IV (1949), 93.

D   Besseler, H. *Dufay, Schöpfer des Fauxbourdons*, in Acta XX (1948), 26.

E   Besseler, H. *Erläuterungen zu einer Vorführung ausgewählter Denkmäler der Musik des späten Mittelalters*, in *Bericht über die Freiburger Tagung für deutsche Orgelkunst vom 27. bis 30. Juli 1926* (1926), 141.

EP   Besseler, H. *Die Entstehung der Posaune*, in Acta XXII (1950), 8.

F   Besseler, H. *Der Ursprung des Fauxbourdons*, in MF I (1948), 106.

M   Besseler, H. *Die Musik des Mittelalters und der Renaissance*, 1931–35.

N   Besseler, H. (ed.). *Altniederländische Motetten*, 1929.

ND   Besseler, H. *Neue Dokumente zum Leben und Schaffen Dufays*, in AfMW IX (1952), 159.

S   Besseler, H. *Studien zur Musik des Mittelalters.*

I   *Neue Quellen des 14. und beginnenden 15. Jahrhunderts*, in AFMW VII (1925), 167; Supp. in VIII (1926), 233.

II   *Die Motette von Franko von Köln bis Philippe von Vitry*, in AFMW VIII (1926), 137.

V   Besseler, H. *Studien zur Musik: Von Dufay bis Josquin*, in ZfMW XI (1928), 1.

BessarA   Bessaraboff, N. *Ancient European Musical Instruments*, 1941.

BezL   Bezdeck, Sister J. J. *The Harmonic and Contrapuntal Style of Orlando Lasso.* Ph.D. dissertation, Eastman School, Rochester, N.Y., 1946, unpublished.

BienS   Bienenfeld, E. *Wolfgang Schmeltzl, sein Liederbuch (1544) und das Quodlibet des XVI. Jahrhunderts*, in SIM VI (1904), 80.

BigM   Bignami, G. *L'Anno di nascita di Luca Marenzio*, in RMI XLII (1938), 46.

BinchC   *Musikalische Denkmäler II: Die Chansons von Gilles Binchois.* Ed. by W. Rehm, 1957.

BirtP   Birtner, H. *Ein Beitrag zur Geschichte der protestantischen Musik im 16. Jahrhundert*, in ZfMW X (1928), 457.

R   Birtner, H. *Renaissance und Klassik in der Musik*, in *Theodor Kroyer-Festschrift* (1933), 40.

BirtS   Birtner, H. *Sieben Messen von Ludwig Senfl*, in AfMF VII (1942), 40.

BlaI   Blaschke, P. *Heinrich Isaaks Choralis Constantinus*, in KJ XXVI (1931), 32.

BleyB   Bleyer, J. *Beheim Mihály élete és müvei a magyar történelem szempontjából*, in *Századok* XXXVI (1902), 21, 131, 215, 347, 444, 528.

D   Bleyer, J. *Demantius Kristóf 'Magyar tábori dob'-ja*, in *Egyetemes Philológiai Közlöny* XXIV (1900), 381.

BlumeE   Blume, F. *Die evangelische Kirchenmusik*, 1931.

G   Blume, F. (ed.). *Geistliche Musik am Hofe des Landgrafen Moritz von Hessen*, 1931.

J   Blume, F. *Josquin des Prés*, in *Der Drachentöter: Jahrbuch des Verlages Georg Kallmeyer, 1929* (1930), 52.

S   Blume, F. *Studien zur Vorgeschichte der Orchestersuite im 15. und 16. Jahrhundert*, 1925.

BlumenS   Blumenfeld, H. *Syntagma musicum of Michael Praetorius, Volume Two, De organographia, First and Second Parts*. English transl., 1949.

BM   *Catalogue of Manuscript Music in the British Museum* by Augustus Hughes-Hughes. 3 vols., 1906–09.

I   *Sacred Vocal Music*, 1906.

II   *Secular Vocal Music*, 1908.

III   *Instrumental Music, Treatises, etc.*, 1909.

BockM   Bote and Bock (Publishers). *Musica sacra*. 16 vols., 1839–96. Commer (*see* CommM) in 1839 began the series *Musica sacra* for Bote and Bock. After providing 4 vols., he shifted to another house, Trautwein, which in due course became the firm of Bahn, and, with Vol. 18, he again shifted, this time to Manz. In all he produced 28 vols. and retained the original series title for all of them. Meanwhile, Bote and Bock continued their own *Musica sacra* series, under various editors, publishing 16 vols. in all. This series and CommM, therefore, have their first 4 vols. in common. The 2 series are often confused with each other.

BoerB   Boer, C. L. W. *Het Anthonius Motet van Anthonius Busnois*, 1940.

C   Boer, C. L. W. *Chansonvormen op het einde van de XVde eeuw*, 1938.

BoettL   Boetticher, W. *Orlando di Lasso und seine Zeit*, 1958.

BogaW   Bogaert, I. *Giaches de Wert: zijn betrekkingen met bekende tijdgenooten*, in *Vlaamsch Jaarboek voor Muziekgeschiedenis* II–III (1940), 61.

WA   Bogaert, I. *De Waelrant's te Antwerpen*, in *Hommage à Charles Van den Borren (Mélanges)* (1945), 72.

BöhA   Böhme, F. M. (ed.). *Altdeutsches Liederbuch*, 1877.

T   Böhme, F. M. *Geschichte des Tanzes in Deutschland*. 2 vols., 1886.

BohH   Bohn, E. *Die musikalischen Handschriften des XVI. und XVII. Jahrhunderts in der Stadtbibliothek zu Breslau*, 1890.

BolC   *Catalogo della Biblioteca del Liceo Musicale di Bologna*. 4 vols., 1890–1905.

BolleE   Bolle, W. *Die gedruckten englischen Liederbücher bis 1600*, in the series, *Palaestra*, XXIX (1903).

BonaB   Bonaventura, A. *Il Boccaccio e la Musica* in RMI XXI (1914), 405.

BonacN   Bonaccorsi, A. *Un nuovo Codice dell' "Ars Nova": Il Codice Lucchese*, in *Atti della Accademia Nazionale dei Lincei: Memorie: Classe di Scienze morali, storiche e filologiche*, Ser. VIII, Vol. I (1948), 539.

BoneJ   Bonelli, L. *Les Joueurs de flûte avignonnais au service de la république de Sienne au XVe siècle*, in *Actes du Congrès d'histoire de l'art, Paris, 1921*, III (*recte* II²) (1924), 802. (In Italian despite title.)

BonnA   Bonnet, J. (ed.). *An Anthology of Early French Organ Music*, 1942.

O   Bonnet, J. (ed.). *Historical Organ Recitals*. 6 vols., 1917–45.

BonninP   Bonnin, T. and A. Chassant. *Puy de musique érigé à Evreux, en l'honneur de madame sainte Cécile; publié d'après un manuscrit du XVIe siècle*, 1837.

BontC   Bontoux, G. *La Chanson en Angleterre au temps d'Elisabeth*, 1936.

BorAI   Van den Borren, C. *L'Apport italien dans un manuscrit du XVe siècle, perdu et partiellement retrouvé*, in RMI XXI (1924), 527.

B   Van den Borren, C. *Les Fragments de messe du manuscrit 222 C. 22 de la Bibliothèque de Strasbourg*, in TVNM XII (1928), 177, 236.

C   Van den Borren, C. *Compositions inédites de Guillaume Dufay et de Gilles Binchois*, in *Annales de l'Académie royale d'archéologie de Belgique* LXX (Ser. 6, X; 1922), 109.

CB   Van den Borren, C. *Le Codex de Johannes Bonadies, musicien du XVe siècle*, in *Revue belge d'archéologie et d'histoire de l'art* X (1940), 251.

CC   Van den Borren, C. *The Codex Canonici 213 in the Bodleian Library at Oxford*, in PRMA LXXIII (1946), 45.

BorD   Van den Borren, C. *Guillaume Dufay: son importance dans l'évolution de la musique au XVe siècle*, 1925.

DO   Van den Borren, C. *Benedictus de Opitiis: Deux de ses oeuvres récemment publiées*, in Musica Sacra: Sancta Sancte XXXIV (1927), 168.

F   Van den Borren, C. *A Light of the Fifteenth Century: Guillaume Dufay*, in MQ XXI (1935), 279.

FA   Van den Borren, C. *Fausses attributions et travestissements musicaux*, in Bulletin de la Classe des beaux-arts de l'Académie royale de Belgique XXII (1941), 7.

GD   Van den Borren, C. *Guillaume Dufay, centre de rayonnement de la polyphonie européenne à la fin du moyen âge*, in Bulletin de l'Institut historique belge de Rome XX (1939), 171.

I   Van den Borren, C. *Inventaire des manuscrits de musique polyphonique qui se trouvent en Belgique*, in Acta V (1933), 66, 120, 177; VI (1934), 23, 65, 116.

IS   Van den Borren, C. *Quelques réflexions à propos du style imitatif syntaxique*, in RB I (1946), 14.

JB   Van den Borren, C. *Les Madrigaux de Jean Brudieu*, in RM VI (1925), 207.

JT   Van den Borren, C. *Johannes Tinctoris*, in Biographie nationale publiée par l'Académie royale . . . de Belgique XXV (1930–32), col. 288ff.

K   Van den Borren, C. *The Sources of Keyboard Music in England*. Transl. by J. E. Matthew, 1914.

L   Van den Borren, C. *Hugo et Arnold de Lantins*, in Annales de la Fédération archéologique et historique de Belgique XXIX (1932), 263.

LI   Van den Borren, C. *Orlande de Lassus et la musique instrumentale*, in RM III (May, 1922), 111.

LN   Van den Borren, C. *En quelle année Roland de Lassus est-il né?*, in Bulletin de la Société "Union musicologique" VI (1926), 51.

M   Van den Borren, C. *La Musique pittoresque dans le manuscrit 222 C. 22 de la Bibliothèque de Strasbourg (XVe siècle)*, in Bericht über den musikwissenschaftlichen Kongress in Basel (1925), 88.

MB   Van den Borren, C. *Les Musiciens belges en Angleterre à l'époque de la Renaissance*, 1913.

MC   Van den Borren, C. *Une "Messe-canzonetta" et un "Magnificat-chanson" d'Orlando di Lasso*, in RMI XXXIV (1927), 603.

MM   Van den Borren, C. *Le Madrigalisme avant le madrigal*, in AdlerF (1930), 78.

MN   Van den Borren, C. *Geschiedenis van de Muziek in de Nederlanden*, 2 vols., 1948, 1951.

O   Van den Borren, C. *Les Origines de la musique de clavier dans les Pays-Bas . . .*, in Annales de la Société d'histoire et d'archéologie de Gand XIII (1914), I.

OL   Van den Borren C. *Orlande de Lassus*, 1920.

P   Van den Borren, C. (ed.). *Polyphonia Sacra: A Continental Miscellany of the Fifteenth Century*, 1932.

PL   Van den Borren, C. (ed.). *Pièces polyphoniques profanes de provenance liégeoise (XVe siècle)*, 1950.

PM   Van den Borren, C. *De quelques aspects de la parodie musicale*, in Bulletin de la Classe des Beaux-Arts de l'Académie royale de Belgique XX (1938), 146.

Q   Van den Borren, C. *Quelques notes sur les chansons françaises et les madrigaux italiens de J. P. Sweelinck*, in Gedenkboek aangeboden aan Dr. D. F. Scheurleer (1925), 73.

QS   Van den Borren, C. *Etudes sur le XVe siècle musical*, 1941.

R   Van den Borren, C. *Deux recueils peu connus d'Orlande de Lassus*, in Actes du Congrès de l'histoire de l'art, Paris, 1921, III (recte II²) (1924), 833.

RL   Van den Borren, C. *Roland de Lassus*, 1944.

S   Van den Borren, C. *Le Manuscrit musical 222 C. 22 de la Bibliothèque de Strasbourg (XVe siècle) brulé en 1870, et reconstitué d'après une copie partielle d'Edmond de Coussemaker*, in Annales de l'Académie royale d'archéologie de Belgique, LXXI (7e Série, Tome II; 1924), 343; LXXII (7e Série, Tome III; 1924), 272; LXXIII (7e Série, Tome III; 1925), 128; LXXIV (7e Série, Tome IV; 1927), 71.

TM   Van den Borren, C. *La Contribution italienne au Thesaurus Musicus de 1564*, in JRB I (1946), 33.

Bibliography

BorVA	Van den Borren, C. *Les Virginalistes anglais*, in *S.I.M. Revue musicale mensuelle* VIII (1912), 13.
BordA	Bordes, C. *et al.* (eds.). *Anthologie des maîtres religieux primitifs*, 1893–95. 3 Années, with a vol. of Masses and a vol. of Motets for each Année.
C	Bordes, C. (ed.). *Chansonnier du XVIe siècle*, 1905.
T	Bordes, C. (ed.). *Trois fantaisies vocales à 4 voix*, n.d.
TC	Bordes, C. (ed.). *Trois chansons du XVe siècle*, n.d.
BöttcM	Böttcher, T. *Musiknoten auf Kupferstichen*, in MfMG VIII (1876), 121.
BottrigD	Ercole Bottrigari; *Il Desiderio, 1594*. Ed. by K. Meyer, 1924.
BoutE	Bouton, E. *Esquisse biographique et bibliographique sur Claude le Jeune*, 1845.
BoyceC	Boyce, W. (ed.). *Cathedral Music*. . . . 3 vols., 1760–78; 2nd ed., 1788; 2 new editions by V. Novello (1844) and J. Warren (1849). References in this book are to the 1788 ed.
BoydE	Boyd, M.C. *Elizabethan Music and Musical Criticism*, 1940.
BrS	Brandes, H. *Studien zur musikalischen Figurenlehre im 16. Jahrhundert*, 1935.
BraM	Branberger, J. *Musikgeschichtliches aus Böhmen* I, 1906.
BragL	Bragard, R. *Lambert de Sayve 1549–1614. Etude biographique et bibliographique*, 1934.
BraunV	Braungart, S. *Die Verbreitung des reformatorischen Liedes in Nürnberg in der Zeit von 1525–1570*, 1939.
BraunfA	Braunfels, W. (ed.). *Altdeutsche geistliche Chorlieder aus dem 16. Jahrhundert*, n.d.
BreidS	Breidert, F. *Stimmigkeit und Gliederung in der Polyphonie des Mittelalters*, 1935.
BrenD	Brenet, M. *Deux comptes de la chapelle-musique des rois de France*, in SIM VI (1904), 1.
E	Brenet, M. *Essai sur les origines de la musique descriptive*, in RMI XIV (1907), 725; XV (1908), 457, 671.
EA	Brenet, M. *Un Poète musicien français du XVe siècle, Eloy d'Amerval*, in *Revue d'histoire et de critique musicales* I (1901), 46.
FA	Brenet, M. *Les Concerts en France sous l'ancien régime*, 1900.
G	Brenet, M. *Claude Goudimel*, 1898.
H	Brenet, M. *L'Homme armé*, in MfMG XXX (1898), 124 (German transl. of article published in French in the Nov. 19, 1898, issue of the less accessible *Journal musical*).
JM	Brenet, M. *Jean Mouton*, in TSG V (1899), 323.
M	Brenet, M. *Les Musiciens de la Sainte-Chapelle du Palais*, 1910.
N	Brenet, M. *Notes sur l'histoire du luth en France*, in RMI V (1898), 637; VI (1899), 1. Also pr. as a monograph, 1899. References in this book are to RMI.
P	Brenet, M. *Palestrina*, 1905.
PM	Brenet, M. *Les Poésies de Jehan Molinet*, in *Bulletin de la Société française de musicologie* I (1917), 21.
V	Brenet, M. *Musique et musiciens de la vieille France*, 1911.
Z	Brenet, M. *Deux traductions françaises inédites de Zarlino*, in *L'Année musicale* I (1911), 124.
BrennM	Brennecke, E. *John Milton the Elder and his Music*, 1938.
P	Brennecke, E. *"Parthenia Inviolata": The Second Book of Keyboard Music Printed in England*, in *The Musical Times* LXXV (1934), 701.
S	Brennecke, E. *A Singing Man of Windsor*, in M&L XXXIII (1952), 33.
BridgeT	Bridge, J. C. *Town Waits and their Times*, PMA LIV (1928), 63.
BridgmB	Bridgman, N. *Eustorg de Beaulieu, Musician*, in MQ XXXVII (1951), 61.
M	Bridgman, N. *Un manuscrit italien du début de XVIe s. . . .*, AM I (1953), 269.
BrigiB	Brigidi, A. *Cenni sulla vita e sulle opere di Giulio Belli*, 1865.
BrooA	Brooks, C. V. *Antoine Busnois, Chanson Composer*, in JAMS VI (1953), 111.
B	Brooks, C. V. *Antoine Busnois as a Composer of Chansons* (including transcriptions of all the pieces). Ph.D. dissertation, New York University, 1951, unpublished.
D	Brooks, C. V. *Some Aspects of the Music Drama before 1600*. Master's thesis, Columbia University, 1937, unpublished.
BruA	Bruger, H. D. (ed.). *Pierre Attaingnant (1529), zwei- und dreistimmige Solostücke für die Laute*, 1927.
D	Bruger, H. D. (ed.). *Deutsche Meister des ein- und zweistimmigen Lautensatzes*, 1926.

BruJD   Bruger, H. D. (ed.). *John Dowland's Solostücke für die Laute*, 1923.

L   Bruger, H. D. (ed.). *Alte Lautenkunst aus drei Jahrhunderten.* 2 vols., 1923.

S   Bruger, H. D. *Schule des Lautenspiels*, 1926.

BrudieuM   *Joan Brudieu: Els Madrigals i la Missa de Difunts.* Ed. by F. Pedrell and H. Anglès, 1921.

BruinS   Bruinsma, H. A. *"Souterliedekens" and its Relation to Psalmody in the Netherlands.* Ph.D. dissertation, University of Michigan, 1949, unpublished.

BrumO   *Antoine Brumel: Opera omnia.* Ed. by A. Carapetyan, 1951–   .

BruynD   Bruyn, J. de. *Ghisilinus Danckerts, kapelaanzanger van de pauselijke kapel van 1538 tot 1565. Zijn leven, werken en onuitgegeven tractaat*, in TVNM XVI (1946), 217; XVII (1949), 128.

BuH   Burney, C. *General History of Music.* 4 vols., 1776–89. Ed. with notes by F. Mercer, 2 vols., 1935. References in this book are to the 1st ed.

BukB   Bukofzer, M. *The Book of the Courtier on Music*, in MTNAP, Ser. 38 (1944), 230.

CR   Bukofzer, M. *Caput Redivivum: A New Source for Dufay's Missa Caput*, in JAMS IV (1951), 97.

E   Bukofzer, M. *Geschichte des englischen Diskants und des Fauxbourdons nach den theoretischen Quellen*, 1936.

FR   Bukofzer, M. *Fauxbourdon Revisited*, in MQ XXXVIII (1952), 22.

MB   Bukofzer, M. *Music in the Baroque Era*, 1947.

MC   Bukofzer, M. *Two Mensuration Canons*, in MD II (1948), 165.

ML   Bukofzer, M. *The Music of the Laudes*, in Ernst H. Kantorowicz, *Laudes Regiae: A Study in Liturgical Acclamations and Mediaeval Ruler Worship*, University of California Publications in History, XXXIII (1946), 188.

MR   Bukofzer, M. *Studies in Medieval and Renaissance Music*, 1950.

OH   Bukofzer, M. *The Music in the Old Hall Manuscript*, in MQ XXXIV (1948), 512; XXXV (1949), 36.

P   Bukofzer, M. *Popular Polyphony in the Middle Ages*, in MQ XXVI (1940), 31.

R   Bukofzer, M. *On the Performance of Renaissance Music*, in MTNAP XXXVI (1942; for 1941), 225.

T   Bukofzer, M. *The Beginnings of Polyphonic Choir Music*, in PAMS for 1940 (1946), 23.

U   Bukofzer, M. *An Unknown Chansonnier of the 15th Century (The Mellon Chansonnier)*, in MQ XXVIII (1942), 14.

BullMG   *John Bull, edited for the pianoforte. . . .* Ed. by M. Glyn, 1920.

BurbE   Burbure, L. de. *Etude sur un ms. du 16ème siècle*, in *Mémoires publiés par l'Académie royale des Sciences, des Lettres et des Beaux-Arts de Belgique* XXXIII (1882).

L   Burbure, L. de. *Charles Luython, compositeur de musique de la Cour impériale (1550–1620). Sa Vie et ses ouvrages*, 1880.

M   Burbure, L. de. *La Musique à Anvers aux XIVe, XVe et XVIe siècles*, in *Annales de l'Académie royale d'archéologie* LVIII (1906), 159.

BurgL   Burger, C. P. *Lofzangen en prenten ter verheerlijking van Keizer Maximilianus*, in *Het Boek* XVII (1928), 23.

BushC   Bush, H. E. *The Emergence of the Chordal Concept in the Polyphonic Period.* Ph.D. dissertation, Cornell University, Ithaca, N.Y., 1939. Abstract published.

CF   Bush, H. E. *The Recognition of Chordal Formation by Early Music Theorists*, in MQ XXXII (1946), 227.

L   Bush, H. E. *The Laborde Chansonnier*, in PAMS for 1940 (1946), 56.

BuszL   Buszin, W. E. *Luther on Music*, in MQ XXXII (1946), 80.

BuxO   *Das Buxheimer Orgelbuch . . .* Facs., ed. by B. A. Wallner (in *Documenta musicologica*), 1955.

ByrdF   *William Byrd: Forty-five Pieces for Keyboard Instruments.* Ed. by S. D. Tuttle, 1939.

OB   *William Byrd: The Byrd Organ Book. A collection of pieces . . . fit for the pianoforte. . . .* Ed. by M. Glyn, 1923.

P   *William Byrd. 14 Pieces for Keyed Instruments.* Ed. by J. A. Fuller Maitland and W. Barclay Squire, 1923.

W   *The Collected Works of William Byrd.* Ed. by E. H. Fellowes. 20 vols., 1937–50.

CaP   Campbell, F. C. *The Polychoral Motets of Adam Gumpelzhaimer (1559–1625) with Special Emphasis on Modulation, Part I.* Master's thesis, Eastman School, Rochester, N.Y., 1942, unpublished.

CafS   Caffi, F. *Storia della Musica sacra nella già Cappella Ducale di S. Marco in Venezia dal 1318 al 1797.* 2 vols., 1854–55; reprinted, 1931.

CamC   Cametti, A. *Le Case di Giovanni Pierluigi da Palestrina in Roma*, in RMI XXVIII (1921), 419.

D   Cametti, A. *Due "canoni" commemorativi di Giovanni M. Nanino*, in RMI XXXV (1928), 583.

F   Cametti, A. *Il Compositore piemontese Costanzo Festa*, in Bollettino Bibliografico Musicale VI, No. 4 (1931), 5.

L   Cametti, A. *Firmino Lebel, Maestro in S. Luigi dei Francesi a Roma*, in RMI XXXII (1925), 196.

M   Cametti, A. *Nuovi contributi alle biografie di Maurizio e Felice Anerio*, in RMI XXII (1915), 122.

N   Cametti, A. *Un nuovo Documento sulle origini di Giovanni Pierluigi da Palestrina. Il Testamento di Jacobella Pierluigi (1527)*, in RMI X (1903), 517.

P   Cametti, A. *Palestrina*, 1925.

PA   Cametti, A. *Giovanni Pierluigi da Palestrina e le sue alleanze matrimoniali*, in RMI XXX (1923), 489.

PC   Cametti, A. *G. P. da Palestrina e il suo commercio di pelliccerie*, 1922.

CanM   Canal, P. *Della Musica in Mantova*, in Memorie del R. Istituto Veneto di Scienze, Lettere ed Arti XXI (1879), 655.

CaraC   Carapetyan, A. *The Concept of the "Imitazione della natura" in the Sixteenth Century*, in JRB I (1946), 47.

M   Carapetyan, A. *The Musica Nova of Adriano Willaert*, in JRB I (1946), 200.

CaravI   Caravaglios, N. *Una nuova "Intavolatura di Cimbalo" di Antonio Valente Cieco*, in RMI XXIII (1916), 491.

CarpenR   Carpenter, N. C. *Rabelais and the Chanson*, in Publications of the Modern Language Association LXV (1950), 1212.

CarrH   Carriazo, Juan de Mata (ed.). *Hechos del Condestable Don Miguel Lucas de Iranzo*, 1940.

CarvO   *Robert Carver: O bone Jesu, [1546]*. Ed. by J. A. Fuller Maitland, 1926.

CasAP   Casimiri, R. (ed.). *Antologia polyphonica*. 2 vols., 1932.

C   Casimiri, R. *Il Codice 59 dell'Archivio musicale lateranense*, 1919.

CP   Casimiri, R. *Musica e Musicisti nella Cattedrale di Padova nei sec. XIV, XV, XVI*, in NA XVIII (1941), 1, 101, 181.

D   Casimiri, R. *G. P. da Palestrina: Nuovi Documenti biografici*, 1918.

F   Casimiri, R. *Firmin le Bel di Noyon, Maestro in Roma di Giov. Pierluigi da Palestrina*, in NA I (1924), 64.

L   Casimiri, R. *Orlando di Lasso, Maestro di Cappella al Laterano nel 1553*, 1920.

MD   Casimiri, R. *Una "Missa Dominicalis" falsamente attribuita a Tommaso Ludovico de Victoria*, in NA X (1933), 185.

MP   Casimiri, R. *Memorie Musicali Prenestini del secolo XVI*, in NA I (1924), 7.

R   Casimiri, R. (ed.). *Societatis Polyphonicae Romanae Repertorium*. 3 vols., 1925–26.

S   Casimiri, R. *I "Diarii Sistini,"* in NA I (1924), 85, 149, 267; III (1926), 1, 169, 257; IV (1927), 256; IX (1932), 53, 150, 260; X (1933), 45, 149, 261, 326; XI (1934), 76, 300; XII (1935), 55, 126, 249; XIII (1936), 59, 147, 201; XIV (1937), 19, 73, 128, 298; XV (1938), 42, 129, 200, 281; XVI (1939), 74; XVII (1940), 65.

SV   Casimiri, R. *Simone Verovio da Hertogenbosch*, in NA X (1933), 189.

V   Casimiri, R. *Il Vittoria*, 1934.

CastP   Castellani, C. *I Privilegi di stampa e la proprietà letteraria in Venezia*, 1888.

CatM   Catelani, A. *Memorie della Vita e delle Opere di Claudio Merulo*, 1859, revised by G. Benvenuti, 1931. Also in Bollettino Bibliografico Musicale V, No. 12 (1930), 7; VI, No. 1 (1931), 5. References in this book are to the revision, monograph form.

CauC   Cauchie, M. *Les Chansons à trois voix de Pierre Cléreau*, in RdM VIII (1927), 77.

D   Cauchie, M. *Documents pour servir à une biographie de Guillaume Costeley*, in RdM VII (1926), 49.

G   Cauchie, M. *Clément Janequin, chapelain du duc de Guise*, in Le Ménestrel LXXXIX (1927), 21.

J   Cauchie, M. *Clément Janequin: recherches sur sa famille et sur lui-même*, in RdM IV (1923), 13.

M   Cauchie, M. *La Pureté des modes dans la musique vocale franco-belge du XVIe siècle*, in Theodor Kroyer-Festschrift (1933), 54.

N   Cauchie, M. *Les Véritables Nom et Prénom d'Ockeghem*, in RdM VII (1926), 9.

P   Cauchie, M. *Les deux plus anciens recueils de chansons polyphoniques imprimés en France*, in RdM V (1924), 72.

CauPJ   Cauchie, M. *Les Psaumes de Janequin*, in *Mélanges de musicologie offerts à M. Lionel de la Laurencie* (1933), 47.

Q   Cauchie, M. (ed.). *Quinze Chansons françaises du XVIᵉ siècle*, 1926.

CaulM   Caullet, G. *Musiciens de la Collégiale Notre-Dame à Courtrai*, 1911.

CazaT   *Francesco Caza: Tractato vulgare de canto figurato*. Facsimile ed. with German transl. and notes by J. Wolf, 1922.

CDMI   *I Classici della Musica Italiana* (*Raccolta Nazionale*). Ed. by G. d'Annunzio. 36 vols. (152 quaderni), 1918–21.
     Quad. 1–3 *Adriano Banchieri: Musiche corali*. Ed. by F. Vatielli, 1919.
     Quad. 23–27 *G. Cavazzoni. Composizioni*. Ed. by G. Benvenuti, 1919.
     Quad. 59–62 *Carlo Gesualdo, Principe di Venosa: Madrigali a 5 voci*. Ed. by I. Pizzetti, 1919.
     Quad. 82–84 *Pier Luigi Sante da Palestrina: Madrigali a 4 e 5 voci*. Ed. by C. Perinello, 1919.

CE   *Catholic Encyclopedia*. 17 vols. and index, 1907–22.

CelaCP   Celani, E. *I Cantori della Cappella Pontificia nei secoli XVI–XVII*, in RMI XIV (1907), 83, 752; XVI (1909), 55.

CelleF   Cellesi, L. *Documenti per la storia musicale di Firenze*, RMI XXXIV (1927), 579; XXXV (1928), 553.

S   Cellesi, L. *Storia della più antica banda musicale senese*, 1906.

CerfI   Le Cerf, G. and E.-R. Labande (eds.). *Instruments de musique du XVᵉ siècle. Les Traités d'Henri-Arnaut de Zwolle et de divers anonymes*, 1932. (Includes 23 plates of facsimiles.)

CeroM   *Domenico Pietro Cerone: El Melopeo y Maestro*, 1613.

CesB   Cesari, G. *L'Archivio musicale di S. Barbara in Mantova ed una messa di Guglielmo Gonzaga*, in *Theodor Kroyer-Festschrift* (1933), 118.

E   Cesari, G. *Die Entstehung des Madrigals*, 1908. (Published in Italian in RMI XIX [1912], 1 380.)

M   Cesari, G. *Musica e Musicisti alla Corte sforzesca*, in F. Malaguzzi Valeri, *La Corte di Lodovico il Moro* IV (1923), 183. Printed also, but with fewer music exx., etc., in RMI XXIX (1922), 1. References in the present book are to the 1923 ed.

ChamM   Chambers, E. K. *The Mediaeval Stage*. 2 vols., 1903.

ChappP   Chappell, W. (ed.). *Old English Popular Music*. New ed., revised by H. E. Wooldridge. 2 vols., 1892. (1st ed., *Popular Music of the Olden Time*. 2 vols., 1859.) References in this book are to the revised ed.

S   Chappell, W. *Some Account of an Unpublished Collection of Songs and Ballads by King Henry VIII and his Contemporaries*, in *Archaeologia* XLI (1865–67), 371.

ChaseG   Chase, G. *Guitar and Vihuela: A Clarification*, abstract printed in BAMS, No. 6 (1940), 13.

J   Chase, G. *Juan del Encina, Poet and Musician*, in M&L XX (1939), 420.

M   Chase, G. *The Music of Spain*, 1941.

N   Chase, G. *Juan Navarro Hispalensis and Juan Navarro Gaditanus*, in MQ XXXI (1945), 188.

O   Chase, G. *Origins of the Lyric Theater in Spain*, in MQ XXV (1939), 292.

ChavM   Lopez-Chavarri, E. *Música popular española*, 1940.

ChierZ   Chiereghin, S. *Zarlino*, in RMI XXXVII (1930), 21, 204.

ChilB   Chilesotti, O. (ed.). *Biblioteca di Rarità musicali*. 9 vols., 1884–1915.
    I   *"Nobiltà di Dame" del . . . Caroso . . . ; "Le gratie d'amore" di . . . Negri . . .* , [1884?]
    II   *"Balli d'Arpicordo" di Giovanni Picchi . . .* , [1884?]
    V   *Arie, Canzonette e Balli . . . di Horatio Vecchi . . .* , [1892]
    VII   *Airs de Court . . . dal "Thesaurus Harmonicus" di J. B. Besard . . .* , [1914]
    IX   *Madrigali, Villanelle ed Arie di danza . . . dalle opere di J. B. Besard . . .* , [1915]

C   Chilesotti, O. *Una Canzone celebre nel cinquecento: "Io mi son giovinetta" del Ferabosco*, in RMI I (1894), 446.

CB   Chilesotti, O. *Gli Airs de cour di Besard*, in *Atti del Congresso Internazionale di Scienze Storiche*, VIII for 1903 (1905), 131.

CI   Chilesotti, O. *Chansons françaises du XVIᵉ siècle en Italie (transcrites pour le luth)*, in *Revue d'histoire et de critique musicales* II (1902), 63, 202.

CP   Chilesotti, O. *Una Canzone popolare del Cinquecento*, in RMI XXII (1915), 113.

ChilF — Chilesotti, O. *Francesco da Milano*, in SIM IV (1903), 382.

G — Chilesotti, O. *Trascrizioni da un Codice musicale di Vincenzo Galilei*, in *Atti del Congresso Internazionale di Scienze Storiche* VIII for 1903 (1905), 135.

GB — Chilesotti, O. *Di Giovanni Battista Besardo e del suo Thesaurus Harmonicus*, in an offprint from the *Gazetta musicale di Milano*, 1886.

J — Chilesotti, O. *Jacomo Gorzanis, Liutista del Cinquecento*, in RMI XXI (1914), 86.

L — Chilesotti, O. (ed.). *Da un codice Lauten-Buch del Cinquecento*, 1890.

LI — Chilesotti, O. *Note circa alcuni liutisti italiani della prima metà del Cinquecento*, in RMI IX (1902), 36, 233.

LS — Chilesotti, O. (ed.). *Lautenspieler des 16. Jahrhunderts*, 1891.

LV — Chilesotti, O. *Il primo Libro di liuto di Vincenzo Galilei*, in RMI XV (1908), 753.

N — Chilesotti, O. *Notes sur les tablatures de luth et de guitare*, in EC, *Partie I*, II, 636.

P — Chilesotti, O. *Il Pater noster di Adriano Willaert*, in SIM III (1902), 468.

S — Chilesotti, O. *Saggio sulla Melodia popolare del Cinquecento*, 1889.

SM — Chilesotti, O. *Savonarola musicista*, in RMI VI (1898), 792.

T — Chilesotti, O. *"Toujours bien" di Jo. Martini*, in RMI XXIII (1916), 66.

V — Chilesotti, O. *Villanella a 3 voci dal "Thesaurus harmonicus" di J. B. Besard (1603)*, in RieF (1909), 287.

ChorP — Choron, A. E. (ed.). *Principes de composition des Ecoles d'Italie*. 6 vols. (2nd ed.), 1816.

ChrysZ — Chrysander, F. *Lodovico Zacconi als Lehrer des Kunstgesangs*, in VfMW VII (1891), 337; IX (1893), 249; X (1894), 531.

ChybB — Chybiński, A. *Do biografji Wacława z Szamotuł (zm. 1572)*, in *Kwartalnik Muzyczny*, No. 12–13 (1931), 427.

D — Chybiński, A. *Die deutschen Musiktheoretiker im 16.–18. Jahrhundert und die polnische Musik*, in ZIM XIII (1911), 56.

JL — Chybiński, A. *Tabulatura organowa Jana z Lublina*, 1911–14.

K — Chybiński, A. *Die Musikbestände der Krakauer Bibliotheken von 1500–1650*, in SIM XIII (1912), 382.

M — Chybiński, A. *Z Dziejów muzyki polskiej do 1800 roku (Muzyka wielogłosowa)*, in *Muzyka Polska* (1927), 31.

P — Chybiński, A. *Polnische Musik und Musikkultur des 16. Jahrhunderts in ihren Beziehungen zu Deutschland*, in SIM XIII (1912), 463.

R — Chybiński, A. *Materjały do dziejów Królewskiej Kapeli Rorantystów*. I, 1910; II, 1925.

S — Chybiński, A. *Do biografji Sebastjana z Felsztyna*, in *Kwartalnik Muzyczny*, No. 14–15 (1932), 594.

T — Chybiński, A. *Teorja mensuralna w polskiej literaturze muzycznej pierwszej połowy XVI-go wieku*, 1911.

TP — Chybiński, A. *Trzy przyczynki do historji muzyki w Krakowie, w pierwszej połowie XVII wieku*, in *Prace filologiczne* XII (1927), 94.

U — Chybiński, A. *Über die polnische mehrstimmige Musik des XVI. Jahrhunderts*, in RieF (1909), 340.

W — Chybiński, A. *Bogurodzica pod względem historyczno-muzycznym*, 1907.

ClemensO — *Jacobus Clemens non Papa: Opera omnia*. Ed. by K. Ph. Bernet Kempers, 1951– .

ClementC — Clement, M. L. *The Approach to the Cadence in High Renaissance Music*. Master's thesis, University of California, Berkeley, 1943, unpublished.

ClercxB — Clercx, S. *Introduction à l'Histoire de la musique en Belgique*, in RB V (1951), 9, 114.

ClosB — Closson, E. *L'Origine de Gilles Binchois*, in RdM V (1924), 149.

BD — Closson, E. (ed.). *Le Ms. dit des Basses Danses de la Bibliothèque de Bourgogne*, 1912. Facsimile ed. with commentary.

D — Closson, E. *La Structure rythmique des basses danses du ms. 9085 de la Bibliothèque royale de Bruxelles*, in SIM XIV (1913), 567.

CMI — I Classici Musicali Italiani, 1941–

I — *M. A. Cavazzoni, J. Fogliano, J. Segni ed Anonimi: Composizioni per organo*. Ed. by G. Benvenuti, 1941.

V — *A. Gabrieli: Musiche di chiesa da cinque a sedici voci, 1587*. Ed. by G. d'Alessi, 1941.

CoatesP — Coates, H. *Palestrina*, 1938.

CocliC — Coclico, A. P. *Compendium musices*, 1552. Facs., ed. by M. F. Bukofzer (in *Documenta musicologica*), 1954.

CoelhoT   *P. Manuel Rodrigues Coelho: 5 Tentos, extraidos das "Flores de Musica para o instrumento de tecla e harpa," 1620.* Ed. by S. Kastner, 1936.

CohenA   Cohen, Albert. *The Vocal Polyphonic Style of Juan de Anchieta.* Master's thesis, New York University, 1953, unpublished.

ColE   Collet, H. *Contribution à l'étude des théoriciens espagnols de la musique au XVI*e *siècle,* in *L'Année musicale* II (1912), 1.

M   Collet, H. *Le Mysticisme musical espagnol au XVI*e *siècle,* 1913.

T   Collet, H. *Un Tratado de Canto de Organo (siglo XVI),* 1913.

V   Collet, H. *Victoria,* 1914.

ColeT   Cole, E. *In Search of Francis Tregian,* in M&L XXXIII (1952), 28.

CollB   Collins, H. B. *Byrd's Latin Church Music,* in M&L IV (1923), 254.

L   Collins, H. B. *Latin Church Music by Early English Composers,* in PMA XXXIX (1913), 55; XLIII (1917), 97.

M   Collins, H. B. (ed.). *Missa "O quam suavis,"* with introductions by H. B. Collins and Dom Anselm Hughes, 1927.

T   Collins, H. B. *John Taverner's Masses,* in M&L V (1924), 322; VI (1925), 314.

TT   Collins, H. B. *Thomas Tallis,* in M&L X (1929), 152.

ComesO   *Obras musicales de J. B. Comes. . . .* 2 vols. Ed. by J. B. Guzmán, 1888.

CommB   Commer, F. (ed.). *Collectio operum musicorum Batavorum saeculi XVI.,* 12 vols., 1844–58.

M   Commer, F. (ed.). *Musica sacra.* 28 vols., 1839–87. (*See also* BockM)

CompèreO   *Loyset Compère: Opera omnia.* Ed. by L. Finscher, 1958– .

ComteR   Comte, C. and P. Laumonier. *Ronsard et les musiciens du XVI*e *siècle,* in *Revue d'histoire littéraire de la France* VII (1900), 341.

ConfB   *Giovanni Luca Conforto: Breve et facile maniera d'essercitarsi a far passaggi, 1593 (1603?).* Facsimile ed. with German transl. by J. Wolf, 1922.

CoopI   Cooper, G. M. *Italian Instrumental Music of the 16th Century,* in PMA LVI (1929), 55.

CopM   *The Manner to Dance Bace Dances* [translation, printed 1521, from an unspecified French source]. Reprint, 1937.

CoperarioR   Coperario, G. *Rules How to Compose.* Facsimile ed. with commentary by M. Bukofzer, 1952.

CordD   Cordero di Pamparato, S. *Guglielmo Dufay alla Corte di Savoia,* in *Santa Cecilia* XVII (1925), 19, 34.

CornazL   *Il libro dell'Arte del Danzare di Antonio Cornazano.* Ed. by C. Mazzi, in *La Bibliofilia* XVII (1916), 1.

CortP   Cortés, N. A. *Diego Pisador, Algunos datos biográficos,* in *Boletin de la Biblioteca Menéndez y Pelayo* III (1921), 331.

CorteA   Corte, A. della. *Antologia della Storia della Musica,* 4th ed., 1945.

S   Corte, A. della and G. Pannain. *Storia della Musica.* 2 vols., 1936. 2nd ed. in 3 vols., 1942 (reprinted 1944). References are to the 2nd ed.

CosterA   Coster, A. *Juan de Anchieta et la famille de Loyola,* in *Revue hispanique* LXXIX (1930), 1.

CouG   Coussemaker, C. E. H. de. *Chansons religieuses de Théodoric de Gruter, Moine de Doesburg au XV*e *siècle,* in *Dietsche Warande* III, *Partie française* [Part 2], (1857), 29.

H   Coussemaker, C. E. H. de. *Histoire de l'Harmonie au moyen-âge,* 1852.

N   Coussemaker, C. E. H. de. *Notice sur les collections musicales de la Bibliothèque de Cambrai . . . ,* 1843.

S   Coussemaker, C. E. H. de (ed.). *Scriptorum de Musica medii aevi nova series.* 4 vols., 1864–76; facsimile ed., 1931.

T   Coussemaker, C. E. H. de (ed.). *Joannis Tinctoris Tractatus de Musica,* 1875.

CowM   Cowling, G. H. *Music of the Shakespearean Stage.* 1913.

CP   *Capolavori polifonici del secolo XVI.* Ed. by B. Somma, 1939– .

I   Adriano Banchieri: *Festino nella sera del Giovedì grasso avanti Cena,* 1939.

II   Orazio Vecchi: *Le Veglie di Siena,* 1940.

III   Giovanni Croce: *Triaca musicale,* 1942.

IV   Alessandro Striggio: *Il cicalamento delle donne al bucato,* 1947.

CPC   *Collection de Polyphonie classique.* Ed. by J. Delporte.

CPM   *Choice of Polish Music,* 1944 [?].

CreAC   Crevel, M. van. *Adrianus Petit Coclico, Leben und Beziehungen eines nach Deutschland emigrierten Josquinschülers,* 1940.

C   Crevel, M. van. *Het sterfjaar van Clemens non Papa,* in TVNM XVI (1942), 177.

CreS   Crevel, M. van. *Secret Chromatic Art in the Netherlands Motet?*, in TVNM XVI (1946), 253.

V   Crevel, M. van. *Verwante Sequensmodulaties bij Obrecht, Josquin en Coclico*, in TVNM XVI (1941), 107.

CrockerC   Crocker, E. C. *An Introductory Study of the Italian Canzona for Instrumental Ensembles*. Ph.D. dissertation, Radcliffe College, 1943, Cambridge, Mass., unpublished.

CrollW   Croll, G. *Gaspar van Weerbeke, An Outline of his Life and Works*, in MD VI (1952), 67.

CsánM   Csánky, D. *Mátyás udvara*, in *Századok*, XVII (1883), 515, 617, 750.

CuttsR   Cutts, J. P. *A Reconsideration of the* Willow Song, in JAMS X (1957), 14.

CuylerCC   Cuyler, L. E. *The Choralis Constantinus Book III (1555)* Ph.D. dissertation. Eastman School of Music, Rochester, N.Y., 1948; text section unpublished (music section = IsaacC).

S   Cuyler, L. *The Sequences of Isaac's Choralis Constantinus*, in JAMS III (1950), 3.

CW   *Das Chorwerk*. Small vols. of music, under general editorship of F. Blume. 1929– .

I   *Josquin des Prés: Missa Pange lingua*. Ed. by F. Blume, 1929.

II   *Jacobus Vaet: Sechs Motetten*. Ed. by E. H. Meyer, 1929.

III   *Josquin des Prés und andere Meister [Compère, Pipelare, Pierre de la Rue]*. Ed. by F. Blume, 1930.

IV   *Johannes Ockeghem: Missa Mi-Mi*. Ed. by H. Besseler, 1930.

V   *Adrian Willaert und andere Meister [Arcadelt, Verdelot, Rore], Italienische Madrigale*. Ed. by W. Wiora, 1930.

VI   *Thomas Stoltzer: Der 37. Psalm, "Erzürne dich nicht."* Ed. by O. Gombosi, 1930.

VII   *Heinrich Isaac: Missa Carminum*. Ed. by R. Heyden, 1930.

VIII   *Adrian Willaert und andere Meister [Lasso, Castellino, Nola, Cimello, Perissone, Corneti], Volkstümliche italienische Lieder*. Ed. by E. Hertzmann, 1930.

IX   *Heinrich Finck: Acht Hymnen*. Ed. by R. Gerber, 1931.

X   *Giovanni Gabrieli: Drei Motetten*. Ed. by H. Besseler, 1931.

XI   *Pierre de la Rue: Requiem und eine Motette*. Ed. by F. Blume, 1931.

XIII   *Orlando Lasso: Madrigale und Chansons*. Ed. by H. Besseler, 1931.

XIV   *Lasso, Hassler, Schein, Sweelinck, Hieronymus Praetorius: Sieben chromatische Motetten*. Ed. by F. Blume, 1931.

XV   *Johannes Lupi: Zehn weltliche Lieder*. Ed. by H. Albrecht, 1932.

XVIII   *Josquin des Prés: Vier Motetten*. Ed. by F. Blume, 1932.

XIX   *Guillaume Dufay: Zwölf geistliche und weltliche Werke*. Ed. by H. Besseler, 1932.

XX   *Josquin des Prés: Missa Da pacem*. Ed. by F. Blume, 1932.

XXI   *Heinrich Finck: Missa In summis*. Ed. by K. Hasse, 1933.

XXII   *Gilles Binchois: Sechzehn weltliche Lieder zu 3 Stimmen*. Ed. by W. Gurlitt, 1933.

XXIII   *Josquin des Prés: Drei Evangelien-Motetten*. Ed. by F. Blume, 1933.

XXIV   *Melchior Franck: Fünf Hohelied-Motetten*. Ed. by A. A. Abert, 1933.

XXVIII   *Gallus Dressler: Fünf Motetten*. Ed. by M. Ruëtz, 1934.

XXIX   *Peter Schöffer: Fünfzehn deutsche Lieder*. Ed. by K. Hasse, 1934.

XXX   *Josquin et al: Acht Lied- und Choralmotetten*. Ed. by H. Osthoff, 1934.

XXXI   *Aulen: Missa*. Ed. by H. Birtner, 1934.

XXXII   *[Von Fulda, Finck, Florigal, Hartzer, Kungsperger:] Zwölf Hymnen*. Ed. by R. Gerber, 1935.

XXXIII   *Josquin des Prés: Drei Psalmen*. Ed. by F. Blume, 1935.

XXXIV   *Orlando Lasso: Busstränen des Heiligen Petrus*, Part I. Ed. by J. Therstappen, 1935.

XXXV   *Nordische Schüler Giovanni Gabrielis: Johann Grabbe, Mogens Pedersön, Hans Nielsen. . . .* Ed. by R. Gerber, 1935.

XXXVII & XLI   *Orlando Lasso: Busstränen des Heiligen Petrus*, Parts II and III. Ed. by J. Therstappen, 1935, 1936.

XLII   *Josquin des Prés: Missa de Beata Virgine*. Ed. by F. Blume, 1936.

XLIII   *[H. Isaac, M. Pesenti, L. Compère, J. B. Zesso, P. Scotus, Jac. Fo., J. D. da Nola, G. da Nola:] Karnevalslieder der Renaissance*. Ed. by K. Westphal, 1936.

XLIV   *Johannes Hähnel (Galliculus): Ostermesse*. Ed. by F. Blume and W. Schulze, 1937.

CW XLV   [*Magister Alanus, Egidius de Rhenis, Pyllois, Egolfus Koler:*] *Deutsche Lieder aus fremden Quellen.* Ed. by H. Funck, 1937.

XLVI   *Johannes Martini: Drei geistliche Gesänge.* Ed. by R. Gerber, 1937.

XLVII   *Balthasar Harzer (Resinarius): Summa Passionis secundum Johannem.* Ed. by F. Blume and W. Schulze, 1937.

XLVIII   *Orlando Lasso: Prophetiae Sibyllarum.* Ed. by H. J. Therstappen, 1937.

XLIX   *Guillaume Dufay: Sämtliche Hymnen.* Ed. by R. Gerber, 1937.

LI   *Lambert de Sayve und Michael Praetorius: Teutsche Liedlein.* Ed. by F. Blume, 1938.

DaA   David, H. T. (ed.). *The Art of Polyphonic Song,* 1940.

F   David, H. T. (ed.). *French Chansons of the Sixteenth Century for Two High Voices,* 1944.

T   David, H. T. *Themes from Words and Names,* in *A Birthday Offering to Carl Engel* (ed. by G. Reese [1943], 67).

DahnkM   Dahnk, E. *Musikausübung an den Höfen von Burgund und Orléans während des 15. Jahrhunderts,* in *Archiv für Kulturgeschichte* XXV (1934), 184.

DanisP   Daniskas, J. *Een bijdrage tot de geschiedenis der parodie-techniek,* in TVNM XVII (1948), 21.

DannS   Dannemann, E. *Die spätgotische Musiktradition in Frankreich und Burgund vor dem Auftreten Dufays,* 1936.

DartC   Dart, T. *The Cittern and its English Music,* in *The Galpin Society Journal,* No. 1 (1948), 46.

CL   Dart, T. *Morley's Consort Lessons of 1599,* in PMA LXXIV (1947), 1.

M   Dart, T. *Simone Molinaro's Lute-Book of 1599,* in M&L XXVIII (1947), 258.

DaveyA   Davey, H. *Die ältesten Musikhandschriften auf englischen Bibliotheken,* in MfMG XXXIV (1902), 30, 47, 63, 79, 93, 124, 144.

H   Davey, H. *History of English Music,* 1895. 2nd ed., 1921. References in this book are to the 2nd ed.

DDT   *Denkmäler deutscher Tonkunst.* Erste Folge, 65 vols. Ed. under direction of R. von Liliencron, H. Kretzschmar, H. Abert, and A. Schering, 1892–1931. (*See also* DTB.)

II   *Hans Leo Hassler: Werke I, Cantiones sacrae* for 4 to 12 voices. Ed. by H. Gehrmann, 1894.

VII   *Hans Leo Hassler: Werke II, Messen.* Ed. by J. Auer, 1902.

XVI   *Melchior Franck und Valentin Haussmann: Ausgewählte Instrumentalwerke.* Ed. By Franz Bölsche, 1904.

XXIII   *Hieronymus Praetorius: Ausgewählte Werke.* Ed. by H. Leichtentritt, 1905.

XXIV & XXV   *Hans Leo Hassler: Werke III, Sacri concentus* for 4 to 12 voices. Ed. by J. Auer, 1906.

XXXI   *Philippus Dulichius: Prima pars Centuriae. Octonum et Septenum vocum (1607).* Ed. by R. Schwartz, 1907.

XXXIV   *Newe deudsche geistliche Gesenge für die gemeinen Schulen (Rhau, 1544).* Ed. by J. Wolf, 1908.

XLI   *Philippus Dulichius: Secunda pars Centuriae. Octonum et Septenum vocum (1608).* Ed. by R. Schwartz, 1911.

LXV   *Thomas Stoltzer: Sämtliche lateinische Hymnen und Psalmen.* Ed. by H. Albrecht and O. Gombosi, 1931.

DeffÜ   Deffner, O. *Über die Entwicklung der Fantasie für Tasteninstrumente,* 1927.

DehnC   Dehn, S. W. *Compositionen des XVI. Jahrhunderts zu weltlichen Texten,* in *Caecilia, eine Zeitschrift für die musikalische Welt,* XXV (1846), 29.

S   Dehn, S. W. (ed.). *Sammlung älterer Musik aus dem 16. und 17. Jahrhundert.* Lieferungen 1–12, 1837.

DelétP   *Aulcuns pseaulmes et cantiques mys en chant, 1539.* Facsimile ed. with supplementary comment by D. Delétra, 1919.

DelpA   Delporte, J. *L'École polyphonique franco-flamande: Alexandre Agricola,* in *Revue liturgique et musicale* XV (1932), 102.

C   Delporte, J. *L'École polyphonique franco-flamande: Loyset Compère (14.– 1518),* in *Revue liturgique et musicale* XVI (1932), 19.

F   Delporte, J. *L'École polyphonique franco-flamande: Antoine de Févin,* in *Revue liturgique et musicale* XVIII (1934), 27, 42; (1935), 54; Addendum, 75.

M   Delporte, J. *L'École polyphonique franco-flamande: Jean Mouton,* in *Revue liturgique et musicale* XVI (1932), 72; (1933), 109, 144; XXI (periodical renamed *Musique et liturgie,* 1937), 7.

DentA   Dent, E. J. *Notes on the "Amfiparnaso" of Orazio Vecchi,* SIM XII (1911), 330.

DentB   Dent, E. J. *William Byrd and the Madrigal*, in *Festschrift für Johannes Wolf* (1929), 24.

L   Dent, E. J. *The Laudi Spirituali in the XVIth and XVIIth Centuries*, in PMA XLIII (1917), 63.

DèzB   Dèzes, K. *Van den Borrens "Dufay,"* in ZfMW IX (1927), 294.

E   Dèzes, K. *Der Mensuralcodex des Benediktinerklosters Sancti Emmerami zu Regensburg*, in ZfMW X (1927), 65.

M   Dèzes, K. (ed.). *Messen- und Motettensätze des 15. Jahrhunderts*, I, 1927.

S   Dèzes, K. *Das Dufay zugeschriebene Salve Regina, eine deutsche Komposition*, in ZfMW X (1928), 327.

DieL   Dieckmann, J. *Die in deutscher Lautentabulatur überlieferten Tänze des 16. Jahrhunderts*, 1931.

DietG   Dietrich, F. *Geschichte des deutschen Orgelchorals im 17. Jahrhundert*, 1932.

DisK   Dischner, O. (ed.). *Kammermusik des Mittelalters. Chansons der 1. u. 2. niederländischen Schule für drei bis vier Streichinstrumente herausgegeben*, 1927.

DiseC   Disertori, B. *Campane in un Mottetto del Quattrocento*, in RMI XLIV (1940), 106.

G   Disertori, B. *Un libro italiano su Carlo Gesualdo*, in RMI XLV (1941), 20.

J   Disertori, B. *Il Manoscritto 1947–4 di Trento e la Canzone "i' ay prins amours,"* in RMI XLVIII (1946), 1.

L   Disertori, B. *La leutista di Brera o del sonare a libro*, in RMI XLIII (1939), 640.

M   Disertori, B. *Le Canzoni strumentali da sonar a quattro di Claudio Merulo*, in RMI XLVII (1943), 305.

P   Disertori, B. *L'Epistola all'Italia del Petrarca musicata nei Codici Tridentini*, in RMI XLVI (1942), 65.

V   Disertori, B. *Un Incunabolo di assolo per il Violone*, in RMI XLVI (1942), 455.

DoA   Dodge, J. *Les Airs de cour d'Adrien Le Roy*, in *Revue musicale S.I.M.* III (1907), 1132.

L   Dodge, J. *Lute music of the XVIth and XVIIth centuries*, in PMA XXXIV (1908), 123.

DoflS   Doflein, E. (ed.). *Spielmusik für Violine: Alte Musik*. Heft II, 1932.

DohrnI   Dohrn, E. *Marc'Antonio Ingegneri als Madrigalkomponist*, 1936.

DolS   Dolmetsch, A. (ed.). *Select English Songs & Dialogues of the 16th and 17th Centuries*, 1898.

DonIN   Donington, R. and T. Dart. *The Origin of the In Nomine*, in M&L XXX (1949), 101.

DoorB   Van Doorslaer, G. *Noël Baudoin, maître de chapelle-compositeur*, in *De Gulden Passer (Le Compas d'or)*, n.s. VIII (1930), 167.

C   Van Doorslaer, G. *La Chapelle musicale de l'empereur Rudolphe II en 1594, sous la direction de Philippe de Monte*, in Acta V (1933), 148.

CL   Van Doorslaer, G. *Nicolas et Jacques Champion, dits Liégeois*, in *Mechlinia* VIII (1930), 4.

CM   Van Doorslaer, G. *Aperçu sur la pratique du chant à Malines au XVe siècle*, in *Annales du Congrès d'Archéologie de Belgique en Anvers en 1930*, 465.

D   Van Doorslaer, G. *Antonius Divitis, maître de chapelle-compositeur, 1475?–1526?*, in TVNM XIII (1929), 1.

E   Van Doorslaer, G. *Ludovicus Episcopus: Kapelmeester-Componist (1522–1595)*, in *De Muziek* III (1929), 337.

H   Van Doorslaer, G. *Georges de la Hèle, maître de chapelle-compositeur, 1547–1587*, in *Bulletin de l'Académie royale d'archéologie de Belgique* (1924), 108.

HB   Van Doorslaer, G. *Herry Bredemers, organiste et maître de musique, 1472–1522*, in *Annales de l'Académie royale d'archéologie de Belgique* LXVI (Ser. 6, VI; 1914), 209.

J   Van Doorslaer, G. *Jean Lestainnier, organiste-compositeur, 1520(?)–1551*, in *Mechlinia* for 1921.

L   Van Doorslaer, G. *Ludovicus Episcopus, maître de chapelle-compositeur 1520?–1595*, in *Bulletin du Cercle royal archéologique, littéraire et artistique de Malines* XXXVI (1935).

M   Van Doorslaer, G. *La Chapelle musicale de Philippe le Beau*, in *Revue belge d'archéologie et d'histoire de l'art* IV (1934), 21, 139.

MR   Van Doorslaer, G. *Die Musikkapelle Kaiser Rudolphs II. i. J. 1582, unter der Leitung von Ph. de Monte*, in ZfMW XIII (1931), 481.

P   Van Doorslaer, G. *Jacobus Peetrinus, compositeur malinois*, in *Bulletin du Cercle royal archéologique, littéraire et artistique de Malines* XXVII (1922), 23.

DoorPM   Van Doorslaer, G. *La Vie et les oeuvres de Philippe de Monte*, 1921.

R   Van Doorslaer, G. *Jean Richafort, maître de chapelle-compositeur 1480?–†1548*, in *Bulletin de l'Académie royale d'archéologie de Belgique, 1929* (1930), 103.

RM   Van Doorslaer, G. *René de Mel*, in *Annales de l'Académie royale d'archéologie de Belgique* LXIX (1921), 221.

SC   Van Doorslaer, G. *Séverin Cornet, compositeur, maître de chapelle, 1530–†1582*, in *De Gulden Passer (Le Compas d'or)*, n.s. III (1925), 163.

T   Van Doorslaer, G. *Jean van Turnhout, compositeur-maître de chapelle à Malines et à Bruxelles (1545? †après 1618)*, in *Musica Sacra* (Malines) (1935), 218.

DorezM   Dorez, L. *Francesco da Milano et la musique du Pape Paul III*, in RM XI (1930), 104. (Also in Dorez's *La Cour du Pape Paul III* I [1932], 221.)

DouM   Douen, O. *Clément Marot et le Psautier huguenot*. 2 vols., 1878–79.

DowlL   *John Dowland: Lachrymae, or Seven Tears, figured in Seven Passionate Pavans (1605)*. Ed. by P. Warlock, 1927.

LM   *The Lute Music of John Dowland*. Transcr. and ed. for piano by P. Warlock, 1927.

DowlgP   Dowling, M. *The Printing of John Dowland's "Second Booke of Songs or Ayres,"* in *The Library*, Ser. 4, XII (1932), 365.

DPLSER   *Documenta polyphoniae liturgicae Sanctae Ecclesiae Romanae.* (Ser. I. *Ordinarium missae;* II. *Proprium missae;* III. *Divinum officium;* IV. *Motecta*). Ed. by L. Feininger, 1947– .

Ser. I
No. 1   G. Dufay: *Fragmentum Missae*, 1947.
2   L. Power: *Missa super Alma Redemptoris Mater*, 1947.
3   G. Dufay: *Et in terra "ad modum tube,"* 1948.
4   G. Dufay: *Missa de Sanctissima Trinitate*, 1949.
5   G. Binchois: *Missa de Angelis*, 1949.
7   G. Dufay: *2 Kyrie et 1 Gloria in Dominicis diebus*, 1949.
10   G. Dufay: *Et in terra de Quaremiaux*, 1951.
Ser. I B
No. 1   P. de la Rue: *Missa Ave Sanctissima*, 1950.

DrinM   Drinker, S. *Music and Women*, 1948.

DrozB   Droz, E. *Guillaume Boni de Saint-Flour en Auvergne, musicien de Ronsard*, in *Mélanges offerts à M. Abel Lefranc* (1936), 270.

C   Droz, E. *Les Chansons de Nicolas de la Grotte*, in RdM VII (1927), 133.

M   Droz, E. *Musiciens liégeois du XVe siècle*, in RdM X (1929), 284.

N   Droz, E. *Notes sur Me Jean Cornuel, dit Verjus, petit vicaire de Cambrai*, in RdM VII (1926), 173.

P   Droz, E. and G. Thibault (eds.). *Poètes et musiciens du XVe siècle*, 1924.

T   Droz, E., G. Thibault, and Y. Rokseth (eds.). *Trois Chansonniers français du XVe siècle*, 1927.

U   Droz, E. and G. Thibault. *Un Chansonnier de Philippe le Bon*, in RdM VII (1926), 1.

DTB   *Denkmäler deutscher Tonkunst.* Zweite Folge (*Denkmäler der Tonkunst in Bayern*). 36 vols. Ed. under direction of A. Sandberger, 1900–31.

V1   Bd. 8. *Hans Leo Hasslers Werke*, 2. Teil, Lief. 1. Biography and music history of Nuremberg and Augsburg in 16th century and early 17th by A. Sandberger, 1904.

V2   Bd. 9. *Hans Leo Hasslers Werke*, 2. Teil, Lief. 2. *Canzonette (1590) und Neue Teutsche Gesang (1596)*. Ed. by R. Schwartz, 1904.

X1   Bd. 18. *Gregor Aichinger: Ausgewählte Werke I*. Ed. by T. Kroyer, 1909.

X2   Bd. 19. *Adam Gumpelzhaimer: Ausgewählte Werke*. Ed. by O. Mayr, 1909.

XI1   Bd. 20. *Hans Leo Hassler, Werke III*. Ed. by R. Schwartz, 1910.

XXVI   Bd. 34. *Jacobus de Kerle: Preces speciales . . . (1562)*. Ed. by O. Ursprung, 1926.

XXIX–XXX   Bd. 36. *Andreas Raselius: Cantiones sacrae*. Ed. by L. Roselius, 1931.

DTO   *Denkmäler der Tonkunst in Österreich.* Editor-in-chief, Guido Adler, 1894.

V1   Bd. 10. *Heinrich Isaac: Choralis Constantinus liber 1, 1550*. Ed. by E. Bezecny and W. Rabl, 1898.

VI1   Bd. 12. *Jakob Handl (Gallus): Opus musicum, I. Teil*. Ed. by E. Bezecny and J. Mantuani, 1899.

DTO VII   Bd. 14 & 15. *Sechs Trienter Codices. Erste Auswahl.* Ed. by G. Adler and O. Koller, 1900.

XI¹   Bd. 22. *Sechs Trienter Codices. Zweite Auswahl.* Ed. by G. Adler and O. Koller, 1904.

XII¹   Bd. 24. *Jakob Handl (Gallus): Opus musicum, II. Teil.* Ed. by E. Bezecny and J. Mantuani, 1905.

XIV¹   Bd. 28. *Heinrich Isaac: Weltliche Werke.* Ed. by J. Wolf, 1907.

XV¹   Bd. 30. *Jakob Handl (Gallus): Opus musicum, III. Teil.* Ed. by E. Bezecny and J. Mantuani, 1908.

XVI¹   Bd. 32. *Heinrich Isaac: Choralis Constantinus liber II.* Ed. by A. von Webern; also Supplement to XIV¹: *Weltliche Werke.* Ed. by J. Wolf, 1909.

XVIII²   Bd. 37. *Österreichische Lautenmusik im 16. Jahrhundert.* Ed. by A. Koczirz, 1911.

XIX¹   Bd. 38. *Sechs Trienter Codices. Dritte Auswahl.* Ed. by O. Koller and others, 1912.

XX¹   Bd. 40. *Jakob Handl (Gallus): Opus musicum, IV. Teil.* Ed. by E. Bezecny and J. Mantuani, 1913.

XXIV   Bd. 48. *Jakob Handl (Gallus): Opus musicum, V. Teil.* Ed. by E. Bezecny and J. Mantuani, 1917.

XXVI   Bd. 51 & 52. *Jakob Handl (Gallus): Opus musicum, VI. Teil.* Ed. by E. Bezecny and J. Mantuani, 1919.

XXVII¹   Bd. 53. *Sechs Trienter Codices. Vierte Auswahl.* Ed. by R. Ficker and A. Orel, 1920.

XXXI   Bd. 61. *Sieben Trienter Codices. Fünfte Auswahl.* Ed. by R. Ficker, 1924.

XXXVII²   Bd. 72. *Das deutsche Gesellschaftslied in Österreich 1480–1550.* Ed. by L. Nowak, A. Koczirz, and A. Pfalz, 1930.

XXXVIII¹   Bd. 73. *Blasius Amon: Kirchenwerke I.* Ed. by P. C. Huigens, 1931.

XL   Bd. 76. *Sieben Trienter Codices. Sechste Auswahl.* Ed. by R. Ficker, 1933.

XLI   Bd. 77. *Italienische Musiker und das Kaiserhaus, 1567–1625.* Ed. by A. Einstein, 1934.

XLII¹   Bd. 78. *Jakob Handl (Gallus): Sechs Messen.* Ed. by P. Pisk, 1935.

DuZ   Dunicz, J. J. *Do biografji Mikołaja Zieleńskiego,* in *Polski Rocznik Muzykologiczny* II (1936), 95.

DufayO   *Guglielmi Dufay: Opera omnia.* 6 vols. Vols. 1–4, in original numbering, ed. by G. de Van. These subsequently renumbered, 1 and 2 forming I, 3 and 4 forming II. In our footnote references, the 4 divisions become I¹, I², II¹, and II². Vols. III–VI being ed. by H. Besseler. 1948– .

DufoD   Dufourcq, N. *Documents inédits relatifs à l'orgue français (XIVᵉ–XVIIIᵉ siècles).* 2 vols., 1934–35.

DC   Dufourcq, N. *A propos d'Eustache du Caurroy,* in RdM XXIX (1950), 94.

E   Dufourcq, N. *Esquisse d'une histoire de l'orgue en France du XIIIᵉ au XVIIIᵉ siècle,* 1935.

DuyL   Van Duyse, F. (ed.). *Het oude nederlandsche lied.* 4 vols., 1903–08.

NL   Van Duyse, F. (ed.). *Oude nederlandsche liederen: melodieen uit de Souterliedekens,* 1889.

EB   *Encyclopaedia Britannica,* 14th ed., 1929.

EberM   Eberth, F. *Die Minne- und Meistergesangweisen der Kolmarer Liederhandschrift,* 1935.

EC   *Encyclopédie de la musique et Dictionnaire du Conservatoire.* Ed. by A. Lavignac and L. de la Laurencie, 1913–31. *Partie I: Histoire de la musique* appears in 5 vols.; *Partie II: Technique, pédagogie et esthétique,* in 6 vols.; *Partie III: Dictionnaire alphabétique* has not appeared, but a partial index has been compiled by R. Bruce for the Music Library Association, 1936.

EccG   *Johannes Eccard: Geistliche Lieder auf den Choral . . . ,* 2 vols. Ed. by G. W. Teschner, n.d.

GL   *Johannes Eccard: Geistliche Lieder auf den Choral . . . ,* Part I. Ed. by F. von Baussnern, 1928.

P   *Johannes Eccard: Preussische Festlieder.* Ed. by G. W. Teschner, 1858.

EckB   Eckhardt, S. *Balassi Bálint irodalmi mintái,* in *Irodalomtörténeti Közlemények,* XXIII (1913), 171.

EDMR   *Das Erbe deutscher Musik. Reichsdenkmale.* 1935– .

IV   *Das Glogauer Liederbuch,* Erster Teil: *Deutsche Lieder und Spielstücke.* Ed. by H. Ringmann and J. Klapper, 1936.

EDMR V	*Ludwig Senfl: Sämtliche Werke,* Bd. I: *Sieben Messen zu vier bis sechs Stimmen.* Ed. by E. Löhrer and O. Ursprung, 1937.
VIII	*Das Glogauer Liederbuch,* Zweiter Teil: *Ausgewählte lateinische Sätze.* Ed. by H. Ringmann and J. Klapper, 1937.
X	*Ludwig Senfl: Sämtliche Werke,* Bd. II: *Deutsche Lieder, Erster Teil.* Ed. by A. Geering and W. Altwegg, 1938.
XIII	*Ludwig Senfl: Motetten, Erster Teil.* Ed. by W. Gerstenberg, 1939.
XV	*Ludwig Senfl: Deutsche Lieder, Zweiter Teil.* Ed. by A. Geering and W. Altwigg, 1939.
XVI	*Caspar Othmayr: Ausgewählte Werke,* Teil 1: *Symbola.* Ed. by H. Albrecht, 1941.
XX	*Georg Forster: Frische teutsche Liedlein (1539–1556),* Teil 1. Ed. by K. Gudewill and W. Heiske, 1942.
XXII	*Thomas Stoltzer: Ausgewählte Werke.* Ed. by H. Albrecht, 1942.
XXIII	*Sixt Dietrich: Ausgewählte Werke,* Teil 1: *Hymnen (1545),* Erste Abteilung. Ed. by H. Zenck, 1942.
XXXVII–VIII	*Das Buxheimer Orgelbuch,* ed. by B. A. Wallner, 1958.
XLII	*Adrian Petit Coclico: Consolationes piae, Musica reservata (1552).* Ed. by M. Ruhnke, 1958.
EEH	*Early English Harmony.* Vol. I (facsimiles, selected and with short notes by H. E. Wooldridge), 1897; Vol. II (transcriptions, with notes, by H. V. Hughes), 1913.
EhmA	Ehmann, W. *Adam von Fulda,* 1936.
M	Ehmann, W. *Das Musizierbild der deutschen Kantorei im 16. Jahrhundert,* in *Musik und Bild. Festschrift Max Seiffert* (1938), 69.
EhrS	Ehrmann, R. *Die Schlüsselkombinationen im 15. und 16. Jahrhundert,* in SzMW XI (1924), 59.
EIF	*Exposition internationale: La Musique dans la vie des nations, Francfort-sur-le-Mein, Juin-Août 1927: Catalogue de la Section française,* 1927.
EIM	*English Instrumental Music of the 16th and 17th Centuries from MSS in the New York Public Library.* 1st ed., 1937–42; 2nd ed., 1947–
II-1st ed.	*Four In Nomines in five parts.* Ed. by H. T. David, 1937.
II-2nd ed.	*Nine Fantasias in four parts. . . .* Ed. by S. Beck, 1947.
VII-1st ed	*Four Suites in 3 parts with organ by John Coperario.* Ed. by S. Beck, 1942.
EinA	Einstein, A. *Augenmusik im Madrigal,* in ZIM XIV (1912), 8.
AA	Einstein, A. *Ancora sull' 'Aria di Ruggiero'* in RMI XLI (1937), 163.
AAC	Einstein, A. *Andrea Antico's "Canzoni Nove" of 1510,* in MQ XXXVII (1951), 330.
AD	Einstein, A. *The 'Dialogo della Musica' of Messer Antonio Francesco Doni,* in M&L XV (1934), 244.
AR	Einstein, A. *Die Aria di Ruggiero,* in SIM XIII (1912), 444.
B	*Bibliography of Italian Secular Vocal Music printed between the years 1500–1700, by Emil Vogel,* revised and enlarged by A. Einstein, in *Notes* II (1945), 185, 275; III (1945), 51, (1946), 154, 256, 363; IV (1946), 41, (1947), 201, 301; V (1947), 65, (1948), 277, 385, 537.
C	Einstein, A. *Claudio Merulo's Ausgabe der Madrigale des Verdelot,* in SIM VIII (1907), 220, 516.
CC	Einstein, A. *Eine Caccia im Cinquecento,* in *Festschrift [für]. . . Rochus Freiherrn von Liliencron* (1910), 72.
D	Einstein, A. *Das Madrigal zum Doppelgebrauch,* in Acta VI (1934), 110.
DM	Einstein, A. *Dante, on the Way to the Madrigal,* in MQ XXV (1939), 142, 507.
EM	Einstein, A. *The Elizabethan Madrigal and Musica Transalpina,* in M&L XXV (1944), 66.
F	Einstein, A. *Das Elfte Buch der Frottole,* in ZfMW X (1928), 613.
GA	Einstein, A. (ed.). *The Golden Age of the Madrigal,* 1942.
GG	Einstein, A. *The Greghescha and the Giustiniana of the Sixteenth Century,* in JRB I (1946), 19.
H	Einstein, A. *Werke Hans Leo Hassler's (1564–1612),* in ZIM XII (1911), 309.
I	Einstein, A. *Italian Madrigal Verse,* in PMA LXIII (1937), 79.
IK	Einstein, A. *Italienische Musik und italienische Musiker am Kaiserhof . . . ,* in SzMW XXI (1934), 3.
IM	Einstein, A. *The Italian Madrigal.* 3 vols., 1949.
L	Einstein, A. *La prima "Lettera Amorosa" in Musica,* in *La Rassegna Musicale* X (1937), 45.

EinMD	Einstein, A. *Dante im Madrigal*, in AfMW III (1921), 405.
N	Einstein, A. *Narrative Rhythm in the Madrigal*, in MQ XXIX (1943), 475.
OV	Einstein, A. *Un Libro di Canzoni spirituali di Orfeo Vecchi*, in *La Bibliofilia* XL (1938), 38.
P	Einstein, A. *Annibale Padoanos Madrigalbuch*, in AdlerF (1930), 121.
PM	Einstein, A. *Filippo di Monte als Madrigalkomponist*, in *International Society for Musical Research, First Congress, Liége, September 1–6, 1930, Report*, 102.
SH	Einstein, A. *A Short History of Music*, 2nd ed., 1938.
SP	Einstein, A. *Un Sonetto del Petrarca nella Musica del Cinquecento*, in *La Rassegna Musicale* IX (1936), 81.
U	Einstein, A. *Ein unbekanntes Madrigal Palestrinas*, in ZfMW VII (1925), 530.
V	Einstein, A. *Die Parodie in der Villanella*, in ZfMW II (1920), 212.
VG	Einstein, A. *Vincenzo Galilei and the Instructive Duo*, in M&L XVIII (1937), 360.
VK	Einstein, A. *Anfänge des Vokalkonzerts*, in Acta III (1931), 8.
VR	Einstein, A. *Vincenzo Ruffo's Opera nova di musica*, in JAMS III (1950), 233.
W	Einstein, A. *Die mehrstimmige weltliche Musik von 1450–1600*, in AdlerH I, 358.
Z	Einstein, A. *Zur deutschen Literatur für Viola da Gamba im 16. und 17. Jahrhundert*, 1905.
EisZ	Eisenring, G. *Zur Geschichte des mehrstimmigen Proprium Missae bis um 1560*, 1913.
EitA	Eitner, R. *Jacob Arcadelt*, in MfMG XIX (1887), 122, 129, 137, 153.
AW	Eitner, R. *Adrian Willaert*, in MfMG XIX (1887), 81, 97, 113.
B	Eitner, R. (ed.). *Das Buxheimer Orgelbuch*, in MfMG XIX (1887), Supp. 2, 1, and XX (1888), Supp. 2, 41.
C	Eitner, R. *Cipriano de Rore*, in MfMG XXI (1889), 41, 57, 73.
D	Eitner, R. (ed.). *Das deutsche Lied des XV. und XVI. Jahrhunderts*. 2 vols., 1876–80. Also publ. in instalments: Vol. I in MfMG VIII (1876), Supp., 1; IX (1877), Supp., 73; X (1878), Supp., 145. Vol. II in MfMG XII (1880), Supp., 1; XIII (1881), Supp., 93; XIV (1882), Supp., 167; XV (1883), Supp., 243.
F	Eitner, R. and R. Schlecht. *Hermann Finck über die Kunst des Singens, 1556*, in MfMG XI (1879), 129, 135, 151.
HL	Eitner, R. *Chronologisches Verzeichniss der gedruckten Werke von H. L. von Hassler und Orlandus Lassus*, in MfMG, Supps. to V and VI (1874).
J	Eitner, R. *Jachet da Mantua und Jachet Berchem*, in MfMG XXI (1889), 129, 143.
Q	Eitner, R. *Biographisch-bibliographisches Quellenlexikon der Musiker und Musikgelehrten der christlichen Zeitrechnung bis zur Mitte des 19. Jahrhunderts*. 10 vols., 1899–1904. Additions and corrections published from 1912 in a quarterly, *Miscellanea Musicae Bio-bibliographica*, ed. by H. Springer, M. Schneider, and W. Wolffheim. (Reprint ed. of EitQ, including the *Miscellanea*, with other additions and corrections, 1947.)
S	Eitner, R. *Bibliographie der Musik-Sammelwerke des XVI. und XVII. Jahrhunderts*, 1877.
T	Eitner, R. (ed.). *Tänze des 15. bis 17. Jahrhunderts*. Supp. to MfMG VII (1875).
EKMV	*Schott's Anthology of Early Keyboard Music. English Virginalists.* Ed. by F. Dawes.
I	*Ten pieces by Hugh Aston and others*, 1951.
II	*Twelve pieces from Mulliner's Book (c. 1555)*, 1951.
III	*Seven Virginal Pieces (from B. M. Add. 30486)*, 1951.
IV	*[Eight] Pieces from the Tomkins Manuscript*, 1951.
V	*Fifteen pieces from Elizabeth Rogers's Virginal Book (1656)*, 1951.
EL	*The English School of Lutenist Song Writers.* Ed. by E. H. Fellowes, 2 series, 16 vols., 1920–32.
Ser. I	
I–II	*John Dowland: First Book of Airs*, 1920–21.
III	*Thomas Ford: Airs to the Lute, from Musicke of Sundrie Kindes*, 1921.
IV	*Thomas Campion: Songs from Rosseter's Book of Airs*, Part 1, 1922.
V–VI	*John Dowland: Second Book of Airs*, 1922.
VII	*Francis Pilkington: First Book of Songs or Airs*, Part 1, 1922.
VIII–IX	*Philip Rosseter: Songs from Rosseter's Book of Airs*, 1923.

EL X–XI	*John Dowland: Third Book of Airs*, 1923.
XII	*John Dowland: A Pilgrimes Solace*, Part 1, 1924.
XIII	*Thomas Campion: Songs from Rosseter's Book of Airs*, Part 2, **1924.**
XIV	*John Dowland: A Pilgrimes Solace*, Part 2, 1925.
XV	*Francis Pilkington, First Book of Songs or Airs*, Part 2, 1925.
XVI	*Thomas Morley: First Book of Airs (1600)*, 1932.
Ser. II	
I	*Thomas Campian: First Book of Airs*, 1925.
II	*Thomas Campian: Second Book of Airs*, 1925.
III	*John Bartlet: A Booke of Ayres*, 1925.
IV	*Robert Jones: First Booke of Songes and Ayres*, 1925.
V	*Robert Jones: Second Booke of Ayres*, 1926.
VI	*Robert Jones: Ultimum vale, Third Booke of Ayres*, 1926.
VII	*Songs included in Michael Cavendish's Booke of Ayres and Madrigalles*, 1926.
VIII	*John Danyel: Songs for the Lute, Viol and Voice*, 1926.
IX	*John Attey: First Booke of Ayres*, 1926.
X	*Thomas Campian: Third Booke of Ayres*, 1926.
XI	*Thomas Campian: Fourth Booke of Ayres*, 1926.
XII	*William Corkine: First Book of Ayres*, 1926.
XIII	*William Corkine: Second Booke of Ayres*, 1927.
XIV	*Robert Jones: A Musicall Dreame, or Fourth Booke of Ayres, 1609*, 1927.
XV	*Robert Jones: The Muses Gardin for Delights, or Fifth Booke of Ayres, 1610*, 1927.
XVI	*Alfonso Ferrabosco the Younger: Ayres*, 1927.
ELAM	*Edition Laudy. [Twelve] Albums of Madrigals.* Ed. by L. Benson.
I	*Palestrina: Four Madrigals*, Ed. Laudy No. 171.
II	*Lasso: Seven Madrigals*, Ed. Laudy No. 172.
III	*Marenzio and Vecchi: Five Madrigals*, Ed. Laudy No. **173.**
IV	*Wilbye: Five Madrigals*, Ed. Laudy No. 174.
V	*Bateson and Weelkes: Six Madrigals*, Ed. Laudy No. 175.
VI	*Jannequin and Costeley: Six Madrigals.* Ed. Laudy No. 176.
VII	*Various Composers: Seven Madrigals (English School)*, Ed. Laudy No. 177.
VIII	*Various Composers: Six Madrigals (Italian School)*, Ed. Laudy No. 178.
IX	*Various Composers: Six Madrigals (French School)*, Vol. I, Ed. Laudy No. 179.
X	*Various Composers: Six Madrigals (French School)*, Vol. II, Ed. Laudy No. 180.
XI	*Various Composers: Seven Madrigals (Dutch School)*, Ed. Laudy No. 181.
XII	*Various Composers (German School)*, Ed. Laudy No. 182.
EllgM	Elling, C. *Die Musik am Hofe Christians IV. von Dänemark*, in VfMW IX (1893), 62.
EllinT	Ellinwood, L. *Tallis' Tunes and Tudor Psalmody*, in MD II (1948), 189.
ElsU	Elsner, E. *Untersuchungen der instrumentalen Besetzungspraxis der weltlichen Musik im 16. Jahrhundert in Italien*, 1935.
ElúsA	Elústiza, D. J. B. de and G. C. Hernandez (eds.). *Antologia musical, Siglo de Oro de la Música litúrgica de España. Polifonia Vocal Siglos XV y XVI*, 1933.
EmC	Emmanuel, M. *The Creation of the Violin and its Consequences*, in MQ XXIII (1937), 509.
EMS	*English Madrigal School*, Ed. by E. H. Fellowes. 36 vols., 1914–24.
I	*Thomas Morley: The First Book of Canzonets to two voices*, 3rd ed., 1921.
II	*Thomas Morley: First Book of Madrigals to four voices*, 2nd ed., 1921.
III	*Thomas Morley: Canzonets or Little Short Airs to five and six voices*, 2nd ed., 1921.
IV	*Thomas Morley: First Book of Ballets to five voices*, 2nd ed., 1921.
V	*Orlando Gibbons: First Set of Madrigals and Motets of five parts*, 2nd ed., 1921.
VI	*John Wilbye: First Set of Madrigals to three, four, five, and six voices*, 1914.
VII	*John Wilbye: Second Set of Madrigals to three, four, five, and six voices*, 2nd ed., rev., 1920.
VIII	*John Farmer: First Set of Madrigals to four voices*, 1914.
IX	*Thomas Weelkes: Madrigals to three, four, five, and six voices*, 1916.
X	*Thomas Weelkes: Ballets and Madrigals to five voices*, 1916.
XI	*Thomas Weelkes: Madrigals of five parts*, 1916.

EMS XII	*Thomas Weelkes: Madrigals of six parts,* 1916.
XIII	*Thomas Weelkes: Airs or Fantastic Spirits to three voices,* 1916.
XIV	*William Byrd: Psalms, Sonnets, and Songs of Sadness and Piety to five parts,* 1920.
XV	*William Byrd: Songs of Sundry Natures to three, four, five, and six parts,* 1920.
XVI	*William Byrd: Psalms, Songs, and Sonnets, some solemn, others joyful, to three, four, five, and six parts,* 1920.
XVII	*Henry Lichfild: First Set of Madrigals of five parts,* 1922.
XVIII	*Thomas Tompkins: Songs of three, four, five, and six parts,* 1922.
XIX	*John Ward: Madrigals to three, four, five, and six parts,* 1922.
XX	*Giles Farnaby: Canzonets to four voices,* 1922.
XXI	*Thomas Bateson: First Set of Madrigals,* 1922.
XXII	*Thomas Bateson: Second Set of Madrigals,* 1922.
XXIII	*John Bennet: Madrigals to four voices,* 1922.
XXIV	*George Kirbye: Madrigals to four, five, and six voices,* 1922.
XXV	*Francis Pilkington: First Set of Madrigals and Pastorals of three, four, and five parts,* 1923.
XXVI	*Francis Pilkington: Second Set of Madrigals and Pastorals of three, four, five, and six parts,* 1923.
XXVII	*Richard Carlton: Madrigals to five voices,* 1923.
XXVIII	*Henry Youll: Canzonets to three voices,* 1923.
XXIX–XXXI	*Michael East: Madrigals,* 1923.
XXXII	*Thomas Morley and twenty-three others: The Triumphs of Oriana,* 1923.
XXXIII	*Richard Alison: An Hour's Recreation in Music,* 1924.
XXXIV	*Thomas Vautor: Songs of Divers Airs and Natures,* 1924.
XXXV	*Robert Jones: The First Set of Madrigals,* 1924.
XXXVI	*Michael Cavendish, Thomas Greaves, William Holborne, Richard Edwards: Madrigals. . . ,*1924.
EnI	Engel, E. *Die Instrumentalformen in der Lautenmusik des 16. Jahrhunderts,* 1915.
EncC	*Cancionero de Juan del Encina, 1496.* Facsimile ed. issued by the Real Academia Española, 1928.
EngB	Engel, H. *Luca Marenzio, saggio biografico,* in *La Rassegna Musicale* III (1930), 185, 278.
M	Engel, H. *Marenzios Madrigale,* in ZfMW XVII (1935), 257.
MV	Engel, H. *Madrigal und Villanelle,* in *Neuphilologische Monatsschrift* III (1932), 257.
EngelkeM	Engelke, B. *Musik und Musiker am Gottorfer Hofe,* 1930.
EppN	Eppstein, H. *Nicolas Gombert als Motettenkomponist,* 1935.
EsL	Eslava, Don H. (ed.). *Lira sacro-hispana.* 10 vols., 1869.
EvJ	Evans, W. M. *Ben Jonson and Elizabethan Music,* 1929.
ExA	Expert, H. (ed.). *Anthologie chorale des Maîtres musiciens de la Renaissance française,* 1938.
CL I–VI	Expert, H. (ed.). String Fantasy by Claude Le Jeune and five by Eustache Du Caurroy, published separately. Ed. by H. Expert. (Sénart Nos. 2644–49).
F	Expert, H. (ed.). *La Fleur des musiciens de Pierre de Ronsard,* 1923.
FR	Expert, H. (ed.). *Florilège du Concert vocal de la Renaissance,* 8 vols., 1928–29.
I	*Janequin,* 1928.
II	*Lassus,* 1928.
III	*Janequin,* 1928.
IV	*Costeley,* 1928.
V	*Pierre Bonnet,* 1929.
VI	*Le Jeune,* 1929.
VII	*Mauduit,* 1928.
VIII	*Duos,* 1928.
P	Expert, H. (ed.). *Le Pseautier huguenot du XVIᵉ siècle, publié sur un plan nouveau,* 1902.
R	Expert, H. *A propos de la Musique française à l'époque de la Renaissance,* in EC, *Partie I,* III, 1261.
FallerW	Fallersleben, A. H. Hoffmann von, *Weimarische Liederhandschrift vom Jahre 1537,* in *Weimarisches Jahrbuch für deutsche Sprache, Litteratur, und Kunst* I (1854), 100.

FarkU   Farkas, G. *Zur Frage der ungarischen Spielleute*, in *Deutsch-ungarische Heimatsblätter* V (1933), 208.

FarmS   Farmer, H. G. *A History of Music in Scotland*, 1948.

FarnSP   *Giles Farnaby, Selected Pieces*. Ed. by M. Glyn, 1927.

FedM   Federmann, M. *Musik und Musikpflege zur Zeit Herzog Albrechts; zur Geschichte der Königsberger Hofkapelle in den Jahren 1525–1578*, 1932.

FederhA   Federhofer, H. *Ein Beitrag zur Biographie von Giovanni Francesco Anerio*, in MF II (1949), 210.

B   Federhofer, H. *Biographische Beiträge zu Erasmus Lapicida und Stephan Mahu*, in MF V (1952), 37.

Q   Federhofer, H. *Eine neue Quelle der Musica Reservata*, in Acta XXIV (1952), 32.

FédorovB   Fédorov, V. *Peut-on parler d'une école bourguignonne de musique au XVe siècle?* in *Les Cahiers techniques de l'art* II (1949), 29.

FeiM   Feicht, H. *O mszy wielkanocnej Marcina Leopolity (zm. 1589)*, in *Kwartalnik Muzyczny*, No. 6–7 (1930), 109.

FeinK   Feininger, L. K. J. *Die Frühgeschichte des Kanons bis Josquin des Prez (um 1500)*, 1937.

FelCT   Fellowes, E. H. *The Catalogue of Manuscripts in the Library of St. Michael's College, Tenbury*, 1924.

E   Fellowes, E. H. *The English Madrigal Composers*, 1921.

EE   Fellowes, E. H. *English Cathedral Music from Edward VI to Edward VII*, 1941.

JW   Fellowes, E. H. *Wilbye*, in PMA XLI (1915), 55.

OG   Fellowes, E. H. *Orlando Gibbons*, 1925.

S   Fellowes, E. H. (ed.). *Songs and Lyrics from the Plays of Beaumont and Fletcher*, 1928.

SG   Fellowes, E. H. *Organists and Masters of the Choristers of St. George's Chapel in Windsor Castle*, 1939.

TW   Fellowes, E. H. *Thomas Weelkes*, in PMA XLII (1915), 117.

V   Fellowes, E. H. *English Madrigal Verse, 1588–1632, from the original Song Books*, 1920.

WB   Fellowes, E. H. *William Byrd*, 1936; 2nd ed., 1948. References in this book are to the 2nd ed. (FelWB supersedes Fellowes' earlier book on Byrd [1923].)

FeldC   Feldmann, F. *Der Codex Mf 2016 des Musikalischen Instituts bei der Universität Breslau*. 2 vols., 1932.

M   Feldmann, F. *Musik und Musikpflege im mittelalterlichen Schlesien*, 1938.

Q   Feldmann, F. *Ein Quintenorganum aus einer Breslauer Handschrift des frühen 16. Jahrhunderts*, in KJ XXVII (1932), 75.

FellC   Fellerer, K. G. *Das Credo in Palestrinas Messe "Ecce Sacerdos,"* in *Gedenkschrift für Hermann Abert* (1928), 44.

P   Fellerer, K. G. *Palestrina*, 1930.

FerandF   Ferand, E. T. *Two unknown Frottole*, in MQ XXVII (1941), 319.

H   Ferand, E. T. *The "Howling in seconds" of the Lombards*, in MQ XXV (1939), 313.

M   Ferand, E. T. *Die Improvisation in der Musik*, 1938.

S   Ferand, E. T. *"Sodaine and Unexpected" Music in the Renaissance*, in MQ XXXVII (1951), 10.

FernanF   *Farsas y églogas al modo y estilo pastoríl, fechas por Lucas Fernandez, salmantino*. Ed. by M. Cañeti, 1867.

FestaM   *Madrigali scelti di Costanzo Festa, a 3 e 4 voci*. Ed. by P. G. Pistone, 1935.

FétB   Fétis, F. J. *Biographie universelle des musiciens*. . . . 2nd ed., 8 vols., 1860–65. References in this book are to that ed. Two-vol. supp. by A. Pougin, 1878–80.

FiB   Ficker, R. *Beiträge zur Chromatik des 14. bis 16. Jahrhunderts*, in SzMW II (1914), 5.

F   Ficker, R. *Die frühen Messenkompositionen der Trienter Codices*, in SzMW XI (1924), 3.

K   Ficker, R. *Die Kolorierungstechnik der Trienter Messen*, in SzMW VII (1920), 5.

Z   Ficker, R. *Zur Schöpfungsgeschichte des Fauxbourdon*, in Acta XXIII (1951), 93.

FiciF   *Supplementum Ficinianum* [Marsilio Ficino]. Ed. by P. O. Kristeller. 2 vols., 1937.

FiscS   Fischer, H. *Musikalische Formen*, Vol. 18: *Die Sonata . . .* , 1936.

FischerI   Fischer, W. *Instrumentalmusik von 1450–1600*, in AdlerH I (1929), 382.

FitzI	Fitzgibbon, H. M. *Instruments and their Music in the Elizabethan Drama*, in MQ XVII (1931), 319.
L	Fitzgibbon, H. M. *Two Lute Books of Ballet and Dallis*, in M&L XI (1930), 71.
FloodB	Flood, W. H. Grattan. *Gilbert Banaster, Master of the Children of the English Chapel Royal (1478–1490)*, in SIM XV (1913), 64.
C	Flood, W. H. Grattan. *The English Chapel Royal under Henry V and Henry VI*, in SIM X (1909), 563.
CR	Flood, W. H. Grattan. *The Beginnings of the Chapel Royal*, in M&L V (1924), 83.
E	Flood, W. H. Grattan. *Early Tudor Composers*, 1925.
I	Flood, W. H. Grattan. *Irish Ancestry of Garland, Dowland, Campion and Purcell*, in M&L III (1922), 59.
R	Flood, W. H. Grattan. *Entries Relating to Music in the English Patent Rolls of the Fifteenth Century*, in MAn IV (1913), 225.
S	Flood, W. H. Grattan. *Master Sebastian of Paul's* in MAn III (1912), 149.
FlorM	Florimo, F. *La Scuola musicale di Napoli ed i suoi Conservatorii*. 4 vols., 1880–84.
FlowM	Flower, D. *On Music Printing 1473–1701*, in *The Book Collector's Quarterly* [London], No. 4 (Oct.–Dec., 1931), 76.
FogL	Fogel, J. *II. Lajos udvartartása*, 1917.
FőkM	Főkövi, L. *Musik und musikalische Verhältnisse in Ungarn am Hofe von Matthias Corvinus*, in KJ XV (1900), 1.
ForkA	Forkel, J. N. *Allgemeine Geschichte der Musik*. 2 vols., 1788–1801.
L	Forkel, J. N. *Allgemeine Literatur der Musik . . .* , 1792.
FosA	Foschini, G. F. *Antologia classica italiana*, 1931.
FoxA	Fox, C. W. *Accidentals in Vihuela Tablatures*, abstract in BAMS, No. 4 (1938), 22.
F	Fox, C. W. *Ein Fröhlich Wesen . . .* , in PAMS for 1937 (1938), 56.
M	Fox, C. W. *The Masses of Cristóbal Morales*, abstract in BAMS, No. 5 (1941), 16.
NQ	Fox, C. W. *Non-Quartal Harmony in the Renaissance*, in MQ XXXI (1945), 33.
P	Fox, C. W. *A Pleasant and Very Useful Book (1529)*, abstract in BAMS, No. 2 (1937), 22.
R	Fox, C. W. *The Polyphonic Requiem before about 1600*, abstract in BAMS, No. 7 (1943), 6.
FrakL	Fraknói, V. *II. Lajos udvara*, 1878.
FratC	Frati, L. *Un Capitolo autobiografico di Orazio Vecchi*, in RMI XXII (1915), 71.
S	Frati, L. *Per la Storia della Musica in Bologna dal secolo XV al XVI*, in RMI XXIV (1917), 449.
V	Frati, L. *La Vita privata di Bologna dal secolo XIII al XVII*, 1900.
FreitC	Freitas-Branco, L. de. *Les Contrepointistes de l'école d'Evora*, in *Actes du Congrès d'histoire de l'art, Paris, 1921* III (recte II²) (1924), 846.
FrereA	*Antiphonale Sarisburiense*, 1901–25. Facsimile ed. with introduction, etc., by W. H. Frere.
B	Frere, W. H. *Bibliotheca musica liturgica*, 1901.
G	*Graduale Sarisburiense*, 1894. Facsimile ed. with commentary by W. H. Frere.
FrieV	Friederich, B. *Der Vokalstil des Hieronymus Praetorius*, 1932.
FrotO	Frotscher, G. *Geschichte des Orgelspiels und der Orgelkomposition*. Vol. I, 1935.
V	Frotscher, G. *Die Volksinstrumente auf Bildwerken des 16. und 17. Jahrhunderts*, in *Musik und Bild. Festschrift Max Seiffert* (1938), 61.
FullerBC	Fuller Maitland, J. A. (ed.). *Twenty-five Pieces for Keyed Instruments from Benjamin Cosyn's Virginal Book*, 1923.
C	Fuller Maitland, J. A. (ed.). *English Carols of the Fifteenth Century*, 1891.
F	Fuller Maitland, J. A. and W. Barclay Squire (eds.). *The Fitzwilliam Virginal Book*. 2 vols., 1894–99.
S	Fuller Maitland, J. A. *A Scottish Composer of the 16th Century*, in *Gedenkboek aangeboden aan Dr. D. F. Scheurleer* (1925), 119.
FunA	Funck, H. *Martin Agricola, Ein frühprotestantischer Schulmusiker*, 1933.
C	Funck, H. *Eine Chanson von Binchois im Buxheimer Orgel- und Locheimer Liederbuch*, in Acta V (1933), 3.
GabrC	Gabrieli, G. *Canzoni per sonar a quattro*, in *Antiqua, eine Sammlung alter Musik*. Ed. by A. Einstein, 1933.
GabriR	*Andrea Gabrieli: Three four-part Ricercari*. Ed. by H. T. David, 1940.

GafT   *Franchino Gafori: Theorica musica, 1492.* Facsimile ed. with preface by G. Cesari, 1934.

W   *Franchinus Gafurius: Collected Musical Works.* Ed. by L. Finscher, 1955– .

GaillB   Gaillard, P. A. *Loys Bourgeoys: sa vie, son oeuvre comme pédagogue et compositeur,* 1948.

GalD   *Vincenzo Galilei: Dialogo della Musica antica et moderna* (1581). Facsimile ed., 1934.

DM   *Vincenzo Galilei: Dialogo della Musica antica e della moderna,* 1947. (Partial reprint, with commentary by F. Fano.)

Z   *Vincenzo Galilei: Discorso intorno alle opere di Gioseffo Zarlino et altri importanti particolari attenenti alla musica, MDLXXXIX.* Facsimile ed., 1933.

GalpO   Galpin, F. W. *Old English Instruments of Music,* 1910.

GanF   Gandolfi, R. *Intorno al Codice membranaceo N. 2440 esistente nella Biblioteca del R. Istituto musicale di Firenze,* in RMI XVIII (1911), 537.

L   Gandolfi, R. *Lettere inedite scritte da musicisti e letterati appartenenti alla seconda metà del secolo XVI, estratte dal R. Archivio di Stato di Firenze,* in RMI XX (1913), 527.

GanaF   *Silvestro Ganassi: Opera intitulata Fontegara . . . , 1535.* Facsimile ed., 1934.

R   *Silvestro Ganassi: Regola Rubertina, 1542–43.* Facsimile ed. with preface by Max Schneider, 1924.

GárB   Gárdonyi, A. *A Báthoryak és a zeneművészet,* in *Muzsika* I (1929), 33.

GarsC   Garside, C. *Calvin's Preface to the Psalter: A Re-Appraisal,* in MQ XXXVII (1951), 566.

GasA   Gastoué, A. *L' "Alarme" de Grimache (vers 1380–1390) et les chansons polyphoniques du moyen âge,* in *Actes du Congrès d'histoire de l'art, Paris, 1921* IV (1924), 784.

BC   Gastoué, A. *Manuscrits et fragments de musique liturgique à la Bibliothèque du Conservatoire à Paris,* in RdM XIII (1932), 1.

MA   Gastoué, A. (ed.). *Le Manuscrit de musique polyphonique du Trésor d'Apt (XIVe–XVe s.),* 1936.

GaspI   Gasperini, G. *La Musique italienne au XVe siècle,* in EC, *Partie I,* II, 620.

GastB   *Giovanni Giacomo Gastoldi: Balletti a tre voci* [1600]. Ed. by W. Herrmann, 3 Hefte, 1927.

S   *Giovanni Giacomo Gastoldi: Spielstücke für zwei Melodieinstrumente.* Ed. by E. Kiwi, 1933.

GeH   Gerber, R. *Die Hymnen des Apelschen Kodex,* in *Festschrift Arnold Schering* (1937), 76.

GeerP   Geering, A. (ed.). *Psalmen und geistliche Gesänge von Johannes Wannenmacher und Cosmas Alder,* 1934. (Fasc. III in *Musikalische Werke Schweizerischer Komponisten des XVI., XVII., und XVIII. Jahrhunderts.* Ed. by K. Nef.)

V   Geering, A. *Die Vokalmusik in der Schweiz zur Zeit der Reformation,* in SJ VI (1933).

GeiB   Geiger, A. *Bausteine zur Geschichte des iberischen Vulgär-Villancico,* in ZfMW IV (1921), 65.

E   Geiger, A. *Juan Esquivel: Ein unbekannter spanischer Meister des 16. Jahrhunderts,* in *Festschrift . . . Adolf Sandberger* (1918), 138.

GerS   Gerbert, M. (ed.). *Scriptores ecclesiastici de musica.* 3 vols., 1784. Facsimile ed., 1931.

GerhW   C. Gerhardt. *Die Torgauer Walter Handschriften,* 1949.

GéroB   Gérold, T. (ed.). *Le Manuscrit de Bayeux,* 1921.

C   Gérold, T. *Chansons populaires des XVe et XVIe siècles avec leurs mélodies,* in *Bibliotheca romanica* Nos. 190–192, n.d.

L   Gérold, T. *Monodie et Lied,* in EC, *Partie II,* V, 2757.

P   Gérold, T. *Les Premiers Recueils de mélodies religieuses protestantes à Strasbourg,* in RdM VI (1925), 49.

S   Gérold, T. and E Wagner. *Les plus anciens chants de l'église protestante de Strasbourg et leurs auteurs,* 1928.

GesualdoM   *Gesualdo da Venosa: Madrigale.* Ed. by W. Weismann, 1931.

GeutU   Geutebrück, R. *Über Form und Rhythmus des älteren deutschen Volksgesanges,* in AfMW VII (1925), 337.

GhiA   Ghisi, F. *Un Frammento musicale dell'Ars Nova italiana,* in RMI XLII (1938), 162.

B   Ghisi, F. *Bruchstücke einer neuen Musikhandschrift der italienischen Ars Nova und zwei unveröffentlichte Caccien der zweiten Hälfte des 15. Jahrhunderts,* in AfMF VII (1942), 17.

GhiC	Ghisi, F. *Carnival Songs and the Origins of the Intermezzo Giocoso*, in MQ XXV (1939), 325.
CC	Ghisi, F. *I Canti carnascialeschi nelle fonti musicali del XV e XVI secolo*, 1937.
F	Ghisi, F. *Frammenti di un nuovo Codice musicale della "Ars Nova" italiana e due saggi inediti di "Cacce" del secondo Quattrocento*, in *La Rinascita* V (1942), 72.
FM	Ghisi, F. (ed.). *Feste musicali della Firenze Medicea (1480–1589)*, 1939.
I	Ghisi, F. *Italian Ars-Nova Music, the Perugia and Pistoia fragments of the Lucca Codex and other . . . early 15th century sources*, in JRB I (1946), 173.
IM	Ghisi, F. (ed.). *Italian Ars-Nova Music.* Musical Supp. to JRB I (1947).
MI	Ghisi, F. *Le Musiche di Isaac per il San Giovanni e Paolo di Lorenzo il Magnifico*, in *La Rassegna Musicale* XVI (1943), 264.
SF	Ghisi, F. *A Second Sienese Fragment of Italian Ars Nova*, in MD II (1948), 173.
SL	Ghisi, F. *Strambotti e Laude nel Travestimento Spirituale della Poesia Musicale del Quattrocento*, in *Collectanea historiae musicae* I (1953), 45.
GibC	*Orlando Gibbons: Complete Keyboard Works.* Ed. by M. H. Glyn. 5 vols., 1925.
F	*Orlando Gibbons: 9 Fantasies for 3 and 2 for 4 instruments.* Ed. by E. H. Fellowes. 3 vols., 1924–25.
MG	*Orlando Gibbons edited for the Pianoforte.* Ed. by M. H. Glyn, 1920.
T	*Ten pieces arranged for Modern Organ from the Virginal Book of Benjamin Cosyn, Composed by Orlando Gibbons.* Ed. by J. A. Fuller Maitland, 1925.
GiebG	Gieburowski, W. *Choral Gregorjański w Polsce od XV do XVIII wieku*, 1922.
M	Gieburowski, W. *Die Musica Magistri Szydlovite*, 1915.
GiesA	Giesbert, F. J. (ed.). *Pierre Attaingnant: Pariser Tanzbuch aus dem Jahre 1530*, 1950.
S	Giesbert, F. J. (ed.). *Ein altes Spielbuch, Liber Fridolini Sichery*, 1936.
GläB	Gläsel, R. *Zur Geschichte der Battaglia*, 1931.
GlarD	Glareanus (Heinrich Loris). *Dodecachordon*, 1547.
GleC	Gleason, H. *The Cracow Tablature of 1548*, abstract in BAMS, No. 3 (1939), 14.
S	Gleason, H. *Arnold Schlick, Organ Expert and Composer*, abstract in BAMS, No. 1 (1936), 8.
GlynE	Glyn, M. H. (ed.). *Early English Organ Music*, 1939.
F	Glyn, M. H. *Famous Books on Elizabethan Virginal Music . . . Discovered in the New York Public Library*, in *Musical Courier* LXXVIII (1919), 12.
N	Glyn, M. H. *The National School of Virginal Music in Elizabethan Times*, in PMA XLIII (1917), 29.
NV	Glyn, M. H. *The Nevill Virginal Book*, in *Musical Standard* XVI (1920), 188.
P	Glyn, M. H. (ed.). *Twenty-one Old English Compositions . . . Parthenia*, 1927.
T	Glyn, M. H. *Two Forgotten Virginal Books*, in *Musical Standard* XIII (1919), 30.
V	Glyn, M. H. *About Elizabethan Virginal Music and its Composers*, 1924. New ed., "embodying recent . . . discoveries," 1934. References in this book are to the 1934 ed.
VP	Glyn, M. H. (ed.). *Thirty Virginal Pieces*, 1927.
GmelchU	Gmelch, J. *Unbekannte Reimgebetkompositionen aus Rebdorfer Handschriften*, in *Peter Wagner-Festschrift* (1926), 69.
GoehlG	Goehlinger, F. *Geschichte des Klavichords*, 1910.
GoetM	Goetze, E. *Monographie über den Meistersänger Adam Puschman*, 1877.
GoldI	Goldschmidt, H. *Die italienische Gesangsmethode des XVII. Jahrhunderts und ihre Bedeutung für die Gegenwart*, 1890.
GomA	Gombosi, O. *Die Musikalien der Pfarrkirche zu St. Aegidi in Bártfa*, in *Festschrift für Johannes Wolf* (1929), 38.
B	Gombosi, O. *Bemerkungen zur "L'homme armé"-Frage*, in ZfMW X (1928), 609.
C	Gombosi, O. *Ghizeghem und Compère. Zur Stilgeschichte der burgundischen Chanson*, in AdlerF (1930), 100.
CF	Gombosi, O. *The Cultural and Folkloristic Background of the Folia*, in PAMS for 1940 (1946), 88.
D	Gombosi, O. *About Dance and Dance Music in the late Middle Ages*, in MQ XXVII (1941), 289.
E	Gombosi, O. *Some Musical Aspects of the English Court Masque*, in JAMS I, No. 3 (1948), 3.
F	Gombosi, O. *Zur Frühgeschichte der Folia*, in Acta VIII (1936), 119.

GomH   Gombosi, O. *Der Hoftanz*, in Acta VII (1935), 50.

I   Gombosi, O. *Italia, Patria del Basso Ostinato*, in *La Rassegna Musicale* VII (1934), 14.

J   Gombosi, O. *Jacob Barbireaus letzte Lebensjahre*, in ZfMW XII (1930), 378.

MB   Gombosi, O. *Quellen aus dem 16.–17. Jahrhundert zur Geschichte der Musikpflege in Bartfeld (Bártfa) und Oberungarn*, in *Ungarische Jahrbücher* XII (1932), 331.

O   Gombosi, O. *Jacob Obrecht, eine stilkritische Studie*, 1925.

Q   Gombosi, O. *Quellenmässige Belege über den Einfluss der Chansonkunst auf die deutsche Liedmusik in der zweiten Hälfte des fünfzehnten Jahrhunderts*, in *Beethoven Zentenarfeier, Wien, . . . Internationaler musikhistorischer Kongress* (1927), 152.

SF   Gombosi, O. *Ein neuer Sweelinck-Fund*, in TVNM XIV (1932), 1.

U   Gombosi, O. *Die ältesten Denkmäler der mehrstimmigen Vokalmusik aus Ungarn*, in *Ungarische Jahrbücher* XI (1931), 84.

V   Gombosi, O. *Vita musicale alla Corte di Re Mattia*, in *Corvina*, XVII (1929), 110.

VB   Gombosi, O. *Bakfark Bálint élete és müvei (Der Lautenist Valentin Bakfark, Leben und Werke) (Musicologia Hungarica*, Vol. II) (Hungarian and German text), 1935.

VD   Gombosi, O. *Violenduette im 15. Jahrhundert*, in Acta IX (1937), 57.

VT   Gombosi, O. *Zur Vorgeschichte der Toccata*, in Acta VI (1934), 49.

W   Gombosi, O. Review of *Adrian Willaert in der weltlichen Vokalmusik seiner Zeit* by Erich Hertzmann, in ZfMW XVI (1934), 54.

WG   Gombosi, O. *Zur Biographie Wolfgang Greffingers*, in Acta IX (1937), 54.

GombertO   *Nicolai Gombert: Opera omnia*. 12 vols. Ed. by J. Schmidt-Görg, 1951–   .

GoovH   Goovaerts, A. *Histoire et bibliographie de la typographie musicale dans les Pays-Bas*, 1880.

GordM   Gordon, P. *The Morley-Shakespeare Myth*, in M&L XXVIII (1947), 121.

GossR   Gosslau, W. *Die religiöse Haltung in der Reformationsmusik, nachgewiesen an den "Newen deudschen geistlichen Gesengen" des Georg Rhaw 1544 . . .*, 1933.

GostL   *Giovanni Battista della Gostena: Intavolatura di Liuto*. Ed. by G. Gullino, 1949.

GoudP   *Claude Goudimel: Les Pseaumes mis en rime françoise par Clément Marot et Théodore de Bèze. Mis en musique à quatre parties, . . . 1565*. Facsimile ed. with introductions by P. Pidoux and K. Ameln, 1935.

GradenMI   Gradenwitz, P. *The Music of Israel, Its Rise and Growth Through 5000 Years*, 1949.

Graduale   *Graduale Romanum*, 1924. (Desclée edition)

GrafcP   Grafczyńska, M. *Die Polyphonie am Hofe der Jagellonen*, in *Beethoven Zentenarfeier, Wien, . . . Internationaler musikhistorischer Kongress* (1927), 164.

GravA   Gravisi, A. *Andrea Antico da Montona*, in *Atti e Memorie della Società Istriana di Archeologia e Storia Patria* I (1885), 141.

GrayG   Gray, C. and P. Heseltine. *Carlo Gesualdo, Prince of Venosa, Musician and Murderer*, 1926.

V   *Carlo Gesualdo, Prince of Venosa; Musician and Murderer*, in *Contingencies and other Essays* by Cecil Gray (1946), 157.

GreC   Greene, R. L. *The Early English Carol*, 1935.

GrégoL   Grégoir, E. G. J. *Littérature musicale*. 4 vols., 1872–76.

GreuB   Greulich, M. *Beiträge zur Geschichte des Streichinstrumentenspiels im 16. Jahrhundert*, 1934.

GrösG   Grössel, H. *Georgius Otto. Ein Motettenkomponist des 16. Jahrhunderts (1550–1618)*, 1933.

Grove   *Grove's Dictionary of Music and Musicians*, 1st ed. 1879–89; 3rd ed. (5 vols. and supp.), 1928. Ed. by H. C. Colles. References in this book are to the 3rd ed.

GrunN   Grunzweig, A. *Notes sur la musique des Pays-Bas au XVe siècle*, in *Bulletin de l'Institut historique belge de Rome* XVIII (1937), 73.

GuerrC   Guerrini, P. *Un Codice piemontese di teorici musicali del Medioevo*, in RMI XXXIV (1927), 63.

GC   Guerrini, P. *Giovanni Contino di Brescia*, in NA I (1924), 130.

GuglielT   *Trattato dell'Arte del Ballo di Guglielmo Ebreo pesarese [De Praticha seu Arte Tripudii]*. Ed. by F. Zambrini, in *Scelta di Curiosità Letterarie inedite o rare dal secolo XII al XVII*. Dispensa CXXXI, 1873.

GurB   Gurlitt, W. *Burgundische Chanson und deutsche Liedkunst . . .*, in *Bericht über den Musikwissenschaftlichen Kongress in Basel* (1925), 153.

GurJ   Gurlitt, W. *Johannes Walter und die Musik der Reformationszeit*, in *Lutherjahrbuch* XV (1933), 1.

K   Gurlitt, W. *Johannes Kotter und sein Freiburger Tabulaturbuch von 1513*, in *Elsass-Lothringisches Jahrbuch* XIX (1941), 216.

L   Gurlitt, W. *Ein Lütticher Beitrag zur Adam von Fulda-Frage*, in *International Society for Musical Research, First Congress, Liége, September 1–6, 1930*, Report, 125.

HaasA   Haas, R. *Aufführungspraxis der Musik*, 1930.

M   Haas, R. *Musik des Barocks*, 1928.

Z   Haas, R. *Zu Walther's Choralpassion nach Matthäus*, in AfMW IV (1922), 24.

HabA   Haberl, F. X. *Das Archiv der Gonzaga in Mantua*, in KJ I (1886), 31.

D   Haberl, F. X. *Wilhelm Dufay*, in VfMW I (1885), 397. Published also as *Bausteine zur Musikgeschichte I*, 1885. References in this book are to the *Bausteine*.

FA   Haberl, F. X. *Felice Anerio, Lebensgang und Werke*, in KJ XVIII (1903), 28.

FS   Haberl, F. X. *Francesco Soriano*, in KJ X (1895), 95.

GA   Haberl, F. X. *Giovanni Francesco Anerio . . .*, in KJ I (1886), 51.

GC   Haberl, F. X. *Giovanni Croce, Eine bio-bibliographische Skizze*, in KJ III (1888), 49.

I   Haberl, F. X. *Marcantonio Ingegneri, Eine bio-bibliographische Studie*, in KJ XIII (1898), 78.

K   Haberl, F. X. *Die Kardinalskommission von 1564 und Palestrina's Missa Papae Marcelli*, in KJ VII (1892), 82.

LM   Haberl, F. X. *Luca Marenzio, eine bio-bibliographische Skizze*, in KJ XV (1900), 93.

M   Haberl, F. X. *Eine Komposition des Cardinals Jo. de Medicis . . .*, in KJ III (1888), 39.

MW   Haberl, F. X. *Messen Adrian Willaert's gedruckt von Franc. Marcolini da Forlì*, in MfMG III (1871), 81.

N   Haberl, F. X. *Giovanni Maria Nanino . . .*, in KJ VI (1891), 81.

OV   Haberl, F. X. *Orpheo Vecchi*, in KJ XX (1907), 167.

R   Haberl, F. X. *Die römische "schola cantorum" und die päpstlichen Kapellsänger bis zur Mitte des 16. Jahrhunderts*, in VfMW III (1887), 189. Published also as *Bausteine zur Musikgeschichte III*, 1888. References in this book are to the *Bausteine*.

RMS   Haberl, F. X. (ed.). *Repertorium musicae sacrae ex auctoribus saeculi XVI et XVII*. 2 vols., 22 fascicles (1886–1925).

S   Haberl, F. X. and G. Lisio. *Una Stanza del Petrarca musicata da Guillaume du Fay*, in RMI I (1894), 257.

T   Haberl, F. X. *Ein unbekanntes Werk des Johannes Tinctoris*, in KJ XIV (1899), 69.

V   Haberl, F. X. *Biographischer und thematischer Musikkatalog des päpstlichen Kapellarchives im Vatikan zu Rom*. Supp. to MfMG XIX–XX (1887–88). Published also as *Bausteine zur Musikgeschichte II*, 1888.

W   Haberl, F. X. *Matthias Hermann Werrecorensis*, in MfMG III (1871), 197; IV (1872), 4 (with Supp.).

HadlW   Hadland, F. A. *The Waits*, in *Music Record* XLV (1915), 93.

HäfnE   Häfner, R. *Die Entwicklung der Spieltechnik und der Schul- und Lehrwerke für Klavierinstrumente*, in *Schriftenreihe des Musikwissenschaftlichen Seminars der Universität München* II (1937), 45.

HajM   Hajek, E. *Die Musik, ihre Gestalter und Verkünder in Siebenbürgen einst und jetzt*, 1927.

HalbG   Halbig, H. (ed.). *Geistliche Musik bis zum Ausgang des 16. Jahrhunderts* (Bd. 5 in *Musikalische Formen in historischen Reihen*, ed. by H. Martens), 1930.

H   Halbig, H. *Ein handschriftliche Lautentabulatur des Giacomo Gorzanis*, in *Theodor Kroyer-Festschrift* (1933), 102.

K   Halbig, H. (ed.). *Klaviertänze des 16. Jahrhunderts*, 1928.

HallC   *Hall's Chronicle. The union of the two noble and illustrate famelies of Lancastre and Yorke*, reprint, 1809.

HAM   Davison, A. T. and W. Apel (eds.). *Historical Anthology of Music*, I, 1946.

HambF   Hamburger, P. *Die Fantasien in Emanuel Adriansens Pratum Musicum (1600)*, in ZfMW XII (1929), 148.

HamilD   Hamilton, J. A. *His Celebrated Dictionary*, 1849.

HammN — Hammerich, A. *Niederländische Musiker in Dänemark im 16.–17. Jahrhundert*, in *Gedenkboek aangeboden aan Dr. D. F. Scheurleer* (1925), 135.

HanA — Hannas, R. *Cerone's Approach to the Teaching of Counterpoint*, in PAMS for 1937 (1938), 75.

C — Hannas, R. *Cerone, Philosopher and Teacher*, in MQ XXI (1935), 408.

E — Hannas, R. *Cerone's Exposition of Mensural Notation*, abstract in BAMS No. 3 (1939), 8.

MC — Hannas, R. *Concerning Deletions in the Polyphonic Mass Credo*, in JAMS V (1952), 155.

HandAT — Handschin, J. *Anselmi's Treatise on Music Annotated by Gafori*, in MD II (1948), 123.

MG — Handschin, J. *Musikgeschichte*, 1948.

U — Handschin, J. *Über Estampie und Sequenz*, in ZfMW XII (1929), 1; XIII (1930), 113.

WB — Handschin, J. *Über William Byrd und den Begriff der Fortgeschrittenheit*, in *Schweizerische Musikzeitung* LXXXV (1945), 453.

ZP — Handschin, J. *Zur Frage der melodischen Paraphrasierung im Mittelalter*, in ZfMW X (1928), 513.

HansenL — Hansen, P. *Liber Secundus Mutetarum by Dominico Phinot, a Modern Transcription with an Introduction*. Master's thesis, Eastman School of Music, Rochester, N.Y. 1935, unpublished.

P — Hansen, P. *The Life and Works of Dominico Phinot*. Ph.D. dissertation, University of North Carolina, Chapel Hill, No. Car., 1939, unpublished.

HarZ — Harich-Schneider, E. and R. Boadella. *Zum Klavichordspiel bei Tomás de Santa Maria*, in AfMF II (1937), 243.

HaraD — Haraszti, E. *Les Rapports italo-transylvains de Il Transilvano de Girolamo Diruta*, in *Mélanges de musicologie offerts à M. Lionel de la Laurencie* (1933), 73. Published also in *Archivum Europae centro-orientalis* VI (1940), 312. References are to the earlier publication.

F — Haraszti, E. *Mattheo Flecha le jeune, abbé de Tyhon*, in Acta VII (1935), 22.

L — Haraszti, E. *Un grand luthiste du XVIᵉ siècle: Valentin Bakfark*, in RdM X (1929), 159.

M — Haraszti, E. *Marie de Hongrie et son Ungarescha*, in RdM XI (1930), 176.

PB — Haraszti, E. *Pierre Bono, luthiste de Mathias Corvin*, RdM XXVIII (1949), 73.

S — Haraszti, E. *Sigismond Báthory, prince de Transylvanie et la musique italienne*, in RdM XII (1931), 190.

HarrnC — Harrison, F. L. *An English "Caput,"* in M&L XXXIII (1952), 203.

E — Harrison, F. L. *The Eton Choirbook*, in AM I (1953), 151.

HasK — *Hans Leo Hassler: Kirchengesäng: Psalmen und geistliche Lieder . . . , 1608.* Ed. by R. von Saalfeld, 1927.

P — *Hans Leo Hassler: Psalmen und Christliche Gesäng . . . , 1607.* Ed. by R. von Saalfeld; Folge 1, 1926 (references in this book are to the 3rd ed., 1935); Folge 2, 1928; Folge 3, 1933.

PG — *Hans Leo Hassler: Psalmen und Christliche Gesäng . . . , 1607.* [Ed. by J. P. Kirnberger;] Breitkopf, 1777.

HaverH — Havergal, W. H. *A History of the Old Hundredth Psalm Tune, with Specimens,* 1854.

HawkH — Hawkins, J. *A General History of the Science and Practice of Music.* 5 vols., 1776. New ed., 3 vols., 1853, 1875. References are to the orig. ed.

HayE — Haydon, G. *The Evolution of the Six-Four Chord*, 1933.

HayesM — Hayes, G. R. *Musical Instruments and their Music, 1500–1750.* 2 vols. (1928–1930).

HelmH — Helm, E. B. *Heralds of the Italian Madrigal*, in MQ XXVII (1941), 306.

I — Helm, E. B. *Italian Traits in the English Madrigal*, in *The Music Review* VII (1946), 26.

M — Helm, E. B. *The Beginnings of the Italian Madrigal and the Works of Arcadelt.* Ph.D. dissertation, Harvard University, 1939, unpublished.

S — Helm, E. B. *The Sixteenth-Century French Chanson*, in MTNAP XXXVI (1942; for 1941), 236.

HelmhS — Helmholtz, H. *On the Sensations of Tone.* Transl. and ed. by A. J. Ellis, 1930.

HenryS — *Henry VIII, King of England: Songs, Ballads and Instrumental Pieces. Reproduced from the British Museum MS 31922.* Ed. by Lady Mary Trefusis, 1912.

HenryT | Henry VIII: Three Songs of his own Composition. Ed. by A. Lewis, 1936.

HernánV | Hernández, D. F. La cuna y la escuela de Tomás L. de Victoria, in Ritmo XI, Num. Extraordinario (1940), 27.

HerrT | Herrero, J. J. and C. de Roda López. Tres músicos españoles: Juan del Encina, Lucas Fernandez, Manuel Doyagüe, y la cultura artística de su tiempo, 1912.

HertzC | Hertzmann, E. Trends in the Development of the Chanson in the Early 16th Century, in PAMS for 1940 (1946), 5.

M | Hertzmann, E. Zur Frage der Mehrchörigkeit in der ersten Hälfte des 16. Jahrhunderts, in ZfMW XII (1929), 138.

S | Hertzmann, E. Studien zur Basse danse im 15. Jahrhundert, mit besonderer Berücksichtigung des Brüsseler Manuskripts, in ZfMW XI (1929), 401.

W | Hertzmann, E. Adrian Willaert in der weltlichen Vokalmusik seiner Zeit, 1931.

HeuW | Heurich, H. John Wilbye in seinen Madrigalen, 1931.

HewMM | Hewitt, H. Malmaridade and Meshouwet, in TVNM XVII (1951), 181.

O | Hewitt, H. (ed.). Harmonice Musices Odhecaton A, 1942.

HillM | Hill, A. G. Medieval Organs in Spain, in SIM XIV (1913), 487.

HilleR | Hillemann, W. Ricercari, Canzonen und Fugen des 17. und 18. Jahrhunderts, 1932.

HirB | Hirsch, P. Bibliographie der musiktheoretischen Drucke des Franchino Gafori, in Festschrift für Johannes Wolf (1929), 65.

HirzD | Hirzel, B. Dienstinstruktion und Personalstatus der Hofkapelle Ferdinand's I. aus dem Jahre 1527, in SIM X (1909), 151.

G | Hirzel, B. Anton Gosswin . . . ein Beitrag zur Geschichte der Hofkapellen in München und Freising, 1909.

HMS | Hymn Melodies for the Whole Year (from the Sarum Service Books and other Ancient English Sources together with Sequences), 2nd ed., 1903.

HofL | Hofmann, G. Leonhart Schröter, ein lutherischer Kantor zu Magdeburg (1532–1601), 1934.

S | Hofmann, G. Die freien Kompositionen Leonhart Schröters, in ZfMW XVI (1934), 344.

HögZ | Högler, F. Bemerkungen zu Zarlinos Theorie, in ZfMW IX (1927), 518.

HolA | Hol, J. C. L'Amfiparnaso e le Veglie di Siena, in RMI XL (1936), 3.

H | Hol, J. C. Horatio Vecchi et l'évolution créatrice, in Gedenkboek aangeboden aan Dr. D. F. Scheurleer, (1925), 159.

HV | Hol, J. C. Horatio Vecchi, in RMI XXXVII (1930), 59.

R | Hol, J. C. Cipriano de Rore, in Festschrift für Karl Nef (1933), 134.

S | Hol, J. C. Le Veglie di Siena di Horatio Vecchi, in RMI XLIII (1939), 17.

V | Hol, J. C. Horatio Vecchi als weltlicher Komponist, 1934.

HorsE | Horsley, I. Improvised Embellishment in the Performance of Renaissance Polyphonic Music, in JAMS IV (1951), 3.

HouH | Houdoy, J. Histoire artistique de la cathédrale de Cambrai, 1880.

HowesB | Howes, F. William Byrd, 1928.

HR | The Harrow Replicas. 1942–   .

III | Parthenia . . . Composed by William Byrd, John Bull and Orlando Gibbons, 1611. Facsimile ed., 1942.

VI | Encomium Musices. By Philippe Galle, Jaen van der Straet and Joannes Bochius c. 1590. Facsimile ed., 1944.

HuD | Huber, K. Die Doppelmeister des 16. Jahrhunderts, in Festschrift . . . Adolf Sandberger (1918), 170.

I | Huber, K. Ivo de Vento, 1918.

HughEM | Hughes, Dom A. The Eton Manuscript, in PMA LIII (1927), 67.

IF | Hughes, Dom A. An Introduction to Fayrfax, in MD VI (1952), 83.

RF | Hughes, Dom A. The Works of Robert Fayrfax, in M&L XXX (1949), 118.

S | Hughes, Dom A. Sixteenth Century Service Music, in M&L V (1924), 145, 335.

HughesD | Hughes, C. W. Richard Deering's Fancies for Viols, in MQ XXVII (1941), 38.

L | Hughes, C. W. An Elizabethan Self-Instructor for the Lute, in The Guitar Review IX (1949), 29.

P | Hughes, C. W. Peter Philips, an English Musician in the Netherlands, in PAMS for 1940 (1946), 35.

PPM | Hughes, C. W. Porter, Pupil of Monteverdi, in MQ XX (1934), 278.

HuigA | Huigens, P. C. Blasius Amon, in SzMW XVIII (1931), 3.

HunC | Hunt, J. E. Cranmer's First Litany, 1544, and Merbecke's Book of Common Prayer, 1550, 1939.

HuschL   Huschke, J. *Orlando di Lassos Messen,* in AfMF V (1940), 84, 153.

HutchV   Hutchinson, L. *The Vihuela Music of Diego Pisador.* Master's thesis, Eastman School of Music, Rochester, N.Y. 1937, unpublished.

HuttC   Hutter, J. *Česká Notace: Nota Choralis,* in *Universita Karlova, Prague. Filozofická fakulta. Sbírka pojednání a rozprav* XVII (1930).

IdD   Idelsohn, A. Z. *Deutsche Elemente im alten Synagogengesang Deutschlands,* in ZfMW XV (1933), 385.

J   Idelsohn, A. Z. *Jewish Music,* 1929.

IISM   *Pubblicazioni dell'Istituto italiano per la Storia della Musica.*

     A   *Antologie e Raccolte,* 1941–   .

        I   *Villanelle alla Napolitana a tre voci di musicisti baresi del secolo XVI.* . . . Ed. by S. A. Luciani, 1941.

     M   *Monumenti,* 1942–   .

        I   *Madrigali di Carlo Gesualdo, Principe di Venosa.* Ed. by F. Vatielli, 1942.

       II   *Madrigali di Pomponio Nenna.* Ed. by E. Dagnino, 1942.

IllM   Illing, C.-H. *Zur Technik der Magnificat-Komposition des 16. Jahrhunderts,* 1936.

IM   *Instituta et Monumenta*

   Ser. I   *Monumenta*

       I   *Le Frottole nell'Edizione principe di Ottaviano Petrucci, Libri I, II, e III.* Ed. by G. Cesari, 1954.

IMAMI   *Istituzioni e Monumenti dell'Arte Musicale Italiana.* 1931–   .

     I-II   *Andrea e Giovanni Gabrieli e la Musica strumentale in San Marco.* I ed. by G. Benvenuti, 1931; II by Benvenuti with pref. by G. Cesari, 1932.

     IV   *La Camerata fiorentina: Vincenzo Galilei.* Ed. by F. Fano, 1934.

     V   *L'Oratorio dei Filippini e la Scuola musicale di Napoli.* Ed. by G. Pannain, 1934.

     VI   *La Musica in Cremona nella seconda metà del secolo XVI e i Primordi dell'Arte monteverdiana.* Ed. by G. Cesari with pref. by G. Pannain, 1939.

   Ser. II

       I   *La Cappella Musicale del Duomo di Milano I.* Ed. by F. Fano, 1956.

ImelS   Imelmann, R. *Zur Kenntnis der vor-Shakespeare'schen Lyrik,* in *Jahrbuch der deutschen Shakespeare-Gesellschaft* XXXIX (1903), 168.

IsaacC   Isaac, H. *Choralis Constantinus Book III, 1555.* Ed. by L. Cuyler, 1950.

IsozK   Isoz, K. *Körmöczbánya XV–XVI, századi zenészeiről,* 1908.

JaC   Jamot, P. *"Le Champion des Dames" de Martin le Franc, Manuscrit de la Bibliothèque de Grenoble,* in *Les Trésors des bibliothèques de France* V (1935), 117.

JachH   Jachimecki, Z. *Historja muzyki polskiej,* 1920.

     M   Jachimecki, Z. *Muzyka na dworze króla Władysława Jagiełły, 1424–1430,* 1915.

   MPH   Jachimecki, Z. *Muzyka Polska w Rozwoju Historycznym* . . . , I, 1948.

   MPJ   Jachimecki, Z. *Muzyka Polska w epoce Piastów i Jagiellonów,* in *Polska, jej dzieje i Kultura,* I (c. 1931), 531.

   MPR   Jachimecki, Z. *Muzyka Polska od roku 1572 do roku 1795,* in *Polska, jej Dzieje i Kultura,* II (ca. 1931), 529.

   MWP   Jachimecki, Z. *Muzyka w Polsce,* in *Polska: Obrazy i opisy* II (1909), 535.

     P   Jachimecki, Z. *Eine polnische Orgeltabulatur aus dem Jahre 1548,* in ZfMW II (1920), 206.

     T   Jachimecki, Z. *Tabulatura organowa z biblioteki klasztoru św. Ducha w Krakowie z r. 1548,* 1913.

     Z   Jachimecki, Z. *W kole zagadnień Bogurodzicy,* in *Księga pamiątkowa ku czci Leona Pinińskiego* I (1936), 403.

JahD   Jahn, F. *Die Nürnberger Trompeten- und Posaunenmacher im 16. Jahrhundert,* in AfMW VII (1925), 23.

JamesC   James, M. *Catalogue of the Manuscripts in the Library of Eton College,* 1895.

JAMS   *Journal of the American Musicological Society,* 1948–

JanequinD   *Clément Janequin: Deux chansons à 5 voix.* Ed. by M. Cauchie, 1924.

     T   *Clément Janequin: Trente chansons à 3 et 4 voix.* Ed. by M. Cauchie, 1928.

JasE   James, P. *Early Keyboard Instruments from the Beginnings to the Year 1820,* 1930.

JepCP   Jeppesen, K. *Counterpoint,* 1935. Transl. by G. Haydon, 1939.

     F   Jeppesen, K. *Über einige unbekannte Frottolenhandschriften,* in Acta XI (1939), 81.

     G   Jeppesen, K. *Die 3 Gafurius-Kodizes der Fabbrica del Duomo, Milano,* in Acta III (1931), 14.

JepI	Jeppesen, K. (ed.). *Die mehrstimmige italienische Laude um 1500*, 1935.
K	Jeppesen, K. (ed.). *Der Kopenhagener Chansonnier*, 1927.
KC	Jeppesen, K. *Eine musiktheoretische Korrespondenz des früheren Cinquecento*, in Acta XIII (1941), 3.
L	Jeppesen, K. *Die neuentdeckten Bücher der Lauden des Ottaviano dei Petrucci und andere musikalische Seltenheiten der Biblioteca Colombina zu Sevilla*, in ZfMW XII (1929), 73.
M	Jeppesen, K. *Wann entstand die Marcellus-Messe?* in AdlerF (1930), 126.
MP	Jeppesen, K. *The Recently Discovered Mantova Masses of Palestrina*, in Acta XXII (1950), 36.
O	Jeppesen, K. *Die italienische Orgelmusik am Anfang des Cinquecento*, 1943.
P	Jeppesen, K. *Marcellus-Probleme, einige Bemerkungen über die Missa Papae Marcelli*, in Acta XVI-XVII (1945), 11.
PS	Jeppesen, K. *The Style of Palestrina and the Dissonance*, 1st Eng. ed., 1927; 2nd Eng. ed., 1946. References in this book are to the 2nd ed.
U	Jeppesen, K. *Über einen Brief Palestrinas*, in *Peter Wagner-Festschrift* (1926), 100.
V	Jeppesen, K. *Ein venezianisches Laudenmanuskript*, in *Theodor Kroyer-Festschrift* (1933), 69.
VF	Jeppesen, K. *Venetian Folk-Songs of the Renaissance*, in PAMS for 1939 (1944), 62.
JespG	Jesperssøn, N. *Graduale*, 1573. Facsimile ed., 1935.
JirS	Jireček, C. *Staat und Gesellschaft im mittelalterlichen Serbien, III. Teil*, in *Denkschriften der Kaiserlichen Akademie der Wissenschaften in Wien, Philosophisch-historische Klasse, Band 58, Abhandlung 2*, 1915.
JoaC	Joaquim, M. (ed.). *O Cancioneiro Musical e Poético da Biblioteca Públia Hortênsia*, 1940.
M	Joaquim, M. *Em Louvor do grande Polifonista Estêvão Lopes Morago*, in *Brasil Cultural* II (1948), 16.
N	Joaquim, M. *Nótulas sôbre a Música na Sé de Viseu*, 1944.
P	Joaquim, M. *A propósito dos livros de polifonia existentes no Paço Ducal de Vila Viçosa (Portugal)*, in *Anuario Musical* II (1947), 69.
U	Joaquim, M. *Um Inédito musical: O "Te Deum" do licenciado Lopes Morago*, in *Brotéria* XXX (1940), 497.
JödeC	Jöde, F. (ed.). *Chorbuch*. 6 vols., 1927-31.
Josq	*Josquin des Prés: Werken*. Ed. by A. Smijers. In progress, 1921– .
K	*Klaagliederen op den Dood van Josquin*, 1921.
MS	*Missen*, 1931– .
MT	*Motetten*, 1926– .
WW	*Wereldlijke Werken*, 1925– .
JP	*Le Jardin de plaisance et fleur de rethoricque* (publ. c. 1501 by Antoine Vérard), facsimile ed.; I. Facsimile (1910); II. *Introduction et notes* (by E. Droz and A. Piaget, 1925).
JRB	*Journal of Renaissance and Baroque Music*, 1946-47. (See MD.)
JulD	Julian, J. *A Dictionary of Hymnology*, 5th ed., 1925.
JulbeM	Julbe, V. G. *Maestros españoles del Siglo de Oro de la Polifonía vocal* (n.d.; 1947?).
KabisM	Kabis, Sister M. E. *The Marian Tropes*, in *The Catholic Choirmaster* XXXVIII (1952), 149.
KadAC	Kade, O. *Adrian Petit Coclicus (1500-1555/6). Ein Beitrag zur Musikgeschichte des 16. Jahrhunderts*, in MfMG XXIX (1897), 1.
B	Kade, O. *Biographisches zu Antonio Squarcialupi, dem Florentiner Organist im XV. Jahrhundert*, in MfMG XVII (1885), 1.
M	Kade, O. *Mattheus le Maistre*, 1862.
P	Kade, O. *Die älteren Passionskompositionen bis zum Jahre 1631*, 1893.
KadeC	Kade, R. *Christoph Demant. 1567-1643*, in VfMW VI (1890), 469.
S	Kade, R. *Antonius Scandellus (1517-1580); Ein Beitrag zur Geschichte der Dresdener Hofkantorei*, in SIM XV (1914), 535.
KahF	Kahmann, B. *Antoine de Fevin—A Bio-bibliographical Contribution*, in MD IV (1950), 153; V (1951), 143.
KalG	Kallenbach, H. *Georg Forster's Frische Teutsche Liedlein*, 1931
KastH	Kastner, J. *Humanizmus és régi magyar irodalom*, in *Győri Szemle* IV (1933), 19.
KastenC	Kastendieck, M. M. *England's Musical Poet, Thomas Campion*, 1938.
KastnCE	Kastner, S. *Contribución al Estudio de la Música española y portuguesa*, 1941.

KastnCP   Kastner, S. (ed.). *Cravistas portuguezes*, 1935.
M   Kastner, S. *Música hispânica: O Estilo musical de Padre Manuel R. Coelho . . . ,* 1936.
MM   Kastner, S. *Los manuscritos musicales n⁸ 48 y 242 de la Biblioteca General de la Universidad de Coimbra,* in *Anuario Musical* V (1950), 78.
KeinM   Keiner, F. *Die Madrigale Gesualdos von Venosa,* 1914.
KelM   Kellogg, K. *Die Messen von Ludwig Daser (1525–1589),* 1938.
KemJC   Kempers, K. P. Bernet. *Jacobus Clemens non Papa und seine Motetten,* 1928.
M   Kempers, K. P. Bernet. *Muziekgeschiedenis,* 1943.
S   Kempers, K. P. Bernet. *Die "Souterliedekens" des Jacobus Clemens non Papa . . . ,* in TVNM XII (1928), 261; XIII (1929), 29; (1931), 126.
W   Kempers, K. P. Bernet. *Die wallonische und die französische Chanson in der ersten Hälfte des 16. Jahrhunderts,* in *International Society for Musical Research, First Congress, Liége, September 1–6, 1930, Report,* 76.
KenM   Kendall, R. *The Life and Works of Samuel Mareschall,* in MQ XXX (1944), 37.
N   Kendall, R. *Notes on Arnold Schlick,* in Acta XI (1939), 136.
KennO   Kenney, S. W. *Origins and Chronology of the Brussels Manuscript 5557 in the Bibliothèque royale de Belgique,* in RB VI (1952), 75.
KentonN   Kenton, E. F. *A Note on the Classification of 16th-century Music,* in MQ XXXVIII (1952), 202.
KermanA   Kerman, J. *Elizabethan Anthologies of Italian Madrigals,* JAMS IV (1951), 122.
M   Kerman, J. *The Elizabethan Madrigal. A comparative study.* Ph. D. dissertation, Princeton University, 1950, Princeton, N.J., unpublished.
MA   Kerman, J. *Master Alfonso and the English Madrigal,* MQ XXXVIII (1952), 222.
MT   Kerman, J. *Morley and "The Triumphs of Oriana,"* in M&L XXXIV (1953), 185.
KiS   Kiwi, E. *Studien zur Geschichte des italienischen Liedmadrigals im XVI. Jahrhundert; Satzlehre und Genealogie der Kanzonetten,* 1937.
KiesC   Kiesewetter, R. G. *Galerie der alten Contrapunctisten,* 1847.
G   Kiesewetter, R. G. *Geschichte der europäisch-abendländischen oder unserer heutigen Musik,* 1834.
S   Kiesewetter, R. G. *Schicksale und Beschaffenheit des weltlichen Gesanges,* 1841.
T   Kiesewetter, R. G. *Die Verdienste der Niederländer um die Tonkunst,* 1829.
KillK   Killing, J. *Kirchenmusikalische Schätze der Bibliothek des Abbate Fortunato Santini,* 1910.
KinDT   Kinkeldey, O. *Dance Tunes of the Fifteenth Century,* in *Instrumental Music* (Isham Library Papers I), 3, 89.
G   Kinkeldey, O. *Franchino Gafori and Marsilio Ficino,* in *Harvard Library Bulletin* for Autumn 1947, 379.
J   Kinkeldey, O. *A Jewish Dancing Master of the Renaissance,* in *A. S. Freidus Memorial Volume,* 1929.
L   Kinkeldey, O. *Luzzasco Luzzaschi's Solo-Madrigale mit Klavierbegleitung,* in SIM IX (1908), 538.
O   Kinkeldey, O. *Orgel und Klavier in der Musik des 16. Jahrhunderts,* 1910.
P   Kinkeldey, O. *Music and Music Printing in Incunabula,* in *Papers of the Bibliographical Society of America* XXVI (1932), 89.
R   Kinkeldey, O. *Thomas Robinson's "Schoole of Musicke,"* abstract in BAMS, No. 1 (1936), 7.
T   Kinkeldey, O. *Fausto Torrefranca's Theory of the Villota,* abstract in BAMS, No. 6 (1942), 7.
KinsP   Kinsky, G. *A History of Music in Pictures,* 1930.
S   Kinsky, G. *Schriftstücke aus dem Palestrina Kreis,* in *Peter Wagner Festschrift* (1926), 108.
KJ   *Kirchenmusikalisches Jahrbuch,* 1886–   .
KlefA   Klefisch, W. *Arcadelt als Madrigalist,* 1938.
KnappC   Knapp, J. M. *The Canzone Francese and its Vocal Models.* Master's thesis, Columbia University, 1941, New York, unpublished.
KoczA   Koczirz, A. *Die Auflösung der Hofmusikkapelle nach dem Tode Kaiser Maximilians I.,* in ZfMW XIII (1931), 531.
D   Koczirz, A. *Die Gitarrekompositionen in Miguel de Fuenllana's Orphénica lyra (1554),* in AfMW IV (1922), 241.
G   Koczirz, A. *Zur Geschichte des Luython'schen Klavizimbels,* in SIM IX (1908), 565.
J   Koczirz, A. *Der Lautenist Hans Judenkünig,* in SIM VI (1905), 237.
LO   Koczirz, A. *Lauten und Orgeltabulaturen,* in AdlerH I (1930), 398.

KoczM   Koczirz, A. *Die Fantasien des Melchior de Barberis für die siebensaitige Gitarre*, in ZfMW IV (1921), 11.

KodS   Kodály, Z. *Sajátságos dallamszerkezet a cseremisz népzenében*, 1934. (In series, *Magyar Zenei Dolgozatok*, No. 11. Reprinted from *Balassa Emlékkönyv*.) Contains abstract in German.

KörL   Körte, O. *Laute und Lautenmusik bis zur Mitte des 16. Jahrhunderts*, 1901.

KornH   Kornmüller, U. *Johann Hothby, eine Studie zur Geschichte der Musik im 15. Jahrhundert*, in KJ VIII (1893), 1.

T   Kornmüller, U. *Die alten Musiktheoretiker: Johannes Tinctoris*, in KJ XVIII (1903), 1.

KorteH   Korte, W. *Die Harmonik des frühen XV. Jahrhunderts in ihrem Zusammenhang mit der Formtechnik*, 1929.

S   Korte, W. *Studie zur Geschichte der Musik in Italien im ersten Viertel des 15. Jahrhunderts*, 1933.

KosackL   Kosack, H.-P. *Geschichte der Laute und Lautenmusik in Preussen*, 1935.

KrE   Kroyer, T. *Dialog und Echo in der alten Chormusik*, in *Jahrbuch der Musikbibliothek Peters* XVI (1909), 13.

I   Kroyer, T. *Die Anfänge der Chromatik im italienischen Madrigal des XVI. Jahrhunderts*, 1902.

MR   Kroyer, T. *Von der Musica reservata des 16. Jahrhunderts*, in *Festschrift Heinrich Wölfflin zum 70. Geburtstag* (1935), 127.

V   Kroyer, T. (ed.). *Der vollkommene Partiturspieler* . . . Vol. I, 1930.

ZC   Kroyer, T. *Zur Chiavettenfrage*, in AdlerF (1930), 107.

KrausB   Kraus, H. *Jacob Buus, Leben und Werke*, in TVNM XII (1926), 35, (1927), 81, (1928), 221.

KrebsD   Krebs, C. *Girolamo Dirutas Transilvano*, in VfMW VIII (1892), 307.

K   Krebs, C. *Die besaiteten Klavierinstrumente bis zum Anfang des 17. Jahrhunderts*, in VfMW VIII (1892), 91.

KrenekO   Krenek, E. *Johannes Ockeghem*, 1953.

KretM   Kretzschmar, H. *Musikgeschichtliche Stichproben aus deutscher Laienliteratur des 16. Jahrhunderts*, in *Festschrift [für]* . . . *Rochus Freiherrn von Liliencron* (1910), 116.

S   Kretzschmar, H. *Führer durch den Konzertsaal* . . . *Die Orchestermusik: I Sinfonie und Suite*. Ed. by F. Noack, 1932.

Z   Kretzschmar, H. *Lodovico Zacconis Leben auf Grund seiner Autobiographie*, in *Jahrbuch der Musikbibliothek Peters* XVII (1910), 45.

KristM   Kristeller, P. O. *Music and Learning in the Early Italian Renaissance*, in JRB I (1947), 255.

KuV   Kuhn, M. R. A. *Die Verzierungs-Kunst in der Gesangs-Musik des 16.–17. Jahrhunderts (1535–1650)* . . . , 1902.

KühD   Kühner, H. *Ein unbekannter Brief von Guillaume Dufay*, in Acta XI (1939), 114.

KühnR   Kühn, A. *Rhythmik und Melodik Michael Behaims*, 1907.

LachOM   Lach, R. *Studien zur Entwickelungsgeschichte der ornamentalen Melopöie*, 1913.

LafC   La Fage, J. A. L. de. *Extraits du Catalogue critique et raisonné d'une petite bibliothèque musicale*, n. d.

E   La Fage, J. A. L. de. *Essais de diphthérographie musicale*. 2 vols., 1864.

LafonK   Lafontaine, H. C. de. *The King's Musick*, 1909.

LamE   Lamson, R. *English Broadside Ballad Tunes of the 16th and 17th Centuries*, in PAMS for 1939 (1944), 112.

LandL   Land, J. P. N. *De luit en het wereldlijk lied en Duitschland en Nederland*, in TVNM IV (1892), 17.

T   Land, J. P. N. *Het Luitboek van Thysius* . . . , in TVNM I (1884), 129, (1885), 205; II (1885), 1, (1886), 109, (1887), 177, 278; III (1888), 1.

LangM   Lang, P. H. *Music in Western Civilization*, 1941.

N   Lang, P. H. *The so-called Netherlands Schools*, in MQ XXV (1939), 48.

LangeZ   Lange, G. *Zur Geschichte der Solmisation*, in SIM I (1900), 535.

LassoS   *Orlando di Lasso: Septem Psalmi poenitentiales*. Ed. by H. Bäuerle, with analytical study. 7 vols., 1906.

W   *Orlando di Lasso. Sämtliche Werke*. First Series, ed. by F. X. Haberl and A. Sandberger, 1894–1953, 21 vols.; New Series begun with Vol. I, ed. W. Boetticher, 1956.

LauC   Laurencie, L. de la, A. Mairy, and G. Thibault (eds.). *Chansons au luth et airs de cour français du XVIᵉ siècle*, 1934.

L   Laurencie, L. de la. *Les Luthistes Charles Bocquet, Antoine Francisque et Jean-Baptiste Besard*, in RdM VII (1926), 69, 126.

LauLL   Laurencie, L. de la. *Les Luthistes*, 1928.

M   Laurencie, L. de la. *La Musique à la Cour des Ducs de Bretagne aux XIVe et XVe siècles*, in RdM XVII (1933), 1.

LaudP   Laudon, R. T. *Poetry and Music of the Polyphonic Chanson, circa 1520–1535*. Master's thesis, University of Minnesota, Minneapolis, 1950, unpublished.

LawrM   Lawrence, W. J. *Music in the Elizabethan Theatre*, in MQ VI (1920), 192.

MM   Lawrence, W. J. *Notes on a Collection of Masque Music*, in M&L III (1922), 49.

LdnL   Van der Linden, A. *La Légende d'un psautier perdu de Samuel Mareschall*, in *Hommage à Charles van den Borren (Mélanges)* (1945), 308.

M   Van der Linden, A. *La Musique dans les Chroniques de Jean Molinet*, in *Mélanges Ernest Closson* (1948), 167.

LechnerD   *Leonhard Lechner: Deutsche Sprüche von Leben und Tod*. Ed. by W. Lipphardt and K. Ameln, 1929.

H   *Leonhard Lechner: Das Hohelied Salomonis*. Ed. by W. Lipphardt and K. Ameln, 1928.

L   *Leonhard Lechner: Das Leiden unseres Herren Jesu Christi, aus dem Evangelisten Johannes (1594)*. Ed. by W. Lipphardt and K. Ameln, 1927.

TL   *Leonhard Lechner: Neue teutsche Lieder (1582)*. Ed. by E. F. Schmid, 1926.

LedH   Lederer, V. *Über Heimat und Ursprung der mehrstimmigen Tonkunst*, 1906.

LeiE   Leichtentritt, H. *The Reform of Trent and its Effect on Music*, in MQ XXX (1944), 319.

G   Leichtentritt, H. *Geschichte der Motette*, 1908.

M   Leichtentritt, H. *Claudio Monteverdi als Madrigalkomponist*, in SIM XI (1910), 255.

MR   Leichtentritt, H. *Musica Riservata*, abstract in BAMS, No. 6 (1942), 18.

LejP   *Claude Le Jeune: Three-part Psalms . . .* Ed. by H. David, 1945.

LenAW   Lenaerts, R. B. M. *Voor de biographie van Adriaen Willaert*, in *Hommage à Charles van den Borren (Mélanges)* (1945), 205.

C   Lenaerts, R. B. M. *La Chapelle de Saint-Marc à Venise sous Adrian Willaert (1527–1562)*, in *Bulletin de l'Institut historique belge de Rome* XIX (1938), 205.

MT   Lenaerts, R. B. M. *De zesstemmige mis "Mente tota" van Adriaen Willaert*, in *Musica Sacra: Sancta Sancte* LXII (1935), 153.

N   Lenaerts, R. B. M. *Het nederlands polifonies lied in de 16de eeuw*, 1933.

P   Lenaerts, R. B. M. *La Chanson polyphonique néerlandaise aux 15e et 16e siècles*, in *International Society for Musical Research, First Congress, Liége, September 1–6, 1930, Report*, 168.

PM   Lenaerts, R. B. M. *The 16th-Century Parody Mass in the Netherlands*, in MQ XXXVI (1950), 410.

W   Lenaerts, R. B. M. *Notes sur Adrien Willaert, maître de chapelle de Saint-Marc à Venise de 1527 à 1562*, in *Bulletin de l'Institut historique belge de Rome* XV (1935), 107.

LenzB   Lenzinger, G. *Domorganist Hans Buchner*, in *Verein für Geschichte des Bodensees und seiner Umgebung: Schriften* LXIII (1936), 54.

LesA   Lesure, F. *Pierre Attaingnant, notes et documents*, in MD III (1949), 33.

AC   Lesure, F., N. Bridgman, I. Cazeaux, M. Levin, K. Levy, and D. P. Walker *Anthologie de la Chanson parisienne au XVIe siècle*, 1952.

C   Lesure, F. *La Communauté des "Joueurs d'instruments" au XVIe siècle*, in *Revue historique de droit français et étranger* I (1953), 79.

E   Lesure, F. and G. Thibault. *Bibliographie des éditions musicales publiées par Nicholas du Chemin (1549–1576)*, in AM I (1953), 269.

G   Lesure, F. *Claude Goudimel, étudiant, correcteur et éditeur parisien*, in MD II (1948), 225.

GF   Lesure, F. *La Guitare en France au XVIe siècle*, in MD IV (1950), 187.

J   Lesure, F. *Clément Janequin*, in MD V (1951), 157.

LeviA   Levitan, J. S. *Adrian Willaert's Famous Duo "Quidnam ebrietas,"* in TVNM XV (1938), 166.

O   Levitan, J. S. *Ockeghem's Clefless Compositions*, in MQ XXIII (1937), 440.

LevrJ   Levron, J. *Clément Janequin, musicien de la Renaissance*, 1948.

LevyS   Levy, K. J. *"Susanne un jour." The History of a 16th Century Chanson*, in AM I (1953), 375.

LewisS   Lewis, A. (ed.). *William Shakespeare. Two Songs from The Tempest*, n. d.

Liber   *Liber usualis: Missae et Officii pro dominicis et festis cum cantu Gregoriano*, 1934. (Desclée edition)

LiberR   *Liber responsorialis . . . ,* 1895. (Desclée edition)

LichtD   Lichtenthal, P. *Dizionario e Bibliografia della Musica*, 3 vols., 1826.

LiliC	Liliencron, R. von. *Die Chorgesänge des lateinisch-deutschen Schuldramas im XVI. Jahrhundert*, in VfMW VI (1890), 309.
D	Liliencron, R. von. *Deutsches Leben im Volkslied um 1530*, 1884.
H	Liliencron, R. von. *Die Horazischen Metren in deutschen Kompositionen des 16. Jahrhunderts*, in VfMW III (1887), 26.
V	Liliencron, R. von. *Die historischen Volkslieder der Deutschen vom 13. bis 16. Jahrhundert*, 4 vols., 1865–69. (Music exx. pr. in an appendix to Vol. 4.)
LindM	Lindsey, E. S. *The Music of the Songs in the Elizabethan Drama*. Ph.D. dissertation, University of North Carolina, Chapel Hill, No. Car., 1923, unpublished.
S	Lindsey, E. S. *The Music of the Songs in Fletcher's Plays*, in *Studies in Philology* XXI (1924), 325.
LindenR	Lindenburg, C. W. H. *Het leven en de werken van Johannes Regis*, 1939.
LippGZ	Lipphardt, W. *Gesellige Zeit*, 1933.
P	Lipphardt, W. *Die Geschichte des mehrstimmigen Proprium Missae*, 1950.
LisioM	Lisio, G. *Musica e Poesia. Osservazioni alla Stanza del Petrarca musicata dal Du Fay*, in RMI I (1894), 267.
U	Lisio, G. *Una Stanza del Petrarca musicata dal Du Fay, tratta da due Codici antichi*, 1893.
LittC	Littleton, A. H. *A Catalogue of One Hundred Works Illustrating the History of Music Printing . . .*, 1911.
LiuO	Liuzzi, F. *L'Opera del Genio italiano all'Estero—I Musicisti in Francia*, I, 1946.
Q	Liuzzi, F. *Notes sur les Barzelette et les Canzoni a ballo du Quattrocento italien . . .*, in PAMS for 1939 (1944), 193.
LivS	Livermore, A. *The Spanish Dramatists and their Use of Music*, in M&L XXV (1944), 140.
LiviF	Livi, G. *The Ferrabosco Family*, in MAn IV (1913), 121.
LivingS	Livingston, N. *The Scottish Metrical Psalter of 1635*, 1864.
LöK	Löwenfeld, H. *Leonhard Kleber und sein Orgeltabulaturbuch*, 1897.
LobS	Łobaczewska, S. *O utworach Sebastjana z Felsztyna (XVI wiek)*, in *Kwartalnik Muzyczny*, No. 3 (1929), 227; No. 4 (1929), 346.
LoboC	*Duarte Lôbo: Composições polifónicas*. Ed. by M. Joaquim, Vol. I, 1945.
LoepL	Loepelmann, M. *Die Liederhandschrift des Cardinals de Rohan*, in *Gesellschaft für romansche Literatur* XLIV (1923).
LöhM	Löhrer, E. *Die Messen von Senfl: Beitrag zur Geschichte des polyphonen Messordinariums um 1500*, 1938.
LongS	Long, J. H. *Shakespeare and Thomas Morley*, in *Modern Language Notes* LXV (1950), 17.
———	Lopez-Chavarri, E. *Historia de la Música*. 2 vols. 3rd ed., 1929.
LowA	Lowinsky, E. *Zur Frage der Deklamationsrhythmik in der a-cappella-Musik des 16. Jahrhunderts* in Acta VII (1935), 62.
BV	Lowinsky, E. *A Newly Discovered Sixteenth-century Motet Manuscript in the Biblioteca Vallicelliana in Rome*, in JAMS III (1950), 173.
C	Lowinsky, E. *Secret Chromatic Art in the Netherlands Motet*, 1946.
G	Lowinsky, E. *The Goddess Fortuna in Music*, in MQ XXIX (1943), 45.
L	Lowinsky, E. *Das Antwerpener Motettenbuch Orlando di Lasso's und seine Beziehungen zum Motettenschaffen der niederländischen Zeitgenossen*, 1937. (Also in TVNM XIV [1935], 185; XV [1939], 1, 94.)
M	Lowinsky, E. *Music in the Culture of the Renaissance*, in *Journal of the History of Ideas* XV (1954), 531.
MS	Lowinsky, E. *The Concept of Physical and Musical Space in the Renaissance*, in PAMS for 1941 (1946), 57.
S	Lowinsky, E. *The Function of Conflicting Signatures in Early Polyphonic Music*, in MQ XXXI (1945), 227.
SS	Lowinsky, E. *On the Use of Scores by Sixteenth-Century Musicians*, in JAMS I, No. 1, (1948), 17.
LuD	Luther, W. M. *Gallus Dressler: Ein Beitrag zur Geschichte des protestantischen Schulkantorats im 16. Jahrhundert*, 1941.
LückS	Lück, S. (ed.). *Sammlung ausgezeichneter Kompositionen für die Kirche*, 2nd ed. 4 vols., 1884–85.
LudD	Ludwig, F. *Die mehrstimmige Messe des 14. Jahrhunderts*, in AfMW VII (1925), 417.
G	Ludwig, F. *Die geistliche nichtliturgische, weltliche einstimmige und die mehrstimmige Musik des Mittelalters bis zum Anfang des 15. Jahrhunderts*, in AdlerH I, 157.
GM	Ludwig, F. *Geschichte der Mensuralnotation von 1250–1460*, in SIM VI (1905), 597. (A review of WolfG)

LudQ   Ludwig, F. *Die Quellen der Motetten ältesten Stils*, in AfMW V (1923), 185, 273.

LukO   *Ivan Lukačić: Odabrani Moteti (1620)*. Ed. by D. Plamenac, 1935.

LunI   Lunelli, R. *Iconografia monteverdiana*, in RMI XLVII (1943), 38.

T   Lunelli, R. *Contributi trentini alle relazioni musicali fra l'Italia e la Germania nel Rinascimento*, in Acta XXI (1949), 41.

LupP   Luper, A. T. *Portuguese Polyphony in the Sixteenth and Early Seventeenth Centuries*, in JAMS III (1950), 93.

LütgG   Lütgendorff, W. L. von. *Die Geigen- und Lautenmacher vom Mittelalter bis zur Gegenwart*. 2 vols., 1922.

LuthD   *Martin Luther. Deutsche Messe, 1526*. Facsimile ed., with preface by J. Wolf, 1934.

W   *Martin Luther. Werke. Kritische Gesamtausgabe. Bd. 35*, 1923. Bibliographical and text-critical part by W. Lucke; musical part by H. J. Moser.

LyG   Lyon, C. *Jean Guyot dit Castileti, célèbre musicien wallon du 16e siècle . . . né à Châtelet en 1512*, 1876.

LyderP   Lyder, P. *Polyphonic Techniques in the Motets of Peter Philips as Illustrated in Thirty Examples*. Master's thesis, New York University, 1950, unpublished.

M&L   *Music & Letters*. 1920– .

MaH   Machabey, A. *Histoire et évolution des formules musicales du 1er au XVe siècle*, 1928.

MachM   Guillaume de Machaut: *Musikalische Werke*. Ed. by F. Ludwig. in PubAMD Vol. 1 (*Ballades, Rondeaux*, and *Virelais*), 1926; Vol. 2 (Commentary), 1928; Vol. 3 (Motets), 1929; Vol. 4 (Mass and *Lais*), 1943 (ed. destroyed), 1954.

MacmE   MacMillan, J. B. *An Historical Sketch of the Tune set by Matthias Greiter to "Es sind doch selig alle die"* . . . Master's thesis, Manhattan School of Music, New York, 1953, unpublished.

MaddV   Maddison, A. R. *A Short Account of the Vicars Choral, Poor Clerks, Organists and Choristers of Lincoln Cathedral, from the 12th c. to the Accession of Edward 6th*, 1878.

MaiM   Maier, J. J. *Die musikalischen Handschriften der k. Hof- und Staatsbibliothek in München, Erster Theil*, 1879.

MalCM   Malipiero, G. F. *Claudio Monteverdi*, 1929.

D   Malipiero, G. F. *Antonfrancesco Doni Musico*, 1946.

M   Malipiero, G. F. *Monteverdi*, in MQ XVIII (1932), 383.

Mald   Maldeghem, R. van. (ed.). *Trésor musical*. 1865–93.

P   *Musique profane*. 29 vols., 1865–93.

R   *Musique religieuse*. 29 vols., 1865–93.

MAn   *The Musical Antiquary*. Oct. 1909–July 1913.

MangF   Mangeot, A. (ed.). *Three Fancies for String Quartet* [Coperario, Jenkins, Ward; printed separately], 1936.

MannL   Manning, R. J. *Lachrymae: A Study of John Dowland*, in M&L XXV (1944), 45.

MantN   Mantuani, J. *Über den Beginn des Notendrucks*, in *Vorträge . . . herausgegeben von der Leo-Gesellschaft, Nr. 16*, 1901.

MarG   Marix, J. *Hayne van Ghizeghem, Musician at the Court of the 15th-century Burgundian Dukes*, in MQ XXVIII (1942), 276.

H   Marix, J. *Histoire de la musique et des musiciens de la cour de Bourgogne sous le règne de Philippe le Bon*, 1939.

M   Marix, J. *Les Musiciens de la cour de Bourgogne au XVe siècle (1420–1467)*, 1937.

MarchiP   Marchi, L. and G. Bertolani. *Inventario dei Manoscritti della R. Biblioteca Universitaria di Pavia* I, 1894.

MarenM   *Luca Marenzio: Motetten*. Ed. by H. Engel, 1926.

V   *Luca Marenzio: Villanellen für drei Stimmen*. Ed. by H. Engel, 1928.

W   *Luca Marenzio: Sämtliche Werke*. Ed. by A. Einstein. In PubAMD. Vol. 1 in Jahrg. IV¹, 1929; Vol. 2 in Jahrg. VI, 1931.

MarieV   Sister Lucy Marie. *Tomás Luis de Victoria, Priest-Composer*, in *The Catholic Choirmaster* XXXII (1946), 149.

MarkG   Mark, J. *The Orlando Gibbons Tercentenary, Some Virginal MSS in the Music Division of the N. Y. Public Library*, 1926.

J   Mark, J. *The Jonsonian Masque*, in M&L III (1922), 358.

MarpB   Marpurg, F. W. *Kritische Briefe über die Tonkunst*. 3 vols., 1759–63.

MarquS   Marquardt, H. *Die Stuttgarter Chorbücher, unter besonderer Behandlung der Messen*, 1936.

MarrF   Marrocco, W. T. *Fourteenth-Century Italian Cacce*, 1942.
MarriF   Marriage, E. *Georg Forsters Frische Teutsche Liedlein in fünf Teilen*, 1903.
MartiniE   Martini, G. B. (ed.). *Esemplare ossia Saggio fondamentale pratico di Contrappunto*. 2 vols., 1774–75.
S   Martini, G. *Storia della Musica*. 3 vols., 1757–81.
MarxC   Marxer, O. *Zur spätmittelalterlichen Choralgeschichte St. Gallens*, 1908.
MaryO   Mary, A. *L'Orchésographie de Thoinot Arbeau*, in *Les Trésors des bibliothèques de France* V (1935), 85.
MAS   *Musical Antiquarian Society*. 19 vols., 1840–47.
I   *William Byrd: A Mass for Five Voices*. Ed. by E. F. Rimbault, 1841.
II   *John Wilbye: The First Set of Madrigals*. Ed. by J. Turle, 1841.
III   *Orlando Gibbons: Madrigals and Motets for Five Voices*. Ed. by Sir G. Smart, 1841.
V   *Thomas Morley: The First Set of Ballets for Five Voices, 1595*. Ed. by E. F. Rimbault, 1842.
VI   *William Byrd: Book I of Cantiones Sacrae for Five Voices*. Ed. by W. Horsley, 1842.
VIII   *Thomas Weelkes: The First Set of Madrigals*. Ed. by E. J. Hopkins, 1843.
IX   *Orlando Gibbons: Fantasies in Three Parts composed for Viols*. Ed. by E. F. Rimbault, 1843.
XI   *The Whole Book of Psalms . . . in four parts* [by Farmer, Farnaby, Dowland, Kirbye, *et al.*], published by Thomas Este. Ed. by E. F. Rimbault, 1844.
XII   *John Dowland: The First Set of Songs*. Ed. by W. Chappell, 1844.
XIII   *John Hilton: Airs or Fa las*. Ed. by J. Warren, 1844.
XIV   *M. Este, T. Ford, Weelkes and Bateson: A Collection of Anthems*. Ed. by E. F. Rimbault, 1845.
XV   *John Bennet: Madrigals for Four Voices*. Ed. by E. J. Hopkins, 1845.
XVI   *John Wilbye: The Second Set of Madrigals*. Ed. by G. W. Budd, 1846.
XVII   *Thomas Bateson: The First Set of Madrigals*. Ed. by E. F. Rimbault, 1847.
XVIII   *W. Byrd, J. Bull and O. Gibbons: Parthenia, or the first music ever printed for the Virginals*. Ed. by E. F. Rimbault, 1847.
MassonB   Masson, P.-M. *La Musique espagnole au Congrès de Barcelone*, in RdM XVII (1936), 113.
C   Masson, P.-M. (ed.). *Chants de carnaval florentins*, 1913.
H   Masson, P.-M. *Le Mouvement humaniste*, in EC, *Partie I*, III, 1298.
M   Masson, P.-M. *Jacques Mauduit et les Hymnes latins de Laurence Strozzi*, in RdM VI (1925), 6, 59.
MayV   May, H. von. *Die Kompositionstechnik T. L. de Victorias*, 1943.
MB   *Monumenta musicae belgicae*. Ed. by J. Watelet. 1932–   .
IV   *Charles Guillet, Giovanni (de) Macque, Carolus Luython*, 1938.
McalS   McAlpine, C. L. *A Study of the Chansons of Antoine Busnois*. Master's thesis, Eastman School of Music, Rochester, N.Y., 1943, unpublished.
MD   *Musica Disciplina*. (This title succeeds *Journal of Renaissance and Baroque Music*), 1948–   .
MeK   Meyer, K. *Das Konzert*, 1925.
L   Meyer, K. *The Liturgical Music Incunabula in the British Museum. Germany, Italy, and Switzerland*, in *The Library* Ser. 4, XX (1939), 272.
M   Meyer, K. *Michel de Toulouze*, in *The Music Review* VII (1946), 178.
N   Meyer, K. *New Facts on the Printing of Music Incunabula*, in PAMS for 1940 (1946), 80.
P   Meyer, K. *The Printing of Music 1473–1934*, in *The Dolphin* II (1935), 171.
MeistK   Meister, K. S. (ed.). *Das katholische deutsche Kirchenlied in seinen Singweisen von den frühesten Zeiten bis gegen Ende des siebzehnten Jahrhunderts* I, 1862.
MendD   Mendel, A. *Devices for Transposition in the Organ before 1600*, in Acta XXI (1949), 24.
P   Mendel, A. *Pitch in the 16th and Early 17th Centuries*, in MQ XXXIV (1948), 28, 199, 336, 575.
MeneN   *Les Théoriciens de la musique au temps de la Renaissance: Michel de Menehou —Nouvelle Instruction Familière (1558)*. Ed. by H. Expert, 1900.
——   Ménil, F. de. *L'École contrapuntique flamande au XVe et au XVIe siècle*, 1905.
MerG   Merian, W. (ed.). *Geistliche Werke des XVI. Jahrhunderts* (Fasc. I in *Musikalische Werke schweizerischer Komponisten des XVI., XVII., und XVIII. Jahrhunderts*, ed. by K. Nef), 1927.

MerM   Merian, W. *Gregor Meyer*, in SJ I (1924), 138.

O   Merian, W. *Die Tabulaturen des Organisten Hans Kotter*, 1917.

T   Merian, W. *Der Tanz in den deutschen Tabulaturbüchern*, 1927.

MerbO   *The Office of the Holy Communion as set by John Merbecke*. Ed. by E. H. Fellowes, 1949.

MercF   Mercati, A. *Favori di Paolo III a Musici (Giacomo Archadelt—Ivo Barry—Bartolomeo Crotti—Francesco [Canova] da Milano)*, in NA X (1933), 109.

MerrM   Merritt, A. T. *The Motet at the Time of Gombert*, abstract in BAMS No. 7 (1943), 19.

MeruC   *Claudio Merulo: Canzonen*, 1592. Ed. by P. Pidoux, 1941.

O   *Claudio Merulo: Livre IV des Oeuvres d'Orgue . . . , Venise, 1568*. Ed. by J. B. Labat [1865?].

MeyMM   Mey, K. *Von den Meistersingern und ihrer Musik*, in *Neue Zeitschrift für Musik*, Jahrgang LXXI, Bd. 100 (1904), 2, 17, 33, 53, 69.

MeyeE   Meyer, E. H. *English Chamber Music*, 1946.

F   Meyer, E. H. *Form in the Instrumental Music of the 17th Century*, in PMA LXV (1938), 45.

M   Meyer, E. H. *Die mehrstimmige Spielmusik des 17. Jahrhunderts in Nord- und Mitteleuropa*, 1934.

N   Meyer, E. H. *The In Nomine and the Birth of Instrumental Style*, in M&L XVII (1936), 25.

S   Meyer, E. H. *Spielmusik des Barock, I*, 1934.

MF   *Die Musikforschung*, 1948–

MfMG   *Monatshefte für Musikgeschichte*, 1869–1905.

MGG   *Die Musik in Geschichte und Gegenwart*. Ed. by F. Blume, 1949–

MichW   Michaelis, O. *Johann Walter (1496–1570), der Musiker-Dichter in Luthers Gefolgschaft*, 1939.

MichelD   Michel, A. *The Earliest Dance Manuals*, in *Mediaevalia et humanistica III* (1945), 117.

MiesL   Mies, O. H. *Dowland's Lachrymae Tune*, in MD IV (1950), 59.

MilánL   *Luys Milán: Libro intitulado El Cortesano*, in *Colección de Libros españoles raros ó curiosos* VII, 1874. Facsimile ed.

M   *Luys Milán: Musikalische Werke*. Ed. by L. Schrade. In PubAMD II¹, 1927.

MillB   Miller, H. M. *John Bull's Organ Works*, in M&L XXVIII (1947), 25.

D   Miller, H. M. *The Earliest Keyboard Duets*, in MQ XXIX (1943), 438.

P   Miller, H. M. *"Pretty Wayes: For Young Beginners to Looke On,"* in MQ XXXIII (1947), 543.

S   Miller, H. M. *Sixteenth-Century English Faburden Compositions for Keyboard*, in MQ XXVI (1940), 50.

MilleGD   Miller, C. A. *Henricus Glareanus: Dodecachordon*. Ph. D. dissertation, University of Michigan, Ann Arbor, Mich., 1950, published in microfilm.

MillerL   Miller, H. C. *Introductory Euing Lectures on Musical Bibliography and History*, 1914.

Min   Mincoff-Marriage, E. *See also* MarriF.

S   Mincoff-Marriage, E. (ed.). *Souterliedekens: Een nederlandsch psalmboek van 1540, met de oorspronkelijke volksliederen die bij de melodieën behooren*, 1922.

U   Mincoff-Marriage, E. *Unveröffentlichtes aus der Weimarer Liederhandschrift v. J. 1537*, in *Tijdschrift voor nederlandsche taal- en letterkunde* XXXVIII (New Ser. XXX), 81.

Z   Mincoff-Marriage, E. (ed.). *Zestiende-eeuwsche dietsche volksliedjes, De oorspronkelijke teksten met de in de Souterliedekens vans 1540 bewaarde melodieën*, 1939. (Publisher's previously unbound copies of MinS, bound with a new title.)

MinorM   Minor, A. C. *The Masses of Jean Mouton*. Ph. D. dissertation, University of Michigan, Ann Arbor, Mich., 1950, unpublished.

MissaleR   *Missale Romanum*, 1920. (Dessain edition).

MitC   Mitjana, R. *Comentarios y apostillas al "Cancionero poético y musical del siglo XVII" recogido por I. Jesus Aroca*, in *Revista de Filología Española* VI (1919), 14, 233.

E   Mitjana, R. *Estudios sobre algunos Músicos españoles del siglo XVI*, 1918.

G   Mitjana, R. *Francisco Guerrero*, 1922.

I   Mitjana, R. *Don Fernando de las Infantas, Teólogo y Músico*, 1918.

MitM   Mitjana, R. *La Musique en Espagne*, in EC, *Partie I*, IV, p. 1913.

N   Mitjana, R. *Nuevas Notas al "Cancionero musical de los siglos XV y XVI" publicado por el Maestro Barbieri*, in *Revista de Filología Española* V (1918), 113.

U   Mitjana, R., J. Bal y Gay, and I. Pope (eds.). *Cancionero de Upsala*, 1944. (I. Pope's prefatory essay is printed in English, in less developed form, in PopeV.)

MLAC   Modern Language Association. *Collection of Photographic Facsimiles, 94: British Museum MS. Add. 5665*, 1927.

MllrC   Miller, C. K. *Early English Carol*, in *Renaissance News* III (1950), 61.

MlrS   Miller, P. *The Augmented Sixth Chord: Its Historical and Theoretical Origin and Development to the Era of Key-Feeling*, in *Journal of Musicology* I (1939), 17.

MME   *Monumentos de la Música Española*. Ed.-in-chief, H. Anglés. 1941–

I   *La Música en la Corte de los Reyes Católicos: Polifonia religiosa I*. Ed. by H. Anglés, 1941.

II   *La Música en la Corte de Carlos V*. Ed. by H. Anglés, 1944.

III   *Luys de Narváez. Los seys Libros del Delphin de Música de Cifra para tañer Vihuela*. Ed. by E. Pujol, 1945.

IV   *Juan Vásquez: Recopilación de Sonetos y Villancicos a quatro y a cinco, 1560*. Ed. by H. Anglés, 1946.

V   *La Música en la Corte de los Reyes Católicos: Polifonia profana—Cancionero musical de Palacio I*. Ed. by H. Anglés, 1947.

VII   *Alonso Mudarra: Tres Libros de Música en Cifra para Vihuela, 1546*. Ed. by E. Pujol, 1949.

VIII   *Cancionero musical de la Casa de Medinaceli (siglo XVI)*. Ed. by M. Q. Gavaldá, 1949.

X   *La Música en la Corte de los Reyes Católicos: Polifonia profana—Cancionero musical de Palacio II*. Ed. by H. Anglés, 1951.

MMFTR   *Les Monuments de la musique française au temps de la Renaissance*. 10 vols. Ed. by H. Expert, 1924–1930. (*See also* ExA.)

I   *Claude Le Jeune: Octonaires de la vanité du Monde (I–VIII)*, 1924.

II   *Pierre Certon: Messes à 4 voix*, 1925.

III   *Didier le Blanc: Airs de plusieurs musiciens reduits à quatre parties*, 1925.

IV   *Anthoine de Bertrand: Premier livre des Amours de P. de Ronsard*, Part I, 1926.

V   *Anthoine de Bertrand: Premier livre des Amours de P. de Ronsard*, Part II, 1926.

VI   *Anthoine de Bertrand: Second livre des Amours de P. de Ronsard*, 1927.

VII   *Anthoine de Bertrand: Troisième livre de chansons de P. de Ronsard*, 1927.

VIII   *Claude Le Jeune: Octonaires de la vanité du Monde (IX–XII); Pseaumes des Meslanges de 1612; Dialogue à sept parties (1564)*, 1928.

IX   *Claude Goudimel: Messes à 4 voix*, 1928.

X   *Paschal de l'Estocart: Premier livre des Octonaires de la vanité du Monde*, 1929.

MMRF   *Les Maîtres musiciens de la Renaissance française*. 23 vols.; also supplementary vols. Ed. by H. Expert, 1894–1908.

I   *Orlande de Lassus: Meslanges (1576)*, Part I, 1894.

II   *Claude Goudimel: 150 Psaumes de David (1580)*, Part I, 1895.

III   *Guillaume Costeley: Musique (1570)*, Part I, 1896.

IV   *Claude Goudimel: 150 Psaumes de David (1580)*, Part II, 1896.

V   *Trente et une chansons musicales (Attaingnant, 1529)*, 1897.

VI   *Claude Goudimel: 150 Psaumes de David (1580)*, Part III, 1897.

VII   *Clément Janequin: Chansons (Attaingnant, 1529)*, 1898.

VIII   *Antoine Brumel: Missa de Beata Virgine; Pierre de la Rue: Missa Ave Maria (1516)*, 1898.

IX   *Jean Mouton: Missa Alma Redemptoris; Antoine de Févin: Missa Mente tota (1516)*, 1899.

X   *Jacques Mauduit: Chansonnettes mesurées de I. A. de Baïf (1586)*, 1899.

XI   *Claude Le Jeune: Dodécacorde (1598)*, Part I, 1900.

XII   *Claude Le Jeune: Le Printemps (1603)*, Part I, 1900.

XIII   *Claude Le Jeune: Le Printemps*, Part II, 1901.

XIV   *Claude Le Jeune: Le Printemps*, Part III, 1901.

XV   *François Regnard: Poésies de P. de Ronsard et autres poètes*, 1902.

XVI   *Claude Le Jeune: Meslanges*, Part I, 1903.

MMRF XVII	*Eustache Du Caurroy· Mélanges,* 1903.
XVIII	*Guillaume Costeley:Musique (1570),* Part II, 1904.
XIX	*Guillaume Costeley: Musique (1570),* Part III, 1904.
XX	*Claude Le Jeune: Psaumes mezurez à l'antique,* Part I, 1905.
XXI	*Claude Le Jeune: Psaumes mezurez à l'antique,* Part II, 1905.
XXII	*Claude Le Jeune: Psaumes mezurez à l'antique,* Part III, 1906.
XXIII	*Claude Gervaise, Estienne du Tertre, et Anonymes: Danceries,* Part I, 1908.
BT, III	*Bibliographie thématique: Trente et une chansons musicales (Attaingnant 1529),* 1900.
BT, VIII	*Bibliographie thématique: Trente et sept chansons musicales (Attaingnant 1530),* 1900.
O	Separate octavo numbers, some taken from the main MMRF series (see above) and some consisting of pieces that do not appear there. The former are not cited separately in this book, the latter are referred to by the symbol MMRFO with the Sénart catalogue number added.
R	*Répertoire de la Société des Concerts du Conservatoire de Paris, extraits des Maîtres musiciens de la Renaissance française,* I, 1905.
MMSP	*Monumenta musices sacrae in Polonia.* 4 vols. Ed. by Jos. Surzynski, 1887.
MoD	Morelot, S. *Notice sur un manuscrit de musique ancienne de la Bibliothèque de Dijon,* in *Mémoires de la Commission des Antiquités du Département de la Côte-d'Or* IV (1856), 133. (Also published separately as *De la musique au XVᵉ siècle. Notice. . . .*)
MobergU	Moberg, C. A. *Über die schwedischen Sequenzen,* 1927.
ModF	*Jacques Moderne: Fröhliche Musik (Musique de joye). . . .* Ed. by F. J. Giesbert, 1934.
MohrA	Mohr, E. *Die Allemande.* 2 vols., 1932.
MolD	Molitor, R. *Deutsche Choral-Wiegendrucke,* 1904.
T	Molitor, R. *Die Nach-Tridentinische Choral-Reform zu Rom.* 2 vols., 1902.
MolinL	*Simone Molinaro: Intavolatura di Liuto, Lib. primo.* Ed. by G. Gullino, 1940.
MolnM	Molnár, G. *Magyar táncok a 16. századból,* 1908.
MomV	Mompellio, F. *Pietro Vinci, Madrigalista Siciliano,* 1937.
MonteO	*Philippe de Monte: Opera.* Ed. by C. van den Borren and J. van Nuffel, 1927– .
MontevO	*Claudio Monteverdi: Tutte le Opere.* Ed. by F. G. Malipiero. 14 vols., 1926–42.
MontiV	Monti, G. M. *Le Villanelle alla napoletana e l'antica Lirica dialettale a Napoli,* 1925.
MorL	Morphy, G. (ed.). *Les Luthistes espagnols du XVIᵉ siècle.* 2 vols., 1902.
MoraledaS	Moraleda y Esteban, J. *Los Seises de la Catedral de Toledo,* 1911.
MoralesO	*Cristóbal de Morales: Opera omnia.* Ed. by H. Anglés, 1952– .
MorlF	*Thomas Morley: Nine Fantasies for Two Viols, 1595.* Ed. by E. H. Fellowes, 1928.
P	*Thomas Morley: A Plaine and Easie Introduction to Practical Musicke, 1597.* Facsimile ed. with introduction by E. H. Fellowes, 1937.
PE	*Thomas Morley, A Plain and Easy Introduction to Practical Music.* Ed. by R. A. Harman, 1952.
MorrC	Morris, R. O. *Contrapuntal Technique in the Sixteenth Century,* 1922.
MosC	Moser, H. J. and F. Piersig (eds.). *Carmina. Ausgewählte Instrumentalsätze des 16. Jahrhunderts,* 1929.
DK	Moser, H. J. *Das deutsche monodische Kunstlied um 1500,* in *Peter Wagner-Festschrift* (1926), 146.
F	Moser, H. J. (ed.). *Frühmeister der deutschen Orgelkunst,* 1930.
G	Moser, H. J. *Geschichte der deutschen Musik.* 3 vols. I, 1920; II, 1922; III, 1924, 5th ed., 1930. References are to the 5th ed.
GR	Moser, H. J. (ed.). *Gassenhawerlin und Reutterliedlin (1535).* Facsimile ed., with missing discant supplied from a later ed. of the work, 1927.
H	Moser, H. J. *Hans Ott's erstes Liederbuch,* in Acta VII (1935), 1.
I	Moser, H. J. *Instrumentalismen bei Ludwig Senfl,* in *WolfF* (1929), 123.
JC	Moser, H. J. *Johannes de Cleve als Setzer von zehn Lutherischen Melodien,* in TVNM XVI (1940), 31.
K	Moser, H. J. (ed.). *Die Kantorei der Spätgotik,* 1928.
L	Moser, H. J. and E. Bernoulli (eds.). *Das Liederbuch des Arnt von Aich,* 1930.
LC	Moser, H. J. *Lutheran Composers in the Hapsburg Empire 1525–1732,* in MD III (1949), 3.

MosLL	Moser, H. J. *Leben und Lieder des Adam von Fulda*, in *Jahrbuch der Staatlichen Akademie für Kirchen- und Schulmusik* I (1929), 7.
M	Moser, H. J. *Zur mittelalterlichen Musikgeschichte der Stadt Cöln*, in AfMW I (1918), 135.
O	Moser, H. J. *Eine Trienter Orgeltabulatur aus Hofhaimers Zeit*, in AdlerF, (1930), 84.
PH	Moser, H. J. *Paul Hofhaimer*, 1929.
TS	Moser, H. J. *Thomas Stoltzers Psalm "Noli aemulari,"* in ZfMW XIV (1932), 241.
V	Moser, H. J. *Die mehrstimmige Vertonung des Evangeliums I*, 1931.
VC	Moser, H. J. *Vestiva i colli*, in AfMF IV (1939), 129, 376.
ZL	Moser, H. J. *Der Zerbster Lutherfund*, in AfMW II (1920), 337.
MoserGV	Moser, A. *Geschichte des Violinspiels*, 1923.
MottaM	Motta, E. *Musici alla Corte degli Sforza*, in *Archivio Storico Lombardo*, Ser. Seconda IV (1887), 29, 278, 514.
MPI	*Monumenta polyphoniae italicae*. Ed. by R. Casimiri and E. Dagnino. 1930– .
I	*Missa Cantantibus organis, Caecilia . . .* (Palestrina, Stabile, Soriano, Dragoni, Giovanelli, Mancini, Santini). Ed. by R. Casimiri, 1930.
II	*Costanzo Festa: Sacrae cantiones 3–6 vocibus*. Ed. by E. Dagnino, 1936.
MPLSER	*Monumenta polyphoniae liturgicae Sanctae Ecclesiae Romanae.* (Series I. *Ordinarium missae;* II. *Proprium missae;* III. *Divinum officium;* IV. *Motecta*). Ed. by L. Feininger, 1947– .
Ser. I	
I	Published in 10 fascicles, each containing a different *L'Homme armé* Mass (Dufay, Busnois, Caron, Faugues, Regis, Ockeghem, de Orto, Basiron, Tinctoris, Vaqueras), 1948.
II	*Missae octo cum duobus fragmentis* [4 works ascribed to Dufay in the sources, 4 anon. in the sources but ascribed by the editor to Dufay on stylistic grounds, 2 not so ascribed, but included because of stylistic similarities to *Missa Se la face ay pale*]. Ed. by L. Feininger, 1951–53.
Ser. II	
I	*Auctorum anonymorum missarum propria XVI quorum XI Guglielmo Dufay auctori adscribenda sunt*, 1947.
MQ	*The Musical Quarterly*, 1915–
MrS	Meyer, B. van den Sigtenhorst. *Jan P. Sweelinck en zijn instrumentale muziek*, 1934; 2nd ed., 1946. References in this book are to 2nd ed.
V	Meyer, B. van den Sigtenhorst. *De vocale muziek van Jan P. Sweelinck*, 1948.
MTNAP	*Proceedings of the Music Teachers National Association*. 1906–
MülleI	Müller-Blattau, J. *Über Instrumentalbearbeitungen spätmittelalterlicher Lieder*, in *Festschrift für Arnold Schering* (1937), 151.
L	Müller-Blattau, J. *Die Weisen des Locheimer Liederbuchs*, in AfMF III (1938), 277.
S	Müller-Blattau, J. *Die musikalischen Schätze der Staats- und Universitätsbibliothek zu Königsberg i. Pr.*, in ZfMW VI (1924), 215.
MüllerM	Müller, E. H. *Die Musiksammlung der Bibliothek zu Kronstadt*, 1930.
MünzerS	Münzer, G. (ed.). *Das Singebuch des Adam Puschman, nebst den Originalmelodien des M. Behaim und Hans Sachs*, 1907.
MusB	*Musica Britannica*. Ed. by Anthony Lewis. 1951–
I	*The Mulliner Book*. Ed. by Denis Stevens, 1951.
IV	*Mediaeval Carols*. Ed. by John Stevens, 1952.
MusiolR	Musiol, J. *Cyprian de Rore*, 1932.
MusetS	Muset, J. (ed.). *Early Spanish Organ Music*, 1948.
MyG	Meyer, C. *Geschichte der Mecklenburg-Schweriner Hofkapelle*, 1913.
NA	*Note d'Archivio*, 1924–43.
NagA	Nagel, W. *Annalen der englischen Hofmusik 1509–1649*, 1894.
G	Nagel, W. *Geschichte der Musik in England*. 2 vols., 1894–97.
SM	Nagel, W. *Studien zur Geschichte der Meistersänger*, 1909.
NayE	Naylor, E. W. *An Elizabethan Virginal Book, being a critical essay on the contents of a manuscript in the Fitzwilliam Museum at Cambridge*, 1905.
H	Naylor, E. W. *Jacob Handl (Gallus) as Romanticist*, in SIM XI (1909), 42.
M	Naylor, E. W. *Music and Shakespeare*, in MAn I (1910), 129.
SM	Naylor, E. W. *Shakespeare and Music, with illustrations from the music of the 16th and 17th centuries*, 1931.

NeS   Newman, W. S. *The Origins and First Use of the Word Sonata*, in *The Journal of Musicology* V (1947), 31.

NedK   Nedden, Otto zur. *Zur Musikgeschichte von Konstanz um 1500*, in ZfMW XII (1930), 455.

P   Nedden, Otto zur. *Zur Frühgeschichte der protestantischen Kirchenmusik in Württemberg*, in ZfMW XIII (1931), 309.

Q   Nedden, Otto zur. *Quellen und Studien zur oberrheinischen Musikgeschichte im 15. und 16. Jahrhundert*, 1931.

NefB   Nef, K. *Die Musik in Basel. Von den Anfängen im 9. bis zur Mitte des 19. Jahrhunderts*, in SIM X (1909), 532.

I   Nef, K. *Die Intraden von Alexander Orologio*, in *Gedenkboek aangeboden aan Dr. D. F. Scheurleer* (1925), 219.

O   Nef, K. *An Outline of the History of Music*. Transl. by C. F. Pfatteicher, 1935.

V   Nef, K. *Seb. Virdungs Musica getutscht*, in *Bericht über den musikwissenschaftlichen Kongress in Basel* (1925), 7.

NejC   Nejedlý, Z. *Dějiny české hudby*, 1903.

H   Nejedlý, Z. *Dějiny husitského zpěvu za válek husitských, II*, in *Královská česká společnost náuk*, XX (1913).

P   Nejedlý, Z. *Dějiny předhusitského zpěvu v Čechách*, 1904.

Z   Nejedlý, Z. *Magister Záviše und seine Schule*, in SIM VII (1905), 41.

NelsV   Nelson, R. U. *The Technique of Variation*, 1948.

NeriS   Nerici, L. *Storia della Musica in Lucca*, 1879.

NeuV   Neudenberger, L. *Die Variationstechnik der Virginalisten im Fitzwilliam Virginal Book*, 1937.

NewL   Newton, R. *English Lute Music of the Golden Age*, in PMA LXV (1939), 63.

NewmM   Newman, J. *Francesco Canova da Milano, a lutenist of the sixteenth century*. Master's thesis, New York University, 1942, unpublished.

NeyR   Ney, N. J. (Prince de la Moskowa) (ed.). *Recueil des morceaux de musique ancienne, executés aux concerts de la Société de musique vocale religieuse et classique. . . .* 10 vols., n. d.

NfO   Nef, W. R. *Der St. Galler Organist Fridolin Sicher und seine Orgeltabulatur*, in SJ VII (1938), 1.

NieS   Niemann, W. *Studien zur deutschen Musikgeschichte des XV. Jahrhunderts*, in KJ XVII (1902), 1.

V   Niemann, W. *Die Virginalmusik . . .* , 1919.

NijM   Nijhoff, W. *Een merkwaardig muziekboek te Antwerpen nij Vorsterman uitgegeven, 1529*, in *Het Boek* XXII (1934), 267.

NorG   Norlind, T. *Zur Geschichte der Suite*, in SIM VII (1906), 172.

H   Norlind, T. *Die schwedische Hofkapelle in der Reformationszeit*, in *Festschrift für Johannes Wolf* (1929), 148.

S   Norlind, T. *Schwedische Schullieder im Mittelalter und in der Reformationszeit*, in SIM II (1901), 552.

T   Norlind, T. *Zur Geschichte der polnischen Tänze*, in SIM XII (1911), 501.

NorthG   *Roger North: The Musicall Gramarian*. Ed. by Hilda Andrews with a pref. by R. R. Terry, 1925.

M   *Roger North: Memoirs of musick*. Ed. by E. F. Rimbault, 1846.

NowakH   Nowak, L. *Paul Hofhaymers "Nach willen dein" in den Lautentabulaturen des 16. Jahrhunderts. Ein Vergleich*, in *Festschrift Adolf Koczirz* (1930), 25.

Z   Nowak, L. *Zur Geschichte der Musik am Hofe Kaiser Maximilians I.*, in *Mitteilungen des Vereines für Geschichte der Stadt Wien* XII (1932), 71.

NuffM   Nuffel, J. van. *Philippe de Monte*, in PMA LVII (1931), 99.

OberM   Obertello, A. *Madrigali italiani in Inghilterra*, 1949.

V   Obertello, A. *Villanelle e Madrigali inediti in Inghilterra*, in *Italian Studies* III (1947), 97.

Obr   *Jakob Obrecht: Werken*. Ed. by J. Wolf, 1912–21.
MS   *Missen*
MT   *Motetten*
P   *Passio Domini Nostri Jesu Christi . . .*
WW   *Wereldlijke Werken*

OckW   *Johannes Ockeghem: Sämtliche Werke:* I (PubAMD I²), 1927 (to be republished in SAMS); *Collected Works:* II (SAMS I), 1947; III (SAMS, in preparation). Ed. by D. Plamenac.

OEE   *Old English Edition.* 25 vols. Ed. by G. E. P. Arkwright, 1889–1902.

I   *Campion, Lupo and Giles: Masque for Lord Hayes's Marriage,* (*1607*), 1889.

X   *Christopher Tye: Mass to Six Voices, "Euge bone,"* 1893.

XI   *Alfonso Ferrabosco: Nine Madrigals to Five Voices from Musica Transalpina,* 1894.

XII   *Alfonso Ferrabosco: Five Madrigals to Six Voices from Musica Transalpina,* 1894.

XXI   *R. White, G. Kirbye, J. Wilbye, W. Daman: Anthems and Motets,* 1898.

XXII   *John Milton: Six Anthems,* 1900.

Officium   *Officium majoris hebdomadae et octavae Paschae,* 1932. (Dessain edition)

OH   *Oxford History of Music,* 1901–34. 7 vols. Ed. by Sir Henry Hadow. Introductory Volume added and 2nd ed. of Vol. 1 issued, 1928; 2nd ed. of Vol. 2 issued, 1932. 1929 and 1932 vols. edited or revised by P. C. Buck. Introductory Volume contains chapters of unequal merit by 9 authors. Vols. 1 and 2 (*The Polyphonic Period*), by H. E. Wooldridge, excellent in their day, have, in the revisions, been brought up to date in some respects and not in others, with confusing results. New material by G. M. Cooper and J. A. Westrup. Vol. 3 (*The Seventeenth Century*) by C. H. H. Parry. (Other vols. outside range of present book.) *New Oxford History of Music* in preparation.

OliM   Oliphant, T. *La Musa madrigalesca,* 1837.

OpieJ   Opieński, H. *Jacob polonais et Jacob Reys,* in RieF (1909), 349.

P   Opieński, H. *La Musique polonaise,* 1918.

R   Opieński, H. *Quelques Considérations sur l'origine des Ricercari pour luth,* in *Mélanges de musicologie offerts à M. Lionel de la Laurencie* (1933), 39.

S   Opieński, H. *Sześć listów lutnisty Bekwarka,* in *Kwartalnik Muzyczny,* No. 6 (1930), 158.

OpitiisL   *G. en B. de Opitiis: Lofzangen ter eere van Keiser Maximiliaan en zijn zoon Karel den vijfde, 1515.* Facsimile ed. with introduction by W. Nijhoff, 1925.

S   *Benedictus de Opitiis: Sub tuum praesidium; Summae laudis, O Maria.* Ed. by W. Nijhoff, 1927.

OppelF   Oppel, R. *Einige Feststellungen zu den französischen Tänzen des 16. Jahrhunderts,* in ZIM XII (1911), 213.

J   Oppel, R. *Jakob Meiland,* 1911.

OrM   Orel, A. *Die mehrstimmige geistliche (katholische) Musik von 1430–1600,* in AdlerH I, 295.

OrbaN   Orbaan, J. A. F. *Notizie inedite su Luca Marenzio,* in *Bolletino Bibliografico Musicale* III, No. 2 (1928), 11.

NL   Orbaan, J. A. F. *Notizie inedite su Luzzasco Luzzaschi,* in *Bolletino Bibliografico Musicale* IV (1929), 9.

OrelH   Orel, D. *Hudebné prvky svatovaclavské,* 1937.

P   Orel, D. *Počátky uměĺého vícehlasu v Čechách,* in *Universita Komenského v Bratislave. Filozofická fakulta. Sborník* I (1922), 145.

R   Orel, D. *Die alttschechischen Roratelieder,* 1922.

S   Orel, D. *Stilarten der Mehrstimmigkeit des 15. und 16. Jahrhunderts in Böhmen,* in AdlerF (1930), 87.

OrtizT   *Diego Ortiz: Tratado de glosas sobre clausulas y otros generos de puntos en la música de violones (1553).* Ed. by Max Schneider, 1913.

OsG   Osthoff, H. *Der Lautenist Santino Garsi da Parma,* 1926.

J   Osthoff, H. *Besetzung und Klangstruktur in den Werken von Josquin des Prez,* in AfMW IX (1952), 177.

N   Osthoff, H. *Die Niederländer und das deutsche Lied (1400–1640),* 1938.

U   Osthoff, H. *Eine unbekannte Schauspielmusik Jacob Regnarts,* in *Festschrift für Johannes Wolf* (1929), 153.

OsiaG   *Das erste evangelische Choralbuch* [*Osiander: 50 geistliche Lieder und Psalmen auf Kontrapunktweise, 1586.*] Ed. by F. Zelle, 1903.

OthmayrR   *Caspar Othmayr: Reutterische und Jegerische Liedlein (1549).* Ed. by F. Piersig, 1928.

PaL   Pastor, C. P. *Escrituras de Concierto para imprimir Libros,* in *Revista de Archivos, Bibliotecas y Museos* I (1897), 363.

PachtaP   Pachta, J. *Poznámky a vysvětlivky k Rorátním zpěvům,* in *Cyrill* VIII (1881).

PadovanoR   *Annibale Padovano: 13 Ricercari for Organ, 1556.* Ed. by N. Pierront and J. P. Hennebains, 1934.

PalO   *Giovanni Pierluigi da Palestrina: Le Opere Complete.* Ed. by R. Casimiri and others, 24 vols. to date (1958), 1939– .

R   *Giovanni Pierluigi da Palestrina: Ricercari sopra li Tuoni a quattro voci,* in *Antiqua, eine Sammlung alter Musik,* 1933.

W   *Giovanni Pierluigi da Palestrina: Werke: Erste kritisch durchgesehene Gesammtausgabe.* Ed. by F. Espagne, F. X. Haberl, *et al.* 33 vols., 1862–1907.

PAMS   *Papers read by Members of The American Musicological Society.* 1936–41 (printed 1937–46).

PannOM   Pannain, G. *Le Origini della Scuola musicale napoletana,* 1914.

T   Pannain, G. *La Teoria musicale di Jo. Tinctoris,* 1913.

PanofE   Panofsky, E. *Who is Jan van Eyck's Tymotheos?* in *Journal of the Warburg and Courtauld Institutes* XII (1949), 80.

PaoM   Paoli, D. de. *Claudio Monteverdi,* 1945.

PaoluA   Paolucci, G. *Arte pratica di contrappunto dimostrata con Esempi di vari Autori.* 3 vols., 1765–72.

ParisC   Paris, G. and A. Gevaert, *Chansons du XVe siècle,* 1875; reimpression, 1935.

ParrishM   Parrish, C. and J. F. Ohl. *Masterpieces of Music before 1750,* 1951.

PäslC   Päsler, C. *Fundamentbuch von Hans von Constanz,* in VfMW V (1889), 1.

PatLM   Pattison, B. *Literature and Music in the Age of Shakespeare,* in PMA LXI (1933), 67.

MP   Pattison, B. *Music and Poetry of the English Renaissance,* 1948.

P   Pattison, B. *Notes on Early Music Printing,* in *The Library,* Ser. 4, XIX (1939), 389.

PeaC   Pearce, C. W. *A Collection of Songs and Madrigals of English Composers of the Close of the Fifteenth Century,* 1891.

M   Pearce, C. W. and C. F. Abdy Williams (eds.). *Madrigals by English Composers of the Close of the Fifteenth Century,* 1893.

PedA   Pedrell, F. *Musichs vells de la terra: Joan Carlos Amat,* in *Revista Musical Catalana* II (1906), 1, 21.

AO   Pedrell, F. (ed.). *Antología de Organistas clásicos españoles.* 2 vols., 1908.

C   Pedrell, F. *Catàlech de la Biblioteca Musical de la Diputacià de Barcelona. . . .* 2 vols., 1908–09.

CP   Pedrell, F. (ed.). *Cancionero musical popular español.* 4 vols., 1919–20.

E   Pedrell, F. *La Festa d'Elche,* in SIM II (1901), 203.

F   Pedrell, F. *Folk-lore musical castillan du XVIe siècle,* in SIM (1900), 372.

H   Pedrell, F. (ed.). *Hispaniae schola musica sacra.* 8 vols., 1894–98.

J   Pedrell, F. *Jean I d'Aragon, compositeur de musique,* in RieF (1909), 229.

M   Pedrell, F. *Les Échanges musicaux entre la France et la Catalogne au moyen âge. Le français Jean Brudieu, musicien catalan,* in *Actes du Congrès d'histoire de l'art, Paris, 1921* III (recte II²) (1924), 823.

O   Pedrell, F. *Emporio científico y histórico de Organografía musical antigua española,* 1901.

T   Pedrell, F. *Tomás Luis de Victoria,* 1919.

PederV   *Vaerker af Mogens Pedersøn (Dania Sonans, Tomus I).* Ed. by K. Jeppesen, 1933.

PeliP   Pelicelli, N. *Musicisti in Parma nei secoli XV–XVI,* in NA VIII (1931), 132, 196, 278; IX (1932), 41, 112.

PeluzV   Peluzzi, E. *Chi fu l'Inventore del Violino,* in RMI XLV (1941), 25.

PerG   Pereyra, M. *Elzéar Genet dit Il Carpentrasso, par le Chanoine Requin,* in *Bulletin de la Société française de musicologie* II (1918), 139.

L   Pereyra, M. *Les Livres de virginal de la Bibliothèque du Conservatoire de Paris,* in RdM VII (1926), 204; VIII (1927), 36, 205; IX (1928), 235; X (1929), 32; XII (1931), 22; XIII (1932), 86; XIV (1933), 24.

PerinA   Perinello, C. *L' "Amfiparnaso" di Horatio Vecchi,* in RMI XLI (1937), 1.

PerleB   Perle, G. *The Chansons of Antoine Busnois,* in *The Music Review* XI (1950), 89.

PetrF   *Ottaviano Petrucci: Frottole, Buch I und IV,* in PubAMD VIII. Edited by R. Schwartz, 1935.

O   *Ottaviano Petrucci: Odhecaton (Venice, 1501).* Facsimile ed., 1932. Petrucci, O. *See also* HewO.

PfatJ   Pfatteicher, C. F. *John Redford, Organist and Almoner of St. Paul's Cathedral in the Reign of Henry VIII . . . ,* 1934.

PflU   Pfleger, M. C. C. *Untersuchungen am deutschen geistlichen Lied des 13. bis 16. Jahrhunderts,* 1937.

PicM   Picard, I. *La Musique dans le culte protestant,* in EC, Partie 2, IV, 2399

PicotC   Picot, E. *Catalogue des livres composant la bibliothèque de feu M. le baron James de Rothschild.* 5 vols., 1884–1920.

PietzschD   Pietzsch, G. *Mscr. Dresd. A 52,* in *Festschrift Martin Bollert* (1936), 167.

P   Pietzsch, G. *Pflege der Musik an den deutschen Universitäten im Osten bis zur Mitte des 16. Jahrhunderts,* in AfMW I (1936), 257, 424.

PiqM   Piqueras, F. R. *Música y Músicos toledanos,* 1922.

PirA   Pirro, A. *Musiciens allemands et auditeurs français au temps des rois Charles V et Charles VI,* in AdlerF (1930), 71.

AO   Pirro, A. *L'Art des Organistes,* in EC, Partie 2, II, 1181.

B   Pirro, A. *Dokumente über Antoine Brumel, Louis van Pullaer und Crispin van Stappen,* in ZfMW XI (1929), 349.

C   Pirro, A. *Les Clavecinistes,* 1925.

D   Pirro, A. *Deux danses anciennes,* in RdM V (1924), 7.

E   Pirro, A. *L'Enseignement de la musique aux Universités françaises,* in Acta II (1930), 26, 45.

F   Pirro, A. *Les "frottole" et la musique instrumentale,* in RdM III (1922), 3.

G   Pirro, A. Review of C. van den Borren's *Guillaume Dufay . . . ,* in RM VII (1926), 321.

GM   Pirro, A. *Gilles Mureau, chanoine de Chartres,* in *Festschrift für Johannes Wolf* (1929), 163.

H   Pirro, A. *Histoire de la musique de la fin du XIVe siècle à la fin du XVIe,* 1940.

JC   Pirro, A. *Jean Cornuel, vicaire à Cambrai,* in RdM VII (1926), 190.

L   Pirro, A. *Leo X and Music,* in MQ XXI (1935), 1.

M   Pirro, A. *La Musique à Paris sous le règne de Charles VI (1380–1422),* 1930.

MC   Pirro, A. *Un Manuscrit musical du XVe siècle au Mont-Cassin,* in *Casinensia (Miscellanea di studi cassinesi . . .)* I (1929), 205.

NB   Pirro, A. *Notes sur Jean Braconnier, dit Lourdault,* in RM IX (1928), 250.

P   Pirro, A. *Pour l'histoire de la musique,* in Acta III (1931), 49.

R   Pirro, A. *Remarques sur l'exécution musicale de la fin du XIVe siècle au milieu du XVe siècle,* in *International Society for Musical Research, First Congress, Liége, September 1–6, 1930, Report,* 55.

RM   Pirro, A. *Robinet de la Magdalaine,* in *Mélanges de musicologie offerts à M. Lionel de la Laurencie* (1933), 15.

T   Pirro, A. *Les Organistes français du XVIIe siècle: Jean Titelouze,* 1898.

PirrD   Pirrotta, N. *Dulceto e subtilitas nella pratica polifonica franco-italiana al principio del '400,* in RB II (1948), 125.

E   Pirrotta, N. *Il codice Estense lat. 568 e la Musica francese in Italia etc.,* in *Atti della Reale Accademia di Scienze, Lettere e Arti di Palermo* V (1946), 11.

L   Pirrotta, N. and E. Li Gotti *Il Codice di Lucca,* in MD III (1949), 119; IV (1950), 111; V (1951), 115.

PiscaerO   Piscaer, A. *Jacob Obrecht, geboortendatum en andere bijzonderheden,* in *Mens en Melodie* VII (1952), 329.

PiskP   Pisk, P. *Das Parodieverfahren in den Messen des Jacobus Gallus,* in SzMW V (1918), 35.

PistR   Pistone, P. G. (ed.). *Raccolta di Musiche corali italiane antiche e moderne,* 1941.

PlamA   Plamenac, D. *Autour d'Ockeghem,* in RM IX (1928), 26.

C   Plamenac, D. *Toma Cecchini, kapelnik stolnih crkava u Splitu i Hvaru u prvoj polovini XVII stoljeća,* in *Rad Jugoslavenske Akademije Znanosti i Umjetnosti,* Knjiga 262 (1938), 77.

D   Plamenac, D. *Music of the 16th and 17th Centuries in Dalmatia,* in PAMS for 1939 (1944), 21.

DP   Plamenac, D. *Deux pièces de la Renaissance tirées de fonds florentins,* in RB VI (1952), 12.

F   Plamenac, D. *Keyboard Music of the 14th Century in Codex Faenza 117,* in JAMS IV (1951), 179.

H   Plamenac, D. *La Chanson de "L'Homme armé" et le manuscrit VI E 40 de la Bibliothèque nationale de Naples,* in *Annales de la Fédération archéologique et historique de Belgique, Congrès jubilaire* (1925), 229.

J   Plamenac, D. *Johannes Ockeghem als Motetten- und Chansonkomponist.* Ph. D. dissertation, University of Vienna, 1924, unpublished.

PlamJO   Plamenac, D. *A Postscript to Volume II of the Collected Works of Johannes Ockeghem*, in JAMS III (1950), 33.

M   Plamenac, D. Answer to GomB, pr. under *Miszellen*, in ZfMW XI (1929), 376.

S   Plamenac, D. *A Reconstruction of the French Chansonnier in the Biblioteca Colombina, Seville*, in MQ XXXVII (1951), 501; XXXVIII (1952), 85, 245.

V   Plamenac, D. *An Unknown Violin Tablature of the Early 17th Century*, in PAMS (1941), 144.

PlattD   Platt, P. *Dering's Life and Training*, in M&L XXXIII (1952), 41.

PM   *Paléographie musicale*. Begun under the editorship of Dom Mocquereau.

VII   *Le Codex H. 159 de la Bibliothèque de l'École de médecine de Montpellier (XIᵉ siècle): Antiphonarium tonale missarum* (commentary), 1901–05.

IX   *Le Codex 601 de la Bibliothèque capitulaire de Lucques (XII siècle): Antiphonaire monastique*, 1906–09.

PMA   *Proceedings of the Musical Association*. 1874– . (See also PRMA.)

PolD   Polinski, A. *Dzieje muzyki polskiej w zarysie*, n. d.

PopeS   Pope, I. *The "Spanish Chapel" of Philip II*, in *Renaissance News* V (1952), 1, 34.

V   Pope, I. *The Musical Development and Form of the Spanish Villancico*, in PAMS for 1940 (1946), 11.

PorchC   Porcher, J. and E. Droz. *Le Chansonnier de Jean de Montchenu*, in *Les Trésors des bibliothèques de France* V (1935), 100.

PraF   Pratt, W. S. *The Importance of the Early French Psalter*, in MQ XXI (1935), 25.

M   Pratt, W. S. *The Music of the French Psalter of 1562*, 1939.

S   Pratt, W. S. *The Significance of the old French Psalter begun by Clément Marot in 1532*, 1933.

PraetM   Praetorius, E. *Die Mensuraltheorie des Franchinus Gafurius*, 1905.

PraetoS II   Praetorius, M. *Syntagma musicum*, Part II. Facsimile ed. with postscript by W. Gurlitt, 1929.

III   Praetorius, M. *Syntagma musicum*, Part III. Ed. by E. Bernoulli, 1916.

PrenT   Prendergast, A. H. D. *Tallis and the "Et incarnatus,"* in ZIM IX (1907), 65.

PRMA   *Proceedings of the Royal Musical Association*. (The name of the former *Musical Association* appears as *Royal Musical Association* beginning with Vol. LXXI.)

ProcessionaleM   *Processionale monasticum*, 1893. (Solesmes edition)

ProdE   Prod'homme, J.-G. *Écrits de musiciens*, 1912.

M   Prod'homme, J.-G. *Guillaume Morlaye, éditeur d'Albert de Ripe, luthiste et bourgeois de Paris*, in RdM VI (1925), 157.

ProsM   Proske, K. *et al.* (eds.). *Musica divina*. 8 vols., 1853–69.

P   Proske, K. (ed.). *Missa Papae Marcelli . . .* [Palestrina's original *a 6* with Anerio's and Suriano's arrgts. *a 4* and *a 8*, respectively], 1850.

S   Proske, K. (ed.). *Selectus novus missarum*. 2 vols., 1855–59.

ProtaN   Prota-Giurleo, U. *Notizie sul Musicista belga Jean Macque*, in *International Society for Musical Research, First Congress, Liége, September 1–6, 1930, Report*, 191.

PruB   Prunières, H. *Le Ballet de cour en France*, 1914.

CM   Prunières, H. *Monteverdi: His Life and Work*. Transl. by M. D. Mackie, 1926.

M   Prunières, H. *La Musique de la chambre et de l'écurie sous le règne de François I*, in *L'Année musicale* I (1912), 215.

P   Prunières, H. *Un Portrait de Hobrecht et de Verdelot par S. del Piombo*, in RM III, No. 8 (1922), 193.

PubAMD   *Publikationen älterer Musik . . . der Deutschen Musikgesellschaft*, 1926–40.

PubAPTM   *Publikation älterer praktischer und theoretischer Musikwerke. . . .* Ed. by R. Eitner. 29 vols., 1873–1905.

I–III   *Johann Ott: Ein hundert fünfzehn weltliche und einige geistliche Lieder . . .*, 1544. Ed. by R. Eitner *et al.*, 1873–75.

IV   Eitner, R. *et al. Einleitung, Biographieen, Melodieen und Gedichte zu Johann Ott's Liedersammlung von 1544 . . .*, 1876.

V   Schubiger, Anselm. *Musikalische Spicilegien über das liturgische Drama, Orgelbau und Orgelspiel, das ausserliturgische Lied und die Instrumentalmusik des Mittelalters*, 1876.

VI   *Josquin Després: Eine Sammlung ausgewählter Compositionen. . . .* Ed. by F. Commer, R. Schlecht, and R. Eitner, 1877.

VII   *Johann Walther: Wittembergisch geistlich Gesangbuch von 1524.* Ed. by O. Kade, 1879.

PubAPTM VIII *Heinrich Finck: Eine Sammlung ausgewählter Kompositionen.* . . . Ed. by R. Eitner, 1879.

IX *Erhart Oeglin: Liederbuch zu 4 Stimmen (1512).* Ed. by R. Eitner and J. J. Maier, 1880.

XI *Sebastian Virdung: Musica getutscht* . . . *(1511),* facsimile ed. with an index by R. Eitner, 1882.

XIII *Michael Praetorius: Syntagmatis musici Tom. II de Organographia* . . . *(1618).* Ed. by R. Eitner, 1884.

XV *Lustgarten. 50 Lieder* . . . *nebst einigen Instrumentalwerken von Hans Leo Hassler (1601).* Ed. by F. Zelle, 1887.

XVI *Glareani Dodecachordon.* Transl. by Peter Bohn, 1888.

XIX *Jacob Regnarts deutsche dreistimmige Lieder (1576–79).* Ed. by R. Eitner, 1895.

XX *Martin Agricola: Musica instrumentalis deudsch (1528, 1545),* ed., partly facsimile, by R. Eitner, 1896.

XXI *Johannes Eccard: Neue geistliche und weltliche Lieder* . . . *(1589).* Ed. by R. Eitner, 1897.

XXII *Joachim von Burck: 20 deutsche geistliche vierstimmige Lieder (1575), Die Passion nach dem Evangelisten Johannes* . . . *(1568),* and *Die Passion nach dem 22. Psalmen Davids (1574).* Ed. by A. Halm and R. Eitner, 1898.

XXIII *60 Chansons zu vier Stimmen aus der ersten Hälfte des 16. Jahrhunderts.* Ed. by R. Eitner, 1899.

XXVI *Orazio Vecchi: L'Amfiparnaso.* Ed. by R. Eitner, 1902.

XXIX *Georg Forster: Der zweite Teil der kurtzweiligen guten frischen teutschen Liedlein* . . . *(1540).* Ed. by R. Eitner, 1905.

PujO *Juan Pujol: Opera omnia.* Ed. by H. Anglès. 2 vols., 1926–32.

PulB Pulver, J. *A Biographical Dictionary of Old English Music,* 1927.

V Pulver, J. *The Viols in England,* in PMA XLVII (1920), 1.

PuliP Pulikowski, J. *Pontificale Lwowskie z XIV wieku pod względem muzycznym,* in *Księga pamiątkowa ku czci Prof. A. Chybińskiego* (1930), 1.

PV *Polifonia vocale sacra e profana sec. XVI.* Ed. by B. Somma. 1940– .

I *Joannes Animucia: Missa Ave maris stella, 1571.* Ed. by B. Somma, 1940.

II *Giovanni Maria Nanino: Il primo Libro delle Canzonette, 1593.* Ed. by A. Schinelli and B. Somma, 1941.

——— Pyne, Z. K. *Giovanni Pierluigi da Palestrina: His Life and Times,* 1922.

QuerC Querol Gavaldá, M. *La Música en las Obras de Cervantes,* 1948.

QuitG Quittard, H. *Elzéar Genet, dit Carpentras,* in TSG V (1899), 161.

I Quittard, H. *Musique instrumentale jusqu'à Lully,* in EC, *Partie I,* III, 1176.

M Quittard, H. *"L'Hortus Musarum" de 1552–53 et les arrangements de pièces polyphoniques pour voix seule et luth,* in SIM VIII (1907), 254.

T Quittard, H. (ed.). *Le Trésor d'Orphée de Francisque,* 1906. (In version for piano.)

RaL Radecke, E. *Das deutsche weltliche Lied in der Lautenmusik des 16. Jahrhunderts,* in VfMW VII (1891), 285.

RadN Radiciotti, G. *Giovanni Maria Nanino,* 1909.

S Radiciotti, G. *Due Musicisti spagnoli del sec. XVI in Relazione con la Corte di Urbino,* in SIM XIV (1913), 185.

RadiA Radino, G. M. *Il primo Libro di Balli d'Arpicordo,* 1592. Ed. by R. E. M. Harding, 1949.

L Radino, G. M. *Intavolatura di Balli per sonar di Liuto.* Ed. by G. Gullino, 1949.

RaheT Rahe, H. *Theme und Melodiebildung der Motette Palestrina's,* in KJ XXXIV (1950), 74.

RamazM Ramazzini, A. *I Musici fiamminghi alla corte di Ferrara,* in *Archivio Storico Lombardo* VI (1879), 116.

RamosM *Musica practica Bartolomaei Rami de Pareia.* Ed. by J. Wolf, 1901.

RamsO *The Old Hall Manuscript.* Ed. by A. Ramsbotham, completed by H. B. Collins and Dom A. Hughes. 3 vols., 1933–38.

RanR Ranke, F. and J. M. Müller-Blattau. *Das Rostocker Liederbuch,* in *Schriften der Königsberger Gelehrten Gesellschaft* IV (1927), 193.

RattM Rattay, K. *Die Musikkultur des deutschen Ostens im Zeitalter der Reformation,* in *Bericht über den 1. Musikwissenschaftlichen Kongress der Deutschen Musikgesellschaft in Leipzig* (1925), 393.

RavenB   *A Reprint of all the Tunes in Ravenscroft's Book with Introductory Remarks.* Ed. by W H. Havergal, 1845.

P   *Thomas Ravenscroft: Pammelia and other Rounds and Catches.* Ed. by P. Warlock, 1928.

RavnE   Ravn, V. C. *English Instrumentalists at the Danish Court in the Time of Shakespeare,* in SIM VII (1906), 550.

RayJP   Ray, Alice. *Double-Choir Music of Juan de Padilla, Seventeenth-Century Composer in Mexico.* Ph.D. dissertation, University of Southern California, 1953, unpublished.

RB   *Revue belge de Musicologie (Belgisch Tijdschrift voor Muziekwetenschap),* 1946– .

RdM   *Revue de Musicologie.* Originally entitled *Bulletin de la Société française de Musicologie.* 1917– .

ReC   Reese, G. and T. Karp. *Monophony in a Group of Renaissance Chansonniers,* in JAMS V (1952), 4.

IN   Reese, G. *The Origin of the English In Nomine,* in JAMS II (1949), 7.

MMA   Reese, G. *Music in the Middle Ages,* 1940.

O   Reese, G. *The First Printed Collection of Part-Music: The Odhecaton,* in MQ XX (1934), 39.

P   Reese, G. *Printing and Engraving of Music,* in O. Thompson, *The International Cyclopedia of Music and Musicians* (1938), 1441.

T   Reese, G. *Maldeghem and his Buried Treasure. A Bibliographical Study,* in *Notes* VI (1948), 75.

ReaneyE   Reaney, Gilbert (ed.). *Early Fifteenth-Century Music,* 1955.

O   Reaney, G. *The Manuscript Oxford, Bodleian Library, Canonici misc. 213,* in MD IX (1955), 73.

RedM   Redlich, H. F. *Das Problem des Stilwandels in Monteverdis Madrigalwerk; ein Beitrag zur Formengeschichte des Madrigals,* 1931.

MLW   Redlich, H. F. *Claudio Monteverdi, Life and Works.* English transl. by K. Dale, 1952.

R   Redlich, H. F. *Monteverdi's Religious Music,* in M&L XXVII (1946), 208.

ReeI   Reeser, E. *Een iso-melische mis uit den tijd van Dufay,* in TVNM XVI (1942), 151; (1946), 312.

N   Reeser, E. *Guillaume Dufay:-Nuper rosarum flores 1436–1936,* in TVNM XV (1939), 137.

RefM   Refardt, E. *Die Musik der Basler Volksschauspiele des 16. Jahrhunderts,* in AfMW III (1921), 199.

RegnD   *Jakob Regnart: Deutsche Lieder mit 5 Stimmen (1580).* Ed. by H. Osthoff, 1928.

T   *Jakob Regnart: "Teutsche Lieder," zu 3 Stimmen.* Ed. by T. Buchleitner, 1925.

ReichB   Reichenbach, H. (ed.). *Bicinia germanica* (selected from G. Rhaw's collection, 1545), 1926.

ReinhH   Reinhardt, C. P. *Die Heidelberger Liedmeister des 16. Jahrhunderts,* 1939.

ReissG   Reiss, J. W. *Nikolaus Gomółka und seine Psalmen-Melodien,* in ZIM XIII (1912), 249.

K   Reiss, J. W. *Książki o muzyce od XV do XVII wieku w Bibljotece Jagiellońskiej,* 1924.

L   Reiss, J. W. *Zwei mehrstimmige Lieder aus dem 15. Jahrhundert,* in ZfMW V (1923), 481.

P   Reiss, J. W. *Pauli Paulirini de Praga Tractatus de musica,* in ZfMW VII (1925), 259.

ReissmA   Reissmann, A. *Allgemeine Geschichte der Musik.* 3 vols., 1863–64.

ReqG   Requin, H. *Elzéar Genet, dit Il Carpentrasso,* in *Mémoires de l'Académie de Vaucluse,* Sér. 2, XVIII (1918), 1.

ReyM   Reyher, P. *Les Masques anglais,* 1909.

RiaC   Riaño, J. F. *Critical and Bibliographical Notes on Early Spanish Music,* 1887.

RieF   *Riemann-Festschrift. Gesammelte Schriften . . . überreicht von Freunden und Schülern,* 1909.

G   Riemann, H. *Geschichte der Musiktheorie im IX.–XIX. Jahrhundert,* 1898; 2nd ed., 1921. References are to the 2nd ed.

H   Riemann, H. *Handbuch der Musikgeschichte.* I, 1923; II[1], 1920; II[2], 1922; II[3], 1922. (Orig. ed.: I[1], 1901; I[2], 1905; II[1], 1907; II[2], 1911; II[3], 1913.)

L   Riemann, H. *Musiklexikon,* 1st ed., 1882; 11th ed., 1929, revised by A. Einstein. References are to the 11th ed.

M   Riemann, H. *Musikgeschichte in Beispielen,* 1912.

MF   Riemann, H. *Das Lautenwerk des Miguel de Fuenllana (1554),* in MfMG XXVII (1895), 81.

RieNA   Riemann, H. *Der Mensural-Codex des Magister Nikolaus Apel* . . . , in KJ XII (1897), 1.

NN   Riemann, H. *Notenschrift und Notendruck*, in *Festschrift zur 50jährigen Jubelfeier des Bestehens der Firma C. G. Röder*, 1896.

R   Riemann, H. *Die rhythmische Struktur der Basses danses der Handschrift 9085 der Brüsseler Kgl. Bibliothek*, in SIM XIV (1913), 349. Addendum in SIM XV (1913), 8.

RiedelL   Riedel, Johannes. *Leisen Formulae: Their Polyphonic Settings in the Renaissance and Reformation*. Ph.D. dissertation, University of Southern California, 1953, unpublished.

RiessM   Riess, K. *Musikgeschichte der Stadt Eger im 16. Jahrhundert*, 1935.

RietschI   Rietsch, H. *Heinrich Isaac und das Innsbrucklied*, in *Jahrbuch der Musikbibliothek Peters* (1917), 19.

RihA   Rihouët [Rokseth], Y. *Note biographique sur Attaingnant*, in RdM V (1924), 70.

M   Rihouët [Rokseth], Y. *Un Motet de Moulu et ses diverses transcriptions pour orgue*, in *Bericht über den Musikwissenschaftlichen Kongress in Basel* (1925), 286.

RimbA   Rimbault, E. F. (ed.). *Ancient Vocal Music of England*, 1847.

B   Rimbault, E. F. *Bibliotheca madrigaliana*, 1847.

C   Rimbault, E. F. *An old Checque Book of the Chapel Royal*, 1872.

CS   Rimbault, E. F. (ed.). *Cathedral Services*, n.d.

P   Rimbault, E. F. *The Pianoforte*, 1860.

S   Rimbault, E. F. *A little Book of Songs and Ballads*, 1851.

RingA   Ringmann, H. (ed.). *Ausgewählte Sätze aus dem Glogauer Liederbuch*, 1927.

G   Ringmann, H. *Das Glogauer Liederbuch (um 1480)*, in ZfMW XV (1932), 49.

RitR   Ritter, A. G. *Die "Ricercari sopra li Toni" von G. P Palestrina*, in MfMG VI (1874), 134.

Z   Ritter, A. G. *Zur Geschichte des Orgelspiels*, 1884.

RM   *Revue musicale*. 1920– .

R   *Numéro spécial: Ronsard et la Musique*, May 1924.

RMI   *Rivista Musicale Italiana*. 1894– .

RobbB   Robbins, Rossell H. *The Burden in Carols*, in *Modern Language Notes* LVII (1942), 16.

RobbinsB   Robbins, Ralph H. *Beiträge zur Geschichte des Kontrapunkts von Zarlino bis Schütz*, 1938.

RobynsJ   Robyns, J. *Pierre de la Rue (circa 1460–1518), een bio-bibliographische Studie*, 1954.

RochaC   *Chansons de P. de Ronsard, Ph. Desportes et autres* . . (1575). Facsimile ed. of Superius by A. de Rochambeau, 1873.

RochlS   Rochlitz, J. F. (ed.). *Sammlung vorzüglicher Gesangstücke*. 3 vols., 1838–40.

Roedi   Roediger, K. E. *Die geistlichen Musikhandschriften der Universitäts-Bibliothek Jena*, 1935.

N   *Notenverzeichnis*.

T   *Textband*.

Roks   Rokseth, Y. *See also* RihA and RihM.

E   Rokseth, Y. *Instruments à l'église au XVe siècle*, in RdM XIV (1933), 206.

F   Rokseth, Y. *Un Fragment de Richafort*, in RdM VII (1926), 28.

I   Rokseth, Y. *Une Source peu étudiée d'iconographie musicale*, in RdM XIV (1933), 74.

J   Rokseth, Y. *Notes sur Josquin des Prés comme pédagogue musical*, in RdM VIII (1927), 202.

MO   Rokseth, Y. *La Musique d'orgue du XVe siècle et au début du XVIe*, 1930.

O   Rokseth, Y. (ed.). *Deux Livres d'orgue édités par Pierre Attaingnant (1531)*, 1925.

T   Rokseth, Y. (ed.). *Treize motets et un prélude pour orgue, édités par Pierre Attaingnant (1531)*, 1930.

RollH   Rolland, R. *Histoire de l'Opéra en Europe avant Lully et Scarlatti (Les Origines du théâtre lyrique moderne)*, 1895; reimpression, 1931.

M   Rolland, R. *Musiciens d'autrefois*, 1908. (Published in English, 1915, as *Some Musicians of Former Days*, transl. by M. Blaiklock; references in this book are to the French ed.)

RoncB   Roncaglia, G. *Intorno ad un Codice di Johannes Bonadies*, in *Reale Accademia di Scienze, Lettere ed Arti, Modena: Atti e Memorie*, Ser. 5, IV (1939), 31.

RoncF   Roncaglia, G. *In Memoria di Ludovico Fogliani nel 4° Centenario della Morte,* in *Reale Accademia di Scienze, Lettere ed Arti, Modena: Atti e Memorie,* Ser. 5, IV (1939), 44.

M   Roncaglia, G. *Simone Molinaro,* in RMI XLV (1941), 184.

OV   Roncaglia, G. *Il Luogo e la Data di nascita di Orazio Vecchi,* in *La Rassegna Musicale* II (1929), 198.

S   Roncaglia, G. *Di J. Fogliani e G. Segni: Documenti,* in RMI XLVI (1942), 294.

RoosO   Roosens, L. *Werd Jan Van Ockeghem te Dendermonde geboren?* in *Musica Sacra: Sancta Sancte* XLIII (1936), 13.

RosaS   Rosa y Lopez, S. de la. *Los Seises de la Catedral de Sevilla,* 1904.

RosenF   Rosenberg, H. *Frottola und deutsches Lied um 1500: Ein Stilvergleich,* in Acta XVIII–XIX (1946–47), 30. (Shorter version, in Italian, in RMI XLVIII [1946], 30.)

L   Rosenberg, H. *Übertragungen einiger bisher nicht aufgelöster Melodienotierungen des Locheimer Liederbuchs,* in ZfMW XIV (1931), 67.

S   Rosenberg, H. (ed.). *Das Schedelsche Liederbuch.* Selected and transc. by H. Rosenberg, 1933.

U   Rosenberg, H. *Untersuchungen über die deutsche Liedweise im 15. Jahrhundert,* 1931.

RossM   *Salomone Rossi (Ebreo): Choix de 22 madrigaux à cinq voix avec accompagnement de Chittarone, Orgue, et Basse continue ou à voix seules.* Ed. by V. d'Indy, 1877.

P   *Salomone Rossi (Ebreo): Psaumes, chants et hymnes à 3, 4, 5, 6, 7 et 8 voix.* Ed. by S. Naumbourg, 1877.

RossiR   Rossi, U. *Lettere di Cipriano de Rore, musico del secolo XVI,* 1890.

RothP   Roth, I. *Leonhard Paminger,* 1935.

RoyM   Royer, L. *Les Musiciens et la musique à l'ancienne collégiale Saint-André de Grenoble du XVe au XVIIIe siècle,* in *Humanisme et Renaissance* IV (1937), 237.

RthG   Roth, F. W. E. *Zur Geschichte der Meistersänger zu Mainz und Nürnberg,* in *Zeitschrift für Kulturgeschichte,* Neue (4.) Folge, Bd. 3 (1896), 261.

RubF   Rubsamen, W. H. *Notes on the Frottola,* abstract in BAMS, No. 5 (1941), 24.

IL   Rubsamen, W. H. *Music Research in Italian Libraries,* in *Notes* VI (1949), 220, 543; VIII (1950), 70.

J   Rubsamen, W. H. *The Justiniane or Viniziane of the 15th Century,* in Acta XXIX (1957), 172.

MM   Rubsamen, W. H. *Some First Elaborations of Masses from Motets,* abstract in BAMS, No. 4 (1940), 6.

RueM   *P. de la Rue: Liber Missarum.* Ed. by A. Tirabassi, 1941.

RunS   Runge, P. *Die Sangweisen der Colmarer Handschrift und die Liederhandschrift Donaueschingen,* 1896.

RybP   Ryb, M. *Notes sur la musique polonaise,* in EC, Partie I, V, 2569.

SaV   *Fray Tomás de Santa Maria: Wie mit aller Vollkommenheit und Meisterschaft das Klavichord zu spielen sei . . . ,* 1937. German transl. by R. Boadella and E. Harich-Schneider (with introduction and notes by the latter's *Libro llamado Arte de tañer fantasia para tecla, vihuela . . . , 1565.*

SaarB   Du Saar, J. *Het leven en de composities van Jacobus Barbireau,* 1946.

SaccR   Sacchetti-Sassetti, A. *La Cappella Musicale del Duomo di Rieti,* in NA XVII (1940), 89, 121.

SachsBD   Sachs, C. *Die Besetzung dreistimmiger Werke um das Jahr 1500,* in ZfMW XI (1929), 386.

CA   Sachs, C. *The Commonwealth of Art,* 1946.

CT   Sachs, C. *Chromatic Trumpets in the Renaissance,* in MQ XXXVI (1950), 62.

DD   Sachs, C. *Doppione und Dulzaina,* in SIM XI (1910), 590.

HI   Sachs, C. *The History of Musical Instruments,* 1940.

MH   Sachs, C. *Our Musical Heritage,* 1948.

MI   Sachs, C. *Handbuch der Musikinstrumentenkunde,* 1920.

PM   Sachs, C. *The Evolution of Piano Music, 1350–1700,* 1944.

R   Sachs, C. *Real-Lexikon der Musikinstrumente,* 1913.

RD   Sachs, C. *Der Rhythmus der basse danse,* in Acta III (1931), 107; shorter version in *Mélanges de musicologie offerts à M. Lionel de la Laurencie* (1933), 57.

RN   Sachs, C. *Some Remarks About Old Notation,* in MQ XXXIV (1948), 365.

RT   Sachs, C. *Rhythm and Tempo, a Study in Music History,* 1953.

SachsW   Sachs, C. *World History of the Dance,* 1937. (English transl. of *Eine Welt-geschichte des Tanzes,* 1933. References are to the transl.)

SalaC   Salazar, A. *Música, Instrumentos y Danzas en las Obras de Cervantes,* in *Nueva Revista de Filología Hispánica* II (1948), 21, 118.

E   Salazar, A. *La Música en la Sociedad europea.* . . . 2 vols., 1942–44.

L   Salazar, A. *El Laúd, la Vihuela y la Guitarra (Notas),* in *Nuestra Música* I (1946), 228.

M   Salazar, A. *Music in the Primitive Spanish Theatre before Lope de Vega,* in PAMS for 1938 (1940), 94.

P   Salazar, A. *Poesía y Música* . . . *en la Edad Media,* in *Filosofía y Letras* (1943), No. 8.

SaliM   Salinas, F. de. *De musica libri septem,* 1577.

SalmL   Salmen, W. *Das Lochamer Liederbuch,* 1951.

SampaA   Sampayo Ribeiro, M. de. *Achegas para a Historia de Musica em Portugal, II: Damião de Goes na divraria Real de Musica,* 1935.

C   Sampayo Ribeiro, M. de. *A Musica em Coimbra,* in *Biblos* XV (1939), 439.

SAMS   *American Musicological Society: Studies and Documents.* 1947– .

SamsP   Samson, J. *Palestrina ou la Poésie de l'exactitude,* 1940.

SanP   Santos, J. E. dos (ed.). *A Polifonia clássica portuguesa. Transcrições* . . . *de trechos dos mestres mais notáveis dos séculos XVI e XVII,* Vol. I, 1937.

SandA   Sandberger, A. *Ausgewählte Aufsätze zur Musikgeschichte,* Vol. I, 1921. (The first essay is published in Italian in RMI I [1894], 678.)

B   Sandberger, A. *Beiträge zur Geschichte der bayerischen Hofkapelle unter Orlando di Lasso.* Vols. I, III, 1894–95.

L   Sandberger, A. *Roland Lassus' Beziehungen zur italienischen Literatur,* in SIM V (1904), 402.

O   Sandberger, A. *Orlando di Lasso und die geistigen Strömungen seiner Zeit (Festrede gehalten in der öffentlichen Sitzung der Bay. Akademie der Wissenschaften zur Feier des 165. Stiftungstages am 13. Juni 1924),* 1926. (Published in Italian in RMI XLIV [1940], 177.)

R   Sandberger, A. *Roland Lassus' Beziehungen zu Frankreich und zur französischen Literatur,* in SIM VIII (1907), 355.

SartC   Sartori, C. *Precisazioni bibliografiche sulle opere di Girolamo Cavazzoni,* in RMI XLIV (1940), 359.

FB   Sartori, C. *A Little Known Petrucci Publication: The Second Book of Lute Tablatures by Francesco Bossinensis,* in MQ XXXIV (1948), 234.

J   Sartori, C. *Josquin des Prés, cantore del Duomo di Milano (1459–1472),* in AM IV (1956), 55.

M   Sartori, C. *Monteverdiana,* in MQ XXXVIII (1952), 399.

MS   Sartori, C. *Bibliografia della Musica Strumentale Italiana Stampate in Italia fino al 1700,* 1952.

P   Sartori, C. *Bibliografia delle opere musicali stampate da Ottaviano Petrucci,* 1948.

Q   Sartori, C. *Il quarto codice di Gaffurio non è del tutto scomparso,* in *Collectanea Historiae Musicae* I (1953), 25.

SaxtonV   Saxton, J. N. *The Masses of Victoria.* Master's thesis, Westminster Choir College, Princeton, N.J., 1951, unpublished.

ScP   Schmid, W. M. *Zur Passauer Musikgeschichte,* in ZfMW XIII (1931), 289.

SchP   Schmid, A. *Ottaviano dei Petrucci da Fossombrone,* 1845.

SchafferR   Schaffer, R. J. *A Comparative Study of Seven Polyphonic Requiem Masses.* Master's thesis, New York University, 1952, unpublished.

ScheerV   Scheer, W. *Die Frühgeschichte der italienischen Villanella,* 1936.

ScherA   Schering, A. *Aufführungspraxis alter Musik,* 1931.

B   Schering, A. *Musikalisches aus Joh. Burckhardts "Liber Notarum" (1483–1506),* in *Festschrift für Johannes Wolf* (1929), 171.

G   Schering, A. (ed.). *Geschichte der Musik in Beispielen,* 1931.

N   Schering, A. *Die Notenbeispiele in Glarean's Dodekachordon (1547),* in SIM (1912), 569.

NO   Schering, A. *Die niederländische Orgelmesse im Zeitalter des Josquin,* 1912.

R   Schering, A. *Ein Rätseltenor Okeghems,* in *Festschrift Hermann Kretzschmar überreicht* . . . (1918), 132.

S   Schering, A. *Studien zur Musikgeschichte der Frührenaissance,* 1914.

T   Schering, A. *Takt und Sinngliederung in der Musik des 16. Jahrhunderts,* in AfMW II (1920), 465.

Z   Schering, A. *Zur alternatim-Orgelmesse,* in ZfMW XVII (1935), 19.

ScherZG   Schering, A. *Zur Geschichte des begleiteten Sologesanges im 16. Jahrhundert*, in ZIM XIII (1912), 190.

ScheurD   Scheurleer, D. F. (ed.). *Een devoot ende profitelyck boecxken, 1539*, 1889.

E   Scheurleer, D. F. (ed.). *Ecclesiasticus . . . ghestelt in liedekens . . . deur Jan Fruytiers, 1565*, 1898.

JS   Scheurleer, D. F. *Sweelinckiana*, in TVNM IX (1914), 224.

S   Scheurleer, D. F. *Die Souterliedekens. Bijdrage tot de geschiedenis der oudste nederlandsche psalmberijming*, 1898.

SchlettM   Schletterer, H. M. *Musikalische Wettstreite und Musikfeste*, in MfMG XXII (1890), 181.

SchlickS   *Arnold Schlick: Spiegel der Orgelmacher und Organisten*. Ed. by E. Flade, 1932; new ed., 1951.

T   *Arnolt Schlick: Tabulaturen etlicher Lobgesang und Lidlein (Mainz, 1512)*. Ed. by G. Harms, 1924.

SchmidlD   Schmidl, C. *Dizionario dei Musicisti*. 2 vols. (pref. dated 1926). Suppl., 1938.

SchmidtgC I   Schmidt-[Görg], J. *Die Messen des Clemens non Papa*, in ZfMW IX(1926), 129.

II   Schmidt-[Görg], J. *Die Messen des Clemens non Papa*, in Gregoriusblatt LII (1928), 169, 183; LIII (1929), 7, 20.

G   Schmidt-Görg, J. *Nicolas Gombert, Kapellmeister Kaiser Karls V: Leben und Werk*, 1938.

I   Schmidt-Görg, J. *Die "Introites de taverne,"* in KJ XXX (1935), 51.

M   Schmidt-Görg, J. *Vier Messen aus dem 16. Jahrhundert über die Motette "Panis quem ego dabo" des Lupus Hellinck*, in KJ XXV (1930), 77, and Supp.

MG   Schmidt-Görg, J. *Die acht Magnifikat des Nicolaus Gombert*, in *Gesammelte Aufsätze zur Kulturgeschichte Spaniens* V (1935), 297.

SchneiM   Schneider, C. *La Musique originelle des psaumes huguenots, d'après les sources de 1562 et de 1565*, 1934.

P   Schneider, C. *Un Problème actuel: la restauration du Psautier huguenot d'après les sources de 1562–1569*, 1930.

R   Schneider, C. *La Restauration du Psautier huguenot*, in SJ IV (1929), 36.

SchneidA   Schneider, Max. *Die Anfänge des Basso Continuo und seiner Bezifferung*, 1918.

L   Schneider, Max. *Eine unbekannte Lautentabulatur aus den Jahren 1537–1544*, in *Festschrift für Johannes Wolf* (1929), 176.

SchneiderH   Schneider, Marius. *Der Hochetus*, in ZfMW XI (1929), 390.

SchnoB   Schnoor, H. *Das Buxheimer Orgelbuch*, in ZfMW IV (1921), 1.

SchöbS   Schöberlein, L. (ed.). *Schatz des liturgischen Chor- und Gemeindegesangs.* 3 vols., 1865–72.

SchofN   Schofield, B. and M. Bukofzer. *A Newly Discovered 15th-century Manuscript of the English Chapel Royal*, in MQ XXXII (1946), 509; XXXIII (1947), 38.

T   Schofield, B. and T. Dart. *Tregian's Anthology*, in M&L XXXIII (1951), 205.

SchöfL   *Peter Schöffers Liederbuch (1513)*. Facsimile ed., 1908.

SchraB   Schrade, L. *Ein Beitrag z. Geschichte der Tokkata*, ZfMW VIII (1926), 610.

C   Schrade, L. *"Choro et Organo" die B. Betazzi*, in RMI XXXVI (1929), 516.

G   Schrade, L. *Eine Gagliarde von Ciprian de Rore?* in AfMW VIII (1927), 385.

I   Schrade, L. *Die handschriftliche Überlieferung der ältesten Instrumentalmusik.* 1931.

M   Schrade, L. *Die Messe in der Orgelmusik des 15. Jahrhunderts*, in AfMF I (1936), 129.

MM   Schrade, L. *Monteverdi, Creator of Modern Music*, 1950.

O   Schrade, L. *The Organ in the Mass of the 15th Century*, in MQ XXVIII (1942), 329, 467.

R   Schrade, L. *Renaissance: the Historical Conception of an Epoch*, in *International Society for Musical Research, Fifth Congress, Utrecht, July 3–7, 1952, Report*, 19.

TI   Schrade, L. *Tänze aus einer anonymen italienischen Tabulatur*, in ZfMW X (1928), 449.

SchreiA   Schreiber, M. *Die Kirchenmusik des Kapellmeisters Leonhard Lechner Athesinus (1553–1606)*, 1935.

L   Schreiber, M. *Das Leben des Kapellmeisters Leonhard Lechner Athesinus*, 1932.

SchremG   Schrems, T. *Die Geschichte des gregorianischen Gesanges in den protestantischen Gottesdiensten*, 1930.

SchrevB   Schrevel, A. C. de. *Histoire du Séminaire de Bruges*, 1895.

SchröW   Schröder, O. *Zur Biographie Johann Walters*, in AfMF V (1940), 12.

SchulerO Schuler, E. A. *Die Musik der Osterfeiern, Osterspiele und Passionen des Mittelalters,* 1951.

SchünF Schünemann, G. *Zur Frage des Taktschlagens und der Textbehandlung in der Mensuralmusik,* in SIM X (1908), 73.

SchwartzF Schwartz, R. *Die Frottole im 15. Jahrhundert,* in VfMW II (1886), 427.

H Schwartz, R. *Hans Leo Hassler unter dem Einfluss der italienischen Madrigalisten,* in VfMW IX (1893), 1.

N Schwartz, R. *Nochmals "Die Frottole im 15. Jahrhundert,"* in *Jahrbuch der Musikbibliothek* Peters XXXI (1924), 47.

P Schwartz, R. *Zum Formproblem der Frottole Petruccis,* in *Theodor Kroyer-Festschrift* (1933), 77.

SchweiB Schweiger, H. (ed.). *A Brief Compendium of Early Organ Music . . . ,* 1943.

SchzC Schmitz, A. *Ein schlesisches Cantional aus dem 15. Jahrhundert,* in AfMF I (1936), 385.

I Schmitz, A. *Italienische Quellen zur Figuralpassion des 16. Jahrhunderts,* in *Festschrift Max Schneider* (1938), 92.

SCMA Smith College Music Archives. Editor-in-Chief, R. L. Finney. 1935– .

IV *Andrea Antico: Canzoni Sonetti Strambotti et Frottole.* Ed. by A. Einstein, 1941.

V *The Chansons of Jacques Arcadelt,* I. Ed. by E. B. Helm, 1942.

VI *The Madrigals of Cipriano de Rore for 3 and 4 Voices.* Ed. by G. P. Smith, 1943.

VIII *Vincenzo Galilei (1520?–1591): Contrapunti a due voci (1584).* Ed. by L. Rood, 1945.

ScoE Scott, C. K. (ed.). *Euterpe, a Collection of Madrigals and other Music of the 16th and 17th Centuries.* 15 vols., 1905–14. (Published by Breitkopf & Härtel; not to be confused with the *Euterpe* octavo series, also ed. by Scott, published by the Oxford University Press.)

ER Scott, C. K. (ed.). *The Euterpe Round Book, containing 50 English Rounds, Catches and Canons of the 16th and 17th centuries,* 1913.

ScotM Scott, R. H. *Music among the Moravians, Bethlehem, Pa., 1741–1816,* 1938.

SeiffBZ Seiffert, M. *Bildzeugnisse des 16. Jahrhunderts,* in AfMW I (1919), 49.

CS Seiffert, M. *Cornelis Schuijt,* in TVNM V (1897), 244.

G Seiffert, M. *Geschichte der Klaviermusik I,* 1899 (based on K. Weitzmann's *Geschichte des Klavierspiels und der Klavierliteratur,* 1863; 2nd ed., 1879).

M Seiffert, M. *Mattias Mercker. Ein ausgewanderter holländischer Musiker* in *Gedenkboek aangeboden aan Dr. D. F. Scheurleer . . .* (1925), 291.

N *Niederländische Bildmotetten.* 2 vols., 1929. Ed. by M. Seiffert, in *Organum,* Erste Reihe, Nos. 19–20.

SenflW *Ludwig Senfl: Sämtliche Werke.* Ed. by E. Löhrer and O. Ursprung, 1937– .

ShineM Shine, J. *Polyphonic Technique in the Motets of Jean Mouton as Illustrated in Thirty Examples.* Master's thesis, New York University, 1949, unpublished.

MM Shine, J. M. *The Motets of Jean Mouton* (including 107 transcriptions). Ph.D. dissertation, New York University, 1953, unpublished.

ShoreF Shore, S. R. *Robert Fayrfax,* in *The Musical Times* LXI (1920), 526.

SIM *Sammelbände der Internationalen Musikgesellschaft.* Quarterly magazine of the International Musical Society. Oct. 1899–Sept. 1914.

SindH Sindona, E. *È Hubert Naich e non Jacob Hobrecht il compagno cantore del Verdelot nel quadro della Galleria Pitti,* in Acta XXIX (1957), 1.

SJ *Schweizerisches Jahrbuch für Musikwissenschaft,* 1924–33.

SmC Smith, J. S. (ed.). *A Collection of English Songs,* 1779.

M Smith, J. S. (ed.). *Musica antiqua,* 1812.

SmijA Smijers, A. *Algemeene Muziekgeschiedenis,* 1938.

E Smijers, A. *Een kleine bijdrage over Josquin en Isaac,* in *Gedenkboek aangeboden aan Dr. D. F. Scheurleer* (1925), 316.

I Smijers, A. *De Illustre Lieve Vrouwe Broederschap te 's-Hertogenbosch,* in TVNM XI (1925), 187; XII (1926), 40; (1927), 115; XIII (1929), 46; (1931), 181; XIV (1932), 48.

JP Smijers, A. *Josquin des Prez,* in PMA LIII (1927), 95.

KH Smijers, A. *Die kaiserliche Hofmusik-Kapelle von 1543–1619,* in SzMW VI (1919), 139; VII (1920), 102; VIII (1921), 176.

L Smijers, A. *Karl Luython als Motetten-Komponist,* 1923.

M Smijers, A. *Music of the Illustrious Confraternity of Our Lady at 's-Hertogenbosch from 1300 to 1600,* in PAMS for 1939 (1944), 184.

SmijMC   Smijers, A. *De Missa Carminum van Jacob Hobrecht*, in TVNM XVII (1951), 192.

MM   Smijers, A. *Meerstemmige muziek van de Illustre Lieve Vrouwe Broederschap te 's-Hertogenbosch*, in TVNM XVI (1940), 1.

MP   Smijers, A. *De Matthaeus-Passie van Jacob Obrecht*, in TVNM XIV (1935), 182.

MQ   Smijers, A. *Het motet "Mille quingentis" van Jacob Hobrecht*, in TVNM XVI (1942), 212.

O   Smijers, A. (ed.). *Van Ockeghem tot Sweelinck (Nederlandsche Muziekgeschiedenis in Voorbeelden)*. 1939–   . (Published in instalments, of which 6 have appeared to date [1952].)

T   Smijers, A. (ed.). *Treize Livres de motets parus chez Pierre Attaingnant en 1534 et 1535*, 1934–   .

TM   Smijers, A. *Twee onbekende motetteksten van Jacob Obrecht*, in TVNM XVI (1941), 129.

V   Smijers, A. *Vijftiende en zestiende eeuwsche Muziekhandschriften in Italië met werken van Nederlandsche Componisten*, in TVNM XIV (1935), 165.

SmithA   Smith, C. S. *Music of the Ainsworth Psalter and Bay Psalm Book*, abstract in BAMS, No. 5 (1941), 8.

D   Smith, C. S. *Documentos referentes al "Cancionero" de Claudio de la Sablonara*, in Revista de Filología Española XVI (1929), 168.

L   Smith, C. S. *Religious Music and the Lute*, in The Guitar Review IX (1949), 31.

P   Smith, C. S. (ed.). *The Ainsworth Psalter*, 1938.

SmnP   Simon, A. *Polnische Elemente in der deutschen Musik bis zur Zeit der Wiener Klassiker*, 1916.

SmtC   Schmidt, A. W. *Die Calliopea legale des J. Hothby*, 1897.

SnB   Stein, H. *Jean Brudieu et les musiciens français en Catalogne au XVIe siècle*, in Annales du Midi XXXVI (1924), 288.

SolA   Solerti, A. *Gli Albori del Melodramma*. 3 vols., 1905.

M   Solerti, A. and D. Alaleona. *Primi Saggi del Melodramma giocoso*, in RMI XII (1905), 814; XIII (1906), 91, 244.

O   Solerti, A. *Le Origini del Melodramma*, 1903.

P   Solerti, A. *I Precedenti del Melodramma*, in RMI X (1903), 207, 466.

SommiM   Sommi-Picenardi, G. *Claudio Monteverdi a Cremona*, 1895. (Offprint from Gazzetta Musicale di Milano, LI).

SonA   Sonneck, O. G. *A Description of Alessandro Striggio and Francesco Corteccia's Intermedi "Psyche and Amor" 1565*, in MAn III (1911), 40.

M   Sonneck, O. G. *Miscellaneous Studies in the History of Music*, 1921.

SorbM   Sorbelli, A. *Le due Edizioni della Musica Practica di Bartolomé Ramis de Pareja*, in Gutenberg Jahrbuch V (1930), 104.

———   Soriano Fuertes, M. *Historia de la Música española desde la venida de los Fenicios hasta el año de 1850*. 4 vols., 1855–59. (Undependable.)

SowinP   Sowinski, A. *Les Musiciens polonais et slaves anciens et modernes: Dictionnaire biographique . . . ,* 1857.

SpataroD   *Giov. Spataro: Dilucide et probatissime demonstratione . . . contra certe frivole et vane excusatione da Franchino Gafurio (maestro de li errori) in luce aducte, 1521.* Ed. by J. Wolf, 1925.

SpellF   Spell, L. M. *The First Music-Books Printed in America*, in MQ XV (1929), 50.

M   Spell, L. M. *Music in the Cathedral of Mexico in the Sixteenth Century*, in Hispanic American Historical Review XXVI (1946), 293.

SpieT   Spies, H. *Die Tonkunst in Salzburg in der Regierungszeit des Fürsten und Erzbischofs Wolf Dietrich von Raitenau (1587–1612)*, in Mitteilungen der Gesellschaft für Salzburger Landeskunde, Bd. 71 and 72, 1931–32.

SpittaD   Spitta, F. *Benedictus Ducis*, in Monatsschrift für Gottesdienst und kirchliche Kunst XVII (1912), 7.

SquireM   Squire, W. Barclay (ed.). *Ausgewählte Madrigale*. 3 vols., 1903–13.

P   Squire, W. Barclay. *Notes on Early Music Printing*, in Bibliographica II (1897), 99.

S   Squire, W. Barclay. *On an Early Sixteenth Century MS. of English Music in the Library of Eton College*, in Archaeologia LVI (1898), 89.

W   Squire, W. Barclay. *Who Was Benedictus?* in SIM XIII (1912), 264.

StC   Stevens, J. *Carols and Court Songs of the Early Tudor Period*, in PRMA LXXVII (1951), 51.

R   Stevens, J. *Rounds and Canons from an Early Tudor Songbook*, in M&L XXXII (1951), 29.

StaD	Stainer, Sir John, J. F. R., and C. (eds.). *Dufay and his Contemporaries*, 1898.
E	Stainer, Sir John (ed.). *Early Bodleian Music. Sacred and Secular Songs* . . . I, facsimiles, 1901; II, transcriptions by J. F. R. and C. Stainer, 1901; III, *Introduction to the Study of some of the oldest Latin Musical Manuscripts in the Bodleian Library*, by E. W. B. Nicholson, 1913.
StäbK	Stäblein, B. *Die deutschen Kirchenlieder in der Berliner Handschrift Mus. Ms. 40095*, in KJ XXVI (1931), 51.
StainS	Stainer, J. F. R. *Shakespeare and Lassus*, in *The Musical Times* XLIII (1902), 100.
SteB	Stephan, W. *Die burgundisch-niederländische Motette zur Zeit Ockeghems*, 1937.
SteeleE	Steele, R. *The Earliest English Music Printing*, 1903.
SteinG	Stein, H. *Arnoul Gréban, poète et musicien*, in *Bibliothèque de l'École des Chartes* LXXIX (1918), 142.
SteinhV	Steinhardt, M. *Jacobus Vaet and his Motets*, 1951.
StellB	Stellfeld, J. A. *Bronnen tot de geschiedenis van de Antwerpsche clavecimbel- en orgelbouwers in de XVIe en XVIIe eeuwen*, 1942.
BP	Stellfeld, J. A. *Bibliographie des éditions musicales plantiniennes*, 1949.
M	Stellfeld, J. A. *Het muziekhistorisch belang der catalogi en inventarissen van het Plantinsch Archief*, in *Vlaamsch Jaarboek voor Muziekgeschiedenis* XXIII (1940), 5.
P	Stellfeld, J. A. *Andries Pevernage*, 1943.
SternR	Sternfeld, F. W. *Music in the Schools of the Reformation*, in MD II (1948), 99.
StevM	Stevens, D. *The Mulliner Book. A Commentary*, 1952.
O	Stevens, D. *Pre-Reformation Organ Music in England*, in PRMA LXXVIII (1951), 1.
P	Stevens, D. *A Part-Book in the Public Record Office*, in *Music Survey* II (1950), 16.
T	Stevens, D. *A unique Tudor Organ Mass*, in MD VI (1952), 167.
StevensM	Stevens, G. (ed.). *Mediaeval and Renaissance Choral Music*, 1940.
StevnsnC	Stevenson, R. *Cristóbal de Morales (ca. 1500–53). A Fourth-Centenary Biography*, in JAMS VI (1953), 3.
M	Stevenson, R. *John Marbeck's "Noted Booke,"* in MQ XXXVII (1951), 220.
MM	Stevenson, R. *Music in Mexico, a historical survey*, 1952.
P	Stevenson, R. *Thomas Morley's "Plaine and Easie" Introduction to the Modes*, in MD VI (1952), 177.
S	Stevenson, R. *Music Research in Spanish Libraries*, in *Notes* X (1952), 49.
Stn	Stein, E. E. *Twelve [i.e. thirteen] Franco-Flemish Masses of the Early Sixteenth Century*. Ph. D. dissertation, Eastman School, Rochester, 1941, unpublished.
M	Music vol.
T	Text vol.
StokesL	Stokes, E. *Lists of the King's Musicians, from the Audit Office Declared Accounts*, in MAn I (1909), 56; (1910), 119, 182, 249; II (1910), 51; (1911), 114, 174, 235; III (1911), 54; (1912), 110, 171, 229; IV (1912), 55, (1913), 178.
StoltzerO	*Thomas Stoltzer: Octo tonorum melodiae quinque vocibus compositae*. Ed. by O. Gombosi, 1933.
StoneP	Stone, K. (ed.) *Parthenia* . . . , 1951.
StpnW	Stephen, G. A. *The Waits of the City of Norwich through four Centuries to 1790*, in *Norfolk Archaeology* XXV (1933), 1.
StraM	Van der Straeten, Edmond. *La Musique aux Pays-Bas avant le XIXe siècle*. 8 vols., 1867–88.
StraeV	Van der Straeten, Edmond. *The History of the Violin*. 2 vols., 1933.
StrunkH	Strunk, O. *Origins of the "L'Homme armé" Mass*, abstract in BAMS, No. 2 (1937), 25.
M	Strunk, O. *Some Motet-Types of the 16th Century*, in PAMS, 1939 (1944), 155.
OH	Strunk, O. *The Music of the Old Hall Manuscript—A Postscript*, in MQ XXXV (1949), 244.
P	Strunk, O. *Guglielmo Gonzaga and Palestrina's Missa Dominicalis*, in MQ XXXIII (1947), 228.
R	Strunk, O. *Source Readings in Music History*, 1950.
V	Strunk, O. *Vergil in Music*, in MQ XVI (1930), 482.
SubM	Subirá, J. *La Música en la Casa de Alba*, 1927.
SumnO	Sumner, W. C. *A History and Account of the Organs of St. Paul's Cathedral*, 1931.

SünPL   Suñol, Dom G. *Canto español del "Pange lingua,"* in *Revista Montserratina* III (1909), 212, 256, 293, 375, 464.

SurzB   Surzyński, J. *Matka Boska w muzyce polskiej,* 1905.

SusaD   Tylman Susato: *Danserye zeer lustich . . . om spelen op alle musicale instrumenten (1551)* [*Musyck boexken,* No. 3]. Ed. by F. J. Giesbert. 2 vols., 1936.

SutherR   Sutherland, G. *The Ricercari of Jacques Buus,* in MQ XXXI (1945), 448.

SweeW   *Werken van Jan Pieterszn. Sweelinck.* Ed. by M. Seiffert, *et al.* 12 vols., 1895–1903.

SzabE   Szabolcsi, B. *The Eastern Relations of Early Hungarian Folk-Music,* in *Journal of the Royal Asiatic Society,* Present Series (1935), 483. (Published also in Hungarian in *Ethnographia* XXV [1934], 138.)

    L   Szabolcsi, B. and A. Tóth. *Zenei Lexikon.* 2 vols. Vol. I, 1930; Vol. II, 1931.

    M   Szabolcsi, B. *A XVI. Század magyar históriás zenéje,* 1931. (In series, *Magyar Zenei Dolgozatok,* No. 9. Reprinted from *Irodalomtörténeti Közlemények* XXXI [1931].)

    O   Szabolcsi, B. *Die metrische Odensammlung der Johannes Honterus,* in ZfMW XIII (1931), 338.

    S   Szabolcsi, B. *Die ungarischen Spielleute des Mittelalters,* in *Gedenkschrift für Hermann Abert* (1928), 154.

    TS   Szabolcsi, B. *Tinódi Sebestyén dallamai,* 1929. (Reprinted from *Zenei Szemle,* 1929.)

    U   Szabolcsi, B. *Probleme der alten ungarischen Musikgeschichte,* in ZfMW VII (1925), 647; VIII (1925–26), 140, 342, 485.

SzczepD   Szczepańska, M. *Przyczynek do historji polskiej pieśni w XV wieku,* in *Przegląd Muzyczny* n.s. III (1927).

    H   Szczepańska, M. *Do historji muzyki wielogłosowej w Polsce z końca XV wieku,* in *Kwartalnik Muzyczny,* No. 8 (1930), 275.

    L   Szczepańska, M. *O nieznanych Lamentacjach polskich z końca XV wieku,* in *Myśl Muzyczna,* No. 8 (1928).

    M   Szczepańska, M. *Do historji wielogłosowego "Magnificat" w Polsce,* in *Kwartalnik Muzyczny,* No. 9 (1930), 6.

    N   Szczepańska, M. *Nowe źródło do historji muzyki średniowiecznej w Polsce* in *Księga pamiątkowa ku czci Prof. A. Chybinskiego* (1930), 15.

    P   Szczepańska, M. *Do historji polskiej muzyki świeckiej w XV stuleciu,* in *Kwartalnik Muzyczny,* No. 5 (1929), 1.

    U   Szczepańska, M. *O utworach Mikołaja Radomskiego (z Radomia) wiek XV. wtęp,* in *Polski Rocznik Muzyczny* II (1936), 87.

    W   Szczepańska, M. *Wielogłosowe opracowania hymnów marjańskich w rękopisach polskich XV wieku,* in *Kwartalnik Muzyczny,* No. 1 (1928), 1; No. 2 (1929), 107; No. 3 (1929), 219; No. 4 (1929), 339.

    Z   Szczepańska, M. *O dwunastogłosowym Magnificat Mikołaja Zieleńskiego z r. 1611. Do historji stylu weneckiego w Polsce,* in *Polski Rocznik Muzikologiczny* I (1935), 28.

SzMW   *Studien zur Musikwissenschaft.* Issued under the editorship of G. Adler, in conjunction with DTO.

TagA   Tagliapietra, G. (ed.). *Antologia di Musica Antica e Moderna per Pianoforte.* 14 vols., 1931–32.

TapL   Tappert, W. *Die Lautenbücher des Hans Gerle,* in MfMG XVIII (1886), 101.

    S   Tappert, W. (ed.). *Sang und Klang aus alter Zeit,* 1906.

TCM   *Tudor Church Music.* Ed. by P. C. Buck, E. H. Fellowes, A. Ramsbotham, R. R. Terry, and S. T. Warner. 10 vols., 1922–29.

    I   *J. Taverner, Part I,* 1923.

    II   *W. Byrd: English Church Music, Part I,* 1922.

    III   *J. Taverner, Part II,* 1924.

    IV   *O. Gibbons,* 1925.

    V   *R. White,* 1926.

    VI   *T. Tallis,* 1928.

    VII   *W. Byrd: Gradualia,* 1927.

    VIII   *T. Tomkins, Part I: Services,* 1928.

    IX   *W. Byrd: Masses, Cantiones, and Motets,* 1928.

    X   *H. Aston, J. Marbeck, O. Parsley,* 1929.

    A   *Appendix with supplementary notes, by E. H. Fellowes,* 1948.

    O   *Octavo Edition.* This consists of separate issues, some taken from TCM I–X, but some not to be found there.

TebAP   Tebaldini, G. *L'Archivio Musicale della Cappella Antoniana in Padova*, 1895.

TellerM   Teller, F. *Monumenti di Musica sacra nell'Ungheria medievale*, in *Corvina* V (1942), 461.

TerryC I–VII   Terry, R. R. (ed.). Seven Consort Pieces for Strings by Byrd, Cranford, Dering (2 exx.), Forde, Parsons, and Perslye, published separately. (Curwen Nos. 90738, 90790, 90845, 93012–13, 93027–28, resp.)

F   Terry, R. R. *A Forgotten Psalter and Other Essays*, 1929.

M   Terry, R. R. *John Merbecke*, in PMA XLV (1919), 75.

P   *Calvin's first Psalter (1539)*. Ed. with critical notes and modal harmonies to the melodies by R. R. Terry, 1932.

TeuC   Teuscher, H. *Christ ist erstanden. Stilkritische Studie über die mehrstimmigen Bearbeitungen der Weise von den Anfängen bis 1600*, 1930.

ThibL   Thibaut, J.-B. *La Notation musicale*, 1912.

ML   Thibaut, J.-B. *Monuments de la notation ekphonétique et neumatique de l'église latine*, 1912.

ThibaultA   Thibault, G. *Les Amours de P. de Ronsard mises en musique par Jehan de Maletty (1578)*, in *Mélanges de musicologie offerts à M. Lionel de la Laurencie* (1933), 61.

AB   Thibault, G. *Anthoine de Bertrand, musicien de Ronsard, et ses amis toulousains*, in *Mélanges offerts à M. Abel Lefranc* (1936), 282.

B   Thibault, G. and L. Perceau. *Bibliographie des poésies de P. de Ronsard mises en musique au XVIe siècle*, 1941.

D   Thibault, G. *Deux catalogues de libraires musicaux: Vincenti et Gardane (Venise, 1591)*, in RdM X (1929), 177; XI (1930), 7.

F   Thibault, G. *Un Manuscrit de chansons françaises à la bibliothèque royale de la Haye*, in *Gedenkboek aangeboden aan Dr. D. F. Scheurleer* (1926), 347.

Q   Thibault, G. *Quelques chansons de Dufay*, in RdM V (1924), 97.

ThürS   Thürlings, A. *Die Soggetti cavati dalle vocali in Huldigungskompositionen und die Herculesmesse des Lupus*, in *Bericht über den 11. Kongress der Internationalen Musikgesellschaft*, 1907, 183.

TibyR   Tiby, O. *Sebastian Raval: A 16th Century Spanish Musician in Italy*, in MD II (1948), 217.

TierC   Tiersot, J. *Histoire de la chanson populaire en France*, 1889.

E   Tiersot, J. *Elzéar Genet, dit Carpentras, et le chanson "A lombre dung buissonet,"* in TSG V (1899), 207, 236.

R   Tiersot, J. *Ronsard et la musique de son temps*, in SIM IV (1902), 70. Also published separately.

TinctorisT   Tinctoris, J. *Terminorum musicae diffinitorium*. Latin text with French transl. and notes by A. Machabey, 1951.

TiraG   Tirabassi, A. *Grammaire et transcription de la notation proportionnelle*, 1930.

M   Tirabassi, A. *La Mesure dans la notation proportionnelle et sa transcription moderne*, 1924.

ToR   Torri, L. *Vincenzo Ruffo, Madrigalista e Compositore di Musica sacra nel secolo XVI*, in RMI III (1896), 635; IV (1897), 233.

TomasA   Tomasin, Don P. and G. Piber. *Andrea Antico, Chierico di Montona nell'Istria, primo Calcografo musicale*, 1880.

TomkoH   Tomkowicz, S. *Do Historji Muzyki w Krakowie*, in *Rocznik Krakowski* IX (1907), 187.

TorA   Torchi, L. (ed.). *L'Arte musicale in Italia*. 7 vols., 1897–1908 [?].

F   Torchi, L. *I Monumenti dell'antica Musica francese a Bologna*, in RMI XIII (1906), 451, 575.

G   Torchi, L. *Nei Parentali (1614–1914) di Felice Anerio e di Carlo Gesualdo, Principe di Venosa*, in RMI XXI (1914), 492.

M   Torchi, L. *La musica istrumentale in Italia nei secoli XVI, XVII e XVIII*, in RMI V (1898), 64, 281, 455; VI (1899), 255, 693; VII (1900), 233; VIII (1901), 1.

TornC   Torner, E. M. (ed.). *Colección de Vihuelistas españoles del siglo XVI*, 1923.

TorreP   Torrefranca, F. *I Primordii della Polifonia del Cinquecento*, in *Nuova Antologia* CCCLXXVI (Nov.–Dec., 1934), 107.

S   Torrefranca, F. *Il Segreto del Quattrocento*, 1939.

TouA   *L'Art et instruction de bien dancer*, publ. 1496 by M. Toulouze; facsimile ed., 1936, by Royal College of Physicians, London, with bibliographical note by V. Scholderer.

TourC   Catalogue de la Bibliothèque de la ville de Tournai. Ed. by A. Wilbaux, 1860.

TreB   Trend, J. B. Musikschätze auf spanischen Bibliotheken, in ZfMW VIII (1926), 499.

BM   Trend, J. B. Catalogue of the Music in the Biblioteca Medinaceli, Madrid, in Revue hispanique LXXI (1927), 485.

C   Trend, J. B. Salinas: A Sixteenth Century Collector of Folk Songs, in M&L VIII (1927), 13.

CM   Trend, J. B. Cristóbal Morales, in M&L VI (1925), 19.

L   Trend, J. B. Luis Milan and the Vihuelistas, 1925.

M   Trend, J. B. The Music of Spanish History to 1600, 1926.

ME   Trend, J. B. The Mystery of Elche, in M&L I (1920), 145.

N   Trend, J. B. A Note on Spanish Madrigals, in International Society for Musical Research, First Congress, Liége, September 1–6, 1930, Report, 225. (Substantially the same as TreS.)

S   Trend, J. B. Spanish Madrigals and Madrigal-Texts, in AdlerF (1930), 116. (Substantially the same as TreN.)

SC   Trend, J. B. The Mystery of Sybil Cassandra, in M&L X (1929), 124.

SM   Trend, J. B. Spanish Madrigals, in PMA XXVI (1925), 13.

V   Trend, J. B. Thome Luis de Victoria, in The Musical Times LXVI (1925), 311.

TricouL   Tricou, G. Documents sur la musique à Lyon au XVIᵉ siècle, 1899.

TromM   B. Tromboncino and G. Archadelt. Tre Madrigali di Michelangiolo Buonarroti. Ed. by L. Puliti, 1875.

TrzK   Trzciński, X. T. Katalog rękopisów Biblioteki kapitulnej w Gnieźnie, 1910.

TSG   La Tribune de Saint-Gervais. 1895–1922.

TurrA   Turrini, G. L'Accademia Filarmonica di Verona dalla fondazione (Maggio 1543) al 1600 . . . , 1941.

N   Turrini, G. Il Maestro fiammingo Giovanni Nasco a Verona, in NA, Nos. 4–6 (1937).

V   Turrini, G. De vlaamsche Componist, Giovanni Nasco te Verona (1547–1551), in TVNM XIV (1935), 132; XV (1937), 84.

TVNM   Tijdschrift der Vereeniging voor Nederlandsche Muziekgeschiedenis, 1882– .

TyeA   Christopher Tye: The Actes of the Apostles . . . (1553), in Quarterly Musical Magazine and Review IX (1827), after p. 414; X (1828), after p. 134.

UrJ   Ursprung, O. Joan Brudieu, ein Meister der spanischnationalen Kunst des XVI. Jahrhunderts, in Bulletin de la Société "Union musicologique" V (1925), 174.

JP   Ursprung, O. Josquin des Prés, in Bulletin de la Société "Union Musicologique" VI (1928), 11.

K   Ursprung, O. Die katholische Kirchenmusik, 1931–33.

L   Ursprung, O. Neuere Literatur zur spanischen Musikgeschichte, in ZfMW XII (1929), 93.

V   Ursprung, O. Vier Studien zur Geschichte des deutschen Liedes, in AfMW: No. I in IV (1922), 413; No. II in V (1923), 11; No. III in V (1923), 316; No. IV in VI (1924), 262.

VG   Ursprung, O. Der vokale Grundcharakter des diskantbetonten figurierten Stils, in Bericht über den musikwissenschaftlichen Kongress in Basel (1924), 364.

————   Ursprung, O. Musikkultur in Spanien, in P. Hartig and W. Schellberg, Handbuch der Spanienkunde, 1932.

ValC   Valdrighi, L. F. Cappelle, Concerti e Musiche di Casa d'Este, in Atti e Memorie delle Regie Deputazioni di Storia patria per le Provincie modenesi e parmensi, Ser. III, Vol. II (1883), 415.

ValeR   Vale, G. Gli ultimi anni di Vincenzo Ruffo, in NA I (1924), 78.

ValentinT   Valentin, E. Die Entwicklung der Tokkata im 17. und 18. Jahrhundert, 1930.

ValleA   Valle de Paz, G. del. Annibale Padovano, 1933.

VanAM   Van, G. de. A recently discovered Source of Early Fifteenth Century Polyphonic Music, the Aosta Manuscript, in MD II (1948), 5.

B   Van, G. de. Inventory of Manuscript Bologna Liceo Musicale, Q 15 (olim 37), in MD II (1948), 231.

M   Van, G. de (ed.). Les Monuments de l'Ars Nova. Fasc. I. Morceaux liturgiques I, Oeuvres italiennes, 1939.

P   Van, G. de. La Pédagogie musicale à la fin du moyen âge, in MD II (1948), 75.

VasE   Vasconcellos, J. de. El Rey D. João o 4ᵗᵒ, 1900.

J   Vasconcellos, J. de. Primeira Parte do Index da Livraria de Musica do Rey Dom João IV, 1873.

VasM   Vasconcellos, J. de. *Os musicos portuguezes.* 2 vols., 1870.
VatC   Vatielli, F. *Canzonieri musicali del '500,* in RMI XXVIII (1921), 397, 617.
  P   Vatielli, F. *Il Principe di Venosa e Leonora d'Este,* 1941.
  S   Vatielli, F. *Primizia del sinfonismo,* in RMI XLVII (1943), 117.
  V   Vatielli, F. *Vita ed arte musicale a Bologna.* Vol. I, 1927.
VecA   *Orazio Vecchi: L'Amfiparnaso* (1597). 2 vols., facsimile and transcription. Ed.
          by C. Perinello, 1938.
VelA   Velten, R. *Das ältere deutsche Gesellschaftslied unter dem Einfluss der italie-
          nischen Musik,* 1914.
VenA   Venturi, A. *L'Arte a Ferrara nel periodo di Borso d'Este,* in *Rivista Storica
          Italiana* II (1885), 689.
VenteB   Vente, M. A. *Bouwstoffen tot de Geschiedenis van het nederlandse orgel in
          de 16de eeuw,* 1942.
VerhM   Verheyden, P. *De drukker en de componist van het Maximiliaan-boek,* in *Ant-
          werpsch Archievenblad,* Ser. 2, III (1928), 268.
VernO   Vernarecci, A. *Ottaviano de' Petrucci da Fossombrone* (2nd ed.), 1882.
Vesperale *Vesperale Romanum,* 1924. (Desclée edition.)
VfMW   *Vierteljahrsschrift für Musikwissenschaft,* 1884–94.
VicO   *Tomás Luis de Victoria: Opera omnia.* 8 vols. Ed. by F. Pedrell, 1902–13.
VieiM   Vieira, E. *Diccionario biographico de musicos portuguezes,* 1900.
VillaT   Villanis, L. A. *Alcuni Codici manoscritti di Musica del secolo XVI posseduti
          dalla Biblioteca Nazionale di Torino,* in *Atti del Congresso internazionale di
          Scienze storiche, Roma . . . 1903* VIII (1905), 319ff, plus 14 pp. of music.
VincM   Vincent, A. J. H. *Note sur la modalité du chant ecclésiastique et sur son accom-
          pagnement,* in *Revue archéologique* XIV (1857), 620, 662.
  R   Vincent, A. J. H. *Rapport sur un ms. musical du XVe siècle,* in *Bulletin du
          Comité de la langue, de l'histoire et des arts de la France* IV (1857), 393.
VirdungM *Sebastian Virdung: Musica getutscht (1511).* Facsimile ed. with supplementary
          comment by L. Schrade, 1931.
VNM   *Vereeniging voor Nederlandsche Muziekgeschiedenis. Uitgaven.* 1869– .
  V   *Cornelis Schuÿt: Drie madrigalen; Jan Pieters Sweelinck, Twee chansons.* Ed.
          by R. Eitner, 1873.
  VI   *Jan Pieters Sweelinck: Acht zesstemmige Psalmen.* Ed. by R. Eitner, 1876.
  IX   *Jacob Obrecht: Missa Fortuna desperata.* Ed. by R. Eitner, 1880.
  XII   *Jan Pieters Sweelinck: Zes vierstemmige Psalmen.* Ed. by R. Eitner, 1883.
  XXII   *Cornelis Boscoop: 50 Psalmen Davids (1568).* Ed. by M. Seiffert, 1899.
  XXVI   *Een duytsch musyck boek (1572).* Ed. by F. van Duyse, 1903.
  XXIX   *Tielman Susato: Het ierste musyck boexken (1551).* Ed. by F. van Duyse,
          1908.
  XXX   *25 driestemmige oud-nederlandsche liedern.* Ed. J. Wolf, 1910.
  XXXV   *Adrian Willaert: Missa super Benedicta.* Ed. by A. Averkamp, 1915.
  XXXVIII *Philippus de Monte: Missa ad modulum Benedicta en.* Ed. by A. Smijers, 1920.
  XLIV   *J. Obrecht, Josquin des Prés, Jacobus Clemens non Papa: Drie oud-neder-
          landsche motetten.* Ed. by E. Reeser and S. Dresden, 1936.
  XLV   *Cornelis Schuÿt: Vijfstemmige madrigalen.* 2 parts. Ed. by A. Smijers, 1937–
          38.
VoE   Vogel, A. *The English Part-Song around 1500,* abstract in BAMS, No. 4
          (1940), 10.
VogQ   Vogeleis, M. *Quellen und Bausteine zu einer Geschichte der Musik und des
          Theaters im Elsass,* 1911.
VogelG   Vogel, E. *Marco da Gagliano. Zur Geschichte des florentiner Musiklebens von
          1570–1650,* in VfMW V (1889), 396.
  M   Vogel, E. *Claudio Monteverdi: Leben, Wirken im Lichte der zeitgenössischen
          Kritik und Verzeichniss seiner im Druck erschienenen Werke,* in VfMW III
          (1887), 315.
  V   Vogel, E. *Bibliothek der gedruckten weltlichen Vokalmusik Italiens aus den
          Jahren 1500–1700.* 2 vols., 1892.
VP   *Variae preces,* 1901. (Solesmes edition.)
WaA   Waldapfel, J. *Adalékok Balassi istenes énekeinek mintáihoz,* 1927.
WackerK   Wackernagel, P. *Das deutsche Kirchenlied von den ältesten Zeiten bis zum
          Anfang des 17. Jahrhunderts.* 5 vols., 1863–77.
WagCR   Wagner, P. (ed.). *Fr. Petrarcas Vergini in der Komposition des Cyprian de
          Rore,* 1893.

WagE   Wagner, P. *Einführung in die gregorianischen Melodien*, 1st ed., 1895; 2nd ed., Part 1, 1901–05; 3rd ed. 1911, as *Ursprung und Entwicklung der liturgischen Gesangsformen bis zum Ausgange des Mittelalters;* Part 2, *Neumenkunde*, 1905, 2nd ed., 1912; Part 3, *Gregorianische Formenlehre; eine choralische Stilkunde*, 1921. Part 1 appeared in English, 1907, as *Introduction to the Gregorian melodies: Part 1, Origin and Development of the Forms of the Liturgical Chant up to the end of the Middle Ages.* References to Part 1 are to the English ed.

G   Wagner, P. *Geschichte der Messe. 1. Teil: Bis 1600*, 1913.

MP   Wagner, P. *Das Madrigal und Palestrina*, in VfMW VIII (1892), 423.

PK   Wagner, P. *Palestrina als weltlicher Komponist*, 1890.

T   Wagner, P. (ed.). *Das Graduale der St. Thomaskirche zu Leipzig (14. Jahrhundert) als Zeuge deutscher Choralüberlieferung.* Vol. 1, 1930. In PubAMD V.

Z   Wagner, P. *Zur Musikgeschichte der Universität*, in AfMW III (1921), 1.

WagenM   Wagenseil, J. C. *Von der Meister-singer holdseligen Kunst*, appendix to *De Sacri Rom. Imperii libera civitate Noribergensi commentatio*, 1697.

WalB   Wallner, B. A. *Die Bilder zum achtzeiligen oberdeutschen Totentanz*, in ZfMW VI (1923), 65.

H   Wallner, B. A. *Die Gründung der Münchener Hofbibliothek durch Albrecht V und Johann Jakob Fugger*, in ZfMW II (1920), 299.

I   Wallner, B. A. *Ein Instrumentalverzeichnis aus dem 16. Jahrhundert*, in *Festschrift . . . Adolf Sandberger . . .* (1918), 275.

M   Wallner, B. A. *Musikalische Denkmäler der Steinätzkunst des 16. und 17. Jahrhunderts nebst Beiträgen zur Musikpflege dieser Zeit*, 1912.

S   Wallner, B. A. *Sebastian Virdung von Amberg*, in KJ XXIV (1911), 85.

U   Wallner, B. A. *Urkunden zu den Musikbestrebungen Herzog Wilhelms V von Bayern*, in *Gedenkboek aangeboden aan Dr. D. F. Scheurleer . . .* (1925), 369.

WaldN   Waldner, F. *Nachrichten über die Musikpflege am Hofe zu Innsbruck. 1. Unter Kaiser Maximilian 1. von 1490–1519*, in MfMG XXIX (1897); XXX (1898), Supp.

WalkB   Walker, D. P. *The Aims of Baïf's Académie de Poésie et de Musique*, in JRB I (1946), 91.

I   Walker, D. P. *The Influence of Musique mesurée à l'antique, Particularly on the Airs de Cour of the Early Seventeenth Century*, in MD II (1948), 141.

J   Walker, D. P. and F. Lesure. *Claude le Jeune and Musique Mesurée*, in MD III (1949), 151.

M   Walker, D. P. *Musical Humanism in the 16th and Early 17th Centuries*, in *The Music Review* II (1941), 1, 111, 220, 288; III (1942), 55.

WalkerH   Walker, E. *A History of Music in England*, 1st ed., 1907; 3rd ed., revised and enlarged by J. A. Westrup, 1952. References are to the 3rd ed.

O   Walker, E. (ed.) *An Oxford Book of Fancies* in MAn III (1912), 65.

WarA   Warlock, P. *The English Ayre*, 1926.

C I–V   Warlock, P. and A. Mangeot (eds.). Five Consort Pieces for Strings by Johnson, Parsley, Parsons, and Woodcocke, published separately. (Curwen Nos. 90824–28)

EA   Warlock, P. and P. Wilson (eds.). *English Ayres, Elizabethan and Jacobean.* 6 vols. Vols. 1–3, 1927; 4–6, 1931.

ES   Warlock, P. (ed.). *Elizabethan Songs . . . for one voice . . . and four stringed instruments.* 3 vols., 1926.

WardD   Ward, J. M. *"Dolfull Dumps,"* in JAMS IV (1951), 111.

L   Ward, J. M. *The Lute in 16th-Century Spain*, in *The Guitar Review* IX (1949), 27.

T   Ward, J. M. *Trumpets in the Elizabethan and Early Stuart Theaters (1584–1642).* Master's thesis. University of Washington, 1942, unpublished.

TT   Ward, J. M. *Trumpets and the Tudor Theater*, abstract in BAMS, No. 8 (1945), 32.

U   Ward, J. M. *The Use of Borrowed Material in 16th-Century Instrumental Music*, in JAMS V (1952), 88.

V   Ward, J. M. *The Vihuela de mano and its Music (1536–1576).* Ph.D. dissertation, New York University, 1953, unpublished.

VH   Ward, J. M. *The Editorial Methods of Venegas de Henestrosa*, in MD VI (1952), 105.

WasG	Wasielewski, J. W. von. *Geschichte der Instrumentalmusik im 16. Jahrhundert*, 1878.
I	Wasielewski, J. W. von (ed.). *Instrumentalsätze vom Ende des XVI. bis Ende des XVII. Jahrhunderts*, 1874.
WauG	Wauters, E. *Jean Guyot de Châtelet, musicien de la Renaissance; sa vie et son oeuvre*, 1944.
WDMP	*Wydawnictwo dawnej muzyki polskiej (Publications de la musique ancienne polonaise)*. Ed. by A. Chybinski, 1928– .
VIII	*Anonymous (s. XVI): Duma*. Ed. by M. Szczepańska and T. Ochlewki, 1929.
IX	*Wacław z Szamotuł: In te Domine speravi (Psalmus XXX)*. Ed. by M. Szczepańska and H. Opieński, 1930.
XII	*Mikołaj Zieleński (c. 1611): Vox in Rama*. Ed. by A. Chybinski and B. Rutkowski, 1933– .
WeckB	*Balet comique de la royne (Paris, 1582)*. Ed. with piano reduction by J.-B. Weckerlin, 1882.
C	Weckerlin, J.-B. *Bibliothèque du Conservatoire national de musique et de déclamation: Catalogue bibliographique*, 1885.
CP	Weckerlin, J.-B. *La Chanson populaire*, 1886.
WeelP	*Thomas Weelkes: Pieces for Keyed Instruments*. Ed. by M. H. Glyn, 1924.
WeinK	Weinmann, K. *Das Konzil von Trient und die Kirchenmusik*, 1919.
KK	Weinmann, K. *Eine Komposition des Kardinals Joh. de Medici, des nachmaligen Papstes Leo X.*, in *Gedenkboek aangeboden aan Dr. D. F. Scheurleer . . .* (1925), 379.
T	Weinmann, K. *Johannes Tinctoris und sein unbekannter Traktat "De inventione et usu musicae,"* 1917.
U	Weinmann, K. *Ein unbekannter Traktat des Johannes Tinctoris*, in RieF (1909), 267.
WerR	Werner, L. *Una Rarità musicale della Biblioteca Vescovile di Szombathély*, in NA VIII (1931), 89.
WernH	Werner, T. W. *Die im herzoglichen Hausarchiv zu Zerbst aufgefundenen Musikalien aus der zweiten Häifte des 16. Jahrhunderts*, in ZfMW II (1920), 681.
J	Werner, T. W. *Anmerkungen zur Kunst Josquins und zur Gesamt-Ausgabe seiner Werke*, in ZfMW VII (1924), 33.
M	Werner, T. W. *Die Magnificat-Kompositionen Adam Rener's*, in AfMW II (1920), 195.
WestC	West, J. E. *Cathedral Organists*, 1899.
E	West, J. E. *Old English Organ Music*, in SIM XII (1911), 213.
O	West, J. E. (ed.). *Old English Organ Music*, Novello Ed., Nos. 14, 24, 25, 31.
WestrB	Westrup, J. A. *William Byrd (1543–1623)*, in M&L XXIV (1943), 125.
WeyF	Weyler, W. *Documenten betreffende de muziekkapel aan het hof van Ferrara*, in *Vlaamsch Jaarboek voor Muziekgeschiedenis* I (1939), 81.
WhitB	Whittaker, W. G. *Byrd's Great Service*, in MQ XXVII (1941), 474.
W	Whittaker, W. G. *Byrd's and Bull's "Walsingham" Variations*, in *The Music Review* III (1942), 270.
WidmK	Widmann, B. *Die Kompositionen der Psalmen von Statius Althof*, in AfMW V (1889), 290.
WidmaM	Widmann, W. *Die 6-stimmigen Messen Palestrinas*, in KJ XXVIII (1934), 10.
WienM	Wienpahl, R. W. *Modal Usage in Masses of the Fifteenth Century*, in JAMS V (1952), 37.
WillO	*Adrian Willaert: Opera omnia*. Ed. by H. Zenck and W. Gerstenberg, 1950– .
R	*Adrian Willaert: Ricercari a 3 voci*. Ed. by R. Zenck, 1933.
W	*Adrian Willaert: Sämtliche Werke*. Ed. by H. Zenck. Vol. I (no more issued) in PubAMD IX, 1927.
WinR	Winter, C. *Ruggiero Giovanelli (1560–1625), Nachfolger Palestrinas zu St. Peter in Rom*, 1935.
WintG	Winterfeld, C. von. *Johannes Gabrieli und sein Zeitalter*. 3 vols., 1834.
K	Winterfeld, C. von. *Der evangelische Kirchengesang und sein Verhältnis zur Kunst des Tonsatzes*. 3 vols., 1843–47.
WmsH	Williams, C. F. Abdy. *A Historical Account of the Degrees in Music at Oxford and Cambridge*, 1893.
WolfAL	Wolf, J. *Altflämische Lieder des 14./15. Jahrhunderts . . .* , in *Bericht über den musikwissenschaftlichen Kongress in Basel* (1925), 377.

WolfBA   Wolf, J. *Ein Brief Pietro Arons an Giovanni del Lago*, in *Von Büchern und Bibliotheken*. Ed. by G. Abb (1928), 65.

CE   Wolf, J. *Der Choraltraktat des Christoual de Escobar*, in *Gedenkboek aangeboden aan Dr. D. F. Scheurleer* (1925), 383.

DL   Wolf, J. *Deutsche Lieder des 15. Jahrhunderts*, in *Festschrift [für]* . . . *Freiherrn Rochus von Liliencron* (1910), 404.

DQ   Wolf, J. *Eine deutsche Quelle geistlicher Musik aus dem Ende des 15. Jahrhunderts*, in *Jahrbuch der Musikbibliothek Peters* XLIII (1936), 30.

EA   Wolf, J. *Ein alter Lautendruck*, in ZIM I (1899), 29.

F   Wolf, J. *Florenz in der Musikgeschichte des 14. Jahrhunderts*, in SIM III (1902), 599.

G   Wolf, J. *Geschichte der Mensural-Notation von 1250–1460*. 3 vols., 1904.

GM   Wolf, J. *Geschichte der Musik*. 3 vols., 1929–30. 2nd ed. of Vol. II, 1934.

H   Wolf, J. *Handbuch der Notationskunde*. 2 vols., 1913, 1919.

L   Wolf, J. *Luther und die musikalische Liturgie des evangelischen Hauptgottesdienstes*, in SIM III (1902), 647.

ME   Wolf, J. (ed.). *Music of Earlier Times (13th Century to Bach)*, 1946. (American reprint of *Sing- und Spielmusik aus älterer Zeit*, the collection of music examples for WolfGM.)

MS   Wolf, J. (ed.). *Musikalische Schrifttafeln*, 1923.

N   Wolf, J. *Der niederländische Einfluss in der mehrstimmigen gemessenen Musik bis zum Jahre 1480*, in TVNM VI (1900), 197; VII (1904), 154.

Q   Wolf, J. *Eine neue Quelle zur mehrstimmigen kirchlichen Praxis des 14. bis 15. Jahrhunderts*, in *Festschrift zum 60. Geburtstag von Peter Wagner* (1926), 222.

QM   Wolf, J. *Eine neue Quelle zur Musik des 15. Jahrhunderts*, in *Juhlakirja Ilmari Krohn'ille (Festschrift* for Ilmari Krohn) (1927), 1951.

TL   Wolf, J. *Zwei Tagelieder des XIV. Jahrhunderts*, in *Mittelalterliche Handschriften* (1926), 325.

WoodG   Woodward, G. R. *The Genevan Psalter of 1562. Set in Four-Part Harmony by Claude Goudimel, in 1565*, in PMA XLIV (1918), 167.

P   *Piae cantiones, 1582.* Ed. by G. R. Woodward, 1910.

WoodfillM   Woodfill, W. L. *Musicians' Companies in England 1500–1640*, abstract in JAMS IV (1951), 278.

Wool   Wooldridge, H. E. *See also* OH.

S   Wooldridge, H. E. *Studies in the Technique of Sixteenth-Century Music*, in MAn III (1912), 87, 142, 191; IV (1912), 31; IV (1913), 87, 175.

T   Wooldridge, H. E. *The Treatment of the Words in Polyphonic Music*, in MAn I (1910), 73, 177.

WotC   Wotquenne-Plattel, A. *Chansons italiennes de la fin du XVIme siècle*, n.d.

WüllnC   Wüllner, L. *Chorübungen*, new ed. of E. Schwickerath. 3 vols., 1931.

WustM   Wustmann, R. *Musikgeschichte Leipzigs* I, 1909.

WustmannA   Wustmann, G. *Elias Ammerbach*, in SIM XI (1909), 137.

YaF   Yates, F. A. *The French Academies of the Sixteenth Century*, 1947.

ZahnM   Zahn, J. *Die Melodien der deutschen evangelischen Kirchenlieder*. 6 vols., 1889–93.

ZarI   Zarlino, G. *Istitutioni harmoniche*, 1558, 1562, 1573, 1589. References are to the 1573 ed.

ZenA   Zenatti, A. *Andrea Antico da Montona*, in *Archivio Storico per Trieste, l'Istria e il Trentino* I (1881), 167.

N   Zenatti, A. *Nuovi appunti su A. Antico da Montona*, in *Archivio Storico per Trieste, l'Istria e il Trentino* III (1886), 249.

S   Zenatti, A. *Una Stanza del Furioso musicata da Bart. Tromboncino*, 1889.

ZenckN   Zenck, H. *Nicola Vicentinos L'Antica Musica (1555)*, in *Theodor Kroyer-Festschrift* (1933), 86.

S   Zenck, H. *Sixtus Dietrich*, 1928.

SS   Zenck, H. *Adrian Willaert's "Salmi Spezzati,"* in MF II (1949), 97.

Z   Zenck, H. *Zarlinos "Istitutioni harmoniche" als Quelle zur Musikanschauung der italienischen Renaissance*, in ZfMW XII (1930), 540.

ZfMW   *Zeitschrift für Musikwissenschaft*. 1918–35.

ZIM   *Zeitschrift der Internationalen Musikgesellschaft*. Monthly magazine of the International Musical Society. Oct. 1899–Sept. 1914.

ZuthH   Zuth, J. *Handbuch der Laute und Gitarre*, 1926.

Index

◆§In alphabetizing titles, the definite article is not considered unless it is declined; the indefinite article, however, is alphabetized, except in English. ◆§An abbreviation consisting of doubled letters represents a recurring word in its plural form, e.g., cc. = chansons. ◆§If no composer's or author's name is given after a title, the work is anonymous. ◆§Proper names in parentheses immediately following a title indicate printers or editors. ◆§Abbreviated symbols used for people's names in the bibliography are given in parenthesis after the full names they represent. ◆§Cities are entered under the name of the country to which they belong. ◆§MSS are grouped geographically, according to location of libraries, under the general heading: Manuscripts; separate entries (cross-references) are provided only for MSS with distinctive titles, e.g., Laborde Chansonnier. ◆§Printed collections, mostly of the anthology type, are listed only if they are especially important or bear distinctive titles. ◆§Complete Masses are listed under *Missa . . .* , and readers seeking all references to an independent melody upon which Masses may be based should look there as well as in the normal place for its title. ◆§Readers interested in Palestrina's Masses are referred to pp. 470ff, since, unless discussed elsewhere in the book, the Masses tabulated there are not indexed below. ◆§Grouping several compositions under their common titles does not imply a musical relationship, though this may sometimes exist. ◆§*Contrafacta* are equated to their models, but no attempt is made to list, under the name of a model, all the pieces based on it. ◆§Although empresses and queens are listed as "consorts" if they did not rule in their own right, no such distinction has been attempted for women of lesser rank, nor has any attempt been made to index every minor reference to subjects that recur frequently. ◆§Regarding plates, see list at front of book.

a cappella performance, 38, 161, 818f
A ce matin, Lassus, 392
A che tormi il ben mio, Monteverdi, 438f (incl. Ex. 106)
A cui giova, Marenzio, 421f (incl. Ex. 100)
A la audienche, Hayne, 100
A la bataglia, Isaac, 172
A la dolc'ombra, Rore, 332
A la fontaine du prez, Willaert, 351
A le guancie di rose, A. Gabrieli, 414f
A l'ombre d'ung buissonet, the melody, 214, 286; see also: *En l'ombre*
A los baños, 583
A madamme playsant et belle, Hugho de Lantins, 41
A Patri unigenitus, Greg. Chant, 361
A qui vens tu tes coquilles, Busnois, 104 (Ex. 26a)
A solis ortus cardine: Greg. Chant, 90; Binchois, 90
A toi mon Dieu mon coeur monte: Genevan mel., 503; Goudimel, 2 settings, 503

A une dame, Busnois, 106, 255
A virtutis—Ergo beata—Benedicta, Césaris, 21, 23
A vous non autre, La Rue, 272
A vous sans autre, Busnois, 102, 105
Abbott, Edwin A., 878
Abelard, 217
Aber, Adolf, 655, 677, 681
Abert, Anna Amalie, 687f, 696
Abgesang, 15; see also: *Bar* form
Abondante, Julio, 527
Abrégé de l'art poétique françois, Ronsard, 382
Absalon fili mi, Josquin, 257
Abyngdon, Henry, 767f, 850
Académie de poésie et musique, 382f
Académie du Palais, 385
Accademia de' Floridi, 436
Accademia di Santa Cecilia (= *Compagnia dei Musici di Roma*), 424ff
Accademia Filarmonica, Verona, 326, 400f
accentuation, quantity, declamation, 159, 245,

accentuation, etc. (*continued*)
253, 315, 322, 339, 350, 354f, 372, 374, 381ff, 450, 461, 475, 705, 709, 788, 797, 827, 829, 836, 839, 841
Accepit Jesus calicem, Palestrina, 464
accidentalism, 16, 24, 41, 195, 292, 328, 376, 406, 410, 423, 659, 802, 827, 858; see also: chromaticism; degree inflection
accidentals, their uniform indication recommended, 182; see also: *Musica ficta*
accordatura, see under name or type of instrument; see also: intonation (= tuning)
Accueillie m'a la belle, Caron, 111
Ach edler hort, Hofhaimer, 641
Ach hülf mich leid, Adam von Fulda, 639
Ach Jupiter, Adam von Fulda, 639
Ach lieb mit leyd, Hofhaimer, 641
Ach meyden du vil sene pein, 634
Acordés moy, Busnois, 103, 105f, 196
acrostics, 52, 63, 87, 101f, 228, 707
Actes and Monuments, Foxe, 769
Actes of the Apostles, Tye, 798f (incl. Ex. 185)
Actors Remonstrance, The (a tract), 883
Ad cantus laetitiae, 712
Ad coenam Agni providi (the melody = *Nunc Sancte nobis Spiritus; Aurora lucis rutilat; Aurora coelum*): Greg. Chant, 83, 467, 470, 604; Dufay, 83; Palestrina, 467; Victoria, 604
Ad te levavi: Lassus, 509 (incl. Ex. 118); Rore, 376
Adam, 35
Adam de St. Victor, 217
Adam von Fulda, 35, 179, 639, 646, 649f, 655, 705
Adami da Bolsena (Adami), 362
Adams, H., 773
Adesto nunc (= stanza 2 of *Salvator mundi,* q.v.): anon., 773; Tallis (instr. ensemble), 786
Adew, J. Dowland, 847
Adieu ces bons vins de Lannoys, Dufay, 49
Adieu les damez de vaillance, 151
Adieu m'amour, adieu ma ioye, Dufay, 54
Adieu m'amour et ma maistresse, Binchois, 88
Adieu mes amours: the melody, 195f, 205f, 232; Josquin, 232; Mouton, 281
Adieu mon amoureuse joye, Binchois, 88
Adieu naturlic leven myn, Lannoy, 115
Adieu quitte le demourant, Dufay, 45 (Ex. 7a)
Adiew sweet Amarillis, Wilbye, 830
Adiew you kind and cruel, Morley, 826
Adjuva nos, John IV of Portugal, 598
Adler, Guido, 35, 643, 689
Adoramus te: Palestrina, 469; Rosselli, 469; Ruffo, 490
Adrian VI, Pope, 362
Adriansen, Emanuel (= Hadrianus), 555f (incl. Ex. 128)
Adson, John, 873, 874
Aeterna Christi munera, Greg. Chant, 470
Affektenlehre, 695
Afflictus sum, Coclico, 516 (Ex. 119a)

Afflitti spirti, Festa, 319
after-dance (= *Nachtanz, Auff und nider;* incl. *pas de Brabant, piva, saltarello,* etc.), 37, 152, 177, 523, 553, 665, 671
Agenda defunctorum, Vasquez, 612
Agnus Dei (outside of complete Masses), see various Agnus settings under: Mass sections
Agora que soy niña, Vasquez, 612
Agricola, Alexander: biogr. and sec. voc. mus., 169f, 207ff (incl. Ex. 38), 244, 261, 266, 273; sacr. mus., 201, 210f, 740; see also 93, 100, 137, 184, 212, 220, 222, 250, 262f, 276, 278, 286, 580, 663
Agricola, Martin, 656ff, 669, 679, 689, 757
Aguilera de Heredia, Sebastian de, 629
Ah dear heart, Gibbons, 819
Ah dolente partita, Wert, 410
Ahi chi mi rompe, Monte, 407
Ahi come soffri, Wert, 410
Ahi tormento, Orazio Vecchi, 433
Aichinger, Gregor, 667, 699 (incl. Ex. 156), 702
Ailly, Pierre d', 8
Ain frelich wesen, Isaac, 644, 648; see also: *Een vroylic wesen*
Ainsi qu'on oit le cerf bruire: Genevan mel., 503; Le Jeune, 503
Ainsworth, Henry, 808
air de cour, 389, 557f
Airs de plusieurs musiciens, Le Blanc, 390
Ajolla, Francesco, see: Layolle, François (the Elder)
Al alba venid, 583
Al mormorar, Gastoldi, 427
Al vag'e incerto gioco di primiera, Striggio, 436
Alain (= Alanus?), 22
Alaleona, Domenico (Ala), 453f, 485, 592
Alamire, 337
Alanus (= Alain?), 632f
Alarme, alarme, Grimace, 12
Alas! it is I that wote nott what to say, Turges, 768f
Alas what hope of speeding, Kirbye, 829 (incl. Ex. 196); Wilbye, 829 (incl. Ex. 195)
Albanus Domini laudans mirabile nomen, Sarum Chant, 775
Albergona, L', Mortaro, 545
Albert, Prince of Prussia, 719, 721, 724
Albert, Archduke (co-ruler of Netherlands), 398, 793, 809
Albert III, Duke of Bavaria, 658
Albert V, Duke of Bavaria, 376, 395, 414, 449, 511ff, 690
Albini, Eugenio (Albi), 548
Albrecht, Hans (Alb), 306f, 682
Albrecht, Otto E., 97
Alder, Cosmas, 679
Aldobrandini, Cardinal Cinzio, 420, 425f
Aldomar, 585
Alectorius, see: Hähnel, Joh.
Aleman, Cardinal Louis, 49
Ales regrets, A. Agricola, 210

Alessandro, Organista da Firenze, 170
Alessi, Giovanni d' (Ales), 140, 174, 285, 326, 368, 373, 493
Alexander VI, Pope, 584
Alexander (= Agricola?), 222
Alfieri, Pietro (Alfi), 286, 362, 484
Alfonsina, La, Ghiselin, 266
Alfonso V, King of Naples and Sicily (*"el Magnánimo"*), 139, 576f
Alfonso I, Duke of Ferrara, 260, 266, 327
Alfonso II, Duke of Ferrara, 327, 329, 372, 409, 411, 430
Alford, John, 842
Algorithmus Proportionum, Scriptor, 746
Alison, Richard, 807f, 819, 874ff (incl. Ex. 214)
All mein Gedanken: the melody, 638; Brahms, 638
All people that on earth do dwell (= Old Hundredth), W. Parsons, 801
All the French Psalm Tunes with English Words (1632), 361
Alla riva del Tebro, Palestrina, 402
Allégez moy, Josquin, 233
Alleluia Christus surrexit, F. Anerio, 484
Alleluia Tulerunt Dominum, Palestrina, 462
Alleluia Veni Sancte Spiritus, Dufay, 77
Alleluias: several anon. (some by Dufay?), 77; Contino, 493
allemandes (= almans, etc.): instr. ensemble: in Susato print (1551), 564; Cranford, 873; Deering, 873; J. Dowland, 874; A. Ferrabosco II, 871; Ford, 873; keyboard: in Engl. MSS, 863, 866; B. Schmid the Elder, 668; lute: in Engl. MSS, general, 844f; J. Dowland, 847; in masques, 882
Alleregres, Longaval, 275
Allez regretz, Hayne, 100, 210, 224, 244, 275
Allez souspirs, Sermisy, 292
Allon gay, gay, gay, bergères, Costeley, 388
Alma Nemes, Lassus, 404
Alma Redemptoris Mater: Greg. Chant, 66, 81 (incl. Ex. 21), 121f, 185, 191, 254, 284, 345, 463, 471, 605; Aichinger, 699; Dufay, 81 (incl. Ex. 21); Dunstable, 24; Josquin, 254, 256; Obrecht, 191; Ockeghem, 121f (incl. Ex. 29); Palestrina, 2 settings, 463; Philips, 794; Victoria, 605, 607f
Almighty God who by the leading of a star (= Starre Anthem), Bull, 810
Alons ferons nos barbes, Compère, 224
Alouette, L', Janequin, 297, 299, 383
Also heilig ist der Tag: the melody, 706; Senfl, 706; see also 751f
Alta, La Torre, 619
Alte Jahr vergangen ist, Das, de Fine, 713
alternation Masses and Mass sections: Dufay, 59f; Isaac, 647; Palestrina, 474; see also next entry
alternation practices: monophony-polyphony, 23, 77, 83ff, 91, 216f, 223, 264, 346, 363, 474, 590, 604f, 647, 649f, 662, 693, 744, 764, 774, 780, 784, 790f; organ-plainsong, 536, 560, 662, 854f; soloists-chorus, 23f,

28, 766, 804; see also: alternation Masses
Altro non è il mio amor, Sermisy, 292
altus (derivation of term), 108
Alwood, Richard, 851, 854
Amadeus VIII, Duke of Savoy (= Felix V, antipope), 50
Amadino, 521
Amans amés, Cordier, 14
Amans doublés, Vide, 43
Amarilli, Caccini, 835
Amat, Juan Carlos, 625
Amati, Andrea, 548
Amati, Antonio, 548
Amati, Hieronymus, 548
Amati, Nicola, 548
Ambra d', Francesco, 568
Ambros, August W. (Amb) 26, 57, 72f, 87f, 100, 107, 110f, 119ff, 133, 147, 149, 158, 164, 170, 178, 180, 187, 189ff, 202, 208ff, 214, 216, 218f, 221f, 224, 230, 232, 234, 244f, 253, 257, 261f, 264ff, 270, 272, 275ff, 285f, 305, 337, 343, 346, 350, 370, 374, 486, 499, 501, 525, 568, 570f, 591, 602, 641, 646, 648f, 677f, 680, 682ff, 688, 690, 707ff, 724, 843
Ambrosian liturgy, 227, 731
Ameln, Konrad (Ame), 634, 636ff, 675, 677f, 680ff, 686ff, 706, 708
Amerbach, Bonifacius, 663, 680
Amerval, Eloy d', 116, 263
Amfiparnaso, L', Orazio Vecchi, 433ff (incl. Ex. 105)
Aminta, Tasso, 569
Ammerbach, Elias Nicolaus, 665ff
Amon, Blasius, 699
Amor amaro, 30
Amor che mi consigli, Festa or Gero, 319
Amor che sospirar, A. Agricola, 170, 208
Amor ecco colei, 696
Amor io fallo, Wert, 410
Amor mi sento, Gero, 327
Amorosi ardori, Li, 433
Amour de moy, L': the melody, 206f, 270; anon. setting a 4, 270; Bruhier, 278
Amoureux suy, Binchois, 88
Amours, Les, Ronsard, 298f, 389
Amours, amours, trop me fiers de tes dars! Hayne, 100
Amours, amours, vous me faictes grant tort, Gombert, 304
Amsfortius, Franciscus Marcellus, 713
Amye a tous, L', Josquin, 233
An Wasserflüssen Babylon, Wannenmacher, 683
Ana, Francesco d', 158, 165, 175
Anchieta, Juan de, 578f, 584
Anchor che col partire, Rore, 332, 434, 538, 698, 703; keyboard transcr. by A. Gabrieli, 538
Ancina, Padre Giovenale, 454, 600
Ancona, Alessandro d' (Anco), 171ff
Ancona, Francesco d', 726
Anders kein freud, Heinrich Finck, 640

Andreas Christi famulus, Morales, 591

Andrews, Hilda (And), 850f, 853, 859f, 862ff, 881

Andryan, 771

Anerio, Felice, 425f, 447, 458, 482ff, 825 (incl. Ex. 192)

Anerio, Giovanni Francesco, 425f, 482, 484f, 532, 544

Anerio, Maurizio, 426

Angelicum ac divinum opus musicae, Gafori, 181

Angelus ad pastores ait: A. Gabrieli, 497f; Palestrina (lute intab. by Terzi), 521 (Ex. 120)

Angelus Domini ad pastores: Clemens, 353; Gombert, 345

Anglès Higini (= Anglés, Higinio) (Ang), 98, 149, 177, 187, 190, 192, 196, 575ff, 582f, 586f, 591f, 611, 614ff, 618f, 623, 625, 627, 631

Anglican Church music with English text, 781, 795ff; A. chanting, 804

Angoulême, Marguerite d', 292

Anima mea Dominum, G. Gabrieli, 498

Anima mea liquefacta est: the text, 117; Greg. Chant, 82; Busnois, 108f; Dufay, 82; Martini, 221

Animuccia, Giovanni, 449, 453ff

Anna of Hungary, Duchess of Württemberg, 722

Anne of Brittany, Queen of France (consort of Louis XII), 283

Anne of Cyprus, Duchess of Savoy, 50

Anonymous X, 645

Anonymous XI, 727

Anselmi, Georgius, 180

Anselmo da Parma, 727

Anselmus of Brno, 727

Antegnati, family, 175f

Antegnati, Costanzo, 492, 530, 542

anthem-adaptations of Latin pieces, 797, 800

anthem (= motet), Anglican, 798ff; see also: verse anthem

Anthon, Carl (Anth), 316

Anthoni usque limina, Busnois, 109

Antica musica, L', Vicentino, 328f, 364, 513, 541

anticipation (= portamento), 460f

Antico, Andrea, 156, 161, 234, 281, 284, 289, 295, 314, 519, 528, 534

antimasque, 883

antiphonal writing, see: *decani* and *cantoris* sides; dialogue treatment; echo pieces; polychoral writing; vocal orchestration, contrasting subgroups of voices

Antiquis, Giovanni de, 443f, 549

Antoine (son of Philip the Good), 90

Antonello (= Amarotus) da Caserta, 31, 33

Antoniano, Antonio, 490

Antonio da Cividale del Friuli (= Antonius de Civitate Austriae), 25, 28, 31

Antonio Romano, 26

Antonowytsch, Myroslaw (Antono), 371

Antony, Marc, 771

Antwerp motet book, Lassus, 506ff

Apel, Nikolaus, 645

Apel, Willi, 11f, 14, 16, 19, 20, 30f, 33, 35, 38, 41, 45, 52, 82, 119, 121, 134, 141, 144ff, 165, 179f, 197, 245, 521f, 528f, 534ff, 540, 553, 559, 620, 622, 626, 658f, 661ff, 665, 667ff, 849f, 853, 861f, 865ff

aperto (= *ouvert*) ending, 30

Apiarius, Matthias, 706

Apollo aller Kunst, Adam von Fulda, 639

Apologia . . . adversus Joannem Spatarium, Gafori, 180, 587

Apostolo glorioso—Cum tua doctrina—Andreas, Dufay, 77f, 189

Appearance of Our Lady to Thomas, 877

Appenzeller, Benedictus, 234, 305f, 308, 340, 555, 679

appoggiaturas, 441f, 861

"apt" for singing or playing, 292, 308, 362, 709, 827, 876; see also: performance practice

Apuleius, 568

Aqua vale al mio gran foco, L', Michael, 159

Aquila, Marco d', 520

Aquila, Serafino dall', 157, 229, 311

Aquila è gita al ciel, L', Ruffo, 416

Araiz Martínez, Andrés (Ara), 591f, 595, 611

Araldo, L', see: Ottonaio, Battista dell'

Arbeau, Thoinot (= Tabourot, Jehan), 554, 564f, 866, 880

Arcadelt, Jacques: biogr. and madrigals, 313, 321f (incl. Ex. 68), 696, 816; chansons, 356, 380f, 392; Masses, 501; motets, 364; see also 293, 309, 314, 316f, 319, 324, 387, 401, 413, 416f, 420, 422, 433, 439, 456, 461, 523, 554, 629, 666

Arcadia: Sannazaro, 313, 415, 568; Sir Philip Sidney, 313

Archilei, Antonio, 570

Archilei, Vittoria, 570

Architectonice musices, Decorus (= Schonsleder), 533

arcicembalo, 530, 861

arciorgano, 530

arciviolata lira, 570

Ardo sì, ma non t'amo, Porta, 416

Aretusa, Lollio, 568

Argenti, Agostino, 568

aria, see: *canzonetta*

Aria di cantar in ottava rima, G. M. Nanino, 447

Aria di cantar sonnetti, G. M. Nanino, 447

Aria di Firenze, 325; *A. di Genova,* 325; *A. di Ruggiero,* see: *Ruggiero,* the melody

Arianna, Monteverdi, 441

Arie di canzon francese per sonar, Ingegneri, 550

Ariosto, Lodovico, 157, 311, 313, 322, 404, 424, 567, 818, 820

Arise gett upp my deere, Morley, 823

Arise O Lord, Byrd, 805

Aristides Quintilianus, 180

Aristotle, 435
Aristoxenos, 141
Arkwright, Godfrey E. P. (Ark), 313, 778, 791f, 802, 817, 832, 840, 880
Arlt, Gustave O., 705
Armonia celeste, Ruffo, 513
Armonia di scelti autori (Scotto), 433
Arnaut, Henricus, 36
Arnold, Denis M. (Arld), 826
Arnold, Frank T. (Arnd), 487, 489, 500, 529, 545, 634
Arnold, Friedrich W. (Ar), 634, 637, 658
Arnt von Aich (= of Aachen), 275, 638f, 649, 706
Aroca, D. Jesús, 616f
Aron (= Aaron), Pietro, 63, 73, 93, 120, 148, 160, 178, 181ff, 370, 530ff, 534, 547
Ars musicorum, Despuig, 577
ars nova, 11, 30, 52, 633
Art et instruction de bien dancer, L', Toulouze, 37
Art poétique, Sibilet, 381
Arte de canto llano, Bizcargui, 587
Arte de música teórica y práctica, Montanos, 592f
Arte de tañer fantasia, Sancta Maria, 630
Arte organica, L', Antegnati, 530
Artusi, Giovanni M., 329, 441, 494
Artusi overo delle imperfettioni della moderna musica, L', Artusi, 441
As it befell upon a Penticost day, 766
Ascanio, Jusquin d', see: Josquin des Prez
Ascendens Christus in altum, Victoria, 600, 608
Ascendit Deus: Clemens, 355; G. Gabrieli, 498; Philips, 794
Ascendo ad Patrem meum, Palestrina, 462, 471, 477f (incl. Ex. 112d)
Aseneste, Hans, 771
Ashbee, E. W., 883
Ashwell, Thomas, 768
Asinaria, Plautus, 158, 173, 567
Asola, Giovanni Matteo, 426f, 493, 536
Asolani, Gli, Bembo, 312f
Asperges me, Domine: Mendes, 598; Schiavetto, 761f (incl. Ex. 175)
Aspice Domine: Byrd, 788; Gombert, 588; Jaquet of Mantua, 366, 470; Monte, 703; Sermisy, 339; anon. keyboard transcr. thereof, 560; Vaet, 366
Asproys, Jo. (= Hasprois), 13, 16
Assumpta est Maria, Palestrina, 462, 472, 477f (incl. Ex. 112c)
Aston, Hugh, 777, 779, 853f, 857
asymmetry, predilection for, 119, 344, 346, 375
Atalante, 153
Atkins, Sir Ivor (Atk), 809, 811
Attaingnant, Pierre (Attain), 269, 289ff, 293ff, 298, 300f, 303, 305, 307f, 314, 335, 339ff, 348, 370, 381, 391, 553ff, 557ff, 561ff, 670, 761, 771, 835, 852, 868
Attamasch, 635

Attey, John, 838, 841
attributions, the problem of conflicting, 42, 307; false aa., 101, 220
Au feu d'amour: La Rue, 272; Monte, 396
Au hault de la roue de fortune, Cornuel, 137
Au joly jeu, Janequin, 298
Au povre par necessité, Busnois, 107
Au travail suis: Barbingant, 116, 129, 224; Compère, 224
Aubigné, Agrippa d', 566
Aubry, Pierre (Au), 14, 35, 98, 205
Auclou, Robert, 63
Auda, Antoine, 25, 38, 41, 138, 147, 180, 308, 473
Audivi media nocte: Tallis, 786; Taverner, 777, 780
Auff und nider, see: after-dance
Augé-Chiquet, Mathieu (Augé), 382
Augenmusik, see: eye music
augmented second, 752, 858, 872; third, 328; fourth, 24, 47, 143; fifth, 595; sixth, 390, 565, 701, 752, 789; triad, 435
Aulen, Johannes, 646
Aultre jour, L', 368
Aure che'l verde lauro, L', Marenzio, 421
Aurea luce: Greg. Chant (= *Decora lux*), 83, 467; Dufay, 83; Palestrina, 467
Aurora coelum, Greg. Chant, 467
Aurora lucis rutilat (pars II = *Tristes erant apostoli*, q. v.; stanza 2 of pars II = *Sermone blando*, q. v.): Lassus, 693; Greg. Chant, 467, 604; Sarum Chant, 604, 856; keyboard settings thereof: anon., 856; Redford, 856
Aus fremden Landen komm ich her, the melody, 675
Aus tiefer Not: the melody, 131, 675 (incl. Ex. 152); Dietrich, 680 (Ex. 153); Hassler, 3 settings, 684
Austria: in general, 303; Graz, 415; Innsbruck, 212, 221, 721; Salzburg, 491; Vienna, 207, 212, 304, 374, 457, 720, 737
Autant en emporte le vent, La Rue, 272
Author of light, Campion, 839
authority of sources, 41
Auto del Repelón, Encina, 583
Autre d'antan, L', Ockeghem, 120
auxiliary note, 460
Avalos, Alfonso d', 416
Ave Christe immolate, Josquin, 257
Ave Dei Matris, Merbecke, 781
Ave Dei Patris filia: Fayrfax, 775, 778; Tallis, 785; Taverner, 780
Ave dulce tu frumentum (= *Je loe amours*), Binchois, 634
Ave gratia plena, Merulo, 496
Ave Maria . . . benedicta tu: Greg. Chant, 254f, 265, 268, 276, 345, 374, 471, 580, 589, 601, 794; Arcadelt (*Nous voyons que les hommes*), 381, 501; Felstin, 747; G. Fogliano, 471; Josquin, 254; Mouton, 2 settings, 282; Ockeghem, 121f, 124; de

Ave Maria . . . benedicta tu (continued)
Orto, 265; Parsons, 786; Philips, 794; Regis, 114; van Stappen, 276; Victoria, 2 settings, 601; Willaert, 374
Ave Maria, gemma virginum, Mouton, 282
Ave Maria . . . Virgo serena: Greg. Chant, 192, 253; Josquin, 253, 256, 279, 690; Senfl, 690
Ave maris stella: Greg. Chant, 223, 241, 345, 494f (incl. Ex. 115), 562, 565, 589, 595, 605, 628; Cabezón, 628f (incl. Ex. 140*b*); Du Caurroy (*Fantaisies* XIV, XV), 565; Dufay, 83f; Josquin, 241; Jo. Martini, 222f; Porta, 494f (incl. Ex. 115), 345; Titelouze, 562
Ave Mater, O Maria, 743
Ave Mater omnium, Weerbecke, 219
Ave mundi spes Maria—In Gottes namen faren wir, 645
Ave nobilissima, Josquin, 255
Ave Regina: Greg. Chant, 21, 76, 82, 90, 254, 345, 464, 471; Aichinger, 3 settings, 699; F. Anerio, 484; Dufay: 2 settings *a 3*, 82; setting *a 4*, 51, 76, 82, 113; Gesualdo, 486; Palestrina, 4 settings, 464; de Silva, 501; Victoria, 607f
Ave Regina . . . Mater Regis: Greg. Chant, 90; Binchois, 90; Frye, 93ff (incl. Ex. 24), 98, 123, 191, 200f, 372; Obrecht, 191, 200f, 372; Willaert, 372
Ave rosa sine spinis: Senfl, 690; Tallis, 785
Ave sanctissima Maria, Verdelot, 269f, 365
Ave sidus clarissimum (= *Helas que pourra devenir*), Caron, 110
Ave verum corpus: Greg. Chant, 255; Byrd, 790; Josquin, 255; Philips, 794; Viadana, 489; Weerbecke, 2 settings, 219
Ave Virgo Cecilia, Manchicourt, 351
Ave Virgo gloriosa, Crecquillon, 350
Ave Virgo, lux Maria, Franchois, 42, 78, 189
Ave Virgo, quae de coelis, Dufay, 82
Ave Virgo sanctissima, Guerrero, 595
Ave virtus—Prophetarum—Infelix, Grenon, 22
Aveuglé Dieu, L', Janequin, 340
Ay me, poore heart, Farnaby, 859
ayre, 817, 832, 835ff
Ayres or Phantasticke Spirites, Weelkes, 828
Azzaiolo, Filippo, 445, 691, 859

Baccusi, Ippolito, 831
Bach, Johann Sebastian, 133, 199, 256, 563, 565, 628, 643, 683, 686, 711
Bacher, Joseph, 549
Bacon, Sir Francis, 815
Badajoz, 586
bagpipe, 57, 631, 759
Bagpipes, The, 842
Baïf, Jean Antoine de, 296, 382f, 385f, 504, 553, 569, 571, 839
Baillie, Hugh, 96
Baines, Anthony, 147
Baini, Giuseppe (Bai), 286, 457, 468, 471, 480

Baisés moy: the melody, 278; see also: *Basiés moy*
Baix, François, 50
Bakfark, Michael, 721
Bakfark, Valentin, 554, 719ff (incl. Ex. 164), 748, 756, 842
Bal y Gay, Jesús (Bal), 394, 596, 616f, 620f, 623
Balassi Valentin, 716, 726
Balbi, Ludovico, 416, 493, 495, 520
Baldassare da Imola, 414
Baldwin (= Baldwyne), John, 851, 870
Baldwin, Thomas W., 879
ballad, English, 766, 833f, 848, 878, 881
ballade, 12, 14ff, 18, 27, 32, 53, 88, 205, 232, 634; see also: *formes fixes; b.* with Latin text, 32; *b. equivoquée,* 55; *b.* style (the term), 17
Ballard, Pierre, 386
Ballard, Robert, 289, 386, 561; see also: Le Roy and Ballard
Ballarino, Il, (= *Nobiltà di dame*), Caroso, 525
ballata, 26, 29f, 766; the literary *b.,* 312f; *b.* style, 17
Ballestra, Reimundo, 514
Ballet, William, 843f, 848
ballet, English, 824ff
Ballet comique de la royne, Beaujoyeulx, 571
ballet de cour, 570f, 882
Ballet des Polonais, Le, 571
balletto, 445f, 711, 824f
Balli d'arpicordo, Picchi, 716
ballo, 177
Balmer, Lucie (Balm), 140f, 696
Balogh, Louis (Balo), 140
Banastre, Gilbert, 767, 773
Banchieri, Adriano (Banch): biogr. and sec. voc. mus., 433, 436f; sacr. mus., 487, 500; instr. mus., 543, 550; see also 401, 413, 536f
bands, civic, 174, 545f; see also: *Stadtpfeiffer; Waits*
banduria, 626
Bannister, Henry M., 52
Baños de Argel, Los, Cervantes, 631
Banquet of the Oath of the Pheasant, 57ff, 150
Bar form, 15, 636, 642, 653, 709, 734
Barbé, Antoine, 308, 310
Barberiis, Melchiore de, 522, 526, 528
Barbetta, Giulio, 523
Barbieri, Francisco A., 156, 222, 230, 576ff, 613, 621
Barbingant, 115f, 129, 210, 223f, 263
Barbireau, Jacobus, 109, 116f, 187, 196, 266, 275, 644, 648, 662, 723
Barbour, J. Murray (Barb), 617f
Barca di Venezia, Banchieri, 437
Barclay, Alexander, 882
Barclay Squire, William, 154f, 298, 305f, 321, 393, 396, 409, 420, 424f, 427, 433, 445, 616, 773, 794, 815

Bardi, Count Giovanni, 420, 570
Barges, Antonio, 760
Barilli, Arnaldo (Bari), 417
Barker, E. Phillips (Bark), 564
Barley, William, 792, 808, 842f, 846f, 849
Barnard, John, 798, 803, 805
Barone, Nicola, 145, 576
baroque elements, 418, 440, 552, 563, 569, 686, 832
Barré, Antonio, 326f, 403
Barré, Leonardo, 456
barring in sources, 487, 557, 559
Bartha, Dénes von, 273, 294, 298, 300, 304ff, 309f, 340, 727
Bartlet, John, 838
Bartoli, Cosimo, 259, 546
Bartoli, Romeo, 426, 436, 446f
Bartolomeo, Organista da Firenze, 170
Bartolomaeus de Brolis, see: Brolo, Bartolomeo
Bartolomeo da Bologna, 26, 28, 30, 33
Bartolucci d'Assisi, Fra Ruffino, 238, 285
Bartók, Béla, 714
Barwick, Steven, 593
barzelletta (= *frottola*), 155f, 158
Barycz, Henryk, 741
bas, see *instruments bas*
Basiés moy, Josquin, 2 settings, 232f; see also: *Baisés moy*
Basiron (= Barizon), Philippe, 115, 117, 136, 263
Baskervill, Charles R. (Bas), 881
bass (or low contratenor), character of, 27, 31, 67, 106, 160, 273, 323, 331, 352, 374, 396, 423, 590, 640, 646, 678, 830, 836
Bassano, Giovanni (Bassa), 394, 403, 412, 465, 499, 545, 550
basse dance (= *bassadanza, baxa*), 36ff, 176f, 521, 553, 564f, 619, 634, 665
Basselin, Olivier, 205
basso continuo, 418, 440f, 489, 699, 793; *b. figurato*, 483, 529ff, 835; *b. ostinato*, see: *ostinato; b. seguente*, 489, 753; see also: organ bass
bassus (derivation of term), 108
Baston, Josquin, 308
Bataglia Taliana, Werrecore, 327, 550
Bataille, Gabriel, 558
Bataille de Marignan, La, Janequin, see: *Guerre, La*
Batcheler, Daniell, 844
Bateson, Thomas, 811
Báthori, King Stephen, 721, 725f, 748, 755
Báthori, Prince Andrew, 721
Báthori, Prince Sigismund, 721f, 725f
Batist, 771
Batka, Richard (Bat), 728f, 732
Batten, Adrian, 806
battle pieces: anon., 172; Barberiis, 526; Barbetta, 526; *Bogurodzica*, 742; Brudieu, 614; Byrd, 866; Costeley, 388; Demantius, 722; on Elizabethan stage, 879; A. Gabrieli: voc., 415, 526; instr., 550; Heredia, 629; Hussite, 734; Isaac, 172; Janequin, see: *Guerre, La*;

Las Infantas, 609, 614; Marcantonio del Pifaro, 526; Padovano, 550; Palestrina, 403, 614; Werrecore, 327, 550
battle symbolism in love songs, 12, 56
Battre, H., 42
Bäuerle, Hermann (Bäu), 695
Bauldewyn (= Baudouin), Noel, 279, 285, 337f, 347
Baumann, Otto A. (Baum), 643, 651, 707
Baumgartner, see: Paumgartner
Bäumker, Wilhelm (Bäumk), 8, 356, 514, 651, 679, 706
Bautier-Regnier, Anne-Marie (Baut), 366f, 409, 488
Bavaria: in general, 414; Augsburg, 451, 721; Dillingen, 451; Munich, 329, 376, 391, 416, 418, 510, 513; Nuremberg, 391, 512, 721, 810
Baxter, J. H., 252
Bayeux MS, see: Manuscripts—Paris
Beata Barbara, Palestrina, 462
Beata Dei Genitrix, Compère, 229
Beata es, Maria: Greg. Chant, 75, 192; Obrecht, 192, 253
Beata es, Virgo: G. Gabrieli, 498; L'Héritier, 337
Beata Mater, Greg. Chant, 345
Beata progenies, Gafori, 181
Beati omnes, Gombert, 347
Beati pacifici, Greg. Chant, 276
Beati quorum remissae sunt, A. Gabrieli, 497
Beatrice of Aragon, later Queen of Hungary (consort of Matthias Corvinus), 139, 145, 148f, 157, 221f, 717, 719, 723
Beatus homo, Rore, 376
Beatus Laurentius, Greg. Chant, 472
Beaujoyeulx, Balthasar de (= Baldasarre da Belgioioso), 570f
Beaulieu, Eustorg de, 300, 561
Beaulieu, Lambert de, 571
Beaumont, Francis, 881f
Beauvoys, N., 284
Beaux yeux, Sweelinck, 399 (incl. Ex. 92)
Bebrleyn, 635
Beccari, Agostino, 568
Becherini, Bianca (Becher), 58f, 544
Beck, Sydney, 875
Becker, Adolf (Bec), 651
Becker, Georg (Be), 300, 362, 393, 396, 505
Bedbrook, Gerald S. (Bedb), 552, 867
Bedingham, Johannes, 30, 93, 635, 658
Beethoven, Ludwig van, 4, 552
Behaim, Michel, 652, 654, 716, 718
Behold, O God, Byrd, 805
Behr, Ludwig, 709
Bel Acueil, Busnois, 105 (incl. Ex. 27)
Bela III, King of Hungary, 716
Bel'aronde, La, Le Jeune, 383 (incl. Ex. 86)
Belcari, Feo, 453
Belgioioso, Baldassare da (= Balthasar de Beaujoyeulx), 570f
Bell, Charles F., 882
bell, 109

Bella, La, Vicentino, 550
Bella man, La, Marenzio, 420
Bella pargoletta, La, A. Gabrieli, 415
Bellasio, Paolo, 425
Belle, Jan, 308
Belle Margarite, La, Clemens, 301
Belle que vous ai je mesfait, Dufay, 57
Belle se siet, La: the melody, 265; Dufay, 54f, 188, 265f
Belle vueilles moy vengier, Dufay, 57
Bellengues, Richard de (= Cardot), 6, 90
Bellère, Jean, see: Phalèse and Bellère
Bellermann, Heinrich (Beller), 138, 140, 266, 492, 531f
Belles sur toutes—Tota pulchra es, A. Agricola, 208
Bell'Haver, Vincenzo, 419f, 499, 542, 544
Belli, Girolamo, 411, 488, 493
Belli, Giulio, 493, 495
Bellini, Gentile, 546
Bellini, Giovanni, 497
Bells, The, Byrd, 867
Bembo, Elena, 544
Bembo, Cardinal Pietro, 161, 312f, 322, 403, 406, 413, 534f, 544, 820
Bendidio, Lucrezia, 409, 411
Benedicam Dominum, A. Gabrieli, 496
Benedicamus Domino, Dufay, 72
Benedicite, Almechtiger got, Hermann der Münch von Salzburg, 634
Benedicite omnia opera, Josquin, 258
Benedicta es, coelorum Regina: Greg. Chant, 251f (incl. Ex. 49), 475, 565; Guyot (Castileti), 511; Josquin, 251f (incl. Ex. 49), 282f, 371, 472, 475, 511, 588, 703; Le Jeune, 565; Mouton, 283 (incl. Ex. 58), 588; Willaert, 371f
Benedicta semper sancta sit Trinitas, the melody, 251
Benedicta sit sancta Trinitas, Victoria, 600
Benedicta viscera—Ave Mater, Velut, 23
Benedictus, see: Appenzeller; Ducis
Benedictus, Isaac, 212
Benedictus Dominus Deus Israel, Anglican Canticle, 798
Benedictus Dominus Deus Israel: Greg. Chant, 366, 488; Corteccia, 366; A. de Févin, 283; Perez, 610; Tallis, 800; Orazio Vecchi, 488
Benedixisti, G. Gabrieli, 498
Benndorf, Kurt (Bennd), 687
Bennet, John, 808, 823
Berberich, Ludwig, 647
Berchem, Jachet, 309, 327, 341, 366f, 416, 703
Berg, Adam, 697, 700
Berg, Johann vom (= Montanus), see: Montanus and Neuber
bergamasca, 445
Bergier et la bergiere, Le, Gombert, 304, 356, 696
bergerette, 15f, 92, 102, 117, 119, 208, 232; see also: *formes fixes*

Bergerette savoy(si)enne: the melody, 207; Josquin, 232, 261
Bergmans, Paul (Berg), 147, 290, 292, 335, 356, 398, 427, 511, 517, 794
Bermudo, Fray Juan (Bermu), 531, 620, 624ff, 629f
La Bernardina, Josquin, 230
Bernal, Juan, 592
Bernet Kempers, Karel P. (Kem), 294f, 300, 303, 352, 354ff, 514
Bernhard, B. (Bernh), 7, 566
Bernoulli, Eduard (Ber), 210, 232, 281, 343, 679, 705f
Bertha, Alexandre de, 729
Bertoldo, Sperindio, 542
Bertolotti, Antonio (Bertol), 156, 222, 229, 326, 409, 457, 462
Bertrand, Anthoine de, 389
Berzeviczy, Albert, 139, 221
Besard, Jean-Baptiste, 527, 554f, 558, 755f, 844, 848
Beschaffenes Glück (= Il me suffit), 696
Bessaraboff, Nicholas (Bessar), 548
Besseler, Heinrich (Bes), 6, 8ff, 14, 16, 19, 27, 35, 40ff, 48ff, 53, 59, 61, 63ff, 69, 78ff, 82, 84, 91f, 94, 98, 107, 112ff, 122, 131, 157, 187, 204, 210, 225, 251, 258, 267, 334, 454, 470, 546, 559, 575, 619, 634, 656, 691
Bevin, Elway, 851, 870
Bezdeck, Sister John Joseph (Bez), 695f
Bèze, Théodore de, 359f, 503, 726
Bianchini, Domenico, 522, 525, 527
Bianco e dolce cigno, Il: Arcadelt, 306, 313, 321, 816; Orazio Vecchi, 433
bicinia: in Rhaw (1545), 678; Bruhier, 278; Galilei, 549; Gastoldi, 549; Lassus, 672, 691; Lupachino, 549; Morley, 825; Sermisy, 292; J. M. Tasso, 549; Whythorne, 871
Bien doy servir, Dufay, 45 (Ex. 7c)
Bienenfeld, Elsa (Bien), 707
Biggle, Lloyd, 260
Bignami, Giovanni (Big), 420
binary rhythm, predilection for, 52, 56f, 99, 258, 294, 308, 338, 867
Binchois, Gilles (Binch): biogr. and chansons, 36, 44 (incl. Ex. 6c), 58, 86ff (incl. Ex. 23), 100, 102, 105, 128, 196, 209, 214f, 253, 634; sacr. mus., 91f, 94, 181; see also 6, 8, 13, 34, 40, 51, 56, 59, 65, 93, 98, 115, 118, 121, 142, 145, 205, 263, 646, 658, 763
Birtner, Herbert (Birt), 481, 686, 689
Bisth, Johannes, 723
Blahoslav, Bishop Jan, 735
Blame I confes, Byrd, 817 (incl. Ex. 190)
Blancks, Edward, 807f
Blaník, Smetana, 734
Blas de Castro, Juan, 616f, 631
Blaschke, Paul (Bla), 217
Blessed be Thy name, Tallis, 800
Bleyer, Jakob (Bley), 718, 722
Blitheman, William, 809, 851f, 854f, 857
Bloch, Suzanne, 847

Blume, Clemens, 504
Blume, Friedrich, 37, 178, 229, 294, 553, 559, 563ff, 675f, 678, 680, 684, 686, 688
Blumenfeld, Harold (Blumen), 684
Boccaccio, Giovanni, 162, 312f, 322, 400, 429
bocedisation, see: solmisation
Boer, C. L. Walther, 107, 109, 208, 210, 220, 231, 234, 265
Boethius, 141, 180, 577, 586
Boetticher, Wolfgang, 391
Bóg wieczny a wszechmocny, "M. H.", 748
Bogaert, Irène (Boga), 396, 409
Bogurodzica, 742
Bohemia (outside Chap. 14): in general, 414; Prague, 395, 451, 491, 698, 700
Böhme, Franz M (Böh), 193, 633, 666, 669, 675, 678, 756f
Bohn, Emil (Boh), 746
Boleyn, Anne, 778, 841
Bolle, Wilhelm, 815
Bolte, Johannes, 881
bombarda (= tenor *tibia*), 147
Bon jour, bon mois, Dufay, 56
Bona of Savoy, 181
Bonaventura, Arnaldo (Bona), 313
Bonaccorsi, Alfredo (Bonac), 25, 29f
Bonadies, Johannes, 178
Bonelli, Luigi (Bone), 174
bonifantes, 731
Bonjour et puis, Lassus, 395
Bonnet, Joseph (Bonn), 538, 565, 858
Bonnin, Théodore, 389
Bono, Pietro, 148, 719
Bonté, bialté, Césaris, 16
Bontoux, Germaine (Bont), 841, 848
Bonum est, Palestrina, 466
Booke of Common Praier noted, Merbecke, 782, 796
Bordes, Charles (Bord), 224, 232, 248, 253, 257, 270, 286, 295f, 298f, 355, 383, 388, 391, 452, 483ff, 489, 493, 496f, 500, 502, 588, 591, 595, 599, 696
Bordet, Louis, 453
Borek, Christopher, 753
Borghini, Vincenzo, 171
Borgia, Lucrezia, 157, 312
Borote (= Torote), 585
Borromeo, Cardinal Carlo, 449, 490
Borrono, Pietro P., 522f, 525
Boscán Almogaver, Juan, 612
Boschop (= Boscoop), Cornelis, 505
Bossinensis, Franciscus, 160f, 163f (incl. Ex. 33b), 522, 759
Boteauville, Michel de, 382
Böttcher, Theodor (Böttc), 517
Bottrigari, Ercole (Bottrig), 546f
Bourgeois, Louis, 36off (incl. Ex. 80)
bourgeoisie, influence of, 6, 53, 87, 288, 655
Bouton, Ernest (Bout), 383
Bovicelli, Giovanni B., 412
Bow thine ear, Byrd, 789
Bowle, Raphe, 842
Bowman, Robert, 850

Boyce, William, 798, 800, 802, 805f
Boyd, Morrison C., 781, 800, 808ff, 816, 839ff, 844
Brack, Jörg, 638f
Braconnier, Jean (= Lourdault), 224
Bracos traygo, Los, Vasquez, 612
Bragard, Roger (Brag), 702
Brahms, Johannes, 119, 638, 643, 674, 709
Braittenstein, Johann, 651
Branberger, Jan (Bra), 739
Brandes, Heinz (Br), 695
Brandolini, Aurelio, 153
Brandolini, Rafaelle, 153, 325
Brandt, Jan, 753
Brandt, Jobst vom, 682, 707
branle (= *brando;* brawle), 525, 554, 563, 567, 863, 868
Brassart, Jean, 38, 633
Braunfels, Walter (Braunf), 687, 709
Braungart, Siegfried (Braun), 678
Bravo, Juan (= Count Juan of Ureña?), 612
Braxatoris, W., 633
Bredemers, Herry, 561, 719
Bref à vous, Sweelinck, 399
Breidert, Fritz (Breid), 133, 135, 191
Breitengraser, Wilhelm, 706
Brelles, Georget de, 227, 263
Brenet, Michel (Bren), 6, 8, 115, 118, 121, 131, 137, 146, 172, 263, 268, 274, 276, 285, 291, 296, 298f, 305, 327, 377, 383, 386f, 465, 501f, 504, 553f, 565
Brennecke, Ernest (Brenn), 808, 851f
Breve . . . maniera . . . a far passaggi, Conforto, 412
Breve regnum, 745
Brewster, 868
Briard, Etienne, 289
Bridge, Sir Frederick, 793, 833
Bridge, Joseph C., 772
Bridgman, Nanie (Bridgm), 159, 300
Brigidi, A. (Brigi), 495
Brignoli, Giacomo, 542
Briquet, see: Villeroye, Jean de
Brissac, Marshal de, 570
broadsides, 651, 833
Brocco, Giovanni, 158, 161
broken consort, see: consort
Brolo, Bartolomeo, 26, 30f, 53, 153, 635, 658
Brooks, Catherine V. (Broo), 102, 106f, 109, 270, 280, 571
Browne, John, 768
Browning Madame, 845 (Ex. 201)
Browning (= *The leaves be greene*) pieces: general, 845; Byrd (keyboard variations), 870
Bruck, Arnoldus de, 678f, 680, 706, 708
Bruder Conrat (= *Frater Conradus*), the melody, 214, 755
Brudieu, Joan, 614f
Bruger, Hans D. (Bru), 158, 318, 447, 521ff, 525ff, 553ff, 661, 668f, 847
Bruhier, Antoine, 278
Bruinsma, Henry A. (Bruin), 356

Brumel, Antoine (Brum): biogr. and Masses, 260ff; motets and chansons, 192, 240, 262f (incl. Ex. 51), 559; see also 137, 184, 235, 243, 246, 273, 285, 452, 522, 663
Brumel, Jachet, 260
Brunelleschi, Filippo, 79, 171
Brünlein die do fliessen, Die, the melody, 647
Bruyn, J. de, 364
Buccinate in neomenia tuba, Croce, 500
Buchberger, Michael, 504
Buchner, Hans (= Hans of Constance), 662ff, 754
Bueno, Juan José, 597
buffone, 173
Buglhat, Giovanni de, 314
Bukofzer, Manfred (Buk), 14, 19, 22, 24, 26f, 29f, 32, 37ff, 41, 53, 56, 61, 68f, 78, 82, 87, 90ff, 98f, 103f, 106f, 111, 113, 119, 137, 149, 158, 160, 165f, 177, 196, 206, 264, 394, 398, 440, 489, 501, 521, 524, 635, 715, 763f, 816, 855f, 858
Bull, John, 563, 809f, 851f, 857f (incl. Ex. 207), 860ff (incl. Ex. 209), 865ff, 871
Bullen, Arthur H., 880, 882
Bullinger, Heinrich, 358
Buoh všemohúcí, Jan of Jenštejn, 731
Buonaccorsi, Filippo, 743
Burald, Jacques, 505
Burbure, Léon de (Burb), 48, 116, 118, 265, 702
Burck, Joachim a (= Moller), 686, 688
burden in carol, 765f
Burgaud des Marets, Henri, 100, 293
Burger, Combertus P. (Burg), 265
Burgkmair, Hans, 655f
Burgundian court as cultural center, 4ff
Burgundian court musicians, 98ff
Burgundian school (the term), 8f, 53
Burgundy, Duchy of (outside Chaps. 1–3), 656
Burmeister, Joachim, 695
Burney, Charles (Bu), 235, 244f, 250, 261, 279, 283f, 301, 305, 319, 321, 331, 334, 364, 385, 404, 424, 431, 443, 446, 494, 502, 763ff, 768f, 775f, 778, 780, 784, 799, 802, 825, 843
Burning of the Vanities, 170
Burzio, Nicolo, 155, 178, 587
Bush, Helen E., 54, 98, 102, 182, 264, 578
Busnois, Antoine: biogr. and chansons, 101ff (incl. Exx. 25–27), 196, 201, 203, 210f, 214, 255, 559, 843; sacr. mus., 73, 107ff, 136, 197, 248; see also 7, 15, 98, 115, 118f, 121, 141ff, 145, 155, 189, 220, 227, 263, 278, 634ff, 663, 763
Busto (= Busti), Pietro, 726
Buszin, Walter E. (Busz), 674, 677
Buus, Jacques, 327, 374f, 529, 537, 540, 547, 629, 667, 700
Buxheimer Orgelbuch, see: Manuscripts— Munich
Buyten, Martin van, 447

By painted words (= O the syllye man), Edwards, 816
Byrd, Thomas, 702
Byrd, William: biogr. and sacr. mus. with Latin text, 702, 784f, 787ff (incl. Ex. 183); sacr. mus. with Engl. text, 803ff (incl. Ex. 186), 809; sec. voc. mus., 817ff (incl. Ex. 190), 833; keyboard mus., 851ff, 857ff (incl. Ex. 210), 874, 881; instr. ensemble mus., 873f; see also 287, 395, 767, 786, 820f, 824, 843, 846
Byron, George Gordon, Lord, 26, 49
Byzantium, 49, 77

Cabezón (= Cabeçón), Antonio de, 615, 625ff (incl. Ex. 140), 853, 857, 862, 866
Cabezón, Hernando de, 627, 629
Cabezón, Juan de, 629
Caccia, La, Morley, 873
caccia and *caccia* style, 14, 17, 22, 26ff, 32, 41, 56, 59f, 169, 435
Cacciando per gustar, Zacharia, 32, 632
Cacciando un giorno, Ciconia, 30
Caccini, Giulio, 570, 835, 841
Cadéac, Pierre, 307, 341, 348, 471, 475, 478 (Ex. 112a), 629, 696
cadences: Burgundian, 44 (Ex. 6), 47, 103; leading-tone-to-tonic, 47 (Ex. 13b), 103; octave-leap, 44 (Ex. 5), 95f, 103, 160; Phrygian, 44f (incl. Ex. 7), 47, 200, 603; under-third, 44 (Ex. 5a, c), 103, 281, 363, 636, 679; V-I c. replacing *fauxbourdon*-like c., 99; "drive" to the c., 113, 122, 126, 132; c. extensions, 259, 603f; figuration at c. 59, 65, 91, 103
Caffi, Francesco (Caf), 175, 368, 374, 499, 544
Caimo, Gioseppe, 432, 447
Calami sonum ferentes, Rore, 331 (incl. Ex. 72), 404
Calandria, La, Bibbiena, 567
Calderon de la Barca, Pedro, 631
calendar changes, 155, 290
Calendimaggio, 168, 171
Caligaverunt oculi mei, Victoria, 603
Call to remembrance: Hilton, 802; R. Farrant, 802
Callino casturame: the melody, 862; Byrd, 862
Calliopea legale, Hothby, 178
Calvez, Gabriel, 471
Calvin, Jean, 311, 358f, 362, 502, 683
Calvinism and Calvinist music, 358ff, 782, 796
Calvisius, Seth, 684, 687
cambiata, nota, 75, 461
Cambio, Perissone, 334
Cambrai as musical center, 7f, 51, 110, 306
Cambridge, the melody, 807
Cambridge University, see: degrees
Camden, William, 813
Cametti, Alberto (Cam), 319, 362, 364, 425f, 455f, 483
Camilla of Aragon, 174
Campbell, Frank C. (Ca), 688

Campion, Thomas, 836f (incl. Ex. 198), 839, 883
Canal, Pietro (Can), 148, 173, 222, 409, 436, 442, 457, 546f
Cañas, Las, Brudieu, 614
Cancionero de Upsala, 582, 585, 613; for other cancioneros (or cancioneiros), see: Manuscripts—Elvas, Madrid, Munich, Seville, Turin
cancrizans (= retrograde) writing, 62, 74, 198, 236f, 263, 580; see also: canon; crab
Cani, I, Ciconia, 30
Canis, Cornelius, 301, 350, 512, 629
Canite tuba: Greg. Chant, 192; Palestrina, 462
canon: extensive or distinctive use of c., 120, 231, 256, 464, 482, 609f, 869; decline in use of c. in cinquecento, 294, 304; crab c., 11, 22, 30, 788; c. Masses, 111, 133ff, 136, 245, 261, 269, 477ff; multiple c., 38, 61, 124, 133ff, 232f, 239, 250f, 256, 261, 282, 289, 304, 309, 480, 602, 608, 650, 785, 870; mensuration c., 19f, 81, 237, 269, 647, 761; mirror c., 11, 282, 610, 788; c. with varying time-interval, 20, 189, 204, 213, 231, 870; see also: catch; round
canon, verbal, 11, 22, 26, 30, 64f, 70, 107, 125, 219f, 483, 586, 647; see also: puzzle pieces
Cantabo Domino, Orazio Vecchi, 488
Cantai; hor piango, Lassus, 404
Cantai, mentre nel cor, Cara, 158
Cantai un tempo: Monteverdi, 440; Padovano, 415
cantata, 409, 440
Cantate Domino: A. Gabrieli, 496; Gallus, 738; G. M. Nanino, 482f; Viadana, 489
Cantemus Domino, Las Infantas, 609, 614
Canterbury, the melody, 807
Canti B (Petrucci), 155, 185, 208, 219, 222, 256, 261, 265
Canti C (Petrucci), 104, 111, 155, 185, 191, 202, 208, 213f, 218ff, 231, 234, 261, 265, 270, 276, 284, 289, 295, 300, 304
Cantiam, Marenzio, 421
Canticles, Morning and Evening (Anglican), 796, 798
cantilena: = carol, 765; = chanson, 140; c. style (the term), 17; see also: treble-dominated style
Cantionale of Jistebnice, 734
canto carnascialesco, 167ff, 208, 214, 570
Canto de' facitori d'olio, A. Agricola, 208; C. de' sartori, C. della malmaritata, etc., 168; C. dei lanzi, C. delle palle, 170
canto de órgano (= mensural music), 577, 619
canto llano (= plainsong; cantus firmus), 579, 585
Cantollano del Cavallero, El: the melody, 585; Cabezón (diferencias), 628
cantus (= treble; the term), 16
cantus firmus: c.f. in canon form, 136, 191, 228, 235, 242, 254ff, 285, 335, 589; choice of c.f. (how made), 29, 66f, 69, 126, 234f; decline in use of c.f. in 16th c., 347, 351; c.f. in instr. mus., 174f, 854ff, 862, see also: In nomine pieces; Miserere instrumental pieces, etc.; late entry of c.f., 67, 194, 754; c.-f. (= tenor) Masses, 66ff, 92f, 95f, 107f, 117ff, 125ff, 136, 149f, 192f, 210f, 214ff, 218, 223, 228, 236ff, 260f, 263, 265, 268f, 275, 283ff, 286, 335f, 342f, 347f, 351, 375, 469ff, 588, 611, 647, 689f, 696, 775ff, 779f, 782, 784; migrating c.f., 32, 66, 193, 196, 210, 235ff, 265, 275, 647, 664, 681, 683, 695, 775, 788, 790, 853, 862; c.f. (= tenor) motets, 21ff, 67, 77ff, 82f, 108, 114f, 121ff, 190ff, 215ff, 222f, 227, 248, 253ff, 271, 275, 336, 350, 482f, 591, 648f, 690, 695f, 746f, 761f, 773, 777, 780, 784, 788, 794; multiple c. firmi, 114f, 195f, 216, 218, 222, 255, 268, 345, 689, 799; partitioning of c.f., 129f, 193ff, 198ff, 203f; permeation by c.f., 72, 76, 82, 123, 210, 237, 241f, 264, 268f, 284, 588; position of c.f., 35, 59, 67, 80, 92, 94, 122, 126, 264, 636, 649, 746; c.f. in secular vocal music, 159, 176, 233f, 678, 701, 706f; c.f. with original text retained, 75, 116, 195, 218, 268
cantus regalis, 147
Cantzler, 652
Canzon ariosa, A. Gabrieli, 538
canzona (= canzone): the frottolistic type of c., 156, 164, 286, 315; c. a ballo, 168; c. cycles, 332, 403; c. francese and c. da sonar, 291, 435, 520, 534ff, 538f, 550f, 871; c. alla napolitana, 445; c. spirituale, 403f, 406, 435; the literary form, 52, 332, 403; individual instrumental cc.: Banchieri, 543; Brignoli, 542; A. Gabrieli, 538f; G. Gabrieli, 545, 551 (incl. Ex. 127); Guami, 543; Luzzaschi, 542; Malvezzi, 543; Maschera, 550f; Merulo, 540; Mortaro, 545; Pellegrini, 542f
canzonet, 824ff, 828
canzonetta (= aria), 446f, 711, 825f
Canzoniere, Petrarch, 312
Capet, Hugh, 118
Capirola, Vincenzo, 521ff
capilla española, 592; c. flamenca, 579f, 592
capitolo, 156, 162
cappella grande, c. piccola, 330, 370
Cappello, Bianca, Grand Duchess of Tuscany, 419f
capriccio, 520, 543 (incl. Ex. 126)
Capricciosa, La, Pellegrini, 543
Caprioli, Antonio, 158
Capitán, Maestro (= Mateo Romero), 616f
Captaine Digorie Piper His Galiard (melody = If my complaints), J. Dowland, 874
Caput: the cantus firmus, from Sarum Chant, 68, 126, 196, 773; see also: Missa Caput
Caquet des femmes, Le, Janequin, 296
Cara, Marco, 157ff, 161, 163 (incl. Ex. 33a), 165, 167, 314, 522, 759
Cara la vita mia, Wert, 496, 703

Carapetyan, Armen (Cara), 316, 323f, 377
Caravaglios, Nino (Carav), 541
Cardoso, Manuel, 599
Cardot, see: Bellengues, Richard de
Carewe, Sir Peter, 769
Carité (= Charité?), Jehan, 7
Carleton, Nicholas, 855
Carlton, Richard, 819
Carman's Whistle, The: the melody, 862; Byrd, 862
Carmen, Johannes, 12f, 21f
Carmen saphicum, 747
Caro mea, Manchicourt, 351
carol, English, 731, 764ff
Carole magnus erat, Crecquillon, 350
Carole sceptrigeri patris, Cleve, 701
Carolus (= Charles Fernand), 148
Caron, Firmin or Philippe: biogr. and sec. voc. mus., 109ff (incl. Ex. 28), 117, 202 (incl. Ex. 36a), 213; sacr. mus., 111, 136; see also 101, 107, 142ff, 227, 635
Caron, Jehan, 110
Caroso, Fabritio, 523, 525, 628
Carpaccio, Vittorio, 167
Carpenter, Nan Cooke (Carpen), 100
Carpentras (= Genet, Elzéar), 285f, 289f, 303, 501, 532
Carreira, Antonio, 629
Carretto, Galeotto del, 157f, 161
Carriazo, Juan de Mata (Carr), 577f
Cartellieri, Otto, 6, 87
Carver, Robert (Carv), 777
Casa, Girolamo dalla, 412
Casimir IV, King of Poland, 746
Casimiri, Raffaele (Cas), 220, 253, 362, 364, 447, 452, 455ff, 467f, 481f, 485, 489f, 493, 500, 600f
Casina, Plautus, 173
Cassandre, La, Francisque, 554
Cassola, Luigi, 313, 322
Casteliono, Antonio, 522f
Castellani, Carlo (Cast), 155
Castellanus, Petrus, 581
Castiglione, Baldassare, 157f, 160, 311, 435, 547, 620
Castileti, see: Guyot, Jean
Castilleja, Pedro Fernandez de, 587, 594, 596
Castillo, Fructus del, 593
Castro, Jean de, 390
catch, 833f, 881
Catelani, Angelo (Cat), 317, 417, 541, 569
Cathalogus illustrium virorum Germaniae, Trithemius, 138
Cathedral Music, Boyce, 798
Catherine of Aragon, Queen of England (consort of Henry VIII), 362
catholicon, 120, 133, 237
Cato, Diomedes, 756
Cattaneo, Claudia, 438
Cauchie, Maurice (Cau), 118, 272, 289, 291, 294ff, 299, 340, 381, 387f, 564
Caulery, Jean, 505
Caullet, G. (Cau), 267

Caus, Salomon de, 436
Caussin, Ernoul, 220
Caustun, Thomas, 796f, 801
Cavaccio, Giovanni, 541f
Cavalieri, Emilio de', 569f
Cavazzoni, Girolamo, 535ff (incl. Ex. 123), 754
Cavazzoni, Marco Antonio, 520, 534f, 559
Cavendish, Michael, 807f, 838
Caymo, Paolo, 490
Caza, Francesco, 155f, 178
Ce me semblent choses perdues, Layolle the Younger, 300
Ce jour de l'an, Dufay, 54, 56
Ce jour le doibt, Dufay, 55
Ce moys de mai, Janequin, 298
Ce n'est pas jeu, La Rue, 272
Cease mine eyes, Morley, 823
Cease sorrowes now, Weelkes, 824, 826
Ceballos (= Cevallos), Francisco, 592
Ceballos (= Cevallos), Rodrigo, 592, 612
Cecchi, Giovanmaria, 566
Cecchini, Tomaso, 760ff
Cecil, Sir Robert, 810
Cedan l'antiche tue chiare vittorie, Marenzio, 422
Cefalo, Niccolò da Correggio, 173
Cela sans plus: Josquin, 234; Lannoy, 115, 189, 222, 234, 286; Leo X, 286; Obrecht, 189
Celani, Enrico (Cela), 362
Célébrons sans cesse, Lassus, 391
celimela (= shawm), 147
Cellesi, Luigia (Celle), 174
Celliers, Nicole des, see: Hesdin
Cellini, Benvenuto, 326, 545f
Celsa sublimatur—Sabine presul, Hugho de Lantins, 41
Celsus nuntiat, Greg. Chant, 195
Celtes, Konrad, 705, 747
Cent mille escus, Busnois or Caron, 57, 107
Cent mille regretz, La Rue (not Josquin), 273
Cent nouvelles Nouvelles, 48
Cento concerti ecclesiastici, Viadana, 489, 545, 762
Ceretto, Scipione, 549
Cerone, Domenico Pietro (Cero), 148, 350, 532, 618f
Certaine notes set forthe, Day, 797
Certon, Pierre, biogr. and chansons, 299f; sacr. works, 335, 339f, 554; see also 502
Cervantes Saavedra, Miguel de, 630f
Cesari, Gaetano (Ces), 158, 181, 218ff, 223, 314, 457
Césaris, Jean, 12f, 16f, 21ff
C'est a grand tort, Crecquillon, 302
C'est assez, Binchois, 89
C'est bien maleur, Busnois, 102, 104
C'est bien raison, Dufay, 49
C'est une dure departie: Sermisy, 294; basse dance, 564
chace, 14
chain-canzona, 550f, 871
chain-verse, 162

Chambers, Sir Edmund K. (Cham), 850, 876f, 879

Champion, Jacques (= Jacobus Scampion), 308, 338, 517

Champion, Nicolas, 338

Champion des dames, Le, Le Franc, 12, 51, 86

Chandieu, Antoine, 384, 390

Channey, Jean de, 289f

chanson, French, see Chaps. 1–3, 5, 6, 8, *passim;* cc. with Dutch or Flemish texts, 8, 187, 273

chanson au luth, see: lute songs

chanson de geste, 325

Chansonnier Cordiforme, see: Manuscripts— Paris

chansonniers, see: Manuscripts—Berlin, Bologna, Brussels, Cambridge, Chantilly, Copenhagen, Dijon, Escorial, Florence, New Haven, Oxford, Paris, Pavia, Porto, Rome, Seville, Tournai, Vatican City, Washington, Wolfenbüttel

Chant, Gregorian, *passim* throughout book; decline in its prestige, 59, 450, 491; late 16th-c. revision, 458, 474, 609; after Constance use, 216f; after Cracow use, 746; after Mantuan use, 474; after Sarum use, see separate entry; see also: *cantus firmus;* paraphrase Masses; alternation Masses; alternation practices

Chant des oiseaux, Le: Gombert, 304f; Janequin, 296f

Chant du rossignol, Le, Janequin, 383

Chanter je veux, Lassus, 393

Chantons, sonnons, trompetes, Janequin, 295

Chapels, 6; Papal (at Avignon), 10, 13, 575; Papal (at Florence), 50; Papal (at Rome), 31, 38; Imperial, 303f, 699ff; Burgundian, 6f, 48, 98f, 109, 580, see also: *capilla flamenca;* Danish, 712f; English (Chapel Royal), 767f, 774, 877, 880; French (Sainte Chapelle), 8; Hungarian (Royal Chapel), 723; Spanish (Chapel Royal), 575, see also: *capilla española; c. flamenca*

Chappell, William (Chapp), 768f, 841, 843, 845, 861ff, 875, 878

characterization: anon., 159; Busnois, 106f; Guerrero, 596; Maistre Jhan, 366; Lassus, 393; Rore, 376; Soriano, 485; see also: madrigals, quasi-dramatic m. cycles; vocal orchestration

Chardavoine, Jehan, 206, 389f

Chardon, H., 278

Chargé de deul, 214

Chariteo (= Gareth, Benedetto), 153

Charles IV, Emperor (= Charles I, King of Bohemia), 729ff.

Charles V, Emperor, 265, 267, 303, 338, 343, 350f, 506f, 561, 568, 578, 585, 591f, 609, 627, 649, 690, 725

Charles I, King of England, 792, 813

Charles V, King of France, 5ff, 13

Charles VI, King of France, 5, 7, 43

Charles VII, King of France, 36, 118

Charles VIII, King of France, 118, 148, 208, 223

Charles IX, King of France, 382, 388, 391, 561, 570

Charles, Archduke of Austria, 701

Charles, Duke of Bourbon, 118

Charles the Bold, Duke of Burgundy, 5ff, 36, 98ff, 108f, 148

Charles, Duke of Orléans, 87

Charles Emmanuel, Duke of Savoy, 428

Chartier, Alain, 87, 205, 391

Chase, Gilbert, 584ff, 591, 593, 600, 620, 631

Chasse, La, Janequin, 296

Chasse de lievre, La, Gombert, 304

Chaucer, Alice, 86

Chaucer, Geoffrey, 86

Che debb'io far, Pisano, 313f

Che fa la ramacina: the melody, 159; Compère, 224

Che fara la, che dira la, M. Vicentino, 292

Cheshire: the melody, 807; Farmer (Ex. 187), 807

Chesney, Kathleen, 99

chest of viols, 868; see also: consort

Chi fara fed'al cielo: Striggio, 436, 859; keyboard transcr. by Philips, 859

Chi la gagliarda, Donato, 443

Chi passa, Azzaiolo, 445, 691, 859

Chi salirà per me, Wert, 409

Chi vole, Ciconia?, 30

Chiare, fresche e dolci acque, Palestrina, 403

chiarenzana, Marcantonio del Pifaro, 525f

chiavette, chiavi naturali, chiavi trasportati, see: clef combinations

Chiereghin, Salvino (Chier), 379

Child, Francis J., 834

Children of the Chapel Royal, 767f, 877, 880; C. of Blackfriars, C. of Pauls, C. of the Revells to the Queene, 880f

Chilesotti, Oscar (Chil), 158, 170, 222, 234, 313, 326, 374, 420, 443, 445f, 520, 523, 525ff, 551, 555, 558, 669, 716, 755f, 847

Ch'io non t'ami, Luzzaschi, 412 (incl. Ex. 97)

Chipre, 13

chitarrone, 570

chiterna (= guitar), 740

chiuso (= *clos*) ending, 16, 30

Choice of Valentines, Nashe, 841

choir schools (= *maîtrises*), 8, 25, 43

Chomiński, Jozef M., 756

choral recitative, 415, 434, 440f, 820, 832

choral singing of polyphony, early, 24, 28

Choralis Constantinus, Isaac, 216f, 648ff, 689, 724

chord inversion, theory of, 839

chord progressions: dominant-subdominant, 407, 692; c.p. with roots moving by thirds, 160, 324, 423, 642, 737; c.p. with roots moving by fifths, 257, 423, 830

Choreae polonicae, Cato, 756

Chorearum molliorum collectanea (Phalèse), 565, 716

Chori Sacrae Virginis Marie Cameracensis, Jo. Lupi, 341

Choron, Alexandre E. (Chor), 373, 424, 432, 455, 495, 590, 592f

chorus (the term), 24, 766

Chounter, Anthony, 850

Christ der ist erstanden, the melody, 633, 679, 751

Christ ist erstanden: the melody, 633, 648f, 674, 681, 751; anon. settings, 633; Amsfortius, 2 settings, 713; Brassart, 633; Heinrich Finck, 639; Isaac, 679; Leopolita, 751; Senfl, 679, 751

Christe Dei soboles, Lassus, 695

Christe du Lamm Gottes (= Agnus in German Mass), 676

Christe Jesu, Taverner, 780

Christe qui lux es: Sarum Chant, 870; anon. setting, 649; Byrd, 791; White, 5 settings, 784; see also: *Precamur; Te lucis*

Christe Redemptor . . . Conserva: Greg. Chant (= *Jesu, Redemptor*), 84f; Dufay, 84f; Palestrina, 467

Christe Redemptor . . . Ex Patre: Greg. Chant (= *Jesu Redemptor*), 84; F. Anerio, 484; Dufay, 83ff (incl. Ex. 22); Palestrina, 467; Victoria, 604

Christe Redemptor, O Rex omnipotens, Mouton, 283

Christe sanctorum, Greg. Chant (= *Iste confessor*), 83

Christian IV, King of Denmark and Norway, 713, 810

Christine of Lorraine, 569

Christine de Pizan (= Pisan), 15, 87

Christoforus de Monte (= Cristoforo da Feltre), 26

Christum ducem (= Pars VI of *Qui velatus facie fuisti,* q. v.), Josquin, 252, 257

Christum wir sollen loben schon, derivation from *A solis ortus cardine,* 674

Christus filius Dei (= *Virgo prudentissima*), Isaac, 649

Christus mortuus, Josquin, 255

Christus natus est, Compère, 227

Christus resurgens: Sarum Chant, 777; Redford, 777; Richafort, 337, 371

Christus vincit, H. de Lantins, 41

chromaticism, 16, 321, 328ff, 353, 364, 384, 400, 402, 423, 430ff, 616, 709, 737, 818, 828, 847, 871; see also: accidentalism; degree inflection

Chronique, Mathieu d'Escouchy, 57

Chroniques, Molinet, 137

Chrysander, Friedrich (Chrys), 412

Chrystus Pan zmartwychwstał, the melody, 750 (Ex. 171a)

Chrystus zmartwychwstał jest, the melody, 750 (Ex. 171a)

Chrzanowita, Nicolaus, 747, 754

Chybiński, Adolf (Chyb), 741ff, 746ff, 753ff

Cibavit eos, Leopolita, 750

Cicalamento delle donne, Il, Striggio, 435f

Ciconia, Johannes, 25ff (incl. Ex. 3), 39, 53, 79, 743

Cigne je suis, Le Jeune, 384

Cima, Gian Paolo, 541

Cimello, Tomas, 334

Cingari siamo, Willaert, 334

Cini, Giovanni Battista, 568

Cinzio, Giraldi, 568

Circumdederunt me: Sarum Chant, 255; Josquin's *cantus firmus* thereon in canon form, 235, 255f (incl. Ex. 50), 335f; Gombert's use of the melody, 255, 305

Cisneros, Cardinal Ximenez de, 597

Cittadella, Luigi N., 117

cittern (= citole), 148, 488, 566, 848ff, 873

clairon, 57

Clangat plebs, Regis, 114

Clare sanctorum, Sermisy, 339

Clarifica me Pater, Greg. Chant, 858; see also: *Miserere* pieces

Clark, Andrew, 810

Claudin, see: Sermisy, Claudin de

Claus, Hans, 751

clavicembalum, 529

clavichord (= *jeu de manichorde, manacordo, manicordion, monachordio, monacordo*), 529, 558, 561, 630, 667

Clavijo, Bernardo de, 629

clef combinations, 249, 267, 325, 357, 531ff, 611

Clemens non Papa, Jacobus (= Jacob Clement): chansons and biogr., 301ff, 308, 557, 696; Masses and motets, 351ff (incl. Ex. 78), 486, 510, 629, 666; *Souterliedekens,* 355ff (incl. Ex. 79); see also 307, 343, 459, 461, 507, 509, 588, 700, 712, 720, 738, 749

Clemens of Piotrków, 746

Clement, Mary L., 122

Clement VII, Pope (= Giulio de' Medici), 362, 545f

Clement VIII, Pope, 426, 483

Clement XI, Pope, 362

clerc de matines (the term), 8

Clercx(-Lejeune), Suzanne, 9, 25, 118, 229

Cléreau, Pierre, 294, 297, 340

Cleve, Johannes de, 700ff

Clinkscale, Edward, 278f

clos (= *chiuso*) ending, 16, 30

Closson, Ernest (Clos), 36f, 86, 152

Coates, Henry, 455f

Cobbold, William, 807

Cobham, Sir Henry, 810

Cock, Symon, 355f

Coclico, Adriaen Petit, 229, 338, 512, 514ff (incl. Ex. 119), 682, 713

Coeleste beneficium, Ockeghem, 123f

Coelho, Manuel Rodrigues, 629f

Cofanaria, La, d'Ambra, 568

Cohen, Albert, 579

Cohen, Gustave, 152

Cohn, Albert, 881

Cole, Elizabeth, 851

Colinet, see: Lannoy, Colinet de

Collebaudi, Jacobus, see: Jaquet of Mantua
Collectorium super Magnificat, de Gerson, 154
Collegium Germanicum, 599; C. Musicum, 740; C. Rorantistarum, 748
Collet, Henri (Col), 587, 599ff, 608, 619
Collier, John P., 882
Collins, Henry B., 719, 721, 765, 770, 774f, 778f, 782ff, 786, 791, 794
Colmar school, see: Meistersinger
Colombina Chansonnier, see: Manuscripts—Seville
Colonna, Vittoria, 49, 413
color (the term), 22; see also: isorhythmic motet
coloration, 664ff (incl. Ex. 149), 754; see also: diminution; keyboard ornamentation; lute ornamentation
colorists, 665ff
Columba, Giovanni Battista, 156
Columbus, Christopher, 578
Columbus, Ferdinand, 578, 582
Columna es immobilis, Palestrina, 464
Come clap thy hands, Weelkes, 827 (incl. Ex. 193)
Come haro dunque ardire, Tromboncino, 158, 314
Come la cera, Lassus, 405
Come tread the paths, 817
Come wofull Orpheus, Byrd, 818
Coment peult haver joye, Josquin, 256
Comes, Juan Bautista, 611
Comme femme desconfortée: A. Agricola, 2 settings, 209; Binchois, 87, 102, 209, 215, 253, 690; text incipit, 207
commedia dell'arte, 434, 444, 686
Commer, Franz (Comm), 117, 231ff, 247f, 250, 255, 257f, 283, 294ff, 299, 301f, 304, 307f, 331, 346, 349ff, 353, 372ff, 381, 482f, 485f, 488f, 491, 493, 495f, 498ff, 506, 517, 541, 595, 679, 682f, 687, 690, 694ff, 701ff, 708, 791
commiato (= envoy), 164, 314, 332, 421, 441
Commodo, Il, Landi, 567
Commodye of pacient and meeke Grissill, The 878
Communiones totius anni, Zieleński, 753
Compagnia dei Musici di Roma (= *Accademia di Santa Cecilia*), 424ff
companies of musicians, 7, 424ff, 566, 772; see also: guilds
Compendiolo, Aron, 181
Compendium musices, Coclico, 229, 512, 515
Compendium of Practical Musick, A, Simpson, 834
Compère, Loyset: biogr. and sec. mus., 223ff; sacr. mus., 118, 190, 225ff (incl. Ex. 42), 559, 689; see also 100, 121, 137, 164, 184, 235, 263f, 275, 277f, 285f, 663
Complainte de la dame (at the Banquet of the Oath of the Pheasant), Dufay(?), 58
Compleat Gentleman, The, Peacham, 822, 831

Complexus effectuum musices, Tinctoris, 140, 146f, 187
Compositions-Regeln, Sweelinck, 377
Comte, Charles, 382
Con lagrime e sospir, Verdelot (and transcr. for voice and lute by Willaert), 318, 523, 835
Con lei foss'io: Ponte, 539; keyboard transcr. by A. Gabrieli, 539
Con qué la lavaré, Vasquez, 613
conceit, 835
Concentus novi, Kugelmann, 678
Conceptio tua, Marenzio, 482
concert giving, 382, 409, 880
concertante style, 409
Concerti ecclesiastici: Banchieri, 487; Belli, 495; Viadana, 489, 545, 762
Conclusioni nel suono dell'organo, Banchieri, 537
Concupivit rex, Greg. Chant, 77
Condamnation des banquets, La Chesnaye, 100
Conde Claros: the melody, 584, 623; anon. (*glosas*), 584; Encina, 584; Narváez (*diferencias*), 621
Conditor (= *Creator*) *alme siderum:* Greg. Chant, 83, 252; Genevan derivative, 361; Du Caurroy (*Fantaisies* XIX, XXV), 565; Dufay, 83f; Palestrina, 467
Condolmieri, Cardinal Gabriel, see: Eugene IV, Pope
conducting, 179, 546
conductus style, 17, 23, 28, 646, 659f, 744, 764
Confitebor tibi: Lassus, 703; Palestrina, 466, 470
Confitemini (*Pars II* of *Haec dies*), Gombert, 345
conflicting rhythms, see: rhythmic conflict
conflicting attributions, see: attributions, conflicting
conflicting signatures, see: key signatures; time signatures
Conforto, Giovanni Luca (Conf), 412
Congregati sunt inimici nostri: Crecquillon, 350; Janequin, 340
congregational singing, 358ff, 676, 683f, 689
Congregazione dell'Oratorio, 453f
Conradus, in Lublin Tablature, 755
Conscendit iubilans, Florigal, 649
Conseil, Jean, 300
Consomo (= *Consummo*) *la vita mya,* Prioris, 264; anon. keyboard transc., 559
consort (= instrumental ensemble), 547, 883; whole c., 868ff; broken c., 868, 873; c. songs, 809
Constans de Languebroek, 98, 115
Constantinople, Fall of, 57
contests, 389, 616, 652f
Contino, Giovanni, 420, 492f
contrafacta, 28, 167, 170, 256f, 291, 356f, 361, 395, 453, 596, 632, 674f, 696, 793; see also: *sainctes chansonnettes*
Contrainct je suis, Crecquillon, 302
Contrappunto, Galilei, 528

Contrappunto bestiale, Banchieri, 437
contrappunto inverso (the term), 494
contrapunctus (the term), 142
contrapuntally accompanied solo song, 817ff,
    841, 874, 882
Contrapunti, Galilei, 549
Contreros, Fernando de, 587
Conversi, Girolamo, 445, 874
Convito musicale, Orazio Vecchi, 433
Conviviorum deliciae, Demantius, 756
Cooper, Gerald M. (Coop), 552
Cooper, John (= Giovanni Coperario), 809,
    811, 836, 839, 871
Cooper (= Cowper), Robert, 768, 770
Copenhagen Chansonnier, see: Manuscripts—
    Copenhagen
Copin, 115
copla (the term), 581f
Coplande, Robert (Cop), 882
Coppinus, Alexander, 169f
Cor meum, A. Gabrieli, 496
Corante du roy, Schmid the Elder, 564
Corbet (= Courbet), 227
Cordero di Pamparato, Stanislas (Cord), 50
Cordier, Baude, 13f, 23
Córdoba, Alonzo de, 582
Cordouval, Jehan de, 51
Corkine, William, 838
Cornago, Johannes, 119, 139, 576f
Cornaro, Francesco, 534
Cornazano, Antonio (Cornaz), 176f, 215
Cornet, Pieter, 563
Cornet, Severin, 398
Cornetto, Antonio da, 546
cornetto (= zink), 366, 495, 499, 545ff, 551,
    567, 569, 655, 672, 676, 721, 873f; *c. grosso,*
    546
Cornuel, Jean (= Verjust), 137, 220, 723
Cornysh, William, 768ff (incl. Ex. 176), 773,
    835, 868
coro spezzato, 372f; see also: polychoral writ-
    ing
Corona aurea, Palestrina, 462
Corps, Le—Corpusque meum, Compère, 225
Corps digne—Dieu quel mariage, Busnois,
    104 (Ex. 26b)
Corps femenin, Solage, 12
Corrado da Pistoia, 26f
Corte, Andrea della, 444f, 691
Corteccia, Francesco, 325f (incl. Ex. 70a),
    364ff (incl. Ex. 82), 428, 567f
Cortegiano, Il, Castiglione, 158, 160, 547, 620
Cortes de Jupiter, Vicente, 581
Cortes, Narciso A. (Cort), 623
Così suav'è'l foco, Festa, 320
Costeley, Guillaume, 388ff (incl. Ex. 89), 561
Coster, Adolphe, 578
Cosyn, Benjamin, 851, 866
Cosyn, John, 807
Cotarelo y Mori, Emilio, 583, 619, 631
Couillart, 351
Council of Basle, 736; C. of Constance, 31,

644; C. of Trent, 60, 130, 242, 251, 364,
    448f, 696, 703
Counter-Reformation, 448ff, 698, 736ff
counterpoint of rhythms, see: rhythmic conflict
counterpoint rules: Tinctoris, 144; Gafori, 179;
    Cerone, 618f
Countrie and Citie Conceits, Ravenscroft, 835
Country Cryes, Deering, 833
Couperin, François, 289, 566
courantes (= corantos): in masques, 882; for
    instr. ensemble: in *Orchésographie,* 564; for
    keyboard: Byrd, 863; Schmid the Elder,
    564; in Engl. sources, general, 863, 866; for
    lute: Francisque, 554; in Engl. sources, 844f
Courbet (= Corbet), 227
Couronne et fleur de chansons, La (Antico),
    234, 286
Court of Love, 7
Courtois, Jean, 300
Courville, Thibaut de (= Joachim Thibaut),
    382
Coussemaker, Ch. Edmond H. de (Cou), 8,
    31, 56, 86, 93, 101, 109ff, 120, 138, 140ff,
    178, 182, 187, 295, 306, 337, 632, 727, 763
Coverdale, Myles, 781
Cowling, George H. (Cow), 879
Cowper, see: Cooper, Robert
Cracovia civitas, 743, 745
Cracoviensis, Nicolaus, 747, 754
Cracow Gradual, 750
Cracow tablature, see: Manuscripts—Warsaw
Craen, Nicolas, 276, 663
Craindre vous vueil (= *Quel fronte signorille*),
    Dufay, 52
Crampe, The, the melody, 834
Cranford, William, 873
Cranmer, Thomas, Archbishop of Canterbury,
    795, 800
Crastina die, Greg. Chant, 192
Creator alme siderum, see: *Conditor . . .*
Creator omnium Deus: Lassus, 510; Willaert,
    510
Crecquillon, Thomas: chansons and biogr.,
    301ff (incl. Ex. 61), 538, 628, 738; sacr.
    mus., 202, 350f, 511, 591, 753; see also 353,
    507, 557, 629, 666, 706, 712
Credidi propter, Lassus, 696
Credo, Greg. Chant: Cr. I, 29, 32, 39, 130,
    228, 242, 268f, 282, 470, 689; Cr. II, 29,
    244; Cr. IV, 472, 580; Cr. V, 29, 239; Cr.
    VI, 29; *Cr. Paschale,* Cracow use, 750; Cr.,
    Mantuan use, 470; for polyphonic Credos
    outside of complete Masses, see various
    Credos under: Mass sections
Credo excisions: on Continent, 69, 95, 112;
    in England, 773f, 780, 782
Crema, Giovanni Maria da, 522, 527
Crétin Guillaume, 99, 115ff, 124, 137, 263,
    266, 293
Crevel, Marcus van (Cre), 195, 230, 255, 257,
    303, 353, 395, 512ff, 701
Cris de Paris, Les, Janequin, 296

Index

Cristoforo da Feltre, 26
Croce, Benedetto, 139
Croce, Giovanni: biogr. and sec. mus., 436; sacr. mus., 499f; see also 433, 487, 493, 545, 810, 826, 831
Crocker, Eunice C., 552
Croll, Gerhard, 218f
cromorne (= dolzaine, douchaine, dulcina), 36, 57, 146f, 546, 567, 655, 721
Cromwell, Oliver, 793
Cromwell, Thomas, 778
Crónica del Condestable Miguel Lucas de Iranzo, Pedro de Escavais (?), 577f
Cronica, Tinódi, 718
cross relation (= false relation), 297, 534f, 601, 621, 693, 700f, 752, 783, 794, 802, 824, 858, 872
Crowley, Robert, 796
Crucifige, Compère, 225f (incl. Ex. 42)
Cruda Amarilli: Monteverdi, 441; Wert, 410 (incl. Ex. 96)
Cruda mia nemica, La, Palestrina, 402
Crudel perche mi fuggi, Monteverdi, 440
Crudelis (= *Hostis*) *Herodes*, Greg. Chant, 83
Crux fidelis: F. Anerio, 484; John IV, 598
Crux triumphans, Compère, 225
Csánky, Dezsö (Csán), 722f
Cueur est bon, Le, basse danse, 564
Cueur langoureux, Josquin, 233
Cueurs désolez, Appenzeller (?), 234; Josquin, 234f
Cueurs désolez—Dies illa, dies irae, La Rue (?), 272
Cum beatus Ignatius, Victoria, 600
Cum invocarem, Willaert, 373
Cum ortus fuerit, Palestrina, 464
Cum sit omnipotens rector Olympi, Monte, 703
Cum transisset, see: *Dum transisset*
Cunliffe, John W., 878
Cutting, Francis, 842, 848
Cutts, John, 841
Cuvelier (= Cunelier), 16
Cuyler, Louise E., 217
Cyprus MS, see: Manuscripts—Turin
Czech Brethren (= Moravian Brethren), 735
Czech musical societies, 739

Da Jakob nun das Kleid ansah, Senfl, 679
Da le perle e rubini, Merulo, 417
Da pacem Domine (= *Accueillie m'a*), Caron, 111
Da pacem in diebus nostris: Greg. Chant, 90, 216, 223, 242, 350, 509f; Binchois, 90; Lassus, 509f; Martini, 223
Dafne: Giampietro della Viola, 173; Rinuccini, 569
Dahnk, Emilie, 6
Dalle belle contrade, Rore, 332 (incl. Ex. 74)
Dalle più alte sfere, Malvezzi, 570
Dallis, Thomas, 844
Dalza, Joan Ambrosio, 161, 521ff, 525, 621, 671
Daman (= Damon), William, 807

Dame doucement, Vaillant, 12
Dammene un poco, Isaac, 214
Dammonis, Innocentius, 167, 253
Damon and Pithias, the melody, 878
D'amours je suis desheritée, Richafort, 301
D'amours me plains, Pathie, 299
Danceries, d'Estrées, 564
Danckert, Werner, 552
Danckerts, Ghiselin, 364
Daniel, Arnaut, 332
Daniel, Jean (= Maître Mitou), 278
Daniel, Magister, 722
Daniel, Samuel, 820
Danish music, 712f
Daniskas, John (Danis), 116
Dannemann, Erna (Dann), 7, 10f, 16ff, 22, 24, 61
danse mesurée, 571
Dante Alighieri, 312, 400, 424
Danyel, John, 838, 844
Dart, R. Thurston, 445, 536, 774, 824, 849, 873f
Daser, Ludwig, 690, 696
Davey, Henry, 772f, 795, 852
David, Hans T. (Da), 215, 234, 253, 256, 281, 290, 295, 299, 307, 429, 551f, 792, 809
Davy, Richard, 773
Day, John, 797, 799, 801
Daye, Stephen, 809
Daza, Esteban, 594, 596, 612, 624
De accentibus . . . linguae hebraicae, Reuchlin, 705
De arte canendi, Heyden, 219
De bien amer, Fontaine, 35
De harmonia musicorum instrumentorum, Gafori, 180
De institutione harmonica, Aron, 181, 185
De inventione et usu musicae, Tinctoris, 140, 147f
De l'oeil de la fille du roy, La Rue, 272
De los álamos vengo, madre, Vasquez, 2 settings, 613
De mon triste deplaisir, Richafort, 302, 356
De musica: Adam von Fulda, 639; St. Augustine, 746
De musica figurata, Kromer, 747
De musica libri septem, Salinas, 252, 579, 617f
De plus en plus, Binchois, 86f, 128
De profundis: A. Gabrieli, 497; Josquin, 2 settings, 249f; Lassus, 695; Sweelinck, 518
De tous biens plaine (= *playne*): A. Agricola, several settings, 209f; anon. (not Busnois), 101; Hayne, 98, 100f, 198, 205, 209, 219, 224f, 227, 251, 276, 580; Japart, 219; Josquin, 233; D'Oude Scheure, 295; Tinctoris, 149
De tous biens plaine—Beati pacifici, van Stappen, 276
De voltate in qua, 159
Decameron, Boccaccio, 313
decani and *cantoris* sides, 118, 799, 802f
Decet huius cunctis horis, Jan of Ienštein, 731

declamation, see: accentuation, quantity, declamation
Declaración de instrumentos musicales, Bermudo, 630
Decora lux (= Aurea luce), Greg. Chant, 83
decoration, see: ornamentation
Decorus, Volupius (= Schonsleder, Wolfgang), 532f
Deducto se', 86
Deepe lamenting, Morley, 822f
Deering, Richard, 793, 833, 872f
Déesse Venus, La, Monte, 396
Deffense et Illustration de la langue françoise, Du Bellay, 381f
Deffner, Oskar (Deff), 539, 630
Defyled is my name, Johnson, 778
degree inflection, 16, 311, 321, 328, 331, 384, 402, 404, 413, 420, 431, 438, 441, 481, 603, 791, 793f, 802, 827, 839, 847, 874; see also: accidentalism; chromaticism
degrees: Bachelor of Music, 767, 775, 783, 792, 809, 813; Doctor of Music, 770, 774, 809, 813
Deh, come trista, Arcadelt, 322
Dehn, Siegfried W., 376, 447, 488, 491, 494, 499, 609, 687f, 702, 709, 791
Dei Mater alma, Gombert (correctly Ave maris stella, Porta), 345
Deitatis aures: Greg. Chant, 467; Palestrina, 467
Del Tuppo, Francesco, 147
Delétra, D. (Delét), 359
Deliciae Phoebi, Lassus, 506
Delicta juventutis, La Rue, 272
Deliette, mignonette, Du Caurroy, 386
Delitiae musicae, Van den Hove, 556, 756, 844, 847
Della prattica musica, Ceretto, 549
Delle imperfettioni della moderna musica, Artusi, 494
Delporte, Jules (Delp), 207f, 223, 278, 280
Demantius, Christoph, 712, 722, 756f
Denham, Henrie, 807
Denmark: in general, 712f, 810; Copenhagen, 713
Dent, Edward J., 67, 167, 434, 453, 568, 711, 816, 818, 883
Dentice, Luigi, 546
Deo gratias: ex. in Tinctoris, 143; Ockeghem?, 124, 250
Déploration, Crétin, 99, 115, 118, 137, 263, 266
déplorations in musical setting, see: laments; dumps
Der nunnentantz, Newsidler, 671 (Ex. 151)
Der pawir schwanz, Rubinus, 48
Der pfoben schwanz, Barbingant, 116, 200, 223
Des kleffers neyden, the melody in the versions of the Lochamer Liederbuch and Buxheimer Orgelbuch and Paumann's setting of it, 660 (Ex. 147a)
Des Prez, Josquin, see: Josquin

Descende in hortum meum, A. de Févin, 279, 338
Descendi, Greg. Chant, 261
Descendit angelus: Penet, 285, 471; Victoria, 600
Descendit de coelis, Byrd, 789
Deschamps, Pierre, 26
Desiderio di Pavia, 378
Desiderio, Il, Bottrigari, 546f
Desleaulx, Les, Ockeghem, 120
Deslouges, Philippe, see: Verdelot
Despuig, Guillermo (= Guillermus de Podio), 577
Dessus le marché d'Arras, Lassus, 393, 697f
Deudsche Messe (= German or Lutheran Mass), 776
Deus creator, Greg. trope, 95
Deus deorum Pluto, Zachara da Teramo, 32f
Deus Deus meus, G. Gabrieli, 498
Deus in adjutorium meum, Lassus, 697f
Deus in nomine tuo, Josquin, 247
Deus misereatur nostri, A. Gabrieli, 497
Deus tuorum militum (the melody = Nunc Sancte nobis Spiritus; Aurora lucis rutilat; Aurora coelum): Greg. Chant, 467; Palestrina, 467
Deus ultionum, Gombert, 346
Deuteromelia, Ravenscroft, 769, 833f, 845
Deutsche Volkslieder, Brahms, 638
devozione, 164f, 171
Dèzes, Karl (Dèz), 38, 51f, 59, 63, 82ff, 633, 743
Di moy, mon coeur, Lassus, 395
Dialoghi: Dentice, 546; Troiano, 487
Dialogo della musica, A. Doni, 316, 325, 401, 546
Dialogo della musica antica e della moderna, Galilei, 377, 420
Dialogue du Gendarme et de l'Amoureux, Molinet, 12, 87
dialogue treatment, 54, 106f, 317, 405, 408, 415, 436, 484, 769f
Diarii Sistini, 362
Diario, Sorranzo, 760
diatonicism, predilection for, etc., 119, 297, 322, 353, 459, 820
Diaz, Gabriel, 616f
Dictes moy toutes vos pensées, Compère, 284
Dido's lament, see: Dulces exuviae
Dieckmann, Jenny (Die), 671
Dies est laetitiae: the melody, 674; Heinrich Finck, 650
Dies illa, dies irae: Greg. Chant, 272; Du Caurroy, 404f (incl. Ex. 117)
Dies irae, dies illa, Jacopone da Todi, 121, 130, 262, 272
Dies sanctificatus, Palestrina, 464, 471
Dietrich, Fritz (Diet), 668
Dietrich, Sixtus, 662, 679ff (incl. Ex. 153), 706
Dieu gard de mal, Mouton, 280f
Dieu gard la bone sans reprise, Dufay, 57

diferencias: Cabezón, 628, 862; Narváez, 621f; Mudarra, 622f; Valderrábano, 623
Diffinitorium musicae, Tinctoris, 140f
Diffusa est gratia: G. M. Nanino, 483; Porta, 494
Dignus es, Pevernage, 517
Diletto spirituale (Verovio), 447
Diliges Dominum, Byrd, 788
Dilucide . . . demonstratione, Spataro, 587
diminished fifth, d. triad, 47, 143, 321, 422, 435, 812
diminished fourth, 63, 82, 410, 431, 435, 601, 793, 799
diminished seventh chord, 423, 752
diminution (= "division" of long notes), 394 (incl. Ex. 91), 403, 411f (incl. Ex. 97), 544, 548, 566; see also: coloration; d. (= opposite of augmentation), see: proportional system
Dimmi lume del mondo, Monte, 408
Dimostrationi harmoniche, Zarlino, 378, 417
Diobono, Pompeo, 570
Diomedes of Venice, 844
Directiones musicae ad cathedralis, Felstin, 746
Diruta, Girolamo, 416, 541f, 544f, 722
Disant adieu, Compère, 224
discant, English, 45, 64f, 96, 745
discant-tenor technique, 54
discantus (= treble; the term), 16
Dischner, Oskar (Dis), 24, 35, 41, 43, 59, 65, 86, 92
Discorsi delli triumphi, Troiano, 691
Discorso intorno alle opere di . . . Zarlino, Galilei, 377
Disertori, Benvenuto (Dise), 27, 31, 101, 111, 190, 262, 430, 529, 540, 843
dissonance, extensive or unusual use of, 16, 43, 355, 438, 515f, 534f, 624, 640, 739, 752; see also: appoggiaturas; suspensions; etc.; and names of dissonant intervals
dissonance, unregulated, 23, 62, 535
dissonance, tendency toward stricter use, 3f, 143, 425, 459ff
Diversi diversa orant, Gombert, 345
Divini occhi sereni, Verdelot, 317
Divitis, Antonius, 276f, 285, 335f
Dixerunt discipuli, Greg. Chant, 263
Dixit Joseph, Lassus, 697
Dizen a mi: the melody, an anon. setting, and that of Vasquez, 613
Długoraj, Albert, 755
Do ciebie panie (Psalm XXV), 752 (incl. Ex. 172)
Dobrucki, Matthaeus, 753
Doctor bonus, Victoria, 602
Doctor egregie: Greg. Chant, 467; Palestrina, 467
Dodecachordon, Glareanus, 136, 185f, 197, 249, 276, 280, 282, 598, 639, 680f
Dodge, Janet (Do), 523, 557
Doflein, Erich (Dofl), 549, 871
Dohrn, Ellinor, 438

Dolce, Lodovico, 569
Dolce fortuna, Ciconia, 30
Dolce mio ben, Vicentino, 328f (incl. Ex. 71)
Dolce vista a me, La, Monte, 703
Dolce vista del tuo viso, La, Dufay, 52
Dolcissimi legami, Monteverdi, 440
Dolmetsch, Arnold (Dol), 836, 841, 872
Domenico da Ferrara, 30
Domenico da Piacenza, 176
Domine da nobis, Crecquillon, 202
Domine Deus conteris bella, Crecquillon, 350
Domine Deus in simplicitate, Palestrina, 467
Domine, Dominus noster, Josquin, 248
Domine exaudi: Byrd, 789; G. Gabrieli, 498
Domine fac mecum, Morley, 792
Domine in virtute tua, Johnson, 778
Domine Jesu Christe, fons bonorum omnium, Merbecke, 781
Domine Jesu Christe qui cognoscis, Lassus, 389
Domine Jesu Christe qui hora diei, Anchieta, 579
Domine non est exaltandum, Lassus, 508
Domine non secundum peccata nostra: Greg. Chant, 254, 265; Josquin, 254; de Orto, 265; Vaqueras, 136
Domine non sum dignus, Victoria, 602
Domine ostende nobis Patrem, Las Infantas, 609f
Domine probasti me, Willaert, 373 (Ex. 85)
Domine quid multiplicati sunt, Goudimel, 502
Domine quis habitabit, White, 784
Domine salvum fac regem, Mouton, 282f
Domingos, I. Leroy, 365, 703
Dominus regnavit, Josquin, 249f (incl. Ex. 48), 257
Domitor Hectoris, Binchois, 90
Domynyk, 771
Donato, Baldissera, 415ff, 420, 436, 443, 499
Doni, Antonfrancesco, 316, 323, 325, 401, 546f
Doni, Giovanni Battista, 329
Donington, Robert (Don), 779
Donna bella, Verdonck, 427
Donna di dentro dalla tua casa, Isaac, 214
Donna gentil'e bella, Dufay, 53
Donna i ardenti ray, Dufay, 52
Donna leggiadr'e bella, Verdelot, 317, 319
Donna ne fu ne fia, Festa, 320
Donne, John, 815, 820
Donnés au Seigneur gloire, Monte, 511
Donnez l'assault, Dufay, 56
Doomsday (a play), 877
Doorslaer, Georges van, 7, 98, 101, 218, 265, 267, 276, 303, 308, 335, 337f, 350, 395, 398, 429, 447, 511, 561, 700
Doppelmeister, see: identity problems
Dorez, Léon, 527
Dorian Service, Tallis, 800
Dorico, Valerio, 314
Dormend'un giorn'a Bai, Verdelot, 317f, 595
Dormoli, Virginia, 458
D'où (dont) vient cela: Sermisy, 294f, 356f, 564; *basse dance,* 564

double (= ornamented version of piece), 556
double counterpoint, 106, 254, 258, 336, 351, 377, 477, 754, 824
Douce mémoire, Sandrin, 299, 696
douchaine, see: cromorne
Douen, Orentin (Dou), 299, 339f, 358ff, 362, 503f, 554
Doutfull state that I posses, The, Whythorne, 816
Doutrepont, Georges, 58
Dovro dunque morire, Caccini, 835
Dowland, John (Dowl): biogr. and sacr. mus., 810; ayres, 832, 839ff. (incl. Exx. 199, 200), 865; lute mus., 846ff (incl. Exx. 203, 204); instr. ensemble mus., 873f; see also 180, 554, 639, 713, 807ff, 815, 820f, 835, 838, 852, 876
Dowland, Robert, 835, 840, 844, 846f
Dowland's Adew, J. Dowland, 847
Dowling, Margaret (Dowlg), 840
Down in a flow'ry vale (= *Quando ritrovo la mia pastorella*), Festa, 320
Dragan of Prizren, 759
Dragoni, Giovanni Andrea, 425, 482, 485
dramatic presentations with music: England, 876ff; France, 150ff, 570ff; Germany, 655; Italy, 566ff; Spain, 584, 630f
dramatic-type Passion (defined), 165
Drayton, Michael, 769, 820, 831
Dressler, Gallus, 682
Drinker, Sophie (Drin), 409, 547
Droz, Eugénie, 6, 25, 38, 87, 97, 100ff, 109, 111, 120f, 137f, 149, 223f, 264, 305, 382, 389
drum, 146, 152, 656, 721, 867, 878, 879
Drusina, Benedikt de, 669
Držić, Džore, 758
Du Bellay, Joachim, 381f, 389, 392
Du Boulay, César, 148
Du Cange, Charles, 93
Du Caurroy, Eustache, 386f, 389, 504f (incl. Ex. 117), 565
Du Chemin, Nicolas, 290, 300, 341, 387, 502
Du Lot, F., 351
Du mien amant, Josquin, 231 (incl. Ex. 43a)
Du Saar, Johannes (Saar), 48, 116f, 220, 223, 266, 275, 307, 648
Du Tertre, Etienne, 564
Du tout m'estoie, Dufay, 57
Du tout plongiet—Fors seulement, Brumel, 262 (incl. Ex. 51)
Du trist' hyver, Le Jeune, 384f (incl. Ex. 87)
Ducis, Benedictus, 266, 305f, 679f
Dueil angoisseux, Binchois, 87, 152
Dufay, Caterine (= Cateline), 52
Dufay, Guillaume: biogr. and early works, 48ff; sec. voc. mus., 44f (incl. Exx. 5c; 7a, c), 52ff, 112f, 121, 153, 188, 224, 265, 271, 332, 576, 635, 646, 659; sacr. mus., 59ff (incl. Exx. 14–17, 19–22), 109, 113, 118, 122, 125f, 145, 181, 189, 196f, 216, 230, 251, 363, 467, 588, 645, 773; see also 6, 8, 10, 13, 34f, 40ff, 90f, 95ff, 102, 107f, 113, 115,

119, 138, 142, 145, 227, 239, 263, 380, 461, 577, 633, 644, 658, 763
Dufourcq, Norbert (Dufo), 386, 561
Dulces exuviae (= Dido's lament): Josquin, 253, 281; Lassus, 695; Mouton, 281; de Orto, 265; Willaert, 374
Dulci sub umbra, Lassus, 695
dulcina, see: cromorne
Dulcis amica Dei, Prioris, 264
Dulichius, Philippus, 688
Dum aurora finem daret, Crecquillon, 350
Dum committeret bellum, Sarum Chant, 114
Dum complerentur: Josquin, 255; Palestrina, 471; Victoria, 608
Dum esset summus pontifex, Greg. Chant, 471
Dum sacrum mysterium, Greg. Chant, 114
Dum (= *Cum*) *transisset*: Greg. and Sarum Chant, 778; Johnson, 778; Tallis, 785; Taverner, 780
Dum vagus, Gallus, 738
Duma, 756f (incl. Ex. 174)
dumps (= *déplorations*), 853, 868
D'ung aultre amer: A. Agricola, 3 settings, 209; Ockeghem, 117, 120, 209, 224, 245, 251; Tinctoris, 149
D'ung desplaisir, La Rue, 272
D'ung petit mot, Crecquillon, 350
Dunicz, Jan J. (Du), 753
Dunstable, John, 6, 10, 13, 24, 30, 48, 65f, 86, 92f, 115, 119, 142, 145, 263, 577, 635, 644, 658, 763f, 775, 849
duo of upper voices at opening as 15th-c. trait, 39, 68, 93, 108, 126
Duo Seraphim, Victoria, 603
Dupire, Noël, 12, 101
Dupuis, Nicaise, 90
Dura mia pietra viva, Galilei, 420
Durandarte, Milán, 621 (incl. Ex. 137)
durchkomponiert, see: through-composed music
Dürer, Albrecht, 655
Dusart, 111, 202, 227
Dutch texts, chansons with, see: chanson
dux and *comes* (the terms), 687
Duyse, Florimond van (Duy), 189, 356
Dvořák, Antonín, 734
Dyce, Alexander, 881, 883
Dygon, John, 774, 777
dynamics indicated in sources, 437, 498, 521, 551

E ben ragion, Caimo, 432
E s'altri non m'inganna, Wert, 410
Ea judíos, the melody, 578f
Earle of Darby, His Galliard, J. Dowland, 847 (incl. Ex. 203)
Earl of Salisbury Pavan and Galiard: Byrd, 865; Gibbons, 865
Early Renaissance, characteristic traits, 3, 68, 105, 250, 583, 635, 769, 775, etc.
East (= Este), Michael, 811, 822
East (= Este), Thomas, 787, 792, 811, 827ff, 841, 869

Eberth, Friedrich (Eber), 653
Eccard (Ecc), Johann, 680, 685f (incl. Ex. 154), 688, 696
Ecce ancilla Domini, Greg. Chant, 75, 115
Ecce apparebit Dominus, Vaet, 297, 700f (incl. Ex. 157)
Ecce beatam lucem, Striggio, 487
Ecce Dominus veniet, Victoria, 600
Ecce quam bonum, Clemens, 351
Ecce quomodo moritur justus, Gallus, 738
Ecce sacerdos magnus: Greg. Chant, 347, 470, 472, 601; Porta, 494; Victoria, 601f
Ecce tu pulchra es, Josquin, 258
Ecce video coelos, Craen, 276
Ecclesiastici concentus, Balbi, 495
Ecclesiasticus, Fruytiers, 355
Ecclesie militantis—Sanctorum arbitrio—Bella canunt—Ecce nomen Domini—Gabriel, Dufay, 79ff
Ecco, d'oro l'età, Arcadelt, 322
Ecco l'aurora, A. Gabrieli, 414
Ecco mormorar l'onde, Monteverdi, 440
Ecco, o mia dolce pena, Nenna, 432
echo pieces, 422, 444, 563, 571
Eck, Johann M., 678
Eckhardt, Sandor (Eck), 726
ecloga (= *farsa*), 173
Edward VI, King of England, 781, 796, 802, 815, 850
Edwards, Richard, 801, 816, 851
Een devoot ende profitelijck boecxken (Cock), 356f
Een duytsch musyck boeck (Phalèse), 308, 357
Een vroylic wesen: Barbireau, 117, 266, 275, 644, 648, 662; Ghiselin (*Een vrowelic wesenn*), 266; Pipelare, 275; see also: *Ain frelich wesen*
effects of music as named by Tinctoris, 146
Egardus, 743
Egenolf, Christian, 706f
Egidius de Rhenis, 632
Ego dixi, G. Gabrieli, 498
Ego flos campi: Clemens, 353; Gallus, 738
Ego sum, ego Dominus Deus tuus (= *Alma Redemptoris*), Obrecht, 191
Ego sum panis vivus, Philips, 794
Ego sum pastor bonus, Szamotułczyk, 749
Egregie Doctor Paule, Greg. Chant, 467
Egressus Jesus, Wert, 488
Eheu sustulerunt Dominum meum, Morley, 792
Ehmann, Wilhelm (Ehm), 646, 690
Ehrmann, Richard (Ehr), 532
Ein feste Burg: the melody, 675, 684, 781; Le Maistre, 682; 9 settings, 684
Ein Kind geborn zu Bethlehem (= *Puer natus in Bethlehem*), the melody, 674
Ein Korbelmacher in eim Dorff, Lassus, 709
Ein new künstlich Lautten Buch, Newsidler, 755
Ein vrouleen edel von naturen, 634, 636
Einr junckfrau zart, Hofhaimer, 642
Einstein, Alfred (Ein), 156ff, 164f, 168, 170,

173, 187, 214, 229, 260, 285, 293, 299f, 307, 311ff, 316ff, 330ff, 381, 400, 403f, 406, 408ff, 413ff, 427, 431ff, 435ff, 440f, 443ff, 469, 490, 498, 513, 515, 523, 538, 540, 543, 549, 568, 616, 671, 690, 707f, 711, 818, 821, 831
Eisenring, Georg (Eis), 216, 343, 649, 690
Eitner, Robert (Eit), 48, 111, 115f, 136f, 218, 223, 264, 275f, 285, 289f, 307, 310f, 321, 332, 340, 352, 364, 366, 375, 412, 416, 445, 482, 485, 488, 492, 499, 528, 559, 563f, 616, 621, 634f, 659, 663, 666ff, 684, 687, 694, 707, 717
Eleanor, Queen of France (consort of Francis I), 561
Elegi abjectus esse, Philips, 794
Eleonora of Toledo, 325, 365, 567
Eleonora of Aragon, Duchess of Ferrara, 139, 719
Elizabeth I, Queen of England, 766, 781, 784, 791, 797, 807, 809, 815, 831, 850, 879
Elizabeth Rogers hir Virginall Booke, see: Manuscripts—London
Elle est à vous, Sweelinck, 399
Elling, Chatharinus (Ellg), 713
Ellinwood, Leonard (Ellin), 332, 800
Ellis, Alexander J., 617, 878
Eloge, Mersenne, 386
Elsner, Emilie (Els), 174, 545ff, 569, 571
Elústiza, Juan B. de (Elús), 470, 578ff, 587f, 590ff
Elvinus, 716
embellishment, see: ornamentation
Emendemus in melius: Greg. Chant, 591; Morales, 591; Richafort, 281, 337, 471
Emeric, King of Hungary, 716
Emmanuel, Maurice (Em), 570f
Emperor Soliman's Fight with Kazul Pasha, Tinódi, 718 (Ex. 163)
emyolia, see: hemiola
En atendant, Selesses, 12
En avois (= *Une fois*), the melody, 658
En douleur, en tristesse: the melody, 338; Bauldeweyn, 338; Willaert, 338
En espoir d'avoir, Gombert, 351
En espoir vis, Lassus, 393
En l'ombre d'un(g) buyssonet: the melody, 206; Gombert, 304 (incl. Ex. 62); Josquin, 3 settings, 234, 261, 286, 304; see also: *A l'ombre*
En l'ombre—Una musque—Sustinuimus pacem, Isaac, 214
En m'oyant chanter, Lassus, 393
En non saichant, Josquin, 234
En passant par la Lorraine, the melody, 381
En son temple sacré, Mauduit, 504
En venant de Lyon (= *Lourdault, lourdault*), the melody, 206
En vos adieux, Rore, 311, 343
Enchiridion, Despuig, 577
Enchiridion of Erfurt, 675
Encina, Juan del (Enc), 583ff (incl. Ex. 130)
Encomium musices (Galle), 517

Engel, Carl, 19
Engel, Egon (En), 521, 523, 525, 669
Engel, Hans (Eng), 420, 423f, 444f
Engelke, Bernhard, 876
England (outside Chaps. 15, 16), 23, 65, 67, 69, 71, 86, 93, 266, 395, 428, 436, 511, 627, 713
English Bible, 781; concordance to E.B., 782
English influence on French music, 7, 9, 13, 65; on German music, 644, 876, 881; on continent generally, 881
Englitt, 851
engraving, copperplate, 447
enharmonic microtones, see: microtones
Enojado esta el Abril, Navarro, 593
Enrique, 585
ensalada (= quodlibet), 580, 586, 615
Entré je suis, Josquin, 232
Entre vous filles de quinze ans, Clemens, 302, 696
entremes (= intermezzo), 631
envoi of *ballade*, 55; *e.* of French *sestina*, 385
envoy, see: *commiato; envoi*
epic singers, 714, 717, 719
Episcopius, Ludovicus, 308, 357, 394
epithalamium, 26, 49, 52, 77, 419
Epithoma utriusque musices practice, Monetarius, 727, 746
Epitre des dames de Paris, Marot, 564
Eppstein, Hans (Epp), 255, 303, 344, 346, 348
equal temperament, see: intonation (= tuning)
Erano i capei d'or, G. M. Nanino, 447
Erasmus, Desiderius, 118, 123, 187, 296, 339, 448, 598
Erat Jesus, Orazio Vecchi, 488
Erbach, 667
Eremita, 831
Ergo ne conticuit, J. Lupi, 118
Eripe me, Maillard, 470
Errant par les champs, Goudimel, 387
Erunt prava, Greg. chant, 192
Erzürne dich nicht, Stoltzer, 724 (Ex. 165)
Es het ein Baur ein Töchterlein, Isaac, 643f
Es leit ein Schloss in Österreich, 637 (Ex. 141b)
Es sind noch selig (= *O Mensch, bewein dein' Sünde gross*), the melody, 683
Es spricht, Hassler, 684
Es taget vor dem Walde: the melody, 638; Franz, 638
Esaltazione della Croce, Cecchi, 566
Escavias, Pedro de, 577
Esclarecida madre (= *Esclarecida Juána*), Guerrero, 596
Escobar, André de, 598
Escobar, Cristóbal de, 579
Escobar, Pedro de, 579, 587
Escobar (identity uncertain), 584
Escobedo, Bartolomé, 591, 599
Escouchy, Mathieu d', 57

Escribano, Juan, 587
Eslava, Don Hilarion (Es), 580, 587, 591ff, 595f, 600, 609, 611, 617
espinette, see: spinet
Espinosa, Juan de, 587
Espoir m'est venu, Vide, 44f (incl. Exx. 5a, 7b)
Esquivel, Juan de, 610
Este, Alfonso d', 157, 378; Beatrice d', 526; Eleonora d', 430; Ercole I d', 139, 148, 157, 187, 221, 229, 236, 248, 342, 375, 719; Ercole II d', 311, 327, 329, 342f, 375f, 690; Hugo d', 49; Cardinal Ippolito d', 328, 370, 457, 527, 591; Isabella d', 120, 157, 222, 526; Cardinal Luigi d', 420
Estéban, Fernando, 577
Estote fortes, Marenzio, 481
Estrées, Jean d', 564
estribillo (the term), 581f
Estrinez moy, Dufay, 54
Et in terra (outside of complete Masses), see various Glorias under: Mass sections
Et que feront povres gendarmes, 205
Et qui la dira, Isaac, 212f (incl. Ex. 39a, b)
Eugene IV, Pope, 50, 78f, 596
Euripides, 878
Europa, Madama, 442
Evans, Marshall B., 705
Evans, Willa M. (Ev), 882
Evening Service (Anglican), Parsley, 803
Ewarger (= Ewargeris), 744
Exaltabo te: Croce, 500; Palestrina, 466
examinations for professional competence, 7, 48, 619
Exercitationes Musicae duae, Calvisius, 687
Exhortation to all Kynde of Men . . . (lute book), 843
Expert, Henry (Ex), 282, 285, 292f, 295f, 298f, 327, 340, 357, 359ff, 382, 384ff, 393, 503f, 511, 518, 565
Expositio manus, Tinctoris, 140f
Exsultet orbis gaudiis, Greg. Chant, 467
Exsurge Domine, Byrd, 789 (incl. Ex. 183)
Exultate Deo, Palestrina, 465
Exultate justi, Viadana, 489
Exultent et laetentur, G. M. Nanino, 482
Exultet coelum laudibus: Greg. Chant, 361, 467; Palestrina, 467
Eya dulcis—Vale placens, Tapissier, 21
Eyck, Jan van, 5, 36, 86
eye-music (= *Augenmusik*), 43, 132, 134, 159, 235, 311, 406, 422
Eytelwein, Heinrich, 638

Fa ch'io riveggia, Monte, 406
fa fictum (= f" flat), 89, 126
"fa la" refrains, 446, 711, 824, 827
Faber, Gregor, 261f
Faber, Heinrich, 333
Fabri, Pierre, 15
faburden (type of English *cantus-firmus* technique), 854f
Factor orbis, Obrecht, 191f

Factum est silentium: Sarum Chant, 114; F. Anerio, 484; Deering, 793; Mouton, 282 (incl. Ex. 57)
Faignient, Noel, 308, 398, 427
Faire, if you expect admiring, Campion, 837 (Ex. 198)
Fairfax Book, see: Manuscripts—London
Fais que je vive, Pevernage, 397
Falcone, Achille, 616
Fall of Lucifer, The (play), 877
Fall of the Leafe, Peerson, 867
Falla, Manuel de, 613
Fallamero, Gabriele, 523
false-relation, see: cross-relation
falsobordone, 91, 166, 215, 248, 274, 286, 488, 491ff (incl. Ex. 114), 611, 804
Fammi una gratia, Isaac, 170
fantasias (= fancies): general, 526, 539, 620, 845, 870; anon., 847f (incl. Ex. 204); Abondante, 527; Antiquis, 549; d'Aquila, 520; Bakfark, 720 (incl. Ex. 164); Banchieri, 550; Barberiis, 528; Bassano, 550; Bull, 871; Byrd, 870; Cabezón, 282; Cooper, 871; Costeley, 561; Daza, 624; Deering, 872; J. Dowland, 847; Du Caurroy, 565; Farnaby, 861; A. Ferrabosco II, 871; Francesco da Milano, 527 (incl. Ex. 122), 555; Francisque, 554; Fuenllana, 623f (incl. Ex. 139a); A. Gabrieli, 539 (Ex. 124); G. Gabrieli, 541; Gibbons, 871f (incl. Ex. 212); Gintzler, 555; Gostena, 528; Guillet, 561f, 565; Henestrosa, 627; Kotter, 664f; Laurencinus Romanus, 527; C. Le Jeune, 565; H. Le Jeune, 566; T. Lupo, 873; Milán, 620, 622, 630; Morley, 870f; Mudarra, 626; Mundy, 861; Narváez, 621; Perino, 527; Philips, 860; Rotta, 555; Santa Cruz, 625; Segni, 550; Stoltzer, 725; Sweelinck, 563; Tomkins, 873; Valderrábano, 623; Valente, 539; Van den Hove, 556; Orazio Vecchi, 539; Ward, 873; Weelkes, 872 (incl. Ex. 213); Willaert, 550
Faragoa de Amor, Vicente, 581
Fardyng, Thomas, 770, 868
Farewell, J. Dowland, 847
Farewell, deere love, Jones, 838
Farewell disdainfull, Morley, 823
Farkas, Gyula (Fark), 715
Farlati, 758
Farmer, Henry G. (Farm), 777f
Farmer, John, 807f, 823, 830, 877
Farnaby, Giles (Farn), 807f, 823, 852, 855, 859, 861f, 865ff
Farnabye's Conceit, Farnaby, 867
Farnese, Alexander, Duke of Parma, 397; Ottavio, Duke of Parma, 322
Farrant, John, 802
Farrant, Richard, 802, 817, 880
Farrenc, Louise, 852
farsa (= *ecloga*), 173
Farsa del Juego de Cañas, La, Sanchez de Badajoz, 631

Fasciculus chorodiarum, Demantius, 756
Fattorini, Gabriele, 541
Faugues, Guillaume or Vincent: Masses, 109, 111ff, 116f, 133; see also 136, 142ff, 198, 202, 204, 227
Faulte d'argent: the melody, 284; Beauvoys, 284; Cavazzoni (*canzone*), 536; A. de Févin, 284; Josquin, 231f (incl. Ex. 43b), 284, 335f, 536
fauxbourdon, 45, 64f, 78, 83ff, 90f, 107f, 142, 165f, 744, 854; with added part on top, 90
fauxbourdon-like writing, 64, 90f, 323, 346, 355, 363, 375; see also: six-three writing
Fayrfax, Robert: biogr. and sacr. mus., 774ff (incl. Ex. 177); see also 764, 768, 773, 785f, 846, 868
Fays, Guillaume de (= Dufay?), 48
Fedé, Jehan, 115, 263
Federhofer, Hellmuth (Federh), 426, 514, 679, 641
Federmann, Maria (Fed), 677f
Féderov, Vladimir, 9
Feicht, Hieronim (Fei), 750
Feininger, Laurence K. J. (Fein), 42, 63, 111, 124, 261, 269, 285
Fekete, Andrew, 721
Feldmann, Fritz (Feld), 633, 644ff, 649, 657, 741, 743, 746
Felis, Stefano, 443
Felix V, antipope (= Amadeus VIII, Duke of Savoy), 50
Felix es, Virgo Maria, Felstin, 747
Felix namque: Sarum Chant, 855f; Tallis, 856f (incl. Ex. 206)
Fellerer, Karl G. (Fell), 458, 465, 473, 482
Fellowes, Edmund H. (Fel), 787ff, 791, 795ff, 799f, 802ff, 806, 811, 814f, 821, 826ff, 831, 833, 836, 841, 846, 860, 867, 869f, 872f, 880, 882
Felstin (= Felsztyn), Sebastian de, 746f, 749
Ferabosco, Domenico Maria, 312, 325, 428f, 456f, 470, 472; see also: Ferrabosco
Feraguti, Beltrame, 26f
Ferand, Ernst T., 36, 91, 142f, 145, 156, 158, 163, 166, 178f, 182, 334, 522, 568, 571
Ferdinand I, Emperor (also King of Hungary and Bohemia, etc.), 449, 592, 641, 701, 722, 725
Ferdinand I (= Ferrante), King of Naples, 138f, 141, 145, 149, 576
Ferdinand II, King of Aragon (= Ferdinand V, King of Castile and León), 208, 578ff
Ferdinand, Archduke of Austria, 514
Ferdinand II, Archduke of the Tyrol, 711
fermata-marked block-chords, 28, 40, 55, 60, 78, 81f, 90, 258, 281, 779, 782
Fermoselle, Diego de, 583
Fermoselle, Juan de, 583
Fernand, Charles (= Carolus), 148
Fernand, Jean (= Johannes), 148
Fernandes, Jehan, 51
Fernández, Lucas (Fernan), 585

Ferrabosco I, Alfonso, 428, 791, 821, 868f
Ferrabosco II, Alfonso, 792, 808, 838, 848, 868, 871
Ferrabosco III, Alfonso, 792
Ferrabosco, Henry, 792
Ferrabosco, John, 792
Ferrabosco, see also: Ferabosco
ferraresa, 445
Ferrari, Gaudenzio, 546
Ferretti, Giovanni, 445
Ferretti, Paolo, 450
Festa, Costanzo: biogr. and madrigals, 313, 319ff (incl. Exx. 66, 67); sacr. mus., 279, 362ff (incl. Ex. 81), 501, 693; see also 285, 316f, 324, 327, 365, 417, 483, 759
Festino nella sera del giovedi grasso, Banchieri, 437
Festivis resonent, Greg. Chant, 470
Festum nunc celebre, Greg. Chant, 471; Heinrich Finck, 649
Fétis, François J. (Fét), 340, 360
Feu couvert, Le, Verdonck, 398
Feuillerat, Albert, 880
Févin, Antoine de, 220, 257, 278ff (incl. Ex. 56), 283ff, 337, 372, 522, 559f (incl. Ex. 129), 670, 680
Févin, Robert de, 278f
Fezandat, Michel, 553
Fiamma Gabriele, 404
Ficino, Marsilio (Fici), 180
Ficker, Rudolf (Fi), 16, 26, 29, 32, 43, 45, 59ff, 65f, 87, 91, 158
fiddle (= *fydel*), 656, 658, 715, 717, 719
Fidi amanti, Torelli, 433
Field of the Cloth of Gold, 291, 775
fifths, consecutive (= parallel), 72, 93, 333f, 434, 444, 590, 618, 644
fifths, see also: diminished fifth
figured bass, see: *basso figurato*
Figurenlehre, 695
Files à marier, anon., 88; Binchois, 88
Filiae Jerusalem, A. Gabrieli, 496
Filippo da Caserta, 31, 33
Finck, Heinrich: biogr. and sec. voc. mus., 639f (incl. Ex. 142); sacr. mus., 242, 646f (incl. Ex. 144), 649f; see also 638, 641ff, 663, 665, 674, 677, 707, 713, 724, 754
Finck, Hermann, 110, 344, 346, 412, 640, 665
Fine, Arnoldus de, 713
Finland, 712
Finley, Lorraine Noel, 297
Fior angelico di musica, Angelo da Picitono, 179
Fischer, Hans (Fisc), 552
Fischer, Wilhelm, 176, 538
Fitzgibbon, H. Macaulay (Fitz), 848, 879
Fitzwilliam Virginal Book, see: Manuscripts— Cambridge
flat before f″ (= *fa fictum*), 89, 126; double flat, 370
flat, see also: chromaticism; key signatures; *musica ficta*
flauto grosso, 546; *f. d'Alemana*, 546

Flecha (the Elder), Mateo, 615
Flecha (the Younger), Mateo, 615f, 700
Flemish School (the term), 9
Flemish texts, chansons with; see under: chanson
Fletcher, Jefferson B., 312
Fletcher, John, 831f
Flood, W. H. Grattan, 767, 773ff, 777f, 810, 877
Flora, wilt thou torment mee, Morley, 825 (incl. Ex. 192b)
Flores de Musica, Coelho, 629f
Flori morir debb'io, F. Anerio, 825 (incl. Ex. 192a)
Florigal, 649
Florimo, Francesco (Flor), 139
Flos florum, Dufay, 81f
Flow my tears (= *Lachrimae*), J. Dowland, 840f (incl. Ex. 200), 843, 847, 865, 874
Flower, Desmond (Flow), 155
flute (= *traversa*), 37, 146ff, 323, 487f, 545ff, 566, 568f
Fogel, Josef (Fog), 723
Fogliano, Giacomo (= Jacobo), 158, 167, 471, 537
Fogliano, Ludovico, 158f, 224, 377
Főkövi, Ludwig (Fők), 148, 221, 722f
folia, 524f (incl. Ex. 121), 625, 628, 631
Foliot (contemp. of Josquin), 38
Foliot (= Philippe de la Folie), 38, 43, 90
folk songs, 54, 73, 189, 206, 256, 355ff, 381, 613, 618, 637, 644, 714f, 718, 729, 732, 740, 821, 861ff
Folz, Hans, 654
Fonde youthe is a bubble (= *Purge me, O Lord*), Tallis, 816
Fontaine, Pierre, 6, 13, 34f, 36, 38, 43f (incl. Ex. 6b), 90
Fontana, Vincenzo, 334
Fontegara, La, Ganassi, 548
For 2 Basses, Weelkes, 872 (incl. Ex. 213)
Ford, Thomas, 809, 811, 838, 873
Forestier, Colinet, 575f
Forestier, Mathurin, 278
Foresto, Matteo, 726
Forkel, J. Nicolaus (Fork), 140, 178, 192, 229, 250, 262, 271
Forlorne hope, J. Dowland, 847
formes fixes, 14ff, 156; decline or absence of *f. f.*, 53, 188, 205, 213, 272, 288, 299; see also: *ballade; bergerette; rondeau; virelai*
Formschneider, Hieronymus, 648, 706
Formula Missae et Communionis, Luther, 676
Fors seulement contre ce que ay promis, Ockeghem, 120
Fors seulement l'attente: Ghiselin, 266; Ghiselin or Josquin, 234; Josquin, 234; La Rue, 272; Obrecht, 187f; Ockeghem, 119f, 126ff, 188, 201, 234, 262, 266, 272, 275; Pipelare, 275
Forster, Georg, 357, 679, 706ff
Fortem virili pectore, Greg. Chant, 467
Forti qui celebres, Cleve, 701

Fortis cum quaevis actio, Brassart, 38
Fortuna (the goddess), 137
Fortuna desperata: anon., 2 settings, 663, 706; Busnois, 102, 201, 214, 240, 559 (anon. keyboard transcr.), 663, 683, 706, 843; Isaac, 214 (2, possibly 3, settings), 663 (another setting)
Fortuna d'un gran tempo, the melody, 159, 214; Josquin (?), 230
Fortunae cantilena anglica, Scheidt, 843
Fortune my foe: the melody, 843; Byrd, 863
Fortune par ta cruaulté, Vincenet, 137
Fortunio, Gian Francesco, 312
Foscari, Francesco, 26, 41
Foschini, Gaetano F. (Fos), 541ff
Fossa, Johann de, 696
fourths, 64, 142, 160, 179, 461, 643; see also: augmented fourth; diminished fourth; non-quartal writing
Fox, Charles Warren, 104, 117, 130, 179, 264, 276f, 335, 555, 588ff, 623, 643, 648, 662
Foxe, John, 769
Foxwell, Agnes K., 770
Fragmenta missarum (Petrucci), 245, 265
Fraknói, Vilmos (Frak), 723
Franc cueur gentil, Dufay, 56
Franc, Guillaume, 360, 503
France (outside Chaps. 1–3, 5–10): in general, 575, 719, 721, 729, 809; Avignon, 575; Béthune, 719; Bordeaux, 225; Lyons, 656, 719; Paris, 716, 731, 810
Francesco (Canova) da Milano, 520, 522, 526ff (incl. Ex. 122), 555
Francesco d'Ancona, 726
Franchois, Johannes, 42, 78, 189, 658
Franci (= Raynaldino?), 220
Franciosio of Florence, 546
Francis I, King of France, 273, 280, 283, 290ff, 296, 298, 359, 527, 553, 561, 570, 591
Francisque, Antoine, 554
Franck (= Marcello Silber), 156
Franck, Melchior, 672, 684, 712
Franco, Fernando, 593
Franco-Flemish School (the term), 9
Franco-Netherlandish influence on English music, 818; on German music, 632, 634, 644, 673, 685, 702, 707; on Italian music, 149ff, 184f, 372, 409, 455; on Spanish music, 579f
Franco-Netherlandish School (the term), 9
François, Duke of Guise, 296
Françon, Marcel, 270
Franz, Robert, 638
Frappier, Jean, 150
Frater Conradus (= *Bruder Conrat*): the melody, 755; Isaac, 755
Frati, Ludovico (Frat), 174, 433
Fraticello si leva, Lo, Razzi, 453
Fratres enim ego accepi, Palestrina, 472
Frauenlob, Heinrich, 652, 675 (incl. Ex. 152), 728, 731
Frederick III, Emperor, 148, 633

Frederick the Wise, Elector of Saxony, 649, 677
free-treble style (the term), 17; see also: treble-dominated style
freely composed Masses, 131f, 480, 787f
freemen's songs, 769
Freitas-Branco, Luiz de (Freit), 598
Fremuit spiritu Jesus: Clemens, 353, 510; Lassus, 510
French influence on English music, 763; on German music, 632ff, 658, 673; on Italian music, 13f, 16, 26f, 30, 33, 291f; on Spanish music, 575f
French Mass, Shepherd, 784
Frere, Walter H., 90, 95, 114, 255, 777ff, 856
Frescobaldi, Girolamo, 411, 848
Fresneau, Jehan, 137
frets, 520; their use on bowed instruments, 548
Freu dich sehr, O meine Seele (the melody = *Ainsi qu'on oit le cerf bruire*), 503
Frey, H. W., 483, 485
fricassée (= quodlibet), 291
Friederich, Bruno (Frie), 688
Frische teutsche Liedlein, Forster, 706
Frisque et galliard, Clemens, 302
Frog he went a-courting, 834
Frog's Galliard, The (= *Now, O now, I needs must part*), the melody, 845
Fröliche polnische Täntze, Demantius, 756
Fronimo, Il, Galilei, 420, 487, 523, 526, 528, 594
Frotscher, Gotthold (Frot), 175, 537ff, 544f, 550, 656f, 664f, 668
frottola, 155ff, 176, 181, 214, 218, 230, 286, 311, 313ff, 322, 643; see also: *barzelletta; canzona; capitolo; oda; strambotto; villota*
frottolists, 158f
Frowe all myn hoffen, 657
Fruytiers, Jan, 355
Frye, Walter, 92ff (incl. Ex. 24), 98, 123, 191, 200f, 209, 244, 281, 372, 635, 658
Fuchswild, Johann, 638, 663
Fuenllana, Miguel de, 594, 612f, 616, 623f (incl. Ex. 139), 627
Fuga a l'unisono, Galilei, 528; *F. al contrario,* Cabezón, 627; *F. del IX tono,* G. Gabrieli, 541; *F. trium vocum* (= *Prennez sur moi*), Ockeghem, 120, 157
Fugger family, 571, 699, 727; Johann Jakob, 690; Octavian II, 687
Fuggir non posso, Caron, 110
Fuhrmann, Georg, 669, 844
Fuions (= *Fuyons*) *tous d'amour le jeu:* Certon, 299; Lassus, 391
Fuit homo missus, Palestrina, 462, 692
Fulgens iubar—Puerpera pura—Virgo post partum, Dufay, 80
Full fathom five, Johnson, 882
Fuller Maitland, John A. (Fuller), 777, 850f, 853, 855ff
Füllsack and Hildebrand, 876
Funck, Heinz (Fun), 634, 676, 689

Fundamenta in *Buxheimer Orgelbuch:* 2 anon., 658f; 2 attrib. to Paumann, 659
Fundamentum, Buchner, 662ff, 754
Fundamentum organisandi, Paumann (in Berlin, Öff. wiss. *40613*), 658ff, 664, 708, 850
Funeral Anthem, Händel, 738
Furnivall, Frederick J., 766, 882
Fust, Johann, 154
Fux, Egidius, 512
Fux, Johann J., 75, 459, 619
fydel, see: fiddle
Fyer, fyer, my hart!, Morley, 824
Fyner, Conrad, 154

Gabriel, 585
Gabriel archangelus, Verdelot, 365, 470
Gabrieli, Andrea (Gabri): biogr. and sec. voc. mus., 413ff (incl. Ex. 98), 419f, 427, 445; sacr. mus., 496ff; instr. mus., 537ff (incl. Ex. 124); mus. for dramatic presentations, 414, 569; see also 373, 401, 418, 544, 667, 687, 699.
Gabrieli, Giovanni (Gabr): biogr. and madrigals, 418f (incl. Ex. 99); sacr. voc. mus., 414, 497ff; instr. mus., 539ff, 545, 551f (incl. Ex. 127); see also 373, 401, 413, 420f, 496, 537, 544, 667, 687, 712f, 753
Gafori (= Gafurius), Franchino (Gaf): biogr. and treatises, 178ff, 587; sacr. voc. mus., 180f; see also 148f, 727, 746; also: Manuscripts—Milan
Gagliano, Marco da, 437, 569
Gaillard, Paul A. (Gaill), 360, 362
gajd (oboe or horn), 715
Galilei, Vincenzo (Gal), 306, 313, 326, 377f, 420, 487, 523, 526, 528, 530, 549, 551, 594, 849
galliards (= *gagliarde*): instr. ensemble: Cooper, 871; J. Dowland, 874, 876; Parsons, 873; keyboard: in Engl. sources, general, 866; in *Parthenia,* 852; Bull, 865; Byrd, 865; Philips, 863, 865; Tomkins, 865; lute: in Engl. sources, 844f; in Ger. sources, general, 671; in Ital. sources, general, 523ff; Adriansen, 556 (incl. Ex. 128); G. F. Anerio, 544; Cato, 756; J. Dowland, 847 (incl. Ex. 203); Francisque, 554; Galilei, 526; Garsi, 526; Molinaro, 526; Terzi, 526; Wecker, 671
Galliculus, Joannes, see: Hähnel, Joh.
Gallicus, Joannes, 182
Gallus (organ builder), 722; see also: Handl, Jacob; Le Cocq, Jehan
Galpin, Francis W. (Galp), 771, 850, 868
Gamez, Diego de, 577
Ganassi, Silvestro di (Gana), 548f
Gandolfi, Riccardo (Gan), 158, 170, 172, 314, 435f
Ganiere, Henri de, 553
Garcilaso de la Vega, 612
Gardane (later Gardano), Antonio, 292, 314, 319, 494, 527, 529, 534, 760

Gardano, Angelo, 401, 410, 415, 434, 495, 538, 616
Garden of Esperance, The, Cornysh, 768
Gárdonyi, Albert (Gár), 721ff, 726
Gareth, Benedetto (= Chariteo), 153
Garison sçay, 106
Garnier, 300
Garsi, Santino, 523, 526
Garside, Charles (Gars), 360
Gascoigne, George, 877f
Gascoing, Johannes, 273
Gascongne, Matthieu, 273, 278, 283, 300, 348, 559
Gaspar (= Jaspar; Jaspart), 219; see also: Weerbecke, Gaspar van
Gasparo, 218
Gaspary, Adolf, 312
Gasper, 771
Gasperini, Guido (Gasp), 157f, 545
Gassenhawerlin und Reutterliedlin (Egenolff), 706
Gastoldi, Giovanni Giacomo (Gast): biogr. and sec. voc. mus., 426f, 445f (incl. Ex. 108), 824f; sacr. mus., 408, 488, 493; instr. mus., 523, 549; see also 711
Gastoué, Amédée (Gas), 61, 84, 576
Gatty, Charles T., 794
Gaude Barbara, 371
Gaude felix Ungaria, 715
Gaude gloriosa, Tallis, 785
Gaude Maria, Okegus (probably = Ockeghem), 123f, 135f
Gaude Mater (= *Quant ce vendra*), Busnois, 107
Gaude mater Polonia, 742
Gaude Virgo . . . quae per aurem concepisti, Battre, 42
Gaude Virgo . . . quia sola meruisti, La Rue, 272
Gaudeamus omnes in Domino . . . Mariae, Greg. Chant, 241, 591
Gaudeamus omnes et laetemur, Gombert, 344
Gauthier, see: Liberti, Gaulterus
Geduld umb Huld, Senfl, 708 (incl. Ex. 159)
Geering, Arnold (Geer), 210, 679, 683
Geiger, Albert (Gei), 585, 610
Geiger (= Konrad von Würzburg), 652
Geiringer, Karl, 223
Geissler, 674
Geloymors (= *Je loe amours*), 634
gemell, see: gymel
genera, Greek, 328f
Genet, Elzéar, see: Carpentras
Gennrich, Friedrich, 332
Gentil dama, Cornago, 577
Gentil galans de gerra, van Stappen, 276
Gentil prince, anon. piece with added altus by Henry VIII, 771
Gentile alma benigna, 30
Genuit puerpera, Compère, 227
Gerardus of Lisa, 140
Gerbert, Martin (Ger), 35, 639

Gerber, Rudolf (Ge), 645
Gerhardt, Carl (Gerh), 677
Gerhardt, Paul, 711
Gerlach, Dietrich, 706
Gerle, Hans, 668f, 671
Germania (the term), 138
Germany (outside Chaps. 12, 13): in general,
    55, 303, 406, 451, 488, 491, 721, 809f;
    Bonn, 482; Cologne, 726; Constance, 212,
    216; Esslingen, 154; Ingolstadt, 747; Mainz,
    154; Schweidnitz, 723; Strasbourg, 359
Germi, 173
Germinavit radix Jesse, Josquin, 259
Gero, Jhan, 319f, 327
Gérold, Théodore (Géro), 55, 205f, 208, 213f,
    233, 265, 270, 338, 381, 683
Geronimo di Bologna, 530
Gerson, Charlier de, 154
Gervaise, Claude, 564
Gesellschaftslieder, 636, 644
Gesius, Bartholomäus, 684, 688
Gesualdo, Carlo, Prince of Venosa: biogr. and
    madrigals, 430ff (incl. Exx. 103, 104);
    sacr. mus., 486f; see also 331, 401, 413, 569,
    838
Gesualdo, Don Fabrizio, 430
Geutebrück, Robert (Geut), 634, 637
Geve not thy minde to heavines, Whythorne,
    816
Geystliche Gesangk Buchleyn, Walter, 674,
    677f, 680
Gheerhart, 308
Gheerkin, 306; see also: Hondt, Gheerkin de;
    Wale, Gheerkin de
Ghequetst ben ick, 565
Ghirlanda di Fioretti Musicali (Verovio),
    447
Ghiselin, Johannes (= Verbonnet), 137, 229,
    234, 266
Ghisi, Federico (Ghi), 25f, 29ff, 167ff, 208,
    420, 567f, 576
Ghizeghem, see: Hayne van Ghizeghem
Già fu chi m'effe cara, Palestrina, 471
Già torna, Marenzio, 421f
Gibbons, Christopher, 813, 852
Gibbons, Edward, 813
Gibbons, Ellis, 813
Gibbons, Orlando (Gib): biogr. and sacr. mus.,
    806, 809, 813f (incl. Ex. 189); sec. voc.
    mus., 819, 832f; instr. mus., 834, 851f,
    857, 860, 865, 868, 871f (incl. Ex. 212);
    see also 811, 815
Gibbons, William, 813
Gieburowski, Wacław (Gieb), 742f, 746
Giesbert, Franz J. (Gies), 103, 120f, 187ff,
    210, 212, 214f, 220, 225, 231, 234, 262f,
    265f, 272, 275, 563, 671
Gigler, Andreas, 701f
Gijón, 585
Giles, Nathaniel, 809, 880
Giles, Thomas, 883
Giles Farnaby's Dreame, His Rest, His Humor,
    Farnaby, 867

Gimel: Migravit Judas, A. de Févin, 279f (incl.
    Ex. 56)
Gintzler, Simon, 555, 669
Gioco della passerina, Banchieri, 437
gioco pieces, 436
Gioie, Le (F. Anerio), 426
Giorgione, 187
Giovanelli, Ruggiero, 425, 447, 482, 485
Giovanni Ambrogio da Pesaro, 176
gipsy music, 717
gittern, see: guitar
Giù per la mala via, 454
Giunto a la tomba, Marenzio, 423f (incl. Ex.
    102)
giustiniana (justiniana), 164f, 445
Giustiniani, Leonardo, 30, 153, 165
Giustiniani, Vincenzo, 528, 569
Giusto, Giovanni di, 575
Glareanus (= Heinrich Loris) (Glar), 120,
    136, 148, 185f, 192, 197, 238, 244, 249,
    256, 259ff, 276, 278, 280, 282, 339, 368,
    377, 481, 532, 562, 639, 680
Gläsel, Rudolf (Glä), 172
Glassenburie, the melody, 807
Gleason, Harold (Gle), 661, 754
Gleut zu Speier, Das (= Trink lang), Senfl,
    707
Glie pur gionto el giorno, Cara, 159
Glogauer Liederbuch, see: Manuscripts—Berlin
Gloria (outside of complete Masses), see vari-
    ous Glorias under: Mass sections
Gloria breve (the term), 60
Gloria, laus et honor: Sarum Chant, 90; Bin-
    chois, 90; Richafort, 336
Gloria tibi Trinitas: Greg. and Sarum Chant,
    779, 833, 845, 857; Blitheman (keyboard),
    857; Bull (keyboard), 857; see also: In
    nomine pieces
Gloriosi principes, Mouton, 281
glosas: general, 581, 619, 627; Cabezón, 628f;
    Coelho, 630; Ortiz, 625; Palero, 627
Glover, Arnold, 882
Glyn, Margaret H., 849ff, 854, 856f, 860, 863ff
Gmelch, Joseph, 651
Gnad kombt oben her, Die, Lassus, 709
Godard, 300, 666
Godebrye, Jacob (= Jacotin), 220
Godefridus, 148
Godendach (= Johannes Bonadies), 178
Goe from my window: the melody, 843, 861f,
    875 (Ex. 214a); Alison (instr. ensemble
    variations), 874ff (incl. Ex. 214b); Byrd
    (keyboard variations), 861f; Engl. lute set-
    tings, 556
Goehlinger, Franz A. (Goehl), 176
Goetze, E. (Goet), 653
Gogos de nuestra Señora, Brudieu, 614
Goís, Damião de, 598
Goldberg Variations, Bach, 133
Goldschmidt, Hugo (Gold), 394
goliard poetry, 301, 764
Gombert, Nicolas: biogr. and sec. voc. mus.,
    255, 303ff (incl. Ex. 62), 696; sacr. mus.,

Gombert, Nicolas (continued)
337f, 341, 343ff (incl. Ex. 77), 352, 500;
G.'s style compared with Lassus's, 507ff;
with Palestrina's, 348, 459; see also 293,
350f, 362, 375, 555, 585, 588, 591, 623,
629, 681, 706, 712, 720, 749, 754
Gombosi, Otto (Gom), 37ff, 57, 73, 100, 111,
115ff, 119ff, 148f, 176f, 187f, 195f, 199ff,
208, 210f, 219, 221, 224, 231, 234, 240,
245, 261ff, 266, 269, 273, 321f, 524, 541,
563, 620, 622, 625, 635, 714, 719f, 722f,
725, 727, 826, 843, 849, 853, 878, 883
Gomólka, Nicholas, 748, 751f (incl. Ex. 172)
Gontrášek, 736, 740
Gonzaga, Duke Guglielmo, 409, 457f, 462,
474; Duke Vincenzo I, 438; Ferdinand,
Viceroy of Sicily, 390; Francesco, 222
Goostly psalmes and spirituall songs, Cover-
dale, 781
Goovaerts, Alphonse, 290
Gordon, Philip (Gord), 792, 874, 882
Gori, Lucrezia, 456, 458
Gorlier, Simon, 561
Gorzanis, Giacomo de, 520, 523, 525
Gossart, A.-M., 150
Gosslau, Werner (Goss), 678, 680
Gosswin, Anton, 709
Gostena, Giovanni Battista dalla (Gost), 432,
528
Gotti, Aurelio, 158, 314, 321
Götz, 658
Goudimel, Claude (Goud): biogr. and chan-
sons, 387; sacr. mus: Catholic, 492. 501f;
Calvinist, 360, 362, 502f (incl. Ex. 116),
683f, 735, 752
Gracuuly (= Gracieulx) et biaulx, Barbireau,
117
Gradenwitz, Peter (Graden), 442, 489
Gradualia, Byrd, 729, 731, 787, 790f
Graduals: anon., 77; Contino, 493; Ockeghem,
130
Grafczyńska, Melania, 744
Grammatica brevis, Niger, 155
Gran Sultana, La, Cervantes, 631
Grand et Vrai Art de plaine rhétorique, Le,
Fabri, 15
Grand Jacques, see: Moderne, Jacques
Granet, Jean, 13
Granjon, Robert, 289
Grans regretz, Les, Hayne, 100, 275
Grates nunc omnes, Greg. Chant, 742
Gratie d'amore, Le, Negri, 525
Grave de l'età, Il, Lassus, 404
Graves, Thornton S., 881
Gravi pene in amor, A. Ferrabosco I, 428
Gravisi, Anteo (Grav), 156
Graw (= Hraw), Andreas, 638
Gray, Cecil, 430
Grazioso da Padova, 26, 28
Grazzini, Anton Francesco (= Il Lasca), 169,
569
Greaves, Thomas, 836, 838
Greban, Arnoul, 150f

Greban, Simon, 151
Greene, Richard L. (Gre), 765f
Greensleeves, the melody, 556, 833, 848,
871
Grefinger, Wolfgang, 663, 706, 722
Greg, Walter W., 879, 881
greghesca, 445
Grégoir, Edouard G. J. (Grégo), 373
Gregory XIII, Pope, 424, 453, 458, 497, 599,
609
Gregory of Sanok (= Grzegorz z Sanoka), 743
Greitter, Matthias, 683
Grenon, Nicolas, 6, 13, 15ff, 22f, 34, 38, 48,
52, 65, 90
Greulich, Martin (Greu), 547f
Greyner zanner, Hofhaimer, 641
Grillo, Carlo, 230
Grillo, El, Josquin, 230
Grillo, Padre Don Angelo, 427
Grimace (= Grimache), 12
Grimpeck, 722
Gritti, Doge Andrea, 368
Groblicz, Martin, 753
Grössel, Heinrich (Grös), 688
Grossin (= Grossim), Estienne, 42f, 92, 743
ground, 539, 845, 853, 862f, 874; see also:
ostinato
Grunzweig, Armand (Grun), 50, 58
Gruyer, Gustave, 221
Gualtier, see: Liberti, Gualterus
Guami, Francesco, 415f
Guami, Gioseffo, 415f, 436, 499, 542ff
Guardan almo pastore, Corteccia, 567
Guárdame las vacas: the melody, 622; Nar-
váez, 622; Mudarra, 622; Valderrábano, 623
Guarini, Giovanni Battista, 415f, 424, 569
Guarino, Battista, 148
Guatemala, 593
Guéroult, Guillaume, 393f
Guerre, La (= La Bataille de Marignan), Jane-
quin, 296ff (incl. Ex. 60), 314, 327, 334,
340, 415, 526, 550, 595, 608, 610, 666
Guerre de Calais, La, Costeley, 366
Guerre de Renty, La, Janequin, 296
Guerrero, Francisco: biogr. and sacr. mus.,
594ff (incl. Ex. 132), 599, 608; adaptations
a lo divino, 592f, 596; see also 597f, 612,
618
Guerrero, Pedro, 594
Guerrero (identity uncertain), 596
Guerrini, Paolo (Guerr), 167, 493
Guglielmo Ebreo (Gugliel), 176
Guiard, 301
Guidiccioni, Giovanni, 313, 322, 404, 569
Guido d'Arezzo, 89f, 587
Guidonian gamut or hand, 35, 89, 360; see
also: solmisation
Guignebert, Charles A. H., 6
guilds of musicians, 80, 877; see also: com-
panies
Guillet, Charles, 561, 565
Guise, Cardinal Charles de, 381; Cardinal Jean
de, 296

guitar (= *chiterna, gittern, quintern*), 148, 528, 555, 557, 566, 620, 625, 656, 740, 851; see also: *vihuela*
Guitarra española, Amat, 625
Güldenton, Hans Sachs, 654
Gumpelzhaimer, Adam, 688
Gurlitt, Wilibald (Gur), 36, 54, 639, 649, 663, 676f
Gusay (= Susay?), 61
Gustate et videte, Lassus, 511
Gustav Vasa, King of Sweden, 712
Gutenberg, Johann, 154, 638
Gutzgauch, Der, Lemlin, 707
Guye, Piero, 771
Guyon, Jean, 341
Guyot (= Castileti), Jean, 301, 511, 629
Guzman, 625
gymel (= *gemell*), 119, 636, 767, 773, 782, 877
Gwynneth, John, 768

Ha que ville et abhominable, Busnois, 101f, 106
Haas, Robert, 394, 568, 571, 689, 691, 701
Haberl, Franz Xaver (Hab), 8, 13, 31, 38, 49f, 52, 79, 82, 84, 107, 109f, 113, 115, 136f, 147, 176, 218, 220, 262, 269, 286, 326f, 368, 371, 420, 425f, 435f, 438, 457, 471, 480ff, 489ff, 494, 499
Hackney, Woodcocke, 873
Hadland, F. A. (Hadl), 772
Hadrianus (= Emanuel Adriansen), 555f
Haec Deum coeli, Obrecht, 191
Haec dies: Sarum Chant, 784; Byrd, 790; Gombert, 345; Shepherd, 784
Haessler, Luise, 358
Häfner, Roland (Häfn), 544, 867
Hahn, see: Han, Ulrich
Hähnel, Joh. (= Galliculus), 182, 681, 688
Hainhofer, Philipp, 669
Hajek, Egon (Haj), 727
Halbig, Hermann (Halb), 79, 481, 525, 559, 663, 666f, 755, 866f
Hall, Edward, 768, 771
Halliwell, James O., 877
Hamburger, Povl, 556
Hamilton, J. A. (Hamil), 140
Hammerich, Angul (Hamm), 713
Han (= Hahn), Ulrich, 154
Händel, Georg F., 738
Handl, Jacob (= Gallus), 301, 700, 736ff (incl. Ex. 168)
Handschin, Jacques (Hand), 8, 14, 17, 39, 61, 180, 252, 365, 772, 818, 849
Hannas, Ruth (Han), 69, 618f, 774
Hans of Constance (= Hans Buchner), 622ff, 754
Hansen, Peter, 350
Happy, O happy he, Wilbye, 830 (incl. Ex. 197)
Harant, Christof, 739, 741
Haraszti, Emile (Hara), 148, 544, 616, 719, 721ff, 725f

Hard by a crystal fountain, Morley, 831
Harich-Schneider, Eta (Har), 630
Harmonia, Flecha the Younger, 615, 626
Harmonia celeste (Phalèse and Bellère), 427
harmonic sequence, 104, 117, 203f, 602
Harmonice Musices Odhecaton A, see: *Odhecaton*
Harmonicorum instrumentorum libri IV, Mersenne, 566
Harmonie Universelle, Mersenne, 386, 504f
Harmonologia Musica, Werkmeister, 377
harmony, see: chord inversion; chord progressions; chromaticism; tonality
harp, 36f, 547, 626, 656, 867
harpsichord (= *clavicembalum*, *cembalo*), 176, 487f, 567, 569, 626, 667, 850
Harrison, Frank Ll. (Harrn), 773, 779
Hartmann, Arnold, 410, 608
Harvest home, the melody, 833
Harzer, see: Resinarius, Balthasar
Has tu point veu, Le Roy, 558
Hashirim Asher Lishlomo, Rossi, 489
Hasprois (= Jo. Asproys), 13, 16
Hassler, Hans Leo (Has): biogr. and sacr. mus., 687f; sec. voc. mus., 711f (incl. Ex. 161); instr. mus., 672, 711; see also 414, 667, 680, 684, 688
Haste thee, O God, Shepherd, 802
Haultin, Pierre, 289
Haussmann, Valentin, 672, 712, 757
haut, see: *instruments hauts*
Have you seen but a whyte lillie grow?, 841
Havergal, William H. (Haver), 503, 801, 810
Hawkins, Sir John (Hawk), 256, 282, 329, 336, 408, 424, 428, 431, 436, 469, 494, 587, 598, 617, 719, 742, 768, 771, 775, 778, 799, 802, 809, 816, 851, 854
Haydon, Glen (Hay), 69, 290
Hayduczky, 716
Hayes, Gerald R., 625, 868
Hayes, Lord (= Sir James Hay), 883
Hayne van Ghizeghem: biogr. and chansons, 99ff, 107, 121, 198, 209f, 219, 224f, 227, 233, 244, 251, 275, 336, 580, 635; see also 6, 98, 228, 263, 286
Hé compaignons, Dufay, 54
Hé logerons nous, Isaac, 212f
head-motif (= motto, *motif de tête, Kopfmotiv*, etc.), 27, 39f, 42, 68, 71f, 76, 108, 114, 196, 237, 347, 646, 774, 787f
Heare the voyce and prayer, Tallis, 799
Heath, John, 797
Hebreo, see: Rossi, Salomone
Heckel, Wolf, 669, 716
Heer Liederbuch, see: Manuscripts—St. Gall
Heidelberg school of *lied* composers, 707
Heinrich (lutenist), 148
Heinricus de Libero Castro (= Louffenberg, Heinrich?), 645
Hektorović, Peter, 758
Helas, Tinctoris, 149
Helas, comment voulés vous, Rore, 311
Helas Madame, Henry VIII, 771

Helas mon bien, Obrecht, 188
Helas mon dueil, Dufay, 53
Helas que devera mon cuer, Isaac, 212f
Helas que pourra devenir, Caron, 110f (incl. Ex. 28), 213
Helas Seigneur, Le Jeune, 503
Hellas Olivier Bachelin, 205
Hellinck, Lupus, 306ff, 342f (incl. Ex. 46), 350, 352, 470, 477, 486, 678ff, 706
Helm, Everett B., 162, 291, 322, 815
Helmholtz, Hermann (Helmh), 617
Hémart, 121, 227
Hembold, Ludwig, 686
Hémeré, 228
hemiola (= *emyolia*), 18, 104, 145f, 216, 711f
Hemmel, Sigmund, 683f
Henestrosa, Luis Venegas de, 625ff
Henrietta Maria, Queen of England (consort of Charles I), 793, 813
Henry IV, King of Castile, 578
Henry V, King of England, 767
Henry VI, King of England, 767
Henry VII, King of England, 769, 850
Henry VIII, King of England, 291, 362, 768, 770ff, 781, 796, 815, 842, 850, 867f, 880, 882
Henry II, King of France, 291, 570
Henry III, King of France, 385, 389, 391, 414, 569, 571
Henry IV, King of France, 383, 566
Henry IV, Shakespeare, 393, 841
Henry V, Shakespeare, 862
Henslowe's Diary, 879
Hentzner, Paul, 881
Heptaméron, Marguerite d'Angoulême, 292
Hérault, Louis, 291
Hercules I and II, Dukes of Ferrara, see under Este, Ercole d' (I and II)
Herford, Charles H, 883
Heribald, 714
Hermann der Münch von Salzburg, 632, 634
Hermannus Contractus, 81
Hernández, D. Ferreol, 599
Herod (play from York Cycle), 877
Heroides, Ovid, 161
Heroldt, Johannes, 688
Héron, A., 15
Heroum soboles, Lassus, 506, 509
Herrero, José J. (Herr), 585
Hert, 119
Hertzmann, Erich (Hertz), 36, 38, 288f, 292, 309f, 320, 324, 334, 349
Herzlich thut mich verlangen (the melody = *Mein gmüth ist mir verwirret*), 711
Herzlieblich Lieb durch Scheiden: the melody, 638; Schoenberg, 638
Herzliebstes Bild, Hofhaimer, 642
Hesdin (= Nicolle des Celliers?), 299, 348, 371, 475, 629
Hesse, Johann, 643
Hessemann, Henricus, 645
Heure e venue, L'—Circumdederunt, Agricola, 208
Heurich, Hugo (Heu), 424, 829

heurier (the term), 7
Hewitt, Helen (Hew), 54f, 100f, 103, 106f, 110f, 120, 137f, 147, 149, 155, 187, 189f, 205f, 208ff, 219f, 223ff, 230ff, 260, 262, 265f, 272, 275, 278, 280, 581, 771
hexachord Masses, see: *Missa ut re mi fa sol la; Missa La sol fa mi re ut*
hexachord variations, 861, 871, 873
Hey ho to the Greenwood, Byrd, 833
Hey Robyn, Joly Robyn, Cornysh, 769f (incl. Ex. 176)
Heyden, Sebald, 110, 219
Heyducken Tantz, 716f
Heyns, Cornelius, 136
Heywood, John, 850, 877
Heywood, Thomas, 881
Hic est beatissimus Evangelista, G. M. Nanino, 482
Hide not thou thy face, R. Farrant, 802
Hill, Arthur G., 619
Hillemann, Willi (Hille), 541
Hilton (the Elder), John, 802
Hilton (the Younger), John, 824, 832
Hindemith, Paul, 656, 707
Hinunter ist der Sonnenschein, Vulpius, 684
Hirsch, Paul (Hir), 179
Hirzel, Bruno (Hirz), 680, 709
Hoboecken dans, the melody, 565
hoboy, 879
Hobrecht, see: Obrecht
Hoby, Sir Thomas, 158
Hoc est praeceptum meum, Morales, 591
hocket, 23, 61, 106, 210f, 744, 856
Hodie Christus natus est: Comes, 611; G. M. Nanino, 483; Palestrina, 472; Rore, 376; Sweelinck, 518
Hodie completi sunt, G. Gabrieli, 498
Hodie nobis de Virgine, Compère, 227
Hodie sanctus benedictus, Philips, 794
Hoeber, Karl, 634
Hoffmann von Fallersleben, August H. (Faller), 356
Hofgreff, 718
Hofhaimer, Paul (= Messer Paolo): biogr. and sec. voc. mus., 640ff (incl. Ex. 143), 670, 705, 722; instr. mus., 662 (incl. Ex. 148); see also 221, 638f, 643, 656, 663, 666, 677, 707, 724
Hofmann, Gertrude (Hof), 682
Högler, Fritz (Hög), 379
Hol, Johannes C. (Hol), 332, 433, 435, 445
Holborne, Anthony, 844, 849, 873, 876
Hole, Robert, 852
Hollander, Christian, 700, 702, 738
Hollandrinus (= Olendrinus; Valendrinus), 743
Homme armé, L', the melody, 73 (incl. Ex. 18), 101, 107, 111, 114, 117, 125, 136, 146, 149f, 196, 228, 233, 237f, 261, 265, 269, 275, 285, 470, 689; anon. setting, 73, 75, 99; Josquin, 233f; Morton, 99
Homme banni, L': Agricola, 210; Barbingant, 210

Homme inconstant, L' (= *Si par souffrir*), Monte, 396
Homo natus de muliere, Wilbye, 792
Hond, de, see: Canis, Cornelius
Hondt, Gheerkin de, 301, 306
Honesta defensio, Spataro, 587
Honterus, Johann, 726
Hooper, Edmund, 807
Hopkins, John, 796, 801
Hoquetus David, Machaut, 23
Hor chi mai, Corteccia, 567
Hor ved' amor, Arcadelt, 322
Horace, 143, 369f, 381, 430, 435, 657
Höre, Gott, meine Stimm', Luther?, 673
horn, 448
Hornepype, Aston, 853
Horsley, Imogene (Hors), 394, 412
Hortus conclusus, Greg. Chant, 345
Hortus musarum (Phalèse), 303, 555, 557
Hosanna to the Son of David: Gibbons, 813f (incl. Ex. 189); Weelkes, 806
Hospodine pomiluj ny, Bishop Adalbert?, 728, 730
Hostis (= *Crudelis*) *Herodes*: Greg. Chant, 83, 467; Dufay, 83; Palestrina, 467
Hothby, John, 110, 178
Houdoy, Jules (Hou), 8, 13, 50, 65, 110, 113, 227
Howes, Frank, 791
Howre's Recreation in Musicke, Alison, 819
Hoyda, hoyda, joly rutterkyn, Cornysh, 771
Hraw (= Andreas Graw), 638
Huber, Kurt (Hu), 306, 327, 366, 514, 710
Hubertus de Salinis, 22
Huc me sydereo—Plangent eum, Josquin, 255
Hucher, Antonio, 314
Hughes, Dom Anselm (Hugh), 765, 768, 773ff
Hughes, Charles W., 794, 831f, 842f, 873
Huigens, P. Caecilianus (Huig), 699
Huizinga, Johan, 6
Humanism, its effect on music: in Dalmatia, 758; in England, 839, 877f; in France, 381ff; in Germany, 639, 679, 705f; in Hungary, 725ff; in Italy, 310f, 328f, 378, 450, 458, 474f; in Poland, 743, 747f
Hume, Captain Tobias, 836, 873f
Hund, Der, Isaac, 671
Hungary, incl. Transylvania (outside Chap. 14), 116, 147, 221, 370, 438, 639
Hunnis, William, 796
Hunt, J. Eric (Hun), 795f
Hunt, Thomas, 811
Hunting Galliard, Tompkins, 865
Hunyadi, John, 722
Hupff auff, see: after-dance
Huschke, Joachim (Husch), 696f
Husitska, Dvořák, 734
Huss, Jan, 729, 732f
Hussites and Hussite music, 730, 732ff; see also: Taborites; Utraquists
Hutchinson, Loving (Hutch), 623
Hutter, Josef, 729
Hygons, Richard, 773

Hykaert (= Bernardo Ycart), 149
Hylaire (= Hilaire Penet), 285
hymn cycles: Corteccia, 365; Dufay, 83ff; J. Martini, 222; Palestrina, 467; Porta, 494f; Victoria, 604
hymn settings (individual): in vocal polyphony, 90f, 363, 494f, 649, 693, 724, 784, 786, 791; in keyboard mus., 536, 562, 628f, 854f; in instr. ensemble mus., 565, 869f; see also: processional-hymn form
Hymnodia, Porta, 345
Hymns of Mesomedes, 420
Hymnus de septem doloribus (= *Memorare Mater Christi*), Pipelare, 275
Hystorigraphi aciem, Nicholas of Radom, 744

I smyle to see howe yow devyse, 816
I will exalt thee, Tye, 798
Iam sol recedit (= *O lux beata Trinitas*), Greg. Chant, 83
Ic en hebbe gheen ghelt, Obrecht, 189
Ich far dahin: the melody, 638; Brahms, 638
Ich hab heimlich ergeben mich, Hofhaimer, 641
Ich hab vermeint, Regnart, 726
Ich schell mein Horn: anon., 638; Brahms, 638
Ich stund an einem Morgen: Arnoldus de Bruck, 708; Heinrich Finck, 640 (incl. Ex. 142); Senfl, 707
Ich weiss mir ein meidlein, Lassus, 709f (incl. Ex. 160)
Ick seg adieu, Clemens, 357
Ick weedt een molenarinne, Pipelare, 275
iconography, musical, 36f, 86, 179, 187, 229, 270, 376, 464, 546, 655f, 690f; see also: marquetry
Idelsohn, Abraham Z. (Id), 442, 489, 705
identity problems, 32, 220, 300, 305ff, 327, 341, 579, 802, 813
If my complaints (the melody = *Captaine Digorie Piper His Galliard*), J. Dowland, 876
If the deepe sighs, Ward, 831
If ye love mee, Tallis, 799
Ihesu Criste rex superne, Polish sequence, 742
Il est bel et bon: Passereau, 299; G. Cavazzoni (*canzone*), 536
Il estoit une religieuse, Lassus, 393
Il fait bon fermer son huys, 206
Il faut que de tous mes esprits, Sweelinck, 517f
Il me suffit, Sermisy, 295, 356, 564, 696
Il m'est si grief, Vide, 43f (incl. Ex. 6a)
Il n'est sy doulce vie, Richafort, 302
Ileborgh, Adam, 535, 657f; see also: Manuscripts—Philadelphia
Illae dum pergunt, Tallis, 786
Illibata Dei Virgo, Josquin, 228, 256
Illing, Carl-Heinz (Ill), 363, 590, 649
Ilumina oculos meos, Palestrina, 466; de Silva, 471
Ilz sont bien pelez (the melody = *Adieu mes amours*), 206
Im Mayen, Lassus, 738

Imelmann, Rudolf (Imel), 816
imitation, early extensive uses, 27, 42, 56, 82, 105f, 123f, 128, 241; early exx. of pervading i., 88, 105, 224, 249f; gradual adoption of i. as a structural element, 27, 88, 105, 249f, 344; late adoption of i. by English, 773, 775; decline of exact i., 405, 488, 508f, 692; anticipatory i. of the *c.f.*, 76, 93, 108, 112, etc.; 5 types of paired i., 257f; rhythmic i., 61, 63, 407, 509; i. with varying time-intervals, 110f, 213, 279, 606, 870; tonal i., see: tonal answer
imperial measure, 37
Imperii proceres, Isaac, 649
Improperia: Palestrina, 468; Victoria, 604
Improperium expectavit cor meum: Lassus, 693; Palestrina, 466
improvisation, 38, 42, 64, 142ff, 153, 166, 176f, 325, 412, 529, 545, 562, 571, 616, 621, 625, 630, 766; see also: ornamentation; *sortisatio*
In Christi Jesu thalamo, 651
In convertendo: Rore, 511; Ruffo, 490
In darknesse let mee dwell, J. Dowland, 840 (Ex. 199)
In Deo speravit, Merulo, 496
In die tribulationis: Guami, 499; Jaquet of Mantua, 696
In dulci jubilo, 674, 712
In ecclesiis, G. Gabrieli, 499, 552
In exitu Israel: Binchois, 90; Galilei, 487; Willaert, 373
In goinge to my naked bedde, Edwards, 816
In Gottes Namen fahren wir: the melody, 674; Isaac, 643
In hora ultima, Lassus, 694
In hydraulis, Busnois, 108f, 118, 248
In illo tempore loquente Jesu, Gombert, 344f (incl. Ex. 77), 500
In illo tempore Maria Magdalene, Mouton, 281
in medio chori (the term), 806
In Monte Oliveti: Croce, 500; Lassus, 695; Zieleński, 753
In nomine pieces: anon., 845f; Blitheman, 857; Brewster, 868; Bull, 858 (incl. Ex. 207); Byrd, 868f; A. Ferrabosco I and II, 868; Gibbons, 833, 857, 868; Parsons, 868; Picforth, 869; Tallis, 868; Taverner's basic *I. n.* and direct adaptations, 779f (incl. Ex. 179), 797, 845f, 868; Tye, 868f (incl. Ex. 211); Weelkes, 868; White, 846 (incl. Ex. 202), 868; Whytbroke, 868
In nomine Jesu, Josquin, 256
In principio erat verbum, Josquin, 254
In qual parte del ciel, Monte, 407 (incl. Ex. 95)
In questo dì giocondo, Monte, 407
In seculum (tenor from Greg. Chant), 100
In te Domine speravi: Josquin, 230, 583; Lupus, 341, 471; Szamotułczyk, 749 (incl. Ex. 170)
In te speravi, Palestrina, 466f

Incarnacion, Greban, 151
Incessament livré, Josquin, 233
Incessament mon povre coeur: La Rue (not Josquin), 273; lute transcr., 557
Incipite Domino, Croce, 500
Inclina cor meum, Monte, 703
Inclita stella maris, Dufay, 81
incunabula containing music, 37, 154f, 335, 577, 586f
Infelix ego, Rore, 376
Inferno, Dante, 400, 413
Infunde unctionem, 754
Ingegneri, Marc'Antonio: biogr. and madrigals, 437f, 490; sacr. mus., 469, 491; instr. mus., 550; see also 500, 666
Ingeniosa Comparación, Villalón, 579
Ingredere foelicissimis auspiciis urbem tuam, Corteccia, 365 (Ex. 82)
initial motif, see: Head-motif
Innocentes pro Christo: Marenzio, 482; Palestrina, 464
Innsbruck ich muss dich lassen, see: *Isbruck . . .*
Institution harmonique, Guillet, 562
Instruction de partir toute musique facilement en tabulature de luth, Le Roy, 554, 558; Eng. transls., 842
instrumental ensembles and ensemble music: England, 867ff; France and Low Countries, 563ff; Germany, 672; Hungary, 721f; Italy, 546ff; Poland, 756f; Spain, 615, 626; see also: bands, civic; consort
instrumental solo music, see under name of instrument, also: keyboard music
instruments, see under name of instrument; see also: consort; instrumental ensembles; keyboard instruments; performance practice
instruments hauts, bas, 13, 37, 99, 152, 174
instruments in theatrical performances, 151f, 172, 174, 567ff, 877ff, 883ff, see also: dramatic presentations; instrs. with other sec. voc. mus., 35f, 54, 120, 160, 366, 411, 636, etc., see also: ayre; instrs. (except organ) with sacr. voc. mus., 22, 40, 42f, 67, 181, 216, 486ff, 497, 499, 610, 725, 740, 808f
integer valor (the term), 70
Integer vitae, 161
Intellige, Morago, 598
Intemerata Dei Mater, Ockeghem, 123
Inter natos mulierum: Sarum Chant, 90; Binchois, 2 settings, 90
intermedi (= *intermezzi*), 173, 437, 567ff, 882
Intermedii et Concerti, Malvezzi, 570
intonation (= tuning): equal temperament, 379, 423, 531, 850, 861; just intonation, 158, 377, 586; mean-tone tuning, 530f, 617f, 850; Pythagorean tuning, 377, 586
intonations in plainsong for Mass sections, 23, 39, 64f, 90, 130
intonazioni, A. and G. Gabrieli, 539f

Intonuit de coelo, Aichinger, 699 (incl. Ex. 156)
intrade: Hassler, 672; Orologio, 672
Introductory to Wryte and to Pronounce Frenche, The, Barclay, 882
Introduxit me rex, Palestrina, 465
Introits: anon., 77; Contino, 493; Porta, 494
introitus (= introduction), instrumental or vocal, 22, 42
Invention for two to play upon one lute (= *My Lord Chamberlaine his Galliard*), J. Dowland, 847
inversion, see: chord inversion; mirror canon
Inviolata integra: Greg. Chant, 251, 338, 345, 470; Bauldeweyn, 338; Josquin, 251; Willaert, 372
Io che l'onde raffreno, Malvezzi, 570
Io dico e dissi e dirò, Corteccia, 325f (incl. Ex. 70a)
Io mi credea scemare, Gero, 327
Io mi son giovinetta: D. Ferabosco, 312, 470, 472; Sweelinck, 429
Io non son però morto, Wert, 410
Io piango, Marenzio, 421, 423 (Ex. 101)
Io son ferito: Nola, 696; Palestrina, 403, 444, 471, 490, 696
Io son l'ocello che non pò volare, Tromboncino, 162 (Ex. 32)
Io tacerò, Gesualdo, 431
Io vidi amor, Macque, 411, 430
Iocundare Ierusalem, Mouton, 281
Iranzo, Miguel Lucas de, 577f
Isaac, Heinrich (= Yzak; Arrigo Tedesco): biogr., 169f, 212, 229, 642; sec. voc. mus. with Ger. text, 643f, 684, 706; other sec. voc. mus., 168ff, 172, 212ff (incl. Ex. 39), 286, 755; sacr. mus., 117, 214ff (incl. Ex. 40), 647ff (incl. Ex. 145), 650, 679, 723; instr. mus., 662, 671; see also 54, 175, 184, 220, 639, 666, 677, 681, 689, 707f, 724
Isabella of Portugal, Empress (consort of Charles V), 592
Isabella, Queen of Hungary (consort of John Zápolya), 721
Isabella of Castile, Queen of Spain, 208, 578, 583
Isabella, Archduchess (co-ruler of the Netherlands), 398, 793
Isabella of Portugal, Duchess of Burgundy, 51
Isagoge in artem testudinariam, Besard, 844
Isbruck ich muss dich lassen: the melody (= *O Welt ich muss dich lassen; Nun ruhen alle Wälder*), 643; Isaac, 2 settings, 643f, 647, 684
Isidore of Seville, 141
Isnardi, Paolo, 488
isomelic writing, 80, 92f, 765
isorhythmic motet, 21f, 27, 41f, 63, 77ff, 89f, 565; i. rondeau, 16; i. sequence, 16, 61
Isoz, Kálmán, 722
Issacs, J., 880
Ista est speciosa, Greg. Chant, 268
Iste confessor: Greg. Chant (mode 8), 191,

467, 470; Greg. Chant (= *Ut queant laxis*), 83; Greg. Chant (= *Christe sanctorum*), 83; Dufay, 83, 467; Obrecht, 191; Palestrina, 467
Iste Sanctus, Victoria, 601
Istitutioni harmoniche, Zarlino, 377, 475
istromento (= *instromento*) *perfetto* (the term), 529; *i. piano e forte,* 530; see also: *strumento*
It doth me good when Zeph'rus rains, Whythorne, 816
It was a lover and his lass, Morley, 835, 882
Italian influence: on English music, 815f, 819ff, 829, 831f, 841f, 847, 853, 860; on French music, 7, 9, 14, 16, 21, 33, 52, 84, 161, 184, 208, 211, 288, 291f, 387, 400; on German music, 643, 673, 685, 687f, 690, 698f, 710f; on Spanish music, 576f, 612
Italo-Burgundian School (the term), 53
Italian Madrigalls Englished, Watson, 818, 821, 874
Italy, incl. Trent (outside Chaps. 1, 4, 6–10): in general, 49f, 52, 59, 80, 86, 119, 263, 576, 594, 642, 713, 719, 721, 726, 810f, 816; Bergamo, 618; Bologna, 222, 586f; Cremona, 190; Ferrara, 49, 187, 212, 229, 260, 266, 656, 719; Florence, 51, 184, 207, 212, 229; Loreto, 276; Mantua, 208, 222, 658, 726; Milan, 207, 217f, 220, 223, 228f, 658; Modena, 229; Naples, 139ff, 149, 576f, 592, 617f, 723; Padua, 276, 285, 720f, 726; Palermo, 616; Rome, 218, 229, 260, 263f, 265f, 276, 285, 584, 586f, 594, 598f, 609, 616f, 698, 730; Urbino, 616; Venice, 656, 663, 721
Ite caldi sospiri, Brocco, 161
Ite, missa est, Greg. Chant, 593
Ite, rime dolenti, Rore, 696
Itinerarium Germaniae, Hentzner, 881
Ivo de Vento, 666, 710
Ivo (not de Vento), 327
I'vo piangendo, A. Gabrieli, 414f (incl. Ex. 98)

J.S., 747
Ja que lui ne s'i attende, Busnois, 101
jácara, 631
Jachet, see: Jaquet
Jachimecki, Zdzisław (Jach), 742ff, 749ff
Jacob (lutenist), 554, 755f
Jacqueline d'Hacqueville, 101
Jacomi (3 homonyms; 1 = Selesses), 575
Jacopo da Bologna, 52
Jacotin, 220, 285; see also: Godebrye; Le Bel
Jagiełło, Cardinal, son of Casimir IV, 746
Jagiełło, King of Poland, 745
Jahn, Fritz (Jah), 656
Jakoubek of Stříbra, 733
Jam Christus astra ascenderat, Greg. Chant, 470
Jam lucis orto sidere, Lassus, 695
Jamais tant que je vous revoye, Binchois, 89
Jambe-de-Fer, Philibert, 504

James I, King of England, 832, 882
James, Montagu, 772
James, Philip (Jas), 529f, 850
Jamès, jamès, jamès, Mouton, 280
Jamès je n'auré envie (= L'amour de moy), 206
Jamès que là ne peut estre, Brumel, 263
Jamot, Paul (Ja), 12
Jan of Jenštejn, Archbishop of Prague, 731
Jan of Lublin, 716, 754
Jane Pickering's Lute Book, see: Manuscripts —London
Janequin, Clément: biogr. and sec. voc. mus., 291, 295ff (incl. Ex. 60), 305, 314, 319, 327, 334, 340, 361, 363, 539; sacr. mus., 340; see also 293, 299ff, 362, 388, 390, 415, 550, 554, 595, 608, 610, 614, 629, 666, 712, 754
Jankowska, Duchna, 744
Japart, Johannes, 219f, 663
Jaquet (= Jachet) of Mantua, 327, 366f (incl. Ex. 83), 373, 470, 480, 696, 703
Jardin de Plaisance, Le, 54, 97, 207, 392
Jardin musiqual (Waelrant and Laet), 505
J'ay bien cause de lamenter, Josquin, 234
J'ay bien choisi, Hayne or Busnois, 100
J'ay cherché la science, Lassus, 391
J'ay mis mon coeur, Arcadelt, 356
J'ay pris amours a ma devise: anon. (3 settings with same S and T but different Contra-tenors), 100f; reworkings of the pre-existent material: general, 205; by Busnois, 107; by Isaac, 214 (3 settings), 649; by Japart, 219; by Obrecht, 188; text incipit in quodlibet, 207
J'ay pris amours tout au rebours, Busnois, 107
J'ay pris ung poul en ma chemise, 101
J'ay veu le cerf, Manchicourt, 351
J'ayme bien celui qui s'en va, Fontaine, 35
J'ayme trop souffrir la mort, Costeley, 388
Je cuide, Japart?, 219
Je file, Van Wilder, 873
Je loe amours, Binchois, 87, 634, 658
Je me complains de mon amy, Josquin, 233
Je me complains piteusement, Dufay, 54
Je me recommande humblement, Binchois, 88
Je ne demande autre degré, Busnois, 103, 203, 210f
Je n'ay dueil: Agricola, 209, 261, 266; Ocke-ghem, 119f, 209, 266
Je ne demande lialté, Busnois, 103
Je ne puis plus—Unde veniet, Dufay, 55
Je ne puis vivre ainsi, Busnois, 102ff (incl. Ex. 25)
Je ne vis oncques la pareille, Dufay or Binchois, 58, 196, 211, 233, 263, 266, 271
Je prends en gré, Clemens, 302
Je sey bien dire, Josquin, 232
Je suis Amour: La Grotte, 389; transcr. for voice and lute, 558
Je suis desheritée: Cadéac or Lupus, 307, 341, 471, 475, 478 (Ex. 112a), 565, 696; Jacotin, 307

Je suis tellement amoureux, Bertrand, 389
Je suis venut, Busnois, 100, 107
Jean II, Duke of Bourbon, 100
Jean de Montchenu Chansonnier, see: Manu-scripts—Paris
Jeppesen, Knud (Jep), 45, 54, 75, 98ff, 104, 106f, 117, 120, 137, 142f, 149, 159ff, 165ff, 175, 177f, 180f, 195, 212, 214, 219, 227, 238, 253, 258, 264, 286, 314, 354, 402, 457, 460f, 467, 469ff, 474f, 480, 483, 492, 529, 532, 534f
Jerusalem Delivered, Tasso, 400, 409
Jerusalem surge, Clemens, 353
Jesaja dem Propheten das geschah (in Ger-man Mass), 676
Jesperssøn, Niels (Jesp), 713
Jesu corona Virginum (the melody = Nunc Sancte nobis Spiritus; Aurora lucis rutilat; Aurora coelum): Greg. Chant, 467; Pales-trina, 467
Jesu, Jesu (= Visin, visin), 167
Jesu dulcis memoria: anon. (not Victoria), 601; Deering, 793
Jesu nostra redemptio (= Salutis humanae sator): Greg. Chant, 83, 467, 470; Dufay, 83; Palestrina, 467
Jesu Redemptor omnium (melody = Christe Redemptor . . . Conserva; Christe Re-demptor . . . Ex Patre), Greg. Chant, 85
Jesus Christus unser Heiland, the melody, 676
Jesus dulcedo cordium, Deering, 793
Jesus ist ein süsser Nam, the melody, 679, 696
Jewell, A. H., 794
Jezusa Judasz przedał, 745
Jhan of Ferrara, Maistre, 327, 366, 376
Jhan of Verona, Maistre, see: Nasco, Giovanni
jig (= gigge): general, 863, 866, 868; Bull, 866; Farnaby, 866
Jireček, Constantin (Jir), 758
Jižt mne vše radost ostává, Záviš (incl. Ex. 166)
Joan of Arc, 5, 263
Joanna, Queen of Castile, 208
Joannis Lelandi . . . Collectanea, 767
Joaquim, Manuel, 584, 598
Jobin, Bernhard, 716
Jocasta, Euripides, 878
joculatores, 715, 721
Jöde, Fritz, 638f, 641ff, 677ff, 686ff, 691, 699, 702, 706ff
Jodelle, Étienne, 571
Johanna of Austria, 568
Johannes (= Jean Fernand), 148
John I, King of Aragon, 575
John II (the Good), King of France, 5
John III, King of Portugal, 594, 598
John IV, King of Portugal, 598, 793
John of Luxemburg, King of Bohemia, 729
John (= Juan), Prince (son of Ferdinand and Isabella), 578, 583
John Sigismund, Prince of Transylvania, 720ff, 726
John V, Duke of Brittany, 7

John the Fearless, Duke of Burgundy, 5f, 43
John the Steadfast, Elector of Saxony, 655
Johnson, Alvin, 252, 375
Johnson, Edward, 807
Johnson, John, 844
Johnson, Robert (d. 1554), 777f, 785, 796, 851, 873
Johnson, Robert (d. 1634), 882
Jones, Inigo, 815, 882
Jones, Robert (fl. 1530), 768
Jones, Robert (fl. 1600), 835, 838, 880
jongleurs and jongleresses, 7
Jonson, Ben, 841, 880, 882f
Jorges, (= Georget de Brelles), 227, 263
Joseph, lieber Joseph mein (= Resonet in laudibus): the melody, 674; Calvisius, 687
Josquin des Prez (= Jusquin d'Ascanio): biogr., 228ff; J.'s historical position, 4, 459, 506; Bartoli's opinion of J., 259f; sec. voc. mus., 118, 165, 205, 230ff (incl. Ex. 43), 266, 284, 286, 304f, 536, 583, 588; sacr. mus., 73, 102, 235ff (incl. Exx. 45-50), 262, 270, 279, 336, 342f, 371, 475, 511, 565, 675 (incl. Ex. 152), 690, 703ff; J.'s style compared with Palestrina's, 460, 466, 468, 481; traits of J.'s style mentioned elsewhere, 4, 76, 106, 188, 355, 461; see also 93, 100, 123, 137, 147, 181, 184ff, 190f, 219ff, 223, 227, 273, 277f, 285, 293, 303, 308f, 335f, 338, 344, 368, 372, 375, 401, 409, 450, 472, 512, 517, 532, 591, 618, 623, 629, 645, 662f, 666, 674, 679, 681, 689, 697, 724, 726, 754, 774f
Jour s'endort, Le (= Ce jour le doibt), Dufay, 55
Jouissance vous donneray: Sermisy, 292f (incl. Ex. 59), 310, 557; Willaert, 310 (incl. Ex. 63)
Joye, Gilles, 98, 115
Joye me fuit, Busnois, 105, 196
Juan of Ureña, Count, see: Bravo, Juan
Jubilate Deo: G. Gabrieli, 498; Marenzio, 482; Morales, 591, 608; Palestrina, 465f
Judas mercator, Victoria, 603
Judenkünig, Hans, 668ff
Julbe, Vicente G., 593, 595f, 600, 610f
Julian, John (Jul), 735, 796
Julius II, Pope, 285
Julius III, Pope, 456
Julius de Modena, see: Segni, Giulio
July and Julian (a play), 842
Jung, Anton, 727
Junckfraw, dein schöne gstalt, Hassler, 711
Jussona, La, Merulo, 540
Just, H., 833
just intonation, see: intonation (= tuning)
Juvenis qui puellam, Dufay, 78f

K.H. [King Henry's] Mirth or Freeman's Songs, 769
Kabis, Sister Mary Elise, 60

Kade, Otto (Kad), 51, 165, 274, 327, 333, 339, 366, 376, 493, 515, 596, 604, 682, 689, 708, 757
Kahmann, B. (Kah), 278
Kallenbach, Hans (Kal), 706
Kalwitz, see: Calvisius, Seth
Kan ich nit über werden, 636
Kapassa (= Kypassa; Kypascie), see: Chi passa; Qui passe
Kargel, Sixt, 669
Karp, Theodore C., 226, 846, 869
Karpeles, Maud, 834
Kastendieck, Miles M. (Kasten), 840
Kastner, J. (Kast), 726
Kastner, M. Santiago (Kastn), 615, 620, 626ff
Kaufmann, Paul, 706
Keiner, Ferdinand (Kein), 432
Kellogg, King (Kel), 690
Kemp, Will, 881
Kempa, Bishop Jan, 742
Kempers, see: Bernet Kempers, K. P.
Kemps Nine Daies Wonder, Kemp, 881
Kendall, Raymond (Ken), 661, 683
Kenney, Sylvia W. (Kenn), 95f
Kentish (= Rochester), the melody, 807
Kenton, Egon F., 537
Kerle, Jacobus de, 397, 449, 451f, 473, 698, 700, 756
Kerman, Joseph, 428, 815, 819, 821, 824f, 831
Kethe, William, 797
Kettenton, Folz, 654
kettledrum, 721, 878
key signatures: conflicting k. ss., 18, 45ff (incl. Exx. 8-13), 230, 611, 681, 854; uniformity recommended, 182; unusual k. ss. for the period, 41, 54, 272
keyboard accompaniment, 176f, 411f, 447, 604f, 607f, 676, 753, 803, 805f, 812, 836, 871; k. duets, 544, 855; k. ornamentation and figuration, 174, 533f, 537f, 544f, 559f, 627, 661, 664ff, 754, 850, 854ff, 859ff, 866f; other aspects of k. performance practice, 529ff, 537, 544f, 565, 629, 663, see also: musica ficta; k. transcriptions, 55, 161, 174, 291, 536, 538f, 559f, 628, 658, 662f, 666f, 754, 816, 851, 859f; k. variations, 536, 562, 628, 861ff
keyboard instruments, stringed: makers, 176, 180, 529f, 561, 850; structure, 36, 530f, 667f
keyboard music (organ and stringed): England, 849ff; France, 558ff; Germany, 657ff; Hungary, 716f, 722f; Italy, 174ff, 528ff; Low Countries, 562ff; Poland, 753ff; Spain, 625ff; see also: suites; also under names of various dances
keyboard tablature: English, 853; French, 559; German, 659, 663ff; Italian, 528f; Spanish, 626
Kicher (= Kiejcher), Bartholomaeus, 753
Kiesewetter, Raphael (Kies), 8f, 56, 59, 101, 104, 107, 111, 114, 158, 192, 230, 262f, 334, 416, 424, 432, 532, 568, 570

Killing, Joseph (Kill), 225, 336, 368, 469, 481ff, 488, 492, 497, 501
King's Hunt, Bull or Cosyn, 866
Kinkeldey, Otto (Kin), 37, 135, 155, 164, 174, 176f, 180, 411f, 447, 493, 500, 528ff, 537f, 540f, 544, 547, 559, 569f, 605, 619, 626, 629f, 844
Kinsky, Georg (Kins), 154f, 426, 447, 512, 529f, 544f
Kirbye, George, 807f, 829 (incl. Ex. 196)
Kittridge, George L., 834
Kiwi, Edith, 444
Kleber, Leonhard, 662ff (incl. Ex. 149), 754
Klefisch, Walter (Klef), 321ff, 400
Klein, Valentin, 722
Kleine Schlacht, Die, 668
Klingende Ton, Hans Sachs, 654f (incl. Ex. 146)
Klingenstein, Bernhard, 699, 702
Klingsohr, 652
Knapp, J. Merrill, 536
Knell, A, Johnson, 873
Knights of the Golden Fleece, 57
Knox, John, 801
koboz (lute), 715
Kochanowski, Jan, 751f
Koczirz, Adolf, 421, 528, 623, 656, 667f, 689
Kodály, Zoltán (Kod), 714
koleda, 731, 733
Komm Gott Schöpfer, heiliger Geist, derivation from *Veni Creator Spiritus,* 674
Komm heiliger Geist, Eccard, 685 (incl. Ex. 154)
Konrad von Würzburg (= Geiger), 652
Kopfmotiv, see: Head-motif
Kornmüller, Utto (Korn), 140, 145, 178
Körte, Oswald (Kör), 157, 521, 525, 553, 661, 668f
Korte, Werner, 25ff, 31ff, 69
Kosack, Hans-Peter, 299, 699, 671, 755
Kotter, Hans, 662ff, 754
Kraus, Hedwig, 375, 537
Krebs, Carl G., 530, 542, 544f
Krenek, Ernst, 135
Kretzschmar, Hermann (Kret), 412, 552, 757
Kriesstein, Melchior, 300, 304, 681
Kristeller, Paul O. (Krist), 180
Kromer, Martin, 747
Kroyer, Theodor von (Kr), 158, 323, 325, 328f, 332, 346, 422f, 431f, 445ff, 514, 532, 592, 611, 690, 702, 707
Ktož jsú boží bojovníci, 734 (incl. Ex. 167)
Kugelmann, Johann, 678
Kühn, Alfred, 652
Kuhn, Max R. A. (Ku), 394
Kühner, Hans (Küh), 50, 58
kürt (horn), 715
Kurtzweilige teutsche Lieder, Regnart, 710
Kurtzweiligen guten frischen teutschen Liedlein, Forster, 357
Kurzweil ich hab, Heinrich Finck, 640
Kyrie (outside of complete Masses), see various Kyries under: Mass sections; omission

of K. from polyphonic Masses, 95, 227, 765, 773ff, 780, 782
Kyrie as Anglican response, 797
Kyrleisen (= *Kyrioleisen*), see: *Leisen*

La Chesnaye, Nicole de, 36, 100
La Croix, Barthélemy de, 554
La Fage, J. Adrien L. de, 25, 106, 139, 153, 175, 222, 232, 262, 366, 455
La Folie, Philippe de, see: Foliot
La Grotte, Nicolas de, 305, 389f, 558
La Hèle (= Helle), George de, 375, 389, 510f, 592
La, la, la, je ne l'ose dire, Certon, 299
La, la, la, l'oysillon du boy, Mouton, 281
La, la, maistre Pierre, Clemens, 302
La Laurencie, Lionel de (Lau), 7, 289f, 294f, 554ff, 756
La Marche, Olivier de, 57
La Pole, William de, Earl (later Duke) of Suffolk, 86
La Rue, Pierre de: biogr. and Masses, 266ff (incl. Ex. 52), 611; motets, 270ff (incl. Ex. 53); sec. voc. mus., 187, 272f, 396, 557; see also 119, 184, 220, 225, 235, 263, 276, 278, 517, 580, 674
La Torre, Francisco de, 585, 619
La ver l'aurora: Lassus, 692; Palestrina, 692
Lacen adieu, Obrecht, 189
Lach, Robert, 394
Lachrymae pieces (based on J. Dowland's *Flow, my teares*): Barley, 843, 846; Besard, 847f (incl. Ex. 204); Byrd, 865; J. Dowland, 846, 873ff; Farnaby, 865; Morley, 865
Ladislaus V, King of Hungary, 718, 721
Ladmirant, J., 125
Lady your words doe spite mee, Wilbye, 830
Laet, Jean, 290, 505; see also: Waelrant and Laet
Laet uns met herten reyne, Bull, 858
Laetabundus: Greg. Chant, 22, 83; Dufay, 83
Laetamini in Domino: G. M. Nanino, 482; Verdelot, 364
Laetania, Byrd, 790
Laetatus sum, Victoria, 608
Laetetur plebs—Pastor, Zacharia, 32
Lafage, 278, 285, 339, 348
Lafontaine, Henry C. de (Lafon), 771, 867
Lagarto, 585
Lago, Giovanni del, 181
Lagrime d'amante, Monteverdi, 441
Lagrime di San Pietro, Lassus, 406
Lambertus (= Pseudo-Aristotle), 727
Lamentabatur Jacob, Morales, 591
Lamentatio sanctae matris Ecclesiae constantinopolitanae, Dufay, 58f
Lamentations: Greg. Chant formula, 58, 219, 254, 279f (incl. Ex. 56); anon. setting, 745; Arcadelt, 501; Carpentras, 286, 501; Cornago, 576; Contino, 492; de Orto, 265; Festa, 501; A. de Févin, 278ff (incl. Ex. 56); Galilei, 487; La Rue, 267; Lapicida, 165; Lassus, 698; Luython, 702; Mahu, 679;

Massaini, 491; Nasco, 368; Palestrina, 462, 468 (incl. Ex. 111); Phinot, 349; Szamotułczyk, 749; Tallis, 785; Tinctoris, 149; Tromboncino, 165; Weerbecke, 165, 219; White, 783f (incl. Ex. 181); Ycart, 149; see also 121

laments on the death of musicians: Appenzeller for Josquin, 305; Baston for Lupus, 308; Gombert for Josquin, 305, 336; Josquin for Ockeghem, 118, 235, 245; Lupi for Ockeghem, 306; Mouton for Févin, 280; Ockeghem for Binchois, 86, 121; Vaet for Clemens, 700; Vinders for Josquin, 308

Lamson, Roy (Lam), 833, 878

Land, Jan P. N., 117, 556, 783, 881

Landi, Antonio, 567

Landini, Francesco, 10, 52, 174f

Landini sixth (the term), 44; see also: cadences, under-third

Laneham, Robert, 766; *Laneham's Letter*, 766, 882

Lanfranco, Giovanni Maria, 179, 547f

Lang, Paul H., 8f

Lange, Georg, 396

languages, relative prestige in sec. mus., 33, 52, 98, 187

Languir en mille distresse, the melody, 634

Languir me fais, Sermisy, 295, 301, 351, 356

Languir my fault, Clemens, 351

Lannoy, Colinet de, 115, 189, 222, 234, 286, 740

Lantins, Arnold de, 39ff (incl. Ex. 4), 60

Lantins, Hugho de, 41f

Lapicida, Erasmus (= Rasmo; Steinschneider), 159, 165, 641, 707

Lapidabant Stephanum, G. M. Nanino, 482

L'Araldo (= Ottonaio?), 171f

Las Infantas, Fernando de, 609f (incl. Ex. 135), 614, 618

Las j'ay perdu mon espincel, Vide, 43

Las je me plains, Bertrand, 389

Las je n'yray plus, Costeley, 388

Las! que feray?, Dufay, 44 (Ex. 5c), 54

Lasca, Il (= Anton F. Grazzini), 169, 569

Lascia fare mi (= *Lassa fare a mi*), 238 (incl. Ex. 44)

Lasciatemi morire, Monteverdi (solo and setting *a 5*), 441ff (incl. Ex. 107)

Lasson, M., 352, 368, 470

Lassus, Ferdinand, 691

Lassus, Roland de (= Orlando di Lasso): biogr., 389ff, 414, 690f; L.'s historical position, 459, 506f; sec. voc. mus.: in French, 390ff (incl. Exx. 90, 91), 399, 538, 554, 616, 823, 859 (Ex. 208); in Ger., 709f (incl. Ex. 160), 738; in Ital., 404ff (incl. Ex. 94), 443f; in Lat., 506f, 509, 691; sacr. mus., 307, 352, 449, 465, 506ff (incl. Ex. 118), 511, 691ff (incl. Ex. 155), 696ff, 703; instr. mus., 672, 691; mus. for ballet, 571; L.'s style compared with Gombert's, 507ff; with Palestrina's, 404, 406, 481, 692ff, 697; traits of L.'s style mentioned elsewhere, 125,

407, 452, 516, 700, 794; see also 184, 287, 380, 401, 418, 512f, 517, 629, 666, 685ff, 712, 720

Lassus, Rudolph, 691, 697f

Late Renaissance, characteristic traits, 3f, 105, 184f, 188, 190, 230, 250, 294, 378, 481, 585, 778, etc.

Lattre, Joan de, 308

lauda and *laudesi*, 80f, 166f, 172, 218f, 258, 452ff, 592, 596, 766

Lauda anima mea, La Rue, 271

Lauda Deum tuum Syon, Porta, 495

Lauda pia Dominum, Pevernage, 517

Lauda Sion: Greg. Chant, 262, 463; Brumel, 262; Palestrina (2 settings *a 8*), 463 (setting *a 4*), 463, 470

Laudabit usque, Lassus, 405

Laudate Dominum: Greg. Chant, 610; Brumel, 262; Las Infantas, 610 (incl. Ex. 135); Lassus, 695; Palestrina, 466, 472

Laudate pueri, Josquin, 247f

laudes Regiae, 41, 715

Laudon, Robert T. (Laud), 293

Laumonier, Paul, 298f, 387

Laura soave vita, Martoretta, 325

Laurencinus Romanus (= Lorenzini del liuto), 527, 554, 844

Lauro verde, Il, Wert, 411

lavoltas, 863

Lawes, William, 866, 883

Lawrence, W. J. (Lawr), 879f, 883

Lawry, Eleanor M., 521

Layolle (the Elder), François (= Francesco Ajolla), 170, 300

Layolle (the Younger), François (= Francesco) de, 300, 326, 343

Le Bé, Guillaume, 289

Le Bel, Firmin, 364, 456

Le Bel (= Level?), Jacotin, 307

Le Blanc, Didier, 390

Le Cerf, Georges (Cerf), 36, 850

Le Cocq, Jehan (= Gallus), 301, **327**

Le Franc, Martin, 12, 51, 65

Le Heurteur, Guillaume, 348

Le Jeune, Claude: biogr., 383; sec. voc. mus.: in French, 296, 383ff (incl. Exx. 86, 87); in Ital., 427; sacr. mus.: in French, 503f; in Lat., 504; instr. mus., 565; see also 386, 390, 557, 839

Le Jeune, Henri, 566

Le Maistre, Matthaeus, 327, 333, 666, 682, 708f

Le Pelé, Robert, see: Robinet de la Magdalaine

Le Petit, see: Ninot le Petit

Le Rouge, Guillaume, 92; see also: Ruby, Guillaume

Le Roy, Adrian, 289, 296, 389, 391, 554, 557, 559, 842

Le Roy and Ballard, 289, 296, 300f, 310, 335, 340, 380f, 391, 501f, 553, 555, 557

Lea, Kathleen M., 691

Lealtat! O lealtat, 577

Leaves be greene, The, see: *Browning* pieces

Lebertoul, François, 48
Lechner, Leonhard, 666, 686ff, 710f
Lectio Actuum Apostolorum, Josquin, 255
Lectiones, Lassus, 698
Lederer, Victor (Led), 93, 99
legato and non-legato, earliest occurence, 521
Legend of Thomas Cromwell, Drayton, 769
Legrant, Guillaume, 13, 23f, 658
Legrant, Jean, 24
Leich, 730f
Leichtentritt, Hugo (Lei), 350, 441, 448, 450ff, 485, 494, 497, 514, 600f, 687f, 696
Leighton, William, 809f, 874
leisen, 633, 645, 674, 679, 681
Leisentritt, Johann, 651
Lemlin, Lorenz, 707
Lenaerts, René B. M. (Len), 8, 102, 115ff, 206, 275, 303, 306, 308f, 369f, 372
Lenzinger, Gustav (Lenz), 662
Leo VIII, Pope, 652
Leo X, Pope, 169, 215, 260, 280, 285f, 306, 319, 362, 368f, 534, 546, 567, 580, 656
Leo XI, Pope, 483
León, J. de, 585
León, Ponce de, 578
Leonel, see Power, Leonel
Leoni, Leone, 426f, 493
Leopolita (= Marcin Lwowczyk), 748ff (incl. Ex. 171*b*)
Lepanto, Battle of, 403, 609, 614
Lestainnier, Jean, 350
L'Estocart, Paschal de, 390
Lesure, François (Les), 220, 266, 280, 289, 291f, 294ff, 298f, 307, 311, 340, 360, 382, 385ff, 555, 557, 566
Level (= Le Bel?), Jacotin, 307
Levitan, Joseph S. (Levi), 120, 133, 325, 370
Levron, Jacques (Levr), 296
Levy, Kenneth J., 394
Lewis, Anthony, 882
L'Héritier, Jean, 285, 337, 364, 470
Li Gotti, Ettore, 86
Liber de arte contrapuncti, Tinctoris, 140ff
Liber de natura, Tinctoris, 101, 140f
Liber generationis: anon. settings, 651, 745f; Josquin, 254; Stolzer, 673
Liber imperfectionum notarum, Tinctoris, 140f
Liber musicalium, Pseudo-Vitri, 727
Libera me: Greg. Chant, 272; Byrd, 788
Liberti, Gualterus (= Gualterius Liberth, etc.), 38, 93
Libreria, A. Doni, 316
Libro de Cifra Nueva para tecla, harpa y vihuela, Henestrosa, 626f
Libro de la Cámara, Oviedo, 578
Lichtenthal, Peter (Licht), 140, 181
Liebert, Reginaldus, 65f, 68
lied, sacr. and sec., 632ff, 674ff, 705ff
Liégeois, see Champion, Jacques
Lieto godea, G. Gabrieli, 418f (incl. Ex. 99)
Like two proud armies, Weelkes, 827
Liliencron, Rochus von (Lili), 635, 638f, 643, 680, 682f, 705ff. 719

Limburgia, Johannes de, 42
Lindenburg, Cornelis W. H. (Linden), 113ff
Lindsey, Edwin S. (Lind), 882
Lipphardt, Walter (Lipp), 77, 216, 343, 467, 649, 677, 681ff, 686, 688, 694, 707, 709, 711
Lisio, Giuseppe, 52
Lissa, Zofia, 756
Litany (Anglican), 795f; L. (Catholic), 362f, 467f, 633
Litta, Pompeo, 41, 49
Littleton, Alfred H. (Litt), 154f
Liuzzi, Fernando (Liu), 33, 554
Livermore, Ann (Liv), 584, 631
Livi, Giovanni, 313, 428
Livingston, Neil (Living), 781, 796, 801
Livre de la Deablerie, Eloy d'Amerval, 263
Livre plaisant et tres utile, anon., 555f
Lloyd, John, 774
Lo Spagna (= Giovanni di Pietro), 167
Łobaczewska, Stefanja (Lob), 747
Lobet den Herren, alle Heiden, Dressler, 683
Lobo, Alfonso, 611
Lôbo, Duarte, 598
Lobwasser, Ambrosius, 683
Lochamer (= *Locheimer*) *Liederbuch,* see: Manuscripts—Berlin
Lodi della Musica (Verovio), 447
Loepelmann, Martin (Loep), 54, 102, 205, 207
Löffelholtz, Christoph, 665f, 668, 755
Loft, Abram, 7
Loga, Valerian von, 594
Lohet, Simon, 562, 668
Löhrer, Edwin (Löh), 689
Lollio, 568
Long, John H., 792
Long Tone, Mülich of Prague, 729
Longaval (= Antoine de Longueval; Johannes à la Venture), 273ff (incl. Ex. 54), 285
Lopez-Chavarri, Eduardo (Chav), 619
Lopez de Yanguas, Fernán, 586
Loqueville, Richard de, 7, 13, 18 (incl. Ex. 1), 22f, 34, 48, 52
Lord, for thy tender mercies' sake, Tye or Hilton the Elder (not R. Farrant), 802
Lord Willobies Welcome Home: the melody, 881; Byrd, 881
Lorenzini, see: Laurencinus Romanus
Los Rios, Alvare de, 616
Loscos, Francisco Martinez di, 486
L'oserai-je dire, the melody, 284
Lotto, Lorenzo, 187
Louffenberg, Heinrich (= Heinricus de Libero Castro?), 645
Louis XI, King of France, 36, 48, 118
Louis XII, King of France, 181, 229, 234, 264, 273, 276, 278, 280, 283, 285, 291, 311, 343
Louis II, King of Hungary, 719, 722f
Louis, Duke of Orleans, 553
Louis, Duke of Savoy, 50
Lounay, Carlo di, 222
Lourdault (= Jean Braconnier), 224
Lourdault: the melody, 206; Compère, 224

Louys, Jean, 505
Love me not for comely grace, Wilbye, 830
Lovers made Men, Ben Jonson, 883
Lover's Progress, John Fletcher, 882
Low Countries (outside Chaps. 1, 3, 5, 7–10):
    Flanders, 87, 616; Hainaut, 86; Duchy of
    Limburg, 42; Antwerp, 809; Brussels, 616,
    809; Mons, 505; Ypres, 698
Low Mass, 227
Löwenfeld, Hans (Lö), 663
Lowinsky, Edward (Low), 4, 45ff, 89, 137, 160,
    167, 180, 182, 222, 230, 257, 306, 317, 326,
    332, 337, 341f, 350f, 353, 355, 365, 370,
    374, 505f, 510, 513ff, 533, 538, 695
Lowndes, 840
Luca, Antonio da, 546
Lucca, Lorenzo da, 546
Lucidario, Aron, 93
Lück, Stephan, 367, 374, 482ff, 488ff, 495,
    497, 500, 598
Luculentum theatrum musicum, 555
Lucy Marie, Sister, 600
Ludford, Nicholas, 774
Ludovico (harpist), 626
Ludovico da Rimini, 26f
Ludwig, Friedrich (Lud), 10f, 19, 31, 61, 654,
    743f
Lugebat David Absalon, Josquin, 257
Lukačić, Ivan (Luk), 761f
Lully, Jean-Baptiste, 289, 566
Lunelli, Renato (Lun), 438, 641, 662
Lupachino, Bernardino, 549
Luper, Albert T. (Lup), 598f
Lupi, Johannes, active at Antwerp, 306; J. L. of
    Cambrai, 306f, 343, 471 (No. 42), 475,
    478 (incl. Ex. 112c), 696; J. L. of Nivelles,
    306, 337; J. L. of Nivelles (?), 118, 341ff,
    471 (No. 61)
Lupi Second, Didier, 307, 393
Lupo, Ambrose (= Lupus Italus), 771
Lupo, Thomas, 869, 873, 883
Luprano, Filippo da, 158, 167
Lupus, identity uncertain, 351, 465, 471 (No.
    41), 478 (Ex. 112a)
Luscinius (= Ottmar Nachtgall), 656, 663
Lusitano, Vicente, 329, 364, 591, 598
Lust hab ich ghabt zuer Musica, Senfl, 707
Lustgarten neuer teutschen Gesäng, Hassler,
    672, 711
lute, 36f, 58, 146, 148, 153, 155, 176, 323,
    487f, 520ff, 546f, 550, 552, 566ff, 656, 658,
    717, 719, 753, 759, 842ff, 867, 873
lute makers, 520, 753
lute music: England, 842ff; France, 552ff;
    Germany, 668ff; Hungary, 717ff; Italy,
    521ff; Low Countries, 555f; Poland, 755f;
    Spain, 620; l. accompaniment, 153, 160,
    325, 333, 339, 447, 522f, 557f, 566, 670,
    717f, 758, 808, 832, 835ff; l. duets, etc.,
    528, 555f, 670, 847; l. ornamentation and
    figuration, 521, 527, 670, 720, 844ff; l. songs,
    160f, 163f, 339, 523, 557f, 670, see also:
    ayre; l. transcriptions, 161, 163f, 291, 299,

339, 521ff, 554, 558, 670, 846; see also:
    suites; also under names of various dances
lute tablature: Italian, 520f; French, 553,
    555f; German, 669
Lütgendorff, Willibald L. von (Lütg), 176,
    520, 753, 757
Luther, Martin (Luth), 356, 649, 673ff (incl.
    Ex. 152), 681ff, 685, 709, 724
Luther, W. M. (Lu), 683
Lutheran liturgy, 676, 681f
Lutheran music: 673ff; in Scandinavia, 712f
Luython, Charles (= Carl), 562, 667, 700, 702
Luzzaschi, Luzzasco: biogr., 411; solo mad-
    rigals with instr. accomp., 411f (incl. Ex.
    97), 440, 545; other madrigals, 411, 413;
    sacr. mus., 488; instr. mus., 541f; see also
    375, 530, 544
Lwowczyk, Marcin (= Leopolita), 748ff
Lyder, Péguy, 593, 794f
Lyffe of Sir Peter Carewe, The, 769
Lyke as the dolefull dove, Tallis, 816
Lyly, John, 879f
Lyon, Clément (Ly), 301
lyra (= *lira*) family, 148, 546f, 549, 568, 570

M. H., 747f (incl. Ex. 169)
Ma bouche rit: text, 207; Josquin, 234; Ocke-
    ghem, 120, 223, 234
Ma fin, Machaut, 30
Ma maistresse, Ockeghem, 116, 120, 129
Ma seulle dame, 205
MacClintock, Carol, 408
Macedo, 629
Machado, Manuel, 616
Machaut, Guillaume de (Mach), 10ff, 14ff, 23,
    30f, 34, 39f, 44, 53, 60, 68, 87, 174, 390,
    577, 593, 729, 743f
Machiavelli, Niccolò, 311
Macmillan, John B. (Macm), 683
Macon, Jehan, 6
Macque, Giovanni de, 411, 425, 430, 486, 543
    (incl. Ex. 126)
Madame helas, Josquin, 234
Maddison, Arthur R. (Madd), 867
Madonna io v'amo, Festa or Gero, 319
Madonna non so dir, Verdelot, 318
Madonna poi ch'uccidermi volete, Merulo, 417
Madonna qual certezza, Verdelot, 318
Madonna voi mi fare, Nola, 333
Madrid (composer), 577, 585
madrigal, 14th c., 26f, 59, 312, 322
madrigal, 16th c.: Italian m., see Chaps. 6 and
    8; Italian m. outside Italy, 408ff, 711, 760;
    English m., 819ff; Spanish m., 612ff; quasi-
    dramatic m. cycles, 409, 433ff; see also: solo
    madrigals
Maessens, Petrus, 700
Maestro, El, Milán, 620f
Magalhães, Felipe de, 598
Maggi, 173
Magnanimae gentis laudes, Dufay, 50
Magnificats (incl. Protestant settings): gen-
    eral, 59; Greg. Chant formulas, 85; Mm. in

an Attaingnant print (keyboard), 560; in Eton MS, 772; in Paumann *Fundamentum* (keyboard), 658; in Polish MS, 744; Animuccia, 455; Binchois, 91; Busnois, 108; Byrd, 803; G. Cavazzoni (keyboard), 536; Compère, 227; Divitis, 276f; Dufay, 85; Esquivel, 610; Fayrfax, 775; Festa, 362f (incl. Ex. 81); A. de Févin, 278f; Franco, 593; G. Gabrieli, 498; Gafori, 181; Gascoing, 273; Gombert, 346; Guerrero, 594f; La Rue, 272; Lassus, 697f; Le Jeune, 504; Lôbo, 598; Ludford, 774; Mahu, 679; J. Martini, 222f; Monte, 702; Morales, 590, 594; Nicolas of Radom, 744; Obrecht, 190; Palestrina, 468f; Pasche, 777; Pipelare, 275; Prioris, 264; Rener, 649; Richafort, 335, 560; Ruffo(?), 416; Scandello, 708; Tallis, 785f; Taverner, 780; Titelouze (keyboard), 562; Vaet, 700; Victoria, 605; Weelkes, 806; White, 783; Whytbroke, 777; Willaert, 372; Zieleński, 753
Magnificentia Parthenopolitana, J. Vulpius, 676
Magnum opus musicum, Lassus, 404, 506, 691ff
Magnus es tu, Domine, Josquin, 258
Mahnung an die Jugend, Hindemith, 656
Mahu, Stephen, 679, 706, 708
Mai mit lieber zal, Der, Oswald von Wolkenstein, 12
Maid of Honour, The, Massinger, 840
Maids Tragedy, The, Beaumont and Fletcher, 882
Maier, Julius J. (Mai), 94, 227, 271, 634, 645
Maillard, Jean, 300, 341, 470, 475
Main, Alexander, 279
Maintenon, Mme. de, 566
Maio, Giovan Tommaso di, 334
Mais que ce just, Compère or Pietrequin, 224
Maitland, see Fuller Maitland, John A.
maîtrises, see: choir schools
major and minor, tendency towards; see: tonality, feeling for
mal mariée as a song subject, 214
Malatesta, Carlo, 49, 55
Malatesta, Cleofe, 41, 49, 77
Malbecque, Guillaume, 38
Malchinger (= Malchier), 638, 666
Maldeghem, Robert van (Mald), 100, 119, 192, 208ff, 220, 224f, 231, 233ff, 250, 253f, 261ff, 270ff, 275, 283, 290, 292, 295, 298f, 300ff, 304ff, 311, 317, 321ff, 327, 331f, 336f, 341, 345f, 350f, 355, 364f, 367, 373f, 376, 381, 383, 387, 390ff, 396ff, 404, 408, 411, 427f, 430, 444, 482, 502, 506f, 517, 539, 611, 682, 691, 695, 698, 700f, 703f
Malebouche—Circumdederunt me viri mendaces, Compère, 225
Maler, Laux, 520
Malheur me bat, Ockeghem (?), 120, 199, 210, 239f, 368
Malheureux cueur, Dufay, 53f, 57, 224
Malin, Nicolas, 48

Malipier, Francesco, 27
Malipiero, G. Francesco (Mal), 316, 438, 441
Mallapert, Robin, 455
Malvezzi, Cristofano, 425, 543, 569f
Malvicino, Marchese of Piacenza, 323
manacordo, manicordion, see: clavichord
Mañana de San Juan, La, Pisador (not Mudarra), 622
Manchicourt, Pierre de, 301, 351, 510, 592, 629
Mancini, Curzio, 485
Mancini Codex, see: Manuscripts—Lucca
Mane nobiscum, Clemens, 354
Maner of dauncynge of bace daunces, The, 882
Mangeot, André (Mang), 871, 873
Mann, Arthur H., 851
Mannerists and Manneristic style, 11, 17
Manning, Rosemary J. (Mann), 810
mantovana, 445
Mantuani, Josef (Mant), 155
Manuale ad usum per celebris ecclesia Sarisburiensis (1526 ed.), 255
Manuel II, Byzantine Emperor, 41
Manuscripts: **Aosta,** Seminario, 10, 41, 66; **Apt,** Trésor de Ste. Anne *16 bis (IV),* 14, 61, 84; **Basle,** Univ. Bibl. *F.IX.22 (Kotter tablature),* 662ff; *F.X.1–4,* 281; **Berlin,** Öff. wiss. Bibl. *40021 (Z.21),* 645f; *40026 (Z.26; Kleber tablature),* 662ff; *40034 (Z.34; Löffelholtz tablature),* 665f, 668; *40089 (Z.89; Nörmiger tablature),* 666ff, 716; *40098 (Z.98; Glogauer Liederbuch),* 48, 107, 123, 268, 634ff, 671; *40613 (Lochamer Liederbuch; olim* Wernigerode Fürstl. Stolberg'sche Bibl. *Zb 14),* 634ff, 652, 658, 660, 708; *Theol. lat. quart. 290 (Winsem),* 657ff, 661; Kupferstichkabinett *78 B 17 (Rohan Chansonnier),* 54; **Bologna,** Liceo mus. (renamed Conservatorio di Musica G. B. Martini) *Q 15 (olim 37),* 10, 13, 31ff, 35f, 38ff, 52, 61f, 64, 91f; *Q 16 (chansonnier),* 177; *Q 19 (Rusconi),* 211, 220, 261, 341, 367f; Bibl. Univ. *2216,* 41, 52, 92, 743; **Breslau,** Diocesan Archive *58,* 746; Univ. Lib. *I.F. 386,* 746; *I.F. 391,* 644; *I.F. 459,* 650; *I.Qu 438 (Sagan),* 657, 659, 661; Univ., Mus. Inst. *MF. 2016,* 645f; *Lute MS of 1544,* 716; **Brussels,** Bibl. roy. *228 (chansonnier),* 225, 262, 269f, 272, 275; *4147,* 140ff; *5557,* 95, 108, 136; *9085,* 36f; **Cambrai,** Bibl. comm. *6,* 62; *20,* 285; *124,* 264, 309, 336f, 371; **Cambridge,** Fitzwilliam Mus. *32 G 29 (Fitzwilliam Virg. Book),* 556, 727, 855, 858, 861, 866f; Gonville and Caius College *667,* 776; Magdalene College *Pepys 1236,* 93, 773; *Pepys 1760 (chansonnier),* 264, 278, 280f, 301; Trinity College, *O.3.58 (olim 1230),* 765; Univ. Lib. *Dd. 2.11,* 844; *Dd. 4.23,* 849; *Dd. 5.78,* 844; *Dd. 9.33,* 844; *Nn. 6.36,* 844; **Chantilly,** Musée Condé *1047 (chanson-*

nier), 10ff., 19f., 22, 31, 575; **Chicago,** Newberry Lib. *Capirola Lute Tablature,* 521ff; *Lute MS,* 669; **Coimbra,** University Lib. *Mus. 43,* 629; **Copenhagen,** Kongelige Bibl. *Thott 291*[8] (*chansonnier*), 97f, 117, 264; **Cracow,** Academy of Fine Arts *2216,* 745; Academy of Sciences *1716* (*Jan of Lublin tablature*), 716, 753ff; Jagiellońska Lib. *1619,* 742; *2464,* 742f, 745; **Dijon,** Bibl. Publique *517* (*chansonnier*), 97, 99ff, 103, 105, 111, 120, 244, 264; **Dresden,** Sächs. Landesbibl. *A 52,* 745f; **Dublin,** Archbishop Marsh's Lib. *Lute MS,* 844; Trinity College *William Ballet Lute MS,* 843f, 848; *Thomas Dallis Lute MS,* 844; **Elvas,** Bibl. Públ. Hortênsia *11973,* 582, 584f; *Escorial IV.a.24* (*chansonnier*), 97f, 633; *V.III.24* (*chansonnier*), 35, 98; **Eton,** Eton College *178,* 767, 772f; **Faenza,** Bibl. Com. *117,* 149, 174, 178, 534; **Florence,** Bibl. Med. Laur. *Pal. 87* (*Squarcialupi Codex*), 51; Bibl. naz. centr. *II.I, 232* (= *Magl. XIX, 58*), 274; *Banco rari 229* (= *Magl. XIX, 59; chansonnier*), 202, 222, 635; *Banco rari 230* (= *Magl. XIX, 141*), 169; *Magl. XIX, 164–167* (*chansonnier*), 275; *Magl. XIX, 176* (*chansonnier*), 101; *Panc. 27,* 266; Bibl. Riccardiana *2794* (*chansonnier*), 94, 275; Conserv. *B. 2439* (*chansonnier*), 209, 264, 266, 278; *B. 2440,* 170, 300; *B. 2442* (*chansonnier*), 284; **Gniezno,** Cathedral *94–97,* 746; *149, 741;* **Hradec Králové,** Museum, *Speciálník Codex,* 740; **Jena,** Univ. Bibl. *2,* 269; *31,* 215; *32,* 196; *36,* 647; **Leipzig,** Stadtbibl. *ii. 6.15,* 716; Univ. Bibl. *1494* (*Nik. Apel Codex*), 645f; **Leyden,** Gemeentearchief, *863,* 245; Univ. Bibl. *Thysius Lute-Book,* 556, 847, 881; **London,** Brit. Mus. Add. *5465* (*Fairfax Book*), 768, 775; *5665* (*Ritson*), 765, 768; *10337* (*Elizabeth Rogers hir Virginall Booke*), 852, 867; *10444,* 883; *15117,* 841; *17492,* 769f; *17786–91,* 842; *17802–5,* 773, 778; *23623,* 858; *23624,* 702; *28550* (*Robertsbridge*), 659, 849; *29246,* 845f; *29247,* 846; *29996,* 855; *30486,* 862; *30513* (*Mulliner Book*), 816, 849, 851, 854f, 858; *31390,* 868f; *31922,* 768ff, 843, 866f; *31992,* 846; *36526,* 870; *Cotton, Julius B. xii,* 767; *Egerton 2046* (*Jane Pickering's Lute Book*), 844, 847; *Egerton 2461,* 471; *Egerton 3307,* 764f, 772; *Harley 978,* 11; *Lansdowne 462,* 474; *Roy. II E. II,* 773; *Roy. App. 45–48,* 774; *Roy. App. 58,* 768, 842, 853f; *Stowe 389,* 842; *Benjamin Cosyn's Virginal Book,* 851, 866; *Will. Forster's Virginal Book,* 852, 859, 866; *My Ladye Nevell's Booke,* 851, 853, 864, 866; **Lucca,** Arch. di Stato *Mancini Codex,* 29; Bibl. Cap. *601,* 345; **Madrid,** Bibl. Medinaceli *13230* (= *Tonos Castellanos A*), 596, 616; *13231*

(= *Tonos castellanos B*), 616; Bibl. Nac. *M. 1370–72* (*Romances y letras . . .*), 616; Bibl. del Pal. Real *2.I.5* (*Cancionero de Palacio*), 99, 576f, 580ff, 619; **Milan,** Arch. del Duomo *2267–69* (*Gafori Codices*), 180f, 195, 219, 223, 227; **Modena,** Bibl. Estense α.*M.1, 11–13* (= *Lat. 454–6; also V.H.11,* 9, 10), 28, 165f, 223; α.*M.5, 24* (= *Lat. 568; also IV.D.5*), 10, 12, 31; α.*X.1, 11* (= *Lat. 471; also VI.H.15*), 21, 82, 92, 767; **Montecassino** *871N,* 93, 139, 576; **Munich,** Bay. Staatsbibl. *Mus. A* (*Lassus*), 690, 695; *Mus. B* (*Rore*), 376; *Mus. E 200* (*Cancionero de Sablonara*), 616f, 631; *Cgm 4997* ("*Colmar*"), 729, 731; *Mus. 3154,* 83, 108, 221f, 268, 645f; *Cim. 351*ª (= *Mus. 3232, also Cgm 810; Schedelsches Liederbuch*), 94, 634ff, 658, 671, 708; *Mus. 3232a,* 52, 632f, 743; *Cim. 352*ᵇ (= *Mus. 3725; Buxheimer Orgelbuch*) 55, 94, 658ff, 664, 708; **Naples,** Bibl. naz. *VI.E.40,* 73, 149, 204, 672; **New Haven,** Yale Univ. *Mellon Chansonnier,* 53, 73, 87, 92f, 97ff, 103, 105, 107, 153; **New York,** New York Public Library *Drexel 4030,* 768; *Drexel 4180–85,* 871; *Drexel 4302* (*Sambrooke*), 428f, 795; *Drexel 5609,* 852, 866f; *Drexel 5611,* 852, 866; *Drexel 5612,* 852, 865ff; **Old Hall** (Herts.), St. Edmund's College *Old Hall MS,* 19, 22, 32, 39, 61, 763, 765; **Oxford,** Bodleian Lib. *Ashmole 831* (*chansonnier*), 581; *Canonici misc. 213,* 7, 10, 13f, 18, 22, 29f, 34f, 38f, 40ff, 48f, 52, 54, 82, 92, 98, 205, 378; *E. 420–2* (*Wanley*), 786, 797, 799; *Selden B 26,* 765; *26356–60* (*D 212–16*), 857, 868; Christ Church College *984–8,* 817; *1113,* 865; **Padua,** Bibl. Univ. *fragments,* 29; **Paris,** Bibl. nat. *f. fr. 9346* (*Bayeux Chansonnier*), 152, 205ff, 213f, 233f, 265, 270, 278, 284, 286; *f. fr. 12744* (*chansonnier*), 152, 205ff, 210, 214, 224, 233, 261, 263, 270; *f. fr. "15103,"* 149; *f. fr. 15123* (*Pixérécourt Chansonnier*), 97f, 100f, 110, 149, 214; *nouv. acq. fr. 4379* (*chansonnier*), 30, 97, 100f, 206, 634; *nouv. acq. fr. 6771* (*Reina MS; chansonnier*), 10, 12, 19f, 31, 175; *Rés. Vm*⁷ *676,* 159; *Jean de Montchenu Chansonnier* (*Cordiforme*), 97f, 153; Bibl. du Conservatoire, *Rés. 1122, 1184–1185, 1186, 1186 bis* (= *18547, 18548, 18546, 18570*), 852; Bibl. G. Thibault, *Nivelle de la Chaussée Chansonnier,* 97f; **Parma,** Arch. di Stato *fragment,* 29; **Pavia,** Bibl. Univ. *Ald. 362* (*chansonnier*), 54, 97f; **Perugia,** Bibl. Com. *431* (*G 20*), 99, 177, 286; *fragment of Lucca-Mancini,* 29; **Philadelphia,** Curtis Inst. of Music *Ileborgh tablature,* 657ff, 661; **Pistoia,** Arch. Capit. *fragment,* 29; **Porto,** Bibl. Municip. *714* (*chansonnier*), 30; **Regensburg,** Bibl.

Proske, *B. 216–219*, 602, 646; *C. 120* (*Pernner*), 262; **Rome** (see also **Vatican City**), Bibl. Casanatense *2856* (*chansonnier*), 111, 202, 222; Arch. of St. John Lateran *59*, 468; Bibl. Vallicelliana *S. Borr. E. II, 55–60*, 341, 364; **Rostock,** Univ. Bibl. *Phil. 100/2* (*Rostocker Liederbuch*), 651f; **St. Gall,** Stiftsbibl. *461* (*Sicher Liederbuch*), 120, 210, 234, 262, 275, 671; *462* (*Heer Liederbuch*), 706; *463* (*Tschudi Liederbuch*), 219; *530* (*Sicher organ tablature*), 663ff, 671; *546, 650*; **Segovia,** Cathedral, 102, 149, 187, 196, 202; **Seville,** Bibl. Colombina *5-I-43* (*chansonnier*), 97f, 153, 219, 234; *5-5-20*, 578; *7-1-28* (*cancionero*), 582; **Siena,** Arch. di Stato *fragment,* 29; **Strasbourg** Bibl. *222 C.22*, 55f, 632f, 645; **Tarazona,** Cathedral *3*, 578; **Tenbury,** St. Michael's College *340*, 806, *791* (*Organ Book of Adrian Batten*), 806; **Toledo,** Cathedral *25*, 611; **Tournai,** Bibl. de la Ville *94* (*chansonnier*), 206, 634; **Trent,** Trent Codices: Castello del Buon Consiglio *87–92* & Arch. Capit. *93*, 10, 30, 32, 35, 38f, 41f, 59f, 62f, 66,, 68, 77, 87, 91f, 98, 101, 107f, 110ff, 126, 223, 268, 576, 633, 635, 645, 663, 708, 763f; Bibl. Civica *1947–4*, 101; **Turin,** Bibl. Naz. *J II 9* (*Cyprus*), 14, 50; *Ris. mus. I.14* (*qm III, 36; cancionero*), 616; *Ris. mus. I.27* (*qm III, 59*), 100; **Vatican City,** Bibl. Ap. Vat. *Capp. Giulia XIII, 27* (*chansonnier*), 119, 222, 286; *Capp. Sist. 14*, 109, 112; *15*, 84; *34*, 269; *35*, 125, 195, 223; *36*, 270; *42*, 262; *51*, 136; *160*, 284; *Chigi C. VIII. 234*, 125, 131, 219; *Pal. lat. 457*, 746; *Pal. lat. 1982*, 261; *S. Pietro B. 80*, 82, 92; *Urb. lat. 1411* (*chansonnier*), 30, 52; **Venice,** Bibl. Marciana *Ital. IX, 145*, 166f, 743; **Vienna,** Nationalbibl. *18825*, 337; **Warsaw,** Krasiński Lib. *52*, 743ff; State Arch. *Cracow tablature,* 753f; Univ. Lib. MS., formerly St. Petersburg Imp. Lib. *F. I. 378*, 743ff; **Washington,** Folger Shakespeare Lib. *1610.1* 844; *4448.16*, 841f; Lib. of Congress *M.2.1 L. 25 Case* (*Laborde Chansonnier*), 93f, 97f, 100, 264; **Wolfenbüttel,** Herzog August-Bibl. *287 extrav.* (*chansonnier*), 97f, 120, 153, 264, 338; *677* (*olim Helmst. 628*), 252; **Wrocław** (see **Breslau**); **Zwickau,** Ratschulbibl. *16*, 727
Manuzzi, Giuseppe, 517
Marbeck, see: Merbecke, John
Marcantonio del Pifaro, 522, 526
Marcellus II, Pope, 456, 462, 480
Marches in Byrd's *Battell*, 866
Marchi, Luigi de, 98
Marenzio, Luca: biogr., 420, 748; sec. voc. mus., 419ff (incl. Exx. 100–102), 426f, 443, 445; *canzonette spirituali*, 447; sacr. mus., 481f; traits of style mentioned elsewhere, 826; see also 400f, 411, 413, 416, 430, 440, 492, 569, 667, 810, 821f, 828, 832

Mareschall, Samuel, 683
Margaret of Austria, Duchess of Parma, 322, 330, 690
Margaret of Austria, Duchess of Savoy, Regent of the Netherlands, 36, 109, 267, 272f, 322
Margaret of Flanders, Duchess of Burgundy, 5
Margarita dai corai, Orazio Vecchi, 446
Margarite fleur de valeur, Binchois, 88f (incl. Ex. 23)
Margot labourés les vignes: the melody, 381; Arcadelt, 381, 392; Lassus, 392, 859; keyboard transcr. thereof by Philips, 859 (incl. Ex. 208)
Maria ein reisz des paradeisz, Luython, 702
Maria, Empress (consort of Maximilian II), 600, 608, 615
Maria Magdalene, Du Lot, 351
Maria uns tröst, Aichinger, 699
Mariä Wiegenlied, Reger, 674
Maria zart: the melody, 193f (incl. Ex. 34a), 645, 662; Schlick, 662
Marian tropes, 60, 242, 261, 452, 473, 589, 595, 606; see also: tropes and troping
Marini, Giambattista, 435
Marix, Jeanne (Mar), 6f, 10, 13, 15ff, 22, 34, 36, 38, 43ff, 48, 58, 86ff, 98ff, 107, 110, 121
Mark, Jeffrey, 852, 883
Marle, Nicolas de, 341
Marner, 652f
Marot, Clément, 288, 295f, 298, 311, 339, 359f, 381, 391, 394, 398, 503, 505, 511, 561, 564, 726, 796
Marot, Jean, 288
Marpurg, Friedrich W. (Marp), 178
Marquardt, Hans (Marqu), 683
marquetry, music in, 120, 157
Marriage, Elizabeth (Marri), 706; see also: Mincoff-Marriage, Elizabeth
Marriage of the Frogge and the Mouse, The, Ravenscroft?, 834
Marrocco, W. Thomas (Marr), 32
Mars in a furie, Weelkes, 827
Marston, John, 880
Martial, 381
Martin V, Pope, 31, 49f
Martin I, King of Aragon, 576
Martin, E., 505
Martin (= Martini), Thomas, 221
Martin menoit, Janequin, 539; A. Gabrieli (*canzone*), 539
Martinella, La, Jo. Martini, 222
Martinengo, Giulio Cesare, 500
Martinez de Bizcargui, Gonzalo, 587
Martini, Giambattista, 75, 178, 373, 424, 432, 455, 494f, 532, 590, 592f
Martini, Jean (= Johannes), of Noyen, 575f
Martini, Johannes (= Giovanni), 157, 220ff (incl. Ex. 41), 575, 662
Martini (= Martin), Thomas, 221
Martino d'Alemagna, Don, 221
Martinus, Petrus, 221
Martoretta, Giandomenico, 325

Marulić, Marko, 758
Marxer, Otto (Marx), 650
Mary, André, 564
Mary I, Queen of England, 395, 781, 784, 797, 815, 850
Mary, Queen of Hungary (consort of Louis II; later Regent of the Netherlands), 299, 303, 340f, 719, 722ff
Mary of Burgundy (daughter of Charles the Bold), 109
Marzio, Galeotto, 717
Mascarate piacevoli, Croce, 436
Maschera, Fiorenzo, 550
mascherata, 333f
mask (dance type), 863
masque, England, 571, 771, 839, 879, 881ff
Mass, see main entry under: *Missa*
Mass for the Dead, see: Requiem Mass
Mass, German (= *Deudsche Messe*), 676, 682; Taborite M., 733; Utraquist M., 735
Mass Proper cycles: anon., 77; Byrd, 787, 790f; Gallus, 738; Isaac, 648f, 689; see also 343
Mass sections, Greg. Chant (Ordinary, except for Credo, q. v.): I (*M. Lux et origo*): K., 116, 211; G., 211; II (*M. Fons bonitatis*): K., 472; S., 472; IV (*M. Cunctipotens Genitor*): K., 32, 91, 579; S., 242, 260; A., 242, 260, 472; VIII (*M. de Angelis*): K., 91; S., 261, 579; IX (*M. de Beata Virgine: Cum jubilo*): K., 91, 242, 470, 646; G., 60, 242, 470, 579; S., 39, 260; A., 62, 243, 579; X (*M. de Beata Virgine: Alme Pater*): A., 275; XI (*M. Orbis factor*): K., 59, 131, 185, 470; G., 60, 470; XII (*M. Pater cuncta*): G., 689; S., 470; A., 470; XV (*M. in Festis Simplicibus*): K., 689; G., 130, 239, 578, 580; S., 91; A., 91; XVI (*M. in Feriis per annum*): K., 130; XVII (*M. in Dominicis Adventus et Quadragesimae*): S., 39, 91, 243, 260, 470, 647; A., 29, 39; XVIII (*M. in Feriis Adventus et Quadragesimae*): S., 245, 470; A., 91, 245; Gloria I, *ad lib.,* 472
Mass sections (Ordinary), polyphonic: **Kyrie,** anon., 32; Binchois, 91; Bonadies, 178; Dufay: K. *Orbis factor,* 2 settings, 59f; other Kk., 62, 64, 67; de Orto, *K. de Beata Virgine,* 265; **Gloria,** anon., in Sagan MS (keyboard), 657; Antonio da Cividale, 28; Bartolomeo da Bologna, 28, 33; Binchois, 91; Ciconia, 28f (incl. Ex. 3), 39; Cooper, 770; Dufay: *G. ad modum tubae* 6of, 109, 181; *G. de Quaremiaux,* 60; other Gg., 6off; Dufay (?), 41; Dunstable, 66; Franchois, 42; Grazioso da Padova, 28; Grossin, 42; Hugho de Lantins (?), 41; Legrant, 24; Matteo da Perugia, 29; Nicholas of Radom, 744; Pevernage, 517; Poignare, 38; Power, 39; Pycard, 61; Zacharia, 32; **Credo,** anon., in Winsem MS (keyboard), 657; A. Agricola, 208; Bartolomeo da Bologna, 28; Binchois, 91; Ciconia, 29, 39; Dufay, 61f (incl. Ex. 14); Dunstable, 66; Franchois, 42; Gombert, 348f. 352; La Rue, *Patrem L'Amour de moy,* 270f; Legrant, 24; Loqueville, 18; Nicholas of Radom, 744; Ockeghem, 118; Pipelare, *C. de Sancto Johanne evangelista,* 275; Power, 39; Pycard(?), 19; Zachara da Teramo, *Patrem du vilage* = *Patrem dominicale* = Z's *Deus Deorum,* 32f, 59; **Sanctus,** anon., in Winsem MS (keyboard), 657; Binchois, 91; Dufay, *S. Papale,* 62; Grazioso da Padova, 28; Obrecht, 195; Power, 39; **Agnus,** Binchois, 91; Dufay, 62; Morley, 792; Power, 39. Related pairs, etc.: **Gloria-Credo,** Binchois, 91; Ciconia, 29, 39; Dufay, 62; Franchois, 42; Legrant, 24; Power, 39; **Sanctus-Agnus,** Binchois, 91; **Kyrie-Gloria-Credo,** Binchois, 91f; **Gloria-Credo-Sanctus,** Dufay, 62
Massaini (= Massaino), Tiburtio, 420, 426, 491, 831
Massarello, Angelo, 449
Massinger, Philip, 840
Masson, Paul-Marie, 168ff, 382f, 386, 504, 575
Mastičkář, 732
Matelart I, Jean, 523, 528, 588
Matelart II, Jean, 482
Mater digna Dei, Weerbecke, 218
Mater Patris, Brumel, 240, 262
Matković, 760
Matona mia cara, Lassus, 444
Matteo da Perugia, 16, 26, 29, 31
Mattheson, Johann, 398
Matthew of Austria, Emperor, 702
Matthias Corvinus, King of Hungary, 139, 145, 207, 221f, 717, 719, 722f
Mauduit, Jacques, 386 (incl. Ex. 88), 389, 504
Maximilian I, Emperor, 109, 116, 138, 170, 212, 221, 265, 267, 641f, 649, 655f, 689, 723
Maximilian II, Emperor, 457, 600, 615, 690
May, Hans von, 467, 600ff, 606, 608
Mayer, August L., 594
Maynard, John, 836, 844
Mayshuet, 22
Mazzone, Marc'Antonio, 400
McAlpine, Carlotta L., 107
McPeek, Gwynn S., 764
Me stesso incolpo (= *Sancta Maria ora pro nobis*), Cara and Tromboncino, 167
mean-tone tuning, see: intonation (= tuning)
meane (the term), 853
Meane, Blitheman, 854
mechanical reproduction of music, 436, 687
Media vita: Greg. Chant, 347, 668; Gombert, 347; Lohet, 668
Mediatrix nostra, Greg. Chant, 195
Medici, Alessandro de', 322; Catherine de', 571; Cosimo I de', 325, 365, 436, 567; Ferdinando de', 425, 569; Francesco de', 419, 425, 568; Giovanni de' (son of Cosimo the Elder), 58; Giovanni de' (son of Lorenzo

the Magnificent; = Leo X, q. v.); Giulio de' (= Clement VII), 362, 545f; Lorenzo de' (the Magnificent), 51f, 153, 168ff, 172f, 176, 185, 208, 212, 215, 286, 322, 453, 567; Lucrezia de', 453; Piero de', 51, 58; Pietro de', 222
Medicean edition of the Chant, 260, 458
Medulla, 869
Megli, Domenico, 835
Megnier, D., 561
Meiland, Jacob, 682, 712
Mein gmüth ist mir verwirret, Hassler, 711f (incl. Ex. 161)
Mein hercz jn hohen frewden ist, Georg von Putenheim, 658
Mein herz in hohen freuden stet, Senfl, 708
Mein herz in steten treùen: the melody, 638; Schoenberg, 638
Mein herz ist mir gemenget: the melody, 638; Schoenberg, 638
Mein höchste frucht, Rener, 639
Mein müterlein, Isaac, 643
Mein traut gesell, 636f (incl. Ex. 141a)
Meins traurens ist, Hofhaimer, 642 (Ex. 143)
Meister, Karl S. (Meist), 679
Meistersinger, 642, 651ff, 718
Meistersinger, Die, Wagner, 652, 708
Mel, René de (= Rinaldo del), 220, 357, 427ff, 482
Melanchthon, Philipp, 677, 681f
Meldert, Leonardo, 411
Melismata, Ravenscroft, 833f
Mellon Chansonnier, see: Manuscripts—New Haven
Melodia Olympica, 427f, 430
melodic idioms or formulas, 104, 123, 206, 314, 317f, 321, 816; see also: narrative formula; also last items under: *ostinato*
melodic-nucleus technique, 26, 29
melodic sequence, 16, 104, 195, 215, 246f (incl. Ex. 46), 265, 355, 363 (Ex. 81), 432 (incl. Ex. 104), 602, 620, 792, 830 (incl. Ex. 197), 875 (Ex. 214)
Melodie spirituali, Peetrino, 447
Melopeo y Maestro, El, Cerone, 350, 618f
Memento salutis, Compère, 227
Memmo (= Memo), Dionisio, 663, 771f
Memoirs, North, 869
Mémoires, Olivier de la Marche, 57
Memor esto verbi tui: Josquin, 246f (incl. Ex. 46), 259, 262; Palestrina, 471
Memorare, Peñalosa, 580
Memorare Mater Christi (= *Hymnus de septem doloribus*), Pipelare, 275
Menčetić, Šiško, 758
Mendel, Arthur (Mend), 529f, 532, 661, 813
Mendes, Manuel, 598
Menehou, Michel de (Mene), 294
Menghini, Mario, 157
mensura (a keyboard form), 657
Mente tota (= Pars V of *Vultum tuum*, q. v.), Josquin, 257, 279, 372
Mentre che'l cor, Willaert, 324 (incl. Ex. 69)

Mentre fiamma d'orgoglio, Monte, 407f
Mentre io mirava fiso, Monteverdi, 440
Mentre sperai, Monte, 408
Merbecke (= Marbeck), John, 781, 795ff
Mercati, Angelo (Merc), 527
Mercè, mercè, o morte, 30
Merian, Wilhelm (Mer), 564, 662, 665ff, 681, 683, 690, 717
Merker (= marker), 652
Merritt, A. Tillman, 75, 344
Mersenne, Marin, 386, 504f, 555f
Merulo, Claudio (Meru): biogr. and madrigals, 417, 419; sacr. mus., 496; instr. mus., 537, 540f (incl. Ex. 125); mus. for dramatic presentations, 569; M. as printer, 317, 319, 417, 494; see also 378, 490, 544f, 726
Mes pensées, Compère, 224
Meskin es hu, Obrecht, 189
Metamorfosi musicale, Banchieri, 437
Methodius, 728
Metzger, Ambrosius, 655
Mexico, 593
Mey, Kurt, 653
Meyer, Clemens (My), 656
Meyer, Ernst H. (Meye), 565, 834, 868ff
Meyer, Gregor, 681
Meyer, Kathi (Me), 37, 154f, 335, 338
Meyer, see also: Sigtenhorst Meyer
Meyere, Jacques de, 207, 221, 725
Mi fa lasso languire, Marenzio, 422
Mi larés vous tousjours languir, Josquin, **234**
Mia benigna fortuna, Rore, 332
Michael (= Pesenti? Vicentino?), 159
Michael, Rogier, 684
Michaelis, Otto (Mich), 677
Michel, Artur, 37, 176
Michel, Francisque, 150
Michelangelo Buonarroti, 158, 259f, 313f, 321f, 413
Micheli, Domenico, 413
Micrologus, Ornithoparchus, 180, 639, **810**, 844
microtones, 328f, 389
Middleton, Thomas, 881
Mielich, Hans, 376, 691
Mies, Otto H., 847
Mignonne, allon voir, Costeley, 388 (incl. **Ex. 89**)
Mignonne, je me plains, Le Jeune, 384
Migravit Judas, A. de Févin, 279f
Mihi autem, Leopolita, 750
Mijn hert heft: 2 anon. settings, 273; La Rue, 273
Mikołaj z Radomia, see: Nicholas of Radom, 743
Milán, Luis, 620ff (incl. Ex. 137), 630
Milano, Francesco da, 555, 627, 842
Mille quingentis (= *Requiem*; not a Mass), Obrecht, 186, 191, 245
Mille regretz, Josquin, 588
Miller, Catharine K. (Mllr), 765
Miller, Hugh M. (Mill), 855, 858
Miller, Poland (Mlr), 390

Milton, John (father of the poet), 808f
Min frow, min frow, Alanus, 632
Min herz, Alanus, 632
Mincoff-Marriage, Elizabeth (Min), 356f; see also: Marriage, Elizabeth
Minieri-Riccio, Camillo, 145
Minnesinger, 632, 635, 652ff
Minnesinger tradition, 635, 728f
Minor, Andrew C., 282ff
minuta (the term), 545; see also: ornamentation
Miodoński, 743
Mirabile mysterium, Gallus, 737f (incl. Ex. 168)
Mirabiles elationes, Merulo, 496
miracle plays, see: dramatic presentations
Miscellany, Tottel, 771
Misereatur mei, Richafort, 336
Miseremini mei, Mouton, 282
Miserere mei Deus: G. Gabrieli, 498; Josquin, 248 (incl. Ex. 47), 336, 462; Lassus, 694; Tye, 783
Miserere mihi, Domine, Byrd, 788
Miserere nostri, Tallis, 785 (incl. Ex. 182)
Miserere instrumental pieces: general, 846; i. ensemble, 869; keyboard, 857f; lute, 848
Miséricorde, Clemens, 2 settings, 351
Missa A Battaglia, Annibale, 700; *M. A la fontaine du prez*, Clemens, 351f; *M. A la Incoronation*, Gombert, 347; *M. A l'ombre d'un(g) buysonet*, Brumel, 261; *ditto*, Carpentras, 286; *M. a note negre*, Rore, 375; *M. Accueillie m'a*, Caron, 111; *M. ad fugam*, Josquin, 245; *M. ad placitum*, Cadéac, 341; *M. Adieu mes amours*, Layolle, 343; *ditto* I (= *M. diversorum tonorum*), Obrecht, 195f; *ditto* II, Obrecht, 196; *M. Adjuva me*, Certon, 339; *M. Albanus*, Fayrfax, 775ff (incl. Ex. 177); *M. Alleluya*, Mouton, 283f; *M. Allez regrets*, Compère, 228; *ditto*, Josquin, 244; *M. Alma Redemptoris Mater*, Mouton, 284; *ditto*, Power, 66, 95; *ditto*, Victoria, 607f; *M. L'Ami Baudichon*, Josquin, 244; *M. Amor ecco colei*, Lassus, 696; *M. Anchor che col partire*, Monte, 703f; *M. Apon ye square*, Whytbroke, 777; *M. Ascendens Christus*, Victoria, 608; *M. Ascendo ad Patrem*, Palestrina, 477f; *M. Aspice Domine*, Monte, 366, 703; *ditto*, Morales, 588; *ditto*, Palestrina, 366; *M. Assumpta est Maria*, Palestrina, 477f; *M. Au travail suis*, Ockeghem, 128ff; *M. Audi filia*, Goudimel, 502; *M. Ave Domine Jesu Christe*, Compère, 227; *M. Ave Maria*, A. de Févin, 279, 559; *ditto*, La Rue, 268f (incl. Ex. 52); *ditto*, Morales, 589 (incl. Ex. 131); *ditto*, Peñalosa, 580; *M. Ave maris stella*, Animuccia, 455; *ditto*, Josquin, 241f, 244f; *ditto*, Morales, 589f; *ditto*, Victoria, 605; *M. Ave Regina*, Arcadelt, 501; *ditto*, Dufay, 72, 76; *ditto*, Victoria, 607f; *ditto*, Weerbecke, 218; *M. Ave Regina* (= *A. R. . . . Mater Regis*), Obrecht, 198, 200f; *M. Ave sanctissima*

Maria, La Rue, 269f; *M. L'aveuglé dieu*, Janequin, 340; *M. Baise moy*, Forestier, 278; *M. Basse danse*, Faugues, 111; *M. Bataille de Marignan*, Guerrero, 595; *ditto*, Janequin, 340; *M. Batalla*, Esquivel, 610; *M. Beati omnes*, Gombert, 347; *M. La belle se sied*, Ghiselin, 266; *ditto*, de Orto, 265; *M. Benedicam Dominum*, Merulo, 496; *M. Benedicta es coelorum Regina*, La Hèle, 511; *ditto*, Monte, 703ff (incl. Ex. 158); *ditto*, Morales, 588; *ditto*, Palestrina, 475, 480; *ditto*, Willaert, 371; *M. Benedictus Dominus Deus*, Mouton, 283f; *M. Bergerette savoyene*, Brumel, 261; *M. Le bergier et la bergiere*, Lassus, 696; *M. Beschaffenes Glück*, Lassus, 696; *M. Le bien que j'ai*, Goudimel, 502; *M. Bon temps*, Brumel, 261; *M. brevis*, see separate subject entry; *M. Caça*, Morales, 588; *M. Cantabo Domino*, Viadana, 489; *M. Cantantibus organis*, jointly by Dragoni, Giovanelli, Mancini, Palestrina, Santini, Soriano, and Stabile, 485; *M. Caput*, Dufay, 67ff, 126, 196f, 773; *ditto*, Obrecht, 196f, 773; *ditto*, Ockeghem, 125f, 196f, 773; *M. Cara la vita mia*, Merulo, 496; *ditto*, Monte, 703f; *M. super carmen italicum*, Fossa, 696; *M. carminum*, Isaac, 647f, 650; *ditto* (= *M. diversorum tenorum*), Obrecht, 195f; *M. Caro mea*, Clemens, 351f; *M. Cela sans plus*, Martini, 223; *M. Chargé de deul*, Isaac, 214f; *M. Christus resurgens*, Pasche, 777; *ditto*, Pulaer, 337; *ditto*, Willaert, 371; *M. Christus surrexit*, Dufay (?), 63; *M. Coda de pavon*, Martini, 223; *M. Comme femme*, Isaac, 214; *M. Conceptio tua*, La Rue, 268f; *M. Conditor alme siderum*, Animuccia, 455; *M. Confitebor tibi*, Monte, 703; *M. Corona spinea*, Taverner, 778f; *M. Cortilla* (= *M. super Fa re ut fa sol la*), Morales, 588; *M. Credidi propter*, Lassus, 696; *M. Cucu*, Martini, 223 (incl. Ex. 41); *M. Cuiusvis toni*, Ockeghem, 131, 133; *M. Cum sit omnipotens rector Olympi*, Monte, 703; *M. Cunctipotens*, anon., 560; *M. Cunctorum plasmator* (= *M. L'Homme armé*), Tinctoris, 149; *M. Da pacem*, Gombert, 347; *ditto*, Josquin, 241f; *M. de Alamania* (= *M. Regina mearum*), Mouton, 284; *M. de Beata Virgine* (see also *M. de Nuestra Señora*), Animuccia, 455; *ditto*, Arcadelt, 501; *ditto*, Brumel, 243f, 260f; *ditto*, Cavazzoni, 536 (incl. Ex. 123); *ditto*, Heinrich Finck, 646f (incl. Ex. 144); *ditto*, Guerrero, 595; *ditto*, Josquin, 241ff (incl. Ex. 45), 260f; *ditto*, Kerle, 452; *ditto*, 2 settings, Morales, 589, 605; *ditto*, 2 settings, Palestrina, 473; *ditto*, Rodio, 486; *ditto*, Victoria, 605; *M. de doloribus*, La Rue, 268f; *M. de Feria*, A. de Févin, 279; *ditto*, La Rue, 269; *ditto*, Mendes, 598; *ditto*, Pipelare, 275; *ditto*, Ruffo, 490 (incl. Ex. 113); *M. de Franza*, Basiron, 117; *M. de la mapa mundi*, Cornago, 576; *M. De mes en-*

nuys, Goudimel, 502; M. *de Nuestra Señora*, Anchieta and Escobar, 578f; M. *De plus en plus*, Ockeghem, 87, 128; M. *de Sancta Anna* (= M. *Felix Anna*), La Rue, 270; M. *de Sancta Cruce*, La Rue, 268; M. *De silde al cavallero*, Morales, 588; M. *de Spiritu Sancto*, Rhaw, 678; M. *De tous biens plaine* (= M. *sine nomine*), Obrecht, 198f (incl. Ex. 35); M. *Der Pfoben, Swancz*, Obrecht, 200; M. *Descendi*, Brumel, 261; M. *Descendit angelus*, Palestrina, 285; M. *Deus in adjutorium*, Lassus, 697; M. *Di dadi*, Josquin, 244; M. *Dictes moy toutes vos pensées* (= M. *sine nomine*), Mouton, 284; M. *Dies est laetitiae*, Szadek, 753; M. *diversorum tenorum* (= M. *carminum*; M. *Adieu mes amours I*), Obrecht, 195f; M. *Dixerunt discipuli*, Brumel, 263; M. *Dixit Joseph*, Lassus, 696f; M. *La dolce vista*, Monte, 703f; M. *Domine, da nobis*, Paix, 202; M. *Domine quis habitavit*, Sermisy, 338; M. *dominicalis*, Heinrich Finck, 647; *ditto*, de Orto, 265; *ditto*, Palestrina, 474; *ditto*, Senfl, 689; *ditto*, Victoria (?), 601; M. *Dormend' un giorn'*, Guerrero, 595; M. *Douce mémoire*, Lassus, 696; M. *Dringhs*, Brumel, 261; M. *duarum facierum*, Moulu, 277 (incl. Ex. 55); M. *Dulcis amica*, Lassus, 696; M. *Dueil angoisseux*, anon., 87; M. *Dum complerentur*, Victoria, 608; M. *D'ung aultre amer*, Josquin, 245, 258, 270; M. *D'ung petit mot sine pausa*, Crequillon, 350; M. *Ecce ancilla Domini*, Dufay, 72, 75f, 107; *ditto*, Regis, 115; M. *Ecce nunc benedicite*, Daser, 696; *ditto*, Lassus, 696; M. *Ecce quam bonum*, Clemens, 351f; M. *Ecce sacerdos magnus*, Palestrina, 456, 472; M. *Ego sum panis*, Cadéac, 341, 348; M. *Elisabethae impletum est tempus*, Gallus, 739; M. *En douleur, en tristesse*, Bauldeweyn, 338; M. *En espoir*, Clemens, 351; M. *Entre vous filles*, Lassus, 696; M. *Et ecce terraemotus*, Brumel, 261; M. *Euge bone*, Tye, 782; M. *Faulte d'argent*, Mouton, 284; M. *Faulx perverse*, Barbireau, 116; M. *Faysant regrets*, Josquin, 244; M. *La fede non debbe esser corrotta*, Jaquet of Mantua, 367; M. *Felix Anna* (= M. *de Sancta Anna*), La Rue, 270; M. *festivale* (= M. *Je n'ay dueil*), Brumel, 261; M. *Filipina*, Cardoso, 599; M. *Flos regalis*, Frye, 95; M. *Fons bonitatis*, anon., 560; M. *Forseulement*, Gombert, 347f; *ditto*, Obrecht, 201; *ditto*, Ockeghem, 112, 126ff, 135, 198; *ditto*, Pipelare, 275, 347; M. *Fortuna desperata*, Josquin, 240; *ditto*, Obrecht, 201, 240; *French Mass*, Shepherd, 784; M. *Frölich wesen*, Isaac, 117, 648; M. *Galeazescha*, Compère, 227; M. *Gaude Barbara*, Willaert, 371; M. *Gaude lux Donatiane*, Clemens, 352; M. *Gaudeamus*, Josquin, 241, 244, 259; *ditto*, Victoria, 608; M. *Gloria tibi Trinitas*, Taverner, 778f (incl. Ex. 179), 845; M. *Gustate et videte*,

Lassus, 511; M. *Hercules [I] Dux Ferrariae*, Josquin, 236f, 239, 342f; M. *Hercules [II] Dux Ferrariae*, Lupus, 342f; two Hercules II Masses differently entitled, Rore, 375; M. *Hodie Christus natus est*, Palestrina, 477; M. *Hodie nobis*, Compère, 227; M. *L'Homme armé*, anon. of Naples, Bibl. naz. VI. E. 40 (set of 6 Masses), 149f, 204, 723; *ditto*, Basiron, 117; *ditto*, Brumel, 261; *ditto*, Busnois, 73, 107, 109; *ditto*, Caron, 109, 111; *ditto*, Carver, 777; *ditto*, Compère, 228; *ditto*, Dufay, 72, 74f (incl. Ex. 19), 109; *ditto*, Faugues, 109, 111ff, 117, 133; *ditto*, Forestier, 278; *ditto* (*sexti toni*), Josquin, 238f; *ditto* (*super voces musicales*), Josquin, 236ff; *ditto*, 2 settings, La Rue, 269; *ditto*, 2 settings, Morales, 588; *ditto*, Mouton, 285; *ditto*, Obrecht, 196ff, 239; *ditto*, Ockeghem, 72, 125f; *ditto*, de Orto, 265; *ditto*, 2 settings, Palestrina, 473, 618; *ditto*, Pipelare, 275; *ditto*, Regis, 109, 114; *ditto* (= M. *Cunctorum plasmator*), Tinctoris, 149; *ditto*, Vaqueras, 136; M. *Hor le tue forze adopra*, Anerio, 484; M. *In convertendo*, La Hèle, 511; M. *In die tribulationis*, Lassus, 696; M. *In illo tempore*, Monteverdi, 344, 500; M. *In myne zyn*, A. Agricola, 210; M. *in summis*, Heinrich Finck, 647; M. *Inclina cor meum*, Monte, 703; M. *Inviolata integra*, Bauldeweyn, 338; M. *Io ne tengo*, Martini, 223; M. *Io son ferito*, Lassus, 696; M. *Ista est speciosa*, La Rue, 268; M. *Ite, rime dolenti*, Lassus, 696; M. *J'ay pris amours*, de Orto, 265; M. *Jay veu le cerf*, Clemens, 351; M. *Je n'ay dueil*, Brumel, 261; *ditto*, de Orto, 266; M. *Je ne demande*, A. Agricola, 210f; *ditto*, Obrecht, 203f (incl. Ex. 37), 461, 869; M. *Je suis desheritée*, Gombert, 341, 347; *ditto*, Guyon, 341; *ditto*, Lassus, 307, 696; *ditto*, Maillard, 341; *ditto*, Marle, 341; *ditto* (= M. *sine nomine*), Palestrina, 307, 475, 478; M. *Jesus ist ein süsser Nam'*, Lassus, 696; M. *La sol fa mi re ut*, Vinci, 492; M. *La sol fa re mi*, Josquin, 238f; M. *Laetatus sum*, Victoria, 608; M. *Languir my fault*, Clemens, 351f; M. *Laudate Dominum*, Palestrina, 484; M. *Levavi oculos*, Cadéac, 341; M. *Libenter gloriabor*, Obrecht, 195, 204, 341; M. *L'oserai-je dire*, Mouton, 284; M. *Ma bouche rit*, Martini, 223; M. *Malheur me bat*, A. Agricola, 210f; *ditto*, Josquin, 239f; *ditto*, Obrecht, 198ff, 202, 204; *ditto*, de Silva, 368; M. *Maria Magdalena*, N. Champion, 338; M. *Maria zart*, Obrecht, 193ff (incl. Ex. 34*b*), 199, 202; M. *La Martinella*, Martini, 223; M. *Mater Christi*, Taverner, 778; M. *Mater Patris*, Josquin, 240, 262; M. *Media vita*, Gombert, 347; M. *Mente tota*, A. de Févin, 257, 279, 372; *ditto*, Willaert, 257, 372; M. *Mi-Mi* (= M. *Quarti toni*), Ockeghem, 131ff (incl. Ex. 30), 204, 675; *ditto* (= M. *Petite camusette*), Pipelare, 275; M. *Mijn hert heft*, Gascoing, 273; M. *Mille regretz*,

Morales, 588; *M. Miséricorde*, Clemens, 351f;
M. Misericordias Domini, Isaac, 214f (incl.
Ex. 40); *M. Mittit ad Virginem*, Willaert,
372; *M. La mort de Saint Gothard*, Dufay,
63, 66, 68f, 71; *M. Mort e merci*, Berchem,
341; *M. Mortuorum*, Porta, 494; *M. N'as
tu pas*, Weerbecke, 218; *M. Nasce la pena
mia*, Monte, 703; *M. Nigra sum sed formosa*,
La Hèle, 511; *M. Nobilis et pulchra*, Frye,
95; *M. Noé Noé*, Arcadelt, 282, 501; *M. Nos
autem gloriari*, Soriano, 485; "*Messe Notre
Dame*," Machaut, 39f; *M. Nunca fué pena
mayor*, Peñalosa, 580; *M. O altitudo divitiarum*, Monte, 703; *M. O bone Jesu*, Fayrfax,
777; *M. O crux lignum*, Busnois, 107; *M. O
Dei genitrix*, Richafort, 336; *M. O gloriosa
Margaretha*, La Rue, 267; *M. O magnum
mysterium*, Victoria, 606f (incl. Ex. 134*a*);
M. O Michael, Taverner, 778f; *M. O passi
sparsi*, Sermisy, 292; *M. O praeclara*, Isaac,
215, 648; *M. O quam glorifica*, Fayrfax, 776;
M. O quam gloriosum, Victoria, 606; *M. O
quam suavis*, Brumel, 261; Lloyd, 774;
M. O rosa bella, 3 Masses, anon., 93, 774;
M. O salutaris hostia, La Rue, 269; *M. O
Venus banth*, Weerbecke, 218; *M. Octavi
toni*, Asola, 493; *Officium Auleni*, Aulen
(?), 646; *M. Or combien*, Clemens, 351f; *M.
O Regem coeli*, Palestrina, 368; *M. Pange
lingua*, Josquin, 241, 244; *M. Panis quem
ego dabo*, Clemens, 352; *ditto*, "Lupus"
(Hellinck?), 342; *ditto*, Palestrina, 477,
598; *ditto*, Roy, 486; *M. Papae Marcelli*,
Palestrina, 452, 480; *ditto* arranged *a 4* by
Anerio, 485; *ditto* arranged *a 8* by Soriano,
485; *M. Paschale*, Barbireau, 116; *ditto*,
La Rue, 268; *M. Paschalis*, Isaac, 647f (incl.
Ex. 145); *ditto*, Leopolita, 750 (incl. Ex.
171*b*); *M. Paschalis* (*super Je ne vis oncques*)
A. Agricola, 211; *M. Pastores quidnam
vidistis*, Clemens, 351; *M. Pater peccavi*, A.
Gabrieli, 496; *M. Per arma justitiae*, Mer-
becke, 781; *M. Petite camusette* (= *M.
Petita camuseta*), de Orto, 265; *ditto* (=
M. Mi-Mi), Pipelare, 275; *M. Philomena
praevia*, Gombert, 347; *ditto*, Verdelot or
Sermisy, 337; *M. Pis ne me peult venir*,
Crecquillon, 753; *ditto*, Szadek, 753; *M.
Playn Song*, Taverner, 778f; *Playnsong
Mass for a Mene*, Shepherd, 784; *M. plurium
motettorum*, Sermisy, 338; *M. Pour quelque
paine*, Heyns, 136; *M. Praeter rerum seriem*,
La Hèle, 511; *ditto*, Rore, 375; *M. prima
Sexti toni*, Croce, 499; *M. Primi toni*, A.
Agricola, 210f; *M. Princesse d'amorettes*,
Weerbecke, 218; *M. pro defunctis*, see: Requiem Mass; *M. pro victoria*, 608ff; *M. Pro-
lationum*, Ockeghem, 131, 133ff (Ex. 31),
294, 479; *M. Puis que je vis*, Dufay (?), 63;
M. Quaeramus cum pastoribus, Morales, 282,
588; *ditto*, Willaert, 371; *M. Qual donna
attende*, Lassus, 696; *M. Qual è il più
grand'amor*, Palestrina, 476, 478; *M. Quam

pulchra es, Clemens, 351; *ditto*, Gombert,
338, 347; *M. Quam pulchri sunt*, Victoria,
608; *M. Quand'io penso*, Lassus, 696; *M.
Quando lieta sperai*, Monte, 703; *M. Quant
ce vendra*, anon., 107; *M. Quant j'ay au cor*,
Isaac, 214f; *M. Quarti toni*, Ockeghem, see *M.
Mi-Mi*; *ditto*, Victoria, 608; *M. Quem dicunt
homines*, Divitis, 276f, 336; *ditto*, Josquin,
336; *ditto*, Morales, 336, 588; *ditto*, Mouton,
284, 336; *ditto*, Palestrina, 336; *M. Quinti toni*, Ockeghem, 131; *M. Regali*, Fayrfax, 776;
M. Regina mearum (= *M. De Alamania*),
Mouton, 284; *M. Regnum mundi*, Certon,
339; *M. Repleatur os meum*, Palestrina, 366,
477, 479f; *M. Reviens vers moy*, Monte, 703;
M. Rex saeculorum, Power or Dunstable, 66;
M. Rosa playsant, Obrecht, 202f (incl. Ex.
36*b*); *M. Salve diva parens*, Obrecht, 187;
M. Salve intemerata, Tallis, 786; *M. Salve
Regina*, Victoria, 607f; *M. Salvum me fac*,
Palestrina, 366; *M. Sancta Maria*, Gombert,
347; *M. Sancta Trinitas*, Févin, 279; *ditto*,
Mouton, 284; *M. Sancti Anthonii de Padua*,
Dufay, 63, 77; *M. Sancti Anthonii Viennen-
sis*, Dufay, 63; *M. Sancti Jacobi*, Dufay, 60,
63ff (incl. Ex. 15), 68; *M. Scarco di doglia*,
Lassus, 696; *M. Se la face ay pale*, Dufay,
68, 69ff (incl. Exx. 16 and 17), 145; *M.
Secundi toni*, A. Agricola, 210f; *M. Le
serviteur*, anon., 112; *ditto*, A. Agricola,
210f; *ditto*, Faugues, 112f, 115, 143, 198;
M. Si bona suscepimus, Morales, 588; *M.
Si dedero*, Divitis, 276; *ditto*, Obrecht,
201f; *M. Sicut spina rosam*, Obrecht, 204;
M. Sidus ex claro, Lassus, 697; *M. Simile
est regnum caelorum*, Victoria, 608; *M. sine
cadentia*, Mouton, 285; *M. sine nomine*,
Mouton, 283; *ditto* (a different work),
Mouton, see: *M. Dictes moy*; *ditto*, Obrecht,
see: *M. De tous biens plaine*; *ditto*, Palles-
trina, see: *M. Je suis desheritée*; other Masses
without titles: anon. (in Breslau MS), 646;
anon. (in Egerton *3307*), 765; Adam von
Fulda, 646; Brumel, 2 Masses, 261; Byrd,
3 Masses, 787f; Dufay, 60, 63; Grossin, 43
(*M. with trumpet*); Josquin, 245; Arnold de
Lantins, 39, 60; Liebert, 65, 68; Johannes
de Limburgia, 42; Ludford, 7 Masses, 774;
Monte, 4 Masses, 703, 705; Ockeghem, 2
Masses, 130f; Tallis, 786; Taverner, 778,
780; Tinctoris, 3 Masses, 149; Viadana, 489;
Willaert, 371; *M. Small Devotion*, Taverner,
778; *M. Soyez aprantiz*, Rouge, 92; *M. La
Spagna*, Isaac, 214f; *M. Spem in alium*,
Palestrina, 366; *M. Spes salutis*, Clemens,
351f; *M. Sub tuum praesidium*, Obrecht,
195f; *M. Summae Trinitati*, Frye, 95; *M.
Super voces musicales*, Soriano, 485; *M. Sur
le pont d'Avignon*, Certon 339; *M. Surge
et illuminare*, Manchicourt, 351; *M. Surge
propera*, Victoria, 608; *M. Susanne un jour*,
Lassus 696; *M. Tant plus ie metz*, Goudimel,
502; *M. Te Deum*, Aston, 777; *M. Tempore

paschali, Gombert, 347; *M. Teribilment,* Barbingant, 115f; *M. Trahe me post te,* Victoria, 608; *M. Tristezas me matan,* Morales, 588; *M. Trombetta,* Gafori, 181; *M. Tu es Petrus,* Mouton, 284; *M. Tua est potentia,* Mouton, 284; *M. Ultimi miei sospiri,* Monte, 703; *M. Un gay bergier,* Gallus, 738; *M. Una musque de Buscaya,* Josquin, 244; *M. Upon the Square,* Mundy, 786; *M. Ut re mi fa sol la,* Esquivel, 610; *ditto,* Morales, 588; *ditto,* Palestrina, 473; *M. Veni sponsa Christi,* Lupi, 342; *M. Verbum bonum,* Mouton, 284; *ditto,* Ruffino, 285; *M. Vestiva i colli,* Giovanelli, 485; *ditto,* Monte, 703f; *ditto,* Nanino, 483; *M. Veterem hominem,* Dufay(?), 63; *M. Victimae paschali,* Brumel, 261; *M. Videte manus meas,* Aston, 777; *M. Vidi speciosam,* Victoria, 606f; *M. Vinum bonum,* Lassus, 696f; *M. Virgo parens Christi,* Barbireau, 116; *M. Virgo prudentissima,* Isaac, 649; *M. Virtute magna,* Clemens, 352; *M. Vivat felix Hercules secundus,* Rore, 375; *M. Vulnerasti cor meum,* Morales, 588; *M. Western Wynde,* Shepherd, 784; *ditto,* Taverner, 778f; *ditto,* Tye, 782

Missa brevis type: general, 450, 491; anon., 765; G. F. Anerio, 485; Croce, 499; A. Gabrieli, 496; Gafori, 181; Ockeghem, 130; Palestrina, 470; Weerbecke, 218

Missus est Gabriel angelus, Josquin, 2 settings, 254f

Mit ganczen willen, the melody and Paumann's setting, 660 (Ex. 147*b*)

Mitjana, Rafael (Mit), 577, 580ff, 585, 587f, 591f, 594ff, 600, 608ff, 613, 616f

Mitou, Maître, see: Daniel, Jean

Mitten wir im Leben sind: the text (= *Media vita*), 674; Resinarius, 679

Mittit ad Virginem, Josquin, 252

Moberg, Carl A., 742

Mocenigo, Tommaso, Doge of Venice, 26

Mocht ich dein begeren, 636

Mock-Nightingall, 867

Moderne, Jacques (= Grand Jacques), 290, 300, 341, 343, 381, 564

modes, 141, 182f, 185f, 377, 384, 562, 654, 858; see also: modulation; tonality

modulation and transition, 195, 257, 370, 404, 423, 440, 508, 525, 704, 839, 861ff

Mögeling (= Mügling), Heinrich von, 652f, 728f

Mohr, Ernst, 564, 668

Molinaro, Simone, 431ff, 489, 523, 526, 528

Molinet, Jean, 12, 87, 101, 118, 137, 213, 227

Molino, Antonio, 445

Molins, Pierre des, 12

Molitor, Raphael (Mol), 154, 458, 609

Moller, see Burck, Joachim a

Molmenti, Pompeo, 25

Molnár, Géza (Moln), 716

Molza, Tarquinia, 409, 546

Mompellio, Federico (Mom), 413

Mon cuer chante, Binchois, 87

Mon cueur a demy, Prioris, 264

Mon cueur et moi, Prioris, 264

Mon cueur me fait, Dufay, 56

Mon coeur se recommande à vous: setting *a 4,* attrib. to Lassus (incorrectly?), 395; setting *a 5* by Lassus, 395

Mon doulx amy tenés, Fontaine, 34f

Mon doulx espoir, Binchois, 87

Mon mignault—Gracieuse, Busnois, 103, 196

Mon père m'a donné mari, Isaac, 214

Mon petit cueur: anon., 309; Willaert, 309

Mon seul plaisir, 206f

Mon souvenir, Hayne, 336

monacordo, monachordio, see: clavichord

Mone, Franz J., 94

Monetarius, see: Münzer, Stephan

monody and monodic style, 160, 410, 413, 442, 489, 620, 762; see also: ayre; contrapuntally accompanied solo song; lute accompaniment; lute songs; solo madrigal; *vihuela* songs

monophony, 205ff, 355f, 358ff, 650ff, 683, 717f, 730ff

Montagna, Bartolomeo, 546

Montanari, Giovanni Battista, 425

Montanos, Francisco de, 592f

Montanus (= Berg) and Neuber, 256f, 344, 365, 373, 516, 682, 706

Monte, Joannes de, 586

Monte, Philippe de: biogr., 395f, 406, 457, 511, 726, 737, 788; historical position, 380, 406, 413, 702; sec. voc. mus., 395f, 406ff (incl. Ex. 95), 411; sacr. mus., 366, 792ff (incl. Ex. 158); traits of M.'s style mentioned elsewhere, 405, 409, 420, 692; see also 287, 397, 401, 427, 430, 516, 666, 670, 700

Montella, Gian Domenico, 486

Monteverdi, Claudio (Montev): biogr., 437f, 491, 500; sec. voc. mus., 413, 437ff (incl. Exx. 106, 107), 446f; sacr. mus., 344, 500f; traits of M.'s style mentioned elsewhere, 831, 838; see also 401, 409, 460, 832

Monti, Gennaro M., 333

Morago, Estêvão Lopes, 598

Moraleda y Esteban, Juan, 597

Morales, Cristóbal de: biogr., 364, 587f; sec. voc. mus., 588; sacr. mus., 282, 336, 472, 588ff (incl. Ex. 131), 595; see also 594, 600

Moralia, Gallus, 739

morality plays, see: mystery plays

Morata, Gines de, 598

Moravian Brethren (= Czech Brethren) and their hymns, 735

More, Sir Thomas, 850

Morelot, Stephen (Mo), 97, 100, 121, 244

moresca (= morris), 173, 567, 864

moresca (villanella type), 444

Morì quasi il mio core, Palestrina, 402 (incl. Ex. 93), 409

Moribus—Virgo, Dufay, 80

Morlaye, Guillaume, 553f

Morley, Thomas (Morl): biogr., 792, 810; sec. voc. mus., 446, 822ff (incl. Exx. 191, 192*b*), 831f, 835, 882; sacr. mus. with Lat. text, 792f; sacr. mus. with Engl. text, 805, 808; instr. mus., 851, 861, 865, 867, 870f, 873, 874f (incl. Ex. 214); traits of M.'s style mentioned elsewhere, 820, 828f; M. as theorist, 148, 182, 532f, 792; see also 787, 806, 815, 819, 834, 839, 844, 880

Moro lasso al mio duolo, Gesualdo, 431

Moroni, Cardinal Giovanni, 449

Morphy, Guillermo (Mor), 588, 592, 594, 596, 612ff, 620ff, 626, 628

Morra, La, Isaac, 212

Morris, Reginald O. (Morr), 212, 480

morris, see: moresca

Mort ou merci vous requiers, Caron, 110

Mort tu as navré, Ockeghem, 121

Mortaro, Antonio, 545

Morton, Robert, 6, 98, 110, 244, 635, 763

Moser, Andreas, 548

Moser, Hans J. (Mos), 94, 148, 165, 175, 217, 271, 274f, 481, 483ff, 634, 636, 638f, 641f, 645, 647, 653f, 656f, 659, 662f, 671, 673, 683, 688, 690f, 702, 705ff, 711, 724, 746

Mosto, Giovanni Battista, 726f

motet: the term, 20f, 140; early use, in the m., of Bible texts generally, 40; of psalm texts, 246ff (incl. Exx. 46–48), 262, 271; of gospel texts, 254; special types: ceremonial and political mm., 21, 25ff, 41, 50, 79, 90, 215, 263, 265, 283, 365, 590f, 599, 609, 649; isorhythmic m., see: isorhythmic; responsory m., see: responsory; song-m., 22, 55, 94f, 98, 140, 225; tenor-m., see: *cantus firmus;* m.-chanson, 55, 58, 208, 225, 233ff, 272; see also: "substitution" Mass; variation-chain sequence

motet-type Passion (defined), 165f

Motetti de la Corona (Petrucci), 246, 337, 368f

Motetti del Fiore (Moderne), 341

Motetti del Frutto (Gardano), 367

motif de tête; motif initial; see: head-motif

motifs generating other motifs, 282, 342, 350

Motta, E, 148, 174, 207, 217f

motto, see head-motif

Moulu, Pierre, 277f (incl. Ex. 55), 283, 471, 559, 662

Mouton, Jean: biogr. and sec. voc. mus., 280f; sacr. mus., 279, 281ff (incl. Exx. 57, 58), 371, 501, 588; see also 184, 309, 335, 337, 623, 629, 663

Moxica, 585

Moytié de Basse dance (= *Il me suffit*), Sermisy, 564

Mrs. Katherin Tregians Pavan (= *Pavana chromatica*), Tisdall, 865

mudanza (the term), 581

Mudarra, Alonso de, 594, 596, 622f, 626ff, 866

Mügling, see Mögeling, Heinrich von

Mülich of Prague, 729

Müller, Erich H., 725, 727

Müller-Blattau, Josef (Mülle), 634, 658, 675

Mulliner, Thomas, 784, 851; see also: Manuscripts—London

Münch von Salzburg, see Hermann

Mundy, John, 811, 819, 861

Mundy, William, 786f, 802, 851

Münzer, Georg, 652, 654

Münzer, Stephan (= Monetarius), 727, 746

Mureau, Gilles, 138, 263

Muris, Jean de, 729

Musae Jovis, Gombert, 305

Musae Sioniae, M. Praetorius, 680, 684

Muset, Joseph, 615, 626, 629

music of the spheres, 141

Musica (treatises): Adam von Fulda, 179; Szydlovita, 743

Musica Dei donum: Clemens, 352f (incl. Ex. 78); Lassus, 352

Musica Deo Sacra, Tomkins, 811ff

Musica divina (Phalèse and Bellère), 427, 821

Musica enchiriadis (treatise), 120

musica ficta, 13, 18f, 89, 230, 297, 353, 586, 665, 858; see also: accidentals; transcription into modern notation

Musica getutscht, Virdung, 555, 656

Musica instrumentalis deudsch, M. Agricola, 656, 757

Musica nova, Willaert, 324

Musica nova . . . per cantar et sonar (Pozzo), 537

Musica practica, Ramos de Pareja, 586f

musica reservata, 511ff

Musica reservata (motet collection), Coclico, 512, 516

Musica . . . sopra le canzone del Petrarcha, Pisano, 313

Musica theorica, L. Fogliano, 158

Musica transalpina (Yonge): Bk. I, 428, 818f, 821, 823; Bk. II, 822

musica vera, 89

Musicall Banquet, R. Dowland, 835, 840, 844

Musicall Gramarian, North, 869

Musicall Humors, Hume, 874

Musices Opusculum, Burzio, 155, 587

Musices practicae erotematum, Faber, 261f

Musiciens qui chantez, Waelrant, 396

Musicke of Sundrie Kindes, Ford, 838

Musiol, Josef, 311, 330ff, 375f, 404, 470, 478

Musique de Joye (Moderne), 564

musique mesurée, 383ff, 504, 839

Musyck Boexken (Susato): Bks. I and II, 308; Bk. III, 564; Bks. IV–VII (= *Souterliedekens,* Clemens), 355ff

My Country, Smetana, 734

My flocks feed not, Weelkes, 826

My frindes, 816

My Lady Carey's Dompe, 853f

My Ladye Nevells Booke, see: Manuscripts—London

My Ladye Nevels Grownde, Byrd, 863

My little sweete darling, Byrd, 817

My Lord Chamberlaine his Galliard (= *Invention for two to play*), J. Dowland, 847
My woeful hart in paynful weryness, Sheryngham, 768
Myn hert, La Rue (not Obrecht), 187
Mystère de la Passion, A. Greban, 150f
Mystère de Roy Advenir, 151
Mystère de Saint Louis, 150ff
Mystère des Actes des apostres, A. and S. Greban, 151
Mystery of Elche, 587, 610
Mystery of Sybil Cassandra, 610
mystery plays, 150f, 716, 877
Myszkowski, Bishop Peter, 751

N. C. (= Nicolaus Cracoviensis), 747, 754
Nach willen dein, Hofhaimer, 670 (Ex. 150a and b)
Nachtgall, Ottmar (= Luscinius), 656, 663
Nachtanz, see: after-dance
Nagel, Willibald (Nag), 652, 771f, 803, 842, 867, 871
Naich, Hubert, 187, 326
Naldi, Antonio, 570
Namque triumphanti, 646
Nanino, Giovanni Bernardino, 424f, 482f
Nanino, Giovanni Maria, 424ff, 447, 482f, 490, 616
napolitana (= *villanella*), 445, 816
N'aray-je jamais mieulx, Morton, 99, 244
narrative formula in chansons and madrigals, 292f, 320, 403, 435
Narváez, Luis de, 613, 621ff (incl. Ex. 138), 627f, 630
Náš milý Svatý Václave, 740
N'as tu pas, 218
Nasce la gioia mia, Primavera, 35
Nasce la pena mia, Striggio, 703
Nasco, Giovanni (= Maistre Jhan of Verona), 326, 368, 400
Nashe, Thomas, 841
Nata est grata polo, Pevernage, 517
Navagero, Cardinal Bernardo, 449
Navarro, Francisco, 593
Navarro, Juan (of Cadiz), 593
Navarro, Juan (of Seville), 593
Naylor, Edward W. (Nay), 738, 768, 770, 844, 849, 851, 853, 867, 879
Ne Geneive, Tristan, Yssout, Cuvelier, 16
Ne irascaris, Byrd, 789
Ne je ne dors, Dufay, 57
Ne più bella di queste, Isaac, 170
Ne reminiscaris, Wilbye, 792
Ne timeas, Greg. Chant, 115
Nedden, Otto zur (Ned), 216, 644, 683
Nef, Karl, 446, 656, 672, 681
Nef, Walther R. (Nf), 663
Nef de Santé, La, La Chesnaye, 36
Negri, Cesare, 523, 525
Nejedlý, Zdenék (Nej), 728, 730ff, 734f, 740
Nelson, Robert U. (Nels), 628, 861
Nenna, Pomponio, 430, 432, 443f, 486
Neri, St. Philip, 452ff

Nerici, Luigi (Neri), 416
Nervi d'Orfeo (Haestens), 427
Nesciens mater virum: Mouton, 282; Wright, 786
Nessun visse giammai: Lassus, 692; Palestrina, 692
Nestor's *Chronicle*, 714
Netherlands (the term), 9; Netherlands Schools (the terms), 8f
Neudenberger, Lucia (Neu), 851, 861
Neüe teütsche Gesang nach art der welschen Madrigalien und Canzonetten, Hassler, 711
Neuschel, Hans, 656
New Booke of Tabliture, A, Barley, 842f, 848f
New Interlude and Mery of the Nature of iiij Elements, A (a play), 878
New Way of Making Fowre Parts in Counterpoint, Campion, 839
Newark, William, 767f, 835
Newe deudsche geistliche Gesenge (Rhaw), 678ff
Newman, Joel (Newm), 527
Newman, William S., 520
Newsidler, Hans, 668ff (incl. Exx. 150, 151), 717, 721, 755
Newsidler, Melchior, 632, 669, 721
Newton, Richard (New), 843f, 847f, 881
Ney, Napoléon J. (Prince de la Moskowa), 431, 469, 484
Niccolo da Perugia, 424
Nicholas V, Pope, 587
Nicholas III of Ferrara, Marquis of Este, 49
Nicholas of Radom (= Mikołaj z Radomia), 743f
Nicholson, Richard, 811, 817
Nicolaus Cracoviensis (= Nicolaus Chrzanowita?), 754
Nicolaus de Zagabria, 759
Nicoll, Allardyce, 883
Nicolo, D., 167
Nielsen, Hans, 713
Niemann, Walter, 646, 649, 852f
Niger, Franciscus, 155
Nightingale, The, Philips, 831
Nightingall, 867
Nigra sum sed formosa: Crecquillon, 511; L'Héritier, 470; Victoria, 600
Nijhoff, W., 356, 555
Nimphes nappés, Josquin, 235, 255
Ninot (= Nynot) le Petit, 190, 207, 278
ninths: melodic, 423, 789; harmonic (unprepared), 441
nio, 164
Nisi Dominus, Asola, 493
Nivelle de la Chaussée Chansonnier, see: Manuscripts—Paris
Noah's Flood (a play), 877
Nobil Accademia delli pittori, 424
Nobilis, Sarum Chant, 95
Nobiltà di dame (= *Il Ballarino*), Caroso, 525
Nobis datus, 611
Nobis post hoc, Kotter, 662
Nobis Sancti Spiritus, A. Agricola, 211

Nobodyes Gigge, The, Farnaby, 866

Nodler, Wenzel, 635

Noe, noe, psallite noe, Mouton, 282, 501

Noel, Henry, 810

Nola, Giovane Domenico da, 333f, 420, 430, 445, 696

Nolo mortem peccatoris, Morley, 805

Non al suo amante: Jacopo da Bologna, 52; Macque, 430

Non derelinquet Dominus, Coclico, 516

Non giacinti o narcisi, Monteverdi, 439

Non moriar sed vivam, Luther, 673

Non nobis Domine, Mouton or Gascongne, 283

non-quartal style, 57, 103f, 142, 643

Non salvatur rex, Coclico, 516 (Ex. 119*b*)

Non si levava, Monteverdi, 440

Non val aqua al mio gran foco, Tromboncino, 159

Norlind, Tobias (Nor), 523, 525, 712, 757

Nörmiger, Augustus, 665ff, 716, 755

North, Roger, 869

Nos autem gloriari, Palestrina, 464

Nos qui sumus in hoc mundo, Lassus, 694

notation: types and procedures, 11, 19, 31, 36f, 133ff, 141, 154f, 289f, 294, 328f, 654, 741, 745; format, 24, 28, 123, 155, 290, 314, 340f, 544, 557, 562, 635, 836; see also: *chiavette;* keyboard tabl.; lute tabl.; proportional system; puzzle pieces; score

note nere (= small time values), 320, 324f, 327, 330, 334

Notker Balbulus, 217, 347

Nous sommes de l'ordre de Saint Babouin, Compère, 224

Nous vous verens bien, Binchois, 87

Nous voyons que les hommes font tous vertu d'aimer (= *Ave Maria*), Arcadelt, 381

Nouvelle Instruction familière, Menehou, 294

Nova musica, Ciconia, 25

Nova vobis gaudia, Grenon, 22

Nove cantum melodie, Binchois, 89, 92

Novum et insigne opus musicum (Montanus and Neuber), 344

Novum pratum musicum, Adriansen, 555

Novus Partus sive Concertationes Musicae, Besard, 555

Now is the month of Maying, Morley, 824

Now must I dye recurelesse, Morley, 823 (Ex. 191*b*)

Now, O now, I needs must part (= *The Frog's Galliard*), the melody, 845

Nowak, Leopold, 641, 670

Nozze di Psiche e Cupidine, Carretto, 158

Nuffel, J. van (Nuff), 395

Nuict froide et sombre, La, Lassus, 392 (incl. Ex. 90)

Nul ne l'a tele, Basiron, 117

Nun bitten wir den heiligen Geist, the melody, 674, 676

Nun freut euch, lieben Christen gmein, Ducis, 680

Nun komm der Heiden Heiland, derivation from *Veni Redemptor gentium,* 674

Nun ruhen alle Wälder (= *Isbruck ich muss dich lassen*), 643

Nunc dimittis: Festa, 362; Tallis, 786

Nunc dimittis: Anglican Canticle, 798; Weelkes, 806

Nunc Sancte nobis Spiritus, Greg. Chant, 83, 467, 469

Nunca fué pena mayor, Wreede, 275, 581

Nuntius celso veniens, Adam von Fulda, 649f

Nuove Inventioni di Balli, Negri, 525

Nuove Musiche, Le, Caccini, 835

Nuper rosarum flores, Dufay, 79f (incl. Ex. 20)

Nympha, refer qual sit vox, Gallus, 738

Nymphes des bois, Josquin, 235

O admirabile commercium: Compère, 227; Josquin, 259; Palestrina, 471; Regis, 114

O altitudo divitiarum, Rore, 376, 703

O beate Basili, Obrecht, 191

O begli anni dell'oro, Corteccia, 568

O bone et dulcis Domine Jesu—Pater noster—Ave Maria, Josquin, 255

O bone Jesu, exaudi me, Palestrina, 2 settings, 469

O bone Jesu, illumina oculos meos, Compère, 225

O bone Jesu, miserere nostri, Palestrina (??), 469

O bone Jesu . . . O dulcissime Jesu, Carver, 777

O bone Jesu, . . . O Jesu plene misericordia, Palestrina, 469

O care thou wilt dispatch mee, Weelkes, 824, 827f (Ex. 194)

O celestial lume, Brolo, 30, 53

O clap your hands, Gibbons, 813

O Crux benedicta, Vinci, 492, 502

O Crux viride lignum, Werrecore, 368

O death rock me asleep, 841

O devotz cueurs—O vos omnes, Compère, 190, 225; anon. keyboard transc., 559

O dolce compagno, Domenico da Ferrara, 30

O Domine Jesu Christe, adoro te: G. Gabrieli, 498; Josquin, 258

O Domine Jesu Christe, pastor bone, Brumel, 262

O felici occhi, Arcadelt, 322f

O felix templum, Ciconia, 27, 53

O filii, Greg. Chant, 281

O flos fragrans, Brassart, 38

O give thanks unto the Lord, Tomkins, 812

O gloriosa Domina: Greg. Chant, 621; Narváez, 621

O gloriosa Regina, Touront, 98

O happye dames, Shepherd, 816

O Haupt voll Blut und Wunden, the text, P. Gerhardt, 711

O invida fortuna, Tinctoris, 149

O Jesu fili David (= *Coment peult haver joye*), Josquin, 256

O Jesu mi dulcissime, G. Gabrieli, 498

O la, o che bon eccho, Lassus, 444
O Leyda gratiosa, Schuyt, 429
O Lord, increase my faith, Gibbons, 814
O Lord, the maker of all thing, W. Mundy, 802
O Lord turn thy wrath, Byrd, 789
O lux beata Trinitas: Greg. Chant (= *Iam sol recedit*), 83, 467; Dufay, 83; Palestrina, 467
O Lux on the faburden, Redford, 854
O magnum mysterium: G. Gabrieli, 498; Palestrina, 470; Victoria, 602, 606f (incl. Ex. 134*a*)
O Mensch, bewein dein' Sünde gross (= *Es sind noch selig*), 683
O Mistress Mine: the melody, 861; Byrd, 861; Morley, 874
O morte, eterno fin, Rore, 331 (Ex. 73)
O nachbar Roland: the melody, Byrd's setting (as *Lord Willobies Welcome Home*) and Scheidt's setting, 881
O najdrozszy kwiatku, 745
O pastor aeterne, Philips, 794
O potores exquisiti, 764
O praise the Lord, all ye heathen, Tomkins, 812
O pray for the peace of Jerusalem, Tomkins, 812
O primavera, Wert, 410
O pulcherrima mulierum: Bauldeweyn, 337; Févin, 279; Arnold de Lantins, 40 (incl. Ex. 4)
O quam glorifica luce: Greg. Chant, 211; A. Agricola, 211
O quam gloriosum, Marenzio, 481
O quam suavis: Greg. Chant, 593; Sarum Chant, 261, 774; G. Gabrieli, 498
O Regem coeli, de Silva, 368, 470
O Rex gloriae: Marenzio, 482; Palestrina, 471
O rosa bella: the text, 30, 153; Ciconia, 30; Dunstable, 30, 93, 146, 774; Hert, 119; Ockeghem, 119
O sacrum convivium: Morales, 472; Viadana, 489
O salutaris hostia (= verse 5 of *Verbum supernum*, q.v.): La Rue, 270; Lassus, 693; Mouton, 281
O the syllye man (= *By painted words*), Edwards, 816
O triste ennuy, Monte, 396
O tu che fra le selve, Marenzio, 422
O vaghe de Jesù (= *O vaghe montanine*), 172
O Venus bant, Josquin, 219
O Virgo Genitrix (= *Plusieurs regrets*), Josquin, 256f
O Virgo simul et Mater, Palestrina, 471
O virum mirabilem, Philips, 794
O virum omnimoda—O lux—O beate Nicholaë, Ciconia, 27
O voi che sospirate, Marenzio, 423
O vos omnes: Compère, see: *O devotz cueurs;* Deering, 793; Gesualdo, 486; Victoria, 591, 603
O Welt ich muss dich lassen (= *Isbruck, ich muss dich lassen*), 643
O wretched man, Wilbye, 830
Obertello, Alfredo (Ober), 815, 819, 821f, 824

Obras de musica, Cabezón, 627ff
Obrecht (= Hobrecht), Jacob (Obr): biogr., 186f, 270; historical position, 186, 205; sec. voc. mus., 187ff; sacr. mus., 102, 186, 190ff (incl. Exx. 34*b*, 35, 36*b*, 37), 240, 245, 253; traits of O.'s style mentioned elsewhere, 125, 230, 246, 281, 341, 461; see also 8, 100, 108, 147, 184f, 219f, 239, 263, 273f, 278, 372, 374, 522, 559, 645, 663, 689, 773, 869
Obrecht, Willem, 186
Ochsenkhun, Sebastian, 550, 669
Ockeghem, Johannes (Ock): biogr., 100, 118f, 147; historical position, 34, 118; Bartoli's opinion of O., 259; sec. voc. mus., 86, 116f, 119ff, 157, 201, 209, 223f, 232, 234, 239, 245, 251, 258, 275, 368; sacr. mus., 72f, 121ff (incl. Exx. 29–31), 250, 675 (incl. Ex. 152); traits of O.'s style mentioned elsewhere, 97, 105, 112f, 196ff, 202, 211, 246, 281; see also 9, 87, 95, 99f, 108, 141f, 144f, 155, 188, 204, 208, 227, 235, 262ff, 272f, 293f, 309, 346, 479, 576f, 580, 635, 645, 763, 768, 773
Octo tonorum melodiae, Stoltzer, 725
Octonaires de la vanité: Le Jeune, 384; L'Estocart, 390
ocular music, see: eye music
oda, 156, 162, 165, 293
Odae cum harmoniis, Honterus, 726
Odarum quas vulgo madrigales appellamus, Vila, 615
Odenoch de Flandria, Raynaldus, 220
Odhecaton (= *Harmonice Musices Odhecaton A*; Petrucci), 141, 155, 185, 208, 211, 219, 224, 230, 262, 265, 280, 284, 521, 581, 671, 771
Oedipus Rex: Sophocles, 569; choruses by A. Gabrieli, 414
Oeil trop hardy, L', Cadéac, 307
Offertory cycles: Lassus, 465, 694; Palestrina, 465ff; Zieleński, 753
Office: Christmas, 681; Easter, 681; Holy Week, 603f
Office for the Dead: Guerrero, 596; Morales, 590; Viadana, 489; Victoria, 609
Officium Paschale, Hähnel, 681
Ofterdingen, Heinrich von, 652
Öglin, Erhard, 705; O. *Liederbuch*, 638, 640
Oimè, dov'è'l mio ben, Marenzio, 422
Oimè, il bel viso, Marenzio, 421f; Monteverdi, 441
Oimè, il cor: Cara, 163 (incl. Ex. 33*a*); Bossinensis, 163 (incl. Ex. 33*b*)
Ojos claros y serenos, Guerrero, 596
Ojos morenos, Vasquez, 612
Okeland, 796
Old Dutch: the melody, 807; Blancks, 807
Old Hundredth, the melody (= *Or sus, serviteurs du Seigneur*, q.v.; see also *All people that on earth do dwell*)
Olendrinus (= Hollandrinus), 743
Olid, Juan de, 577

Oliphant, Thomas (Oli), 320, 824
Olthoff, Statius, 705
Omnes gentes, Tye, 783 (incl. Ex. 180)
Omnia tempus habent, Lassus, 694f
Omnium bonorum plena, Compère, 118, 227, 251
On a beau sa maison bastir, Sweelinck, 518
On freyd verzer ich, Hofhaimer, 641
On the plains fairy trains, Weelkes, 826
Opdycke, Leonard E., 158
Opieński, Henri (Opie), 526, 743, 748f, 752f, 755f
Opitiis, Benedictus de, 265f, 679, 771
Oppel, Reinhard, 563ff, 683
Optime pastor, Isaac, 215f
Opus aureum, Wollick, 334
Opus chronographicum, Opmeer, 229
Opus musicum: Gallus, 737f; Paminger, 681
Opusculum musices, Felstin, 746
Or combien, Sermisy, 351
Or ouez les introites de taverne, Guiard, 301
Or sus, serviteurs du Seigneur, the melody by Bourgeois(?), 361 (Ex. 80); the text, 361, 503f; Goudimel, 503 (incl. Ex. 116); Sweelinck, 517; see also: *Old Hundredth*
Or sus, vous dormés trop, 299
Oraison à la Vierge Marie, Molinet, 87
Orationes, Utendal, 702
Oravi Dominum Deum, Porta, 494
Orbaan, J. A. (Orba), 413, 420
Orbecche, Cinzio, 568
Orchésographie, Arbeau, 554, 564f, 866
Ordellafi, Giorgio, 26
Ordinarium (Augustinian; Mexico, 1556), 593, 689
Ordinarium missae, see: Mass, Ordinary; see also: Mass sections
Ordonez, Pedro, 591
Or'è di Maggio, Isaac, 170
Orel, Alfred (Or), 94
Orel, Dobroslav, 736, 740, 742
Orfeo, Politian, 173, 567
organ-bass, 484, 545; see also: *basso continuo; b. figurato; b. seguente*
organ makers, 417, 561, 619
organ-Mass, 174f, 536f, 560, 659f, 855
organ music, see: keyboard music (organ and stringed)
organ-point, see: pedals and double pedals
organ, portative (= chamber organ, *organetto, organino, organo di legno*), 36, 529, 567
organ, structure, 36, 175, 180, 529f, 562, 567
Organo suonarino, L', Banchieri, 536
organum and organum style, 20, 23f, 38, 644, 651, 659f, 665, 745
Orlando furioso, Ariosto, 157, 313, 325ff, 428
Orliennaise (a *basse dance?*), 152
ornamentation (incl. figuration), 32, 42f, 174, 209ff (incl. Ex. 38), 272f, 460f, 514, 544f, 589, 719; see also: coloration; diminution; keyboard o.; lute o.
Ornithoparchus, Andreas (= Vogelmaier or Vogelsang), 180, 182, 639, 810, 844

Orologio, Alexander, 672, 810, 831
orpharion, 842, 848f, 873
Orphénica Lyra, Fuenllana, 594, 612, 623f
Ortiz, Diego, 299, 322, 486, 592, 625ff, 630, 852
Orto, Marbriano de, 195, 264f
Osculetur me: Barbireau, 117; Pevernage, 517
Osiander, Lucas, 684, 705
Ostermayer, Georg, 727
Ostermayer, Hieronymus, 727
Osthoff, Helmuth (Os), 38, 245, 394, 513, 525f, 632ff, 643ff, 649, 680, 682, 688, 702, 707, 709ff
ostinato, 61, 79, 108f, 181, 200, 209, 242, 248f, 254, 355, 364, 392f, 510, 524, 591, 608, 622, 625, 681, 701; see also: *folia;* grounds; *passamezzo antico; passamezzo moderno; romanesca; Ruggiero*
Ostrorog, N. de, 743
Oswald von Wolkenstein, 12, 632, 634, 716, 743
Otep myrrhy, 731
Othello, Shakespeare, 841
Othmayr, Caspar, 681f, 707
Ott, Johann, 242, 244, 706f, 709
ottava rima, 162, 325
Otto I, Emperor, 652
Otto, Georgius, 677, 688
Ottonaio, Battista dell' (= L'Araldo?), 169, 172
Ou doy je secours, Vincenet, 136
Oublier veuil tristesse, A. Agricola, 210
Out of the deepe, Morley, 805
ouvert (= *aperto*) ending, 30
Ovid, 161
Oviedo, Gonzalo Fernandez de, 578
Oxford, the melody and settings by Kirbye and J. Dowland, 807
Oxford University, see: degrees

Pachta, J., 736
padovana (= *padoana*): in lute tablatures, 524f, 670f; Bianchini, 525; Gorzanis, 525; Rotta, 524; Wecker, 671
Padovano, Annibale, 415, 417, 496, 537, 540, 544, 550, 700
Paiva, Heliodoro de, 598, 629
Paix, Jakob, 202, 665f, 716f (incl. Ex. 162)
Palafox, Cardinal, 597
Palaiologos, Theodore, 41, 49
Paleotti, Cardinal Gabriele, 429
Palestrina, Pierluigi da (Pal): biogr., 364, 409, 424ff, 449, 455ff, 598, 721; historical position, 246, 459ff, 506; sec. voc. mus., 322, 401ff (incl. Ex. 93), 419, 426, 435, 437, 444, 447, 483, 490, 696, 703; sacr. mus., 73, 133, 336, 366, 368, 462ff (incl. Exx. 109–112), 483, 521 (Ex. 120), 608, 610, 618; instr. mus., 541; P.'s style compared with Clemens', 354f; with Gombert's, 348, 459; with Josquin's, 460, 466, 468, 481; with Lassus', 404, 406, 481, 692ff, 697; with Victoria's, 467, 481; traits of P.'s style men-

tioned elsewhere, 125, 258, 422, 425, 440, 507, 614; see also 52, 184, 287, 326, 350, 363, 371, 452, 485, 491, 493, 499, 532, 599f, 604

Palestrina, Angelo, 456, 458; Iginio, 457f; Rodolfo, 456, 458; Silla, 458

Paligonius, 753

Pallavicino, Benedetto, 438, 488

Pallavicino, Bishop Carlo, 242

Palle, palle, Isaac, 170, 286

Palmer, George H., 255

Paminger, Leonhard, 681f, 688, 706

Pammelia, Ravenscroft, 833f

Pan divino, gracioso, sacrosancto (= *Prado verde y florido*), Guerrero, 596

pandore (= *pandora; bandora; bandurion?*), 566, 842, 848f, 873, 878

Pange lingua: Greg. Chant, 581, 693, 706; Spanish Chant, 581, 599, 604, 611, 628; Cabezón, 628; Dufay, 84; Victoria, 2 settings, 604; Wreede, 581, 628; see also: *Tantum ergo*

Panis angelicus (= verse 6 of *Sacris solemnis,* q.v.), Greg. Chant, 83

Panis quem ego dabo, Hellinck, 342f (incl. Ex. 76), 350, 352, 470, 477

Pannain, Guido (Pann), 139f

Panofsky, Erwin, 86

Pantagruel, Rabelais, 286, 293

Paoli, Domenico de (Pao), 438, 501

Paolucci, Giuseppe (Paolu), 379, 493ff, 532

Papa, Jacobus, 303

Par droit je puis, Dufay, 56

Par le regart: the text, 207; Dufay, 224, 271

Par maintes foy, Vaillant, 12

Par ung jour de matinée, Isaac, 213

Parabosco, Girolamo, 319, 325, 417, 537, 544

Paradyse of Daynty Devises, The, 816

Parangon des chansons (Moderne), 290, 300

paraphrase Masses (incl. P. Mass sections), 32, 59ff, 64ff, 68, 130ff, 244, 260f, 264, 267, 284, 336, 351, 455, 470ff, 473ff, 504f, 589, 646ff, 689f; other uses of p. technique, 40, 81, 83ff, 90f, 109, 119, 121f, 128f, 136, 174f, 191, 194, 200, 203, 210f, 214, 219, 223, 228, 242ff, 247, 251ff, 262, 269, 271, 336, 339, 345, 362f, 369, 463f, 467, 484f, 494f, 536, 560, 579, 604f, 724, 777, 794

Paraza, Francisco de, 629

Parce Domine: Franci, 220; Obrecht, 192; anon. keyboard transcr. thereof, 559

Parfons regretz, Josquin, 233

Paris, Gaston, 150, 205f, 214, 232, 234, 338

Paris-type chanson, 291ff, 299ff

Parker, Archbishop Matthew, 800

Parks, Edd W., 288, 382

Parma, Anselmo da, 727

Parnaso, El, Daza, 624f

parody (= travesty of texts), 301, 333, 434

parody-Mass: general, 202, 240f; anticipatory and sporadic uses of the technique, 28, 33, 76, 112f, 116, 128, 201ff (incl. Ex. 36), 211, 239f, 284, 648; individual works: F. Anerio,

484; Arcadelt, 501; Clemens non Papa, 351f, 486; Crecquillon, 350; Esquivel, 610; A. de Févin, 279; Gallus, 738f; Gascoing, 273; Giovanelli, 485; Gombert, 347f; Goudimel, 501f; Guerrero, 595; Josquin, 240f; La Hèle, 511; La Rue, 269f; Lassus, 696f; Merulo, 496; Monte, 703ff; Monteverdi, 500; Morales, 588; G. M. Nanino, 485; Paix, 202; Palestrina, 469, 475ff (incl. Ex. 112), 486, 628; Palestrina in collaboration with 6 others, 485; Roy, 486; Senfl, 689; Soriano, 485; Tallis, 786; Victoria, 605ff (incl. Ex. 134); Whytbroke, 777; Willaert, 371f

Parrish, Carl, 88, 192, 254, 538, 692

pars (plural, *partes;* the term), 38

Parsley (= Persleye), Osbert, 786, 803, 869, 873

Parsons, Robert, 786, 802, 817, 868ff, 873

Parsons, William, 801

part-song in England (secular, nonmadrigalian), 768ff, 815f, 835

Parthenia . . . (Lowe), 852, 860, 872

Parthenia In-violata (Hole), 852

partial signatures, see: key signatures, conflicting

Partite sopra Ruggiero, Macque, 543

pas de Brabant, see: after-dance

Pasche, William, 777

Paseábase el rey moro: Fuenllana, 623f; Narváez, 623; Pisador, 623

Päsler, Carl (Päsl), 662f

Pasquin, 115

passamezzo antico, defined, 524 (Ex. 121)

passamezzo-gagliarda pairs: Molinaro, 526; Philips, 865, Terzi, 526

passamezzo moderno (= *comune*), defined, 524 (incl. Ex. 121)

passamezzo-pavana pairs, Philips, 865

passamezzo (= *passemaize,* passinge mesures, passy-measure) pieces: instr. ensemble: in Phalèse print, 565; Gervaise, 564; keyboard: in tablature of Schmid the Elder, 716; Byrd, 864f; A. Gabrieli, 539; Philips, 864f; lute: in Engl. MSS, 844f; in Ger. books, general, 670; Bakfark, 720; Barbetta, 526; Cato, 756; Francisque, 554; in tablature of Jobin, 716; Laurencinus Romanus, 527; Molinaro, 526; Terzi, 526; Wecker, 671; vihuela: Narváez, 622; viol: Ortiz, 625; see also: *quadran pavan*

Passan vostri triomphi, Lassus, 405

Passando con pensier: Marenzio, 424; Niccolo da Perugia, 424

Passereau, 295, 299, 536

Passerose de biaulté, 19f (incl. Ex. 2)

Passinge Mesures, The: the Nynthe Pavian, Byrd, 864f (incl. Ex. 210)

Passio Sacra, d'Ana, 165

Passion plays, German, with music, 705

. . . Passiones Christi Domini, Navarro, 593

Passions, German, monophonic: 650; polyphonic: anon., 689; Bach, 711; Burck, 688;

Galliculus, 688; Gesius, 688; Heroldt, 688; Lechner, 688; Scandello, 689; Walter, 689
Passions, Latin, monophonic (= Greg. Chant), 165f (incl. key to abbreviations), 226, 271, 274, 339; polyphonic: anon., 165f, (incl. def. of motet and dramatic types), 339, 764f (earliest known exx.); Asola, 493; Claudin, 339; Davy, 773; Guerrero, 596; Maistre Jhan, 366, 376; Lassus, 697; Longaval (not Obrecht), 190, 273ff (incl. Ex. 54); Rore, 376; Soriano, 485; Victoria, 604
Passions en nouvelle maniere, Binchois, 89
Pastor, Cristóbal P. (Pa), 627
Pastor Fido, Il, Guarini, 415, 569; see also: *Ah dolente partita; Cruda Amarilli; O primavera*
Pastor gregis, Ostrorog, 743
pastoral style, 415, 424, 568
Pastorella si leva, La, Razzi, 453
Pastores quidnam vidistis, Clemens, 351
Pastyme with good companye, Henry VIII, 771
Pater noster: Greg. Chant, 255, 472; Arcadelt, 501; Gombert, 345; Paminger, 681; Philips, 794; Schiavetto, 761; Willaert (not Obrecht), 190, 374, 761
Pater peccavi: Clemens, 353; Manchicourt, 351; Morales, 591
Pathie, Rogier, 299
Patrem (outside of complete Masses), see various Credos under: Mass sections; also Credo
Patres nostri peccaverunt, Cornago, 576
Patricio (= Petris), Andrea, 760
Patricio, Francesco, 760
Patrick, Nathaniel, 811
Patrocinium musices (Montanus and Neuber), 697, 700
Pattison, Bruce (Pat), 155, 755, 815, 819, 824, 839, 841
Pauer, Ernst, 852
Paul III, Pope, 312, 359, 362, 455, 527, 587, 591
Paul IV, Pope, 456
Paulirinus, Paulus, 667
Paulomimes, 662ff
Paulus de Broda (= Rhoda?), 635
Paumann, Conrad, 535, 635, 658ff (incl. Ex. 147), 669, 850
Paumgartner (= Baumgartner), 658
pausa (special meaning), 346
pavans (individual dances): instr. ensemble: in Engl. sources, general, 868; in Ital. sources, 523f; in Attaingnant prints, general, 563; in *Orchésographie,* 564; in *Musique de Joye,* 564; in Susato print (1551), 564; Deering, 873; J. Dowland, 873f; Gervaise, 564; keyboard: in Engl. sources, general, 863, 866; in *Parthenia,* general, 852; Bull, 865; Byrd, 865; Cabezón, 628; Morley, 865; Philips, 850, 865; Tisdall, 865; Tomkins, 850; lute: in Engl. sources, 844; in Ger. sources, 671; Besard (after Dowland), 847f;

Dalza, 523; Francisque, 554; *vihuela:* Milán, 621; see also: *Lachrymae* pieces
pavan-galliard pairs: instr. ensemble: in Engl. sources, general, 845f; in Attaingnant prints, 564; in *Booke of Consort Lessons,* 874; Byrd, 873; Gibbons, 873; Holborne, 876; Philips, 876; keyboard: in Engl. sources, 864, 866; Byrd, 864f (incl. Ex. 210); Bull, 865; Philips, 864; lute: in Engl. sources, 845; in French sources, 553; in Ital. sources, 523f
pavana-saltarello pairs, Barberiis, 526
Pavaniglia: the melody, 525; Bull, 865f; Cabezón, 628; Mudarra, 628
Pavlovsky, Jan, 737
Payen, Nicolas, 350, 512
Pazzia senile, La, Banchieri, 436
Peacham, Henry, 793, 822, 831
Pearce, Charles W. (Pea), 768, 770f
Pearson, John, 881
Peccantem me quotidie: Gesualdo, 486; Palestrina 464
Pecorina, Polissena, 323f
pedal-points and double pedals, 160, 218, 248, 308, 405, 693, 830
pedals (on organs), 175, 529, 562, 657f, 661, 754
Pedersøn, Mogens (Peder), 713
Pedrell, Felipe (Ped), 575, 590f, 593, 595f, 600, 610, 613ff, 622ff
Pedro de Urdemalas, Cervantes, 631
Peerson, Martin, 808, 836, 838, 867
Peetrino, Jacopo (= Jacob Pieters), 447
Peignot, Etienne G., 289
Pelicelli, Nestore (Peli), 220
Pellegrini, Vincenzo, 542
Peluzzi, Euro (Peluz), 548
Peñalosa, Francisco de, 579f
Penet, Hilaire (= Hylaire), 285, 471
Peni, Luca, 546
Penitential Psalms, Lassus, 513
Peperara, Laura, 409, 411
Per illud ave, (not Mouton), see: *Benedicta es . . . ,* Josquin, 282f
Perch'al visa, Arcadelt, 322
Perche la vista, Randulfo, 30
Percy, Thomas, 843
Perenotto, Antonio, 507
Pereyra, Marie-Louise (Per), 286, 852
Perez, Francisco Palero, 626f
Perez, Juan Ginés, 610
performance practice, 36ff, 42f, 57, 60, 67, 75, 160f, 174f, 176f, 323f, 436, 488, 519, 522, 533f, 546ff, 565f, 569f, 661, 665, 690f, 725f, 813, 820, 833, 858, 874; see also: *a cappella;* alternation practices; *chiavette;* choral singing; congregational singing; instrumental ensembles; keyboard accompaniment, etc.; lute accompaniment, etc.; *musica ficta*
Peri, Jacopo, 425, 569f
Perinello, Carlo (Perin), 434f

Perino Fiorentino, 522, 527
Perissone, see Cambio, Perissone, 334
Perle, George, 107
Pernette, La, the melody, 54
Pernner MS, see: Manuscripts—Regensburg
Perotin, 34, 716
Perslis Clocke, Parsley, 873
Peru: Lima, 600
Pesenti, Michele, 158, 292
Peter I, King of Cyprus, 14
Peter of Chelčic, 735
Petite camusette: the melody, 275, 361; Josquin, 232, 309; Ockeghem, 119f, 131, 196, 232, 265, 309; Willaert, 2 settings, 309
Petite nymphe folâtre, François Regnart, 390
Petrarca, Francesco (= Petrarch), 28, 52, 161, 292, 311ff, 316, 322, 324, 330, 332, 400, 403f, 406, 414, 417, 424, 429, 447, 453, 820, 831
Petre tu pastor omnium, Josquin, 675
Petreius, Johann, 124, 277, 319, 648, 706
Petri, Theodoricus, 712
Petris, see: Patricio, Andrea
Petrucci, Ottaviano de', 101, 111, 117, 124, 147, 149, 155ff, 167, 185, 191f, 199, 208, 210f, 214f, 218ff, 222, 224, 226, 230, 235, 238, 245f, 248, 250, 258, 262, 265f, 276, 278, 282ff, 289, 300, 311, 313, 337, 341, 368, 452, 521f, 535, 583, 588, 641, 646, 665, 671, 759
Petrus Apostolus, Greg. Chant, 281
Pevernage, Andries, 397, 427f, 517
Pfatteicher, Carl F. (Pfat), 777, 803, 850, 854ff, 860
Pfleger, Maria C. C. (Pfl), 674
Phalèse, Pierre, 290, 303, 357, 510, 555, 557f, 565, 666, 793, 821
Phalèse and Bellère, 511
Philidor, André Danican, 564
Philip the Handsome (= Philip I, King of Spain), 109, 208, 218, 267, 276, 338
Philip II, King of Spain, 395f, 511, 592, 600, 609, 614, 618, 623, 627, 702
Philip III, King of Spain, 592, 608, 617f
Philip IV, King of Spain, 599
Philip the Bold, Duke of Burgundy, 5f
Philip the Good, Duke of Burgundy, 5f, 12, 36, 38, 43, 48, 51, 57f, 87, 90, 98f, 109
Philip of Rouvre, Duke of Burgundy, 5
Philip of Luxemburg, Count of St. Pol, 8
Philippon, 117, 202; see also: Basiron, Caron
Philips, Peter: biogr., 793; sec. voc. mus., 428, 831; sacr. mus., 793ff (incl. Ex. 184); instr. mus., 850, 859f (incl. Ex. 208), 863, 865, 874, 876
Philips, Sir Thomas, 768
Philomena praevia, Richafort, 337, 347
Phinot, Dominique, 349f, 373
Piae Cantiones (Petri), 712
Piaget, Arthur, 7
Pibrac, Guy Du Faur de, 385

Picard, Isaac, 362, 503
Picchi, Giovanni, 716
Picforth, 869
Picitono, Angelo da, 179
Picot, Emile, 98
Picquigny (=Pikyni), Jean de, 20
pictures containing musical compositions, 93f, 167, 292, 464, 517, 594
Pietà, cara signora, Cara, 159
Pietà chiuso ha le porte, La, Tromboncino, 159
Pieters, Jacob (= Jacopo Peetrino), 447
Pietosi affetti, 427
Pietrequin (= Petrequin), Guillaume, 225
Pietro da Vienna, 207
Pietzsch, Gerhard, 741f, 745
Pifaro, Marcantonio del, 522, 526
piffari, pifferi, etc., see: pipes
Piissimae ac sanctissimae Lamentationes, 501
Pikyni, see Picquigny
Pilgrimes Solace, A, J. Dowland, 810
Pilkington, Francis, 809, 811, 824, 830, 838f, 844
Pinheiro, Antonio, 598
Pinturicchio (= Bernardino Betti), 229
Piombo, Sebastiano del, 187, 317
Pipelare, Matthaeus, 225, 275, 347, 663
Piper's Galliard (= Captaine Digorie Piper His Galiard), J. Dowland, 876
pipes (= *piffari, pifferi, pifare, rauschpfeiffe*), 174, 323, 448, 545, 567, 656, 658, 758
Piqueras, F. Rubio, 588
Pirro, André (Pir), 6ff, 12f, 16, 18, 35, 38, 40, 43, 48f, 51f, 55, 58, 61f, 85f, 94, 99, 101, 106, 115, 118, 123, 131, 133, 137f, 145, 147f, 150ff, 156, 161, 172, 174, 186f, 207, 209ff, 218f, 224, 228f, 238f, 244f, 260, 262ff, 270ff, 276, 278, 285f, 291f, 299, 315, 330, 337, 339, 346, 351, 355, 372, 375, 381, 390, 455, 481, 501, 529, 551, 561f, 565, 576, 588, 591, 633, 656, 683, 691, 705, 723, 850, 856, 860, 866
Pirrotta, Nino (Pirr), 10, 25, 29, 32f
Pis ne me peult venir, the melody, 753
Pisador, Diego, 613, 622f
Pisano, Bernardo, 170, 313f, 317
Piscaer, Anny, 186
Pisk, Paul A., 739
Pistone, Pier G. (Pist), 424, 445ff
pitch (letter-symbol system used in this book), 35, 850
pitch (of pipes; of keyboard instruments), 530ff, 813
pitch-level, relative, 35
piva, see: after-dance
Pixérécourt MS, see: Manuscripts—Paris
Più vagha et più bella, La, Isaac, 214
Plaine and Easie Introduction to Practicall Musicke, Morley, 532, 792, 824, 839
Plaine de dueil, Josquin, 233
Plaine d'ennuy—Anima mea, Compère (not Pipelare), 225
plainsong Mass (the term), 68

Plamenac, Dragan (Plam), 32, 43, 73, 90, 93f, 98, 107, 110, 112, 116, 119f, 122, 124, 136, 149f, 163, 174, 209f, 212, 214, 234, 280, 392, 548, 633, 741, 757, 760ff

Plange, Ingegneri, 491

Plantin, Christophe, 511

Planxit autem David, Josquin, 254, 262

Plasanche ortost acux, Picquigny, 20

Plato, 141, 180

Platt, Peter, 793

Plautus, 158, 173, 567

Pléiade, 382, 391, 569, 571

Plorans ploravit in nocte, Greg. Chant, 235

Plorer, gémir—Requiem, La Rue, 272

Plummer, John, 767

Plura modulatione genera, Las Infantas, 610

Plus belle et doulce figure, La, Grenon, 15

Plus des plus, La, Josquin, 232

Plus grant chiere, La, 99

Plus n'en aray, Hayne, 100

Plus n'estes ma maistresse, Josquin, 232

Plus nulz regretz, Josquin, 231, 233

Plus onques dame, anon. (not Matteo da Perugia), 31

Plusieurs regrets (= O Virgo Genitrix), Josquin, 233, 257

Podio, Guillermus de (= Guillermo Despuig), 577

poesia per musica, 161, 313, 315, 400, 820, 824

Poésies de P. de Ronsard & autres Poëtes, F. Regnart, 390

Poeticall Musicke, Hume, 873

poetry, predilections of English composers, 819f, 832; French composers, 87, 288; Italian composers, 157, 311ff; Spanish composers, 581ff, 585, 617

Poi che volse la mia stella, Trombombino, 161

Poi ch'el ciel e la fortuna, 159

Poignare, Barthélemy, 38

Poland (outside Chap. 14): in general, 420, 426, 639, 663; Cracow, 639

Pole, Cardinal Reginald, 507

Polinski, Aleksander (Pol), 742, 745, 749ff, 753, 755

polische Geige, 757

Polish dances, 755f (incl. Ex. 173)

Poliziano, Angelo (= Politian), 153, 161, 170, 173, 214, 311, 567f

Poll, Hermann, 529

Polnisch Tantz, Der, 755

Polnische Art Täntze, Demantius, 756f

Polonais, Jacob (= Jacobus Reys?), 755f, 844

Polumier (= John Plummer?), 767

polychoral writing, 28, 174, 285, 349, 372f, 395, 418f, 463, 477, 483, 497f, 502, 511, 599, 604, 607f, 611, 679, 688, 694f, 698f, 737f, 749, 753; see also: antiphonal writing; *decani* and *cantoris* sides

polytextuality and polytextual style, 17, 21, 75, 114ff, 121, 192, 195, 218, 255, 263, 268, 275, 588, 591, and *passim*; see also: motets, bilingual; quodlibets

Pominoczky, Philip, 718

Ponce, Juan, 578

Ponnelle, Louis, 453

Pontano, Giovanni, 139

Ponte, Giaches de, 539

Pontifici decori speculi, Carmen, 22

Pontormo, Jacopo da, 326

Ponzio, Pietro, 542

Pope, Isabel, 585, 592

popolaresca lirica, 169, 291

popular music, 61, 69, 73, 159, 164, 213f, 244. 355f, 360, 613f, 636, 769f, 779, 793, 833ff, 843, 845, 848, 855

Por las sierras, Peñalosa, 580

Porcher, Jean (Porch), 98

Porcio mea Domine, White, 784

Porta, Costanzo, 345, 415f, 419, 427, 493ff (incl. Ex. 115)

portamento (= anticipation), 460f

portative, see: organ, portative

Porter, Walter, 832

Portiforium secundum usum Sarum, 795

Portinaro, Francesco, 415, 417

Portugal (outside Chap. 11), 51

Portugaler (= Portigaler), Dufay, 51, 659

Postquam consummati essent, Vaet, 701

Postquam consummati sunt, Lupus or Lupi, 341

Pour ce que j'ay jouy, Hayne, 100

Pour courrir en poste, Lassus, 394

Pour entretenir mes amours, Busnois, 107

Pour l'amour de ma doulce amye, Dufay, 56

Pour quelque paine, 136

Pour quoy tournés vous vos yeux, Janequin, 298

Pour vous tenir, Fontaine, 34f

Pouray-je avoir vostre mercy, Dufay, 56

Pourquoy non, La Rue, 272

Potter, Frank Hunter, 841

Power, Leonel, 39, 66, 95

Practica musica, Hermann Finck, 344, 412

Practica musicae, Gafori, 179, 587, 746

Prado verde y florido (= Pan divino . . .), Guerrero, 596

Praeambulum, Kleber, 664 (incl. Ex. 149)

Praeter rerum seriem, Josquin, 252, 375, 511

Praetorius, Ernest (Praet), 179f, 210

Praetorius, Hieronymus, 688

Praetorius, Michael (Praeto), 418, 488, 532f, 566, 667, 677, 680, 684, 702

Praise the Lord, O my soul, Tomkins, 812 (incl. Ex. 188)

Pratt, Waldo S. (Pra), 361f, 801, 808

Prattica di musica, Zacconi, 412, 547

Pratum spirituale, Pedersøn, 713

Prayse ye the Lord, ye children, Tye, 798

Precamur (melody = Te lucis), Byrd, 870

Precamur (= stanza 2 of Christe qui lux es, q.v.)

Preces and Responses: Morley, 805; Tallis, 800; Tomkins, 812

Preces ecclesiasticae, Du Caurroy, 505

Preces speciales pro salubri generalis concilii, Kerle, 449, 451f

Prélude sur chacun ton, 560
preludes, keyboard (= *praeludia; preambula*), 554, 658, 661, 664 (incl. Ex. 149), 658, 754, 851f, 860; see also: *intonazione*
première rhétorique, 87
Prendergast, Arthur H. D. (Pren), 800
Prennez sur moi votre exemple amoreux (= *Fuga trium vocum*), Ockeghem, 120, 157
Presque transi, Ockeghem, 224
Pretty Wayes: for young beginners to looke on (in Brit. Mus. Add. MS 29996), 855
Preussische Festlieder, Eccard and Stobäus, 686
Prez, Josquin des, see: Josquin des Prez
Primavera, Giovanni Leonardo, 445, 470
Prince de la Moskowa, see: Ney, Napoléon J.
Printemps, Le, Le Jeune, 383
printing of music: England, 768, 784f, 787, 792, 852, 872; France, 37, 289ff, 335, 562; Germany, 706; Italy, 140, 147, 153ff, 327; Spain, 577, 627; see also: quantities in printings
Prioris, Johannes, 137, 263f, 266ff, 559
Prise d'Alexandrie, La, Machaut, 14
Prise du Havre, La, Costeley, 388
Private Musicke, Peerson, 411, 836
processional-hymn form, 336, 766
Procul recedant, Tallis, 786
Prod'homme, Jacques-Gabriel (Prod), 50f, 370, 554
program music, 32, 57, 165, 295ff, 339, 433ff, 485, 569, 596, 603f, 631, 650, 668, 688f, 823, 866f, 873; see also: battle pieces
prolations, see: proportional system
Promptuarium musicum, Schadeus, 532
Prophetiae Sibyllarum, Lassus, 695
proportional system, 19f, 70, 133ff, 145f, 619
Proportionale musices, Tinctoris, 60, 140, 144ff
Proportz, see: after-dance
Proprium Missae, see: Mass, Proper
prosa, see: sequence
Prose della volgar lingua, Le, Bembo, 312
Proske, Karl (Pros), 186, 355, 458, 469, 481ff, 492ff, 500, 517, 590, 592, 599f, 681, 688, 691, 694, 696ff
Prota-Giurleo, Ulisse (Prota), 430, 486
Proverbes de Salomon, Janequin, 340
Prudenza giovenile, La (= *La Saviezza giovenile*), Banchieri, 437
Prunières, Henry (Pru), 173, 187, 291, 438, 440f, 500f, 567, 570f
Prussz, Lasarus, 650
Przez thwe szwyęte szmarthwywstanije, 754
Psallite felices, Sampson, 778
psalm numbers; psalm-number systems, Catholic and Jewish-Protestant, 90, 359
psalm-tones, 90, 247f, 271, 373 (incl. Ex. 85), 491f (incl. Ex. 114), 627, 695f, 724 (incl. Ex. 165), 804f
Psalmi Davidis poenitentiales, Lassus, 695
Psalmi Festivales, Anglican, 804f
psalms in *falsobordone,* see: *falsobordone*
Psalterium printed by Fust and Schöffer, 154

psalters (metrical): American, *Bay Psalm Book,* 808; British, Ainsworth P., 808; Alison P., 808f; Anglo-Genevan P., 797; Cosyn P., 807; Crowley P., 796; Daman P., 807; Denham P., 807; Farnaby P., 808; Hunnis P., 796; Parker P. (with music by Tallis), 800; Scottish P., 801, 808; Seager P., 797; *Seven Sobs,* 807; Sternhold-Hopkins P. (= English P.), 796f, 801, 808f; *Whole Book of Psalmes* (Day), 801; *Whole Booke of Psalmes* (Barley), 808; ditto (East), 806f (incl. Ex. 187); ditto (Ravenscroft), 808f; *Whole Psalmes* (Day), 801, 808; Dutch, Bks. IV–VII of *Musyck Boexken* (*Souterliedekens*), 355, 357; Genevan P. (monophonic) with Dutch texts, 808; *Psalmen David,* Boschop, 505; *Souterliedekens* (Cock), 355; Flemish, Flemish P., 360; French, *Dix Pseaumes . . . en forme de Motets,* 503; French P. of Antwerp, 360; Genevan P. (monophonic), Bourgeois, 356, 358ff, 503, 797, 801, 808; Genevan P. (polyphonic), 2 settings by Goudimel, 502f (*1564* and *1565*), 683 (*1565*), 684 (*1564* and *1565*); Janequin P., 340; Lausanne P., 503; *Pseaulmes Cinquante . . . par Maistre Jean Louys* (3 bks.), 505; *Pseaumes en vers mezurez,* 504; German, *Der gantz P. Davids,* 683; Goudimel P. (*1565*) with German texts, 683; *Teutsche geistliche Psalmen,* 698; Polish, *Melodye na Psalterz,* Gomólka, 751f
psaltery, 717
Pseudo-Aristotle (= Lambertus), 727
Pseudo-Vitri, 727
Ptolemy, 180, 377
Puente, José de, 616
Puer natus in Bethlehem, 674
Pueri Hebraeorum, Greg. Chant, 114, 149
Pues que Dios: Cornago, 576; Madrid, 576f
Puisque je voy, Arnold de Lantins, 41
Pujol, Juan Pablo, 611, 616
Pulaer, Louis van, 337
Pulikowski, Juljan (Puli), 741
Pullois (= Pulloys; Pyllois), Jehan, 48, 633, 635, 658, 740
Pulver, Jeffrey (Pul), 767, 802, 807, 809, 850, 867, 874
Purcell, Henry, 814, 845, 870
Purge me, O Lord (= *Fonde youthe is a bubble*), Tallis, 800, 816
Puschmann, Adam, 652ff
Putenheim, Georg von, 658
puzzle pieces, tours de force, etc., 11, 124, 217, 277, 305, 429, 586, 610, 619; decline of p. pieces, 294; see also: canon, verbal; catholicon
Pyamour, John, 767
Pycard, 19, 22, 61
Pygott, Richard, 767f
Pythagorean tuning, see: intonation (= tuning)

quadran (= *quadro*) *pavan,* 843, 864f, 874
Quae pena maior, Bartolomeo da Bologna, 26

Quaeramus cum pastoribus, Mouton, 282, 371, 588

Quaestiones celeberrimae, Mersenne, 504

Quagliati, Paolo, 425, 442f, 482

Quai rime fur sì chiare, Palestrina, 401

Qual dolcezza giammai, Willaert, 323

Qual donna attende, Rore, 695

Qual'è il più grand', o Amor, Rore, 471, 476, 478 (Ex. 112*b*)

Quam pulchra es: Bauldeweyn, 338, 347; Dunstable, 40; Gombert, 338; Lassus, 693; J. Lupi, 342, 351, 465, 471; Mouton?, 283; Sampson, 773, 778

Quam pulchri sunt gressus: Palestrina, 465; Victoria, 600, 608

Quand ce beau printemps je voy, La Grotte, 389

Quand de vous seul, Ockeghem, 120

Quand j'apperçoy, Goudimel, 387

Quand je me trouve (= *I vaghi fiori*), Arcadelt, 323

Quand je vois ma maitresse, Sweelinck, 399

Quand je vous ayme, Arcadelt, 381

Quand mon mari, Lassus, 393

Quand on arrestera, Le Jeune, 557

Quand'io era giovinetto, G. Gabrieli, 418

Quand'io pens'al martire: Arcadelt, 696; Merulo, 417

Quando la sera, Azzaiolo, 445

Quando lieta sperai, Rore, 471, 703

Quando ritrovo la mia pastorella, Festa, 320

Quando'l voler, Lassus, 405

Quant ce vendra, Busnois, 102f, 107

Quant compaignons s'en vont juer, Loqueville, 18 (incl. Ex. 1)

Quant j'ay au cueur, Busnois, 214f

Quant'ahi lasso, Verdelot, 317ff (incl. Exx. 64, 65)

Quanti mercenarii (= *Io son ferito*, Palestrina), Orfeo Vecchi, 490

quantities in printings, 290, 553, 600, 627, 840

quantity, see: accentuation, quantity, declamation

Quanto più m'arde: Festa, 320; Willaert, 323

quarter-tones, see: microtones

quatre prolacions, see: proportional system

quatro de empezar (the term), 583

Que farem del pobre Joan!, 585

Que me servent mes vers, Monte, 396

Quel fronte signorille (= *Craindre vous vueil*), Dufay, 52

Quelque povre homme, Busnois, 106

Quem dicunt homines, Richafort, 276, 284, 336 (incl. Ex. 75); 471f, 588

Quem vidistis pastores: Asola, 493; Compère, 227

Querol Gavaldà, Miguel, 631

Qu'es mi vida: Cornago, 576; Ockeghem, 119

Questa fanciulla, Landini, 175

Qu'est-ce d'amour, Janequin, 298

Qu'est devenu ce bel oeil, Le Jeune, 384

Questo mostrarsi adirata, Isaac, 214

Qui confidunt, Harant, 739

Qui habitat in adjutorio, Josquin, 250

Qui invenit mulierem bonam, Buus, 375

Qui la dira, Crecquillon, 302

Qui ne l'aymeroit, Gombert, 304

Qui ne regrettroit le gentil Févin, Mouton, 280

Qui paraclitus, 649

Qui passe (= *Chi passa*), Byrd, 859

Qui renforcera ma voix, Goudimel, 387

Qui trepidas, Lassus, 691

Qui velatus facie fuisti, Josquin, 257, 259

Qui veult mesdire, Binchois, 44 (Ex. 6*c*)

Qui vult venire post me, G. M. Nanino, 482

Quickelberg, Samuel, 513ff

Quidnam (= *Quid non*) *ebrietas*, Willaert, 369

quintern (= guitar), 656

Quintiani, Lucretio, 545

quintuple meter produced by sequence, 104, 203f (incl. Ex. 37), 215 (Ex. 40), 461, 869 (Ex. 211)

Quis dabit capiti meo aquam, Isaac, 170

Quis dabit oculis, Mouton, 283

Quis mihi det lacrimus gemitus, Lassus, 695

Quis te victorem dicat, Crecquillon, 350f

Quittard, Henri (Quit), 286, 554f, 565ff, 571

Quivi sospiri: the text by Dante, 400; Luzzaschi, 413; Vinci, 413; Micheli, 413

Quod cumque in orbe, Greg. Chant, 467

Quod cumque vinclis: Greg. Chant, 467; Palestrina, 467

Quod jactatur, Ciconia, 26

quodlibet (= *ensalada*, *fricassée*), 146, 159, 192, 196, 206f, 214, 224, 291, 580, 586, 615, 635, 707, 835

Quomodo cantabimus, Byrd, 699, 788, 791

Quoyque Dangier, Binchois, 87

rabel, 626

Rabelais, François, 100, 278, 285, 293, 296

Radecke, Ernst (Ra), 669f

Radiciotti, Giuseppe (Rad), 425, 616

Radino, Giovanni Maria (Radi), 525, 534

Raggionamento di musica, Ponzio, 542

Ragionamenti accademici, Bartoli, 259, 546

Rahe, Heinrich, 463

Rainaldus, Magister, 220

Raisons des forces mouvantes, Les, Caus, 436

Ralegh (= Raleigh), Sir Walter, 819

Ramazzini, Amilcare (Ramaz), 409

Rameau, Jean-Philippe, 839

Ramonez moy ma cheminée, Hesdin, 299

Ramos de Pareja, Bartolomé (Ramos), 93, 107, 148, 158, 178, 182, 396, 547, 577, 586f

Ramsbotham, Alexander (Rams), 19, 39

Randulfo Romano, 30

range, extensions of total, 4, 35, 56, 91, 100, 105f, 109, 116, 119, 123, 128ff, 131f, 175, 240, 249, 267, 316, 320, 331, 405, 410, 418, 435, 533, 619, 658, 667, 693

Ranke, Friedrich (Ran), 651

Rape of Lucrece, The, Heywood, 881

Raphael Sanzio, 499, 567

Rappresentazione de Anima e di Corpo, Cavalieri, 569
Rappresentazione di San Giovanni e Paolo, Lorenzo de' Medici, 172f
Rappresentazione di Santa Eufrasia, 172
Rappresentazione di Santa Margherita, 172f
Raselius, Andreas, 684, 688
Rasmo, see: Lapicida, Erasmus
Rathery, Edme, 100, 293
Rattay, Kurt (Ratt), 656
rauschpfeiffe, see: pipes
Raval, Sebastian, 616
Ravenscroft, Thomas (Raven), 769, 808, 810, 833ff, 845
Ravn, Vilhelm C., 810, 881
Ray, Alice, 593, 617
Raynaldino; Raynaldus de Odena (= de Honderic); Raynaldus francigena; Raynaldo francigene, 220
Raynaud, Gaston, 150
Rayneau (= Reyneau), Gacian, 12, 575f
Razzi, Serafino, 453
Re di Spagna, Il (= La Spagna), 177
Reaney, Gilbert, 10, 11, 14, 16, 21
rebec (= *rabel, rybebe*), 148, 626, 656, 717, 757, 867
rebus form, composers' names in, 40f, 275
Recanetum . . . , Stefano Vanneo, 180
Recherche qui voudra, Pevernage, 397
recitative style, 324, 400, 415, 425, 434, 440f, 568, 820, 832, 883
Recordare, Hofhaimer, 662
recorder, 146, 569, 868, 873f
Red Book of the Exchequer, 767
Redford, John, 777, 803, 851, 854ff, 860, 877
redictae, 144
Redlich, Hans F. (Red), 438, 441, 501
reduction of several voices into one, 42, 78
Reed, Edward B., 768
Reese, Gustave (Re), *passim*
Reeser, Eduard (Ree), 79, 93
Refardt, Edgar (Ref), 705
Reformation, music of the, see: Anglican Church music; Calvinism; Lutheran music
regal, 850
Regali ex progenie, Greg. Chant, 776
Regem archangelorum, Festa, 363
Regem regum, Festa, 362
Regenbogen, 652f
Reger, Max, 674
Reges terrae, Mouton, 281
Regina coeli: Greg. Chant, 109, 195, 262, 471, 794; Aichinger, 2 settings, 699; Brumel, 262; Busnois, 2 settings, 109; Philips, 794; Rousée, 349; Victoria, 605
Regina regnantium (= Au povre par necessité), Busnois, 107
Reginaldus (= Liebert?), 65
Regis, Johannes, 101, 109, 113ff, 142, 144f, 227
Reglas de canto plano, Estéban, 577
Regnart (= Regnard), François, 390
Regnart (= Regnard), Jacques (or Jakob), 390, 666, 700, 710f, 726, 737

Regnum mundi, F. Anerio, 484
Regola Rubertina, Ganassi, 548f
Regole di musica, Rodio, 532
Regretée, La, Hayne, 99f
Regretz sans fin, Josquin, 232
Reichenbach, Hermann, 678
Reige, Mülich of Prague, 729
Reimar von Zweter (= Sigmar der Weise), 652
Reina MS, see: Manuscripts—Paris
Reinhardt, Carl P., 707
Reiss, Josef W., 667, 742, 745ff, 752
Reissmann, August (Reissm), 192, 373, 376
Rejoice in the Lord alway, W. Mundy, 802
relishes (= ornamentation), 845
Remunde, Christophe van, 335
Renaldo, or Renaldino, 220
Rendre me vieng, Binchois, 87
Renée of France, Duchess of Ferrara, 283, 311, 343
Renée of Lorraine, Duchess of Bavaria, 487, 691
Rener, Adam, 639, 649
Renvoy, Le, Compère, 225
repetenda (the term), 766
repetition schemes used in 15th-c. and early 16th-c. secular music to replace *formes fixes,* 188f, 213, 232f, 272f, 275, 287, 294f, 302
Repleatur os meum, Jaquet of Mantua, 366f (incl. Ex. 83), 470, 480
Requiem, Obrecht, see his *Mille quingentis*
Requiem Mass (= Mass for the Dead, Missa pro defunctis): Greg. Chant, 191, 264, 470, 593; G. F. Anerio, 485; Asola, 493; Brudieu, 614f; Brumel, 261f; Certon, 340; Clemens, 351; Cléreau, 340; Du Caurroy, 504f (incl. Ex. 117); Dufay, 76, 118, 130; A. de Févin, 279; Guerrero, 2 Masses, 595f; Josquin (?), 245; Kerle, 452; La Rue, 267, 611; Lassus, 696; Mauduit, 504; Monte, 703; Morales, 2 Masses, 590, 595; Ockeghem, 118, 130f; Palestrina, 475; Prioris, 264; Pujol, 611; Richafort, 335; Sermisy, 338; Vaet, 701; Victoria, 609
Requin, Henri (Req), 286, 290
Rerum Flandriacum tomi X, Jacques de Meyere, 221, 725
res facta (the term), 142
residuum (the term), 15
Resinarius, Balthasar, 678f, 681, 688
Resonet in laudibus, 674
Resplenduit facies eius, Victoria, 602
responsory and responsory motet, 94, 123, 281, 337, 342, 344, 353, 452, 462, 469, 484, 491, 500, 591, 603, 694, 738, 778, 780, 785f, 794f
Rest von Polnischen . . . Täntzen, Haussmann, 757
Resta di darmi noia, Gesualdo, 432 (incl. Ex. 104)
Resurgente, Leopolita, 749
Resurrexi, Isaac, 648ff

Resveillés vous, Dufay, 49, 55, 81
Retractiones de los errores, Espinosa, 587
retrograde writing, see: cancrizans; canon, crab
Reuchlin, Johannes, 705
Reusens, Edmond de, 138
Revenez tous regretz—Quis det ut veniat, A. Agricola, 208
Reviens vers moy, Monte, 703
Rex gloriose Martyrum (the melody = *Nunc Sancte nobis Spiritus; Aurora lucis rutilat, Aurora coelum*): Greg. Chant, 467; Palestrina, 467
Rex virginum (trope), 579
Reyes Católicos, Los, see: Ferdinand II and Isabella of Castile
Reyher, Paul (Rey), 883
Reyneau, see: Rayneau, Gacian
Reys, Jacobus (= Jacob Polonais?), 755f, 844
Rhaw (= Rhau), Georg, 208, 278, 341, 649, 678, 680ff, 684, 688, 724, 727
rhyme, musical, 16
Rhys, Philip ap, 855
rhythmic conflict among parts, 3, 57, 76, 104, 110f (incl. Ex. 28), 212f (incl. Ex. 39), 215 (Ex. 40), 233, 243, 258, 262, 294, 354, 466, 613 (incl. Ex. 136), 624 (incl. Ex. 139*b*), 749 (incl. Ex. 170), 804 (incl. Ex. 186), 812 (incl. Ex. 188); r. c. of macrorhythm and microrhythm, 212f (incl. Ex. 39), 243, 354, 397, 402 (incl. Ex. 93), 461, 466, 496, 733f (incl. Ex. 181), 827 (incl. Ex. 193); see also: accentuation; also some references under: quintuple meter
Riaño, Juan F. (Ria), 111, 579
Ribanje i ribarsko prigovaranje, Hektorović, 758
ribechino (= violin), 547
Ribera, Antonio de, 587, 610, 629
Ribera, Bernardino de, 592
Riccio, Camillo M., 576
ricercari: general, 519f, 526; *ricercare arioso* (the term), 539; *ricercari* in Capirola MS, 522; in Petrucci collections, 522, 535, 658; anon., 520; Antegnati, 542; d'Aquila, 520; Bertoldo, 542; Bianchini, 527; Bossinensis, 522; Buus, 529, 537; Cavaccio, 541f; G. Cavazzoni, 535ff; M. A. Cavazzoni, 534f; Ceretto, 549; Cima, 541f; Crema, 527; Diruta, 541f; Fattorini, 541; J. Fogliano, 537; A. Gabrieli, 537ff; G. Gabrieli, 537, 541; Galilei, 528; Ganassi, 549; Luzzaschi, 541f; Matelart, 528; Merulo, 537, 541; Milano, 526ff; Ortiz (*recercadas*), 630; Padovano, 537f; Palestrina, 541f; Parabosco, 537; Rore, 549; Segni, 537; Tiburtino, 549; Valente, 541f; Willaert, 537, 549
Richafort, Guillaume, 303
Richafort, Jean: biogr., 303; sec. voc. mus., 301ff, 336, 347; sacr. mus., 276, 281, 284, 335ff (incl. Ex. 75), 363, 371, 471, 560, 588; see also 278, 282, 285, 341, 356, 629, 706
Richelieu, Cardinal A. J. du Plessis de, 276

Ridean gia per le piagge, Marenzio, 422
Riedel, Johannes, 633, 674, 679
Riemann, Hugo (Rie), 14, 37f, 92, 120, 124, 136, 144, 155, 158, 179, 182, 211f, 224, 249f, 266, 272, 277, 302, 324, 379, 396, 532, 537ff, 549ff, 587, 591f, 616, 618, 623f, 645f
Riess, Karl, 656
Rietsch, Heinrich, 643, 647
Right Hon. Ferdinando Earle of Darby, his Galliard, J. Dowland, 847 (incl. Ex. 203)
Rihouët, Yvonne (Rih), 278, 289; see also: Rokseth
Rimbault, Edward F. (Rimb), 767f, 803, 815, 850, 852, 857, 866, 882
Rimes françoises et italiennes, Sweelinck, 399, 429
Rimonte (= Ruimonte), Pedro, 616
Ringmann, Heribert (Ring), 635f
Rinuccini, Ottavio, 569
Ripe, Albert de (= Ripa, Alberto da), 553f
Ritson MS, see: Manuscripts—London
Ritter, August G. (Rit), 539ff, 668
Rivaflecha (= Rivafrecha), Martin de, 587
Robbins, Ralph H., 377
Robbins, Rossell H. (Robb), 687
Robert, Duke of Bar, 7
Robertsbridge MS, see: Manuscripts—London
Robin Hood, the melody, 834f
Robinet de la Magdalaine (= Le Pelé, Robert), 48, 263
Robinson, Thomas, 843f, 848f
Robledo, Melchor, 591
Robyns, J., 267
Rochambeau, A. de (Rocha), 389
Rochlitz, Johann F. (Rochl), 469, 483f
Rodio, Rocco, 486, 532
Roediger, Karl E. (Roedi), 116, 131, 192, 196, 215, 218, 228, 236, 238f, 241f, 244f, 261, 264ff, 269ff, 272f, 275ff, 284f, 338, 647, 649
Roettger, B. H., 691
Rogamus te, Isaac, 215, 648
Rogier, Philippe, 611, 617
Rohan, Cardinal Armand G. M. de, 54
roi des ménétriers, 7, 566
Rokseth, Yvonne (Roks), 36, 148, 175f, 192, 225, 230, 262, 264, 278f, 297, 339, 348, 558ff; see also: Rihouët
Rolland, Romain (Roll), 172, 567ff, 571
Rollins, Hyder E., 771, 833
Roman de Fauvel, Le, 652
Roman de la Rose, Le, Guillaume de Lorris and Jean de Meun, 87
Roman School (other than Palestrina), 481ff
Roman Seminary, 426, 457, 599
Romances y letras . . . , see: Manuscripts—Madrid
romanesca, the melody, 436, 524 (incl. Ex. 121), 625
Romanini, Antonio, 723
Romero, Mateo (= Maestro Capitán), 616f
Rommelpot, De, the melody, 834

Roncaglia, Gino (Ronc.), 149, 158f, 178, 433, 526
rondeau, 17, 30, 43, 53f, 56, 88f, 99f, 102, 105, 110f, 119, 188, 205, 208, 225, 232, 264, 272, 299, and *passim;* see also: *formes fixes*
Ronsard, Charles de, 296
Ronsard, Pierre de, 277, 288, 293, 298f, 303, 382, 387ff, 396, 504, 553, 571
Roosens, Laurentius (Roos), 118
Rorantists and Rorate chants, 736, 739, 748, 753
Rorate coeli, Greg. Chant, 736
Rore, Cipriano de: biogr., 309ff, 329f, 375, 411, 691; sec. voc. mus., 311, 330ff (incl. Exx. 72–74), 343, 404, 434, 471, 476ff (incl. Ex. 112*b*), 538, 696, 698, 703; sacr. mus., 375f, 511, 703; instr. mus., 549; traits of R.'s style mentioned elsewhere, 400f, 409, 420; see also 52, 252, 323, 403, 413, 416, 437, 510, 666f
Rosa playsant, Philippon or Caron or Dusart, 111, 117, 202f (incl. Ex. 36*a*)
Rosa y Lopez, Simón de la (Rosa), 597
Rosenberg, Herbert (Rosen), 632, 634, 636, 643
Rosenplüt, Hans, 652
Rosetum Marianum (Klingenstein), 699, 702
Rosselli, Francesco (= Roussel, François), 401, 456, 469
Rosseter, Philip, 838, 843, 847, 880
Rossi (Hebreo), Salomone (Ross), 442, 489
Rossi, Umberto, 330
Rossi, Vittorio, 157
Rossignol, Le, Lassus, 391
Rossignol musical des chansons, Le (Phalèse), 398
Rossignols spirituels, Les, Philips, 793
Rosso, Annibale, 530
Rosso, Il, 449
Rostocker Liederbuch, see: Manuscripts—Rostock
Roth, F. Wilhelm E. (Rth), 652
Roth, Ilse, 681
Rotta, Antonio, 522, 524f, 555
Rouge, W. de, see: Ruby, Guillaume
round, 14, 769f, 833f, 869
Round of three Country dances in one, A, Ravenscroft, 834
Rousée, Jean, 348f
Roussel, François, see: Rosselli, Francesco
Rovigo, Francesco, 438
Rowley, Samuel, 782
Roy, Bartolomeo, 411, 425, 430, 486
Royer, Louis (Roy), 280
Royne des fleurs, A. Agricola, 208
Royne du ciel—Regina caeli, Compère, 225
Rozette, Sweelinck, 399
Rubeis, de, 93
Rubeus, P., 92
Rubinet (= Rubinus?), 48, 635
Rubino (= Rubinet? Rubinus?), 635
Rubsamen, Walter (Rub), 153, 157f, 161f,

164f, 173, 202, 261, 269f, 273, 282f, 311, 314, 316, 339, 365, 367
Rubum quem viderat Moyses: Josquin, 250, 259; Tye, 783
Ruby, Guillaume (= W. de Rouge? G. le Rouge?), 6, 34, 43, 48, 90, 92f, 95, 263, 635
Ruckers family, 561
Rudolph II, Emperor, 511, 698, 737
Ruffino, see: Bartolucci d'Assisi, Fra Ruffino
Ruffo, Vincenzo: biogr., 400, 416, 489; sec. voc. mus., 416; sacr. mus., 416, 489f (incl. Ex. 113); traits of R.'s style mentioned elsewhere, 455; see also 414f, 437, 491, 493, 513
Rufián Viudo, Cervantes, 630
Rugeriis, Ugo de, 155
Ruggiero (= *Aria di Ruggiero*), the melody, 326 (incl. Ex. 70*b*), 428, 524, 625, 818, 848
Ruimonte (= Rimonte), Pedro, 616
Rules how to compose, John Cooper (= Giovanni Coperario), 811
Runge, Paul (Run), 653f
Rupsch, Conrad, 676
Rusconi MS, see: Manuscripts—Bologna
Ruslein, W., 635
Rusticus ut asinum, 159
Ryb, M., 748
rybebe, 656

Sablonara, Claudio de la, 616
Sacchetti, Franco, 424
Sacchetti-Sassetti, Angelo (Sacc), 220
Sacerdos et pontifex, Greg. Chant, 216, 471
Sachs, Curt, 18f, 32, 35ff, 57, 146, 177, 179f, 204, 292, 460, 524f, 530, 547, 585, 631, 667, 766, 850, 863, 865ff
Sachs, Hans, 652, 654f (incl. Ex. 146), 709
sackbut, see: trombone
sacra rappresentazione, 171ff, 567
Sacrae cantiunculae, Monteverdi, 500
Sacrae symphoniae, G. Gabrieli, 498, 551f (incl. Ex. 127)
Sacri di Giove augei, G. Gabrieli, 418
Sacrifizio, Beccari, 568
Sacris solemnis (= *Sanctorum meritis*), Greg. Chant, 83; see also: *Panis angelicus*
Sacro tempio d'honor, G. Gabrieli, 419
Sadeler, Johannes, 517
sainctes chansonettes (= *contrafacta*), 89, 107, 110
St. Adalbert, 728, 742
St. Amour, Sister Mary P. (Amo), 581, 585
St. Anthony, Abbot, 109
St. Augustine, 746
St. Basil, 191
St. Blaise, 758
St. Cecilia, Confraternity of, 389
St. Cyril, 728
St. Elizabeth of Hungary, 715
St. Gellért (= St. Gerard), 715
St. George, 611
St. Gregory, 577
St. Ignatius Loyola, 578, 599
St. John Capistranus, 745

St. John Kanty, 742
St. Julien des Ménétriers, Confraternity of, 7, 566
St. Stanislaus, 742f, 745
St. Stephen, King of Hungary, 715
St. Wenceslaus, 729f
Salazar, Adolfo (Sala), 584ff, 620, 631
Sale, Franciscus, 700
Salinas, Francisco (Sali), 252, 527, 577, 579, 617f, 623, 627
Salisbury, Earl of, 865
Salmen, Walter (Salm), 634
salmi a versi con le sue risposte, 372f
salmi spezzati, 372f
Salmon, Jacques, 571
Salò, Gasparo Bertolotti da, 548
saltarello; s. tedesco; see: after-dance
Salutis humanae sator, Greg. Chant (= *Jesu nostra redemptio*), 83
Salva nos Domine, Mouton, 281
Salvator Deus, G. Gabrieli, 498
Salvator mundi: Sarum text with melody of *Veni Creator Spiritus,* q.v., 773; Byrd (instr. ensemble), 870; Bull (keyboard), 857; see also: *Adesto nunc*
Salve cara Deo tellus, Ludovico da Rimini, 27
Salve crux arbor, Obrecht, 192
Salve crux sancta, Willaert, 372
Salve decus genitoris, Gafori, 181
Salve flos tusce gentis—Vos nunc etrusce—Viri mendaces, Dufay, 78
Salve intemerata, Tallis, 785
Salve mater Salvatoris, Mouton, 282
Salve Regina: Greg. Chant, 8of, 122, 19of, 195, 222f, 253f, 271, 345, 463, 472, 502, 579f, 590, 595, 605, 608, 662, 794; anon. (not Dufay), 83, 645; Aichinger, 3 settings, 699; Anchieta, 579; Byrd, 790; Castilleja, 587; Franco, 2 settings, 593; Goudimel, 502; Guerrero, 595; Hofhaimer, 662 (incl. Ex. 148); Hygons, 773; Josquin, 253f; La Rue, several settings, 271; Jo. Martini, 222f; Morales, 590; Obrecht, 19of; Ockeghem, 2 settings, 121f, 124; Palestrina, 463; Philips, 794; Siculus, 727; Victoria, 4 settings, 605, 608
Salve salutis ianua, Kempa?, 742
Salve service, 8of
Salvum me fac, Jaquet of Mantua, 366, 470
Samber, Johann B., 532
Sambrooke MS, see: Manuscripts—New York
Samotulinus (= Szamotułczyk), Wacław, 748f
Sampayo Ribeiro, Mario de (Sampa), 598
Sampson, Richard, 773, 777f
Samson, Joseph, (Sams), 481
Sanchez de Badajoz, Diego, 631
Sancta et immaculata virginitas, Palestrina, 462
Sancta Maria, Mater Dei, Pasche, 777
Sancta Maria, ora pro nobis: Animuccia, 455; Cara and Tromboncino, 167

Sancta Maria, succurre miseris: Appenzeller, 340; G. Gabrieli, 498; Verdelot, 347; Victoria, 601 (incl. Ex. 133a)
Sancta Maria, Tomás de, 629f
Sancta Trinitas, A. de Févin, 284, 559 (incl. Ex. 129; anon. keyboard transcr.), 670 (Ochsenkhun's lute transcr.), 680 (Bruck's reworking)
Sancte Deus, Whytbroke, 777
Sancte Philippe, A. Agricola, 211
Sancte Sebastiane, Mouton, 281
Sancti et justi, Merulo, 496
Sanctorum meritis (= *Sacris solemnis* or *Panis angelicus*): Greg. Chant, 83, 467, 471; anon., 150; Dufay, 83; Palestrina, 467; Torrentes, 592
Sanctus (outside of complete Masses), see various Sanctus settings under: Mass sections
Sandberger, Adolf (Sand), 391, 393, 395, 404, 418, 512ff, 547, 656, 690f, 709
Sandley, 92
Sandrin, Pierre, 299, 696, 754
Sannazaro, Jacopo, 139, 313, 400, 406, 415, 421, 424, 568
Sans faire de vous departie, Fontaine, 36, 38, 44 (Ex. 6b)
Santacroce, Francesco, 285
Santa Cruz, Antonio de, 625
Santini, Prospero, 485
Santos, Julio E. dos (San), 598f
Sanuto, Marin, 158
Sargent, Helen C., 834
Sarto, Andrea del, 326
Sartori, Claudio (Sart), 155, 161, 222, 228f, 235, 438, 522, 528, 535
Sartorius, Thomas, 708
Sarum use, 68f, 90, 95, 114, 255f, 604, 765, 773f, 777ff, 784, 856, 870
sauterelle, see: after-dance
Sauvegarde de ma vie, 58
Saviezza giovenile, La (= *La Prudenza giovenile*), Banchieri, 437
Savonarola, Fra Girolamo, 170, 212, 364f, 453
Savorgnano, Girolamo, 760f
Savoy, Court of, 49f, 428
Saxton, J. Niles, 588, 595, 599, 608
Sayve, Lambert de, 700, 702
Sçais tu dire l'Ave, Lassus, 393
Scaldava il sol, Marenzio, 420
Scam (= Seam), Walterus, 635
Scampion, Jacobus, see: Champion, Jacques
Scandello (= Scandellus), Antonio, 666, 689, 708, 710
Scandinavian music, 712f
Scapulis suis, Palestrina, 466
Scaramella: the melody, 230; Compère, 224, 230, 277; L. Fogliano, 159; Josquin, 230
Scarco di doglia, Rore, 696
Scarlatti, Domenico, 862
Schadaeus, Abraham, 532
Schaffer, Robert J., 505
Schedel, Hartmann, 634

Schedelsches Liederbuch, see: Manuscripts— Munich
Scheer, Werner, 333
Scheidt, Samuel, 843, 863, 866, 881
Schein, Hermann, 712
Schering, Arnold (Scher), 22, 26, 40f, 55, 63, 84, 86, 91, 116, 124, 139, 157f, 161, 163, 175, 185, 199, 203, 208, 219ff, 225, 230f, 234, 258, 261, 269f, 282, 307, 319, 322, 332, 334, 347, 365, 411, 423, 432, 441, 453, 464, 478, 480, 489, 520ff, 527, 532, 535, 541, 544, 546, 549ff, 559, 563f, 568, 620f, 627, 634f, 638f, 645, 648, 654, 657ff, 662f, 666f, 669, 672, 676ff, 680, 682f, 686, 690, 705ff, 709ff, 738, 755, 859, 865
Schernito, Lo, Gastoldi, 446 (incl. Ex. 108)
Scherzi musicali, Monteverdi, 441
Scheure, D'Oude, 295
Scheurleer, Daniel F. (Scheur), 356, 398
Schiavetto (= Schiavetti), Giulio, 760ff (incl. Ex. 175)
Schletterer, Hans M. (Schlett), 389
Schlick, Arnolt, 658, 661ff, 668ff, 853
Schmeltzl, Wolfgang, 707
Schmid, Anton (Sch), 154
Schmid (the Elder), Bernhard, 564, 665ff, 716
Schmid (the Younger), Bernhard, 539, 665, 667
Schmid, Wolfgang M. (Sc), 656
Schmidl, Carlo, 181
Schmidt, J. H. (Smt), 178
Schmidt-Görg, Joseph (Schmidtg), 261, 301, 303ff, 317, 337, 341f, 344ff, 351f, 469, 477, 486
Schmitz, Arnold (Schz), 493, 651, 746
Schneider, Charles (Schnei), 362
Schneider, Marius, 23
Schneider, Max (Schneid), 487, 570, 669
Schnoor, Hans (Schno), 659
Schöberlein, Ludwig (Schöb), 484f, 488, 682ff, 686, 688, 708, 710f
Schoenberg, Arnold, 19, 638
Schöffer (the Elder), Peter, 154
Schöffer (the Younger), Peter, 638, 661, 706
Schofield, Bertram (Schof), 518, 764, 767, 851, 873
Schönfelder, Jörg, 638
Schonsleder, Wolfgang (= Volupius Decorus), 532f
Schoole of Musicke, Robinson, 843, 848
Schrade, Leo (Schra), 4, 145, 175, 425, 441, 521, 526, 541, 544, 644, 657ff
Schreiber (= Henricus Scriptor), 746
Schreiber, Maximilian (Schrei), 687
Schrems, Theobald (Schrem), 492, 676
Schrevel, A. Cornelis de, 187
Schröder, Otto (Schrö), 677
Schröter, Leonhart, 677, 682, 688
Schubiger, Anselm, 251
Schuler, Ernst A., 151
Schünemann, Georg (Schün), 180
Schütz, Heinrich, 418, 497, 532f, 569, 677
Schuyt, Cornelius, 429, 517

Schwanendreher, Der, Hindemith, **707**
Schwartz, Rudolf, 157ff, 165, 711
Schweiger, Hertha (Schwei), 866
Scintille di musica, Lanfranco, 179, 548
Scon lief, Barbireau, 117, 196
score, publication in, 332, 432, 529, 538, 752
Scott, Charles K. (Sco), 802, 831, 833
Scott, Ruth H. (Scot), 735
Scotto, Girolamo (= Hieronymus Scotus), 324f, 342, 416, 609, 760, 762
Scotto, Ottaviano, 155f, 314, 321
Scriptor (= Schreiber), Henricus, 746
Scriptum super punctis, Tinctoris, 140f
Scyence of Lutynge, 843
Sdegnosi ardori (Berg), 416
Se bien fait, Obrecht, 189f
Se congié prens, see: *Si congié prens*
Se grato o ingrato, Festa, 321 (incl. Ex. 67)
Se je fays dueil, Le Rouge, 92
Se la face ay pale, Dufay, 54f, 68ff, 70 (Ex. 16)
Se le mie acerbe pene, Porta, 416
Se'l pensier, Marenzio, 421
Se mieulx ne vient: A. Agricola, 210; Compère, 225
Seager, Francys, 797
Seam (= Scam), Walterus, 635
second (melodic minor s.) as expressive device, 257, 320, 355, 600, 603
seconda prattica, 441
seconde rhétorique, 87
seconds (harmonic), consecutive, 179, 615
Secourés moy, Madame: Monte, 396; Sermisy, 294f
Secretum musarum, 556f, 881
Segni, Giulio (= Julius de Modena), 537, 550, 627
Seiffert, Max (Seiff), 429, 485, 517, 544, 713
seises, 596f
Seld, Dr., 395, 511ff, 516
Selectissimae . . . Cantiones (Kriesstein), 300, 304, 681
Selesses (= Senleches), Jacques (or Jacopin) de, 12, 575
Selva di varia ricreatione, Vecchi, 433, 446, 523
semel, 773
Semper Dowland semper dolens, J. Dowland, 875
Senex puerum portabat, Victoria, 608
Senfl, Ludwig: biogr., 217, 642, 674, 679, 689; historical position, 689, 708; sec. voc. mus., 638, 705ff (incl. Ex. 159); sacr. mus., 678f, 681, 689f, 751; traits of S.'s style mentioned elsewhere, 696; see also 287, 663, 666, 710, 713, 749, 754
Senleches, see: Selesses, Jacques de
sennet, 879
Señor cual soy venido, Cornago, 577
Sento che nel partire, Gesualdo, 431
Senza te alta Regina, Nicolo (= *Vengo a te*, G. Fogliano), 167
Sepulto Domino, Victoria, 603
sequence (liturgical), 22, 83, 217; see also:

variation-chain sequence;—also harmonic sequence; isorhythmic sequence; melodic sequence

Sermisy, Claudin de (= Claudin): biogr., 291, 383; sec. voc. mus., 291ff (incl. Ex. 59), 301, 337, 351, 356, 561, 564; sacr. mus., 335, 338f, 559f, 670; traits of S.'s style mentioned elsewhere, 310, 341, 388; see also 278, 299f, 305, 366, 557, 629, 696, 754

Sermone blando: Sarum Chant, 604; Byrd, 870; see also: *Aurora lucis rutilat*

Serpentina, La, Pellegrini, 542

Services, Anglican: general, 795; individual Ss.: Byrd, 4 Ss., 803f (incl. Ex. 186); Caustun, 2 Ss., 797; Farrant, 3 Ss., 802; Gibbons, 2 Ss., 814; Heath, 797; Merbecke (*B. of Common Praier*), 796f; Morley, 6 Ss., 805; Paisley, 803; Patrick, 811; Shepherd, 801; Tallis, 4 Ss., 800; Tomkins, 7 Ss., 812; Weelkes, 10 Ss., 805f

Serviteur, Le, Dufay, 54, 56, 112f, 649

sesquialtera, 145f, 776

sesquitertia, 243

sestina: literary, 312, 332; musical, 332, 385, 404, 419, 421, 429, 441

Seule esgarée, Binchois, 88

Seven Last Words, 274

Seven Sobs . . . , Hunnis, 807

sevenths: harmonic (unsuspended), 69, 181, 441, 752; melodic leaps, 258f, 396, 410

Seys libros del Delphin de música, Los, Narváez, 621f

Sfogava con le stelle, Monteverdi, 440

Sfortunato, Lo, Lollio, 568f

Sforza, Cardinal Ascanio, 229f, 238; Bona, 719; Costanza, 174; Francesco, 327; Galeazzo Maria, 174, 181, 207, 217, 229; Gian Galeazzo, 181, 227; Lodovico, 178, 181, 229

Shakespeare, William, 393, 769, 792, 815, 820, 841, 843, 865, 879, 881f

Shaking of the Sheets, The, 848

Sharp, Cecil J., 834

sharps: in signature, 54; see also: chromaticism

shawm (= *celimela*), 37, 146f, 598

Shepherd, John, 779, 782, 784, 796, 801f, 816, 851

Sheryngham, 768

Shine, Josephine M., 227, 281ff, 285

Shirley, James, 881, 883

Shoote false love, Morley, 825

Shore, S. Royle, 777

Short, Peter, 837

Short measure off My Lady Wynkfyld's Rownde, 853f (incl. Ex. 205)

short octave, 850

Si ambulavero, Palestrina, 466 (incl. Ex. 110)

Si ambulem: Greg. chant, 130, 264, 703; in the Requiems of Monte, 703; Ockeghem, 130, 264; Prioris, 264

Si ascendero, Craen, 276

Si bona suscepimus: Sermisy, 670; Verdelot, 588, 627

Si c'est amour, Arcadelt, 381

Si congié prens (with various spellings): the melody, 207, 210, 233; A. Agricola, 210; Josquin, 233

Si dedero, A. Agricola, 201, 211, 276

Si j'ai esté vostre amy, Janequin, 298

Si liet'e grata morte, Verdelot, 318

Si mon travail, Crecquillon, 302 (Ex. 61)

Si oblitus fuero, Ninot le Petit, 190, 278

Si par souffrir, Monte, 396

si placet voice-parts, 100, 103, 110; *s.p.* sections, 485

Si qua tibi obtulerint, Lassus, 510

Si sumpsero, Obrecht, 192

Si tantos halcones, Narváez, 622 (incl. Ex. 138)

Si tus penas no pruebo (= *Tu dorado cabello*), Guerrero, 596

Sibilet, Thomas, 381

Sic Deus dilexit, Josquin, 255f

Sic Patres vitam (= *Ut queant laxis*), Greg. Chant, 83

Sicher, Fridolin, 662ff, 671

Sicher Liederbuch, see: Manuscripts—St. Gall

Siculus, Petrus, 727

Sicut cedrus, F. Anerio, 484

Sicut cervus: Greg. Chant, 130, 267; La Rue, 267; Ockeghem, 130, 267; Palestrina, 462 (incl. Ex. 109)

Sicut lilium: Brumel, 262; anon. keyboard transcr. thereof, 559; Palestrina, 470

Sicut malus, Moulu, 278

Sidney, Sir Philip, 313, 815, 819f

Sidus ex claro, Lassus, 697

Sieben und siebentzig . . . Art Täntze, Demantius, 756

Siège de Metz, Le, Janequin, 296

Sies, Johannes, 638f

Sigismund, Emperor, 78, 657

Sigismund I, King of Poland (= Sigismund the Elder), 719, 748

Sigismund II, King of Poland (= Sigismund Augustus), 719, 748

Sigismund III, King of Poland, 420, 426, 702, 712, 748

Sigismund, Archduke of Austria, 221

Sigmar der Weise (= Reimar von Zweter), 652

Sigmund, Archbishop, 641

signatures, see: key signatures; time signatures

Signora, io penso, Nenna, 444

Sigtenhorst Meyer, Bernhard van den (Mr), 398, 563

Silber, Marcello (alias Franck), 156

Silberweise, Hans Sachs, 654

silete, 151

Silva, Andreas de, 285, 326, 352, 368, 469ff, 501, 681, 706

Silva, Tristano de, 93

Silva de Sirenas, Valderrábano, 613, 623

Silver Swan, The, Gibbons, 819

Simile est regnum coelorum, Guerrero, 608

Simon, Alicia (Smn), 666f, 669, 755, 757

Simon, Jehan, 13

Simpson, Christopher, 834

Simpson, Percy, 882f
Simulacra gentium, Willaert, 373
Since first I saw your face, Ford, 838
Sindona, Enio (Sind), 187
Sinfonia d'Istromenti . . . , Banchieri, 550
Sing we and chaunt it, Morley, 824
Sing we merrily, C. Gibbons, 813
Singer, Alan, 202
singer, qualifications, 147, 370, 653
Singet frisch und wohlgemut (= *Resonet in laudibus; Joseph, lieber Joseph*), the melody, 674
Singleton, Charles, 169
S'io sedo a l'ombra, Cara, 161
síp (pipe), 715, 721
Sir Henry Umpton's Funerall, Dowland, 875
six-four chord, 69, 432, 441, 602, 618, 794
six-three writing, 41, 45f, 56, 59, 64, 88, 91, 211, 646f, 744f, 750, 856; see also: discant, English; fauxbourdon
sixths: harmonic (attitude of Tinctoris), 143; leaps, 259, 355, 396, 429, 789
Sixtus V, Pope, 494
Skoczek, J., 741
slide-trumpet, see: trombone
Sluter, Claus, 5
Smetana, Bedřich, 734
Smijers, Albert (Smij), 100, 104, 107ff, 111, 117, 119f, 123, 125, 149, 186f, 189f, 192, 195f, 202, 204, 209, 213ff, 218f, 224f, 228ff, 232, 234, 240, 251, 262, 265, 267, 269ff, 273ff, 282f, 335ff, 339, 341, 346, 348, 351, 365, 368, 371f, 374, 469, 643, 700, 702
Smith, Carleton Sprague, 554, 616, 808
Smith, James H., 288, 382
Smith, John S. (Sm), 301, 310, 327, 337, 339, 341, 426, 435, 488, 588, 765, 768, 771, 853f
Smith, L. T., 877
Smout, Adriaan J., 556
So lang sie mir in meinem sinn, Braxatoris or Pullois, 633
So ys emprentid (= *Sois emprantis; Soyez* . . .), Frye, 92f
Soares, Manuel, 598
Soave fia il morir, Palestrina, 402
soggetto cavato dalle vocali, 234, 236, 343, 375, 701
Sohier, Matthieu, 348
Sois emprantis (= *So ys* . . . ; *Soyez* . . .), Frye, 92f
Sola angioletta, Marenzio, 421
Sola soletta, Conversi, 445, 874
Solage, 12
Solerti, Angelo (Sol), 172, 379, 435, 551, 567f, 570f
Sol mi trafigge'l cor, Zacharia, 32
solmisation and solfeggio: based on hexachord, 141, 360; based on octave, 182, 396, 586; solmisation figures and puns, 131, 215, 234, 238f, 255f, 318, 422, 693, 873; see also: *soggetto cavato* . . . ; hexachord variations; *Missa Ut re mi fa sol la*

Solo e pensoso, Marenzio, 423
solo madrigals, 411f (incl. Ex. 97), 440, 442f, 545, 567, 570
Sommi-Picenardi, Giorgio (Sommi), 438
Son quest'i bei crin d'oro, Patricio, 760
sonata, suonata, 520, 525, 543, 551
Sonata con tre violini, G. Gabrieli, 552
Sonata pian e forte, G. Gabrieli, 551
Song of the Sybil: Córdoba, 582; Triana, 582
Sonneck, Oscar G. (Son), 569
sonnet, 156, 161, 165, 324, 408
Sonno che gli animali, Cara, 161
Sophia, Duchess of Saxony, 666
Sophocles, 569
Sopplimenti musicali, Zarlino, 378f
Sorbellini, Albano, 586f
Soriano (= Suriano), Francesco, 425f, 447, 458, 482, 485, 599, 616
Sorranzo, Jacopo, 760
Sortez regretz, Monte, 396
Sortie des gendarmes, La, Le Jeune, 296
sortisatio, 334; see also: improvisation
Sospitati dedit, Frye, 93
Soto de Lanza, Francisco, 454, 591, 596, 629
Soto, Pedro de (organist), 626
Soto, Petrus de (theologian), 451
Sourdés regrets, Compère, 225
Souterliedekens, 355ff; settings by Clemens (= Bks. IV–VII of *Musyck Boexkens*), 308, 355, 358 (Ex. 79)
Southwell, the melody, 807
Souvenir de vous, Le, Morton, 99
Souvent amour ne sçay pourquoy, Arcadelt, 381
Souviegne vous de la douleur, 244
sovrano (= soprano), 177
Sowinski, Albert, 752
Soyez aprantiz (= *Sois emprantis; So ys* . . .), Frye, 92f
Spain (outside Chap. 11): in general, 208, 265, 267, 276, 303, 350, 451, 481, 698; Barcelona, 12; Madrid, 304, 510f
Spagna, La (= *Il Re di Spagna*), 177, 215, 266, 521, 619, 665
Spaniol Kochersperg, Kotter, 665
Spanish Paven, Bull, 865
spartitura, 487
Spataro, Giovanni, 63, 178, 180f, 370, 534, 587
Spell, Lota M., 593
Spem in alium: Jaquet of Mantua, 366, 470; Tallis, 785
Spenser, Edmund, 819f
Spes salutis, Lupus, 351
Spiegel der Orgelmacher, Schlick, 661
Spies, Hermann (Spie), 656
Spinaccino, Francesco, 519, 521, 523, 525, 528, 620
spinet (= *espinette*), 488, 523, 530, 558, 561, 566, 850, 852
Spiritata, La, G. Gabrieli, 545, 551
Spiritus et alme (trope), 60
Spirto real, Padovano, 415
Spitta, Friedrich, 305

Sprüche von Leben und Tod, Lechner, 687
Sprung, see: after-dance
Squarcialupi, Antonio, 51, 153, 169, 175, 217
Squarcialupi Codex, see: Manuscripts—Florence
Squire, Laurence, 767
Squire, see also: Barclay Squire, William
Stabat Mater: a lost melody, 253; Aichinger, 699; Dammonis, 253; Gafori, 181; Josquin, 253f, 690; Lassus, 694; Palestrina, 463; Weerbecke, 219, 253
Stabile, Annibale, 425, 447, 482, 485
Stäblein, Bruno, 651
Staden, Johann, 712
Stadtpfeiffer, 655
Stainer, J. F. R. (Stain), 393
Stainer, Sir John (Sta), 6f, 10, 12, 15, 17, 21ff, 28, 30, 35, 38, 41, 43f, 52, 54ff, 59, 65, 86f, 89f, 92, 210, 265, 581
Standomi un giorno, Mel, 429
Stangetta, La, Obrecht or Weerbecke, 187, 190, 219
Stanley, Edward, 850
Stanley, William, Earl of Derby, 880
Stappen, Crispin van (= Crispiaenen), 275f
Starre Anthem (= *Almighty God*), Bull, 810
Stat felix Austriae, Vaet, 701
Staynes Moris, 848
Steele, Robert, 768, 811, 815, 878
Stefano da Salerno, 722
Stein, Edwin E. (Stn), 306, 336, 338, 341f, 347f, 350f
Stein, Henri, 151, 614
Steinhardt, Milton (Steinh), 352, 701
Steinschneider, see: Lapicida, Erasmus
Stella del nostro mar, Monte, 408
Stellfeld, Jean-Auguste (Stell), 397, 428, 511, 517, 561
Steno, Michele, Doge of Venice, 25
Stephan, Wolfgang (Ste), 55, 79, 81, 98, 108ff, 114, 122, 124, 137, 223, 268
Stephen, George A. (Stpn), 772
Sternfeld, Frederick W. (Stern), 705
Sternhold, Thomas, 796
Stet quicunque volet potens, Lassus, 507
Stevens, Denis (Stev), 765, 777f, 803, 816, 849, 851, 853, 855, 858
Stevens, Mother Georgia, 81, 198
Stevens, John, 768, 770
Stevenson, Robert (Stevnsn), 472, 587f, 590f, 593, 792, 796
Stillò l'anima, Marenzio, 422
Stimmtausch, 318, 396, 712, 745; see also: double counterpoint
Stirps Jesse, Greg. Chant, 108
Sto core mio, Lassus, 444
Stobäus, Johann, 686
Stokes, E., 771
Stokhem, Johannes, 147, 663, 723
Stoll, 652
Stollen, 15
Stoltzer (= Stolzer), Thomas, 679, 706, 723ff (incl. Ex. 165), 727

Stone, Kurt, 852, 864ff
Stoninge, Henry, 870
Stopes, C. C., 767, 880
stops on keyboard instruments, 530, 850
storta, 546
Stradivari, Antonio, 520
strambotto, 156, 161f, 167, 333
strambotto texts, 316
stravaganze, Macque, 543
street cries, English, 832f
Strife is o'er, The (after Palestrina), 469
Striggio, Alessandro: biogr., 436, 546, 570; sec. voc. mus., 426, 435f, 703, 859; sacr. mus., 487; mus. for dramatic presentations, 568f; traits of S.'s style mentioned elsewhere, 413; see also 401, 433, 666
stringed instrument makers (other than of s. keyboard instrs.), 520, 547f, 753
Strogers, Nicholas, 851, 869
stromenti (= keyboard instruments, stringed), 323
Strozzi, Giovambattista, 567
strumento di penna (the term), 546; see also: *istrumento . . .*
Strunk, Oliver, 19f, 61, 71, 73, 105, 107, 120, 141, 145, 150, 158, 160, 182, 185, 197, 228, 240, 251, 253, 262, 269, 275, 281, 293, 360, 377, 420, 441, 451, 458, 469f, 474f, 502, 586, 618, 677, 705, 763, 795, 806
Sub tuum praesidium: Greg. Chant, 195; de Opitiis, 265
Subirá, José, 584, 617, 625
"substitution" Mass, 227, 245, 270
Sufficiebat, Richafort, 336
Suis venu (= *Je suis venut*), Busnois, 100, 107
suites, 523ff, 553, 668, 671, 871
Summae laudis, O Maria, de Opitiis, 265
Summe Trinitati, Sarum Chant, 95
Summer, Der, 636
Summum sanctus, 657
Sumner, William C., 867
Suñol, Dom Gregorio, 581
Super flumina Babylonis: Byrd, 788; Gombert, 346; Monte, 702; Palestrina, 464; Victoria, 599
super librum cantare (the term), 141f
Super montem, Crecquillon, 350
Super ripam Jordanis, Clemens, 354
superius (= treble; the term), 16
Supplicamus nos, Greg. Chant, 195
Suppositi, I, Ariosto, 567
Supremum est mortalibus, Dufay, 78, 80f
Sur le pont d'Avignon, Sermisy, 295
Sur tous regretz, Richafort, 301, 347
Surge illuminare Jerusalem, present liturgical text of *Jocundare Jerusalem,* 281
Surge Petre, Philips, 794f (incl. Ex. 184)
Surge propera: Palestrina, 465, 608; adaptation of Palestrina's *Vestiva i colli,* Orfeo Vecchi, 490
Suriano, see: Soriano, Francesco
Surrexit Christus, G. Gabrieli, 552

Surrexit pastor bonus: Lassus, 692; Palestrina, 692

Surzyński, Jozef (Surz), 742

Sus: tous ses servants, Mauduit, 504

Susanna, Willaert, 374

Susanne un jour (incl. *Susanna faire* and *Susannen frumb*): Coelho (glosas), 630; Episcopius, 394; Farnaby (*Susanna faire*), 823; D. Lupi?, 393; Lassus, 393f (incl. Ex. 91), 538, 554, 616, 823; Lassus (*Susannen frumb*), 709; Monte, 396; Pevernage, 397; Sweelinck, 399; Turnhout, 394. Reworkings of the Lassus chanson: Bassano (diminution), 394 (Ex. 91); Francisque (lute), 554; A. Gabrieli (*canzona*), 538; Lassus: parody-Mass, 696; parody-Magnificat, 697

Susato, Tielman, 290, 296, 300ff, 308, 335, 353, 355, 357, 370, 510, 564

Susay, Jehan de, 61

Susay, Pierre de, 61

suspensions, 257, 262, 268, 441, 461, 692, 831, 837, 858; ss. created out of passing or auxiliary notes, 322, 355, 461

Sutherland, Gordon (Suther), 529, 537, 549

Svátý Václave, 729, 740

Swedish music, 712

Sweelinck, Jan P.: biogr., 398, 505; sec. voc. mus., 398ff (incl. Ex. 92), 429; sacr. mus., 517f; instr. mus., 562f; traits of S.'s style mentioned elsewhere, 410, 430; S. as theorist, 377; see also 8

Sweete, come away, my darling, Jones, 838

Switzerland: in general, 358; Basle, 705; Geneva, 359f, 362; Lausanne, 503; Lucerne, 705

Symbola, Othmayr, 682

symbolism, 12, 43, 58, 114f, 121, 227, 235, 251, 253ff, 268, 275, 335f, 352, 371, 580, 588, 610, 614; see also: eye music

Symonds, John Addington, 171, 546, 567

Symonet le Breton (= Maistre Symon), 75, 90

Symphonia angelica (Waelrant), 427f

synagogue music, etc., 489, 705

Syntagma musicum, Praetorius, 532f, 667, 684

Szabolcsi, Benedict (Szab), 714f, 718, 726

Szadek, Thomas, 753

Szalkai, Ladislaus, 727, 743

Szamosközi, 723

Szamotułczyk, Wacław (incorrectly called Szamotulski), 748f (incl. Ex. 170)

Szapolyai, John, 719

Szczepańska, Marja (Szczep), 741, 743ff, 753

Szydłovita, Magister, 743

Ta bonne grace, Canis, 301

tablature, see under name or type of instrument

Tábor, Smetana, 734

taboret (= tabor), 867

Taborites, 733f

Tabourot, Jehan, see: Arbeau, Thoinot

Tabulatur (= *Meistersinger* rules), 652f

tactus, 180

Tag der ist so freudenreich, Der (the text = *Dies est laetitiae*), 674

Taglia, Pietro, 328

Tagliapietra, Gino (Tag), 318, 332, 523, 535, 538ff, 549, 551, 620, 861, 863, 865ff

Tailhandier, 13

talea, the term, 21f; see also: isorhythmic motet

Tallis, Thomas: biogr., 784f, 787; historical position, 785; sacr. mus. with Lat. text, 785f (incl. Ex. 182); sacr. mus. with Engl. text, 799ff, 808; sec. voc. mus., 816; instr. mus., 856ff (incl. Ex. 206), 868; see also 782, 792, 798, 851, 870

tambura, 148, 174

Taming of the Shrew, Shakespeare, 792

Tamquam ad latronem, Victoria, 603

T'Andernaken: anon., 671; Brumel, 263; Obrecht, 189

Tannhäuser, 728

Tansillo, Luigi, 406

Tant que j'estoys, 558

Tant que nostre argent dura, Obrecht, 190

Tanto l'affanno, Caron, 110

Tantum ergo (= stanzas 6–7 of *Pange lingua,* q.v.): Span. Chant, 599, 604; Cardoso, 599

Tapissier, Jean, 6, 12f, 21, 23

Tappert, Wilhelm (Tap), 318, 521ff, 525f, 549, 553, 620, 661, 666ff, 755

tárogató (military oboe), 721

Tart ara: Isaac, 213; Molinet, 137, 213

Tasso, Joan Maria, 549

Tasso, Torquato, 400, 403, 409, 415, 420, 422ff, 430, 569, 820

tastar de corde, 522

tasti scavezzi, 175

Taverner, John: biogr. and sacr. mus., 777ff (incl. Ex. 179); Engl. adaptations of T.'s sacr. mus., 796f; T.'s relation to *In nomine* pieces, 779, 845, 857, 868; traits of T.'s style mentioned elsewhere, 773, 784; see also 768, 785f, 851

Te Deum: Anglican Canticle, 798; Shepherd, 801f; Tallis, 800; Weelkes, 800

Te Deum, Roman Canticle: Greg. Chant, 150, 362, 471, 560, 698, 855; troped text of *T. D.,* 149; *T. D.* in an Attaingnant print (keyboard), 560; G. F. Anerio, 2 settings, 485; Binchois, 90, 181; Blitheman (keyboard), 855; Festa, 362; Kerle, 2 settings, 698; Morago, 598; Resinarius, 679; Taverner, 780

Te lucis (several melodies; 1 = *Christe qui lux es*), 870; Byrd settings (1 called *Precamur*) of 2 diff. *T. 1.* melodies, 870

Te merito, Lassus, 692

Te spectant, Lassus, 507

Teach me, O Lord, Byrd, 804

Teach me Thy way, O Lord, Hooper, 807

Teares or Lamentacions of a Sorrowfull Soule, Leighton, 809, 811, 874

Teatro armonico spirituale, G. F. Anerio, 484

Tebaldeo, Antonio, 311

Tebaldini, Giovanni (Teb), 285, 411, 416, 447, 495

tecla (= keyboard), 625
tedesca (= *todesca*), 445
Teller, F., 715
temperament, see: intonation (= tuning)
Tempest, The, Shakespeare, 866
Tempio armonico, Ancina, 454
Templeuve, Jacques de, 43
tempo, 179f, 622, 813
Temps peut bien, Le, Lassus, 370
Temptation, The (a play), 877
Tems passé, Le, Lassus, 393
Tenebrae factae sunt: Croce, 500; Ingegneri (not Palestrina), 469, 491; Victoria, 603
Tenez moy en vos bras, Josquin, 232
Tenori e Contrabassi intabulati, Bossinensis, 759
tenths (parallel): Gafori's recommendation, 179; as style characteristic, 104, 129, 189, 191, 362, 579, 836
Terminorum musicae diffinitorium, Tinctoris, 723
ternary rhythm, predilection for, 52, 56, 88, 766
Terribilis est locus iste, Greg. Chant, 79
Terrible dame, Busnois, 106
Terriblement suis fortunée, 115f
Terry, Charles Sanford, 212
Terry, Sir Richard Runciman, 359, 786, 794, 796, 801, 869f, 873
Terzi, Giovanni, 521 (Ex. 120), 523, 526, 528, 551
Tessier, Charles, 835
Testagrossa, Gian Angelo, 526
Testudo gallo-germanica, Fuhrmann, 844
Teuscher, Hans (Teu), 633, 679
Teutsch Kirchenamt, 675
Teutsch Lautenbuch, Newsidler, 669f
Teutsche Liedlein, L. de Sayve, 702
text distribution among parts, 41, 54, 126, 160, 636, 638
text-substitution, see: *contrafacta; sainctes chansonettes*
text underlaying in sources, 34f, 75, 289; Zarlino's rules for t. u., 377f
texts by composers themselves, 78, 87, 99, 101, 159, 228, 263, 433, 711; see also: *Meistersinger*
theater music, see: dramatic presentations
Theiner, Augustin, 449
Thelamonius Hungarus, 727
Theophilactus, 714
theorbo, 488, 528, 566
Theorica musica, Gafori, 179
theorists, treatises, 25, 31, 35f, 63, 73, 110, 137ff, 178ff, 185f, 219, 256, 259f, 294, 328f, 350, 364, 376ff, 412, 436, 441, 483, 512ff, 526, 530ff, 536, 544ff, 553ff, 566, 577, 586f, 592f, 598, 617ff, 625f, 630, 639, 656, 658, 661ff, 667, 684, 687, 727, 746f, 754, 792, 811, 824, 834, 839, 844
Therache, Pierkin, 284f
Thesaurus harmonicus, Besard, 527, 554, 558, 755f, 844, 847

Thesaurus musicus (Montanus and Neuber), 256, 365, 372f, 708
Thibault, Geneviève, 57, 98, 308, 382, 389f, 401
Thibaut, Jean-Baptiste (Thib), 742f
Thibaut, Joachim (= de Courville), 382
Thiel, Carl, 694
Think'st thou, Kate, to put me down?, Jones, 838
third as consonance, 586, 754
third of chord at end of cadence (presence or absence), 45, 64, 102, 129, 144, 217, 259, 603f, 701, 800
This is the record of John, Gibbons, 814
This sweet and merry month of May, Byrd, 818
Thomas, E., 334
Thomson, James C., 213, 215
Thomson, Samuel H., 728, 741
thorough bass, see: *basso continuo*
Though choler cleapt the hart about, Whythorne, 816
Three Blind Mice, Ravenscroft(?), 834
Three Kings, The (a play), 877
Three Ravens, The, Ravenscroft(?), 834
Three virgin Nimphes, Weelkes, 826
through-composed music, 29, 52, 234f, 315, 322, 392, 636, etc.
Thule the period of Cosmographie, Weelkes, 827
Thürlings, Adolf (Thür), 343, 375, 701
Thurzó, George, 727
Thysius, Johann, 847, 881; see also: Manuscripts—Leyden
Tibi Christe splendor Patris: Greg. Chant, 467; Palestrina, 467
Tibi laus, tibi gloria, Lassus, 695
tibia, 146ff
Tiburtino, 549
Tiby, Ottavio, 616
Tieffenbrucker family, 520
tientos: Cabezón, 627; Milán, 620f; Vila, 626; see also: fantasias
Tiersot, Julien (Tier), 205f, 215f, 234, 261, 270, 286, 298f, 382, 387, 504
Tigrini, Orazio, 182
Tilley, Arthur A., 6
time-signatures, conflicting, 20, 57, 70, 134ff, 214, 473; adoption of common t. s., 320
time-unit, 188, 320, 402, 813; see also: *note nere*
Timor et tremor: G. Gabrieli, 498; Lassus, 695
Tinctoris, Johannes: biogr., 137ff, 221, 723; historical position, 148f; T. as theorist, 63, 101, 109, 139ff, 176, 183; T. on contemp. musicians, 86, 107, 110ff, 116, 120, 187, 763; sacr. and sec. voc. mus., 149; see also 93, 178, 180, 227, 263, 635, 727, 740
Tinódi, Sebastian, 718 (incl. Ex. 163)
Tintoretto (= Jacopo Robusti), 497, 546
Tirabassi, Antonio (Tira), 146, 180, 327, 500, 550
Tirsi morir volea: A. Gabrieli, 415; Gesualdo, 431; Marenzio, 424

Tisdall, William, 865
Titelouze, Jean, 562
Titian (= Tiziano Vecellio), 157, 499
Titus Andronicus, Shakespeare, 843
Titus Andronicus's Complaint (ballad), 843
Tityre, tu patulae, Lassus, 695
toccata (= *tochata*) and *toccata* style, 520, 540ff, 562, 664, 860
Toccata a modo di Trombette, Macque, 543
toccate: Bell'Haver, 542; Cavaccio, 542; Diruta, 542; G. Gabrieli, 541; Guami, 542; Luzzaschi, 542; Macque, see above; Merulo, 540f; Padovano, 537f; Romanini, 723
Toffanin, Giuseppe, 312
Tomasin, Pietro, 156
Tomboy, the melody, 834
Tomek, 736, 740
Tomkins, Thomas: biogr. and sacr. mus., 806, 808, 811ff (incl. Ex. 188); sec. voc. mus., 824, 832; instr. mus., 850, 852, 865, 869, 873; see also 814, 855
Tomkowicz, Stanislaw (Tomko), 753
tonal answer, 56, 106, 249, 345, 350f, 367, 399, 530, 698
tonality, feeling for; tendency toward major and minor, 185f, 188, 204, 259, 287, 348, 351, 361, 377, 384, 398, 400, 410, 418, 429, 467, 562, 578, 642, 650, 692, 699, 707, 740, 801, 808, 820, 824f, 828, 830, 837, 843, 847, 858, 86off
Tonos Castellanos A and *B*, see: Manuscripts—Madrid
Tonus peregrinus, Greg. Chant, 90
Torchi, Luigi (Tor), 10, 165, 180, 319, 325, 327, 333, 362ff, 366, 379, 413ff, 423ff, 432ff, 443, 446, 455f, 482f, 485, 488, 490, 492f, 495ff, 500, 535, 538ff, 825
Torelli, Gasparo, 433
Torner, Eduard M., 621
Torrefranca, Fausto (Torre), 110, 147, 158f, 164f, 172, 220, 224, 230, 232, 238
Torrentes, Andres, 592
Torres Naharro, Bartolomé de, 586
Torri, Luigi (To), 416
Tortorella, La, Obrecht, 187
toscanella, 445
Toscanello in musica, Il, Aron, 73, 182
Tota pulchra es: the text, 117; Arnold de Lantins, 40; Vargas (?), 594; Weerbecke, 219
Tota scriptura, Ghiselin, 266
Totote (= Barote), 585
Tottel, Richard, 771
Toujours bien, Jo. Martini, 222
Toulouze, Michel de, 37, 154, 177
Touront, Johannes, 98, 635, 658
Tous les regrets: Brumel, 263; La Rue, 272
Tout a par moy: A. Agricola: *a 3*, 209 (Ex. 38); *a 4*, 244; Frye, 93, 209, 244
Toutes les nuitz, Lassus, 392
Tower Hill, the melody, 862; Byrd, 862
toy(e), 835, 847, 867; see also: conceit
Toye, A, 867
Tra quante regione, Hugho de Lantins, 41

Trabaci, Giovanni Maria, 486
Tractato vulgare de canto figurato, Caza, 178
Tractatus alterationum, Tinctoris, 140f
Tractatus de musica, Paulirinus, 667
Tractatus de notis, Tinctoris, 140f
Tractatus de regulari valore, Tinctoris, 140f
Tragedia (a pasticcio), 569
Tragedie of Gorboduc (a play), 877
Trahe me post te: Guerrero, 595 (Ex. 132); Victoria, 602, 608
Trame, Albert, 553
transcription into modern notation (problems and procedures), 18f, 35, 94, 111, 179, 202, 520f, 854
Transilvano, Il, Diruta, 544f, 722f
transposition, 530ff, 545, 850; see also: clef combinations
Tratado de canto llano, C. de Escobar, 579
Tratado de cifra nueva, Valderrábano, 623
Tratado de glosas, Ortiz, 625f, 852
Trattato della natura . . . di tutti gli tuoni . . ., Aron, 182
traversa, see: flute
trayn (= *traynour*), 31f; see also: rhythmic conflict
Tre ciechi siamo, Nola, 333
treble-dominated style in early 15th-c. French music, 16f (the term), 23, 27f, 40, 54, 59, 63, 81, 88f, 91; see also: superius
Trebor, Jean, 19, 575f
Tregian, Francis, 851
Treg[ian's Ground], Aston, 853
Treibenreif, Peter, see: Tritonius, Petrus
Trend, John B., 581, 584, 587f, 591, 594, 596, 600, 610f, 615ff, 620, 629
Trent Codices, see: Manuscripts—Trent
Tres breve et familiere introduction (Attaingnant), 553f, 557, 56of
Tres libros de música en cifra, Mudarra, 622f
Trésor d'Orphée, Le, Francisque, 554
Treze Motetz musicaulx avec ung Prelude (Attaingnant), 558, 560
Triaca musicale, Croce, 436
Triana, 582
Tribularer si nescirem, Palestrina, 462
Tribulatio et angustia, Josquin, 250, 259
Tribus miraculis: Gallus, 738; Lassus, 692; Palestrina, 692
Tricinia (Rhaw), 727
tricinia, instrumental, 212, 230
Tricou, Georges, 300, 326
trillo, 545
trills, 521, 534, 545
Trink lang (= *Das gleut zu Speier*), Senfl, 707
trionfi (= pageants), 173, 567, 570, 882
Trionfo d'Arianna e Bacco, Lorenzo de' Medici, 168
Trionfo della Morte, 170
Trionfo di Dori, Il (Gardano), 426f, 831
Trionfo di musica (Scotto), 419
tripla, see: after-dance
Triste plaisir: a melody, 205; Binchois, 36, 87, 205

Tristes erant apostoli (the melody = *Nunc Sancte nobis Spiritus, Aurora lucis rutilat, Aurora coelum*): Greg. Chant, 467, 604; Palestrina, 467; Victoria, 604; concerning text, see also: *Aurora lucis rutilat*
Tristezas me matan, 588
Tristis est anima mea: Croce, 500; Lassus, 692 (incl. Ex. 155)
Tristitia, Byrd, 789
Trithemius, 138f, 145
Tritonius, Petrus (= Peter Treibenreif), 705, 726, 747
Tritt auff den rigel, Lassus, 709
Triumph of Peace (a play), Shirley, 883
Triumphes of Oriana (East), 426, 831
Troche, Guillam, 771
Troiane, Dolce, 569
Troiano, Massimo, 445, 487, 691
Trolly lolly lolly lo, Cornysh, 771
Trombetti, Ascanio, 546
Trombetti, Girolamo, 546
Tromboncino, Bartolomeo (Trom), 157ff, 161ff (incl. Ex. 32), 165, 167, 173, 314, 321, 522, 567, 754, 759
Trombone, Bartolomeo, 546
trombone (= sackbut, slide-trumpet, *tuba*), 22, 27, 35f, 37, 40, 42f, 60, 67, 147, 366, 487, 499, 545ff, 550ff, 568f, 655f, 672, 676, 715, 721, 867
Trop plus secret, La Rue, 272
tropes and troping, 40, 61f, 82, 261, 729, 765; see also: Marian tropes
Trost, J. C., 377
trouvère tradition, 7, 15, 53
Truchsess von Waldburg, Cardinal Otto von, 451, 599, 698
trumpet, 57, 146, 152, 448, 545, 626, 658, 721f, 759, 867, 878f, 883
trumpet style, see: *tuba* style
Trzciński, X. T. (Trz), 742
Trzycielski, Andreas, 751f
T'saat een meskin, Obrecht, 189
Tschudi Liederbuch, see: Manuscripts—St. Gall
Tu as tout seul: Janequin, 298; Sweelinck, 398
Tu dorado cabello (= *Si tus penas no pruebo*), Guerrero, 596
Tu es pastor ovium, Palestrina, 471
Tu es Petrus: Greg. Chant, 284, 471; Byrd, 791; Clemens, 355; Palestrina: *a 6,* 462, 472; *a 7,* 462
Tu lumen, see: *Christe Redemptor . . . Ex Patre*
Tu m'uccidi, Gesualdo, 431 (Ex. 103)
Tu pauperum refugium (= *Pars II* of *Magnus es tu, Domine,* q. v.), Josquin, 258
Tu pers ton temps, Gombert, 304
Tu solus qui facis mirabilia, Josquin, 245, 258, 364
Tua est potentia, Mouton, 282, 284
tuba, see: trombone
tuba style, 21f, 60f, 645, 689
Tudway, Thomas, 798
Tui sunt coeli, Lassus, 695

Tulerunt Dominum meum (music = *Pars I* of *Lugebat David,* q. v.), Josquin, 257
Tullia of Aragon, 319
tuning, see: intonation (= tuning)
Tunstede, Simon, 727
Turbarum voces, Byrd, 790
Turges, Edmond, 768
Turnhout, Gerardus, 308, 394
Turnovský, Jan T., 739
Turrini, Giuseppe (Turr), 326, 400, 616
Tutti i Trionfi, Grazzini (Il Lasca), 169
Tuttle, Stephen, 860
Twelfth Night, Shakespeare, 769, 865, 881
twelve-mode system, 185, 377, 384, 503, 562
Tye, Christopher: biogr., 782; sacr. mus. with Lat. text, 779, 782f (incl. Ex. 180); sacr. mus. with Engl. text, 798f (incl. Ex. 185), 802; instr. mus., 851, 868f (incl. Ex. 211); see also 803
Tye, Ellen, 783
Tyme to pas with goodly sport, 878 (Ex. 215)
Tympanum Militare Ungerische Heerdrummel . . . , 722

Ubi caritas et amor, 167
Udite lagrimosi spirti d'Averno: Marenzio, 422f; Wert, 411
Ugolini, Baccio, 153
Ulenberg, Caspar, 698
Ulrich of Württemburg, 638f, 647
Ultimi miei sospiri, Verdelot, 317f, 703
Umor allegro, L', Orazio Vecchi, 435
Umor misto, L', Orazio Vecchi, 435
Un di lieto giamai, Lorenzo de Medici, 170
Un Enfant du ciel, Du Caurroy, 386
Un(g) gay bergier: Crecquillon, 302, 538, 628, 738; keyboard transcrs. thereof: anon., 628; Cabezón, 628; A. Gabrieli, 538
Un jour je m'en allai, Wert, 445
Un jour l'amant, Lassus, 395
Un jour vis un foulon, Lassus, 393
Una hora, Ingegneri, 491
Un'amiga tengo, hermano, Encina, 583f (incl. Ex. 130)
Une fillette, Clemens, 302
Une fois avant que mourir (= *En avois*), 634, 658
Une jeune fillette, the melody, 565; Du Caurroy, 5 settings, 565
Une mousse (= *musque*) *de Buscaye:* the melody, 214; Josquin, 232
Ung franc archier, Compère, 224
Ungaresca; Ungarischer Tanz; Ungarischer Aufzug, 716f (incl. Ex. 162)
Ungaro, Franco, 530
Unus (as term with special meaning), 24
Unus ex discipulis, Victoria, 603
Urban IV, Pope, 597
Urban VI, Pope, 731
Urban VIII, Pope, 83
Urbano, Fra, 175
Urbs beata Jerusalem, Greg. Chant, 649
Ureda (= Urrede), see: Wreede, Johannes

Ursprung, Otto (Ur), 68, 81, 235, 254, 257, 451, 514, 611, 614f, 634, 651, 691
Ut heremita solus, Ockeghem, 99, 124
Ut Phoebi radiis, Josquin, 256
Ut queant laxis (= *Iste confessor, Sic Patres vitam*): Greg. Chant, 83, 90, 191, 467; Binchois, 90; Dufay, 83; Lassus, 693; Palestrina, 467
Ut re mi fa sol la, Bull, 861 (incl. Ex. 209)
Utendal, Alexander, 700, 702
Utilis . . . introductio, Judenkünig, 668
Utraquists, 735

Va t'ent souspier, Grossin, 43
Vadam et circuibo, Victoria, 601
Vaet, Jacob, 297, 366, 488, 700f (incl. Ex. 157), 738
Vaghi fiori, I (= *Quand je me trouve*), Arcadelt, 323
Vaillant, Jean, 12
Valderrábano, Enriquez de, 613, 623, 627
Valdrighi, Luigi F. (Val), 221, 229
Vale, Giuseppe, 416
Vale, vale, de Padoa, o sancto choro, van Stappen, 276
Valendrinus (= Hollandrinus), 743
Valente, Antonio, 539, 541f
Valentin, Erich, 541
Valentinian, Fletcher, 882
Valenzuela (= Valenzola), Pedro, 616
Valle de Paz, Giacomo del, 415, 538
Vallet, Nicolas, 556, 881
Van, Guillaume de, 8, 10f, 28, 31, 43, 61, 66, 90
Van den Borren, Charles (Bor), 8ff, 12, 18, 21ff, 30, 32f, 35, 38ff, 48, 50ff, 55ff, 62, 69, 76, 78f, 85, 91, 96, 105, 107ff, 115f, 124, 126, 131, 133, 138ff, 142, 145, 147, 149, 178, 195, 208ff, 224f, 227, 261ff, 270, 272ff, 305, 308, 319, 327, 344, 366, 381, 390, 394, 399, 427, 445, 563, 614, 645, 691, 696ff, 708f, 771, 850f, 853, 856f, 860ff
Van den Hove, Joachim, 556, 756, 844, 847
Van den Vaerwere, 138
Van der Linden, Albert (Ldn), 51, 137, 683
Van der Straeten, Edmond (Stra), 43, 118, 138f, 148f, 187, 207, 215, 218f, 229, 260, 299, 301, 340, 346, 351, 370, 374, 376, 447, 575, 581, 723
Van der Straeten, Edmund (Strae), 548
Vanneus, Stephanus, 180
Vaqueras, Bertrandus (= Bernardus), 136
Vargas, Luis de, 594
variation-chain sequence, 251ff, 339, 369, 372, 463, 605, 694
variations (English or Italian) for lute or keyboard: general, 526, 855f, 862f; use of popular and dance tunes as basis, 861f; individual pieces: anon., 853; Alison, 874f (incl. Ex. 214); Aston, 853; Baldwyne, 870; Byrd, 853, 870; Casteliono, 523; Dalza, 523; Farnaby, 862; A. Gabrieli, 539; Molinaro, 526;

Stoninge, 870; Terzi, 526; Woodcocke, 870; see also: *diferencias, glosas*
Varietie of Lute Lessons, R. and J. Dowland, 844, 846f
Vasari, Giorgio, 317
Vasconcellos, Josquim de (Vas), 598f
Vasilissa ergo gaude, Dufay, 49, 77
Vasquez, Juan, 612ff (incl. Ex. 136), 624 (incl. Ex. 139)
Vater unser: Dietrich, 680; Lassus, 709
Vatielli, Francesco (Vat), 61, 430, 437, 444, 550
Vattene pur crudel, Monteverdi, 440
Vaughan Williams, Ralph, 206, 270, 800
Vautor, Thomas, 832
vaux-de-vire, see: *voix-de-ville*
Vecchi, Orazio (Vec): biogr. and sec. voc. mus., 420, 426, 433ff (incl. Ex. 105), 446, 523; sacr. mus., 487f; instr. mus., 539; traits of V.'s style mentioned elsewhere, 413, 826; see also 401
Vecchi, Orfeo, 435, 490f
Vega, Lope de, 596, 617, 631
Veggi'or con gli occhi, Festa, 320 (incl. Ex. 66)
Veglie di Siena, Le, Orazio Vecchi, 435
Vehe, Michael, 651
Velociter exaudi me, Orazio Vecchi, 487
Velten, Rudolf (Vel), 443, 445f, 707, 710
Velum templi, Croce, 500
Velut, Gilet, 22f
Venegas, see: Henestrosa, Venegas de
venetiana, 445
Venez regrets, Compère, 224, 228
Veneziani, Vittore, 446
Vengo a te, madre Maria, G. Fogliano (= *Senza te alta Regina,* Nicolo), 167
Veni Creator Spiritus: Greg. Chant, 150, 363, 472, 649, 773, 786, 857; Byrd (keyboard), 857; Festa, 363; Philips, 794; see also: *Adesto nunc; Salvator mundi*
Veni Creator Spiritus—Veni Sancte Spiritus, Heinrich Finck, 649
Veni Domine, Greg. Chant, 192
Veni Redemptor gentium: Luther's transl. of the text, 674; Redford, 854
Veni Sancte Spiritus: Greg. Chant, 83, 223, 251, 372, 463, 649; Dufay, 83; Josquin, 251; Palestrina, 463; Victoria, 605; Willaert, 372
Veni sponsa Christi: Palestrina, 464, 471, 602; Victoria, 601f (incl. Ex. 133b)
Veni, veni, dilecte mi, Palestrina, 465
Venit ad Petrum, Sarum Chant, 68
Venite, Anglican Canticle, 798
Vente, M. A., 561
Venture, Johannes à la, see: Longaval
Venturi, A. (Ven), 174
Venus tu m'a pris, de Orto, 265
Venusblümlein, Metzger, 655
Venusgarten, Haussmann, 757
Vérard, Antoine, 74
Verbonnet, see: Ghiselin, Johannes
Verbum bonum: Greg. Chant, 284, 369;

Therache, 284; Willaert, 368f (incl. Ex. 84), 372; see also: *Vinum bonum*
Verbum caro: anon. melody, 114; Lassus, 693; Weerbecke, 219, 258
Verbum supernum: Greg. Chant, 693; Redford, 854; see also: *O salutaris hostia*
Verdelot, Philippe (= Philippe Deslouges?): biogr., 270, 316f, 364; historical position, 316; sec. voc. mus., 317ff (incl. Exx. 64, 65), 417, 523, 595, 703, 835; sacr. mus., 269, 337, 347, 364f, 470, 588, 627; traits of V.'s style mentioned elsewhere, 324; see also 93, 285, 296, 309, 321, 327, 352, 623, 629, 706f, 754
Verdi, Giuseppe, 26, 124
Verdonck, Corneille, 397f, 427f, 517
Vere lang̲ ores, Victoria, 600
Verel, Robin, 87
Vergebliches Ständchen, Brahms, 709
Vergil, 153, 253, 381, 583, 695
Vergiliana Opuscula, Niger, 155
Vergine bella: Dufay, 52f, 188; Merulo, 417; Palestrina, 403; Rore, 332, 403, 698
Vergine madre, figlia del tuo figlio, Merulo, 417
Verginella si leva, La, Razzi, 453
Verheyden, P. (Verh), 265
Veri almi pastores, Corrado da Pistoia, 27
Verjust, see: Cornuel, Jean
Vernarecci, Augusto, 154, 222
Vero modo di diminuir, Il, dalla Casa, 412
Verovio, Simone, 447, 543f
Vers lyriques, Du Bellay, 389
vers mesurés à l'antique, 382f, 386, 504f; *v. m. à la lyre*, 382
verse anthem: Byrd, 805; Gibbons, 813f; Morley, 805; Tomkins, 812
Versè, Marion L., 336, 344, 367, 495, 516
versicle, double (the term), 216
Versillos del primer tono, 627f (incl. Ex. 140a)
Vestiva i colli, Palestrina, 403, 435, 437, 465, 471, 490, 703
Vetranović, Mavro, 759
Vexilla Regis: Greg. Chant, 150, 223, 271; Festa, 363
Vexilla Regis—Passio Domini, La Rue, 271
Vezzosette ninfe belle, Gastoldi, 446
Viadana, Ludovico Grossi da, 416, 427, 488f, 545, 753, 762
Viaje de Jerúsalem, Guerrero, 594
vicaire (the term), 7
Vicente, Gil, 581, 586
Vicentino, Michele, 158, 292
Vicentino, Nicolò, 323, 328ff (incl. Ex. 71), 364, 377, 513, 515f, 530, 541, 550, 586, 591
Vich, Luis, 610
Victimae paschali: Greg. Chant, 77, 251, 281, 361, 372, 463, 609, 681; anon. setting, 77, 83; Busnois, 109; Josquin, 245, 251; Las Infantas, 609; Palestrina, 463; Willaert, 372
Victoria (= Vittoria), Tomás Luis de (Vic): biogr., 599f, 617; historical position, 481; sacr. mus., 591, 599ff (incl. Exx. 133, 134),

629, 693; traits of V.'s style mentioned elsewhere, 467, 615; see also 287, 594, 610, 618
Vidal, Peire, 716
Vide, Jacques, 43ff (incl. Exx. 5a, b; 6a; 7b), 48
Videntes stellam, Lassus, 692
Vidi impium, Coclico, 516
Vidi speciosam: F. Anerio, 484; Victoria, 606f (incl. Ex. 134b)
Vie et passion de Mgr. Sainct Didier, La, Greban, 150
Vieira, Ernesto (Viei), 598
Vienn' Himeneo, G. M. Nanino, 425
Vigilate, Byrd, 788
vihuela: the instrument, 160, 619ff; tablature, 620ff; solo music, 620ff; *v.*-accompanied song, 613, 620ff
Vila, Pedro Alberch, 615, 626
Vilanella non è bella, La, the melody, 61 (incl. Ex. 14)
Viletti, Jacobus, 658
Villalar, Andrés de, 592
Villalón, Cristóbal de, 579
villancico, 581ff, 612f, 765f
villanella, 316, 443ff, 558, 709, 755, 816
villanesca, 165, 313, 320, 326, 332ff, 443f
Villanis, Lui█████ (Villa), 100
Villeroye, Jehan de (= Briquet), 7
Villon, François, 100
villota, 164, 445
Vince con lena, Bartolomeo da Bologna, 28, 30, 33
Vincenet, 136, 635
Vincenot, Johannes, 137
Vincent, Alexandre J. H. (Vinc), 94f, 98, 117, 264
Vincenti, Giacomo, 401, 545
Vincentius, Caspar, 532
Vinci, Leonardo da, 153, 157, 292
Vinci, Pietro, 453, 492, 502
Vindella, Giovanni, F., 522
Vinders, Jerome, 308
Vinum bonum et suave (travesty of *Verbum bonum*): Lassus, 697; Richafort, 301
viol family, bowed (incl. *viola da braccio*, *violone*, etc.), 36, 148, 160, 176, 323f, 370, 487f, 546ff, 550f, 566ff, 625f, 671, 753, 792, 809, 836, 852, 867, 871f, 873f, 877
viol tablature, 548f, 848
Viola, Alfonso della, 324f, 546, 568f
Viola, Andrea della, 568
Viola, Francesco, 324f, 329, 378
Viola, Giampietro della, 173
violin, 495, 499, 528, 547f, 551, 570f, 757; see also: *ribechino*
Virdung, Sebastian, 124, 555, 638f, 656f, 667, 669, 707
virelai, 12, 14f, 17, 20, 53, 102, 205; see also: *bergerette; formes fixes*
virginal, 667, 850ff
Virginalis flos vernalis, 634
Virginella, La, Byrd, 428, 818
Virgini Mariae laudes, Felstin, 747

Virgo caelesti, Compère, 225
Virgo et Mater, Anchieta, 579
Virgo Maria, Weerbecke, 218
Virgo parens Christi, Greg. Chant, 116
Virgo prudentissima: Greg. Chant, 255, 379; Isaac, 649; Josquin, 255
Virgo rosa venustatis (= *C'est assez*), Binchois, 89
Viri Galilei: Couillart, 351; Palestrina, 471
Viri mendaces, Greg. Chant, 78
Virtute magna, Lasson, 352, 368, 470
Visin, visin (= *Jesu, Jesu*), 167
Vit encore ce faux Dangier, Vide, 43f (incl. Ex. 5b)
Vita dulcedo, Ghiselin, 266
Vitellozzo, Cardinal Vitello, 449f
Vitri, Philippe de, 19f, 133, 577, 633, 652
Vittoria, see: Victoria, Tomás Luis de
Viva el gran Re Don Fernando, 155
Vive le roy, Josquin, 234
Viver lieto voglio, Gastoldi, 825
Vivian, S. Percival, 883
Vivray-je tou(s)jours: Josquin, 234; Sermisy, 295
Vobis datum est, Porta, 494
vocal orchestration, contrasting subgroups of voices, 76, 103, 126, 128, 218, 238, 243, 261, 294, 308, 366, 376, 591, 606, 649, 775, 779f, 783, 785, 812
vocal orchestration, contrasting of successive sections, 85, 236, 238, 255, 647, 777
vocal orchestration, subdivision of individual voice-parts, 62, 81
voces musicales (the term), 237
Vogel, Arthur (Vo), 768
Vogel, Emil, 165, 319, 437f, 441f, 445
Vogeleis, Martin (Vog), 645, 666f, 669, 688
Vogelmaier or Vogelsang, see: Ornithoparchus, Andreas
Voglie e l'opre mie, Le, Lassus, 405 (incl. Ex. 94)
Voi mi poneste in foco, Palestrina, 403
Voi ve n'andate, Arcadelt, 321f (incl. Ex. 68)
voix-de-ville (= *vaux-de-vire*), 205, 389f, 558
Volante, James D., 696
voluntaries: Alwood, 854; Byrd, 860; Gibbons, 860; Redford, 860; Weelkes, 860
Vom Himmel hoch da komm ich her (the melody = *Aus fremden Landen*), 675
Von Gott will ich nicht lassen, Bach, 565
Vorria morire per uscir, Waelrant, 427
Vos me matastes, Vasquez, 613 (incl. Ex. 136), 624 (incl. Ex. 139b)
Vostr'acuti dardi, I, Verdelot, 318
Vostre alée, Binchois, 88, 100, 105
Vostre amour est vagabonde, Sweelinck, 399
Vostre bargeronette, Compère, 224
Vostre bruit, Dufay, 54, 56
Vostre regart, Tinctoris, 149
Vostre tarin je voudrois estre, Mauduit, 386 (incl. Ex. 88)
Vous me tuez si doucement, Mauduit, 386
Vox dilecti mei, Palestrina, 465

Vox in Rama: Clemens, 355; Deering, 793
Vray amy, Le, Lassus, 370
Vray dieu d'amours: the melody, 206, 263; Brumel, 263
vuelta (the term), 581
Vulnerasti cor meum: anon., 588; Palestrina, 465
Vulpius, J., 676
Vulpius, Melchior, 684
Vultum tuum deprecabuntur, Josquin, 257, 279, 372

Wach auf mein hort, von Wolkenstein, 634
Wackernagel, Philipp (Wacker), 193
Wäckinger, Regina, 690
Waelrant, Hubert, 290, 396f, 427, 505ff, 510
Wagenseil, Johann Christoph (Wagen), 652f
Wagner, Peter (Wag), 29, 60, 62, 69, 75, 77, 94, 122, 130, 191, 210, 215, 218, 245, 261, 264, 270, 302, 317, 319f, 323, 327, 332, 336, 338ff, 352, 372, 375, 404, 450, 455, 469, 473, 481, 484, 489, 496, 498, 588f, 605, 608, 646ff, 688f, 696f, 741f
Wagner, Richard, 463, 652, 659
Waissel (= Waisselius), Matthäus, 669, 671, 755
waits, 772
Wald hat sich entlaubet, Der, 636
Waldapfel, Jozsef (Wa), 726
Waldner, Franz (Wald), 656
Wale, Gheerkin de, 306
Walker, D. P. (Walk), 382f, 558
Walker, Ernest (Walker), 783, 871
Wallace, Charles W., 880
Waller, A. R., 882
Wallner, Bertha Antonia (Wal), 438, 656, 681, 690f
Walpole, Horace, 881
Walsingham: the melody, 862, 870; Bull, 862; Byrd, 862
Walter, Johann, 657, 674, 676ff, 681f, 684, 688f
Walter von der Vogelweide, 652
Walterus de salice, 635
Wanley MS, see: Manuscripts—Oxford
Wannenmacher, Johannes, 683
Ward, Charles F., 263
Ward, John, 808f, 831, 851, 873
Ward, John M., 160, 428, 523ff, 620ff, 627f, 768, 854, 859, 866, 876, 879
Warlock, Peter, 771, 810, 816f, 836, 839ff, 873
Warner, G. F., 879
Warren, Edwin B., 777
Was mein Gott will das gscheh' allzeit: the melody (= *Il me suffit*), 696; Eccard, 696
Wasielewski, Joseph W. von (Was), 521f, 527f, 534, 537ff, 550ff, 556, 668f
Watson, Thomas, 818, 821, 874
Wauters, Edgar (Wau), 301
Weber, Veit, 652
Weck, Johann, 665
Wecker, Hans Jacob, 669, 671

Weckerlin, Jean-Baptiste (Weck), 224, 234, 261, 433, 447, 571
Weelkes, Thomas (Weel), 805f, 809, 815, 819ff, 824, 826ff (incl. Exx. 193, 194), 831ff, 851f, 860, 868, 872 (incl. Ex. 213)
Weepe, weepe, mine eyes, Wilbye, 830
Weerbecke, Gaspar van, 137, 147, 165, 190, 205, 218ff, 253, 258, 663
Weet ghij wat mynder jonghen herten deert? Obrecht, 187
Weinmann, Johannes, 679
Weinmann, Karl (Wein), 140, 147, 176, 286, 449f, 480
Welsford, Enid, 883
Wenceslaus II, King of Bohemia, 729
Wenceslaus of Prachatitz, 729
Wer hat gemeint, Heinrich Finck, 640
Werkmeister, Andreas, 377
Werner, Luigi (Wer), 726
Werner, Theodor W. (Wern), 253, 649, 683, 687
Werrecore, Hermann Matthias, 327, 333, 368, 550, 682
Wert, Giaches de: biogr., 327, 408f, 438; sec. voc. mus., 409ff (incl. Ex. 96), 445, 496, 703; sacr. mus., 488; traits of W.'s style mentioned elsewhere, 413, 430; see also 401, 426f, 490, 566
Wesoły nam dzień nas tął, the melody (= *Also heilig ist der Tag*), 750f (incl. Ex. 171a)
West, John E., 854, 858, 860, 865ff
Westcote, Sebastian, 877
Western Wynde, The, the melody, 779 (incl. Ex. 178)
Weston, Father William, 787
Westrup, Jack A. (Westr), 818
Weyler, Walter W. (Wey), 311, 327
What ayles my darling? Morley, 822f (incl. Ex. 191a)
What if I seeke for love of thee? Jones, 838
What is our life? O. Gibbons, 819
When David heard that Absalom was slain, Tomkins, 812
When grypinge griefes, Edwards(?), 816
When shall my sorowful sygheinge, Tallis, 816
When shall my wretched life, Wilbye, 830
When You See Me You Know Me, Rowley, 782
Where most my thoughts, Wilbye, 830
Where the bee sucks, R. Johnson, 882
Whethamstede, Abbot of St. Albans, 850
White, Robert, 783f (incl. Ex. 181), 791, 802, 846 (incl. Ex. 202), 869
Whittaker, W. Gillies (Whit), 804, 862
Whittingham, William, 797
Who shall have my fayre lady, 771
Why aske you? Farnaby, 862
Whytbroke, William, 777, 796, 869
Whythorne, Thomas, 816f, 871
Widmann, Benedikt (Widm), 705
Widmann, Wilhelm (Widma), 481
Wie lieflich is der mai, Egidius de Rhenis, 632
Wienpahl, Robert W., 186
Wigthorpe, William, 817

Wilbye, John, 792, 809, 819f, 824, 828ff (incl. Exx. 195, 197), 874
Wilder, Philip van, 771, 873
Wilkin, Ludolf of Winsem, 657
Will Forster's Virginal Book, see: Manuscripts —London
Willaert, Adrian (Will): biogr., 280, 309, 368, 725; historical position, 323, 343, 348; sec. voc. mus.: in Dutch, 308; in French, 309f (incl. Ex. 63), 338, 351; in Ital., 316, 323f (incl. Ex. 69), 334; in Lat., 374; sacr. mus., 190, 257, 282, 368ff (incl. Exx. 84, 85), 475, 510, 761; instr. mus., 537, 549f; W. as arranger for solo voice and lute, 318, 523, 835; W.'s relation to polychoral mus., 28, 285, 349; see also 293, 328ff, 336, 378, 403, 408, 413, 416, 450, 459, 469, 515, 534f, 588, 600, 623, 629
Willekommen, herre Christ, 633
William V, Duke of Bavaria, 487, 691, 700
Williams, C. F. Abdy (Wms), 774
Willow Song, anon., 841
wind instrument makers, 656, 753
Windsor, the hymn tune, 798
Winsem MS, see: Manuscripts—Berlin
Winter, Carl (Win), 425
Winter will hin weichen, Der, 636
Winterfeld, Carl von (Wint), 175, 295, 377, 379, 423, 498, 540, 551f, 677ff, 682ff, 686, 688, 690, 696, 706, 708
Wir glauben all an einem Gott (= Credo in German Mass), 676
Wirthmann, F., 691
Witch, The, Middleton, 882
Wladislaus II, King of Hungary, 641, 722f
Władysław of Gielniow, 745
Wohlauf, gut g'sell, von hinnen, 256
Wohlauf, ihr lieben Gäste, Sartorius, 708
Wol kumpt der May, Senfl, 708
Wolf, Johannes (Wolf), 8, 10f, 13f, 16, 19, 24ff, 34, 37, 41f, 67, 78, 84, 88, 90, 92, 98, 115, 120, 146, 149, 155, 157f, 162, 170, 175, 181, 191f, 195f, 210, 231, 276, 286, 310, 338, 411, 432, 443, 446f, 489, 491, 520ff, 527f, 534, 544f, 548f, 553, 565, 575, 579, 616, 623, 626, 634, 641, 644f, 650f, 657ff, 663, 668f, 676ff, 707, 711, 757, 849, 852f
Wolff, Martin, 638
Wolfram von Eschenbach (= Wolfgang Rohn), 652
Wollick, Nicolas, 334
Wolsey's Wild: the melody, 862; Byrd, 862
Woltz, Johann, 668
Wonder of Women, The, Marston, 880
Wood, Anthony, 810
Woodcocke, Clement, 870, 873
Woodfill, Walter M., 772
Woodward, George R. (Wood), 361, 712
Woods so wilde, The, Byrd, 863
Wooldridge, H. Ellis, 379
Worde, Wynken de, 768
Wotquenne-Plattel, Alfred (Wot), 447
Wreede (= Urrede), Johannes, 581, 628

Wright, Thomas, 786, 877
Wstał Pan Chrystus Zmartwych, the melody, 750 (incl. Ex. 171*a*)
Wüllner, Ludwig (Wülln), 469
Würzburg, Theodor von, 155
Wustmann, Gustav, 666
Wustmann, Rudolf (Wust), 666, 675, 684, 687
Wyatt, Sir Thomas, 769f
Wyssenbach, Rudolf, 668
Wyt and Sience, Redford, 877

Xilobalsamus, 635

Yates, Frances A. (Ya), 382f, 385
Ycart (Hykaert), Bernardo, 149
Yolanda of Aragon, Queen of Sicily (consort of Louis II), 13
Yonge, Nicholas, 821
Youll, Henry, 824
Yzak, see: Isaac, Heinrich

Zabaione musicale, Il, Banchieri, 437
Zacar, see: Zachara da Teramo, Antonio
Zacconi, Lodovico, 409, 412, 414, 547
Zachara da Teramo (= Zacar), Antonio, 31ff, 59
Zacharia (Zachariis), Cesare, 491f (incl. Ex. 114)
Zacharia, Nicola, 31f, 632
Zacharia, Nicola?, 743f
Zahp Johannes, 680

Zakythinos, Dennis A., 41, 49
Zambeccara, La, Merulo, 540 (incl. Ex. 125)
Zamojski, Chancellor Jan, 751
Zanni, Lassus, 444
Zarlino, Gioseffo (Zar): biogr., 323, 376f; Z. as theorist, 182, 329, 376ff, 530f, 617; Z.'s ten rules for text-underlaying, 378, 450, 475, 507; dissemination of Z.'s theories, 377, 562, 617, 687; Z. as composer, 379; see also 148, 234, 368, 370, 372, 374, 398, 416f, 421, 429, 436, 499, 503, 551
Zarotus, Michael, 154
zarzuela, 631
Záviš, Magister, 730f (incl. Ex. 166)
Zeltenpferd, 645
Zenatti, Albino (Zen), 156
Zenck, Hermann, 329, 373, 379, 681
Zerata, La, Merulo, 540
Zeuner Tantz, 717
Zieleński, Nicholas, 753
Zirler, Stephan, 707
zink, see: *cornetto*
Zoilo, Annibale, 425, 458
Zuccarini, Giovanni B., 419
Zucchelli, Giovanni B., 447
Zucchetto, 25
Zúñiga, Don Antonio de, 612
Zuth, Josef, 520
Zuylen van Nyevelt, Willem van, 357
Zwick, Jean, 359
Zwingli, Ulrich, 358, 683
Zwischen perg und tieffe tal, Isaac, 643